Praise for *The Handbook of Global Education Policy*

"This is a remarkable editorial achievement. By bringing together some of the best known writers on global education policy, this volume does the international educational community an invaluable service. Those wishing to deepen their understanding of the complex mechanisms and processes that drive education policy in this new global era will find much in this book that will engage, challenge, and provoke them. An essential overview for students and seasoned researchers alike."

       Ronald G. Sultana, *Euro-Mediterranean Centre for Educational Research, University of Malta*

"This authoritative Handbook, edited by leading international scholars, brings together a veritable Who's Who from the world of comparative education. It also includes chapters by promising young scholars from many parts of the world. Core issues relating to education's role in the global polity, key actors, and future directions are elegantly knitted together with a thought-provoking commentary for each section by the four editors."

       Ruth Hayhoe, *Ontario Institute for Studies in Education, University of Toronto*

"A cutting-edge resource for Chinese education researchers and policy-makers supporting interaction with the international education community. At a time when China is receiving more and more attention worldwide, there is an urgent need for us to better understand and then contribute to global education governance. It also shows the special value of developing comparative education in China since we are moving toward more international and development studies."

       Teng Jun, *Faculty of Education, Beijing Normal University*

"The editors and contributors are eminent scholars, who have been working in the research of the education policies for years. They profoundly understand and are able to write about global changes in the field. This book is essential reading for everyone with an interest not only in education policy research but also more widely across education policy and international policy."

       Risto Rinne, *Center for Research on Lifelong Learningand Education and Department of Education, University of Turku*

Handbook of Global Policy Series

Series Editor
David Held
Master of University College and Professor of Politics and International Relations at Durham University

The Handbook of Global Policy series presents a comprehensive collection of the most recent scholarship and knowledge about global policy and governance. Each Handbook draws together newly commissioned essays by leading scholars and is presented in a style which is sophisticated but accessible to undergraduate and advanced students, as well as scholars, practitioners, and others interested in global policy. Available in print and online, these volumes expertly assess the issues, concepts, theories, methodologies, and emerging policy proposals in the field.

Published

The Handbook of Global Climate and Environment Policy
Robert Falkner

The Handbook of Global Energy Policy
Andreas Goldthau

The Handbook of Global Companies
John Mikler

The Handbook of Global Security Policy
Mary Kaldor and Iavor Rangelov

The Handbook of Global Health Policy
Garrett Brown, Gavin Yamey, and Sarah Wamala

The Handbook of Global Science, Technology, and Innovation
Daniele Archibugi and Andrea Filippetti

The Handbook of Global Education Policy
Karen Mundy, Andy Green, Bob Lingard, and Antoni Verger

The Handbook of Global Education Policy

Edited by

Karen Mundy, Andy Green, Bob Lingard, and Antoni Verger

WILEY Blackwell

This edition first published 2016
© 2016 John Wiley & Sons, Ltd
Except chapters 4 and 18, © Elsevier

Registered Office
John Wiley & Sons, Ltd, The Atrium, Southern Gate, Chichester, West Sussex, PO19 8SQ, UK

Editorial Offices
350 Main Street, Malden, MA 02148-5020, USA
9600 Garsington Road, Oxford, OX4 2DQ, UK
The Atrium, Southern Gate, Chichester, West Sussex, PO19 8SQ, UK

For details of our global editorial offices, for customer services, and for information about how to apply for permission to reuse the copyright material in this book please see our website at www.wiley.com/wiley-blackwell.

The right of Karen Mundy, Andy Green, Bob Lingard, and Antoni Verger to be identified as the authors of the editorial material in this work has been asserted in accordance with the UK Copyright, Designs and Patents Act 1988.

All rights reserved. No part of this publication may be reproduced, stored in a retrieval system, or transmitted, in any form or by any means, electronic, mechanical, photocopying, recording or otherwise, except as permitted by the UK Copyright, Designs and Patents Act 1988, without the prior permission of the publisher.

Wiley also publishes its books in a variety of electronic formats. Some content that appears in print may not be available in electronic books.

Designations used by companies to distinguish their products are often claimed as trademarks. All brand names and product names used in this book are trade names, service marks, trademarks or registered trademarks of their respective owners. The publisher is not associated with any product or vendor mentioned in this book.

Limit of Liability/Disclaimer of Warranty: While the publisher and authors have used their best efforts in preparing this book, they make no representations or warranties with respect to the accuracy or completeness of the contents of this book and specifically disclaim any implied warranties of merchantability or fitness for a particular purpose. It is sold on the understanding that the publisher is not engaged in rendering professional services and neither the publisher nor the author shall be liable for damages arising herefrom. If professional advice or other expert assistance is required, the services of a competent professional should be sought.

Library of Congress Cataloging-in-Publication Data
Names: Mundy, Karen E. (Karen Elizabeth), 1962– editor of compilation. | Green, Andy, 1954– editor of compilation. | Lingard, Bob, editor of compilation. | Verger, Antoni, 1975– editor.
Title: The handbook of global education policy / edited by Karen Mundy, Andy Green, Bob Lingard, and Antoni Verger.
Description: Chichester, Uk ; Malden, MA : John Wiley & Sons, 2016. | Includes bibliographical references and index.
Identifiers: LCCN 2015046807 (print) | LCCN 2015050575 (ebook) | ISBN 9781118468050 (cloth) | ISBN 9781118468036 (Adobe PDF) | ISBN 9781118468043 (ePub)
Subjects: LCSH: Education–International cooperation. | Education and state–United States. | Educational change–Government policy.
Classification: LCC LC71 .H3635 2016 (print) | LCC LC71 (ebook) | DDC 379–dc23
LC record available at http://lccn.loc.gov/2015046807

A catalogue record for this book is available from the British Library.

Cover image: mygueart/Getty

Set in 10/12.5pt Sabon by SPi Global, Pondicherry, India

Printed in the UK

Contents

Notes on Contributors ix

Acknowledgements xix

List of Acronyms xx

Introduction: The Globalization of Education Policy – Key Approaches and Debates 1
Karen Mundy, Andy Green, Bob Lingard, and Antoni Verger

Part I Education and a Global Polity **21**

    Introduction 22
    Andy Green

  1 Educational Policies in the Face of Globalization: Whither the Nation State? 27
    Martin Carnoy

  2 World Society and the Globalization of Educational Policy 43
    Francisco O. Ramirez, John W. Meyer, and Julia Lerch

  3 The Global Diffusion of Education Privatization: Unpacking and Theorizing Policy Adoption 64
    Antoni Verger

  4 Economic Growth in Developing Countries: The Role of Human Capital 81
    Eric A. Hanushek

  5 Education, Poverty, and the "Missing Link": The Limits of Human Capital Theory as a Paradigm for Poverty Reduction 97
    Xavier Bonal

6	Gender and Education in the Global Polity *Elaine Unterhalter*	111
7	The Global Educational Reform Movement and Its Impact on Schooling *Pasi Sahlberg*	128
8	Global Convergence or Path Dependency? Skill Formation Regimes in the Globalized Economy *Marius R. Busemeyer and Janis Vossiek*	145

Part II Educational Issues and Challenges — 163

	Introduction *Bob Lingard*	164
9	Education and Social Cohesion: A Panglossian Global Discourse *Andy Green and Jan Germen Janmaat*	169
10	Policies for Education in Conflict and Post-Conflict Reconstruction *Sarah Dryden-Peterson*	189
11	Human Rights and Education Policy in South Asia *Monisha Bajaj and Huma Kidwai*	206
12	Early Childhood Education and Care in Global Discourses *Rianne Mahon*	224
13	Education for All 2000–2015: The Influence of Global Interventions and Aid on EFA Achievements *Aaron Benavot, Manos Antoninis, Nicole Bella, Marcos Delprato, Joanna Härmä, Catherine Jere, Priyadarshani Joshi, Nihan Koseleci Blanchy, Helen Longlands, Alasdair McWilliam, and Asma Zubairi*	241
14	The Politics of Language in Education in a Global Polity *M. Obaidul Hamid*	259
15	The Global Governance of Teachers' Work *Susan L. Robertson*	275
16	The Global Construction of Higher Education Reform *Simon Marginson*	291

Part III Global Policy Actors in Education — 313

	Introduction *Antoni Verger*	314
17	The Historical Evolution and Current Challenges of the United Nations and Global Education Policy-Making *Francine Menashy and Caroline Manion*	319

	18	The World Bank and the Global Governance of Education in a Changing World Order *Karen Mundy and Antoni Verger*	335
	19	The Changing Organizational and Global Significance of the OECD's Education Work *Bob Lingard and Sam Sellar*	357
	20	The Policies that Shaped PISA, and the Policies that PISA Shaped *Andreas Schleicher and Pablo Zoido*	374
	21	Dragon and the Tiger Cubs: China–ASEAN Relations in Higher Education *Rui Yang and Jingyun Yao*	385
	22	An Analysis of Power in Transnational Advocacy Networks in Education *Ian Macpherson*	401
	23	The Business Case for Transnational Corporate Participation, Profits, and Policy-Making in Education *Zahra Bhanji*	419
	24	New Global Philanthropy and Philanthropic Governance in Education in a Post-2015 World *Prachi Srivastava and Lianna Baur*	433
Part IV		**Critical Directions in the Study of Global Education Policy**	**449**
		Introduction *Karen Mundy*	450
	25	Rational Intentions and Unintended Consequences: On the Interplay between International and National Actors in Education Policy *Timm Fulge, Tonia Bieber, and Kerstin Martens*	453
	26	Policy and Administration as Culture: Organizational Sociology and Cross-National Education Trends *Patricia Bromley*	470
	27	Ethnography and the Localization of Global Education Policy *Amy Stambach*	490
	28	Global Education Policy and the Postmodern Challenge *Stephen Carney*	504
	29	Policy Reponses to the Rise of Asian Higher Education: A Postcolonial Analysis *Fazal Rizvi*	519

30 Joined-up Policy: Network Connectivity and Global Education Governance 535
Carolina Junemann, Stephen J. Ball, and Diego Santori

31 A Vertical Case Study of Global Policy-Making: Early Grade Literacy in Zambia 554
Lesley Bartlett and Frances Vavrus

32 Global Indicators and Local Problem Recognition: An Exploration into the Statistical Eradication of Teacher Shortage in the Post-Socialist Region 573
Gita Steiner-Khamsi

Name Index 590

Place Index 592

Subject Index 595

Notes on Contributors

Monisha Bajaj is Associate Professor of international and multicultural education at the University of San Francisco, where she directs the MA program in human rights education. She is also Visiting Professor and Research Fellow at the Institute for Reconciliation and Social Justice, University of the Free State, South Africa. Dr Bajaj is the editor and author of multiple books, including the award-winning *Schooling for Social Change: The Rise and Impact of Human Rights Education in India* (Bloomsbury, 2012) and *Peace Education: International Perspectives* (Bloomsbury, 2016), as well as numerous articles. She has also developed curriculum for non-profit organizations and inter-governmental organizations, such as the Unted Nations Children's Fund (UNICEF) and the United Nations Educational, Scientific and Cultural Organization (UNESCO).

Stephen J. Ball is Professor of sociology of education at the UCL Institute of Education, University College London, and Fellow of the British Academy. His work uses sociology in the analysis of education policy. Recent books include *Global Education Inc.* (Routledge, 2012) and *The Education Debate* (second edition) (Policy Press, 2012).

Lesley Bartlett is Associate Professor in educational policy studies at the University of Wisconsin-Madison. Her teaching and research interests include anthropology of education, literacy studies, and international and comparative education. She is the author, co-author, or co-editor of *Refugees, Immigrants, and Education in the Global South: Lives in Motion* (2013), *Teaching in Tension: International Pedagogies, National Policies, and Teachers' Practices in Tanzania* (2013), *Additive Schooling in Subtractive Times: Bilingual Education and Dominican Immigrant Youth in the Heights* (2011), *The Word and the World: The Cultural Politics of Literacy in Brazil* (2010), and *Critical Approaches to Comparative Education: Vertical Case Studies from Africa, Europe, the Middle East, and the Americas* (2009).

Lianna Baur is a graduate student at the School of International Development and Global Studies, University of Ottawa. She has worked as a Junior Policy Analyst on education with the Government of Canada's Department of Foreign Affairs, Trade and Development (DFATD). She has conducted field research on private foundations in education in Uttar Pradesh, Rajasthan, and New Delhi, India for her Master's thesis. She has published on the privatization of Indian higher education in the graduate student journal, *Canadian Journal of Globalization*, and has assisted with publications on education for the UK's Department for International Development (DFID) and DFATD.

Zahra Bhanji is Director, Office of the Vice-Principal Research at the University of Toronto Scarborough. She has previously worked as the Director, Research, International Initiatives and Knowledge Mobilization at the Ontario Institute for Studies in Education at the University of Toronto, the Policy and Research Manager at The Learning Partnership, and was a Research Fellow at the Lee-Chin Institute for Corporate Citizenship at the Rotman School of Management, UT. Zahra's publishing record includes articles in *Comparative Education Review*, *Globalisation, Societies and Education*, and the *Journal of International Business Studies*. Her research expertise includes the study of transnational non-state actors, community engagement, and partnerships in education policy and practice.

Tonia Bieber is Postdoctoral Fellow in the Kolleg-Forschergruppe "The Transformative Power of Europe" at the Freie Universität Berlin. Previously, she was a Senior Researcher in the research project "Internationalization of Education Policy" at the Collaborative Research Centre 597 "Transformations of the State" at the University of Bremen. Specializing in international relations and comparative public policy, she has published widely in the field of European integration and internationalization processes in social policy, especially education policy, in Western democracies. In particular, she is interested in policy diffusion and convergence research, as well as empirical research methods in this field. Tonia holds a PhD in political sciences from the University of Bremen and Jacobs University Bremen.

Xavier Bonal is a Special Professor of education and international development at the University of Amsterdam and an Associate Professor in sociology at the Autonomous University of Barcelona (UAB). He is the Director of the Globalisation, Education and Social Policies (GEPS) research center and Coordinator of the GLOBED Erasmus + Master's on education policies for global development. He has widely published on sociology of education, education policy, and education and development. He has worked as a consultant for several international organizations. Between 2006 and 2010, he was the Deputy Ombudsman for Children's Rights at the Office of the Catalan Ombudsman.

Patricia Bromley works at Stanford University as an Assistant Professor of international and comparative education. Conceptually, her research focuses on the rise and globalization of a culture emphasizing rational, scientific thinking and expansive forms of rights. Empirically, she draws on two settings – education systems and organizations – to show how the institutionalization of these new cultural emphases transforms societies worldwide. Recent publications appear in *Administration and Society*, *Sociological Theory*, and the *American Sociological Review*.

NOTES ON CONTRIBUTORS

Marius R. Busemeyer is Professor of political science at the University of Konstanz, Germany. Busemeyer studied political science, economics, public administration, and public law at the University of Heidelberg and the Harvard Kennedy School of Government. He received his PhD (Dr. rer. pol.) in political science from the University of Heidelberg in 2006 and worked as a Senior Researcher at the Max Planck Institute for the Study of Societies in Cologne before coming to Konstanz in 2011. His research focuses on comparative political economy, education and training policies, welfare states, public spending, public opinion, and welfare state attitudes, as well as theories of institutional change. Recent publications include an edited volume (with Christine Trampusch) entitled *The Political Economy of Collective Skill Formation* (Oxford University Press), a special issue of the *Socio-Economic Review* co-edited with Torben Iversen on *The Political Economy of Skills and Inequality*, as well as a book on *Skills and Inequality* (Cambridge University Press). He has published in journals such as the *British Journal of Industrial Relations*, the *Socio-Economic Review*, the *British Journal of Political Science*, the *Journal of European Social Policy*, and the *European Journal of Political Research*.

Stephen Carney is an Associate Professor of education policy at Roskilde University, Denmark. His research concerns theorizing global educational reform and has involved extensive ethnographic work in Denmark, England, Nepal, and China. He has been active in the US Comparative and International Education Society (CIES), first, as chair of the 'Globalization and Education' thematic group and, more recently, the 'Post-foundational theory and method' group, which he was instrumental in founding. He is Vice-President of the Comparative Education Society of Europe and Co-editor of the journal, the *Comparative Education Review*.

Martin Carnoy is Vida Jacks Professor of education and economics at Stanford University. He was trained at Caltech and the University of Chicago, and writes on the underlying political economy of educational policy. Much of his work is comparative and international, and investigates the impact of global economic and social change on educational systems. Examples of this are his books, *Sustaining the New Economy: Work, Family and Community in the Information Age* (Harvard, 2000), *Cuba's Academic Advantage* (2007), and *The Low Achievement Trap* (2012). His latest book compares higher educational expansion, financing, and quality in Brazil, China, India, and Russia – *University Expansion in a Changing Global Economy* (2013).

Sarah Dryden-Peterson leads a research program focused on connections between education and community development, specifically the role that education plays in building peaceful and participatory societies. Her work focuses on conflict and post-conflict settings in sub-Saharan Africa and African diaspora communities. She is concerned with the interplay between local experiences of children, families, and teachers, and the development and implementation of national and international policy. She is Assistant Professor at the Harvard Graduate School of Education. Previously, she taught middle school in Madagascar, South Africa, and the USA, and founded non-profits in South Africa and Uganda.

The **Education for All (EFA) Global Monitoring Report** (GMR) monitors progress toward the six EFA goals, to which more than 160 countries agreed as part of the *Dakar Framework for Action*, adopted during the World Education Forum held in April 2000 at Dakar, Senegal. The following GMR team members were authors of the GMR chapter: **Aaron Benavot**, Director; **Manos Antoninis**, Senior Policy Analyst; **Nicole Bella**, Senior Statistician and Policy Analyst; and Research Officers **Marcos Delprato, Joanna Härmä, Catherine Jere, Priyadarshani Joshi, Nihan Koseleci Blanchy, Helen Longlands, Alasdair McWilliam**, and **Asma Zubairi**.

Timm Fulge is a Research Fellow and doctoral candidate at the University of Bremen in Germany. He is a member of the research project "Internationalization of Education Policy" at the Collaborative Research Centre 597 "Transformations of the State." His research interests include international relations and the political economy of education.

Andy Green is Professor of comparative social science at the UCL Institute of Education, University College London, and Director of the ESRC Centre for Research on Learning and Life Chances in Knowledge Economies and Societies (LLAKES). His major books include: *Regimes of Social Cohesion: Societies and the Crisis of Globalisation* (Palgrave, 2011), *Education and Development in a Global Era: Strategies for "Successful" Globalisation* (DFID, 2007), and *Education, Equality and Social Cohesion* (Palgrave, 2006). His influential volume, *Education and State Formation* (Macmillan, 1990), has recently (2013) been published in a revised and extended second edition. Andy Green was elected as an Academician of the Academy of Social Science in 2010.

M. Obaidul Hamid, PhD, is a Lecturer in Teaching English to Speakers of Other Languages (TESOL) education at the University of Queensland, Australia. Previously he worked at the University of Dhaka, Bangladesh. His research focuses on the policy and practice of TESOL education in developing societies. He is the co-editor of *Language Planning for Medium of Instruction in Asia* (Routledge, 2014).

Eric A. Hanushek is the Paul and Jean Hanna Senior Fellow at the Hoover Institution of Stanford University. He is a leader in the development of economic analysis of educational issues. He has authored numerous, highly cited studies on the effects of class size reduction, high stakes accountability, the assessment of teacher quality, and other education related topics. He introduced the idea of measuring teacher quality through the growth in student achievement that forms the basis for the development of value-added measures for teachers and schools. Most recently, Hanushek shows that the quality of education is closely related to national economic growth. He has authored or edited 20 books along with over 200 articles. He is a Distinguished Graduate of the United States Air Force Academy and completed his PhD in economics at the Massachusetts Institute of Technology.

Jan Germen Janmaat is Reader in comparative social science at the UCL Institute of Education, University College London, and founder member of the ESRC LLAKES Centre. He co-edited *The Dynamics and Social Outcomes of Education Systems* and is the author of *Nation-Building in Post-Soviet Ukraine: Educational Policies and the Response of the Russian-Speaking Population*.

Carolina Junemann is a Researcher at the Institute of Education, University of London. Her research interests focus on education policy analysis, the social impacts of policy, and more broadly the relationship between educational and social inequalities. She is co-author (with Stephen Ball) of *Networks, New Governance and Education* (Policy Press, 2012).

Huma Kidwai is an education consultant with the World Bank's East Asia Division (Education – Global Practice). She recently graduated with a doctoral degree (EdD) from Teachers College-Columbia University, where she was studying the relationship between the state and madrassas in India. In 2013, she was awarded the American Institute of Indian Studies fellowship for her study. Her professional experience includes working at the World Bank in New Delhi as a research analyst with the Poverty Reduction Group, supporting projects related to health, education, and other civil rights at the Praxis Institute for Participatory Practices in New Delhi, and overseeing the educational programs and research at Columbia University's Global Center in Mumbai on their Model Districts Education Project.

Julia Lerch is a doctoral candidate in international comparative education in the Graduate School of Education at Stanford University. Her research interests are situated at the intersection of the study of globalization in education and the field of education and conflict. She currently studies why, how, and where education sectors in conflict-affected countries are increasingly becoming spaces of targeted global intervention. In addition, she examines cross-national and longitudinal variations in school curricula and textbooks.

Bob Lingard is a Professorial Research Fellow in the School of Education at the University of Queensland. Bob's research interests are educational policy framed by a sociological approach and focus on globalization and education policy, the Organisation for Economic Co-operation and Development (OECD), international testing, and social justice and schooling. His most recent book is *Politics, Policies and Pedagogies in Education* (Routledge, 2014). He is an editor of the journal, *Discourse: Studies in the Cultural Politics of Education*, and the book series, *Key Ideas and Education* (Routledge, New York). Bob is a Fellow of the Academy of Social Science in Australia.

Ian Macpherson is currently an Education Specialist with the Global Partnership for Education, however during the writing of this volume, he worked with the Open Society Foundations. He has conducted and managed research in education in over 25 countries and managed education programs in Africa, South Asia, and Latin America for over 12 years. In addition to a core concern with social justice and human rights issues in education, he is particularly interested in the international and transnational dynamics of advocacy in and around education and the role of civil society organizations in education policy reform. He holds several postgraduate degrees and gained his doctorate in education studies from Oxford University (UK).

Rianne Mahon holds a Centre for International Governance Innovation (CIGI) chair at the Balsillie School of International Affairs and is a Professor in the Department of Political Science, Wilfrid Laurier University. She is co-editor of *The OECD and Transnational Governance* (with S. McBride), *Leviathan Undone?* (with R. Keil), and *Feminist Ethics and Social Politics* (with F. Robinson), and has written numerous articles on the politics of childcare policy as part of a broader, gendered process of redesigning welfare regimes. Her current work focuses on the role of international organizations in disseminating ideas and the (contested) translation of such traveling ideas.

Caroline Manion is an Adjunct Professor in the Department of Leadership, Higher and Adult Education, teaching in the collaborative program in comparative, international and development education at the Ontario Institute for Studies in Education, University of Toronto. Her research focuses on global education policy, international organizations, educational governance, and gender in education.

Simon Marginson is Professor of international higher education at the UCL Institute of Education, University College London, and joint Editor-in-Chief of the journal *Higher Education*. He is a member of Academia Europaea, a fellow of the Academy of Social Sciences Australia and the Society for Research into Higher Education in the UK, and the 2014 Clark Kerr Lecturer in Higher Education at the University of California. Recent scholarly works include sole and jointly authored books and papers on higher education and globalization, international education and cross-border students, intercultural learning, university ranking, science, technology, engineering, and mathematics (STEM) policies and programs, and higher education in Vietnam.

Kerstin Martens is an Associate Professor of international relations at the University of Bremen, Germany. Her research interests include education policy, international organizations, in particular the OECD and the United Nations (UN), and non-governmental organizations (NGOs). She heads the research project on "Internationalization of Education Policy," a 12-year project financed by the German Research Foundation as part of the Collaborative Research Centre 597 "Transformations of the State." Kerstin holds a PhD in social and political science from the European University Institute in Florence.

Francine Menashy is an Assistant Professor in the Department of Leadership in Education at the University of Massachusetts, Boston. Her research focuses on aid to education, private sector engagement, and the policy-making processes of international organizations.

John W. Meyer is Professor of sociology (and, by courtesy, education), emeritus, at Stanford. He has contributed to organizational theory, comparative education, and the sociology of education, developing sociological institutional theory. Since the 1970s, he has studied global impacts on national societies (some papers are in G. Kruecken and G. Drori (eds) *World Society: The Writings of John W. Meyer*, Oxford University Press, 2009). A recent collaborative project is on global impacts on organizational structures (Drori *et al.* (eds) *Globalization and Organization*, Oxford University Press, 2006). He now studies the world human rights regime, and world curricula in mass and higher education.

Karen Mundy is a Professor of international and comparative education at the University of Toronto (on leave) and the Chief Technical Officer and Director of Strategy, Policy and Performance for the Global Partnership for Education (2014–2017), a multi-stakeholder partnership whose mission is to ensure good quality education for children in the developing world. Her published research has focused on the global politics of "Education for All" programs and policies, educational policy and reform in sub-Saharan Africa, and the role of civil society organizations in educational change. She has published five books and more than 50 articles and chapters.

Francisco O. Ramirez is Professor of education and (by courtesy) sociology at Stanford University. His current research interests focus on the rise and institutionalization of human rights and human rights education, on the worldwide rationalization of university structures and processes, and on terms of inclusion issues as regards gender and education. His most recent publications may be found in the *American Sociological Review*, *Higher Education*, *Comparative Education Review*, *Comparative Education*, and *Sociology of Education*.

Fazal Rizvi is a Professor of global studies in education at the University of Melbourne, and Emeritus Professor at the University of Illinois in Urbana-Champaign. Born in India and educated in India, Australia, and the UK, he has worked in a number of countries, and has written extensively on issues of identity, culture, and difference in transnational settings, theories of globalization and educational policy studies, and internationalization of education. His most recent books include: *Globalizing Education Policy* (Routledge, 2010) and *Encountering Education in the Global* (Routledge, 2014). His current research deals with issues relating to the pedagogic possibilities of cosmopolitanism, processes of elite formation in the globalizing contexts, and academic and research collaborations across national systems of higher education.

Susan L. Robertson is Professor of sociology of education, Graduate School of Education, University of Bristol, UK. Susan has a long-standing research interest in the transformation of the state, global, and regional processes that materialize and mediate education projects, and teachers' work. She is founding co-editor of the journal, *Globalisation, Societies and Education*. She is also the Director of the *Centre for Globalisation, Education and Societies*, which she established in 2003. Susan has published widely on the political sociology of education.

Pasi Sahlberg is a Finnish educator and scholar. He has worked as a school teacher, teacher educator, and policy advisor in various positions in Finland, and has studied education systems and advised policy-makers globally with the World Bank, the European Commission, and the OECD. His book *Finnish Lessons: What Can the World Learn from Educational Change in Finland* won the 2013 Grawemeyer

Award. He is a former Director General of the Centre for International Mobility and Cooperation (CIMO) at the Finnish Ministry of Education and Culture and currently a Visiting Professor at Harvard University's Graduate School of Education in Cambridge, MA, USA. Twitter: @pasi_sahlberg.

Diego Santori is a Lecturer in sociology of education and education policy analysis, at the UCL Institute of Education. His interests include the relationships between education policy, economics, and subjectivity, and the ways in which their interpenetration produce new cultural forms and practices. His recent publications include: Santori, D., S. Ball, and C. Junemann. 2015. "Education as a Site of Network Governance," in *Mapping Corporate Education Reform: Power and Policy Networks in the Neoliberal State*, edited by W. Au and J. Ferrare. Abingdon: Routledge.

Andreas Schleicher is Director for Education and Skills at the OECD. The Directorate supports countries in their efforts to improve quality, equity, and efficiency in their education systems, to enhance the relevance of skills, and to transform better skills into better jobs and better lives. Major programs include the Programme for International Student Assessment (PISA), the OECD Survey of Adult Skills (PIAAC), the OECD Teaching and Learning International Survey (TALIS), and the development and analysis of benchmarks on the performance of education systems (INES). He studied physics in Germany and received a degree in mathematics and statistics in Australia. He holds an honorary professorship at the University of Heidelberg.

Sam Sellar is a Postdoctoral Research Fellow in the School of Education at the University of Queensland. Sam's research focuses on education policy and social theory. He is currently working on projects investigating the measurement of non-cognitive skills in large-scale assessments, new modes of accountability in schooling, and the changing aspirations of young people. Sam is Associate Editor of *Critical Studies in Education* and *Discourse: Studies in the Cultural Politics of Education*.

Prachi Srivastava is Associate Professor, School of International Development and Global Studies, University of Ottawa, and Visiting Research Fellow, Institute of South Asian Studies, National University of Singapore. She holds a doctorate from the University of Oxford. She has published extensively in the areas of the privatization of education and global education policy. She had provided expertise on global education policy and private schooling for a number of agencies and international NGOs, including the former Canadian International Development Agency, the UK's DFID, and UNESCO. Her latest book is *Low-Fee Private Schooling: Aggravating Equity or Mitigating Disadvantage?* (Symposium Books, 2013).

Amy Stambach is Vilas Distinguished Professor of educational policy studies and anthropology at the University of Wisconsin and Research Affiliate at the Centre for Comparative and International Education Research, University of Oxford. She is the author of *Confucius and Crisis in American Universities* (2014), *Faith in Schools: Religion, Education, and American Evangelicals in East Africa* (2010), and *Lessons from Mount Kilimanjaro: Schooling, Community, and Gender in East Africa* (2000).

Gita Steiner-Khamsi is Professor of comparative and international education of the Department of International and Transcultural Studies at Teachers College, Columbia University, New York. She has published widely on globalization, policy borrowing and lending, and comparative policy studies. Her most recent book is entitled *The Global Education Industry*, co-edited with Antoni Verger and Christopher Lubienski published by Routledge in 2016.

Elaine Unterhalter is a Professor of education and international development at the University College London, Institute of Education. She has published widely on global policy regarding gender, education, and girls' schooling, and participated in a number of research teams investigating policy and practice in these areas in South Asia and Africa.

Frances Vavrus is Professor in comparative and international development education at the University of Minnesota and Co-Director of the University's Interdisciplinary Center for the Study of Global Change. She teaches courses in comparative education, international development, and theoretical foundations in the social sciences. Her current research explores critical geographies of education, teacher education in postcolonial Africa, and transnational knowledge production in international education. Her publications include *Teaching in Tension: International Pedagogies, National Policies, and Teachers' Practices in Tanzania* (2013), *Critical Approaches to Comparative Education: Vertical Case Studies from Africa, Europe, the Middle East, and the Americas* (2009), and *Desire and Decline: Schooling amid Crisis in Tanzania* (2003).

Antoni Verger is an Associate Professor, "Ramon y Cajal" researcher and "Marie Curie" Fellow in the Department of Sociology of the Universitat Autònoma de Barcelona. He has specialized in the study of the relationship between global governance institutions and education policy. His current research looks at the global spread of market education reforms and their re-contextualization and enactment in multiple settings. His most recent publications may be found in *Comparative Education Review*, *Journal of Education Policy*, *Current Sociology*, *Review of International Political Economy*, *Globalisation, Societies and Education*, and *Comparative Education*.

Janis Vossiek holds a diploma in political science from the University of Bremen and is currently a doctoral researcher at the University of Konstanz, where he is writing his dissertation on vocational training reforms in liberal market economies. His main research interests are comparative political economy and welfare state research, and especially the intersection between education and labor market policies.

Rui Yang is Professor of education at the University of Hong Kong and a former Director of the Comparative Education Research Center at that University. He has also taught at the University of Western Australia, Monash University (Australia), and Shantou University (China). He has undertaken many projects in the field of comparative education and is the Editor of the journal *Frontiers of Education in China*.

Jingyun Yao works on research projects based at the Faculty of Education in the University of Hong Kong. She holds a BA in journalism and communication from Hong Kong Baptist University and is completing her MEd studies at the University of Hong Kong with an emphasis on higher education.

Pablo Zoido works at the OECD Directorate for Education and Skills as an analyst. His work focuses on providing advice to countries on how to use international evaluations to improve the quality, equity, and efficiency of education. Prior to joining PISA, he worked at the World Bank and Stanford University. He holds advanced degrees from Johns Hopkins and Stanford universities in international relations and economics.

Acknowledgements

The completion of this volume owes much to Caroline Manion and Robyn Read at the Ontario Institute for Studies in Education, who provided expert editorial support. Each of the Handbook editors conveys their gratitude to family, friends, and colleagues who supported their work on this book. Karen dedicates the book to her family of boys – Niko, Leo, and Konstantin. Andy to his late father, Michael, and to Ye, who has experienced both the best and worst of "global policy." Bob thanks his colleagues Sam Sellar and Aspa Baroutsis, and Carolynn Lingard for her support and forbearance. Toni thanks the *Globalization, Education and Social Policies* research center colleagues for the inspiring discussions on the themes covered by the Handbook, and for the motivating and collaborative work environment they have created. He dedicates the Handbook to Mar and Clara.

The Handbook of Global Education Policy was developed with the support of a research grant from the Social Science and Humanities Research Council of Canada.

List of Acronyms

5DE	five dimensions of exclusion
ADB	Asian Development Bank
AFDB	African Development Bank
ANCEFA	African Network Campaign on Education for All
APEC	Asia-Pacific Economic Cooperation
ASEAN	Association of Southeast Asian Nations
ASER	Annual Status of Education Research
ASPBAE	Asia South Pacific Association for Basic and Adult Education
AUT	Austria
BIBB	Bundesinstitut für Berufsbildung
BIA	Bridge International Academies
BOG	Board of Governors
BRAC	Bangladesh Rural Advancement Committee
BRICS	Brazil, Russia, India, China, and South Africa
BtL	Breakthrough to Literacy
CAN	Canada
CAP	consolidated appeal process
CDA	Critical Discourse Analysis
CDC	CDC Group plc., formerly Commonwealth Development Corporation
CEDAW	Convention on the Elimination of All Forms of Discrimination against Women
CEECIS	Central and Eastern Europe and the Commonwealth of Independent States
CEF	Commonwealth Education Fund
CEI	Center for Education Innovations
CERF	Central Emergency Response Fund
CERI	Centre for Educational Research and Innovation
CH	Switzerland
CIDA	Canadian International Development Agency
CHF	Common Humanitarian Fund
CLADE	Coalition for the Right to Education in Latin America
CME	coordinated market economy

CNN	Cable News Network
COPOME	Cordinatoria Popular de Madres Educadoras
CPE	Cultural Political Economy
CRC	Convention on the Rights of Children
CREATE	Campus for Research Excellence and Technological Enterprise
CSEF	Civil Society Education Fund
DEELSA	Directorate for Education, Employment, Labour and Social Affairs
DFATD	Department of Foreign Affairs, Trade and Development (Canada)
DFID	Department for International Development (UK)
DIBELS	Dynamic Indicators of Basic Early Literacy Skills
EAHEP	EU-Asia Higher Education Platform
ECD	Early Child Development
ECEC	Early Childhood Education and Care
ECTS	European Transfer and Accumulation System
EEPCT	Education and Emergencies and Post-Crisis Transition
EFA	Education for All
EFA-FTI	Education for All Fast Track Initiative
EFTS	Equivalent full-time study
EGRA	Early Grade Reading Assessment
EMI	English as a Medium of Instruction
EPDC	Education Policy and Data Center
EQUIP	Education Quality Improvement Program
ERA	Education Reform Act
ERF	Emergency Response Fund
ESSU	*Education Sector Strategy Update*
EU	European Union
FAWE	Forum of African Women Educationists
FIFA	Fédération Internationale de Football Association
FIMS	First International Math Study
FR	France
G8	Group of Eight
G20	Group of Twenty
GATS	General Agreement on Trade in Services
GAW	Global Action Week
GBCE	Global Business Coalition for Education
GCE	Global Campaign for Education
GEC	Girls' Education Challenge
GEFI	Global Education First Initiative
GER	Germany
GERM	Global Educational Reform Movement
GIIN	Global Impact Investing Network
GNH	Gross National Happiness Index, Bhutan
GPE	Global Partnership for Education
GPS	Global Positioning System
GTER	Gross Tertiary Enrolment Ratio
HCT	Human Capital Theory
HEI	Higher Education Institution
HPS	High Participation System
IAD	Indicators and Analysis Division
IBRD	International Bank for Reconstruction and Development

ICT	information and communications technology
IDA	International Development Agency
IDP	Internally Displaced Person
IEA	International Association for the Evaluation of Educational Achievement
IEG	Independent Evaluation Group (World Bank)
IELTS	International English Language Testing System
IFC	International Finance Corporation
IGO	Intergovernmental Organization
IMF	International Monetary Fund
INEE	Inter-Agency Network for Education in Emergencies
INES	Indicators of Education Systems
INGO	international non-governmental organization
IT	Information Technology
ITA	*Idara-e-Taaleem-o-Aagahi*
ITB	Industrial Training Board
JAP	Japan
KIPP	Knowledge is Power Program
LCPS	Low Cost Private School
LEG	Local Education Group
LME	liberal market economy
LPIP	Learner Performance Improvement Plans
LPP	Language Policy and Planning
MA	Modern Apprenticeship
MAI	Multilateral Agreement on Investment
MDG	Millennium Development Goal
MERCOSUR	Southern Common Market
MET	Measures of Effective Teaching
MOOC	Massive Open Online Course
MPF	Manpower Planning Forecast
MSC	Manpower Services Commission
NAFTA	North-American Free Trade Agreement
NAPLaN	National Assessment Program Literacy and Numeracy
NBTL	New Breakthrough to Literacy
NCF	National Curriculum Framework
NCFTE	National Curriculum Framework for Teacher Education
NCLB	No Child Left Behind
NCP	New Colombo Plan
NGO	non-governmental organization
NPM	New Public Management
NRP	National Reading Panel
NUEPA	National University of Education Planning and Administration, New Delhi
OECD	Organisation for Economic Co-operation and Development
OECD-DAC	Organisation for Economic Co-operation and Development-Development Assistance Committee
OOSC	Out of School Children
PALF	Pearson Affordable Learning Fund
PEAS	Promoting Equality in African Schools
PIAAC	Programme for International Assessment of Adult Competencies
PIRLS	Progress in International Reading Literacy Study

PISA	Programme for International Student Assessment
PPP	public–private partnership
PRES	Pôles de recherche et d'enseignement supérieur
PRSP	Poverty Reduction Strategy Paper
PTA	Parent Teacher Association
RoR	rate of return analysis
ROWITE	OECD working party on the role of women in the economy
RTE	Right to Education Act, India
RTI	Research Triangle Institute International
RTS	Read to Succeed
RWS	Real World Strategies
R&D	Research and Development
SABER	Systems Approach for Better Educational Results
SAGE	Strategies for Advancing Girls' Education
SAP	Structural Adjustment Policy
SAS	Survey of Adult Skills (OECD)
SITAN	UNICEF Situational Analysis
SOCAP	Social Capital Markets
SRGBV	School Related Gender Based Violence
SSA	*Sarva Shiksha Abhiyan*
STEM	science, technology, engineering, and mathematics
SUK	*Schweizerische Universitätskonferenz*
SVP	Swiss People's Party
SWAp	sector-wide approaches
SWE	Sweden
TALIS	Teaching and Learning International Survey
TAN(s)	Transnational Advocacy Network(s)
TEC	Training and Enterprise Council
TFA	Teach for America
TIMSS	Trends in International Mathematics and Science Survey
TNC	transnational corporation
TOEFL	Test of English as a Foreign Language
UCDP	Uppsala Conflict Data Program
UDHR	Universal Declaration of Human Rights
UIS	UNESCO Institute for Statistics
UK	United Kingdom
UN	United Nations
UNDP	United Nations Development Programme
UNESCO	United Nations Educational, Scientific and Cultural Organization
UNFPA	United Nations Population Fund
UNHCR	United Nations High Commissioner for Refugees
UNICEF	United Nations Children's Fund
UNCRC	United Nations Convention on the Rights of Children
UPE	universal primary education
USA	United States of America
USAID	United States Agency for International Development
VAT	value-added tax
VET	vocational education and training
VoC	varieties of capitalism
WCCES	World Council of Comparative Education Societies

WCT	World Culture Theory
WCU	World Class University
WISE	World Innovation Summit for Education
WTO	World Trade Organization
YTS	Youth Training Scheme

Introduction: The Globalization of Education Policy – Key Approaches and Debates

Karen Mundy, Andy Green, Bob Lingard, and Antoni Verger

Education and schooling have long been deeply implicated in processes of internationalization and global economic integration. Throughout the course of modern history, conquering powers, religious movements, and traders each carried with them new approaches to acculturation and learning – perhaps never more prominently than in the 19th and early 20th centuries, when the newly minted educational systems of Western states were carried around the world by colonial powers. Yet it was not until the mid-20th century that education itself became a formal issue arena for international policy-makers and international organizations. The formation of the United Nations Education and Cultural Organization (UNESCO) and the establishment of the Universal Declaration of Human Rights each signaled a new era for global policy-making in education, opening the way to a proliferation of bilateral, multilateral, and non-governmental efforts to influence and transform educational systems and set global educational standards.

Today, governments are increasingly engaged in forms of global educational exchange and policy-making, through membership in such diverse institutions as the Organisation for Economic Cooperation and Development (OECD), the Group of 8 (G8), the World Bank, the European Union (EU), the World Trade Organization (WTO), and the Association of Southeast Asian Nations (ASEAN). International comparison of the performance of education systems is a matter for media headlines, building on the widely accepted view that educational success is a proxy for economic competitiveness. Emerging powers in Asia, the Middle East, and Latin America have created new regional educational organizations and development agencies with keen interest in education policy. Non-state actors and institutions are also increasingly influential – with powerful transnational educational business, professional associations, technology companies, new philanthropies, transnational civil society advocacy networks, and the global business community (e.g. World Economic Forum) each actively participating in the construction of new global "policy spaces" for education.

To understand the increasingly complex and pluri-lateral field of global educational policy, we begin the *Handbook of Global Education Policy* by providing an overview of the actors, policies, and contexts – including processes of globalization – which have spurred the expansion of global policy-making in education. In what follows we first look at historical antecedents to global policy-making in education, before exploring globalization and its impacts on educational systems. We then turn to debates about how best to conceptualize and study the mechanisms and processes that drive education policy in this new global era – reviewing theories of convergence, divergence, coercion, and policy borrowing as frames for understanding global education policy. This chapter concludes with a brief section on key issues and policy actors in global education, and a short overview of the organization of this volume.

Antecedents to Today's Global Education Policy

Education policy has long been understood as the putative domain of the nation state. Sociologists and political scientists, beginning with Max Weber, Emile Durkheim, and John Stuart Mill, recognized that national educational systems arose as part of the apparatus of modern government in the Western world. Education systems complemented the state's legitimate right to exercise power within national territory, providing a mechanism for socializing citizens and allowing for the authoritative allocation of values. Schooling spread rapidly because of popular demand from citizens and communities – who saw education as an opportunity for personal and group progress. Thus, from the 19th and into the 20th centuries, governments in many parts of the world expanded access to schooling: they achieved near universal enrolment at elementary and later secondary levels, and established publicly funded systems for higher education. Early educational systems, which had often been funded and controlled by religious organizations or communities, were gradually absorbed into nationally funded and controlled public systems; leaving governments to play an increasingly authoritative role in childhood socialization. By controlling the allocation of public resources for education; setting national (and sub-national) curricula and standards; hiring and paying teachers and structuring their work; and owning the schools themselves, schooling and school systems played a central role in constructing what Anderson (1991) describes as the "imagined community" of the modern nation state.

In this context, it is perhaps unsurprising that cross-national education policy borrowing emerged as a persistent feature of national educational policy setting. From early in the 19th century, when national or "public" educational systems were first consolidated in Western Europe and North America, education policy makers and reform advocates were active in analyzing developments in other countries, both to provide evidence on what policies to avoid and on what policies might be usefully adopted at home. State-provided elementary education in Prussia in the 1830s, for instance, offered an influential model that was widely studied by reformers in other countries. The Prussian system of free and compulsory state elementary schooling, with professional training for teachers in state Normal schools, and centrally controlled curricula, was used as a basis in the 1830s for the Guizot reforms in France and, in part, for Horace Mann's reforms to the education system in Massachusetts in the USA (Green 2013). Reforms to technical and secondary schooling in England in the late 19th century owed much to the advocacy of continental European policies by leading reformers such as the scientist, Lyon Playfair, and the Schools Inspector, Matthew Arnold, both of whom had conducted extensive research on foreign education policies. When the government in Meiji Japan first developed its national education system in the 1870s, emissaries were dispatched to study the education systems in Germany and the USA, and many of the policies in those countries were subsequently adopted or adapted in the development of the Japanese education system.

Yet while examples from the 19th century, and indeed before, of educational policy borrowing are legion, prior to the mid-20th century there are few examples of organized and sustained international policy setting in education. Apart from modest experiments – such as the creation of the International Bureau of Education at the time of the League of Nations, education remained pre-eminently a national concern. Policy borrowing between states occurred primarily through individual reformers' initiatives, without support from transnational organizations.

The end of World War II marked an important departure from this trajectory. The creation of the United Nations and the first international intergovernmental organization with an educational mandate, UNESCO, as well as the establishment of the Universal Declaration of Human Rights (UDHR), placed education on the agenda of a new kind of multilateralism among post-war governments. Focused on building shared principles and values across nations through stronger economic and political interdependence, the new multilateral architecture helped to construct a form of "embedded liberalism" that married together the objectives of building more inclusive economies (primarily through the recognition of the need for social safety nets and greater access to jobs), with greater civil and political freedoms and a more integrated, and a better managed, world economy (through the creation of the Bretton Woods institutions) (Ruggie 1982; Mundy 1998). It is in the context of "embedded liberalism" that education became recognized as a powerful tool not only for constructing more inclusive national economies, but for ensuring a lasting peace based on common values of individual freedoms and shared prosperity. While education would remain predominantly the preserve of national sovereignty in this new global order, for the first time, the need for global standards and cross-national problem solving in education was recognized as an appropriate and important domain for multilateralism.

The breakdown of colonialism and the emergence of a whole new group of independent states after World War II further spurred the growth of international educational policy-making. By the 1960s, newly formed national programs and agencies for delivering foreign aid, as well as international organizations, such as the United Nations Children's Fund (UNICEF) and the World Bank, had begun to join UNESCO in supporting national educational development in newly independent states. The enormous expansion of international flows of policy-making and exchange in education that followed was marked by the uneven and increasingly polarized power relationships across nation states. Education policies became, especially during the Cold War, a prime arena for competition and influence among the Western and Eastern bloc countries. Thus a fragmented and diverse architecture for international educational policy exchange and influence developed. It included the joint problem solving approach embodied in the educational work of the OECD and other regional organizations; the multilateral (and officially neutral and scientifically driven) activities of such international organizations as UNESCO, UNICEF and the World Bank; and the more self-seeking bilateral flows of aid and advice from richer to newly independent developing countries.

Globalization and the Take-Off of Global Education Policy After 1975

Globalization can be defined as the de-territorialization of social, political, and economic relationships, and the rapid integration of societies across the previously territorially bound units we call "nation states" (Harvey 1989; Ruggie 1993). As noted by Held and colleagues:

> Globalization can be thought of as a process (or set of processes) which embodies a transformation in the spatial organization of social relations and transactions – assessed in terms of their extensity, intensity, velocity and impact – generating transcontinental or interregional flows and networks of activity, interaction, and the exercise of power. (Held et al. 1999, 16)

While globalization processes have been ongoing since at least the 16th century, scholars of global education policy argue that globalization processes over the past 35 years have set the stage for new types of power and complex pluri-lateral forms of influence on domestic educational systems, creating new and more globalized education policy discourses and a more formalized global policy architecture (Rizvi and Lingard 2010). Heightened integration of economies and markets (though profoundly uneven), accelerated mobility and communication across borders, fueled by new technologies, and the end of the Cold War, have each changed the nature of governments' strategic interests and their ability to control and contain domestic social and economic trajectories, allowing for emergence of new global policy spaces for education.

For educational systems, and for other putatively national public policy domains, perhaps the first point of impact from globalization has come from the acceleration of economic integration that has occurred since the 1970s, following the ending of the Bretton Woods system of fixed exchange rates in 1971 and the subsequent movement toward financial de-regulation. The rise of transnational corporations, globally integrated production chains, and markets, and increasingly mobile flows of capital, each contributed to the deepening globalization of national economies and the creation of a global economy (Castells 1996; Green 1997; Harvey 1989; Bourdieu 2003). Although each nation state has followed its own unique trajectory in responding to these changes, it is clear that economic globalization had some common effects on education policy. Globalization shifted post-World War II sources of state power by limiting the historical ability of states to tax capital, and redefining trajectories for national economic development and thereby requirements for skills and human capital.

Economic globalization elicited two key types of educational policy responses from nation states. Beginning in the 1980s, *finance driven reforms* – the search for cost efficiencies, the introduction of new forms of user payments, and other sources of private finance – came to characterize both Western countries and those in the developing world (Carnoy 1999). Alongside these reforms, *competitiveness driven* changes to education systems, including the introduction of new outcomes based performance standards, national and international assessments, new modes of accountability, decentralization of services, and the diversification of service providers, came to characterize a new drive for educational improvement around the world (Carnoy 1999). As Verger (Chapter 3, this volume), Ball (2012), and others have suggested, the introduction of private sector management approaches into the public sector, including through the involvement of private sector organizations, both philanthropic agencies and edu-businesses, became increasingly central to competitiveness driven educational reform.

Perhaps the earliest impact of economic globalization can be found in more limited state capacity to fund the comprehensive and redistributive educational opportunities that had characterized Western welfare states after World War II. Economic globalization also contributed to increasing income inequality within states, in ways that have affected the families and students that education systems serve (Piketty 2014). Yet increasing economic competition between states also put pressure on countries to maintain or improve living standards by raising productivity through ever-greater investments in research, innovation, and skills, as part of the growth of the global knowledge economy (Brown *et al.* 2001). Profits in many economic sectors increasingly depended on the development of high value-added goods and services, leading to increased demand from enterprises for highly skilled labor, as well as from individuals for higher-level education and more qualifications. Ever greater investments were required from governments, not least in some of the most highly developed countries where doubts about the competitiveness of their labor forces were emerging as well as doubts about whether the skills produced by their school and universities systems were sufficient to compete with rapidly developing countries, not least in Asia. This placed increasing strains on public budgets. The major common problem for governments, then, was how to finance the rising costs of meeting the ever growing demand for education and skills, while maintaining globally competitive tax regimes (Carnoy 1999).

Providing higher quality education and training was a major preoccupation of many governments from the 1980s onwards, and particularly after 2000 when the onset of the Programme for International Student Assessment (PISA) surveys appeared to offer a way of comparing the quality of education across countries (Hanushek and Woessmann 2010; Sahlberg 2011). Governments wanted more effective education, but not at greater expense, so measures were sought to improve the efficiency of school systems. From the late 1980s onwards, the USA and the UK strongly promoted the cause of educational marketization. The market logic was simple: schools would be more efficient if they were subject to greater competition. To ensure that market forces had their desired effects, there had to be greater school choice and diversity, more information for consumers, and greater managerial autonomy for schools so that they could respond in innovative ways to competitive pressures. As Salhberg details in Chapter 7 of this Handbook, the 1988 Education Act, brought in by the Thatcher government in the UK, provided the model that many other countries were to follow. Policies on school choice and diversity and on devolution of control to schools followed in many countries, and these in turn led to further requirements for new policies for measuring the outputs and performance of decentralized systems.

Alongside economic globalization, the past 30 years have also seen the acceleration of political globalization – the re-territorialization of the political power of the nation state. Political globalization can be traced both to the rise of joint problem solving across countries facing similar demands from economic globalization, and to the rise and influence of international organizations and other global policy actors. As discussed in several chapters of this volume, international organizations such as the OECD and the World Bank have played a rising role during the past half century as purveyors of policy solutions to national educational (as well as economic) problems, and in so doing have created a common framework for global educational policy discourse or what Novoa (2002) calls "global policyspeak."

International agencies rose to prominence in the context of rapid globalization by offering some novel solutions to dilemmas of globalization. The concept of lifelong learning, sponsored by the OECD, emerged as one of the first over-arching global policy discourses in the realm of education, and was rapidly adopted, at least rhetorically, in both developed and developing countries, to meet two pressing needs (European Commission 1995; 2001; OECD 1996; Green 2003; Jakobi 2009). On the one hand, learning throughout the life course – from cradle to grave – offered a way to meet the challenge arising from the rapid development of new technologies for constant skills upgrading within the work force (Brown et al. 2001; OECD 1996). People would continue to learn new skills throughout their working lives and even beyond, so that they would be able to cope with ever longer periods of retirement resulting from the increasing longevity experienced in most countries. At the same time, lifelong learning provided a way around the problem of the escalating costs for education. Under the new paradigm, learning was to become "life-wide" as well as "life-long," occurring not only in the school and college, but also in the workplace, the family, and the local community (European Commission 2001). This meant that the costs could be spread between the state, which would remain largely responsible for schooling, the employer, and also the individual and his or her family. The concept had immediate appeal to governments, which found themselves unable to resist the political pressure of their electorates for expanded educational provision, but found themselves unable to pay for it, except in the diminishing number of social democratic North West European states that could persuade their electors to pay higher income taxes.

"Neo-liberalism" – the predisposition of governments to increasingly favor free market solutions over governmental intervention, and individual effort over the provision of collective safety nets – has arguably become the vernacular for the global policyscapes elicited by globalization and spread by international organizations (Ball 2013). Arising in the first instance from policy shifts in Anglo-American states (a move that Verger et al. (2012), adopting Boaventura de Sousa Santos terminology, describe as "globalized localisms"), neo-liberal approaches that emerged in Anglo-American states were rapidly picked up in the developing world, and even in putatively socialist societies like China and Vietnam with talk of "market socialism." In education the spread of market choice policies, privatizations of various kinds, new standardized testing regimes (often complementing international testing such as PISA), new test based modes of educational accountability, and an emphasis upon educational standards led to a profound change in the way education systems would be managed – and to policy discourses sharply different from the embedded liberalism and social welfare state norms of the immediate post-World War II era. Technological development reinforced such changes, contributing to the development of globalized technologies of administration – including the technical infrastructure for the globalization of educational data, most notably through the massive increase in cross-national learning assessments, firstly issuing from the surveys conducted by the International Association for the Evaluation of Educational Achievement (IEA) (Trends in International Mathematics and Science Survey (TIMSS) and Progress in International Reading Literacy Study (PIRLS) etc.) and subsequently from the OECD (including main PISA, PISA for Schools, PISA for Development, Teaching and Learning International Survey (TALIS), and the Programme for International Assessment of Adult Competencies (PIAAC)).

Yet it is important to note that the homogenizing influence of new global-level political processes and policy discourses has not circulated in an even or predictable fashion. In part, this is a reflection of the strong role that local context – and in particular local institutions – play in shaping national responses to, and engagement with, global policy processes. It also reflects the profound shifts of power within domestic education systems, where the rise of more complex forms of "networked governance" means that "government is understood to be located alongside business and civil society actors in a complex game of public policy formation, decision-making and implementation" (Koppenjan and Klijn 2004, 25; Ball and Junemann 2012), as modeled in Anglo-American contexts. Cultural and technological globalization has tended to reinforce subnational policy voices, by heightening opportunities for exchange and movement of people and ideas. New opportunities for cross-national policy exchange and contestation among these new non-state actors have emerged. At the same time, new regionalisms have arisen in education – with organizations such as ASEAN, the North-American Free Trade Agreement (NAFTA), the Southern Common Market (MERCOSUR) in Latin America, and the EU each spawning their process and approaches to educational problem solving (Lawn and Grek 2012).

New Approaches to the Study of Education Policy

In order to study the increasingly complex, pluri-lateral, and cross-scalar flow of ideas and power in education policy that have emanated from globalization processes, education policy scholars have coined new terms, employed new theoretical frames, and developed new methodological approaches. As will be seen throughout this volume, vibrant theoretical and methodological debates have accompanied these new efforts to conceptualize research on global education policy.

We have spoken to this point of global education policy, but in fact what has been globalized are mainly policy discourses, whose take-up in nations remains heavily mediated. One of the central concerns in the study of global education policy is the uneven and contested implementation or enactment of global discourse in education systems and organizations. Most scholars of global education policy reject a linear understanding of policy processes as moving in unidirectional fashion from discourse, text, to implementation or enactment. Some, like Luke and Hogan (2006, 171), define educational policy-making "as the prescriptive regulation of flows of human resources, discourse and capital across educational systems towards normative social, economic and cultural ends." Others, such as Ball (1994), have conceptualized a "policy cycle" consisting of multi-directional and non-linear relationships across agenda setting, policy text production, and policy enactment. Ball utilizes the term "enactment" rather than "implementation" (Ball *et al.* 2012) to highlight how the agency and engagement of a variety of actors at global, national, provincial, systemic, and institutional levels of policy processes shape and modify policies as they move between discursive constructions and practice. As Ball (2013, 8) suggests, "Policies are contested, interpreted and enacted in a variety of arenas of practice and the rhetorics, texts and meanings of policy makers do no always translate directly and obviously into institutional practices." Furthermore, there is an important distinction between policies as meta-discourses that shape what can be thought (policyscapes); policies as formalized rules and regulations; and policies as socially constructed enactments that span text and practice. Policy involves all three layers of action, including processes both before and after text production, and sometimes including formal evaluation processes (Taylor *et al.* 1997).

Scholars in the field of comparative and international education and global education policy have sought new theoretical and methodological approaches to help inform their analysis of global education policy. In this volume, chapters by Junemann, Ball, and Santori, and Carney build upon Appadurai's (1996) notion of globalization as the acceleration of different types of flows of people, resources, and ideas, and Foucauldian approaches to discursive power, in elaborating the notion of educational "policyscapes" (see also Carney 2009). Dale and Robertson (2002) and Verger (Chapter 3, this volume) draw on social geography to explore the respatialization of political power, using the notion of policy interplay across "scales" (see also Brenner 2004). Mundy, Verger, Martens, Jones, and others use the term "global governance" as a frame for highlighting the different forms of individual and institutional agency that play a role in constructing a nascent global policy. Drawing on international relations theories and political science, such scholars have attempted to bring greater focus to the organizational architecture that anchors global policy processes.

Researchers have also increasingly focused on the dynamics of policy learning and persuasion that surround global policy discourses, focusing on their uneven and differentiated outcomes (Grek *et al.* 2009; Ball 2012; Mundy and Murphy 2001; Olmedo 2013). Contestation and reinterpretation of policy occur across global/national and national/provincial/local relations in educational systems, and work very differently in relation to developed and developing nations. Networked governance, the localization of global policies, and the continuous reinterpretation and construction of the promise of educational progress by actors at all levels of the global polity are among the key issues raised in this volume.

Convergence, Divergence, Coercion – Borrowing or Learning?

Among the key questions addressed in this volume are why, how, and to what extent national governments have been induced to allow the globalization of policy in an area widely regarded as a national preserve. Empirical research in the global education policy field suggests that national institutions and domestic politics are key to understanding, on the one hand, the uneven level of diffusion and penetration of global education policy ideas in different territories, and, on the other, the re-contextualization and (on occasion) the drastic transformation of such global ideas within local institutions, networks of rules, and local practices. How far policy and practice are actually converging globally as a result of these multiple processes is still much disputed within the literature on global educational change, and judgment depends to some degree on what level of policy and practice is being considered.

Dale (1999) has attempted to document the mechanisms through which policy ideas from international organizations influence national, provincial, and local policies in education, namely, imposition, harmonization, dissemination, standardization, and interdependence. Imposition works through funding conditionalities. International organizationss (as well as powerful states) impose their policy preferences on low-income and/or financially dependent countries via loan conditionalities, debt cancellation, and trade agreements, among other mechanisms (Dale 1999). Harmonization occurs when groups of nations agree to implement common policies in a specific policy domain; think here of the Bologna process in higher education in the EU. Dissemination is the exhortatory or suasion approach to influence and works through examples of best practice and the like (Simons 2014). Standardization is another important mechanism and can be seen in the international comparative testing work of the OECD and the IEA. Tests such as PISA, TIMSS, and PIRLS help constitute the globe as a commensurate space of measurement, creating what we might see as an epistemological mode of global governance through the alignment of global and national epistemic communities and learning standards (Sellar and Lingard 2013a; 2013b; 2014). Interdependence is another mechanism through which the influence of international organizations has effects within national and provincial policies and policy-making, for example, through globally established targets such as with Education for All (Verger *et al*. 2012; Benavot *et al*., Chapter 13, this volume).

One compelling answer to the question of why countries respond to global policies, at least in relation to the more developed countries, is that by the 1980s many national governments were experiencing similar dilemmas with respect to their education systems for which they sought new solutions. Many governments embraced public sector reform ideas developed by international bodies such as the OECD in the hope that they would address these problems, or at least provide the impression that policy-makers had solutions (Pal and Ireland 2009). Here, international organizations, more than imposing policies, would work as forums that, in an apparently technical and neutral way, helped countries to identify (and consequently to emulate) the education strategies of the most successful performers (see Schleicher and Zoido, Chapter 20, this volume). Less developed countries often had less choice in the matter, since aid from international organizations is often tied to the adoption of policies favored by these organizations and their most powerful members. But even, and perhaps especially, in these cases policy-makers have been prone to the voluntary adoption of the discourses of global policy, either because they lacked experience of effective national policy-making themselves and had no other solutions, or because using the language of global policy added political credibility, even where the policies could not, or would not, be actually implemented.

However, such a highly rationalistic and voluntary portrait of national engagement in global policy processes has been much disputed in the empirical literature. Sociological institutionalism and world culture theory agree with the broad argument made by rationalists about global policy convergence, but are skeptical about the mechanisms that drive such convergence. Rather than an aggregation of goal-oriented rational choices by well-informed policy-makers, sociological institutionalism argues that countries adopt global policies not necessarily because they need them, or because they are effective, but as a result of the "transmission of cultural practices" (Hall and Taylor 1996, 14) and the legitimation pressures that governments receive to demonstrate to the international community that they are building a "modern state" (Drezner 2001). In comparative education, world culture theory argues that a single global model of schooling has spread around the world, to a great extent due to the voluntary adhesion of countries to global standards (including human rights, the environment, or transparency) that prescribe for governments the most appropriate ways of organizing their educational systems (see Ramirez *et al.*, Chapter 2, this volume). Despite being criticized for oversimplifying global diffusion dynamics (cf. Carney *et al.* 2012), some of the claims of world culture theory about isomorphism are warranted; countries, for instance, do indeed increasingly adopt globalized curricula and utilize policy discourses that make reference to human rights, accountability regimes, gender equality, norms of international citizenship, environmental sustainability and so on. Bromley, in Chapter 26 of this volume, adopts such an approach to understand the global dissemination of managerialism in education. According to her, important elements of global educational administration and policy are best understood through a cultural lens, including a focus on cultural rationalization processes through which the appropriate and legitimate behavior of individuals in the context of organizations is being redefined globally.

The idea that globalization has spawned policy convergence is one that continues to generate much debate among education policy scholars. Skeptics argue that convergence at the level of discourse does not equate to true enactment of converging policies – that is to say, in common patterns of resource allocation, institution building and reform. For example, Carnoy, in Chapter 1 of this volume, maintains that most countries have more political and financial space to drive how globalization is brought into education than hyperglobalist theories, including world culture theory, claim. Much recent empirical work in comparative education has focused on the ways in which policies change as they travel across different political, social, and geographic contexts, and how they are variously and uniquely taken up in national policy settings. According to Peck and Theodore (2010, 170), global policies mutate during their journeys; they "rarely travel as complete packages, they move in bits and pieces – as selective discourses, inchoate ideas, and synthesized models – and they therefore 'arrive' not as replicas but as policies already-in-transformation."

Steiner-Khamsi (2004 and Chapter 32, this volume) uses the terms "indigenization" and "policy-borrowing" to capture the strong role of national and subnational players in shaping engagement with global policy ideas (Steiner-Khamsi 2004); while others focus on the "vernacularization" of global policies (Rizvi and Lingard 2010; see also Chapters 31 and, 28, this volume). Research on policy borrowing and lending has shown how governments strategically focus on the adoption of those external recommendations that are closest to their particular preferences.

Low-income countries tend to adopt the language of the powerful in order to have access to international resources, and use the supposed neutrality of global policies to legitimate their own political agendas at the domestic level (Steiner-Khamsi 2004; 2012). Such research highlights the fact that it is quite likely that the same globalized policies can lead to continuing policy differentiation between countries, and groups of countries, where national policy-makers adopt only those international policies which are deemed politically and culturally "sympathetic" and which produce the best fit, given their national institutional and political histories and traditions.

Historical institutionalism – an approach that emphasizes the path dependencies locked in by national institutions (Hall and Taylor 1996) – is a framework taken up by many education policy scholars to explore how the political architecture of a country can work in a very different – and even contradictory – way when it comes to retaining new education reform ideas (Fulge et al., Chapter 25 this volume; Takayama 2012; Simola et al. 2013; Verger 2014). In this vein, the "varieties of capitalism" approach adopted by Busemeyer and Vossiek in Chapter 8 of this volume, suggests that "existing socio-economic institutions shape the skill formation strategies of businesses and households, which in turn leads to the development of different kinds of national innovation strategies." Thus, policy convergence has not resulted from common global economic pressures. Particular features of a state's political architecture, including federal or unitary structure, the role and presence of veto points, and the level of independence between the executive and legislative branches of government, can also be key to understanding the uneven adoption of globally supported policy reforms – as for example in the case of voucher reforms, where liberal countries such as the US and the UK (who share an apparent positive ideological predisposition toward market reforms) have taken up less ambitious voucher schemes than a social-democratic country such as Sweden (Klitgaard 2008; Wiborg 2013).

That patterns of convergence or divergence in adoption of global policies are highly idiosyncratic is further highlighted by a recent study of 25 OECD countries by Green and Mostafa (2013). This study found that not only is there no significant convergence in 13 of 25 policy arenas measured, trends were also often not in the direction predicted in global education policy discourses. For instance, countries were converging on greater centralization of decision-making (as opposed to school autonomy); in reducing inequality among learners (in terms of learning outcomes); and in increasing the proportion of schools that were fully publicly funded – while increasing private resourcing of higher education. Overall the authors conclude that, although there are many areas where real convergence has been apparent, there are many others where there has been no convergence, and even in some cases divergence. Much of what is considered as "convergence" in the literature is either only a convergence at the level of general policy rhetoric, or it is a case of countries traveling in the same general direction but, given their different starting points, remaining as far apart from each other as ever on any particular measure.

Key Actors and Debated Issues in Global Education Policy

A large share of the chapters in this volume concentrate on the evolution of international organizations and the global policy architecture and policy flows they anchor. In this section, we provide a brief overview of these organizations and some of the policy ideas – and policy debates – to which they have been central. As we have noted above, perhaps the two most influential global policy actors in education are the World Bank and the OECD. The influence, size, and technical sophistication of the education policy work undertaken by these two organizations far overshadows that conducted by UNESCO, the intergovernmental agency with the key mandate in global education policy.

By the 1980s, the World Bank had emerged as the single largest source of international finance for educational development, and as the most powerful global thought leader in education, particularly for developing countries. Heavily influenced by the USA, the Bank framed educational development as a set of strategic investments in human capital for purposes of economic growth, and has heavily promoted the use of market-like mechanisms and competition to ensure educational efficiency (Jones 1992; Jones and Coleman 2005; Mundy 2002; Resnik 2006; Woods 2000). In the 1980s and 1990s, the Bank was influential in designing a reform agenda for countries facing debt crises due to the loss of cheap international credit, advising governments around the world to restructure their education sectors by lowering subsidies to tertiary level education and introducing user fees at this level; and to introduce efficiency-driven reforms through the use of contract teachers, lowering of repetition rates, and enhanced parental and community "participation" in school level costs (Hinchliffe 1993; World Bank 1988; 1995).

The OECD emerged as a key educational policy player in the context of competition between the Soviet Union and the USA, which helped to produce a strong strategic interest in strengthening educational systems. Education, however, initially had an inferred role in the OECD's work (Papadopoulos 1994) and did not have a separate Directorate (Directorate of Education and Skills) until 2002. Building upon the foundation of voluntary collaboration and mutual problem solving, from the 1970s onward the OECD was able to encourage governments to fund new joint ventures – including the creation of standardized performance benchmarks of education systems, and somewhat later, the development of voluntary programs of international assessment and cross-national comparison among Western educational systems, which members opted into and paid for themselves (Papadopoulos 1994; Lingard and Sellar, Chapter 19, this volume). The ascendance of education at the OECD began in the mid-1990s with the ratification of new policy positions on lifelong learning and knowledge economies and the creation of the Indicators of Education Systems (INES) program and the publication of *Education at a Glance* (Henry et al. 2001). Resnik (2006) has shown how the voluntary membership in intergovernmental organizations like the OECD taught member governments to "think" about the relationship between education and the economy in new ways – in terms of investment in human capital for greater economic growth, rather than as simply a social service. First administered in 2000, the OECD's PISA program, along with the testing work of IEA, pioneered the voluntary engagement of nation states in international benchmarking of educational outcomes, a phenomenon that is spreading rapidly to other regional organizations, such as the EU, where joint educational initiatives have grown substantially (Lawn and Grek 2012; Grek 2013). By modeling a new approach to doing education policy "by numbers" in ways that limit more direct engagement of citizens in educational decision-making, the OECD (many education policy scholars argue) has played a crucial role in the emergence of neo-liberal global policies for education (Dale and Robertson 2002; Henry *et al.* 2001).

Yet, as Lingard and Sellar and Fulge *et al.* show in Chapters 19 and 25 of this volume, it would be wrong to conceptualize the OECD as holding uncontested or unmediated power over educational policies in member and non-member countries. There is both contestation within the OECD itself and mediation in the take-up and impact of its policies. The OECD's policy recommendations can be mediated by strong local policy coalitions to produce enormous variation in the uptake of specific policies (Martens and Jakobi 2010; Martens and Wolf 2009; Bieber and Martens 2011). Furthermore, in the education sector, when compared to the World Bank, the OECD has often taken a stronger stance on equity issues, and appears at times to be more closely aligned to social welfare state democracy than to neo-liberalism – for example, in its championing of the educational systems of Finland and Canada as models for high equity systems;in its work on early childhood education and the education of migrant populations (Mahon, Chapter 12, this volume; see also Mahon 2010; Mahon and McBride 2008; OECD 2006; 2012); and in its advocacy of education as a vehicle for enhancing social capital and social cohesion (see Green and Janmaat, Chapter 9, this volume). In tandem with the European Commission, the OECD also offered a novel solution to the challenges of economic globalization through the development of the concept of lifelong learning (European Commission 1995; 2001; OECD 1996).

Though the OECD and the World Bank form the institutional anchors of the new global policy architecture in education, it is important to recognize that this architecture is thicker – and much more diverse – than a focus on these two organizations might suggest. Among intergovernmental actors, the United Nations and its specialized agencies UNESCO and UNICEF continue to play a critical role in advancing the notion of education as a fundamental human right, often challenging more economistic approaches to education policy. UNICEF developed its own distinctive approach to educational development during the 1960s, targeting marginalized children and developing programs such as its "child friendly schools" initiative, which links education to children's rights and which spawned a large community of non-governmental child rights activities (Black 1996; Phillips 1987; Jolly 1991). These UN agencies are largely responsible – alongside the recently formed Global Partnership for Education – for the development and evolution of a global "education for all" movement that is highlighted in chapters in this volume by Aaron Benevot and members of the UNESCO Education For All Global Monitoring Report team (Chapter 13), as well as by Menashy and Manion (Chapter 17, comparing UNICEF and UNESCO), Unterhalter (Chapter 6, on gender) and Bajaj and Kudwai (Chapter 11, on education rights) (see also, Chabbott 2003; Mundy 2010).

An important aspect of this new era of global educational governance has been the rise of non-state actors as significant players on the global stage. As Mundy and Murphy (2001) and others have shown, transnational advocacy networks on such issues as human rights, debt relief, official development assistance reform, and anti-globalization have frequently taken up the issue of the universal right to education as one part of their broader advocacy efforts. Transnational advocates played substantive roles in pressing OECD governments to support a global debt relief initiative (the Highly Indebted Poor Country Initiative), which provided the fiscal space for many governments to rapidly expand access to primary schooling (Hinchliffe 2004). They have played a critical role in stimulating public awareness of gender equity in education; often working in concert with UN based organizations (see Unterhalter, Chapter 6, this volume). Transnational advocates have been active too in protesting the inclusion of educational services in the liberalization supported by the World Trade Organization's (WTO) General Agreement on Trade in Services (GATS) where, according to Verger (2010), they shaped the degree to which policies promoting the liberalization of international trade in educational services have been adopted by nations. There are also many instances in which national civil society has effectively utilized the global framing of education as a human right to protest the educational policies of their home governments: in Chile, for example, during the 2011 student led movement for equitable access to higher education and in the 2013 movement for social equity in Brazil. Verger and Novelli (2012) provide similar examples in their study of national education coalitions in low and middle-income countries. Chapter 22, by Macpherson in this volume, compares two non-state actors in education – the Global Campaign for Education (GCE) and Inter-Agency Network for Education in Emergencies, the former of which played an important role in a successful campaign to abolish primary school user charges in Tanzania and other African states.

Perhaps in tension with the rising consensus about basic education as a global public good worthy of official intergovernmental action has been the rise of transnational actors engaged in expanding the market for educational services. The creation of the WTO and GATS, alongside the rapid expansion of demand for certain kinds of educational services (particularly technology training, and higher education), have opened new opportunities for cross-border provision by transnational corporations and higher education institutions, which in turn press for liberalized access to educational markets (Verger 2010; Bhanji 2008; 2012; Ball 2012; Au and Ferrare 2015). Robertson *et al.* (2006), among others have noted how the efforts to liberalize higher education dovetail with a new emphasis on international rankings and quality assurance in higher education, spearheaded and supported by both international organizations and private actors (see also Robertson *et al.* 2012). Bhanji has documented the role played in particular by software corporations in shaping a new global marketplace of education and training services (2008; 2012; and Chapter 23 in this volume). Less well known is the development of a significant transnational network promoting low-fee private schooling as an alternative to publicly provided education, which brings together new players, including among others the Pearson corporation (a leading provider of educational services and materials), the Omidyar Foundation, and the private sector arm of the World Bank, the International Finance Corporation (Verger 2012; Ball 2012; Nambissan and Ball 2012; Mundy and Menashy 2012), and which promote the expansion of private education in many parts of the world. In Africa, it is contributing to schooling in rural communities, but mostly through low-quality education services provided by small-scale entrepreneurs. The rise of new, technologically enabled educational services – think, for example, of the Massive Open Online Courses (MOOCs) – will no doubt intensify the opportunities for for-profit entrepreneurship in trans-border educational services, deepening the challenges to territorially based education systems.

The current and potential role of emergent world powers is an area ripe for further attention in the study of global education policy. Since 2000, several of the most powerful emergent economies have established bilateral programs of foreign aid for education – including among others, China, Russia, Brazil, Turkey, India, South Africa, and South Korea, as well as some countries in the Middle East. Many of these emergent powers are also longstanding members of the major multilateral organizations engaged in education, where they have been active in calling for governance reforms to reflect the changing balance of power between Western and non-Western nations. These rising powers are primarily focused on expanding their spheres of geopolitical influence on a bilateral basis. Characterized by sharply differing national approaches to economic and social development, they share a limited appetite for international regimes that constrain national sovereignty (including in such putatively domestic spheres as education).

Yet the growing voice of emergent economies in global decision-making is illustrated by the development of the Group of 20 (G20), which has now replaced the G8 as key global summit on world financial and economic matters. As Kumar (2010) explains, emergent economic powers have insisted that the G20 officially adopt "international development" as a specific area of attention, despite the preference among Western industrialized governments that the G20 concentrate primarily on global financial and economic governance. However, the only reference to education in recent G20 communiques refers to education for economic development and skills formation, reflecting a focus on working together to advance science, technology, and skills to advance their own economic competitiveness. Furthermore, the tendency of emerging powers to tie foreign aid to their own economic self-interest – particularly in resource-rich African countries – suggests that they may contribute more to the erosion of the existing "global compact" than to its amplification (Nordveit 2011; Brautigam 2010; Gu et al. 2008; Bracht 2013; Rodrik 2013; Cammack 2011; Woods 2008).

Overview of the Volume

This Handbook is being launched during a period of world history that has been described as one of "leaderless" globalization – a period in which the USA and the Western world are losing their unique ascendance. Yet as illustrated by chapters throughout this volume, the reach of a distinctly Anglo-American global imaginary for education has retained its power in almost every domain of global educational policy. Because of this context, the Handbook pays particular attention to new actors and new forms of agency and contestation that have the potential to re-envisage and reshape the future of education policies around the world. In doing so, the volume explores not only global level policy discourses, but also regional and national dimensions of policy diffusion, borrowing, learning, and debate.

The Handbook is organized into four sections, each with its own short introduction. In *Section 1: Education and a Global Polity*, chapters focus on broad trends and drivers of educational change over the past half-century. Chapters in *Section 2: Educational Issues and Challenges* look at a range of issue arenas for global educational policy, ranging from early childhood education to higher education, and including such debated topics as teachers' work, social cohesion, and the right to education. *Section 3: Global Policy Actors in Education* takes a closer look at key policy actors, with chapters on the United Nations, the World Bank, the OECD, ASEAN, the private sector, and civil society. A final section, entitled *Critical Directions in the Study of Global Education Policy*, introduces cutting edge approaches to the study of global education policy, highlighting the vibrant theoretical and methodological debates and experimentation that have accompanied new efforts to conceptualize research on global education policy.

References

Anderson, B. 1991. *Imagined Communities: Reflections on the Origin and Spread of Nationalism*. London: Verso.

Appadurai, A. 1996. *Modernity at Large: Cultural Dimensions of Globalization*. Minneapolis: The University of Minnesota Press.

Au, W. and Ferrare, J. (eds). 2015. *Mapping Corporate Education Reform: Power and Policy Networks in the Neoliberal State*. New York: Routledge.

Ball, S.J. 1994. *Education Reform: A Critical and Post-Structural Approach*. Buckingham: Open University Press.

Ball, S.J. 2012. *Global Education Inc.: New Policy Networks and the Neo-Liberal Imaginary*. London: Routledge.

Ball, S.J. 2013. *The Education Debate* (second edition). Bristol: Policy Press.

Ball, S.J. and C. Junemann. 2012. *Networks, New Governance and Education*. Bristol: The Policy Press.

Ball, S.J., A. Braun, and M. Maguire. 2012. *How Schools Do Policy: Policy Enactment in Secondary Schools*. London: Routledge.

Bhanji, Z. 2008. "Transnational Corporations in Education: Filling the Governance Gap Through New Social Norms and Market Multilaterialism?" *Globalisation, Societies and Education*, 6(1): 55–73.

Bhanji, Z. 2012. "Transnational Private Authority in Education Policy in Jordan and South Africa: The Case of Microsoft Corporation." *Comparative Education Review*, 56(2): 300–319.

Bieber, T. and K. Martens. 2011. "The OECD PISA Study as a Soft Power in Education? Lessons from Switzerland and the U.S." *European Journal of Education*, 46(1): 101–116.

Black, M. 1996. *Children First: The Story of UNICEF, Past, Present and Future*. Oxford: Oxford University Press.

Bourdieu, P. 2003. *Firing Back; Against the Tyranny of the Market*. London: Verso.

Bracht, C. 2013, May, 8. "Will the BRICS Delivery a More Just World Order?" *Guardian Weekly*. Retrieved from: www.guardian.co.uk/global-development-professionals-network/2013/may/08/brics-development-bank (accessed November 2, 2015).

Brautigam, D. 2010. China, Africa and the International Aid Architecture. *Working Paper No. 107*. Abidjan, Cote d'Ivoire: African Development Bank Group.

Brenner, N. 2004. *New State Spaces: Urban Governance and the Rescaling of Statehood*. Oxford: Oxford University Press.

Brown, P, A. Green, and H. Lauder. 2001. *High Skills: Globalization, Competitiveness and Skills Formation*. Oxford University Press.

Cammack, P. 2011. "The G20, the Crisis, and the Rise of Global Developmental Liberalism." *Third World Quarterly*, 33(1): 1–16.

Carney, S. 2009. "Negotiating Policy in an Age of Globalization: Exploring Educational 'Policyscapes' in Denmark, Nepal and China." *Comparative Education Review*, 53(1): 63–88.

Carney, S., J. Rappleye, and I. Silova. 2012. "Between Faith and Science: World Culture Theory and Comparative Education." *Comparative Education Review*, 56(3): 366–393.

Carnoy, M. 1999. *Globalization and Educational Reform: What Planners Need to Know.* Paris: UNESCO International Institute for Educational Planning.

Castells, M. 1996. *The Rise of the Network Society, The Information Age: Economy, Society and Culture Vol. I.* Oxford: Blackwell Publishers Inc.

Chabbott, C. 2003. *Constructing Education for Development: International Organizations and Education for All.* London: Routledge Falmer.

Dale, R. 1999. "Specifying Globalization Effects on National Policy: Focus on the Mechanisms." *Journal of Education Policy,* 14(1): 427–448.

Dale, R. and S.L. Robertson. 2002. "The Varying Effects of Regional Organizations as Subjects of Globalization of Education." *Comparative Education Review,* 46(1): 10–36.

Drezner, D.W. 2001. "Globalisation and Policy Convergence." *International Studies Review,* 3(1): 53–78.

European Commission. 1995. *White Paper: Teaching and Learning – Towards the Learning Society.* Brussels: European Commission.

European Commission. 2001. *A Memorandum on Lifelong Learning.* Brussels: European Commission.

Green, A. 1997. *Education, Globalization and the Nation State.* London: Macmillan.

Green, A. 2003. "The Many Faces of Lifelong Learning: Recent Education Policy Trends in Europe." *Journal of Education Policy,* 17(6): 611–626.

Green, A. 2013. *Education and State Formation: Europe, East Asia and the USA. Revised and Extended Second Edition.* Basingstoke: Palgrave MacMillan.

Green, A. and T. Mostafa. 2013. "The Dynamics of Education Systems: Convergent and Divergent Trends, 1990 to 2010," in *The Dynamics and Social Consequences of Education Systems,* edited by J.G. Janmaat, M. Duru-Bellat, A. Green, and P. Mehaut, 160–181. London: Palgrave Macmillan.

Grek, S. 2013. "Expert Moves: International Comparative Testing and the Rise of Expertocracy." *Journal of Education Policy,* 28(5): 695–709.

Grek, S., M. Lawn, B. Lingard, J. Ozga, R. Rinne, C. Segerholm, and H. Simola. 2009. "National Policy Brokering and the Construction of the European Education Space in England, Sweden, Finland and Scotland." *Comparative Education,* 45(1): 5–21.

Gu, J., J. Humphrey, and D. Messner. 2008. "Global Governance and Developing Countries: The Implications of the Rise of China." *World Development,* 36(2): 274–292.

Hall, P.A., and R.C.R. Taylor. 1996. "Political science and the three new institutionalisms." *Political Studies,* 44(5): 936–957.

Hanushek, E. and L. Woessmann. 2010. *The Economics of International Differences in Educational Achievement.* NBER Working Paper 15949. Cambridge, MA: NBER.

Harvey, D. 1989. The Condition of Post-Modernity: An Enquiry into the Conditions of Cultural Change. Oxford: Wiley-Blackwell.

Held, D., A. McGrew, D. Goldblatt, and T. Perraton. 1999. *Global Transformations: Politics, Economics and Culture.* Cambridge: Polity Press.

Henry, M., B. Lingard, F. Rizvi, and S. Taylor. 2001. *The OECD, Globalisation and Education Policy.* Oxford: Pergamon Press.

Hinchliffe, K. 1993. "Neo-Liberal Prescriptions for Education Finance: Unfortunately Necessary or Inherently Desirable?" *International Journal of Educational Development,* 13(2): 183–187.

Hinchliffe, K. 2004. *Notes on the HIPC Debt Initiative on Education and Health Public Expenditure in African Countries.* African Human Development Department. Washington DC: World Bank.

Jakobi, A.P. 2009. "Global Education Policy in the Making: International Organisations and Lifelong Learning." *Globalisation, Societies and Education,* 7(4): 473–487.

Jolly, R. 1991. "Adjustment With a Human Face: A Unicef Record and Perspective on the 1980s." *World Development,* 19(12): 1807–1821.

Jones, P. 1992. *World Bank Financing of Education: Lending, Learning and Development.* New York: Routledge.

Jones, P.W. and D. Coleman. 2005. *The United Nations and Education: Multilateralism and Globalisation.* New York: Routledge Falmer.

Klitgaard, M.B. 2008. "School Vouchers and the New Politics of the Welfare State." *Governance*, 21(4): 479–498.

Koppenjan, J. and E. Klijn. 2004. *Managing Uncertainties in Networks: Public Private Controversies.* London: Routledge.

Kumar, R. 2010. A Development Agenda for the G20. *Policy brief prepared for the European Think-Tank for Global Action (FRIDE).* Retrieved from: http:// fride.org/download/PB_G20_6_eng_A_development_agenda_for_the_G20.pdf (accessed November 2, 2015).

Lawn, M. and S. Grek. 2012. *Europeanizing Education: Governing a New Policy Space.* Oxford: Symposium Books.

Luke, A. and D. Hogan. 2006. "Redesigning What Counts as Evidence in Educational Policy: the Singapore Model," in *World Yearbook of Education 2006: Education Research and Policy: Steering the Knowledge-Based Economy*, edited by J. Ozga, T. Seddon, and T. Popkewitz, 170–184. London: Routledge.

Mahon, R. 2010. "After Neoliberalism? The OECD, the World Bank and the Child." *Global Social Policy*, 10(2): 172–192.

Mahon, R. and S. McBride. 2008. *The OECD and Transnational Governance.* Vancouver: University of British Columbia Press.

Martens, K. and A.P. Jakobi. 2010. *Mechanisms of OECD Governance: International Incentives for National Policy Making?* Oxford: Oxford University Press.

Martens, K. and K.D. Wolf. 2009. "Boomerangs and Trojan Horses: The Unintended Consequences of Internationalising Education Policy through the EU and the OECD," in *European Integration and the Governance of Higher Education and Research*, edited by A. Amaral, G. Neave, C. Musselin, and P. Maassen, 81–107. Dordrecht: Springer.

Mundy, K. 1998. "Educational Multilateralism and World (Dis)Order." *Comparative Education Review*, 42(4): 448–478.

Mundy, K. 2002. "Education in a Reformed World Bank." *International Journal of Educational Development*, 22(5): 483–508.

Mundy, K. 2010. "Paradoxes and Prospects: Moving Beyond the Study of Foreign Aid." *Current Issues in Comparative Education*, 13(1): 51–55.

Mundy, K. and F. Menashy. 2012. "The Role of the International Finance Corporation in the Promotion of Public Private Partnerships for Educational Development," in *Public Private Partnerships in Education: New Actors and Modes of Governance in a Globalising World*, edited by S. Robertson, K. Mundy, A. Verger, and F. Menashy, 81–103. London: Edward Elgar.

Mundy, K. and L. Murphy. 2001. "Transnational Advocacy, Global Civil Society? Emerging Evidence from the Field of Education." *Comparative Education Review*, 45(1): 85–126.

Nambissan, G.B. and S.J. Ball. 2010. "Advocacy Networks, Choice and Private Schooling of the Poor in India." *Global Networks*, 10(3): 324–343.

Nordveit, B.H. 2011. "An Emerging Donor in Education and Development: A Case Study of China in Cameroon." *International Journal of Educational Development*, 31(2): 99–108.

Novoa, A. 2002. "Ways of Thinking about Education in Europe," in *Fabricating Europe: The Formation of an Education Space*, edited by A. Novoa and M. Lawn, 131–155. London: Kluwer.

OECD. 1996. *Lifelong Learning for All.* Paris: OECD.

OECD. 2006. *Measuring the Effects of Education on Health and Civic Engagement.* Proceedings of the Copenhagen Symposium. Paris. OECD.

OECD. 2012. *Better Skills, Better Jobs, Better Lives: A Strategic Approach to Skills Policy.* Paris: OECD.

Olmedo, A. 2013. "Policy-makers, Market Advocates and Edu-businesses: New and Renewed Players in the Spanish Education Policy Arena." *Journal of Education Policy*, 28(1): 55–76.

Pal, L.A. and D. Ireland. 2009. "The Public Sector Reform Movement: Mapping the Global Policy Network." *International Journal of Public Administration*, 32(8): 621–657.

Papadopoulos, G. 1994. *Education 1960–1990: The OECD Perspective*. Paris: OECD.

Peck, J. and N. Theodore. 2010. "Mobilizing Policy: Models, Methods, and Mutations." *Geoform*, 41(2): 169–174.

Phillips, H.M. 1987. *Unicef and Education: A Historical Perspective*. New York: UNICEF.

Piketty, T. (2014) *Capital in the Twenty-First Century*. Cambridge: The Belknap Press of Harvard University Press.

Resnik, J. 2006. "Bringing International Organizations Back in: The 'Education-Economic Growth' Black Box and its Contribution to the World Education Culture. *Comparative Education Review*, 50(2): 173–195.

Rizvi, F. and B. Lingard. 2010. *Globalizing Education Policy*. London: Routledge.

Robertson, S., X. Bonal, and R. Dale. 2002. "GATS and the Education Services Industry: The Politics of Scale and Global Reterritorialisation." *Comparative Education Review*, 46(4): 472–496.

Robertson, S., X. Bonal, and R. Dale. 2006. "GATS and the Education Service Industry: The Politics of Scale and Global Reterritorialization," in *Education, Globalization and Social Change*, edited by H. Lauder, P. Brown, J. Dillabough, and A.H. Halsey, 228–246. Oxford: Oxford University Press.

Robertson, S., K. Mundy, A. Verger, and F. Menashy (eds). 2014. *Public Private Partnerships in Education: New Actors and Modes of Governance in a Globalising World*. London: Edward Elgar.

Rodrik, D. 2013. Leaderless Global Governance. *Project Syndicate: A World of Ideas*. Retrieved from: www.project-syndicate.org/commentary/leaderless-global-governance (accessed November 2, 2015).

Ruggie, J.G. 1982. "International Regimes, Transactions, and Change: Embedded Liberalism in the Postwar Economic Order." *International Organization*, 36: 379–415.

Ruggie, J.G. (1993). "Territoriality and Beyond: Problematizing Modernity in International Relations." *International Organization*, 47: 139–174.

Sahlberg, P. 2011. *Finnish Lessons: What Can the World Learn from Educational Change in Finland?* New York: Teachers' College Press.

Sellar, S. and B. Lingard. 2013a. "Looking East: Shanghai, PISA 2009 and the Reconstitution of Reference Societies in the Global Education Policy Field." *Comparative Education*, 49(4): 464–485.

Sellar, S. and B. Lingard. 2013b. "The OECD and Global Governance in Education." *Journal of Education Policy*, 28(5): 710–725.

Sellar, S. and B. Lingard. 2014. "The OECD and the Expansion of PISA: New Global Modes of Governance in Education," *British Educational Research Journal*, 40(6): 917–936.

Simola, H., R. Rinne, J. Varjo, and J. Kauko. 2013. "The Paradox of the Education Race: How to Win the Ranking Game by Sailing to Headwind." *Journal of Education Policy*, 28(5): 612–633.

Simons, M. 2014. "Governing Education Without Reform: The Power of the Example." *Discourse: Studies in the Cultural Politics of Education*, 36(5): 712–731.

Steiner-Khamsi, G. 2004. *The Global Politics of Educational Borrowing and Lending*. New York: Teachers' College Press.

Steiner-Khamsi, G. 2012. "Understanding Policy Borrowing and Lending: Building Comparative Policy Studies," in *World Yearbook of Education 2012: Policy Borrowing and Lending in Education*, edited by G. Steiner-Khamsi and F. Waldow, 3–17. New York: Routledge.

Takayama, K. 2012. "Exploring the Interweaving of Contrary Currents: Transnational Policy Enactments and Path-Dependent Policy Implementation in Australia and Japan." *Comparative Education*, 48(4): 505–523.

Taylor, S., F. Rizvi, B. Lingard, and M. Henry. 1997. *Educational Policy and the Politics of Change*. London: Routledge.

Verger, A. 2010. *WTO/GATS and the Global Politics of Higher Education*. London and New York: Routledge.

Verger, A. 2012. "Framing and Selling Global Education Policy: The Promotion of PPPs in Education in Low-Income Countries." *Journal of Education Policy*, 27(1): 109–130.

Verger, A. 2014. "Why do Policy-Makers Adopt Global Education Policies? Toward a Research Framework on the Varying Role of Ideas in Education Reform." *Current Issues in Comparative Education*, 16(2): 14–29.

Verger, A. and M. Novelli. 2012. *Campaigning for "Education for All": Histories, Strategies and Outcomes of Transnational Social Movements in Education*. Rotterdam: Sense.

Verger, A., M. Novelli, and H.K. Altinyelken. 2012. "Global Education Policy and international Development: An Introductory Framework," in *Global Education Policy and International Development: New Agendas, Issues and Policies*, edited by A. Verger, M. Novelli, and H.K. Altinyelken, 3–31. London: Continuum.

Wiborg, S. 2013. "Neo-Liberalism and Universal State Education: The Cases of Denmark, Norway and Sweden 1980–2011." *Comparative Education*, 49(4): 407–423

Woods, N. 2000. "The Challenge of Good Governance for the IMF and the World Bank Themselves." *World Development*, 28(5): 823–841.

Woods, N. 2008. "Whose Aid, Whose Influence? China, Emerging Donors and the Silent Revolution in Development Assistance." *International Affairs*, 84(6), 1–17.

World Bank. 1995. *Priorities and Strategies for Education*. Washington, DC: World Bank.

World Bank. 1988. *Education in Sub-Saharan Africa: Policies for Adjustment, Revitalization and Expansion*. Washington, DC: World Bank.

Part I Education and a Global Polity

Part I Introduction

Andy Green

Part I provides an introductory overview of the key contemporary debates concerning educational globalization and global education policy. The chapters consider the origins and drivers of educational globalization from the 1980s onwards; the processes through which global policy discourses emerge and are (selectively) adopted and transformed in national settings; and how far this is leading to convergence in education policy across the world. A number of chapters elaborate and evaluate some of the major theories and concepts that inform global education policy: including human capital theory and the role of skills in economic growth and poverty reduction; notions of educational quality, accountability, and good governance; and the discourses around privatization, cost-efficiency, and cost-sharing in education. Critical perspectives are offered on the dominant global policy discourses on human capital and gender equity in schooling; as well as on the claims made regarding the effectiveness of the policies of the global education reform movement on school accountability, diversity, and choice, and the use of competitive quasi-markets in education. The part ends with an examination of the evolution of the diverse types of skills formation systems found in Europe, thus returning the discussion to the questions raised in the first chapter about the continuing salience of national education policy-making in the face of policy globalization, and thus the limits of policy convergence.

    The first three chapters provide contrasting accounts of the processes of educational globalization. In the first chapter, **Martin Carnoy** explores the origins of educational globalization and the relation of global education policy to national decision-making in education. Assuming that policy-makers act rationally to achieve favored goals within given constraints, and that educational policies and objectives tend to be contested at the national level, Carnoy argues that global policy develops primarily due to different national elites adopting similar solutions to a number of common problems facing education in different countries. Ideological convergence amongst global elites also arises to some extent out of the diffusion of dominant notions of modernity, but only where these are functional to elite interests. Intensified global economic competition since the 1980s, and the rise of the global "knowledge economy," increases the importance of skills, research, and innovation in sustaining the national economic competitiveness upon which government legitimacy rests. At the same time governments face increasing budgetary pressures arising from the ageing of populations and the need to maintain internationally competitive taxation regimes. In order to meet the rising demand for skills and qualifications, from both students and enterprises, governments seek new ways to offset the rising costs of education to the state through various efficiency and cost sharing measures. Global policies for improving educational efficiency and quality – including through accountability regimes, the proliferation of educational testing, and the adoption of new technologies in education delivery – are adopted by national policy-makers as ways to solve these common problems. Yet, as Carnoy reminds us, national elites also have to respond to domestic political pressures, which can vary substantially between countries, and they may respond differently to the proffered global policy solutions. Global policy is thus adopted selectively, and not all policies converge at the national level.

The following chapter provides a quite different perspective on global policy development, which focuses less on different national contexts and attendant power relations that shape national responses to global policy. Writing within the tradition of World Culture Theory, **Francisco Ramirez, John Meyer, and Julia Lerch** present the development of global policy as a process of cultural diffusion, which they say is largely consensual and stateless in form. Global and national policy actors at different levels adopt similar policy discourses out of a desire to conform to global norms of modernity. In this model world society spontaneously develops a global discourse around the virtues of expanded, progressive, and internationalized education systems. Education is globally cast as a key to progress or excellence and justice or equality. Everywhere policy-makers promote increased participation at all levels of education; adopt curricula that seek to foster transnational citizenship and human rights; and adopt "dense" organizational control mechanisms to enhance the efficiency of their systems. A degree of "loose coupling" between global policy rhetoric and actual practice in national states is acknowledged as inevitable, but national variation in educational practice is seen not so much as evidence of continuing nation state efficacy in education policy-making, but rather as a necessary friction involved as powerful global policies are gradually infused into different contexts.

Antoni Verger reviews the variety of different perspectives on the emergence and adoption of global education policy, using privatization policy as a test case. Privatization policy – defined in its broadest terms to include private public partnerships and the contracting out of services, as well as full private ownership of schools – is taken to be an example of a pervasive global education reform approach that induces policy convergence at the national level, albeit around a broad array of policies. National policy-makers are seen to be key players in the process of global policy diffusion but Verger remains skeptical about rationalist claims that they act rationally and in the light of the evidence of what works. The normative emulation thesis of World Culture Theory pays attention to the power of ideas but is also criticized on the grounds that it takes insufficient account of the conflicting political interests at the national level and the processes through which global and national policy-making interact in setting education agendas. Drawing on theories of "critical constructivism" and "cultural political economy," which stress the power relations underlying policy choices, the bounded nature policy rationalism, and the salience of the "semiotics of policy adoption," Verger argues for a more detailed consideration of the interactions involved in the multi-scalar policy process and, particularly, for more attention to be paid to the complexities of policy adoption at the national level, with its key moments of policy selection, variation, and retention.

Chapter 4 addresses the key economic arguments underlying global education policy, in the form of the Human Capital Theory (HCT) claims about the contribution of skills to earnings, productivity, and growth. Reviewing the development of HCT and its impact on education policy since the 1960s, **Erik Hanushek** argues that economists wrongly assumed that schooling was the only source of learning and that the outcomes of learning that promote productivity and economic growth could be adequately measured by levels of school attainment or years of schooling. Substantial variation across countries in the quality of schooling meant that the measures were inadequate and, consequently, models based on them produced inconsistent results and the wrong policy conclusions. However, with the development of direct tests of skills – as in the International Association for the Evaluation of Educational Achievement (IEA) and Programme for International Student Assessment (PISA) surveys – it became possible to model the economic impact of the learning outcomes that matter most: cognitive skills. Summarizing his (and his co-authors') path-breaking findings on skills and growth from 2000 onwards, Hanushek shows that it is the cognitive skills of the adult population, rather than their school attainments, that are most powerfully related to individual earnings, income distribution, and economic growth. Using international data on skills and growth from 1960 to 2000, he shows that the impact of skills on economic growth is much higher than that of school attainment. After controlling for skills, years of higher education have no impact on growth in either developing or developed countries. Claiming that these relationships are causal – despite the still limited skills data for developing countries – Hanushek argues that the results have profound implications for education policy, making the question of school quality the central issue.

Xavier Bonal provides a critique of HCT and its influence on policy in Chapter 5 that ranges well beyond issues of measurement. This chapter provides a detailed account of the evolution of HCT and its effects on global policies for poverty reduction since the 1960s, criticizing many of its core premises and the policies they have supported. From the start, argues Bonal, HCT made unsupported assumptions about human behavior and failed to take due account of the effects of institutions. At the micro level, the rational choice models of individual decision-making it employed ignored the influence of culture and non-instrumental determinants of individual decision-making, consequently underestimating the barriers to rational individual investments in skills. At the macro level, it initially failed to take account of market imperfections and institutional failures, which would also undermine the assumptions on human capital investment. These flawed assumptions, argues Bonal, underpinned the limited range of World Bank polices on education and development – including the narrow priority given to investment in basic education, the heavy promotion of private sector involvement, and the stress on decentralization and cost-recovery policies – which were to have devastating effects. Policies for education and poverty reduction failed to address the central issue of inequality and had little effect. In the era of the "post-Washington consensus," argues Bonal, there has been a growing recognition of market imperfections and of the importance of institutions and good governance, and development policies are more sensitive to issues of inequality and social cohesion. However, there has remained a reluctance to introduce radical changes in policy, with pro-equity measures still based on a flawed market logic.

Chapter 6 shifts the discussion to gender and education and the connected area of girl's schooling, which, according to the author, constitute a field in which a nexus of relationships amongst disparate organizations have formed a global policy discourse stretching over many decades. **Elaine Unterhalter** provides a wide-ranging account of the shifts in policy discourse going back to the late 18th century. The chapter charts three distinct but overlapping phases, each characterized by particular formulations of ideas, and differing relationships of activists, state governments, and transnational organizations, which precipitate particular actions. The first phase, termed the women's rights phase, which stretches from the late 18th century, has its high point around the Beijing Conference on women in 1995 and then fragments into different strands of women's rights movements. The second phase, which concentrates on girls' access to schooling, begins around 1990 with the building of the Education for All (EFA) movement at the Jomtien conference, has a high point around 2000, the year of the adoption of an EFA goal on gender equality and girls' schooling and the presentation of gender parity in schooling as an indicator of women's empowerment in the Millennium Development Goal (MDG) framework. The third phase appears in a policy declaration in 2010, although its roots lie in the 1980s and 1990s. This is termed the "Beyond Access" phase, to signal that it is concerned with issues that emerge beyond the point of access to school. The analysis suggests different meanings of gender equity in education are struggled over, sometimes taking a direction that confronts injustice and the structures of subordination, but sometimes only dealing superficially with these relationships and weakening actions for change.

Next, Chapter 7, by **Pasi Sahlberg,** describes the origins, policies, and impact of what he calls the Global Education Reform Movement (GERM). Like Martin Carnoy, he sees the origins of the globalization of education policy as being located in the 1980s, when the education "superpowers" – including England, the USA, France, Germany, the Netherlands, and Sweden – came to doubt whether their education systems were adequate for them to lead the way in innovation and economic competitiveness. The 1983 *A Nation at Risk* report in the USA sounded the alarm bells, but, according to Sahlberg, it was the 1988 Education Reform Act in the UK that provided the blueprint for further large-scale school reforms in North America, Europe, and the Asia-Pacific, and the English-speaking countries continued to be the main conduit for reforms. These all followed a simple quasi-market logic whereby standards would be driven up by increased competition between schools made possible by greater school diversity and choice, more public information on schools, and greater school autonomy. With greater autonomy for schools, there followed the need for more accountability provided by standardized national testing of students, teacher appraisal, and merit-based pay systems. The paradoxical result of these reforms was a generalized standardization of learning which, argues Sahlberg, narrows the freedom and flexibility of schools to teach in ways which make sense to them, prevents teachers from experimentation, and reduces the use of alternative pedagogic approaches. As evidence that the policies have not worked, Sahlberg invokes the trend data from PISA, which show that in the seven countries that he claims have adopted GERM policies most fully (Australia, Canada, England, the

Netherlands, New Zealand, Sweden, and the USA) average achievements in numeracy declined between 2000 and 2012. The chapter ends by noting that most of the recent educational success stories have been in countries like Finland, South Korea, and Singapore, which have not generally followed the GERM prescriptions for school improvement, and by calling for an alternative reform agenda to promote quality and equity based on teacher professionalism, relations of trust within schools, and collaboration between schools.

The final chapter in Part I, by **Marius Busemeyer and Janis Vossiek**, returns to the dilemma of policy convergence and national system variation raised in the first chapter, arguing that existing institutions and historical legacies prevent full-scale global convergence. Drawing on the theories of institutional path dependency developed within "historical institutionalism" and the Varieties of Capitalism school, the chapter analyses the variant institutional logics that underlie different types of skills formation system. Focusing on the recent developments in the contrasting systems in the "coordinated market economy" of Germany and the "liberal market economy" of the UK, the authors find continuing evidence of path dependent change, even through an era of globalization, indicating a mixed pattern of institutional change and stability. The authors challenge the notion that only neo-liberal institutional forms can flourish in a global world, arguing that globalization is likely to contribute to the rise of new institutional hybrids rather than to full-scale convergence.

Chapter 1

Educational Policies in the Face of Globalization: Whither the Nation State?

Martin Carnoy

The role of the national state in shaping national economic and social policy has, according to both academics and popular thinking, been sharply constrained by economic globalization (e.g. Castells 1997; Friedman 1999; Giddens 2002). Another line of argument is that globalization is producing "convergence" in norms and values (institutional culture) concerning human rights and social policies, such as equity, norms of social efficiency, and democracy (Meyer et al. 1992; 1997). Of particular interest to us is whether and how the constraints and influences imposed by economic globalization and ideological convergence apply to educational policy-making and the shape of educational systems themselves.

In this chapter, I restate an argument I made a number of years ago (Carnoy 2000) that economic globalization does indeed put new pressures on national states. I contend that competition generated by new rising economic players in the system and the specialized skills demanded by high value information technology, financial services, and organizational innovation services induce national states to expand their educational systems, particularly higher education.

Second, I argue that ideological convergence as developed in the world system approach to institutional change is partly the result of spreading elite notions of "modernity," but that these elite notions of modernity develop and spread because they are functional to elite interests, including reproduction of elite power and specific economic interests. Particular reforms of educational systems are also promoted by international agencies representing those interests but also incorporating their own "non-profit" economic interests. That is, "convergence" may appear to emerge from the autonomous diffusion of institutional norms "caused" by increased interaction among individuals in an increasingly globalized and technologically connected environment. Yet, the convergence that does occur is selective, and the selection is the one promoted by powerful global economic interests.

Finally, I make the case that even with all these economic and ideological pressures, there are a great variety of national approaches to educational policy, and these approaches are highly conditioned by how national societies define social efficiency and by the historical paths of national politics.

The National State, Globalization, and the Expansion of Education

Is the power of the national state diminished by globalization? Yes and no. Yes, because increasing global economic competition makes the national state focus on economic policies that improve global competitiveness, at the expense of policies that stabilize the current configuration of the domestic economy or possibly social cohesion (Castells 1997). Yes, because the national state is compelled to promote economic growth to assure its own legitimacy and therefore to make the national economy attractive for the mass of capital that moves globally choosing "winners" over "losers," and that may mean a reduction of public spending and the introduction of monetary policy that favors financial interests rather than workers and consumers (Castells 1997).

But no, because ultimately national states still greatly influence the territorial and temporal space in which most people acquire their capacity to operate globally and where capital has to invest. National states are largely responsible for the political climate in which businesses conduct their activities and individuals organize their social lives. Some analysts have called this underlying context for social and economic interaction "social capital" (Putnam 2000). Others have focused on trust (Fukuyama 1995). National public policy has an enormous influence on social capital and trust. Even the World Bank, supposedly a global institution, has rediscovered the national state as crucial to national economic and social development (World Bank 1997). It makes a major difference to a nation's economic possibilities when the national state is capable of formulating coherent economic and social policies and carrying them out. It makes a major difference if the national state can reduce corruption and establish trust, and it is difficult to imagine achieving greater social capital in most places without a well-organized state.

Ultimately, the state is concerned with its own reproduction. To reproduce its political power, the state bureaucracy seeks political legitimacy even when it is a non-democratic regime. In the past and now even more in a globalized knowledge economy, achieving political legitimacy includes not only stimulating economic growth, but also providing education to the mass of a nation's population.

Increasing Demand for Education in a Globalized Environment

In a globalized environment, the pressure for states to engage with education has increased. Globalization means increased competition among nations in a more closely intertwined international economy, a competition that is continuously enhanced by more rapid communication and computer technology and by a way of business thinking that is increasingly global rather than regional or national. Globalization also means relatively free trade, rather unregulated movement of finance capital, and the increased movement of innovative ideas (knowledge) and labor across national borders.

Major new players have emerged in the world economy, such as China, Korea, Taiwan, Brazil, and India. They are breaking the dominance of the USA, Europe, and Japan in manufacturing, although for the moment, firms (and universities) with their home base in the highly developed countries still have almost total control over the research and development of technical innovations.

One of the main outcomes of such competition and cross-border movements is a worldwide demand for certain kinds of skills – namely language, mathematics reasoning, scientific logic, and programming – associated with higher levels of education. Globalized science-based technology firms are increasingly using scientists and engineers trained at least partially in the emerging economies' universities to staff their innovation activities both in the developed countries and in the emerging economies themselves. At the same time, national states, particularly China, Korea, Taiwan, and Singapore, are increasing their scientific and technological higher education rapidly in the hope of capturing innovation rents as innovation continues to globalize. These forces tend to affect almost all countries in the global economy in the same way.

The tendency for the state in the new competitive global environment is to focus on education policies that enhance its economy's global competitiveness. An important influence of globalization is to increase the relative value of higher educated labor (or decrease the value of less educated labor). Thus, the private rates of return to higher education are rising in most countries and, in many, now exceed the payoff to lower levels of schooling (Carnoy et al. 2013). We need to remember that when the payoffs to higher education rise, this increases the demand not only for places in higher education, but also for lower levels of education and for increased *quality* of lower levels of schooling so students can better compete for university places. The state's legitimacy is entwined with its capacity to expand and improve the educational system as a whole.

More recently, state legitimacy includes improving the quality of mass education, particularly in terms of student scores on international and national assessments. Economists have tried to link higher educational attainment (Barro 1991; Krueger and Lindahl 2001) and educational quality (Hanushek et al. 2013) to economic growth. Such links help governments justify more investment in education, but even if those links prove to be rather vague, the increasing demand for expanding education forces governments to respond. This push for more education has also come to include demands for greatly expanding higher education and, in the larger economies, investing in a prime symbol of knowledge economy prestige, the "world class" university (Altbach et al. 2009).

There are other global economic forces that act similarly across countries. For example, constraints on public spending from aging populations limit educational expansion and attempts to improve educational quality. Increased competition in the global economy has made it more difficult for both developed and developing nations to raise revenue through increased taxation, particularly on corporate profits and individual income, because governments fear the flight of capital or not being able to attract capital investment. Further, many of the world's governments have low capacity to collect income taxes, so rely on excise taxes (value-added tax (VAT), import tariffs, export taxes). Finally, governments are under pressure from international financial institutions, such as the International Monetary Fund (IMF) and the World Bank, to keep public spending low. A major part of the IMF package for countries preparing themselves for "sustained" economic growth is to reduce the size of public deficits and shift national resources from government control to the private sector. This, in turn, means keeping public spending low relative to the size of the private sector.

National Variation in Response to Global Pressures

Nevertheless, there is considerable variation in the way states respond to the growth of demand for higher skills and to the financial constraints imposed by highly mobile capital seeking the best "deal" in terms of low wages and low corporate and income taxes. This suggests that there is an important *national* component to how nations expand their systems and reform them. Two important factors in defining national approaches to education are (a) how much national societies value the social payoffs to education; and (b) how much societies value social equality and how much they view the state as the main force for equalizing opportunity and outcomes.

The social payoffs to education are the positive effects of an educated population on civil society, tolerance for dissenting views, political stability, strengthened democracy, treatment of women and minority groups, and overall economic productivity – more educated people tend to make their co-workers more productive as well. It is therefore generally agreed that primary and basic secondary education should be heavily subsidized if not altogether free, so that no child in the society would be prevented from accessing those levels. Even at the university level and even when university graduates generally belong to a privileged socioeconomic group, the case has been made politically for publicly financing such students to earn higher incomes at public expense. The contention is that high social class individuals increasing their human capital at public expense also increase everyone else's well-being by becoming good doctors, good engineers, and good leaders. These large benefits, it could be claimed, accrue to the society as a whole, not just to the graduates themselves. One of the main arguments used for investing much larger amounts per student in elite or "world class" institutions is that their graduates and the research done there will have large "spillover" effects for society as a whole.

Social equality plays a role in the debate as well: lower social class families may face especially large financial, informational, or other barriers to entry into secondary and higher education. If a society values fairness and places social and political value on ensuring desired levels of equity of access and more equitable economic and social outcomes, the public aspect of education would include financing it in ways that remove such barriers. In addition, taxation and spending policies on public investments would tilt toward greater social equality. This equity/equality argument has been extended to make education as a whole – including higher education – a human right, situating it completely in the public space, available for all at public expense. Again, social preferences for equity/equality are mediated through the state. Depending on power relations in the state, it can interpret how education is to be financed as a public or private good.

Societies vary considerably in how they view the social value of education and social equity and equality. To the degree that states reflect these varying views and are not able to maintain legitimacy by just imposing the views of the global elite, they are likely to vary in their responses to global forces.

Ideological Convergence

One of the most intensive lines of sociological research in the past four decades has revolved around the concept of global ideological convergence across a broad array of social values, including human rights, women's rights, universal primary education (mass schooling), and the importance of science and mathematics. The argument for mass schooling as a world model that infiltrated one nation state after another, rather than the result of local national responses to "solve problems of social order … or to maintain dominance of elites," encapsulates the underlying concept of institutional convergence (Meyer et al. 1992).

The underlying theory of this ideological convergence is that elites implicitly came to agree upon a model of the nation state that had certain features, and one of those features was mass education. Thus, a converging ideological conception of the "modern" nation state was the driving force for defining educational change. Similarly, in the global information society, there is an emerging conception among global/national elites of the institutional nature of "modern" societies. In that sense, national states have "control" over their policies, but they are inexorably driven to "conform" to global institutional norms in order to meet a particular, global elite-defined conception of a "well-functioning, modern" state. State legitimacy in the eyes of global elites has real political meaning and, this theory claims, overrides the power of local economic, social, and ideological forces as an explanation for educational policies.

It is difficult to disagree that changing conceptions of the modern nation state have gradually diffused globally to influence national policies regarding educational expansion, gender equality, and, more recently, notions of educational quality, which include the spread of testing and measurement. To what degree diffusion is the outcome of the "autonomous" spread of ideology or of changing economic conditions that affect the functionality of these policies is an important question, not dealt with satisfactorily by the world system convergence theorists.

Ideological Convergence or Changes in Reproducing State Legitimacy?

In this section of the chapter, I address the interpretation of the ideological convergence argument, mainly to understand why national societal values and politics play such an important role in shaping the impact of these "global" ideologies on education policy. Three important expressions of so-called educational policy convergence in a globalized environment are the expansion of higher education through shifting the costs of that expansion to families through "privatization"; the increasing focus on educational "quality" as an important factor in economic growth and improving social equity; and increasing focus on educational technology (computers/internet) as a key tool for improving teaching and learning and for equalizing educational opportunity.

As noted, in the current era, globalization has increased pressure on many nation states to expand their higher educational systems for very functionalist reasons; that is, the increasing private economic payoff to higher levels of education. Those increasing payoffs have also expanded the possibility for nation states to make families bear an increasing share of the cost of that expansion. This has characterized the expansion, particularly in developing countries, and has been viewed as an ideological shift in the view of higher education as a public to a private good (Altbach *et al.* 2009).

The focus on educational quality and the spread of testing and measurement connected with that focus is intimately connected to elite ideological "convergence" on conceptions of the role of education in economic growth, social mobility, and income inequality. Yet, this ideology also spreads for two types of functionalist reasons – direct reasons, namely the potential for private profits for test and test materials producers associated with the vast education industry; and indirect reasons, namely growing income inequality and the increasing concentration of capital. Would education be the centerpiece of reducing inequality in a globalizing world economy marked by decreasing rather than increasing inequality? Measuring educational quality and using those measurements to fault "bad" education for a host of ills in society is highly functional to maintaining the highly preferred position of the very elites who spread this ideology.

In a similar vein, the diffusion of computers and internet connections into schools as a "solution" to "low schooling quality" and to "achievement gaps" between low- and high social class students is an ideology that has spread rapidly in the past 15 years, much as did the educational television phase of technology-assisted instruction in the 1970s. The most recent manifestation of this ideology is the Massive Open Online Courses (MOOCs). These, again, are posed as a "solution" to providing high quality yet inexpensive teaching-learning opportunities on a global scale to augment (or even replace) localized university classes. Again, the spread of this ideology is situated in the context of its functionality to elite economic interests: large potential profits to hardware and software producers. And, as in the case of testing and measurement, it feeds off growing economic and social inequality and the convenience of seeking solutions to that ill through technology rather than addressing inequality directly.

Education as a Private versus Public Good

As noted by many analysts, there has been a tendency in the past 20 years for governments to shift the cost of higher education to students and their families (e.g. see Altbach and Levy 2005), both through promoting the expansion of fee charging private higher education institutions and the implementation of tuition fees (cost sharing) in public institutions. This has been characterized as a shift in ideology, specifically a change in treatment of higher education from a public to a private good, and also the result of hegemonic neo-liberal influences pushing for markets in education (Marginson and Ordorika 2011).

In assessing these views, it is important to consider that education inherently serves both private and public interests (Levin 1987; Marginson 2007). It serves private interests by enhancing the capacity of individuals to gain economic and social benefits. It also has public value because more highly educated individuals are likely to increase others' productivity (Romer 1994) and to embrace the fundamental tenants of a tolerant democratic society, which benefits all citizens (Mill 1869). However, much of the value of externalities ultimately depends on ideology (what "society" defines as having social value), and ideology, in turn, depends on political power relations. If the political decision process is truly democratic and pluralistic, and full information is equally available to all individuals, the value of externalities could closely reflect the sum of the values individuals living in a society place on them. But this democratic, full information political model is rarely realized. In most societies, economic power and state power are closely entwined. The state (the political system) places a value on externalities that reflect these highly unequal power relations and the asymmetric influence, even in a democracy, of economically powerful groups in defining the value of externalities associated with certain types of higher education.

In the context of our argument that globalization has changed the objective (functionalist) conditions for higher education – greatly increasing the demand for higher educated labor and the payoffs for those who complete university – we contend that such high (and rising) payoffs accentuate the value of higher education as serving private interests. This gives the state the option to shift higher education financing to (mainly elite and higher middle class) families without jeopardizing the state's political legitimacy. Social externalities associated with the expansion of higher education are still likely to be positive, and public pressure continues to keep higher education free. Yet, many national states under pressure to increase higher education access have opted to expand it rapidly through charging tuition in public institutions or allowing low-quality private institutions to take up this new demand with tuition-paying places rather than taking the slower route of free public education.

There could be global-level ideological dimensions to this choice, but the changing private value of higher education is a much more powerful explainer of state moves to directly charging families for the costs of higher education (Carnoy et al. 2013). At the same time, there is considerable variation in whether and how this move is implemented in practice, reflecting national political conditions and historical trends in higher education expansion. For example, Brazil's higher education system was already 60% private in 1970, well before globalization and the recent explosion of enrollment beginning in 1995. Even so, private enrollment grew again after 2000 to almost three-quarters of undergraduates by 2010 and public institutions remained tuition free. India also expanded enrollment mainly through the private higher education sector, but simultaneously implemented cost sharing in public colleges. China's and Russia's systems also expanded rapidly in the same period, but a significant part of the growth was financed by tuition in public institutions – in China's case for all students and in Russia's, only for half the students – those who scored lower on entrance tests. Significantly, China and Russia's states are less democratic and their university systems are more centrally controlled than Brazil's or India's, and the way that financing increased enrollment played out quite differently in part due to these differences.

Focusing on Educational Quality and Testing

Not many years ago, in the 20th century, educational attainment was the main focus of educational policy-makers concerned with economic growth and educational equity. As discussed earlier, the populations of most countries measure their and their children's academic success mainly by how far they go in school, not their scores on tests. For example, one of the ways that higher social class parents improve the success of their less academically able offspring is to make sure that they complete university.

One reason why many higher test-scoring lower social class students do not achieve social mobility is because they fail to continue their education as far as their higher social class counterparts. Logically, attainment and achievement are correlated, but as Samuel Bowles and Herbert Gintis pointed out years ago (Bowles and Gintis 1975), achievement is a far worse predictor of economic success than social class, in part because social class is a far more important predictor of attainment.

However, as average years of schooling expanded in almost every society, and as this did not decrease social and economic differences (although it may have contributed to economic growth), a subtle shift occurred in academic and policy-maker focus from educational attainment to educational quality. Education quality has long been a topic of discussion (see the debate on science education in the USA post-Sputnik), but the new ideological "convergence" on quality of education as an indicator of the wealth of nations, of the possibilities for economic growth, and of state legitimacy, has clearly gone beyond anything in the past.

The new emphasis on educational quality has been accompanied and promoted by the rapid spread of testing and measurement. Measuring and comparing school outcomes across countries and within countries has not occurred spontaneously. Rather, it has been pushed by international organizations such as the International Association for Evaluation of Educational Achievement (IEA) and the Organisation for Economic Co-operation and Development (OECD), by the World Bank, the Inter-American Bank, and the Asian Development Bank, by non-governmental organizations (NGOs) such as the Inter-American Dialogue, and by bilateral agencies such as the US Agency for International Development. All these organizations share a globalized view of education and efficiency, which includes a highly quantitative view of progress. They also share an explicit understanding that "better" education can be measured and that better education translates directly into higher economic and social productivity. With more intensive economic competition among nation states, the urgency of improving productivity is translated by these organizations into spreading the acceptance of inter- and intra-national comparisons on standardized tests of student knowledge (UNESCO 2005; OECD 2011; Hanushek and Kimko 2000; Hanushek and Woessmann 2008). The World Bank and other international and bilateral lenders have also pushed this new emphasis on test score measures of the quality of education through direct monetary incentives of additional foreign assistance for those developing countries that participate in international tests and develop national testing regimes (Kijima 2013).

Nations' average international test performance is playing an increasing role in the way the public in those countries view themselves educationally. The two major players in the international testing universe are the IEA, which began testing internationally in the 1960s and now produces the Trends in International Mathematics and Science Survey (TIMSS), and the OECD, which runs the Programme for International Student Assessment (PISA). The impact of these international tests on national educational policy is steadily increasing, and so is the number of countries that participate in one or the other, or both.

Are testing and measurement and the focus on quality of education (achievement scores) over quantity of education (attainment) the new ideological symbols of national "modernity" in the globalized economy? Is that the reason that more national states are implementing national testing systems, participating in international tests, and putting emphasis on raising those scores? Perhaps. Yet, it is just as likely that national adoption of these "symbols" fulfills two important functions, neither of which is nearly as benign as sending signals to the rest of the world that a nation state has joined a newly defined "global modernity club."

The first of these functions is to reemphasize the role of the family and particularly of "better" schooling as the keys to solving the problems of poverty and social inequality. If it is widely believed that family effort and higher quality schooling can solve these problems, then other measures, such as changing the moral "norms" about how large income differences "should be" in a society and income redistribution through state taxation and spending policies become seen as unnecessary or even harmful to the overall national project of improving people's well-being. The evidence that increasing student test scores per se addresses poverty and social inequality, or even that increasing test scores significantly increases economic growth, is limited to very questionable correlational results. However, the political effect of successfully shifting public consciousness to schooling as the solution to social ills is more believable.

The global movement toward increased educational testing is framed by a long tradition in educational reform dating back to the turn of the 20th century that greater efficiency and control (accountability) is the secret to higher quality. The movement is synonymous with expanding educational access for lower social class youth. As lower social class youth flooded into US urban schools in the later 19th century, reformers such as Ellwood Cubberley called for greater efficiency – a discussion similar to the Taylorism movement taking place in industry (see Cubberley 1910; on Taylorism, see Braverman 1974).

Although articulated and justified in terms of their potential contribution of making education more efficient in terms of improving education, international tests are not necessarily consistent with measures needed for improving schooling. PISA, for example, is not linked to national curriculum standards. Rather, it is a measure of knowledge that experts believe makes youth more functional economically and socially in the current knowledge environment. It is true that cross-nationally PISA results are highly correlated with other test results, but its mathematics portion, for example, would not serve well for writing a mathematics curriculum.

Furthermore, other ways of using testing are linked more directly to school improvement. In the best of cases, school personnel participate in designing and applying the tests, and the tests are directly linked to knowledge transmission goals set either at the national or regional level. Important aspects of school efficiency can certainly be understood through such tests, but efficiency here is less concerned with resource allocation per se than with process and use of resources. In Chile, for example, national testing of fourth and eighth grade students was originally, in the 1980s, used simply as a way to stimulate competition among private and public schools competing for students and the voucher funds attached to each student. Available evidence suggests that this use of tests had no positive effect on student achievement. However, in the 1990s, the use of national testing linked to central government school improvement programs did apparently increase test scores in lower-scoring schools catering to low-income students.

Global notions of efficiency and measurement can therefore have a positive effect on educational output, and improving educational quality may have an effect on economic productivity. For these links to play out, however, policy-makers first have to pass notions of measurement through local filters and have as their specific purpose school improvement even if school improvement requires more resources, which is likely the case in most developing societies. The distinction between this type of application of measurement to raising efficiency and the use of testing to develop national policies for resource use with the intention of avoiding discussions of public resources available for education is subtle and is mainly rooted in how the state, rather than international organizations, interprets the role of measurement in conditioning educational change. In addition, higher test scores must be linked to an improved quality of life for students scoring higher on tests. Although we would all like to believe that better schools will result in better economic and social opportunities for graduates, this may not be the case in highly unequal societies that can only absorb a small percentage of these higher quality graduates into higher paying jobs. The success of any education policy in promoting economic growth and social mobility depends on national state economic and social policies.

One of the ironies of the efficiency movement in education is that test *makers* have a vested economic interest to have educational systems and schools change what they define as academic knowledge or even useful knowledge to fit the particular test they sell. There is big money in testing and in the associated materials related to the curriculum associated with tests, so much so that the test makers have a major incentive in trying to change national curricula to align with their tests.

Globalization and Information and Communications Technology (ICT)

The spread of computers and the internet globally is the most evident manifestation of the information and communications technology foundations of the new global economy. The driving force behind the incorporation of ICT into education is ostensibly to improve student learning and to prepare youth for a global economy in which education contributes to higher productivity. There are strong underlying economic growth motives here, fostered by increased competition in the global economy. Allegedly, nations that have higher scoring students will perform better economically. Nations with students versed in the use of computers and the internet will be more productive. There is a second type of economic driver for the use of ICT in education – one that also motivated the use of educational radio and television a generation earlier: with ICT, the argument goes, it is possible to deliver reasonably high quality teaching to large numbers of students at low cost.

Thus, a case can be made that ICT has an ideological component, particularly in education as a symbol of modernization. However, an important element of the incorporation of ICT into schools is functional to economic growth, potentially lowering costs of schooling (financial functionality), and is a source of profit for the firms that produce ICT – hardware, software, internet connections, advertising on the internet, and schooling itself (privately run distance education). The education industry is an immense source of business opportunity, as we have discussed in the privatization of higher education, the testing and measurement business, and, perhaps most of all, ICT.

It is well to remember, however, that "I" stands for information, and "C" for communications. There is no "L" for "learning" in ICT, and for good reason. Computers were designed to store, access, and process quickly massive amounts of information.

The internet was also designed to access information and communicate it worldwide in real time. Computers as learning devices have proved to be much less effective despite claims that the access and communication functions of computer software could be easily adapted to teaching-learning functions and that they could serve these functions at a lower cost than traditional face-to-face forms of teaching/learning. Indeed, there are many such adaptations. Yet, after many years and many attempts, the promised educational quality improvements and lower costs from computer applications have been elusive (see Carnoy 2012 for a summary).

Perhaps the most appealing use of ICT for teaching and learning and, simultaneously for integrating individuals into a unified conception of culture, is the newest form of virtual higher education and the most recent expression of the combined impact of globalization and ICT on education – the MOOC, or Massive Open Online Course. In theory, MOOCs could make available to a global student clientele courses taught by experts in particular subjects from the very best universities in the world using effective lecture techniques, high level curricula, and well organized evaluation activities (problem sets, tests, etc.). For students who are academically able and disciplined enough to work independently in such courses, they could create the possibility of much higher standards of knowledge transmission worldwide. It is argued that they could also boost the quality of second tier higher education institutions by giving students there the opportunity to study with the very best professors in the world at a distance. However, the main objective of using MOOCs in second tier institutions is likely to be to lower costs per student, not to raise quality. As we discuss below, states are under pressure to decrease the costs of higher education expansion. MOOCs could certainly play a role in accomplishing that goal without necessarily raising higher educational quality.

Is the widespread use of ICT and the increasingly generalized belief in ICTs as the expression of the information age version of modernized, "connected" society (or "network society," in Castells' (1997) terminology) the result of ideological convergence? Or is it functional to both state efforts to increase economic growth and state legitimacy, as well as simply functional to higher profits for computer and peripherals manufacturers?

It makes perfect sense to interpret the use of computers in schools as a product of ideological convergence, particularly since they seem to have little positive impact on children's academic learning (Carnoy 2012). Computers in schools are symbols of the information society – schools with computers and internet connections are certainly viewed by parents as academically innovative, and this view is pushed hard by international agencies, such as the OECD (OECD 2013b, chapter 5).

On the other hand, if we delve carefully into what aspect of "modernization" computers symbolize to parents, it is likely to be the notion that by using "high technology" in schools and at home, their children learn skills that will serve them in the workplace – that is, to help them get better jobs. The use and intensity of use of ICT are positively correlated with gross domestic product, and within a country, with individuals' social class. This correlation does not imply a causal relation between ICT use and higher income or productivity, even though a "semi-causal" study using US data shows a significant relation between hourly wages and computer use at work (Krueger 1993). But before getting too excited that this "proves" that computer use "causes" higher productivity, consider that yet another study using German data duplicated Krueger's positive US results for computer use and hourly wages, but also showed a significant positive relation between hourly wages and the use of pencils and calculators (DiNardo and Pischke 1997).

The public perception that computer skills can benefit young people directly in the form of higher wages is fairly pervasive, and likely it does represent economic reality. In that sense, it is much less the result of a spreading elite conception of modernization (in which computers in schools represent the new modernization) than the result of objective changes in the value assigned to specific skills in a globalized economy. The demand by parents for computers in schools is therefore a functional demand for enhancing their children's employment and wages in the information economy. Similarly, there is an important functionality to supplying more computers to schools. School districts and governments worldwide buy tens of millions of computers for schools. Much, if not most, of this hardware, are earlier years' models. Furthermore, millions of school internet connections are installed annually. This is a major business, along with the production and selling of software, repair and maintenance, and so forth. Even if ICT were never shown to improve academic achievement, parents would demand them and companies would push educational systems to buy them, for very functional reasons.

Despite good functional explanations for why ICT has entered education in such a massive way worldwide, it is marked by a major paradox; namely, that ICT in education is rarely used in the way private business employs it – that is, to manage the quality of output, to raise teacher (worker) productivity, or to reduce costs through analyzing spending and resource allocation.

Beginning in the 1970s, US school districts regularly used computers to store student and personnel data. With the advent of high-speed personal computers in the 1990s, computers became a permanent fixture in school offices. In many school districts in the USA, school administrators have access to data from district computers; in many schools, individual teachers are hooked up to central data files either in the school or district office. Educational administrative offices in most developed countries have ICT, and data collection in the developed world is universally computerized.

Bilateral assistance agencies and international banks put increasing emphasis in the 1980s and 1990s on using ICT to collect educational data and to improve the administration of educational systems in developing countries, particularly through decentralizing educational offices to regions, states, municipalities, and states themselves. As in developed countries, such ICT systems have been used mainly for collecting enrollment data, student attendance, basic information on teachers, and basic information on schools. In other words, ICT mainly helps administrators get a better idea of the size of the educational system, student dropout and repetition, and the number of students per teacher. Yet, ICT is very seldom used to increase student achievement through better allocation of teacher effort or more effective use of other school resources.

Why is ICT used so much less in educational management decision-making than in private business? One argument could be that it is not being used this way because it might be useful for increasing teacher and administrator productivity, and that teachers and school directors, the "production managers" in education, realize this and resist applying ICT to assessing student learning gains at the classroom and school level. If that is the case, this most "modern" of ICT uses is halted from spreading mainly because it is not "functional" to the needs of major actors in the system. The ideology of modernization is not powerful enough to overcome functional rationality. Even as educational assessment reaches down into the most isolated corners of the world, the most common uses of computer technology are not able to implement that assessment to make education more productive and efficient.

National States, Global Convergence, and the Shape of Educational Change

Do the global trends we have described mean that changes in educational systems will converge and that educational improvements will tend to be shaped globally? Given the hype around OECD's PISA reports and the push to find the "common" elements in "excellent" educational systems (OECD 2013a), it seems that this might indeed be the future of education. Assessment, accountability, greater use of ICT for teaching in schools, and increased privatization of schooling, particularly in lower income countries, are all features of the educational system being spread by international agencies intent on "reforming" the delivery of education.

All of these effects of globalization on education are passed through the policy structures of national states, so it is these states that ultimately decide how globalization affects national education. There is much more political and even financial space for the national state to condition the way globalization is brought into education than is usually admitted. Testing and standards are a good example of this space, and ICT is another. States can provide schooling access more equally, improve the quality of education for the poor, and produce knowledge more effectively and more equally for all within a globalized economy.

We see considerable empirical evidence of this in the heterogeneity of approaches to higher educational expansion under resource constraints (Carnoy et al. 2013). Although we observe movement in many countries toward increasingly defining higher education as a private good, there is great variation in this movement, with many European countries maintaining their commitment to providing highly subsidized higher public universities and some nations, such as Chile, on the verge of retreating from extreme versions of university privatization. In each case, national political conditions and the functional driving force of state legitimacy are paramount to defining how the state interprets its reaction to the pressures of global elite ideologies. National educational policy is contested political terrain in most societies (Carnoy and Levin 1985). The current struggles over educational policy in both developed and developing countries suggest that national states are still the terrain on which educational policy is formed, and that attempts to homogenize approaches in the name of global values and norms confront the objective conditions of national educational system histories, and national economic and political conditions.

Despite the dominant global elite drive for greater efficiency and privatization in education, there are increasing examples of national efforts to shift resources to the poor and of making public educational systems more effective for everyone, even if this may appear to be less efficient. There is also evidence that the US educational system, several Latin American systems, and several European systems have improved quality substantially in the past ten years and that they have done so without more privatization (Carnoy and Rothstein 2013). Chile and California have recently shifted major resources to low-income schools, with Chile already showing positive academic returns to that counter-global educational policy (Carrasco 2013). That many states choose to adopt globally induced education policies that lower costs without improving quality (particularly in higher levels of education) is at least partly the result of caving in to "pro-poor" politics in the face of new competitive pressures and new, globalized thinking. Although it is difficult to counter strong, worldwide ideological trends and, indeed, the objective reality of financial globalization, states can and do choose to emphasize more productive, more equal, and more effective public education even in the highly competitive global economic environment, if it is politically functional for them to do so. As Levin and I claimed almost three decades ago (Carnoy and Levin 1985), national educational policies are politically contested within the nation state, and educational policy is the result of how that political contest evolves at the national and local level.

A clear expression of such variation is subnational state and provincial educational policies in federal systems such as the USA, Brazil, Germany, and Mexico. In the USA, states are responsible for their educational policies and even largely for financing education with local and state taxes. Policies and spending levels vary greatly from state to state, and so do educational outcomes (see, for example, Rothstein and Carnoy 2013). Most interesting is the polarized directions that different groups of states are taking in their educational policies, with one the "red" (conservative-run) group pushing for more charter schools, vouchers, anti-teacher union policies, even reducing spending for education, and, in some cases, experimenting with teacher incentives, and the other, "blue" states (governed by left-of-center governors and legislatures), focusing more on improving public education, distributing more resources to lower-income districts and working more cooperatively with the teachers unions. Putting aside the question of which policies will turn out to be more effective, the variation suggests how local (even below nation state) political conditions can influence greatly how the public sector develops the educational system. All this variation suggests that governments have considerable control over how they react to global forces influencing educational policies. That said, globalization has clearly pushed most US states to adopt a common core curriculum and a common evaluation system of those core standards

References

Altbach, P. and D. Levy (eds). 2005. *Private Higher Education: A Global Revolution*. Chestnut Hill: Center for International Higher Education, and Rotterdam: Sense Publishers.
Altbach, P., L. Reisberg, and L. Rumbley. 2009. *Trends in Global Higher Education: Tracking an Academic Revolution*. Chestnut Hill: Boston College Center for International Higher Education.
Barro, R. 1991. "Economic Growth in a Cross-Section of Countries." *Quarterly Journal of Economics*, 106(2): 407–443.
Bowles, S. and H. Gintis. 1975. *Schooling in Capitalist America*. New York: Free Press.
Braverman, H. 1974. *Labor and Monopoly Capital: The Degradation of Work in the Twentieth Century*. New York: Monthly Review Press.
Carnoy, M. 2000. *Sustaining the New Economy: Work, Family, and Community in the Information Age*. Cambridge: Harvard University Press.
Carnoy, M. 2012. "What Does More ICT in the World Economy and in Post-Industrial Societies Mean for Education?" Paper presented at the Foro Valparaiso, Universidad Catolica de Valpariso, June.

Carnoy, M. and H.M. Levin. 1985. *Schooling and Work in the Capitalist State.* Stanford: Stanford University Press.

Carnoy, M., P. Loyalka, M. Dobryakova, R. Dossani, I. Froumin, K. Kuhns, J.B.G. Tilak, and R. Wang. 2013. *University Expansion in a Changing Global Economy: Triumph of the BRICs?* Stanford: Stanford University Press.

Carnoy, M. and R. Rothstein. 2013. *What Do International Test Scores Really Show About U.S. Student Performance?* Washington, DC: Economic Policy Institute.

Carrasco, R. 2014. "Leveling the Playing Field: How Can We Address Educational Inequalities?" Unpublished PhD dissertation, Stanford University.

Castells, M. 1997. *The Network Society.* London: Blackwell.

Cubberley, E. 1910. *Changing Conceptions of Education.* New York: Houghton Mifflin.

DiNardo, J. and J.-S. Pischke. 1997. "The Returns to Computer Use Revisited: Have Pencils Changed the Wage Structure Too?" *Quarterly Journal of Economics,* 112(1): 291–303.

Friedman, T. 1999. *The Lexus and the Olive Tree: Understanding Globalization.* New York: Farrar, Straus, and Giroux.

Fukuyama, F. 1995. *Trust: The Social Virtues and the Creation of Prosperity.* New York: The Free Press.

Giddens, A. 2002. *Runaway World: How Globalisation is Reshaping Our Lives.* London: Profile Books.

Hanushek, E. and D. Kimko. 2000. "Schooling, Labor-Force Quality, and the Growth of Nations." *The American Economic Review,* 90(5): 1184–1208.

Hanushek, E. and L. Woessmann. 2008. "The Role of Cognitive Skills in Economic Development." *Journal of Economic Literature,* 46(3): 607–668.

Hanushek, E., P. Peterson, and L. Woessmann. 2013. *Endangering Prosperity.* Washington, DC: The Brookings Institution.

Kijima, R. 2013. "The Politics of Cross-National Assessment: Global Trends and National Interests." Unpublished PhD dissertation, Stanford University.

Krueger, A. 1993. "How Computers Have Changed the Wage Structure: Evidence from Microdata, 1984–1989." *Quarterly Journal of Economics,* 108(1): 33–60.

Krueger, A. and M. Lindahl. 2001. "Education for Growth: Why and For Whom?" *Journal of Economic Literature,* 39(4): 1101–1136.

Levin, H.M. 1987. "Education as a Public and Private Good." *Journal of Policy Analysis and Management,* 6(4): 628–641.

Marginson, S. 2007. "The Public/Private Divide in Higher Education: A Global Revision." *Higher Education,* 53: 307–333.

Marginson, S. and I. Ordorika. 2011. "'El Central Volumen de la Fuerza': The Hegemonic Global Pattern in the Reorganization of Elite Higher Education and Research," in *Knowledge Matters: The Public Mission of the Research University,* edited by Diana Rhoten and Craig Calhoun. New York: Columbia University Press.

Meyer, J., F. Ramirez, and Y.N. Soysal. 1992. "World Expansion of Mass Education, 1870–1980." *Sociology of Education,* 65(2): 128–149.

Meyer, J., J. Boli, G. Thomas, and F. Ramirez. 1997. "World Society and the Nation-State." *American Journal of Sociology,* 103(1): 144–181.

Mill, J.S. 1869. *On Liberty.* London: Longman, Roberts, & Green.

Putnam, R. 2000. *Bowling Alone.* New York: Simon and Schuster.

Organisation for Economic Co-operation and Development (OECD). 2011. *Lessons from PISA for the United States, Strong Performers and Successful Reformers in Education.* Paris: OECD.

Organisation for Economic Co-operation and Development (OECD). 2013a. *PISA 2012: Results in Focus.* Paris: OECD.

Organisation for Economic Co-operation and Development (OECD). 2013b. *Trends Shaping Education.* Paris: OECD.

Romer, P. 1994. "The Origins of Endogenous Growth." *Journal of Economic Perspectives,* 8(1): 3–22.

Rothstein, R. and M. Carnoy. 2013. "'PISA Day' – An Ideological and Hyperventilated Exercise." Retrieved from: www.epi.org/blog/pisa-day-ideological-hyperventilated-exercise (accessed November 3, 2015).

UNESCO. 2005. *World Education Report 2005*. Paris: UNESCO.

World Bank. 1997. *World Development Report: The State in a Changing World*. New York: Oxford University Press and World Bank.

Chapter 2

World Society and the Globalization of Educational Policy[1]

Francisco O. Ramirez, John W. Meyer, and Julia Lerch

The discursive and organizational structures of educational policy have importantly and rather steadily shifted to a global level in recent decades. There is much more global educational discourse, and many more organizational settings for it, than in any previous period. A number of factors are involved:

First, there are the obvious facts of multidimensional globalization in both realities and perceptions. On every front – economic, political, military, social, and cultural – there is increased worldwide interdependence and awareness of interdependence. National societies are embedded in, and influenced by, their wider contexts. This generates the formation of global models of change and directions of change, and national tendencies to become isomorphic with these models and the directions they emphasize. But beyond this broad cultural influence there are also the direct pressures of increased dependence, as national systems come to be organized to deal with the supra-national environment. Consequently, there is an explosion of efforts at social engineering on a global scale. Supra-national structures arise, and national ones actively participate in them. Shared world goals – most prominently progress and justice – come to the fore. They are frequently framed as complementary goals. And notably, education comes to seem increasingly central to the accomplishment of both of these core goals. Thus, education is globally cast as the key to progress, or excellence, and justice, or equality (Chabbott and Ramirez 2000). Much educational reform discussion insists that one cannot have educational excellence without educational equality (cf. Darling-Hammond 2010).

Second, much of the resultant global structuration focuses on the formation and diffusion of policies and policy talk. Globalization has generated nothing by way of a world state with imperative authority and a monopoly of violence. Even the

European Union (EU), the most advanced of the supra-national structures, is a pale imitation of a state. So instead of the binding authority of hard laws, we find multiple social engineering efforts, responding to interdependence, organized around shared policies, soft laws, and the rise of common standards and rankings. These tend to be organized around the authority of actual or putative scientific knowledge, rather than the constitutional dominance of a state. They tend to be justified by normative global standards like human rights, the environment, or transparency, rather than historical, religious, racial, or dynastic state agendas. In this sort of stateless but culturally integrated system, world standards articulated in international conferences and organizations constitute an influential form of governance without government. In this system, education becomes a central motor through which world standards are to be attained; education is thought to operate both to promote egalitarian norms and to foster rational progress (Meyer et al. 1997).

Third, the emerging world society is built on a changed ontological base. Throughout the modern period, two central social units have been constructed as primordial bases for collective action, broadly reflecting a dualism of the Western religious tradition: the national state and the individual person. These entities, as cultural constructions, reinforce each other (though in practice they may compete), and the political forms of modernity find various balances between individualisms and statisms. The events of the first half of the 20th century undercut such balances: after two world wars, a massive depression, and stunning violations of human rights and welfare, all attributed to aggressive nationalisms, the national state as the charismatic locus of both power and right lost some legitimacy. "My Country, Right or Wrong" lacks currency in the current wider world of transnational standards. In this context, educational reforms are grounded on the premise that countries can learn from other countries and their "best practices." All sorts of educational conferences and workshops (often international in character) are designed to upgrade the quality of schools and universities. Thus, since World War II, an extraordinary explosion in conceptions of society as rooted in individual human persons occurred. The newly imagined person carries both a greatly expanded set of rights (across group identities, like gender and age; and across topics, like health and education and the right to cultural choices). Moreover, this person is imagined to carry enormous capacities, so that whole political systems (with democracy), economic systems (with deregulated choice), and cultural systems (with religious and linguistic freedom), are thought to be the product of empowered choosing persons.

If society increasingly is seen to rest on individual persons, and if society becomes more and more supra-national in character, then it should follow that education becomes a most central global institution. And this has, most dramatically, been increasingly the case over the decades since World War II. National policy agendas have increasingly emphasized education (Jakobi 2011), in part in direct response to globalization (Rosenmund 2006), and a whole supra-national arena of educational policy discourse and organization has arisen. The mantra "Think Globally and Act Locally" emerges in a world in which the activities of individual persons are supposed to be both informed by world society and influence world society developments.

This increasingly institutionalized world society perspective emphasizes the authority of global educational frames and standards and their increasing influence on national educational developments. From this perspective issues of legitimacy and identity are central. Much educational talk and action at the national level is conceptualized as an exercise in the enactment of the legitimate identity of the nation state and of its schools and universities. Such exercises often appear to be ill attuned to the local circumstances or needs that many functionalist theories would emphasize. Nor are these enactments easily accounted for by the power dependency ties emphasized in coercion theories.

To illustrate, consider the plight of Chinese rural school teachers who face ministerial guidelines that call for progressive pedagogy even as they prepare students to cope with a conventional exam structure (Wang 2013). Not surprisingly, the result is an extreme degree of loose coupling. Yet what brings this about is the increasing extent to which Chinese educational policy-makers become more linked to world educational models. In this instance, the increased linkages and their educational ramifications are clearly not driven by economic or related dependencies but instead reflect the deeper embeddedness of China in the wider world of educational reform.

To be sure, local and national factors continue to be important in shaping educational developments (see the papers in Anderson-Levitt 2003, for example; see also Schriewer 2012, and elsewhere). But it is precisely the authority and influence of global educational policy that generates the loose coupling so often noted. Were educational structures and policies only national or local in character, there would be less observable loose coupling (Ramirez 2012). And, it is authority and influence, not solely power and coercion that is often the crucial dynamic (Schofer et al. 2012). Of course, there are powerful organizations that wield extraordinary influence (see, for example, Verger 2010; Dale and Robertson 2002; Edwards 2013). However, these organizations are most influential when they endorse educational reforms that enjoy professional legitimacy; their influence is not solely a matter of muscle flexing. Chinese educational reforms are thus influenced by the legitimacy of ideas about what "quality education" looks like, not compelled by economically powerful actors.

Talk and Action at the National Level

We focus here on the rise of global educational discourse and the organizational frames within which this discourse occurs. However, it is important to emphasize that in the case of education, discursive expansion has been accompanied by, and is in a reciprocal causal relation with, an explosion in practice.

Enrollments

Raw enrollments have expanded rapidly, worldwide. Primary education has expanded almost to universality, even in peripheral countries, in just a few decades, and is now treated as an essential human right (in Article 26 of the Universal Declaration of Human Rights), and one of the least controversial human rights. The old "school leaving" has become "dropout," and even "pushout" (Bradley and Renzulli 2011), and is everywhere seen as a major social problem. Secondary education has expanded even more rapidly everywhere, and in many countries is essentially universal: again, a social movement arises to define it too as a human right. Expansion in higher education is even more extreme, and characterizes every sort of country in the world. Earlier efforts by communist countries to slow it down failed miserably (Lenhardt and Stock 2000), so that enrollment reaches more than 20% of a global cohort of young people (Schofer and Meyer 2005).

All this represents a dramatic change in policy frames, around the world. In the early post-war decades, there was an emphasis on education, but a good deal of concern remained from an earlier modernity about the problem of over-education, especially at the tertiary level (Freeman 1976; Dore 1975). It was understood that education beyond social needs would be inefficient, destructive of stabilizing culture, and inflationary in character: a responsible and authoritative political system would block this inflation. Such concerns have almost completely receded in the world, and low enrollments – for example, of females – are now seen as major social problems.

Curricula

Beyond enrollments, the cultural content of education has expanded greatly, covering more domains of human life and acquiring a globalized character. This is a normative matter, and nationalistic education is strongly criticized (see for instance critiques of nationalistic textbooks in Japan (Nozaki 2002) and Turkey (Çayir 2009)). Schooling touches on a greatly expanded set of domains – sexuality and family life, personal self-expression, multiple cultural frames, and so on. Schooling is notably globalized in content: the universalized sciences are prominent, the universalizing social sciences tend to replace traditional instruction in history, and culture, and cultural and historical materials transcending old civilizational and national boundaries are routinely employed (Frank and Gabler 2006; Wong 1991; Meyer et al. 1992).

Thus, notions that a primary function of education is to create national loyalty are in considerable disrepute. The child should learn to be a good citizen, certainly, but a good citizen of the country is now seen as a good citizen of the world. Dying for one's country is not a main educational goal. Humanity is valorized; respect for diversity within and between countries is emphasized. These normative shifts are reflected in intended curricula, as cross-national textbook studies amply demonstrate (Ramirez et al. 2009; Meyer et al. 2010). The national does not simply disappear but increasingly co-exists with cosmopolitan and multicultural schemas. Global citizenship emerges as a textbook emphasis around the world and is strongly associated with the extent of national linkages to the wider world (Buckner and Russell 2013). These developments are observed and critiqued by scholars with a more nationalistic orientation (Huntington 2004). But it is increasingly evident that the earlier educational transformation of people into national citizens now also emphasizes their transnational personhood (Ramirez 2006; Lie 2004).

Organization

Education has, everywhere, become a main institution. Systems of organizational control become increasingly dense. Local education is tied to national standards, rules, and programs, though often not in a bureaucratically centralized form (Baker and LeTendre 2005). Rather, webs of coordination, testing and measurement, curricular development, teacher training, and the like expand to construct an institution with both national and supra-national missions. Increasingly, these organizational systems link the local and national educational missions, policies, and structures to global ones. This pattern is obviously an ongoing development. A world educational superstructure emerges and impinges on even the once highly localized system of schools in the USA. This superstructure also influences regional and global educational developments. Below we stress the development of the world educational superstructure, filled with organizations and associations and globally legitimated professions.

Global Structure and Discourse

The national-level changes emphasized above are closely linked to the rise of explicit global structures in the educational field. Hegemonic countries (in our period, especially the USA) may operate independently, and indeed may be important sources of global structuration. But for most countries in the world, the global field operates as a set of important sources of influence on the directions of local change. There are endless variations, of course, and every local and national setting has its own history, influence structure, and political or economic agendas. To some extent, the expanding world order encourages and legitimates appropriate localizations – Robertson (1992) coined the useful term *glocalization* to depict the situation. For instance, now more than in any previous period, we might expect students to receive instruction related to their immediately local community. But of course the pictures of the local world they are taught are likely to be highly edited: traditions of child and sexual abuse, for instance, are unlikely to be stressed, and more exotic ones like headhunting are likely to be greatly distanced. Viking raiders, for example, now appear as traders in Scandinavian textbooks and museums, and their raids are seen as intercultural exchanges. On the other hand, textbook emphases on local environments are likely to be framed in global ecological terms (Bromley *et al.* 2011a).

Global Educational Organization

A most striking feature of the emergent global educational policy field is the rise of a dense system of international organizations, each of which may be an arena of policy discourse, and each of which is likely to be a participant in networks of such discourse. Over and above the nationally rooted organizations focusing on international goals, a great many of these are explicitly international, representing multiple national societies.

Most of the organizations involved are non-governmental in character, reflecting religious, or charitable, or more recently, professional missions (Boli and Thomas 1997; Bromley 2010). Figure 2.1, taken from the data of the Union of International Associations, reports a simple count of the international non-governmental education-related organizations (INGOs) over time. For comparison, we also include an overall count of INGOs of all sorts.

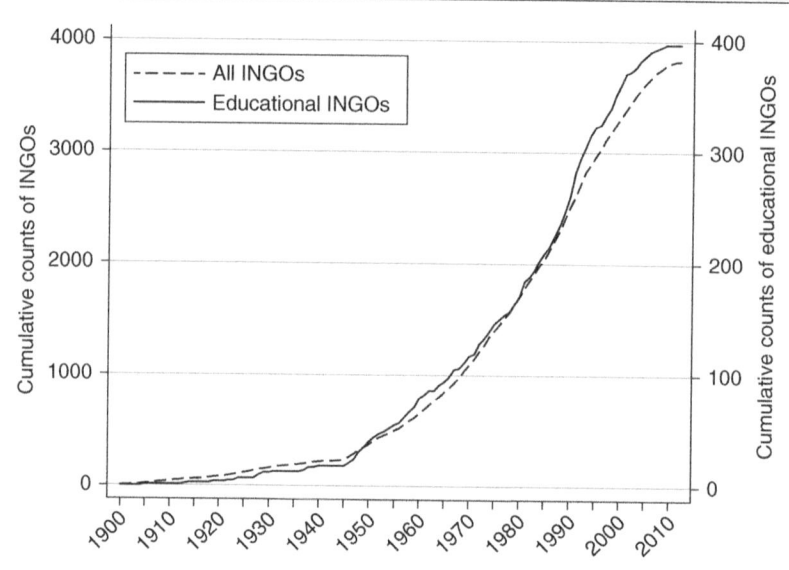

Figure 2.1 Growth in international non-governmental organizations.
Source: Data from UIA (2013).

The count in Figure 2.1 shows explosive growth. Of course, much of this growth parallels the expansion in international organizational life in general. But there is clearly a special dramatic focus on education as a central institution in world society. For both INGOs in general and for educational INGOs in particular, the explosion is especially evident during the latter decades of the past century. Modest increases in foundings earlier on are intensified later.

Bromley (2010) studies this set of organizations, classifying them on their primary missions. She finds a steady shift from traditional religious missions to a more scientific logic. In practice, this means that such organizations are increasingly involved in the policy process, as opposed to simple service delivery. Mundy and Murphy (2001) convincingly show that the international non-governmental system is increasingly involved in transmitting and enforcing policy commitments. The world shifts from a mostly inter-state system characterized by national educational systems to one in which international organizations, with some legitimacy, influence educational developments directly and globally.

Even more central in globalizing policy is the dramatic rise in international governmental organizations. We chart overall figures, also taken from the Union of International Associations, in Figure 2.2. Many of these organizations prominently display education among their foci. And increasingly, as we discuss below, these organizations come to be aggressive in defining proper educational policies worldwide (e.g. in the Education for All movement). This sort of expansion is especially dramatic in Europe, where the EU and related organizations play significant roles and are influential worldwide. The European Bologna Process has had extraordinary impact on a world, not simply a continental, scale.

To summarize, the post-World War II era, and even more the late neo-liberal period, is one in which there has been a sharp increase in international organizations, both governmental and non-governmental. Many of these organizations have a

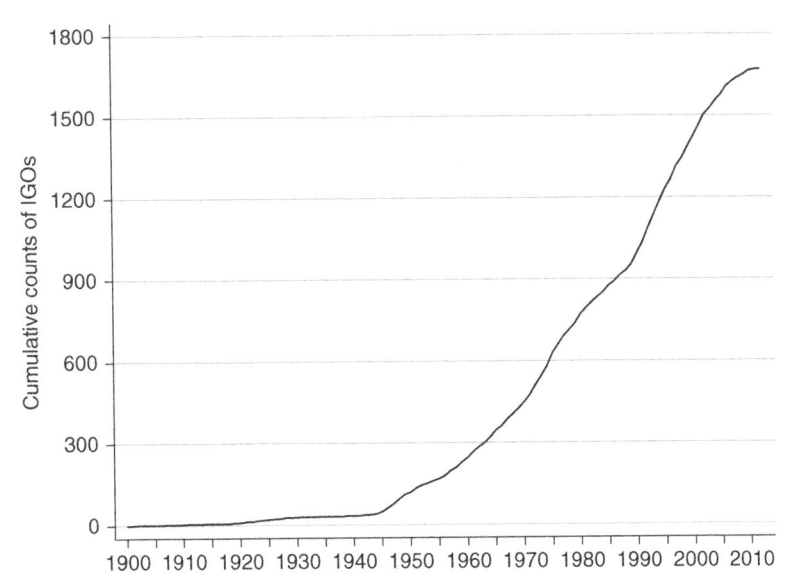

Figure 2.2 Growth in inter-governmental organizations.
Source: Data from UIA (2013).

strong focus on education. The world educational revolution involves both global enrollment growth and the growth of education as a policy domain in international organizations. Increasingly linked to basic goals of progress or justice, education has become a taken-for-granted institution worldwide.

Global Educational Discourse

Organizational expansion generates and reflects discursive expansion. Much of this takes the form of high professionalism, which now occurs in world arenas. Educators of all sorts now function in global communication circles. This is of course greatly facilitated by the rise of modern technologies that lead to the traversing of spatial boundaries. But there is more to it than technological globalization. There is also the growing sense that it is good, perhaps even necessary, to link and "network" across the boundaries. Thus, national educational systems and national professional associations become more receptive to what goes on in other countries and structure themselves accordingly. A strong "best practices" ideology emerges and permeates the world; best practices in turn are often cast as realistic instruments for upgrading education through benchmarking. As one indicator, in Figure 2.3, we track the expansion of the "World Council of Comparative Education Societies." In the 1960 to 1969 period less than ten countries were affiliated with the World Council. Forty years later there are nearly 40 members. These societies themselves have greatly expanded, of course, but the figure shows the growth in the ways they are linked together. Notably, membership in the World Council has also become less exclusive, with more non-Western countries now on board.

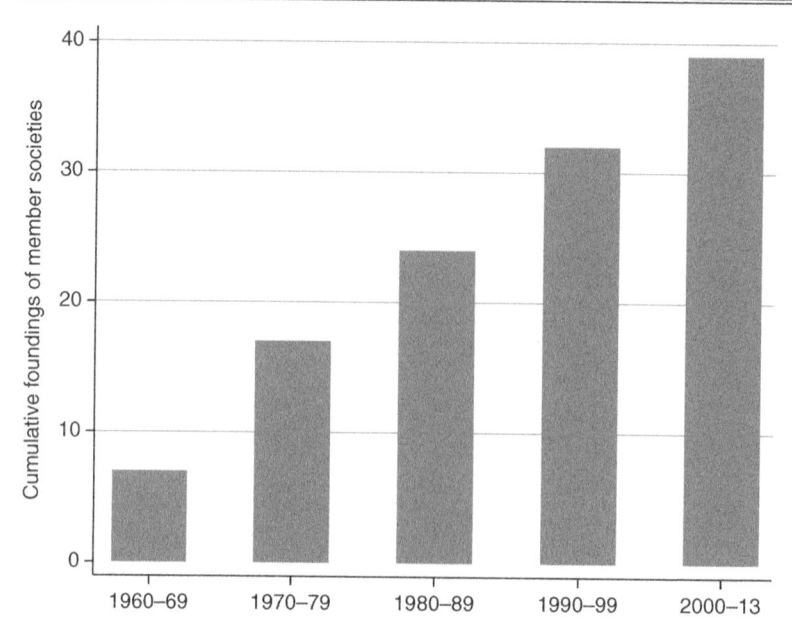

Figure 2.3 An expanding World Council of Comparative Education Societies.
Source: Data from Bray et al. (2008); WCCES (2013).
Notes: Numbers are based on the founding year of societies, not their year of joining WCCES.

Beyond the expansion of the general field of comparative education, we can also note the expansion of global professional discourse in particular educational fields. The economics of education, science education, education for literacy, social science education, educational technology, education for refugees, education in transitional or post-conflict societies – all these sorts of fields come now to be structured supra-nationally, with conferences, journals, and the other apparatuses of professional development. Table 2.1 illustratively lists some of the relevant associations in various educational fields, and their dates of foundation. Some of these associations have organizational aims attuned to the goal of excellence, emphasizing science and technology, for example. However, others seem more linked to equity, focusing on human rights and peace. We reiterate that excellence and equity are diffuse goals that nation states are expected to pursue with education as a driving force.

Professionalized discourse at the global level is structured in an expanding array of academic journals concerned with comparative education. Figure 2.4, based on a limited data set, tracks this growth. The growth pattern is very similar to that displayed in Figure 2.3. For the first time periods there are very few international and comparative education journals. By the 21st century there are many journals in this domain. Education, once imagined in mostly national terms, increasingly evolves to become more comparative in its scope. Furthermore, the reports of the central international governmental organizations increasingly emphasize education. For example, the World Bank generates increasing numbers of reports concerned with education. So do the various

Table 2.1 Associations in various educational fields

Year of foundation	Organization	Organizational aims
1973	International Council of Associations for Science Education	"Extend and improve education in science and technology for all children and youth throughout the world; provide a means of communication among associations of science teachers; foster cooperative efforts to improve science education."
1979	International Organization for Science and Technology Education	"Promote science and technology education as a vital part of the general education of all people of all countries; provide scholarly exchange and discussion and encourage informed debate, reflection and research in the field; continue and strengthen its tradition."
1994	International Association for Citizenship, Social and Economics Education	"Advance theoretical and practical knowledge about children in the areas of their social and economics understanding and learning."
1999	Global Campaign for Peace Education	"Promote the implementation of peace education in both formal and non-formal educational settings around the world."
2000	Inter-Agency Network for Education in Emergencies	"Create an accessible network through which education practitioners working around the world in emergency contexts can interact and engage with one another through the exchange of resources and information which will assists in their individual and organizational efforts to ensure quality education for all persons affected by emergencies, crisis, or chronic instability."
2003	Democracy and Human Rights Education in Europe	"Promote understanding and commitment to human rights and democracy within the enlarged European Union through education."

Source: Data from UIA (2013).

branches of the United Nations Educational, Scientific and Cultural Organization (UNESCO). And so does the EU. Relevant trend data are reported in Figure 2.5. Not surprisingly, UNESCO publishes more educational documents throughout this period. Education is after all a core feature of its mandate. This was not the case with the World Bank, but nevertheless the publication gap between UNESCO and the World Bank shrinks by the period of 2005 to 2009, as education comes to be seen as essential to national and global economic growth. The World Bank has always enjoyed vastly greater resources, but it is only more recently that its resources are substantially focused on education. Again not surprisingly, the EU has a more modest output. Its distinctive mandate was less education-centric. But it, too, experiences dramatic growth in the years since the beginning of the "Bologna Process."

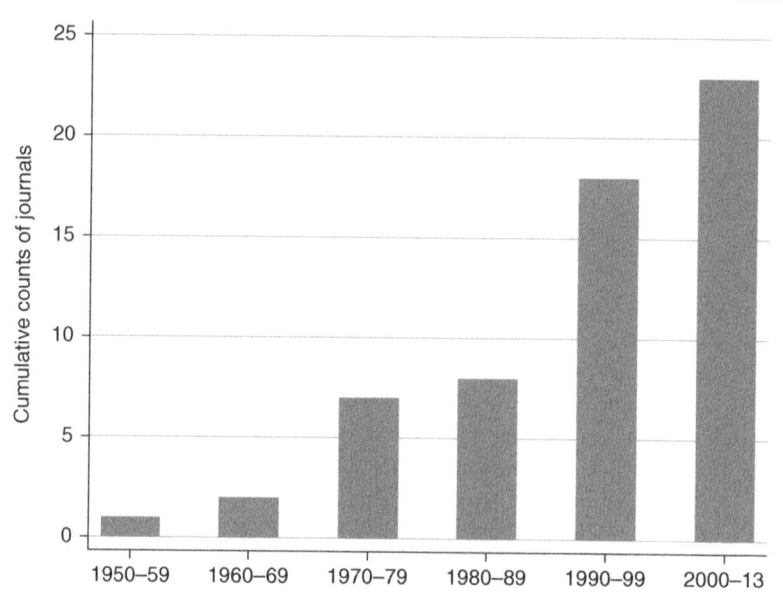

Figure 2.4 Growth in comparative and international education journals.
Source: Data from Bray *et al.* (2008); Stanford University Libraries (2013).

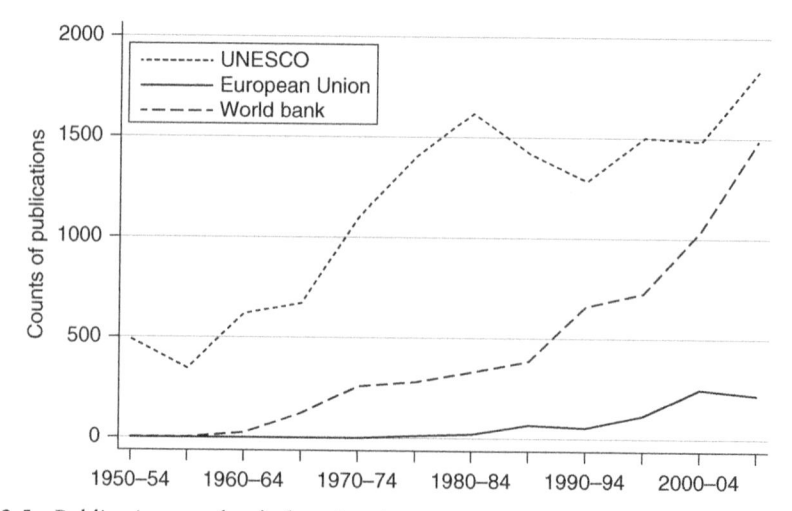

Figure 2.5 Publication trends of education documents.
Source: Data from UNESCO (2013a); World Bank (2013); EU (2013).
Note: Counts represent five-year averages of publications containing the word "education" in the title.

Impact: Global Educational Policies

The sweeping expansion of global-level educational organizational and discursive frames has reflected and produced a great expansion in explicitly global educational policies. By global policies, we mean rules and standards depicting proper national educational systems. Some of these, such as those rooted in human rights treaties, have a standing close to hard law, though of course decoupling is common and enforcement weak. Many others have more of a soft law character, offering prescriptions and models defining proper or best practices. Still others simply lay out standards of virtuous practice and conduct – criteria defining better and worse education, not standards of pre- and proscription.

An important point here is that the contemporary world has generated pervasively influential models defining what a good educational system is. A second point is that these models are formed rather universalistically – good education is good education everywhere. Global discourse often gives lip service to the virtues of local adaptation, variation, and diversity. But uniformity is the general rule – a most striking fact in a world of very great cultural and socioeconomic diversity. It is hard to find international organizations and discourses, for example, that now suggest that impoverished countries delay the creation and expansion of higher education. This was an idea well established just a few decades ago. Earlier World Bank recommendations to restrict the growth of higher education in less developed countries have receded (Heyneman 1995). National salvation outside higher education is now unimaginable.

Much globalized educational policy is ultimately justified under contemporary human rights norms, which are organized universalistically. The child – everywhere covered by such norms – is entitled to education, and will benefit from it. There is no clear depiction of a global social order that functionally requires the child to be schooled. In this the global system differs from the early nationally focused one, in which schooling was both the right of the child and a compulsory obligation to the national state. Thus the world has norms supporting the child's right to an education, but has not yet constructed itself as a corporate body that can make education compulsory. Global society operates to infuse national societies with the sense that they should be embracing education for the widest range of approved goals.

Educational Enrollment

Global policies have increasingly stressed the importance of educational enrollment. Education is forwarded as a human right (in Article 26 of the Universal Declaration of Human Rights). Table 2.2 depicts some crucial dates in the development of this principle, culminating in the worldwide Education for All movement. The Jomtien conference is the first major international educational conference in which non-state actors are given a place at the table. The conference was fostered by an unusual collaboration between the World Bank and UNESCO, a collaboration facilitated by the United Nations Children's Fund (UNICEF) (Chabbott 2003).

Table 2.2 also shows that this general right to education principle is increasingly applied to more and more components of the human population: females (Ramirez and Wotipka 2001), ethnic minorities, refugees, indigenous people (Cole 2011; Tsutsui 2004), pre-school children (Wotipka et al. 2013), post-schooling adults and lifelong learning (Jakobi 2009), disabled persons (Powell 2011), and so on. The universalistic reach of the educational principle is best appreciated by recalling the historical debates about whether this or that category of person was educable – peasants and workers, for example. These debates, in the contemporary context, would be difficult to imagine.

Table 2.2 International instruments recognizing the right to education

Year	Instrument	Adopting body
1948	Universal Declaration of Human Rights	General Assembly of the United Nations
1959	Declaration on the Rights of the Child	General Assembly of the United Nations
1960	Convention against Discrimination in Education	General Conference of UNESCO
1965	International Convention on the Elimination of All Forms of Racial Discrimination	General Assembly of the United Nations
1966	International Covenant on Economic, Social and Cultural Rights	General Assembly of the United Nations
1974	Recommendation on Education for International Understanding and Co-operation and Peace and Education relating to Human Rights and Fundamental Freedoms	General Conference of UNESCO
1978	International Charter of Physical Education and Sport	General Conference of UNESCO
1979	Convention on the Elimination of All Forms of Discrimination against Women (CEDAW)	General Assembly of the United Nations
1989	Convention on Technical and Vocational Education	General Conference of UNESCO
1989	Convention on the Rights of the Child	General Assembly of the United Nations
1990	Jomtien World Declaration on Education for All: Meeting Basic Learning Needs	World Conference on Education for All
1997	Hamburg Declaration on Adult Learning	International Conference on Adult Education
2000	Dakar Framework for Action: Education for All: Meeting our Collective Commitments	World Education Forum
2001	Revised Recommendation concerning Technical and Vocational Education	General Conference of UNESCO
2003	General Comment 13 on the Right to Education (Art. 13 of the International Covenant on Economic, Social, and Cultural Rights)	UNESCO and United Nations Committee on Economic, Social and Cultural Rights
2006	Convention on the Rights of Persons with Disabilities	General Assembly of the United Nations

Source: UNESCO (2013b).

Educational Curricula and Quality

A dramatic aspect of educational policy globalization is to be found in the formation and expansion of curricular and learning standards. The former tend to be implicit, and the latter very explicit.

With respect to mass education, there is the rapid modern expansion of international testing (Kijima 2013; Kamens and McNeeley 2010). PISA tests, rooted in the OECD, have expanded in number. So have the tests of the International Association for the Evaluation of Educational Achievement (IEA). Recently, some regional associations

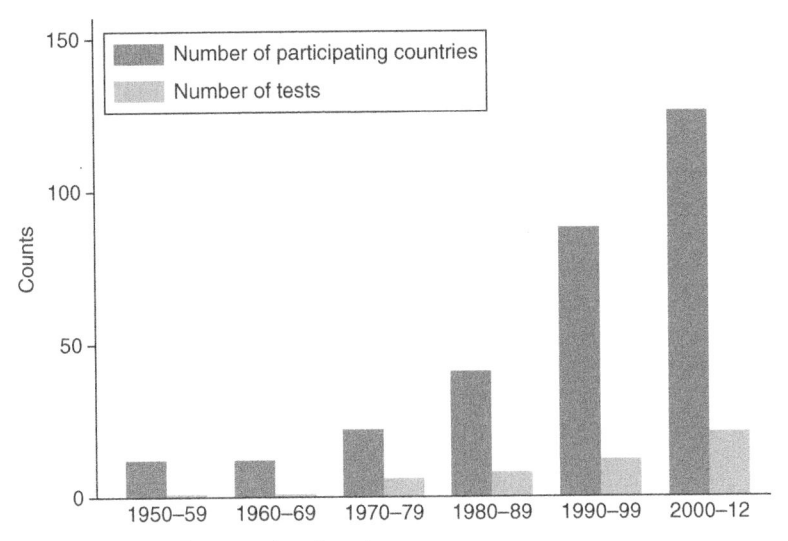

Figure 2.6 Expansion of international testing.
Source: Data from Kijima (2013).

have also constructed tests. Of course, the testing – especially since the results are commonly discussed as scores on single dimensions – carries considerable force in implying a globally common set of standards. In Figure 2.6, we report the expansion in numbers of such international tests, and the expansion in the numbers of countries participating in them. The figure shows the extraordinary increase in testing. Both numbers of tests and the numbers of countries participating in them grow dramatically over time.

International testing has produced an extensive literature at both international and domestic levels. In many countries, national results on international tests have had considerable policy impact. For example, in the USA, a whole policy regime embodied in the document "A Nation at Risk" followed on some test score results. Similar impacts have characterized a despondent educational discourse in Germany and an upbeat one in Finland (but see Rautalin 2013 for a more nuanced assessment of the Finnish educational triumph). New heroes clearly emerge from the widely publicized results of these tests, from "Asian tigers" (Japan, Singapore, South Korea, and Taiwan) to Finland (Takayama 2008) to Shanghai (Sellar and Lingard 2013). It is widely argued, or even assumed, that the country winners in these tests will undergo greater economic development than the laggards (Hanushek and Kimko 2000; but see Ramirez *et al.* 2006, for an alternative perspective).

A similar pattern characterizes the rise of international comparisons in the field of higher education – there is an explosion in the rankings of universities and the formation of national policies to enhance the creation of "world class universities." Table 2.3 reports global rankings that have received attention, and the dates of their creation. Table 2.4 shows a selective list of countries discussed in the literature as having policies related to the creation of world class universities.

The rankings are often and justifiably criticized. But it will not do to pretend that they are inconsequential. The rankings influence higher educational discourse and organization in ways parallel to the influence of the international tests for lower levels of schooling. Both systems, at least as they are commonly employed,

Table 2.3 Global university rankings

Year of launch	Ranking name	Produced by
2003	*Shanghai Academic Ranking of World Universities	Shanghai Academic Ranking Consultancy, China
2004 (ended in 2009)	*Times Higher Education-QS World University Rankings	Times Higher Education and Quacquarelli Symonds, UK
2004	Webometrics Ranking of World Universities	Cybermetrics lab, Centro de Ciencias Humanas y Sociales, Spain
2007	Performance Ranking of Scientific Papers for World Universities	Higher Education Accreditation and Evaluation Council, Taiwan
2007	International Professional Classification of Higher Education Institutions	École des Mines de Paris, France
2008	Leiden Rankings	Leiden University, The Netherlands
2009 (one ranking)	Reitor Global Universities Ranking	Reitor (Реŭмор), Russian Federation
2010	*Times Higher Education World University Rankings	Times Higher Education and Thomson Reuters, UK
2010	*QS World University Rankings	Quacquarelli Symonds, UK
2013	U-Multirank	Funded by the European Commission

Source: Rauhvargers (2011).
Note: The most influential rankings are starred. In 2010, the *Times* and QS ended their collaboration and started producing the Times Higher Education World University Rankings and the QS World University Rankings, respectively.

presuppose universalistic standards that order the standing of local and national schools or universities in the wider world. National policy reactions often imagine that improvement is both possible and necessary. National educational goals are set forth in a comparative mode, to upgrade what one's students know in mathematics and science relative to what students around the world know or to plan to have world class universities like those in other countries (see the papers in Shin and Kehm 2013; Wedlin 2006, as regards business schools).

The Knowledge Society

Central attention to the expansion and quality of both mass and higher education is closely linked to the rise in global discourse of conceptions of society itself as a sort of educational construction, and a product of educational development. Far from an earlier modern depiction of education as producing people for a given (or later, a planned) society, contemporary discourse has a very open-system character. Society – and now, including the economy – is to be built out of creative and entrepreneurial education-produced innovations. This is the "Knowledge Society," or "Knowledge Economy." The conception of society and economy involved is far removed from earlier emphases on material production, material resources, and material human needs. The central

Table 2.4 Selected national excellence initiatives related to world class higher education

Country	Year of launch	Initiative name
Canada	2009	Canada Global Excellence Research Chairs
China	1996	China 211 Project
	1999	China 985 Project
France	2006	Opération Campus
	2006	Pôles de recherche et d'enseignement supérieur (PRES)
Germany	2004	Germany Excellence Initiative
Japan	2002	Japan Top-30 Program (21st Century Centers of Excellence)
	2007	Japan Global Centers of Excellence Program
Republic of Korea	1999	Brain Korea 21 Program
	2008	World Class University
	2008	Humanity Korea Project
	2010	Social Science Korea
Malaysia	2007	National Higher Education Strategic Plan 2020
Saudi Arabia	Opened in 2009	King Abdullah University of Science and Technology
Singapore	1997	Campus for Research Excellence and Technological Enterprise (CREATE)
	2007	Research Centers of Excellence
Taiwan	1998	Program for Promoting Academic Excellence of Universities
	2006	Development Plan for World Class Universities and Research Centers of Excellence

Source: Salmi (2009); Shin and Kehm (2013); Wildavsky (2010); Ramakrishna (2012).

institution in constructing this new world is education – mass education for building both human capital and the expanded human person in general; and elite education, presumably in world class universities, that will generate the innovations and technical developments to enhance competitive progress. In this new model, education, once thought to serve religious and political ends, becomes relevant to every aspect of life and progress, now including an expanded version of the economy.

The Global Educational Model

The literature in comparative education tends to follow its traditional pattern of emphasizing diversity. Case studies abound, and naturally emphasize the unique features of the particular case. This tends to understate the extent to which educational systems reflect common forces – and forces that have become increasingly common through the current period, as we discuss above. Thus, we may here note what seem to be fairly consensual educational virtues in contemporary world society. Of course, as virtues, they are routinely violated in practice, and education is a notorious site for extreme versions of decoupling between policy and practice (Meyer and Rowan 1977; note that Brunsson 1989 speaks of it as hypocrisy). But it is worth attending to the virtues themselves, and what they indicate about world society.

1. Clearly, a virtuous educational system is an expanded one. Mass education should be universal, and secondary education should be near that. Higher education should in some form be available to almost anyone. Particular attention should be given to supplying education to groups earlier barred or discriminated against, for females, ethnic minorities and indigenous peoples, the disabled, very young children, and so on. Almost everyone will benefit from more education (Hout 2012).
2. Education should stress cognitive achievement in all sorts of standard subjects. It should not emphasize ritual knowledge, especially very parochial ritual knowledge in a local culture. The right to education is now framed as the right to learn. This in turn gives rise to a renewed interest in effective teaching that is supposed to lead to deep understanding, not merely rote memorization.
3. Education should be participatory and progressive. Traditional conformity to the rules is not so important. Rote memorization is debunked. The student should develop a capacity for creative initiative and for problem-solving.
4. Education should be emancipatory. The student should learn tolerance for much diversity, including international diversity. The student should become a member of national society, but also a global society within which the nation is to be seen as embedded.
5. Educational systems should be transparent and accountable. Of course, these are faddish terms but they capture the underlying sense that everyone has a right to know what is going on in schools and universities. The latter are under pressure to submit to "report cards" that often take the form of international tests and university rankings.
6. Lastly and most importantly, the virtuous educational system is attuned to world educational standards. These inform the virtues it needs to realize. These also point to successful cases (educational heroes) and cross-national best practices. Educational consulting is increasingly a multi-national enterprise. The emergence and expansion of international tests and transnational rankings facilitates the rise of educational consulting without borders.

Uncertainty, Fashion, and Variations

We have outlined what seem to be consensual features of the contemporary globalized model of education. Yet there is a great deal of variability within and around this model. Some of this arises because of enormous uncertainty in the realities involved. It is not clear what the ideal Knowledge Society is. And it is very unclear what dimensions of education might enhance it: even the established notion that education produces hard-line economic growth rests on very shaky theory and evidence. There is, thus, no good empirical reason to assume that having one world class university is better than having several good ones – or indeed less tertiary education at all. Nor is it clear that it is more important to improve PISA scores than to expand access to more education.

In this context education is understood to be central, but it is unknown what dimensions are important – so waves of fashion arise. These reflect realities or perceptions about dominant or successful countries – here a Finland, there a Singapore, and sometimes a Cuba, but commonly the USA as regards higher education – which should be emulated. And the realities and perceptions involved are the substantive meat of the discourse and organization in the supra-national world. A wave of fashion makes instruction in science and mathematics important, and STEM (science, technology, engineering and mathematics) becomes an international acronym. A related version stresses the importance of female participation in education generally or in engineering particularly. Elsewhere, social movements emphasize expanded participation of marginal populations. Sometimes the focus is on mass education, but currently the attention goes to higher education as the putative source of the golden eggs of "innovation" and "entrepreneurship."

Given all the uncertainties involved, the one certainty is that the whole global educational policy system changes with waves of difficult-to-predict fashion. But another related consequence is a measure of pluralism: ideal models vary, and emulators can copy varying versions. Both the varying international linkages and the domestic policy structures of countries produce variations in what is copied, and in the interpretation of the core models involved. American linkages and models are central in some places, while related European ones dominate elsewhere: and always, path dependencies rooted in earlier (e.g. colonial) systems can retain some effectiveness. Globalized forces may dominate, but they by no means have a unified character: the world society is a stateless one.

Conclusion

In the 18th and 19th centuries mass schooling emerged and expanded as a project of the nation state (Ramirez and Boli 1987). This was a contested project but the advocates of mass schooling triumphed again and again. After 1945 the newly independent countries embraced this project with few of the earlier reservations about who was educable. A contested terrain became an institutionalized domain: all were educable. National education ministries and compulsory school legislation diffused worldwide, creating links between nation states and citizens.

Higher education had earlier medieval roots in Europe, but in the 19th century universities also became laboratories of nation-building (Reisner 1927). Both mass schooling and elite education became closely attuned to the nation state; the production of good national citizens and leaders was their goal. Despite many differences in the organization of schools and universities across countries, these adhered to a nationalizing script that unfolded during the 19th century (Anderson 1991). The script called for the homogenization of the masses: rugged programs for transforming the masses into good Frenchmen, Americans, or Japanese, flourished. Furthermore, subnational loyalties were suspect and to be eradicated. Education was a key institution through which national citizens and elites were to be created.

This dynamic continued into the 20th century. But two world wars later a rethinking of the nationalizing agenda of education emerged. In an earlier era world models privileged national agendas, thereby nudging empires and colonies alike to enact national identities. But these models are changing and increasingly emphasize different conceptions of the good nation state and its virtuous educational system. The ideal citizen is now first and foremost a person with rights, preferences, and capacities that need to be nourished in schools and universities. The good nation state is expected to foster this ideal citizen in terms of broader transnational standards that assist in the project. These standards are reflected in the rise and growth of international achievement tests and university rankings but also in the enormous attention given to the individual learner. The proliferation of tests and rankings presupposes that nation states can upgrade the quality of their educational systems by comparing them against the best in the world. Universalistic world standards influence educational developments not only through national policies but also directly through a web of professional educational organizations and leaders that increasingly use world standards as their reference structures. Thus the virtuous educational system is very much attuned to world standards and their articulation in international organizations and conferences. These transnational standards impose much discipline, but also, reflecting modern individualism, give rise to more student centered curricula (Bromley *et al.* 2011b) and greater choice in university courses (Frank and Gabler 2006). In world society students are conceived not only as potential sources of human capital but also as rights bearing persons with tremendous capacities for transforming the world.

This chapter explores these changing directions – changes in who counts and what counts – by examining global educational structures and trends. These include the growth of international educational organizations, professional associations, publications, and discourse. They also include the growth of international achievement tests and university rankings, and initiatives to create world class universities.

Taken as a whole these developments add up to global policy-making that privileges universalistic and optimistic emphases on high standards and best practices. The virtuous educational system is expected to prepare students to meet world challenges and seize global opportunities. All sorts of educational systems increasingly include references to the world within which they are embedded. The nation state continues to be held responsible for the education of its citizens, even as these citizens are increasingly framed in post-nationalist terms. Students are expected to function in and contribute to a Knowledge Society that is itself a creature of world standards, scripts, and statistics. Thus, the individual person is increasingly linked to the wider world not just through nation states with increasingly more similar structures and policies, but also more directly through processes that emphasize world citizenship and a global economy. The national era now co-exists with a post-nationalist global agenda, and national educational policy-making coexists with much global educational policy.

To come to terms with these developments, one needs to engage in long-term and large-scale comparative educational research. This means prioritizing longitudinal instead of cross-sectional research designs and examining changes over extended time periods. Much of what we now take for granted – women in higher education, for example – was unthinkable in many countries at the beginning of the 20th century and even well into it. Moreover, much of what we often "explain" with this or that local societal need or cultural tradition becomes problematized when we explicitly compare many countries and find common developments over time. Furthermore, one can also estimate the clout of the global versus the local only by examining the comparative weights of their influence over time. A core world society insight supported in numerous analyses is that the global weight is greater in the more recent era. A related insight is that as countries become more closely linked to world society their educational talk and action will be more attuned to global scripts. Lastly, a world society research perspective compels one to go beyond world economy emphases and to recognize the role of global authority and influence in shaping legitimate identity and proper discourse, policy, and action.

Note

1 Work on this chapter was partially funded by the National Research Foundation (Korea).

References

Anderson, B. 1991. *Imagined Communities: Reflections on the Origins and Spread of Nationalism*. London and New York: Verso.
Anderson-Levitt, K. (ed.). 2003. *Local Meanings, Global Schooling: Anthropology and World Culture Theory*. New York: Palgrave Macmillan.
Baker, D. and G.K. LeTendre. 2005. *National Differences, Global Similarities: Current and Future World Institutional Trends in Schooling*. Stanford: Stanford University Press.
Boli, J. and G.M. Thomas. 1997. "World Culture in the World Polity: A Century of International Non-Governmental Organization." *American Sociological Review*, 103: 171–190.
Bradley, C.L. and L.A. Renzulli. 2011. "The Complexity of Non-Completion: Being Pushed or Pulled to Drop Out of High School." *Social Forces*, 90: 521–545.
Bray, M., M. Manzon, and V.L. Masemann. 2008. *Common Interests, Uncommon Goals: Histories of the World Council of Comparative Education Societies and its Members*. Hong Kong, China: Comparative Education Research Centre, University of Hong Kong.
Bromley, P. 2010. "The Rationalization of Educational Development: Scientific Activity among International Nongovernmental Organizations." *Comparative Education Review*, 54: 577–601.
Bromley, P., J.W. Meyer, and F.O. Ramirez. 2011a. "The Worldwide Spread of Environmental Discourse in Social Science Textbooks, 1970–2010." *Comparative Education Review*, 55: 517–545.
Bromley, P., J.W. Meyer, and F.O. Ramirez. 2011b. "Student-Centeredness in Social Science Textbooks, 1970–2008: A Cross-National Study." *Social Forces*, 90: 547–570.
Brunsson, N. 1989. *The Organization of Hypocrisy: Talk, Decisions and Actions in Organizations*. London: Wiley.
Buckner, E. and S. Garnett Russell. 2013. "Portraying the Global: Cross-National Trends in Textbooks' Portrayal of Globalization and Global Citizenship." *International Studies Quarterly*, 57: 738–750.
Çayir, K. 2009. "Preparing Turkey for the European Union: Nationalism, National Identity and 'Otherness' in Turkey's New Textbooks." *Journal of Intercultural Studies*, 30: 39–55.
Chabbott, C. 2003. *Constructing Education for Development. International Organizations and Education for All*. London: Routledge.
Chabbott, C. and F.O. Ramirez. 2000. "Development and Education," in *Handbook of the Sociology of Education*, edited by M. Hallinan, 163–187. New York: Kluwer Academic/Plenum Publishers.
Cole, W. 2011. *Uncommon Schools: The Global Rise of Postsecondary Institutions for Indigenous Peoples*. Stanford: Stanford University Press.
Dale, R. and S.L. Robertson. 2002. "The Varying Effects of Regional Organizations as Subjects of Globalization of Education." *Comparative Education Review*, 46: 10–36.
Darling-Hammond, L. 2010. *The Flat World and Education: How America's Commitment to Equity Will Determine Our Future*. New York: Teachers College Press.
Dore, R. 1975. *The Diploma Disease: Education, Qualification, and Development*. Berkeley: University of California Press.
Edwards Jr, D.B. 2013. "International Processes of Education Policy Formation: An Analytic Framework and the Case of Plan 2021 in El Salvador." *Comparative Education Review*, 57: 22–53.
European Union (EU). 2013. "EU Bookshop." Retrieved from: https://bookshop.europa.eu/en/home/ (accessed November 3, 2015).
Frank, D. and J. Gabler. 2006. *Reconstructing the University: Worldwide Shifts in Academia in the 20th Century*. Stanford: Stanford University Press.

Freeman, R.B. 1976. *The Overeducated American*. New York: Academic Press.

Hanushek, E.A. and D.D. Kimko. 2000. "Schooling, Labor-force Quality, and the Growth of Nations." *American Economic Review*, 90: 1184–1208.

Heyneman, S.P. 1995. "Economics of Education: Disappointments and Potential." *Prospects*, 25: 559–583.

Hout, M. 2012. "Social and Economic Returns to College Education in the United States." *Annual Review of Sociology*, 38: 379–400.

Huntington, S.P. 2004. *Who Are We? The Challenges to America's National Identity*. New York: Simon and Schuster.

Jakobi, A.P. 2011. "Political Parties and the Institutionalization of Education: A Comparative Analysis of Party Manifestos." *Comparative Education Review*, 55: 189–209.

Jakobi, A.P. 2009. "Global Education Policy in the Making: International Organizations and Lifelong Learning." *Globalisation, Education and Societies*, 7: 473–487.

Kamens, D. and C.L. McNeely. 2010. "Globalization and the Growth of International Educational Testing and National Assessment." *Comparative Education Review*, 54: 5–25.

Kijima, R. 2013. *The Politics of Cross-National Assessments: Global Trends and National Interests*. Unpublished doctoral dissertation, Stanford University.

Lenhardt, G. and M. Stock. 2000. "Hochschulentwicklung und Bürgerrechte in der BRD und der DDR." *Kölner Zeitschrift für Soziologie und Sozialpsychologie*, 52: 520–540.

Lie, J. 2004. *Modern Peoplehood*. Cambridge: Harvard University Press.

Meyer, J.W. and B. Rowan. 1977. "Institutionalized Organizations: Formal Structure as Myth and Ceremony." *American Journal of Sociology*, 83: 340–363.

Meyer, J.W., D. Kamens, and A. Benavot (with Y.-K. Cha and S.-Y. Wong). 1992. *School Knowledge for the Masses: World Models and National Primary Curricular Categories in the 20th Century*. London: Falmer Press.

Meyer, J.W., J. Boli, G.M. Thomas, and F.O. Ramirez. 1997. "World Society and the Nation-State." *American Journal of Sociology*, 103: 144–81.

Meyer, J.W., P. Bromley, and F.O. Ramirez. 2010. "Human Rights in Social Science Textbooks, 1970–2008." *Sociology of Education*, 83: 111–134.

Mundy, K. and L. Murphy. 2001. "Transnational Advocacy, Global Civil Society: Emerging Evidence from the Field of Education." *Comparative Education Review*, 45: 85–126.

Nozaki, Y. 2002. "Japanese Politics and the History Textbook Controversy, 1982–2001." *International Journal of Educational Research*, 37: 603–622.

Powell, J. 2011. *Barriers to Inclusion: Special Education in the United States and Germany*. Boulder: Paradigm Publishers.

Ramakrishna, S. 2012. "Building a World-Class University System: Singapore's Experience and Practices." *Journal of International Higher Education*, 5: 79–82.

Ramirez, F.O. 2006. "From Citizen to Person: Rethinking Education as Incorporation," in *The Impact of Comparative Education Research on Institutional Theory*, edited by D. Baker and A. Wiseman, 367–388. Amsterdam: Elsevier.

Ramirez, F.O. 2012. "The World Society Perspective: Concepts, Assumptions, and Strategies." *Comparative Education*, 48(4): 423–439.

Ramirez, F.O. and J. Boli. 1987. "The Political Construction of Mass Schooling: European Origins and Worldwide Institutionalization." *Sociology of Education*, 60: 2–17.

Ramirez, F.O. and C.M. Wotipka. 2001. "Slowly but Surely? The Global Expansion of Women's Participation in Science and Engineering Fields of Study, 1972–92." *Sociology of Education*, 74: 231–251.

Ramirez, F.O, X. Luo, E. Schofer, and J.W. Meyer. 2006. "Student Achievement and National Economic Growth." *American Journal of Education*, 113: 1–29.

Ramirez, F.O., P. Bromley, and S. Garnett Russell. 2009. "The Valorization of Humanity and Diversity." *Multicultural Education Review*, 1: 29–54.

Rautalin, M. 2013. *Domestication of International Comparisons: The Role of the OECD Programme for Student Assessment in Finnish Educational Policy*. Unpublished dissertation. School of Social Sciences and Humanities, University of Tampere, Finland.

Rauhvargers, A. 2011. *Global University Rankings and their Impact*. Brussels: European University Association.

Reisner, E.H. 1927. *Nationalism and Education since 1789*. New York: MacMillan.

Robertson, R. 1992. *Globalization: Social Theory and Global Culture*. London: Sage.

Rosenmund, M. 2006. "The Current Discourse on Curriculum Change," in *School Curricula for Global Citizenship*, edited by A. Benavot and C. Braslavsky, 173–194. Hong Kong: Comparative Education Research Center, University of Hong Kong/Springer.

Salmi, J. 2009. *The Challenge of Establishing World Class Universities*. Washington, DC: World Bank Publications.

Schriewer, J. 2012. "Meaning Constellations in World Society." *Comparative Education*, 48: 411–422.

Schofer, E. and J.W. Meyer. 2005. "The Worldwide Expansion of Higher Education in the Twentieth Century." *American Sociological Review*, 70: 898–920.

Schofer, E., A. Hironaka, D. Frank, and W. Longhofer. 2012. "Sociological Institutionalism and World Society," in *The Wiley-Blackwell Companion to Political Sociology*, edited by E. Amenta, K. Nash, and A. Scott, 57–68. Malden: Wiley-Blackwell.

Sellar, S. and B. Lingard. 2013. "Looking East: Shanghai, PISA 2009 and the Reconstitution of Reference Societies in the Global Education Policy Field." *Comparative Education*, 49: 464–485.

Shin, J.C. and B. Kehm (eds). 2013. *Institutionalization of World-Class University in Global Competition*. New York: Springer.

Stanford University Libraries. 2013. "SearchWorks." Retrieved from: http://searchworks.stanford.edu (accessed November 3, 2015).

Takayama, K. 2008. "The Politics of International League Tables: PISA in Japan's Achievement Crisis Debate." *Comparative Education*, 44: 387–407.

Tsutsui, K. 2004. "Global Civil Society and Ethnic Social Movements in the Contemporary World." *Sociological Forum*, 19: 63–87.

Union of International Associations (UIA). 2013. *Yearbook of International Organizations*. Online version.

United Nations Educational, Scientific and Cultural Organization (UNESCO). 2013a. "UNESDOC Database." Retrieved from: www.unesco.org/new/en/unesco/resources/online-materials/publications/unesdoc-database (accessed November 3, 2015).

United Nations Educational, Scientific and Cultural Organization (UNESCO). 2013b. "Education Standard Setting." Retrieved from: www.unesco.org/new/en/education/themes/leading-the-international-agenda/right-to-education/normative-action/standard-setting (accessed November 3, 2015).

Verger, A. 2010. *WTO/GATS and the Global Politics of Higher Education*. New York: Routledge.

Wang, D. 2013. *The Demoralization of Teachers: Crisis in a Rural School in China*. Lanham: Lexington Books.

Wedlin, L. 2006. *Ranking Business Schools: Forming Fields, Identities, and Boundaries in International Management Education*. Cheltenham: Elgar Publishing.

Wildavsky, B. 2010. *The Great Brain Race: How Global Universities are Reshaping the World*. Princeton: Princeton University Press.

Wong, S.-Y. 1991. "The Evolution of Social Science Instruction, 1900–86." *Sociology of Education*, 64: 33–47.

World Bank. 2013. "Documents and Reports." Retrieved from: http://documents.worldbank.org/curated/en/home (accessed November 3, 2015).

World Council of Comparative Education Societies (WCCES). 2013. "Member Societies." Retrieved from: www.wcces.com/alphbetical.html (accessed November 3, 2015).

Wotipka, C., B. Jarillo Rabling, M. Sugawara, and P. Tongliemnak. 2013. "The Worldwide Expansion of Early Childhood Education, 1985–2005." (Under review).

Chapter 3

The Global Diffusion of Education Privatization: Unpacking and Theorizing Policy Adoption

Antoni Verger

Introduction

Education privatization is a global policy process with multiple manifestations in different world locations. Both industrialized and developing countries, and nations with very different administrative traditions and regulatory frameworks, are adopting privatization policies of a different nature as a way to address a range of social, political, economic and educational challenges. Among the most internationalized and emblematic education privatization policies we find charter schools, school choice policies, and voucher schemes.

The objective of this chapter is twofold. First, the chapter reflects on the multiple policy manifestations of the privatization phenomenon in different educational settings. Second, and more importantly, the chapter analyzes the global diffusion of education privatization policies and, in particular, the reasons why privatization has played such a central role in education reform processes in a broad range of world locations.

Theoretically speaking, rationalistic and normative approaches have dominated the policy diffusion debate (see Jacoby 2000; Meseguer 2006; Meyer and Rowan 1977). However, as I argue in this chapter, these approaches provide an incomplete understanding of global education policy and, therefore, are not the most useful approaches to understand why and how education privatization, as a policy program, disseminates globally. Too often, rationalistic and normative approaches reach the conclusion that policy convergence is happening, but neglect the diverse factors and dynamics of convergence, including the complex political interplay between the international and the domestic policy fields. Moreover, these approaches focus on the formal adoption of external policy models, but de-problematize to what extent converging policies are effectively retained and enacted in domestic networks of rules and practices.

The Handbook of Global Education Policy, First Edition.
Edited by Karen Mundy, Andy Green, Bob Lingard, and Antoni Verger.
© 2016 John Wiley & Sons, Ltd. Published 2016 by John Wiley & Sons, Ltd.

Alternatively, I consider critical constructivism and cultural political economy (e.g. Hay 2001; Jessop 2010, Schmidt 2010) to be better equipped for this endeavor. They allow us to scrutinize global education policies and problematize key moments in the policy process that, too often, mainstream theories on policy diffusion take for granted (or only consider very superficially). In particular, these approaches contribute to look more in depth and more critically at the politics and semiotics of policy adoption, as well as at the role of ideas and strategic actors operating at a range of scales in the selection and retention of new educational policies.

To elaborate on this argument, this chapter is structured in three main parts. In the first part, I develop the different faces of education privatization and show that the privatization agenda develops into multiple and quite diverse educational policies. In the second part of the chapter, I reflect on how both rationalism and normative approaches understand the globalization of education policies. I present the main premises for each of the approaches and specifically show how they apply to the diffusion of education privatization policies. After having identified the main weaknesses of the two mentioned approaches, in the third part of the chapter, on the basis of critical constructivism and cultural political economy studies, I elaborate an alternative approach to understand education policy diffusion. To this purpose, I unpack policy adoption in three key evolutionary mechanisms (namely, variation, selection, and retention), and illustrate how education privatization reforms disseminate, work, and evolve through each of them.

The Multiple Faces of Privatization

Education privatization cannot be considered as a policy in itself, since it has multiple policy manifestations. Education privatization needs to be seen as a process by which private actors participate more actively in a range of education activities that have traditionally been the responsibilities of the state.

Education privatization does not necessarily mean a drastic transfer of the "ownership" of the education service from public to private hands – in contrast to what we have witnessed in other widely privatized sectors like telecommunications or energy. At least, this is not the most important way education privatization develops in most parts of the world. Privatization is a process that tends to happen more at the levels of services provision and funding, than at the level of ownership in a strict sense. According to Fitz and Beers (2002, 139), education privatization is "a process that occurs in many modes but in one form or another involves the transfer of public money or assets from the public domain to the private sector."

Education privatization can emerge by default (i.e. because of states' passivity in front of a growing education demand), but it also tends to happen because of governments proactively promoting it through the adoption and implementation of specific policies. The education privatization agenda covers policies like voucher schemes, charter schools, education sector liberalization, contracting out educational services, and so on. All of them are measures that introduce higher levels of private sector participation, especially in the delivery of services that were provided by the public sector.

Ball and Youdell (2007) have famously distinguished between two main types of privatization policies: (a) Privatization *of* public education (or "exogenous" privatization), which involves "the opening up of public education services to private sector participation [usually] on a for-profit basis and using the private sector to design, manage or deliver aspects of public education"; and (b) Privatization *in* public education (or "endogenous" privatization), which involves the "importing of ideas, techniques and practices from the private sector in order to make the public sector more like businesses and more business-like" (Ball and Youdell 2007, 9). This latest modality implies deconcentrating managerial responsibilities at the school level, allowing users more scope for choice and exit, and introducing outcomes based management techniques, among other policy measures (Maroy 2009).

More recently, Ball (2012) has referred to a third modality of privatization: privatization *through* education policy, which refers to the increasingly active role of private actors in the process of education policy-making (e.g. by selling or advocating policy solutions to governments).

To make the conceptualization of the privatization phenomenon even more complex, public–private mixes are becoming increasingly central in the organization of educational systems in many places. In policy terms, public–private mixes or "public–private partnerships" (PPPs), tend to translate into more or less stable contracts between the public and the private sector. Through this contract, the public sector buys a service from the private sector for a certain period of time at a certain price and depending on results. Both the private and the public are expected to assume risks in the delivery of the service (Patrinos *et al.* 2009).

In one way or another, many of these policies are being adopted and applied in countries and regions with very little in common, for very different reasons (Verger *et al.* 2016). To start with, this is the case in countries like the UK, New Zealand, and Chile, where education privatization policies have advanced drastically as part of a broader strategy of state reform under neo-liberal principles (Ball 2007; Mizala 2007). This is also the case in Nordic European countries, which have traditionally enjoyed a strong public intervention in education provision, and where privatization and pro-market measures started being adopted in the 1990s as a way to debureaucratize and modernize the welfare state (Wiborg 2013). On their part, North American states are gradually advancing charter school legislation and local voucher experiences under the pressure of the persistent and influential school-choice movement (DeBray-Pelot *et al.* 2007). In Central and Southern Europe and in Latin America, many governments tend to contract education services to religious providers on a large scale as both a cost-efficient measure, but also as a historical compromise between the State and the Church (Bonal 2000). Finally, privatization is also expanding in South Asian and sub-Saharan countries, where the so-called "low-fee private schools" seem to be mushrooming and many governments and donors are considering their incorporation into PPP frameworks as an efficient way to expand education (Srivastava 2014).

Main Approaches to Policy Diffusion

As the previous section shows, the education privatization agenda is very diverse and translates into a range of different policy programs (i.e. PPPs, school choice policies, charter schools, and so on). Nevertheless, and independently from the final form they take, we are also witnessing a global convergence around the idea of privatization as a desirable policy option and, consequently, the enactment of this policy idea in multiple settings. In the following sections, and before I provide an alternative account, I reflect on how mainstream theories on policy diffusion (namely rationalism and normative-emulation) would explain such levels of convergence around education privatization.

Rationalism

Rationalism considers that reality has an intrinsically logical structure and agents reproduce such structure by taking rational or utilitarian decisions through which to pursue their interests. Rationalism is an epistemological approach grounded on strong ontological claims, the main one probably being that of human beings as primarily benefit maximizers. When applied to policy-making, rationalism considers that decision-makers are goal-oriented and engage in strategic interactions as a way to maximize their utilities (or those of the constituency they represent) on the basis of pre-given interests and preferences (Risse 2000)

Rationalist scholars assume that, when confronted with a new education problem, policy-makers will scan the international environment in search of policies that have "worked well" elsewhere; process the obtained information through a thorough cost–benefit analysis; and pick the most optimal policy, i.e. the one that better demonstrates that it can contribute to maximizing its utility in the country in question (Meseguer 2006; Weyland 2005). Rationalist scholars would consider that education privatization policies are spreading because evidence shows that such policies work or have worked well elsewhere. In other words, according to rationalism, policy-makers embrace privatization policies once it has been demonstrated that these policies can contribute to, among other aspects, improving students' academic performance and/or the efficiency of education systems.

Research on the diffusion of education privatization that adopts an explicit rationalist approach is uncommon. However, despite this fact, several agencies advocating education privatization seem to subscribe to rationalist assumptions when they engage with local policy-makers. For instance, international organizations like the World Bank seem to assume that, by systematizing worldwide evidence and/or doing impact evaluations of a range of interventions (such as PPPs, teachers' incentives schemes and so on), they demonstrate to national policy-makers which policies "work" and, accordingly, the latter will opt to adopt and implement them (see, for instance, Bruns et al. 2011; Patrinos et al. 2009).

Normative Emulation

Normative approaches are skeptical about the idea of policy diffusion as the result of an aggregation of goal-oriented rational choices by self-interested policy-makers. According to these approaches, countries adopt global policies not necessarily because they need them, or because they know that they work well, but rather due to the legitimation pressures that governments receive to demonstrate to the international community that they are a modern and responsible state (Drezner 2001). Adopting the categories made famous by March and Olsen (1998), normative-emulation scholars believe that, in global politics, the logic of appropriateness predominates over the logic of expected consequences.

In comparative education, this approach is strongly represented by World Culture Theory (WCT) (Meyer *et al.* 1992; 1997; see also Ramirez, Meyer, and Lerch, Chapter 2, this volume). This theory argues that a single global model of schooling has spread around the world as part of the diffusion of a more general culturally embedded model of the modern nation state. The need for nation states to conform to an international ideal of the rationalized bureaucratic state has led to a process of institutional isomorphism and convergence in education (Meyer *et al.* 1992). In this view, international organizations and international non-governmental organizations (NGOs) are key transmitters of modernization ideas and Western values at a global scale.

WCT also understands policy diffusion as the result of the misleading attraction that some new global policy ideas generate – even when there is not enough international evidence supporting the effectiveness of such policies. According to this theoretical current, once a new policy reaches a certain threshold of adoption in different countries, more and more policy-makers become inclined to "take the policy for granted as necessary and will adopt it whether or not they have need of it"; consequently, such policies will "spread to polities for which they were not originally designed" (Dobbin *et al.* 2007, 454). Such an "irrational" modality of policy dissemination is seen as especially problematic in low-income countries, which end up assigning their scarce resources to adopt external policies that do not fit within their more urgent needs and implementation capacities (Jakobi 2012).

According to WCT, more and more policy-makers would implement privatization policies like PPPs because they are normatively accepted by the international community and/or because these policies have become a sort of international policy fad – with "partnerships" being perceived as an inherently positive policy approach in a range of policy sectors (see Cornwall 2007).

Several pieces of research on education privatization apply this theoretical approach explicitly. This is the case, for instance, of Komatsu (2013), according to whom the government in Bosnia-Herzegovina adopted a school-based management reform to present itself as a reformer in tune with European standards, thereby responding to the citizens' aspirations for European integration. Following a similar argumentation, Rinne (2000) considers that, in the 1990s, Finland adopted endo-privatization ideas and abandoned equity as a core educational goal[1] as a consequence of its integration into the European Union (EU):

> Finland has adapted the general lines of a globalising world in its educational policy, and as one of the "model students" of the European Union, wants to continue being seen very clearly as a good students who can be trusted and who is in the front ranks of those achieving the goals set for Europe. (Rinne 2000, 139)

In this volume, Patricia Bromley also uses WCT to understand the global diffusion of privatization and related managerial practices in education. According to her, administrative practices in education, like New Public Management ideas, would "diffuse as a cultural matter. As culture, formal structures spread beyond functional requirements and in ways that are not obvious reflections of aggregated self-interests or to the benefit of elites and not necessarily most efficient" (Bromley, Chapter 26, this volume, p 471).

Overall, WCT offers a very solid alternative to rationalism, but is still incomplete for providing us with a more nuanced and situated understanding of global education policy processes. From an ontological point of view, WCT prefers to err on the side of *ideationalism* (i.e. it does not sufficiently introduce material and economic factors in its explanations of policy change (Dale 2000)), *structuralism* (does not pay attention to actors' preferences and strategies, and does not reflect enough on whose interests are being served by policy convergence (Carney *et al.* 2012)), and *de-contextualization* (looks at the world polity with self-sufficiency and, accordingly, does not provide a rich account of political interactions at the national and subnational levels (Steiner-Khamsi 2004; Carney *et al.* 2012; Verger 2014)).

As a consequence of such an ontological strait-jacketing, WCT scholars tend to see *policy adoption* as a black box or, at least, as a moment that is not relevant from both an analytical and empirical point of view. At the same time, in methodological terms, they adopt a macro-sociological approach that requires the availability of world indicators to build their arguments, which allows them to do indirect analysis without directly inquiring into specific policy adoption dynamics. In the following section, I argue it is important to pay more in-context attention to policy adoption mechanisms to understand the gradual, and also uneven and erratic evolution of global education policies and agendas, particularly in education privatization.

The Politics and Semiotics of Policy Adoption

Focusing on policy adoption is fundamental to understanding, on the one hand, why and under which conditions global policy ideas spread and, on the other, the transformation processes these ideas suffer once they penetrate different territories and policy fields (what many call "re-contextualization"). Analyzing policy adoption implies paying closer attention to the processes, reasons, and circumstances that reflect how and why policy-makers embrace new education policies, usually coming from outside, and aim to apply them in their educational realities (Verger 2014).

Policy adoption is a multi-scalar process that does not necessarily materialize in a simple direction. Policy adoption is about international organizations influencing member states' policies; however, it also involves dynamics of emulation and influence in different directions, and between actors that may operate at a similar scale – see, for instance, Grek's (2012) work on the noticeable impact of the Organisation for Economic Co-operation and Development (OECD) in the EU educational agenda, or Renzulli and Roscigno (2005)'s research on the influence between US states when it comes to the adoption of charter school legislation. Maybe more counter-intuitively, policy adoption also involves bottom-up dynamics; such was the case of the World Bank adopting the conditional cash transfer idea from local governments in Mexico and Brazil – and transforming it, only afterwards, in global education policy (Peck and Theodore 2010).

Despite its relevance, policy adoption is an under-researched and under-theorized stage in education policy diffusion studies. As I have argued before, both rationalism and neo-institutionalism are not well equipped to look (and, to a great extent, not particularly interested in looking) at policy adoption. Nevertheless, in international studies and in comparative politics, there are other theoretical currents much better suited to conducting research on the policy adoption stage. I refer, in particular, to critical constructivism and to cultural political economy.

Critical constructivism has many commonalities with conventional constructivism, but "adds a belief that constructions of reality reflect, enact, and reify relations of power" (Finnemore and Sikkink 2001, 398). Critical constructivism advocates a more dialectical understanding of the relationship between ideas, social change, and strategically selective contexts and social structures (Béland 2010; Hay 2006). For its part, Cultural Political Economy (CPE) is interested in the study of economic and political imaginaries, their translation into hegemonic strategies and projects, and their institutionalization into specific structures and practices (Jessop 2010; Robertson and Dale 2015). CPE adds to conventional political economy a clear focus on semiosis (understood as all forms of social production of inter-subjective meaning) and a rich account of the semiotic dimension of economic and political orders (Jessop 2008).

There is a great deal of potential cross-fertilization between these two approaches since they share core ontological claims, including that human interests and preferences are not objectively pre-given (instead they are constructed to a great extent), and that human agents have an incomplete and often precarious understanding of the environment where they intervene (see Hay 2006). The most direct implication for policy analysis of these claims is that paying closer attention to the mobilization of ideas, and to political actors' perceptions, is key to understanding the nature and results of policy dynamics. In most occasions, policy-makers intervene in policy fields where uncertainty prevails and, as a consequence, they need to resort to inferential shortcuts and external inputs to figure out how to position themselves (Jessop 2010; Weyland 2005). Here is where the role of experts – including external advisers, policy entrepreneurs, consultancies, knowledge-brokers, etc. – and the mechanisms of persuasion and construction of meaning, should be seen and analyzed as key variables in processes of policy change (Risse 2000; Schmidt 2010).

Both CPE and critical constructivism consider power relations as consubstantial to policy processes, and that an important dimension of power in policy-making has an ideational nature. "Soft power," in interaction with the material or political dimensions of power, is considered as a key component and driver of policy change. In Jessop's words (2008, 16), "semiosis is causally effective as well as meaningful. Events and processes and their emergent effects can be interpreted and, at least in part, explained by semiosis."

However, how can all these theoretical premises on semiosis and the role of ideas be operationalized in political analysis, and in the study of policy adoption in particular? There is not a straightforward answer to this question, but Jessop's development of CPE is particularly insightful in this respect. According to him, in all institutional transformations, material and semiotic factors interact through the evolutionary mechanisms of *variation* (which relates to the contingent emergence of new practices), *selection* (which relates to the subsequent privileging of these practices), and *retention* (their ongoing realization) (Jessop 2010). This conceptual framework can contribute to moving beyond conceptions of policy adoption as a concrete and isolable stage in policy processes, or moving past the notion of policy adoption as the simple act in which policy-makers take a specific decision and/or buy (into) a new policy solution. Furthermore, this framework is especially valuable from both a heuristic and analytical point of view. The variation, selection, and retention categories can contribute to identifying more systematically the sequence of contingencies, events, forms of agency and technologies of power involved in policy adoption, as well as the specific mechanisms – of both a semiotic and non-semiotic nature – that conduct or inhibit policy change. In other words, a careful analysis of each of these categories separately can contribute to building more complex explanations of why certain policies are adopted in particular settings.

As I aim to show below, this categorization of evolutionary mechanisms is particularly useful to analyze education policy changes and, specifically, to scrutinize the worldwide adoption of education privatization reforms.

Variation

Variation starts when dominant policy discourses and practices need to be revisited due to a range of circumstances that can go from the perception of persistent educational problems (which may be related to internal dissatisfaction with the appropriateness of the education offer, or rather induced externally by the bad results of a country in international standardized evaluations such as the Programme for International Student Assessment (PISA) (Phillips and Ochs 2003) to more systemic phenomena (e.g. global pressures to become a "knowledge economy," or the responses to economic crisis or related challenges (Robertson 2005). All these elements and circumstances would put pressure on policy-makers to introduce substantive changes into their education systems.

In general, national or international economic crises tend to disorient political actors and are conducive to variation in different policy sectors (Hay 2001). In periods of crises, policy-makers are more open to reforming their education systems or importing new policies from elsewhere. This is especially true when the narratives of the crisis draw education as part of the problem and/or the solution (Ball 1990).

Global political imaginaries, like Education for All (EFA), also work in a similar way. Privatization advocates use the insufficient resources available for many low-income countries to achieve the globally agreed EFA goals as an argument to introduce urgency to pro-private reform pressure. Specifically, privatization advocates try to convince governments and donors that they should perceive the private sector as a key ally to develop their educational systems; and, if they want to achieve the EFA goals, then governments and donors need to bring the private sector into education delivery (Srivastava 2010). It is also well documented that the confusion generated by "natural disasters" or violent conflict derive in moments of variation, which some agents strategically use to advance policy reforms that otherwise would be difficult to carry out. For instance, both post-earthquake Haiti and post-Katrina New Orleans have become laboratories for neo-liberal education reformers to advance privatization and ambitious school choice reforms (Atasay and Delavan 2012; DeBray-Pelot et al. 2014).

Overall, economic crises or the global emergence of new political and economic imaginaries are constitutive of critical junctures and, as such, represent moments of disruption to typical operating procedures that expose underlying structures and mechanisms of influence (Danermark et al. 2002). Occasionally, "external" shocks generate policy convergence because, in a more globalized policy environment, policy-makers from different countries tend to give similar policy responses to similar "problems" they face (Knill 2005, see also Carnoy, Chapter 1, this volume).

However, moments of crises are also conducive to competition and conflict between different views. They tend to be perceived and used as a window of political opportunity by policy entrepreneurs and advocates operating on a range of scales with a conflicting understanding of which (global) policy programs, including privatization, are the most appropriate and suitable policy options in certain contexts.

Selection

The selection of particular policy solutions by politicians and policy-makers is another key moment in education policy change. It implies the identification of the most suitable interpretations of existing problems, as well as the most complementary policy solutions.

Neo-institutionalist scholars tend to explain countries' selection of external polices by resorting to factors of an institutional nature like the so-called "institutional fit" (i.e. diffusion tends to happen between countries that share similar institutional arrangements; Lejano and Shankar 2013). For instance, according to this view, the promotion of PPP schemes is more likely to succeed in a country with a well-established tradition of private schools (religious schools, community schools, NGO-based schools, etc.), than in a country where private sector participation is very marginal.

Despite the importance of institutional factors in the selection moment, a range of ideational factors of a different nature (including frames, ideologies, public sentiments, and policy paradigms) also plays a determinant role. To start with, for a particular policy solution to be selected (usually among a broader range of competing options) the way this policy is framed and packaged matters. Policy entrepreneurs need to frame their programs in a way that makes these programs appear to be empirically credible and consistent with the problems that are expected to address. At the same time, policy-makers need to perceive these programs as sound, based on accepted ideas for public sector reform, and fitting within the budgetary and technical capacities of their government (Verger 2012).

Increasingly, as a means to convince policy-makers, policy reform advocates try to frame the desirability of their preferred solutions in a scientific and evidence-based way. In relation to contentious themes (as education privatization clearly is), the use of research is more susceptible to politicization, with privatization advocates tending to use evidence in a very selective way (Ball 2007). For instance, using bibliometric techniques, Lubienski *et al.* (2014) show that several American foundations as a way to create momentum around privatization reform produce a sort of "echochamber effect" around a small, usually low-quality and unrepresentative sample of studies produced by like-minded research centers. It is also documented that in both Australia and in Spain neo-liberal think-tanks use evidence in a selective and tendentious way to advance pro-school choice legislation at the federal level (Olmedo and Grau 2013; Windle 2014). In the context of low income countries, it has been also analyzed how a network of international agencies, including the World Bank, the Asian Development Bank and the Council for British Teachers have instrumentalized scientific evidence similarly to try to convince low-income countries to adopt PPPs in education (Verger 2012).

Government ideologies also mediate in the selection of specific policies among a range of policy alternatives. In relation to the education privatization debate, right-wing governments are expected to be more inclined to privatize educational services than left-wing governments; with the latter more willing to manage services directly. Elinder and Jordahl (2013) conducted a study on education privatization in Swedish municipalities, on the basis of a complete database on local governments outsourcing of public services. Contradicting habitual explanations of outsourcing like the transaction cost model (which explains outsourcing by the contracting difficulties of the services in question) or the patronage model (according to which decisions on outsourcing would be subordinated to governments – irrespective of their political hat – aiming at receiving support from public employees and their unions), they found that right-wing governments are more prone to use outsourcing than left-wing governments (Elinder and Jordahl 2013).

According to Le Grand (2003), such different positions concerning privatization are related to the main assumptions regarding human motivation that different political ideologies hold. In short, right-wing governments consider teachers, principals, and families to be primarily motivated by their own self-interest and, accordingly, the introduction of quasi-markets is necessary to make public education more effective. Contrarily, social-democrats and socialists have traditionally conceived public sector workers as altruistic or public-spirited and, accordingly, there is no apparent reason to challenge the bureaucratic organization of the educational system.

Nevertheless, the left-wing vs right-wing cleavage is not always so clear-cut in relation to the privatization debate. In fact, in many places, social-democratic and labor parties are well-known for having advanced pro-market reforms, although apparently for different reasons than those of neo-liberal or conservative parties. For instance, in nordic European countries, where there is a long tradition of welfare state politics, social-democrats have advanced market reforms in many social sectors (including education) as not a way to promote competition, but to respond to middle class demands of more choice and diversification in public services. By doing so, they did not expect to undermine the welfare state, but rather the opposite: to be protecting the universal welfare state in the face of its public legitimacy crisis (Klitgaard 2008).

Beyond the political color of the ruling party, there are more stable institutions, such as welfare state regimes or policy paradigms, which are also expected to influence governmental positions and choices in the framework of the education privatization debate. A "policy paradigm" is an ideational-based structure with the capacity to work as a powerful lens through which policy-makers interpret their reality and act accordingly (Hall 1993). Policy paradigms are selective in nature since they discriminate for and against particular policy ideas and discourses (Hay 2001). In developing countries, for instance, the prevailing developmental policy paradigm is the so-called Post-Washington Consensus. This paradigm is especially conducive to privatization measures as it encourages governments to explore non-bureaucratic ways of coordinating economic and social activities, and to create an environment that favors the private sector acquiring a more dynamic role in economic and societal issues (Van Waeyenberge 2006).

Public opinion and societal values are also variables of an ideational nature that mediate in the selection of particular policies. In societies that have embraced strong consumerist values and/or that tolerate better the existence of socio-economic inequalities, policy ideas that promote school choice and competition will be more resonant than in societies with a strong public sentiment around the idea of education as a public good (Boyd 2007).

Many of the variables affecting policy selection identified here should not be seen as working in an isolated or exclusionary manner. Campbell (2004) theorizes on how different types of ideas (including policy paradigms, policy programs, frames, and public sentiments, which interpellate to very different domains of reality) interact in processes of institutional change. Paraphrasing him, new policy proposals, including privatization, will be more likely to penetrate education systems if policy advocates can present them in a way that appears to translate well into the prevailing regulatory framework and policy paradigm, and into the normative sentiments of decision-makers and key stakeholders.

Finally, it is important to remark that the selection of external policies is not always a free or voluntary decision (Dolowitz and Marsh 2000; Edwards 2013). It is well documented that many countries, especially developing countries, have adopted privatization measures in different educational levels due to the loan conditionalities imposed by international financial organizations like the World Bank and the International Monetary Fund (IMF) (Mundy 1998), or due to having to comply with international binding agreements (such as the General Agreement on Trade in Services of the World Trade Organization) that many countries have been forced to subscribe in multilateral negotiations (Robertson et al. 2002).

Retention

Retention represents a final and necessary step for the realization of policy adoption. There are many policies that are selected by decision-makers, but end up not being finally retained in their particular settings. Retention of new education policies means their institutionalization and inclusion into the regulatory framework, and into the network of educational technologies and practices of a system (Colyvas and Jonsson 2011).

Of all the adoption moments described here, retention is the most potentially contentious. This is due to the fact that it represents the materialization of a policy change and, as such, policy retention is also often the crystallization point of conflicts and oppositional movements. Once a government announces its education reform plans, political actors and key stakeholders of a different nature tend to position themselves around the new proposals and, according to their level of (dis)agreement with them, they articulate strategies of opposition or support. The consequent negotiation and conflict may result in the transformation, or partial or total "displacement" of government plans (Bardach 2006).

The prevailing political architecture in countries mediates determinately in the final retention of new policy proposals. Political institutions and systems of rules can work in very different – and even contradictory – ways when it comes to retaining education reform ideas. For instance, in some countries, like Denmark or the Netherlands, the political party realm is so fragmented that governments usually need to be formed by multiple party coalitions (Kjaer and Pedersen 2001). These coalitions can be so ideologically diverse that it tends to be more difficult for them to agree on the final adoption of drastic measures, as education privatization can be. Overall, the role and presence of veto points and veto players – both within and outside the government - in policy processes can also be vital to understand the uneven adoption and retention of education privatization policies in different settings (Klitgaard 2008).

In contrast to the previous moments of policy adoption in which international influences are more visible, retention is more clearly determined by interactions happening in the domestic arena. Nevertheless, as a way to legitimate policy preferences and/or to neutralize internal opposition, it is common for governments to resort to external or global education models and institutions in order to guarantee the retention of new policies (Steiner-Khamsi 2012). Several European governments, for instance, have used the Bologna process in this particular way to advance privatization policies in higher education (Huisman and Van der Wende 2004). It is also well documented that many governments have perceived the OECD/PISA results as a political opportunity to advance their pre-established policy preferences (see Fulge *et al.*, Chapter 25, this volume). In Catalonia, for instance, key education decision-makers have repeatedly evoked – and actively transformed to their convenience – recommendations coming from OECD/PISA to legitimate the adoption of school-based management and related endogenous privatization measures in education (Verger and Curran 2014).

It has been also documented that policy entrepreneurs and policy-makers (as a way to ensure the retention of privatization measures) tend to avoid the use of the privatization concept in their public talk on education reform. As a sign of their "discursive abilities" (cf. Schmidt 2010), they prefer to resort to more appealing, vague and euphemistic concepts such as public–private *partnerships*, *free* schools, *innovative* forms of provision, or school *autonomy* (Srivastava 2014; Verger 2012).

It is important to mention that once the new policy programs are retained, there is a *lock-in effect* resulting from the fact that these policies are usually associated with the creation of new constituencies and interests, and to periods of policy stability (Bardach 2006; Dale 2012).

Due to its political connotations, retention is apparently a more materially and institutionally inscribed moment than the moments of variation and especially selection. However, policy retention also has very important semiotic connotations. In Jessop's words:

> The greater the range of sites (horizontally and vertically) in which resonant discourses are retained, the greater is the potential for effective institutionalization and integration into patterns of structured coherence and durable compromise. The constraining influences of complex, reciprocal interdependencies will also recursively affect the scope for retaining resonant discourses. (Jessop 2010, 341)

Conclusion: The Politics and Semiotics of Policy Adoption

Both exogenous and endogenous forms of education privatization are converging in the reform agendas of multiple countries. Education privatization is thus a suitable phenomenon to look at from a policy diffusion perspective. Nevertheless, the dominant approaches to policy diffusion (specifically, rationalism and normative emulation) are not sufficient to explain the dynamics of global education privatization in its complexity. Of course, while both approaches represent an advance in relation to explanations that simply focus on external imposition or on exogenous shocks, they still adopt a globalist stance to diffusion. This results in highly deterministic explanations of policy change and convergence, and makes them understate the complex, multi-scalar, and even contradicting political interactions that gear around the advance of most global education policies. Such a flat ontology of the global polity is especially problematic in relation to the study of education privatization processes for two main reasons; first, due to the multiple and even divergent motives why countries adopt privatization as an educational reform approach; and second, due to the very diverse policy measures through which privatization ends up being regulated and enacted in different educational realities.

On the basis of theoretical currents like critical constructivism and CPE, I have elaborated an alternative approach that focuses on the "politics and semiotics of policy adoption." This approach is better suited to explain the global education privatization phenomenon because it looks at relevant moments and variables that are often neglected in other sources of policy diffusion literature. According to this approach, we cannot understand policy dissemination without understanding policy adoption and, at the same time, we cannot understand policy adoption without unpacking it into three main dimensions, namely variation, selection, and retention. Focusing on policy adoption requires a good comprehension of domestic politics, power relations, negotiation, and resistance. It also requires leaving rationalistic and linear conceptions of the policy process apart, since the moments of variation, selection, and retention interact dialectically and are usually loosely coupled. This is especially true when it comes to explaining the selection and retention of contentious policies like education privatization, as well as the final form privatization adopts in particular country settings.

Applying this suggested approach to the study of education policy diffusion means scrutinizing dynamics of persuasion, deliberation, the construction of political interests and values and, more broadly speaking, the generation of meaning at all stages of policy adoption. Although ideas do not determine education change in an isolated manner, they intervene crucially in policy decisions by shaping the perceptions of decision makers, providing them with rationales for action, or filtering interpretations of the external world. It is fundamental, as Colin Hay (2006) argues, to focus on ideas, and on the carriers of those ideas, because policy-makers make decisions according to their views and beliefs about the social and political environment they inhabit.

Finally, the "politics and semiotics of policy adoption" approach advocates for a more comprehensive, but also respectful understanding of the role of local actors in global policy processes, in the sense that it infuses these actors with agency. When studying policy adoption, we need to see education policy decision-makers, including those operating at the national and subnational levels, as key political agents and active generators of meaning. To some extent, their policy options are related to the complementary (symbolic, political and material) gains that certain global policies come with, but also to the way these policies fit within their technical capacities, policy preferences and, certainly, their political agendas.

Note

1 Rinne's argument was produced before OECD/PISA consecrated Finland as an "international good practice" of how effectiveness and equity are compatible goals.

References

Atasay, E. and G. Delavan. 2012. "Monumentalizing Disaster and Wreak-Construction: A Case Study of Haiti to Rethink the Privatization of Public Education." *Journal of Education Policy*, 27(4): 529–553.

Ball, S.J. 1990. *Policy and Policy Making in Education*. London: Routledge.

Ball, S.J. 2007. *Education plc: Understanding Private Sector Participation in Public Sector Education*. New York: Routledge.

Ball, S.J. 2012. *Global Education Inc. New Policy Networks and the Neoliberal Social Imaginary*. Didcot: Routledge.

Ball, S.J. and D. Youdell. 2007. *Hidden Privatisation in Public Education*. Brussels: Education International.

Bardach, E. 2006. "Policy Dynamics," in *Oxford Handbook of Public Policy*, edited by M. Moran, M. Rein, and R.E. Goodin, 336–366. Oxford: Oxford University Press.

Béland, D. 2010. "The Idea of Power and the Role of Ideas." *Political Studies Review*, 8: 145–154.

Bonal, X. 2000. "Interest Groups and the State in Contemporary Spanish Education Policy." *Journal of Education Policy*, 15(2): 201–216.

Boyd, W.L. 2007. "The Politics of Privatization in American Education." *Educational Policy*, 21(1): 7–14.

Bruns, B., D. Filmer, and H. Patrinos. 2011. *Making Schools Work: New Evidence on Accountability Reforms*. Washington, DC: The World Bank Group.

Campbell, J.L. 2004. *Institutional Change and Globalisation*. Princeton: Princeton University Press.

Carney, S., J. Rappleye, and I. Silova. 2012. "Between Faith and Science: World Culture Theory and Comparative Education." *Comparative Education Review*, 56(3): 366–393.

Colyvas, J.A. and S. Jonsson. 2011. "Ubiquity and Legitimacy: Disentangling Diffusion and Institutionalization." *Sociological Theory*, 29(1): 27–53.

Cornwall, A. 2007. "Buzzwords and Fuzzwords: Deconstructing Development Discourse." *Development in Practice*, 17(4/5): 471–484.

Dale, R. 2000. "Globalisation and Education: Demonstrating a 'Common World Educational Culture' or Locating a 'Globally Structured Educational Agenda'?" *Educational Theory*, 50(4): 427–448.

Dale, R. 2012. "Global Education Policy: Creating Different Constituencies of Interest and Different Modes of Valorisation," in *Global Education Policy and International Development*, edited by A. Verger, M. Novelli, and H.K. Altinyelken, 287–300. London: Bloomsbury.

Danermark, B., M. Ekstrom, L. Jakobsen, and J.C. Karlsson. 2002. *Explaining Society: Critical Realism in the Social Sciences*. New York: Routledge.

DeBray-Pelot, E., C. Lubienski, and J. Scott. 2007. "The Institutional Landscape of Interest Group Politics and School Choice." *Peabody Journal of Education*, 82(2–3): 204–230.

DeBray-Pelot, E., J. Scott, C. Lubienski, and H. Jabbar. 2014. "Intermediary Organizations in Charter School Policy Coalitions: Evidence from New Orleans." *Educational Policy*, 28(2): 175–206.

Dobbin, F., B.A. Simmons, and G. Garrett. 2007. "The Global Diffusion of Public Policies: Social Construction, Coercion, Competition or Learning?" *Annual Review of Sociology*, 33: 449–472.

Dolowitz, D. and D. Marsh. 2000. "Learning from Abroad: The Role of policy Transfer in Contemporary Policy-Making." *Governance*, 13(1): 5–24.

Drezner, D.W. 2001. "Globalisation and Policy Convergence." *International Studies Review*, 3(1): 53–78.

Edwards, D.B. 2013. "International Processes of Education Policy Formation: An Analytic Framework and the Case of Plan 2021 in El Salvador." *Comparative Education Review*, 57(1): 22–53.

Elinder, M. and H. Jordahl. 2013. "Political Preferences and Public Sector Outsourcing." *European Journal of Political Economy*, 30: 43–57.

Finnemore, M. and K. Sikkink. 2001. "Taking Stock: The Constructivist Research Program in International Relations and Comparative Politics." *Annual Review of Political Science* 4(1): 391–416.

Fitz, J. and B. Beers. 2002. "Education Management Organisations and the Privatisation of Public Education: A Cross-National Comparison of the USA and Britain." *Comparative Education*, 38(2): 137–154.

Grek, S. (2012). "Learning from Meetings and Comparison: A Critical Examination of the Policy Tools of Transnationals," in *World Yearbook of Education 2012: Policy Borrowing and Lending in Education*, edited by G. Steiner-Khamsi and F. Waldow, 41–61. New York: Routledge.

Hall, P. 1993. "Policy Paradigms, Social Learning and the State. The Case of Economic Policymaking in Britain." *Comparative Politics* 25(3): 275–296.

Hay, C. 2001. "The 'Crisis' of Keynesianism and the Rise of Neoliberalism in Britain: An Ideational Institutional Approach," in *The Rise of Neoliberalism and Institutional Analysis*, edited by J.L. Campbell and O.K. Pedersen, 193–218. Princeton: Princeton University Press.

Hay, C. 2006. "Constructivist Institutionalism… Or Why Ideas Into Interests Don't Go." Paper presented at the APSA Conference, Philadelphia, August 31, 2006.

Huisman, J. and M. Van Der Wende, M. 2004. "The EU and Bologna: Are Supra- and International Initiatives Threatening Domestic Agendas?" *European Journal of Education*, 39(3): 349–357.

Jacoby, W. 2000. *Imitation and Politics*. New York: Cornell University Press.

Jakobi, A. 2012. "Implementing global Policies in African Countries: Conceiving lifelong Learning as Basic Education," in *Global Education Policy and International Development*, edited by A. Verger, M. Novelli, and H.K. Altinyenken, 119–140. London: Bloomsbury.

Jessop, B. 2008. "Cultural Political Economy of Competitiveness and its Implications for Higher Education," in *Education and the Knowledge-Based Economy in Europe*, edited by B. Jessop, N. Fairclough, and R. Wodak, 13–39. Rotterdam: Sense.

Jessop, B. 2010. "Cultural Political Economy and Critical Political Studies." *Critical Policy Studies*, 3(3–4): 336–356.

Kjaer, P. and O.K. Pedersen. 2001. "Translation Liberalization: Neoliberalism in the Danish Negotiated Economy," in *The Rise of Neoliberalism and Institutional Analysis*, edited by J.L. Campbell and O.K. Pedersen, 219–248. Princeton: Princeton University Press.

Klitgaard, M.B. 2008. "School Vouchers and the New Politics of the Welfare State." *Governance*, 21(4): 479–498.

Knill, C. 2005. "Introduction: Cross-National Policy Convergence: Concepts, Approaches and Explanatory Factors." *Journal of European Public Policy* 12(5): 764–774.

Komatsu, T. 2013. "Why Do Policy Leaders Adopt Global Education Reforms? A Political Analysis of School Based Management Reform Adoption in Post-Conflict Bosnia and Herzegovina." *Education Policy Analysis Archives*, 21(62): 1–16.

Le Grand, J. 2003. *Motivation, Agency, and Public Policy: Of Knights and Knaves, Pawns and Queens*. Oxford: Oxford University Press.

Lejano, R.P. and S. Shankar. 2013. "The Contextualist Turn and Schematics of Institutional Fit: Theory and a Case Study from Southern India." *Policy Sciences* 46(1): 83–102.

Lubienski, C., J. Scott, and E. DeBray-Pelot. 2014. "The Politics of Research Production, Promotion, and Utilization in Educational Policy." *Educational Policy*, 28(2): 131–144.

March, J.G. and J.P. Olsen. 1998. "The Institutional Dynamics of International Political Orders." *International Organization* 52(4): 943–969.

Maroy, C. 2009. "Convergences and Hybridization of Educational Policies Around 'Post-Bureaucratic' Models Of Regulation." *Compare* 39(1): 71–84.

Meseguer, C. 2006. "Rational Learning and Bounded Learning in the Diffusion of Policy Innovations." *Rationality and Society*, 18(1): 35–66.

Meyer, J.W. and B. Rowan, 1977. "Institutionalized Organizations: Formal Structure as Myth and Ceremony." *American Journal of Sociology*, 83: 340–363.

Meyer, J.W., F.O. Ramirez, and Y.N. Soysal. 1992. "World Expansion of Mass Education, 1870–1980." *Sociology of Education*, 65: 128–149.

Meyer, J.W., J. Boli, G. Thomas, and F.O. Ramirez. 1997. "World Society and the Nation-State." *The American Journal of Sociology*, 103(1): 144–181.

Mizala, A. 2007. "La Economía Política de la Reforma Educacional en Chile." *CIEPLAN Serie Estudios Socio-Económicos* 36.

Mundy, K. 1998. "Educational Multilateralism and World (Dis)Order." *Comparative Education Review*, 42(4): 448–478.

Olmedo, A. and E.S.C. Grau. 2013. "Neoliberalism, Policy Advocacy Networks and Think Tanks in the Spanish Educational Arena: The Case of FAES." *Education Inquiry*, 4(3): 473–496.

Patrinos, H., F. Barrera-Osorio, and J. Guaqueta. 2009. *The Role and Impact of PPPs in Education*. Washington, DC: The World Bank Group.

Peck, J. and N. Theodore. "Recombinant workfare, across the Americas: Transnationalizing 'Fast' Social Policy." *Geoforum*, 41(2): 195–208.

Phillips, D. and K. Ochs. 2003. "Processes of Policy Borrowing in Education: Some Explanatory and Analytical Devices." *Comparative Education*, 39(4): 451–461.

Renzulli, L.A. and V.J. Roscigno. 2005. "Charter School Policy, Implementation, and diffusion across the United States." *Sociology of Education*, 78(4): 344–366.

Rinne, R. 2000. "The Globalisation of Education: Finnish Education on the Doorstep of the new EU Millennium." *Educational Review*, 52(2): 131–142.

Risse, T. 2000. "Let's Argue!: Communicative Action in World Politics." *International Organization*, 54: 1–39.

Robertson, S. 2005. "Re-imagining and Rescripting the Future of Education: Global Knowledge Economy Discourses and the Challenge to Education Systems." *Comparative Education*, 41(2): 151–170.

Robertson, S. and R. Dale. 2015. "Toward a 'Critical Cultural Political Economy' Account of the Globalising of Education." *Globalisation, Societies and Education*, 13(1): 149–170.

Robertson, S., X. Bonal, and R. Dale. 2002. "GATS and the Education Services Industry: The Politics of Scale and Global Reterritorialisation." *Comparative Education Review*, 46(4): 472–496.

Schmidt, V. 2010. "Taking Ideas and Discourse Seriously: Explaining Change Through Discursive Institutionalism as the Fourth 'New Institutionalism'." *European Political Science Review*, 2(1): 1–25.

Srivastava, P. 2010. "Privatization and Education for All: Unravelling the Mobilizing Frames." *Development*, 53(4): 522–528.

Srivastava, P. 2014. "Contradictions and the Persistence of the Mobilizing Frames of Privatization: Interrogating the Global Evidence on Low-Fee Private Schooling." Paper presented at the 2014 CIES Conference, Toronto, March 10–15, 2014.

Steiner-Khamsi, G. 2004. "Blazing a Trail for Policy Theory and Practice," in *The Global Politics of Educational Borrowing and Lending*, by G. Steiner-Khamsi, 201–220. New York: Teachers' College Press.

Steiner-Khamsi, G. 2012. "Understanding Policy Borrowing and Lending: Building Comparative Policy Studies," in *World Yearbook of Education 2012: Policy Borrowing and Lending in Education*, edited by G. Steiner-Khamsi and F. Waldow, 3–17. New York: Routledge.

Van Waeyenberge, E. 2006. "From Washington to Post-Washington Consensus," in *The New Development Economics: After the Washington Consensus*, edited by Ben Fine, 21–46. London: Zed Books.

Verger, A. 2012. "Framing and Selling Global Education Policy: The Promotion of PPPs in Education in Low-Income Countries." *Journal of Education Policy*, 27(1): 109–130.

Verger, A. 2014. "Why Do Policy-Makers Adopt Global Education Policies? Toward a Research Framework on the Varying Role of Ideas in Education Reform." *Current Issues in Comparative Education*, 16(2): 14–29.

Verger, A. and M. Curran. 2014. "New Public Management as a Global Education Policy: Its Adoption and Re-Contextualization in a Southern European Setting." *Critical Studies in Education*, 55(3): 253–271.

Verger, A., C. Fontdevila, and A. Zancajo. 2016. The Privatization of Education: A Political Economy of Global Education Reform, New York: Teachers College Press.

Weyland, K.G. 2005. "Theories of Policy Diffusion: Lessons from Latin American Pension Reform." *World Politics*, 57(2): 262–295.

Wiborg, S. 2013. "Neo-Liberalism and Universal State Education: The Cases of Denmark, Norway and Sweden 1980–2011." *Comparative Education*, 49(4): 407–423.

Windle. J. 2014. "The Rise of School Choice in Education Funding Reform: An Analysis of Two Policy Moments." *Educational Policy*, 28(2): 306–324.

Chapter 4

Economic Growth in Developing Countries: The Role of Human Capital*

Eric A. Hanushek

The role of improved schooling has been a central part of the development strategies of most countries and of international organizations, and the data show significant improvements in school attainment across the developing world in recent decades. The policy emphasis on schooling has mirrored the emphasis of research on the role of human capital in growth and development. Yet, this emphasis has also become controversial because expansion of school attainment has not guaranteed improved economic conditions.[1] Moreover, there has been concern about the research base as questions have been raised about the interpretation of empirical growth analyses. It appears that both the policy questions and the research questions are closely related to the measurement of human capital with school attainment.

Recent evidence on the role of cognitive skills in promoting economic growth provides an explanation for the uncertain influence of human capital on growth. The impact of human capital becomes strong when the focus turns to the role of school quality. Cognitive skills of the population – rather than mere school attainment – are powerfully related to individual earnings, to the distribution of income, and most importantly to economic growth.

A change in focus to school quality does not by itself answer key questions about educational policy. Other topics of considerable current interest enter into the debates: should policy focus on basic skills or the higher achievers? Also should developing countries work to expand their higher education sector? The currently available research indicates that both basic skills and advanced skills are important, particularly for developing countries. At the same time, once consideration is made

*This chapter was originally published as Eric A. Hanushek, "Economic Growth in Developing Countries: The Role of Human Capital," in Economics of Education Review, 37, December 2013, pp. 204–212. Used with permission from Elsevier.

of cognitive skills, the variations in the amount of tertiary education have no discernible impact on economic growth for either developed or developing countries.

This chapter puts the situation of developing countries into the perspective of recent work on economic growth. When put in terms of cognitive skills, the data reveal much larger skill deficits in developing countries than generally derived from just school enrollment and attainment. The magnitude of change needed makes clear that closing the economic gap with developed countries will require major structural changes in schooling institutions.

The Measurement of Human Capital in Economic Growth

In the late 1980s and early 1990s, empirical macroeconomists turned to attempts to explain differences in growth rates around the world. Following the initial work of Barro (1991), hundreds of separate studies – typically cross-sectional regressions – pursued the question of what factors determined the very large observed differences. The widely different approaches tested a variety of economic and political explanations, although the modeling invariably incorporated some measure of human capital.

The typical development is that growth rates (g) are a direct function of human capital (H), a vector of other factors (X), and a stochastic element (ε) as in:

$$g = rH + X\beta + \varepsilon \quad (4.1)$$

where r and β are unknown parameters to be estimated. The related empirical analysis employs cross-country data in order to estimate the impact of the different factors on growth.[2]

From a very early point, a number of reviews and critiques of empirical growth modeling went to the interpretation of these studies. The critiques have focused on a variety of aspects of this work, including importantly the sensitivity of the analysis to the particular specification (e.g. Levine and Renelt 1992). They also emphasized basic identification issues and the endogeneity of many of the factors common to the modeling (e.g. Bils and Klenow 2000).

In both the analysis and the critiques, much of the attention focused on the form of the growth model estimated – including importantly the range of factors included – and the possibility of omitted factors that would bias the results. Little attention was given to measurement issues surrounding human capital. This oversight in the analysis and modeling appears to be both explicable and unfortunate.

A short review of the history of human capital modeling and measurement helps to explain the development of empirical growth analysis. Consideration of the importance of skills of the workforce has a long history in economics, and the history helps to explain a number of the issues that are pertinent to today's analysis of economic growth. Sir William Petty (1676 [1899]) assessed the economics of war and of immigration in terms of skills (and wages) of individuals. Adam Smith (1776 [1979]) incorporated the ideas in the *Wealth of Nations*, although ideas of specialization of labor dominated the ideas about human capital. Alfred Marshall (1898), however, thought the concept lacked empirical usefulness, in part because of the severe measurement issues involved.

After languishing for over a half century, the concept of human capital was resurrected by the systematic and influential work of Theodore Schultz (1961),

Gary Becker (1964), and Jacob Mincer (1970; 1974), among others. Their work spawned a rapid growth in both the theoretical and empirical application of human capital to a wide range of issues.

The contributions of Mincer were especially important in setting the course of empirical work. A central idea in the critique of early human capital ideas was that human capital was inherently an elusive concept that lacked any satisfactory measurement. Arguing that differences in earnings, for example, were caused by skill or human capital differences suggested that measurement of human capital could come from observed wage differences – an entirely tautological statement. Mincer argued that a primary motivation for schooling was developing the general skills of individuals and, therefore, that it made sense to measure human capital by the amount of schooling completed by individuals. Importantly, school attainment was something that was frequently measured and reported. Mincer followed this with analysis of how wage differentials could be significantly explained by school attainment and, in a more nuanced form, by on-the-job training investments (Mincer 1974). This insight was widely accepted and has dictated the empirical approach of a vast majority of empirical analyses in labor economics through to today. For example, the Mincer earnings function has become the generic model of wage determination and has been replicated in over 100 separate countries (Psacharopoulos and Patrinos 2004).

Owing in part to the power of the analysis of Mincer, schooling became virtually synonymous with the measurement of human capital. Thus, when growth modeling looked for a measure of human capital, it was natural to think of measures of school attainment.

The early international modeling efforts, nonetheless, confronted severe data issues. Comparable measures of school attainment across countries did not exist during the initial modeling efforts, although readily available measures of enrollment rates in schools across countries were a natural bridge to changes in school attainment over time. The early data construction by Barro and Lee (1993), however, provided the necessary data on school attainment, and the international growth work could proceed to look at the implications of human capital.[3]

In this initial growth work, human capital was simply measured by school attainment, or S. Thus, Equation (4.1) could be estimated by substituting S for human capital and estimating the growth relationship directly.[4]

Fundamentally, however, using school attainment as a measure of human capital in an international setting presents huge difficulties. In comparing human capital across countries, it is necessary to assume that the schools across diverse countries are imparting the same amount of learning per year in all countries. In other words, a year of school in Japan has the same value in terms of skills as a year of school in South Africa. In general, this is implausible.

A second problem with this measurement of human capital is that it presumes schooling is the only source of human capital and skills. Yet, a variety of policies promoted by the World Bank and other development agencies emphasize improving health and nutrition as a way of developing human capital. These efforts reflect a variety of analyses into various health issues relative to learning including micronutrients (Bloom *et al.* 2004), worms in school children (Miguel and Kremer 2004), malaria, and other issues. Others have shown a direct connection of health and learning (Gomes-Neto *et al.* 1997; Bundy 2005).

This issue is in reality part of a larger issue. In a different branch of research, a vast amount of research has delved into "educational production functions." This work has considered the determinants of skills, typically measured by achievement tests.[5] Thus, this line of research has focused on how achievement, A, is related to school inputs (R), families (F), other factors such as neighborhoods, peers, or general institutional structure (Z), and a stochastic element (η):

$$A = f(R, F, Z, \eta) \qquad (4.2)$$

Much of the empirical analysis of production functions has been developed within individual countries and estimated with cross-sectional data or panel data for individuals. This work has concentrated on how school resources and other factors influence student outcomes (Hanushek 2003). However, as reviewed in Hanushek and Woessmann (2011a), a substantial body of work has recently developed in an international context, where differences in schools in other factors are related to cross-country differences in achievement.

The analysis of cross-country skill differences has been made possible by the development of international assessments of math and science (see the description in Hanushek and Woessmann 2011a). These assessments provide a common metric for measuring skill differences across countries, and they provide a method for testing directly the approaches to modeling growth, as found in Equation (4.1).[6]

The fundamental idea is that skills as measured by achievement, A, can be used as a direct indicator of the human capital of a country in Equation (4.1). And, as described in Equation (4.2), schooling is just one component of the skills of individuals in different countries. Thus, unless the other influences on skills outside of school are orthogonal to the level of schooling, S, the growth model that relies on only S as a measure of human capital will not provide consistent estimates of how human capital enters into growth.

The impact of alternative measures of human capital can be seen in the long-run growth models displayed in Table 4.1. The table presents simple models of long-run growth (g) over the period 1960–2000 for the set of 50 countries with required data on growth, school attainment, and achievement (see Hanushek and Woessmann 2012a).

Table 4.1 Alternative estimates of long-run growth models

	(1)	(2)	(3)
Cognitive skills (A)		2.015	1.980
		(10.68)	(9.12)
Years of schooling 1960 (S)	0.369		0.026
	(3.23)		(0.34)
GDP per capita 1960	−0.379	−0.287	−0.302
	(4.24)	(9.15)	(5.54)
No. of countries	50	50	50
R^2 (adj.)	0.252	0.733	0.728

Source: Hanushek and Woessmann (2012a).
Note: Dependent variable: average annual growth rate in GDP per capita, 1960–2000. Regressions include a constant. t-statistics in parentheses.

The first column relates growth to initial levels of GDP and to human capital as measured by school attainment.[7] This basic model shows a significant relationship between school attainment and growth and explains one-quarter of the international variation in growth rates. The second column substitutes the direct measure of skills derived from international math and science tests for school attainment. Not only is there a significant relationship with growth but also this simple model now explains three-quarters of the variance in growth rates. The final column includes both measures of human capital. Importantly, once direct assessments of skills are included, school attainment is not significantly related to growth, and the coefficient on school attainment is very close to zero.

These models do not say that schooling is worthless. They do say, however, that only the portion of schooling that is directly related to skills has any impact on cross-country differences in growth. The importance of skills and conversely the unimportance of schooling that does not produce higher levels of skills have a direct bearing on human capital policies for developing countries.

Finally, the estimated impacts of cognitive skills on growth are very large. The cognitive skills measure is scaled standard deviations of achievement. Thus, one standard deviation difference in performance equates to 2% per year in average annual growth of GDP per capita. The importance of human capital indicated by these estimates combined with the deficits of developing countries (below) identifies the policy challenges.

Improvement in School Attainment of Developing Countries

With this background on human capital and growth, it is possible to assess the position of developing countries and their prospects for the future. To provide perspective, this discussion begins with the traditional measure of human capital, school attainment.

International development agencies have pursued the expansion of schooling as a primary component of development. Growing out of a 1990 international conference in Jomtien, Thailand, UNESCO and the World Bank began a movement to achieve "Education for All (EFA)"[8] While this conference developed some fairly general goals, a follow-on conference became much more specific. A central element of the goals for EFA is achieving compulsory and universal primary education in all countries. The 2000 conference included a commitment to achieving the specific goals by 2015.

The United Nations in 2000 established the Millennium Development Goals (MDGs).[9] The second MDG was universal primary education, to be achieved by 2015 and consistent with EFA. To be sure, both the MDGs and the EFA goals recognize that quality is an issue, and both suggest that quality should be monitored. But, the ease of measurement of school completion and the ability to assess progress toward the specific goals imply that qualitative issues of schooling receive considerably less attention.

The data on school attainment show dramatic growth and improvement of developing countries. Table 4.2 charts the progress since 1991 in school attainment across the developed and developing world.

The developed world has maintained high levels of net enrollment at about 95%. Transitional economies have slightly improved over these two decades. But

Table 4.2 Expansion of primary education

	1991	1999	2008
Net enrollment in primary school			
Developed	96.2	96.6	95
Countries in transition	89.0	85.4 (89)[a]	91
Developing	79.5	83.2 (80)[a]	87
School expectancy			
Developed	14.2	15.7	15.9
Countries in transition	12.2	11.9	13.5
Developing	8.4	9.1	10.4

Source: UNESCO (2006, 2011).
Note: [a] Alternative estimate from UNESCO (2011) as opposed to UNESCO (2006).

developing countries have closed half of the gap of their enrollment rates compared to those in developed countries.

A similar picture holds for school expectancy. All countries have on average increased school expectancy over the period 1991–2008. And, again, the largest gains are in developing counties that on average added 2 years to their average school completion, reaching 10.4 years in 2008. Developed countries also made significant gains, moving to 15.9 years by 2008, so the closing of schooling gaps has been relatively slow. But, there is no doubt that there have been steady gains in developing countries.

These are the data typically used to judge the progress and the challenges facing the developing world. But the previous discussion of the measurement of human capital suggests that the data on school attainment – the focus of international monitoring – may be misleading without consideration of how much students are learning.

Better Measures of the Human Capital Deficit in Developing Countries

International data on skills are most readily available for developed countries, but in recent years their availability in developing countries has expanded dramatically. There are two current sources of assessments: the International Association for the Evaluation of Educational Achievement (IEA), which has produced the Trends in International Mathematics and Science Study (TIMSS) assessments and related tests;[10] and the Organisation for Economic Co-operation and Development (OECD), which has produced the Programme for International Student Assessment (PISA) assessments.[11] These assessments, which were used in the skill measures that went into Table 4.2, have somewhat different test developments, age coverage, and country sampling. Nevertheless, they provide a clear indication of the skill differentials across countries that were absent from the prior discussion of school attainment.

Table 4.3 provides basic measures of math competencies for a sample of developing countries that have participated in the 2009 PISA assessment of mathematics. The PISA assessments of performance of 15 year olds categorize students in Levels 1–6. Level 1, which includes scores 0.8 standard deviations or more below the OECD mean, relates to the most rudimentary knowledge. The performance levels are described in OECD (2010): "Students proficient at Level 1 can answer questions

Table 4.3 Performance at or below Level 1 on the PISA Mathematics Assessment, 2009: selected countries (%)

	Below Level 1	Level 1	Level 1 or less
Kyrgyzstan	64.8	21.8	86.6
Panama	51.5	27.3	78.8
Indonesia	43.5	33.1	76.7
Qatar	51.1	22.7	73.8
Tunisia	43.4	30.2	73.6
Peru	47.6	25.9	73.5
Colombia	38.8	31.6	70.4
Brazil	38.1	31.0	69.1
Albania	40.5	27.2	67.7
Jordan	35.4	29.9	65.3
Argentina	37.2	26.4	63.6
Kazakhstan	29.6	29.6	59.1
Montenegro	29.6	28.8	58.4
Trinidad and Tobago	30.1	23.1	53.2
Thailand	22.1	30.4	52.5
Uruguay	22.9	24.6	47.6
Bulgaria	24.5	22.7	47.1
Romania	19.5	27.5	47.0
Azerbaijan	11.5	33.8	45.3
Serbia	17.6	22.9	40.6

Source: OECD (2010).

involving familiar contexts where all relevant information is present and the questions are clearly defined. They are able to identify information and to carry out routine procedures according to direct instructions in explicit situations. They can perform obvious actions that follow immediately from the given stimuli." At this level of knowledge, students will have a difficult time participating in a modern workforce that includes new technologies, and they will have trouble adjusting to changes in these technologies. Such students are likely to have serious difficulties using mathematics to benefit from further education and learning opportunities throughout life.

Across OECD countries, an average of 14% of students perform at Level 1, and 8% perform below Level 1. But Table 4.3 illustrates the plight of a number of countries where over 40% of the students (who are still in school at age 15) are performing at Level 1 or below in 2009.[12] Restricting the assessments to those who are still in school at 15 is also an important caveat, since many still drop out before Grade 9. If the less able students tend to be the earliest dropouts, the data on achievement of 15 year olds will overstate the performance of children in these countries.

The deficit of developing countries can be better illustrated by considering the full distribution of outcomes for countries, i.e. by merging the typical school attainment data with the achievement data from the international assessments. A graph that highlights the alternative perspectives of the traditional focus on attainment and the achievement focus can be found in Figure 4.1. In the separate panels, the pattern of school attainment – taken from recent household surveys – is combined for a subset

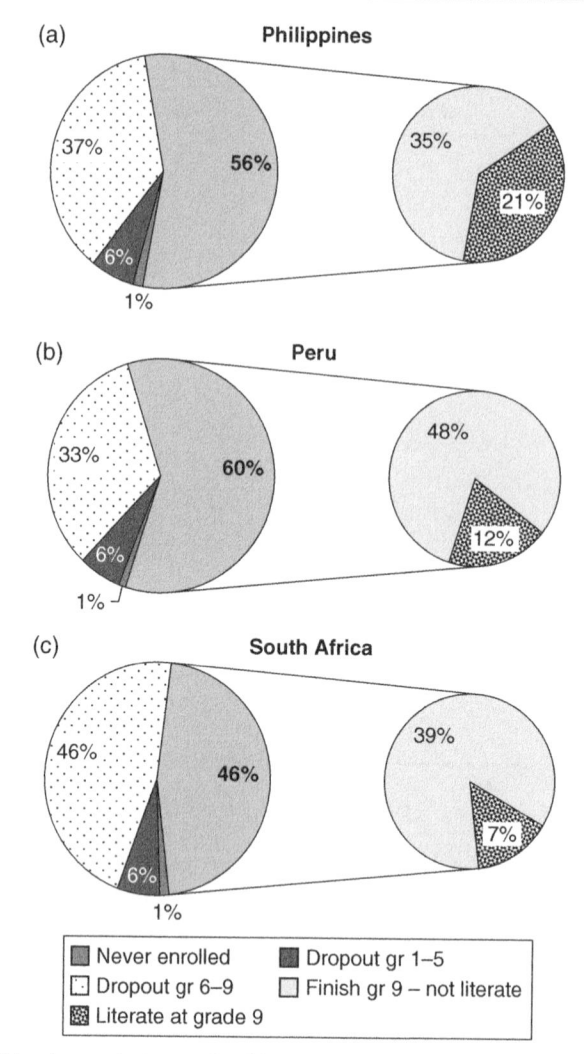

Figure 4.1 Combined completion and achievement outcomes, selected countries.

of countries with the minimal skill achievement from PISA.[13] PISA tests achievement for a representative sample of 15 year olds in each country and thus can be taken as a measure of the competencies of the subset of students in each country that completes Grade 9.

Take Peru as an example.[14] Sixty percent of students make it at least through Grade 9. Assuming that the students with the highest achievement levels complete the most schooling and applying an even looser definition of "modern literacy" – scoring within one standard deviation of the OECD average – shows that only 20% of Grade 9 completers and only 12% of the population is fully literate.[15] Comparable calculations for full literacy yield 21% in the Philippines and just 7% in South Africa. Thus, the performance in terms of school attainment may show some success and promise, but this stands in contrast to the performance in terms of internationally competitive skills. The general narrowing of the human capital deficit shown in Table 4.2 is far less evident in Table 4.3 and Figure 4.1.

International agencies have not completely ignored the possibility that there are school quality differences across countries. Indeed both EFA and the MDGs include mention of quality in their goals. But when they have developed measures of quality to parallel the attainment data, they have employed school input measures. Thus, for example, the quality measures in the United Nations Educational, Scientific and Cultural Organization (UNESCO) (2006) include: pupil/teacher ratio, percentage female teachers, percentage trained teachers, public current expenditure on primary education as a percentage of GDP, and public current expenditure per pupil on primary education. Unfortunately, the large volume of studies that have looked at educational production functions in both developed and developing countries has shown little relationship between any of these measures and student achievement.[16] As a result, the focus of much of the international attention to human capital development appears less successful than commonly available reports might suggest.

In terms of the growth analysis, one standard deviation in achievement is related to long-run growth that is two percentage points higher. While one standard deviation is a large skill difference, the a significant number of developing countries participating in the PISA 2009 assessments were more than this far behind the OECD average: Argentina, Jordan, Brazil, Colombia, Albania, Tunisia, Indonesia, Qatar, Peru, Panama, and Kyrgyzstan.

Varying Human Capital Approaches for Developing Countries

It is useful to look deeper into the relationship between human capital (as measured by achievement) and growth. To begin with, simply because of the different technologies that are being employed, the overall relationship between skills and growth may be more important to OECD countries than in developing countries. Moreover, given the more basic and less technologically advanced technologies in developing countries, there may a stronger demand for basic skills and a weaker demand for high level skills in developing countries.

To assess these, Table 4.4 expands on the modeling of long-run growth contained in Table 4.2. The first column provides a direct test about whether cognitive skills are more important in developed as opposed to developing countries. The point estimate on the interaction of cognitive skills and OECD countries is slightly negative – indicating that skills are *more* important in developing countries. Nonetheless, the differences are not statistically significant.

The previous growth models have uniformly considered just country-average skills. But, particularly in developing countries there is often a large variance in performance with some very high performers and many very low performers (see Hanushek and Woessmann 2008). In fact, given resource constraints, many developing countries frequently feel it is necessary to make decisions about whether to spread resources broadly across their population to provide as great a coverage as possible for its schools or to concentrate resources on those students identified as the best.

To judge the efficacy of these alternative strategies, it is possible to measure the proportion of high performers and the proportion with basic literacy as assessed by the cognitive skills tests.[17] Column (2) of Table 4.4 provides an estimate of the impact on long-run growth of having a broad basic education versus having more high

Table 4.4 Extensions of basic models for developing countries

	(1)	(2)	(3)	(4)
Cognitive skills	1.978			1.923
	(7.98)			(9.12)
Share of students reaching basic literacy		2.644	2.146	
		(3.51)	(2.58)	
Share of top-performing students		12.602	16.536	
		(4.35)	(4.90)	
OECD	0.859		−0.659	
	(0.32)		(0.44)	
OECD × cognitive skills	−0.203			
	(0.36)			
OECD × basic literacy			2.074	
			(0.94)	
OECD × top-performing			−13.422	
			(2.08)	
Years of non-tertiary schooling				0.076
				(0.94)
Years of tertiary schooling				0.198
				(0.16)
Initial years of schooling	0.080	0.066	0.070	
	(1.07)	(0.87)	(0.94)	
Initial GDP per capita	−0.313	−0.305	−0.317	−0.325
	(5.61)	(6.43)	(5.63)	(6.81)
No. of countries	50	50	50	50
F (OECD and interaction)	0.10		1.62	
R^2 (adj.)	0.723	0.724	0.734	0.728

Source: Hanushek and Woessmann (2011b).
Note: Dependent variable: average annual growth rate in GDP per capita, 1960–2000. Regressions include a constant. *t*-statistics in parentheses. Basic literacy is a score of 400 or above on the PISA scale, which is one standard deviation below the OECD mean. Top performing is a score of 600 or above on the PISA scale, which is one standard deviation above the OECD mean.

achievers. Importantly, both broad basic skills ("education for all" in terms of achievement) and high achievers have a separate and statistically significant impact on long term growth. Interestingly, column (3), which allows for different impacts in the OECD and non-OECD countries, indicates that high performers are more important for growth in developing countries than in the OECD countries. This somewhat surprising result suggests the importance of high skills for adapting more advanced technologies to developing countries, particularly when the overall proportion of high performers is small.

These estimates of the varied impact of basic literacy and of top performers, while suggestive, do not answer the overall policy question about where to invest resources. To address that question, it is necessary to know more about the relative costs of producing more basic and more high performers. In fact, no analysis is available to describe the costs of producing varying amounts of skills.

An additional issue about the level of investment in developing countries revolves around the development of tertiary education. A variety of developing countries have contemplated expanding their systems of higher education, both in terms of broad access institutions (generally two-year colleges) and higher level institutions. Column (4) provides estimates of the separate impact of tertiary education on long-run growth. Consistent with the prior analysis, once the level of cognitive skills is considered, years of tertiary schooling – like years of earlier schooling – in the population has no independent effect on growth. This result also holds for just developing countries or for just OECD countries (not shown).[18]

Finally, the form of education institutions is an issue that has not been adequately addressed, particularly for developing countries. A common issue is how much of education should be general in nature and how much should be vocational. Vocational education is designed to provide students with the specific job-related skills that will allow them to move easily into employment. This type of education appears very attractive when there are large youth unemployment problems as is the case in many developing countries. But, there may well be a trade-off with vocational education. If students have a limited set of skills, even if very appropriate for today's jobs, they might find that they are less adaptable to new technologies that are introduced.[19] Such an issue is particularly important for developing countries that frequently experience very rapid growth and significant changes in production technologies.

Some evidence in developing countries suggests that the trade-off of easy labor market entry versus potential disadvantages later in the life cycle because of less adaptability can be significant (Hanushek, Schwerdt, Woessmann and Zhang 2017). Unfortunately, this evidence comes just from developed countries. No similar analysis exists for developing countries, and it is unclear whether the trade-off holds across different development levels.

Issues of Causation

An analytical concern is that the growth relationships discussed do not measure causal influences but instead reflect reverse causation, omitted variables, cultural differences, and the like. This concern has been central to the interpretation of much of the prior work in empirical growth analysis.

An obvious issue is that countries that grow faster have the resources to invest in schools so that growth could cause higher scores. However, the lack of relationship across countries in the amount spent on schools and the observed test scores that has been generally found provides evidence against this (Hanushek and Woessmann 2011a). Moreover, a variety of sensitivity analyses show the stability of these results when the estimated models come from varying country and time samples, varying specific measures of cognitive skills, and alternative other factors that might affect growth (Hanushek and Woessmann 2012a). Finally, other work has considered a series of analyses aimed at eliminating many of the other natural concerns about the identification of the causal impacts of cognitive skills (Hanushek and Woessmann 2012a, 2015).[20]

Each of the analyses points to the plausibility of a causal interpretation of the basic models. Nonetheless, with our limited international variations, it is difficult to demonstrate identification conclusively. But, even if the true causal impact of cognitive skills is less than suggested in Table 4.1, the overall finding of the importance of such skills is unlikely to be overturned.

Some Conclusions

Much of the motivation for human capital policies in developing countries is the possibility of providing economic growth that will raise the levels of incomes in these countries. The focus on alleviating poverty in developing countries relates directly to economic growth because of the realization that simply redistributing incomes and resources will not lead to long-run solutions to poverty.

The direct analysis of growth in developing countries adds a much more specific focus than has existed in much of the current policy discussions. Differences in economic growth across countries are closely related to cognitive skills as measured by achievement on international assessments of mathematics and science. In fact, once cognitive skills are incorporated into empirical growth models, school attainment has no independent impact on growth.

The general focus on universal school attainment underlying the campaigns of EFA and the MDGs, while seemingly reasonable and important, has not put the developing countries in a good position for growth. Specifically, while emphasizing school attainment – a readily available quantitative measure – they have not ensured that the quality of schools has had a commensurate improvement. The data on improvements in school attainment have been impressive, but the very large gaps in achievement lead to a different interpretation of progress.

In terms of cognitive skills, little closing of the gaps between developed and developing countries has occurred.[21] A surprisingly large proportion of students completing nine years of schooling is uncompetitive in terms of international skill levels.

A focus on quality does, however, complicate decision-making. It appears to be generally easier to understand how to expand access than to improve quality. Simple approaches to improving quality have not proved very effective. Past research has indicated that simply providing more resources to schools is generally ineffective.[22] Political problems may also accompany an emphasis on quality. For any given amount of funds, if resources are focused on a smaller set of schools in order to improve quality, it implies that less access to schooling can be provided.

Certainly, in order to provide quality schooling, there must be both infrastructure and access. However, the evidence from the growth analysis indicates that providing schools that fail to teach basic skills does no good. Therefore, slowing the pace of the provision of schools to a rate that also permits the development of quality schools appears to be a good solution.

One other element enters into the calculations. The rapid expansion of new digital technologies – both as blended learning with teachers and technology and as stand-alone approaches – suggests that many of the past decisions both on access and on quality might rapidly change.[23] The potential in developing countries appears especially large.

Acknowledgements

This analysis is closely related to work on international growth and development done jointly with Ludger Woessmann. Helpful comments were received from Bruce Chapman and the participants at the ANU-DPU International Conference on the Economics of Education Policy.

Notes

1. See, for example, Easterly (2001) or Pritchett (2006).
2. Detailed discussion of this growth model and of variants of it can be found in Hanushek and Woessmann (2008, 2015).
3. There were some concerns about accuracy of the data series, leading to alternative developments (Cohen and Soto 2007) and to further refinements by Barro and Lee (2010).
4. A variety of different issues have consumed much of the empirical growth analysis. At the top of the list is whether Equation (4.1) should be modeled in the form of growth rates of income as the dependent variable, or whether it should model the level of income. The former is generally identified as endogenous growth models (e.g., Romer 1990), while the latter is typically thought of as a neoclassical growth model (e.g. Mankiw et al. 1992). The distinction has received a substantial amount of theoretical attention, although little empirical work has attempted to provide evidence on the specific form (see Hanushek and Woessmann 2008).
5. See, for example, the general discussion in Hanushek (2002).
6. This approach to modeling growth as a function of international assessments of skill differences was introduced in Hanushek and Kimko (2000). It was extended in Hanushek and Woessmann (2008, 2015) and a variety of other analyses identified there.
7. The inclusion of initial income levels for countries is quite standard in this literature. The typical interpretation is that this permits "catch-up" growth, reflecting the fact that countries starting behind can grow rapidly simply by copying the existing technologies in other countries while more advanced countries must develop new technologies. Estimating models in this form permits some assessment of the differences between the endogenous and neo-classical growth models discussed previously (see Hanushek and Woessmann 2011b).
8. See the history and framework at: http://en.wikipedia.org/wiki/Education_For_All (accessed November 4, 2015).
9. See the history and framework at: http://en.wikipedia.org/wiki/Millennium_Development_Goals (accessed November 4, 2015].
10. The IEA tests were the first such assessments, begun with the First International Math Study (FIMS) in 1964 and continuing through the most recent Trends in Mathematics and Science Study (TIMSS) in 2011.
11. PISA started in 2000 and has continued at three-year intervals through 2015. It has expanded country coverage significantly over time.
12. Note that these are not all of the developing countries. These are the countries that both participated in PISA 2009 and had such substantial numbers performing at the bottom levels. The vast majority of developing countries have never participated in the PISA examinations. Although a somewhat larger number of developing countries have participated in the TIMSS assessments, their performance relative to developed countries is not noticeably better.
13. See the description in Hanushek and Woessmann (2008). These figures rely on household surveys generally done around 2000; the achievement data use the closest international assessment data.
14. Peru is actually illustrative of a much larger problem in Latin America where achievement has lagged significantly behind the expansion of school attainment. This lag in fact can fully explain why growth rates in Latin American countries have been disappointingly small (Hanushek and Woessmann 2012b).
15. One standard deviation away from the OECD average on PISA tests is 400 points. The top of the Level 1 range illustrated previously was 420 points in mathematics in 2009.
16. The evidence for developed countries is summarized in Hanushek (2003). For developing countries, similar evidence is found in Hanushek (1995) and Glewwe et al. (2013). The direct cross-country studies are analyzed in Hanushek and Woessmann (2011a).
17. Basic literacy for this purpose is a score one standard deviation below the OECD mean. Top performing is a score one standard deviation above the OECD mean.

18 This result, particularly for developed countries, is somewhat surprising. A variety of models such as those of Vandenbussche *et al.* (2006) or Aghion and Howitt (2009) suggest that tertiary education is particularly important for countries near the technological frontier where growth requires new inventions and innovations.
19 In a series of macro models of employer adoption of new technologies, Krueger and Kumar (2004a; 2004b) suggest that relying on more vocational training may explain the lower growth in Europe as opposed to the USA.
20 To rule out simple reverse causation, Hanushek and Woessmann (2015) separate the timing of the analysis by estimating the effect of scores on tests conducted until the early 1980s on economic growth in 1980–2009, finding an even larger effect. Three further direct tests of causality were also devised to rule out certain alternative explanations based on unobserved country-specific cultures and institutions confirm the results. The first one considers the earnings of immigrants to the USA and finds that the international test scores for their home country significantly explain US earnings but only for those educated in their home country and not for those educated in the USA. A second analysis takes out level considerations and shows that changes in test scores over time are systematically related to changes in growth rates over time. A third causality analysis uses institutional features of school systems as instrumental variables for test performance, thereby employing only that part of the variation in test outcomes emanating from such country differences as use of central exams, decentralized decision-making, and the share of privately operated schools. These results support a causal interpretation and also suggest that schooling can be a policy instrument contributing to economic outcomes.
21 While some developing countries have made significant gains in achievement – e.g. Latvia, Chile, and Brazil – there is little overall tendency for developing countries to gain more than developed countries on international assessments (Hanushek *et al.* 2012).
22 Hanushek (1995), Hanushek and Woessmann (2011a), Glewwe *et al.* (2013).
23 Christensen *et al.* (2008).

References

Aghion, P. and P. Howitt. 2009. *The Economics of Growth*. Cambridge: MIT Press.
Barro, R.J. 1991. "Economic growth in a Cross Section of Countries." *Quarterly Journal of Economics*, 106(2): 407–443.
Barro, R.J. and J.-W. Lee. 1993. "International Comparisons of Educational Attainment." *Journal of Monetary Economics*, 32(3): 363–394.
Barro, R.J. and J.-W. Lee. 2010. "A New Data Set of Educational Attainment in the World, 1950–2010." NBER Working Paper 15902. Cambridge: National Bureau of Economic Research (April).
Becker, G.S. 1964. *Human Capital: A Theoretical and empirical Analysis, With Special Reference to Education*. New York: National Bureau of Economic Research.
Bils, M. and P.J. Klenow. 2000. "Does schooling Cause Growth?" *American Economic Review*, 90(5): 1160–1183.
Bloom, D.E., D. Canning, and D.T. Jamison. 2004. "Health, Wealth and Welfare." *Finance and Development*, 41(1): 10–15.
Bundy, D. 2005. "School Health and Nutrition: Policy and Programs." *Food and Nutrition Bulletin*, 26(2) (Supplement 2): S186–S192.
Christensen, C.M., M.B. Horn, and C.W. Johnson. 2008. *Disrupting Class: How Disruptive Innovation Will Change the Way the World Learns*. New York: McGraw-Hill Book Company.
Cohen, D. and M. Soto. 2007. "Growth and Human Capital: Good Data, Good Results." *Journal of Economic Growth*, 12(1): 51–76.

Easterly, W. 2001. *The Elusive Quest for Growth: An Economist's Adventures and Misadventures in the Tropics.* Cambridge: The MIT Press.

Glewwe, P., E.A. Hanushek, S.D. Humpage, and R. Ravina. 2013. "School Resources and Educational Outcomes in Developing Countries: A Review of the Literature from 1990 to 2010," in *Education Policy in Developing Countries*, edited by P. Glewwe. Chicago: University of Chicago Press.

Gomes-Neto, J.B., E.A. Hanushek, R.H. Leite, and R.C. Frota-Bezzera. 1997. "Health and Schooling: Evidence and Policy Implications for Developing Countries." *Economics of Education Review*, 16(3): 271–282.

Hanushek, E.A. 1995. "Interpreting Recent Research on Schooling in Developing Countries." *World Bank Research Observer*, 10(2): 227–246.

Hanushek, E.A. 2002. "Publicly Provided Education," in *Handbook of Public Economics, Vol. 4*, edited by A.J. Auerbach and M. Feldstein, 2045–2141. Amsterdam: Elsevier.

Hanushek, E.A. 2003. "The Failure of Input-Based Schooling Policies." *Economic Journal*, 113(485): F64–F98.

Hanushek, E.A. and D.D. Kimko. 2000. "Schooling, Labor Force Quality, and the Growth of Nations." *American Economic Review*, 90(5): 1184–1208.

Hanushek, E.A. and L. Woessmann. 2008. "The Role of Cognitive Skills in Economic Development." *Journal of Economic Literature*, 46(3): 607–668.

Hanushek, E.A. and L. Woessmann. 2011a. "The Economics of International Differences in Educational Achievement," in *Handbook of the Economics of Education, Vol. 3*, edited by E.A. Hanushek, S. Machin, and L. Woessmann, 89–200. Amsterdam: Elsevier.

Hanushek, E.A. and L. Woessmann. 2011b. "How Much Do Educational Outcomes Matter in OECD Countries?" *Economic Policy*, 26(67): 427–491.

Hanushek, E.A. and L. Woessmann. 2012a. "Do Better Schools Lead to More Growth? Cognitive Skills, Economic Outcomes, and Causation." *Journal of Economic Growth*, 17(4): 267–321.

Hanushek, E.A. and L. Woessmann. 2012b. "Schooling, Educational Achievement, and the Latin American Growth Puzzle." *Journal of Development Economics*, 99(2): 497–512.

Hanushek, E.A. and L. Woessmann. 2015. *The Knowledge Capital of Nations: Education and the Economics of Growth.* Cambridge, MA: MIT Press.

Hanushek, E.A., P.E. Peterson, and L. Woessmann. 2012. "Is the U.S. Catching Up? International and State Trends in Student Achievement." *Education Next*, 12(3): 32–41.

Hanushek, E.A., S. Link, and L. Woessmann. 2013. "Does school Autonomy Make Sense Everywhere? Panel Estimates from PISA." *Journal of Development Economics*, 104: 212–232.

Hanushek, E.A., G. Schwerdt, L. Woessmann, and L. Zhang. forthcoming. "General education, vocational education, and labor-market outcomes over the life-cycle." *Journal of Human Resources* (Winter 2017).

Krueger, D. and K.B. Kumar. 2004a. "Skill-Specific Rather Than General Education: A Reason for US-Europe Growth Differences?" *Journal of Economic Growth*, 9(2): 167–207.

Krueger, D. and K.B. Kumar. 2004b. "US-Europe Differences in Technology-Driven Growth: Quantifying the Role of Education." *Journal of Monetary Economics*, 51(1): 161–190.

Levine, R. and D. Renelt. 1992. "A Sensitivity Analysis of Cross-Country Growth Regressions." *American Economic Review*, 82(4): 942–963.

Mankiw, N.G., D. Romer, and D. Weil. 1992. "A Contribution to the Empirics of Economic Growth." *Quarterly Journal of Economics*, 107(2): 407–437.

Marshall, A. 1898. *Principles of Pconomics.* Vol. 1. London: Macmillan and Company.

Miguel, E. and M. Kremer. 2004. "Worms: Identifying Impacts on Education and Health in the Presence of Treatment Externalities." *Econometrica*, 72(1): 159–217.

Mincer, J. 1970. "The Distribution of Labor Incomes: A Survey With Special Reference to the Human Capital Approach." *Journal of Economic Literature*, 8(1): 1–26.

Mincer, J. 1974. *Schooling, Experience, and Earnings.* New York: NBER.

Organisation for Economic Co-operation and Development (OECD). 2010. *PISA 2009 Results: What Students Know and Can Do – Student Performance in Reading, Mathematics and Science (Volume I)*. Paris: OECD.

Petty, Sir W. 1676 [1899]. "Political Arithmetic," in *The Economic Writings of Sir William Petty*, edited by C.H. Hull, 233–313. Cambridge: Cambridge University Press.

Pritchett, L. 2006. "Does Learning to Add Up Add Up? The Returns to Schooling in Aggregate Data," in *Handbook of the Economics of Education*, edited by E.A. Hanushek and F. Welch, 635–695. Amsterdam: Elsevier.

Psacharopoulos, G. and H.A. Patrinos. 2004. "Returns to Investment in Education: A Further Update." *Education Economics*, 12(2): 111–134.

Romer, P. 1990. "Endogenous Technological Change." *Journal of Political Economy*, 99(5) pt. II: S71–S102.

Schultz, T.W. 1961. "Investment in Human Capital." *American Economic Review*, 51(1): 1–17.

Smith, A. 1776 [1979]. *An Inquiry into the Nature and Causes of the Wealth of Nations*. Oxford: Clarendon Press.

UNESCO. 2006. *Literacy for Life: EFA Global Monitoring Report*. Paris: UNESCO.

UNESCO. 2011. *The Hidden Crisis: Armed Conflict and Education*. Paris: UNESCO.

Vandenbussche, J., P. Aghion, and C. Meghir. 2006. "Growth, Distance to Frontier and Composition of Human Capital." *Journal of Economic Growth*, 112: 97–127.

Chapter 5

Education, Poverty, and the "Missing Link": The Limits of Human Capital Theory as a Paradigm for Poverty Reduction

Xavier Bonal

Introduction

When visiting the World Bank's website the first thing one can see is the banner "Working for a World Free of Poverty." And a click on "What we do" identifies two main goals of the organization for 2030:

- End extreme poverty by decreasing the percentage of people living on less than $1.25 a day to no more than 3%.
- Promote shared prosperity by fostering the income growth of the bottom 40% for every country.

These incontestable and ethical goals tell us how important poverty reduction is today for the leading organization in the field of financing economic development in developing countries. Of course, poverty reduction has always been an important goal of the Bank, particularly since Robert MacNamara assumed the World Bank's Presidency in 1968 and assumed the "Basic needs" approach to development as a clear priority of the organization (Jones 1997). It is not by chance that 1968 was also the first year in which the World Bank started giving credits to the education sector (Psacharopoulos and Woodhall 1985).

The "Basic needs" approach coincided with important debates in development economics that questioned the centrality of physical capital for economic growth and attached more importance to the "residual factor"; i.e. human development and human capital. Assuming human capital theory as the central paradigm for economic development progressively placed education as a key sector to boost growth, which had an obvious impact on the role that many thought education should play in poverty reduction. By developing personal skills and competencies, education became the privileged investment that could bring private and social returns. Under this paradigm, access to education is understood as a means for achieving two central goals: economic growth and poverty reduction. More than 40 years later little has changed in terms of the goals – although there have been important changes in the means to achieve poverty reduction (Jones 2006) – and nothing has changed in terms of human capital theory's position as the fundamental paradigm for economic development and poverty reduction.

Despite the central importance that education policy has today in the World Bank's agenda for poverty reduction, the evidence does not provide uncontestable support to human capital theory as the *only* and the *best* framework for ensuring poverty reduction. I have argued elsewhere that there are both technical and political omissions in the conceptualization of the relationship between education and poverty (Bonal 2007). These omissions are clamorous silences indicating the inability of mainstream economics of education theories to explain the unprecedented levels of educational expansion but only modest levels of poverty reduction, or the behavior of educational demand of the poor. Unpleasantly for many scholars and policy-makers, reality has not perfectly fit into the model. Interestingly, instead of investigating why poverty reduction has been clearly less than expected and reformulating their models, most continue to wait patiently for reality to change.

This chapter aims to account for some reasons why human capital theory, in its "hard" version, is unable to respond to those factors that explain the weak effects of education in poverty reduction; reasons that are crucial to understanding the complex relationship between education and poverty. Two main arguments are presented here. In the first part of the chapter, I identify the weaknesses of human capital theory for understanding human behavior and the multiple rationalities that can guide the educational investments of the poor. In the second part of the chapter, I argue that the focus on poverty reduction has resulted in education policies that completely ignore educational inequalities and have failed to recognize the importance of educational inequalities in mediating the effects between educational expansion and poverty reduction.

A Brief Critical History of Human Capital Theory as a Paradigm of Educational Development

The success of the human capital theory as the mainstream paradigm in educational development cannot be understood without referring to the political and economic context of post-war Europe. In fact, and somewhat unexpectedly after witnessing the evolution of the theory and its centrality in endogenous growth models of development (Romer 1990), the human capital theory came about in times of a Keynesian view of development, focusing on the benevolent intervention of the state. After World War II, there was an urgent need for national reconstruction in developed economies, but even more so in those developing countries that had become politically independent. In these contexts, human capital theory appeared to be a fundamental tool to promote development. The concept of education as investment (rather than a consumption), combined with human capital's theoretical relationship between education, productivity, and income, became powerful driving forces which guided decision-making in education policy. Interestingly, the pressing need for states to intervene in the economy opened the door to a theory that offers a complete scientific rationalization for this intervention. The confluence of these two phenomena – a demand for scientifically supported information for decision-making and the appearance of a theory that could respond to it – explain, as Mark Blaug said, why no education minister could even dream of making a decision without having an economist on his advisory team (Blaug 1985).

The rise of Keynesianism and the subsequent need for economic planning justified, in its very beginnings, human capital theory's focus on Manpower Planning Forecast (MPF) as a method to identify investment priorities. Assessing the needs of the labor force for economic growth was a consistent logic in Western countries, but even more so in developing countries. In a context of hegemonic theories of modernization and the need to support newly independent countries, the ability to calculate the needs of the workforce for each economic sector became a crucial tool for development. The MPF was actually the methodology used by the World Bank to give the first loans in education in 1968. Among other things, MPF led to the prioritization of vocational education and training, and made the Bank less careful about educational policies for fighting poverty and reducing social inequalities.

The failure of most systems of MPF is documented by Heyneman (2003) in his evaluation of the programmes promoted by the World Bank at this stage. Incorrect planning and the business interests of American firms explain why most programs did not reach the expected results. But the MPF also failed because it assumed that educational demand would always react to the signs of the labor market. Thus, it was assumed, for example, that more training provision in agriculture should compensate for the lack of skilled technicians in this area. And it was also assumed that the social demand for education would respond to this new supply because the labor market would provide job opportunities in this sector. The absence of a sociological or anthropological approach became increasingly evident, especially when the demand for education was concentrated in programs of study that could ensure access to civil servant jobs that provided a stable salary and the possible survival of the extended family (Williamson 1979).

So, the statist logic that accompanied the human capital theory in its early days as a planning tool led to an economic-centered approach to development, while other social sciences were excluded from the scene. Predictions made without considering the different social structures, and the specific institutional and cultural characteristics of the population led to strategies that were often inefficient in fostering educational and economic development.

However, the marriage between human capital theory and Keynesianism soon came to an end. There is no doubt that Keynesianism suffered the most in this divorce. The end of the post-war boom and the economic crisis of the 1970s opened the door to monetarism and new classical economics. Prior to this point, the state had been considered to be a fundamental economic actor for macroeconomic equilibrium and fiscal and monetary policy, but by the 1970s the state had come to be considered as a source of inefficiency and a disruption to the market equilibrium. This change, as noted by Ben Fine (2009), not only affected the emergence of a new macroeconomic theory, but also included a new conception of microeconomics, according to which the state was not even the corrector of market and institutional imperfections.

There are two particularly significant reductive effects of this new microeconomics. The first is the restriction of human behavior to utility functions and the pursuit of individual self-interest. Under conditions of perfect markets, this means that rational decision-making is guided solely by instrumentalism. The second is the capacity that new economic imperialism has on what Ben Fine (2001) considers to be the colonization of other social sciences, which is more evident today than ever. Despite its obvious theoretical and empirical weaknesses, the new economic imperialism has a strong influence on other social sciences, which make use of methodological individualism and rational action theory as key analytical frameworks of agents' behavior. This extraordinary sociological reductionism eliminates concepts such as power, conflict, or structures and replaces them with market imperfections.

This new context explains the rapid relocation of the human capital theory, which moved from going hand in hand with Keynesianism to becoming the best example of applying the principles of neo-classical economics in a "non-economic" area such as education. The consequence of this change was crucial for the development of a new rationale of educational investment and new policy priorities in developing countries. In the context of an economic science increasingly based on microeconomic modelling and empiricism supported by sophisticated quantitative techniques, the human capital theory abandoned the MPF method and introduced new calculation techniques of educational investment based on the signs of the market. The best illustration of this step is the calculation of rates of return on educational investment and its automatic translation into investment priorities (Psacharopoulos 1994).

The Hegemony of the Microeconomic Version of Human Capital

It is precisely in its neo-classical version that the theory of human capital reinforces its hegemony. In fact, during the 1970s, critiques of human capital theory from institutionalism (Thurow 1979) and credentialism (Arrow 1973; Collins 1979), specifically questioned the macroeconomic side of the theory. That is, they challenged the alleged effects of educational expansion on economic growth (questioning the productivity gains resulting from education or the functioning of the labor market and the demand of employment). However, these critiques did not focus on the microeconomic principles of human capital theory, which are based on methodological individualism and agents' rational action in making decisions.

In developing countries, the dominance of this hard version of human capital theory greatly influenced educational investment priorities and policy agendas. The rates of return on educational investment became the new dogma from which states should prioritize public investment in education (hence, for example, the changing priorities from vocational education to basic education). But above all, it was assumed that rates of return should be the signal for people to follow when making investment decisions in education. It was taken for granted that the actors perform with instrumental rationality, and that human capital theory provided the best methods and models to guide and interpret this rationality.

Thus, human capital theory incorporates two key absences as a framework for policy-making: at the macro level, it ignores the functioning of the institutions (both education and the labor market); at the micro level, it ignores alternative determinants of human action other than instrumental rationality.

In developing countries, the volume of policy decisions resulting from this framework was huge. It also became the only method used by the World Bank to establish investment priorities in education. During the years of structural adjustment, and under the leadership of the World Bank, education policies focused on what Stephen Heyneman called "the short education policy menu" (Heyneman 2003). Investment priorities in basic education, the prominent role of the private sector in secondary and higher education, decentralisation or cost-recovery policies (even including fees in basic education) are undoubtedly the best examples of this limited menu. Poor countries had little room for autonomy in implementing externally imposed agendas. Generally speaking, these policies had devastating social effects, including, in some cases, drawbacks in access to primary schooling, as was the case in sub-Saharan Africa (Reimers 1994).

The blunder of such policies is another example of the above-mentioned absences. Today, their failure is explained by both institutional and market imperfections. This explanation clearly exonerates policy-makers from responsibility: the policies are good, but institutional deficiencies, corruption, and agents' misinformation are the reasons behind the poor results. The potential failure of these policies is not therefore in the hands of the policy-makers, but in the hands of those who are responsible for implementing them. Taking this into consideration it is not uncommon, therefore, that one of the most significant developments of economic imperialism under the Post Washington Consensus was the colonization of what is called "governance" – if possible, without government (Rosenau and Czempiel 1992). Within this view of economics there is no discussion about which are the best policies, or about which optimal institutional conditions need to be added to the model in order to ensure its proper implementation (regardless of the power relations or cultural roots of these institutions). The use and perversion of the concept of social capital is perhaps the best example of how non-economic concepts were included into microeconomic models. In this case, social capital, a concept originally coined in sociology, especially from the work of Bourdieu, was appropriated to refer to positive social relations to improve institutional governance (Fine 2001).

The co-optation of the concept of social capital is a good example of the capacity of neo-classical economics and neo-liberalism as the associated ideology to manage its crises of hegemony and to maintain the dominant paradigm within the field of education for development. Paradoxically, these forms of paradigm maintenance, far from eroding it, have reinforced the colonization character of economics over other social sciences. The complexity of social relations and the functioning of the institutions are reduced by the invasion of econometric models that make predictions about human behavior that rarely occur. This capacity of neo-classical economics to transform itself by invading other social sciences has been referred by Ben Fine (2009) as the era of Zombieconomics. In his words:

> This is because [neoclassical economics] is both alive and dead at the same time. It is alive in the sense not only of aggressively and crudely, if not savagely, occupying its own territory and subject matter to the exclusion and absorption of competing paradigms but also through its increasing appetite for the flesh of other disciplines that both it infects and converts to its own nature with only limited traces remaining of what has been destroyed. By the same token, it is intellectually dead, having nothing new to offer other than parasitic extension of its principles to new applications. (Fine 2009, 888).

The expression "all other things being equal" becomes probably the most repeated formula in the comparative analysis of educational systems, or in the use of methodologies to evaluate educational policies (Verger and Bonal 2012). "All other things being equal" assumes that the effect of a given variable on a dependent variable is "scientifically true" if other variables that could interfere with the behavior of the dependent variable do not change. Of course, in social sciences things are never equal. However, this "all other things being equal" technique continues to be applied in developing countries to evaluate the effects of the introduction of quasi-market reforms in education (e.g. to evaluate the impact of voucher systems or the promotion of low cost private schools), as it is also applied to simulations on educational resource allocation mechanisms. The methodological bias of this "all other things being equal" technique is related both to the implicit assumptions in the equations, and to the exclusion of factors that are not included in the model because they are not quantifiable or because they are simply not considered. The obsession with what Bourdieu (1973) called "scientism" characterizes the current alienation of social sciences to economic methods.

Failing to Explain the Poor's Educational Demand

As has been previously stated, human capital theory includes an implicit conceptualization and interpretation that reduces human behavior to instrumental motivation and the ability of individuals to act only as utility maximizers. This understanding of human behavior is fundamental for interpreting the reactions of education to changes in the different signs *sent* by markets (either represented by educational or labor institutions). Thus, neo-classical economics (and human capital theory as its version in the education field) assumes that utility functions are appropriate patterns for expecting changes in the behavior of individuals, independently of their social and cultural origin or their economic situation.

Moreover, if human beings are guided by instrumental rationality, calculating rates of return to education is undoubtedly the best methodology to identify the signs sent by both education and the labor market. The principle of *wage competition* states that educational demand will mainly react to how different educational levels will be rewarded in the labor market. Thus, if getting better education is certainly compensated by a better salary, incentives for educational demand would encourage individuals to invest in their education. By calculating the difference between benefits and costs, individuals can instrumentally foresee whether it is convenient spending more time at school instead of entering the labor market or whether it can be a good strategy getting a loan to complete a degree.

The wage competition principle has been questioned by the job-competition theory (Thurow 1979), which puts job characteristics, not wages, as the main causal factor of decision-making and likelihood of employment. But even in the job-competition theory, although the signs to follow in the market are different, incentives for investing in education would remain high or would be even greater. Since education reduces the costs of trainability and increases the likelihood of being employed, people would generally prefer investing in education and positioning themselves in the queue of potential jobs for their qualifications. Different factors would certainly intervene in the possible job mismatches (Wolbers 2003), but getting a good position in the queue highly depends on an individual's level of qualification (all other things being equal such as gender, race, or class).

What both human capital theory and job-competition theory fail to explain is which other factors can play a decisive role in shaping the educational demand of certain social groups. In both theories there is a clear understanding of individual's rationality that is based on the ability to project the future, and especially on the capacity to overcome present impediments and barriers to ensure educational investment. But of course this is never homogeneously distributed. While certain groups are in a position to visualize educational investment strategies in the medium and long term, the most excluded groups do not have access to the resources required for an investment of this nature. Thus, although the rates of return corresponding to completion of each educational level are positive with the benefits therefore exceeding the costs, this assessment hides the obstacle represented by the short-term availability of financial resources in poor homes. The greater the amount of investment required in education, the harder it is for these homes to fund it, and there can be no return if one cannot even begin to invest. Unfortunately, the average rates of return hide the fact that it is impossible for poor homes to invest in the medium term, or that their level of "risk aversion" is higher than the average (Van de Werfhorst and Andersen 2005).

Significantly, policy decisions associated with rates of return analyses (or any other approach assuming instrumental rationality of the poor), ignore other forms of rationality that may guide people's actions and expectations (Boudon 2003). For instance, let's take the argument of cost recovery, which is mainly due to the need to offset falling public spending in education. It is argued, on the basis of simulations, that increases in academic fees can provide the benefits of increased supply without a significant fall in demand (due to its inelasticity), obtaining improvements from a point of view of both efficiency and equality. It is also argued that cost-recovery policies allow public spending to be redirected toward the most needy sectors (Albrecht and Ziderman 1991). However, the theses on which this argument is based can be easily questioned. For example, according to Colclough (1996) the idea of the inelasticity of demand is not correct if one considers falls in family income or reductions in the expected benefits of investing in education. Furthermore, levels of elasticity in the demand for education differ substantially depending on income levels. Elasticity increases as the proportion of cost recovery becomes greater (Colclough 1996, 596). Other factors, such as differences in the levels of information regarding the potential benefits of investing in education among different social groups, or the negative impact on the incomes of the poorest families whose ability to pay for their basic needs is affected as a result of increased private education costs, reflect the potential social inequalities that can result from cost-recovery policies (Colclough 1996, 597).

Ignoring the reactions of the poorest families to increases in the cost of private education means underestimating the impact that the cost of schooling may have on students abandoning their studies early; a circumstance that is particularly common in secondary education (Van der Berg 2008). If we add to this the fact that a reduction in a particular family's income will increase the need for the children of the house to provide financially,[1] the effects of higher costs of schooling on children and adolescents (particularly girls) abandoning their studies become even greater.

Differences in the quality of schooling can also make significant differences in the way educational demand reacts to the *signs* of the market. Thus, low quality education makes it impossible for a student to gain the knowledge required in order to guarantee a good educational career and opportunities for social mobility, but it is also the basis on which social groups build their educational aspirations. In other words, the way a particular society perceives the quality of education available will have a clear influence on the educational investment strategy of individual families. Nevertheless, possible options are, of course, different depending on the financial and cultural capital available. In other words, while the middle classes can respond to problems of teaching quality by turning to the various alternatives available in the market place (opting out), the poor have to decide whether or not they can continue to send their children to school.

The arguments presented are just a selection of reasons that challenge the assumptions embedded in human capital theory and its policy prescriptions about the poor's demand for education. These arguments question the instrumental rationality of the poor as maximizing choosers of schooling. But the arguments presented fall strictly into what we can consider economic rationalities in decision-making processes. Another set of arguments, mainly related to cultural and political aspects, would definitely add complexity to the analysis of why and how the poor behave in the way they do. Arguments such as girls' exclusion of access to schooling (Stromquist 1989), cultural norms around child labor, or significant differences in conditions of educability of the poor (Bonal *et al.* 2010) are powerful determinants not only of the poor's educational demand, but also of their behavior and the likelihood they finish their studies.

Conferring uncritical effectiveness to policies based on a single and simplistic rationality of the poor is a clear political mistake which can have critical consequences for the opportunities of the poor. Ignoring other determinants of educational demand and behavior tells us many things about the limited effects of some educational policies to reduce poverty.

Fighting Poverty by Ignoring Inequality?

The World Bank's 2001 World Development Report focused on policy strategies for fighting poverty. The report was explicitly entitled *Attacking Poverty* and symbolized a turn in World Bank priorities (putting poverty even before growth, though strictly related) in context of the new Comprehensive Development Framework under James Wolfensohn's mandate. Chapter 3 of this report is especially interesting. The chapter, titled "Growth, inequality and poverty," is an extensively documented chapter, which assesses the relationship between these three variables on the basis of questions such as "Why are similar rates of growth associated with different rates of poverty reduction?" (World Bank 2001, 51). Far from offering an unequivocal reply to this question, the World Bank's discourse abandons the classic and almost taken for granted incompatibility between growth and equality, acknowledging that:

> Recent thinking – and empirical evidence – weakens the case for such a trade-off: lower inequality can increase efficiency and economic growth through a variety of channels. Unequal societies are more prone to difficulties in collective action, possibly reflected in

dysfunctional institutions, political instability, a propensity for populist redistributive policies, or greater volatility in policies – all of which can lower growth. And to the extent that inequality in income or assets coexists with imperfect credit markets, *poor people may be unable to invest in their human and physical capital, with adverse consequences for long-run growth.* (World Bank 2001, 56)

Even so, in the same chapter, the World Bank asserts that:

> This is not to say that every pro-equity policy will have such desired effects. If the reduction in inequality comes at the expense of the other factors conducive to growth, the gains from redistribution can vanish. Expropriation of assets on a grand scale can lead to political upheaval and violent conflict, undermining growth. And sometimes attempts to redistribute income can reduce incentives to save, invest, and work. (World Bank 2001, 56–57)

The chapter is a good example of how policies for fighting poverty (and education policies in particular) have always been designed to be acceptable for, and compatible with, mainstream development policy. The evolution of the World Bank's agenda in setting priorities for fighting poverty provides further evidence of this trend (Bonal 2007; Jones 2006; Mundy and Verger 2014). The confidence about the *trickle down* effect of economic growth to reduce poverty illustrates how, under the Washington Consensus paradigm, poverty reduction would be an expected effect of growth. Thus, under this paradigm, there was no need for specific policies aimed at poverty reduction, since growth-oriented policies benefit all society, including the poorest. Again, positive expectations about economic growth and rational choice would be conducive to optimal levels of educational investment. The poorest would escape poverty by foreseeing the value of investing in education.

Interestingly enough, the many critiques of the high social cost of adjustment led to the need to review a development policy paradigm that was hurting rather than helping the poor. Targeting the poor became the new *mantra* in policy development. Actually, the new language of development policy included concepts like "emergency social funds" or "fast social policy" for the most needy (Whitehead 1995; Peck and Theodore 2010). In education, conditional cash transfers, initiated in Brazil and Mexico, rapidly became a global education policy that perfectly fit the new mainstream development agenda, which added a priority to tackle poverty to the unchanged pro-growth policies (Bonal *et al.* 2012).

By prioritizing targeting, it was assumed that market imperfections would be corrected, without the need to challenge a development model focusing exclusively on growth-oriented policies. This is basically what the Post-Washington Consensus brought to the structural basis of the economic policy for development. Under this new model, recognizing market imperfections in development policy simply meant giving room to anti-poverty policies without questioning the unlimited virtues of the market for generating incentives and for resource allocation and distribution.

There are two main consequences of the neo-liberal reconfiguration that clearly affected the evolution of development policies in the following years. The first was a growing interest in the emphasis on good governance as a new field of study and the increasing interest in institutionalism as a functional approach to development. The increasing interest of the World Bank in institutional design and reform, for example, enabled it to maintain a discourse that defended market-oriented policies and focused on issues such as corruption or incorrect policy implementation as causes of development failure (Bonal 2004). The positive disposition of the World Bank toward targeting policies also had to do with the possibility to bypass bureaucratic bad governments (incapable of reducing poverty) and directly empower individuals to find their way out of poverty (Bonal et al. 2012).

The second main characteristic of mainstream development policy was its ability to add poverty to the objective of growth by keeping inequality outside of the picture (Wade 2004). Even in a context of growing evidence of the positive effects of equity for reducing poverty (Ravaillon 2001), mainstream models of development did not focus on equity as a *causal* variable for poverty reduction, but only as a *mediating* variable to understand differences in poverty reduction given the same levels of growth. Indeed, even when distributional change was understood as something positive for poverty reduction, policy prescriptions for redistribution included market-friendly approaches as valid as state-led redistribution policies (Ferreira 2010, 26). Interestingly, there is some movement in mainstream development discourses from positions that resisted considering inequality as something intrinsically bad for development (or simply spurious in relation to the objective of poverty reduction), to a position that, despite giving importance to inequality, prescribes market-oriented policies to enhance redistribution. This is especially visible in some of the recent debates on globalization, poverty, and inequality, where some positions even argue that lack of sufficient trade openness and financial liberalization can explain why some regions do not benefit enough from globalization and cannot reduce poverty. That is, globalization still has to go further to help the poor (Agénor 2004).

There is no doubt that development policies have shown an increasing receptivity toward the danger of inequality for economic growth and social cohesion. A special issue of *The Economist* alerted that "inequality has reached a stage where it can be inefficient and bad for growth" or that "social spending is often less about helping the poor than giving goodies to the relatively wealthy".[2] The same publication refers also to education when stating, "even the sort of inequality produced by meritocracy can hurt growth. If income gaps get wide enough, they can lead to less equality of opportunity, especially in education." The recent book by Thomas Piketty, *Capital in the Twenty-First Century*, is probably the best example of an immense empirical research that alerts about the dangers of growing inequalities in today's global capitalism (Piketty 2014).

However, there is an evident resistance pushing to introduce radical changes in development policies. Policy prescriptions identify the existence of monopolies and vested interests as main barriers toward a real liberalization that would help the poor. At the same time, focusing funds to the poor is also understood as the best "redistributive" policy. In education, the same type of policy prescriptions is applied to combat teacher union monopolies (Moe 2011). This mindset is also used to frame policies such as targeting, *vouchers*, and other forms of non-state educational provision as symbols of pro-equity policies (World Bank 2011). Despite several critiques to these forms of reductionism (Ginsburg 2012; Verger and Bonal 2012), today pro-poor and pro-equity mainstream education policies are conceived from a position that claims less rather than more state intervention. Paradoxically, the assumed numerous deficiencies of state's ownership and provision of services do not only affect efficiency allocation. It is also understood that equality of opportunities and the distribution of these opportunities themselves are better achieved by market means, especially through the direct involvement of the private sector (even the for-profit one) in educational provision (Patrinos *et al.* 2009).

Despite the lack of consistency about the positive effects of introducing market mechanisms in education in terms of educational quality and performance (Waslander *et al.* 2010), public–private partnerships in education have become today one of the most significant global education policies (Robertson *et al.* 2012).

We are therefore in front of a discourse that radically transforms the means through which welfare and equity must be achieved. "State failures" become much more relevant than "market failures" as the basis to construct pro-poor education policy. It is by giving more choice to the poor and by making schools compete for their clients that equity will be achieved. In this context, lack of evidence is not at all an impediment for prescribing these policies. Breaking vested interests of teacher unionism and introducing systems of incentives to providers are powerful ideological tools to compensate for the absence of rigorous analyses on the supposed virtues of market mechanisms.

In fact, the extreme reductionism in which education inequality is understood means that current global education policies ignore the potential impact of reducing educational inequalities for increasing the performance of educational systems (Wilkinson and Pickett 2009). Despite that, even the Organisation for Economic Co-operation and Development (OECD) is today recognizing the crucial importance of equity for achieving excellence in educational systems (OECD 2013), mainstream discourses on education policies ignore a systemic approach to educational inequalities to tackle poverty and to improve academic performance. Possibly, the best example of this ignorance is the contempt toward school segregation as a central phenomenon in today's educational systems. Fighting school segregation requires an option for state intervention on educational planning, and some form of political action of free school choice regulations (Bonal 2012). Certainly, these are clear taboos as educational policy tools.

Conclusions

In spite of the centrality of anti-poverty policies in educational priorities and discourses today, mainstream educational policies usually tend to overestimate the capacity of certain educational policies to tackle poverty. This chapter has focused on two different types of arguments to respond to this limitation. On the one hand, human capital theory provides a framework full of assumptions about human behavior that do not always happen in real life. Implicit notions of rational choice and consumer's instrumental preferences cannot be uncritically assumed when understanding the poor's educational demand. Different forms of rationality (not necessarily instrumental) can lead to forms of decision-making that do not always follow the expected pattern of maximizing educational investment. Furthermore, there are many restrictions that generate specific circumstances that might prevent individuals from achieving a Pareto optimal investment in education. Mainstream formal models of education policy usually underestimate many of these restrictions, such as differences in the educational quality available to the poor or opportunity costs of school attendance. Needless to say, the prevalence of market-oriented policies is the clearest example of biased assumptions of human behavior reactions to those signs provided by the market.

On the other hand, this chapter has also argued that ignorance of educational inequality as a crucial aspect of educational policy agendas explains why educational policies have been less effective than expected in tackling poverty. Education inequalities widen the distance with regard to the educational levels achieved by different social groups; usually they make the poor poorer and increase the necessary investments (in material, human, and cultural resources) to facilitate children's real learning at school. Ignorance of educational inequalities is actually consistent with the disdain for social inequalities in the agenda for development. Undoubtedly, the centrality of growth and poverty and the absence of inequality is an appealing option for both international organizations and national governments in policy-making. They avoid facing fiscal reforms and direct confrontations with wide segments of the middle class, which have been increasingly encouraged to look for quality services in the market and ignore the public ones.

Today's economic crisis in the developed world and in middle income world regions is showing the limitations of social and educational policies to facilitate poor's inclusion, and to ensure social stability for the middle class. These conditions might shape a new scenario in which the impoverished, but increasingly influential middle classes use their voice to claim their right to better social services. Recent protests in Brazil, for example, show that middle classes unite to poorer sectors to protest for the insufficiency and low quality of the public services. Somewhat paradoxically, social inequalities and the splintering of the middle class might activate new claims for extensive and quality public services that will cause new problems of legitimation of the state. These potential changes will deserve a careful analysis, with education being one of the crucial sectors to observe.

Notes

1 In calculating rates of return it is common practice to assume that there is no opportunity cost in primary education. See a critique of the calculation method in Bennell (1996).
2 *The Economist.* "True Progressivism. The New Politics of Capitalism and Inequality." October 13–19, 2012. Retrieved from: www.economist.com/node/21564556 (accessed 5 November 2015).

References

Agénor, P.-R. 2004. "Does Globalization Hurt the Poor?" *International Economics and Economic Policy*, 1(1): 21–51.
Albrecht, D. and A. Ziderman. 1991. *Deferred Cost Recovery for Higher Education: Student Loan Programs in Developing Countries*. Washington, DC: The World Bank.
Arrow, K.J. 1973. "Higher Education as a Filter." *Journal of Public Economics*, 2(3): 193–216.
Bennell, P. 1996. "Using and Abusing Rates of Return." *International Journal of Educational Development*, 16: 235–248.

Blaug, M. 1985. "Where Are We Now in the Economics of Education?" *Economics of Education Review*, 4(1): 17–28.

Bonal, Xavier. 2004. "Is the World Bank Education Policy Adequate for Fighting Poverty? Some Evidence from Latin America." *International Journal of Educational Development*, 24(6): 649–666.

Bonal, X. 2007. "On Global Absences: Reflections on the Failings in the Education and Poverty Relationship in Latin America." *International Journal of Educational Development*, 27(1): 86–100.

Bonal, X. 2012. "Education Policy and School Segregation of Migrant Students in Catalonia: the Politics of Non-Decision-Making." *Journal of Education Policy*, 27(3): 401–421.

Bonal, X., A. Tarabini, M. Constans, F. Kliczkowski, and O. Valiente. 2010. *Ser pobre en la escuela. Habitus de pobreza y condiciones de educabilidad*. Buenos Aires: Miño y Dávila.

Bonal, X., A. Tarabini, and X. Rambla. 2012. "Conditional Cash Transfers in Education for Development: Emergence, Policy Dilemmas and Diversity of Impacts," in *Global Education Policy and International Development: New Agendas, Issues and Programmes*, edited by A. Verger, M. Novelli, and H. Kosar-Altinyelken, 141–160. New York: Continuum.

Boudon, R. 2003. "Beyond Rational Choice Theory." *Annual Review of Sociology*, 29 (1): 1–21.

Bourdieu, P. 1973. *Le Métier de Sociologue (second edition)*. Paris: Mouton.

Colclough, C. 1996. "Education and the Market: Which Parts of the Neoliberal Solutions are Correct?" *World Development*, 24: 589–610.

Collins, R. 1979. *The Credentialist Society*. New York: Academic.

Ferreira, F. 2010. "Distributions in Motion: Economic Growth, Inequality, and Poverty Dynamics." *World Bank Policy Research Working Paper Series 5424*.

Fine, B. 2001. *Social Capital Versus Social Theory: Political Economy and Social Science at the Turn of the Millennium*. London: Routledge.

Fine, B. 2009. "Development as Zombieconomics in the Age of Neoliberalism." *Third World Quarterly*, 30(5): 885–904.

Ginsburg, M. 2012. "Teachers as Learners: A Missing Focus in 'Learning for All'," in *World Bank and Education: Critiques and Alternatives*, edited by S. Klees, J. Samoff, and N. Stromquist, 83–94. Rotterdam: Sense Publishers.

Heyneman, S.P. 2003. "The History and Problems in the Making of Education Policy at the World Bank 1960-2000." *International Journal of Educational Development*, 23: 315–337.

Jones, P.W. 2006. *Education, Poverty and the World Bank*. Rotterdam: Sense Publishers.

Jones, P.W. 1997. "On World Bank Education Financing." *Comparative Education*, 33(1): 117–130.

Moe, T.M. 2011. *Special Interest: Teachers Unions and America's Public Schools*. Washington, DC: Brookings Institution Press.

Mundy, K. and A. Verger. 2015. "The World Bank and the Global Governance of Education in a Changing World Order." *International Journal of Educational Development*, 40: 9–18.

OECD. 2013. *Excellence Through Equity: Giving Every Student the Chance to Succeed*. PISA 2012 Results Vol. II. Paris: OECD.

Patrinos, H.A., F. Barrera Osorio, and J. Guáqueta. 2009. *The Role and Impact of Public-Private Partnerships in Education*. Washington, DC: The World Bank.

Peck, J. and N. Theodore. 2010. "Recombinant Workfare, Across the Americas: Transnationalizing 'Fast' Social Policy." *Goforum*, 41(2): 195–208.

Piketty, T. 2014. *The Capital in the Twenty-First Century*. Boston: Harvard University Press.

Psacharopoulos, G. 1994. "Returns to Investment in Education: A Global Update." *World Development*, 22(9): 1325–1343.

Psacharopoulos, G. and M. Woodhall. 1985. *Education for Development: An Analysis of Investment Choices*. Oxford: Oxford University Press.

Ravallion, M. 2001. "Growth, Inequality and Poverty: Looking Beyond Averages." *World Development*, 29(11): 1803–1815.

Robertson, S.L., K. Mundy, A. Verger, and F. Menashy. 2012. *Public Private Partnerships in Education: New Actors and Modes of Governance in a Globalizing World*. Cheltenham: Edward Elgar Publishing.

Romer, P. 1990. "Endogenous Technological change." *Journal of Political Economy*, XCVIII: 71–102.

Rosenau, J.N. and E.-O. Czempiel. 1992. *Governance Without Government: Order and Change in World Politics*. Cambridge: Cambridge University Press.

Reimers, F. 1994. "Education and Structural Adjustment in Latin America and Sub-Saharan Africa." *International Journal of Educational Development*, 14(2): 119–129.

Stromquist, N.P. 1989. "Determinants of Educational Participation and Achievement of Women in the Third World: A Review of the Evidence and a Theoretical Critique." *Review of Educational Research*, 59(2): 143–183.

Thurow, L. 1979. "A Job-Competition Model", in *Unemployment and Inflation*, edited by M. Piore, 17–32. White Plains: ME Sharpe.

Van der Berg, S. 2008. "Poverty and Education". *Education Policy Series, International Academy of Education and International Institute for Education Planning*. Paris: UNESCO.

Van de Werfhorst, H.G. and R. Andersen. 2005. "Social Background, Credential Inflation and Educational Strategies." *Acta Sociologica*, 48: 321–340.

Verger, A. and X. Bonal. 2012. "'All things being equal?' Policy Options, Shortfalls, and Absences in the World Bank Education Strategy 2020," in *World Bank and Education: Critiques and Alternatives*, edited by S. Klees, J. Samoff, and N. Stromquist, 125–142. Rotterdam: Sense Publishers.

Wade, R. 2004. "Is Globalization Reducing Poverty and Inequality?" *World Development*, 32(49): 567–589.

Waslander, S., C. Pater and M. van der Weide. 2010. "Markets in Education: An Analytical Review of Empirical Research on Market Mechanisms in Education." OECD Education Working Papers, No. 52, OECD Publishing.

Whitehead, C. 1995. "Emergency Social Funds: The Experience of Bolivia and Peru." *Development in Practice*, 5(1): 53–57.

Williamson, B. 1979. *Education, Social Structure and Development*. London: MacMillan.

Wilkinson, R. and K. Pickett. 2009. *The Spirit Level: Why More Equal Societies Almost Always Do Better*. London: Allen Lane.

Wolbers, M. 2003. "Job Mismatches and their Labour-Market Effects Among School-Leavers in Europe." *European Sociological Review*, 19(3): 249–266.

World Bank. 2001. *World Development Report 2000/2001. Attacking Poverty*. New York: Oxford University Press.

World Bank. 2011. *Learning for All. Education Sector Strategy 2020*. Washington, DC: The World Bank.

Chapter 6

Gender and Education in the Global Polity

Elaine Unterhalter

Gender and education, and the connected area of girls' schooling, constitute a field in which a nexus of relationships amongst disparate organizations have formed a global policy discourse stretching over decades. Historically, clear shifts in this discourse and associated actions can be delineated. The chapter charts three distinct phases, each characterized by particular formulations of ideas, and differing relationships of activists, state governments, and transnational organizations, which precipitate particular actions. The analysis suggests different meanings of gender equity in education are struggled over, sometimes taking a direction that confronts injustice and the structures of subordination, but sometimes only dealing superficially with these relationships and weakening actions for change.

Several starting points suggest themselves for this history. In 1993 Lawrence Summers, then Chief Economist at the World Bank, wrote a Foreword to an influential set of essays on girls' schooling (King and Hill 1993) in which he asserted "investment in the education of girls may well be the highest-return investment available in the developing world" (Summers 1993). This phrase has been much repeated over the ensuing decades. In 2012, Kavita Ramdas, Executive Director for Programs on Social Entrepreneurship at Stanford University, and former CEO of the Global Fund for Women, wrote that enthusiasm for girls' schooling was becoming the new microfinance (Ramdas 2012), seen as a kind of silver bullet that would slay all demons associated with underdevelopment. Although Summers' assertion is confident and Ramdas' critical, they agree on the significance of concern with gender, girls' schooling, and education.

However, this arc of consensus starts before 1993, and, as Ramdas notes, is likely to persist. This chapter charts how ideas about gender, education, and girls' schooling appear in the policy discourses and associated actions of global organizations in

The Handbook of Global Education Policy, First Edition.
Edited by Karen Mundy, Andy Green, Bob Lingard, and Antoni Verger.
© 2016 John Wiley & Sons, Ltd. Published 2016 by John Wiley & Sons, Ltd.

different periods, looking back to a long history that helped shape Summers' formulation. It considers what was included and excluded from the discourse in different periods, and the institutional arrangements that might explain this. In concluding, it evaluates some gains and losses, particularly for the present context of extreme global inequalities, with particular gendered configurations.

Defining Gender Equity in Education

Disputed definitions regarding the nature of gender equity in education are a key component of this history. Four formulations can be distinguished (Unterhalter 2005; 2007; 2012a; 2014a), although sometimes policy discourses are not as clear-cut as this taxonomy might suggest, and there is some overlap between categories and positions.

First, gender can be thought of as a noun that delineates different groups defined in terms of sex – girls and boys or women and men. In this approach, concerns with gender equality are largely with numbers, for example, getting girls in increasing numbers to school and ensuring they finish at least a primary cycle. Sometimes this approach is expressed in terms of concern at the high numbers of boys who drop out of school in some contexts (UNESCO 2014, 104–105). Gender equity is understood in terms of gender parity; that is, equal numbers of girls and boys enrolling, progressing, completing, or attaining adequate learning outcomes.

A second approach to gender works like an adjective. From this perspective gendered forms of power, gendered structures, such as the law or the labor market, or gendered discursive frames of thinking or talking constitute the social relations of schooling. Gendered configurations are evident in the shape of the curriculum, the assumptions teachers communicate in their pedagogy, the language children use, and the organization of work in a school. Sometimes gendered power intersects with other configurations of inequality, associated with race, class, or ethnicity. Sometimes, racialized boundaries will include girls and boys of one dominant racialized group, but exclude those of a subordinated group. Connell's notion of hegemonic masculinity (2005) is associated with this formulation. From this perspective, gender equity concerns exposing and transforming the inequalities inscribed in curricula or policy, developing feminist or critical pedagogies, challenging and changing the gendered structure of pay, work conditions, or management, and addressing the gendered conditions of society associated with school-related gender based violence.

A third approach I have termed "gender as a verb." This links with ways of doing or performing gender, articulating particular ways of speaking, embodying, or signaling gender identities, and the sliding forms the relationship takes. Doing gender may be associated, for example, with forms of dress, talk or behaviors required of girls and boys at school, or of women and men teachers and the relational dynamic that expresses this. Pedagogies may limit or expand the ways in which students can explore doing, thinking, or transforming gender, and foster relationships of tolerance and equality or denial, subordination and control. The social relations of a school may enable or constrain teachers' gendered embodiment and allow pupils space to express or explore aspects of sexuality. Girls' or boys' clubs may be created as safe spaces to examine gender norms or epistemologies and build networks to support change. Gender equity in education here is concerned with tolerating and supporting diverse ways of doing gender.

In an emerging fourth approach, I use the metaphor that gender works as a gerund (Unterhalter 2014a). I seek to signal with this certain features of the present conjuncture, where gender, and girls' schooling, work in policy discourses and school processes in multiple, and sometimes contradictory, ways. A gerund is a verb that works as a noun, and through this I want to highlight how gender can operate as a social justice project associated with the expansion of women's rights, a broad human rights agenda, and *at the same time* gender concerns can operate to sanction or sanitize relations of commodification, exploitation, or continued inequalities. Thus education agents (learners, teachers, managers, policy negotiators, parents) may "do gender" and the historical location of the process may turn the action sometimes into a commodity, sometimes into a form of social projection and engagement with justice, sometimes into a different way of reading or acting in the world, but not necessarily always concerned to undo inequalities. Forms of Public–Private Partnership (PPP) for girls' education are an example, when aid, raised from taxes, is partnered with corporate initiatives, which do not allow for any scrutiny of the relations of production or consumption associated with corporate enterprise. Another is government policy discourses, which support halting violence against women globally, while at home enacting austerity programs, cutting benefits for poor women, squeezing housing provision, and doing little to regulate or ameliorate very low pay. Addressing this formation of gender as a gerund requires particular conceptual and practice moves to anchor ideas about gender equality and empowerment in education (Unterhalter 2016, forthcoming).

A History of Consensus Building

Three periods are evident in the emergence of a global project regarding gender equality in education and girls' schooling. These overlap slightly and the end of one period tends to blend into the emergence of a subsequent phase. The first period, which I have termed the women's rights phase, stretches from the late 18th century and has its high point around the Beijing Conference on women in 1995, subsequently fragmenting into different strands of women's rights movements. The second period I have termed the girls' access to school phase. This begins around 1990 with the building of the Education for All (EFA) movement at the Jomtien conference, has a high point around 2000, the year of the adoption of an EFA goal on gender equality and girls' schooling and the presentation of gender parity in schooling as an indicator of women's empowerment in the Millennium Development Goal (MDG) framework. The third phase appears in a policy declaration in 2010, although its roots lie in the 1980s and 1990s. I term this the Beyond Access phase, to signal that it is concerned with issues that emerge beyond the point of access to school.

The Women's Rights Phase

The women's rights phase of a global policy discourse on gender equality, education, and girls' schooling begins in the late 18th century. It is linked to the anti-slavery movement, political associations that questioned the authority of kings and aristocrats, and articulates themes about rationality, embodiment, and the social circumscription of women through art, literature, music, and religion. As Stamatov (2014) has argued, this transnational humanitarian discourse is not disconnected from the mercantile interests associated with free trade and economic exchanges between Europe, Africa, and the Americas, and, as work on British feminism and empire explores (Midgeley 2004), it is not always unambiguously critical of imperialism. Initially the networks that articulated, created, and sustained ideas linking together women's rights and the importance of education for girls, were global relationships of friendship, between individuals, sometimes enhanced by connection to a particular cause, such as the anti-slavery movement or opposition to racial exploitation (Midgeley 1993; Guy-Sheftall 1995; May 2007). The early 18th- and 19th-century history of ideas about gender equality and girls' education circulated primarily through associations formed at lectures and meetings, and many of their practices entailed writing and reading to draw in global networks of like-minded women and men. Initial action did not seek to engage with the practical political terrain of writing laws, taking office, or shaping state or supra-state level institutions. The discourse was chiefly moral, focusing on how education can reframe identities and norms, and how resources for this can be distributed to schools, or local authorities. It is thus concerned with gender as an adjective and the ways that education or rationality or work may help reform ways of doing gender.

In the 19th century women's networks engaged with colonial governments, missionaries, or traders to try to secure more education for girls. Frequently these global women's education networks were critical of states' confirmation of women's exclusion and subordination (Kartini 1920; Leach 2008; Gaitskell 2003; Snaith 2014). The women's suffrage movement at the end of the 19th century opened to these educated, politically interested, and globally connected networks opportunities to engage on a different terrain. The campaigns for women to gain the vote, side by side with access not just to schooling, but also higher education, linked with ideas of reforming the state. This was reconfigured in discourse and practical action taking on social protection, laws on marriage and property, engagement with peace, questioning ideas about colonial rule and the content of education. National identity was an important site for articulating political struggles, often supported by transnational connections (Edwards and Roces 2006; Ferree and Tripp 2006). These spaces allowed for an engagement with gender as an adjective, challenging existing forms of power, and gender as a verb, suggesting how women might talk or act differently. In this process of explicit political involvement with the state articulating demands for schooling or higher education for women, the notion of gender as a noun was introduced.

Late 19th-century women's organizations, concerned with expanding the suffrage, set out explicitly to build links across different kinds of polities, forging women's peace congresses, and movements to expand higher education opportunities for women (Rupp 1997). World War I put many of these networks and organizations under strain, dividing some irreconcilably. For some, transnational women's rights and education demands came to be obscured by nationalist sentiment. For others, the horror of the war and its aftermath made cross-national organizations and aspirations for peace even more urgent.

After World War II, states and the newly forming United Nations (UN) organizations came to be seen as the source of protection for women's rights and gender equality in education. Girls' schooling and women's education were positioned by women's rights activists, not as niche enclaves to protect and advance minority views, but as human rights, to be extended to all. In this discursive frame, working with gender as a noun was imbued with moral authority associated with universal rights. Article 26 of the Universal Declaration of Human Rights (UDHR) sets out the universal right to education, irrespective of gender. It also sets out a universal right to free and compulsory schooling at the "elementary and fundamental stages",[1] while technical and professional education are to "be made generally available" and higher education "shall be equally accessible to all on the basis of merit"[2] (UDHR 1948, Article 26). In these formulations, education rights according to Goetz (2007, 19) express an "enabling paradigm" for gender justice associated with minimal entitlements and choices for well-being (Goetz 2007, 19). This provides for actions which ensure entitlements to minimal levels of education, but little participation for women in decision-making or engagements with the content and practices of schooling. The assumption in UDHR and later declarations, including the International Covenant on Economic, Social and Cultural Rights (1976), the Convention on the Elimination of Discrimination against Women (1979), and the Convention on the Rights of the Child (1989) was that the public sphere of the school would not replicate the subordination of women associated with the family or the household. School, it was assumed, once access was provided, would be gender equitable and this drove actions on expanding access without addressing gender inequalities (Unterhalter 2007; Maslak 2007). The formulations associated with "gender as an adjective" and "gender as a verb," which had been such strong currents in the early phases of the global policy discourses regarding girls' education associated with women's rights networks, appeared to recede.

However, a different strand in transnational women's rights activism used networks built through the international women's rights movement's convening initiatives to develop more expansive meanings of gender equality and more diverse sites for realization. This network, met in Mexico (1980), in Nairobi (1985) and built toward the Beijing Declaration in 1995 (Sen and Grown 1986). Activists attending these meetings identified multiple sites of gender inequalities that were personal, emotional, embodied, political, economic, social, and cultural. In this discourse, there is a presentation of gender as a noun, an adjective, and a verb, delineating the multiple sites of gendered power that needed to be addressed through policy-making and practice in the global polity.

The Beijing Declaration and Platform of Action of 1995 adopted at the UN-convened Beijing conference, with a very large presence of state and non-state actors, is the fullest statement by a global polity of how girls' and women's education, women's rights, and gender equality connect. The Platform of Action's strategic objective 2 on education sits next to objectives that deal with poverty, health, violence against women, participation in decision-making, and in institutions. Under the education objective detailed attention is given to gender equality and women's rights to access, progression, and completion of different levels of schooling. Content and organization of schooling and aspects of inequities are noted. Women's participation is to be encouraged in leadership, decision-making, information flows, sport, and arts. A separate strategic objective addresses girls' schooling looking at aspects of health, vulnerability to violence, child labor, and discriminatory attitudes (UN 1995). The Declaration and Platform for Action can be read as marking the high point of the long women's rights phase. They also, despite the clear policy platform articulated, appear to bring to a close a period of bottom-up networking and collaborative partnership activities of women's rights movements working with governments and multilateral organizations. After 1995 some of these links start to become more formalized and less organic (Sen and Mukherjee 2014). Education becomes detached from much women's rights campaigning.

The period from the end of World War II had seen the articulation of a broad women's rights agenda, in which access to education blended with access to the vote and for improved pay and social recognition. Education was seen as a key space for the assertion of women's dignity and capacity to participate socially, politically, and economically, and was considered a space in which gender equality, as a lived set of relations, could be articulated and experienced. Peppin Vaughan's (2013) work on women's rights activists in India shows how they navigated between the structures of the newly independent state, international organizations, like the United Nations Educational, Scientific and Cultural Organization (UNESCO), and networks of local political activists to advance their agenda. Similar dynamics are evident in the way women's groups, often led by highly educated women, operated in Kenya (Maathai 2004) and Uganda (Tripp 2000).

The women's rights period spans two centuries and a transformation of political relations regarding the franchise and women's work outside the home. It is associated with the emergence of nation states and multilateral organizations, both of which provide openings, but also closures with regard to advancing gender equality in education and other areas. It sees a considerable expansion of education and literacy, but this is unevenly distributed, and women and girls predominate amongst those who are excluded or have very unequal and often gender-biased provision (King and Hill 1993; Unterhalter 2007). The women's rights period is one in which the specifics of formal educational content, organization, and pedagogical dynamics, initially an important thread in the moral and political argument for women's education, come to be obscured by more general arguments about women's social, political, and economic recognition and participation. Education *in general* is seen to underpin this and the detailed discussion of what gender equitable education might look like and how it is to be delivered intermingles with these other threads. After World War II, education became a major area of global policy formation by international organizations, and the major discourse deployed was one where education rights were to be advanced. Gender equality was a component of those rights, but the contours of gender equality rights in education were rather broadly formulated. The positions associated with the women's rights phase did not disappear after the Beijing Conference, but increasingly, after that date, they came to focus on aspects of economic and political discrimination against women, and schooling became a site of separate global initiatives, largely led by the education sector, particularly three large UN organizations, which had a narrower interpretation of gender equality.

The Get Girls in School Phase

The get girls in school phase of global policy-making started to emerge in the 1970s, associated with the correlations that were observed between the level of women's education and reductions in population growth (Rindfuss *et al.* 1980; Schultz 1993).

However, the dynamics of differing responses by UN organizations to the debt crises and structural adjustment in the 1980s, meant that population policy was only one amongst many global initiatives with a bearing on gender equality and girls' schooling. The end of the Cold War, and the inauguration, from 1990 of a decade of global convening and policy development, had the effect of distilling out getting girls into school, as a single issue, where the benefits in terms of health, economic growth, and political cohesion could be easily documented (Unterhalter 2000; 2007). The moves that made this possible were largely associated with the politics of global organizations. Unlike the women's rights phase, with alliances and positions developing over centuries as a bottom-up movement, the get girls to school phase was characterized by powerful global organizations formulating policy positions and using aid and other forms of political leverage to bring member states into forms of alliance on the issue. In this process, the meaning of gender was narrowed to focus largely on gender as a noun, while gender equality became highly attenuated, used chiefly to denote gender parity.

This phase is very clearly driven by UN organizations, who use girls' and women's education, an area of overlapping concern, to help them build a consensus across differences, and link them through aid and policy dialogue to the governments of member states. Two conferences in 1990 set this agenda: the Jomtien conference, which launched the EFA movement as a strategic partnership of certain governments and UN organizations, with limited civil society engagement, and the United Nations Children's Fund (UNICEF) conference, which linked education with children's health, and identified monitoring and evaluation, as key components of advancing global policy agendas.

The Declarations adopted at these two events show how access to education is the dominant trope, with only a small amount of attention focused on participation, and nothing said about gender equality, pedagogy, and links to wider areas of women's rights. The Jomtien Declaration proclaims:

> The most urgent priority is to ensure access to, and improve the quality of, education for girls and women, and to remove every obstacle that hampers their active participation. All gender stereotyping in education should be eliminated. An active commitment must be made to removing educational disparities. Underserved groups: the poor; street and working children; rural and remote populations; nomads and migrant workers; indigenous peoples; ethnic, racial, and linguistic minorities; refugees; those displaced by war; and people under occupation, should not suffer any discrimination in access to learning opportunities. (Inter-Agency Commission 1990).

In this period, quality is broadly sketched with no reflection on equality. Gender inequality is not considered in any depth, placed next to a call to attend to "underserved" groups portrayed as marginal, even though they may constitute majorities. No delineation of the structural inequalities is made, including those implicated in schooling. While the justification for improving access draws on the earlier rights discourse, there is a falling away of the broader integrated framing of rights, where many social political and economic processes were intertwined, and gender as an adjective and verb were addressed (Sen and Grown 1986). Enhancing access to education was intended, in the discourse of Jomtien, to revitalize economic growth and development, to protect the environment, to prevent the spread of fatal and crippling diseases, and to achieve greater social and economic justice (Article 1). But how education in school might do this was not much addressed.

The Declaration adopted at the end of the UNICEF conference linked rights and education access, but said little on gender equality or women's rights, framing the objectives in terms of benefits for children:

> Strengthening the role of women in general and ensuring their equal rights will be to the advantage of the world's children. Girls must be given equal treatment and opportunities from the very beginning. At present, over 100 million children are without basic schooling, and two-thirds of them are girls. The provision of basic education and literacy for all are among the most important contributions that can be made to the development of the world's children. (UNICEF 1990)

Women's rights to education access are to provide "advantage" and "development" for children. This view that women's education was not for women themselves, but for others – driving health, economic, or other social benefits – was to become a major aspect of the discourse of this period (Unterhalter 2000).

Studies of the implementation of EFA in the 1990s show how national ministries of education worked with UN organizations to develop policies on enhancing access to school (King and Hill 1993; Mundy and Manion 2015; Strutt and Kepe 2010). While there was considerable concern to improve access for girls, the actual implementation of EFA policies neglected gender inequalities associated with poverty, discriminatory curricula, failures to protect indigenous rights, and silence on violence against women and girls (Heward and Bunwaree 1999).

During this decade, policy interventions by the World Bank identified two key messages: primary schooling should be prioritized as the rate of return was higher than that on other phases (World Bank 1995), and girls' education was one of the best investments for development. The empirical material to support this was provided in the volume edited by King and Hill (1993), which highlighted the economic benefits of girls' schooling, and the Lawrence Summers' Foreword, quoted at the beginning of this chapter, and distilled this to a succinct policy message. Throughout this decade the World Bank, drawing on these perceptions, came to take a key role steering global education policy and policy-making. It used its financial resources and policy leadership to endorse actions in countries like Malawi, Ethiopia, and Bangladesh that facilitated getting girls into primary school, often regardless of the quality or capacity to support girls to learn (Aikman and Unterhalter 2005a; Jones 2007; Klees *et al.* 2012)

An attempt to resolve differences emerging in global education policy-making on EFA was expressed in the Dakar Framework of Action adopted in 2000, and supported by all the main UN organizations, many governments, and a large civil society presence (Mundy 2007). This presented a wider perspective on gender equality in education than that articulated by the World Bank or the Jomtien Declaration. Goal 6 identified the importance of working for "integrated strategies for gender equality in education" that recognized the need for change in "attitudes, values and practices" (Dakar Framework 2000, 19). The goal aims to address institutional constraints on gender equality, engaging with gender as an adjective, as well as working to get girls into school and support participation. At Dakar the UN Girls' Education Initiative (UNGEI) was launched with a remit to mobilize a wide partnership to support work on gender equality and girls' education (UNESCO 2000). UNGEI (expanded from the UNICEF African Girls' Education Initiative (AGEI)) (Chapman and Miske 2007) saw its remit as "a wider call to action on the part of United Nations Member States to partner in promoting girls' education and gender equality" (UNGEI 2010). Unfortunately, this specific education focus meant that many of the broader contextual themes articulated in the Beijing Declaration were pushed to the side. Nonetheless, UNGEI and the Dakar Platform still represented opportunities both to develop policy processes to get girls into school and to widen ambition to larger gender equality goals (Aikman and Unterhalter 2005b; Unterhalter 2007).

However, the ways in which the Dakar initiative had set the question of girls' education within a wider policy context of gender equality was to be narrowed by another initiative of 2000, the Millennium Declaration, which in 2001 was given specific form, to effect particularly focused actions, in the shape of the Millennium Development Goals (MDGs). The MDGs, an attempt to steer development initiatives through results based management, had two goals with a bearing on education. MDG 2 dealt with schooling and had indicators concerned with all children completing primary schooling and an expansion of youth literacy. MDG 3 on women's empowerment, conceived gender parity in primary, secondary, and tertiary education as the major route to achieving all the other MDGs (Unterhalter 2007; Sen and Mukherjee 2014). An effect of the MDGs and their indicator framework was that activity drawing from the wider Dakar agenda tended to be circumscribed; ambition in governments and non-governmental organizations (NGOs) was all too often limited just to getting girls in school, and the wider questions of the articulation with the women's rights agenda was pushed to the side, as detailed research on implementing this policy framework in Kenya, South Africa, and Ghana indicates (Unterhalter 2012b; 2014b).

The strength and the weakness of the MDGs was that they encouraged top-down leadership around simple messages. From 2002, the EFA Global Monitoring Report had looked at gender in schooling largely in terms of gender as a noun. Although work was published on gendered education processes in schools and policy enactment (Heward and Bunwaree 1999; Aikman and Unterhalter 2005a; 2007; Maslak 2007; Fennell and Arnot 2007), the major policy initiatives, with money and influence behind them, concerned girls' access to school and the financial and other arrangements, such as cash or kind incentives, expansion of school building, or abolition of fees, that would support this. Governments, particularly those who were receiving large aid packages, were key players, but so too were large global NGOs that harnessed development assistance funds and income from the private and charitable sectors to establish programs in girls' education. In 2010, when UNGEI held a 10-year review conference, a number of large initiatives on girls' education had emerged. These included large NGOs like ActionAid and Camfed, aid programs, such as the United States Agency for International Development (USAID) Strategies for Advancing Girls' Education (SAGE), the Department for International Development's (DFID) Girls' Education Challenge (GEC), and work on girls' schooling associated with the Forum of African Women Educationists (FAWE). Gender parity was a key monitoring and evaluation indicator for the Fast Track Initiative, which dispensed funds for EFA (FTI 2009). A number of private sector donors, like the Nike Foundation, were in partnership with large donors on girls' education projects (Fennell 2012; Moeller 2013). The terrible attack in 2012 by Taliban militants on the schoolgirl education activist, Malala Yousafzai in Pakistan, gave this movement to get girls into school a potent symbol and an articulate spokesperson.

Monkman and Hoffman (2013) have conducted a critical discourse analysis of the policy documents of 14 organizations engaged in global policy-making on the theme of girls' education and gender equality between 1995 and 2008. They identified the kinds of arguments made for educating girls, some linked with justice, rights, equality, and inclusion, but many associated with sustaining unexamined gender inequitable family relationships, superficial delineations of empowerment, and a frequent conflation of sex and gender. The trends they identify suggest that the inclusion of gender in global policy-making, is partly linked to a depoliticization of the notion of gender as a noun, but also suggests that gender has become a place marker, in which it is used to stand for concern with all other inequalities, obscuring the specificities and contextual dynamics, both of gender and other kinds of social division.

This discursive framing needs to be read together with the detailed monitoring from government reports and household surveys of gender and the numbers in and out of school (UNESCO 2014). In 2010, the authors of the UNESCO Global Monitoring Report introduced the innovation of drawing on household level data to show how inequalities intersect, and how gender, rurality, ethnicity, and income quintiles amplified each other for some children who had very limited access to education, compared to others in higher income groups, urban settings, and belonging to dominant racial or ethnic groups (UNESCO 2010, 138–156). While this was a much more sophisticated deployment of ideas about gender compared to the simple approach based on gender parity, it still framed the major policy dynamic in terms of getting girls into school and did little to expand the exploration of how gender inequalities might work in different spaces and the reasons for these intersections.

What remained outside this discourse to get girls into school were feminist concerns with the wide range of sites of gender inequalities and how they might connect with schooling. Thus gender inequalities in families, violence against women, discrimination against women in the labor market, at work, in health provision, and in political, cultural and social representation were not taken up. In addition, what children learned in school and how forms of femininities and masculinities that might perpetuate gender inequalities were validated by school cultures were not the focus of global policy-making, and the actions to engage with these issues tended to be local, small-scale, and not well documented (Unterhalter et al. 2014).

This period of policy-making around an EFA consensus may be characterized as one of elite circulation in which there was a flow of ideas, policy frameworks, and financial resources between a connected group of policy brokers, in which certain global NGOs came to participate. This consensus differs from that associated with a grassroots mobilization around women's rights, which built up in the previous phase. There were few efforts made to reach down to grassroots women's organizations or education activists. The detailed studies I have participated in of how the MDGs and EFA were interpreted and acted on in global organizations and at different levels by governments and NGOs in Kenya and South Africa show how these processes of making a singular policy at the top came to be detached from the concerns of teachers and education activists and were interpreted very narrowly and often in ways that undermined inclusion by actors working on middle level initiatives (Unterhalter 2012b). Research in Bangladesh, Niger, and Gambia confirms this pattern regarding how policy is interpreted and the actions that follow (Dejaeghere and Wiger 2013; Greany 2008; Manion 2012).

A gulf now opened up between education and women's rights activists. The discursive and political links that had existed at national and transnational level from the previous phase of global activism were often difficult to sustain. Batliwala (2007) describes a process in India by which simple technical messages about women's participation in microfinance became detached from a wider empowerment and social justice orientation concerned with education and addressing connected inequalities. In South Africa, Hassim (2006) documents a process where feminists entered government ministries, effecting some important political shifts, but fragmenting their connection with an integrated women's rights mobilization. Dieltiens *et al.* (2009) and Karlsson (2010) show how feminists working in the education department in South Africa at national and provincial level could only act on substantive issues of gender equality and women's rights in quite superficial ways.

The simplicity of the MDG focus on gender parity and access to schooling and the process of implementing this through the EFA consensus of elite partnership between governments, large NGOs, and UN organizations meant that gender as a noun was the major trope in policy-making. This sometimes led to actions to improve gender equalities, for example, where governments linked policies to get girls into school with a wider social reform agenda, enhancing women's local representation in governance structures, such as Village Education Committees in India, or reforming land law, supporting maternal and child health provision, or addressing some of the gendered dimensions of poverty, nutrition, and limited access to reproductive and sexual health interventions in Bangladesh. But all too often global policy on getting girls into school was implemented by governments with minimal capacity to take forward a wider gender equality and women's rights agenda and was accompanied by virtually no attention to other areas of women's lack of rights or processes that maintained gender inequalities.

The Beyond Access Phase

A third period begins around 2010, when fault lines begin to emerge in the EFA consensus, although this remains in place, shifting to accommodate new concerns and policy actors. The complex issue of School Related Gender Based Violence (SRGBV) begins to displace the simple policy focus on getting girls into school, while alliances shift to accommodate the presence of large corporate and philanthropic organizations, and new technologies. A dispersed landscape of issues suggests politics may be dubious, but consensus should form around technically robust interventions regarding what works.

On one level, the appeal to a global policy community of the multi-dimensional area of SRGBV (Parkes 2015) is difficult to understand. Work on this theme had been published in the previous period (Leach and Mitchell 2006; Dunne *et al.* 2006; Morrell *et al.* 2009), but was not immediately used to guide action, possibly partly because it questioned some of the clear actions associated with getting girls into school. In 2010, the UNGEI review conference identified violence, together with poverty and quality, as key areas for deepening work on gender equality and education (UNGEI 2010). While the concern with quality quickly became incorporated into discussions of measuring learning outcomes, and little attention was given to explicit work on poverty, a number of meetings of donors, large NGOs, and multilateral organizations took place, leading to the funding of some large-scale projects, and research on SRGBV (UNGEI 2013; 2014). Many of the organizations, which had engaged with the EFA consensus focusing on gender as a noun, were now reflecting, through their concern with SRGBV, on gender as an adjective and verb. Why this switch of focus took place requires investigation, but it may be that an interpretation of SRGBV, focusing on acts of violence, rather than the structural dimensions of inequality and poverty associated with violence (Parkes and Unterhalter 2015), accommodates well to the current era and the slippery dimensions of gender as a gerund. Large donors working on SRGBV might *both* be working with and against wider gender equalities at home and abroad.

A second area where some of the twofold features of gender as a gerund are apparent are the alliances with the private sector. In a number of countries for-profit organizations, sometimes linked with new information technologies, and sometimes through their corporate social responsibility arms, have taken up the issue of girls' education. In 2013, the Discovery TV Channel became a key partner with DFID in Kenya, Ghana, and Nigeria to use new media to train teachers and support girls to develop national broadcast programs on gender and marginaliszation (DFID 2014). The global multinational Pearson entered into a partnership with the NGO Camfed under DFID's GEC to develop learning resources for young girls in Tanzania and Zimbabwe, linked to their post-school needs (Camfed 2013). The private sector had a presence in grant making to girls' education and gender equality in both previous eras, but these two examples signal a new aspect. Both instances show companies with commercial interests in the lucrative, growing African market for broadcast media using access to public aid money to help them grow their businesses producing learning materials while they engage in philanthropic work. Both initiatives are "doing gender" and attending to girls' voice. However, project documentation suggests that only certain features of voice and "doing gender" will be heard, as neither aims to look critically to the transnational connections that might cause marginalization and the gendered social, political, and economic relations, in which these corporations are enmeshed and which might limit meeting girls' post-school needs. These initiatives signal shifts away from investments in public education systems and attending to inequalities in delivery. The private sector, it is assumed, will do better with gender, although their experience of this work thus far has been limited.

Why the corporate media sector may be positioned as so influential at the policy table in the current period is suggested in an infographic created by participants, many of them donors, governments, NGOs, multilaterals, and the private sector taking part in a conference held in Brussels in 2014 to secure replenishment of aid funds for the Global Partnership for Education. The infographic portrays gender inequalities as positioned beyond access to school linked with questions of safety, relations in the home, low aspirations and imbalances between economic and cultural issues (GPE 2014). What is striking about this portrayal is that the dispersed centers of action that characterized the women's rights phase are reprised.

But violence and early marriage are the only sites of gender inequality represented. The political, economic, social, and cultural language of rights and gender as an adjective has disappeared. Gender as a verb and a gerund must do work in a fragmented policy landscape that does not have a clear narrative about inequalities and their intersections. Thus the media presentations of voice may be what this group of actors considers appropriate, because there is no connective tissue explaining how gender inequalities might work with forms of power and structures of national and global injustice.

Conclusion

This chapter has mapped the emergence of three different periods of global policy-making on girls' education and gender equality with three different kinds of consensus and implications for action. A broad-based, bottom-up consensus built up over centuries around women's rights and education, deployed meanings of gender as a verb, adjective, and noun. This movement weakened, around 2000, ceding leadership of the global policy community concerned with gender and girls' schooling, built on a narrow consensus driven by elites, primarily focused on gender as a noun and getting girls into school. From around 2010, this elite partnership has given a particular welcome to global corporations, notably in the media sector, and has stressed the importance of engaging with SRGBV.

There are gains and losses in each period. The long women's rights phase saw the articulation of a broad global policy agenda with many diverse sites of negotiation, enactment, and a stress on inter-connection between gender and other kinds of inequalities. However, it was difficult for activists from this position both to maintain an integrated stance on multiple forms of subordination of women and gender injustice, and to take leadership of education sector reform. It may be partly because of the complexity of this process, and its uneven results that the simple message associated with "get girls in school" appeared so compelling.

Political will was exhorted to lead this policy process from the front through governments' partnerships with multi-lateral organizations to effect a simple menu of actions to support girls into school. From the perspective of key policy actors in this period, the question of inequalities was primarily a question of gender barriers to school access and progression. The more diverse political, economic, and social interactions that had been articulated in the earlier period to challenge multi-dimensional gender inequalities were often overlooked.

In the third period, the elite partnership of the previous phase has broadened to include a wider range of players, and SRGBV has gained a welcome prominence. But, the new policy actors, while appropriately "on message" regarding girls' education and questions of quality beyond access, are silent on other salient matters. The world in which this new phase is unfolding is marked by excessive global inequalities linked with widening income gaps, and particular gendered forms of precarious livelihoods. Economic growth in OECD and developing countries concentrates wealth amongst the rich and super-rich, dismissing majorities to suffer grossly inadequate health and education provision, and dangerous environmental vulnerabilities, which energy policies exacerbate. Because gender inequalities permeate all social sectors, these inequalities intersect. The expanded community of global policy brokers on girls' education and gender equality has not yet made clear statements addressing poverty, injustice, exploitation, and the global lines of connection, through corporations, and government deregulation that sustain this.

However, these elite partnerships are not the only actors concerned with gender equality and girls' education as a global project. A new generation of young, educated women and men, engaged in different forms of social and political networking has grown, building on previous phases of policy-making and action. They have the potential to formulate new discourses and actions concerning gender, education, and social justice as a trans-national project. But, at the time of writing, they remain outside the consensus. Theirs is a set of judgments waiting to be heard.

References

Aikman, S. and E. Unterhalter (eds). 2005a. *Beyond Access: Developing Gender Equality in Education* Oxford: Oxfam Publishing.

Aikman, S. and E. Untehalter. 2005b. "Conclusion: Policy and Practice Change for Gender Equality," in *Beyond Access: Developing Gender Equality in Education*, edited by S. Aikman and E. Unterhalter, 245–249. Oxford: Oxfam Publishing.

Aikman, S. and E. Unterhalter (eds). 2007. *Practising Gender Equality in Education: Programme Insights* Oxford: Oxfam.

Batliwala, S. 2007. "Taking the Power out of Empowerment: An Experimental Account." *Development in Practice*, 17(4–5): 557–565.

Camfed. 2013. "Camfed and Pearson Launch Partnership for Girls' Education". Cambridge: Camfed online. Retrieved from: https://camfed.org/latest-news/camfed-and-pearson-Launch-Partnership (accessed November 5, 2015).

Chapman, D. and S. Miske. 2007. "Promoting Girls' Education in Africa," in *The Structure and Agency of Women's Education*, edited by M. Maslak, 87–105. Albany: State University of New York Press.

Connell, R.W. and R. Connell. 2005. *Masculinities*. Berkeley: University of California Press.

Dakar Framework. 2000. *The Dakar Framework for Action*. Paris: UNESCO.

DeJaeghere, J. and N. Wiger. 2013. "Gender Discourses in an NGO Education Project: Openings for Transformation Toward Gender Equality in Bangladesh." *International Journal of Educational Development*, 33(6): 557–565.

DFID. 2014. *Girls' Education Challenge* London: DFID. Retrieved from:https://www.gov.uk/girls-education-challenge (accessed November 5, 2015).

Dieltiens, V., E. Unterhalter, S. Letsatsi, and A. North. 2009. "Gender Blind, Gender-lite: A Critique of Gender Equity Approaches in the South African Department of Education." *Perspectives in Education*, 27(4): 365–374.

Dunne, M., S. Humphreys, and F. Leach. 2006. "Gender Violence in Schools in the Developing World." *Gender and Education*, 18(1): 75–98.

Edwards, L. and M. Roces (eds). 2006. *Women's Suffrage in Asia: Gender, Nationalism and Democracy*. Abingdon: Routledge.

Fennell, S. 2012. "Why Girls' Education Rather Than Gender Equality? The Strange Political Economy of PPPs in Pakistan," in *Public Private Partnerships in Education*, edited by S. Robertson, K. Mundy, T. Verger, and F. Menashy, 259–276. Northampton: Edward.

Fennell, S. and M. Arnot (eds). 2007. *Gender Education and Equality in a Global Context* Abingdon: Routledge.

Ferree, M. and A. Tripp (eds). 2006. *Global Feminism* New York: New York University Press.

FTI. 2009. *Annual Report Education for All Fast Track Initiatives* Washington, DC: Fast Track Initiative Secretariat.

Gaitskell, D. 2003. "Rethinking Gender Roles: The Field Experiences of Women Missionaries in South Africa," in *The Imperial Horizons of British Protestant Missions, 1880–1914*, edited by A. Porter, 131–157. Cambridge: Eerdmans.

Goetz, A.M. 2007. "Gender Justice, Citizenship and Entitlements. Core Concepts, Central Debates and New Directions for Research," in *Gender Justice, Citizenship and Development*, edited by M. Mukhopadhyay and N. Singh, 15–57. New Delhi: Zubaan.

Global Partnership for Education (GPE). 2014. *Moving Beyond Access for Girls' Education*. Infographic developed for replenishment conference, Brussels of Global Partnership for education. Retrieved from: www.globalpartnership.org/blog/moving-beyond-access-girls-education (accessed December 3, 2015).

Greany, K. 2008. "Rhetoric Versus Reality: Exploring the Rights-Based Approach to Girls' Education in Rural Niger." *Compare*, 38(5): 555–568.

Guy-Sheftall, B. (ed.). 1995. *Words of Fire: An Anthology of African-American Feminist Thought*. New York: The New Press.

Hassim, S. 2006. *Women's Organizations and Democracy in South Africa: Contesting Authority*. Madison: University of Wisconsin Press.

Heward, C. and S. Bunwaree, S. (eds). 1999. *Gender, Education and Development* London: Zed.

Inter-Agency Commission. 1990. *World Declaration on Education for All and Framework for Action to Meet Basic Learning Needs*. Jomtein: UN Inter-Agency Commission.

Jones, P. 2007. *World Bank Financing Of Education: Lending, Learning and Development*. Abingdon: Routledge.

Karlsson, J. 2010. "Gender Mainstreaming in a South African Provincial Education Department: A Transformative Shift or Technical Fix for Oppressive Gender Relations?" *Compare*, 40(4): 497–514.

Kartini, R.A. 1920. *Letters of a Javanese Princess*. New York: CPSIA.

King, E. and A. Hill (eds). 1993. *Women'S Education in Developing Countries: Barriers, Benefits and Policies* Baltimore: Johns Hopkins University Press.

Klees, S., J. Samoff, and N. Stromquist (eds). 2012. *The World Bank and Education: Critiques and Alternatives*. Dordrecht: Springer.

Leach, F. 2008. "African girls, Nineteenth-Century Mission Education and the Patriarchal Imperative." *Gender and Education*, 20(4): 335–347.

Leach, F and C. Mitchell (eds). 2006. *Combating Gender Violence in and Around Schools*. Stoke-on-Trent: Trentham Books.

Maathai, W. 2004. *The Green Belt Movement: Sharing the Approach and the Experience*. New York: Lantern.

Manion, C. 2012. "Power, Knowledge and Politics: Exploring the Contested Terrain of Girl-Focused Interventions at the National Launch of the United Nations Girls' Education Initiative in The Gambia." *Theory and Research in Education*, 10(3): 229–252.

Maslak, M. (ed.). 2007. *The Structure and Agency of Women's Education* Albany: State University of New York Press.

May, V. 2007. *Anna Julia Cooper, Visionary Black Feminist: A Critical Introduction*. New York: Routledge.

Midgeley, C. 1993. "Anti-Slavery and Feminism in Nineteenth-Century Britain." *Gender and History*, 5(3): 343–362.

Midgeley, C. 2004. *Women Against Slavery: The British Campaigns, 1780–1870*. Abingdon: Routledge.

Moeller, K. 2013. "Proving 'The Girl Effect': Corporate Knowledge Production and Educational Intervention." *International Journal of Educational Development*, 33(6): 612–621.

Monkman, K. and L. Hoffman., L. 2013. "Girls' Education: The Power of Policy Discourse." *Theory and Research in Education*, 11(1): 63–84.

Morrell, R., D. Epstein, E. Unterhalter, D. Bhana, and R. Moletsane. 2009. *Towards Equality? Gender in South African schools During the HIV and AIDS Epidemic* Durban: University of Kwazulu Natal Press.

Mundy, K. 2007. "Global Governance, Educational Change." *Comparative Education*, 43(3): 339–357.

Mundy, K. and C. Manion. 2015. "The education for all initiative," in *Education and International Development: Practice, Policy and Research*, edited by T. McCowan and E. Unterhalter. London: Bloomsbury.

Parkes, J. (ed.). 2015. *Gender Violence in Poverty Contexts: The Educational Challenge.* Abingdon: Routledge.

Parkes, J. and E. Unterhalter. 2015. "Hope and History: Education Engagements with Poverty, Inequality and Gender Violence," in *Gender Violence in Poverty Contexts: The Educational Challenge*, edited by J. Parkes. Abingdon: Routledge.

Ramdas, K. 2012. "What's Sex Got to Do With It?" *Stanford Social Innovation Review*, 39. Retrieved from: www.ssireview.org/articles/entry/whats_sex_got_to_do_with_it (accessed November 5, 2015).

Rindfuss, R., L. Bumpass, and C. St. John. 1980. "Education and Fertility: Implications for the Roles Women Occupy." *American Sociological Review*, 45: 431–447.

Rupp, L. 1997. *Worlds of Women: The Making of an International Women's Movement.* Princeton: Princeton University Press.

Schultz, T.P. 1993. "Returns to Women's Education," in *Women's Education in Developing Countries: Barriers, Benefits and Policies*, edited by E. King and A. Hill, 51–99. Baltimore: Johns Hopkins University Press.

Sen, G. and C. Grown. 1986. *Development Crises and Alternative Visions* London: Earthscan.

Sen, G. and A. Mukherjee. 2014. "No Empowerment without Rights, No Rights without Politics: Gender-equality, MDGs and the post-2015 Development Agenda." *Journal of Human Development and Capabilities*, 15(2–3): 188–202.

Snaith, A. 2014. *Modernist Voyages; Colonial Women Writers in London, 1890–1945* Cambridge: Cambridge University Press.

Stamatov, P. 2014. *The Origins of Global Humanitarianism: Religion, Empires, and Advocacy.* Cambridge: Cambridge University Press.

Strutt, C. and T. Kepe. 2010. "Implementing Education for All – Whose Agenda, Whose Change? The Case Study of the Ghana National Education Campaign Coalition." *International Journal of Educational Development*, 30(4): 369–376.

Summers, L. 1993. "Foreword," in *Women's Education in Developing Countries: Barriers, Benefits and Policies*, edited by E. King and A. Hill, v–vii. Baltimore: Johns Hopkins University Press.

Tripp, A. 2000. *Women and Politics in Uganda* Oxford: James Currey.

UN. 1995. *Fourth World Conference on Women, Held at Beijing* New York: United Nations.

UNESCO. 2000. *Girls Education, Action Now. The Ten Year UN Girls' Education Initiiative* Concept Paper prepared for Dakar meeting, Paris: UNESCO.

UNESCO. 2010. *Education for All Global Monitoring Report 2010: Reaching the Marginalized* Paris: UNESCO.

UNESCO. 2014. *Education for All Global Monitoring Report 2013/4: Teaching and Learning: Achieving Quality for All.* Paris: UNESCO.

UNGEI. 2010. "Dakar Declaration on Accelerating Girls' Education and Gender Equality." Retrieved from: www.ungei.org/index_2527.html (accessed November 30, 2015).

UNGEI. 2013. *UNGEI Annual Report*. New York: UN Girls' Education Initiative.

UNGEI. 2014. *International Partners Meeting on School Related Gender Based Violence* New York: UNGEI. Retrieved from: www.ungei.org/247_5737.html (accessed November 5, 2015).

UNICEF. 1990. *World Declaration on the Survival, Protection and Development of Children* New York: United Nations Children's Fund.

Unterhalter, E. 2000. "Transnational Visions of the 1990s. Contrasting Views of Women, Education and Citizenship," in *Challenging Democracy: Feminist Perspectives on the Education of Citizens*, edited by M. Arnot and J.A. Dillabough, 87–102. London: Routledge.

Unterhalter, E. 2005. "Fragmented Frameworks: Researching Women, Gender, Education and Development," in *Beyond Access: Developing Gender Equality in Education*, edited by S. Aikman and E. Unterhalter, 15–35. Oxford: Oxfam Publishing.

Unterhalter, E. 2007. *Gender, Schooling and Global Social Justice* Abingdon: Routledge Taylor Francis.

Unterhalter, E. 2012a. "Mutable Meanings: Gender Equality in Education and International Rights Frameworks." *Equal Rights Review*, 8: 67–84.

Unterhalter, E. 2012b. "Silences, Stereotypes and Local Selection: Negotiating Policy and Practice to Implement the MDGs and EFA," in *Global Education Policy and International Development: New Agendas, Issues and Policies*, edited by A. Verger, H. Altinyelken, and M. Novelli, 79–100. London: Continuum.

Unterhalter, E. 2014a. "Thinking About Gender in Comparative Education." *Comparative Education*, 50(1): 112–126.

Unterhalter, E. 2014b. "Measuring Education for the Millennium Development Goals: Reflections on Targets, Indicators, and a Post-2015 Framework." *Journal of Human Development and Capabilities*, 15(1–2): 176–187.

Unterhalter, E. 2016 forthcoming. "Balancing Pessimism of the Intellect and Optimism of the Will: Some Reflections on the Capability Approach, Gender, Empowerment, and Education," in *The Capability Approach, Empowerment and Participation: Concepts, Methods and Applications*, edited by D.A. Clark, M. Biggeri, and A. Frediani. London: Palgrave.

Unterhalter, E. and A. North. 2010. "Assessing Gender Mainstreaming in the Education Sector: Depoliticised Technique or a Step Towards Women's Rights and Gender Equality?" *Compare*, 40(4): 389–404.

Unterhalter, E., A. North, M. Arnot, C. Lloyd, L. Moletsane, E. Murphy-Graham, J. Parkes, and M. Saito. 2014. *Interventions to Enhance Girls' Education and Gender Equality. Education Rigorous Literature Review*. London: DFID. Retrieved from: http://r4d.dfid.gov.uk/pdf/outputs/HumanDev_evidence/Girls_Education_Literature_Review_2014_Unterhalter.pdf (accessed November 5, 2015).

Vaughan, R.P. 2013. "Complex Collaborations: India and International Agendas on Girls' and Women's Education, 1947–1990." *International Journal of Educational Development*, 33(2): 118–129.

World Bank. 1995. *Priorities and Strategies for Education* Washington, DC: World Bank.

Chapter 7

The Global Educational Reform Movement and Its Impact on Schooling

Pasi Sahlberg

Globalization and School Reforms

Globalization is normally interpreted as the process of opening doors to international exchange, whether commercial, cultural, or demographic. In many parts of the world, globalization has diminished the role of nation states and, in the opinion of many, forfeited independence in the name of trade. This has been visible throughout Europe as *Europeanization* resulting from the integration brought about by the European Union (EU) (Lawn and Grek 2012). As a consequence, standardization in economies, policies, and culture has become a new normal for nations, corporations, and public services in open and competitive environments.

Globalization has paradoxical effects on our daily lives, including schools. While competition has become the normal state of life, strategic alliances and cooperation between competing parties remains a necessary condition for sustainable success. Economic markets have become open and flexible because of diminishing barriers of trade and lower labor regulations. Subregional and global agreements have increased the mobility of goods, services, money, and intellectual capital. Competition to expand markets, promote innovations, enhance efficiency of services, and develop skilled workforces defines globalization. Corporations and schools alike are regularly employing accountability policies that commit them to management strategies based on performance appraisal of both staff and leaders.

These changes necessarily affect teaching and learning in schools. As the other chapters of this handbook on global policy-making in education illustrate, it is obvious that there is no single view of the consequences that globalization has for schooling. Although globalization has created some new opportunities to transform education from an industrial model, i.e. organization of schooling according to age

The Handbook of Global Education Policy, First Edition.
Edited by Karen Mundy, Andy Green, Bob Lingard, and Antoni Verger.
© 2016 John Wiley & Sons, Ltd. Published 2016 by John Wiley & Sons, Ltd.

and ability groups, traditional disciplines, 50-minute lessons, and textbook-based study, to more dynamic models of schooling, this chapter focuses on some problematic implications of globalization evident in current education reform thinking described in recent professional literature (e.g. Ball 2012; Hargreaves and Fullan 2009; Malone 2013; Meyer and Benavot 2013).

The failure of education systems to meet expectations has brought corporate management to schooling. Standardization of teaching and learning in schools, frequent external testing of students and teachers, and alternative forms of providing education to children have come to challenge conventional public education policies and practices in many countries. International student assessments such as the Programme for International Student Assessment (PISA), Trends in International Mathematics and Science Study (TIMSS), and Progress in International Reading Literacy Study (PIRLS) have driven much of the reform discussion (Breakspear 2012; OECD 2013; Sahlberg 2015). While these international comparisons are helpful in a sense that they provide a benchmark in some school subjects to national policy-makers, they can take on too much importance in defining educational success.

Some argue that globalization with its truly international labor markets requires "globally benchmarked standards" for teaching and learning in the core subjects that are same in schools around the world in order to enhance competitiveness of both individuals seeking employment and national economies fighting over world's markets (Barber et al. 2012). Others insist that what is needed instead in a globalized world is personalization, creativity, and the ability to differentiate teaching and learning in schools to match the interests, curiosity, and passion of students (Wagner 2012; Zhao 2012). This tension concerning the ends of education also influences how education policies and reforms in different education systems look. This is clear from a survey of how globalization has shaped education reform thinking since the 1980s.

The Origin Of Global Educational Reform Agenda

In the 1980s, the global geography of education was very different than it is today. Although international tests to compare what students knew existed then, there was not a commonly accepted index to compare the educational performance of nations and jurisdictions. In practically every country there were world class schools that educated champions in international academic Olympics and other competitions. Often because of that success of individual students in international competitions, some policy-makers thought their education systems were among the best in world (typically, the former socialist systems of Eastern Europe). At that time, the performance of educational systems was also determined by student enrolment and graduation statistics, educational attainment levels, or simply by the reputation that country had in other fields, such as university education, innovation and technology, or prosperity. On the same basis, there were people, like the Finns for example, who believed their schools were mediocre, at best, when compared to other nations. In the 1990s, the international education superpowers included the UK, the USA, France, Germany, The Netherlands, and Sweden. East Asian education systems, many parts of Canada, and Finland, which now dominate international benchmarking, didn't receive much global attention at that time.

The origin of the global educational reform agenda dates back to the 1980s when many developed nations realized that their education systems would not able to lead the way in economic, technological, and social transformations that were emerging globally. Since it was difficult to compare the quality of education systems due to the absence of reliable global data, the motivation to reform education systems primarily came from national studies and research projects. One significant and frequently cited report was *A Nation at Risk* (1983) in the USA during the Ronald Reagan administration. The other one that received much more global attention was the *Education Reform Act* (ERA) of 1988 in England. This large-scale reform legislation became so important – not only for that country but also for much of the rest of the world – that Levin and Fullan (2008) call it "a watershed event in international educational reform movement." The public sector policies of Margaret Thatcher constituted a particular approach to educational change that built on free-market inspired competition and parental choice as the key principles of raising the quality of schools. There had been earlier attempts to transform education systems through free market principles elsewhere (e.g. Chile), but ERA became the most well-known and globally researched act of its kind (Carnoy 1998; Levin and Fullan 2008). Several other large-scale school system reforms in North America, Europe, and Asia-Pacific were inspired by it, both ideologically and educationally.

The reason for the issuance of ERA and its unexpected survival under Tony Blair's Labour government in the 1990s in England was the common-sense logic of its initial architecture. Levin and Fullan (2008, 289) describe it through the following four operational principles:

- Competition among schools would lead to better outcomes for students.
- Autonomy for schools is necessary in order for schools to properly compete.
- Freedom for parents to choose schools for their children.
- Information for the public based on comparable measures of student achievement and on a single national curriculum.

These assumptions of whole-system educational reform soon became the driving ideas of education policies in other countries. International development organizations, consultants, philanthropies, and especially private corporations engaged in education policy change adopted the reform thinking that has its origins in ERA. Education reforms in many parts of the USA, Canada, and Australia adopted variations of this reform logic. School competition and choice, standardization of teaching and learning in schools, systematic management of data through standardized testing, and privatization of public education soon spread to other countries, as well, including countries in developing parts of the world.

When the emergence of market-based education reforms became evident worldwide, Boston College professors Andy Hargreaves and Dennis Shirley (2009) developed a framework to analyze the evolution of the global education reform agenda in more systematic ways. They use the metaphor of Change Ways in describing different phases in the history of educational change. The ethos of educational reform thinking arising in the wake of ERA evolves into the Third Way of educational change in the Hargreaves and Shirley model of Four Ways of Change. The Third Way is a way of market competition and standardization of schooling in which professional autonomy is gradually replaced by the ideals of efficiency, productivity, and rapid service delivery. New terms such as "standards," "accountability" and "delivery" appeared as commonplace in education policy discourse and occupied much of the technical attention of education consultancy and policy advocacy communities. Marketplace education ideology promised to governments efficiency and transparency, and to consumers diversity and quality. They were soon trumped by uniformity and standardization instead. Hargreaves and Shirley (2009, 9) write:

> [I]n the United States, statewide high-stakes tests were increasingly administered to all students – even those who were newly arrived from abroad without the barest rudiments of English. Standards were easy to write, inexpensive to fund and they spread like wildfire. They were revered in administrative and policy circles but by-passed or resisted in classrooms. However, as scripted and paced literacy programs were then imposed in many districts and on their schools, the bureaucratic screw tightened with increased ferocity.

Early lessons from the large-scale education reforms in England, the USA, New Zealand, Australia, and Sweden became widely available to all through new communication technologies and the internet in the 1990s. These reform lessons were particularly influential in the transition and developing countries – Central and Eastern Europe, the former Soviet Union, and Latin America – where the externally determined educational standards and national testing were adopted as the key drivers of educational change in circumstances that often lacked capacity and resources to steer foreign-designed reforms. The success or failure of these change efforts was not adequately judged and many reform efforts created more debates on their actual impacts than evidence-supported lessons for further improvement. In the 1990s, whole-system school reform introduced mechanisms to increase parental choice regarding their children's education that, in turn, placed schools in a new situation where they were competing against other schools for student enrolment.

But there were some who were not convinced that this reform movement was the best way to enhance teaching and learning in schools. Many European countries, including France, Germany, Denmark, Norway, Belgium, and Japan and South Korea in East Asia were among those countries where school policies remained distant to the idea that market-based reform ideology suited reforming education systems. Finland, which Cable News Network (CNN) humorously called the education world's ultimate slacker because of its relaxed and unorthodox approach to schooling, outperformed the other countries in the Organisation for Economic Cooperation and Development (OECD) in the first three PISA surveys with policies diametrically opposed to those embraced in the USA, the UK, and other countries that followed the path of marketization and privatization. Finland was for a long time seen as a stranger and educational lone wolf. The international consulting firm McKinsey, which analyzed the success factors in the best performing education systems after the third PISA survey didn't even include Finland as a high-achieving system due to its non-conservative policies and reforms (Moursed *et al.* 2010). This being the case, it is especially surprising that Finland's system is now regarded as the educational holy grail, particularly due to its superior teachers.

The Global Educational Reform Movement

We know much more about how different countries score in international league tables than we know about how education reforms in these countries have been designed and implemented. The literature indicates that the focus of education policies in many parts of the world has shifted from structural reforms – e.g. changes in length of schooling, governance structures, or institutional arrangements – to improving the quality and relevance of education (Darling-Hammond 2009; Hargreaves *et al.* 2010; Zajda 2010). As a result, global reform efforts focus increasingly on developing new standards for schools, introducing more frequent assessments and examinations to test students and teachers, allocating resources to teacher professional development, investing in technology-assisted teaching and learning, and finding more efficient ways to provide high quality teaching and learning for all students. Sometimes these reforms are designed by applying solutions designed in other countries (e.g. curriculum reforms in some parts of the Middle East) and occasionally by imitating foreign education policy principles found in books and journals (e.g. system-wide reforms in South-Eastern Europe). The transfer of education policies across country borders has become so common that it can be called a *Global Movement*. Some of the consequences of this movement have benefited schools, such as more systematic focus on student learning instead of just instruction, high expectations for all students rather than just some, and integration of technology as part of teaching and learning in schools. Other consequences of this global movement have not always been beneficial for teachers' work and students' learning in schools; for example, narrowed focus on curriculum and over-reliance on test scores as the only criteria for quality of education.

The original idea for the Global Educational Reform Movement, or GERM, is from Andy Hargreaves and his research on how standardization affected teachers' work in schools in the late 1990s. In *Learning to Change: Teaching Beyond Subjects and Standards* (Hargreaves *et al.* 2001), he presented a critique of the standards-based reform movement that became prevalent from the 1990s. Emotional and intellectual aspects of educational change have been commonly known characteristics of successful education reforms. GERM, however, brought new change forces to national policy-making. Hargreaves and colleagues claimed:

> [A] new, official orthodoxy of educational reform is rapidly being established in many parts of the world. This is occurring primarily in predominantly Anglo-Saxon countries but through international funding organizations such as the World Bank and the global distribution of policy strategies, elements of this orthodoxy are increasingly being exported in many parts of the less-developed world as well. (Hargreaves *et al.* 2001, 1)

The inspiration for GERM comes from three sources in the 1980s and the 1990s. The first was the then new paradigm of learning that challenged existing behaviorist conceptions of how people learn. The breakthrough of constructivist approaches to learning gradually shifted the focus of education reforms from the teacher to the student and learning. According to this paradigm, intended outcomes of schooling emphasize deeper conceptual understanding, problem-solving, recognition of multiple intelligences, and advancement of social skills.

The second inspiration was the public demand for guaranteed, effective learning for all pupils. The worldwide campaign of Education for All insisted not only that every child must have access to school, but also that common learning standards for all must be offered as means to promote the ideal of universal education. Centrally mandated learning standards in tandem with aligned national standardized student assessments became the main means proposed to improve the quality of educational performance in many parts of the world during the 1990s. Learning standards and aligned testing of student achievement were often limited to the core subjects in national curricula, i.e. reading literacy, mathematics, and, more recently, science.

The third source feeding the expansion of GERM was the demand to move decision-making authority from central offices to local governments. Decentralization of governance enhanced school autonomy and thereby also brought with it stronger accountability for schools and teachers. A common means to hold schools and teachers accountable for learning in school was to link that accountability to externally employed standardized test results. This, in turn, shifted the focus from school-based assessments to external standardized tests that radically changed the nature of teaching and learning in schools. Various forms of test-based accountability have emerged where school performance and raising the quality of education are closely tied to processes of accreditation, promotion, sanctions, and financing. Strengthening the role of test-based accountability in national education policies has remained a controversial area subject to continual debates in education systems affected by GERM.

GERM has several manifestations that vary from one education system to another. As mentioned earlier, some of the elements of this international education agenda have been welcomed and have improved teaching and learning in schools. Thanks to the international student assessments, particularly the OECD's PISA study, we now know much better than in the 1990s what seem to be the drivers of successful reforms and strong performance in education. For the purposes of this chapter, I have identified the five most common features of education policies since the 1990s that education authorities in different countries have chosen to improve the quality – and more recently also equity – of their education systems. Next is a brief description of these common policy features.

First, and perhaps the most visible common feature, is increased *competition* between schools for enrolment. Almost all education systems within OECD have enhanced alternative forms of schooling – private schools, independent schools, international schools, charter schools, and home schooling – to offer parents more *choice* regarding their children's schooling (OECD 2013). The voucher system in Chile in the 1980s, free schools in Sweden in the 1990s, charter schools in the USA in the 2000s, and secondary academies in the UK in the 2010s are examples of faith in market-like competition as an engine of advancement. At the same time, the proportion of more advantaged students studying in private schools or independent schools has grown in OECD countries' education systems (OECD 2013). In Australia, for example, nearly every third primary and secondary school student studies in a non-governmental Catholic or private school (Jensen 2013). School league tables that rank schools based on their performance in national standardized assessments have further increased competition between schools. OECD data show that according to school principals across OECD countries more than three-quarters of the students assessed by PISA attend schools that compete with at least one other school for enrolment (OECD 2010, 72). Finally, students especially in many Asian countries, experience stronger pressure to perform better than their peers due to the tough race to get into the best high schools and universities (Dang and Rogers 2008).

Increased focus on competitiveness as a main driver of overall prosperity in our societies has made it a key success factor in government policies around the world. Because global economic competitiveness rankings also measure some aspects of national human capital, they bring education policies close to economic policy discourse. As a response to national economic competitiveness policies some education authorities have concluded that raising competitiveness requires that education sector also becomes part of competitiveness campaign. Schools racing against other schools, measuring teacher effectiveness against among teachers, and pushing students to try harder by competing against one another for examination results are thought to have a positive affect on the quality of schooling. As a consequence, however, schools collaborate less with one another, teachers don't share their best ideas with colleagues, and students perceive cooperation with other students as a threat to their own success. The most harmful consequences of such unhealthy competition in education are increased suspicion, distrust, anxiety, and fear in schools and classrooms. As I have argued elsewhere, economic competitiveness that is fueled by individuals' habits of mind, risk-taking abilities, and creativity won't be enhanced by education policies that lead to such unhealthy competition (Sahlberg 2006).

The second is *standardization* of teaching and learning in schools. Shifting the focus from inputs to outcomes in education in the 1990s led to the popularity of standards-based education policies, especially in the English-speaking part of the world. These reforms initially aimed to have a stronger emphasis on learning outcomes and school performance instead of content and structures of schooling. It has been a generally unquestioned belief among policy-makers and education reformers that the presence of clear and sufficiently high performance standards for schools, teachers, and students is a precondition to improved quality of teaching and better overall performance of schools. Enforcement of external standardized testing and school evaluation systems to judge how these standards have been attained emerged originally from these standards-driven education policies. Standardization draws from an assumption that all students should be educated to the same, ambitious learning targets, which, in turn, has led to prevalence of prescribed curricula and homogenization of curriculum policies worldwide. The National Curriculum in England and in Australia, New National Education Standards in Germany, and Common Core State Standards in the USA are examples of attempts to bring coherence and quality to teaching and learning in all schools.

Standardization that is too tight narrows the freedom and flexibility in schools and classrooms to do things that are truly meaningful to them. It also prevents teachers from experimentation, reduces the use of alternative pedagogical approaches, and limits risk-taking in schools and classrooms. Research on educational systems that have adopted policies emphasizing steering education through pre-determined standards and prioritized core subjects, suggests that teaching and learning are narrower and teachers focus on "proven methods," "guaranteed content" and "predetermined scripts" to best prepare their students for the high-stakes tests (Au 2009).

The consequence is that the higher the stakes of student tests, the lower the degree of freedom, risk-taking, and creativity in classroom teaching and learning.

The third common feature of the global education reform movement is an *increased emphasis on reading literacy, mathematics, and science* in schools. These are sometimes called the core subjects in the school curriculum. The importance of these disciplines means that they also are elevated as prime targets of required improvement in national education reforms. According to the OECD and research on national education policies in a number of countries, national education policies are increasingly influenced by the international student assessments, especially PISA (Ball 2012; Wiseman 2013). Breakspear (2012, 27) summarizes PISA's policy influence:

> The results make clear that PISA is becoming an influential element of education policymaking processes at the national level. Furthermore, the findings provide preliminary evidence that PISA is being used and integrated within national/federal policies and practices of assessment and evaluation, curriculum standards and performance targets.

Reading, mathematics, and science have now become the main determinants of perceived success or failure of pupils, teachers, and schools in many education systems. Literacy and numeracy strategies that increased instructional time for the core subjects in England and in Ontario (Canada) are concrete consequences of GERM. Several independent studies in the USA have shown how the *No Child Left Behind* legislation caused most school districts in the country to shift teaching time from other subjects, especially from social studies, arts, and music, to teaching reading, mathematics, and science so that schools were better prepared for tests that measure student performance and hold schools accountable in these subjects.

The fourth globally observable phenomenon in educational reforms is the *borrowing of change models from the corporate world* as a main means of improvement. Tougher competition, firing poorly performing staff, performance-based pay, and priority on measurable results are some of the most common examples of corporate style principles in education. A clear example of corporate-inspired education policies is Pearson's attempt to mold global education policies and reforms through their new corporate strategy. They adopted the term "efficacy" from the pharmaceutical industry, where "demonstrating the efficacy of medical interventions through systematic trials is essential" (Barber and Rizvi 2013, 12). Pearson's definition of efficacy is that "an education product has efficacy if it has a measurable impact on improving people's lives through learning" (Barber and Rizvi 2013, 12). The implementation of this efficacy framework first by the company (Pearson), and then in education systems through its products and services, includes "setting clear efficacy goals," "developing products underpinned by evidence," "build and use effective data systems," and "employ iterative processes" (Barber and Rizvi 2013, 48–49). The singular focus is on learning outcomes independent of who provides the education and what happens during teaching (or delivery as they call it), and learning opens access to new players in public education, including the advocates of these alternative models.

Faith in educational change that is built on reform ideas brought from outside the system undermines two important elements of successful change. First, it often limits the role of national policy development and the enhancement of an education system's own capability to maintain continuous renewal. Second, it paralyzes teachers' and schools' attempts to learn from the past and also to learn from one another other how to improve their schools. Change models brought to education systems from the corporate world, accordingly, prevent schools from enhancing professional capital within the system when the reforms are driven by ideas from outside the community of schools.

The fifth global trend is the adoption of *test-based accountability policies* that hold teachers and schools to account for students' achievement in schools. School performance – especially raising student achievement – is intimately tied to the processes of evaluating, inspecting, and rewarding or punishing schools and teachers. Merit-based pay, data walls in teachers' lounges, and school league tables in newspapers are examples of new accountability mechanisms that often draw their data primarily from external standardized student tests and teacher evaluations (Springer 2009). The problem with test-based accountability is not holding students, teachers, and schools accountable per se, but rather how accountability is arranged and how the related mechanisms affect teachers' work and students' studying in school. Whenever school accountability relies high-stakes for schools and low-stakes for students on poor-quality and low-cost standardized tests, accountability becomes what is left when responsibility is subtracted. In other words, strengthening accountability for student achievement is weakening the responsibility that students take for their own learning.

Since its emergence in England and the USA in the late 1980s, the features of GERM have become evident in education policies in Chile, Australia, New Zealand, South Africa, and more recently Central and Eastern Europe, the Middle East and to a lesser degree also Sweden, Spain, and East Asia. It is also a movement because it is a coordinated group action focused on a political and social issue, i.e. enhancing productivity and quality of education systems. Figure 7.1 illustrates the spread of GERM in 2015.

Figure 7.1 Prevalence of GERM in 2015.

Impacts of GERM on Education Systems

GERM has dual consequences for teachers and students and what they do in schools. On the one hand, it brings more autonomy to schools to craft some of the structures, like allocating time, utilizing spaces, and managing staff as is best for the school. On the other hand, it increases external control of the school through tighter standards, more frequent testing, and stronger accountability. An important question is: Have the countries that have followed GERM closely been able to enhance the quality of education? Table 7.1 illustrates some of the consequences of GERM for teaching and learning in schools (adapted from Sahlberg 2011).

Table 7.1 shows that GERM may have significant consequences for teachers' work and students' learning in schools wherever it has been a dominant driver of change (Ravitch 2013). The most visible consequence is standardization of educational and pedagogical processes. Performance standards set by the educational authorities and consultants have been brought to the lives of teachers and students. Assessments and testing that have been aligned to these standards have often been disappointments and brought new problems to schools.

GERM has gained global popularity because it emphasizes some fundamental new orientations to learning and educational administration. It suggests strong guidelines to improve quality, better education for more students, and the effectiveness of education such as putting priority on learning, seeking high achievement for all students, and making assessment and testing integral parts of the teaching and learning process. However, it also strengthens market-like logic and mechanisms in the governance of education. First, and most importantly, GERM assumes that school choice combined with external performance standards measured by standardized tests, leads to better learning for all. By concentrating on the basics and defining explicit learning targets for students and teachers, such standards place strong emphases on mastering the core skills of reading, writing, and mathematical and scientific literacy.

Second, GERM assumes that the most effective way to improve educational systems is to bring well-developed innovations to schools and classrooms from outside, often from the business world. The systematic training of teachers and staff, or recruitment of "better and smarter" people to schools, is an essential element of this approach.

Third, GERM relies on an assumption that competition between schools, teachers, and students is the most productive way to raise the quality of education. This requires that parents choose schools for their children, that schools have enough autonomy, and that schools and teachers are held accountable for their students' learning.

What Does the Evidence Suggest?

The OECD's PISA is, in many ways, both a product of GERM as described in this chapter and, at the same time, it has been used as the primary driver of it. International standardized student assessments, especially PISA, are becoming global curriculum standards for many education reforms (Breakspear 2012), and prevalence of PISA has spawned the move toward standardized testing in many nations (Ravitch 2013),

Table 7.1 Five common features of GERM and their impacts on schooling

Global Educational Reform Movement

Feature of Global Educational Reform Movement	Impact on schooling
Competition and choice School choice is the main vehicle to enhance competition between schools. Opening school markets for various providers, such as charter schools, free schools, independent schools, and private schools has increased competition between those and public schools. The basic assumption is that competition works as a market mechanism that will eventually improve quality and lower the cost of education	Increasing competition between schools that is almost always linked to race for resources limits opportunities to cooperate, share ideas, and help one another. When schools compete it affects the cultures of teaching in these schools so that cooperative learning and collaborative professional development will not be core values. Increasing school choice often leads to segregation of students and teachers that is harmful to equity in education
Standardization of teaching and learning Setting clear, high, centrally prescribed performance standards for all schools, teachers, and students to improve the quality and equity of outcomes. Standardizing teaching and curriculum in order to have coherence and common criteria for measurement and data. Generic aim of standardization often is to educate all students to be similar according to same expectations	Changes the nature of teaching from an open-ended, non-linear process of mutual inquiry and exploration to linear process with causal outcomes. This minimizes risk-taking in teaching and learning and therefore reduces creativity. Often narrows teaching to desired content only and promotes use of teaching methods beneficial to attaining preset results. Standardization is a counterforce to innovation
Focus on reading, mathematics, and science Basic knowledge and skills in reading, writing, mathematics, and the natural sciences serve as prime targets of education reform. These subjects are the ones that determine a country's position in the international education league tables. The key assumption is that since a student's performance in reading and mathematics highly correlates with her or his overall academic achievement, it justifies the focus on these "core subjects"	Curricula and standards in most parts of the world give more room to reading, mathematics, and science at the expense of non-academic subjects and social studies. The ethos of schools in many countries has become academic rather than comprehensive. When educational performance is determined by students' test scores in reading, mathematics, and science, it reduces focus on whole-child development due to decreasing time for arts, music, drama, and sports

Corporate models of change
Sources of educational change are external models or innovations brought to schools from the corporate world through legislation or national programs. Increasing role of private funds through philanthropy and commercial interests in education reforms has increased the infusion of market principles in national education policies

Running schools according to measured results narrows the purpose of school education from educating good citizens to training young people to produce acceptable academic results. This distances teachers from the moral purpose of their profession. Competition, efficiency, and productivity may demoralize teachers and jeopardize the attractiveness of the teaching profession

Test-based accountability
School performance and raising student achievement are closely tied to the processes of evaluation, inspection, and rewarding schools and teachers. Standardized tests have a central role as a source of data. Winners normally gain fiscal rewards whereas struggling schools and individuals are punished

Increases teaching-to-the-test when stakes of accountability are high. May also increase malpractice in testing and reporting if the stakes include rewards or sanctions for teachers or the school. This has increased bureaucracy in many schools because the management of data requires more resources. May increase teaching that aims to showcase good practices rather than help students to learn. This narrows the focus on pedagogy and encourages standardized and predictable behaviors

Source: Adapted from Sahlberg (2011)

and envy of education systems with superior scores regardless of the inhumane means used to achieve them (Zhao 2014). Introduction of the PISA Test for Schools by the OECD (and administered by McGraw-Hill educational firm) is another push toward testing-driven school policies. Those who see international student assessments as global competitions on standardized achievements make sure that schools, teachers, and students are well prepared to teach these standards and take those tests. Learning materials are adjusted to fit to the style of these assessments and teaching is geared more to success in these tests. As a consequence, lives in many schools around the world are unevenly split between the important academic study that these tests measure and other "not-so-important" study, which these academic measurements don't cover.

At the same time, however, it is due to a more mindful use of the PISA data that we now have more aspects to look at when we analyze cross-country education policies worldwide. There are two questions that are much better answered through PISA data than without them. The first one is: What are the performance trends in reading, mathematics, and science in countries that have built their school policies on the five features of GERM described above? In other words, is there evidence that competition, choice, standardization, testing, and accountability in education policies have improved student learning in international comparisons since the 1990s? The second question is: What are the lessons from the OECD PISA study for countries that hope to enhance their school systems? In other words, does the evidence that the PISA database provides enforce the features of GERM or not?

The first part of the evidence of the impact of GERM-related education policies comes from the first four cycles of the PISA study since its launch in 2000. OECD member countries that have notable elements of GERM in their education policies in the 1990s and the 2000s include the USA, England, Canada, Australia, New Zealand, The Netherlands, and Sweden. Figure 7.2 shows the national average scores of 15-year-old students in the mathematics test in PISA since its inauguration in 2000. None of these countries was able to consistently improve mathematics performance despite the promises made when competition, choice, and more frequent testing of students were introduced in these countries or jurisdictions. Indeed, quite the opposite. Declining performance has been the destiny of each of them. It seems obvious, at least in the light of the PISA data, that GERM has failed to fulfill the expectation that policy-makers had when they assumed that education reforms will succeed with these change logics.

The second source of evidence is the latest PISA study, released in late 2013. In 2012 when the OECD collected the data for that study from 65 education systems, GERM had spread globally. School competition and choice (Heyneman 2009), increasing governance of education systems by data collected through standardized student assessments and examinations (OECD 2013), common use of accountability systems that require schools' test results to be made public (Meyer and Benavot 2013), and the growing role of the private sector in funding education reforms and providing education (Ravitch 2013) have been evident trends throughout the world. In its recent reports of the 2012 PISA findings, which include all of the most developed nations and much of the rest of the world, the OECD made this determination (OECD 2013):

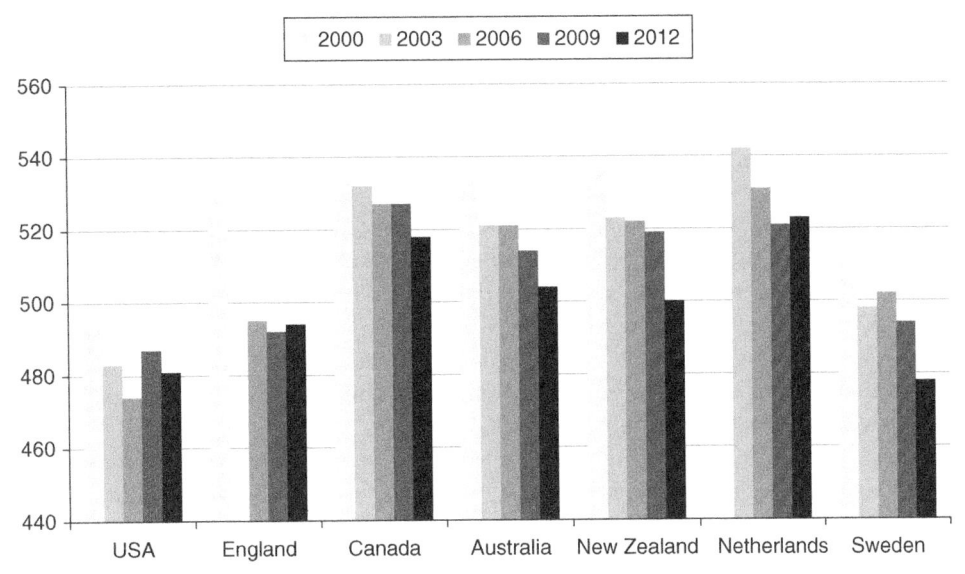

Figure 7.2 National averages of 15-year-old students' mathematics achievement measured by PISA between 2000 and 2012.
Source: Data from PISA database, OECD (www.pisa.oecd.org)

- Since the early 1980s, reforms in many countries have granted parents and students greater choice in the school the students will attend (p. 54).
- Between 2003 and 2012 there was a clear trend towards schools using student assessments to compare the school's performance with district or national performance and with that of other schools (p. 159).
- On average across OECD countries with comparable data from 2003 to 2012, students in 2012 were 20 percentage points more likely than their counterparts in 2003 to attend schools where the use of tests or assessments of student achievement are used to monitor teacher practice (p. 160).

Many countries have carried out their own studies to understand how market mechanisms affect the quality of their education systems. Wiborg (2010) studied the impact of 20 years of the free school system (government-funded private schools) in Sweden and drew the following conclusion:

> [T]he Swedish experiment (using for-profit private providers) has proved expensive and has not led to significant learning gains overall. At the same time the Swedish reforms, albeit on a small scale, appear to have increased inequality, even in the context of this very egalitarian system. (Wiborg 2010, 19)

The Australian Grattan Institute examined how market mechanisms, especially school competition, choice, and autonomy, impact schools' performance. The conclusion was that relying on markets is not the best way to improve student learning. The report stated that

> by increasing competition, government policies have increased the effectiveness of many sectors of the economy. But school education is not one of them. (Jensen 2013, 35)

An inevitable question emerges: Do PISA findings reinforce the premises of GERM being right? Let's take a look at three key findings of PISA 2012 to see how the elements of GERM believed to be the drivers of successful reforms resonate with that global evidence.

The first finding is that education systems that give schools autonomy over curricula and student assessments often perform better. This contradicts the basic premise of GERM which assumes that externally set teaching standards and aligned standardized testing are preconditions for success. PISA shows how success is often associated with professional autonomy balanced with a collaborative culture in schools. Evidence also shows how high performing education systems engage teachers to set their own teaching and learning targets, to craft productive learning environments, and to design multiple forms of student assessments to best support student learning and school improvement.

The second finding is that high average learning outcomes and system-wide equity are often interrelated. Equity in education means that students' socioeconomic status has little impact on how well they learn in school. Equity is high on the agenda in all successful school systems. Focus on equity means to give high priority to universal early childhood programs, comprehensive health, and special education services in schools, and a balanced curriculum that has equal weight in arts, music, and sports, and academic studies. Fairness in resource allocation is important for equity, too. PISA 2012 shows that fair resourcing is related to the success of the entire school system: high student performance tends to be linked to more equitably resource allocation between advantaged and disadvantaged schools.

The third finding is that school choice and competition do not improve the performance of education systems. In the OECD countries, school choice and competition between schools are related to greater levels of segregation in the education system. That, in turn, may have adverse consequences for equity in learning opportunities and outcomes. Indeed, successful education systems do better than those that have expanded school choice. All successful school systems have a strong commitment to maintain their public schools and local school control. PISA 2012 data show that the prevalence of charter and free schools with related competition for students has no discernible relationship with student learning.

PISA 2012 also reaffirms the appeal of teachers in many parts of the world that they should be paid better. While paying teachers well is only part of the story, higher salaries can help countries to attract more young people to choose teaching as their lifelong career. PISA results show that more successful countries tend to pay more to their teachers relative to their per capita GDP pay, and give them higher status in society (OECD 2013, 191).

Lastly, the overall picture of the consequences of GERM becomes clearer when we look at lessons from some of the most successful education systems: Finland, Alberta, Singapore, and South Korea. Finland has been a consistent high performer of PISA through to the latest PISA study in 2012 (Sahlberg 2015). Significantly, none of the elements of GERM mentioned in Table 7.1 has been adopted in Finland. This, of course, does not imply that competition, choice, standardized testing, or accountability per se are harmful and therefore should be avoided in education policies and reforms. But the evidence is very clear that market-based education policies that rely on these elements of GERM are the wrong way as has also been endorsed by the OECD (OECD 2013). Finland, Alberta, Singapore, and South Korea all have some of these elements in their current school policies, but none of these education systems treats them as primary drivers of change. The conclusion is that a good educational system can be built using policies averse to the market principles promoted by GERM.

References

Au, W. 2009. *Unequal by Design. High-Stakes Testing and the Standardization of Inequality* New York: Routledge.

Ball, S. 2012. *Global Education Inc. New Policy Networks and the Neo-Liberal Imaginary* Abingdon: Routledge.

Barber, M. and S. Rizvi. 2013. *The Incomplete Guide to Delivering Learning Outcomes* London: Pearson.

Barber, M., K. Donnelly, and S. Rizvi. 2012. *Oceans of Innovation. The Atlantic, the Pacific, Global Leadership and the Future of Education* London: The Institute for Public Policy Research.

Breakspear, S. 2012. *The Policy Impact of PISA: An Exploration of the Normative Effects of International Benchmarking in School System Performance*. OECD Education Working Papers, No. 71, OECD Publishing. Retrieved from: 10.1787/5k9fdfqffr28-en (accessed November 9, 2015).

Carnoy, M. 1998. "National Voucher Plans in Chile and Sweden: Did Privatization Reforms Make for Better Education?" *Comparative Education Review*, 42(3): 309–337.

Dang, H.-A. and F. Halsey Rogers. 2008. "The Growing Phenomenon of Private Tutoring: Does It Deepen Human Capital, Widen Inequalities, or Waste Resources?" *The World Bank Research Observer*, 23(2): 161–200.

Darling-Hammond, L. 2009. "Teaching and the Change Wars: The Professionalism Hypothesis," in *Change Wars*, edited by A. Hargreaves and M. Fullan, 45–70. Bloomington: Solution Tree.

Hargreaves, A. and M. Fullan (eds) 2009. *Change Wars* Bloomington: Solution Tree.

Hargreaves, A. and D. Shirley. 2009. *The Fourth Way. The Inspiring Future of Educational Change* Thousand Oaks: Corwin.

Hargreaves, A., L. Earl, S. Moore, and S. Manning. 2001. *Learning to Change. Teaching Beyond Subjects and Standards* San Francisco: Jossey-Bass.

Hargreaves, A., A. Lieberman, M. Fullan, and D. Hopkins (eds). 2010. *Second International Handbook of Educational Change* New York: Springer.

Heyneman, S. 2009. "International Perspectives on School Choice," in *Handbook of Research on School Choice*, edited by M. Berends, M.G. Springer, D. Ballou, and H.J. Walberg, 79–96. New York: Routledge.

Heyneman, S. and B. Lee. 2014. "Impact of International Studies of Academic Achievement on Policy and Research," in *Handbook of International Large Scale Assessments*, edited by L. Rutkowski, M. von Davies, and D. Rutkowski, 37–75. Boca Raton: Taylor and Francis.

Jensen, B. 2013. *The Myth of Markets in School Education*. Melbourne: Grattan Institute.

Lawn, M. and S. Grek. 2012. *Europeanizing Education* Oxford: Symposium Books.

Levin, B. and M. Fullan. 2008. "Learning About System Renewal." *Educational Management, Administration and Leadership*, 36(2): 289–303.

Malone, H. (ed.) 2013. *Leading Educational Change. Global Issues, Challenges, and Lessons on Whole-System Reform* New York: Teachers College Press.

Meyer, H.-D. and A. Benavot (eds). 2013. *PISA, Power, and Policy: The Emergence of Global Educational Governance* Oxford: Oxford Studies in Comparative Education.

Mourshed, M., C. Chijioke, and M. Barber. 2010. *How the World's Most Improved School Systems Keep Getting Better* London: McKinsey.

OECD. 2010. *PISA 2009 Results: What Makes a School Successful? Resources, Policies and Practices* Volume IV. Paris: OECD.

OECD. 2013. *PISA 2012 Results: What Makes Schools Successful? Resources, Policies and Practices* Volume IV. Paris: OECD.

Ravitch, D. 2013. *Reign of Error. The Hoax of the Privatization Movement and the Danger to America's Public Schools* New York: Alfred A. Knopf.

Sahlberg, P. 2006. "Education Reform for Raising Economic Competitiveness." *Journal of Educational Change*, 7(4): 259–287.

Sahlberg, P. 2011. "The Fourth Way of Finland" *Journal of Educational Change*, 12(1): 173–185.

Sahlberg, P. 2015. *Finnish Lessons 2.0. What Can the World Learn from Educational Change in Finland* New York: Teachers College Press.

Springer, M. 2009. *Performance Incentives: Their Growing Impact on American K-12 Education* Washington, DC: Brookings Institution Press.

Wagner, T. 2012. *Creating Innovators. The Making of Young People Who Will Change the World* New York: Scribner.

Wiborg, S. 2010. *Swedish Free Schools: Do They Work?* London: Centre for Learning and Life Chances in Knowledge Economies and Societies.

Wiseman, A. 2013. "Policy Responses to PISA in Comparative Perspective," in *PISA, Power, and Policy. The Emergence of Global Educational Governance*, edited by H.-D. Meyer and A. Benavot, 303–322. Oxford: Symposium Books.

Zajda, J. (ed.) 2010. *Globalization, Ideology and Education Policy Reforms* Dordrecht: Springer.

Zhao, Y. 2012. *World Class Learners. Educating Creative and Entrepreneurial Students.* Thousand Oaks: Corwin.

Zhao, Y. 2014. *Who's afraid of the Big Bad Dragon? Why China Has the Best (and the Worst) Education System in the World.* San Francisco: Jossey-Bass.

Chapter 8

Global Convergence or Path Dependency? Skill Formation Regimes in the Globalized Economy

Marius R. Busemeyer and Janis Vossiek

Introduction

Without doubt, the internationalization of education has proceeded and intensified significantly in the last decades, resulting in a certain convergence of governance structures, most prominently in the higher education sector (Knill *et al.* 2013). The literature has identified a number of causal mechanisms that drive policy diffusion and transfer (Holzinger *et al.* 2007; Voegtle *et al.* 2011), e.g. coercion, emulation, or joint problem-solving and transnational communication. In contrast to these arguments, the purpose of this chapter is to highlight the limits of global convergence of education policies and institutions. More specifically, we argue that existing institutional arrangements create strong feedback effects and path dependencies, which make full-scale convergence unlikely. However, this does not preclude processes of transformative change in skill formation regimes. What we observe in the real world is likely to be a mix of both continuity and change, the latter being mostly path-dependent and reflecting the legacies of existing institutions.

The chapter is divided into three parts: in the following subsection, we explain how and why institutional path dependencies delimit global convergence. We approach the topic from the perspective of comparative political economy, i.e. we highlight the importance of socioeconomic institutions as factors shaping skill formation strategies of businesses and individual households. Next, we present a typology of skill formation regimes in post-industrial Western democracies. The observed variety of skill regimes reflects, in our view, the existence of institutional path dependencies identified in the previous section. Finally, we discuss concrete cases representing the different regime types: Germany and the UK. In both cases, we can observe a mixture of stability and change in the institutional set-up of the skill system.

The Handbook of Global Education Policy, First Edition.
Edited by Karen Mundy, Andy Green, Bob Lingard, and Antoni Verger.
© 2016 John Wiley & Sons, Ltd. Published 2016 by John Wiley & Sons, Ltd.

Institutional Path Dependencies and the Limits of Global Convergence

Proponents of path dependency theory argue that once established, institutions are increasingly hard to change (Pierson 2000; 2004). Institutions can be regarded as the "building-blocks of social order," involving "mutually related rights and obligations" (Streeck and Thelen 2005, 9), which constrain actors' behavior in certain ways. However, from the actors' perspective, institutions are not merely constraints, but can also be regarded as resources (namely when they constrain the behavior of others in a way that is favorable to the interests of a particular actor). Therefore, institutions also influence the distribution of material and political resources across social groups. This in turn makes conflicts about the design of institutions a highly political matter (Hall and Thelen 2009).

The mechanism by which institutions create path dependencies are "positive feedback effects" (Pierson 2000, 252). The idea is that when two cases start from a similar starting point, deviations in a particular direction will not correct themselves (negative feedback), but reinforce their movement away from each other, because actors start to develop an interest in the maintenance of existing institutions. For example, many education systems started with a similar institutional structure, namely segmented secondary school systems with early tracking of students and elitist higher education. Those countries that moved away from this path early on (e.g. the USA) by opening up access to higher levels of education are likely to move even further in this direction, because more actors start to develop an interest in opening up access to education. Vice versa, elitist education systems will likely remain unchanged for a longer period of time because those benefitting from the segmented system have an interest in its continued survival. Of course, path dependency does not preclude any kind of change and actors who "lost" in one round will likely continue to mobilize against existing institutions in the hope of changing the system in the future. However, the longer the system remains on a particular development path, the less likely are fundamental changes.

The early generation of historical institutionalism (Hall and Taylor 1996; Steinmo et al. 1992; Thelen 1999) – the school of thought that emphasizes the importance of institutional legacies – argued that, because of path dependencies, large-scale change is likely to happen only at "critical junctures," which can be regarded as windows of opportunity that open up as a result of exogenous shocks (e.g. wars, economic crises, etc.). More recent contributions, however, emphasize that the contrast between phases of radical change at critical junctures and complete stability in between is too simplistic (Streeck and Thelen 2005). Instead, Streeck and Thelen (2005) argue that seemingly minor changes can also accumulate to major institutional transformations in the long run.

For the purpose of the present chapter, we concentrate on one particular type of positive feedback: economic benefits created by existing institutions. Here, it is helpful to make the connection to the varieties of capitalism (VoC) literature (Hall and Soskice 2001; Estévez-Abe et al. 2001; Iversen 2005). A core argument of VoC-scholars is that existing socioeconomic institutions shape the skill formation strategies of businesses and households, which in turn leads to the development of different kinds of innovation strategies. Hall and Soskice (2001) identify two "institutional equilibria," i.e. different types of capitalism: liberal market economies

(LMEs, mostly the Anglo-Saxon countries) and coordinated market economies (CMEs, mostly Continental and North-Western Europe). Southern European as well as East Asian countries are less straightforward to classify, leading to discussions as to whether they constitute a separate type of capitalism (Amable 2003).

Hall and Soskice (2001) identify five institutional spheres, which represent the central institutional pillars of political economies: the relationship between trade unions and employers' associations, the relationship between individual employers and employees, corporate governance system, the nature of connections between different firms, and – last, but not least – the education and training systems. The crucial difference between LMEs and CMEs is whether coordination among employers happens via markets or via non-market mechanisms (e.g. coordination via associations and chambers).

LMEs combine flexible and deregulated labor markets with shareholder capitalism and antagonistic relationships between employers and employees, both at the firm level and beyond (Hall and Soskice 2001, 27–31). In this institutional environment, the incentives for individual employers to invest in skill formation are weakly developed. Each employer who does so faces the risk of poaching, i.e. competing firms luring trained workers away with higher wages. Because there is little non-market based coordination between firms, individual employers cannot effectively prevent this from happening. The result is an underinvestment of employers in training (see Finegold and Soskice (1988) for an early application of this argument for the UK). When employers are not involved intensely in the training of workers, the rational reaction of households is to invest in general, transferable skills instead. Therefore, in LMEs academic higher education at colleges and universities is the predominant form of post-secondary education, whereas vocational education and training (VET) is institutionally underdeveloped. According to the VoC argument, the prevalence of academic general skills, combined with deregulated labor markets and a shareholder-oriented form of corporate governance and company financing, sets strong incentives for firms to engage in radical innovation strategies, specializing and excelling in product markets for things like high-level consulting, biotech, IT, and pharmaceutical industries.

In CMEs, employers have more positive incentives to invest in skill formation. One important example of such an institutional incentive is collective wage bargaining between unions and employers' associations, which equalizes wages within, but to a certain extent also between different sectors of the economy. Then the risk of poaching is lower for employers who invest in skill formation, because competing firms cannot offer higher wages (Acemoglu and Pischke 1998; 1999). Competition for skilled workers between firms is also reduced by the social networks that develop between employers (i.e. non-market based forms of coordination). Moreover, collective wage bargaining works as a "beneficial constraint" (Streeck 1989), to a certain extent forcing employers to raise the productivity of those in the lower half of the skills distribution by means of training since the structure of wages is more egalitarian. Employer involvement in skill formation in combination with "beneficial constraints" leads to a certain overinvestment in skills, which might seem irrational in the short term, but creates significant payoffs in the long term: Having a highly skilled workforce allows employers to react swiftly to changes in the socioeconomic environment without having to invest in re-training of workers.

These kinds of "polyvalent skills" (Streeck 1996, 141) constitute the foundation for the competitiveness of CMEs in "diversified quality production" (Streeck 1992), i.e. high-end manufacturing goods such as cars, chemicals, and machine-building. Skill formation strategies aiming at maximizing long-term rather than short-term payoffs are complemented by a reliance on "patient" forms of corporate financing (i.e. stakeholder instead of shareholder capitalism). Furthermore, the cooperation between unions and employers' associations also helps to promote joint investments in skills (Thelen 2004).

The VoC paradigm identifies two mechanisms that create positive feedback effects. The first results from the effect of existing institutions on production and innovation strategies of firms. Although they might try to change existing institutions in the long term, individual firms have to consider them as a given in the short term and adjust their strategies accordingly ("strategy follows structure;" Hall and Soskice 2001, 15). Over time, this leads to the development of "comparative institutional advantages" (Hall and Soskice 2001, 37), i.e. competitive advantages of firms in different types of capitalism. Recognizing these advantages, firms come to support the continued maintenance of existing institutions in order to maintain their competitive edge. In Germany, for example, employers are strong supporters of the dual apprenticeship training system (Hassel 2007), although it imposes considerable constraints on them in the short term. In the UK, in contrast, the government's attempts to get employers involved in apprenticeship training have regularly failed (Finegold and Soskice 1988; King 1997; Fuller and Unwin 2011).

A second positive feedback mechanism results from the interplay between the different institutional spheres. Hall and Soskice (2001, 17) talk about institutional complementarities in this context, which are defined as such: "[Two] institutions can be said to be complementary if the presence (or efficiency) of one increases the returns from (or efficiency of) the other." That is, institutions are not independent from each other, but their functioning depends on the presence of complimentary institutions in adjacent spheres. Once a political economy reaches a particular institutional equilibrium (LME or CME), institutional complementarities stabilize the institutional arrangement, because even if for some reason one institutional sphere undergoes a process of change, institutional complementarities between the spheres ensure that the system reverts to the long-term equilibrium.

Empirically, Hall and Soskice (2001) claim (further elaborated in and supported by Hall and Gingerich 2009) that the economic performance of "pure" types of capitalism is superior to the performance of mixed types or hybrids. This means that, according to Hall and Soskice (2001), there are two ways of dealing successfully with the challenges of globalization: either by relying on the power of markets, or by doing the exact opposite, i.e. resorting to non-market forms of coordination among firms via the state and/or associations. This argument is powerful, because it challenges the predominance of the neo-liberal economic paradigm, which claims that only the liberal model could successfully deal with globalization. In an important extension of the original VoC paradigm, Iversen and Soskice (2001) develop an argument as to why large welfare states in CMEs are not an impediment to competitiveness, but support prevailing patterns of comparative institutional advantages by helping employers to convince workers to invest in specific skills (Estévez-Abe *et al.* 2001; Iversen 2005).

One thought-provoking implication of this argument is that globalization will not reduce the differences between different varieties of capitalism, but enhance them for several reasons. First, firms who have developed production strategies associated with the different comparative institutional advantages may be hesitant to move abroad because they risk losing these advantages (Hall and Soskice 2001, 56). Second, international businesses may actually have an interest in cultivating different "varieties of capitalism" in order to able to engage in "institutional arbitrage" (Hall and Soskice 2001, 57), i.e. choosing to locate parts of their businesses in different countries depending on which institutional advantage best suits their particular needs.

Despite its merits, the VoC paradigm has been criticized on many fronts (Becker 2003; Crouch 2009; Jackson and Deeg 2006; Hancké 2009; Streeck 2009; 2010; 2012). For example, some doubt the fact that idealtypical LMEs or CMEs indeed perform better in economic terms compared to mixed types (Kenworthy 2006). Denmark might be an institutional hybrid combining elements of LMEs and CMEs which performs better than their "pure" types (Campbell and Pedersen 2007). Furthermore, although Hall and Soskice (2001) discuss Germany and the USA as real-world examples of a coordinated and liberal market economy, respectively, it remains somewhat unclear whether Scandinavian countries would not be closer to the idealtypical CME than Germany (see for a similar argument, Crouch 2009). Therefore, many have argued that Nordic economies represent a third type of capitalism (see e.g. Amable 2003). Finally, the VoC argument is fundamentally based on the idea that rational actors recognize the comparative advantages associated with a prevailing institutional framework. This does not only imply strong assumptions about the rationality of actors, but also downplays the political and ideological conflicts associated with the design of socioeconomic institutions and underestimates the implications of a general trend of liberalization in all advanced political economies, including CMEs (Streeck 2009; 2010).

The most relevant criticism for the purpose of this chapter is the discussion about the concept of skill specificity (Busemeyer 2009a; Emmenegger 2009; Streeck 2012; Tåhlin 2008). In Hall and Soskice (2001, 17), the notion of asset specificity is applied in a broad sense. In CMEs, according to the authors, actors are more willing to invest in specific assets ("assets that cannot readily be turned to another purpose and assets whose returns depend heavily on the cooperation of others"), whereas actors turn to "switchable assets" ("assets whose values can be realized if diverted to other purposes") in LMEs. This broad definition of asset specificity also includes human capital, i.e. skills. In a related publication, Iversen and Soskice, drawing on Becker, look at the distinction between general and specific skills more narrowly defined: "Specific skills are valuable only to a single firm or a group of firms (whether an industry or a sector), whereas general skills are portable across all firms" (Iversen and Soskice 2001, 876). This distinction between general and specific skills can be regarded as the cornerstone for the whole VoC framework, because differences in skills across countries determine production and innovation strategies. However, as stated above, the comparative advantage of education systems such as the German or the Japanese one is that skilled workers in the manufacturing and similar industries are particularly well trained. They do not have a narrow skill set applicable only in one particular firm, but command a broad set of skills, which combines general with firm-specific skills as well as theoretical with practical knowledge. Most importantly, this broad skillset could in theory also be applied in different firm settings (i.e. a worker at one car firm could apply many of her skills working at a different car firm) if other labor market institutions did not effectively restrict worker mobility. Hence, the content of skills (general or specific) is only one aspect in the political economy of skill formation: the real portability of these skills from one company context to another is a different one (Busemeyer 2009a; Streeck 2012). In countries with strong dual apprenticeship training such as Germany, labor market institutions do allow for a certain degree of mobility in occupational labor markets, whereas employees are more tied to internal labor markets in segmentalist skill regimes such as Japan (see below).

If this caveat is accepted, then the real question is how to get employers involved in the provision of skills that are transferable in theory and broader than the firm's immediate job requirements. Thelen's influential work (2003, 2004, 2007) on the history of VET in Britain, the USA, Germany, and Japan provides an answer to this question. She investigates skill formation from a historical-institutionalist perspective, paying close attention to the conflicts of interests between organized labor market interests such as unions or employers' associations at critical junctures in the historical development of education and training systems. Her core argument is that the crucial variable was whether the issue of skill formation was contested across the class divide or not (Thelen 2004, 19–22). In Britain, for example, trade unions' membership profiles are typically defined by particular crafts or occupations. Unions then used training policies and regulations to limit access to skilled labor markets, driving up wages, and in the long run triggering employers to develop production strategies with a reduced input from skilled workers ("Taylorism"). In contrast, unions organize members in a particular economic sector or region in Germany, which is typically a broader category than belonging to an occupation or craft. Therefore, unions were more willing and able to coordinate and cooperate with employers on issues of training as well as wage policy in corporatist countries, which set incentives for employers to stay involved in the provision of skills. Thus, according to Thelen, the particular outcome of political conflicts over the issue of skill formation in the critical period of early industrialization in the late 19th and early 20th century had important long-term implications for the institutional and political survival of firm-based vocational education and training in the contemporary period (see Iversen and Soskice 2009; Martin and Swank 2008; 2012; Martin 2012 for similar arguments). However, crucial decisions about the institutional design of education and training institutions were taken in later periods as well, in particular in the decades following World War II. Furthermore, these decisions did not only depend on the guise of socioeconomic institutions, but were deeply affected by the prevailing distribution of power between different parties in government (Ansell 2010; Busemeyer 2015; Iversen and Stephens 2008). As a consequence, the variety of skill formation regimes is larger than the simple distinction between LMEs and CMEs suggests, as will be shown in the following section.

The Variety of Skill Formation Regimes in Post-Industrial Democracies

The VoC school of thought suggests the existence of two different types of skill regimes: one centering on the production of general (academic) skills to be found in LMEs, the other with a particular emphasis on specific (vocational) skills to be found in CMEs.

This dichotomous classification of countries is already broadened by Estévez-Abe *et al.* (2001), who distinguish between CMEs with a focus on firm-specific skills (e.g. Japan) and those with a strong reliance on occupation-specific skills (e.g. Denmark). Others have pointed out the striking similarity in terms of institutions and political origins between existing welfare state regimes and education systems (Busemeyer 2015; Hega and Hokenmaier 2002; Iversen and Stephens 2008; West and Nikolai 2012; Willemse and de Beer 2012), which suggests the existence of at least three different "worlds of human capital formation" (Iversen and Stephens 2008).

In this chapter, we follow the typology of Busemeyer and Trampusch (2012; see also Busemeyer 2009a for an earlier version of this typology, as well as Busemeyer and Iversen 2012, Busemeyer and Schlicht-Schmälzle 2014, and Martin 2012 for concrete applications). This typology builds on previous typologies that classify skill formation regimes (Allmendinger 1989; Blossfeld 1992; Crouch *et al.* 1999; Green 2001). The term skill formation regime captures the *institutional set-up of education and training systems at the post-secondary educational level and its connections to labor market institutions such as collective wage bargaining and labor market policies*. Whereas the VoC framework classifies skill regimes along one dimension (from general to specific skills), we argue that (at least) two dimensions are needed in order to cover the most significant differences between existing education and training regimes.

The first dimension relates to the *involvement of employers* in initial vocational education and training. On the one extreme, employers can be deeply involved in the skill formation process, e.g. by training apprentices and promoting the acquisition of a broader set of "polyvalent" skills (Streeck 1996) that can be applied in different contexts. At the other end of the spectrum, employer involvement is limited when employers do not invest in the skills of their workforce beyond the immediate needs for a particular job. Here, the responsibility for skill formation falls to individual workers/employees and the training market more generally speaking.

The second dimension captures the extent of *public commitment* to VET, which can take different forms. One example would be the provision of public subsidies to employers to encourage them to hire apprentices or subsidies to individual youths with similar intentions. Another aspect is the extent to which the education system establishes institutions for the "authoritative certification of vocational skills" (Busemeyer 2009a, 376). Blossfeld (1992) called this the "vocational specificity" of the education system.

The possible combinations of the two dimensions yield four idealtypical skill formation regimes (see Table 8.1). The first is the *liberal skill formation regime*, which is characterized by a low degree of employer involvement as well as a low public commitment to VET. Real-world examples could be the USA, Canada or the UK (although the UK is actually more of a mixed case, see below). The US secondary education system does not have any strong mechanisms for the authoritative certification of vocational skills. At the end of compulsory schooling, all graduating students receive a general high school degree. Of course, students have specialized in different subjects and have taken different classes, but the "vocational specificity" of a high school degree is very low compared to one of the more than 300 recognized occupational profiles in the German dual apprenticeship training system. Because of low public commitment to VET and the associated low vocational specificity of the system, the

Table 8.1 The variety of skill formation systems in advanced industrial democracies

Public commitment to vocational training			
	High	Statist skill formation system (SW, FR)	Collective skill formation system (GE, CH, AU)
	Low	Liberal skill formation system (USA, CAN, UK)	Segmentalist skill formation system (JAP)
		Low	High
		Involvement of firms in initial vocational training	

Source: Busemeyer and Trampusch (2012), 12.

focus of post-secondary education is on higher education at universities or colleges. Of course, some types of skill formation at colleges (e.g. at community colleges) have a more applied "vocational" character, but the extent of employer involvement in these courses is very limited compared to the deep involvement of firms in the administration, financing, and organization of VET in some European countries.

The second is the *statist skill formation regime*, which combines low involvement of employers in VET with a high degree of public commitment. Real-world examples are Sweden or France. Compared to the liberal regime, VET plays a more important role in the statist regime, indicated by a higher degree of vocational specificity of educational credentials. In the French education system, for example, the general university entrance examination (*Baccalauréat général*) is complemented by a *Baccalauréat professionelle* with a more vocational character. The degree of vocational specificity is even higher in the Swedish case, where students in the vocational track of the upper secondary education system can choose between 13 vocationally oriented programs. In both countries, however, various attempts to increase the involvement of employers in the provision of training have largely failed (Culpepper 2003; Lundahl 1997). Because of the extensive involvement of the state in education, employers seem to be less pressed to take matters into their own hands.

The third regime is the *segmentalist skill regime* – a term coined by Thelen (2004) and Swenson (2002) to describe a configuration in which the interests of particular firms or sectors dominate over collective interests of businesses or workers. Japan (one could also include other East Asian countries) is typically mentioned as a real-world example of the segmentalist regime (Thelen 2004; Busemeyer 2009a). Because workers are usually tied to a particular employer for the long term, firms are more willing to invest in the skills of their employees. In part, this is driven by the constraints that existing labor market institutions – often referred to as the Japanese model of lifetime employment – impose on firms (Jackson 2007). However, Japanese firms also use private social policies, e.g. housing, health, or pension benefits, to enhance the dependency of the worker on the firm. Unions are typically weak in segmentalist skill regimes, because it is the interests of particular employers or economic sectors that dominate.

Finally, the fourth type has been called the *collective skill formation regime* (Busemeyer and Trampusch 2012; Thelen 2004). This regime is characterized by both a high involvement of employers in the provision of VET and a significant public commitment to the promotion of VET as an alternative to academic higher education. Typical examples are countries with strong dual apprenticeship training schemes such as Austria, Denmark, Germany, or Switzerland. Compared to statist skill regimes, the involvement of state actors is less hierarchical and dominant. Instead, state actors play a largely supportive role, facilitating cooperation between organized labor market interests (trade unions and employers' associations). Therefore, collective skill formation regimes have developed strong institutions and procedures of corporatist conflict mediation. In contrast to liberal regimes, the issue of skill formation is not contested across the class divide, i.e. unions and employers are willing and able to forge alliances and compromises to promote joint investments in skills. Another important characteristic of collective skill formation regimes is a high degree of vocational specificity in the system of educational certificates, which is also a consequence of the involvement of employers in the process of defining and reforming occupational profiles.

How sustainable are these regimes in the face of globalization pressures? Will path dependencies continue to dominate or will there be a convergence of policies and institutions in the long run? Can we observe the emergence of institutional hybrids combining elements from different skill formation regimes? In order to address these questions more thoroughly, we look at two cases from the opposing ends of the spectrum in the next section: Germany and the UK.

Two Case Studies: Germany and the UK

In the following section, we look at Germany and the UK in greater detail with the aim of identifying dominant patterns of continuity and change. How strong are path dependencies really and to what extent can we observe movement in directions different from institutional legacies?

Germany

The German VET system is often treated as a role model in international comparisons (Culpepper 1999; Finegold and Soskice 1988), because it achieves both low levels of youth unemployment and a high standard of training for skilled workers on the intermediate skill level across a range of economic sectors, including services. As hinted at above, the corporatist collective skill formation regime of the 1980s was characterized by three defining features: the combination of practical learning in firms with theoretical education in vocational schools – usually referred to as the dual apprenticeship training model, the dominance of the "occupational principle" (*Berufsprinzip*) in the design of occupational profiles, and a corporatist style of policy-making based on compromises between trade unions, employers' associations and state actors. At first sight, there is little movement on all three fronts. Dual apprenticeship training remains a popular alternative to academic higher education for youths, and employers are still committed to the system and willing to get involved in training (Hassel 2007). If new skill needs arise, employers can voice their demands via their associations. The Federal Institute for Vocational Education and Training (*Bundesinstitut für Berufsbildung*) – itself a corporatist body – provides additional research support for identifying emerging skills gaps. Proposals for the creation of new occupational profiles or reforms of existing ones are negotiated in a corporatist framework between employers, unions, and state actors, often involving input from academic researchers.

This picture of apparent stability may be misleading, however. Looking from the long-term perspective, the German system has undergone a number of significant changes, which may seem incremental at the outset, but could accumulate to transformative changes in the long run (Busemeyer 2009b; Thelen and Busemeyer 2012).

The first of these changes is the rise of the so-called transition system (Baethge *et al.* 2007). This is a complex arrangement of labor market and school-based training measures that is meant to smooth the transition of youths from school to training and employment. Various measures and programs were set up in the early 1980s to deal with a temporary shortage of training places at that time (e.g. the *Berufsvorbereitungsjahr* or the *Berufsgrundbildungsjahr*). Over time, however, these programs developed their own path dependencies (e.g. training providers developed an interest in their long-term maintenance) and short-term scarcities of training places turned into long-term structural deficiencies. In the Eastern *Länder* where the shortage of training places was particularly acute in the 1990s, external training centers have become a well-established part of the VET system, diverting apprentices away from firm-based dual training. Nowadays, about a third of all youths in the VET sector are in the transition system broadly defined, even in times when labor market conditions are very favorable as in the recent period (Autorengruppe BIBB and Bertelsmann Stiftung 2011, 7). Therefore, the share of youths going through the traditional dual apprenticeship training scheme is significantly lower than in the 1980s.

A second example of change is the transformation of the occupational principle. The *Berufsprinzip* is both a practical guideline and a normative orientation in the reform of occupational profiles. It can be regarded as a compromise solution between employer demands for specific skill profiles and union demands for broadly defined occupations that ensure the portability of vocational skills. Thus, the *Berufsprinzip* signifies a combination of broad occupational skills with firm-specific components. In the 1980s, the bulk of recognized occupational profiles did not provide for opportunities to gain specialized or differentiated skills. In a way, dual apprenticeship training had the character of a "one size fits all" model, which usually required training of three or three and a half years before graduation as a skilled worker. Since the mid-1990s, however, a large number of occupational profiles have been reformed in order to allow for more differentiation and specialization toward the end of training. This allows employers (and to a lesser extent apprentices) to achieve a closer match between their specific skill needs and the content of apprenticeship training. Another example of this trend is the discussion of moving parts of the final apprenticeship examination from the responsibility of Chambers of Industry and Commerce to the firm context (Busemeyer 2012; Thelen and Busemeyer 2012). This would again allow certain employers, namely those with the capacities to administer firm-based examinations, to achieve a tighter fit between their firm-specific needs and the content of training.

Finally, a third indicator of change is the partial breakdown of the corporatist principle in the reform of occupational profiles. A telling example for this (and the second type of change mentioned previously) is the reintroduction of shorter two-year apprenticeships in 2003 by the then Federal Minister for Labor and Economic Affairs, Wolfgang Clement, from the social democratic party. The reintroduction of theoretically less ambitious two-year apprenticeships catered to new skill demands of employers in the electrical and car industry (Clement and Lacher 2007), who wanted to create new occupational profiles below the level of a recognized skilled worker. Unions had opposed this for a long time, because they feared that the introduction of a new type of apprenticeship below the level of a traditional apprenticeship would contribute to promote a further spread in wages. The government, however, decided to side with employers in this case against the vocal opposition of unions and created new two-year apprenticeships (Busemeyer 2009b; 2012). Despite the bitter conflict about two-year apprenticeships, unions and employers acted together in other areas of training policy; for example, in their joint opposition against state intrusion into the regulation of apprenticeship training during a reform of the federal law on VET in 2005.

UK

The UK is a paradigmatic example of a liberal skill formation regime in many respects. Higher education is strongly geared toward general academic education and to a significant degree privately financed via tuition fees. In contrast to tertiary education, VET plays a much smaller role for skill formation and has historically been based on voluntarist cooperation between employers, unions, and the state (King 1993; 1997). Public commitment to vocational training is low, with little state involvement in the provision and regulation of vocational training. For example, apprenticeships, which had traditionally been the main form of skill formation, are only lightly regulated with strongly varying sectoral standards and training quality. There are few "collective" approaches by the state, employers, and unions toward training regulation, and training standards are mainly developed by (semi-)private institutions such as registered training organizations and, in turn, approved by governmental agencies. While employers exert a certain influence on training standards via Sector Skills Councils, unions play a negligible role. Furthermore, since the beginning of the 1980s, state funding for vocational training mainly takes the form of financing youth employment programs or is distributed among private and public training providers, which compete in a training market.

Another important contrast to Germany is that firm involvement in the financing and provision of initial vocational training is low. While practical training is often provided on the job, the skill content of training has a more narrow scope and the volume of training is lower than in segmentalist or collective training systems, due to poaching problems between training and non-training firms (Stevens 1999). The British labor market is also less densely regulated: the coverage of collective wage agreements above the firm level is narrow and employment protection is low. These two factors have been found to act as safeguards against the poaching of skilled employees in the form of "beneficial constraints" (Streeck 1989) in other countries, increasing employer commitment in training provision.

The low degree of firm involvement and, more generally, the development of a liberal skill formation regime in the UK and other liberal market economies such as the USA can be attributed to the fact that training was historically contested across the class divide between capital and labor (Thelen 2004). However, despite the contested history of training and its liberal institutional legacy, apprenticeships in the UK did not decline as early as in the USA (Gospel 1994). It was the training reforms of the Thatcher governments in the 1980s that finally consolidated the liberal approach to skill formation in Britain (King 1993; Busemeyer 2015). Despite the predominantly liberal character of vocational training in the UK, we can also identify governmental attempts toward developing more collective approaches to skill formation.

Against the background of a voluntarist tradition of training and the concomitant underinvestment in vocational skills, two initiatives were taken in the 1960s and 1970s. In 1964, 27 statutory and tripartite Industrial Training Boards (ITBs) were introduced that organized employers and unions on an industry-wide basis and were given the right to impose a training levy in their respective industrial sector to increase training investments. Moreover, in 1973, the tripartite Manpower Services Commission (MSC) was founded and given the responsibility to formulate a national training policy. However, while these initiatives helped to shore up apprenticeships to a certain degree, they had a limited impact compared to the reforms under the Thatcher governments.

First, the tripartite ITBs and, subsequently, the MSCs as central institutions of training policy were abolished and replaced by Training and Enterprise Councils (TECs). These were sectoral, employer-led bodies without statutory union representation, and responsible for the provision of training, while the task of training development was reassigned to the Department of Employment. This resulted in an exclusion of unions from training policy, but also in a first move towards a training market as they were state-funded according to training achievements (certifications, apprentice placements), and competed inter-sectorally for the public training budgets (Wood 1999).

Second, the introduction of the Youth Training Scheme (YTS) had a profound effect on training provision. YTS was an unemployment program with a training component, heavily criticized for its low requirements in terms of educational content (Finegold and Soskice 1988; Marsden and Ryan 1990). Under YTS, trainees received allowances and were no longer covered by volutarist agreements between employers and unions, which gave individual firms much leeway on training provision at the workplace (Gospel 1995; King 1993) or enabled training by specialized training providers. It contributed to a further decline of traditional apprenticeships as training take-up moved from being demand-driven by employers' skill needs toward being supply-driven by the number of youth receiving government allowances (King 1993).

In an effort to resuscitate employer involvement and to increase the quality of vocational training, the Modern Apprenticeship (MA) Programme was introduced in the 1990s. It set the formal learning requirements of apprenticeships at a higher level than YTS and entailed a minimum duration of three years. Apprentices were normally covered by an employment contract. However, employers still remained entitled to a government subsidy for training costs, and competency standards were set by sectoral training organizations with little union involvement, which led to strong variations in skill levels and standards in different sectors (Ryan and Unwin 2001). While apprenticeship numbers have increased in the 2000s, this can be mostly attributed to the growth of apprenticeships with a shorter duration and lower training standards, partly used to certify the skills of already employed adult workers. Generally, despite many additional reform efforts and institutional re-engineering in the past two decades (most recently under the Coalition government), the institutional arrangements established by the Thatcher reforms have remained remarkably resilient (Keep 2006; Rainbird 2010). Vocational training in the UK is still characterized by little union representation in training governance, state funding for a competitive market between public and private training providers, and government subsidies for trainees in employment programs.

Conclusions: Stability and Change in Skill Formation Regimes

To conclude, the case studies have demonstrated a mixed picture of stability and change in skill formation regimes. From the broadly comparative perspective that we adopted in the second section of this chapter, the continuing differences between skill formation regimes are more obvious than potentially emerging similarities. This is particular true for the field of vocational education and training. In contrast to higher education, where we do see a lot of evidence for convergence related to internationalization (Knill *et al.* 2013), convergence is less pronounced in VET, probably because the latter is more embedded in existing socioeconomic and labor market institutions (cf. Bieber 2010, for a comparison of the internationalization of VET and higher education in Switzerland). The VoC framework – in particular the notion of comparative institutional advantages – can help to understand the nature of this link between firms' production and innovation strategies and existing skill formation regimes.

However, observing strong path dependencies should not detract from the fact that transformative change can and does happen. The German VET system, for example, is moving away from its collective heritage toward a more segmentalist variety (Thelen and Busemeyer 2012), as the particularistic interests of some parts of the economy, in particular the export-oriented sectors, gain more influence. Still, path dependencies are strong; the central pillars of the system (dual training, the occupational and the corporatist principle) are still largely intact, although they are being modified in important ways. Path dependencies are also strong in the UK, where various governments have repeatedly tried to resuscitate apprenticeship training schemes without success. The "tenacity of voluntarism" (King 1997) has made collective approaches to skill formation based on the cross-class cooperation between unions and employers' associations difficult to sustain in the long term. In the future, we dare to speculate in closing, we may observe more cases of institutional hybrids, in which existing institutions are combined and enriched with elements from other skill regimes.

References

Acemoglu, D. and J.-S. Pischke. 1998. "Why Do Firms Train? Theory and Evidence." *Quarterly Journal of Economics*, 113: 79–119.

Acemoglu, D. and J.-S. Pischke. 1999. "Beyond Becker: Training in Imperfect Labour Markets." *Economic Journal*, 109: F112–F142.

Allmendinger, J. 1989. "Educational Systems and Labor Market Outcomes." *European Sociological Review*, 5: 231–250.

Amable, B. 2003. *The Diversity of Modern Capitalism*. Oxford, New York: Oxford University Press.

Ansell, B.W. 2010. *From the Ballot to the Blackboard: The Redistributive Political Economy of Education*. Cambridge: Cambridge University Press.

Autorengruppe BIBB, and Bertelsmann Stiftung. 2011. *Reform des Übergangs von der Schule in die Berufsausbildung: Aktuelle Vorschläge im Urteil von Berufsbildungsexperten und Jugendlichen*. Bonn, Gütersloh: BIBB, Bertelsmann Stiftung.

Baethge, M., H. Solga, and M. Wieck. 2007. *Berufsbildung im Umbruch: Signale eines überfälligen Aufbruchs*. Berlin: Friedrich-Ebert-Stiftung.

Becker, U. 2007. "Open Systemness and Contested Reference Frames and Change: A Reformulation of the Varieties of Capitalism Theory." *Socio-Economic Review*, 5: 261–286.

Bieber, T. 2010. "Europe à la Carte? Swiss Convergence towards European Policy Models in Higher Education and Vocational Education and Training." *Swiss Political Science Review*, 16: 773–800.

Blossfeld, H.-P. 1992. "Is the German Dual System a Model for a Modern Vocational Training System?" *International Journal of Comparative Sociology*, 33: 168–181.

Busemeyer, M.R. 2009a. "Asset Specificity, Institutional Complementarities and the Variety of Skill Regimes in Coordinated Market Economies." *Socio-Economic Review*, 7: 375–406.

Busemeyer, M.R. 2009b. *Wandel trotz Reformstau: Die Politik der beruflichen Bildung seit 1970*. Frankfurt a.M., New York: Campus.

Busemeyer, M.R. 2012. "Business as a Pivotal Actor in the Politics of Training Reform: Insights from the Case of Germany." *British Journal of Industrial Relations*, 50: 690–713.

Busemeyer, M.R. 2015. *Skills and Inequality: The Political Economy of Education and Training Reforms in Western Welfare States*. Cambridge, New York: Cambridge University Press.

Busemeyer, M.R. and T. Iversen. 2012. "Collective Skill Systems, Wage Bargaining, and Labor Market Stratification," in *The Political Economy of Collective Skill Formation*, edited by M.R. Busemeyer and C. Trampusch, 205–233. Oxford, New York: Oxford University Press.

Busemeyer, M.R. and R. Schlicht-Schmälzle. 2014. "Partisan Power, Economic Coordination and Variations in Vocational Training Systems in Europe." *European Journal of Industrial Relations*, 20: 55–71.

Busemeyer, M.R. and C. Trampusch. 2012. "Introduction: The Comparative Political Economy of Collective Skill Formation," in *The Political Economy of Collective Skill Formation*, edited by M.R. Busemeyer and C. Trampusch, 3–38. Oxford, New York: Oxford University Press.

Busemeyer, M.R. and C. Trampusch. 2013. "Liberalization by Exhaustion: Transformative Change in the German Welfare State and Vocational Training System." *Zeitschrift für Sozialreform*, 59: 291–312.

Campbell, J.L. and O.K. Pedersen. 2007. "The Varieties of Capitalism and Hybrid Success: Denmark in the Global Economy." *Comparative Political Studies*, 40: 307–332.

Clement, U. and M. Lacher. 2007. "Kompetenzentwicklung in ganzheitlichen Produktionssystemen: Globale Herausforderungen – europäische Lösungen?" *BWP*, 4: 32–36.

Crouch, C. 2009. "Typologies of Capitalism," in *Debating Varieties of Capitalism: A Reader*, edited by B. Hancké, 75–94. Oxford, New York: Oxford University Press.

Crouch, C., D. Finegold, and M. Sako. 1999. *Are Skills the Answer? The Political Economy of Skill Creation in Advanced Industrial Countries*. Oxford, New York: Oxford University Press.

Culpepper, P.D. 1999. "Still a Model for the Industrialized Countries?" in *The German Skills Machine: Sustaining Comparative Advantage in a Global Economy*, edited by P.D. Culpepper and D. Finegold, 1–34. New York, Oxford: Berghahn Books.

Culpepper, P.D. 2003. *Creating Cooperation: How States Develop Human Capital in Europe*. Ithaca, London: Cornell University Press.

Emmenegger, P. 2009. "Specificity vs. Replaceability: The Relationship between Skills and Preferences for Job Security Regulations." *Socio-Economic Review*, 7: 407–430.

Estévez-Abe, M., T. Iversen, and D. Soskice. 2001. "Social Protection and the Formation of Skills: A Reinterpretation of the Welfare State," in *Varieties of Capitalism: The Institutional Foundations of Comparative Advantage*, edited by P.A. Hall, and D. Soskice, 145–183. Oxford, New York: Oxford University Press.

Finegold, D. and D. Soskice. 1988. "The Failure of Training in Britain: Analysis and Prescription." *Oxford Review of Economic Policy*, 4: 21–53.

Fuller, A. and L. Unwin. 2011. "Vocational Education and Training in the Spotlight: Back to the Future for the UK's Coalition Government?" *London Review of Education*, 9: 191–204.

Gospel, H. 1994. "The Survival of Apprenticeship Training: A British, American, Australian Comparison." *British Journal of Industrial Relations*, 32: 505–522.

Gospel, H. 1995. "The Decline of Apprenticeship Training in Britain." *Industrial Relations Journal*, 26: 32–44.

Green, A. 2001. "Models of High Skills in National Competition Strategies," in *High Skills: Globalization, Competitiveness, and Skill Formation*, edited by P. Brown, A. Green, and H. Lauder, 56–160. Oxford, New York: Oxford University Press.

Hall, P.A. and D.W. Gingerich. 2009. "Varieties of Capitalism and Institutional Complementarities in the Political Economy: An Empirical Analysis." *British Journal of Political Science*, 39: 449–482.

Hall, P.A. and D. Soskice. 2001. "An Introduction to Varieties of Capitalism," in *Varieties of Capitalism: The Institutional Foundations of Comparative Advantage*, edited by P.A. Hall and D. Soskice, 1–68. Oxford, New York: Oxford University Press.

Hall, P.A. and R.C.R. Taylor. 1996. "Political Science and the Three New Institutionalisms." *Political Studies*, 44: 936–957.

Hall, P.A. and K. Thelen. 2009. "Institutional Change in Varieties of Capitalism." *Socio-Economic Review*, 7: 7–34.

Hancké, B. 2009. *Debating Varieties of Capitalism: A Reader*. Oxford, New York: Oxford University Press.

Hassel, A. 2007. "What Does Business Want? Labor Market Reforms in CMEs and its Problems," in *Beyond Varieties of Capitalism: Conflict, Contradictions, and Complementarities in the European Economy*, edited by B. Hancké, M. Rhodes, and M. Thatcher, 253–277. Oxford, New York: Oxford University Press.

Hega, G.M. and K.G. Hokenmaier. 2002. "The Welfare State and Education: A Comparison of Social and Educational Policy in Advanced Industrial Societies." *German Policy Studies*, 2: 143–173.

Holzinger, K., H. Jörgens, and C. Knill. 2007. "Transfer, Diffusion und Konvergenz: Konzepte und Kausalmechanismen." *Politische Vierteljahresschrift, Sonderheft*, 38: 11–38.

Iversen, T. 2005. *Capitalism, Democracy, and Welfare*. Cambridge: Cambridge University Press.

Iversen, T. and D. Soskice. 2001. "An Asset Theory of Social Policy Preferences." *American Political Science Review*, 95: 875–893.

Iversen, T. and D. Soskice. 2009. "Distribution and Redistribution: The Shadow of the Nineteenth Century." *World Politics*, 61: 438–486.

Iversen, T. and J.D. Stephens. 2008. "Partisan Politics, the Welfare State, and Three Worlds of Human Capital Formation." *Comparative Political Studies*, 41: 600–637.

Jackson, G. 2007. "Employment Adjustment and Distributional Conflict in Japanese Firms," in *Corporate Governance in Japan: Institutional Change and Organizational Diversity*, edited by M. Aoki, G. Jackson, and H. Miyajima, 282–309. Oxford, New York: Oxford University Press.

Jackson, G. and R. Deeg. 2006. "How Many Varieties of Capitalism? Comparing the Comparative Institutional Analyses of Capitalist Diversity." *MPIfG Discussion Paper*, 06.

Keep, E. 2006. "State Control of the English Education and Training System: Playing with the Biggest Train Set in the World." *Journal of Vocational Education and Training*, 58: 47–64.

Kenworthy, L. 2006. "Institutional Coherence and Macroeconomic Performance." *Socio-Economic Review*, 4: 69–91.

King, D.S. 1993. "The Conservatives and Training Policy 1979–1992: From a Tripartite to a Neoliberal Regime." *Political Studies*, 41: 214–235.

King, D.S. 1997. "Employers, Training Policy, and the Tenacity of Voluntarism in Britain." *Twentieth Century British History*, 8: 383–411.

Knill, C, E.M. Vögtle, and M. Dobbins. 2013. *Hochschulpolitische Reformen im Zuge des Bologna-Prozesses*. Wiesbaden: Springer.

Lundahl, L. 1997. "A Common Denominator? Swedish Employers, Trade Unions and Vocational Education." *International Journal of Training and Development*, 1: 91–103.

Marsden, D. and P. Ryan. 1990. "Institutional Aspects of Youth Employment and Training Policy in Britain." *British Journal of Industrial Relations*, 28: 351–369.

Martin, C.J. 2012. "Political Institutions and the Origins of Collective Skill Formation Systems," in *The Political Economy of Collective Skill Formation*, edited by M.R. Busemeyer and C. Trampusch, 41–67. Oxford, New York: Oxford University Press.

Martin, C.J. and D. Swank. 2008. "The Political Origins of Coordinated Capitalism: Business Organizations, Party Systems and State Structure in the Age of Innocence." *American Political Science Review*, 102: 181–198.

Martin, C.J. and D. Swank. 2012. *The Political Construction of Business Interests: Coordination, Growth and Equality*. Cambridge, New York: Cambridge University Press.

Pierson, P. 2000. "Increasing Returns, Path Dependence, and the Study of Politics." *American Political Science Review*, 94: 251–267.

Pierson, P. 2004. *Politics in Time: History, Institutions, and Social Analysis*. Princeton, Oxford: Princeton University Press.

Rainbird, H. 2010. "Vocational Education and Training in the United Kingdom," in *Vocational Training: International Perspectives*, edited by J.G.C. Bosch, 242–270. New York: Routledge.

Ryan, P. and L. Unwin. 2001. "Apprenticeship in the British Training Market." *National Institute Economic Review*, 178: 99–124.

Steinmo, S., K. Thelen, and F. Longstreth. 1992. *Structuring Politics: Historical Institutionalism in Comparative Analysis*. Cambridge: Cambridge University Press.

Streeck, W. 1989. "Skills and the Limits of Neo-Liberalism: The Enterprise of the Future as a Place of Learning". *Work, Employment and Society*, 3: 89–104.

Streeck, W. 1992. "On the Institutional Conditions of Diversified Quality Production," in *Beyond Keynesianism: The Socio-Economics of Production and Full Employment*, edited by W. Streeck and E. Matzner, 21–61. Aldershot, Brookfield *et al.*: Edward Elgar.

Streeck, W. 1996. "Lean Production in the German Automobile Industry: A Test Case for Convergence Theory," in *National Diversity and Global Capitalism*, edited by S. Berger and R. Dore, 138–170. Ithaca, London: Cornell University Press.

Streeck, W. 1998. "Beneficial Constraints: On the Economic Limits of Rational Voluntarism," In *Contemporary Capitalism: The Embeddedness of Institutions*, edited by J. Rogers Hollingsworth and R. Boyer, 197–219. Cambridge: Cambridge University Press.

Streeck, W. 2009. *Re-Forming Capitalism: Institutional Change in the German Political Economy*. Oxford, New York: Oxford University Press.

Streeck, W. 2010. "E Pluribus Unum? Varieties and Commonalities of Capitalism." *MPIfG Discussion Paper*, 10.

Streeck, W. 2012. "Skills and Politics: General and Specific," in *The Political Economy of Collective Skill Formation*, edited by M.R. Busemeyer and C. Trampusch, 317–352. Oxford, New York: Oxford University Press.

Streeck, W. and K. Thelen. 2005. "Introduction: Institutional Change in Advanced Political Economies," in *Beyond Continuity: Institutional Change in Advanced Political Economies*, edited by W. Streeck and K. Thelen, 1–39. Oxford, New York: Oxford University Press.

Stevens, M. 1999. "Human Capital Theory and UK Vocational Training Policy." *Oxford Review of Economic Policy*, 15: 16–32.

Swenson, P.A. 2002. *Capitalists against Markets: The Making of Labor Markets and Welfare States in the United States and Sweden*. Oxford, New York: Oxford University Press.

Tåhlin, M. 2008. *Asset Specificity, Labor Market Outcomes, and Policy Preferences*. Stockholm: Swedish Institute for Social Research, unpublished manuscript.

Thelen, K. 1999. "Historical Institutionalism in Comparative Politics." *Annual Review of Political Science*, 2: 369–404.

Thelen, K. 2003. "How Institutions Evolve," in *Comparative Historical Analysis in the Social Sciences*, edited by J. Mahoney and D. Rueschemeyer, 208–240. Cambridge: Cambridge University Press.

Thelen, K. 2004. *How Institutions Evolve: The Political Economy of Skills in Germany, Britain, the United States and Japan*. Cambridge, New York, Melbourne: Cambridge University Press.

Thelen, K. 2007. "Skill Formation and Training," in *The Oxford Handbook of Business History*, edited by G. Jones, and J. Zeitlin, 558–580. Oxford, New York: Oxford University Press.

Thelen, K. and M.R. Busemeyer. 2012. "Institutional Change in German Vocational Training: From Collectivism toward Segmentalism," in *The Comparative Political Economy of Collective Skill Formation Systems*, edited by M.R. Busemeyer and C. Trampusch, 68–100. Oxford, New York: Oxford University Press.

Voegtle, E. Maria, C. Knill, and M. Dobbins. 2011. "To What Extent does Transnational Communication Drive Cross-National Policy Convergence? The Impact of the Bologna-Process on Domestic Higher Education Policies." *Higher Education*, 61: 77–94.

West, A. and R. Nikolai. 2013. "Welfare Regimes and Education Regimes: Equality of Opportunity and Expenditure in the EU (and US)." *Journal of Social Policy*, 42: 469–493.

Willemse, N. and P. de Beer. 2012. "Three Worlds of Educational Welfare States? A Comparative Study of Higher Education Systems across Welfare States." *Journal of European Social Policy*, 22: 105–117.

Wood, S. 1999. "Building a Governance Structure for Training? Employers, Government and the TEC Experiment in Britain," in *The German Skills Machine. Sustaining Comparative Advantage in a Global Economy*, edited by P.D. Culpepper and D. Finegold, 363–402. New York; Oxford: Berghahn Books.

Part II Educational Issues and Challenges

Part II Introduction

Bob Lingard

The chapters in this part deal with some challenges facing education policy in the context of the multiple impacts of globalization. These challenges result from contested policy pressures emanating from global policy actors (e.g. the Organisation for Economic Co-operation and Development (OECD), the World Bank), which are the focus of Part III of this Handbook. Part II chapters deal with the impacts of multiple kinds of globalization in relation to economics, politics, policy discourses, culture, languages, conflict, and other aspects of social life, which have implications for education policy. The specific issues covered include consideration of the broader social purposes of education that complement human capital approaches. Specifically, the chapters deal with education and social cohesion (Green and Janmaat), policy issues facing education in reconstruction agendas in conflict and post-conflict societies (Dryden-Peterson), human rights and education policy focusing on the nations of South Asia (Bajaj and Kidwai), global early childhood and care policy (Mahon), an evaluation of progress toward the Education for All (EFA) goals, 2000–2015 by Aaron Benavot and colleagues, the politics of language policies in the global polity (Hamid), teacher quality in global education policy discourses (Robertson), and finally, global reform agendas in higher education (Marginson). A major challenge facing all education systems today is how to ensure quality provision and socially just outcomes and achieve this at a time of economic difficulties and tight funding. These matters are dealt with in various chapters of the Handbook.

Andy Green's chapter with Jan Germen Janmaat (Chapter 9) considers the contribution of education to social cohesion within nations, including in relation to the more ethnically diverse populations that result from the global flows of people and growth in inequality arising from policies of austerity after the 2008 global financial crisis. The OECD, a major global actor in contemporary education policy, argues the centrality of education for human capital development as a driver of national economic competitiveness, but engages strongly on issues of social cohesion and social equity purposes of education. Of course, Green and Janmaat's title suggests that they see some naïve optimism in such discourses, given the reality of education as a positional good, advantaging some and in the process disadvantaging others. They also consider the different policy mixes between these multiple goals for

The Handbook of Global Education Policy, First Edition.
Edited by Karen Mundy, Andy Green, Bob Lingard, and Antoni Verger.
© 2016 John Wiley & Sons, Ltd. Published 2016 by John Wiley & Sons, Ltd.

education in both developed and developing nations. They acknowledge that skills formation – the human capital framing of education policy – often takes precedence over social cohesion and civic and citizenship functions of schooling. Yet they also point out that today national governments often want to "monetarize the social benefits of learning" in relation to reduced cost claims on the state in respect of health policy, policing, criminal justice, etc. Macro policy frames, including those of the OECD, also suggest more inequality and social divisions have adverse impact on economic growth, and competitiveness. The research on the social benefits of education, Green and Jermaant show, demonstrates great social benefits to individuals; for example, the better educated have better health and are more socially tolerant. The argument of their chapter is that we do not know how such individual benefits translate into social benefits. In addressing this issue, they document and analyze four approaches for understanding how education generates social benefits, namely, "absolute direct effects," "cumulative effects," "positional or relative effects," and "distributional effects." Global policy frames in respect of social cohesion, Green and Jermaant demonstrate, most often rest on the simplistic assumption that individual benefits that flow from more education automatically aggregate to ensure social benefits and more cohesive and tolerant societies.

Sarah Dryden-Peterson (Chapter 10) deals with what educational policies are necessary in the various phases of reconstruction in conflict and post-conflict societies. The United Nations' (UN) report on the Post-2015 Development Agenda outlines what needs to be done to end poverty and ensure "no one is left behind." Dryden-Peterson notes that almost half the children "left behind" educationally live in conflict situations, thus arguing that education policy's role in post-conflict reconstruction should be very important in the UN's Post-2015 agenda. She shows how the causes of conflict and definitional issues are important for policy responses and traces the phases of conflict (latent, emergency, protracted, reconstruction) and the different policy responses for learners and teachers in these phases. It is also shown how the nature of armed conflict has changed since the end of the Cold War. Conflicts are now more protracted, are more deadly for civilians, especially children, and are played out within national borders with international troop support. Dryden-Peterson documents the massive educational disadvantages facing children in conflict situations. Within this group, the poor, females, and ethnic and linguistic minorities are the most marginalized.

Three major policy approaches to education in conflict societies are outlined by Dryden-Peterson: humanitarian, development, and security. The humanitarian approach emphasizes the provision of education as an emergency response in conflict situations and also as a human right. The development approach stresses institution building and strengthening of fragile states. Today these two approaches are usually intertwined, as in the policies of the United Nations High Commissioner for Refugees (UNHCR) and the Global Partnership for Education (GPE). The security approach links to the security focus of contemporary aid programs and building stable societies. Dryden-Peterson concludes by noting two tensions in education policy agendas for conflict societies. The first is the focus on access to education and the neglect of curriculum and pedagogy. The second is the gap between global policy frames and the lived realities of teachers and students in conflict societies.

Human rights and education policy are the focus of Monisha Bajaj and Huma Kidwai's chapter (Chapter 11). Set against the rise of human rights frameworks in global educational policy making based on the cornerstone 1948 Universal Declaration of Human Rights (UDHR), they focus specifically on these issues in eight South Asian countries. These are Afghanistan, Bangladesh, Bhutan, India, Maldives, Nepal, Pakistan, and Sri Lanka, and they note that this region accounts for 20% of the world's population. The adoption of Right to Education policies and the move to Education for All mandates in the region are traced and the strengthening of such discourses is documented for the period from the 1990s. While national adoption of a human rights approach results from the circulation of global discourses and UN agreements and targets, national uptake also results from bottom-up pressure from civil society activists, who utilize these global discourses for political ends. We might see this as globalization from above meeting globalization from below. Bajaj and Kidwai also show how such rights discourses have local, national, and regional origins in the anti-colonial and independence movements dating back to the turn of the 20th century. They also juxtapose a human rights focus with the more dominant human capital and returns on investment approaches in education policy.

Rianne Mahon (Chapter 12) considers the place of Early Childhood and Care (ECEC) in the global education policy agenda. Her focus is on the policies of three international organizations (global policy actors): the World Bank, the OECD and the United Nations Educational, Scientific and Cultural Organization (UNESCO). One policy frame focuses on early childhood development as enabling parents and children to participate in the future in work and global markets. The second policy position emphasizes early childhood and care as a universal social right. The chapter suggests that the World Bank has adopted the first position and the OECD the second, while UNESCO policy seeks to adjudicate between the two. Mahon also notes how international non-governmental organizations (INGOs) such as the Bernard van Leer Foundation, the Aga Khan Foundation, Save the Children, the Christian Children's Fund, and the Soros Foundation have been very important in focusing the policy attention of international organizations on ECEC. A focus on early childhood education is also central to equity arguments and attempts to overcome the effects of socioeconomic disadvantage on the educational opportunities available to young people.

Aaron Benavot and colleagues from the EFA Global Monitoring Report Team at UNESCO (Chapter 13) provide a granular and salutary documentation and analysis of the achievements of the Education for All (EFA), 2000–2015, intervention, focusing on global strategies and aid effectiveness. Specifically, an account is provided of progress toward achievement of the six EFA goals. In providing this analysis, the significance of political commitment at all levels, effective coordination of efforts, appropriate targets and targeting of funding, and availability of reliable data for measuring progress are shown to be very important factors for effective policy interventions aimed at achieving quality schooling for all young people globally. Some progress has been made toward the achievement of the EFA goals, or at least progress has been faster than trends up to the production of the 2000 Dakar Framework for Action. However, much remains to be done, particularly in sub-Saharan Africa, and in South and West Asia. It is shown how the emphasis in the complementary Millennium Development Goals on the provision of universal primary education took the focus away from some other significant EFA targets, demonstrating again the necessity of effective coordination across relevant agencies. Girls and the poorest remain the most disadvantaged, particularly in fragile states, which are home to 36% of all out-of-school children globally. Importantly, this chapter demonstrates how policies are as much political as technical instruments.

Language policy in the global polity is the topic of Obaidul Hamid's chapter (Chapter 14). One of the effects of globalization has been the rise of English as the global language of business and the reframing of language learning in instrumental terms, at the same time as language learning has been constructed as a form of cultural capital to advantage some in terms of educational outcomes and labor market and career opportunities. Hamid begins by asking whether or not language should be considered as an "ontological reality" or a "cultural construct," and accepts that the politics of language refers to "ideological representations of language"; thus, he acknowledges that language is political in all ways. The chapter attempts to provide an answer to the question: "what are the discourses that frame macro-level language policy decisions and implementation in our globalized world?" The tentative answer of the chapter is that it is various features of neo-liberalism (language as capital, de-politicization of languages, commercialization and privatization of language teaching, and the globalization of language policies) that frame at the meta level language policy across the globe, but are played out in specific nations in vernacular ways, as are the precepts of neo-liberalism.

Chapter 15 by Susan Robertson examines the focus on "quality teachers" in the recent education policy work of the OECD and the World Bank, and by multinational edu-businesses, private consultants, and global philanthropists. The chapter argues that the global governance of teachers' work is not new, but has been strengthened from the turn of this century. From World War II until the early 2000s, there was what Robertson calls a "thin" global governance of teachers, framed by a concept of the professional teacher. Since that time, Robertson argues, there has been a "thickening" in this global governance of teachers. Here the OECD and the World Bank have promoted new tools for the governing of teachers, including their work conditions and their pedagogical practices, potentially linked to student learning outcomes as a mode of accountability. Important here as well is that teacher quality has become the focus in a decontextualized fashion at a moment of growing economic inequality. The chapter specifically explores what is at stake for teachers and their work through an examination of three tools for governing teachers globally, namely, the OECD's *Teaching and Learning International Survey* (TALIS), the OECD's Education GPS and the World Bank's SABER-Teacher (Systems Approach for Better Education Results).

Simon Marginson in the final chapter in Part II (Chapter 16) deals with the global construction of higher education reform. He also deals with important theoretical and methodological issues to do with researching, theorizing, and understanding the globalizing world today. He notes that what we have is an incompletely globalized higher education system; yet at the same time he argues we must reject "methodological nationalism" in researching global/nation policy relations in higher education, an approach that underestimates global effects in higher education reforms. He utilizes instead the framework he developed with Rhoades that suggests all higher education institutions and the individuals involved participate in local, national, and global dimensions of action. To pick up on this, they coined the awkward neologism, *glonacal,* to denote these multiple imbrications as the basis for policy and action, with glonacal connoting global + national + local. Marginson argues that looking at developments in higher education policy from multiple viewpoints – what he calls a "transpositional sensibility" – provides a more adequate account of what is actually occurring. Marginson's chapter focuses on three worldwide tendencies in higher education reform: the growth of high participation systems, the rise of a one-world science system and related growth of "world-class universities," and finally the implementation in higher education of quasi-business organizational features and practices. The expansion of participation across the globe he shows is precipitated as much by social pressures, as by economic and labor market demand. Accompanying higher participation rates is differentiation of institutions within national higher education systems, but he also shows, as in the Nordic countries, that such differentiation can be limited through state policy interventions and targeted expenditure of public monies. With the emergence of a one-world science system, Marginson documents the creation of a single global research conversation within the now dominant global English-language science system. Global rankings of universities have been developed, based on metrics framed around the world science system. He also demonstrates the new administrative, managerial, and organizational approaches in higher education worldwide, manifesting an ecumenical move of these forms and practices from the business sector. Marginson emphasizes that political and cultural factors ensure vernacular representations of these policy trends regionally and in nations.

Chapter 9

Education and Social Cohesion: A Panglossian Global Discourse

Andy Green and Jan Germen Janmaat

Introduction

Promoting social cohesion is widely seen by policy-makers as a major purpose of education policy. National governments frequently cite it as one of the twin overarching objectives – along with enhancing national competitiveness – of public investment in education. Global education discourses promoted by international policy agencies frequently echo the same theme. The Organisation for Economic Co-operation and Development (OECD) produces numerous policy reports not only on education and economic performance but also on the importance of education for social capital and social cohesion (see, for instance, OECD 2001; 2006; 2007). The European Council famously declared in its 2000 Lisbon Goal a ten-year target to make the EU "the most competitive and dynamic knowledge-based economy in the world, capable of sustained economic growth with more and better jobs and *greater social cohesion*" (European Council 2000); the European Commission later made those twin objectives the major themes of its education policy in the *Lifelong Learning Memorandum* (European Commission 2000). Similar declarations about the importance of education for enhancing societal outcomes (including in health, democratic engagement and citizenship, and social cohesion more broadly) can be found in any number of policy documents from national and international bodies.

It is often argued that, despite the rhetoric, policy-makers treat social cohesion objectives as subordinate to economic objectives when it comes to education policy. This may often be true when the two are seen to conflict, particularly in the developed countries. In newly formed or newly developing states, education for nation-building is necessarily a top priority, particularly where national identity is contested or not yet securely established, and where public and state institutions, which intermediate

The Handbook of Global Education Policy, First Edition.
Edited by Karen Mundy, Andy Green, Bob Lingard, and Antoni Verger.
© 2016 John Wiley & Sons, Ltd. Published 2016 by John Wiley & Sons, Ltd.

conflicts and underpin social cohesion, are still fragile (Brown 2000; Green 2013; Hill and Lian 1995). But in the older states, where state formation has long since established more robust institutions and identities, skills formation for economic activity often takes precedence over value- formation for citizenship (Green 1997). Nevertheless, many countries, including older ones, have adopted new policies for civic and citizenship education in recent years. Nor are the social benefits of learning considered simply as an add-on or a "luxury" in developed countries. Evidence of increasing inequality and declining social cohesion causes some anxiety to governments in the richer countries, not only because it presents potential or actual social and political challenges, but also because it can have adverse effects on economic competitiveness (OECD 2007). Beyond this it is also recognized that adverse social outcomes – such as poor health, increased crime, and civil conflict – involve direct economic costs. Hence the appetite of various governments for research which monetarizes the social benefits of learning in terms of the reduced costs to the state for public health, policing, and criminal justice systems (McMahon 1999).

So while it may be that economic objectives predominate over social objectives in much education policy, it is not the case that social objectives are absent in policy. There are countless education initiatives aimed at societal improvements around the world. These include "peace education" programs in countries during or after periods of civil strife (Novelli and Smith 2011); sex and relationship education programs in both developing and developed countries; environmental education programs and civic education programs to promote tolerance, gender equality, and active citizenship. Some of these are known to work in certain contexts. Education on relationships and birth control has been shown to be highly effective, along with increasing girls' education generally, in bringing down birth rates in some developing countries, with all the attendant economic and social benefits this may bring (Sen 1999). However, the problem with much of the global policy on education, social benefits, and social cohesion more broadly is that it is often not clear if it works, and if so how it works.

The starting point for most policy analysis of education and social outcomes is the social benefits that learning brings to individuals. Studies for various countries demonstrate that more educated people tend to show higher levels of social and political trust; civic and political engagement; democratic values and tolerance; and are less prone to committing acts of violent crime (Nie et al. 1996; Stubager 2008; Hagendoorn 1999; Emler and Frazer 1999; Putnam 2000; McMahon 1999). Analyses of British longitudinal data show that the size of these effects can be substantial. For instance, compared with those educated only to lower secondary level, higher education graduates in the UK are: 70–80% more likely to report excellent health and 55% less likely to suffer from depression in the case of males (females: 35%). They are also 30–40% more likely to hold positive attitudes to race and gender equality, 50% more likely to vote, and, in the case of males, 3.5 times more likely to be a member of a voluntary association (females: 2.5×) (Feinstein et al. 2008). Not all of the social advantages associated with higher levels of education can be attributed to the individuals' experiences of upper secondary and higher education programs, since there may also be selection effects. Those staying on longer in education may already have characteristics which dispose them to be more tolerant or politically engaged. However, studies which control for other factors do still show strong effects from education of social outcomes for individuals (Campbell 2006).

Robert Putnam (2000), for instance, claims on the basis of his analysis of US data that education is the strongest predictor of most of the characteristics – like trust, tolerance, and civic engagement – that he associates with social capital.

The problem for analyses of education and social benefits, however, is that we don't know much about how individual benefits associated with education translate into societal benefits. First of all, although we know that there is a strong association between levels of education and social outcomes for individuals in various countries, we don't always know if the relationships are causal and, if so, what is the mechanism of causation and what educational processes are involved. The process by which learning affects individual attitudes and behaviors remains something of a black box (Campbell 2006). More problematic still is how these individual effects aggregate into societal effects. Better educated people may tend to be more trusting, tolerant, and politically engaged in various countries, but more educated societies are not necessarily more tolerant and politically engaged in the aggregate (Green *et al.* 2006). Furthermore, in many developed countries, education levels have been rising at the same time as levels of tolerance, trust, and engagement in mainstream politics (including voting) have been in decline (Campbell 2006; Green *et al.* 2011; Putnam 2000).

What these societal characteristics may mean for that elusive property, social cohesion, is also often not at all clear, since social cohesion may mean different things in different countries and rely on different institutions and values in each case. Definitions of social cohesion tend to be highly normative and vary widely in the policy and academic literature (see, for instance, Beauvais and Jenson 2002; Berger-Schmitt 2000 and Chan *et al.* 2000). In some cases they stress common identity and a sense of belonging (Heydt 2003); in others an active civil society (Putnam 2000), and in the more "republican" forms, equality and social solidarity (Bernard 1999; Maxwell 1996). In the most inclusive definition, social cohesion refers to the property by which whole societies, and the individuals within them, are bound together through the action of specific attitudes, behaviors, rules, and institutions, where the latter rely more on consensus than pure coercion (Green and Janmaat 2011). Taking a broad definition like this allows us to analyze empirically how social cohesion functions in a range of different societies, but does not settle the normative questions about what forms are most "desirable." Manifestations of social cohesion in specific national contexts can be, for instance, more or less egalitarian and more or less democratic. Here we are less concerned with disentangling these normative issues than with examining in general the processes by which education generates societal effects.

A number of different theories have been proposed to explain potential links between the effects on education on individual attitudes and behaviors and on society as a whole. In each case these involve stipulating a pathway or mechanism through which learning affects individuals and an aggregation mechanism through which individual effects translate into societal effects. These can be characterized as: (a) absolute direct effects; (b) cumulative effects; (c) positional or relative effects; and (d) distributional effects. This chapter will briefly consider the underlying logics of these theories and then examine in more detail how they may be used to explain the processes by which education effects occur at the societal level in terms of specific aspects of social cohesion. We focus here on tolerance, political engagement, and social and political trust as the key aspects of social cohesion in a number of theories.

Absolute Direct Effects

Absolute direct effects are said to occur when learning impacts individual attitudes and behaviors directly, without being mediated by other factors, and when the impact of education on an individual is not affected by his or her education level relative to other people's education level. In this scenario the effects of education on individuals are simply aggregated together in societies so that if education has a positive effect on, for instance, tolerance, at the individual level, increasing average levels of education will have a positive effect on average levels of tolerance in that society. A number of writers (Nie *et al.* 1996; Hagendoorn 1999) argue that the relation between education and tolerance takes this form in various countries because education increases knowledge and cognitive ability. More educated individuals are said to acquire a greater breadth of knowledge and understanding of the diversity of human conditions, which makes them more sympathetic to different lifestyles and beliefs. They also acquire higher cognitive abilities, for instance in sifting information and evaluating arguments, so that they can see through false stereotypes and irrational prejudices. Other studies focus on the socializing effects of particular forms of learning. Stubager's (2008) analysis of Danish voters aged 18–75 in 2004, for instance, which distinguishes between different types of education received, finds that the strongest effects on tolerance comes from higher education in medium and long programs, particularly in social and caring fields of study, suggesting a dominant socializing process. Controlling for income level does not reduce the impact of higher education on tolerance, thus leading the author to conclude that education has an absolute effect on individual tolerance, rather than a positional effect mediated through occupation.

Theories of direct and absolute effects from education on social outcomes assume an unproblematic relationship between individual effects and societal effects. If education makes individuals more tolerant, more educated societies, other things being equal, will be more tolerant. The problem is that this is not always the case. Historically, there are obvious examples of highly educated societies that have not been very tolerant, as Inglehart reminds us with respect to highly educated Nazi Germany (Inglehart 1990). Some studies of contemporary societies, for instance, Peri (1999) on Italy, do not find a significant positive relationship between education and tolerance at the individual level, and other studies comparing across countries (Green *et al.* 2006) find no significant correlation between levels of education and levels of tolerance. The last clearly does not necessarily mean that education has no positive effect. It could simply mean that its influence is overwhelmed by other factors in cross-country analysis. Likewise if, as Nie *et al.* (1996) note, rising levels of education in some countries are not accompanied by rising levels of tolerance, this could simply be because other factors are counteracting the positive effects of education. However, where there is a disconnect between the individual level associations and the cross-national associations, it does mean that there remains a lot to explain in terms of the other national contextual factors which may be impinging on the relationships.

Cumulative Effects

Direct effects, as in the above example, are not incompatible with indirect or mediated effects. It is quite possible, for instance, that education has an indirect effect on tolerance in the longer term as well as an immediate direct effect. Certain types of education may socialize learners into more tolerant attitudes, as Stubager (2008) argues, and these may persist over time. At the same time, over the longer term, education may lead to a higher occupational status, and this may also be conducive to more tolerant attitudes if those in more privileged positions feel a greater sense of security and less threatened by others. This may be considered as a mediated effect or, as Stubager argues for tolerance, a complementary effect. In his analysis, social class has a limited impact and does not reduce the direct impact of education on tolerance when occupation and income are put into the same model. Another case where both direct and mediated effects occur simultaneously, according to Campbell (2006), is with educational influences on social trust. According to his analysis an individual's level of social trust is enhanced by education and also by the education of others. The educational "environment" surrounding an individual acts as mediating factor so that education has both a direct effect and a "cumulative effect."

Positional Effects

In the examples above, the effects of education are aggregative or multiplicatory. That is to say, if you increase the levels of education of individuals in a society those individuals will be more tolerant, and that will increase levels of tolerance in the society as a whole. By contrast, where effects of education are relative or "positional," individual effects may not translate into societal effects at all. This is because it is an individual's level of education relative to others that matters, not his or her level of education *per se*. Education is acting as a positional good and not everyone can be highly positioned relative to everyone else.

The study by Nie *et al.* (1996) on the effects of education on political engagement and "political enlightenment" provides the classic examination of the difference between absolute and positional effects. Their analysis of longitudinal and cross-sectional US data in *Education and Democratic Citizenship in America*, suggests different processes for the two types of outcome. The effect of education on political enlightenment (which they take to be respect for civil liberties, and toleration of freedom of speech for unpopular minorities) is absolute. Education makes people more tolerant and in the aggregate more educated people will, ceteris paribus, make society more tolerant. The reason for this, they say, is that tolerance is not a positional or competitive good. There is no limit to the amount of tolerance available in society. My being tolerant does not make you less so. On the other hand, they find that the effect of education on political engagement is positional. What affects the political engagement of the individual is his or her level of education relative to others.

The explanation provided for this by Nie *et al.* is that many of the activities which constitute political engagement are essentially competitive and "zero-sum." As they argue:

> certain aspects of democratic citizenship are in fact bounded, or limited, by their essentially competitive nature. The instrumental behaviors and cognitions of political engagement can be seen as … a zero-sum game, bounded by finite resources and conflict, where one's gain will necessarily be another's loss. Elected representatives can vote only one way on a proposed piece of legislation, and bureaucrats cannot regulate to everyone's satisfaction. (Nie *et al.* 1996, 101)

According to their theory access to influential positions where you can make your voice heard is limited and a product of what they call "network centrality." Those located centrally within the right networks have a better chance of having political influence than those who are on the periphery and they therefore have a greater incentive to become politically engaged. Network centrality is largely determined by occupational status, which is in turn influenced by education. But because education acts primarily as a sorting mechanism, it is not your absolute level of education which determines your occupational status so much as your educational level relative to others. Education is considered a positional good which impacts indirectly on political engagement primarily through its effects on occupational status.

The study provides one answer to the problem of aggregation – or what might be called the paradox of levels. There is a wealth of research for the USA and other countries which shows that more educated people tend to more politically engaged. They are more likely to discuss politics, to join and be active in political parties, to campaign for parties, petition, write letters to political representatives, and to vote. However, more educated societies do not necessarily show higher levels of political engagement in the aggregate. As countries like the USA become more educated they do not necessarily become more politically engaged, and the better educated younger cohorts do not exhibit more political engagement than less educated older cohorts, at least in the traditional forms of political activity (Putnam 2000). The reason for this non-correspondence of education effects at different levels, according to Nie et al. (1996), is that the opportunities for political engagement are limited and essentially zero-sum, and that education effects are only relative.

Education and Democratic Citizenship in America provides one neat solution to the problem of aggregation, but it also begs a number of questions. One relates to exactly which types of political activity can be considered to be competitive and zero-sum. Another has to do with the nature of educational positionality and exactly what constitutes the reference group with whom the individual is competing. A number of other studies have examined these questions more closely and in so doing refine the theory developed by Nie et al.

Campbell's study (2006) extends the analysis in a number of different ways. First, while Nie et al. only test the positional effects thesis with US data, this analysis uses cross-sectional European Social Survey data on education levels and social attitudes and behaviors for a number of countries. Second, the study differentiates between types of political engagement that are deemed to be competitive in the way Nie et al. suggest and other types which may not be. Political activities like contacting political leaders and working for political parties or "action groups" are categorized as "competitive" because the more people contact a political leader, the less the impact made by each individual contact, and the more people volunteer for a party, the less the relative value of each individual volunteer. Activities like boycotting consumer products, marching in demonstrations and signing petitions are labeled "Expressive Political Activities" and considered to be essentially non-competitive because they are mass activities where the more the people taking part, the greater the effect as a whole and the impact of the individual's actions. Such collective action may involve contest between social groups but it is non-competitive, in Campbell's sense, at the individual level. Third, Campbell adopts a narrower definition of the group with whom the individual is deemed to be competing regarding their educational credentials. Rather than assuming as Nie *et al.* do that the individual is competing with all adults, Campbell assumes the competition is with people in the same cohort. The education environment variable, therefore, is the mean level of education of those in the individual's age cohort in the country in question (where there are four age cohorts). To test for absolute and relative effects Campbell uses a random coefficient (mixed effects) model with controls for gender and household income, and where the relationships between the dependent variable and both education level and educational environment are permitted to vary cross-nationally. Where the education variable has a significant positive effect and the education environment variable has a non-significant effect, this is deemed to provide strong evidence for the absolute effects model. On the other hand, if there is a negative coefficient for the education environment variable, particularly where the coefficient is larger than for the education level variable, this is deemed to show that the effect of education is relative or positional.

Campbell's analysis leads him to say that the relationship between education and competitive political activities is, as Nie *et al.* claim, best explained by the relative effects model. For non-competitive political activities, however, he finds evidence for both absolute and relative effects. In the case of voting, the coefficient for the education environment is negative and greater in magnitude than the positive coefficient for education, which suggests relative effects, but the coefficient is not significant, so the effect is only weak. Campbell's findings are largely confirmed in another study by Persson (2011), which tests the relative effects model on data for Sweden from the Swedish Election Survey (1985–2006). Like Campbell, Persson finds that the relative effects model works for certain types of political engagement but not for others. There is no evidence of positional effects from education on communicating with political representatives. However, for voting, membership of political parties, and activism in political parties, there is clear evidence that education effects are positional.

The statistical methods for testing the relative effects are complex in both studies, but the results seem quite intuitive. Neither study finds evidence of positional effects for activities such as writing to political representatives, boycotting, petitioning, or marching. These are not essentially competitive activities and are certainly not zero-sum in as much as there are no limits on how many can take part. However, both studies find evidence of positional effects where the activity is competitive or where there is a limit on how many can take an active or influential part. Most political parties in democracies will allow anyone to join but in many countries those with relatively low levels of education and income are least likely to find their own interests represented in the political agendas of the main parties and therefore will be least likely to join them. Small parties may reflect their interests better but they are unlikely to get into office or to have an impact (except perhaps in coalition governments in systems with proportional representation), so the relatively less educated may still not feel an incentive to join. Not everyone can take on significant roles in party organization and activities. All eligible voters can vote but those with relatively lower qualifications and incomes are least likely to see their vote getting candidates or parties into office who will change things in the way they would like.

Distributional Effects

So far we have considered aggregation mechanisms where the effects of education are initially conceptualized at the individual level. Theoretical suppositions are then made about how these individual level effects may be aggregated at the societal level. The three models of absolute effects, cumulative effects, and relative effects are the ones most often discussed in the literature. However, there is a fourth possible mechanism for effects at the societal level that is often considered in relation to the effects of income distribution but less often in relation to the effects of education and skills. This is the model of distributional effects.

Distributional effects differ from the other kinds of effects because they cannot be conceptualized at the individual level. An individual does not have a distribution. These are societal effects which concern the relations between individuals but which are in principle irreducible to individuals. Durkheim famously characterized such properties as characteristics of the collectivity, which are more than the sum of the individual parts. Economists and psychologists who favor an epistemology of methodological individualism tend to be suspicious of distributional effects precisely because you cannot conceptualize them at the level of the individual. In this way of thinking, societal phenomena that can't be explained statistically as a result of the aggregation of individual actions do not have a real existence, they are simply abstractions. But to most sociologists collectivities are real and have real properties, which Durkheim (1982) referred to as "social facts."

Distributional effects are certainly widely considered in the debates around the effects of income inequality. The social epidemiologist, Richard Wilkinson, for instance, has argued that income inequality has measurable negative effects on a wide range of societal phenomena, from public health, life expectancy, obesity rates, and child well-being, to social trust, political engagement, social mobility, and crime (Wilkinson and Picket 2009). Inequality is strongly associated with negative values on all these social outcomes in cross-national bivariate correlations. There has been much debate about whether these associations imply causal relationships between income inequality and the negative social outcomes, or whether the latter are independent of each other and both caused by other underlying societal factors (Salverda *et al.* 2014). In fact, Wilkinson has put forward some compelling psychosocial arguments about why income inequality may affect individuals in ways that lead to negative social outcomes at the societal level. High levels of income inequality in societies may generate various kinds of high-stakes competition, which can become a source of conflict or stress and anxiety for individuals, which in turn leads to negative health and attitudinal, behavioral outcomes. However, it has often been difficult to show statistically the mechanisms by which societal characteristics (such as income inequality) are mediated at the individual level in such a way as to aggregate to a societal effect.

Distributional models are less common in the literature on education effects, although they have been used to try to explain the effects of skills inequality on social trust, for instance (Green *et al.* 2006). In principle, however, they are no less plausible than distributional models of the effects of income inequality. For one thing, education and skills inequality (whether measured by distributions of tested skills or years of education) have been shown to be closely related to income inequality (Bedard and Ferrall 2003; Green et al. 2006; Nickel and Layard 1998). So it is quite possible that skills inequality may have distributional effects on societal outcomes indirectly through income inequality. It is also possible that skills inequality has independent effects on social outcomes, as has been argued in relation to social trust (Green et al. 2006) but through similar mechanisms as have been postulated for income inequality. Skills inequality may, for instance, engender greater social distance between groups of individuals. It may also raise levels of anxiety and stress as a result of more intense competition. But the problems in demonstrating causality remain the same. Plausible theories are needed to show the mechanisms through which societal properties act on individual attitudes and behaviors in ways that can be shown to aggregate into societal effects. Statistical models then must be developed to test these relationships.

Such relationships cannot necessarily be adequately tested through the use of interaction terms in multi-level models. Interaction terms are used when effects of two variables acting simultaneously on a third variable are not additive because one independent variable modifies the effects of another independent variable on the dependent variable. So, in the case of the model discussed above for the positional effects of education on political engagement, the lower the level of the educational environment, the stronger the effect of education on engagement. The education environment variable diminishes the effect of the education variable. However, distributional effects do not necessarily work in this way. In the case of education and social trust, for instance, education may enhance the level of trust of the individual. At the same time the distribution of skills at the macro level may affect the level of trust of the individual. A higher level of skills inequality may reduce individual level trust. This is not necessarily because of any interaction between skills inequality and the education effect. There may be no reduction in the education effect. But skills inequality may be having an independent negative effect through a quite different mechanism. If skills inequality reduces individual trust by increasing social distance and conflicts between people it may have this effect on everyone whatever their level of education relative to others. In a positional effects model greater skills inequality might increase the trust of the most educated both absolutely and relative to that of the less educated by interacting positively with the education effect.

Education and Social Trust – Multiple Effects

Interpersonal or "social" trust has often been considered one of the key measures of social cohesion (Green et al. 2006; Uslaner 2002; Reeskens 2007). It relates to people's willingness to place their confidence in a wide range of others, including people they do not know. And it is widely considered to be an important precondition for the functioning of modern societies where there is a highly evolved division of labor and where everyday activities often involve interactions with strangers. Trust is necessary for the legitimacy of democratic systems which require that we trust the politicians we elect to deliver their pledges. It is a precondition for welfare states, which redistribute resources toward the needy because they depend on people trusting that if they pay their taxes to support others in need, others in turn will pay theirs to support them if they are in need. Trust is also essential for efficient economic activity, which depends on people sticking to what they have agreed. The higher the levels of trust and trustworthiness the less need for legal contracts and lawyers for every transaction and thus the lower the transaction costs (North 1990). Above all, trust is what allows people to go about their daily business without constant fear of being let down or cheated. This general form of trust has been widely identified as necessary for a substantial range of private and public goods in society. If we believe the correlational evidence, it is closely associated with economic and social outcomes as diverse as economic growth (Knack and Keefer 1997), innovation (Osberg 2003), public health (Wilkinson 1996), better government (Putnam 2000), and general well-being and happiness (Wilkinson and Pickett 2009).

Social trust is usually measured by the World Values Survey question which asks "Generally speaking, would you say that most people can be trusted or that you can't be too careful in dealing with people?" It can be objected that the question is not entirely clear about the range of people in question, but factor analysis suggests that respondents do indeed interpret the question in terms of how much they trust strangers (Uslaner 2002). Other statistical tests that have been applied also suggest that the measure is relatively robust. "Dropped wallet" experiments conducted in different countries show that in countries with high levels of measured trust more of these wallets are returned. There is also a strong correlation between measured levels of trust in particular countries, and the perception of people in other countries as to how far people can be trusted in these countries, suggesting that trust and trustworthiness are closely related (Green et al. 2006). Results from repeated surveys in different countries over 50 years do show considerable consistency in their patterns. There are very large differences between countries in how far people say they trust each other and these differences remain relatively stable over time.

We know relatively little about how trust arises. Putnam has argued (2000) that trust relates to participation in groups; that it arises out of the repeated interactions between individuals in associations bound by collective norms. We learn to trust through successful cooperation with others in pursuing common objectives. He supports this with evidence from the USA that people who join associations are more likely to be trusting. However, as others have shown, this correlation does not hold in all countries (Newton 1999), let alone across countries (Green et al. 2006; Uslaner 2002). There is no significant relation between levels of trust in a country and the frequency with which its people join organizations. Uslaner (2002), on the other hand, argues that trust is built on "moral foundations," which are learnt in early childhood, and is only partially affected by later experiences. It is not necessarily enhanced by membership of organizations, although trusting people are perhaps more likely to join organizations. Generalized trust is not a matter of strategic calculations to trust particular persons because you have had good experiences with them. It is about a more general disposition to have faith in strangers. This, says Uslaner, is basically a question of optimism. "Collectively," he writes, "the most optimistic person – who wants a fulfilling job, thinks about the future, and believes that she can make it regardless of luck, connections, or current circumstances – is 36 % more likely to trust others than the most convinced pessimist" (Uslaner 2002, 13).

It is not at all clear how the individual's propensity to trust changes throughout the life cycle. Uslaner's research suggests that it is quite stable, which supports his hypothesis that trust is a deep character trait that is acquired in childhood. Other studies have found different patterns. Cross-country data for 1959 provided by

Almond and Verba (1963) suggested that older and younger people were equally likely to trust. However, Hall (1999), using data from the repeated waves of the World Values Survey (WVS), found that people over 30 years were more trusting in 1981 than people under 30 and that the age differential had increased by 1990. It is notoriously difficult to disentangle life cycle, cohort, and period effects in the data, and it may well be that the effects of age on trusting vary in time and place.

What we do know – and what must considerably qualify any explanation of trust based purely on the effects of early parenting – is that levels of trust vary massively across countries, from less than 10% in Brazil and Turkey, for instance, to over 60% in Norway and Sweden (Delhey and Newton 2005). Aggregate levels of trust in different countries do change over time, but the pattern across countries shows considerable regularity. We also know that average levels of trust tend to vary by social class, with the more affluent more inclined to trust than others lower down the income scale (Hall 1999). These social variations suggests that although being trusting is an individual disposition, which may well be a quite deep-seated personality trait, it is also strongly influenced by societal contexts. People are more likely to trust as adults if others are trustworthy. So trust is not only fundamental to the functioning of societies. It is also a product of how societies function.

One of the social contexts that appears to have a strong effect on trusting is inequality. In more unequal societies, it is argued, trusting others becomes much more difficult. The social and cultural distance between individuals tends to be larger, making common understanding and communication more difficult. As Dorling writes: "As inequality rises people begin to treat others less and less as people, and begin to behave towards others as if some are different species" (Dorling 2010, 126). Furthermore, a high level of inequality in society creates high-stakes competition for access to resources and life chances. This can cause conflict between individuals and groups, and increased incidence of status anxiety and general stress. It is not hard to see how any of these might make trusting others more difficult (Green *et al.* 2011; Wilkinson and Pickett 2009). Most of the cross-country analyses of social trust show that mean levels of trust are strongly negatively correlated with income inequality (Delhey and Newton 2005; Green *et al.* 2006; Green and Janmaat 2011; Uslaner 2002; Rothstein and Uslaner 2005; Wilkinson and Picket 2009). More unequal societies tend to be less trusting on average. In a study using the US General Social Survey for 1960 to 1998, Rothstein and Uslaner also show how over time changes in income inequality correlate with changes in levels of trust. The higher the Gini measure of income inequality, the lower the proportion of other people say they can trust. Using a test for causality, Rothstein and Uslaner argue that it is income inequality that is affecting trust and not the other way around (2008, 45). As Uslaner has argued (2002), relative equality promotes solidarity because people feel more or less in the same boat.

How, then, may the relationships between education and trust be conceptualized? What are the mechanisms by which education affects trust at the individual level and how do individual level effects translate into societal effects? Are the relationships best characterized as absolute direct effects, cumulative effects, positional effects, or distributional effects?

Evidence for a number of countries suggests that more educated people tend to be more trusting (Campbell 2006; Putnam 2000). Some of the analyses point toward this being both an absolute direct effect and a cumulative effect

(Campbell 2006; Helliwell and Putnam 1999). This would fit, to some extent, with Uslaner's contention that one form of trust, which he terms "moral trust," is a deep character trait which is learned early on in childhood. Some children learn from their parents and from early schooling to view the world as optimists and to expect the best out of other people and life in general. They are more likely to be trusting as adults. This is more likely in more affluent families and, as Green et al. (2011) show, there is a strong positive correlation between parental social class and trust at 33 years and 34 years, respectively, in the National Child Development Study and British Cohort Study 70 longitudinal data for Britain. Campbell (2006) and Helliwell and Putnam (1999) also claim to find a cumulative effect. Individuals are more trusting because of the education they have received but they also trust more when others around them are well educated. According to Campbell this may be because individuals may be more inclined to trust when others are also trusting or when they deem that others are more trustworthy.

However, it would seem equally plausible that education has an indirect effect on trust through adult occupation, income, and status. Uslaner shows that one element of trust is a character trait which is learnt early on and which is likely to be lasting over the life course. But the propensity to trust is also shaped by experience and may change over the life course. Adverse events may diminish an individual's level of trust, or the accumulated advantages stemming from education may enhance it. The latter would be consistent with the idea that trust is related to general well-being and what psychologists call "locus of control" (Layard 2005; Wilkinson and Picket 2009). More educated individuals are more likely to acquire higher status jobs as adults. They will experience a greater sense of control over their lives, and be more likely to think that things will work out well in their encounters with others. This is likely to encourage an attitude of trust. The effect of education in this case may be both direct and indirect (as mediated by occupation). An indirect effect through occupation is likely to have a positional dimension to it because jobs are acquired through a process of selection. However, this may be counterbalanced by the positive effect of others being well educated and more trusting or trustworthy, so that being more educated than others may be a mixed blessing for one's capacity to trust. Campbell's multilevel analysis across countries, for instance, finds no evidence of a positional effect of education on trust. This is supported by the evidence that better educated and richer countries tend to have higher average levels of trust. It is true that trust has declined in many of the more affluent countries in recent decades (Green et al. 2011) at the same time as education levels have risen, but this may be because factors other than education are undermining trust.

Various reasons have been advanced as to why trust may be declining in some countries despite higher levels of education and wealth. One popular idea is that globalization and increasing ethnic and cultural diversity reduce levels of trust. In series of cross-national and cross-area analyses, Alesina and La Ferrara (2003), Knack and Keefer (1997), Putnam (2000, 2007), and Uslaner (2002) all find that increasing diversity reduces average levels of trust. Putnam claims, in his analyses across areas in the USA (2007), that diversity reduces trust both within and across "racial" groups, even when we control for other factors, such as inequality. However, he restricts his analysis to diversity across four "racial" groups in the USA, and says nothing about ethnic diversity more broadly. Other studies, using appropriate controls, have found no relation between ethnic diversity and trust, either at the cross-national level (Green *et al.* 2006) or in cross-area analyses in Canada (Johnson and Soroka 1999) and the UK (Letki 2006).

The most likely societal source of declining trust in many countries would seem to be rising inequality. Virtually all cross-national and multi-level analyses of the determinants of social trust find that inequality has a strong negative effect, as discussed above. In as much as educational inequality contributes to income inequality it seems likely that there may be a distributional effect of education on trust as well as absolute and cumulative effects. It may also be the case that skills inequality diminishes societal levels of trust independently of income inequality as some previous studies have found (Green *et al.* 2006; 2011). These distributional effects may occur at the same time as absolute direct effects of education on individual level trust.

Our analysis of the data from the OECD's recently published *Survey of Adult Skills* (SAS) (OECD 2013), shows exactly this. Adult numeracy and literacy skills have a significant positive effect on trusting at the individual level. In addition to this, there is a distributional effect on mean levels of trusting in society, at least for Western countries. Inequality of adult skills is negatively correlated with levels of trust, and significantly so in the case of numeracy.

SAS contains publicly available data for 24 countries and regions on the tested skills of 16–65 year olds in literacy, numeracy, and problem solving. The survey also asks respondents about their health, volunteering activities, political efficacy and social attitudes. There are two questions on trust which are relevant here. The survey asks:

To what extent do you agree or disagree with the following statements?

a. There are only a few people you can trust completely.
b. If you are not careful, other people will take advantage of you.

[1 strongly agree; 2 agree; 3 neither agree nor disagree; 4 disagree; 5 strongly disagree]

In this analysis a combined measure for trust for 22 countries was calculated by adding up the responses to these two items and subtracting the total by 1. As a result the scale of the measure ranges between 1 (maximum distrust) and 9 (maximum trust). The value 5 is the midpoint representing a neutral response. The measure was assumed to be a coherent indicator of social trust as the two items composing it are strongly correlated in each of the participating countries. Figures 9.1, 9.2, and 9.3 show the mean values across countries on the two separate questions and on the combined measure.

As other studies have shown, levels of trust vary significantly across countries, with the Scandinavian countries, Japan, and The Netherlands showing quite high levels of trust and southern and eastern European countries in this sample showing rather low levels of trust.

If we look at the correlations across countries for skills inequalities and the aggregates for trust, we begin to see some relationships emerge. Table 9.1 shows correlations between the inequality measures (of both income and skills) and mean levels of trust for all 22 countries and for Western countries only (see Figure 9.4). It also includes GDP per capita as one of the predictor variables because economic

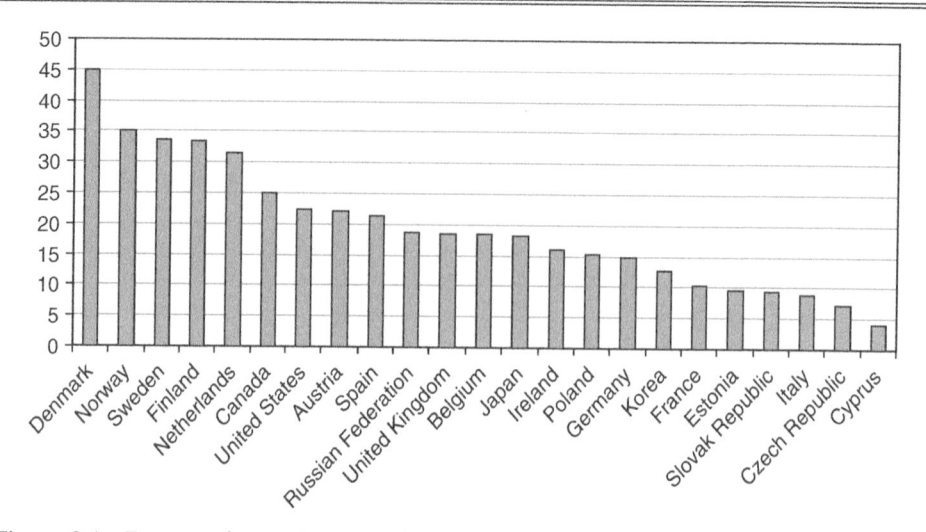

Figure 9.1 Few people can be trusted completely (percentage disagreeing plus strongly disagreeing).
Source: Data from OECD (2013), *OECD Skills Outlook 2013: First Results from the Survey of Adult Skills*. OECD, Paris.

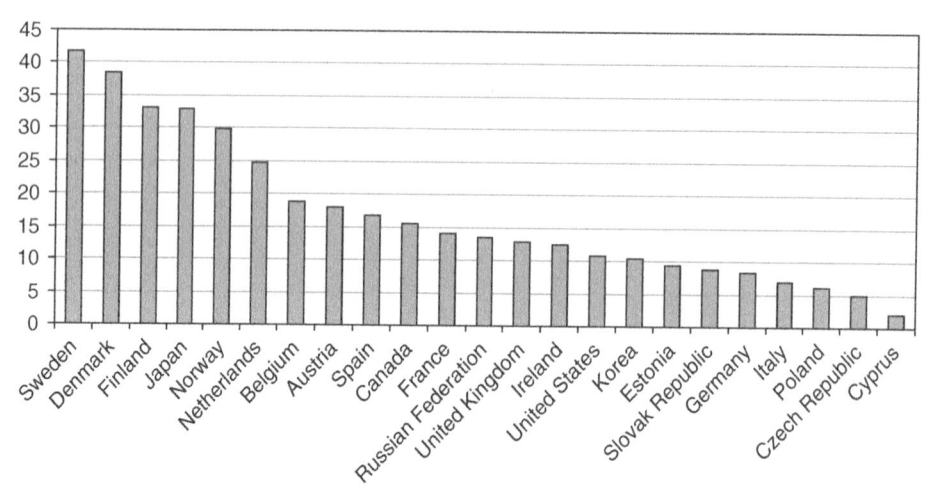

Figure 9.2 Other people take advantage of you (percentage disagreeing plus strongly disagreeing).
Source: Data from OECD (2013), *OECD Skills Outlook 2013: First Results from the Survey of Adult Skills*. OECD, Paris.

prosperity has been shown to be a strong determinant of trust (e.g. Delhey and Newton 2005). The predictor variables appear to be linked in quite different ways to mean levels of trust depending on the group of countries examined. If all the countries are included in the analysis non-relationships prevail between the inequality measures and trust, while GDP per capita shows a strong positive correlation with trust (see Figure 9.4). However, amongst the Western countries skills inequality is negatively related to trust (see Figure 9.4). This is consistent with the findings of

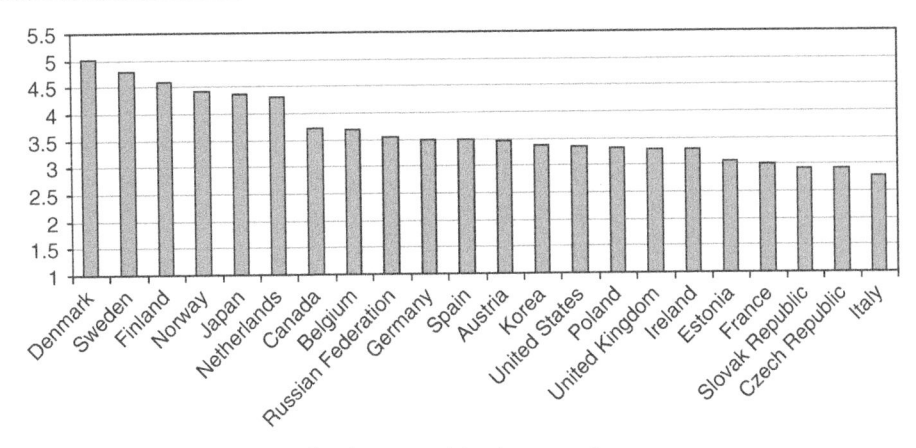

Figure 9.3 Social trust (mean levels on combined measure).
Source: Data from OECD (2013), *OECD Skills Outlook 2013: First Results from the Survey of Adult Skills*. OECD, Paris.

Table 9.1 Correlations of inequality and GDP per capita with social trust

	Social trust All countries (N = 22)	Social trust Western countries (N = 15)
Income inequality (2009 gini household income)	−0.14	−0.34
Inequality of literacy skills	0.11	−0.33
Inequality of numeracy skills	−0.12	−0.59*
GDP per capita ppp (2012)	0.52*	0.38

*$P < 0.05$; **$P < 0.01$; ***$P < 0.001$
Source: Data from OECD (2013), *OECD Skills Outlook 2013: First Results from the Survey of Adult Skills*. OECD, Paris.

Table 9.2 The determinants of social trust (coefficients of multiple regression)

	All countries (N = 22)	Western countries (N = 15)
Inequality of numeracy skills	−0.39	−0.55*
GDP per capita ppp (2012)	0.69**	0.31

*$P < 0.05$; **$P < 0.01$; ***$P < 0.001$
Source: data from OECD (2013), *OECD Skills Outlook 2013: First Results from the Survey of Adult Skills*. OECD, Paris.

earlier research based on data from the International Survey of Adult Skills (IALS) data, the 1990s predecessor of SAS (Green *et al.* 2006). For inequality in numeracy skills this negative correlation is significant at the 0.05 level. Interestingly, skills inequality thus shows a stronger link to trust than income inequality. GDP per capita is no longer significantly correlated to trust once the analysis is restricted to Western countries.

These relationships are confirmed in a regression analysis on trust including numeracy skills inequality, and GDP per capita as predictors, and thus as each other's controls (see Figure 9.5).

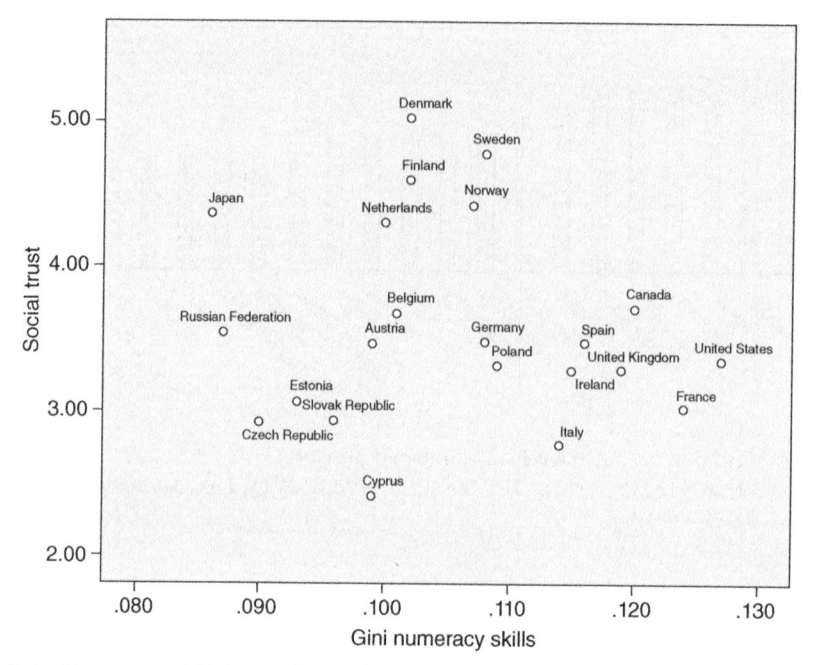

Figure 9.4 Numeracy skills inequality and social trust (22 countries).
Source: Data from OECD (2013), *OECD Skills Outlook 2013: First Results from the Survey of Adult Skills*. OECD, Paris.

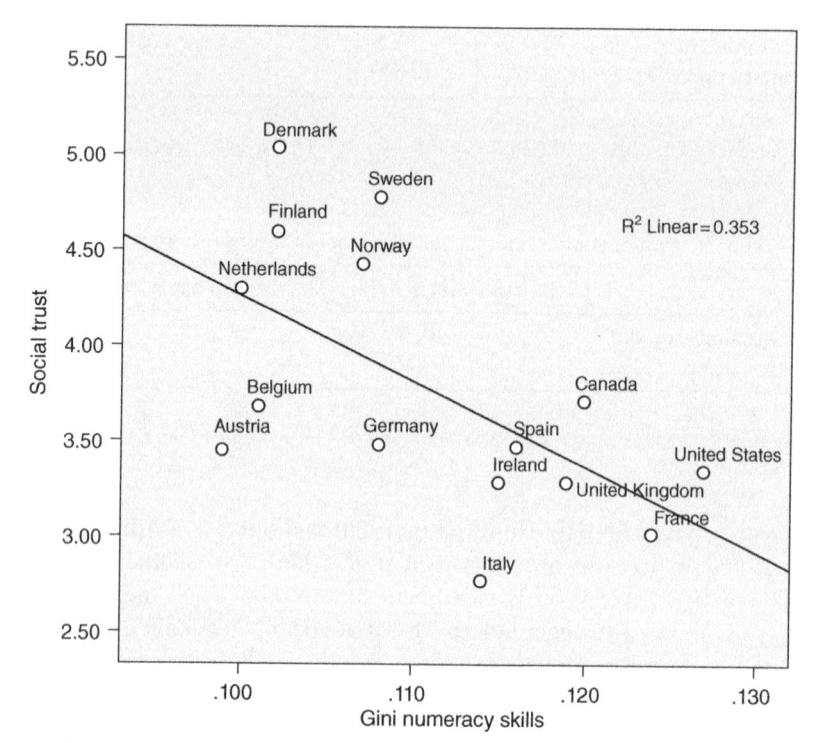

Figure 9.5 Numeracy skills inequality and social trust in Western countries.
Source: Data from OECD (2013), *OECD Skills Outlook 2013: First Results from the Survey of Adult Skills*. OECD, Paris.

As in all cross-country correlations the results are highly sensitive to which countries are included. Wealth is strongly associated with trust across a large group of countries. Richer countries tend to have higher levels of trust, whereas poorer countries, like the central and eastern European countries (CEE) countries in this sample, tend to have lower levels of trust. If you restrict the sample to the richer countries the variation in wealth is not very large and ceases to be significant.

Skills inequality is negatively associated with trust in Western countries. This relationship disappears if you include the CEE countries, because, unlike the Western countries, they combine low levels of skills inequality with low levels of trust. These features are likely to be a legacy of communism, as communist rule in eastern bloc countries has been associated with egalitarian outcomes *and* an erosion of trust (Schöpflin 2000). The Latin American countries are not included in SAS so we can't include them in this analysis. But were we able to include them, along with the other 22 countries, it is likely that a negative correlation between skills inequality and trust would again emerge in a larger group of countries, since Latin American countries all combine very high levels of income inequality with very low levels of trust (according to the WVS data).

Conclusions

Research on the social outcomes of learning clearly shows that education brings substantial benefits to individuals in many countries in terms of improved health and general well-being, and higher levels of social trust, civic involvement, and political engagement. However, not all of these individual benefits translate into societal benefits. This is because they are often positional benefits or because they depend on how education and skills are distributed as much as on the mean levels of education and skills. More educated societies, for instance, are not necessarily more politically engaged, partly because the effects of education on many forms of political engagement are positional rather than absolute. Richer and more educated societies do tend to be more trusting, but the full benefits of education on social trust are dependent on how education and skills are distributed. Amongst equally affluent and educated societies, it is the more egalitarian ones which have higher levels of social trust. This is particularly important for social cohesion, however we define this, because social trust is widely considered to be the single most important characteristic of socially cohesive societies of whatever type.

Global policy on education, social benefits, and social cohesion tends to rest on the rather simplistic assumption that individual benefits automatically aggregate into societal benefits but, as we have seen, this is not always the case. This Panglossian approach produces a number of misunderstandings. On the one hand, it leads to an overly optimistic assessment of the social benefits of education for societies as a whole, and consequent disillusionment when these are not realized. On the other hand, it leads to a failure to realize the full societal benefits of education, particularly in terms of social cohesion. Many factors contribute toward the development of more trusting and cohesive societies, not least reducing inequalities in wealth and incomes. Education can also play a significant role. But it is not just the overall levels of education that matter. A more equal distribution of educational opportunities, and consequent reduction in skills inequalities, is equally important for promoting more cohesive societies.

References

Alesina, A. and E. La Ferrara. 2002. "Who Trusts Others?" *Journal of Public Economics*, 85: 207–234.

Almond, G. and S. Verba. 1963. *The Civic Culture*. Princeton: Princeton University Press.

Beauvais, C. and J. Jenson. 2002. *Social Cohesion: Updating the State of Research*. CPRN Discussion Paper, F/22. Ottawa: Canadian Policy Research Network.

Bedard, K. and C. Ferrall. 2003. "Wage and Test Score Dispersion: Some International Evidence." *Economics of Education Review*, 22: 31–34.

Berger-Schmitt, R. 2000. *Social Cohesion as an Aspect of the Quality of Societies: Concept and Measurement*. EuReporting Working Paper No. 14. Manheim: Centre for Survey Research and Methodology.

Bernard, P. 1999. *Social Cohesion: A Critique*. CPRN Discussion Paper No. F/09. Ottawa: Canadian Policy Research Networks.

Brown, D. 2000. *Contemporary Nationalism: Civic, Ethnocultural and Multicultural Politics*. London: Routledge.

Campbell, D. 2006. "What is Education's Impact on Civic and Social Engagement?" in *Measuring the Effects of Education on Health and Civic Engagement. Proceedings of the Copenhagen Symposium*. Paris: OECD.

Chan, J., H.-P. To, and E. Chan. 2006. "Reconsidering Social Cohesion: Developing a Definition and Analytical Framework for Empirical Research." *Social Indicators Research*, 75: 273–302.

Delhey, J. and K. Newton. 2005. "Predicting Cross-National Levels of Social Trust: Global Pattern or Nordic Exceptionalism?" *European Sociological Review*, 21: 331–327.

Dorling, D. 2010. *Injustice: Why Social Inequality Persists*. Bristol: Policy Press.

Durkheim, E. 1982. *The Rules of Sociological Method*. London: Macmillan.

Emler, N. and E. Frazer. 1999. "Politics: The Education Effect." *Oxford Review of Education*, 25(1 and 2): 271–272.

European Commission. 2000. *A Memorandum on Lifelong Learning*. Retrieved from: http://europa.eu.int/comm/education/life/memoen.pdf (accessed November 10, 2015).

European Council. 2000. *Declaration of the European Council Lisbon Goal*. Retrieved from: www.europarl.europa.eu/summits/lis1_en.htm (accessed November 10, 2015).

Feinstein, L., D. Budge, J. Vorhaus, and K. Duckworth. 2008. *The Social and Personal Benefits of Learning: Summary of Key Findings*. London: Wider Benefits of Learning Centre, Institute of Education.

Green, A. 1997. *Education, Globalization and the Nation State*. London: Macmillan.

Green. A. 2013. *Education and State Formation: Europe, East Asia and the USA (second edition)*. Basingstoke: Palgrave.

Green, A. and J.-G. Janmaat. 2011. *Regimes of Social Cohesion: Societies and the Crisis of Globalization*. Basingstoke: Palgrave.

Green, A., G. Janmaat, and H. Cheng. 2011. "Social Cohesion: Converging and Diverging Trends." *National Institute Economic Review*, 215: 7–23.

Green, A., J. Preston, and J.-G. Janmaat. 2006. *Education, Equality and Social Cohesion*. Basingstoke: Palgrave.

Hagendoorn, L. 1999. "Introduction: A Model of the Effects of Education on Prejudice and Racism," in *Education and Racism: A Cross-National Inventory of Positive Effects on Education and Racial Tolerance*, edited by L. Hagendoorn and S. Nekuee, 1–20. Aldershot: Ashgate.

Hall, P. 1999. "Social Capital in Britain." *British Journal of Policy*, 29: 417–461.

Helliwell, J. and R.D. Putnam. 1999. "Education and Social Capital." *NBER Working Paper* (W7121).

Heydt, J.-M. 2003. *Education for Democratic Citizenship and Social Cohesion: A Background Study*. Strasbourg: Council of Europe.

Hill, M. and K.F. Lian. 1995. *The Politics of Nation-Building and Citizenship in Singapore*. London: Routledge.

Inglehart, R. 1990. *Culture Shift in Advanced Industrial Society*. Princeton: Princeton University Press.

Johnson, R. and S. Soroka. 1999. "Social Capital in a Multicultural Society: The Case of Canada." Paper presented at the Annual Meeting of the Political Science Association, Sherbrooke, QC.

Knack, S. and P. Keefer. 1997. "Does Social Capital Have an Economic Pay-off? A Cross-Country Investigation." *Quarterly Journal of Economics*, CX11: 1251–1288.

Layard, R. 2005. *Happiness: Lessons from a New Science*. London: Penguin Books.

Letki, N. 2006. "Does Diversity Erode Social Cohesion? Social Capital and Race in British Neighbourhoods." Unpublished paper. Oxford: Nuffield College.

Maxwell, J. 1996. *Social Dimensions of Economic Growth*. Eric John Hanson Memorial Lecture Series, Volume VI. Edmonton: II, University of Alberta.

McMahon, W. 1999. *Education and Development*. Oxford: Oxford University Press.

McMahon, W. 2009. *Higher Learning Greater Good: The Private and Social Benefits of Higher Education*. Baltimore: Johns Hopkins University Press.

Newton, K. 1999. "Social and Political Trust in Established Democracies," in *Critical Citizens*, edited by P. Norris. Oxford: Oxford University Press.

Nickel, S. and R. Layard. 1998. *Labour Market Institutions and Economic Performance*. London: Centre for Economic Performance, LSE.

Nie, N., J. Junn, and K. Stahlik-Barry. 1996. *Education and Democratic Citizenship in America*. Chicago: University of Chicago Press.

North, A. 1990. "A Transaction Theory of Politics." *Journal of Theoretical Politics*, 2: 355–356.

Novelli, M. and A. Smith. 2011. *The Role of Education in Peace-Building: A Synthesis Report of Findings from Lebanon, Nepal and Sierra Leone*. New York: United Nations.

OECD. 2001. *The Well-Being of Nations*. Paris: CERI, OECD.

OECD. 2006. *Measuring the Effects of Education on Health and Civic Engagement*. Proceedings of the Copenhagen Symposium. Paris: OECD.

OECD. 2007. *Societal Cohesion in and the Globalising Economy: What does the Future Hold?* Paris: OECD.

OECD. 2013. *OECD Skills Outlook 2013: First Results from the Survey of Adult Skills*. Paris: OECD.

Osberg, L. (ed.). 2003. *The Economic Implications of Social Cohesion*. Toronto: Toronto University Press.

Peri, P. 1999. "Education and Prejudice against Immigrants," in *Education and Racism: A Cross-National Inventory of Positive Effects on Education and Racial Tolerance*, edited by L. Hagendoorn and S. Nekuee. Aldershot: Ashgate.

Persson, M. 2011. "An Empirical Test of the Relative Education Model in Sweden." *Political Behaviour*, 333: 455–478.

Putnam, R. 2000. *Bowling Alone: The Collapse and Revival of American Community*. New York: Simon and Schuster.

Putnam, R. 2007. "E Pluribus Unum: Diversity and Community in the Twenty-First Century." *Scandinavian Political Studies*, 20: 139–174.

Reeskens, T. 2007. "Defining Social Cohesion in Diverse Societies." Paper presented at the 103rd Annual Meeting of the American Political Science Association. August 30–September 2, 2007, Chicago.

Rothstein, B. and E. Uslaner. 2005. "All for All: Equality, Corruption and Social Trust." *World Politics*, 58: 41–72.

Salverda, W., B. Nolan, D. Checchi, I. Marx, A. McKnight, I.V. Tóth, and H. van de Werfhorst (eds). 2014. *Changing Inequalities in Rich Countries: Analytical and Comparative Perspectives*. Oxford: Oxford University Press.

Schöpflin, G. 2000. *Nations, Identity, Power: The New Politics of Europe*. London: C. Hurst and Co. Publishers.

Sen, A.K. 1999. *Development as Freedom*. Oxford: Oxford University Press.

Stubager, R. 2008. "Education Effects on Authoritarian-Libertarian Values: A Question of Socialization." *British Journal of Sociology*, 59(2): 327–350.

Uslaner, E. 2002. *The Moral Foundations of Trust*. Cambridge: Cambridge University Press.

Wilkinson, R. 1996. *Unhealthy Societies: The Affluence of Inequality*. London: Routledge.

Wilkinson, R. and K. Pricket. 2009. *The Spirit Level: Why More Equal Societies Almost Always Do Better*. London: Allen Lane.

Chapter 10

Policies for Education in Conflict and Post-Conflict Reconstruction

Sarah Dryden-Peterson

Introduction

Despite remarkable progress toward universal primary education, 59 million children remain out of school globally. More than half of these children live in conflict-affected settings. Compared with children in other low-income countries, children living in conflict are less likely to survive to school age; they more rarely attend school and complete a full basic education; and they are far less likely to access secondary education. Only 79% of youth and 69% of adults are literate in conflict-affected settings, as compared with 93% and 85% in other countries. Conflict disrupts teacher education systems, destroys physical infrastructure, and promotes a culture of violence that impacts classroom pedagogy, contributing to poor quality of teaching and learning (Lewin 2009; UNESCO 2011; UNESCO 2014; Dryden-Peterson 2010c). Children in conflict who are poor, female, and from ethnic and linguistic minority groups are multiply marginalized, and they access and persist in school at much lower rates than do children in countries not affected by conflict. In Nord-Kivu, a conflict-affected area of the Democratic Republic of Congo, young people are twice as likely to have had under two years of education as compared to young people in other parts of the country. Poor women in this area are three times as likely to have had this little education (UNESCO 2011).

The United Nations High Level Panel report on the Post-2015 Development Agenda identifies five big, transformative shifts in order to end poverty and promote sustainable development. The first is to "leave no one behind" (United Nations 2013). Given that more than half of the children who are "left behind" from educational opportunities globally live in conflict settings, education in conflict and post-conflict reconstruction is an urgent policy priority.

The Handbook of Global Education Policy, First Edition.
Edited by Karen Mundy, Andy Green, Bob Lingard, and Antoni Verger.
© 2016 John Wiley & Sons, Ltd. Published 2016 by John Wiley & Sons, Ltd.

This chapter provides an overview of the origins and implications of policies for education in conflict and post-conflict reconstruction. First, I begin by defining conflict, surveying the criteria for identifying conflict-affected countries, and outlining the implications of definitional issues for policy. Second, I examine the nature and causes of conflict and the implications of these understandings on the design of global policy. Third, I outline the phases of conflict and the different policy responses required in each phase to meet the needs of learners and teachers. Fourth, I trace the history of the rise of policy for education in conflict. Fifth, I present three principal policy approaches to education in conflict – humanitarian, development, and security – providing examples of the actors who work within each approach. Finally, I explore two significant tensions in current policies for education in conflict and post-conflict reconstruction – access/learning and global/local – and I suggest ways in which the field might move forward through addressing these tensions.

Defining Conflict

Conflict-affected settings are generally defined by the use of armed force and the number of battle-related deaths. The Uppsala Conflict Data Program (UCDP) is the most widely used and respected resource in the identification and characterization of conflicts. It defines an armed conflict as a "contested incompatibility that concerns government or territory or both where the use of armed force between two parties results in at least 25 battle-related deaths in a year." They note that at least one of the parties to the conflict must be the government of a state. UCDP divides conflicts into two categories based on their intensity: armed conflicts involve at least 25 battle-related deaths in a year (but fewer than 1000) and wars involve at least 1000 battle-related deaths in a year.

In 2012, there were 32 armed conflicts globally, in 26 countries. In this same year, there were six ongoing wars (see Table 10.1). UCDP identifies the best estimate of battle-related deaths in 2012 as 37,941, with the war in Syria resulting in, at best

Table 10.1 2012 countries with active conflict

Europe	*Middle East*	*Africa*	*Asia*	*Americas*
<u>Azerbaijan</u>	Iraq	Algeria	Afghanistan	Colombia
Russia	Israel	<u>Central African Republic</u>	India	<u>United States of America</u>
	Syria	<u>Democratic Republic of Congo</u>	Myanmar	
	Turkey		Pakistan	
	Yemen	Ethiopia	Philippines	
		Mali	Thailand	
		Nigeria		
		Rwanda		
		Somalia		
		South Sudan		
		Sudan		

Source: Data from Themnér and Wallensteen (2013).
Note: *Italics* indicates engagement in an interstate conflict. <u>Underline</u> indicates engagement in an internationalized conflict.

estimate, 15,055 deaths. The number of conflicts in 2012 was at a relative low for the post-World War II period. Between 1979 and 2000, for example, there were around 40 conflicts in any given year (Themnér and Wallensteen 2013).

Given that impacts of conflict persist many years after the cessation of violence or peace accords are signed, some agencies define as conflict situations those settings in which there is not active armed conflict but where there has been in the past. For example, the United Nations Environmental, Scientific and Cultural Organization (UNESCO) Global Monitoring Report included on its list of conflict-affected states Angola, Liberia, and Sierra Leone, where there was no longer acute conflict (UNESCO 2011). For the purposes of this chapter, I refer to these situations as post-conflict, a phase of conflict that is discussed in more detail below.

In characterizing education in conflict and post-conflict settings, the concept of "fragility" is also used, often interchangeably with conflict. The concept of fragility is typically much broader, however, such as in the Organisation for Economic Co-operation and Development (OECD) definition of those countries that are "failing to provide basic services to poor people because they are unwilling or unable to do so" (OECD 2007). While the term fragility has conceptual value, I do not use it here; the causes and dimensions of conflict are multiple, often-contested, and recent evidence suggests that conflict and fragility may have divergent impacts on education (Shields and Paulson 2014). In this chapter, I use the term "conflict-affected" to mean countries that are impacted by violent and armed conflict, resulting in weak governance and inequality in resource allocation that negatively affect the lives and livelihoods of children and the provision of education (see Mundy and Dryden-Peterson 2011).

The Nature and Causes of Conflict

The nature of armed conflict has changed since the end of the Cold War. As related to education policy, there are four particularly important ways in which conflicts have changed over this time. First, conflicts are increasingly protracted. The average conflict lasts for 12 years in low income countries and 22 years in middle income countries (UNESCO 2011, 138), and the average length of displacement is 17 years (UNHCR 2006, 109). Some conflicts persist for much longer, such as Afghanistan (33 years), Colombia (36 years), Democratic Republic of Congo (19 years), and Somalia (23 years). Second, contemporary conflicts are more deadly for civilians, especially children, and more destructive of civilian infrastructure, including schools. Between 1998 and 2008, over 2 million children were killed in conflicts; 6 million were disabled; 300,000 were recruited as child soldiers; and 20 million were refugees or Internally Displaced Persons (IDPs), having fled their homes (UNICEF 2008). Children also constitute the majority of casualties of landmines, remnants of cluster munitions, and other explosive remnants of war (UNICEF 2013, 55). In 2012, 69 teachers were killed and 2445 schools damaged in Syria (General Assembly Security Council 2013, para. 157). Third, conflicts play out increasingly within national borders rather than between states. The one interstate conflict – Sudan–South Sudan – is indicated with italics in Table 10.1. Fourth, 25% of conflicts in 2012 were internationalized, meaning that they involved troop support from an external state; this number is unprecedented in the post-World War II period. These countries are underlined in Table 10.1.

These four dimensions of contemporary conflicts interact with three primary understandings of the causes of conflict, with implications for the design of global policies for education in conflict (for more on these three theories as they relate to education, see Novelli and Lopes Cardozo 2008). The *modernization theory*, championed by Samuel Huntington, is global in outlook (Huntington 1996). It is premised on a "clash of civilizations," particularly perceived irreconcilable cultural and religious differences both within states (such as between Hindu and Muslim in India) and among states (such as between what he calls Islamic and non-Islamic civilizations). Modernization theory can lead global policy in education to focus on elimination of radical intolerance and countering anti-Western ideology through "winning hearts and minds," which harkens back to Lyndon B. Johnson's call for winning popular Vietnamese support during the Vietnam War. US troop involvement in the building of schools in Afghanistan is an explicit example of such an approach (Fishstein and Wilder 2012). Less explicit are activities such as US President Barack Obama's Global Engagement Initiative, which includes a component to engage youth in the Muslim world through education as a peacebuilding and counter-terrorism endeavor (USAID 2009).

The other two schools of thought on the causes of contemporary conflicts are centered on the state. The *structural inequalities theory* relates social, economic, and political inequalities to ongoing violence (Stewart *et al.* 2008; Duffield 2001; Brown 2010). These inequalities are evident in the education sector. For example, in conflict-affected Guinea, Kosovo, and Nepal, 40% of government spending on education reached the richest quintile of the population, with less than 10% going to the poorest quintile (World Bank, 2004 in Lewis and Lockheed 2006, 71). Understanding conflict as caused by structural inequalities leads educational policy to focus on reducing exclusion and, as a consequence, decreasing intergroup grievances. One policy intervention that follows from this understanding is increasing the availability of school for the marginalized. In Chad, for example, 80% of enrolled children came from the 8% of villages that had schools located in them. Three kinds of distance were relevant to marginalization: the physical distance in kilometers; the time distance, which included obstacles such as mountains and rivers and how they impact travel time; and, most neglected, the cultural distance, "the drop-off that occurs as children are expected to leave their own community to go to a community that may be considered foreign or unfriendly" (Lehman 2003). This cultural distance appears to be particularly pronounced, even between villages that are geographically close, in countries and regions that have experienced years of violent conflict.

The *opportunity theory* of conflict also emphasizes existing socio-political conditions, but with an emphasis on the weakness of the state, the availability of "lootable" resources, and human nature as inherently greedy (Collier 2007; Collier and Hoeffler 2004). The 2009 Education for All (EFA) Global Monitoring Report concluded that good governance was essential to address persistent inequalities in access that limit progress on EFA and Millennium Development Goals (MDG) (UNESCO 2008), the greatest of which exist in conflict-affected settings. With this understanding of conflict, educational policy focuses on the strengthening of the state, both through educating moral and productive citizens and training in good governance. The idea is that schools can model good governance. The Sudan Basic Education Program, funded by USAID, for example, linked financial management training for Parent

Teacher Associations (PTAs), school Board of Governor (BOG) members, and the administrators of teacher training institutions to the maintenance of peace in what was then southern Sudan (Kirk 2011, 28).

Phases of Conflict

The roots and trajectories of each conflict are unique. Yet mapping several distinct "phases" of conflict is conceptually useful, particularly in defining broadly the educational needs and policy responses. Conflicts are generally divided into four phases: the build-up to conflict (latent phase); escalation of conflict (emergency phase); continuation of conflict (protracted phase); and cessation of conflict and building of peace (reconstruction phase). Of course, these phases are idealized. They do not substitute for context-specific analysis of a given conflict, and moreover, there are often no clear distinctions between one phase and another: they usually overlap and are frequently cyclical (see Figure 10.1).

In the *latent phase* of conflict, conflict can be simmering beneath the surface or hidden. Often the indications of rising conflict are recognized only in retrospect. In the latent phase, education is often an important driver of conflict. Davies argues that there are five key drivers of conflict: problems of governance, lack of security, weak economy, cultural barriers to change or cohesion, and environmental degradation (Davies 2011). Problems of governance and cultural barriers to change or cohesion often interact with the unequal distribution of the resource of public education. In Sierra Leone, for example, central demands of the rebel Revolutionary United Front (RUF) army related to redressing a public education system that was geographically unequal and divided by class. The consequences of unequal access to education can be stark. In 2001 in Nepal, the literacy rate among the ruling Brahmins was 70% compared with only 10% among the lower/excluded castes (Novelli and Smith 2011). In the latent phase, especially in countries that have a propensity for

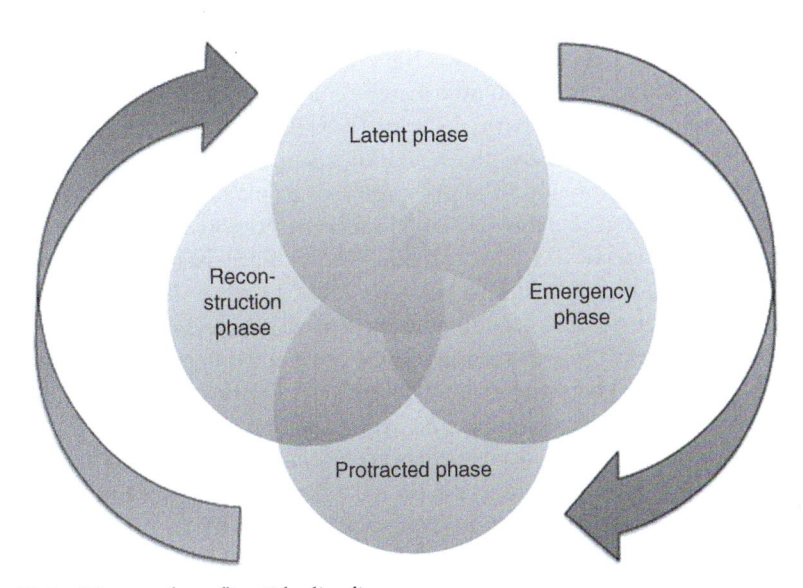

Figure 10.1 Phases of conflict (idealized).

conflict, educational policies and programming focus on conflict prevention through the protection of children's rights in national legislation, ongoing conflict analysis and evaluation of the conflict sensitivity of education, and the building of resilience through curriculum and pedagogy.

The *emergency phase* of conflict is the period that follows the onset of high intensity fighting. It is often accompanied by massive displacement of people who either flee across borders to become refugees or to another area of their own country as IDPs. Humanitarian action is at its highest during this phase of conflict, with rapid responses by international and national agencies. Education was once marginalized during emergencies, with priority placed on "life-saving" interventions in health, shelter, food, and water and sanitation. Now, policies of the United Nations High Commissioner for Refugees (UNHCR), the lead agency in emergencies, articulate commitment to "quality education as an integral part of the planning and provision of humanitarian response" (UNHCR 2012, 7), with the rationale that education is "life-sustaining," especially in the physical, psychosocial, and cognitive protection it provides. Research demonstrates that education in the emergency phase provides more than protection: it provides hope for the future and a bridge to aspirations for livelihoods (Dryden-Peterson 2011a; Winthrop and Kirk 2008). Education often takes the form of temporary learning spaces in the emergency phase, with attempts at reestablishing formal schooling as soon as possible. Despite strategic commitment to education during emergencies, humanitarian aid to education has remained shockingly low, hovering at around 2% for the past decade (UNESCO 2011). In this phase, access to education can drop precipitously. For example, while primary school enrolment in Syria before the crisis had been almost universal, at 97%, and secondary enrolment had been 67%, only about 56% of school-age Syrian children (ages 5 to 17), both inside and outside of Syria, had access to school in December 2013 (UNICEF et al. 2013).

The *protracted phase* of conflict encompasses all conflict after the initial onset. Increased attention to education in the emergency phase is due in large part to understanding the nature of contemporary conflict as protracted, meaning that it persists for more than five years. As noted above, the average conflict lasts for 12 years in low income countries and 22 years in middle income countries (UNESCO 2011, 138), and the average length of displacement is 17 years (UNHCR 2006, 109). This means that the education that children receive during conflict is not a stop-gap measure but their one shot at education. Humanitarian aid continues to play a critical role during the protracted phase of conflict; the Global Monitoring Report concludes that "more than half of humanitarian aid goes to countries where it has represented at least 10 percent of total aid of at least nine years" (UNESCO 2011, 201–202).

The *reconstruction phase* of conflict occurs after the cessation of conflict and represents a shift toward longer-term planning. Dismantling inequitable systems of education, which may have been contributors to conflict, and rebuilding new systems that ensure equity, requires the strengthening of planning capacity for dimensions of the education system such as monitoring, financial management, and teacher recruitment and training. Reconstruction is often an opportunity for building anew, with possibilities for innovation and reform that are more challenging in entrenched systems (Nicolai 2009). Decisions about what should be taught – curriculum – prove an especially contentious part of this process, especially for sensitive subjects such as history (Tawil and Harley 2004; Pingel 2010). While long-term planning is essential during reconstruction, short-term and visible outcomes – schools being open and accessible – become paramount as indicators to parents and communities of the stability and legitimacy of a new government (Practical Action Consulting *et al.* 2012), often referred to as "peace dividends" (United Nations Peacebuilding Support Office 2012).

The Rise of a Field of Policy

Education in conflict and post-conflict settings is often described as a new field. However, its roots stretch back at least as far as World War II, when communities as well as organizations such as Save the Children set up schools for evacuees and refugee children (Dryden-Peterson 2011b). From World War II until 1990, education in conflict was a field of practice, a loose collection of educational programs deeply embedded in local contexts (see Dryden-Peterson 2011b). Much of the education was community-based, with schools started by Eritreans and Tigreans in exile in Sudan in the 1970s and Nicaraguans living in Honduras in the 1980s (Dodds and Inquai 1983). Education in conflict settings at this time was also connected to processes of decolonization and liberation movements, such as the African National Congress' Solomon Mahlangu Freedom College in Tanzania (Serote 1992).

From the mid-1990s, education in conflict has become a field of policy, increasingly coordinated at the global level by a wide range of actors (see Dryden-Peterson 2011b). The main actors have included UN agencies UNHCR and UNICEF; multi-stakeholder collaborations such as the Inter-Agency Network for Education in Emergencies (INEE) and the Education for All Fast Track Initiative (EFA FTI), now the Global Partnership for Education (GPE); bilaterals, particularly the UK's Department for International Development (DFID), the Canadian International Development Agency (now Global Affairs Canada), and the US Agency for International Development (USAID); and non-governmental organizations (NGOs), notably the International Rescue Committee, Save the Children, and the Norwegian Refugee Council. Winthrop and Matsui call this first stage "proliferation" and the second "consolidation" (2013, 14–15). What are the origins of these policies in education in conflict that "consolidated" the field? There are four key dimensions of this development: the articulation of a universal rights-based framework for education; growing recognition of the need to protect children in armed conflict; the massification of access to education for all globally; and the creation of normative standards for education in conflict settings.

Articulation of the *right to education* in conflict settings has its roots in the aftermath of World War II, in international instruments that proliferated at that time. The 1948 Universal Declaration of Human Rights recognized compulsory primary education as a universal entitlement. The 1979 Convention on the Elimination of All Forms of Discrimination Against Women (United Nations 1979) called for no discrimination in educational provision for men and women, and the 1989 Convention on the Rights of the Child (CRC) affirmed the right of all children, regardless of status, to free and compulsory primary education, to available and accessible secondary education, and to higher education on the basis of capacity

(United Nations 1989, Article 28). The right to education for refugees was articulated in Article 22 of the 1951 Convention relating to the Status of Refugees, which stated that signatory states "shall accord to refugees the same treatment as is accorded to nationals with respect to elementary education … [and] treatment as favourable as possible … with respect to education other than elementary education" (UNHCR 2010). The right to education for all, including in conflict settings, has become the centerpoint of education strategies of the main actors in this field. Both UNHCR and UNICEF, for example, center their education strategies, and associated programming and advocacy, on the right to education. The concept of "right to education" is invoked 25 times in the 20-page UNICEF Education Strategy, of which the stated purpose is to define "the contribution of UNICEF to national efforts to fulfil children's right to education" (United Nations Economic and Social Council 2007). The institutional structure of UNHCR also reflects increasing centrality of a rights-based approach to education. The Education Unit historically has been within the Department of Operational Support and the Division of Programme Support and Management, indicating a service-delivery approach to education. In 2010, the Education Unit was moved to the Division of International Protection, reflecting education as a tool in UNHCR's core mandate of protection of the rights of refugees (Dryden-Peterson 2011b).

The changing nature of conflict, in which children were increasingly casualties, was a direct challenge to the CRC. The *protection of children* in settings of armed conflict came to the fore, especially out of the Bosnia Herzegovina Conflict and the Rwanda Genocide. The killing of children who were outside playing in Sarajevo, for example, captured international attention and raised the profile of the needs of children living in conflict settings. Graça Machel's 1996 report, *The Impact of Armed Conflict on Children*, was highly critical of the international humanitarian system for inattention to these needs (Machel 1996; see also, United Nations 1993). Her report highlighted the role for education in the "psychosocial recovery" of war-affected children and the reconstruction of societies, which paved the way for a policy space for education within humanitarian response. As noted above, education now resides within the Department of International Protection of UNHCR, and Action 2 of the UNHCR Education Strategy 2012–2016 is "schools will protect children and young people" (UNHCR 2012, 5). In refugee and other conflict-affected situations, NGOs have also increasingly had a protection focus in their programming. The flagship educational program of the International Rescue Committee (IRC), for example, is Healing Classrooms, launched in 2004 and premised on the role of education in protecting teachers' and students' physical and psychosocial well-being (Kirk and Winthrop 2007; Winthrop and Kirk 2008). Through partnerships and an eLearning program, this initiative has been widely adopted by other agencies, including as mandatory training for UNHCR Education Officers.

The third dimension of the development of a field of policy in education in conflict was broader changing expectations for education, represented by the EFA movement and the inclusion of universal access to education as an MDG. The *massification of education* extended to children in conflict settings. The 1990 Jomtien World Declaration on EFA identified "war, occupation, [and] civil strife" as some of the "daunting problems" that "constrain efforts to meet basic learning needs"

(World Conference on Education for All 1990). By the Mid-Decade EFA meeting in Amman, Jordan in 1996, education was presented as critical to humanitarian response:

> Given escalating violence caused by growing ethnic tensions and other sources of conflict, we must respond by ensuring that education reinforces mutual respect, social cohesion and democratic governance; We must learn how to use education to prevent conflict and, where crises do occur, ensure that education is among the first responses, thereby contributing to hope, stability and the healing of the wounds of conflict. (UNESCO 1996)

By the 2000 reconvening of Ministers of Education in Dakar, education in conflict was more fully on the agenda. The 2000 World Education Forum included a background thematic study, *Education in Situations of Emergency and Crisis*; a special strategy session on education in emergencies; and the outcome document, the Dakar Framework for Action, highlighted the ways in which conflict acts as a barrier to education and outlined a commitment to "meet the needs of education systems affected by conflict, national calamities and instability and conduct educational programmes in ways that promote mutual understanding, peace and tolerance, and help to prevent violence and conflict" (UNESCO 2000, Article 8v). At this time, education in emergency situations became one of nine EFA flagship programs.

Recognition of conflict settings as an important space in the global movement toward universal education led to the creation of a set of *normative standards* to guide policy and practice in this domain. INEE was conceived at a November 2000 workshop hosted at UNCHR, as a follow-up to the World Education Forum in 2000. When the Sphere Project, which laid out standards for humanitarian action in health, water, food, and shelter did not include education, INEE developed the Minimum Standards for Education, first published in 2004 (INEE 2004) and revised and updated in 2010 (INEE 2010). These Standards are now a companion to the Sphere Project Humanitarian Charter; Winthrop and Matsui call this partnership with other sectors the "collaboration" phase. INEE has also developed a range of tools that now serve as a robust technical framework for the field, including the INEE Minimum Standards for Education and the INEE Guiding Principles on Integrating Conflict Sensitivity in Education. The Minimum Standards are widely used at both the policy level and the field level. They guide the UNHCR Education Strategy, for example, and several bilateral donors, including USAID and Global Affairs Canada, require their contractors to show familiarity with them and to use them in their programming and evaluation.

The establishment of education in conflict as a field of policy in these four ways has led to several recent high-level developments that continue to shape current approaches to global policy. In 2010, the United Nations General Assembly passed a resolution on the right to education in emergencies, which urges concerted international effort to ensure that all children living in conflict have access to education (United Nations 2010). In 2012, Secretary General Ban Ki-moon established the Education First Initiative, which identifies sustaining education in humanitarian crises, especially conflict, as a key action to addressing the global education emergency. And, in 2013, the Global Partnership for Education (GPE) – a multilateral partnership of 60 developing country and donor governments; international, civil society, NGO, and private sector organizations; and teachers – released its Fragile States Policy, which for the first time creates the opportunity for systemic international investment in education in conflict and post-conflict settings (see Global Partnership for Education 2012a). The "New Deal" on Aid Effectiveness, agreed to in Busan in December 2011, paved the way for this type of commitment to investment in conflict settings.

Current Policy Approaches to Education in Conflict and Post-Conflict Reconstruction

Understandings of conflict – how it is defined, its nature, its phase – have impacted the historical development of this field of policy. These understandings also inform the contemporary approaches to education policy in conflict and post-conflict reconstruction adopted by global actors. The humanitarian approach and the development approach have dominated the field for the past several decades, with a security approach proliferating after the attacks of September 11, 2001. Below I define each of these approaches and trace the ways in which they are interrelated.

The humanitarian approach conceptualizes education as one component of a rapid emergency response. While the focus of humanitarian work is generally on saving lives, advocacy for humanitarian aid to education describes education fitting into this approach through its "life sustaining" characteristics. The humanitarian approach emphasizes education as a human right to be realized as well as being protective against human rights abuses. The UN Committee on Economic, Social and Cultural Rights has outlined four essential elements of the right to education: availability, accessibility, acceptability, and adaptability (the "Four As"). Through accessing an education that is available, acceptable, and adaptable, the right to education becomes an "enabling right," permitting the activation of other civil and political rights. Yet the humanitarian approach is necessarily emergency-driven and short-sighted, which results in the provision of only minimal education, often focused on building schools and enrolling children without concerted attention to the content and pedagogy that make education relevant and engaging. The humanitarian approach often involves little, if any, coordination with governments and a lack of focus on long-term institution-building.

The development approach to education, on the other hand, takes institution-building as its starting point. It recognizes education as an investment both for individuals and for society and is integrally connected to broader development goals of poverty alleviation and economic development. As such, the lack of quality education, even in a crisis, holds back development potential. The development approach takes a long-term view of education, with priority on current access to quality education but with a sense of future relevance toward individual livelihoods and societal advancement. Ministries of Education take the lead on education within a development approach and international actors support the existing system or develop capacity for transformation.

Understanding of the nature of contemporary conflicts as protracted and the causes of conflict as inextricably linked to education have led to a growing overlap between humanitarian and development approaches in education, as in the relief to development continuum across sectors. The humanitarian approach and the development approach are increasingly difficult to separate. Policies of UNHCR and GPE demonstrate these linkages.

UNHCR, for example, as the UN agency mandated with the provision of education for refugees is a humanitarian organization. Education for refugees was, until recently, very much aligned to a humanitarian approach. The UNHCR Education Strategies, both 2007–2009 and 2010–2012, conceived of education as a way to restore normalcy to children (UNHCR 2007; 2009). The implication of this strategic approach was that getting children into school was what was important, rather than the content of learning. Access was indeed prioritized over quality in these Strategies, with indicators of quality being about the provision of education not its outcomes of teaching and learning (Dryden-Peterson 2011b). The UNHCR Education Strategy, 2012–2016, however, takes a decidedly development approach, with its priority as "access to quality education" and its key principle of "integration of learners within national systems" (UNHCR 2012, 8). In this new Strategy, a humanitarian approach persists, however, in tandem to the development approach. In an emergency response, the Strategy advocates temporary learning spaces immediately, but with simultaneously attention to the "establishment of formal schooling, both through integration of refugee learners into national systems and support for certified, quality education in the home country curriculum, where appropriate and feasible" (UNHCR 2012, 7).

The Global Partnership for Education, which was previously called the Education for All Fast Track Initiative (FTI), is a multilateral organization founded in 2002 with the mandate to fund education globally toward meeting EFA and MDG targets. It has recently evolved policies that take a development approach in what were previously conceived of as humanitarian contexts. Initially, the GPE did not invest in conflict-affected states, what it calls "fragile states," as governments were often unable to meet "good performance" criteria. With the understanding that almost half of children out of school globally live in conflict settings, and with increased demand from conflict-affected states, the GPE experimented with mechanisms to support the development and implementation of education sector plans in these settings. One policy, employed for a short time, was the Education Transition Fund (ETF), established by UNICEF and the Dutch government, that treated conflict states separately (Sperling 2008). The 2010 Strategic Review, however, concluded that "[f]ragile states should not be seen as a separate category. In reality there is always a continuum of 'fragility' with states moving back and forth. There needs to be one common process that all countries follow, but with support tailored to circumstances" (Cambridge Education *et al.* 2010, xxiv).

The 2013 release of the GPE Fragile States Policy is a major turning point in this endeavor, as is the 2012–2015 Strategic Plan, which prioritizes conflict-affected states (Global Partnership for Education 2012c). Now part of one flexible fund, the GPE has synthesized humanitarian and development approaches. As a result of the new policy approach, the number of conflict-affected countries supported by the GPE climbed from 1 in 2002 to 5 in 2007 to 10 in 2011 and to 28 by 2014 (Global Partnership for Education 2012b, 47). Further, while between 2002 and 2012 only one-third of funds went to countries affected by conflict and fragility (Global Campaign for Education and Oxfam International 2012, 12), by 2014, 52% of the overall allocations were to these settings (Menashy and Dryden-Peterson, 2015).

An increasingly security-oriented aid agenda has also influenced the global policy approach to education in conflict and post-conflict settings, reflecting the internationalized nature of contemporary conflicts. This securitization of education in conflict settings can be traced to donor focus on connections between terrorism and education in the aftermath of the September 11, 2001 attacks. It also mirrors a general trend in conceptualizing aid as a "tool for fighting the war on terror" (Novelli 2011, 50). OECD Development Assistance Committee (DAC) documented in 2006 that 50% of Overseas Development Assistance (ODA) went to just five of what they classified as the 48 fragile and conflict-affected states: Iraq (23%), Afghanistan (9.9%), and Ethiopia, Pakistan, and Sudan (sharing 17% of the total) (see Novelli 2011, 51–53). The main focus of this work is statebuilding and peacebuilding, once the domain of political and security specialists. This approach reflects both the modernization theory of conflict, in its focus on radical Islam, and the opportunity theory of conflict, with its emphasis on good governance as a key element of conflict mitigation.

Education increasingly figures in global policy aimed at building the foundations for stability during and after conflict. On the one hand, government's provision of education is viewed as restoring or building trust in the new state (Practical Action Consulting *et al.* 2012; United Nations Peacebuilding Support Office 2012). In a more substantive way, the content of education can contribute to changing social and political norms toward what Galtung describes as "positive peace." Positive peace involves not only minimizing the ways in which education can exacerbate conflict but also maximizing the ways in which it can mitigate it (Galtung 1969). This policy approach has been evident in the infusion of conflict resolution and peace education into curricula in post-conflict Lebanon, Nepal, and Sierra Leone, for example (Novelli and Smith 2011). It is also the focus of the Back on Track and the Education and Emergencies and Post-Crisis Transition (EEPCT) programs, partnerships between UNICEF, the Dutch government, and the European Commission. These initiatives aim to support the transformation of conflict through the development of policy and programs at country-level that operationalize the idea of peacebuilding: "multidimensional measures to reduce risk of a lapse or relapse into conflict by addressing causes and consequences of conflict" (UNICEF 2012, 11). Peacebuilding represents the coming together of development and security approaches, toward the consolidation of peace and the prevention of recurrence of conflict.

Ways Forward: Resolving Tensions

There remain two major tensions in education policies in conflict and post-conflict settings that need to be addressed to meet the needs of the millions of children and young people living in conflict settings. The first is the gap between access to education and good quality teaching and learning. The second is a gap between global policies and local realities.

Education policies in conflict settings continue to be largely focused on *access* to education (Novelli and Lopes Cardozo 2008; Paulson and Rappleye 2007; Dryden-Peterson 2010c; 2011b; Smith 2009; Winthrop and Matsui 2013). The most blatant example is the USAID Education Strategy 2011–2015. This Strategy is laudable in its direct attention to conflict settings. However, it specifies a clear focus on learning in stable contexts – "improved reading skills for 100 million children in primary grades by 2015" (Goal One) – while limiting work in conflict settings to access – "increased equitable access to education in crisis and conflict environments for 15 million learners by 2015" (Goal Three) (USAID 2011). Children living in conflict settings are very clear that the low quality education they access is not meeting their needs (Winthrop and Kirk 2008). My data from extended participant observation and interviews with refugees and returnees in Uganda, Kenya, Democratic Republic of Congo, and Afghanistan, for example, coalesce around learning of skills and knowledge that will allow them access to livelihoods and, often, the ability to act on social injustice. Children state that they wish to become a "nurse," a "judge who will rule fairly on land conflicts," to become educated to help my family, to be a leader so I can "rescue the country from bad fortunes" (Dryden-Peterson 2010a; 2010b; 2011a). Yet the focus on access rather than content and pedagogy has meant limited learning for children in conflict settings. In two Eritrean refugee camps in Ethiopia, less than 5% of children reached benchmark reading fluency by Grade 4 (Anastacio 2011). In DRC, more than half of children in Grade 4 do not meet minimum math benchmarks (UNESCO 2012). Learning outcomes for girls in conflict settings are among the worst in the world (OECD 2009). The economic and social benefits of education that global policy explicitly aims toward do not accrue when children are simply in classrooms. To create conditions for development and sustainable peace, a focus on teaching and learning is essential.

The second is a gap between global education policies and local realities of teachers and learners in conflict settings. Global policy can be effective in bettering structures and strengthening institutions. It is less effective at engaging with the local-level relationships and interactions that enable learning. The policy to integrate refugees children from DRC into national schools in Uganda in the early 2000s, for example, focused on how many children, how to pay school fees to the Ugandan government for refugee children, and the economic benefits for a refugee-hosting district of this joint development strategy for refugees and nationals. There was no attention paid at policy level to the curricular aspects of integration – the lack of possibility for Congolese children to learn the history of their country or the challenges of transitioning from a French language school system to an English one. Nor was there attention at policy level to the social aspects of integration. How would refugee and national children develop relationships with each other? How would Ugandan national teachers interact with refugee children? What would it mean to Congolese refugee children to stand around the Ugandan flag every morning and sing "Oh, Uganda!... We lay our future in thy hand"? (Dryden-Peterson 2011a; Dryden-Peterson and Hovil 2003). Despite the exciting developments with global policy on education in conflict and post-conflict settings over the past decade, the imposition of global policy without processes of adapting it to the needs and realities of local situations can reinforce inequalities and runs the risk of exacerbating conflict conditions.

References

Anastacio, A. 2011. "Crisis and Post-Crisis Context Reading Assessments: Ethiopia Case Study." *Presented at CYPD Meeting*. New York: International Rescue Committee.

Brown, G.K. 2010. "Education and Violent Conflict: Background Paper for EFA Global Monitoring Report 2011." Paris: UNESCO.

Cambridge Education, Mokoro, and Oxford Policy Management. 2010. "Mid-Term Evaluation of the EFA Fast Track Initiative, Final Synthesis Report Volume 1 – Main Report." Cambridge: Cambridge Education, Mokoro, and Oxford Policy Management.

Collier, P. 2007. *The Bottom Billion: Why the Poorest Countries are Failing and What Can Be Done About It*. Oxford, New York: Oxford University Press.

Collier, P. and A. Hoeffler. 2004. "Greed and Grievance in Civil War." *Oxford Economic Papers*, 56(4): 563–595.

Davies, L. 2011. "Can Education Interrupt Fragility? Towards the Resilient and Adaptable State," in *Educating Children in Conflict Zones: Research, Policy, and Practice for Systemic Change (A Tribute to Jackie Kirk)*, edited by K. Mundy and S. Dryden-Peterson, 33–48. New York: Teachers College Press.

Dodds, T. and S. Inquai. 1983. "Education in Exile: The Educational Needs of Refugees." Cambridge: International Extension College.

Dryden-Peterson, S. 2010a. *Barriers to Accessing Education in Conflict-Affected Fragile States: Afghanistan*. London: Save the Children.

Dryden-Peterson, S. 2010b. *Barriers to Accessing Education in Conflict-Affected Fragile States: Democratic Republic of Congo*. London: Save the Children.

Dryden-Peterson, S. 2010c. *Barriers to Accessing Primary Education in Conflict-Affected Fragile States: Literature Review*. London: Save the Children.

Dryden-Peterson, S. 2011a. "Refugee Children Aspiring toward the Future: Linking Education and Livelihoods," in *Educating Children in Conflict Zones: Research, Policy, and Practice for Systemic Change (A Tribute to Jackie Kirk)*, edited by K. Mundy and S. Dryden-Peterson, 85–99. New York: Teachers College Press.

Dryden-Peterson, S. 2011b. *Refugee Education: A Global Review*. Geneva: UNHCR.

Dryden-Peterson, S. and L. Hovil. 2003. "Local Integration as Durable Solution: Refugees, Host Populations and Education in Uganda." *New Issues in Refugee Research*, 93.

Duffield, M. 2001. *Global Governance and the New Wars: The Merging of Development and Security*. London: Zed Books.

Fishstein, P. and A. Wilder. 2012. *Winning Hearts and Minds? Examining the Relationship between Aid and Security in Afghanistan*. Medford: Feinstein International Center, Tufts University.

Galtung, J. 1969. "Violence, Peace, and Peace Research." *Journal of Peace Research*, 3: 167–191.

General Assembly Security Council. 2013. *Children and Armed Conflict: Report of the Secretary General*. New York: United Nations Security Council.

Global Campaign for Education, and Oxfam International. 2012. *A More Ambitious, Effective Global Partnership for Education: Three Priorities for the Next Phase of Reform, Briefing by Civil Society Organisations*. London: Global Campaign for Education.

Global Partnership for Education. 2012a. *Annex 2. Strategic Direction for Education in Fragile States*. Washington, DC: Global Partnership for Education.

Global Partnership for Education. 2012b. "The Education Challenge in Fragile and Conflict-Affected Contexts," in *Results 4 Learning*. Washington, DC: Global Partnership for Education.

Global Partnership for Education. 2012c. *Strategic Plan 2012–2015*. Washington, DC: Global Partnership for Education.

Huntington, S.P. 1996. *The Clash of Civilizations and the Remaking of World Order*. New York: Simon & Schuster.

INEE. 2004. *Minimum Standards for Education in Emergencies, Chronic Crises and Early Reconstruction*. Paris: UNESCO.

INEE. 2010. *Minimum Standards for Education: Preparedness, Response, Recovery*. New York: INEE.

Kirk, J. 2011. "Education and Fragile States," in *Educating Children in Conflict Zones: Research, Policy, and Practice for Systemic Change (A Tribute to Jackie Kirk)*, edited by K. Mundy and S. Dryden-Peterson, 15–31. New York: Teachers College Press.

Kirk, J. and R. Winthrop. 2007. "Promoting Quality Education in Refugee Contexts: Supporting Teacher Development in Northern Ethiopia." *International Review of Education/Internationale Zeitschrift für Erziehungswissenschaft*, 53(5): 715–723.

Lehman, D. 2003. *Bringing the School to the Children: Shortening the Path to EFA*. Washington, DC: World Bank.

Lewin, K.M. 2009. "Access to Education in Sub-Saharan Africa: Patterns, Problems and Possibilities." *Comparative Education*, 45(2): 151–174.

Lewis, M. and M. Lockheed. 2006. *Inexcusable Absence: Why 60 Million Girls Still Aren't in School and What to Do About it*. Washington, DC: Center for Global Development.

Machel, G. 1996. *The Impact of Armed Conflict on Children*. New York: United Nations.

Menashy, F. and S. Dryden-Peterson. 2015. "The Global Partnership for Education's Evolving Support to Fragile and Conflict-Affected States." *International Journal of Educational Development*, 44: 82–94.

Mundy, K. and S. Dryden-Peterson. 2011. "Educating Children in Conflict Zones: An Overview and Introduction," in *Educating Children in Conflict Zones: Research, Policy, and Practice for Systemic Change (A Tribute to Jackie Kirk)*, edited by K. Mundy and S. Dryden-Peterson. New York: Teachers College Press.

Nicolai, S. 2009. *Opportunities for Change: Education Innovation and Reform During and After Conflict*. Paris: IIEP.

Novelli, M. 2011. "Are We All Soldiers Now? The Dangers of the Securitization of Education and Conflict," In *Educating Children in Conflict Zones: Research, Policy, and Practice for Systemic Change (A Tribute to Jackie Kirk)*, edited by K. Mundy and S. Dryden-Peterson, 49–65. New York: Teachers College Press.

Novelli, M. and M.T.A. Lopes Cardozo. 2008. "Conflict, Education and the Global South: New Critical Directions." *International Journal of Educational Development*, 28(4): 473–488.

Novelli, M. and A. Smith. 2011. *The Role of Education in Peacebuilding: A synthesis report of findings from Lebanon, Nepal and Sierra Leone*. New York: UNICEF.

OECD. 2009. *PISA 2009 Results: Overcoming Social Background Equity in Learning Opportunities and Outcomes (Volume II)*. Paris: OECD.

OECD. 2011. *Glossary of Statistical Terms: Fragile States*. OECD 2007. Retrieved from: http://stats.oecd.org/glossary/detail.asp?ID=7235 (accessed November 10, 2015].

Paulson, J. and J. Rappleye. 2007. "Education and Conflict: Essay Review." *International Journal of Educational Development*, 27(3): 340–347.

Pingel, F. 2010. "The Power of the Curriculum," in *Even in Chaos: Education in Times of Emergency*, edited by K.M. Cahill, 109–135. New York: Fordham University Press, Center for International Humanitarian Cooperation.

Practical Action Consulting, Save the Children, and CfBT Education Trust. 2012. *Synthesis Research Report: State-building, Peace-building and Service Delivery in Fragile and Conflict-affected States*. London: Practical Action Consulting, Save the Children, CfBT Education Trust.

Serote, P. 1992. "Solomon Mahlangu Freedom College: A Unique South African Educational Experience in Tanzania." *Transformation*, 20: 47–60.

Shields, R. and J. Paulson. 2014. "'Development in Reverse'? A Longitudinal Analysis of Armed Conflict, Fragility and School Enrolment." *Comparative Education*: 1–19.

Smith, A. 2009. *Education and Conflict: Think Piece Prepared for the Education for All Global Monitoring Report 2011*. Paris: UNESCO.

Sperling, G. 2008. *A Global Education Fund: Toward a True Global Compact on Universal Education*. Washington, DC: Council on Foreign Relations, Center for Universal Education.

Stewart, F., G.K. Brown, and A. Langer. 2008. "Major Findings and Conclusions on the Relationship Between Horizontal Inequalities and Conflict," in *Horizontal Inequalities and Conflict: Understanding Group Violence in Multiethnic Societies*, edited by F. Stewart, 285–300. Basingstoke, New York: Palgrave Macmillan.

Tawil, S. and A. Harley. 2004. "Education and Identity-based Conflict: Assessing Curriculum Policy for Social and Civic Reconstruction," in *Education, Conflict and Social Cohesion*, edited by S. Tawil, A. Harley, and C. Braslavsky, 1–36. Geneva: UNESCO, International Bureau of Education.

Themnér, L. and P. Wallensteen. 2013. "Armed Conflict, 1946–2012." *Journal of Peace Research*, 50(4): 509–521.

UNESCO. 1996. *The Amman Affirmation, Mid-Decade Meeting of the International Consultative Forum on Education for All*. Amman: UNESCO.

UNESCO. 2000. *The Dakar Framework for Action: Education for All: Meeting our Collective Committments*. Paris: UNESCO.

UNESCO. 2008. *Education for All Global Monitoring Report 2009, Overcoming Inequality: Why Governance Matters*. Paris: UNESCO.

UNESCO. 2011. *Education for All Global Monitoring Report 2011: The Hidden Crisis: Armed Conflict and Education*. Paris: UNESCO.

UNESCO. 2012. *EFA Global Monitoring Report 2012: Youth and Skills: Putting Education to Work*. Paris: UNESCO.

UNESCO. 2014. *EFA Global Monitoring Report 2013–14, Teaching and Learning: Achieving Quality for All*. Paris: UNESCO.

UNHCR. 2006. *State of the World's Refugees 2006*. Oxford: Oxford University Press.

UNHCR. 2007. *Education Strategy, 2007–2009: Policy, Challenges and Objectives*. Geneva: UNHCR.

UNHCR. 2009. *Education Strategy: 2010–2012*. Geneva: UNHCR.

UNHCR. 2010. *Convention and Protocol Relating to the Status of Refugees*. Geneva: UNHCR.

UNHCR. 2012. *Education Strategy 2012–2016*. Geneva: UNHCR.

UNICEF. 2011. *Child Protection from Violence, Exploitation and Abuse: Children in Conflict and Emergencies*. UNESCO 2008. Retrieved from: www.unicef.org/protection/index_armedconflict.html (accessed November 10, 2015).

UNICEF. 2012. *Conflict Sensitivity and Peacebuilding in UNICEF, Technical Note*. New York: UNICEF.

UNICEF. 2013. *State of the World's Children 2013: Children with Disabilities*. New York: UNICEF.

UNICEF, World Vision, UNHCR, and Save the Children. 2013. *Syria Crisis: Education Interrupted, Global Action to Rescue the Schooling of a Generation*. New York: UNICEF, World Vision, UNHCR, and Save the Children.

United Nations. 1979. *Convention on the Elimination of All Forms of Discrimination Against Women*. New York: United Nations.

United Nations. 1989. *Convention on the Rights of the Child*. New York: United Nations.

United Nations. 1993. *Protection of Children Affected by Armed Conflicts*. New York: United Nations General Assembly.

United Nations. 2010. *The Right to Education in Emergency Situations*. New York: United Nations General Assembly.

United Nations. 2013. *A New Global Partnership: Eradicate Poverty and Transforma Economies through Sustainable Development, The Report of the High-Level Panel of Eminent Persons on the Post-2015 Development Agenda*. New York: United Nations.

United Nations Economic and Social Council. 2007. *UNICEF Education Strategy (E/ICEF/2007/10)*. New York: United Nations.

United Nations Peacebuilding Support Office. 2012. *Peace Dividends and Beyond: Contributions of Administrative and Social Services to Peacebuilding*. New York: United Nations Peacebuilding Support Office.

USAID. 2010. *Global Engagement on Entrepreneurship*. USAID 2009. Retrieved from: www.usaid.gov/press/factsheets/2009/fs091116.html (accessed November 10, 2015).

USAID. 2011. *USAID Education Strategy 2011–2015: Education: Opportunity through Learning*. Washington, DC: USAID.

Winthrop, R. and J. Kirk. 2008. "Learning for a Bright Future: Schooling, Armed Conflict, and Children's Well-Being." *Comparative Education Review*, 52 (4): 639–661.

Winthrop, R. and E. Matsui. 2013. "A New Agenda for Education in Fragile States," in *Center for Universal Education Working Paper*. Washington, DC: Brookings.

World Conference on Education for All. 1990. *World Declaration on Education for All*. Jomtien: World Conference on Education for All.

Chapter 11

Human Rights and Education Policy in South Asia

Monisha Bajaj and Huma Kidwai

Introduction

The rise of the human rights framework over the past seven decades has influenced diverse sectors including education. The forces of globalization and human rights are reflected differentially in educational policy discussions, textbook revisions, teacher education, and in the everyday life of schools across the South Asian region, comprising the diverse nations of Afghanistan, Bangladesh, Bhutan, India, the Maldives, Nepal, Pakistan, and Sri Lanka. The adoption of the Universal Declaration of Human Rights (UDHR) in 1948, arguably the cornerstone document of the global rights framework, occurred around the same time as the independence of many South Asian nations from British rule. Three South Asian nations were among the original 40 signatories to the UDHR (Afghanistan, India, and Pakistan), preceding the independence of most nations in sub-Saharan Africa and elsewhere in the global South. In more recent years, rights discourses, referred to in this chapter synonymously as "rights talk," have influenced donor aid as well as local movements towards policy reform in education in the region (see also Bajaj 2012; 2014).[1]

One of the most common shifts in international educational policy discourse is the assertion of rights-based claims that education, in and of itself, is an entitlement alongside the decades-old conditional and cost–benefit analyses of schooling – namely, human capital theory and rate of return analyses (Perkins 2001; Psacharopoulos 1996; Schultz 1961; 1980). Rights-based approaches emphasize marginalized and hard-to-reach populations, such as ethnic minorities, certain religious groups, and disabled children, viewing their access to schooling as a fundamental component of their guarantees as citizens and human beings (UNESCO 2010). International documents increasingly count out-of-school children in global, rather

The Handbook of Global Education Policy, First Edition.
Edited by Karen Mundy, Andy Green, Bob Lingard, and Antoni Verger.
© 2016 John Wiley & Sons, Ltd. Published 2016 by John Wiley & Sons, Ltd.

than purely national, terms, highlighting the efforts towards Education for All (EFA) launched through the 1990 (Jomtien) and 2000 (Dakar) summits, the Millennium and Sustainable Development Goals (2000; 2015) and subsequent meetings.

In this chapter, we seek to chart the rise of rights talk in global educational policy and map it onto educational development and national policy formation in the diverse nations of South Asia. Discourses of educational rights circulate globally and have been shaped through international meetings and conventions; as they circulate, government actors, non-governmental organizations (NGOs), and local activists anchor such discourses in unique ways resulting in distinct localized meanings when examined closely. Looking past the similar language utilized, the nation states of South Asia have varied histories and trajectories – as well as different relationships with donor countries due to geopolitical shifts during the Cold War and, soon after its demise, the post-September 11, 2001 influx of aid to parts of the region. We argue that education reforms are deeply linked to nation states' integrations and alliances in the global community, as is evidenced through policy-making and educational development across and within each country discussed in this chapter.

For this chapter, we relied on various sources to frame our argument and analysis. First, we each drew on our many years of experience as educational scholars and practitioners in the South Asian region. Second, we identified key policy documents to review from each of the eight nations in South Asia. We noted how, where, and when human rights discourses were (and were not) utilized, hypothesizing together on "why" such language was engaged. There is a lack of available, organized, and rigorous evidence on the impact of the human rights framework on education policies in South Asian countries. To overcome this lacunae in organized research on the subject, we drew from a variety of sources, including: (a) *government:* policy reports, research publications, and briefs, as well as the content from their official websites; (b) *civil society:* reports, petitions, blogs, white papers, policy reviews, and the like; (c) *bi- and multi-lateral organizations:* education reviews, project reports, thematic case studies, statistical databases; (d) *media:* news reports and articles; and (e) *academic research and literature,* such as published articles, books, and dissertations.

The sections that follow offer perspectives on how rights discourses influence contemporary educational policy-making in South Asia. We have given primacy to the policy and discursive level in order to substantiate comparisons across the eight nations of the subcontinent that currently constitute over one-fifth of the world's population. Without sustained investigation at the local levels in each nation, it would be unfair to offer evidence on implementation or divergence between policy and practice. Instead, we seek to compare policy, with an eye toward continuities and discontinuities vertically from the global to the national, and horizontally from nation to nation in the region.[2]

The Rise of Rights Talk in Global Education Policy

Over the past seven decades, education has increasingly been framed as a human right in global policy discussions, valuable in and of itself, as opposed to solely an instrumental mechanism for economic development. The modern rise of human rights in the post-World War II era can be traced to the establishment of the United Nations (UN) in 1945 and the adoption of the Universal Declaration of Human

Rights (UDHR) in 1948. The right to free and compulsory primary education provided by national governments was enshrined in this seminal document:

> Article 26: (1) Everyone has the right to education. Education shall be free, at least in the elementary and fundamental stages. Elementary education shall be compulsory. Technical and professional education shall be made generally available and higher education shall be equally accessible to all on the basis of merit. (2) Education shall be directed to the full development of the human personality and to the strengthening of respect for human rights and fundamental freedoms. It shall promote understanding, tolerance and friendship among all nations, racial or religious groups, and shall further the activities of the United Nations for the maintenance of peace. (3) Parents have a prior right to choose the kind of education that shall be given to their children. (UDHR, UN 2014)[3]

Subsequent conventions and agreements, such as the UN International Covenant on Economic, Social and Cultural Rights (1976), the UN Convention on the Rights of the Child (1989), the Education for All Frameworks (1990 and 2000), and the Millennium and Sustainable Development Goals (MDGs and SDGs), have further elaborated the conditions and benchmarks for access, quality, equity, and accountability in educational provision.

Globalization and the global flow of ideas have resulted in rights-based approaches infusing, at least discursively, national education policies worldwide over the past several decades through various "top-down" inter-governmental meetings and "bottom-up" strategies by civil society advocates seeking to expand and improve educational access and quality (Bajaj 2012; Mundy and Murphy 2001; Mundy 2008). Human rights are largely discussed vis-à-vis education in three interrelated ways: (a) education *as a* human right; (b) education *with* human rights and dignity; and (c) education *for* human rights (Bajaj 2014).

Positing access to schooling as a human right has provided rights-bearers the ability, at least in theory, to hold governments accountable. Rights frameworks also facilitate the agency of children and their families in demanding their right to schooling as opposed to being passive beneficiaries or targets of interventions (typically framed in larger efficiency terms rooted in arguments for economic development) (McCowan 2013; Robeyns 2006).

Critiques of the rights framework in education often focus on the limited entitlement offered by international declarations and meetings, "access to primary schooling," rather than a more comprehensive vision of rights to further secondary and tertiary education, food, work, social security, etc. Additionally, the inordinate focus on *access*, at least in the MDGs, has also been critiqued for its myopia to questions of overcrowding, lack of resources in schools, and consequent poor quality education that does not benefit children (and may actually put them at heightened risk, particularly girls, as they attend crowded schools with limited adult supervision) (Mirembe and Davies 2001). Still, the contemporary framing of access to education as a human right demonstrates the potential of globalization to diffuse ideas and frameworks internationally. International organizations, such as the United Nations Children's Fund (UNICEF), have declared and promoted the view that, "Education is not a static commodity to be considered in isolation from its greater context; it is an ongoing process and holds its own inherent value as a human right" (UNICEF 2007, xii, as cited in Bajaj 2014).

From the vantage point of the global South, in the years after independence from colonial rule, access to schooling shifted from an elite concern to part of broader national visions for advancing integration and social cohesion (however slowly and partially realized) (Meyer *et al.* 1992). Post-World War II, as the process of decolonization began in parts of Asia and Africa, the deepening of Western schooling in newly independent nations corresponded with international calls for equitable and broad access to schooling regardless of whether rights justifications were utilized locally for such decisions (Boli *et al.* 1985; Fuller 1991). For example, India's first Prime Minister Jawaharlal Nehru governed a largely illiterate populace (only 16.7% of Indians could read or write basic texts at the time of independence in 1947); he thus advocated for schooling as an engine of economic growth, national cohesion, and self-reliance, resonating with global discourses of schooling as an integral factor in human capital development (Becker 1964) and human rights.

Educational Development in South Asia

South Asia has experienced rapid and robust economic growth since the early 1990s. Manifestations of this growth can be seen in declining poverty rates and significant improvements in human development (Dreze and Sen 2013). The percentage of people living on less than US$1.25 a day fell in South Asia from 61% in 1981 to 36% in 2008 (World Bank 2013a). This progress in relation to the mounting pressure to view development from a rights-based approach, and donor aid conditioned on policies that reflect this, has created a receptive political environment for adopting EFA goals and policies. Given the plethora of challenges facing the South Asian region – a large proportion of the world's population, the largest number of poor and undernourished children, and several "fragile" states of geopolitical significance (World Bank 2013a) – South Asia has and will continue to play an important role in the global development story providing new dimensions to both discourse and implementation related to educational provision.

South Asian countries have espoused diverse responses to political and economic realities since the end of the Cold War and notably post-9/11, with foreign funding being channeled to Pakistan and Afghanistan along with military involvement in those countries. While some countries, like India, previously asserted their "nonalignment," others, such as Afghanistan, have had education and curriculum closely tied to the political realities of distinct historical moments, ranging from Soviet rule to the Taliban to current US influences on educational reforms. From early on, nations of the subcontinent have recognized the value of education, despite differences in how schooling has been mandated legally.

Global commitments to education through landmark meetings and declarations have incrementally provided a strong push towards education becoming a key component of policy discourse locally. In India, *Sarva Shiksha Abhiyan* (SSA) – operational since 2000 and with a near US$10 billion budget in 2013 – is the overarching program under which different education programs are designed and implemented at the central as well as the state levels, where the majority of educational planning occurs. While some attention has been paid to improving the quality of education in schools, the predominant focus of SSA has been to increase enrollments in primary schools.

Education surveys from the 1990s show abysmally low levels of achievement for most countries in South Asia (De et al. 2011, UNICEF 2011; Dreze and Sen 2013; World Bank 2015). However, the decades following the Jomtien Education for All Declaration (1990) have witnessed tremendous change in the landscape of education, with the number of out-of-school children being halved between 1999 and 2010 in the region (UNESCO 2010); from 2002 to 2005 alone, the number of out-of-school children went from 43 to 26 million – by about 11.5 million in India, 3 million in Afghanistan, 2 million in Pakistan, and 1 million in Bangladesh. There was also a substantial increase in enrollment rates at the secondary level, though the overall numbers still remain low (see Table 11.1). At the tertiary level, enrollment rates in the region increased to 10% on average (World Bank 2013b).

Similar to many nations across the globe whether in the global North or global South, education has historically been a much lower development priority as evidenced from most South Asian countries' limited financial inputs into the sector (SIO 2013). Barring the Maldives, every other country in the region reports investing an average of 3.3% of GDP as public spending on education (see Table 11.1), placing the entire region among those with *low human development* on this indicator according to the United Nations (UNDP 2015a). In effect, a large share of this very limited spending is earmarked for teachers' salaries, leaving few resources for learning materials or other expenditures (De et al. 2011; World Bank 2013b). In fact, many countries, including India, Pakistan, Bangladesh, and Sri Lanka, have over the years *reduced* their spending on education in the face of budgetary deficits and increased spending on military functions (Chopra 2012; Shaukat 2012; UNDP 2015a). Low or reduced funding for education often goes unnoticed due to poor or unvoiced public demand for quality education that characterizes most countries in the region (Satya 2011). Recent legislation in the region, such as India's Right to Education Act, recasts citizens as rights-bearers, as opposed to passive beneficiaries of state services, yet vibrant social movements with marginalized citizens acting together to demand their rights have yet to emerge on a broad scale. The mismatch between policy discourse and actual implementation is beyond the scope of this chapter, but suffice to note that despite rights talk infusing policy documents, greater citizen-led accountability efforts are still required.[13]

While South Asian countries have issued national educational policies and frameworks periodically since Independence, rights talk began to infuse these documents in the 1990s, coinciding with the Jomtien Education for All Summit (1990) and the ratification by all eight South Asian nations of the UN Convention on the Rights of the Child (Bhutan and Bangladesh were among the first 20 nations to both sign and ratify the Convention in 1990).

Transnational Advocacy Networks in Education

A useful framework for understanding and interpreting the diverse manifestations and forms of rights discourses in South Asian educational policies is political scientists Margaret Keck and Kathryn Sikkink's (1998) notion of the boomerang effect of transnational advocacy networks. In their conceptualization, the authors

Table 11.1 Education in South Asia

	Afghanistan	Bangladesh	Bhutan	India	Maldives	Nepal	Pakistan	Sri Lanka
Population (millions) 2014	31.3	158.5	0.77	1267.4	0.35	28.1	185.1	20.70
Urbanized population (%), 2014	26	34	38	32	44	18	38	18
Pop. below poverty line of US$1.25/day (%) 2006–2012	–	43.3	2.4	23.6	–	23.7	12.7	7
Human Development Index category, 2014	Low	Medium	Medium	Medium	Medium	Low	Low	High
Total adult literacy rate (%) 2007–2011, male/female	39.5/12.5	61/52	65/38.7 (2005)	66/60	98.4/98.4	73/48	69/40	93/90
Mean years of schooling, 2014	3.21	5.07	2.3	4.43	5.84	3.24	4.73	10.8
Primary gross enrolment ratio (%) 2008–2012, male/female	114/81	98/106 (2004)	110/112	116/116	111/107	–	104/85	99/99
Primary completion ratio (%), 2009/2013, male/female	48/19	70/80	96/101	96/97	111/103	97/107	79/67	98/97
Secondary gross enrolment ratio (%) 2008–2011, male/female	60/30	48/55	69/71	66/60	71/75 (2005)	46/41	40/30	90/100
Government spending on education as a % of GDP, 2011–2013	4.6	2.2	4.7	3.3	7.2	4.1	2.2	2.0
Constitutional guarantees for the right to free and compulsory education	Partial guarantee	Partial guarantee	Partial guarantee	Full guarantee	Partial guarantee	Partial guarantee	Partial guarantee	Full guarantee
Constitutional status of the right to free and compulsory education[4]	Article[5] since 2003	Act since 1990[6] (primary only)	Article[7] since 2007	Act since 2009[8]	Article[9] since 2008	Article[10] since 2007	Article[11] amended in 2010	Act since 1945[12]

Source: Right to Education Project 2013; UNDP 2015a; 2015b; UNICEF 2013; World Bank 2015.

posit that nation states may express initial reluctance for reforms, but that pressure from civil society actors in their own country who have powerful transnational alliances with international organizations and global solidarity movements can impel governments to adopt human rights-friendly policies. In the field of education, Mundy and Murphy (2001) have explored "the emergence and evolution of non-governmental organizational forms and actors engaged in transnational advocacy" to advance education for all (2001, 125). The authors cite various reasons for this rise, such as new entrants into the field of education, new coalitions among local and global organizations, and "unprecedented levels of interaction ... between non-governmental actors and intergovernmental bodies like UNESCO, UNICEF, and the World Bank" (2001, 126).

In the diverse cases of rights-based policies in South Asia – whether still under discussion and deliberation or already adopted – the boomerang effect and analyses of educational transnational advocacy networks provide useful frameworks to account for the influence of colonial legacies, historic and new foreign aid relationships, the rise of civil society actors throughout the subcontinent, and South–South cooperation across the globe and among the nations of South Asia. While it is beyond the scope of this chapter to trace the genealogy of educational policies and the diverse influences upon them in each South Asian nation, it is of significance to note the multiple roles and influences of civil society actors, donor organizations, intergovernmental agencies, and national discourses on educational policy-making in each of the country case studies that follow.

Notably, evidence of pressures from above (the international community), below (civil society and local social movements), and the effects of circulating policy discourses can be found in the trajectory of contemporary educational policy-making in South Asia. In India, the largest South Asian nation with a population of over one billion, the early 1990s, when policies adopted more rights talk, also marked a shift in economic policy, with the liberalization of trade and greater integration into the global economy. In Sri Lanka, despite having legislation on the right to education since 1945 and boasting an almost 92% adult literacy rate, national and international policy documents on education credit the international EFA movement for the revival of their commitment to improving the quality of education. Similar references are made to EFA declarations and to the MDGs in almost all the documents reviewed that were sourced from local and international NGOs, bi- and multi-lateral organizations, and academic literature for the various South Asian nations. In utilizing the same language and references, national- and local-level policy actors, as well as local social movements and NGOs, build pressure to be placed on policy decisions from above, below, and in the multi-directional way that transnational networks operate. This, however, does not mean that rights talk is used in the same way across contexts.

While human rights discourses, particularly the right to education, are influenced by global discourses that circulate, rights talk has a long history on the South Asian subcontinent. Human rights discourses have been an underlying feature of resistance and liberation movements in these countries, dating back to the anti-colonial struggles in the early- to mid-1900s. Much of the ways in which rights continue to be envisioned as something to be fought for and as platforms for social activism in South Asian countries draw from the anti-imperialist traditions from which they emerged (Cornwall and Nyamu-Musembi 2004). Given this historical context of rights, the role of civil society and local activists in pushing governments from below – despite adoption of rights language in policy texts given global influences – offers a complex dynamic of how local actors shape and deepen the many meanings of rights domestically.

The role of civil society in both the Constitutional Amendment and the drafting and passage of India's Right to Education Act (RTE) in 2009 offers a glimpse into how civil society actors (some of whom sat on the legislation's drafting committee) indigenize international rights discourses to make them locally meaningful and legitimate (Bajaj 2014). For example, India's Right to Education Act includes provisions not necessarily commonly associated with this right: 25% of private school seats must be made freely accessible to poor children, schools must have libraries with local periodicals such as newspapers and magazines, and parent–teacher committees must include proportional representation of women and marginalized groups (Bajaj 2014). These local interpretations may diverge from common understandings globally, but have given policy actors legitimacy for advocating these measures by subsuming a variety of reforms under the umbrella of educational rights.

In most other South Asian nations, efforts to make the right to education an enforceable right under domestic law are still underway. Although confined to primary schooling, Bangladesh enacted the right to education in its Compulsory Primary Education Act in 1990. The country has made significant improvement since then in raising school participation. Compared to 71% in 1980, the gross enrollment rate in primary schools increased to over 100% in 2004. However, the primary school completion rate is the lowest in the region at 70% for male students and 80% for female students (see Table 11.1). Nevertheless, Bangladesh has shown enormous progress in closing the gender gap in primary and secondary enrollment to the extent that girls' enrollment has exceeded that of boys' (see Table 11.1). Although this development in raising gender parity cannot be underestimated, it points to the high prevalence of child labor that often explains poor enrollment among boys across the region (Asadullah and Chaudhury 2009). In addition, Bangladesh has sought to address female education through conditional cash transfer programs over the years, and many NGOs have worked on girls' access to education, resulting in the current reverse gender gap. The gender gap has been found to be more prominent among poor households where the female stipend programs appear to have had the most impact (Ahmed et al. 2009). Overall, poverty in Bangladesh, the highest in South Asia, is seemingly the single largest factor explaining why outcomes fail to match policy discourses on the right to (primary) education in the country.

Local actors have been central to advancing discussions on the right to education in Pakistan. Under Pakistan's 18th Constitutional amendment in 2010, Article 25A guarantees free and compulsory education, but legal frameworks and mechanisms for redress have yet to be developed (Idara-e-Taaleem-o-Aagahi 2011). A local campaign, spearheaded by *Idara-e-Taaleem-o-Aagahi* (ITA), one of Pakistan's leading educational organizations, has developed plans and coordinated a petition of over a million signatures to influence government policy. Additionally, a Draft Bill was prepared by the United Nations Educational, Scientific and Cultural Organization (UNESCO) and presented to the Pakistan government (UNESCO 2012). This Draft Bill was open to the public for critical review and comparative analysis, using India's recently ratified RTE Act as an example. Pakistan's right to education campaign has provided greater visibility for human rights discourses at the grassroots level as opposed to government pronouncements and official usage of rights talk. Young educational activist and Nobel Peace Prize Laureate (2014), Malala Yousafzai's role as an advocate and spokesperson in local and international media has highlighted gender discrepancies in educational access, further strengthening the call for a constitutional right to education nationally.

Another mechanism through which local policy-making in Pakistan is often linked with rights discourses in global agreements on education is the significant presence of international NGOs and aid agencies in the country. In 2011, Pakistan was the fourth largest recipient of US foreign aid (Center for Global Development 2012). In 2010, the United States Agency for International Development's (USAID) education program in Pakistan was its largest in the world with budgeted funds of more than US$330 million (Birdsall 2010). Security considerations have been used to justify the prioritization of US aid to Pakistan's education sector (Birdsall 2010). The strategic use of rights talk for security-related initiatives in US foreign policy is an area that requires further scholarly attention, but it is worth noting here that rights language often infuses the rationale for military interventions as has been seen in Afghanistan and Pakistan since 2001.

Educational Rights Amidst Social and Political Conflict

Similarly positioned as a recipient of significant global aid for education, the Afghan Ministry of Education has been working in close collaboration with international agencies towards EFA goals by 2020, an extended date from the usual 2015 target given the severity of challenges facing Afghanistan's achievement of universal access and gender parity in education (Islamic Republic of Afghanistan 2011). Striving to increase enrollment and tackle profound barriers to girls' schooling, the government also faces a significant rural–urban divide (see Table 11.1).

The Afghan government is making simultaneous attempts to design a curricular policy that acknowledges local cultures and diverse realities across the country within a wider global discourse on peace and human rights. In her research on Afghan education, Jones (2007) traces the school curriculum in Afghanistan from the period of Soviet rule through the Taliban, following it to the present. She illustrates the destruction of the education system in Afghanistan for decades, partly in the name of a radical version Islam, by numerous wars fought in the country, and partly by different international and political groups trying to gain control over the nation. During this period, schools were either shut down or used to promote a curriculum ridden with the political ideologies of the ruling regime; for example, in what is now an oft-cited example, USAID funded the publication of textbooks during the Cold War with violent examples such as "My uncle has a weapon" and "'J' is for 'Jihad,'" and offered US financial support for the extremist *mujahedeen* in their bid to overthrow Soviet rule in the 1980s (*The Economist* 2012).

Despite the tumultuous history of Afghanistan's political transformations, significant changes in the education system have been brought about since the downfall of the Taliban in 2001. Efforts to revise the national curriculum have sought to link ideals of peace and human rights with concepts in Islam. The initial input for this revision was from NGOs working with and on behalf of the new government. In December 2002, at a national workshop facilitated by USAID, over 120 education experts from Afghanistan and other countries participated in drafting the new national curricular framework. By 2003, the government framework was approved by the Ministry of Education's Compilation and Translation Department. The new curriculum has been hailed by education researchers (Jones 2007; Georgescu 2007) for acknowledging the need for integrating new learning areas, such as "peace education, life-skills, human rights education, mine awareness, environmental education, [and] gender issues," among others (Georgescu 2007, 437). The preface to the Curriculum Framework Afghanistan (Department of Compilation and Translation 2003) reiterates that the new curriculum is based on the Afghan cultural context and that, while it notes the trauma of war particularly among children, it no longer focuses on war as it did in previous textbooks and curricular approaches.

Similarly emerging from violent conflict, Sri Lanka provides a unique example in the region from the perspective of human rights discourse and high levels of educational access and literacy, an indicator of quality. Much planning for EFA in Sri Lanka is consistent with many of the Jomtien and Dakar expectations (Little 2003, 83). As noted in Table 11.1, Sri Lanka is the only country in the region to be on a par with nations with high human development in education given its near-universal literacy rate (92%), high gross primary enrollments (99%), and regional record for the greatest mean years of schooling (9.3 years). Arguably, in the regions most affected by the civil war and ethnic conflict, access and quality education is harder to assess given that government reports may not disaggregate data by region. While the Universal Declaration of Human Rights was adopted in 1948 with provisions for the right to education, Sri Lanka had *already* instituted free education for all children from primary to university (tertiary) levels in 1945 through a bill passed by then-Education Minister Dr Kannangara prior to the nation's full political independence from Britain in 1948 (Rajapaksa 2009; Little 2010). Since the passage of the 1945 bill, it has been compulsory by law for Sri Lankan children aged 5–14 to attend school (Right to Education Project 2013); in 1997, this provision was further extended to make not only enrollment mandatory, but for attendance and completion to be as well (National Education Commission 2003).

It is difficult to trace a direct influence of global agreements on the policy and planning of Sri Lanka given their historic record of education access and attainment. According to Angela Little (2003), this was perhaps because Sri Lanka had already made considerable progress in enrollments by the time of the Jomtien EFA Conference (1990). Crediting the "democratic socialism of the pre-independence period" (2003, 10), which had a cumulative impact on the social development of the country, Little posits that "By the mid-1990s, national policies for primary education, especially quality improvements in primary education, were gaining ground both within the work of the high profile National Education Commission and the Ministry of Education and Higher Education. While the policies were consistent with EFA Goals, they appear not to have been influenced by them. The policy dialogue revolved around a discourse that was generated nationally and had national and intra-national referents" (2003, 19). Such independence in policy-making and localization within the context of the right to education, particularly given Sri Lanka's high rates of access and completion, offer a perspective that international discussions merely provided an echo of local efforts rather than an external impetus for educational policy reform, differing markedly from other nations in the region.

By contrast, Nepal has a very recent history of mass education and has made remarkable progress in increasing access despite political shifts and turmoil that have affected the provision of education. However, the expansion of mass schooling in the country has not yet sufficiently addressed the diversities of caste, language, gender, class, and recently, political affiliation. With frequent shifts in the political system over the past 70 years, the country has not had a consistent priority and policy in education. Historically, the monarchy in Nepal considered education the prerogative of the ruling elite and made no attempts to extend schooling to all citizens.

After the downfall of the Rana regime in 1951, mass schooling began to expand (IREWOC 2007). With the assistance of the United States Overseas Mission, in 1956 the Nepal National Educational Planning Commission suggested that the government of Nepal make primary education free and universal once the necessary infrastructure and the requisite teaching force was developed (Tuladhar n.d.). The Commission favored linguistic and cultural assimilation and suggested the Nepali language as the medium of instruction. In a country with over 97 languages and numerous other dialects, having a common language as the medium of instruction has continued to be a major impediment to facilitating the school attendance of children with diverse linguistic backgrounds (Tuladhar n.d.). These assimilationist policies excluded large sections of the population in the name of national integration until 1990 when the country transitioned from an absolute monarchy to a multi-party system (Singh and Jensen 2006). Influenced simultaneously by the EFA discussions globally, the National Education Commission of 1991, for the first time, considered the linguistic and cultural diversity of Nepal and suggested that primary education be offered in the mother tongue (Tuladhar n.d.). Donor aid for various projects, and shifting priorities by diverse regimes, has shaped Nepal's recent policy trajectory within a largely rural educational system.

Localizing Educational Discourses in Small South Asian nations

Small nations in South Asia often adopt reforms similar to their larger neighbors, in addition to – as seen in the cases of Bhutan and the Maldives – infusing educational policy and provision with the flavor of local values, customs, and religious ideals.

The trajectory of education in Bhutan presents an interesting manifestation of human rights and development relevant to the cultural values and traditions of Buddhism. Placing happiness at the core of public policy, decisions on education and other social rights are guided by the principles of Bhutan's Gross National Happiness (GNH) Index. GNH was designed in the 1970s in an attempt to define an indicator and concept that measures the quality of life or social progress in more complete terms than the commonly used gross domestic product (GDP), striking a balance between the spiritual and material values of well-being. The GNH indicators recognize nine components of happiness: (1) psychological well-being, (2) ecology, (3) health, (4) education, (5) culture, (6) living standards, (7) time use, (8) community vitality, and (9) good governance (Centre for Bhutan Studies and GNH Research 2013). This vision of holistic development is far beyond most international interpretations of human rights and education.

Education is a key indicator and increasingly a high priority for the country. Despite the low overall literacy rates noted in Table 11.1 (65% male and 38% female), when disaggregated by age, Bhutan's youth literacy rate (15–24 years) is 80% for young men and 68% for young women (UNICEF 2013), suggesting a trend toward greater educational attainment. Bhutan's education mission aspires to "build a broadly liberal, culturally sensitive, forward-looking, standards-based education system that combines the best of received wisdom of successive generations and the results of innovation and enterprise in the diverse fields of human endeavor" and envisions an "educated and enlightened society ... at peace with itself, at peace with the world" (Royal Government of Bhutan 2012).

The Bhutan Ministry of Education recognizes EFA goals and MDGs as a means to achieve the nation's development philosophy of enhancing "gross national happiness" (Centre for Educational Research and Development 2009). Bhutan has advanced its goal of universal access to primary education with a reported net primary enrollment ratio of 96% in 2012, up from 62% in 2000. Gender parity at both primary and secondary levels has also significantly improved. The ratio of girls to boys at the primary level increased from 82% in 2000 to 99% in 2012 (Royal Government of Bhutan 2012, 2013). Having nearly achieved EFA goals, the government is now focusing on strengthening the quality of teaching and learning (Royal Government of Bhutan 2012). Rights talk has influenced Bhutan, given the spur in educational expansion and enrollments arguably linked to the country's commitments under EFA and the MDGs, but local concepts such as happiness and psychosocial well-being also have permeated Bhutanese educational discourses.

The Maldives is another example of a small country in the region, like Bhutan, that has had recent successes in the expansion of primary education. The Maldives, with near universal rates of access, has sought to address the challenge of improving the quality of education. This multi-island nation is second in the region to Sri Lanka in its human development index and economic well-being (UNDP 2013; World Bank 2012). Made up of nearly 1200 islands, the smallest South Asian country is faced with the serious challenge of reaching out to all children with consistent quality standards amidst recent political turmoil and the real possibility of climate change subsuming the entire nation under water this century (Aljazeera 2013; Carrington 2013). Additionally, the training of teachers and their deployment across the islands is a major factor impeding the quality of education in the country, leading to a decline in enrollment over the past few years (World Bank 2012). Given this situation, most policy documents and reviews of education in the Maldives emphasize the need to invest in *human capital* in order to sustain its provisions for quality education for all (Republic of Maldives 2013; World Bank 2011; 2012). This presents another example of the strategic use of various discourses – human capital, human rights, and capabilities – in the formulation and circulation of educational policy in the South Asian region.

Horizontal Dimensions of Rights-Based Educational Policies in South Asia

As smaller South Asian nations often feel the ripple effects of policy shifts of their larger neighbors, cases of cross-learning among South Asian countries on policy related to educational rights are on the rise. For example, the Department of

Education in Nepal has been actively collaborating with the National University of Education Planning and Administration (NUEPA) in India in devising plans for effective decentralization (Singh and Jensen 2006). The Bangladeshi NGO, the Bangladesh Rural Advancement Committee (BRAC), the largest NGO in the world, has been active in designing flexible and adaptable schooling for marginalized and conflict-affected communities in Afghanistan and Sri Lanka in the region – as well as in East Africa – building on their over 40 years of success in improving educational outcomes in Bangladesh. Furthermore, active sections of civil society in India and Pakistan have been making an attempt to create avenues for cross-learning on development issues. The education communities in the two countries have been recognizing the similarities in their cultural and historical contexts of schooling.

While the right to education and educational access are a key area of horizontal collaboration in South Asia, there is considerable cross-learning in the area of accountability as well. One such example of a civil society partnership is the work of the Annual Status of Education Research (ASER) Centers in India and Pakistan, which conduct comprehensive research on education processes and outcomes to support evidence-based advocacy for education rights and quality. Such collaboration is greatly facilitated by donor aid. The horizontal dimensions of educational policy-making and the sharing of tools for state accountability – utilizing rights talk to galvanize aid and public support – is a particularly clear example of the "boomerang effect" in South Asia (Keck and Sikkink 1998). The international instrument – developed in one South Asian nation but circulated and exported to another country in the region through international aid and advocacy linkages with private foundations, the World Bank, and other donors – is utilized by subnational actors to pressure their own governments for reform and change.

Similar attempts at linkages and the creation of regional advocacy networks have been made to connect across borders by India and Bangladesh. In 2011, during the Global Action Week in Bangladesh, education practitioners from India and Bangladesh exchanged their experiences with opportunities and challenges in implementing their respective Right to Education Acts (CREATE 2011). Increased transnational advocacy networks on the subcontinent – regionalizing Keck and Sikkink's (1998) boomerang concept – utilize similar rights language and provide a useful example of how new coalitions and networks are connecting and growing in innovative ways on the South Asian subcontinent.

Concluding Thoughts

The impact of globalization and the framing of rights language in education policy in South Asia operate in complex and diverse ways. Rights-based claims to education of course have their critiques, particularly from international and comparative education scholars writing from a capabilities perspective (Robeyns 2006; Unterhalter 2003). Robeyns finds that, despite its justice orientation, the rights framework "sounds overtly rhetorical" with governments adopting guarantees while millions of children still languish out of school (2006, 76). Similarly, she notes that the reduction of the right to education to merely a legal right standing alone, without any connection to a moral imperative or comprehensive plan for implementation, risks confining the right to political discourse. Where cultural or social impediments to educational access exist, significant racial, caste, religious, or gender gaps may still persist if rights are limited to laws on paper to be enacted by governments and absent engagement with unequal social structures and hierarchies (Bajaj 2014).

Yet, rights frameworks have become the primary organizing force for diverse actors in educational policy-making. The localization of rights talk in diverse nation states in South Asia offers a window into how policy actors make sense of globally circulating discourses as well as how civil society actors pressure national governments to respond to educational demands on the ground. A unique example of this is the drafting committee of India's Right to Education Act, which included civil society actors in the core committee that put together to draft the bill alongside policy-makers (Bajaj 2014). As neighboring countries use the framework and example of India's legislation as a model and through conversations across their borders, diverse visions of educational rights infuse new legislative forms. Rights talk is mobilized differentially by diverse actors, and may shift over time and when examined at distinct levels (international, national, local) in diverse nations. Nevertheless, the increase and permanence of rights discourses in educational policy in the region are certainly worthy of further scholarly attention (Bajaj 2014).

Rights-based arguments for educational access, quality, equity, and accountability have rivaled the efficiency and rate of return arguments of decades past (and present) in calling for the expansion of schooling worldwide. South Asian nations' experiences with codifying the Right to Education (India, Bangladesh, Pakistan), juxtaposed with historic records of educational advancement prior to global declarations (the Maldives, Sri Lanka), and nations emerging from or currently facing civil and/or political unrest (Afghanistan, Nepal, Sri Lanka), suggest diverse and powerful relationships among education, citizenship, and human development. Many nations have not met the targets set forth in the EFA and MDG agreements (nor the recently launched Sustainable Development Goals set forth). While intergovernmental agencies, NGOs, and research institutes discuss strategies post-2015, questions remain about what rights and justice claims do for families and communities. Further exploration of educational policy, particularly those mandates that espouse universal notions of human rights, is needed to better understand gaps between policy and practice and the lived experiences of youth in complex and diverse regions such as South Asia.

Notes

1. Sections of this chapter are adapted from text that originally appeared in "The Productive Plasticity of Rights: Globalization, Education and Human Rights," in *Globalization and Education: Integration and Contestation Across Cultures* (second edition), edited by N. Stromquist and K. Monkman, 55–69. Lanham: Rowman and Littlefield.
2. This is akin to the vertical case study approach developed by Vavrus and Bartlett (2008), though, in this case, we are comparing *across* (not within) nations.
3. There have been debates over parents' right to choose the form of education that children will receive and the framing of education as a fundamental right. These debates are important to keep in mind in terms of how they impact tensions and contestations in the conceptualization of the right to education. For the purposes of this chapter, however, these debates have not significantly influenced the way South Asian policy-makers have engaged discourses of education.

4   Status to be determined by three stages: (1) Insertion/amendment of an Article in the Constitution, (2) Approval of the Bill by the Government, and (3) Passing of an Act, thereby making it a legal right.
5   Article 43: "Education is the right of all citizens of Afghanistan, which shall be provided up to the level of the B.A., free of charge by the state."
6   Article 17: "The State shall adopt effective measures for the purpose of establishing a uniform, mass-oriented and universal system of education and extending free and compulsory education to all children to such stage as may be determined by law."
7   Article 9(16). "The State shall provide free education to all children of school going age up to tenth standard (grade) and ensure that technical and professional education shall be made generally available and that higher education shall be equally accessible to all on the basis of merit."
8   Article 21A: "The State shall provide free and compulsory education to all children of the age of six to fourteen years in such manner as the State may, by law, determine."
9   Article 36(b): "Primary and secondary education shall be freely provided by the State."
10 Article 17(2): "Every citizen shall have the right to receive free education from the State up to secondary level as provided for in the law."
11 Article 25A: "The State shall provide free and compulsory education to all children of the age of five to sixteen years in such a manner as may be determined by law."
12 Article 27: "...complete eradication of illiteracy and complete assurance to all persons of the right to universal and equal access to education at all levels."
13 An NGO in India, the ASER Centre, which is part of the larger educational organization Pratham, developed a learning tool for language and mathematics to assess the quality of learning (as opposed to just rates of access). "Aser" means "impact" in Hindi and also stands for the Annual Status of Education Reports conducted by the organization. These annual reports have found that less than 50% of 5th standard (grade) students are able to read a simple standard two-level passage. Since launching the first annual report in 2005, ASER's model has been replicated in other parts of South Asia, such as Pakistan, and sub-Saharan Africa, offering communities greater information about how government schools fare. Citizen activists and policy-makers then have the ability to use this information for interventions and reform, which many have begun to do (Russell and Bajaj 2014).

References

Ahmed, M., S.A. Kazi, N.I. Khan, and R. Ahmed. 2007. "Access to Education in Bangladesh: Country Analytic Review of Primary and Secondary Education." *Consortium for Research on Educational Access, Transitions and Equity (CREATE)*. Retrieved from: www.create-rpc.org/pdf_documents/Bangladesh_CAR.pdf (accessed November 10, 2015).

Aljazeera. November 11, 2013. "Maldives Sinks into Greater Political Crisis." Retrieved from: www.aljazeera.com/news/asia/2013/11/maldives-sinks-into-deeper-political-crisis-2013111185028484704.html (accessed November 10, 2015).

Asadullah, M.N. and N. Chaudhury. 2009. "Reverse Gender Gap in Schooling in Bangladesh: Insights from Urban and Rural Households." *Journal of Development Studies*, 45(8): 1360–1380.

Bajaj, M. 2012. *Schooling for Social Change: The Rise and Impact of Human Rights Education in India*. New York, London: Bloomsbury.

Bajaj, M. 2014. "The Productive Plasticity of Rights: Globalization, Education and Human Rights," in *Globalization and Education: Integration and Contestation Across Cultures (second edition)*, edited by N. Stromquist and K. Monkman, 55–69. Lanham: Rowman and Littlefield.

Becker, G. 1964. *Human Capital*. Chicago: University of Chicago Press.

Birdsall, N. 2010. "U.S. Development Assistance to Pakistan's Education Sector (Fifth Open Letter to Ambassador Richard Holbrooke)." *CGD*. Retrieved from: www.cgdev.org/

publication/us-development-assistance-pakistan%E2%80%99s-education-sector-fifth-open-letter-ambassador (accessed November 10, 2015).

Boli, J., J. Meyer, and F. Ramirez. 1985. "Explaining the Origins and Expansion of Mass Education." *Comparative Education Review*, 29(2): 145–170.

Carrington, D. 2013. "The Maldives, a Fledgling Democracy at the Vanguard of Climate Change." *The Guardian*, September 26, 2013. Retrieved from: www.theguardian.com/environment/2013/sep/26/maldives-democracy-climate-change-ipcc (accessed November 10, 2015).

Centre for Bhutan Studies and GNH Research. 2013. "Gross National Happiness." Retrieved from: www.grossnationalhappiness.com (accessed November 10, 2015).

Centre for Educational Research and Development. 2009. "Quality of Education in Bhutan: Proceedings of National Seminar." Retrieved from: www.pce.edu.bt/sites/default/files/Quality%20of%20Education%20II.pdf (accessed November 10, 2015).

Center for Global Development. 2012. "Aid to Pakistan by the Numbers." *CGD*. Retrieved from: http://international.cgdev.org/page/aid-pakistan-numbers (accessed November 10, 2015).

Chopra, R. December 17, 2012. "India's Education-for-All Dream Comes to a Halt as Cash-Strapped Government Slashes RTE Budget." *India Today*. Retrieved from: http://indiatoday.intoday.in/story/cash-strapped-government-shaves-right-to-education-budget-hrd/1/238105.html (accessed November 10, 2015).

Cornwall, A. and C. Nyamu-Musembi. 2004. "Putting the 'Rights-Based Approach' to Development into Perspective." *Third World Quarterly*, 25(8): 1415–1437.

CREATE. 2011. "Round Table on Right to Education: Ensuring Access with Equity and Quality." Retrieved from: www.create-rpc.org/events/reports/BangladeshconferencereportMay2011.php (accessed November 10, 2015).

De, A., R. Khera, M. Samson, and S. Kumar. 2011. *Probe Revisited: A Report On Elementary Education In India*. New Delhi: Oxford University Press.

Department of Compilation and Translation. 2003. *Curriculum Framework Afghanistan*. Retrieved from: www.academia.edu/2914344/The_Curriculum_Framework_for_Primary_and_Secondary_Education_Afghanistan_ (accessed November 10, 2015).

Dreze, J. and A. Sen. 2013. *An Uncertain Glory: India and its Contradictions*. New Delhi: Penguin/Allen Lane.

Fuller, B. 1991. *Growing Up Modern*. New York, London: Routledge.

Georgescu, D. 2007. "Primary and Secondary Curriculum Development in Afghanistan." *Prospects*, 37: 427–448.

IREWOC. 2007. "Deprived Children and Education: Nepal." Retrieved from: www.crin.org/docs/Nepal_Education.pdf (accessed November 10, 2015).

Islamic Republic of Afghanistan. 2011. "Response to EFA Global Monitoring Report – 2011." Ministry of Education. Retrieved from: http://moe.gov.af/Content/files/077_GMR_ResponseV,%20English.pdf (accessed November 10, 2015).

Idara-e-Taleem-o-Aagahi. 2011. "Report on 'Right to Education' in Pakistan: A Draft for Discussion." Retrieved from: www.itacec.org/document/Right%20to%20Education_Report%20final%20ITA.pdf (accessed November 10, 2015).

Jones, A.M.E. 2007. "Muslim and Western Influences on School Curriculum in Post-War Afghanistan." *Asia Pacific Journal of Education*, 27(1): 27–40.

Little, A.W. 2003. "Education for All: Policy and Planning: Lessons from Sri Lanka." Department for International Development. Retrieved from: www.ioe.ac.uk/about/documents/educationforalledpaper46.pdf (accessed November 10, 2015).

Little, A.W. 2010. "The Politics and Progress of Basic Education in Sri Lanka." Retrieved from: www.create-rpc.org/pdf_documents/PTA38.pdf (accessed November 10, 2015).

Keck, M.E. and K. Sikkink. 1998. *Activists Beyond Borders: Advocacy Networks In International Politics*. Ithaca: Cornell University Press.

McCowan, T. 2013. *Education as a Human Right: Principles for a Universal Entitlement to Learning*. London: Bloomsbury.

Meyer, J., F. Ramirez, and Y. Nuhoğlu Soysal. 1992. "World Expansion of Mass Education, 1870–1980." *Sociology of Education*, 65(2): 128–149.

Mirembe, R. and L. Davies. 2001. "Is Schooling a Risk? Gender, Power Relations, and School Culture in Uganda." *Gender and Education*, 13: 401–416.

Mundy, K. 2008. "Civil Society and its Role in the Achievement and Governance of 'Education for All.'" Background Paper prepared for the Education for All Global Monitoring Report 2009. Paris: UNESCO.

Mundy, K. and L. Murphy. 2001. "Transnational Advocacy, Global Civil Society? Emerging Evidence from the Field of Education." *Comparative Education Review*, 45(1): 85–126.

National Education Commission, Sri Lanka. 2003. "Summary of Recommendations." Retrieved from: http://nec.gov.lk/wp-content/uploads/2014/04/National_Policy_2003.pdf (accessed November 10, 2015).

Perkins, D.H. 2001. *Economics of Development (fifth edition)*. New York: Norton.

Psacharopoulos, G. 1996. *Human Capital Underdevelopment: The Worst Aspects*. Washington, DC: The World Bank.

Rajapaksa, S. 2009. "Human Rights Commission of Sri Lanka: Human Rights Education in Schools Mandate." Asia-Pacific Human Rights Information Center. Retrieved from: www.hurights.or.jp/archives/pdf/education12/hreas-12-03-srilanka.pdf (accessed November 10, 2015).

Republic of Maldives. 2013. "Maldives Enhancing Education Development Project: Environmental and Social Assessment and Management Framework." Ministry of Education. Retrieved from: www.moe.gov.mv/wp-content/uploads/2013/05/MEEDP-ESAMF-March-2013.pdf (accessed November 10, 2015).

Right to Education Project. 2013. "National Constitutional Provisions – Sri Lanka: Education." Retrieved from: www.right-to-education.org/country-node/395/country-constitutional (accessed November 10, 2015).

Robeyns, I. 2006. "Three Models of Education: Rights, Capabilities and Human Capital." *Theory and Research in Education*, 4(1): 69–84.

Royal Government of Bhutan. 2012. "Annual Education Statistics – 2012." Ministry of Education. Retrieved from: www.education.gov.bt/documents/10156/12525/AES+2012-1 (accessed November 10, 2015).

Royal Government of Bhutan. 2013. "SAARC Development Goals: Country Report." Retrieved from: www.gnhc.gov.bt/wp-content/uploads/2013/10/SDG-Country-report-20132.pdf (accessed November 10, 2015).

Russell, S.G. and M. Bajaj. 2014. "Schools, Citizens and Nation-States," in *Education and International Development: Practice, Policy and Research*, edited by E. Unterhalter and T. McCowan, 93–109. London: Bloomsbury.

Satya. 2011. "The Need for Political Innovation to Make Education a Top Political Priority." Education in India. Retrieved from: http://prayatna.typepad.com/education/2011/02/political-innovation-to-make-education-a-top-political-priority.html (accessed November 10, 2015).

Schultz, T. 1961. "Investment in Human Capital." *American Economic Review*, 51(1): 1–17.

Schultz, T. 1980. "Nobel Lecture: The Economics of Being Poor." *The Journal of Political Economy*, 88(4): 639–651.

Shaukat, A. October 16, 2012. "Pakistan Risks Missing Education for all Target." *The Express Tribune*. Retrieved from: http://tribune.com.pk/story/452119/pakistan-risks-missing-primary-education-for-all-target (accessed November 10, 2015).

Singh, R.B. and K. Jensen. 2006. "Nepal Education Sector: Planning for Results in an Unstable Setting." *MfDR Principles in Action: Sourcebook on Emerging Good Practices*. Retrieved from: www.mfdr.org/Sourcebook/3-1stEdition.html (accessed November 10, 2015).

SIO. 2013. "All Political Parties Must Include Education as an Important Subject in their Agenda." Retrieved from: http://sio-india.org/all-political-parties-must-include-education-as-an-important-subject-in-their-agenda-demands-cac-sio-of-india (accessed November 10, 2015).

The Economist. 2012. "Textbooks from Afghanistan: Not yet History." Retrieved from: www.economist.com/blogs/banyan/2012/11/textbooks-afghanistan (accessed November 10, 2015).

Tuladhar, G. (n.d.). "Status of Education in Nepal and Development Plan." Retrieved from: http://web.isc.ehime-u.ac.jp/ice/6-1@Gangalal%20Tuladhar_text%20_8p.pdf (accessed November 10, 2015).

UN. 2014. "The Universal Declaration of Human Rights." Retrieved from: www.un.org/en/documents/udhr/index.shtml (accessed November 10, 2015).

UNDP. 2013. "Country Profiles and Human Development Indicators." Retrieved from: http://hdr.undp.org/en/countries (accessed November 10, 2015).

UNDP. 2015a. "Public Expenditure on Education (% of GDP) (%)." Retrieved from: http://hdr.undp.org/en/content/expenditure-education-public-gdp (accessed November 10, 2015).

UNDP. 2015b. "International Human Development Indicators." Retrieved from: http://hdr.undp.org/en/countries (accessed November 10, 2015).

UNESCO. 2010. "2010 Global Monitoring Report: Reaching the Marginalized." Paris: UNESCO. Retrieved from: www.unesco.org/new/en/education/themes/leading-the-international-agenda/efareport/reports/2010-marginalization (accessed November 10, 2015).

UNESCO. 2012. "UNESCO Hails Passage of Right of Free Education Bill by the Senate in Pakistan." Retrieved from: www.unescobkk.org/education/news/article/unesco-hails-passage-of-right-to-free-education-bill-by-the-senate-in-pakistan (accessed November 10, 2015).

UNICEF. 2011. "Disparities in Education in South Asia: A Resource Tool Kit." UNICEF Regional Office for South Asia. Retrieved from: www.unicef.org/rosa/Countering_Disparities_in_Education_Toolkit__2011.pdf (accessed November 10, 2015).

UNICEF. 2013. "Info by Country: South Asia." Retrieved from: www.unicef.org/infobycountry/southasia.html (accessed November 10, 2015).

Unterhalter, E. 2003. "Education, Capabilities and Social Justice." Retrieved from: http://unesdoc.unesco.org/images/0014/001469/146971e.pdf (accessed November 10, 2015).

Vavrus, F. and L. Bartlett. 2008. *Critical Approaches to Comparative Education: Vertical Case Studies from Africa, Europe, the Middle East, and the Americas.* New York: Palgrave Macmillan.

World Bank. 2011. "Human Capital for a Knowledge Society: Higher Education in the Maldives." Human Development Unit: South Asia Region. Retrieved from: http://siteresources.worldbank.org/INTSOUTHASIA/Resources/Human_capital_for_a_knowledge_society_higher_education_in_the_Maldives.pdf (accessed November 10, 2015).

World Bank. 2012. "Human Capital for a Modern Society: General Education in the Maldives." Human Development Unit: South Asia Region. Retrieved from: www-wds.worldbank.org/external/default/WDSContentServer/WDSP/IB/2012/10/03/000333037_20121003020650/Rendered/PDF/729930WP0Maldi0IC0discloed010010120.pdf (accessed November 10, 2015).

World Bank. 2013a. "South Asia Overview." Retrieved from: www.worldbank.org/en/region/sar/overview (accessed November 10, 2015).

World Bank. 2013b. "Brief on Education in South Asia." Retrieved from: http://web.worldbank.org/WBSITE/EXTERNAL/COUNTRIES/SOUTHASIAEXT/0,,contentMDK:21487829~pagePK:146736~piPK:146830~theSitePK:223547,00.html (accessed November 10, 2015).

World Bank. 2015. "Databank: Education." Retrieved from: http://data.worldbank.org/topic/education (accessed November 10, 2015).

Chapter 12

Early Childhood Education and Care in Global Discourses[1]

Rianne Mahon

Early childhood education and care (ECEC) has come to occupy an important place on the global policy agenda. Although many have endorsed its importance, differences arise in identifying the issues ECEC is designed to address and the recommended course of action. While there are many issues such as public vs. private financing and auspice, center vs. home-based care, a broad distinction can be drawn between two basic positions. The first sees ECEC as simply a part of a larger "early childhood development" (ECD) program. Drawing heavily on Anglo-American knowledge originating in domestic poverty reduction strategies, this version has come to form an important part of the current development discourse, which targets the poor, aiming to enable them (or rather, their children) to participate effectively in globalized markets in the future. The second envisages ECEC as part of a broader set of universal social rights embedded in the welfare state. This version traces its roots to Western European experiences. Its proponents recognize that "childhood contexts and processes are shaped by human action, profoundly social … and at all times mediated by cultural processes, including competing cultural views of young children's needs" (Woodhead 2006, 21).

International non-governmental organizations (INGOs) like the Bernard van Leer Foundation, the Aga Khan Foundation, Save the Children, the Christian Children's Fund, and the Soros Foundation have helped to draw global attention to the importance of ECEC. The focus in this chapter, however, will be on the role of international organizations. Although the United Nations Children's Fund (UNICEF) has played an important role in promoting national ECEC policies in the developing world, its primary contribution has been "on the ground." The chapter focuses instead on the three main international organizations involved in the production and dissemination of policy knowledge in support of ECEC – the World Bank, the Organisation for

The Handbook of Global Education Policy, First Edition.
Edited by Karen Mundy, Andy Green, Bob Lingard, and Antoni Verger.
© 2016 John Wiley & Sons, Ltd. Published 2016 by John Wiley & Sons, Ltd.

Economic Co-operation and Development (OECD), and the United Nations Educational, Scientific and Cultural Organization (UNESCO). The World Bank, which best exemplifies the first position, has come to regard itself "as an important contributor to the debate about childhood" (Penn 2002, 122). Moreover, "the combination of its financing levels and the force with which it promotes its views help account for its emergence as the strongest player in the world of multilateral education" (Jones and Coleman 2005, 94). The OECD has long been an important forum for reflection on common policy concerns of the advanced capitalist countries, although its membership now includes certain Eastern European and Latin American countries and it is involved in outreach programs with other parts of the world. Its conception of ECEC, as reflected in *Starting Strong*, produced through its Education Directorate, is informed by the second position. UNESCO is less directly involved in knowledge production than the first two, but plays a key role in ECEC advocacy as part of its broader concern with children's rights to education. It does, however, commission studies and in this sense can function as a place of encounter between the contending positions.

The chapter opens with an elaboration of the broad distinction outlined above between ECEC as part of ECD programs targeting the poor and ECEC as social right. The second section focuses on ECEC as it appears in the discourses of the World Bank, while the third focuses on the OECD. The final section looks at the ideas that appear in work commissioned by UNESCO especially in its capacity as official monitor of "Education for All." For the World Bank and UNESCO, both of which have offices in the field, I focus on documents produced at, or commissioned by, head offices. This caveat is important, for as Mosse (2004) warns, there is often a gap between policy enunciated in documents and practice in the field.

ECEC as a Traveling Idea

As other contributors to this volume argue, education has only recently moved from being viewed largely as a domestic concern to become a matter for global debate. This is particularly true for ECEC, not surprisingly, given the prevalence of traditional ideas about the early years. International organizations were largely not involved in discussions of the importance of ECEC until the 1970s and initially their interest was limited to preschool education. Very young children (0–3) were assumed to be at home with their mothers. The concept of ECEC had yet to be invented and it was only in the 1990s that ECEC became a global issue. The timing can to some extent be linked to the push-back against the brute neo-liberalism of the 1980s, which, in the North, was represented by the triumph of Thatcher in Britain and Reagan in the USA, and in the South, by the international financial institutions' embrace of the Washington Consensus, which imposed policies of fiscal austerity, privatization, deregulation, and the liberalization of trade and restrictions on foreign direct investment. The inclusion of ECEC and its expansion to encompass the very young can also be traced, however, to the rise to prominence of new (and competing) knowledge claims.

The first set of ideas bases its claims to scientific truth on a mixture of neuro-scientific research highlighting the importance to brain formation of "the early years" (from neonatal to three), and the work of American economists like James

Heckman, whose cost–benefit analysis of investment in human capital at different stages of the lifecycle strongly favors the very young. Emanating largely from US experiments with highly disadvantaged children, this set of ideas has come to hold an important place within the global poverty reduction agenda, where "investment" in the human capital of the very poor aims to enable them (or rather, their children) to participate in globalizing markets.

In the 1990s major American foundations began to distil the domestic policy implications of neuro-scientific research into brain formation. The Carnegie-sponsored study, *Starting Points* (Carnegie Task Force on Meeting the Needs of Young Children 1994) focused attention on the "quiet crisis" affecting American children under three due to inadequate prenatal care, the rising number of lone parents, the substandard daycare available to the adult worker family, and poverty. In 2000, the Committee on Integrating the Science of Early Childhood Development, sponsored by the Board on Child, Youth and Family, the National Research, and the Institute of Medicine, published the oft-cited study, edited by Jack P. Shonkoff and Deborah H. Phillips (2000), *From Neurons to Neighborhoods: the Science of Early Childhood Development*, which conveyed much the same message but added persistent racial and ethnic disparities to the list of problems ECD could address. Heckman's work is similarly very widely cited. Those basing their claims on "neuroscience," however, rarely cite those who contest the too-ready translation of such findings into education policy such as Bruer (1999).

The list of ECD interventions considered appropriate include prenatal care, home visits/parental education programs, and "quality" ECEC – for poor children. As examples of the latter, these studies frequently cite programs targeting poor, and frequently black, American children such as the Carolina Abecedarian project and the High/Scope Perry Pre-School project, which worked with poor black children with low IQ scores and compared the school performance of those who had received cognitive stimulation in the special preschools with those who did not. Heckman's work on early childhood similarly can be traced to his discovery of and reflection on racism in the US south. As he noted in a 2005 interview, "Trying to understand the sources of black-white disparity will occupy me throughout my life. It's actually what led me to my recent work on early childhood, because when one starts looking at gaps in achievement among racial and ethnic groups, one realizes that despite many efforts to improve the circumstances of the African-American population, a lot of progress remains to be accomplished."[2]

While much of the basis for these scientific truth claims is thus rooted in American experiments in poverty reduction at home, as we shall see, the World Bank has been active in extending the message to the Global South. In this it has been aided by the work of the Global Child Development Group and the Early Childhood Development Group, which collaborated on a series of papers for *The Lancet*, documenting "the risks and interventions to improve early childhood development in low resource countries." As the Group's website notes,

> Developmental outcomes for at least 200 million children in resource-starved countries have been severely impacted by multiple risks including poverty, poor nutrition and lack of stimulating environments. Prevalence of the risk factors is often cumulative in these settings, aggravating the adverse effects on the development of one of the world's most

vulnerable groups. Interventions focussing on improved dietary intake of complementary foods and micronutrients, in combination with responsive feeding and early stimulation and care, have shown to improve children's developmental status in conditions of poverty (Global Child Development Group n.d.).

One of the leading – and oft-cited – experts conducting such studies is Sally Grantham-McGregor, Emeritus Professor at the Institute for Child Health, University College London, member of the Group's Secretariat and consultant to a range of international organizations including UNICEF and UNESCO. Grantham-McGregor's research included studies of the impact of home visits and parent education programs on "severely malnourished," "stunted," and "low birth weight" children in Jamaica. Like the US research, this work is motivated by what anthropologist Tanya Li (2007) calls the "will to improve," but in the process it also "renders technical" the problem and the solution. The image of the child conveyed is that of a victim, not of the forces generating global inequality, but of parental ignorance, which is to be combated by parental education in the arts of proper nourishment for the brain as for the belly.

The alternative, rights-oriented discourse also traces its roots to the North, in this case to the Nordic countries and the Emilia Romagna region of Italy. The Nordic countries were among the first to offer integrated ECEC, breaking through the divide between care for young children whose parents were working and preschool education or kindergarten for children of the prosperous middle class. In this system, ECEC is guided by *pedagogues*, who are informed by a vision of the whole child "social, physical, emotional and intellectual" (Cohen *et al.* 2004, 140). Moreover, unlike the US focus on poor children, the Nordic ECEC system aimed at universal coverage from the outset, reflecting its location within a broader welfare system enshrining the social rights of denizens. The embedding of ECEC in such a system is important. As Korpi and Palme's (1998) "paradox of redistribution" suggests, social policy regimes based on the principle of universality tend to be more generous and of better all-round quality, not the least because they include the more vocal middle and upper classes who are in a position to demand quality programs. Conversely, services targeting poor people – the "other" – tend to be poor services.

The Reggio system was developed in Emilia Romagna, one of the richest regions in Italy. This plus the fact that the region has long been a stronghold of the Left provided fertile ground for the development of high quality social services that are atypical of the country as a whole. The Reggio ECEC system is based on the conception of the child articulated by Reggio's founder, Loris Malaguzzi. In contrast to the view of child as victim or object of study discussed above, here the child is understood as the "rich child," rich not in monetary terms but as "an active learner," "seeking the meaning of the world from birth, a co-creator of knowledge, identity, culture and values"; a citizen, the subject of rights, not needs; and born with "a hundred languages" (Moss 2010, 1). While here too the pedagogue has an important role to play, this is tempered by the "understanding that reality is subjective, knowledge is partial and 'different readings of the world' – not only that of the educator – are possible" (Moss 2010, 1).

As Li's analysis of critical politics suggests, those who are active in developing and sharing this second vision are similarly motivated by the will to improve, but also by the will to empower: "Their vision of improvement involves people actively claiming the rights and taking on the duties of democratic citizenship" (2007, 22). They also recognize that all knowledge is partial, provisional, and local. Thus, while the ideals and ideas behind this view of ECEC take their inspiration from Western European examples, those who are inspired by this approach – like Peter Moss[3] (University of London), Gunilla Dahlberg (Stockholm), and John Bennett, former Director of UNESCO's Early Childhood and Family unit and key figure behind the OECD's original *Starting Strong* reviews – are careful to recognize the limits and context-specificity of their knowledge. In addition scholars like Helen Penn (University of East London) have been working with counterparts in "the majority world" to develop context-appropriate alternatives that build on local knowledges. The "rich child" in other words is not to be found only in the North but also resides in the South in the urban barrios and rural areas as well as in leafy upper class suburbs.

As will be clear in the following sections, the division of the ECEC discourse outlined above is real, but can also be overdrawn to the extent that it suggests there is no possibility of dialogue across the two solitudes. In fact, Moss recognizes that "there is considerable diversity within the camps on each side of the divide, which itself is not a total barrier: there are crossing places and observation points" (Moss 2007, 236). Thus, while the Bank has played a key role in the global dissemination of the modernist view and the OECD's *Starting Strong* was inspired especially by the critical alternative, the two UN organizations, UNESCO in a sense represents a space where these ideas co-exist.

From Structural Adjustment to Investing in Children: The World Bank

Of all the international organizations, the World Bank is best placed to promote its vision of ECEC through its spending power. In 2006 alone it approved US$22.3 billion in loans and grants. While in the 1980s it used loan conditionality to promote harsh neo-liberal structural adjustment policies, by the end of the decade it had begun to adopt "adjustment with a human face." With James Wolfensohn's Presidency in 1995, the balance clearly shifted in favor of a "softer" version that included "investing in (poor) people." A key figure who helped convince the Bank of the importance of investing in early childhood development was Robert Myers of the Consultative Group on Early Childhood Care and Development. In response to criticisms of its structural adjustment policies, the Bank commissioned Myers to write a report (Myers 1987), which Bank insiders used to make ECD part of the Bank's broader social investment project. The emphasis on ECD was reinforced with the 1989 hiring of paediatrician Mary Eming Young as Child Development Specialist in the Human Development Network. By 1992 ECD components began to appear in Bank educational projects and numerous studies of the issue were commissioned between 1998 and 2002. The Bank also hosted two major international ECD conferences (1996, 2000), as well as several regional conferences, on ECD and became involved in several ECD projects in partnership with other international organizations like UNICEF, and INGOS such as Save the Children and the Bernard van Leer Foundation.

The Bank's ECD research draws heavily on the Anglo-American research discussed above, filtered through its "investing in people" lens. For instance Young's first public report (Young 1995) referred to the Carnegie and Rand studies, while later publications drew on Heckman's argument for the efficiency of investment in the early years. Subsequent studies, such as *Investing in Young Children* (World Bank 2011a) and *No Small Matter: The Impact of Poverty, Shocks and Human Capital Investment* (World Bank 2011b) similarly refer to Heckman's work, the Shonkoff and Phillips publication, and evaluations of the High/Scope Perry Preschool and Abecedarian programs. The primary interest is in promoting human capital formation, by improving "school readiness" and laying the foundations for success in school to subsequent labor market performance. In line with the American social model that underlies much of the US research on which it draws, the Bank argues that ECD investments should target the very poor. In this it projects the "will to improve" the lot of poor children in the South. Thus, investment in ECD is partly cast as "the right thing to do." In making the normative case, Bank experts draw not only on the global child rights discourse referred to above, but also on liberal philosophers like Rawls and Sen. The liberal developmentalist lens is reflected in the following statement:

> a minimum notion of what constitutes "social justice" would exclude any state in which some groups of children are deprived of having a reasonable chance to live a productive life just because they are born poor. Even societies that are unable, or unwilling, to provide a "level playing field" … may want to put policies in place that allow all who have reasonable talents and are willing to use them, a chance to enjoy at least a minimum level of well-being. (van der Gaag and Tan 1998, 32).

In other words, ECD for poor children may contribute to equality of opportunity, at least for the children of the poor.

The normative claims are incorporated into a renewed development paradigm, which has been modified in some of its detail but not in the basic perspective. Expert knowledge is thus brought to bear in identifying the "failures" of those to be developed and prescribing the "appropriate" (technical) solution. Thus *Investing in Young Children* notes that in low and middle income countries, poor children fall behind their better-off counterparts "in part because poor children tend to receive less speech directed toward them and because the speech they do hear tends to have reduced lexical richness and sentence complexity" (World Bank 2011a, 16). That is, their parents are assumed to be ignorant of the "right way" to nourish and to raise children. In the absence of ECD, poor parents are thus likely to pass poverty onto their children because "they are also more likely to have low productivity and income, to provide poor care for their children, and to contribute to the intergenerational transmission of poverty and less likely to contribute to the growth of their country" (2011a, 17). The document does recognize in passing that the higher exposure of poor children to "risk factors" like malnutrition, poor health, "unstimulating" home environments, and even child maltreatment (2011a, 17) may be partly due to "supply side" factors such as "unequal distribution of resources and services for young children," but it leaves largely unexplored the unequal class, gender, and race/ethnicity relations that reproduce such inequalities, not to mention the way in which its own economic advice has reinforced these. Instead, the main weight of the evidence cited places the blame on the poor themselves and their "parenting failures." A paper by Bank staffer, Katrina Kosec (2011), did explore the impact of local power structures on patterns of expenditure but such examples are rare.

Recognizing that "few budgets are reallocated after a finance minister has had a conversion on the road to Davos" (World Bank 2011a, 3), more recent Bank documents include evidence from the Global South – evidence, however, produced from within the same paradigm. For instance, to establish the "universality" of its truth claims with regard to child development, the Bank cites (and supports) the work of Grantham-McGregor and others, like Patrice Engle and Susan Walker, associated with the Global Child Development Group based at the University of West Indies in Jamaica. While the site of the experiments has shifted from the USA to the Global South, the basic assumptions about child development have not. Thus Grantham-McGregor and her team evaluated the impact of nutrition programs and home visits on "stunted," "malnourished" children in the South, undervaluing local knowledges about child-raising. Their solutions focus on treating the individual, while ignoring the wider web of relationships within which s/he is embedded.

What role does ECEC play in Bank-favored ECD programs? In their contribution to *No Small Matter*, Alderman and Vegas recommend the extension of conditional cash transfers – a Bank-promoted program that provides incentives to keep children in school – to preschool education for children from three and up. As elsewhere (a point rarely acknowledged in the Bank's studies), the Bank recognizes that there is little ECEC for children under three even though urbanization and the rise in mothers' labor force participation will generate increasing demand in the future. In these circumstances, the Bank advocates support for non-formal programs like Bolivia's *Proyecto Integral de Desarrollo Infantil* or Colombia's *Programa Hogares Communitarios de Bienestar*. Such programs enlist local mothers as caregivers, providing them with training in proper nutrition, hygiene, and techniques of cognitive and socio-emotional stimulation. For instance *Investing in Children* argued that:

> Mothers can be effective ECD providers in home-based programs, such as in Colombia and Bolivia. The women receive training and minimum assistance, on credit, to meet facility standards. They are "accredited" as eligible to provide day-care services. Such efforts enable providers to benefit from public subsidies while also participating in a competitive, choice-based system of ECD programs. In addition, they benefit parents by increasing the number and type of care options to choose from (e.g., based on convenience, proximity, flexibility of hours). By helping to create new providers locally, government helps consolidate the players, power, position, and perception of early child development, primarily at the local level. (Young 1995, 386–387)

Yet such programs do not offer local women the kind of employment opportunities they hoped for. For example, one of the Bank's "exemplary" programs in Medellin, Colombia, "has almost petered out in disarray as women who had been hired as childminders objected to lack of employment benefits and security in the projects" (Penn 2002, 128), while the Bank-supported Bolivian project was terminated before completion (Alderman and Vegas 2011). The Bank's advice to the Brazilian government – to focus on such programs rather than expanding universal preschool – has supported the informalization of care work, undoing years of effort to integrate daycare and preschools in a unified ECEC system (Rosemberg 2006).

ECEC thus forms a part of the World Bank's post-Washington Consensus development discourse, in which the child holds a central position. In this discourse, impoverished parents threaten to pass their poverty onto their "malnourished" and "stunted" children through their inadequate parenting practices – unless governments, the private sector, NGOs, and international donors invest in ECD. Scientific support is claimed for the benefits of targeted prenatal care, parent education, and preschool programs, designed by experts. Such programs promise a better future through enhanced school readiness, school performance, and, in the longer run, better jobs, higher incomes, and a stronger contribution to the nation's economy.

ECEC for OECD Countries: Gender Equality ... and Children's Rights

Unlike the Bank, the OECD has historically focused its attention on the policy challenges facing the advanced capitalist countries that constitute the majority of its members. While also relying on experts, the relationship between the Secretariat and its member states is based on a liberal mode of governance, typified by its renowned peer review process (Mahon and McBride 2008; Porter and Webb 2008). Peer review works to generate (and to structure) dialogue among "peers" – representatives of the member countries – facilitated by experts in the Secretariat. Through these meetings "the national representatives bring their own experiences together, complemented with reports, at a central location, where relationships from around the globe are condensed to a manageable size and studied, a form of experimentation that can generate new relationships" (Porter 2012, 542–543). As we shall see, in conducting its research into ECEC, *Starting Strong* utilized the peer review technique, taking care to enlist not only the relevant officials within each of the participating countries, but also ECEC experts to conduct the reviews.

Under the influence of John Bennett, who had been deeply involved in the UN Committee on the Rights of the Child, *Starting Strong* viewed ECEC as a right for all children. It therefore rejected the targeted approach favored by the Bank and its associated view of the "child as human-capital-in-the-making," stressing instead a view of children as active learners and citizens in the here and now. The background study, prepared by Sheila Kamerman, highlighted the need to balance between adequate financial and other supports from central governments and strong local, including parental and community, involvement. This would be echoed in the final report, where it emphasized the potential role for the national government as "guarantor of democratic discussion and experimentation at the local level" (OECD 2006, 220). Consistent with the new science of the development of the brain, care for the under threes was flagged as "the major child care issue for the 1990s" (Kamerman 1998, 25), although parental leave also has an important part to play. Kamerman also flagged the European Union's Childcare Network's alternative perspective on "quality":

- "quality is a relative concept, based on values and beliefs;
- defining quality is a process, and this process is important in its own right, providing opportunities to share, discuss and understand values, ideas, knowledge and experience;
- the process should be participatory and democratic, involving different groups including children, parents and families and professionals working in services;
- the needs, perspectives and values of these groups may sometimes differ;
- defining quality should be seen as a dynamic and continuous process, involving regular review and never reaching a final, 'objective', statement." (European Childcare Network 1996, C7–C8).

This approach, which differs markedly from the technical scales developed by experts associated with the modernist paradigm, would be taken up and developed in *Starting Strong*.

From the outset *Starting Strong* placed the child as agent at the center. While this is clear through all the individual country reviews and Volume I of the report, Volume II especially highlighted the importance of placing "the well-being, early development and learning at the core of ECEC work, *while respecting the child's agency and natural learning strategies*" (OECD 2006, 207; emphasis added). Noting that for many countries this remains a challenge, the report singled out the Norwegian and Swedish systems for their recognition of the agency of the child and Reggio Emilia's outstanding work on "listening, project work and documentation as major means of working with young children" (OECD 2006, 207). Critical of the narrow "school readiness" discourse, the report argued "that the early childhood centre should become a community of learners, where children are encouraged to participate and share with others, and where learning is seen as primarily interactive, experiential and social. Echoing the UNESCO Faure report, *Learning to be, learning to do, learning to learn and learning to live together* are each important goals for young children" (2006, 219; emphasis in original). The focus on the child did not mean that gender equality was forgotten. *Starting Strong* underlined the importance of both drawn between "gender equality" – women's right to equal treatment in recruitment and access to work; equal pay for work of equal value, and equal opportunities for advancement – and "gender equity" – "equal sharing of child rearing and domestic work" (OECD 2006, 30). Accordingly, it took a critical view of part time work, long maternal/child care leave, and the lack of genuinely shared "parental" leave.

In contrast to the Bank's "rendering technical" of poverty, *Starting Strong II* recognized that ECEC could only form part of the solution because child poverty was rooted not in the "welfare dependency" of lone parents or parental lack of human capital, but rather in the wider political context that resulted in insufficient transfer payments, the underemployment of parents, and widening income inequalities (OECD 2006, 23). In other words, it located the problem in the wider political economy of "flexibilized" labor markets and restructured welfare states, the product of neo-liberal restructuring. Thus, its solutions also cast the net more widely: "governments need to employ upstream fiscal, social, and labour policies to reduce family poverty and give young children a fair start in life" (OECD 2006, 206). ECEC needs to be situated as part of a broader system of social rights.

Child care staff also received considerable attention. *Starting Strong* was thus critical of the "low recruitment and pay levels ... the lack of certification in early childhood pedagogy...; the feminisation of the workforce; and the failure of pedagogical teams to reflect the diversity of the neighbourhoods they serve" found in many countries (OECD 2006, 17). It argued that appropriate training, fair wages, and good working conditions were critical to the provision of quality care (OECD 2001, 11). *Starting Strong II* devoted a whole chapter to early child pedagogy. Here it highlighted the difference between "school readiness" approaches (France and the English-speaking countries) and the social pedagogy tradition in the Nordic and Central European countries. As it argued, the latter represents "an approach to children combining care, upbringing and learning, without hierarchy" (OECD, 2006, 59).

Although *Starting Strong* recognized the skills required to deliver quality ECEC, it also defined quality in terms of "a participatory approach to quality improvement and assurance" with the stress laid on evaluating "*contextual* (funding, regulation and support by the state), *structural* (e.g. programme standards, stimulating learning environments, teacher certification, strong staff supports, professional development etc.) and *process* variables (the relational and pedagogical skills of educators)" (OECD 2006, 209–210) rather than individual child outcome or performance standards. For *Starting Strong*, as for the European Childcare Network, genuine quality is understood as a moving target, defined through a dialogical, democratic process involving staff, parents, and children. Thus aware of the links between expert knowledge and power, it cautioned:

> In speaking with parents, an awareness of power relations is necessary. Despite the unique interests and knowledge of parents in regard to their children, the tendency to know better than parents is difficult to overcome. Sensitivity to socio-cultural difference is also needed... To avoid prejudice, gender assumptions, class attitudes or ethnocentrism, more anthropological, political and socio-historical analysis of child rearing and early child practice is needed ... and of course more rigorous training of educators and administrators in anti-bias attitudes. (OECD 2006, 215)

In this discourse then, while pedagogues have expertise, so do parents and it is important for the former to enter into genuine dialogue with the latter. This perspective on parents and their knowledge is largely absent from the Bank's discourse.

Starting Strong structured its investigation in such a way as to promote dialogical interaction with officials and others in the countries included in the study. It felt strongly that "the participatory nature of the review process allows national policy makers to debate with the review experts, and become familiar with principles, standards and practices that are current in the early childhood policy field in other countries" (OECD 2006, 237). Such discussion created space for political mobilization for ECEC at multiple scales. The circulation of its country and synthetic reports among childcare advocacy networks in each country was important but the team also designed the research process to include network building among childcare advocates, experts, and public officials. The four international workshops played an important role here. As *Starting Strong II* notes, "this systematic exchange of ideas on policy issues and their implementation was helpful and allowed participants to establish their own 'critical friend' networks" (OECD 2006, 233). To continue the work, the final conference, held in Reggio Emilia in September 2006, passed a resolution designed to give this network an institutional base within the OECD. Housed in the Flemish-speaking Belgian ECEC system (*Kind und Gezin*), the network functioned independently for a couple of years until it was again taken over by the Education and Training Policy Division. While there were concerns that this would lead to a shift in emphasis to "school readiness," examination of *Starting Strong III* suggests that, while it adopted a technical format (a "toolbox"), it incorporated much of the discourse of *Starting Strong II*.

First, *Starting Strong III*, which offers a "quality toolbox for ECEC," hews to the alternative conception of quality. Thus it argues that "defining and assuring quality should be a participatory and democratic process, involving different groups, including children, parents, families and professionals who work with children" (OECD 2012, 38). Moreover, in no small part because of the emphasis on a dialogical view of quality, national – and local – circumstances will affect the way quality is defined: "The way in which quality is developed and the priorities and perspectives which are emphasised may vary across countries; and the enforcement of regulations is more likely to succeed when the authorities engage in consultative policy making and management and build up a general consensus about the need and relevance of standards" (2–12, 39).

While cross-national differences are recognized and respected throughout, *Starting Strong III* continues to favor integrated ECEC systems: "If … childhood is seen as an important stage in life, countries are more likely to integrate 'child care' and 'early education'; which contributes to a more holistic child development and greater clarity in objectives for centres, practitioners, parents and other stakeholders" (2012, 25). It also stresses the importance of qualified staff, good working conditions, and fair pay levels. In making this argument, the report cites Shonkoff and Phillips but it also refers to A. Elliott's (2006) emphasis on "the ability of the staff member to create a better pedagogic environment" (2012, 36), which means involving the child as an active participant in the process. In recommending a national curriculum for children aged 0–6, *Starting Strong III* again stresses that this should facilitate "customised learning and local adaptions … in partnership with staff, families, children and communities" (2012, 10). The benefits of quality ECEC for children living in poverty are by no means ignored. Thus, the report refers to the High/Scope Perry Pre-School and Head Start programs as well as Heckman's work. At the same time, although it acknowledges that such studies are used to support an argument for targeted programs, *Starting Strong III* clearly recognizes that "targeted programmes focused on family income disparity may not be the best way to reach groups most in need… Research suggests that governments should sufficiently invest in pre-primary programmes for children ages 0–6, providing all parents with consistent and affordable options for children" (2012, 38).

Throughout *Starting Strong* used the OECD's peer review process, which stresses dialogue among equals. Accordingly, *Starting Strong*'s team – and now the group within the Education Directorate in which the network is anchored – has remained open to debate among equals and respective of national and local differences. Thus *Starting Strong III* stressed that "what works in one country may not necessarily work in others due to different political, institutional, historical and technical constraints" (OECD 2012, 4) approach.

UNESCO: ECEC as a Critical Component of "Education for All"

As UNESCO constitutes part of the UN firmament and thus has a global reach[4] it is not surprising that it, like the Bank, is inspired by the "will to improve" conditions in the Global South and, in recent years, the "transition" countries of Eastern Europe, although it has not forgotten the childcare system developed in the Soviet era. Its perspectives are thus filtered through UN discourses on the rights of children, in particular as expressed in Education for All (EFA), with which it is charged with monitoring the implementation of. In 1990, delegates from 155 countries and representatives of numerous NGOs met at the World Conference on EFA in Jomtien, Thailand. While the principal aim was universal primary education, the World Declaration on EFA and the Framework for Action took the important step of recognizing that "learning begins at birth." The 2000 Dakar Framework for Action went further: its first goal is to expand and improve comprehensive early childhood care and education, especially for the most disadvantaged. Accordingly, since 2000, UNESCO has commissioned annual reports on progress toward the goals set out in the Dakar Framework. UNESCO also hosted the "first ever world conference dedicated to the area of Early Childhood Care and Education" in Moscow, 2010.

Unlike the Bank and the OECD, UNESCO does not claim to operate as a center for the development of global policy knowledges. Its main role is that of policy advocate at the global scale, distilling and disseminating key policy lessons developed elsewhere. In its role as advocate, it produces material such as its EFA Policy Paper 03, which presents "drastic figures" on underweight births and stunting in developing countries, especially in South and Central Asia and East Africa. At the same time it does play an important role in knowledge mobilization, by commissioning a substantial amount of research. Yet the fact that much of its research is commissioned – and thus published with the disclaimer that such research "does not necessarily reflect the views of the organization" – seems to give it the freedom to recruit experts working from competing paradigms.

Of particular importance here is the work of the teams UNESCO commissions to produce the annual EFA Global Monitoring reports. The team that conducted the 2007 review, which focused on ECEC, included Michelle Neuman, co-author of the first volume of *Starting Strong*, as its special advisor on ECEC. The team also commissioned background papers both from those steeped in the modernist paradigm, like Patrice Engle, and also those more closely associated with the alternative, like Sheila Kamerman and Martin Woodhead. Sources cited in the main document included Gunilla Dahlberg, Peter Moss, and Helen Penn, as well as the standard references to modernist texts such as those by Shonkoff and Phillips and Grantham-McGregor. Thus the report refers to the neuroscience arguments the latter emphasize, but, following Woodhead, the early years are treated as a "sensitive" but not "critical" period (UNESCO 2007, 109). More importantly, *Strong Foundations* does not "render technical" the problem or the solution. For instance it recognizes that the roots of child poverty are political, stemming from "gross inequalities in resources, access, and opportunity – that are shaped by global as well as local factors" (UNESCO 2007, 155). Chapter 6, which lays out the "changing contexts" in which ECE has come to the fore, highlights issues such as migration to urban areas, which often breaks down extended households that previously provided inter-generational care, and women's integration into labor markets marked by insecure low pay employment, frequently in the informal sector.

In addition, despite its concern to help poor children, *Strong Foundations* eschews a targeted approach in favor of programs that include all children as targeting

> is not always free of the patronizing idea that the poor cannot raise their children satisfactorily or the belief that science-based social engineering alone can solve the political issues that generate vulnerability and disadvantage. However there is much scope for levelling the playing field through universal programmes providing the same health and nutritional services, educational experiences and socialization to all young children, whatever their social backgrounds. (UNESCO 2007, 113)

In other words, all children can benefit from high quality ECEC – and quality programs are more likely to be available to poor children if they also include children of the middle class.

Strong Foundations' emphasis on the importance of quality includes classic features such as the qualified staff, fair remuneration, and low child/staff ratio, but it also praises programs that build on traditional childcare practices (i.e. valuing local knowledges) and respect children's linguistic and cultural diversity. The emphasis on quality does not mean that UNESCO seeks to impose a Nordic style model of center-based care on countries that cannot at present afford it. Thus it has supported a pilot program in Tanzania based on "non-formal" education. In contrast to UNICEF's Child to Child pilot program, which targeted countries with "low preschool coverage, low primary school enrolment, poor retention rates and weak learning achievement" (UNICEF 2008), UNESCO selected communities that, while struggling to provide adequate education and care for the very young: (a) "held a rich body of knowledge about how their children best learn" and (b) had made initial efforts to address their challenge by establishing their own community preschools (UNESCO 2009). The aim of the project was to empower local communities to find local ECEC solutions drawing on local knowledges.

In addition to the EFA reports, Yoshie Kaga, who is currently Early Childhood Programme Specialist at UNESCO headquarters, has sought the assistance of critical ECEC experts. Peter Moss was commissioned to write a short policy brief outlining the core principles of the Reggio approach centered on "the rich child" (Kaga *et al.* 2010). Kaga commissioned Moss and Bennett to co-author UNESCO's study of the case for integrating ECEC under ministries of education. Their report emphasized the diverse political paths followed and, while it highlighted the positive aspects associated with this governance structure, the team was careful to point out that "we are unable to give a comprehensive, coherent and conclusive assessment of the consequences. What we are left with is building a partial picture from various pieces and attempted interpretation, which hopefully will open some spaces for productive discussions and focus attention on the evaluation challenge" (Kaga *et al.* 2010, 69).

The 2010 World ECEC conference UNESCO organized, hosted by Russia, offered a mixed picture. On the one hand, there was strong official representation from several "emerging" (China, Indonesia, South Africa) and "developing" (Thailand, Kenya, Democratic Republic of Congo, and Botswana) countries.[5] In addition to a representative from Reggio, the list of consultants included John Bennett, Helen Penn, and Martá Korintus, the Hungarian ECEC expert involved in *Starting Strong*. To some extent, the ideas associated with the critical discourse were reflected in the final document. Thus, the Moscow Action Agenda noted the importance of cultural and linguistic diversity, "especially in regard to indigenous and minority languages." "Quality" was associated with programs that promote "active learning pedagogies that take into account the child's point of view," delivered by qualified ECEC staff using context-sensitive curriculum and material (UNESCO 2011).

On the other hand, the conference title – "Building the Wealth of Nations" – highlighted the "investment in human capital" approach. As the background paper noted, "in the twenty-first century countries' wealth is not defined in terms of material wealth. It depends on the extent to which countries are able to nurture their human capital, with values important in a globalized world..." (UNESCO 2010, 9). Although the paper refers to *Starting Strong*, the latter is read through a modernist lens (UNESCO 2010, 3 and 7), using it to support the utilitarian argument that investment in ECEC pays off. The document is also liberally sprinkled with references to World Bank studies by Eming Young, van der Gaag, and others, as well as the work of Grantham-McGregor, Shonkoff and Phillips, and Heckman. (The heavy reliance on the World Bank and related sources may not be accidental as UNESCO's then-new chief of Basic Education had previously worked at the Bank.) Shonkoff also gave the keynote address. Finally ECEC is clearly framed as a "development imperative" that certain regions – sub-Saharan Africa, South and West Asia, and the Arab countries – have done too little to meet. At the same time the underinvestment in ECEC on the part of countries like Canada and the USA was obscured by merging data on North American and Western Europe.

UNESCO thus can be seen as a space where ideas from both camps co-exist. As Penn notes, "UNESCO is definitely a more open forum in terms of ideas" (email exchange with Penn July 14, 2013). At the moment, however, it does not appear to offer a place where dialogue between the proponents of the two perspectives occurs. The Moscow conference might have provided such an opportunity but such large (1000 participants), "high level" (67 ministers and deputy ministers, embassy staff, and officials from a range of international organizations and INGOS) conferences are not conducive to this. In contrast to the small-scale, confidential peer review process that is the hallmark of much of OECD's work, such public, quasi-diplomatic events do little to encourage exchange of ideas.

Conclusions

As the UNESCO website notes, "the aim is to draw global attention to the critical role of early childhood education in helping children reach their full potential" (UNESCO n.d.). ECEC has made it onto the global agenda in part because it fits well into the contemporary discourse on the needs of the "knowledge based economy" and similarly can readily be configured as an important new "development imperative." It also is sufficiently ambiguous to appeal to neo-liberals, who accept the need for "investment" in human capital formation, social liberals favoring the rights of each individual to develop her/his full capabilities, and those who see ECEC as an important component of a wider system of social rights, available to all.

The existence of such diverse interpretations is matched by division among the experts. Some experts, drawing on neuroscience and economics, see it as part of a "holistic" package (along with nutrition, health, and parent education) of ECD designed to improve the lot of the poor in the Global South as well as in advanced capitalist countries like the USA. There is no reason to doubt that these experts are motivated by the "will to improve," but at the same time they tend to "render technical" the definition of the problem (the inability of "poor" parents to provide the right mental and physical nourishment) and the solution (ECD programs staffed and controlled by experts). In the process, key political and economic determinants are rendered invisible. Those who would challenge this view are motivated by the will to improve but also by the will to empower. Aware of the limits of their knowledge and yet of the power it potentially affords them, they start from the position of the child as the "rich child" embedded in her or his community, a community understood to possess valid language, knowledges, and values.

The World Bank's understanding of ECEC is powerfully informed by the first position, which fits well with its broader developmentalist discourse. The OECD's *Starting Strong* drew much more deeply on the second. To some extent this is consistent with its primary orientation as a policy resource for the core countries of the North and this is reflected in its use of the peer review process. This does not preclude the use of peer review to promote a neo-liberal agenda as an examination of the way the Economics Department has dealt with the Jobs Strategy suggests (McBride and Williams, 2001; Mahon 2011). Yet its peer review process renders it open to different perspectives (Porter, 2012). UNESCO represents an interesting case as a place where competing ideas can co-exist, but it has yet to constitute a place for genuine dialogue between them.

Notes

1 Research for this chapter was financed by a grant from the Social Science and Humanities Council of Canada. I also thank Helen Penn, Peter Moss, and John Bennett for their comments on the very first draft of this chapter.
2 Interview with James Heckman by Douglas Clement, *The Region*, June 2005.
3 Moss headed the European Commission's Childcare Network in the 1990s, which did much to forge an alternative ECEC discourse community. Moss and Dahlberg co-edit an important series, Contesting Early Childhood, published by Routledge. Penn worked with Moss for the Network, drafting "quality targets," which clearly reflected a dialogical view of quality in marked contrast to that which deploys rating scales, checklists, and the like.
4 From 1984–1997, the UK was not a member and the USA also withdrew between 1984 and 2002.
5 There was no official representative of the USA. Moreover, while UNICEF and the key NGOs in the field were well represented, there were only two officials from the World Bank and one from the OECD.

References

Alderman, H. and E. Vegas. 2011. "Convergence of Equity and Efficiency in Early Childhood Development Programs," in *No Small Matter: The Impact of Poverty, Shocks and Human Capital Investment in Early Childhood Development*, edited by H. Alderman, 155–183. Washington, DC: World Bank.
Bruer, J.T. 1999. *The Myth of the First Three years: A New Understanding of Early Brain Development and Life Long Learning*. New York: Simon and Schuster.
Carnegie Task Force on Meeting the Needs of Young Children. 1994. *Starting Points*. New York: Carnegie Corporation.
Clement, C. 2005. Interview with James Heckman. *The Region*, June. Retrieved from: https://www.minneapolisfed.org/publications/the-region/interview-with-james-heckman (accessed November 30, 2015).
Cohen, B., P. Moss, P. Petrie, and J. Wallace. 2004. *A New Deal for Children? Re-forming Education and Care in England, Scotland and Sweden*. Policy Press: Bristol.
Elliott, A. 2006. "Early Childhood Education: Pathway to Quality and Equity for All Children." *Australian Education Review*, 50.
European Commission Childcare Network. 1996. "Quality targets in services for Young children: Proposals for a ten year action programme" reprinted in *Quality in Early Learning*

and Child Care Services: Papers from the European Commission Childcare Network (2004). Toronto: Childcare Resource and Research Unit

Global Child Development Group. n.d. "About Us." Retrieved from: www.globalchilddevelopment.com/about-us (accessed November 10, 2015).

Jones, P. with D. Coleman. 2005. *The United Nations and Education: Multilateralism, Development and Globalisation*. London and New York: Routledge.

Kaga, Y., J. Bennett, and P. Moss. 2010. *Caring and Learning Together: Cross-National Studies of Integration of Early Childhood Care and Education within Education*. Paris: UNESCO.

Kamerman, S.B. 1998. *Early Childhood Education and Care: An Overview of Developments in the OECD Countries*. Paris: OECD.

Kamerman, S.B. 2006. "A global history of Early Childhood Education and Care." Background paper prepared for Education for All Global Monitoring Report 2007. *Strong Foundations: Early Childhood Care and Education*. Paris: UNESCO.

Korpi, W. and J. Palme. 1998. "The Paradox of Redistribution and Strategies of Equality: Welfare State Institutions, Inequality, and Poverty in the Western Countries." *American Sociological Review*, 63: 661–687.

Kosec, K. 2011. "Politics and Preschool: The Political Economy of Investment in Pre-Primary Education." Policy Research Working Paper 5647. World Bank Latin America and Caribbean Region Human Development Department. Washington, DC: World Bank.

Li, T.M. 2007. *The Will to Improve: Governmentality, Development and the Practice of Politics*. Durham: Duke University Press.

Mahon, R. 2011. "The Jobs Strategy: From Neo- to Inclusive Liberalism." *Review of International Political Economy*, 18(5): 570–591.

Mahon, R. and S. McBride. 2008. "Introduction: The OECD and Transnational Governance," in *The OECD and Transnational Governance*, edited by R. Mahon and S. McBride, 3–22. Vancouver: UBC Press.

McBride, S. and R. Williams. 2001. "Globalization, the Restructuring of Labour Markets and Policy Convergence: The OECD 'Jobs Strategy.'" *Global Social Policy*, 1(3): 281–309.

Moss, P. 2007. "Meetings across the Paradigmatic Divide." *Education Philosophy and Theory*, 39(3): 229–241.

Moss, P. 2010. "What is Your Image of the Child?" *Policy Brief on Early Childhood*. UNESCO, 47 January–March.

Mosse, D. 2004. "Is Good Policy Unimplementable? Reflections on the Ethnography of Aid Policy and Practice." *Development and Change*, 35(4): 639–671.

Myers, R.G. 1987. *The Eleven Who Survive: Toward a Re-examination of Early Childhood Development Program Options and Costs*. World Bank Working Paper. Washington, DC: The World Bank.

OECD. 2001. *Starting Strong: Early Childhood Education and Care*. Paris: OECD.

OECD. 2006. *Starting Strong II: Early Childhood Education and Care*. Paris: OECD.

OECD. 2012. *Starting Strong III: A Quality Toolbox for Early Childhood Education and Care*. Paris: OECD.

Penn, H. 2002. "The World Bank's View of Early Childhood." *Childhood*, 9(1): 118–132.

Porter, T. 2012. "Making serious Measures: Numerical Indices, Peer Review and Transnational Actor-Networks." *Journal of International Relations and Development*, 15: 532–557.

Rosemberg, F. 2006. "Multilateral Organizations and Early Childcare and Education Policies for Developing Countries," in *Global Dimensions of Gender and Carework*, edited by M.K. Simmerman, J.S. Litt, and C.E. Bose, 75–85. Stanford: Stanford University Press.

Shonkoff, J.P. and D.A. Phillips. 2000. *From Neurons to Neighborhoods: The Science of Early Childhood Development*. Washington, DC: National Academy Press.

UNESCO. n.d. "Mission." Retrieved from: www.unesco.org/new/en/education/themes/strengthening-education-systems/early-childhood/mission (accessed November 11, 2015).

UNESCO. 2007. *Strong Foundations EFA Global Monitoring Report 2007*. Paris: UNESCO.

UNESCO. 2009. "Early Childhood Care and Education and Non-Formal Education." *UNESCO Policy Brief in Early Childhood*, 45 January–March.

UNESCO. 2010. *The World Conference on Early Childhood Care and Education (ECCE): Building the Wealth of Nations*. Concept paper, Division of Basic Education. Paris: UNESCO.

UNESCO. 2012. *Education for All Global Monitoring Report Policy Paper 03*. Paris: UNESCO.

UNESCO. 2011. *Building the Wealth of Nations: Final Report on the World Conference on Early Childhood Care and Education*. Paris: UNESCO.

UNICEF. n.d. *Early Childhood Development: They Key to a Full and Productive Life*. Retrieved from: www.unicef.org/dprk/ecd.pdf (accessed November 11, 2015).

UNICEF. 2008. *Getting Ready for School: A Child to Child Approach Strategic Framework*. Prepared by ECD consultant Cassie Landia. Revised and Financed by Abhiyan Jung Rana and Cream Wright, Chief Global Education Program, Education Program Officer. New York: UNICEF.

Woodhead, M. 2006. *Changing Perspectives On Early Childhood: Theory, Research and Policy*. A background report commissioned by UNESCO for *Education for All Global Monitoring Report 2007: Strong Foundations*. Paris: UNESCO.

World Bank. 2011a. *Investing in Young Children: An Early Childhood Development Guide for Policy Dialogue and Project Preparation*. S. Nadeau, N. Kataoka, A. Valerio, M.J. Neuman, and L. Kennedy Elder. Human Development Division 57876. Washington, DC: World Bank.

World Bank. 2011b. *No Small Matter: The Impact of Poverty, Shocks and Human Capital Investment in Early Childhood Development*, edited by H. Alderman. Washington, DC: World Bank.

Van der Gaag, J. and J. P. Tan. 1998. "The Benefits of Early Child Development: An Economic Analysis," volume 1. Washington, DC: World Bank.

Young, M.E. 1995. "Investing in Young Children." *World Bank Development Papers 275*. Washington, DC: World Bank.

Young, M.E. 1996. "Early Child Development: Investing in the Future." *Directions in Development*. Washington, DC: World Bank.

Young, M.E. (2002) "Ensuring a Fair Start for All Children – The Case of Brazil." *Investing in Our Children's Future*. Washington, DC: World Bank.

Chapter 13

Education for All 2000–2015: The Influence of Global Interventions and Aid on EFA Achievements[1]

Aaron Benavot, Manos Antoninis, Nicole Bella, Marcos Delprato, Joanna Härmä, Catherine Jere, Priyadarshani Joshi, Nihan Koseleci Blanchy, Helen Longlands, Alasdair McWilliam, and Asma Zubairi

The Education for All Agenda and its Implementation

The Convention on the Rights of the Child, adopted by the United Nations General Assembly in New York in 1989, and the World Declaration on Education for All (EFA) drawn up in 1990 in Jomtien, Thailand, reaffirmed education as a basic human right, as first articulated in the Universal Declaration of Human Rights in 1948. These treaties marked a significant shift toward the promise of a new international environment, one characterized by closer cooperation and solidarity. The realization that education progress was stagnant in many parts of the world, the belief that human development should be at the core of all development, and the optimism generated by the end of the Cold War led to an ambitious call in support of education. The "expanded vision" of the Declaration succinctly articulated education policy concerns, including equity, learning, and non-formal provision (Inter-Agency Commission 1990; Unterhalter 2014).

The EFA agenda rested on the belief that "public policy can radically transform education systems and their relationship to society within a few years, given adequate political will and resources" (UNESCO 2008). Yet, during the 1990s, progress toward EFA was insufficient. Structural adjustment policies severely impeded progress in the poorest countries and participation in pre-primary and primary education barely changed. Two developments in the late 1990s, however, re-energized the global EFA agenda. First, the International Consultative Forum – the inter-agency body responsible for EFA monitoring, advocacy, and partnerships – outlined an ambitious process of national end-of-decade EFA assessments with support from its Paris-based Secretariat. After 180 countries participated in the assessment exercise, the results of which were combined into a global synthesis and a statistical document (UIS 2000; Skilbeck 2000), the importance of the EFA agenda was re-emphasized. Second, civil society, frustrated with the slow pace of progress toward EFA, placed increased pressure on the international community to act. At the forefront of this movement was the Global Campaign for Education (GCE), whose founding members included Action Aid, Oxfam International, the Global March Against Child Labour, and Education International. GCE was established in October 1999 to "mobilise public pressure on governments to fulfil their promises to provide free, quality education for all people, particularly for women."

In April 2000, in the wake of these developments, more than 1100 members of the international community met in Dakar, Senegal, at the World Education Forum. At this meeting, representatives from regional groups, international organizations, donor agencies, non-government organizations (NGOs), civil society groups, and 164 national governments developed the Dakar Framework for Action to deliver on EFA promises.

The Framework consisted of two key elements: six wide-ranging education goals and associated targets to be achieved by all countries by 2015, with one target – gender parity at primary and secondary education level – to be achieved by 2005; and 12 strategies for all stakeholders – global, national, government, or non-government – to contribute to in their different capacities.

The six EFA goals addressed an ambitious set of global education challenges:

- "Goal 1: Expanding and improving comprehensive early childhood care and education, especially for the most vulnerable and disadvantaged children.
- Goal 2: Ensuring that by 2015 all children, particularly girls, children in difficult circumstances and those belonging to ethnic minorities, have access to, and complete, free and compulsory primary education of good quality.
- Goal 3: Ensuring that the learning needs of all young people and adults are met through equitable access to appropriate learning and life-skills programmes.
- Goal 4: Achieving a 50 per cent improvement in levels of adult literacy by 2015, especially for women, and equitable access to basic and continuing education for all adults.
- Goal 5: Eliminating gender disparities in primary and secondary education by 2005, and achieving gender equality in education by 2015, with a focus on ensuring girls' full and equal access to and achievement in basic education of good quality.
- Goal 6: Improving all aspects of the quality of education and ensuring excellence of all, so that recognized and measurable learning outcomes are achieved by all, especially in literacy, numeracy and essential life skills."

Goal 1 was informed by evidence of the fundamental importance, in terms of future well-being, for an individual to receive good early childhood care and education (ECCE). As the Framework did not set specific targets on ECCE, the *EFA Global Monitoring Report*[2] (GMR) has monitored selected available indicators that are closest to key concepts embedded in the goal, including survival, nutrition, and access to learning opportunities. The achievement of Goal 2 – universal primary education – has been seen as the key EFA indicator, despite the fact it represented only part of global ambitions for education. This is partly because of the dominant role that the corresponding second Millennium Development Goal (MDG) has played in the international education agenda. The broad scope of Goal 3 has hampered effective monitoring: learning needs and the ways in which skills are conceptualized vary across cultures and countries, and change over time. Since 2002, the GMR has focused mainly on progress in secondary education as a proxy for foundational skills. Goal 4, which focused on reducing adult illiteracy, was hampered by ambivalent political commitment, contested definitions, and measurement strategies, and the fact that sustained progress in literacy has been more a consequence of expanding access to schooling than short-term literacy campaigns. Goal 5, the gender goal, has been criticized for its narrow understanding of gender equality, which mostly emphasized gender parity and did not adequately specify dimensions of gender equality in education beyond school access (Unterhalter 2007).[3] The final goal – Goal 6 – addressed issues of quality, such as teacher training, access to textbooks, adequate infrastructure, and measurable learning outcomes. The Framework expressed concern at the time that evidence showed a sizeable percentage of children were "acquiring only a fraction of the knowledge and skills they are expected to master," noting that "what students are meant to learn has often not been clearly defined, well-taught or accurately assessed."

Three types of global interventions were proposed to support countries (Figure 13.1):

- *Coordination mechanisms*, some of which already existed, while others were outlined for the first time in the Framework and subsequently modified.

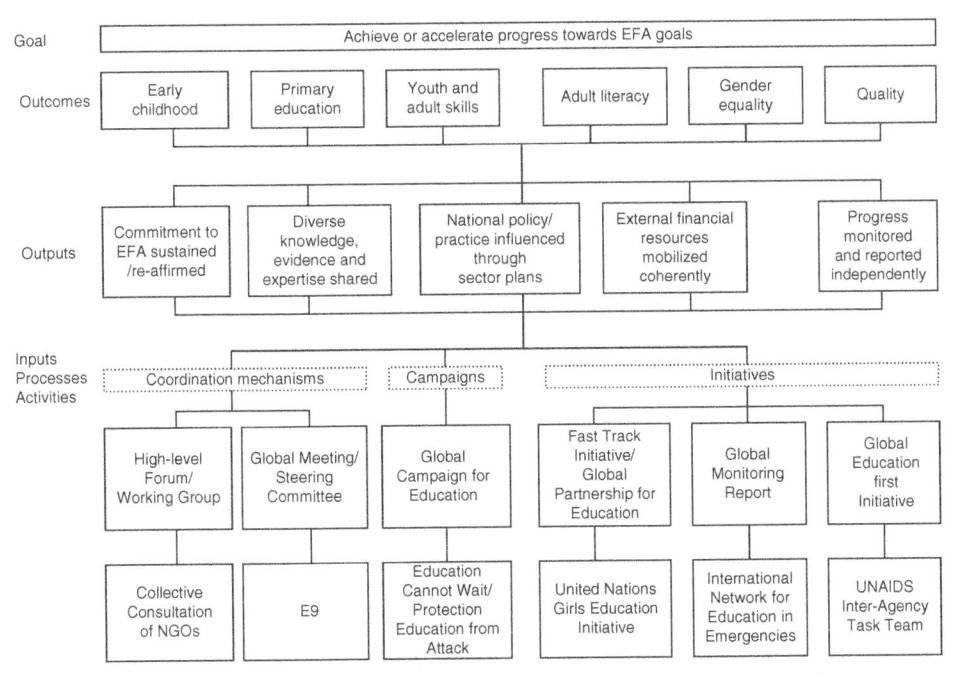

Figure 13.1 Logical framework for the expected effects of the global EFA architecture.
Source: Adapted from 2015 *EFA Global Monitoring Report: Education for All 2000–2015: Achievements and Challenges*. Paris: UNESCO, Figure 0.21, p. 28.

- *Campaigns*, dedicated to particular aspects of EFA, such as adult literacy, or to particular challenges, such as conflict.
- *Initiatives*, some specified in the Framework, while others drew from its authority and were created later.

These interventions overlapped and interacted with one other but had specific organizational and management arrangements. It was hoped that successful implementation would lead to short- to medium-term results, which, in turn, would help speed up the achievement of the EFA goals. However, many of the underlying assumptions that would allow these results to be achieved were not met.

It was hoped, for example, that the Framework and its interventions, although not legally binding, would help *reaffirm and sustain political commitment for EFA*, and provide stakeholders at the national level with sufficient support to push for necessary reforms. In practice, however, progress in this area was limited. Resources for coordination were insufficient and over time agencies reverted to their own agendas, of which EFA was not the only one. Furthermore, new voices outside the designated EFA agencies, such as the Organisation for Economic Co-operation and Development (OECD), increasingly appealed to countries where the EFA agenda may have had less resonance (Bolívar 2011; Sellar and Lingard 2013).

The assumption that *interventions based on information and evidence* would automatically lead to education progress was also flawed. Initially, policy-making was viewed as a technical exercise informed by evidence, and interventions sought to provide opportunities to share such diverse knowledge and expertise. While the concepts of evidence-based policies and results-based management gained currency over the period, there was growing realization of the role of politics (Grindle 2004). Lack of action on the side of national governments did not just reflect lack of information but rather consideration of political opposition or ambivalence. In practice, even countries committed to EFA goals required political support to build their national capacity to seek, absorb, interpret, and apply findings and lessons derived from external sources.

The expectation that various interventions would influence and *strengthen national EFA policy and practice* was also ill informed. For example, the implementation of national EFA plans of action was expected to have positive outcomes. But many countries had existing national mechanisms and planning cycles, and the ways and extent to which action plans have promoted educational development have differed widely. In some cases, the insistence on a separate EFA plan or structure outside the national process of planning and budgeting may have been counterproductive.

A further misplaced assumption was that *financial resources for EFA would be effectively mobilized*. The Dakar signatories believed that developing country efforts to raise more taxes and prioritize basic education in their budgets would be insufficient to achieve EFA. Starting from a concrete estimate of annual resource requirements of US$8 billion, it was expected that various interventions would help close the gap through new coordination schemes. The implicit assumption was that many countries were spending considerably below what would be needed to get every child in school.

In practice, the capacity of countries' financial and education systems to absorb rapid increases in external aid flows was not considered. Neither was the ability of countries to spend effectively. Also, during a period of strong donor coordination and calls for debt relief, it was assumed that no significant shocks would affect aid disbursements (see section on "International Aid for EFA" below). Assuming the accuracy of the estimated cost, the appeal to donors to essentially triple aid to basic education was ambitious yet considered achievable. The subsequent financial crisis in donor countries dampened these expectations.

Finally, the *independent monitoring and reporting of progress* toward the EFA goals has not been easy. Governments choose whether or not to adopt global targets as national targets and their commitments to their citizens are made through national processes. The influence of increasingly authoritative global actors and institutions on national decision-making processes varies over time and by country. Even if countries agree to global targets, independent monitoring could only help countries make progress toward EFA if a formal mechanism designed to measure underperformance had been in place – but none existed.

EFA Coordination and Implementation Strategies

A crucial difficulty facing EFA was that the Dakar Framework did not establish a clear coordination mechanism between the five EFA convening agencies: the United Nations Educational, Scientific and Cultural Organization (UNESCO), the United Nations Children's Fund (UNICEF), the United Nations Population Fund (UNFPA), the United Nations Development Programme (UNDP), and the World Bank. Political wrangling over the leadership of the EFA process diluted substantive discussion on the best way to deliver EFA policies at national level. The participation of several convening agencies in EFA coordination mechanisms gradually diminished after Dakar, and is only being reinstated in 2015 in anticipation of the World Education Forum in South Korea. As EFA convenors such as the World Bank and UNICEF gained influence and finances for education development, they gradually distanced themselves from working with UNESCO.

One serious problem was that the High-Level Group on EFA, the main coordination mechanism, expanded its membership. This had an adverse impact on its effectiveness as a strategic coordinator because accommodating the voices of a large group proved to be problematic, and meetings were not well managed (Burnett 2010). It was also unclear whether appointed countries truly represented their regions at these meetings. In 2011, UNESCO reformed coordination arrangements. A new High-Level Forum was envisaged that would invite leaders and champions of education in the spirit of the Framework that sought political commitment through a group that was high level and flexible. This move came too late, however, and the Forum never met. Meanwhile, during the 2000s other bodies had taken over the role of high-level advocacy. These included the Global Partnership for Education established in 2002, and the UN Secretary-General's Global Education First Initiative, launched in 2012.

The decision in Dakar to assign full responsibility for EFA to UNESCO was made despite concerns about the organization's leadership. And, although UNESCO has retained support for its leadership role among countries, the decision to exclusively assign it the role of global coordinator appears in retrospect to have had a negative impact on its effectiveness, given the financial and governance complexities the organization was already facing. Ultimately, the formal coordination mechanism of EFA has failed to ensure continuous political commitment. Many of the most successful global education mechanisms, initiatives, and campaigns happened despite, rather than because of, attempts to coordinate EFA at a global level.

> **Box 13.1 The 12 EFA strategies established at Dakar (2000).**
>
> 1. Mobilize strong national and international political commitment for Education for All, develop national action plans and enhance significantly investment in basic education
> 2. Promote EFA policies within a sustainable and well-integrated sector framework clearly linked to poverty elimination and development strategies
> 3. Ensure the engagement and participation of civil society in the formulation, implementation and monitoring of strategies for educational development
> 4. Develop responsive, participatory and accountable systems of educational governance and management
> 5. Meet the needs of education systems affected by conflict, natural calamities and instability, and conduct educational programmes in ways that promote mutual understanding, peace and tolerance, and that help to prevent violence and conflict
> 6. Implement integrated strategies for gender equality in education that recognize the need for change in attitudes, values and practices
> 7. Implement education programmes and actions to combat the HIV/AIDS pandemic as a matter of urgency
> 8. Create safe, healthy, inclusive and equitably resourced educational environments conducive to excellence in learning, with clearly defined levels of achievement for all
> 9. Enhance the status, morale and professionalism of teachers
> 10. Harness new information and communication technologies to help achieve EFA goals
> 11. Systematically monitor progress towards EFA goals and strategies at the national, regional and international levels
> 12. Build on existing mechanisms to accelerate progress towards Education for All
>
> Source: 2015 EFA Global Monitoring Report: Education for All 2000–2015: Achievements and Challenges. Paris: UNESCO

To further advance the EFA goals, 12 strategies were identified in the Framework (see Box 13.1). Previous GMR reports have provided partial and rather limited evidence as to the implementation and impact of these 12 strategies. In general it is difficult, if not impossible, to establish a direct link between the implementation of each strategy and the achievement, or lack thereof, of the EFA goals. The 12 EFA strategies were meant to provide a platform for aligning international and national priorities, both governmental and non-governmental – in a more effective and timely manner. National EFA plans were meant to give expression to specific strategies and, in doing so, further improve the coordination and impact of external and internal stakeholders.

The 2015 GMR provided a systematic evaluation of the 12 strategies, and showed that some strategies have been at least partly effective, such as responding to the HIV/AIDS or emergency challenges. These tended to have a strong technical focus, clear objectives, dedicated capacity, and overt political support from influential bodies. But many strategies did not achieve the critical mass of interventions necessary to have an impact (UNESCO 2015). A key lesson is that gaining political influence is essential for realizing the scale of reform and action required to achieve EFA.

Taking Stock of Progress Toward EFA

The EFA movement set forth an ambitious international agenda to improve the provision of equitable quality education for all. Overall EFA progress can be assessed based on the most recent evidence[4]:

- In 2012, 121 million children and adolescents of primary and lower secondary school age, or 12% of this age group globally, were not in school, down from 204 million, or 19%, in 1999.
- While in low and middle income countries as few as one in 20 children may have never attended school in 2015, as many as one in six children will not have completed primary school, and as many as one in three adolescents will not have completed lower secondary school.
- Although globally it is projected that by 2015, gender parity will be achieved in primary and secondary education on average, in practice as many as 3 in 10 countries at the primary level and 5 in 10 countries at the secondary level are projected to not achieve this.
- The adult illiteracy rate will have only fallen by 23% since 2000, instead of the targeted 50%, and most of the fall is due to the transition into adulthood of larger cohorts of better-educated children. At least 750 million adults, nearly two-thirds of whom are women, will not even have rudimentary literacy skills in 2015.

Progress for some of these education indicators has accelerated since 2000 with more children entering school and completing their education than if the pre-2000 rate of progress had been maintained. For example, by 2015 it is anticipated that 20 million more children will have completed primary school in low and middle income countries. However, access to education continues to be unequal. Disadvantaged children still lag behind their peers. For instance, the probability that children from the poorest quintile of households in low and middle income countries were out of school in 2010 was five times higher than the corresponding probability of children from the richest quintile – a gap that has increased compared to 2000.

The following assessments for each EFA goal provide a succinct overview of progress made at the end of the period.

Regarding Goal 1 on early childhood care and education, the rates for under-five mortality, underweight children, and stunting have all fallen. Between 1990 and 2000, the level of child mortality fell globally from 90 to 76 deaths per 1000 live births, and fell further to 46 in 2013. East Asia and the Pacific and Latin America and the Caribbean are expected to achieve a reduction of two-thirds in the child mortality rate by 2015, but in sub-Saharan Africa, in spite of progress, such a reduction is not expected. The proportion of underweight children has also fallen, from 25% in 1990 to 15% in 2013. However, the target of halving the prevalence of underweight children between 1990 and 2015 will be missed. Stunting rates, meanwhile, fell from 40% in 1990 to 24.5% in 2013, but the cognitive and physical development of about 162 million children under the age of five remains at risk, particularly children in sub-Saharan Africa (UNICEF et al. 2014). In terms of the provision of early childhood education services, globally, since 2000, pre-primary education enrolment increased by almost two-thirds, and is projected to reach 8%

by 2015. However, in 2012, while enrolment was 74% in Latin America and the Caribbean, and 89% in North America and Europe, it was only 20% in sub-Saharan Africa and 25% in the Arab States. Furthermore, gaps exist not only between countries but also within countries, especially between rural and urban areas. Overall, the supply of free, publicly provided pre-primary education continues to lag behind the demand for such services. Parents typically have to pay fees for existing government provision or seek services from the private sector whose fees are higher.

In assessing progress toward Goal 2, it is estimated that 57 million children were still out of school in 2015 (although this is significantly down from 106 million in 1999), despite the dominant focus on universal primary education. There are three categories of out-of-school children: children who will eventually go to school; children who will never go to school; and children who were enrolled but left school. Estimates for 2012 indicated that about 43%, or 25 million, out-of-school children will never go to school. Children from poor households are particularly at risk of being out of school, and disparities exist between different groups of children based on, for example, ethnicity, language, and/or gender. Overall, while girls are still more likely than boys never to go to school (48% of the total compared to 37% of boys), boys are more likely than girls to drop out of school early. In addition, the percentage of children who finished primary school in low and middle income countries increased from 77% in 1999 to 81% in 2008. It was expected to reach 84% in 2015. This means that one in six children in those countries – or almost 100 million – had not completed primary school by the 2015 deadline.

In terms of progress toward Goal 3 on learning and life skills, large disparities at both lower and upper secondary education level still exist between regions. The lower secondary gross enrolment ratio in 2012, for example, was above 95% in most regions but only 89% in the Arab States, 81% in South and West Asia, and just 50% in sub-Saharan Africa. The upper secondary gross enrolment ratio, meanwhile, was almost 100% in Central Asia and North America and Western Europe, but only 32% in sub-Saharan Africa. The increase in lower secondary enrolment translates into a reduction in the number of out-of-school adolescents of lower secondary age; in 1999, for example, 99 million adolescents of this age were out of school, but by 2012 this figure had dropped to 63 million. More than half of the total decline is a result of progress in East Asia and the Pacific. However, in spite of progress in enrolment, analysis of attainment rates show far fewer adolescents attain lower secondary school than the number who enrol. By 2015, across all low and middle income countries, one in three young people will not have finished lower secondary school. This means that not only will the learning needs of all young people not be met by 2015, but, as children move into adulthood, their lack of secondary education will also impede their future learning opportunities: adults with secondary education have more chances to benefit from adult education programs than those without.

Assessing the extent of progress for Goal 4 is difficult because the source of literacy data has changed in many countries in sub-Saharan Africa, the region with both the highest illiteracy rates (41%) and the slowest progress in recent years. Data show that while the global adult illiteracy rate fell from 24% to 18% between 1990 and 2000, progress has slowed since. By 2015, it is projected to fall to 14%, well short of the target to halve illiteracy. Furthermore, in 2015, despite the Framework's emphasis on improving literacy rates among women, women still comprise 64% of all illiterate adults – a figure that has remained unchanged since 2000. In order to move toward universal adult literacy, youth literacy rates need to improve. Globally, the most recent youth illiteracy rate stands at 11%, which means that adult illiteracy will remain a policy concern in the years to come. Taking stock of the period since Dakar, it also appears that certain developments that might have contributed to a faster decline in illiteracy rates failed to do so. These include a renewed interest in literacy programs, including those that promoted the use of mother tongue, and more livelihood opportunities that potentially called for the use of literacy skills.

In terms of assessing progress toward Goal 5 targets, while data show significant progress toward gender parity, it is far less clear how much progress has been made towards gender equality. In primary education, there was considerable disparity in 1999, with just 92 girls enrolled for every 100 boys. By 2012, the global average had increased to 97 girls, just above the threshold of parity. At the secondary education level in 1999, 91 girls enrolled for every 100 boys; by 2012, this had likewise increased to almost 97. Comparing data on primary education from 155 countries at three time points shows relatively limited progress: 52% had already achieved gender parity in 1999; 57% reached it by 2005 (the original target deadline); and 65% by 2012. Gender parity, therefore, has not been achieved in far too many countries. Furthermore, progress in reaching gender parity is not a sufficient indicator of progress toward gender equality. Such an assessment requires a systematic look at whether countries have been able to address discriminatory social norms through legislation or policy, remove gender bias from inputs to education such as school textbooks, improve gender equality in education processes, and tackle unsafe learning environments. These aspects of gender equality in education have received less policy attention than gender parity, and such a systematic analysis has yet to be done on a sufficient scale. If the gender gap in learning outcomes is used as a measure of progress toward gender equality, some evidence suggests the relative position of girls has been improving. The gap separating them from boys in mathematics and science has fallen, although some caution is needed, as most of the robust information over time comes from richer countries. On the other hand, the gap in favor of girls in reading has increased.

Finally, an assessment of progress made toward Goal 6 shows that, since 2000, countries have taken increasing interest in the quality of education through improving understanding of the outcomes of education systems. At the time of Dakar, the task of monitoring quality was only conceivable in terms of measuring inputs. In the subsequent period, information on outcomes has been increasingly available. And while learning outcomes are not the only criteria for assessing the quality of education provision, they are nonetheless a major element. In the 1990s, 34% of countries carried out at least one national learning assessment. Since 2000, this has risen to 69% of countries, with significant increases in the Arab States, Central Asia, Central and Eastern Europe, and East Asia and the Pacific – a trend strongly indicating the positive response countries have made to the EFA agenda's quality imperative. At the same time, however, this increasing use of learning assessments has not yet been translated into sufficient information at the global level to assess whether learning outcomes have been improving. In 2015, developments in learning cannot be tracked globally and over time. Moreover, assessments only report the learning outcomes of children who are in school; and thus overestimate the learning achievement of the population.

In terms of other aspects of quality, the Framework acknowledged that teacher shortages had to be addressed. Yet by 2012, 1.4 million additional primary school teachers were still needed in order to achieve universal primary education by 2015. The sub-Saharan African region accounted for well over half (63%) of the additional teachers needed. The Framework also identified additional factors that contribute to quality education including conditions in schools, management of schools, curricula, and the language of instruction. But systematic evidence on global trends for many of these factors is not available.

In summary, as the 2000–2015 EFA era draws to a close, the world remains far from the targets set in Dakar, and wide educational inequalities remain. While many countries are projected to be closer to key targets than if pre-2000 trends had continued, it is difficult to say how much of this improvement is due to EFA efforts. EFA partners have certainly contributed to the monitoring and reporting of developments in education worldwide since 2000: more is known about international progress and inequalities in education than in the past. For example, data are more extensive, accurate and timely, and data sources on school attendance and learning have expanded. Nevertheless, data for many countries are lacking, especially in small and conflict-affected countries.

Changing aspects of the international context since Dakar have also played a role in EFA progress. These include economic growth in low and middle income countries, which created a favorable environment for progress through, for example, enabling governments to increase allocation of resources to education. However, even countries committed to the EFA goals have needed external support to build national capacity for improving education systems.

International Aid for EFA

The Dakar Framework for Action called on national governments and donors to commit to increased financing in order to fulfil the objectives set out in the six EFA goals, stating: "Governments must allocate sufficient resources to all components of basic education. This will require increasing the share of national income and budgets allocated to education, and, within that, to basic education." The Framework also declared "no countries seriously committed to education for all will be thwarted in their achievement of this goal by a lack of resources." Indeed, there was a strong expectation that the donor community would increase its financial support to education. Subsequent global donor commitments to raise aid levels, particularly for Africa, were made in the Gleneagles (2005) G8 summit, while an increased focus on improving aid effectiveness was the subject of high-level forums in Rome (2003), Paris (2005), Accra (2008), and Busan (2011).

Nevertheless, in spite of these global commitments, the lack of resources for financing EFA has persisted throughout the post-Dakar period. The evidence suggests that the total volume of external assistance for all goals fell well short of the assessed need, was insufficiently targeted to countries and levels of education most in need, and declined as a share of recipient governments' budgets over the period. Aid agencies have not been well configured to provide reliable medium- and long-term assurances of aid (OECD 2012). In 2015, education at all levels remains chronically underfunded.

Overall, since Dakar, basic education[5] has attracted the most donor support because it is directly related to poverty reduction and was linked with the second MDG. Between 2002 and 2012, aid to basic education grew, on average, 6% a year, although there are significant regional variations (OECD-DAC 2014). For example, annual growth rates in sub-Saharan Africa during this time only averaged 1%, even though the region had the highest average returns to schooling (Montenegro and Patrinos 2012; Psacharopoulos 2014). Despite this growth in aid for basic education, the share of total aid disbursed for education remained relatively static, not exceeding 10%. Since 2010, however, total aid for education has been in decline, falling 10% between 2010 and 2012, while aid to basic education has fallen 15% (OECD-DAC 2014).

Within basic education, primary education has received the vast majority of international development assistance. Its share increased, on average, from 87% in 2002–2004 to 92% in 2010–2012. On the other hand, the share of total aid disbursements to basic life skills training for youth and adults and early childhood education have decreased, on average, from 10% and 3%, respectively, in 2002–2004 to 6% and 2% in 2010–2012 (OECD-DAC 2014). Donor rhetoric suggesting strong support for early childhood care and education has not translated into increased shares of aid.

Donor support for secondary education has also been limited. A review of donor strategies showed that only Germany, Japan, and the Asian Development Bank treated upper secondary as a priority subsector in their aid programmes (Mercer 2014). Donor strategies have also focused little on other key EFA areas, including adult education, distance learning, non-formal education, and education for children with special needs (Mercer 2014).

In contrast, throughout this period, many donors have continued to prioritize spending on post-secondary education. In the early 2000s, 20 of 28 donor countries spent more on post-secondary education than on secondary education; by the late 2000s, it was 27 of 39 donor countries, indicating little change (OECD-DAC 2014). In 2012, 72% of aid to post-secondary education supported students from developing countries studying in donor countries (OECD-DAC 2014), a practice that does not directly help strengthen higher education systems in low or middle income countries. In the same year, for every US$1 disbursed in direct aid to early childhood care and education, the equivalent of US$58 went to support post-secondary level students studying overseas (OECD-DAC 2014).

The importance of international aid at the country level has declined in the past few years for countries where domestic resources have risen rapidly since Dakar. However, aid remains crucial in low income countries today, despite their growing economies and higher government revenue. Many low income country governments spend well below what is needed to ensure universal access to basic public services, including education (Development Initiatives 2013), and continue to rely on external aid for 10% or more of their total public expenditure on education.[6]

The premise behind aid has been to help poor countries, which has – up until the past decade – meant helping poor people. Since Dakar, however, the correlation between poor countries and poor populations has weakened (Tomasi 2014). While 93% or the world's poor lived in low income countries at the beginning of the 1990s, 72% lived in middle income countries by 2012 (Kanbur and Sumner 2011). More than half of out-of-school children (59%) are concentrated in middle income countries. The share of basic education aid disbursements going to low income countries has declined from 40% to 34% over the past decade. The growth rate of basic education aid disbursements for upper middle income countries during this period was, moreover, double that for low income countries: 10% versus 5% (OECD-DAC 2014), albeit with variations between countries.

The Dakar Framework called on donors to not just increase aid levels but also to improve the effectiveness of aid. The 2005 Paris Declaration on Aid Effectiveness marked an unprecedented shift regarding the delivery of aid by promoting national ownership, alignment of donor priorities with national plans, coordination of donor efforts, and a focus on results and shared accountability for outcomes between donors and recipients (UNESCO 2011). As an indication of how difficult it is to change donor institutional behavior, however, only one of the 13 aid effectiveness targets had been achieved by 2011: aligning and coordinating technical assistance (OECD 2011).

Subsequent to the Paris Declaration, the aid effectiveness agenda has emphasized new partnerships for development cooperation. The 2007 EU Code of Conduct on Complementarity and Division of Labour, and the 2011 New Deal for Engagement in Fragile States, promote coherent development policy through, for example, coordination and more efficient disbursal of international resources by reducing duplication and program proliferation. In addition, the fourth High Level Forum on Aid Effectiveness in Busan, Republic of Korea, in 2011 stressed using multilateral institutions and global funds to reduce aid fragmentation. The first High-Level Meeting of the Global Partnership for Effective Development Cooperation, held in Mexico in April 2014, indicated a shift to more coherence, with "strengthened mobilization of domestic resources and the convergence of efforts of all public and private development stakeholders at all levels" (Global Partnership for Education 2014a).

Nevertheless, current global and country-level coordination mechanisms do not, as yet, seem to have helped aid effectiveness; fragmentation of aid to education remains high, as it does for general development aid (Rose *et al.* 2013). Ineffective global and national coordination means countries most in need of resources for education still lack them.

The Global Partnership for Education (GPE) (previously called the EFA Fast Track Initiative (FTI)), established in 2002, has had potential to play a critical role in the global coordination of international aid for education but developed too slowly to do this effectively so far. The GPE was the first global partnership focusing on education in developing countries. Its emergence constituted the main response to the aspirations of the international community for coherent and adequate funding to countries committed to achieving EFA, and is an example of how independent initiatives emerged outside formal global EFA coordinating bodies.

The GPE was not intended to operate as a new fund but rather placed the onus of responsibility on donors to align their support behind endorsed education sector plans and on governments to mobilize more domestic resources. However, over time, it developed its own fund, which has gradually become increasingly important. In volume terms, relative to other donors, the GPE has become an important source of external financing for basic education in some low and lower middle income countries. In 2004, it was the 22nd largest donor of basic education aid to low and lower middle income countries; by 2007, it was the ninth largest; in 2011 and 2012 it was the fourth largest donor after the UK, the USA, and the World Bank (Global

Partnership for Education 2014b; OECD-DAC 2014). For the 39 countries which received programme implementation grants over 2004–12, the share of GPE aid in total aid disbursements to basic education increased from 4% in 2004-06 to 16% in 2010–12. The influence of the GPE has increased partly due to improved disbursement rates. Its slow rates of disbursement were strongly criticized in a 2010 mid-term evaluation, and in efforts to improve these rates, the number of supervising and managing entities has been diversified. Previously, the World Bank, which now supervises 73% of active grants, supervised 92% of closed program implementation grants, and subjected them to lengthy and slow procedures (Global Partnership for Education 2013a); for example, requiring eligible countries to apply full World Bank project procedures to their trust fund operations, including GPE grants. The GPE also now requires countries seeking support to provide education indicators on disadvantaged groups so that the poorest children are identified and targeted (Australian Aid 2012).

Since the mid-term appraisal in 2010, the GPE's priority focus has also shifted: away from its initial remit to support only a small, select group of countries that had demonstrated commitment, toward all low income countries, including increased support to fragile states, which is now one of its five main objectives. By the end of 2013, more than 40% of GPE disbursements, over US$800 million, went to fragile and conflict-affected countries (Global Partnership for Education 2013b).

Another donor trend is the reduction of general budget support. Bilateral donors reduced average disbursements to general budget support from US$3.2 million in 2007–2009 to US$2.1 billion in 2010–2012, despite the fact that general budget support has provided a substantial increase in the resources available for development spending and basic service delivery. For example, expenditure on so-called "primary development programmes" in the United Republic of Tanzania increased significantly from 27% of the budget in 2004/05 to 46% in 2008/09. This enabled dramatic expansion in provision of education, health, water and sanitation, infrastructure, and agriculture (ICAI 2012). Research suggests governments that received general budget support were twice as likely to report improved access to services compared with countries that did not receive such support (National Audit Office 2008).

In addition to more effective coordination of aid, the Dakar Framework called on donors to "provide flexible development assistance within the framework of sector-wide reforms and support for sector priorities" and "to make longer-term and more predictable commitments." Sector-wide approaches (SWAps), which were already becoming more popular at the time of Dakar, are one way in which donors have allocated funds to education. SWAps involve funds to a defined sector policy led by government authority in partnership with external donors, and marked a change from the project-oriented approach to aid, where hundreds of individual projects put great strain on recipient countries' limited economic and human resources. Education SWAps have, to date, been implemented in 25 low income countries; five of these SWAps are sub-sectoral, focusing on primary and basic education. Some evidence of the success of SWAps includes efficiency and cost savings due to better coordination and flexibility (Boak and Ndaruhutse 2011). SWAps lost their appeal among some donor agencies from around the middle of the 2000s due to political and economic considerations, including a push to demonstrate short-term results and account for every dollar that was spent. Furthermore, some donors' unwillingness or inability to disburse contributions through SWAps has continued to result in high transaction costs for countries where a SWAp arrangement is in place (Boak and Ndaruhutse 2011), and, on occasion, results in the delivery of parallel aid in project form. In 2012, just 7% of total aid for education was delivered in the form of sector-wide budget support (OECD-DAC 2014).

The scope of donor support for education extends to humanitarian aid, and supporting the provision of education in conflict-affected countries remains a priority for donors. The Dakar Framework called on the world to "meet the needs of education systems affected by conflict, natural calamities and instability, and conduct educational programmes in ways that promote mutual understanding, peace and tolerance, and that help to prevent violence and conflict." In the years to come, a large proportion of the poor are likely to be increasingly concentrated in fragile states (OECD-DAC 2014). These countries are home to 36% of the world's out-of-school children. Fragile states are expected to be furthest from reaching the MDGs in 2015, despite 35 fragile states being able to meet at least one of the goals by the set deadline (OECD-DAC 2014).

The majority of international humanitarian assistance goes to long-term recipient countries. In 2012, 66% of humanitarian assistance from OECD donors went to countries that had received above-average shares of aid in the form of humanitarian assistance for eight years or more (Development Initiatives 2014). However, high-impact crises that cause many fatalities in a short period tend to be proportionately better funded than protracted emergencies (Dolan 2011).

With protracted emergencies occurring more frequently, the education sector has, over the past decade, tried to convince the humanitarian aid sector that investment in education is life-saving. Definitions of aid to education in humanitarian situations, however, continue to be narrow. The Central Emergency Response Fund (CERF), a standby pooled funding mechanism that aims to make money available for relief work as soon as the need arises, has particular criteria for funding education, including provision of school-tents, education, and recreational materials, emergency repair of education facilities, teacher training in emergencies, and provision of life-saving skills (CERF 2010).

Education continues to be neglected within an already under-resourced humanitarian aid system (UNESCO 2011). It received one of the smallest proportions of its requests for humanitarian aid, 40%, in 2013, compared with 86% for the food sector and 57% for the health sector. In 2010, a resolution by the UN General Assembly called on member states to increase humanitarian funding to education and to consider diversifying contributions to funding channels (United Nations 2010). In 2012, recognizing the importance of the education sector as life-saving, over 20 stakeholders including governments, UN agencies, the private sector, and CSOs, through the UN consolidated appeal process (CAP) called for doubling the percentage of total humanitarian aid earmarked for education to at least 4% of all funds from humanitarian appeals in the UN (United Nations 2012).

In 2013, this modest target was far from being reached with education receiving just 2% of funds from humanitarian appeals (Office for the Coordination of Humanitarian Affairs 2014). Even if the 4% target had been met, some 19.5 million children would still not have been covered by the CAP (Education Cannot Wait

2014). In 2012, humanitarian aid for education in conflict-affected countries was US$105 million, much less significant than the US$1.1 billion in development aid funding for education. For conflict-affected countries that receive low levels of development aid due to the political turmoil, such as Mali, the low prioritization of education in humanitarian funding is particularly problematic (OECD-DAC 2014; Office for the Coordination of Humanitarian Affairs 2014).

A variety of mechanisms are available for donors to fund education in fragile states, including development (recovery) funding, humanitarian appeals, and multi-donor trust funds. But the Inter-Agency Network for Education in Emergency recommends pooled funding to reduce transaction costs and increase coordination and harmonization. Pooled funding mechanisms include CERF, which covers all countries affected by an emergency; and Common Humanitarian Funds (CHFs) and Emergency Response Funds (ERFs), which are both country-specific and provide country-based pooled and predictable funding for implementing agencies on the ground. The share of total humanitarian funding for education disbursed through these three pooling mechanisms rose steeply in proportionate terms from 6.7% in 2010 to 22.1% in 2012, but fell to 11.7% by 2013.

Conclusion

Since the World Education Forum adopted the Dakar Framework for Action: Education for All in 2000, there has been a major global effort to ensure that every child gains access to and completes a good quality education. The achievements of the EFA movement should not be underestimated. While the comprehensive education vision established at Dakar has not been achieved, there is evidence the world has progressed at a faster rate than it would have done if the trends of the 1990s had continued. However, the extent of progress is less than anticipated in 2000 and has definitely been insufficient to match the scale of the ambition. The most disadvantaged children continue to be the last to benefit from education, tens of millions of children are not reaching minimum learning standards in reading and mathematics, and the acquisition of sustainable literacy skills among adults remains a low priority for governments and donors alike. The educational challenges in much of sub-Saharan Africa and South and West Asia are acute, indicating a plethora of missed opportunities. The world has yet to devise a concrete strategy to support the realization of good quality education for all.

Throughout the post-Dakar period, the evidence suggests that at the global level, the pledges made in the Framework were only partially fulfilled. It is possible that the requirements to fulfil the pledges exceeded the capacity of the international community, particularly to influence major change at the national level. What is clear is that the EFA movement suffered once the MDGs became the dominant development agenda and excessive emphasis was placed on universal primary education (UPE). Although the UPE target appealed to the poorest countries which were furthest from it, and to the richest countries which were prepared to support its achievement, it meant the EFA agenda was less attractive to countries that had already achieved, or were close to achieving, UPE. An exception to this pattern was a growing emphasis on learning and its assessment, which gained considerable traction among multilaterals, donors, and EFA supporters.

In moving forward post-2015, lessons must be learned from the positive aspects of the past period working towards EFA. Areas of progress have been characterized by a strong technical focus. Global mechanisms, initiatives, and campaigns that proved relatively influential have had clear objectives, dedicated strategic and technical capacity, been financed collectively, and had overt political support from influential bodies. They have been evaluated regularly, and in most cases have had clear targets.

In contrast, the impact of interventions requiring coordination, political commitment, and influence has been limited at best. Such interventions tended to be loosely organized, voluntary mechanisms, which may have had technical strength but were politically weak. There has been relatively little scrutiny of the global coordination model, especially within the UN, and issues of accountability have not been adequately addressed. A key lesson to emerge from 2000–2015 is that, while technical solutions are important, gaining political influence and traction is of even greater significance, and is, indeed, essential for realizing the scale of reform and action required to achieve EFA at the national level, and hence globally.

An even more ambitious set of education policy priorities is being embedded in the post-2015 vision of global sustainable development. They are meant to be more universal in application, transformative in intent, and inclusive and equitable in practice than the EFA goals. However, there are several potential risks lurking on the horizon, including the concern that unfinished aspects of the EFA agenda will get sidetracked; targeted funding for the poorest countries and most marginalized populations will decline; and that country commitment to ensuring free, good quality basic education for all will get diverted. Furthermore, placing education priorities in the midst of a broad sustainable development agenda may risk promoting a predominantly instrumentalist view of education, as a driver for economic, political, and environmental change. The potency of these risks remains to be seen.

Notes

1. Detailed evidence for the arguments put forward in this chapter can be found in the 2015 *EFA Global Monitoring Report* (UNESCO 2015).
2. Since, 2002, the *EFA Global Monitoring Report* (GMR), published annually by UNESCO but developed by an independent team, has been an authoritative reference aiming to inform, influence, and sustain genuine commitment toward EFA.
3. Two other goals also made explicit reference to girls and women: Goal 2 specifically mentioned the importance of ensuring girls' access to education, and Goal 4 stressed the importance of improving literacy levels for women.
4. The evidence in this section can also be found in the 2015 *EFA Global Monitoring Report* (UNESCO 2015).
5. In tracking aid to "basic education," this section relies on the OECD-DAC definition, which covers primary education, basic life skills for youth and adults, and early childhood education. In that sense, the term is used in a slightly different way than in the previous section, in which "basic education" is understood to cover primary and lower secondary education.
6. Caution is needed when analyzing aid dependence as it can be influenced by increased domestic spending on education, falling aid levels, or a combination of both.

References

Australian Aid. 2012. *Australian Multilateral Assessment March 2012: Global Partnership for Education (GPE)*. Edited by Australian Aid. Canberra: Australian Aid.

Boak, E. and S. Ndaruhutse. 2011. *The Impact of Sector-Wide Approaches*. Edited by CfBT Education Trust. London: CfBT Education Trust.

Bolívar, A. 2011. "The Dissatisfaction of the Losers," In *Pisa Under Examination: Changing Knowledge, Changing Tests, and Changing Schools*, edited by M.A. Pereyra, H.-G. Kotthoff, and R. Cowen. Rotterdam: Sense Publishers.

Burnett, N. 2010. "How to Develop the UNESCO the World Needs: The Challenges of Reform." *Journal of International Cooperation in Education*, 13(2): 89–99.

CERF. 2010. *Central Emergency Response Fund Life-Saving Criteria*. Geneva: Central Emergency Response Fund.

Development Initiatives. 2013. *Investments to End Poverty: Real Money, Real Choices, Real Lives*. Bristol: Development Initiatives Ltd.

Development Initiatives. 2014. *Global Humanitarian Assistance Report 2014*. Bristol: Development Initiatives.

Dolan, J. 2011. *Making it Happen: Financing Education in Countries Affected by Conflict and Emergencies*. Edited by Save the Children. London: Save the Children.

Education Cannot Wait. 2014. *Financing Education in Emergencies: Challenges and Opportunities*. Edited by Education Cannot Wait. Education Cannot Wait.

Global Partnership for Education. 2013a. *GPE Portfolio Review Report*. Washington, DC: Global Partnership for Education.

Global Partnership for Education. 2013b. *Strategic Plan 2012–2015*. Washington, DC: Global Partnership for Education.

Global Partnership for Education. 2014a. *First High-Level Meeting of the Global Partnership for Effective Development Co-operation: Building Towards an Inclusive Post-2015 Development Agenda*. Mexico City: Global Partnership for Effective Development Co-operation.

Global Partnership for Education. 2014b. *GPE disbursements as of 31st May 2014*. Washington, DC: Global Partnership for Education.

Grindle, M.S. 2004. *Despite the Odds: The Contentious Politics of Education Reform*. Princeton: Princeton University Press.

ICAI. 2012. *The Management of UK Budget Support Operations*. Edited by Independent Commission for Aid Impact. London: Independent Commission for Aid Impact.

Inter-Agency Commission. 1990. *World Conference on Education for All: Meeting Basic Learning Needs – Final Report*. New York: Inter-Agency Commission for the World Conference on Education for All.

Kanbur, R. and A. Sumner. 2011. *Poor Countries or Poor People? Development Assistance and the New Geography of Global Poverty*. Retrieved from: http://kanbur.dyson.cornell.edu/papers/KanburSumnerPoorCountriesOrPoorPeople.pdf (accessed November 30, 2015).

Mercer, M. 2014. "Donor Policies, Practices and Investment Priorities in Support of Education, and Post-2015 Prospects: A Review." *International Journal of Educational Development*, 39: 23–31

Montenegro, C.E. and H.A. Patrinos. 2012. "Returns to Schooling Around the World." *World Development Report 2013*. Washington, DC: World Bank.

National Audit Office. 2008. *Department for International Development: Providing Budget Support to Developing Countries*. Edited by National Audit Office. London: National Audit Office.

OECD. 2011. *Better Aid: Aid Effectiveness 2011: Process in Implenting the Paris Declaration*. Paris:OECD.

OECD. 2012. *The Architecture of Development Assistance*. Paris: OECD.

OECD-DAC. 2014. *International Development Statistics: Creditor Reporting System*. Paris: OECD.

Office for the Coordination of Humanitarian Affairs. 2014. *Financial Tracking Service: Tracking Global Humanitarian Aid Flows*. Geneva: United Nations Office for the Coordination of Humanitarian Affairs.

Psacharopoulos, G. 2014. "Benefits and Costs of the Education Targets for the Post-2015 Development Agenda," in *Education Assessment Paper*, edited by Copenhagen Consensus Center. Copenhagen: Copenhagen Consensus Center.

Rose, P., L. Steer, K. Smith, and A. Zubairi. 2013. *Financing for Global Education: Opportunities for Multilateral Action*. Washington, DC; Paris: Center for Universal Education at Brookings; EFA Global Monitoring Report.

Sellar, S. and B. Lingard. 2013. "The OECD and Global Governance in Education." *Journal of Education Policy*, 28(5): 710–725.

Skilbeck, M. 2000. *Education for All: Global Synthesis*. Paris: Secretariat of the International Consultative Forum on Education for All.

Tomasi, S. 2014. *Does Aid Have a Future?* Edited by OECD. Paris: OECD.

UIS. 2000. *Education for All 2000 Assessment: Statistical Document*. Paris: UNESCO Institute for Statistics – for the International Consultative Forum on Education for All.

UNESCO. 2008. *EDUCAIDS Technical Briefs*. Paris: UNESCO.

UNESCO. 2011. *Beyond Busan: Strengthening Aid to improve Education Outcomes*. Paris: UNESCO.

UNESCO. 2015. *EFA Global Monitoring Report 2015: Education for All 2000–2015 – Achievements and Challenges*. Paris: UNESCO.

UNICEF, WHO, and World Bank. 2014. *Joint Child Malnutrition Estimates*. New York; Geneva; Washington, DC: UNICEF; WHO; World Bank.

United Nations. 2010. *The Right to Education in Emergency Situations*. Edited by United Nations General Assembly. New York: United Nations.

United Nations. 2012. *Global Education First Initiative: An Initiative of the United Nations Secretary-General*. New York: United Nations.

Unterhalter, E. 2007. *Gender Schooling and Global Social Justice*. Abingdon: Routledge.

Unterhalter, E. 2014. "Education Targets, Indicators and a Post-2015 Development Agenda: Education for All, the MDGs, and Human Development." *The Power of Numbers: A Critical Review of MDG Targets for Human Development and Human Rights*. Cambridge; New York: Harvard School of Public Health; The New School.

Chapter 14

The Politics of Language in Education in a Global Polity

M. Obaidul Hamid

Introduction

Although the terms "language" and "politics" are often taken for granted in scholarship, their meanings are both inconstant and contested. For instance, language as a uniquely human endowment can rightly be seen as an essential aspect of the social and political identity of the species, which has facilitated its social and political processes since the beginning of human civilization. Yet it cannot be denied that language, particularly in the sense of something nameable, countable, bounded, distinguishable, and roughly translatable from one into another, was invented in Europe in the interests of nation states (Gal 2006). In other words, whether language should be seen as an ontological entity or a cultural construct (e.g. Makoni and Pennycook 2007) is contentious. If the politics of language is defined as ideological representations of language, a definition preferred in this chapter, language can be seen as political, not only in terms of its origin, but also probably in all conceivable ways – "from top to bottom" (Joseph 2006, 17). And if we agree that "[a]ll language is political; and we all are, or had better become, politicians" (Lakoff 1990, 2), it then becomes difficult to draw a line between language and politics (language is politics, politics is language, as Lakoff argues). Nevertheless, the parallel existence of language and politics is tenable, which is corroborated by the academic edifice of Noam Chomsky whose radical political activism has not affected his linguistic conservatism (Olson and Faigley 1991).

This contested terrain of the politics of language constitutes the background of the chapter in which I do not intend to engage in a philosophical discussion of the subject matter. Rather, my aim is more of an applied nature – which is to provide an overview of language issues in education in a globalized world and to comment on

The Handbook of Global Education Policy, First Edition.
Edited by Karen Mundy, Andy Green, Bob Lingard, and Antoni Verger.
© 2016 John Wiley & Sons, Ltd. Published 2016 by John Wiley & Sons, Ltd.

the underlying discourses or ideologies. The question that I try to explicate is: What are the major discourses that inform macro level language policy decisions and their implementation in the contemporary world? My tentative answer is although the global politics of language is enormously complex, it can be seen to reflect crucial features of neo-liberalism, including an understanding of language as capital, de-politicization of languages, commercialization and privatization of language teaching and learning, globalization of language policies, and an open competition for the linguistic market (Block et al. 2012; Duchêne and Heller, 2011; Holborow 1999; Ricento 2012; Skutnabb-Kangas and Phillipson 2010). More critically, the emphasis on the material outcomes of languages within the ideology of linguistic instrumentalism has led, somewhat paradoxically, to what I call "hyper-languaging," which has tended to undermine the role of non-linguistic factors in the pursuit of material ends through languages. This understanding of language will influence policy-makers and their choices in different ways in different contexts with clear implications for economic and social agenda.

The politics of language has generated scholarly interest from diverse fields, including language policy and planning, politics and political economy, philosophy, communication, and cultural studies. In line with my aim, I concentrate on language in education planning. The major thrust of the chapter is concerned with English, the language of globalization. Whether English is the driver of globalization or vice versa may be unclear, but clearly, the relationship between them is symbiotic: If English provides the linguistic and communicative infrastructure to globalization, the latter promotes the cause of English by representing language as imperative for participation in globalized networks, markets, and resources. It is the marriage of English and globalization, whether arranged (Phillipson 1992) or co-incidental (Crystal 1997), and the bringing together of the underlying discourses of the two (see Graddol 1997; Hamid 2010) that have driven individuals, groups, and societies toward more English.

In the next two sections I discuss conceptual issues. The fourth section provides five examples of languages in a globalized world, which are then discussed in the subsequent section to highlight the underlying politics. The final section concludes the discussion with a brief look into the future of the politics of language in a globalized world.

"Political" in the Politics of Language

The largest body of work on the politics of language refers to questions of languages in national, subnational, or supra-national contexts. Thus, we have the politics of language in Australia (Ozolins 1993), China (Kaske 2008), India (Sarangi 2009), Pakistan (Rahman 1998), Singapore (Wee 2003), South Africa (Alexander 2004), and the USA (Crawford 1998). Supra-national politics refers to transnational spaces, either in geographical or institutional senses, for example, the politics of language in Eastern Europe (Landau and Kellner-Heinkele 2001) and in the European Union (EU) (Ammon 2012). Subnational politics may refer to the politics of specific (minority) languages located in the national territory (e.g. Ashley 1999 for Welsh in Wales). Specific-language focused politics may also refer to a commonwealth of polities, for instance, the politics of language in the Spanish-speaking world (Mar-Molinero 2000).

This literature deals with what is called "macro politics" (Alderson 2009), or politics with a capital P, as opposed to "micro politics" or "small p politics" (Janks 2010), and discusses questions of language conflicts and language rights and choices of languages in education and other domains (Kymlicka and Patten 2003). Whether this literature refers to politics explicitly or implicitly, there is rarely any discussion of the meaning of politics. By the politics of language, Pennycook (2001, 46) refers to "a political understanding of language," which is comparable to "political uses of language" (O'Barr 1976, 2). O'Barr considers language as a political resource which is "used to control, to manipulate, and achieve political ends" (1976, 7–8). While his focus is on the political domain, political ends are relevant to apparently non-political contexts of everyday life as well (Lakoff 1990; Joseph 2006). With the latter focus, Lakoff (1990, 7) understands the politics of language as "the usurpation of language by the powerful, in one way or another, to create, enhance, and justify their power." Lakoff (1990) also argues that the politics of language provides a way of understanding how the forms of language facilitate its functions for specific purposes. Although the functions of language are of primary concern to language pragmatists, what languages are believed to be able to do also depends on how they are discursively constructed in the first place. Thus, Pennycook (2001) argues that the politics of language requires taking into account both the intrinsic (nature of language) and extrinsic (functions of language) qualities. Indeed, if one considers the rise of English over the past centuries beginning with British colonization, it becomes obvious that the focus has not been just on what English can do (functions) compared with local vernaculars in the colonies, but also how English as a language has been constructed and what this can tell us about the civilizational status of the "race" who speak the language (Pennycook 2007; Phillipson 1992). The political use of language refers to the representation of language and its functions – both literal and symbolic (Cameron 2006) – in the interest of individuals, groups, institutions, and polities in ways that may or may not be susceptible to empirical authentication. Thus, the politics of language essentially involves discourses of language or language ideologies (Cameron 2006; Gal 2006).

Discourses of language may draw on different aspects of language and communication, both language-internal and -external. Therefore, the politics of language is enacted in different ways in different domains such as the politics of (a) different ways of speaking; (b) talking to others; (c) what the language is; (d) which language to speak; and (e) policing the language (Joseph 2006). In these micro political contexts of everyday communication, the politics concerns doing language or managing language behavior. Joseph also discusses the politics of language choice, which sheds light on:

> Who has the ability to make choices where language is concerned? Power and politics are fundamentally whose will, whose choices, will prevail. Who has the power to determine what is good and bad in English, or what is grammatically right or wrong in any language? Who should decide on the language or languages of education in a multilingual setting? (Joseph 2006, 17)

Thus, beyond the micro politics, he also refers to macro policy issues by pointing to, among other things, the choice of language in education. My focus in this chapter is this macro context where the politics refers specifically to the (ideological) rationale behind the choice of languages for groups, institutions, and polities.

Discourses of Language

Ruiz's (1984, 2010) model of language planning orientations provides a basis for understanding discourses of language and their functions. As represented in Figure 14.1, it divides language planning orientations into descriptive and normative categories, each of which includes three discourses of language, namely language as: (a) resource, (b) problem, and (c) right, under normative orientations; and language as: (a) a tool, (b) a mediator of culture, and (c) a means of expression, under descriptive orientations. These two sets of orientations present a comprehensive overview of different "worldviews" (Petrovic 2005) of language. While the descriptive orientations appear indisputable, the validity of the normative categories can also be provided by referring to the language policy and planning literature since the emergence of the field in the 1960s. For instance, early language planning in the newly decolonized nations was seen as human resource planning modeled on the positivistic social science paradigm (Kaplan and Baldauf 1997). Its focus was usually a single language, which was seen as a requirement for nation-building following European nation state models (Wright 2012). At the same time, the existence of multiple languages in a polity (multilingualism) was discursively constructed as problematic, calling for an intervention in the form of status planning to prefer usually one official language. The representation of linguistic diversity as a problem can be found in recent discussions as well, particularly from an economic perspective (e.g. Ginsburgh and Weber 2011). Finally, the language-as-right is a relatively recent orientation, which has received much attention in the literature (May 2003; Skutnabb-Kangas 2000; Skutnabb-Kangas and Phillipson 2010).

However, one problem with this model is that it provides a depoliticized view of language and its functions. Crawford (1998, 53) argues that the model may not help in understanding "political and ideological factors that go into language policy decisions." Referring to the legislative background of English-only and bilingual education in the USA, he also argues that language planning orientations rarely act as *determinant* in language policy decisions. For instance, in stressing the instrumentality of language, these orientations have overlooked a key ideological issue: that language has served, first and foremost, the interest of nation states, initially in Europe and subsequently in other parts of the world (Wright 2012).

In critiquing Ruiz's language-as-resource orientation, critics have pointed out that an emphasis on the economic value of languages may devalue language in cultural

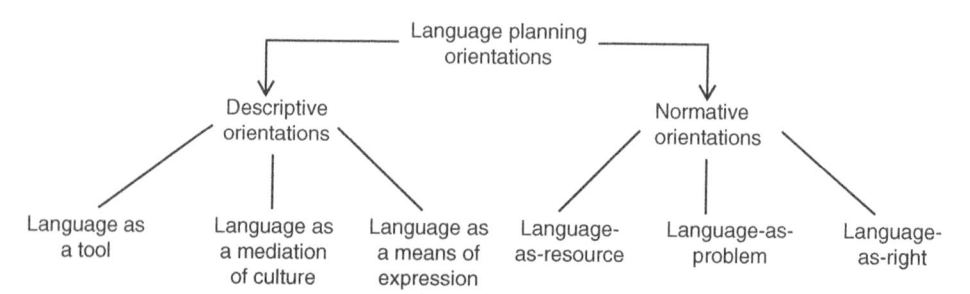

Figure 14.1 Language planning orientations.
Source: Adapted from Ruiz 2010, 163.

terms (May 2003; Petrovic 2005). Moreover, as Petrovic (2005) argues, the emphasis on the economic potential of minority languages may advance the neo-liberal agenda by restoring neo-conservatism. However, whether the promotion of neo-liberalism is intended or unintended, there is no denying that the de-politicization of language in favor of its economics is at the center of the contemporary global politics of languages, as is illustrated in the following section.

Languages in a Global Polity

International languages such as English, French, and Arabic have received scholarly attention for a long time (see Maurais and Morris 2003; Northrup 2013). In particular, the global spread of English has been discussed widely, generating several theories and explanations (Brutt-Griffler 2002; Crystal 1997; Pennycook 1994; Phillipson 1992). Although a conflict between language-as-resource (colonial languages) and language-as-problem (local vernacular languages) underpins much of the discussion, it is the economic and socio-political issues that have been given much explanatory weight (Northrup 2013). For instance, Phillipson's (1992, 47) theory of English linguistic imperialism defined as "the establishment and continuous reconstitution of structural and cultural inequalities between English and other languages" is based on structural questions. Crystal (1997) sees the rise of English as a "natural" outcome of the growing power of the English-speaking nations such as the UK and the USA and the need for a common language for the global econo-cultural system. Brutt-Griffler (2002) also emphasizes this global system in her theorization. However, in place of Phillipson's (1992) argument that English was promoted deliberately by English-speaking countries for their own interests, she locates agency in the masses of the people who have actively sought English for their own interests. Pennycook's explanations are much more complex. While he supports Phillipson's structural explanations, he argues that multiple discourses of English, having their origin in colonialism, contributed to the spread of English since the end of British colonial rule. Maurais and Morris (2003) generate important insights into the global politics and geo-strategies of languages in a globalizing world. Divided into three parts, the volume emphasizes global communication challenges, the major global linguistic domains in terms of regions and institutions, and the languages of wider communication including English, Arabic, German, Russian, Portuguese, and French. The volume illustrates how the fate of languages in a global context has been affected by politics and power relations. It also emphasizes the need for a global language strategy.

However, understanding the global politics of language also requires drawing on language planning issues in national and subnational contexts, which have implications for language issues in transnational contexts. In the remaining part of this section I introduce five examples of language policy of global relevance to base my discussion of the characteristics of the global politics of language.

English in the National Curriculum

There are more non-native speakers of English in the world now than its native speakers. This exponential growth in the English-learning population can be attributed to substantial investment in English learning from both the public and private sectors (e.g. Hamid et al. 2009). Two major language planning reforms that have responded to the globalization of English stand out in the new English-using polities: (a) the early introduction of English (see Baldauf and Nguyen 2012; Kirkpatrick 2012 for Asia and European Commission 2012 for Europe); and (b) adopting English as a medium of instruction (see Doiz et al. 2013; Hamid et al. 2014). The early introduction of English in Asia is driven by national desires to take advantage of English in turning citizens into human capital who can participate in a post-industrial knowledge economy for individual mobility and social and economic development (Hamid 2010). For instance, it is believed that Bangladesh, one of the poorest countries in the world, can change its economic destiny by means of English:

> English in Action will provide the communicative English to *transform the lives of people in Bangladesh* and make a major contribution to the *economic development* of the country [...] It will look to change the lives of up to *25 million people* using new approaches to teaching and learning. (Hamid 2010, 289–290, emphases added)

Vietnam's 2020 project, which is a massive investment in the teaching and learning of English, has comparable policy aspirations. Considering English language education as key to national development, the Vietnamese Ministry of Education and Training aimed to ensure that all young people leaving secondary school by 2020 would have a good command of English, euphemistically called a foreign language (Nguyen 2012).

Although these early English policies are top-down in character (Hamid 2010), they are also responsive to the popularized discourses of English on the ground (Erling and Seargeant 2013).

English and Higher Education

The growing adoption of English as a medium of higher education in Europe and other parts of the world is underpinned by the perceived value of English (Doiz et al. 2013; Hamid et al. 2014). English being the language of knowledge, information, science, and technology, is seen as a natural choice for education in a globalized world (Ammon 2001). One consequence of this choice is the Englishization of higher education (Ammon 2012), which has led to replacing local and national languages. For instance, more and more universities in Europe are opting for English-medium programs as a way of facilitating mobility of academics and students within the EU (Doiz et al. 2013). Higher education institutions in Asian polities, including Singapore, Hong Kong, South Korea, Japan, China, Malaysia, Vietnam, Bangladesh, and Pakistan have relied on English to internationalize higher education and to produce graduates for a globalized job market (Hamid et al. 2014). For instance, Malaysia's national blueprint for higher education called Vision 2020 aims to turn the country into a regional hub of education to attract overseas students in the interest of the national economy (Ali 2013). The Japanese government has called for an increase in the number of English as a Medium of Instruction (EMI) programs to attract more international students into Japanese universities (Bradford 2013). China is also moving toward EMI to meet the challenges of economic globalization and technological revolution and to improve the quality of university and college education (Hu et al. 2014).

Language and Migration

Language and migration is an area that is informed by the economic value of languages in a world that has experienced massive transnational flows of people (Appadurai 1996; Rassool 2012). Proficiency in the dominant language of the migrant society is seen as a necessity for migrants' economic, social, and psychological well-being (e.g. Kim *et al.* 2012). Research in this area is dominated by economic perspectives that examine relationships between migrants' proficiencies in mainstream languages and labor market outcomes (e.g. Chiswick and Miller 2002). State-funded language programs for adult migrants (e.g. Australian Migrant Education Program) and the selection of languages for education of migrant children are informed by the discourses of language, economic well-being, and social integration (e.g. Warriner 2007). This value of language for academic, social, and professional survival of migrants has provided the rationale for the operation of global proficiency tests of English such as the International English Language Testing System (IELTS) and the Test of English as a Foreign Language (TOEFL). For instance, it is common for immigration departments in Western countries to set language proficiency as a requirement for student, work, and residency visas. While on the one hand language and language tests are utilized as social and political tools for managing global flows of people, the nexus between power (political authority to control) and knowledge (measuring language proficiency) has given rise to testing regimes that operate successfully, while hiding their profit-making agenda (Templer 2004). Similarly, the recent policy enthusiasms for introducing citizenship tests, which are essentially language tests, legitimize the value of the dominant language in migrant societies (e.g. McNamara and Ryan 2011).

Minority Languages

Although there have been successful attempts at reviving a small number of endangered languages in some parts of the world, it is widely believed that almost 90% of the world's 6000 plus languages will be extinct in the course of the next century (Skutnabb-Kangas 2000). There are many reasons for language death, but there is no denying that the absence of intergenerational transmission is a crucial one (Clyne and Kipp 2006). Parents may be less interested in transmitting their own (minority) languages to their children based on their assessment of the political economy of languages in the context of the dominance of majority languages (see Villa and Villa 2005, for a shift from Spanish to English in the USA).

The predictable consequences of the loss of linguistic and cultural diversity have given rise to the advocacy for minority language rights and the recognition of these rights in national, regional, and international policy documents (Skutnabb-Kangas 2000). However, advocates of minority language rights have been castigated by their critics, who argue that the recognition of such rights will affect the mobility of minority speakers who also happen to be socially disadvantaged (see May 2003). The construction of "English = mobility" and "minority language = immobility" discourses and their dominance have presented setbacks for proponents of minority language rights including their speakers. For instance, the debate on bilingual education in the USA has its essential focus on the question of language and mobility.

In the face of such critiques, advocates of bilingual education may resort to valorizing minority languages from economic perspectives; for instance, Ruiz's (1984) language-as-resource orientation, as previously discussed.

It is the apparently unassailable economic arguments that have, to a large extent, stood in the way of introducing "mother tongue" as medium of instruction in Africa and other parts of the world (Brock-Utne 2001; Walter and Benson 2012). Despite some scattered examples of reinvigorated mother tongue-based multilingual education, the trend appears to be a continuation of the use of colonial languages as medium of primary education:

> Collectively, more than 2.3 billion people lack access to education in their first language. To the extent that language of instruction matters in education, the data suggests that nearly 40 per cent of the world's population is potentially negatively affected by official policy on language use in education. (Walter and Benson 2012, 282)

While children's education through their first languages is taken for granted in the case of dominant languages such as English, Arabic, Spanish, Chinese, Japanese, and French, the same provision is faced with obstacles in the case of minority languages the world over.

Foreign Languages Other than English

The current status of foreign languages other than English can also be related to linguistic instrumentalism and the economic value of languages (see Chan *et al.* 2011 for Asia). Although foreign languages such as French and German were important cultural capital in the UK and the USA in the past, the global dominance of English may have provided a sense of sufficiency to native speakers of English, who may now be somewhat reluctant to learn foreign languages (Ammon 2012). This may explain why the foreign language teaching scenario in the UK is somewhat different from that in the other EU countries:

> Over the last two decades, Europe has witnessed an increase in the duration of compulsory foreign language teaching [...] Indeed, over the last two decades, all students in general education have had to study a foreign language until the end of upper secondary level, except in Malta and the United Kingdom. (European Commission 2012, 27)

At the same time, the recent interest in certain languages other than English can be attributed to the perceived economic value of these languages. Although, in the USA, Spanish as a second language has been subjected to shifting ideologies, the recent interest in the language can be explained by its potential as a marketable commodity (Leeman 2006). Similarly, the interest in some other languages such as Arabic is due to national security, which is a prerequisite for maintaining political and economic interests (Brecht and Rivers 2012). Australia's inclusion of four Asian languages such as Chinese, Japanese, Korean, and Bahasa Indonesia in the national curriculum has also been guided by the economic rationale (Clyne and Kipp 2006; Djité 2011). Japanese was a favorite language in Australian schools, but Chinese is to take over with the rise of China as a global economic and political power in the so-called Asian century.

Discussion: Neo-liberal and Discursive Politics

An analysis of the global language policy issues discussed in the previous section leads to identifying several aspects of the politics of language. The dominant feature of this politics de-politicizes languages, viewing them as capital – i.e. the economic potential of languages that can be linked to the language-as-resource orientation. This economic imperative underlies instrumentalist and pragmatic views of language (Wee 2003) that consider language as linguistic capital (Bourdieu 1991) required for human capital development (Hamid 2010). For instance, English is represented not only as a tool for economic development (see Erling and Seargeant 2013); the language itself is considered "hard currency" in certain discourses (Nino-Murcia 2003). Indeed, the economic rationale has appeared to be the guiding framework for language management activities in an environment supported by neo-liberalism (Duchêne and Heller 2011). Which languages will be included in education, which ones will be promoted – by extension, which ones deserve to be neglected or merely tolerated or shown *laissez-faire* attitudes – are increasingly guided by the economic rationale (Clyne and Kipp 2006; Djité 2011).

Another key feature, related to the economics of language, is the commercialization of language teaching and the emergence of languages as industries and/or language testing as transnational businesses. Globally, therefore, there is a race for the market share of English in an environment of unfettered capitalism (Kibbee 2003). Although the global English industries are run in the economic and strategic interests of nations – both English-selling and English-buying – privatization is an undeniable feature of the global economy of English. In many parts of Asia, a lot more money is spent on English learning from citizens' private sources than from the public funds, which is attested to by the phenomenal spread of private tutoring in English in the form of cram schools, language centers, one-on-one teaching, and online tutorials (see Hamid *et al.* 2009). Accordingly, privatization of English has taken over the domains traditionally belonging to the public sector. For instance, although in the past English language projects in Bangladesh were implemented by government departments in collaboration with funding agencies, a recent £50 million project called English in Action (2008–2017) funded by the British Department for International Development (DFID) is being managed by a consortium of five partners, without involving government agencies at the level of project implementation. This exemplifies the neo-liberal trend of privatizing education and education policy by outsourcing management to "edu-businesses" (Ball 2009). Related to this, there is the trend of introducing national standardized tests including *No Child Left Behind* (NCLB) in the USA and the National Assessment Program Literacy and Numeracy (NAPLaN) in Australia in the name of ensuring efficiency and accountability. Thus, the global politics of language focuses on the economic value of languages, and the *modus operandi* of this politics is shaped by neo-liberal agendas that characterize contemporary globalization (Block *et al.* 2012; Skutnabb-Kangas and Phillipson 2010).

While the attempts at measuring the economic worth of languages to inform language policy decisions are welcome, such measurements can be tentative at best since it is difficult to measure language outcomes in dollar terms (Kaplan and Baldauf 1997). For instance, the recognition of the role of language in economic and social development has given rise to a fertile area of research (Erling and Seargeant 2013). However, the exact nature of the relationship between language and development remains elusive (Erling and Seargeant 2013). While cost–benefit analysis may contribute to evidence-based language planning (Grin 2003), language policy decisions are often based on perceived, rather than substantiated value of languages. In other words, it is often the discourses of language and its utility that guide language choices for individuals and societies. Construction and dissemination of such discourses about English have been an important strategy behind its global spread and dominance (Pennycook 2000).

The utilitarian view of language in general and English in particular, which dominates the global hierarchy of languages, points to a complex – even contradictory – character of language politics. Materialist critiques of language (e.g. Block et al. 2012; Holborow 1999; Kirk 1994; MacLure 2013) may help deconstruct this politics. This view ignores the value of language for its own sake, as a property of human mind, which constitutes the main focus of Chomskian linguistics. Moreover, it is based on a narrow interpretation of the instrumental role of language, which refers almost exclusively to the economy of language at the expense of the socio-cultural (language as an expression of culture and identity) and political (language for nationalism and national unity) significance of language (see Robichaud and De Schutter 2012). More problematic is the normative relationship between language and material outcomes that underpins the pragmatic view. Language has been valorized in arts and social sciences since the 20th century "linguistic turn" (see Kirk 1994). As a consequence, language has been given a "god-like centrality in the construction and regulation of the worldly affairs" (MacLure 2013, 660), from an epistemological point of view. The ensuing discursive view of social reality underlying post-structuralism and postmodernism has led to undermining the material as an objective reality and to placing a high degree of emphasis on material benefits attributable to language/discourse, particularly for dominant languages such as English. In overvaluing the material benefits of English, it has also emphasized the autonomy of language denying its own materiality and social history. As Holborow (1999, 11) argues:

> Neither language nor English is everything nor determining. Humans are not prisoners of language nor are they, through language, creators of reality. Language is both a social product and a component in the social process of how humans interact and act on the society in which they live.

This materialist view of language allows one to critically examine the material promises of English. For instance, Holborow (1999, 2) argues that "English is either the modernizing panacea or the ruthless oppressor, depending on your place in the world." She does not ignore the potential of English, but she sets some conditionality: whether English gives one a socio-economic lift or leaves one to be doomed depends on one's place in the social world. Indeed, despite the discourse of the popularity of English in a globalized world, who succeeds in learning English and who does not is mediated by socio-economic factors (Hamid 2011). Therefore, the "English-mobility" discourse is political and ideological in the sense that it overlooks the catalyst role played by the material condition of those who seek English and English proficiency. This discursive politics of overvaluing of English can be called "hyper-languaging," which denies not only the materiality of language itself, but also the catalyst role of economic capital in accessing other material and non-material resources including English.

This is not denying the critical role of language in the contemporary text-centric and discourse-saturated deliberative democracies and in a globalized economy in which communication constitutes not only the key to its operation but also its product (Duchêne and Heller 2011; Marazzi 2008). However, if the value of language in the "service" economy lies in communicative efficacy, we need to ask whether it is just language or other things including language that are responsible when communication fails. O'Barr (1976, 22) rightly argues that "the real barriers to effective communication are seldom linguistic." As he explains:

> The real issues are political, not linguistic; and their solutions must lie in the resolution of differentials in power relations. Language is a common medium for the expression of political difficulties; it is the how of many political struggles and manipulations in political systems, but it is not the why. (1976, 19)

Seen from this perspective, it can be argued that advocates of language rights certainly have a great cause, but probably their argument does not have the optimal focus. While language rights are important for maintaining linguistic and cultural diversity and socio-cultural identity, one has to ask whether language rights themselves are enough when the real problem lies elsewhere – in the socio-economic disadvantage and marginalization that happen to be associated with those languages. Political authorities often recourse to the socio-economic marginality of minority groups in defending their denial of language rights in the interest of the latter's mobility.

More crucially, political authorities are guided by their apprehension that recognizing language rights is tantamount to recognizing subnational nationalisms. Similarly, if language rights advocates also consider the recognition of these rights as a first step toward the formation of political nations, the linguistic battle is left with no linguistic substance. In other words, the politics of language has nothing to do with language; it is all about other things that had better not be named (Suleiman 2006).

Conclusions

This chapter has discussed the global politics of language and highlighted its constituent discourses referring to contemporary political, economic, and intellectual paradigms. Discussing how this politics influences education policy-makers in specific contexts and what impact it has on local policy choices in terms of the selection of languages as medium of instruction or curricular provisions, and what implications those choices have for education, development, and socio-cultural diversity and social cohesion was beyond the scope of the chapter. Arguably, the politics manifests in variable forms and has different consequences in different locales, calling for a situated understanding (see Piller and Takahashi 2011).

As has been highlighted, the global politics of language, commensurate with the global linguistic ecology itself, is complex and volatile. While the global dominance of English is a contemporary reality, maintaining the status quo may be difficult due to some recent developments. To some extent, the globalization of English has been punctuated by its simultaneous localization, as embodied by the movements of World Englishes (Kachru 1986) and English as a *lingua franca* (Jenkins, 2009). Similarly, under the impact of new technology in particular, the concept of "translanguaging" (Canagarajah 2012) calls for violating linguistic boundaries of so-called standard languages, including English in favor of "communicative repertoires" to be drawn from multiple languages and other semiotic resources. Furthermore, the potential emergence of Mandarin as a global language under the facilitating condition of the rise of China as a superpower, the establishment of Confucius Institutes in different parts of the world, and the significant increase in the number of people learning Chinese (Zhao and Huang 2010) may also compete with English for the position of global eminence. The growing strength of some other languages of wider communication, including Spanish and Arabic, may also contain the rule of a singular linguistic superpower. At the same time, contemporary efforts at language maintenance, development of awareness of linguistic and cultural diversity, and minority language rights would suggest that some smaller languages may also have some place in the global linguistic ecology, despite the prediction of the loss of many of these languages in the near future.

In the chapter I have made a "political" choice and have bypassed many of these potential aspects of the politics of language to focus on the prevailing discourses of language in a global polity. I have argued, through examples, that the ideology of neo-liberalism, which is also linked to globalization, informs many of the language policy issues of our time. This ideology relates to the discursive view of social reality, which attests to the autonomy of language, taking it out of its material roots to highlight its material promises through the discursive route. I am aware that this reading of the global politics of language is neither uncomplicated nor unproblematic, but to me this constitutes the main plot of the global political narrative of language in a neo-liberal environment, which will probably remain so in the next few decades.

References

Alderson, C.J. 2009. "Setting the Scene," in *The Politics of Language Education: Individuals and Institutions*, edited by C.J. Alderson, 8–44. Clevedon: Multilingual Matters.

Alexander, N. 2004. "The Politics of Language Planning in Post-Apartheid South Africa." *Language Problems and Language Planning*, 28: 113–130.

Ali, L.H. 2013. "A Changing Paradigm in Language Planning: English-Medium Instruction Policy at the Tertiary Level in Malaysia." *Current Issues in Language Planning*, 14: 73–92.

Ammon, U. (ed.). 2001. *The Dominance of English as a Language of Science*. Berlin: Mouton de Gruyter.

Ammon, U. 2012. "Language Policy in the European Union (EU)," in *The Cambridge Handbook of Language Policy*, edited by B. Spolsky, 570–591. Cambridge: Cambridge University Press.

Appadurai, A. 1996. *Modernity at Large: Cultural Dimensions of Globalization*. Minneapolis: University of Minnesota Press.

Ashley, L.R.N. 1999. "Welsh in Wales: Language, Culture, and Politics." *Geolinguistics*, 25: 1–34.

Baldauf, R.B. Jr and H.T.M. Nguyen. 2012. "Language Policy in Asia and the Pacific," in *The Cambridge Handbook of Language Policy*, edited by B. Spolsky, 617–638. Cambridge: Cambridge University Press.

Ball, S.J. 2009. "Privatizing Education, Privatizing Education Policy, Privatizing Educational Research: Network Governance and the 'Competition State.'" *Journal of Education Policy*, 24: 83–99.
Block, D., J. Gray, and M. Holborow. 2012. *Neoliberalism and Applied Linguistics*. London and New York: Routledge.
Bourdieu, P. 1991. *Language and Symbolic Power*. Trans. G. Raymond and M. Adamson. Cambridge: Polity Press.
Bradford, A. 2013. "English-Medium Degree Programs in Japanese Universities: Learning from the European Experience." *Asian Education and Development Studies*, 2: 225–240.
Brecht, R.D. and W.P. Rivers. 2012. "US Language Policy in Defence and Attack," in *The Cambridge Handbook of Language Policy*, edited by B. Spolsky, 262–277. Cambridge: Cambridge University Press.
Brock-Utne, B. 2001. "Education for All – in Whose Language?" *Oxford Education Review*, 27: 115–134.
Brutt-Griffler, J. 2002. *World English: A Study of its Development*. Clevedon: Multilingual Matters.
Cameron, D. 2006. "Ideology and Language." *Journal of Political Ideologies*, 11: 141–152.
Canagarajah, S.A. 2012. *Translingual Practice: Global Englishes and Cosmopolitan Relations*. London: Routledge.
Chan, W.M., K.N. Chin, and T. Suthian (eds). 2011. *Foreign Language Teaching in Asia and Beyond: Current Perspectives and Future Directions*. Berlin: Walter de Gruyter.
Chiswick, B.R. and P.W. Miller. 2002. "Immigrant Earnings: Language Skills, Linguistic Concentrations and the Business Cycle." *Journal of Population Economics*, 15: 31–57.
Clyne, M. and S. Kipp. 2006. "Australia's Community Languages." *International Journal of the Sociology of Language*, 180: 7–21.
Crawford, J. 1998. "Language Politics in the U.S.A.: The Paradox of Bilingual Education." *Social Justice*, 25: 50–69.
Crystal, D. 1997. *English as a Global Language*. Cambridge; New York: Cambridge University Press.
Djité, P.G. 2011. "Language Policy in Australia: What Goes Up Must Come Down?" in *Uniformity and Diversity in Language Policy: Global Perspectives*, edited by C. Norby and J. Hajek, 53–67. Clevedon: Multilingual Matters.
Doiz, A., D. Lasagabaster, and J.M. Sierra (eds). 2013. *English-Medium Instruction at Universities: Global Challenges*. Clevedon: Multilingual Matters.
Duchêne, A. and M. Heller (eds). 2011. *Language in Late Capitalism: Pride and Profit*. Florence: Routledge.
Erling, E.J. and P. Seargeant (eds). 2013. *English and Development: Policy, Pedagogy and Globalization*. Clevedon: Multilingual Matters.
European Commission. 2012. *Key Data on Teaching Languages at School in Europe – 2012*. Brussels: Education, Audiovisual and Cultural Executive Agency.
Gal, S. 2006. "Migration, Minorities and Multilingualism: Language Ideologies in Europe," in *Language Ideologies, Policies and Practices: Language and the Future of Europe*, edited by C. Mar-Molinero and P. Stevenson, 13–27. Basingstoke: Palgrave Macmillan.
Ginsburgh, V. and S. Weber. 2011. *How Many Languages Do We Need? The Economics of Linguistic Diversity*. Princeton: Princeton University Press.
Graddol, D. 1997. *The Future of English?: A Guide to Forecasting the Popularity of the English Language in the 21st Century*. London: British Council.
Grin, F. 2003. "Language Planning and Economics." *Current Issues in Language Planning*, 4: 1–66.
Hamid, M.O. 2010. "Globalization, English for Everyone and English Teacher Capacity: Language Policy Discourses and Realities in Bangladesh." *Current Issues in Language Planning*, 11: 289–310.
Hamid, M.O. 2011. "Socio-Economic Characteristics and English Language Achievement in Rural Bangladesh." *Bangladesh eJournal of Sociology*, 8: 31–50.

Hamid, M.O., H.T.M. Nguyen, and R.B. Baldauf Jr (eds). 2014. *Language Planning for Medium of Instruction in Asia*. London and New York: Routledge.

Hamid, M.O., R. Sussex, and A. Khan. 2009. "Private Tutoring in English for Secondary School Students in Bangladesh." *TESOL Quarterly*, 43: 281–308.

Holborow, M. 1999. *The Politics of English: A Marxist View of Language*. London: Sage.

Hu, G., L. Li, and J. Lei. 2014. "English-Medium Instruction at a Chinese University: Rhetoric and Reality." *Language Policy*, 13: 21–40.

Janks, H. 2010. "Language, Power and Pedagogies," in *Sociolinguistics and Language Education*, edited by N.H. Hornberger and S.L. McKay, 40–61. Bristol: Multilingual Matters.

Jenkins, J. 2009. "English as a Lingua Franca: Interpretations and Attitudes." *World Englishes*, 28: 200–207.

Joseph, J.E. 2006. *Language and Politics*. Edinburgh: Edinburgh University Press.

Kachru, B.B. 1986. "The Power and Politics of English." *World Englishes*, 5: 121–140.

Kaplan, R.R. and R.B. Baldauf, Jr. 1997. *Language Planning: From Practice to Theory*. Clevedon: Multilingual Matters.

Kaske, E. 2008. *The Politics of Language in Chinese Education, 1895–1919*. Boston: Brill.

Kibbee, D.A. 2003. "Language Policy and Linguistic Theory," in *Languages in a Globalizing World*, edited by J. Maurais and M.A. Morris, 47–57. Cambridge: Cambridge University Press.

Kim, S.H.O., J. Ehrich, and L. Ficorilli. 2012. "Perceptions of Settlement Well-being, Language Proficiency, and Employment: An Investigation of Immigrant Adult Language Learners in Australia." *International Journal of Intercultural Relations*, 36: 41–52.

Kirk, N. 1994. "History, Language, Ideas and Postmodernism: A Materialist Critique." *Social History*, 19: 221–240.

Kirkpatrick, A. 2012. "English in ASEAN: Implications for Regional Multilingualism." *Journal of Multilingual and Multicultural Development*, 33: 331–344.

Kymlicka, W, and A. Patten (eds). 2003. *Language Rights and Political Theory*. Oxford: Oxford University Press.

Lakoff, R.T. 1990. *Talking Power: The Politics of Language in Our Lives*. New York: Basic Books.

Landau, J.M. and B. Kellner-Heinkele. 2001. *Politics of Language in the Ex-Soviet Muslim States*. London: Hurst and Company.

Leeman, J. 2006. "The Value of Spanish: Shifting Ideologies in United States Language Teaching." *ADFL Bulletin*, 38: 32–39.

MacLure, M. 2013. "Researching Without Representation? Language and Materiality in Post-Qualitative Methodology." *International Journal of Qualitative studies in Education*, 26: 658–667.

Makoni, S. and A. Pennycook. 2007. *Disinventing and Reconstituting Languages*. Clevedon: Multilingual Matters.

Marazzi, C. 2008. *Capital and Language: From the New Economy to the War Economy*. Trans. Michael Hardt. Los Angeles: Semiotext(e).

Mar-Molinero, C. 2000. *The Politics of Language in the Spanish-Speaking World*. London; New York: Routledge.

Maurais, J. and M.A. Morris (eds). 2003. *Languages in a Globalizing World*. Cambridge: Cambridge University Press.

May, S. 2003. "Rearticulating the Case for Minority Language Rights." *Current Issues in Language Planning*, 4: 95–125.

McNamara, T. and K. Ryan, 2011. "Fairness Versus Justice in Language Testing: The Place of English Literacy in the Australian Citizenship Test." *Language Assessment Quarterly*, 8: 161–178.

Nguyen, H.T. 2011. "Primary English Language Education Policy in Vietnam: Insights from Implementation." *Current Issues in Language Planning*, 12: 225–249.

Nino-Murcia, M. 2003. "'English is Like the Dollar': Hard Currency Ideology and the Status of English in Peru." *World Englishes*, 22: 121–142.

Northrup, D. 2013. *How English Became the Global Language*. New York: Palgrave.

O'Barr, W.M. 1976. "The Study of Language and Politics," in *Language and Politics*, edited by W.M. O'Barr and J.F. O'Barr, 1–27. The Hague; Paris: Mouton.

Olson, G. and L. Faigley. 1991. "Language, Politics, and Composition: A Conversation With Noam Chomsky." *Journal of Advanced Composition*, 11: 1–35.

Ozolins, U. 1993. *The Politics of Language in Australia*. Cambridge; New York: Cambridge University Press.

Pennycook, A. 1994. *Cultural Politics of English as an International Language*. London: Longman.

Pennycook, A. 2000. "English, Politics, Ideology: From Colonial Celebration to Postcolonial Performativity," in *Ideology, Politics and Language Policies: Focus on English*, edited by T. Ricento, 107–109. Amsterdam: John Benjamins.

Pennycook, A. 2001. *Critical Applied Linguistics: A Critical Introduction*. Mahwah: Lawrence Erlbaum.

Pennycook, A. 2007. "ELT and Colonialism," in *International Handbook of English Language Teaching*, edited by J. Cummins and C. Davison, 13–24. New York: Springer.

Petrovic, J.E. 2005. "The Conservative Restoration and Neoliberal Defenses of Bilingual Education." *Language Policy*, 4: 395–416.

Phillipson, R. 1992. *Linguistic Imperialism*. Oxford: Oxford University Press.

Piller, I. and K. Takahashi. 2011. "Linguistic Diversity and Social Inclusion." *International Journal of Bilingual Education and Bilingualism*, 14: 371–381.

Rahman, T. 1998. *Language and Politics in Pakistan*. Karachi: Oxford University Press.

Rassool, N. 2012. "English and Migration," in *The Politics of English: Conflict, Competition, Co-existence*, edited by A. Hewings and C. Tagg, 47–92. Milton Keynes: Open University.

Ricento, T. 2012. "Political Economy and English as a 'Global' Language." *Critical Multilingualism Studies*, 1: 31–56.

Robichaud, D. and H. De Schutter. 2012. "Language is Just a Tool! On the Instrumentalist Approach to Language," in *The Cambridge handbook of language policy*, edited by B. Spolsky, 124–145. Cambridge: Cambridge University Press.

Ruiz, R. 1984. "Orientations in Language Planning." *NABE Journal*, 8: 15–34.

Ruiz, R. 2010. "Reorienting Language-as-Resource," in *International Perspectives on Bilingual Education: Policy, Practice, and Controversy*, edited by J.E. Petrovic, 155–172. Charlotte: Information Age Publishing.

Sarangi, A. (ed.). 2009. *Language and Politics in India*. New Delhi: Oxford University Press.

Skutnabb-Kangas, T. 2000. "Linguistic Human Rights and Teachers of English," in *The Sociopolitics of English Language Teaching*, edited by J.K. Hall and W.G. Eggington, 22–44. Clevedon: Multilingual Matters.

Skutnabb-Kangas, T. and R. Phillipson. 2010. "The Global Politics of Language: Markets, Maintenance, Marginalization, or Murder?" in *The Handbook of Language and Globalization*, edited by N. Coupland, 1–19. Oxford: Blackwell.

Suleiman, Y. 2006. "Constructing Languages, Constructing National Identities," in *Sociolinguistics of Identity*, edited by T. Omoniyi and G. White, 50–74. London: Continuum.

Templer, B. 2004. "High-Stakes Tests as High Fees: Notes and Queries on the International English Assessment Market." *Journal for Critical Education Policy Studies*, 2: 189–226.

Villa, D.J. and J.R. Villa, 2005. "Language Instrumentality in Southern New Mexico: Implications for the Loss of Spanish in the Southwest." *Southwest Journal of Linguistics*, 24: 169–84.

Walter, S.J. and C. Benson. 2012. "Language Policy and Medium of Instruction in Formal Education," in *The Cambridge Handbook of Language Policy*, edited by B. Spolsky, 278–300. Cambridge: Cambridge University Press.

Warriner, D. 2007. "Language Learning and the Politics of Belonging: Sudanese Women Refugees *Becoming* and *Being* 'American.'" *Anthropology and Education Quarterly*, 38: 343–359.

Wee, L. 2003. "Linguistic Instrumentalism in Singapore." *Journal of Multilingual and Multicultural Development*, 24: 211–224.
Wright, S. 2012. "Language Policy, the Nation and Nationalism," in *The Cambridge Handbook of Language Policy*, edited by B. Spolsky, 59–78. Cambridge: Cambridge University Press.
Zhao, H. and J. Huang. 2010. "China's Policy of Chinese as a Foreign Language and the use of Overseas Confucius Institutes." *Educational Research for Policy and Practice*, 9: 127–142.

Chapter 15

The Global Governance of Teachers' Work

Susan L. Robertson

Introduction

Currently unprecedented global attention is being directed at the "quality" of school teachers in education systems around the world (World Bank 2012; OECD 2005; 2009; 2014a) aimed at "revising and strengthening the professional profile of the teaching profession" (European Commission 2014, 4). At one level this refocusing on teacher professionalism is to be welcomed. In many countries, teachers have been at the sharp edge of reforms aimed at promoting global competition and higher student performance. However, many of these reforms have been accompanied by what Maguire and Ball (1994) call a "discourse of derision" – with teachers and their unions viewed as major impediments to modernizing the sector (see OECD 2001; Bruns *et al.* 2011; Kingdon *et al.* 2014). This new focus on teachers is not unproblematic. If anything, there is a new urgency surrounding the call for the reform of teachers' work and workplaces, in that the global competitiveness stakes are regarded as even higher with the rise of China to the East and the economic slowdown in the West. And it is this urgency that is used to legitimate the rescaling of power and authority to a small group of global agencies to advance an ambitious set of projects aimed at governing teachers' work globally. Yet this is not to suggest the global governing of teachers' work is a new phenomenon. Rather I will be arguing that the form, scope, and outcomes of this new global governing of teachers are now very different from that of the post-World War II period. The purpose of this chapter is to explore and explain this difference, and what this means for teachers and for learners.

My point of entry will be through two major political projects focused on teachers: the Organisation for Economic Co-operation and Development's (OECD) Teaching

The Handbook of Global Education Policy, First Edition.
Edited by Karen Mundy, Andy Green, Bob Lingard, and Antoni Verger.
© 2016 John Wiley & Sons, Ltd. Published 2016 by John Wiley & Sons, Ltd.

and Learning International Survey (TALIS) launched in 2007 and which reported in 2008 and 2014; and the World Bank's *SABER-Teacher* launched in 2010 and which has begun to report on a number of the countries in the project. TALIS should be viewed as a parallel data collection project to the OECD's Programme for International Student Assessment – or PISA – which began in 2000 and reports every three years on the learning of 15 year olds (see Grek 2009; Sellar and Lingard 2013). Both in the wings and on center stage is a group of edu-philanthropists, foundations, corporations, and consultants willing to give advice and provide those services that will help teachers and nations compete more effectively in the global economy.

Theoretically, I will be drawing upon the work of Bernstein (1990; 2000) to help grasp the nature of shifts in power and control – as governing moves from what I have called "thin" to "thickening" global governance. I also want to avoid the trap of implying all global processes happen above the nation and national scale. Instead, Sassen's (2006) arguments on "denationalization" are particularly relevant in that we will see these processes operating deep *inside* national territorial spaces and institutional domains, in turn transforming these spaces and social relations into those that face out to the global and embrace its logic.

Governing

Governing is a pedagogical relationship, both in the broadest of senses, as "…a fundamental social context through which cultural reproduction-production takes place" (Bernstein 2000, 3), and, in its more narrow sense, as a pedagogical practice involving teachers and learners. Dale (2008, 1) makes a similar point when he says that "…very basically, education is always part of what I call 'the social contract', the political goals of the wider society, its hegemonic project, to use a different terminology. I shall refer to the way education is organised to make its contribution to the social contract as the ontology of governance […] and that governance always has a pedagogic element." Governance as pedagogy refers to the consequences of the nature and form of the governance of education for identities and their social relations (Dale 2008, 5). In examining the policies and programmes of the global agencies with regard to teachers and their work, we see a concern for governing in both these senses.

I will draw upon the work of Basil Bernstein (1990; 2000) to develop my analysis of transformations in the power to govern teachers in national territorial spaces (see also Robertson 2012). The concepts of "field of symbolic control," "classification," and "framing" are particularly helpful (Bernstein 1990; 2000). By "field of symbolic control," Bernstein (1990, 134–135) means those agents and agencies who specialize in discursive codes that they dominate. In the case of teachers' work, we can place here those agents or organizations who shape teacher policies and regulate teacher practices through the ways in which they determine what is thinkable and doable. In the current environment, this refers to organizations like the OECD, the World Bank, the Bill and Melinda Gates Foundation, global edu-business firms like Pearson Education, Education Fast Forward, and McKinsey and Company. I will be arguing that the denationalization of teachers' work reflects both a recalibration in power relations over who determines the discursive codes in the field of symbolic control and a rescaling of the governing technologies, which in turn produce what is thinkable and doable. By "classification" Bernstein (2000, 6) means "the what and who" of the social division of labor; for instance, the qualified teacher, assistant teacher, head teacher, ministry official, and so on. Each of these categories has a particular identity, voice, and consciousness produced through governing (Robertson 2011, 285). By "framing" Bernstein (2000, 12) is concerned to understand who controls what; in other words, whether the transmitter as opposed to the acquirer (who) has control over the criteria for realizing particular practices (what). For instance, do teachers (as acquirers) claim professional expertise and therefore the right to determine the rules for realizing classroom practices, or do the transmitters (such as the national state or international agencies like the OECD) strongly frame teacher policies in ways that limit the possibilities for teacher interpretation and enactment? I will use these three concepts by Bernstein to trace out changing relations of power and control over teachers and their work over time and space. I'll also be asking what this means for teacher power, education politics, student learning, and wider concerns of democratic accountability in a post-Westphalian world.

Global Governance

There is a tendency in accounts of "global governance" to view it as a phenomenon of the 1990s emerging out of the maelstrom of the 1970s global economic and political crisis. However, the post-war Bretton Woods institutions (such as the World Bank, the International Monetary Fund (IMF), the United Nations Educational, Scientific and Cultural Organization (UNESCO) and the International Labor Organization (ILO)), along with the OECD, had begun to acquire "thin" global governing capability in the post-World War II period. This capacity was to become more crucial from the 1990s onwards, widely viewed as the new global era (Held *et al.* 1999; Mittelman 2004).

The term global governance first emerged in the mid-1970s. Overbeek (2010, 697) argues the early roots of the term were considerably more radical than its current incarnation, which tends to be aligned with the global rule of capital. According to Overbeek (2010, 697–698), early advocates, like Falk (1975), focused "...on the shortcomings of traditional state governments in confrontation with problems that transcended the reach of individual states and on the inherently undemocratic nature of whatever international coordination of policy does occur." This was to change in the 1990s, where it gained currency as a respectable concept following the collapse of the Soviet Union. "The defeat of the Soviet challenge to the Western (primarily United States) claim to represent the common good of all humanity fundamentally altered the terms of debate on international politics. With a global alternative system out of the way, it became possible to promote a depoliticized and watered down version of 'global governance' as the ideal consensual and non-adversarial manner to manage the world's affairs" (Overbeek 2010, 698). Furthermore, the capacities and sovereignty of national states, on the one hand, and the world order on the other, were being transformed as a result of processes broadly associated with globalization (Sassen, 2006). Nation states were no longer the *only* (if they ever were), or *the most* significant, building blocks in the world order. Rather they were being joined by a range of other actors exercising new forms of transnational authority. This development reached its apogee in the report of the international Commission on Global Governance (CGG) published in 1995.

A large and distinct global governance literature emerged out of these debates, with global governance being defined by Rosenau as "governance without government" (cf. Rosenau and Cziempiel 1992). The CGG's own definition of global governance is also highly quoted: as "The sum of the many ways in which individuals and institutions, public and private, manage their common affairs. It is a continuing process through which conflicting or diverse interests may be accommodated and cooperative action may be taken" (CGG 1995, 2). However, this is an apolitical definition in the sense that power is underplayed, there is a pluralist conception of actors and interests, and structural power is absent. However, as we will come to see from this chapter, power is asymmetrical, interests are aligned with capital and big business and the restructuring of teachers' labor can be tied to changes in the strategies and structures of global capitalism.

The "Thin" Global Governance of Teachers' Work

In writing on to the global governance of education, Mundy (2007) argues that in the post-World War II period the ideas of "education as development" and "standard setting" were shared global aspirations. However, the over-riding logic during this period was that it was the sub/national state who would undertake these tasks. Thus, during this period, the role of international organizations like UNESCO and ILO was to help structure a normative understanding of what educational development could and should be about (levels, inputs, processes) around the globe, and, in tandem with bilateral agencies and a weak international federation of teacher unions and associations, to support and boost national education, economic and social development. What was being globalized, however, was a particular "idea" of education, modeled on the one that had come to dominate the Western world; that of modernity, with its commitment to science, progress, individualism, and self-betterment (Meyer *et al.* 1992).

As standard setter, UNESCO was able to develop considerable expertise in education, with education planning a particular strength. With World Bank funding, it set up a statistics branch – the UNESCO Division of Statistics – used to inform education development activities around the right to education. The main objective was to provide member states with internationally comparable data to help them plan and develop national education and literacy programmes (Cusso and D'Amico 2005, 202). Cusso and D'Amico (2005, 200) argue, UNESCO tended to respect the diversity of national education systems, and hence did not publish rankings of countries based on statistical indicators, although technically these would have been possible. The locus of power and authority thus continued to be situated with the Westphalian nation state (Sassen 2006).

This can be seen in the ILO/UNESCO Recommendation concerning the Status of Teachers, adopted on October 5, 1966 (ILO/UNESCO 2008, 8). In 146 paragraphs divided into 13 sections, the Recommendation set out the rights and responsibilities of teachers, including international standards for their initial preparation and further education, recruitment, employment, teaching and learning conditions, security of tenure, disciplinary procedures, participation in education decision-making, and so on.

> ...[T]eaching should be regarded as a profession: it is a form of public service which requires of teachers, expert knowledge and specialised skills, acquired and maintained

through rigorous and continuing stud ... teachers should enjoy academic freedom in the discharge of professional duties to include the choice and selection of teaching materials ... and that their salaries should reflect the importance to society of the teaching function... (2008, 8)

These guidelines were to be the basis of a "national" dialogue between teachers and national educational authorities and unions regarding teaching as a profession, in turn shaping national laws and practices. As a global Recommendation (unlike a Declaration), it was neither subject to national ratification, nor did it have national signatories. In Bernstein's (2000) terms, then, it was strongly classified in that it held a view of teachers with distinctive claims to identity and authority. However, it was weakly framed in that those in national settings (teachers, teacher unions, education departments) were able to significantly shape, and realize, their own conceptions of the good teacher. We can argue, therefore, that the global governance of teachers over the period 1945–late 1990s was "thin" in that though there were global agencies helping shape the terms of the debate, the greatest volume of power and authority lay with the sub/national scale, and in some cases with teachers and the teaching profession.

Teachers and the Race to the Top

The emergence of neo-liberalism as a political project in the 1980s, and its subsequent reshaping of state strategies and spaces over the next three decades, resulted in a series of major reorganizations of public services and the ways in which they were governed. By the early 1990s, it was possible to see deep and far-reaching changes to teachers' work and workplaces in those countries that had embraced market liberalism. Furthermore, not only was the basis of teachers' professional expertise challenged, but those within the system were faced with growing demands around institutional efficiencies and student performance.

Education as a sector was particularly important in the new world order in that it produced the learners and future workers for the putative "knowledge-based economy." And if the future of any country was increasingly dependent upon the ongoing and rapid production of ideas leading to innovation and new products, then learners would need to be active problem solvers, as well as entrepreneurs, whilst teachers would have to learn to teach differently so as to produce a kind new learner.

From early 2000 onward the OECD had become increasingly concerned with the emerging issues with the teaching profession, arguing that teachers continued to favor approaches to teaching that were not necessarily evidence-based, and that their work and workplaces looked much as they had done more than a century before. In 2002 the OECD launched a major project reviewing teacher policy, drawing in 25 member states who committed substantial resources to this review (OECD 2005, 3). A final report, *Teachers Matter*, was published in 2005. This placed teachers' work, and the question of policy to regulate teachers, high on national agendas. Arguing that "[t]his OECD project provides probably the most comprehensive analysis ever undertaken of teacher policy issues at the international level..." (OECD 2005, 3) and that participating countries could learn from each other through "...sharing innovative and successful initiatives, and to identify policy options for attracting, developing and retaining effective teachers..." (OECD 2005, 3) – report was a reaction to wider issues surrounding teacher recruitment (image and status of teachers), the composition of the workforce (growing discipline issues amongst male students, academically weaker students entering teaching), the unequal geographic distribution of good teachers, declining salaries amongst teachers, and a limited incentive structures that might recognize and reward good teachers.

The over-riding concern, however, was the effect of this on pupil performance and national economic competitiveness in the global economy. In the OECD's view this had major implications for realizing globally competitive knowledge economies. The rise of China to the East, and the specter of a declining West, stimulated a growing set of anxieties amongst policy-makers about the capacity of the education system – from schools to universities – to deliver creative, innovative, and entrepreneurial students able to take on this challenge.

In the USA, these anxieties were aired in reports such as *Rising Above the Gathering Storm* published by the National Academies of Sciences in 2005 and *Rising Above the Gathering Storm, Revisited* in 2010. There were worries over where the USA was ranked on the various international competitiveness indicators (National Academies of Sciences 2010, 6), which are placed together in one table; ranked sixth in the world on current innovation-based competitiveness; 11th in the OECD on the percentage of young adults who have graduated from high school; 23rd out of 63 countries (PISA results) on the science proficiency of 15 year olds; 31st out of 63 countries (PISA results) on the mathematics proficiency of 15 year olds; 40th in the world on improvements in innovation-based competitiveness in the past decade, and so on. Worse, the National Academies of Sciences declared that the unanimous decision of the committee members was that the nation's outlook had not improved but had worsened. This global "race to the top," as it was called in, both the UK (Sainsbury Review 2007) and the USA (see program of funding by the US Department of Education 2015), resulted in new funded initiatives around student assessment, data systems to measure learning gains, and a renewed focus on teacher recruitment and capacity, and how to deal with poor performing schools.

But an emerging view began to circulate and settle: that a key strategy of top performing education systems around the globe was recruiting top teachers and keeping them in the system. McKinsey and Company, an influential global consulting firm, produced two reports on top-performing education systems (Barber and Mourshed 2007; Mourshed et al. 2010). Arguing that "the quality of the education system cannot exceed the quality of its teachers" (Barber and Mourshed 2007, 7), the reports highlighted the centrality of effective teachers and systems to support the development of teachers' pedagogical practices. Teachers were also the subjects of a major research and reform initiative launched in 2009 and funded by the corporate philanthropic Bill and Melinda Gates Foundation. Measures of Effective Teaching (MET) represents a huge investment from the foundation – some US$335 million – gathering an unprecedented amount of data on teachers and students in six large school districts in the USA (Robertson 2012). The goal was to create a teacher evaluation system to boost students' educational performance and the performance of the US economy. However another set of facts was evident from the McKinsey and Company reports: that in top performing systems, teachers were well paid, and recruitment into teacher training was highly selective.

Thickening Global Governance of Teachers' Work

The OECD chose to pursue a different route to the well paid, bright teacher solution. Instead of arguing for better wages and changes to the system of selection of teacher trainees, it sought to advance a project that would define the pedagogical attributes of a good teacher and collect data on performance to steer participating countries in this direction. Like a Global Positioning System (GPS) – the OECD had a clear sense of the map of the terrain, the route of travel, and the necessary movements to be made in order to arrive. In 2007, the OECD launched the Teaching and Learning International Survey (TALIS) – a data-gathering and benchmarking project aimed at lower secondary teachers. This could then be linked, though some might argue somewhat tenuously, with the OECD's Programme for International Student Assessment (PISA). And it is the Indicators and Analysis Division (IAD) within the OECD, guided by global policy entrepreneur Andreas Schleicher, now Head of the Education and Skills Directorate, who has most recently set the terms of the debate for what counts as a good teacher, and the scale at which teachers' work will be governed; that is, the global. In 2011, the OECD along with Education International – the global teachers' union, played a major role in shaping the first International Summit on the Teaching Profession. Hosted by the US Department of Education, Andreas Schleicher played the role of "framer" throughout the conference – bringing evidence from the first round of TALIS into a conversation with PISA results and an individual country's performance. A feature of this event was the cast of sponsors; a mix of philanthropic foundations and corporations, all with an interest in the governing of teachers' work. This event is now run annually; a continuing collaboration between the OECD and Education International, and hosted by a participating country partner.

TALIS is the OECD's instrument for providing what it calls "a global selfie" of teachers (OECD 2014a, 7); that is, a mirror on the teaching profession about what the profession looks like. A first round of reporting took place in 2008 on 24 countries (17 OECD countries; seven non-member countries). In 2013, with more signed up participants (and with a significant tranche of funding from the European Commission), the OECD undertook a second round of data collection on teachers, and reported this in 2014. A special report was also prepared on teachers in Europe (European Commission 2014). TALIS collects data from teachers and head teachers regarding their views on student learning, what teachers do in the classroom (hours worked and on what tasks), how school leaders support teachers, teachers engagement with professional development, how schools use teacher appraisals, teachers' views on their own self efficacy and thus confidence as teachers, and whether teachers are satisfied with their work.

At first glance these questions and categories look innocent enough. However, category making, and the materialization of new practices and identities, is *always* political in that it is about power (Bernstein 2000). The question, then, to be addressed here is the degree of interpretation – or control – given to teachers over this process, or indeed what opportunities were given to the teaching profession to participate in shaping this global project? The evidence suggests very little. Those who seem to have a say include a range of global firms who will benefit hugely from any business that might come their way as a result of changing pedagogical practices, learning materials, testing material, ongoing professional development, and so on

(Ball 2012). The launch of TALIS 2013 on June 25, 2014 – a live, two-hour global spectacle – makes this point well. It was hosted by Education Fast Forward, a subsidiary of Promethean – a global supplier of learning materials. Andreas Schleicher from the OECD and Michael Fullan – a global education consultant – were the invited speakers and fielded questions.

The TALIS instrument strongly classifies and frames "the good teacher" in that there is a strong normative view injected into what a good teacher is and advice given to teachers and head teachers in a specially designed teacher booklet as to what they might do to rectify their performance. For instance *A Teachers' Guide to TALIS 2013* (OECD 2014b) provides "insights and advice to teachers and school leaders on how they can improve teaching and learning in their schools." The OECD advises teachers to engage in small group work, use active pedagogy, engage in professional development, use mentoring systems to enhance cooperation and build trust, report daily and weekly inefficiencies in the running of the school, and so on.

We can see from the discussion of the indices in the weighty Technical Annexes (OECD 2009, 268–275; OECD 2014a, 208–256) the OECD's own strong assumptions about teacher pedagogy. Teachers are asked to respond to a series of questions, for instance around teachers' beliefs, indicating how strongly (1 = strongly disagree; 4 = strong agree) they agree with the statement. In relation to teacher beliefs, there are two opposing indices: direct transmission (the implication here is a bad teacher) or constructivism (the implication here is a good teacher). Here the OECD (2009, 269) states: "In short, constructivist beliefs are characterised by a view of the teacher as a facilitator of learning with more autonomy given to students whereas a direct transmission view sees the teacher as the instructor, providing information and demonstrating solutions." In other words, the competent teacher facilitates the learning of the pupil though "making knowledge," while direct transmission approaches to learning are conceptualized as "taking knowledge." That teachers are likely to need a combination of pedagogies depending on what needs to be taught is not thinkable in this framing. The OECD's pedagogical project is thus anchored by constructivism, which in turn fits well with neo-liberalism's concern with the active individual agent. This more constructivist teacher pedagogy, with its emphasis on agency and "social knowledge" as opposed to "disciplinary" or "scientific knowledge" (Rata 2011, 2), links the wider political project of neo-liberalism to the emerging social base of production – the permanently (uncritical?) "creative," entrepreneurial learner for the globally competitive knowledge economy.

Like the PISA tables, countries are compared with others by placing them in rank order. This enables a country to thus make "comparisons with other countries in order to develop more effective policies to improve teaching and learning" (OECD 2014a, 32). And while for the moment no final overall composite figure is given that draws an overall conclusion as to performance, the path to be trod is unequivocal.

Yet there are tensions between this more cooperative and constructivist model of the good teacher, on the one hand, and the use of choice, competition, and accountability mechanisms that structure teachers' work in many countries, on the other. And what do we make of that fact that some countries, like Finland, have excellent students and teachers but do not fit the neat conclusions drawn by the OECD as to the causes. Until recently, Finland had been the poster child in the OECD's Programme for International Student Assessment. But as Finnish education expert, Pasi Sahlberg

(2010) has pointed out, Finland has few, if any, of the elements the OECD believes is part of the formula for successful student and system performance. Similarly, TALIS 2013 findings show that Finnish teachers spend fewer hours in class teaching than the OECD average, have considerable personal autonomy, are not engaged in formal systems of teacher evaluation, do not engage much in continuous professional development, and do not receive merit pay. This has the effect of potentially weakening the strength of the claim as to the dynamics at work in creating "high performing schools" because the rules for realization are made more open regarding which message the acquirer wants to take. This presents the OECD with a paradox in that it cannot fully control the outcomes of its own pedagogic practices.

The World Bank has pursued a rather different strategy regarding the governing of teachers' work – though it is also legitimated in a strong agenda around modernizing the school in order to realize a competitive knowledge-based economy. The World Bank Report, *Lifelong Learning for the Global Knowledge Economy* (LLGKE) (2003) sets out the account of the kinds of challenges knowledge economies present for education and training systems. Teachers are viewed by the Bank as problematic; as unionized, with few incentives to change their performance, and resisting change.

In their 2011 report, *Making Schools Work* (Bruns *et al*. 2011), the Bank dedicates a lengthy chapter (more than 60 pages) to teacher accountability. A key argument is that education policy-makers wishing to recruit, or "groom," great teachers to raise the overall levels of learning amongst pupils confront the reality of education systems where there are weak or no incentives to alter teacher performance. The Report states: "The vast majority of education systems are characterised by fixed salary schedules, lifetime job tenure, and flat labour hierarchies, which create rigid labour environments where extra effort, innovation and good results are not rewarded" (Bruns *et al*. 2011, 142). Criticizing the years of service/credential basis or teacher salaries and promotion, they argue: "The clear implication of available research is that most schools are recruiting and rewarding teachers for the wrong things, failing to encourage the capacities and behaviours that contribute most directly to student learning results, and unable to sanction ineffective performance" (Bruns *et al*. 2011, 143). A further issue emerges: the levels of expenditure on education and the percentage of this allocated to teacher salaries.

> Developing countries today spend an average of 5 percent of GDP on education, and many countries are on track to increase this. The impact of this investment on their subsequent economic growth hangs largely on how they use the 4 percent of GDP (80 percent of total education spending) that goes to pay teachers. In a growing number of countries, the drive to improve student learning outcomes is translated into creative and sometimes radical policy reforms aimed at changing the incentives for teachers. (Bruns *et al*. 2011, 143)

The solution? Teachers should be paid, not by formal recognition of qualifications, or type of service, or geographic location. Rather, they should be placed on contracts for specified periods of employment, with pay tied to student performance, thus establishing a link between teachers' employment conditions and accountability for results. And it is through SABER, the Bank's project to develop a Systems Approach for Better Education Results, that we see the operationalization of what it would mean to have an accountable teacher workforce and competent teachers. Yet the focus of this project – compared with the OECD's is different. SABER-Teachers aims to fill an assumed gap in the availability of data and analysis that could provide policy guidance on teacher policies. Through "...collecting, analysing, synthesising and disseminating comprehensive information on teacher policies in primary and secondary education across a range of different education systems" (World Bank 2011b; 2013), the Bank hopes to "encourage policymakers to learn about how other countries address the same policy challenges related to teacher management and this how to make well informed policy choices that will lead to improved learning outcomes" (World Bank 2011b; 2012). There are three elements at work: policy mapping, policy guidance, and policy comparison.

SABER-Teachers strongly classifies the "good teacher" (defined by ten core policy goals), and uses strong framing rules by specifying ten core teacher policy areas, such as who regulates the requirements for entering and remaining in the teaching field, initial teacher preparation, recruitment and employment, salary and non-salary benefits, and so on. But what is particularly important here are the specific questions to be asked in each of these areas, and an evaluative/moral developmental trajectory – from "latent" to "emerging," "established," "mature" to determine the extent to which the conditions for producing the competent teacher are in place. Questions about the terms and conditions of teachers' labor include: "Is participation in professional development compulsory? What is the burden of teacher compensation? What labor rights do teachers enjoy?" and "Are there monetary sanctions for teacher absenteeism?"

According to the Bank's 2013 Report, information has been collected on 65 education systems in 44 countries – although the quality of information across the different countries is quite varied. A smaller number of countries (13 in all – ranging from Chile and Djibouti, to Egypt, Guatemala, and New Zealand) have acted as case study countries. But it should be noted that the Bank does not simply have a highly normative and preformed view of the good teacher, but an acceptance that the presence of a policy is a sufficiently robust measure of a policy being enacted. There is often a large gap between policy texts and the enactment of policy by those for whom it is intended. For instance, we can compare SABER-Teachers' assessment of a country like Cambodia, which scored reasonably well on its teacher policy profile (such as setting expectations for students and teachers, monitoring teaching and learning), with empirical research on Cambodian teachers by experts such as Brehm and Silova (2014), and we can see a large gap between the two accounts. Brehm and Silova (2014, 160) report a huge shadow schooling industry in Cambodia that in many cases involves school teachers teaching the same class of students in the same buildings, but where a fee is now charged. The extra lessons are where the rest of the national curriculum is delivered and where examination preparation takes place. This seemingly corrupt behavior on the part of teachers, however, can be better understood as the outcome of deeper structural issues in Cambodia: the way the schooling day is organized, the number of subjects to be taught in the national curriculum, large class sizes that limit the capacity of the teacher to teach effectively, low educational expenditures that impact on teacher salaries (Brehm and Silova 2014, 164). In short, being able to "tick off" the presence or absence of teacher policies gives us little real insight into the *real politics* of teachers' work and workplaces.

The Education GPS

In early October 2014, the OECD launched what it calls its Education GPS. GPS, of course, stands for "Global Positioning System." "Education GPS" we are reminded "…is *the* OECD source for internationally comparable data and analysis on education policies and practices, opportunities and outcomes. Accessible any time, in real time, the Education GPS provides you with the latest information on how countries are working to develop high quality and equitable education systems" (OECD 2014c). In short, this Education GPS aims to tell you where you, as a nation, currently are on the global grid, and guide you to your destination. Three services are offered. Users can analyze by a selected country and explore a variety of themes and types of data to create customized country reports. Users are also invited to compare different countries' education systems and their levels of success on providing high quality education. Finally, users can also seek policy advice from the OECD's research and policy archive. For example, we can select Australia and then choose a topic to browse further using the datasets that are part of the OECD's widening data portfolio; this includes Education at a Glance, teachers and teaching conditions (TALIS), student performance (PISA), adult skills (PIAAC) (see Figure 15.1).

Or, we can choose to compare Australia with other countries on TALIS. However, here we can see from Figure 15.2 that there is a limited representation of the countries that might be useful points of comparison for Australia: in this case I chose Canada and the United Kingdom as points for comparison and the entries were N/A. That is likely to change if the current pattern of buy-in to the OECD's TALIS continues.

Finally, we can consider the kinds of policy advice the OECD offers – from that aimed at teachers to advice about the governance of teachers and their work. Again, we can view the specific framing of policies viewed as desirable from this visual representation in Figure 15.3 – with choice, devolution, and a mixed public and private economy of education forming the basic structure of the governance of the education system.

The emergence of the OECD's Education GPS as a guidance tool for countries and their education systems suggests a degree of agency on the part of the user, as choices can be made around what to look at. However like all GPS devices, it has a preferred route based on assumptions about what the terrain looks like, and what the direction

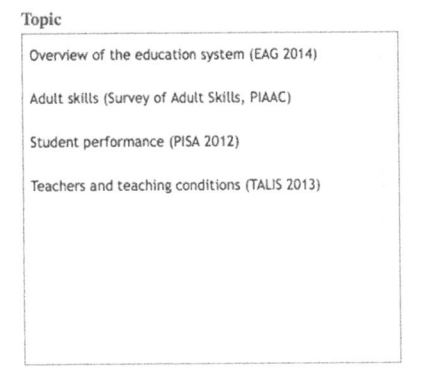

Figure 15.1 OECD's Education GPS by choice of country and theme.
Source: OECD (2014c).

Key facts

OECD | Education GPS
BETTER POLICIES FOR BETTER LIVES | THE WORLD OF EDUCATION AT YOUR FINGERTIPS

Visit our website   Visit the interactive version

TALIS 2013: Full selection of indicators

Recruiting, retaining and developing teachers are vital in ensuring high quality student outcomes in school systems worldwide. The Teaching and Learning International Survey (TALIS) collects internationally comparable data on the learning environment and the working conditions of teachers in schools across the world with the aim to provide valid, timely and comparable information from the perspective of practitioners in schools to help countries review and define policies for developing a high-quality teaching profession. Cross-country analysis from TALIS enables countries to identify other countries facing similar challenges and to learn from other policy approaches.

TALIS examines the ways in which teachers' work is recognised, appraised and rewarded; assesses the degree to which teachers perceive their professional development needs are being met; provides insights into the beliefs and attitudes about teaching that teachers bring to the classroom and the pedagogical practices that they adopt; examines the roles of school leaders and the support that they give their teachers; and examines the extent to which certain factors relate to teachers' reports of job satisfaction and self-efficacy.

DATA TABLE

Indicator	Sort	Australia	Canada	OECD average	TALIS average*	United Kingdom
TEACHERS						
Percentage of female teachers	(2013) Download Indicator	59.2	N/A	67.0	68.1	N/A
Mean age of teachers	(2013) Download Indicator	43.4	N/A	44.0	42.9	N/A
Average years of working experience as a teacher in total	(2013) Download Indicator	16.7	N/A	17.0	16.2	N/A
Completion of teacher education or training programme (%)	(2013) Download Indicator	97.6	N/A	89.2	89.8	N/A
SCHOOL LEADERSHIP						
Female principals (%)	(2013) Download Indicator	38.6	N/A	44.6	49.4	N/A

Figure 15.2 OECD's Education GPS by TALIS dataset and indicators.
Source: OECD (2014c).

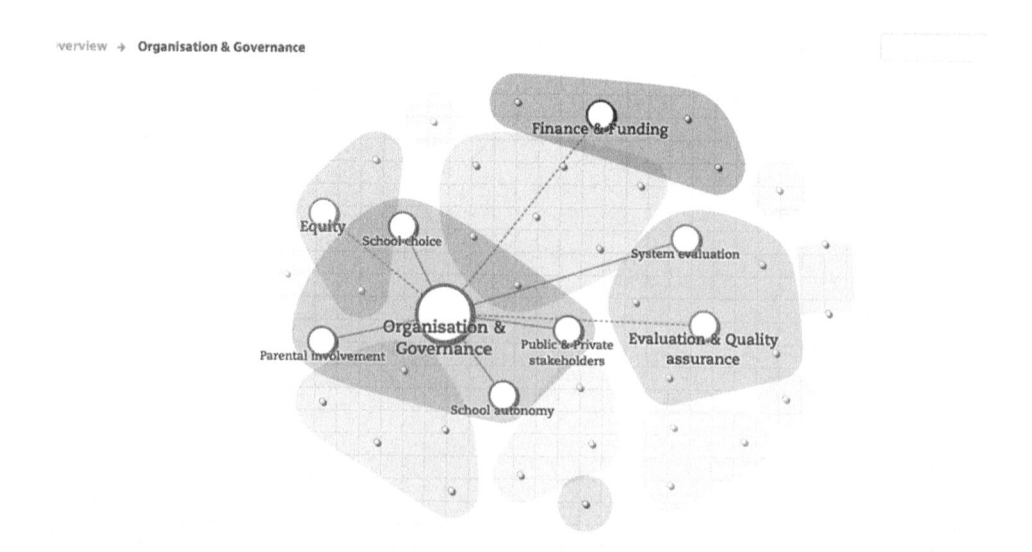

Figure 15.3 OECD's Education GPS policy advice – the lexicon for good governance.
Source: OECD (2014c).

of travel *should* be. The fact that there are alternative routes to be taken, or indeed routes to be taken that are not built into this system and which are perhaps more effective at delivering quality teaching and learning, is made invisible.

Elsewhere I have argued that this kind of global technology has many of the features of unmanned military drones (Robertson 2012, 603) in that they are able to reach deep inside national territorial borders, not only as data collectors but as agents at a distance able to frame, direct, act, and redirect without being physically present, and more importantly, accountable. I also noted that like a GPS system which guides the drone's actions, the OECD – or indeed the World Bank – cannot sufficiently see, or understand, the details that make the difference.

From Thin to Thickening Global Governance of Teachers' Work

I have argued that the global governance of teachers' work is not a new phenomenon. That is, we can see strongly classified, but weakly framed, mechanisms of governing in sub/national territorial states through a focus upon "education as development," and "standard setting" over the period 1960–1990. However these post-war institutions have been eclipsed by a new set of actors – the OECD, the World Bank, and a small group of global education firms – who are not only framing what it means to be a good teacher, but shaping the ongoing realization of this through these new systems of data-driven, direction-given assessment and accountability.

I have also shown that from the late 1990s onwards, there has been a significant transformation in the field of symbolic control, with a small group of global agencies and firms strongly classifying and framing conceptions of the good teacher to be realized in national education settings, and ready and willing to provide the various services that will be for sale to enable a country to arrive there. There is now an intense focus on learning and the learner, and linking this in a causal way to teachers and a specific kind of pedagogy, as the means for developing competitive national economies. Learning as individual development thus displaces education as development. Learning as development takes its logic, development trajectory, and forward momentum not from modernization theory – which assumed a teleology of development, but from neo-liberalism's rawer attention to the individual and their necessary engagement with competition as a means for development. The engine that keeps this governing system moving in a very dynamic, forward-going way is competitive comparison – as it is constantly placing each player in hierarchical relation to the other. It is not a question of striving to reach a state of quality, as much as striving to move ahead of who is in front. This technology for global governing is given an ongoing injection of energy in that global data and rankings structure and trade in "urgency"; in the fear of a loss of height, in shame, and in humiliation. Conversely, countries can follow the path to the "holy grail" by following the policy advice of the OECD and the Bank, and buying the necessary services, which in turn will create vertical movement upward. This only increases the hand of the global agencies, whose diagnosis and prognosis are part of a virtual circle between framing, representing, materializing, institutionalizing, and reproducing the modern teacher.

This denationalization of teachers' work underway has resulted in the globalizing of nationally oriented capabilities aimed at shifting the centre of gravity in the field of symbolic control in the direction of global agencies, such as the OECD, the World

Bank, and global transnational firms. The ILO and UNESCO continue in the wings, but more as voiceless participants rather than noisy protectors of teachers and learners. Yet, like all political projects, the outcomes can also be contested, and thus open to transformation. That we can too easily see the frictions, fissures, and failures in cohering logics at the level of discourse, let alone practice, suggests that these projects might well be stalled as much by their hubris as by an air of nervousness about too much global unaccountability, and too much global edu-business in the world of teaching and learning.

Finally we might reflect on whether or not bringing a number of datasets together – from student learning to teacher pedagogy in the OECD's "Education GPS" – simply tightens the metaphorical "iron cage" for teachers and their laboring that Weber (1978) so famously described in his account of bureaucracy; of a totally rationalized, disenchanted and dehumanized world? We might also wonder whether this level of power and control over teachers' labor – aimed at creating innovative and entrepreneurial workers for the knowledge economy – paradoxically squeezes out, rather than realizes, student imagination. The winners will be those countries, their teachers, and students, who refuse to be players in this global governing game and instead start chart a different course for realizing human potential.

References

Ball, S. 2012. *Global Education Inc*. London and New York: Routledge.
Barber, M. and M. Mourshed. 2007. *How the World's Best-Performing Schools Come out on Top*. McKinsey & Company. Retrieved from: http://mckinseyonsociety.com/downloads/reports/Education/Worlds_School_Systems_Final.pdf (accessed November 30, 2015).
Bernstein, B. 1990. *The Structuring of Pedagogic Discourse: Class, Codes and Control*. London and New York: Routledge.
Bernstein, B. 2000. *Pedagogy, Symbolic Control, and Identity: Theory, Research, Critique* (revised edition). Oxford: Rowman and Littlefield Publishers Inc.
Brehm, W. and I. Silova. 2014. "Ethical Dilemmas in the Education Marketplace: Shadow Education, Political Philosophy and Social (In)justice in Cambodia," in *Education, Privatisation and Social Justice*, edited by I. Macpherson, S. Robertson, and G. Walford, 159–178. Oxford: Symposium Books.
Bruns, B., D. Filmer, and H. Patrinos. 2011. *Making Schools Work: New Evidence on Accountability Reforms*. Washington, DC: The World Bank Group.
Commission on Global Governance (CGG). 1995. *Our Global Neighbourhood*. Oxford: Oxford University Press.
Cusso, R. and S. D'Amica. 2005. "From Development Comparison to Globalization Comparison: Towards More Normative International Education Statistics." *Comparative Education*, 41(2): 119–216.
Dale, R. 2008. *Educational Governance as Ontology and Pedagogy: New Approaches to the Impasse of Educational Reform for Democracy and Social Justice*. GES Working Paper. Bristol: University of Bristol.
European Commission. 2014. *The Teaching and Learning International Survey (TALIS): Main Findings from the Survey and Implications for Education and Training Policies in Europe*. Brussels: European Commission.
Falk, R. 1975. *A Study of Future Worlds*. New York: Free Press.
Grek, S. 2009. "Governing by Numbers: the PISA 'Effect' in Europe." *Journal of Education Policy*, 24(1): 23–37.

Held, D., A. McGrew, D. Goldblatt, and J. Perraton. 1999. *Global Transformations: Politics, Economics, Culture*. Cambridge: Polity Press.

ILO/UNESCO. 2008. *The ILO/UNESCO Recommendation Concerning the Status of Teachers (1966), and the UNESCO Recommendations Concerning the Status of Higher-Education Teaching Personnel (1997) with a Handbook*. Paris: UNESCO.

Kingdon, G., A. Little, M. Aslam, S. Rawal, T. More, H. Patrinos, T. Beteile, R. Banerji, B. Parton, and S. Shama. 2014. *A Rigorous Review of the Political Economy of Education Systems in Developing Countries*. London: DFID.

Maguire, M. and S.J. Ball. 1994. "Discourses of Educational Reform in the United Kingdom and the USA and the Work of Teachers." *British Journal of In-Service Education*, 20: 5–16.

Meyer, J., D. Kamens, and A. Benevot. 1992. *School Knowledge for the Masses: World Models and National Curricula in the Twentieth Century*. London: Falmer.

Mittelman, J. 2004. *Whither Globalization?: The Vortex of Knowledge and Ideology (Rethinking Globalizations)*. New York: Routledge.

Mourshed, M., C. Chijioke, and M. Barber. 2010. *How the World's Most Improved Systems Keep Getting Better*. McKinsey & Company. Retrieved from: http://www.mckinsey.com/~/media/mckinsey/dotcom/client_service/social%20sector/pdfs/how-the-worlds-most-improved-school-systems-keep-getting-better_download-version_final.ashx (accessed November 30, 2015).

Mundy, K. 2007. "Global Governance, Educational Change." *Comparative Education*, 43(3): 339–357.

National Academies of Sciences. 2010. *Rising Above the Gathering Storm: Revisited*. Washington, DC: National Academies of Sciences.

OECD. 2001. *What Schools for the Future: Scenarios*. Paris: OECD.

OECD. 2005. *Teachers Matter: Attracting, Developing and Retaining Effective Teachers*. Paris: OECD.

OECD. 2009. *Creating Effective Teaching and Learning Environments: First Results from TALIS*. Paris: OECD.

OECD. 2011. *OECD Teaching and Learning International Survey (TALIS) TALIS 2013*. Paris: OECD. Retrieved from: www.keepeek.com/Digital-Asset-Management/oecd/education/new-insights-from-talis-2013_9789264226319-en#page1 (accessed November 30, 2015).

OECD. 2014a. *TALIS 2013 Results: An International Perspective on Teaching and Learning*. Paris: OECD.

OECD. 2014b. *A Teachers' Guide to TALIS*. Paris: OECD.

OECD. 2014c. *Education GPS: The World at Your Fingertips*. Retrieved from: http://gpseducation.oecd.org (November 13, 2015).

Overbeek, H. 2010. "Global; Governance: From Radical Transformation to Neo-Liberal Management." *International Studies Review*, 12: 696–719.

Rata, E. 2011. "The Politics of Knowledge in Education." *British Educational Research Journal*, iFirst: 1–22.

Robertson, S. 2005. "Re-imagining and Rescripting the Future of Education: Global Knowledge Economy Discourse and the Challenge to Education Systems." *Comparative Education*, 41(2): 151–170.

Robertson, S. 2011. "The New Spatial Politics of (Re)bordering and (Re)ordering the State-Education-Citizen Relation." *International Review of Education*, 57: 277–297.

Robertson, S. 2012. "Placing Teachers in Global Governance Agendas." *Comparative Education Review*, 56(4): 584–607.

Rosenau, J. and E.O. Czempiel (eds). 1992. *Governance without Government: Order and Change in World Politics*. Cambridge: Cambridge University Press.

Sahlberg, P. 2010. "Rethinking Accountability in a Knowledge Society." *Journal of Educational Change*, 11(1): 45–61.

Sainsbury Review. 2007. *The Race to the Top: A Review of Government's Science and Innovation Policies*. London: HMSO.

Sassen, S. 2006. *Territory, Authority, Rights*. Princeton: Princeton University Press.
Sellar, S. and B. Lingard. 2013. "The OECD and the Expansion of PISA: New Global Modes of Governance in Education." *British Educational Research Journal*, 40(6): 917–936.
US Department of Education. 2015. *Race to the Top Fund*, see full program of funding over several phases at www2.ed.gov/programs/racetothetop/index.html (accessedNovember19, 2015).
Weber, M. 1978. *Economy and Society Volume 1* (edited by Guenther Roth and Chris Wittich), Berkeley: Uuniversity of California Press.
World Bank. 2003. *Lifelong Learning for a Global Knowledge Economy*. Washington, DC: World Bank.
World Bank. 2011a. *Learning for All: Investing in People's Knowledge and Skills to Promote Development, Education Sector 2020 Strategy Report*. Washington, DC: The World Bank Group.
World Bank. 2011b. *SABER – Teachers, Objectives, Rationale, Methodological Approach and Products*. Washington, DC: The World Bank Group.
World Bank. 2012. *What Matters Most in Teacher Policies? A Framework for Building a More Effective Profession*. Washington, DC: The World Bank Group.

Chapter 16

The Global Construction of Higher Education Reform

Simon Marginson

Introduction

This chapter discusses the expansion of, modernization of, and competition in higher education systems and institutions (HEIs) by locating the sector in both its global and national settings. It examines the worldwide spread and variation of neo-liberal marketization reforms, in the context of global systems increasing in weight, patterns of cross-border imitation, and continued national/regional cultural differences. It relativizes higher education on a global basis, while noting the continued centrality of national governments in shaping the sector. Behind this discussion is an empirical question about whether the balance between national and global action is changing, and more subtly, how the global dimension is inflected in the national and vice versa.

To understand this problem – and indeed, to make sense of contemporary higher education in incompletely globalized settings – it is essential to move beyond the "methodological nationalism" (Wimmer and Schiller 2002; Shahjahan and Kezar 2013) that dominates work on both higher education and globalization, and among other things leads to the underestimation of global effects. Wimmer and Schiller (2002, 301) characterize "methodological nationalism" as the assumption "that the nation/state/society is the natural social and political form of the modern world." Marginson and Rhoades (2002) suggest that in higher education, HEIs and human agents (Marginson 2014a) participate in all of national, local, and global dimensions of action. They use the term "glonacal" for this simultaneity (*glonacal* = *glo*bal + *na*tional + lo*cal*). This suggests the need for a synthetic "bird's eye" overview of worldwide higher education space (Marginson and van der Wende 2009), and also suggests there are analytical gains to be made by examining global and national relationality from multiple viewpoints, incorporating different national settings,

The Handbook of Global Education Policy, First Edition.
Edited by Karen Mundy, Andy Green, Bob Lingard, and Antoni Verger.
© 2016 John Wiley & Sons, Ltd. Published 2016 by John Wiley & Sons, Ltd.

languages, disciplines, affiliations, and so on. Sen (1992) suggests "objective inquiry" can be achieved on the basis of a "transpositional" view built as a composite from several positional views (e.g. Marginson and Mollis 2001; Marginson and Ordorika 2011). This chapter is not a joint production, but aims to incorporate a transpositional sensibility.

The contents of the chapter are as follows. First, it isolates three worldwide tendencies that must play out whatever is the policy paradigm of the day: (a) the common growth of high participation systems, which is driven primarily by social rather than economic factors; (b) the spread of "World Class Universities" (WCUs) and research capacity within a one-world science system; and (c) the near-universal implementation in HEIs of quasi-business organization. It provides data and examples, with some attention to China, the new (and large) kid on the block. Second, the chapter identifies political and cultural factors that govern variations at national and regional levels. The common tendencies play out in differing ways. For example, the chapter takes stock of marketization in higher education and finds that there is widespread national competition in social position in higher education, and global competition; but rather than a universal tendency to commodification, there is variation in the political economy of higher education – for example, wide differences in tuition arrangements and in the roles taken by private sectors – between national systems that in other respects are converging or moving in parallel. Such variation, which is partly governed by differences in the nature of states (Green 2013), points to the salience of longstanding, albeit evolving, national/regional political and educational cultures.

Common Trends in Worldwide Higher Education

In *The Birth of the Modern World 1780–1914: Global Connections and Comparisons* (2004), Bayly finds that modern globalization and the modern nation state developed together. In England and Prussia in the late 18th century, followed later by the USA and Meiji Japan, a new kind of nation state emerged. These were "global competition states" (Cerny 1997) that watched closely what other states were doing, especially with military technology, industry, and agricultural productivity. Within the global setting there was an ongoing "process of emulation and borrowing" as each nation strove to secure an advantage (Bayly 2004, 4). This national perspective has been maintained – occasionally leavened by outbreaks of cosmopolitan and collective feeling, for example, at the end of major wars, and in Europe in the first attempt to build something larger than one nation – except that not just state machines, but organizations such as HEIs now engage in continuous surveillance, mimetics, and strategic initiatives. Imitation and competitive advantage are focused on a large range of elements such as business cultures, techniques of government, university design, and the output of research. In the post-1990 era of communicative globalization, in which the internet has brought a new immediacy and potency to cross-border relationships and pooled information (Marginson 2011a), international comparisons like the Programme for International Student Assessment (PISA) (OECD 2014) and university rankings are felt everywhere, the transparency of governments and HEIs is enhanced, and policy borrowing is more rapid. HEIs now have extensive direct relations with institutions across their borders. They are embedded in the global dimension as well as the national. Their global connections are sometimes but not always mediated and articulated by nation states.

More than one kind of global pattern is at work. First, there are global systems, such as disciplinary research and publishing; faculty, student, and doctoral mobility; worldwide comparisons and ranking; with varying impacts in particular nations. Second, from the perspectives of individual nations and HEIs, there are interventions in international relations, and initiatives in global space and systems such as education hubs, education export, or new rankings (Marginson 2011b). Nations (let alone individual HEIs) no longer have sole authority on their own territory, but they retain some scope to articulate or retard global flows and reposition themselves in relation to global systems and cross-border pressures. National policy embraces certain cross-border ideas, adapts and transforms others, and looks to avoid a third group. The modern university is above all a creature of the nation state (Scott 2011). Nations retain agency in the global setting and are still the primary means of funding and regulating higher education and basic research, including private sectors in most countries. Yet within the open ecology of comparison, surveillance, and imitation, to a remarkable degree the voluntary actions of states lead to university and science systems that move in parallel, or replicate each other on the basis of common models. The most important such model is that of the ideal Anglo-American science university.

There are no constant social laws here. There is continuing scope for difference, fragmentation, and off-the-wall initiative by nations and HEIs but it varies in time and place. The purpose and means of agency are always to enlarge its scope for action, and in the global setting the possibilities for action are more open than in the national setting (Marginson 2011a); while at the same time, certain global actions have unforeseen effects in every nation. Consider the transformative impact of global university rankings that began in 2003, and Massive Open Online Courses (MOOCs) that were launched at Stanford in 2011. All else being equal, large and wealthy countries have more resources and strategic options for global action. They can also find it easier to postpone engagement with the global, for a time. Yet some small nations or systems can be very effective in the world, perhaps because they cannot avoid it, when they have the necessary imaginative, financial and cultural resources for global action. Consider Singapore, Hong Kong, Switzerland, Denmark, and Finland.

However, one test of comparative and global higher education studies is whether it can identify social developments. There are three worldwide trends common to all higher education, especially research universities, regardless of national political cultures and state–university relations. These are social trends with broader roots than just states, though states articulate these trends, and can determine the timing.

Tendency to High Participation Systems (HPSs)

The first and strongest of these common trends is the near universal progression toward high participation higher education systems. By "high participation systems" (HPSs) is meant systems in which each school leaver age cohort participates at a rate of 50% or more either on leaving school or in subsequent years, tending eventually toward universal (100%) participation. Typically in such systems, the average labor market value of graduate qualifications falls over time, and some graduate labor moves down the occupational scale, but the graduate premium – the advantage in

Table 16.1 The advance of educational participation: Gross Tertiary Enrolment Ratio by world region, 1995 and 2011

Region	1995	2011
	%	%
North America and Western Europe	60	77
Central and Eastern Europe	33	68
Latin America and the Caribbean	17	42
East Asia and Pacific	10	30
Central Asia	23	24
Arab States	14	23
South and West Asia	6	18
Sub-Saharan Africa	4	8
World	15	30

Source: UNESCO (2014).

wage rates and employment rates enjoyed by graduates relative to school leavers without tertiary education – is maintained (OECD 2013).

In the past 40 years the tendency toward expansion of participation in tertiary education, and within that degree-level studies (OECD type 5A programs),[1] has been universal to all but the poorest countries. The tendency is not linear. In particular countries growth tends to advance by fits and starts, interspersed with periods in which the curve plateaus, and participation may fall a little. Nevertheless, the secular trend is clear and overwhelming. It is readily demonstrated using the UNESCO (2014) database for tertiary education. It is striking that, while age participation rates vary greatly, and only a few systems like South Korea, Taiwan, USA and Canada are near the point where almost the whole age group enrolls at tertiary level, there is no stable resting point halfway along the curve. Over time, participation goes up everywhere. Table 16.1 shows that between 1995 and 2011 (less than one generation) the world Gross Tertiary Enrolment Ratio (GTER) doubled from 15 to 30%. The GTER increased substantially in every world region except Central Asia, though sub-Saharan Africa and South Asia were still far short of 50% participation in 2011. As Figure 16.1 demonstrates, in Europe participation is converging on the basis of near universal levels. It more than doubled in Eastern Europe in 1995–2011. Growth was slow in the USA, which already had a very high GTER in 1995; and in Germany, more resistant to the tendency than most systems. The GTER is moving towards 50% in Latin America and the Caribbean, with Argentina, Venezuela, and Chile over 70%; and in East Asia it exceeds 50% except in China (UNESCO 2014).

The trend to HPS has been advanced by two factors. First, rapid growth in the global middle classes, especially in China, India and Latin America, and the lift in social and educational aspirations that results. Mobility from peasant farming to the cities will continue to drive growth in educational participation. The second factor is facilitation of growth in the policy sphere, especially by global policy agencies. In 2000 the World Bank published a report on higher education, *Peril and Promise* (World Bank 2000), which signaled a shift to encouraging degree-length higher education in emerging states/economies. Previously the Bank had emphasized primary education on the ground that its rates of return were higher, an artifact of the income

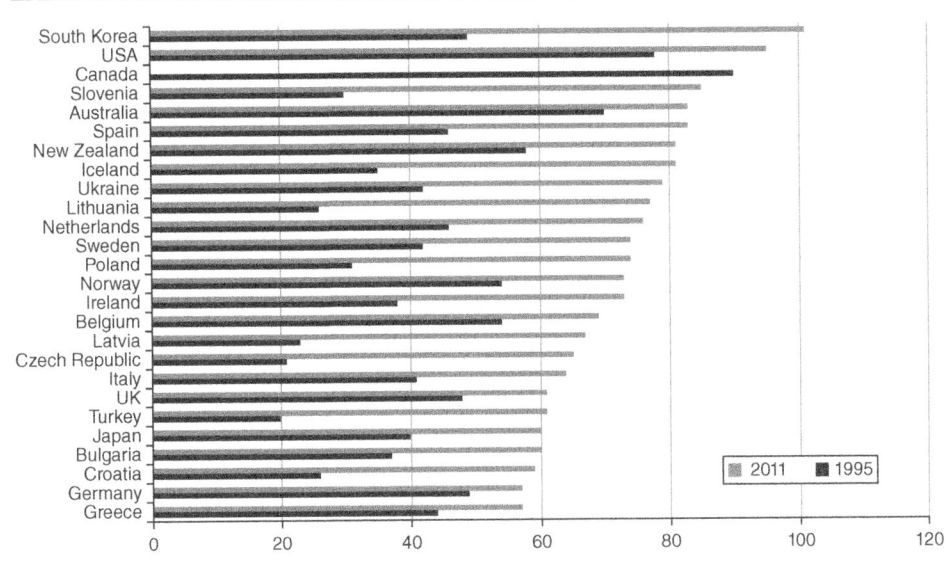

Figure 16.1 High Participation Systems: Gross Tertiary Enrolment Ratio in selected OECD and European nations, 1995 and 2011.
Source: Data from UNESCO (2014).

forgone during periods of extended education. By legitimating mass higher education as part of the development process, rather than as an outcome of it, the Bank encouraged nation building states to meet emerging middle class aspirations, while providing for their own needs for trained personnel.

Social Demand

Policy-makers mostly explain the growth of participation as the outcome of economic modernization and global competition. As they see it, tertiary expansion is driven (not just facilitated) by states, which respond to "natural growth" in the need for high productivity human capital, while providing socially equitable opportunities to take such jobs. It is widely assumed by both governments and social scientists that educational expansion is ultimately driven by economic demand for graduate knowledge, skills, and certified professional competences. But these are merely normative policy rationales for the expansion of participation. They are not empirically grounded. A study of science, technology, engineering, and mathematics (STEM) policies in 12 countries notes that, while higher education improves labor potential, this does not mean participation is shaped by economic demand; and still less that enhanced skills, for example in science, are necessarily used effectively at work (Freeman *et al.* 2015). The notion of economically driven higher education suggests that education expansion is maximized during high economic growth and falls during recessions. Yet recessions are variously associated with increased use of education as a shelter from unemployment or an investment in better options, and reduced educational participation because credentials lose value at the margin. Further, the historical record suggests that in emerging economies, rapid educational growth can precede accelerated economic growth, or operate simultaneously with it, or lag it by five to ten years or more. There is no general law.

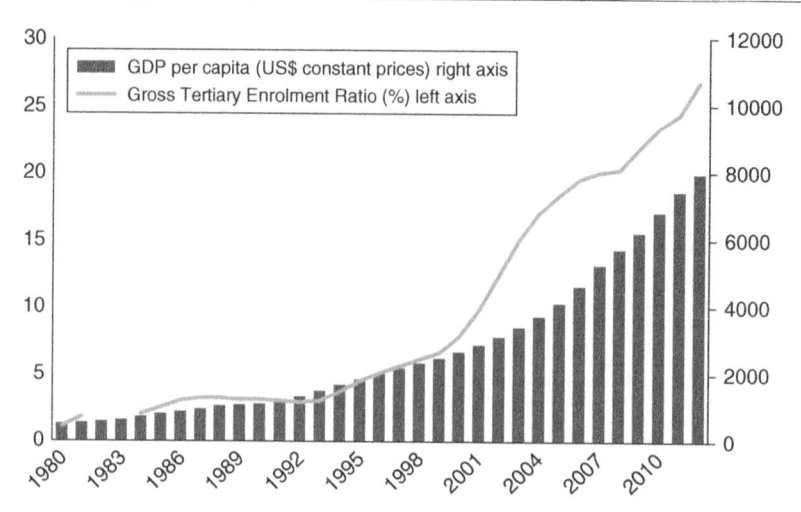

Figure 16.2 No linear correlation between participation and income: trends in per capita GDP (PPP, constant prices) and Gross Tertiary Enrolment Ratio (%), China, 1980 to 2012. Source: Data from World Bank (2014); UNESCO (2014).

Take the case of China. Figure 16.2 for 1980–2012 suggests no linear correlation between tertiary participation and rising national product per head. In the 1980s, a time of rapid economic growth after the opening up of the economy, participation in tertiary education was locked at 2–3%. Participation in secondary education fell sharply after 1982 before returning close to the 1982 level by 1992. Better human capital was not essential for 1980s economic growth, and economic growth failed to trigger early pressures for participation growth. In the 1990s the GTER trends up, with an accelerated take-off from 1999 onwards, with tertiary participation increasing much faster than (rapidly growing) GDP per capita. The late 1990s turning point was determined by the Chinese government's decision to sanction expansion and invest in infrastructure and student support. By then, after two decades of economic expansion, there was enough pent up social demand from the growing middle classes to fully utilize the new opportunities. In fact the growth rate surged ahead of target.

It is true that economic demand fosters expansion of student places in fields short of labor at particular times (e.g. mining engineers in a mining boom), and that some professions maintain a tight fit between training, occupation, and work (e.g. medical training). The proportion of jobs requiring professional qualifications, and the relative weight of high-skill jobs, have both risen – but not as fast as graduate numbers. In the face of the vast growth in educational participation, these instances, and this half correlation, are not sufficient to sustain the human capital narrative. The overall relationship between higher education and the demand for labor appears incoherent. Across the world, many graduates "fail" to work in fields in which they are trained. Many positions requiring specific training are filled by graduates from fields other than the designated occupation. And much graduate labor is generic in character – not only are there graduates in humanities, humanistic social sciences, business studies, and the physical and life sciences, but in some countries many law or engineering graduates work outside the profession. "Graduate jobs" expand but the content is not a constant. Their growth might be more supply driven than demand driven. Credentialism, signaling behavior, and graduates working in erstwhile non-graduate jobs seem to be at least as prominent in the data as the expansion of high-skill work.

The perennial debate about "over-education" versus skill shortage can never be settled. Neither generalization will hold. The education/ economy relationship seems more indirect and less instrumental than human capital theory suggests. Like the rule of law or stable finance, higher education can provide better conditions for production in many economic sectors, without necessarily directly driving value creation.

While the evidence for economic drivers is patchy and inconsistent, the evidence for social drivers is strong and consistent across the world. The secular trend to universal participation is best understood as driven by ever-advancing social demand, whereby aspirations for tertiary education – particularly for university degrees which carry the main status – spread through the population, eventually reaching poor families, remote communities, and others under-represented. Sociological research suggests total aspirations advance over time, both in the spreading of those aspirations through the population and the lifting of the average level of aspiration (e.g. OECD 2013); and also that families aspire to higher education both as a provider of better life opportunities and prospects, and because it provides social distinction in itself. Both motivations can be understood as demand for higher education as a positional good, a source of relative advantage (Hirsch 1976; Marginson 1997). The idea of education as a source of positional advantage encompasses all of economic opportunities, higher social status (Frank and Cook 1995), and cultural distinction (Bourdieu 1988, 1996). The demand for higher education as a positional good extends beyond the boundaries of national systems to include international education (Marginson 2006).

All states must respond to the growing social demand. In enabling participation to grow they release the potential for more social aspirations, the threshold of necessary participation also rises over time, and so it goes. Thus all societies progress toward Korean levels of participation. The main barrier to states enabling social demand is fiscal cost. Nevertheless, in the long run states give way to the pressure from below, often while transferring some of the costs to families. It is easier to persuade some families to share costs (e.g. in East Asia) than others. But while the political economy is variable, expansion is constant. From time to time states play with the notion of "over-education." They rarely accept its logic. Higher education is a primary instrument of social order, especially through the sanctioning of upward mobility as Trow (1973) points out in his essay on the transition from elite to mass to universal higher education.[2] To sustain that role it must be progressively expanded and become more inclusive. Tertiary education is a legitimating mechanism that provides families with hope, and sates ambitions, while channeling aspirations through a mechanism in which they themselves feel partly responsible for their own success/ failure. This reduces the pressure on government to guarantee universal prosperity or genuine fairness. It is as true in electoral democracies as in one-party states such as China. All rest on middle class consent. All governments have strong political incentives to meet social demand.

Social demand for higher education varies by country. It also changes character as participation grows. When the GTER nears 50% it switches from opportunity to obligation. The penalties of non-participation become more severe: not just exclusion from the top of the labor market, but from career work. Globalization enhances this binary by fostering a distinction between globally mobile graduates, and people more locally rooted who lack higher education. Eventually the "schooled society" (Baker 2014) becomes norm and a de facto right, providing self-formation for most citizens. Yet the real universality of HPS is compromised by tuition cost barriers, and the unequal positional value of places in the different institutions and programs, differentiated on a steep hierarchy that ranges from the Harvard Schools of Law and Medicine, to degree mills in developing countries, and online programs without teachers. For some students, the quality of tertiary education is so far collapsed as to be scarcely "participation" at all. The near inevitable accompaniment of HPSs is the enhanced stratification of HEIs.

Stratification of HPSs

The coupling of expansion and stratification is not essential. It is possible for any structural configuration to be associated with HPSs. Nordic systems couple high participation with egalitarian universities all of high standard, and vocational institutions with social esteem. The US couples equally high participation with steep stratification. However, the universalization of participation does contain two intrinsic tendencies to steeper stratification of HEIs within a national system, unless these tendencies are countered by policy, as in the Nordic countries. And in the context of neo-liberal policy and global competition, further elements encourage stratification.

The first intrinsic factor is the economic cost of HPSs. Egalitarian systems with relatively flat value distinctions between HEIs, and in the value of individual places, are typically financed by governments from taxation revenue. In most polities it is not possible to finance free places of standard adequate quality across a whole HPS because of the level of taxation required. As participation expands, governments increasingly favor systems with differentiated value between graduates, and/or shared costs. These two qualities are interdependent. First, once families pay part of the cost, stratification in the value of places follows automatically because families have a varied capacity to pay. Second, once value is differentiated, and places are arranged in a hierarchy of value, willingness to pay is also differentiated.

The second intrinsic factor is the nature of social selection and positional competition in education systems. Bourdieu (1988; 1993; 1996) argues that there is an inherent bifurcation of the social value of cultural and educational goods. The field of production becomes divided between elite goods produced by autonomous institutions and associated with privileged users who erect economic, social, and cultural barriers to protect the circle of privileged consumption and use; and non-elite goods produced by heteronomous institutions driven by states and market demand. Thus, in tertiary education there are elite universities – selective in entry and normally associated with enhanced research performance, that signifies and sustains their value – and low cost mass education institutions, commercial and non-commercial in form. This polarity can be observed in a wide variety of HPSs. While mass institutions vary in character and value, the elite form of university is especially resilient. It also seems that everywhere, social elites are effective in making elite HEIs largely their own. Sometimes elite HEIs are arranged in an Ivy League private sector, more often as well financed state research universities. Even in egalitarian Finland, the University of Helsinki enjoys greater prestige than other HEIs. Many academics in Finland want to work there.

These inherent tendencies toward stratification, generated by the cost of expansion and the dynamics of positional competition, provide favorable conditions for neo-liberal marketization. Marketization can further enhance stratification: by fostering competition in which emphasis on positional objectives tends to increase relative to other goals, and strong HEIs become stronger because of their starting positions; by differentiating access and the value of places on the basis of variable tuition charges; by establishing elite enclaves in private or public sectors; or by using low grade private institutions as the principal medium for the expansion of participation, for example, as in India, Brazil, the Philippines, Korea, and Japan. Global comparisons, ranking, and competition are also associated with enhanced stratification. The development of elite research-intensive universities (see next section) mostly takes place at the expense of the social standing and resource position of other HEIs. At the same time the single world science system, which enhances the standing of all research-intensive HEIs (also see below), tends to exacerbate international stratification between systems, as well as stratification within. Only some nations can support World Class Universities (WCUs).

In sum, in addition to the expansion of participation, there is a common tendency to bifurcation of HPSs. This tendency is exacerbated by – though not caused by – neo-liberal policies. The bifurcated systems consist of on the one hand rising elite WCUs, and on the other hand mass tertiary institutions, mostly local and nation bound, whose relative position is forced down over time by the WCUs. The tendency toward system bifurcation can be modified by compensatory policies that shore up the non-elite sector, but instead many governments are pushing toward steeper hierarchy. Middle HEIs everywhere – those with some standing in research and/or a leading role in servicing local populations, sitting between the elite sector and the mass institutions with low positional value – are placed under growing pressure. However, systems vary, in the steepness of national hierarchies (the degree of inequality between HEIs in their research and the positional value of degrees), the size of the middle layer, and the role of second and third sectors, vocational streaming at school, and other structural factors. System stratification requires empirical study on a case-by-case basis.

The Expanding One-World Science System

The second common tendency is toward the universalization of research science in the top layer of higher education systems. This is both an outcome and catalyst of globalization, with far-reaching consequences for political, economic, and cultural life. It consists of (a) partial subsuming of national science systems into a single world science system, with publication in English, coupled with (b) the spread of indigenous science capacity to an ever-growing number of countries and individual WCUs.

While national systems retain an organizational and instrumental identity, scientific knowledge itself is increasingly combined at global level. This is a long-standing tendency that has become more complete in the internet era, in which English-language science has become the single global conversation and the claims of French, German, and Russian have weakened.³ In the era of communicative globalization, knowledge moves instantaneously with an unprecedented visibility. Academic publications form a single world library. The means of collaboration are much enhanced. The single world science system provides greater resources than any one single national system. To be fully effective research universities and scientists must maximize global connectivity and engagement. Engagement is maximized when HEIs and individuals themselves contribute to the store of research and so function as full partners. Because of the spread of technology in all sectors, including agriculture, and the economically strategic importance of industrial innovation, nations need an indigenous science infrastructure and trained personnel, just as they need clean water, stable governance, and a globally viable financial system. All higher education systems must sustain research capacity, including doctoral training in at least some disciplines. Though not all nations can pay for their own scientific capability, nations lacking the capacity to interpret and understand research, which rests on trained personnel capable of creating research, find themselves in a position of continuing dependence.

Thus the evolution of the one-world science system quickens the roll-out of research capacity in more and more countries. National science systems are partly subsumed in the global dimension, while also becoming more important, both as nodes of the global science system and as bases for autonomous action. National science is yet to become as universal as mass higher education but the spread of research is spectacular. Again the worldwide tendency is from low participation/distribution to high participation/distribution, with no end in sight to the process of growth. Science has moved from a project confined to highly developed North America, Europe/UK, and Japan to part of the normal business of established and emerging states.

In policy circles this tendency takes the competitive form of an arms race in innovation, as nations seek advantages through R&D. Global research rankings continually compare national performance and signify competitive position. In 1995, citizens of 37 nations published over 1000 papers in recognized science journals, a proxy indicator for indigenous capacity in research. By 2011 there were 51 such nations. Figure 16.3 lists the top 25 nations by volume. New science nations also include Croatia, Serbia, Slovenia, Chile, Malaysia, Thailand, and Tunisia. Table 16.2 lists national research systems that have grown rapidly since 1995. In Iran published science grew by 25.2% per annum between 1995 and 2011 (NSF 2014).

The fast-growing science systems include Post-Confucian East and South East Asia: China, Hong Kong special administrative region, South Korea, Singapore, and Taiwan. In 2011 these countries invested US$448 billion in R&D, a third of the global total, just below $453 billion in the USA and Canada. East Asia is becoming the third great region for research and industrial innovation, alongside North America and Western Europe/UK. Three decades ago all Post-Confucian systems except Japan were minor players; in the year 2000, China was the world's tenth largest investor in R&D. Between 2001 and 2011 its R&D rose by 18.1% per year after adjusting for inflation, and it is now second. In 2011 South Korea invested 4.03% of GDP on R&D, second only to Israel. South Korea's total spending at $59.9 billion was fifth, well ahead of France and the UK (NSF 2014).

THE GLOBAL CONSTRUCTION OF HIGHER EDUCATION REFORM

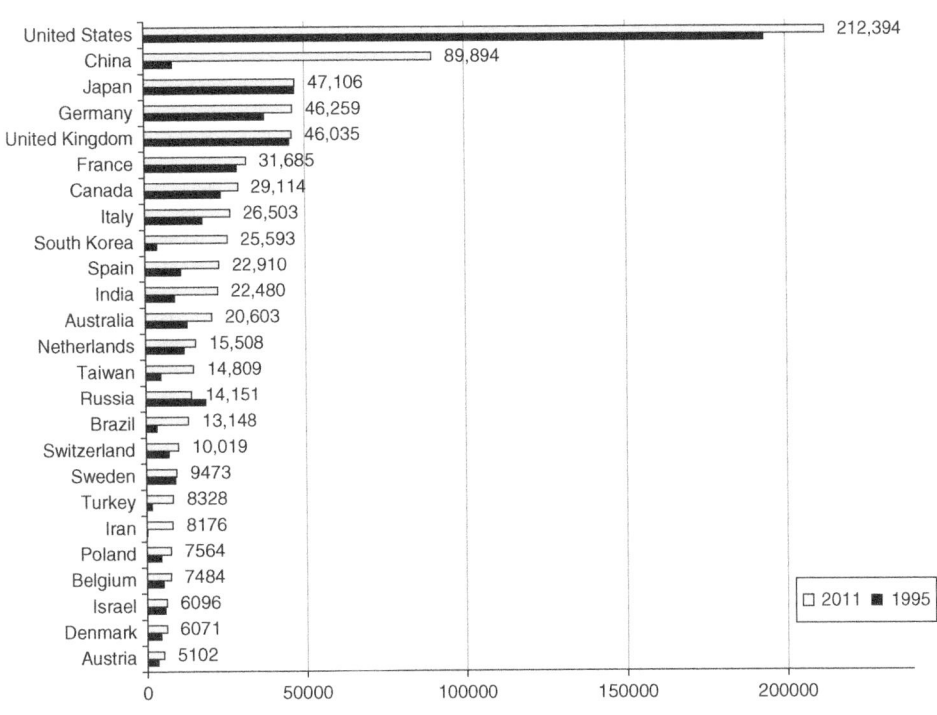

Country	2011
United States	212,394
China	89,894
Japan	47,106
Germany	46,259
United Kingdom	46,035
France	31,685
Canada	29,114
Italy	26,503
South Korea	25,593
Spain	22,910
India	22,480
Australia	20,603
Netherlands	15,508
Taiwan	14,809
Russia	14,151
Brazil	13,148
Switzerland	10,019
Sweden	9473
Turkey	8328
Iran	8176
Poland	7564
Belgium	7484
Israel	6096
Denmark	6071
Austria	5102

Figure 16.3 Spread of capacity in science: number of journal papers in 1995 and 2011, in countries producing more than 5000 papers in 2011.
Source: Data from NSF (2014).

Table 16.2 Fast growing science systems: journal papers 1995 and 2011

	1995	2011	Annual rate of increase 1995–2011
			%
Iran	280	8,176	25.2
China	9,061	89,894	16.5
Tunisia	143	1,016	14.0
South Korea	3,803	25,593	13.6
Thailand	340	2,304	13.6
Malaysia	366	2,092	12.3
Turkey	1,715	8,328	11.1
Portugal	990	4,621	10.8
Pakistan	313	1,268	9.8
Singapore	1,141	4,543	9.6
Brazil	3,436	13,148	9.4
Taiwan	4,759	14,809	7.9
Slovenia	434	1,239	7.2
USA	193,337	212,394	1.0
World	564,645	827,705	2.6

Source: NSF (2014).

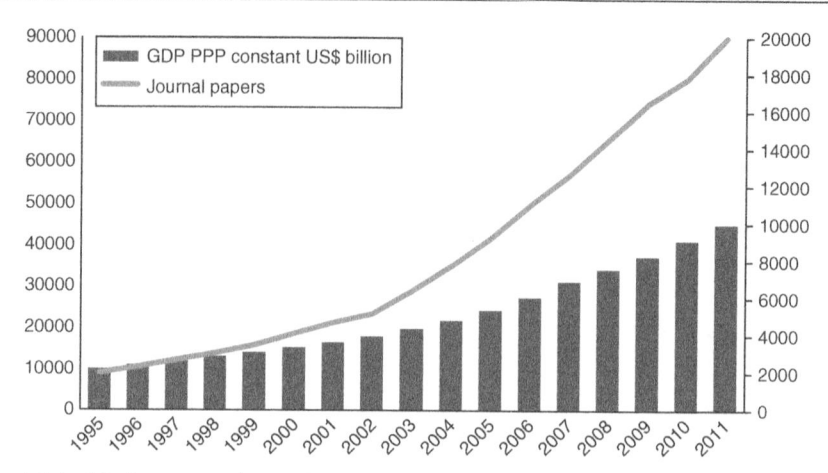

Figure 16.4 No linear correlation between economic growth and scientific output: trends in GDP (US$ billion, PPP, constant prices) and in number of journal papers in science and social science, China, 1995 to 2012.
Source: Data from World Bank (2014); NSF (2014).

Figure 16.4 shows that after 1995 China's scientific output trended upwards much faster than GDP, though the economy grew by world standards. As with educational participation, at the end of the 1990s the Chinese government made a conscious decision to step up research and expand the number of WCUs. It also encouraged international benchmarking and other performance drivers (Wang et al. 2011). Between 2005 and 2013 the number of universities in China ranked in the world top 500 for research jumped from 8 to 28 (ARWU 2014).

Global University Ranking

There is no single world system in teaching or degrees in higher education. There is a collection of separated national systems plus a partial regional system in Europe, where students often cross borders. There are bilateral and occasional multilateral negotiations on the dovetailing of national systems of accreditation, recognition, and quality assurance. There is a partly commercial market in international education, though international students access the same product as domestic students in each country, and except in doctoral training, there is no comprehensive global market in mobile students akin to, say, the national market in mobile students in the USA. The only integrated global competition is in the informal competition between individual HEIs for prestige, especially in research. Here imaginings of a global market have been powerfully advanced by global university rankings, which began in 2003.

Rankings are primarily driven by research publications, citations, and image. The *Times Higher Education* and QS purport to cover all aspects of higher education but their empirical backbone is research reputation and performance. More than two-thirds of the *Times Higher* index derives from various aspects of research and it even influences the survey of teaching reputation. As yet there are no comparative objective measures of teaching (Marginson 2014b). This is consistent with the core role of research in shaping value and reproducing social power in and through competition in higher education. High prestige research-intensive universities offer high value degrees that attract high scoring students, mostly socially advantaged, so drawing the superior resources for both teaching and science that maintain their value. Global league tables are signifiers of both HEI and national standing in higher education and economic innovation, driving national concentration and investment in WCUs. As noted, this magnifies the stratification in national higher education systems; and perversely, more unequal outcomes valorize the market vision by raising the stakes.

At the same time global rankings transform higher education on the basis of a uni-positional blueprint that sustains neo-imperial agendas. Mainstream rankings powerfully normalize the Anglo-American science university model; forcing HEIs everywhere, regardless of their contexts, to conform to that model in order to fulfill its indicators, maximize competitive position, and secure the global status that all desire. Ranking excludes and thereby subordinates non-English language knowledge, the non-quantitative disciplines, and HEIs with predominantly non-research missions.

National/Regional Diversity

The inexorable worldwide growth of participation, the expanding role of world science and spread of national science systems, the global positional competition between HEIs – and the homogenizing tendencies in all three – are articulated through national cultural differences. There is more than one kind of state and more than one kind of university.[4] Political and educational cultures condition the potentials of government and HEIs, shape state–university relations, structure HPS hierarchies and the take on WCUs, and affect the potentials of HEIs as agents in the global setting. Political and educational cultures are often regional clustered, common to several countries. There are Post-Confucian states in East Asia, two approaches (in the Westminster countries UK, Australia and New Zealand, and the USA) in the Anglosphere, and Nordic (Valimaa 2011), Russian (Smolentseva 2003), German, Francophone, Latin American (Marginson 2012), South Asian, Gulf State, and other variations. Space does not permit a full exploration of these distinctions and their foundations and dynamics. The point is that differences in political and educational cultures refract global systems and patterns of global borrowing and policy imitation.

The USA and the Westminster countries draw their notion of the limited liberal state from John Locke and Adam Smith. Freedom is defined as the absence of coercion by the state. Anti-statism is a core principle. Government is seen as separated from and in tension with the economic market and civil society. The US state is federal, exercising central authority in a few areas like defense but not in higher education, though strong national identity unites HEIs offshore. Educational opportunity is framed by a competitive and hierarchical market of HEIs, with fixed diversity between institutional types, facilitated by federal student loans and research funding. In the Westminster countries the state is unitary, more efficient of resources and energy, and exercises an undeclared supervisory power in the sector. National research priorities modify peer judgments about knowledge. The previous regime of centrally managed equality of opportunity has been replaced by fair competition on the basis of a nominally equal playing field (though prior inequalities condition the outcomes of competition). In both kinds of system, university leaders are autonomous and chosen by HEI governing bodies. However, the state steps back further in the US. Westminster systems of higher education are more consistently patterned in terms of the quasi-business models favored by the New Public Management (NPM). Both states leave HEIs free to implement global strategies, but the Westminster governments foster dependence on commercial markets in international education that condition internal organizational cultures. Both kinds of system have substantial numbers of world ranked research universities. There are no official programs of investment in WCUs.

The Anglo-American notion of independent HEIs as part of civil society contrasts with Humboldtian German and Nordic traditions, where professors are understood as state employees autonomous in teaching and research. The Nordic countries do not see higher education systems as markets. Competition is limited except in relation to research support. Institutional hierarchies are compressed, compared to Anglo-American practice, and higher education is understood as a universal citizen right. The state has a larger social role than in the UK and USA, yet on the whole NPM systems are less intrusive. As in the English-speaking countries, HEIs pursue their own global missions and there is little interest in fostering stronger WCUs. Germany, which shares with the Nordic countries' tuition-free systems and moderate use of business models, was likewise indifferent to the WCU project until 2006 when the government-created Excellence Initiative established a more competitive and hierarchical dynamic. In contrast Russia has a pronounced tradition of direct state intervention. Selected NPM mechanisms, including systemic competition, are combined with older Soviet-shaped command structures. HEIs have little autonomy in shaping mission, though tuition fees from about half the student population provide partial financial autonomy. The level of global engagement is weaker than in Europe or East Asia. The state wants WCUs, but is little interested in reforms to install an ongoing dynamic of internationalization.

Higher education in Post-Confucian East Asia and Singapore is different in several respects (Marginson 2011c). The roll-out of participation is sustained by the near universal commitment of families to Confucian self-cultivation through education. Aspirations to participate in higher education are not particularly sensitive to family socio-economic circumstances (Wu and Haiyan forthcoming). With even poor households willing to invest substantial income the state does not need to subsidize enrolment as much as in Europe and the English-speaking world, and the evolution of participation toward universal levels is more readily achieved. The state takes comprehensive social responsibility, but unlike the Nordic state does not exercise it via taxation/spending and high quality universal services, but by fostering social order and intervening in strategic areas. In this era higher education and research are important priorities. Capacity-building in research, and developing WCUs, are major policy priorities. The state regulates the sector closely, influencing or choosing university leaders and partly integrating institutional management into government. The state pursues reforms designed to foster internationalization and speed "catch-up" to the West; for example, through faculty mobility, and benchmarking with comparators. Research universities are encouraged to maintain direct relations with foreign HEIs but there are persistent claims of state interference in scientific decisions about research, especially in China.

How Far has Marketization been Implemented?

These differences in political and educational cultures are clues to the articulation of neo-liberal policies in national systems. Global policy flows in higher education (Rizvi and Lingard 2010) inculcate not only NPM principles of competition between HEIs, executive leadership, goal-driven production, performance management, cost unbundling, customer focus, transparency, and continuous self-evaluation – all part of the common templates of modern organizations in all sectors (Meyer *et al.* 2006) – but also neo-liberal quasi-market models (de Boer *et al.* 2009; Mok 2009). However, NPM and neo-liberal packages are flexible. Different parts can be grafted on to historical traditions, local practices, and state agendas. While enhanced competition, performance cultures, and accountability regimes are near universal, there is wide variation in the extent of marketization.

In an ideal neo-liberal system, full cost commercial prices would mediate supply and demand, consumer decisions would determine HEI profitability, and there would be open competition from diverse possible providers, most in the private sector. No higher education system functions in anything like this manner (Marginson 2013). In the early 2000s the World Trade Organization (WTO) was unsuccessful in its attempt to foster open markets in national education systems via multilateral and bilateral negotiations. States wanted to retain control, except that many agreed to tolerate foreign online education (largely because they could not regulate it). Many countries in the English-speaking world, East Asia, and Eastern Europe have pursued reforms to enhance the role of private education, and/or to significantly increase the proportion of costs paid by students – some joining these changes to a consumerist rhetoric – while others, especially in Western Europe and Latin America, have not.

In 2011 in OECD type 5A programs, private sector enrolments varied from less than 10% of total enrolments in Greece, Denmark, Switzerland, New Zealand, Australia, Ireland, Turkey, Germany, and Sweden, to 75% in Japan and South Korea, 74% in Chile, and 56% in Belgium (OECD 2013, 273). Private HEIs vary markedly on the basis of the degree of commercial orientation, religious denomination, the provision of high prestige professional programs, the cost of tuition fees, and the extent of government subsidies. Though in the OECD as a whole, the private share of students is increasing, there are cases such as Poland where it has declined. Further, in countries with near universal public sectors there is much variation in mixed funding and part-commercial arrangements. Overall, between 2000 and 2010 the proportion of the costs of tertiary education paid from private sources increased from 22.6 to 31.6%, but there was no convergence between countries (p. 207). The growth of commercialization, more transformative than privatization, is largely marginal to first-degree education of domestic students. Even in the USA, while for-profit colleges are the fastest growing part of higher education, they do not compete directly with research-intensive universities and liberal arts colleges. They focus on two specific markets: working students, and adult students who dropped out of formal education as young people. Commercial provision plays a negligible role in Western Europe, and in the Westminster countries except for international education and vocational postgraduate programs. In Japan and Korea many HEIs are nominally commercial institutions but behave more like non-profit private HEIs. Further, in all of East Asia, the USA and Europe international education is largely non-commercial.

Table 16.3 Variations in private cost: average annual tuition fees for full-time students in higher education, first degree programs, OECD nations, 2011.

Country	Public institutions	Independent private institutions	Change in public institutions 2005–2011
	US$ p.a.	US$ p.a.	2005 = 1.00
Ireland	6,450	–	–
Chile	5,885	6,230	–
USA	5,402	17,163	1.16
Korea	5,395	9,383	–
Japan	5,019	8039	1.09
UK*	4,980	–	–
Canada	4,288	–	1.24
Australia	3,924	10,110	1.28
New Zealand	3,645	–	1.35
Slovak Republic	Up to 2,916	–	–
Netherlands	1,966	–	1.13
Italy	1,407	4,406	–
France	200–1402	–	1.16
Spain	1,229	–	–
Switzerland	863	–	–
Austria	860	Up to 11,735	–
Belgium	576–653	–	–
Turkey	332	–	1.36
Norway	0	5,868	–
Mexico	0	5,684	–
Sweden	0	–	–
Finland	0	–	–
Denmark	0	–	–
Poland	–	1,242	–

Source: OECD (2013), 232.
Note:* UK institutions in column 2 are nominally private in legal terms but are regulated like public institutions in other countries. Note that in 2012, one year after the above data, the UK introduced a new high tuition regime in which most universities charged full-time students at the maximum level of £9000 p.a., highest in the OECD.
– Data not available or no institutions in this category.

There are extreme variations in tuition arrangements (Table 16.3). Since £9000 (US$14,000) fees began in the UK in 2012, tuition has been uniformly high in English-speaking systems. US universities set their own fees. In the Ivy League private sector "sticker prices" are very high but there are extensive private and public subsidies that belie price-based competition and allocative efficiency. Only half the students pay full price. In Westminster countries tuition is largely state-regulated and standardized, and underpinned by income-contingent tuition loan arrangements that blunt the impact of market forces and provide back-door state subsidies. It is almost as if Westminster states want to pretend they are more neo-liberal than they actually are. In East Asia also, the state shares funding with the household. The household carries 75% of all costs in Japan and Korea and an increasing share in China. Tuition loans are much less generous than in Westminster countries. This frees government to focus resources in priority areas: research, WCUs, infrastructure, internationalization and recruitment of global talent, and the scholarships for top students in elite HEIs. In contrast there are no fees in the Nordic countries and Mexico. Average fees are very low in Turkey, Belgium, and in Germany (not in Table 16.3). Tuition charges are less than US$2000 per annum in all EU countries in the table except the UK and Ireland (OECD 2013, 232). These variations are joined to a plethora of differing subsidies for student living support. There are four broad groups of nations: low tuition and generous student support (Nordic); high tuition and well developed support (Anglosphere); low tuition and less developed support (much of Europe, and Mexico); and high tuition and less developed support (East Asia and Chile) (OECD 2013, 224–230). The differences derive from varied expectations of state and household responsibilities, varying notions of fairness and opportunity, and varied emphases placed on completion as distinct from entry.

Neo-liberal reform is more specifically national, and less global and homogenizing, than often imagined. Nor is political economy as holistically determining as assumed by advocates and many critics of marketization reform. The differences in the national political economy of higher education have not blocked the near-universal trends to high participation and the spread of research science, nor the formation of global systems and global patterns of imitation and co-evolution. Nor (though the point needs a longer discussion) have these differences led to identifiable variations in overall access to higher education, though marked differences in tuition costs within systems are associated with steep stratification in institutional value and social use.

At the same time it would be unwise to underplay the longer-term transformative potentials of commercialization. Global communications provide wide opportunities to expand not only free public goods in higher education, but free-wheeling commercial distribution. Commercial online delivery, franchising of global chains, and partner-based transnational education are colonizing many developing countries, often with the encouragement of global agencies and cooperation of states thereby relieved of their fiscal obligations (Macpherson et al. 2014). MOOCs have built very large participating communities. They offer prestigious contents from high brand-value HEIs married to free delivery and social networking between students, a successful adaptation to the internet. Like ranking MOOCs augment the neo-imperial global reach of US universities. Like Google MOOCs constitute free global public goods bristling with commercial potential via advertising, and also via credentialing. Their Ivy League sponsors could charge a small unit cost for the second credential, open to all, alongside high value standard degrees. As a distinct product the internet degree would not detract from the value of the parent degree.

Conclusion

The main developments in worldwide higher education are common transitions to HPSs and engagement with global science. In the long run states must implement these tendencies. Participation is driven by social demand for education as a positional good, and the globalization of knowledge sustains the world science system, though funding of R&D and WCUs is also quickened by global competition and imitation. Despite neo-liberal thought, neither participation nor research takes a predominantly commercial form; and in research, a natural public good (Stiglitz

1999), full marketization would largely evaporate the product. In many countries there is intensified social competition in higher education. There is wide use of business models. But genuine markets are absent, except at the margins. There is neither market utopia nor market dystopia.

More important than market metaphors are questions of human agency. The economy is only a means to other ends. Agency and culture are affected by material resources. Poverty is an absolute barrier to self-determination: political economy does matter. At the same time, material development is conditioned by agency freedom. Higher education can foster human agency on a massive scale. In that sense the tendency to HPS is a great step forward for the democratic project. The questions are the cultural contents of higher education, the kind of self-forming persons that it makes possible, and the scope for diverse pathways to freedom. The diversity in national political economy is only a partial break on homogenizing tendencies in the business model, global comparisons, and the world research system. Nor can global homogenization be evaded by eschewing global engagement in research or people mobility – a stance apparent at times in Russia, France, and Japan – as this would condemn national research to obsolescence, weakening agency. (In any case, low rankings puncture national pride.) Yet the networked system of global research universities fails to foster horizontal diversity of mission, contents, and contributions to the common exchange of knowledge. The capacity of a more globally engaged sector to express and learn from its own diversity is in doubt.

Much of the regional, national, subnational, and institutional specificity is centered on humanities and humanistic social science disciplines partly depowered by exclusion from global science and university rankings. As shown by European higher education in the Bologna process, to sustain and develop both open possibility and diversity amid global convergence, and to moderate hierarchies while enhancing both joint and individual agency, requires a deliberate act of political will. The reward is a better kind of globalization. But how could this be negotiated? In the absence of a global democratic process, higher education and science are shaped by those with the strongest capacity for action. Might is right. This is a recipe for neo-imperialism in the sector. There is no lack of examples of that tendency (Marginson and Ordorika 2011; Naidoo 2011). The irony of globalization is this. If diverse national and local agents are to be sustained and to flourish, this diversity can only be fostered by a common system. Glonacal agency will need to commit itself to part-pooled sovereignty, collective relations deeper than multilateralism.

Notes

1   The OECD defines "tertiary" education to include both type 5A programs, degree programs involving at least three years' equivalent full-time study (EFTS), and graduate diplomas; and type 5B programs, sub-degree programs of two years EFTS. These are often but not always vocationally specific. In some countries such as UK, the term "higher education" is normally confined to type 5A. In others such as the USA it encompasses both 5A and 5B. In national tertiary education systems the balance between 5A and 5B varies considerably (OECD 2013), though overall, both have expanded at much the same rate. International differences between systems make it difficult to track the trend to HPS in comparative fashion. This chapter will not untangle the data issues, but see OECD (2013) and Clancy (2013).

2. Trow (1973) said that higher education systems moved from the "elite" to "mass" stage when the school leaver age cohort participation rate reached about 15%. They became "universal" when participation reached 50% or more. Elite HEIs – prestigious research-intensive universities and liberal arts colleges – persist at the mass and universal stages but come under increasing pressure to broaden their missions. Problems of ambiguous standards are rife in mass and universal education. Trow's essay has been very influential in higher education studies.
3. Note, however, that in the humanities, and parts of the social sciences and professional disciplines, nationally bordered conversations remain dominant.
4. The same insight also underpins the comparative studies by Green (2013) and Carnoy et al. (2013), the latter in relation to the BRICS (Brazil, Russia, India, China, and South Africa) countries.

References

Academic Ranking of World Universities (ARWU). 2014. Retrieved from: www.shanghairanking.com/ARWU2013.html (accessed November 13, 2015).
Baker, D. 2014. "Minds, Politics, and Gods in the Schooled Society: Consequences of the education revolution." *Comparative Education Review*, 58(1): 6–23.
Bayly, C. 2004. *The Birth of the Modern World 1780–1914: Global Connections and Comparisons*. Oxford: Blackwell.
de Boer, H., J. Enders, J., and B. Jongbloed. 2009. "Market Governance in Higher Education," in *The European Higher Education Area: Perspective on a Moving Target*, edited by B. Kehm, J. Huisman, and B. Stensaker, 79–104. Rotterdam: Sense Publishers.
Bourdieu, P. 1988. *Homo Academicus*. Cambridge: Polity.
Bourdieu, P. 1993. *The Field of Cultural Production*. New York: Columbia University Press.
Bourdieu, P. 1996. *The State Nobility: Elite Schools in the field of power*. Stanford: Stanford University Press.
Carnoy, M., and P. Loyalka, M. Dobryakova, R. Dossani, I. Froumin, K. Kuhns, J. Tilak, and R. Wang. 2013. "The State and Higher Education Change," in *University Expansion in a Changing Global Economy: Triumph of the BRICS?* Carnoy et al., 1–33. Stanford: Stanford University Press.
Cerny, P. 1997. "Paradoxes of the Competition State: The Dynamics of Political Globalization." *Government and Opposition*, 32(2): 251–274.
Clancy, P. 2013. *High Participation Systems in Comparative Perspective*. Paper to seminar on High Participation Systems, Higher School of Economics, Moscow.
Frank, R. and Cook, P. 1995. *The Winner-Take-All Society*. New York: The Free Press.
Freeman, B., S. Marginson, and R. Tytler (eds). 2015. *The Age of STEM: Educational Policy and Practice Across the World in Science, Technology, Engineering and Mathematics*. New York: Routledge.
Green, A. 2013. *Education and State Formation. Europe, East Asia and the USA*. 2nd Edition. Houndmills: Palgrave Macmillan.
Hirsch, F. 1976. *Social Limits to Growth*. Cambridge: Harvard University Press.
Macpherson, I., S. Robertson, and G. Walford. 2014. *Education, Privatisation and Social Justice: Case Studies from Africa, South Asia and South East Asia*. Oxford: Symposium Books.
Marginson, S. 1997. *Markets in Education*. Sydney: Allen and Unwin.
Marginson, S. 2006. "Dynamics of National and Global Competition in Higher Education." *Higher Education*, 52: 1–39.
Marginson, S. 2011a. "Imagining the Global." in *Handbook of Higher Education and Globalization*, edited by R. King, S. Marginson, and R. Naidoo, 10–39. Cheltenham: Edward Elgar.
Marginson, S. 2011b. "Strategising and Ordering the Global." in *Handbook of Higher Education and Globalization*, edited by R. King, S. Marginson, and R. Naidoo, 394–414. Cheltenham: Edward Elgar.

Marginson, S. 2011c. "Higher Education in East Asia and Singapore: Rise of the Confucian Model." *Higher Education*, 61(5): 587–611.

Marginson, S. 2012. *Global University Rankings: The Strategic Issues*. Keynote address to conference Las Universidades Latinoamericanas ante los Rankings Internacionales: Impactos, Alcances y Límites. UNAM (National University of Mexico), Mexico City, May 17–18.Retrieved from: www.encuentro-rankings.unam.mx/Documentos/ConferenciaMagistralMarginsontexto.pdf (accessed November 13, 2015).

Marginson, S. 2013. "The Impossibility of Capitalist Markets in Higher Education." *Journal of Education Policy*, 28(3): 353–370.

Marginson, S. 2014a. "Student Self-Formation in International Education." *Journal of Studies in International Education*, 18(1): 6–22.

Marginson, S. 2014b. "University Rankings and Social Science." *European Journal of Education*, 49(1): 45–59.

Marginson, S. and M. Mollis. 2001. "'The Door Opens and the Tiger Leaps': Theories and Reflexivities of Comparative Education for a Global Millennium." *Comparative Education Review*, 45(4): 581–615.

Marginson, S. and I. Ordorika. 2011. "'El Central Volumen de la Fuerza': Global Hegemony in Higher Education and Research," in *Knowledge Matters: The public Mission of the Research University*, edited by D. Rhoten and C. Calhoun, 67–129. New York: Columbia University Press.

Marginson, S. and G. Rhoades. 2002. "Beyond National States, Markets, and Systems of Higher Education: A Glonacal Agency Heuristic." *Higher Education*, 43(3): 281–309.

Marginson, S. and M. van der Wende. 2009. In *Higher Education to 2030. Volume 2: Globalisation, The New Global Landscape of Nations and Institutions*, edited by Organisation for Economic Co-operation and Development, Centre for Educational Research and Innovation, 17–62. Paris: OECD.

Meyer, J., G. Drori, and H. Hokyu. 2006. "Conclusion," in *Globalization and Organization: World Society and organizational change*, edited by G. Drori, J. Meyer, and H. Hwang, 258–274. Oxford: Oxford University Press.

Mok K. 2009. *When Neo-Liberalism Colonizes Higher Education in Asia: Bringing the "Public" Back in the Contemporary University?* Book chapter in draft. Hong Kong: University of Hong Kong.

Naidoo, R. 2011. "Rethinking Development: Higher Education and the New Imperialism," in *Handbook of Higher Education and Globalization*, edited by R. King, S. Marginson, and R. Naidoo, 40–58. Edward Elgar, Cheltenham.

National Science Foundation (NSF). 2014. *Science and Engineering Indicators 2014*. Retrieved from: www.nsf.gov/statistics/seind14 (accessed November 13, 2015).

Organisation for Economic Co-operation and Development (OECD). 2013. *Education at a Glance 2013*. Paris: OECD.

Organisation for Economic Co-operation and Development (OECD). 2014. *PISA 2012 Results in Focus. What 15 Year Olds Know and What They Can Do With What They Know*. Paris: OECD.

Rizvi, F. and R. Lingard. 2010. *Globalization and Education Policy*. New York: Routledge.

Scott, P. 2011. "The University as a Global Institution," in *Handbook of Higher Education and Globalization*, edited by R. King, S. Marginson, and R. Naidoo, 59–75. Cheltenham: Edward Elgar.

Sen, A. 1992. *Objectivity and Position*. The Lindley Lecture, The University of Kansas. Lawrence: The University of Kansas.

Shahjahan, R. and A. Kezar. 2013. "Beyond the 'National Container': Addressing Methodological Nationalism in Higher Education Research." *Educational Researcher*, 42(1): 20–29.

Smolentseva, A. 2003. "Challenges to the Russian Academic Profession." *Higher Education*, 45: 391–424.

Stiglitz, J. 1999. "Knowledge as a Global Public Good," in *Global Public Goods: International Cooperation in the 21st Century*, edited by I. Kaul, I. Grunberg, and M. Stern, 308–325. New York: Oxford University Press.

Trow, M. 1973. *Problems in the Transition from Elite to Mass Higher Education*. Retrieved from: http://files.eric.ed.gov/fulltext/ED091983.pdf (accessed November 17, 2015).

United Nations Educational, Scientific and Cultural Organization (UNESCO). 2014. *Educational Statistics*. UNESCO Institute for Statistics. Retrieved from: www.uis.unesco.org/Pages/default.aspx (accessed November 13, 2015).

Valimaa, J. 2011. "The Corporatisation of National Universities in Finland," in *Universities and the Public Sphere: Knowledge Creation and State Building in the Era of Globalization*, edited by B. Pusser, K. Kempner, S. Marginson, and I. Ordorika, 101–119. New York: Routledge.

Wang, Q., Q. Wang, and N. Liu. 2011. "Building World-Class Universities in China: Shanghai Jiao Tong University," in *The Road to Academic Excellence: The making of World-Class Research Universities*, edited by P. Altbach and J. Salmi, 33–62. Washington, DC: The World Bank.

Wimmer, A. and M. Schiller. 2002. "Methodological Nationalism and Beyond: Nation-State Building, Migration and the Social Sciences." *Global Networks*, 4(2): 301–334.

World Bank. 2000. *Higher Education in Developing Countries: Peril and Promise*. Report of the Task Force on Higher Education and Society. Washington, DC: World Bank.

World Bank, 2014. *Data and Statistics*. Retrieved from: http://data.worldbank.org (accessed November 13, 2015).

Wu, C.-L. and B. Haiyan. 2015. "The Effects of Economic Status and Educational Expectations on University Pursuit." *Higher Education*, 69(3): 331–344.

Part III Global Policy Actors in Education

Part III Introduction

Antoni Verger

The chapters in this part focus on the role and impact of global policy actors in the education policy domain. They cover a broad variety of supra-national actors including old and new players, organizations that operate on a regional and/or a global scale, and institutions that are state-centered and others that are rather constituted by non-state forces, among other variables.

Power is a common denominator in all the contributions included in this part. All the chapters reflect, in a more or less explicit way, on the sources of legitimacy and influence of global players, as well as on the particular effects of their actions and strategies in the education policy field. In this respect, most chapters observe that, beyond material power, soft power is becoming increasingly central to understand how most global policy actors operate and currently have impact. As we will observe, many of the international agencies analyzed in this part increasingly resort to the mobilization of ideas, data management and technical assistance to advance what Lingard and Sellar (Chapter 19) conceive as new epistemological modes of global governance.

Overall, the chapters included in this part capture extraordinarily well the predominantly supra-national nature of policy influence in the current global governance scenario. The policy effects and dynamics of influence analyzed by our contributors go from more conventional and well-known inter-scalar policy dynamics (such as international organizations conditioning the policies of their member states) to more intangible dynamics of agenda setting and settlement of educational priorities and policy preferences that emerge at a global scale. The latter tend to be more difficult to capture empirically, but, as our contributors reveal, can be very effective in framing those education policy decisions that policy-makers and practitioners adopt in the different spaces where they intervene.

Nonetheless, the emergence and consolidation of a range of international players in the educational field we are witnessing is not necessarily contributing to the constitution of a coherent and compact "global education agenda." In fact, the contributions to this part make clear that the interests, priorities, and policy preferences of different global actors can differ substantially, and enter into conflict. This contributes to the constitution of a global education policy field that, far from coherent, is loose and contested; a field in which hegemony is constantly disputed.

The Handbook of Global Education Policy, First Edition.
Edited by Karen Mundy, Andy Green, Bob Lingard, and Antoni Verger.
© 2016 John Wiley & Sons, Ltd. Published 2016 by John Wiley & Sons, Ltd.

Francine Menashy and Caroline Manion's chapter (Chapter 17) focuses on two of the most important United Nations institutions involved in global education policy affairs: the United Nations Children's Fund (UNICEF) and the United Nations Educational, Scientific and Cultural Organization (UNESCO). The chapter looks at the evolution of the legitimacy and effectiveness of these two international organizations in the education domain from a historical comparative perspective. Among other results, Menashy and Manion find that UNESCO's centralized, bureaucratic, insular environment, with a state-based guaranteed funding source, has seen both its legitimacy and effectiveness reduced in the past decades. In contrast, UNICEF has become a more successful global education policy entrepreneur due to its decentralized and flexible structure, and to its efficient fundraising machine.

Nonetheless, UNESCO, the international organization with a more explicit and historically grounded education mandate, is not only losing centrality in the politics of education field against UNICEF, but also against other international organizations that were not created to deal with educational affairs initially and are increasingly involved in the sector. In Chapter 18, Karen Mundy and Antoni Verger reflect on how and why the World Bank, despite the fact that its original mandate did not include education, has become the most powerful agency operating in the education for development field. Since the 1960s, the Bank's level of financing and its technical and knowledge-based resources for education tower over those of other international institutions. Nevertheless, due to significant shifts in power in the world system, the competition coming from other international agencies, and issues related to its internal organization, the Bank is going through a period of strategic uncertainty that may end up challenging its current leadership in the education for development field. Beyond the World Bank case study, Mundy and Verger's chapter develops a heuristic framework for understanding agenda-setting processes in international organizations and aid agencies, which focuses on three dynamics: the political opportunities created by geo-political and ideological shifts among the most powerful member governments; the relationships of the international organization with the countries that receive its support; and, finally, the internal dynamics and organizational culture of the international organization'ss own bureaucracy as it aims to reproduce itself and manage shifts in the previous two dynamics.

In Chapter 19, Bob Lingard and Sam Sellar provide an in-depth analysis of another international organization that did not include education in its original mandate and that despite its limited territorial scope and economic resources (if compared to the World Bank) has acquired a great deal of centrality in the global education policy domain. We refer to the Organisation for Economic Co-operation and Development (OECD). After providing a brief history of this international organization, Lingard and Sellar reflect on how the launching of the Programme for International Student Assessment (PISA) in the year 2000 signified a turning point in the OECD's influence in education. The success of PISA has enhanced the OECD's profile in education globally and, at the same time, cemented a place for education within the OECD. To expand and consolidate such a high profile, the OECD has developed a range of new and multiple initiatives which are, to a great extent, grounded on the PISA formula, including *PISA Tests for Schools*, the *Programme for International Assessment of Adult Competencies* (PIAAC) and *PISA for Development*. Despite the fact that the OECD is an international organization whose membership is restricted to industrialized countries, this latter product – PISA for development – shows the organization's ambitions to expand its scope of influence toward the developing world. It remains to be seen if this means that the equity-driven agenda of the OECD in education will dispute the hegemony that the World Bank's finance-driven agenda has enjoyed in the education for development field since the 1980s.

In Chapter 20, Andreas Schleicher and Pablo Zoido reflect more explicitly on the policy influence of PISA globally. Schleicher heads the Directorate of Education and Skills and has been directly involved in the development of the PISA program since its inception; while Zoido is a senior analyst on the OECD PISA team and responsible for the *PISA for Development* program. They review the increasing number of countries that use PISA data as a benchmark in their national educational strategies and reflect on the drivers of such influence. According to these authors, through PISA, the OECD has become a global forum that helps countries to identify and emulate the education strategies and policies of the most successful performers, as well as to find out how different countries deal with and address similar educational problems. In their own words, "the example of PISA shows that data can be more influential than administrative control or financial subsidy through which we traditionally shape education policy and practice."

Rui Yang and Jingyun Yao's chapter (Chapter 21) focuses on the interplay between globalization, regionalization, and higher education. According to these authors, the Association of South-East Asian Nations (ASEAN) is a policy space that, when the necessary circumstances are given, can substantially contribute to the internationalization of higher education and promote more vibrant knowledge economies. The authors frame this argument around an empirical study of one of China's least economically developed provinces and its interconnections with the ASEAN higher education space.

Ian Macpherson's chapter (Chapter 22) inaugurates a series of chapters on the role of non-state actors in the global governance of education. In particular, his chapter focuses on transnational advocacy networks constituted by civil society organizations and how these networks, through a range of semiotic and discursive strategies, aim to influence the actions and decisions of other education stakeholders, including policy-makers, governments, and international organizations. From a Foucauldian perspective, Macpherson wants to prove that discourse is a form of power in the sense that it shapes action and prescribes outcomes both within advocacy networks and externally. He tests this argument using the cases of two of the most active and vibrant networks in the education for development field: the Global Campaign for Education and the Inter-Agency Network for Education in Emergencies.

Zahra Bhanji's chapter (Chapter 23) reviews how transnational corporations are operating as global actors in education policy through a range of corporate social engagement mechanisms. In her view, corporate social activities are increasingly blending business and social goals and are shaping education policies around the world. The chapter presents an overview and categorization of those multilateral mechanisms through which the corporate social approach has entered into the educational field. She illustrates her categories with, on the one hand, concrete global initiatives such as the United Nations Global Compact and the World Economic Forum Global Education Initiative, and, on the other, the education interventions of

The William and Flora Hewett Foundation, the ICICI Foundation, and Pearson Inc. Nonetheless, beyond a thorough description of the emerging and changing field of corporate engagement in education, Bhanji also raises serious concerns on the implications of subordinating education development processes to business partners' strategies.

The latter is, in fact, the main point developed in the last chapter of this part dedicated to global actors. In Chapter 24, Prachi Srivastava and Lianna Baur take an in-depth look at the phenomenon of the "new global philanthropy in education" in the context of the post-2015 development agenda. These authors argue that philanthropic initiatives do not engage sufficiently with the complexity and structural contingencies of educational development processes. Despite their claims of benevolence, goodness, and altruism, these two authors observe that the actions of philanthropic actors are far from neutral. In the face of the education provision problems that the Global South faces, philanthropic actors tend to give priority to market-based solutions and to education privatization policies. By doing so, they alter education governance structures in developing countries, and do not necessarily contribute to the sustainable and equitable development goals they claim to be promoting.

Chapter 17

The Historical Evolution and Current Challenges of the United Nations and Global Education Policy-Making

Francine Menashy and Caroline Manion

Given the deteriorating state of support to education globally, where aid levels to education have decreased by nearly 6% since 2010, the efficacy of international institutions to execute their education policies in the global South is of critical importance (Rose and Steer 2013). As countries are witnessing either reduced or completely cut bilateral support to their education systems, it is crucial we better understand how those institutions that do continue to support education operationalize their policies. In this chapter, we explore two major United Nations (UN) agencies that both have enduring, dedicated, and comparable educational mandates: the United Nations Children's Fund (UNICEF) and the United Nations Educational, Scientific and Cultural Organization (UNESCO). Through an analysis informed by institutional theory, we aim to discern how organizational structures have altered the legitimacy and the effectiveness of the global education policy-making of each institution.

The UN, founded in 1945, is a large and complex organization with a broad mandate that includes the maintenance of peace and security, and the promotion of social progress and human rights. The spectrum of issues it addresses is vast and currently 193 member states sit on its various committees and agencies (UN 2014). Although education figures prominently in international development policies and operations, within the current UN system only three agencies can be assessed as key players in education and development. These are UNICEF, UNESCO, and the World Bank. UNICEF is the only one of the three agencies within the UN system that is accountable to the General Assembly. UNESCO and the World Bank are considered "specialized agencies" and therefore act relatively autonomously. Historically, the United Nations Development Programme (UNDP) also held education as part of its mandate, but since the late 1990s has abandoned most of its educational operations (Jones 2005; 2006; 2007).

The Handbook of Global Education Policy, First Edition.
Edited by Karen Mundy, Andy Green, Bob Lingard, and Antoni Verger.
© 2016 John Wiley & Sons, Ltd. Published 2016 by John Wiley & Sons, Ltd.

Although few UN agencies have explicit education-related mandates, the UN as a whole can be viewed as deeply concerned with improving education globally via its spearheading and support of various international initiatives involving education, including but not limited to the Millennium Development Goals and the current Global Education First Initiative, directed by the UN Secretary-General Ban Ki-moon, who also in 2012 appointed Gordon Brown as the UN Special Envoy for Global Education (Global Education First 2013). Moreover, UN member states have signed several treaties and conventions in which education is integral, including the Declaration of Human Rights (UN 1948), the International Covenant on Economic, Social and Cultural Rights (1966), and the Convention on the Rights of the Child (UN 1989).

In this chapter we provide a historical overview and comparison of UNESCO and UNICEF – two key UN agencies both with broad educational agendas that are central to their mandates. This is not to disregard the significance of the issue of education as it connects to other aspects of and agencies within the UN system. Although UNICEF's key role is that of a humanitarian aid-giving agency, while UNESCO focuses primarily upon providing education policy advice and setting global norms, our choice of these UN agencies stems from their mutual framing of education as a human right and the associated and integral roles both organizations have played in the promotion of Education for All (EFA) for close to quarter of a century (UNICEF and UNESCO 2007). This comparison moreover spurs our interest because of the very different organizational and governance structures that characterize each, in particular how each agency is funded and the degree to which each can be described as centralized. In light of this, in this chapter we ask: How have the organizational structures of UNESCO and UNICEF influenced the ways in which each organization interprets their educational mandates and thereby their legitimacy? Through this examination, we furthermore compare the roles and effectiveness of UNESCO and UNICEF as global educational governors.

A Historical and Sociological Institutional Framework for the Analysis of Legitimacy

Our analysis offers insights into how organizational structures have influenced the nature of these goals, and have affected the ostensible legitimacy of each institution according to external critics from the fields of development and education. In our discussions of legitimacy, we grapple with perceptions of the degree to which each organization is accepted as an authority to operationalize their agendas. According to Keohane (2006), legitimacy for an international organization embodies various dimensions that impact efficacy, which he delineates as normative, epistemic and performative:

> Normative legitimacy requires a consistent pattern of institutional outputs that meet both epistemic and performance tests. The epistemic dimension of legitimacy means that for powerful institutions to be legitimate, they need to generate correct information, both about the problems they purport to solve and about their own practices. They need to be transparent and accountable, and located in the context of independent monitoring agents that can interrogate their behavior. The performance

dimension of legitimacy – what Fritz Scharpf (1999) calls "output legitimacy" – is also crucial since institutions are created, and their costs borne, to solve problems. (2006, 86)

In order to understand the degrees and types of legitimacy held by UNESCO and UNICEF, this chapter uses a theoretical lens derived from a combination of two related approaches that have been used to study the nature of international organizations. Our analysis is informed by sociological and historical institutionalism, both of which target primarily the internal characteristics of organizations and institutional change. Sociological institutionalism takes as its starting point an examination of the dynamics within organizations by studying bureaucratic rules and associated behaviors. It draws our attention to the cultural norms within organizations that shape how the bureaucracy operates and responds to external pressures (Barkin 2006; Schmidt 2008). Under this approach, policy-making processes are argued to be governed primarily by formal rules and procedures, shaping which ideas are considered and selected and thereby what actions are taken by an organization (Campbell 1998; 2002).

Historical institutionalism similarly focuses on norms and procedures as determining factors in organizations' policy development but more precisely examines such elements over time (Hall 2010; Hall and Taylor 1996). Such analyses often conclude that international organizations in particular are subject to "path dependency" where those embedded in bureaucratic structures come to be resistant to change, "where contingent events or decisions result in institutions being established that tend to persist over long periods of time and constrain the range of options available to actors in the future, including those that may be more efficient or effective in the long run" (Campbell 2010, 3). Moreover, "this perspective emphasizes the extent to which institutions are not simply 'rules' but constituted in equal measure by accompanying rituals and symbol systems" (Hall 2010, 23).

Our comparative examination of UNESCO and UNICEF is conducted through the above theoretical lenses, where we expose via an organizational history how the unique structures of each have shaped how the two organizations have come to interpret and take action in service of their educational mandates. By first outlining the historical trajectories of each institution and their current policies, paying particular attention to their educational policies, governance, and organizational structures, we expose key contrasts that have led UNESCO and UNICEF to varied degrees of legitimacy as global education policy actors.

UNESCO as a Global Education Policy Actor and the Struggles of Legitimacy

From its establishment in 1945 as a specialized agency of the United Nations, UNESCO has framed and promoted education as a human right and as a tool and essential ingredient in efforts to create and nurture a more secure and peaceful world order. Beginning with the oft-cited statement that "…since wars begin in the minds of men, it is in the minds of men that the defences of peace must be constructed," UNESCO's Constitution calls on its members to support "full and equal opportunities for education for all" (UNESCO 1945). In the context of the 1948 Universal Declaration of Human Rights, UNESCO called on member states to make elementary education free and compulsory (UN 1948, Article 26). In light of its early consensus-building and thought-leadership roles, UNESCO has sought over the past 65 years to be a leader in educational knowledge production and dissemination, innovation, standard-setting, and capacity building, particularly in the areas of formal basic education and literacy (Engel and Rutkowski 2012; Wagner 2011).

UNESCO's first 40 years of activity in the area of education were rocky (Jones 1988). Despite its strong educational mandate, UNESCO stumbled toward creating a clear educational program in its first two decades (Jones 1998). Forging consensus on its education priorities and programs proved challenging, and the task of building its education portfolio was made more difficult as a result of the preference of donors to channel educational aid bilaterally rather than multilaterally, thereby negatively impacting UNESCO's capacity to pursue its mission and mandate (Mundy 2010). Moreover, as membership grew with the joining of many newly independent countries, and exacerbated by the Cold War politics of the era, UNESCO's reputation for politicization became an increasing concern for some rich countries, including most notably the USA.

UNESCO has long presented itself as a normative leader in several areas, including education. Under the leadership of its first Director, Julian Huxley, UNESCO originally embraced and promoted a universal value system based on scientific humanism: "Thus the general philosophy of UNESCO should, it seems, be a scientific world humanism, global in extent and evolutionary in background" (Huxley 1946, 8). This normative orientation was reflected in the framing of education in UNESCO's early years. First, education was seen as a lifelong process that facilitated individual growth for children and adults; second, the importance of education was understood to extend beyond what it meant for the individual to include the social function of education in processes of cultural production and reproduction; third, education was primarily a technical endeavor and as such could be improved through the application of principles revealed through scientific research (Huxley 1946, 30). These principles informed UNESCO's seminal report, *Learning to Be: The World of Education Today and Tomorrow* (1972) and continued to inform and be promoted in UNESCO's *Learning: The Treasure Within* (1996, see also Burnett 2008).

UNESCO's early championing of scientific humanism as a global ideology that ought to inform policy and practice, including in education, was not without contest and indeed, the longstanding tensions between its philosophical and technical roles and responsibilities is well documented in the literature. For instance, critics have argued that UNESCO's normative leadership has created a slippery slope toward politicization, and its political positions have impacted its financial support and thereby its ability to put its ideals into practice (Burnett 2011; Engel and Rutowski 2012; Pavone 2007). In an early example, the US blocked UNESCO efforts to spearhead a global literacy campaign largely because such an initiative was the idea of the Soviet Union (Jones 1988). Most notably, in 1984/85, the USA, Singapore, and the UK withdrew from UNESCO, in part accusing the organization of being a mere platform for criticizing the West, particularly given the organization's central role in both the New International Economic Order and New World Information and Communication Order movements of the late 1970s and early to mid-1980s – movements that sought to bring about more equitable and democratic economic, social, and political development, but were perceived as a challenge to Western interests.

The withdrawal of these countries had the effect of significantly reducing UNESCO's already inadequate budget, further constraining the organization's policy and programming capacity. The early preference for bilateral aid to education amongst donors and the politicization of UNESCO in the Cold War era can be seen as original contributing factors to one of UNESCO's most longstanding and most oft-cited institutional challenges: the structural imbalance between its program objectives and its resources (Martinez 1995, cited in Heyneman 2011, 314; Mundy 1999). Indeed, by the mid-1980s, moving into the vacuum created by a chronically underfunded and increasingly politicized UNESCO, the World Bank – with a much larger staff and budget – dwarfed UNESCO's role as a lead global governor in education (Mundy 2010).

UNESCO, however, continued to insert itself in a leadership position in the global education policy arena. Under the leadership of Director General Federico Mayor and in response to declining educational enrollments after years of steady expansion in many countries, deteriorating school conditions, poor educational quality, and persistently high levels of illiteracy worldwide, UNESCO, alongside the UNDP, the United Nations Population Fund (UNFPA), UNICEF, and the World Bank, convened the World Conference on Education for All in 1990 in Jomtien, Thailand. As lead agency, UNESCO has been responsible for coordinating international efforts to achieve EFA (UNESCO 2014b). Part of this effort involved building national education reform capacity (see Haddad 1995). As a follow-up, in 2000, along with its UN partners, UNESCO convened the World Education Forum in Dakar, Senegal, where the global community reconfirmed a commitment to achieving quality basic EFA, with UNESCO and others anchoring this commitment on the belief that education is not only a fundamental human right but also an essential ingredient in the promotion of a global culture of peace, sustainable development, equity, and social cohesion. While UNESCO had introduced for the first time the issue of educational quality in 1990 at Jomtien, it would not substantively engage with issues of quality until several years into the second EFA decade when, as a result in part of UNESCO's ideational and technical activities, education quality emerged as a central concern of the international aid community and national governments alike (Wagner 2011, see also UNESCO 2004). Since that time, UNESCO has, as lead global coordinating agency for EFA, sought to provide normative and technical policy leadership on issues concerning quality basic EFA.

Currently, while UNESCO's Education Sector works across 11 thematic areas and coordinates 24 education programs, in the context of EFA the priority areas are: sector wide policy and planning; literacy; teachers; technical and vocational education and training. Current educational initiatives developed or co-developed by the Education Sector focus on literacy, gender equity, social cohesion and development, and health–education intersections (e.g. LIFE: the Literacy Initiative for Empowerment; EDUCAIDS: the Global Initiative on Education and HIV/AIDS; and the Global Partnership for Girls' and Women's Education: "Better Life, Better Future"). More broadly, UNESCO's Education Sector's mission commits it to working on several overlapping fronts: intellectual and policy leadership, technical expertise, knowledge brokerage, partnership building, monitoring, and evaluation (UNESCO 2014d). Toward these goals, UNESCO activities have included convening forums and other spaces for policy dialogue and learning, including several education-related international and regional conferences over the past decade, standard-setting, capacity-building support within national ministries of education, collecting and disseminating national education statistics, and monitoring progress toward EFA, most notably through the annual EFA Global Monitoring Reports published since 2002[1] (Pigozzi 2011).

Structurally, UNESCO's staffing and administrative operations are highly centralized. The General Conference and Executive Board comprise the two apex governance bodies of the organization and together work to define and manage its policies, programs, and budgets (Benavot 2011). The General Conference meets biennially, convening UNESCO's 195 member states, associate members (currently nine of them) and non-state observers, with each member having one vote (UNESCO 2012a). Its Executive Board, comprising 58 member states (elected through the General Conference) meets twice per year and is primarily responsible for the overall management of the organization in line with the decisions of the General Conference.

UNESCO's budget, running on a two-year cycle, is financed through membership dues paid by countries based on wealth, with the USA historically being the largest contributor to UNESCO, averaging just under a quarter of the organization's budget since its establishment. Yet decision-making within UNESCO is based on a one member/one vote system, which has in turn posed problems at times for the largest contributors. The chronic tension that has evolved historically, leading at times as we've discussed to the withdrawal of some of the largest contributors, has meant that the UNESCO budget is quite volatile, dependent as it is on a few key players. For instance, in response to Palestinian membership to UNESCO, in 2011 the USA withdrew its funding, which reduced UNESCO's budget by over 20%.

The Education Sector is bureaucratically structured in line with other UNESCO sectors and organizations. Led by an Assistant Director-General, the Education Sector structure includes an Executive, and four divisions: Basic learning and skills development; Teacher development and higher education; Education for peace and sustainable development; and Education research and foresight division. The sector has approximately 400 staff, with roughly 150 working at headquarters in Paris and the remainder working in the organization's 52 field offices, including four regional bureaus and six education institutes. In these offices education officers are tasked with advancing UNESCO's goals and assisting in designing and implementing programs, as well as raising extra-budgetary support (UNESCO 2014a). The General Conference at its biennial meetings approves the Education Sector's budget. In 2012/13, the Education Sector received approximately 17% of UNESCO's approved budget (US$115,421,300) (UNESCO 2012b). As will be discussed below, it is noteworthy that the Education Sector is set to spend more on staffing (US$63,485,300) than on actual activities (US$51,936,300, with this figure including allocations to UNESCO's six education institutes) (UNESCO 2012b). And while it is important to recognize that almost half of the sector budget goes to staffing and programming in field offices, regional bureaus and institutes, what will be shown is that the percentage of resources allocated to UNESCO's administrative support far exceeds that of UNICEF's administrative budget (Benavot 2011; UNICEF 2012a).

As will be detailed below, much criticism has been levied against UNESCO's inward-oriented governance and related tendency toward excessive bureaucratization with respect to its internal processes. However, it is important to note that the organization has indeed maintained an extensive relationship with hundreds of actors external to the institution, most notably non-governmental organizations (NGOs). And over the past two decades, "the private sector has become an increasingly valuable partner for UNESCO – contributing its core business expertise, creativity, innovative technological solutions, social media outreach, and in-kind contributions to achieve shared objectives in the area of education, culture, the sciences and communication and information" (UNESCO 2014c; see also UNESCO 2012a; 2012c). Current partnerships with the private sector range from fundraising to strategic partnerships. UNESCO is an official partner in a large number of collaborative relationships with the private sector intervening in various degrees from being involved in program delivery arrangements, providing policy guidance, technical assistance and expertise, to playing a strong role in promoting its core ethical and programmatic values through advocacy and awareness-raising (UNESCO 2014c).

Although these relationships indicate a relatively new openness to partnerships, the key structural model of UNESCO (its funding base and staffing models for instance) has not altered for decades. As will be discussed further below, as a global education policy actor, such institutional characteristics have led to a very different level of performative, or "output" legitimacy and normative legitimacy from its counterpart, UNICEF.

UNICEF as a Global Education Policy Actor and the Formation of Legitimacy

For decades, public perception of UNICEF as a development actor has been overwhelmingly positive. As the most recognizable UN agency, with a clear and easily embraced mandate – "to advocate for the protection of children's rights, to help meet their basic needs and to expand their opportunities to reach their full potential" – those within and outside the development arena have widely embraced the work of UNICEF (Jones 2006; UNICEF 2014c). Many scholars indeed agree that this reception of the agency as a whole is well warranted. However, in order to adequately assess and trace the evolution of UNICEF as a global education policy actor, the specific educational policies and operations of UNICEF ought to be treated separately from its broader work, which predominantly focuses on child health. As well, as elucidated below, the funding base, governance, structural organization, and other aspects of its operational structure are clearly as significant as its policies, playing a substantial role in its ability to operationalize its mandate.

UNICEF was initially founded as a temporary agency of the UN that focused upon child survival via the provisioning of supplies for predominantly health and nutrition. Because of its transitory status, it relied exclusively on voluntary contributions. Although in 1953 it became a permanent UN agency, its funding structure remained ostensibly voluntary. And the nature of this resource base – including private corporations, individuals, as well as governments – separates it significantly from other UN agencies with stable committed resources. Fundraising is central to UNICEF, and it therefore has a uniquely "entrepreneurial nature" (Black 1996; Jones 2006; Mundy 2010).

Apart from maternal education programs, UNICEF's initial agenda did not include education, focusing on material assistance including vaccination programs, provision of medication and food supply where scarce. It was not until the 1960s that its mandate broadened to include education. Although initially "resisted by those who regarded UNICEF as having a deliberately humanitarian focus" (Black 1996, 215), it was the growing acceptance of human capital justifications for development that spurred acceptance within the organization of broadening the organization's agenda, under a rationale common to other aid organizations of that era: schooling was seen to contribute to economic and national development, and therefore was deemed to be equally as significant for children's future well-being as immunizations and nutrition. UNICEF trumpeted addressing the needs of the "whole child," and so now provided aid to elementary, vocational, and agricultural education programs (Black 1996, 216). Education programming in the 1960s and into the 1970s sought to bridge two foci, where on the one hand, UNICEF supplied more material needs to schools, including equipment, construction, and training, while on the other hand attempted to take a more policy-level role in advising national governments on educational system improvement (Black 1996; Jones 2006).

But by the mid-1970s, veering in a different direction from UNESCO, UNICEF became much less concerned with improving education systems. The ultimate goal was access, with the aim of universal primary education by 1980 (Black 1996). And although human capital played a role in the organization's initial forays into education, UNICEF increasingly rejected it as the key rationale for aid to schooling, focusing much more on educational deprivation resulting from poverty and disadvantage, and on rural communities. By the mid-1970s, UNICEF began to focus on basic EFA, and its reach included equally non-formal/alternative and formal education systems, due in part to increasingly large donations from Organisation for Economic Co-operation and Development (OECD) countries (Black 1996; Mundy 2010). And by the mid-1980s, the education of women came to the forefront of UNICEF's agenda due to the impact on child survival (Chabbott 1998).

It was under the leadership of Executive Director Jim Grant (1980–1995) that UNICEF's role as a major education promoter took hold, and scholars have widely cited Grant's leadership as the key contributor to its current status as a lead actor in international education (Black 1996; Chabbott 1998; Jones 2006). By the late 1980s, UNICEF's involvement in inter-institutional collective initiatives on education culminated in the World Congress on Education for All. Grant touted UNICEF's previous success with similar campaigns, including its Health for All initiative, lending legitimacy to UNICEF's role in EFA (Chabbott 1998; 2003).

While along with UNESCO, UNICEF was certainly a key player in the establishment of EFA, its role was limited due to a far lower budget than that of the World Bank and the lack of analytical capacity of UNICEF staff in particular at the country office level. As well, Grant had assumed that UNICEF's earlier Health for All initiative could be easily mapped on to education, but this was not the case (Chabbott 1998; 2003; Jones 2006; 2007). Throughout the early 1990s, in spite of rhetorical support to EFA, UNICEF's budgetary support to health and nutrition programs continued to eclipse funding to education (Jones 2006).

Carol Bellamy's leadership of UNICEF (1995–2005) solidified an education policy agenda that focused on both formal and non-formal education, gender equity in education, early childhood education, adult education, and education in emergency contexts. Bellamy advocated increased flexibility in schooling and school administration, which was proposed to increase efficiency and access, most particularly for girls. But most notable was her strengthening of relationships with NGOs, recognizing their crucial roles both politically and operationally in aiding children. As well, during this time UNICEF adopted the role of the lead agency for the United Nations Girls' Education Initiative. The early 2000s also saw a rise in education commitments, and increased staffing particularly in country offices (Jones 2006; Mundy 2010; UNGEI 2014).

As with UNESCO, and significantly departing from the stance put forth by the World Bank, UNICEF's framing of education as a human right solidified in the 1990s, following the adoption of the Convention on the Rights of the Child (CRC) in 1990, and resulted in large part as a response to the advocacy of civil society actors, and its vocal rejection of structural adjustment programs (United Nations General Assembly 1990). Despite some early skepticism and concern on the part of organizational insiders regarding the relative merits associated with the adoption of a rights-based development approach, from this time UNICEF has been an institutional core for the right to education and for the advocacy of rights-based approaches (Black 1996; Mundy 2010; UNICEF 1987; 2014b).

According to its current Education Strategy (2006–2015), UNICEF maintains this rights-based approach, where the organization explicitly frames its policies around the 1989 Convention of the Rights of the Child (2006; see also UNICEF 2013). As well, its current work is contextualized around the Millennium Development Goals and the Education for All Dakar Framework (UNICEF 2012b; 2013a; 2013b) and more recently the post-2015 global development agenda. The scope of UNICEF's educational activities is quite broad, where it claims to impact children from infanthood to 18, in both non-formal and formal education settings, including temporary schooling contexts often found in situations of conflict and crisis (2009; 2012c; 2013a).

UNICEF's policies strongly frame education as an important part of all humanitarian efforts, with an overarching focus on how the organization can support education in conflict-affected and fragile states, and children impacted by crisis. In strategy documents, nearly every key educational goal outlined by the organization – including for instance improving school readiness, reducing gender disparities, increasing retention – is at some point described in the context of emergency or crisis response. Furthermore, UNICEF's policy maintains its earlier stance of advocating an inter-sectoral approach and educating the "whole child" (UNICEF 2009; 2012b; 2013a).

Much like UNESCO, the notion of partnership is central to UNICEF's identity, where it collaborates with other international organizations to achieve educational goals (UNICEF UNAIDS, UNESCO, UNFPA, ILO, WHO, WB, 2011; World Bank and UNICEF 2009). As mentioned, NGO advocacy has historically influenced UNICEF's agenda, and civil society actors remain significant. Yet a newer partner to UNICEF's efforts has come in the form of private sector donors, which have recently been embraced by UNICEF as partners in policy-making but also at the fundraising level (UNICEF 2012c). It is also important to note that UNICEF has maintained until today a relatively diplomatic relationship with the USA, securing voluntary funding year after year (UNICEF 2012c).

There are some key structural elements that most uniquely contribute to the functioning of UNICEF as an institution. It is governed by a relatively small Executive Board comprising 36 members, and representing five regional groups, which reviews all UNICEF policies, and approves country activities and budgets. The Board's work is coordinated by UNICEF's President and four Vice-Presidents; its "Bureau" (UNICEF 2014d). As well, its decentralized staffing structure, with a very small headquarters staff, has resulted in country-by-country educational programming and sizeable country offices. As a result, UNICEF has historically promoted flexibility in program implementation, resisting a one-size-fits-all form of planning. Finally, UNICEF's voluntary funding base, including governments, the private sector and individuals, separates it from other UN agencies with committed resources. Contributions can be directed toward un-earmarked regular (longer-term) voluntary funds, earmarked "other" funds and/or earmarked "trust" funds (UNICEF 2012a). Fundraising, associated with the need for a large degree of responsiveness to the wishes of various contributors, is a central characteristic of UNICEF's identity. Member states are a significant source of revenue for UNICEF, with the USA and the UK being the two largest contributors to the organization, and because of this they hold more decision-making power and influence relative to within UNESCO (even when they were due-paying members). As will be seen below, these characteristics contribute to an organizational structure that resists some of the features that have resulted in critiques of UNESCO.

Discussion

The similarities between UNESCO and UNICEF are clear. Both operate under the auspices of the UN system and are therefore directed by the statutes and declarations made by the UN. Both agencies readily frame education as a human right. The rights-based approaches to education as adopted by both UNESCO and UNICEF informed their joint promotion and formation of the EFA mandate and associated frameworks for action. A cursory rhetorical view of each institution's public statements show very similar institutional education mandates, where UNESCO promotes "…the realization of everyone's right to education, and the belief that education plays a fundamental role in human, social and economic development" (UNESCO 2014a) and UNICEF posits that "Education is a fundamental human right: Every girl and boy in every country is entitled to it. Quality education is critical to development both of societies and of individuals, and it helps pave the way to a successful and productive future" (UNICEF 2014a). Grounded in rights-based rationales, both UNICEF and UNESCO support education for its intrinsic individual and broader societal benefits.

However, as presented in Table 17.1, the organizational and structural attributes of UNICEF and UNESCO differ rather dramatically. The internal organizational features of each, and the fact that such structural characteristics have persisted for decades, can be examined through the theoretical framework described above. Most notably, UNESCO is organizationally characteristic of a highly centralized bureaucracy, where approximately 70% of its staff and nearly 40% of its resources are budgeted toward its administrative headquarters and Northern institutes. On the other hand, with 87% of its staff situated in local country or regional offices and with a very small (8%) administrative budget, UNICEF's most notable organizational feature is its decentralized structure. Such decentralization indicates the likelihood that UNICEF is able to be more responsive to local country contexts and project implementation, and this flexibility thereby lends to its performative, or "output" legitimacy. As described below, critiques of UNESCO as a bloated, ineffectual, and top-heavy institution may be rooted in its centralized structure. In this way, at UNESCO, diverse external

Table 17.1 UNESCO and UNICEF organizational comparison

	UNESCO	UNICEF
Resource base	Committed by member states; weighted by country wealth	Voluntary contribution from states; direct fundraising
Governance	General Conference including 195 member states; one country, one vote	Executive Board including 36 member states; bureau, including President and four Vice-Presidents
Education allocations (2012)	US$115,421,300	US$605,000,000
Staff at headquarters/institutes	70%	13%
Staff in country/regional offices	30%	87%
Resources allocated to headquarters/management	40%	8%

Source: UNESCO (2012c; 2012b); UNICEF (2012a; 2012c).

demands are arguably more difficult to meet. UNESCO, as an insulated bureaucracy, limits external stimuli on its operating structure, whereas the decentralized nature of UNICEF forces upon it a larger degree of responsiveness.

The institutional culture of UNESCO in general and the Education Sector in particular has been singled out in the literature as further contributing to UNESCO's limited and/or uneven impact on international and national education policy and practice (Benavot 2011; Jones 2007; Mundy 2006). Discussing the problem of "closed door syndrome," Benavot talks of a "deep-set, inward-looking organizational culture" maintained within a "conservative bureaucracy" that privileges form and process over substance, problems exacerbated by UNESCO's underfunding (2011). He states: "Also troublesome is the low and muted capacity for organizational learning from past mistakes – and successes. The organization is reluctant – some might say hostile – to critically probe its 'dirty' laundry in public" (Benavot 2011, 560). Such characteristics in the organizational culture of UNESCO have undoubtedly diminished its epistemic legitimacy, where UNESCO has lacked the transparency and accountability expected of an effective global policy entrepreneur.

Critics have noted a lack of commitment to the types of structural changes needed within UNESCO to help it increase the effectiveness and efficiency of its programming – and thereby its performative/output legitimacy – for instance, by focusing on a smaller number of sectors (Benavot 2011; Heyneman 2011). In contrast, UNICEF has a reputation for efficient management and receptiveness to change (Jones 2007; Mundy 2006; 2010). Moreover, UNESCO's governance policy dictating that education budget allocations must be approved by the General Conference has meant that, "priorities often reflect the interest of its members rather than content" (Heyneman 2011, 313). UNICEF, however, is not fiscally dependent on a governing body comprising all member states, and so arguably does not fall prey to similar bureaucratic maneuvering and political push and pull.

Further affecting UNESCO's reputation and legitimacy is its tenuous relationship with the USA; a historical friction that persists today and must be understood within the context of UNESCO's very limited commitments to education relative to its mandate. UNICEF, however, has maintained a depoliticized and generally positive relationship with the USA, likely also enhancing public perception as a normatively legitimate organization (Jones 2006; 2007). Significantly, the funding base of each organization furthermore undoubtedly impacts its effectiveness. While unguaranteed, UNICEF's voluntary resource base potentially acts as a catalyst to its openness and adaptability. UNICEF must be consistently responsive to external actors via its continual fundraising efforts. UNESCO's guaranteed funding from donors arguably works against its adaptability, inhibiting its ability to respond and thereby change.

Compounding the challenges discussed above with respect to UNESCO's bureaucratic structure, institutional culture, and politics, concerns about UNESCO's technical competence have dogged the organization since its establishment. For example, while UNESCO's early spearheading of efforts to collect comparative data on literacy is a key technical impact of the agency's work in the 1950s, speaking to UNESCO's engagement in global literacy policy and assessment Wagner states,

> [T]he statistics provided by UNESCO (now largely through UIS in Montreal) are based today largely on the same methodology (national government estimations, mainly on schooling or indirect self-assessment surveys), and therefore suffer from the same lack of credibility (at least among experts) that has been the case over the years. (2011, 321)

While the EFA Global Monitoring Report – an autonomous wing of UNESCO's Education Sector – is well respected, concerns have been expressed more broadly with respect to the scientific capacity of UNESCO staff to fulfill the agency's mandate and vision, thus contributing to a lack of epistemic legitimacy (Wagner 2011).

To summarize, UNESCO's inward-looking institutional culture is a key structural characteristic that potentially engenders reduced performative legitimacy – possibly magnified by the sheer size of its administrative staff and its centralized structure. Moreover, UNESCO's guaranteed funding results in critiques citing its lack of adaptability and responsiveness to change. Such criticisms are rarely wielded against the decentralized UNICEF, which budgets a much lower percentage to administration and is an organization dependent on fundraising. We argue that UNESCO's guaranteed funding acts as a barrier to its change, while UNICEF must be adaptable and this adaptability guarantees its future funding and continued existence.

Given the overarching aim of this chapter, upon examining these UN agencies in comparison we extrapolate their legitimacy and thereby their abilities to operationalize their educational mandates. The fact that both UNICEF and UNESCO are forthright supporters of rights-based approaches to education makes their contrasting features all the more stark. Advocates of rights-based approaches to education require legitimacy to counter opposing approaches (e.g. the neoclassical model upheld by the World Bank). Based on the analysis presented in this chapter, UNESCO lacks epistemic legitimacy due to, for instance, its scientific capacity, transparency, and accountability. UNESCO's inability – or what some have claimed to be a resistance (Benavot 2011) – to change has impacted its performative legitimacy. UNICEF therefore may have a stronger ability to advocate for a rights-based agenda simply through its claims to performative and epistemic legitimacy associated with flexibility and fiscal efficiency. Its overall normative legitimacy has been historically constituted, where UNICEF's advocacy for children's rights has consistently corresponded with an entrepreneurial, depoliticized, and flexible character.

Conclusion

This chapter has aimed to discern the impacts of the governance and organizational structures of UNICEF and UNESCO on their legitimacy and thereby their capacities to endorse and operationalize their respective educational goals. From first providing a historical backdrop for each institution, focusing in large part on their educational policies and institutional structures, we elucidate some key differences between the two organizations that we argue have informed major divergences in how each operationalizes its education goals. As several critics have noted, UNESCO's centralized, bureaucratic, insular environment, with a state-based guaranteed funding source, has reduced its legitimacy, whereas UNICEF's decentralized and flexible structure, dependent on an efficient fundraising machine, has been far more embraced by external critics who perceive it as more entrepreneurial, adaptable, and legitimate.

This chapter has served as a preliminary analysis and posits a hypothesis that we believe can be supported by institutional ethnographic study. Further research, including interviews with staff at both headquarters and in country offices, can expose what aspects of UNICEF's operational structure most lend themselves to this ostensible legitimacy. Similarly, for UNESCO, the views of staff are crucial to better understand the workings of the organization and the challenges it faces. Observations of the inner workings of each institution are needed to gain a comprehensive understanding of these UN agencies, how they function, and their associated respective impacts on education globally.

This chapter has stopped short of evaluating the work of UNESCO and UNICEF from an ethical standpoint. For instance, in certain geographical regions such as Asia, UNICEF has been more receptive of private sector participation in education, a policy stance with far reaching equity implications (UNICEF and ABD 2011). In light of this, UNICEF may hold more performative legitimacy, but are its decentralized operations more equitable? As well, while UNESCO's centralized bureaucracy and its General Conference may be more cumbersome, it is possible that its one country/one vote governance structure engenders more democratic practices. Moreover, although the politicization of UNESCO's work is often criticized for inhibiting its technical reach, perhaps its political stances exhibit a moral authority that is needed on the international stage.

In light of our exploration and the questions that persist, we moreover believe a rigorous study of lead UN agencies with educational mandates is of particular importance also because of the recent and troubling reduction in aid to education. Issues of legitimacy and responsiveness are particularly pressing in a climate of diminished funding and increased need. Given the current post-2015 international development context, a key question – one that has persisted for decades – is how to make international policies more effective, and therefore understanding the relationships between organizational and governance structures and various forms of legitimacy are crucial. Moving forward, we continue to question how these two major UN agencies can better operationalize education as a human right, perhaps together and more collaboratively.

Note

1 For all reports see www.unesco.org/new/en/education/themes/leading-the-international-agenda/efareport/reports.

References

Barkin, S. 2006. *International Organization: Theories and Institutions*. New York: Palgrave Macmillan.
Benavot, A. 2011. "Imagining a Transformed UNESCO with Learning at its Core." *International Journal of Educational Development*, 31: 558–561.
Black, M. 1996. *Children First: The Story of UNICEF, Past and Present*. Oxford: Oxford University Press.
Burnett, N. 2008. "The Delors Report: A Guide for Education for All." *European Journal of Education*, 43: 181–187.
Burnett, N. 2011. "UNESCO Education: Political or Technical? Reflections on Recent Personal Experience." *International Journal of Educational Development*, 31: 315–318.
Campbell, J.L. 1998. "Institutional Analysis and the Role of Ideas in Political Economy." *Theory and Society*, 27: 377–409.
Campbell, J.L. 2002. "Ideas, Politics, and Public Policy." *Annual Review of Sociology*, 28: 21–38.
Campbell, J.L. 2010. "Institutional Reproduction and Change," in *The Oxford Handbook of Comparative Institutional Analysis*, edited by G. Morgan, J.L. Campbell, C. Crouch, O.K. Pedersen, and R. Whitley. Oxford; New York: Oxford University Press.
Chabbott, C. 1998. "Constructing Educational Consensus: International Development Professionals and the World Conference on Education for All." *International Journal of Educational Development*, 18: 207–218.
Chabbott, C. 2003. *Constructing Education for Development: International Organizations and Education for All*. London: Routledge Falmer.
Engel, L.C., and D. Rutkowski. 2012. *UNESCO Without U.S. Funding? Implications for Education Worldwide*. Bloomington: Center for Education and Evaluation Policy.
Scharpf, F.W. 1999. *Governing in Europe: Effective and Democratic?* Oxford: Oxford University Press.
Global Education First. 2013. "The UN's Global Education First Initiative." Retrieved from: www.globaleducationfirst.org/about.html (accessed 16 November 2015).
Haddad, W.D. 1995. *Education Policy-Planning Process: An Applied Framework*. Paris: UNESCO.
Hall, P.A. 2010. "Historical Institutionalism in Rationalist and Sociological Perspective," in *Explaining Institutional Change: Ambiguity, Agency, and Power*, edited by J. Mahoney and K. Thelen, 204–223. Cambridge: Cambridge University Press.
Hall, P.A., and R.C.R. Taylor. 1996. "Political Science and the Three New Institutionalisms." *Political Studies*, 44: 936–957.
Heyneman, S.P. 2011. "The Future of UNESCO: Strategies for Attracting New Resources." *International Journal of Educational Development*, 31: 313–314.
Huxley, J. 1946. "UNESCO: Its Purpose and Philosophy." Retrieved from: http://unesdoc.unesco.org/images/0006/000681/068197eo.pdf (accessed November 16, 2015).
Jones, P.W. 1988. *International Policies for Third World Education: Unesco, Literacy and Development*. London and New York: Routledge.
Jones, P.W. 1998. "Globalisation and Internationalism: Democratic Prospects for World Education." *Comparative Education*, 34: 143–155.
Jones, P.W. 1999. "Globalisation and the UNESCO Mandate: Multilateral Prospects for Educational Development." *International Journal of Educational Development*, 19: 17–25.

Jones, P.W. 2006. "Elusive Mandate: UNICEF and Educational Development." *International Journal of Educational Development*, 26: 591–604.

Jones, P.W. 2007. "Education and World Order." *Comparative Education*, 43: 325–337.

Keohane, R.O. 2006. "Accountability in World Politics." *Scandinavian Political Studies*, 29: 75–87.

Mundy, K. 1999. "Educational Multilateralism in a Changing World Order: UNESCO and the Limits of the Possible." *International Journal of Educational Development*, 19(1): 27–52.

Mundy, K. 2006. "Education for All and the New Development Compact." *International Review of Education/Internationale Zeitschrift Für Erziehungswissenschaft/Revue Internationale de l'Education*, 52: 23–48.

Mundy, K. 2010. *Who Governs the Globe?* Cambridge: Cambridge University Press.

Pavone, V. 2007. "From Intergovernmental to Global: UNESCO's Response to Globalization." *Review of International Organizations*, 2: 77–95.

Pigozzi, M.J. 2011. "A Commentary on 'Views of the Future of UNESCO'." *International Journal of Educational Development*, 31: 324–325.

Rose, P. and L. Steer. 2013. *Financing for Global Education: Opportunities for Multilateral Action*. Washington, DC: Brookings.

Schmidt, V. 2008. "Discursive Institutionalism: The Explanatory Power of Ideas and Discourse." *Annual Review of Political Science*, 11: 303–326.

UNESCO. 1945. "Constitution of UNESCO." Retrieved from: http://portal.unesco.org/en/ev.php-URL_ID=15244&URL_DO=DO_TOPIC&URL_SECTION=201.html (accessed November 16, 2015).

UNESCO. 1972. *Learning to Be: The World of Education Today and Tomorrow*. Paris: UNESCO.

UNESCO. 1996. *Learning: The Treasure Within*. Paris: UNESCO.

UNESCO. 2004. *Education for All: The Quality Imperative*. Paris: UNESCO.

UNESCO. 2009. "UNESCO Intersectoral Strategy on Philosophy." *Diogenes*, 56: 95–100.

UNESCO. 2012a. *Information Note: Reform of UNESCO's Global EFA Coordination Mechanism*. Paris: UNESCO.

UNESCO. 2012b. *Key Data on UNESCO staff*. Paris: UNESCO.

UNESCO. 2012c. *2012–2013 Approved Budget*. Paris: UNESCO.

UNESCO. 2014a. "About the Education Sector." Retrieved from: www.unesco.org/new/en/education/about-us (accessed November 16, 2015).

UNESCO. 2014b. "Education for All Movement." Retrieved from: www.unesco.org/new/en/education/themes/leading-the-international-agenda/education-for-all (accessed November 16, 2015).

UNESCO. 2014c. "Education Partners: Private Sector." Retrieved from: www.unesco.org/new/en/education/partners/education-partners/private-sector (accessed November 16, 2015).

UNESCO. 2014d. "UNESCO's Mission." Retrieved from: www.unesco.org/new/en/education/about-us/how-we-work/mission (accessed November 16, 2015).

UNICEF. 1987. *Adjustment with a Human Face*. Oxford: Oxford University Press.

UNICEF. 2009. *All Children, Everywhere: A Strategy for Basic Education and Gender Equality*. New York: UNICEF.

UNICEF. 2012a. *Overview of UNICEF's Finance and Budget*. New York: UNICEF.

UNICEF. 2012b. *State of the World's Children Report: Children in an Urban World*. New York: UNICEF.

UNICEF. 2012c. *UNICEF Annual Report*. New York: UNICEF.

UNICEF. 2013a. *State of the World's Children Report: Children with Disabilities*. New York: UNICEF.

UNICEF. 2013b. "Millennium Development Goals." Retrieved from: www.unicef.org/mdg (accessed November 16, 2015).

UNICEF. 2014a. "Basic Education and Gender Equality." Retrieved from: www.unicef.org/education (accessed November 16, 2015).

UNICEF. 2014b. "Human Rights-based Approach to Programming." Retrieved from: www.unicef.org/policyanalysis/rights (accessed November 16, 2015).

UNICEF. 2014c. "Who We Are: Partners." Retrieved from: www.unicef.org/partners (accessed November 16, 2015).

UNICEF. 2014d. "Executive Board." Retrieved from: www.unicef.org/about/execboard (accessed November 16, 2015).

UNICEF and ADB. 2011. *Non-State Providers and Public-Private Partnerships in Education for the Poor*. Bangkok: UNICEF.

UNICEF and UNESCO. 2007. *A Human Rights-Based Approach to Education for All*. New York: UNICEF.

UNICEF, UNAIDS, UNESCO, UNFPA, ILO, WHO, and World Bank. 2011. *Opportunity in Crisis: Preventing HIV from Early Adolescence to Young Adulthood*. New York: UNICEF.

UNGEI. 2014. "The United Nations Girls Education Initiative." Retrieved from: www.ungei.org (accessed November 16, 2015).

United Nations. 1948. "The Universal Declaration of Human Rights." Retrieved from: www.un.org/en/documents/udhr (accessed November 16, 2015).

United Nations. 1966. "International Covenant on Economic, Social and Cultural Rights." Retrieved from: www.ohchr.org/EN/ProfessionalInterest/Pages/CESCR.aspx (accessed November 16, 2015).

United Nations (UN). 1989. "Convention on the Rights of the Child." Retrieved from: www.ohchr.org/EN/ProfessionalInterest/Pages/CRC.aspx (accessed November 16, 2015).

United Nations General Assembly. 1990. *Convention on the Rights of the Child*. New York: United Nations.

United Nations (UN). 2014. "Structure and Organization." Retrieved from: www.un.org/en/aboutun/structure/index.shtml (accessed November 16, 2015).

Wagner, D.A. 2011. "What Happened to Literacy? Historical and Conceptual Perspectives on Literacy in UNESCO." *International Journal of Educational Development*, 31: 319–323.

World Bank and UNICEF. 2009. *Abolishing School Fees in Africa: Lessons from Ethiopia, Ghana, Kenya, Malawi, and Mozambique*. Washington, DC: World Bank.

Chapter 18

The World Bank and the Global Governance of Education in a Changing World Order*

Karen Mundy and Antoni Verger

Introduction

Over the past 50 years, the World Bank has arguably become the epicenter for the global governance of social policy within emerging economies and low-income societies. The Bank is the largest single international provider of development finance to governments. Its staffing and internal resources tower over those of other international institutions, and it is regarded by other providers of international development assistance as a key source of policy evidence and policy advice. For these reasons, the World Bank has often been viewed as holding "a near monopoly on the business of development" (Marshall 2008, xv). Yet like all international institutions, the Bank is both a global governor in its own right, and a member of a larger system of interstate and trans-national relationships.

In this article, we explore the evolution of the World Bank's policies and practices in the field of education to understand how the Bank has come to exert authority in the settlement of global education agendas. Education has long been a significant sectoral focus for the Bank's lending portfolio (smaller but comparable in volume to its efforts in health). Globally, the Bank is the largest single international source of education finance, with a multi-billion dollar budget for education operations. It is also host to several pooled trust funds for education, including funds for education in conflict-affected states, and it is the host of a global "vertical fund" for education, the Global Partnership for Education (formerly the Fast Track Initiative).

---

*This chapter was originally published as Karen Mundy and Antoni Verger, "The World Bank and the Global Governance of Education in a Changing World Order," in *International Journal of Educational Development*, 40, January 2015, pp. 9–18. Used with permission from Elsevier.

The Handbook of Global Education Policy, First Edition.
Edited by Karen Mundy, Andy Green, Bob Lingard, and Antoni Verger.
© 2016 John Wiley & Sons, Ltd. Published 2016 by John Wiley & Sons, Ltd.

As we shall argue, the Bank's formal policies on education are the iterative outcomes of three central dynamics: organizational dynamics, the political opportunities created by geo-political and ideological shifts among its most powerful member governments, and the Bank's relationships with its borrowing (or "client") member governments (on whose willingness to borrow the Bank depends). This article explores how these three dynamics interact in the constitution of the Bank's educational activities and policies in four key periods: from the 1960s to the beginning of the 1980s, when the debt crisis exploded in many developing nations; from 1981 to the mid-1990s, a period marked by structural adjustment lending; from the mid-1990s to 2008, when the Post-Washington consensus emerged; and from 2008 to the present, characterized by a loss of strategic focus and uncertainty at different levels within the Bank.

Conceptual Framework

Three approaches from the field of international relations have dominated the study of international organizations: realism, institutionalism, and constructivism. In conventional realist theories, international organizations are seen as instruments at the service of the interests of powerful states; accordingly, it is assumed that international organizations' policies change and evolve as a consequence of the will of their (most powerful) members. Taking this state-centric approach a step further, neoliberal institutionalism conceives international organizations as rational institutions created by states to reinforce cooperation and reduce transaction costs in an increasingly interdependent world (Rittberger and Zangl 2006).

Constructivism, for its part, is more oriented toward unpacking agency and social relations within international organizations and between international organizations and a broader world polity. This theoretical perspective goes beyond a state-centric approach to international organizations, and focuses on the role played by international bureaucracies and other non-state actors, as well as the cultural and ideational factors that shape political outcomes in the global arena (Barnett and Finnemore 2004). Constructivists observe that even when international organizations are created to serve member states, with the passage of time, they evolve into autonomous sources of power. As bureaucracies, international organizations often have sufficient autonomy to interpret and redefine their own broad mandate and, at the same time, to influence country members' decisions and preferences. *Organizational culture* is a key concept for constructivists when understanding the dynamics of policy change and reproduction in international organizations. It can be defined as the "shared ideologies, norms and routines that shape staff members' expectations about how agendas are set, mandates are operationalized, projects are implemented and evaluated, and what staff behavior will be rewarded or punished in promotions and demotions" (Nielson *et al.* 2006, 109).

In this chapter, we adopt the notion advanced by Nielson *et al.* (2006) of bridging the rationalist–constructivist divide. The rationalist approach contributes to a more sophisticated understanding of principal and agent relationships that influence international organizations' outcomes, and can complement the constructivist framework. To operationalize such an approach, three central dynamics need to be analyzed. These dynamics can be analyzed independently, although they are mutually constitutive and, in ontological terms, they are intertwined in the everyday activities at the Bank.

1. The *first* dynamic is the relationship between the Bank and its most powerful member states. As an organization the Bank was set in motion by the winners of World War II, and has since been dominated by the liberal polities and industrialized economies of the Organisation for Economic Co-operation and Development (OECD). As might be expected within a rationalist/realist paradigm, the Bank has had to respond to these states and to their changing demands and priorities (Abbott and Sindal 2005). However, the rise of new world powers is shifting the constellation of powerful states within the Bank, while the emergence of global civil society advocates, critical of Bank activities, has also added a new complexity to the Bank's external authorizing environment. In this new universe, a "second level" of political responsiveness evolves when civil society pressures powerful governments to mandate new norms for World Bank activities (O'Brien *et al.* 2000; Putnam 1988).

2. At the same time, the Bank bureaucracy has enjoyed considerable autonomy and room for maneuver. The Bank's most powerful member governments have not always converged in their views about development. At important moments they have faced uncertainty about the best ways forward. This creates an important opportunity for autonomy that is amplified by the fact that among development international organizations, the Bank has a unique degree of financial autonomy (derived from its call on initial capital commitments from rich world members) and legitimacy (derived from its claims to scientific rationality and political neutrality) (cf. Finnemore 1996).

    Such autonomy has been used at two levels within the Bank. Starting with Robert McNamara, Bank presidents have played an important role in reshaping both the Bank's mandate as well as the wider global policy agenda for international development. Policy entrepreneurship also thrives at a second level: among technical staff within specific policy fields. Bank staff operate within a context characterized by ingrained organizational imperatives and norms (such as the longstanding dominance of the discipline of economics in decision-making and the "pressure to lend"). Nonetheless, in social policy fields like education, for example, or pension reform, staff often use Bank resources to build both internal (to the Bank) and transnational policy networks and epistemic communities that influence global agenda setting (see Haas 2004; Verger 2012; Ornstein 2008; Broad 2006; Weaver 2008; Finnemore 1996). Thus, the *second set of dynamics* we will explore are the complex patterns of institutional autonomy, organizational culture, and bureaucratic path dependency that have shaped the character of the Bank's education sector work.

3. Finally, we explore the Bank's relationships with middle and low income borrowing countries. From the Bank side, lending conditionality has been a central but evolving mechanism for managing this relationship; the Bank increasingly utilizes soft power mechanisms (like benchmarking, technical assistance, dissemination of ideas) as a way of framing and influencing the preferences of member countries (Stone and Wright 2007; Marshall 2008; World Bank 2005). It should not be assumed however, that the Bank's relationship with borrowing countries is only driven by the Bank. To survive, the Bank must lend and countries must be willing to borrow. Complex patterns of decision-making, involving both rational dimensions on the part of borrowing countries (such as the existence of financing

alternatives and other strategic considerations), and cultural features (such as the match between national policy models and the policy models promoted by the Bank's policy entrepreneurs) shape the Bank's relationships with borrowers.

The combination of these three dynamics constitutes a heuristic framework that fosters structured analysis of the evolution of the World Bank's work throughout this chapter.

The World Bank and Education: Origins of a Mandate

Formed as a kind of credit union among sovereign states in the period after World War II, the International Bank For Reconstruction and Development (IBRD), known today as the World Bank, initially focused on economic reconstruction and development in Europe. The Bank gradually emerged as a global governor in social policy fields during the 1960s, when the organization became a central provider of development finance to newly post-colonial states. Under Robert McNamara's presidency (1968–1981), the Bank adopted its early focus on poverty reduction and increasingly framed its work in social policy around a poverty reduction mandate (Vetterlain 2012, 43).

Dynamics among the Bank's principals fed the development of the Bank's role as a social policy actor. For the past 60 years, agenda-setting at the World Bank has been dominated by Northern countries, which hold the largest number of voting shares. While the Bank's fixed capital base provides it with some autonomy, the historical record suggests that it has been most strongly affected by the policy preferences of the USA, which holds the power of veto and appoints the Bank's president (Woods 2000; Wade 2002). Though other governments have at times worked together to influence the Bank (e.g. Japan in the 1990s; see Wade 1996), American hegemony has been a constant. In the 1960s, concern from the USA and its allies over the advance of communism into newly independent post-colonial nations led to the creation of a new highly concessional financing facility for low-income countries inside the World Bank, the International Development Association (IDA). In this broader geo-political context, McNamara emerged as a successful policy entrepreneur, selling the Bank's role in promoting poverty reduction and the delivery of basic needs as essential to the maintenance of stability in the world system (Vetterlain 2012). The Bank's capital base increased fourfold under McNamara's leadership.

Under McNamara, the Bank's approach to poverty revolved around the idea of redistributing the outputs of growth, through investment projects that targeted the productive capacities of the poor (Kapur et al. 1997). Lending in fields such as integrated rural development for small farmers, water supply, and urban services and infrastructure provided a clever bridge between the Bank's early infrastructure focus and the new poverty agenda. Poverty reduction was also carefully framed as part of the Bank's evolution as a source of expertise on economic growth and development. In the 1960s and 1970s, the Bank became the largest employer of development economists and pioneered the development of country economic reviews and other types of development policy research based in the discipline of economics (Ayres 1983; Finnemore 1996).

Education did not figure as importantly as other social sectors in the Bank's activities during the 1960s, in part because education was not viewed by Bank leadership as directly linked to its focus on improving the material assets of the poor (Stern 1997, 603; Kapur et al. 1997). The Bank's first foray into education was the training components

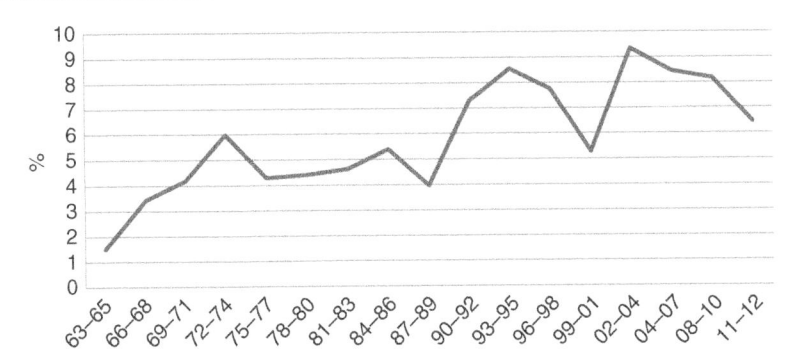

Figure 18.1 Education as percent of World Bank total lending.
Source: Authors with data from the WB education lending figures database (http://go.worldbank.org/PMV1NRBOM1).

of larger infrastructure initiatives in the 1960s. However as more and more newly independent nations joined the Bank, the demand for loans to education increased. In the 1970s, a new Department of Education was created inside the Bank. Education sector efforts led by this new department were framed within theories of manpower planning, endorsed by the dominant country economics teams who controlled lending priorities within the Bank (Heyneman 2003). Projects therefore focused on technical vocational education and providing more "practical" curriculum in secondary education, as a way to train skilled workers and help governments fill skills shortages (Heyneman 2003; Jones 1992). Education projects also focused on infrastructure for education systems: the building of schools, laboratories, workshops, and libraries (Jones 1992). Neither the Bank nor its client governments were interested in loans for recurrent costs such as teachers' salaries or even textbooks (Heyneman 2003).

The McNamara period saw education established as a legitimate sector of Bank activity, one that had considerable attraction for borrowing countries. But perhaps because the link between investing in education and economic growth had not yet been well established, education sector lending during this period rose at only a slightly greater rate than overall bank lending (Mundy 2002, 486). The Bank's Education spending remained less than 5% of total lending (see Figure 18.1). It was only toward the end of McNamara's reign, when a new generation of "human capital" economists were hired at the Bank, that the link between investments in health and education and the increase in the productivity of workers became widely recognized within the institution (World Bank 1980; Kapur et al. 1997, 326–327).[1]

Structural Adjustment and Basic Education: Surprising Bedfellows and a New Economic Argument

The 1980s and early 1990s saw the World Bank develop a distinctive policy agenda for education, which married a new focus on basic education to its broader engagement in mitigating the debt crisis in low and middle income countries. Drawing heavily on the economic theories of human capital, the education sector within the Bank was able to produce a strong internal rationale for the rapid expansion of Bank lending in education (see Figure 18.1), in a way that intersected with its approach to structural adjustment lending during this era.

In the beginning of the 1980s, the specter of massive public debt in the developing world was making it increasingly difficult for the Bank to justify further lending to governments. Among the Bank's most powerful shareholders, there was little appetite for debt relief, and the Bank was increasingly drawn into joint cause with the International Monetary Fund (IMF) as it developed techniques to address debt through fundamental restructuring of national economies and governments. The Reagan administration actively promoted a harsh version of neo-liberal orthodoxy within the Bank and the IMF, and under the US-appointed President, Tom Clausen, and the Bank's American chief economist, Anne Krueger, the focus on poverty in the Bank's corporate level discourse declined (Vetterlain 2012). Structural adjustment policies targeted the downsizing of public expenditure, the liberalization of markets, and the privatization of public utilities as key measures toward achieving macro-economic stabilization. The Bank emerged at the center of a neo-classical resurgence in development economics, more responsible than perhaps any other organization for elaborating what has come to be called the "Washington Consensus" agenda for low and middle income countries (cf. Miller-Adams 1999; Williamson 1993).

It was in this context that the Bank hired a prominent human capital economist previously based at the London School of Economics, George Psacharopoulos (Heyneman 2012). Psacharopoulos' research on wage differentials by level of education in developing countries suggested that investing in primary education produces higher *net* returns on public investment than tertiary education. The technique he helped to popularize in the education domain, "rate of return analysis" (RoR), fell onto fertile ground within the Bank, long dominated by the discipline of economics. For the first time education sector staff had a standard technique for "cost–benefit" estimations of World Bank investments in education (Heyneman 2003).

RoR analysis fit in well with the neo-classical resurgence occurring within the Bank, and particularly with the argument that elite capture of state resources forms the primary barrier to economic restructuring and growth. RoR analysis provided a clear strategy on education policy priorities, arguing for a concentration of public investment in primary education. It also encouraged the privatization of higher education levels, where government subsidies were understood as regressive because they primarily supported the attendance of economically well off students (Colclough 1996). Around the world, governments in the throes of debt crises were advised by the Bank to restructure their education sectors following a rather simple "short policy menu" (cf. Heyneman 2003), which emphasized privatization of tertiary level institutions (cuts to student subsidies, loan schemes and taxes on graduates, etc.), while also encouraging investments in primary education that included greater decentralization of educational systems, increased parental contributions to the basic costs of buildings, books, and materials, and openness to private provision.[2] As captured in the 1986 *Financing Education in Developing Countries*, and the 1995 Policy Paper *Priorities and Strategies in Education*, the Bank's education policy discourse became firmly rooted in the Bank's overarching response to the debt crisis among its client member states (World Bank 1986; 1988a; 1995).[3]

An increasing volume of Bank lending in the structural adjustment era was delivered in larger loans conditioned on policy changes – differing from the project-like investments of the previous period. Certain aspects of structural adjustment loans had clear bearing on education – for example, caps on governments spending, or conditionalities focused on cuts to the size of the civil service. At the same time, wherever a need for structural adjustment emerged in the context of fiscal insolvency (from Africa in the late 1980s, to Mexico and former Soviet states in the early 1990s, and to Asia post-1997), the Bank also offered borrowing countries new "sector adjustment loans" with policy conditionalities aimed at the restructuring of public sector education spending. Common policy recommendations built upon the Bank's epistemic anchor in neo-classical economics to form what Colclough (1996) has described as the *Edlib (education liberalization)* agenda. This included lowering subsidies to tertiary level education and introducing user fees at this level; and encouraging efficiency-driven reforms in kindergarten to Grade 12 level schooling through the use of contract teachers, lowering of repetition rates, and parental "participation" in school level costs (IEG 2011a; World Bank 1986; 1988b; 1995; 2004; Alexander 2002; Hinchcliffe 1993; Jimenez 1987; Mingat and Tan 1984). During this period, Bank investment in secondary vocational schools declined significantly in favor of less expensive non-formal vocational training (Middleton 1988), and Bank work on literacy and adult education further deteriorated (Nordtveit 2012). Borrowing countries, increasingly reliant on international financial institutions for liquidity, had limited ability to contest this new policy agenda.

One of the paradoxes of this period came precisely because the Bank's short policy menu in education focused on primary schooling as the most reasonable public sector investment in education. By the early 1990s, a powerful push back against structural adjustment was emerging within civil society and among United Nations (UN) organizations, which pressed the Bank to implement "structural adjustment with a human face" (see Cornia *et al.* 1988). Bank education sector staff capitalized on this opportunity. On the basis of rates of return analysis, they skilfully argued to the Bank Executive Directors and the Bank's internal country economists that spending in social sectors like education had to be protected and refocused on services that mostly benefit the poor – particularly primary schooling, while at the same time playing to internal expectations among its own economists for a smaller and more efficient public sector (Jones 1992; 2006). Bank education sector staff also mobilized politically, linking up with leaders at the United Nations Children's Fund (UNICEF) and the United Nations Educational, Scientific and Cultural Organization (UNESCO) to host the World Conference on *Education for All* in Jomtien in 1990, which created an important external source of legitimacy and attention for the Bank's role in education at a time when the Bank was under fire and UNESCO itself was faltering under increased political tension (Chabbott 2003).

In summary, an opportunistic technical cadre within the Bank found a way of framing a Bank mandate in education that could be legitimated in the terms of the economic orthodoxy of the period, but also in terms of pro-poor sentiments, building on the context of the Washington Consensus which was actively promoted by the American administration with support from other OECD members. Despite the criticisms of its excessive simplicity, the Bank emerged from this era as the international organization with the most consistent strategy and message in the field of educational development. As can be seen in Figures 18.2 and 18.3, the era of structural adjustment lending contributed to substantial increases in Bank lending activity in education. It also gave an enormous lift to Bank lending to basic education,[4] which came to dominate all other education subsectors (Mundy 2002).

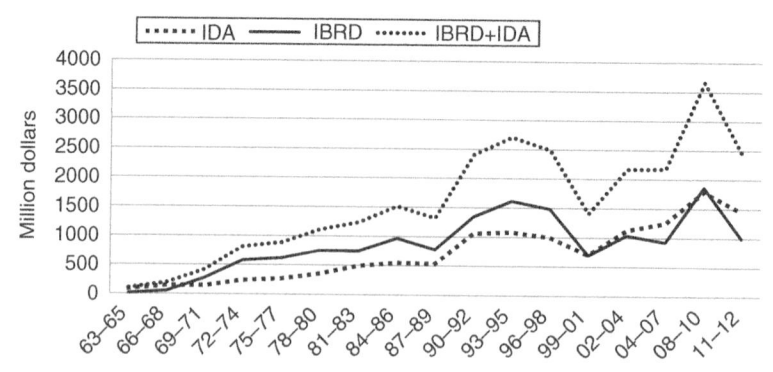

Figure 18.2 Education New Commitments (2011 constant dollars).
Source: Authors with data from the World Bank education lending figures database.

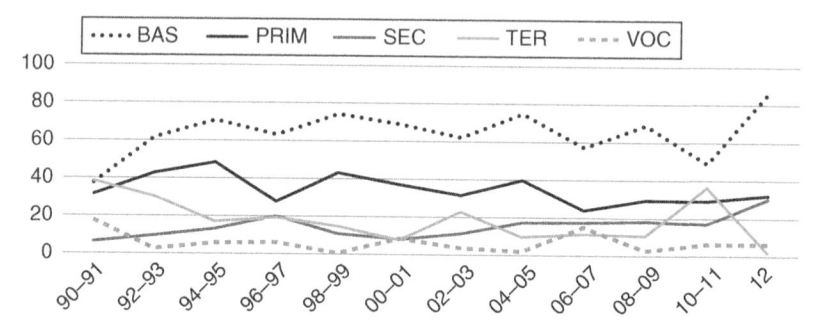

Figure 18.3 World Bank (IBRD+IDA) new education commitments per level (as percentage of total education commitments).
Source: Authors with data from the World Bank education lending figures database.

The Bank and the Global Development Consensus (1996–2008)

The period from the mid-1990s into the first decade of the new millennium saw the Bank face a series of new challenges in its broader authorizing environment. Private financing for development was on the upsurge, challenging the Bank's lending in middle income countries. Civil society advocacy against structural adjustment policies reached its zenith,[5] forcing the Bank into a much stronger campaign to legitimate its practices and activities. At the same time, the decade following the end of the Cold War, saw the Bank's most powerful member states, the Group of Eight (G8) countries, develop a strong consensus about international development, leading to the rise of grant based financing for development at the end of the 1990s captured at its peaks at the Gleneagles G8 summit in 2005.

The new compact on development that began to emerge among OECD governments after 1996 committed them to an expanded program of debt relief, increased levels and harmonization of bilateral aid, and a focus on a handful of top development priorities, including universal education (OECD/DAC 1996). In 2000, the IMF, OECD, World Bank, and the UN also promised closer coordination, more attention to country ownership of development, and a tighter focus on specific development priorities (again including education) in a document entitled *A Better World for All* (IMF et al. 2000). Both agreements fed into the Millennium Development Summit and Millennium Development Declaration, which aligned the UN and its agencies, the Bretton Woods institutions, and OECD governments behind a unifying framework (United Nations General Assembly 2000). This new consensus about international poverty and inequality set out a global "Third Way" between the Washington Consensus and a more pro-poor approach to development, capable of responding to rising international protests against globalization and the aftermath of the East Asian economic crisis of the late 1990s (Stiglitz 2003; Thérien 2002; 2004; Ruggie 2003; Noel, 2005).

Under James Wolfensohn (World Bank president from 1995–2005), the Bank emerged as central to this new development consensus. Wolfensohn quickly announced that the Bank would revitalize its focus on poverty alleviation, and restructure its practices to become more "client centred." The establishment of the Heavily Indebted Poor Country Initiative in 1996 under the IMF and World Bank (enhanced in 1999), created the largest single impetus for expanded national social sector spending in a generation (Hinchcliffe 2004). In this context, the Bank's structural adjustment lending was replaced by "poverty reduction strategy operations," which now provided policy-based tranches of financing for country-led poverty reduction strategies. Such strategies, which became a central policy tool in the context of the Bank but also many other aid agencies, combined macro-economic Washington Consensus-era reforms with enhanced attention to human development, social protection, and governance in what became known as the "post-Washington Consensus" (Tarabini and Jacovkis 2012). Wolfensohn's efforts also included a plan to diversify the Bank's business by becoming "a Knowledge Bank" through renewed emphasis on policy relevant evidence and the provision of technical advice to governments (Stone and Wright 2007).

Education emerged quite centrally within the new post-Washington agenda. Although the education–poverty relationship remained quite weakly conceptualized within the Bank (Bonal 2007), it was attractive to the Bank precisely because it straddled both equity – and productivity – conceptualizations of development, while limiting commitment to stronger redistributive measures that might conflict with neo-classical economic theories. Thus, according to the Bank:

> The expansion of educational opportunity, which can simultaneously promote income equality and growth, is a win-win strategy that in most societies is far easier to implement than the redistribution of other assets, such as land or capital. In short, education is one of the most powerful instruments known for reducing poverty and inequality and for laying the basis for sustained economic growth, sound governance and effective institutions. (World Bank 2002, v)

In keeping with this broad framing, many of the Bank's core ideas from its 1990s education policy statements remained consistent in this period, reflecting the continued dominance of neo-classical economic orthodoxy within the Bank. In the Bank's expanded focus on "good governance" prescriptions for education systems took on an economistic and orthodox coloring. Thus, ideas grounded on public choice and new public management like the decentralization of central state control over basic services, school-based management, local accountability, and the introduction of direct incentives to productivity among user groups emerged across the Bank's K-12 operations. Thess types of policy ideas received perhaps their strongest and most forceful articulation in the 2004 World Development Report *Making Services Work of the Poor* (World Bank 2004; Weaver 2008; Lincove 2006; IEG 2011b; Gershberg et al. 2012). Similarly, in higher education where the Bank sought to expand its lending and diversify its business, much of the earlier logic of the Bank's short policy menu remained intact: most projects retained a preference for private sector provision and cost recovery and advocated the use of competition based incentives to enhance university performance, adding to this agenda new third party "quality assurance" mechanisms (Robertson 2009).

The Bank was able to retain its central role in basic education during the 2000s, especially in primary education, the education subsector most tightly linked to Wolfensohn's resurgent vision of the Bank's poverty mandate and most closely aligned to the Millennium Development Goals. In education, as in health, the Bank successfully promoted a vision of itself as a platform for pooled funding from OECD donor countries, utilizing sector-wide approaches to education anchored with coherent sector plans. The Bank also became a host for sector trust funds from bilateral and private sector donors.[6] At the Dakar World Conference on Education in 2000, Wolfensohn announced that the Bank would allow no country with a coherent education sector plan to be left behind in achieving universal primary education for want of finance. To meet this pledge the Bank became the host of a new multilateral fund for basic education in 2002, called the "Education for All Fast Track Initiative." Wolfensohn's policy entrepreneurship and responsiveness to the broader demands from Bank members resulted in the growth of education sector lending grow both as a share of total World Bank lending (almost doubling to reach over 8% of lending) and in real terms, especially in basic education (see Figures 18.2 and 18.3).

At the same time, the Bank had to rethink its education activities in the face both of more widely available grant financing (for low income countries) and private lending (for middle income countries) as well as the sharpened external critique of its practices from NGO advocates. Bank lending for education declined substantially in the last years of the 1990s, particularly among middle income borrowers eligible under the IBRD (see Figure 18.2). This was, in part, the consequence of increasing private flows of finance for eligible borrowers, but it also reflected a push back against the Education for All agenda (concentrated on primary education) from countries convinced that higher-level skills were most valuable in the global knowledge economy. Bank lending to IDA countries also dipped in the late 1990s, recovering rapidly after 2001 but in a context of increased availability of grant-based aid.

To respond to this decline in demand, the Bank sought to diversify the appeal of its education sector funding to different types of borrowers, focusing on more on client driven lending. Under Director of Education, Maris O'Rourke, it tried to solve the "problematic trends" of decreasing lending to middle income countries by promoting operations in emerging economies, including in Eastern Europe (Jones 2006). Diverting from its "simplified policy" of the 1990s, the Bank offered more expansive policy statements recognizing the need for greater public spending on higher education within the context of a global knowledge economy (World Bank and UNESCO 2000; Samoff and Carrol 2004). Yet despite the move toward client-driven lending with fewer sectoral conditionalities, *ex post* conditions such as indicative benchmarks and numerical objectives were expanded, as another way of incentivizing specific country behavior (World Bank 2005).[7]

Throughout this period of rapid growth in the Bank's authority and scope in the education sector, it is important to note that internal policy entrepreneurship by Bank education sector staff was not always successful, and depended heavily upon wider political opportunities in the Bank's authorizing environment. Two contentious issues in global education policy illustrate how a complex interplay of internal and external factors came to determine World Bank policies and activities in education during this period: free and universal access to primary education, and the private provision of schooling.

In the case of fee-free education, the Bank's policies from the late 1980s to the late 1990s had encouraged parental participation (contributions) to basic education, both to offset gaps in national budgets and to encourage (according to the Bank's 1995 Policies and Strategies) greater parental commitment and engagement in schools. However, in 2001, the Bank changed its longstanding support for parental "participation" in school financing under direct pressure from US-based NGO advocacy organizations. As O'Brien *et al.* (2000), and others have shown, when social movements try to influence the Bank policies, they quite often do so by putting pressure on the US Treasury first. In this instance a powerful transnational campaign to end user fees in education and health, grounded on the case of Tanzania, resulted in a decision by Congress to include language in the foreign aid appropriations bill that required the US Treasury to instruct the US Executive Director at the Bank to oppose any multilateral development loan that included user fees in basic education and health (Alonso i Terme 2002; Mundy 2006). The Bank responded quickly, issuing a policy statement officially opposing school fees in 2001. Soon afterwards the Bank developed a program with UNICEF to promote school fee abolition in low-income countries (Katten and Burnett 2004; Vavrus and Kwauk 2011).

Increasing the share of private education service providers, and promoting the channeling of public funds to private providers, is another policy with longstanding support from among the Bank's economists and education sector specialists. Research and advocacy for this approach flourished alongside the Bank's endorsement of "universal free education/education for all." As documented in Mundy and Menashy (2012) and Verger (2012), private provision of schooling was characterized as inherently desirable in many of the Bank's policy statements and research publications (see World Bank 1999; 2005; Patrinos *et al.* 2009). An influential epistemic community supportive of private provision emerged within the Bank, anchored by a joint program of research and events between the Bank's Economics of Education group and a new group devoted to financing private education at the International Finance Corporation (the Bank's private sector lending arm) (Verger 2012; Mundy and Menashy 2014a; Mundy and Menashy 2014b). In-house policy entrepreneurs hosted regular workshops on private provision and brought leading providers of private schooling and key US-based advocates of privatization (where the trend toward private provision has grown) into the Bank's ambit. Yet despite these efforts, loans that support private sector provision decreased in the Bank's lending portfolio during the 2000s (Mundy and Menashy 2012), as suggested in Figure 18.4. It seems that many client governments were simply not interested in taking public sector loans to support private provision. Drawing on Weaver (2008) we can hypothesize

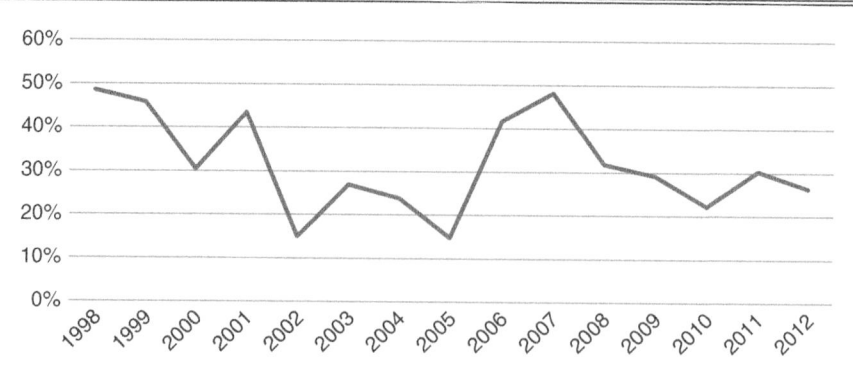

Figure 18.4 Percentage of education projects with privatization components.
Source: Authors with data from the World Bank Education Projects Database (see http://go.worldbank.org/6LRTJRJK30).

that this disjuncture between talk, decisions, and actions became a functional response of the World Bank as it attempted to manage conflicting external agendas arising from the demands of client governments, and the internal institutional preferences derived from pre-existing cultural norms and routines.

In summary, the character of the Bank as a global governor of education changed substantively in the 1996–2008 period. The Bank proved adept at capturing and leading on major parts of the OECD development consensus as it related to primary education, and at the same time, managed to diversify its policy prescriptions while retaining a strong focus on financing efficiencies and private provision in its approach to education. While the Bank's internal culture – especially its reliance on neo-classical economic orthodoxies – led to a degree of consistency in its formal policy setting, and in some dimensions of its lending programs, the "short policy menu" for education of the structural adjustment era clearly gave way to a wider and more diverse approach to education in its actual operations. Here the demands and preferences of borrowing countries played an important role in shaping some surprising disjunctures between the Bank as a setter of a global education agenda, and its role as the single largest global financer of educational reforms.

After Wolfensohn and the Global Financial Crisis: Bank Hegemony Challenged?

Although it is dangerous to speculate, we can use our heuristic focus on the three drivers of change in World Bank policy to explore how geo-political and ideological shifts among the Bank's most powerful member governments and in its borrowing (or "client") countries are likely to interact with the Bank's distinctive organizational culture in the period after 2008. The Bank has a new, reform-minded President, Jim Yong Kim. It is widely seen as no longer enjoying the stable coalition of principals who share a common agenda (see, for example, recent coverage in the media: El-Erian 2014); and its work has been profoundly shaped by the 2008 financial crisis and will likely be affected by rising international insecurity. In this section we ask how such changes internally and in the Bank's wider authorizing environment are affecting or likely to affect its work in the education sector.

In relation to the Bank's longstanding relationship with its most powerful members, the Bank presently operates in a climate of what Rodrik describes as "leaderless globalization" (Rodrik 2012). The G7 governments that have historically been the Bank's most powerful principals, including the USA, continue to face significant economic fall-out from the 2008 financial crisis: they themselves are plagued by high debt and low growth. At the same time, they have been hit by a wave of complex security issues that threaten global stability and the global economy, including recent events in Eastern Europe, the Middle East, and the growth of Islamic fundamentalist militantism. We can speculate that finance for global development is unlikely to emerge high on the policy agendas of G7 countries, though if it does it will likely be linked to areas that directly address these collective geopolitical challenges.

At the same time, rising powers, such as China, India, Brazil, and countries in the Middle East (among others), are increasingly powerful on the global stage. They also became influential development actors: annual concessional flows from emerging economies to low income countries was roughly estimated to be between US$12–15 billion by 2011, equivalent to about 10% and 15% of the aid provided by developed countries (World Bank 2013a). To date the Bank has made much of the opportunity to work with these emerging powers, relying on the innate economic pragmatism of emerging economies, which value access to an expanded, relatively open, and globally integrated world economy, and which in some cases (such as China) remain reliable borrowers of Bank finance (Cammack 2011). The Bank has also gained considerable support from the G20 governments from its responsiveness in rapidly disbursing funds after the financial crisis. However, observers note that it is important to remember that these countries are primarily focused on expanding their spheres of geo-political influence on a bilateral basis. They have sharply different approaches to economic, political, and social development and share a limited appetite for international regimes that constrain national sovereignty (including in such putatively domestic spheres as education); and they are not satisfied with their representation within the Bank (Güven 2012; *The Economist* 2014).

Going forward the Bank will have to address the concerns of rising powers, such as China and India, who are in transition from being "clients" of the Bank to "powerful principals" and who along with Russia and India have expressed dissatisfaction with the pace of reforms in the Bretton Woods institutions (Bracht 2013). As illustrated by the creation of a new international development bank by the BRICS (Brazil, Russia, India, China, and South Africa) at their annual summit in 2013, as well as by the growth of bilateral aid from the BRICS, emerging economies are beginning to destabilize the Bank's hegemony as a development policy setter and lender. The Bank will have to work hard to shape a thicker set of developmental preferences that are endorsed and supported by its emerging market members (Cammack 2011).

In relation to its lower income and lower middle income borrowing members, the Bank faces an equally perplexing set of challenges. As recent analyses suggest, many of the Bank's high performing IDA borrowers are set to graduate into the league of middle income countries. The Bank is under some pressure to redirect its IDA portfolio and find successful new ways of working with a shrinking group of IDA eligible borrowers, which are often conflict-affected or politically fragile (contexts where the Bank's experience has been quite weak) (Severino and Moss 2012). The Bank is in better shape on the IBRD side, with its more secure funding base derived from the proceeds of previous loans. But the IBRD, which focuses lending on middle income countries, faces its own challenges. The rising majority of the world's poor live in middle income countries, creating a natural market for new Bank lending. Yet middle income governments are among the Bank's most discerning and demanding borrowers, and they are not interested in one size fits all policy prescriptions (Güven 2012).

Organizationally the Bank is in a state of flux. Over a relatively short period (2005–2012) it has had three presidents, most recently, Jim Yong Kim, a reform-minded medical doctor who has a background in health sector development. Unlike many previous Bank presidents, Kim is neither an economist nor someone with business/financial sector experience. Kim has introduced a new World Bank Group Strategy (2013b), which commits the Bank to two main goals: ending extreme poverty, and promoting shared prosperity and income growth among the bottom 40% of the population in every country. The strategy promises to reposition the Bank as a "solutions Bank" focused on the science of delivery, results, and the dissemination of global best practices; and to align the work of all three arms of the Bank (IDA/IBRD, the International Financial Corporation, and the Multilateral Investment Guarantee Agency), as well as the multiplying number of donor funded "trust funds" that the Bank manages, around a clearer set of solutions that better leverages the development impact of both public and private actors.

Kim has also instituted a complete organizational restructuring of the Bank's bureaucracy, including the creation in 2014 of 14 global practices groups (through a process in which all senior managers resigned and reapplied for positions) and significant cuts to staffing and the Bank's administrative budget. This restructuring responds to two key problems. First are complaints from donor members and others that the Bank is bloated – for example, the claim by the World Bank Alumni Association, that the Bank "has a very cumbersome inefficient internal structure. It is highly reliant on consultants, in large measure because it has mismanaged its core cadre of experts, and excessively decentralized to the point that the budget is a serious and growing constraint" (quoted in Samerasekera 2012, 16; see also Behar 2012; Lowrey 2014; Talley 2014). Second, the reforms try to reposition the Bank as a purveyor of expertise, especially of expertise on poverty alleviation relevant to middle income countries – responding to the fact that the Bank has not been able to secure a clear role for itself as a *knowledge bank*, and to increasing competition from other expertise providing organizations, such as private consulting firms and other international organizations, including regional banks (Nehru 2012).

Trends in the education sector suggest how the Bank is scrambling to manage these different dynamics. As part of the Bank's response to the financial crisis (2008–2010), its education lending activity spiked in 2008–2009, rising from US$24,702 to 58,747 million "through a combination of additional financing of ongoing projects and approval of large projects in Brazil, Indonesia, Mexico, and Pakistan" (IEG 2011b, xi). Nonetheless, Bank spending on education has fallen off significantly as a share of total Bank lending since it peaked in 2004/5 (Figure 18.1), reflecting a drop in demand for education sector lending. As shown below sub-Saharan African countries have disappeared from the top list of Bank education borrowers – in part because many very low income countries prefer grant-based financing for basic education, such as that provided by the Global Partnership for Education (which the

Table 18.1 Top ten borrowers in education projects (million $)

1987–1995	1996–2007	2008–2012
1. India – 2314.9	1. India – 3918.23	1. Brazil – 5284
2. Mexico – 2009	2. Pakistan – 2394.8	2. Poland – 2631
3. Brazil – 1134.1	3. Indonesia –2019.84	3. India – 2356
4. China – 923.9	4. Brazil – 1907.9	4. Turkey – 2000
5. Indonesia – 871.3	5. Mexico – 1865.2	5. Indonesia – 1821.66
6. Pakistan – 753.7	6. Bangladesh – 1385.7	6. Pakistan – 1771
7. Argentina – 622.5	7. Colombia – 1057.2	7. Mexico – 1320.75
8. Korea – 496.6	8. Uganda – 921.14	8. Colombia – 1001.5
9. The Philippines – 321	9. Ghana – 852	9. Costa Rica – 700
10. Kenya – 249.3	10. Ethiopia – 846.5	10. Bangladesh – 695

Source: Authors, with data from the World Bank Projects and Operations Database.
Note: Projects identified include non-education projects with education components.

Bank hosts) (see Beardmore and Middleton 2012). Thus the financial crisis secured a trend that tilts Bank education lending toward large emerging economies, and away from basic education to secondary and tertiary levels of education, which are in particular demand among emerging market economies (see Table 18.1 and Figure 18.3).

To manage the shifts in external demand for its services, a high profile series of consultations led to the drafting and Board adoption of a new Bank education sector strategy in 2011 (Verger et al. 2014). Focused on "learning for all," the new policy poises the Bank to break with an earlier pattern of funding project inputs, and embraces policy-based lending that is intended to spur the Bank's new results focus by creating incentives for learning outcomes (World Bank 2011a). In its new strategy, the Bank promises to focus on whole-system reform (allowing clients to define different subsectoral investments), while also committing itself to enlarging its role as purveyor of policy knowledge and expertise. Central to this is the creation of standardized benchmarks and policy tools for system development in such areas as teachers' management, national learning assessments, decentralization and accountability, and private provision of services, under its new SABER initiative (Systems Approach for Better Educational Results).

The translation of the ambitious "systemic reform for learning" agenda at the country level may be more challenging than ever, and could feed what the Bank's Independent Evaluation Group has noted is a longer term of decreasing effectiveness in education operations (IEG 2011b).[8] According to Nelson (1999) and to the IEG (2011b) the larger scope of Bank operations in education with respect to the time frame for results and staffing incentives, on the one hand, and the increasing degree of complexity in projects' design in relation to the level of borrower's political commitment and capacity, on the other, create significant problems in implementation and therefore in the delivery of quantifiable results. The Bank has had great difficulty in improving learning outcomes despite a concerted effort over more than a decade to focus on investments that will enhance learning (see for evidence the evaluation of the Bank's support to primary education, IEG 2004). Going forward it will be very interesting to see whether the Bank can sell the idea of borrowing to enhance learning outcomes for the bottom 40% in middle income countries (we suspect the more likely alternative is a continued rise in demand among middle income countries for loans to expand higher education and post-secondary skills training). It will be equally important to monitor the Bank's effectiveness in translating its learning- and results-focused education agenda into results in the shrinking (increasingly conflict affected) group of IDA eligible countries. These are contexts in which the Bank's highly planned and government-focused approach to reform has not proven nimble and responsive. As a lender to governments, the Bank is not well positioned to provide intermediate solutions (such as direct funding of non-state service providers) that are needed as stop-gaps while engaging in system rebuilding (see Pritchett 2014 for a controversial review of this issue).

A strong bid for a scientifically based, simplified framework is the somewhat predictable outcome of the Bank's organizational culture and history, and it fits well with President Kim's call for the Bank to invest in the "science of delivery." But it is an open question whether this highly linear conceptualization of educational development, married as it is to a focus on leveraging system change through the creation of new types of incentives within borrowing country systems, will prove attractive to (and effective for) an increasingly diverse and discerning group of borrowers.

Conclusions

On the basis of its substantial lending capacity, persuasive knowledge production, and transnational political clout, the World Bank has become a key global governance actor in the education for development field. The World Bank entered into the education business in a quite tangential way and without a proper mandate, but education has ended up representing a significant portion of the Bank's lending portfolio. Furthermore, its education policy agenda has become wider and increasingly more complex with the passage of time: it started by providing basic material inputs to education systems, and now is focusing on improving learning outcomes through ambitious systemic reforms.

To understand the evolution of the World Bank education agenda, we have harnessed an approach to understanding international organizations borrowed from the field of political science. In this approach three main dynamics interact and are the focus for our analysis: geopolitical factors and the way most powerful states use the international organization to promote their interests and preferences; the influence exerted by international organization bureaucracies (both at their apex and within their technical divisions); and the way the Bank tries to condition and/or is forced to respond to client –countries demands.

The case of education illustrates how changing external dynamics became opportunities for internal entrepreneurs to develop a strong, simplified agenda for educational reform that bridged core precepts of neo-liberalism and the Washington Consensus. These same staff also proved adept at marrying this agenda, which argued for the concentration of public investment in primary education, to both aspects of the Bank's structural adjustment agenda and to the emergence of a global development consensus focused on poverty reduction and human development in the late 1990s.

Yet while specific parts of this agenda, such as system decentralization and the introduction of performance incentives has spread into most Bank lending programs, some aspects of the agenda have clearly been rejected by borrowers and (often after civil society contestation) by some powerful members. Thus for example, the Bank had to reverse its policies on school fees in elementary education and has had difficulty convincing client countries to borrow for programs that expand private and commercially provided educational services. Clearly, borrowing governments play an important role in conditioning the character of Bank activities, and their preferences are at least partly responsible for disjunctures between the Bank's agenda-setting role and its practical engagement in the financing of educational development.

This article has also raised questions about the future of the Bank in the global governance of education. Until quite recently one could confidently identify the Bank as the pre-eminent global governor of educational policies, particularly influential in emerging and low income country contexts. Today, the Bank's influence in education is less certain, for at least four reasons: the changing composition of its most powerful members; the growing diversity of preferences among Bank borrowers (many of whom prefer membership in the OECD "club" over Bank prescriptions); the rigidity and linearity of Bank prescriptions for educational systems (which are of questionable value in the varied political economies of rapidly transforming emerging economies); and the fact that the Bank's IDA facility must now address the complex needs of conflict affected and politically fragile states, very different from the concentration on "high performing" countries that has anchored its IDA lending over the past decade. Future research on the Bank's role as a global governor in the education sector will need to pay attention to each of these trends to understand what promises to be future decades of instability in the education for development field, during which the Bank's hegemony in education for development is likely to be challenged.

Notes

1 Human capital theory, as developed within the public economics, states that there is a direct relationship between investments in education (usually measured as years of schooling) and the productivity of workers (reflected both on the workers' income and in their countries' economic growth) (Schultz 1971).

2 See the Bank's 1988 education in sub-Saharan Africa report and its 1995 *Policy and Strategies for Education* (World Bank 1988 and 1995).

3 Additional momentum for education sector lending was garnered through the Bank's "discovery" of the East Asian economic miracle in a series of research publications which found that investment in basic education, alongside the development of export oriented markets, had produced rapid economic growth (Mundy 2002; Wade 1996).

4 Basic education is defined by the Bank as the sum of 3/4 × general education + pre-primary education + primary education + 1/2 × secondary education + 3/4 × public administration-education.

5 Former officials from the Bank were also part of this wave of critiques – most notably Joseph Stiglitz - Senior Vice-President and Chief Economist between 1997 and 2000 (see Stiglitz 2003).

6 Many bilateral donors began to set up sector-specific trust funds to support education research and analytical activities including, for example, the Russians, Dutch, and Irish, providing a flexible source

of funding for "knowledge bank" initiatives in education (IEG 2011a). Larger multi-donor trust funds in education focused on conflict-affected states (Sudan and Haiti, for example) were also established inside the Bank rather than in other potential international organization venues. As the IEG evaluation of Bank hosted trust funds notes, the overall value of trust funds between 2003 and 2008 exceeded IDA commitments in the same period (IEG 2011a).

7   A good example of this can be found in the Bank's Poverty Reduction Strategy Paper (PRSP) Handbook, which provided prescriptive arguments and policy benchmarks in education that were quite clearly in tension with the *participatory* and *bottom-up* processes putatively intended to accompany PRSPs (Robertson et al. 2007).

8   According to a recent IEG review, only 57% of education sector board projects had satisfactory Bank performance ratings, a 29% decline from FY05–07. Bank performance ratings at the institutional level, without education, would increase to 79% (IEG 2011b).

References

Abbott, K.W. and D. Sindal. 2005. "Why States Act Through Formal International Organizations," in *The Politics of Global Governance: International Organizations in an Interdependent World*, edited by P.F. Dihel, 25–59. London: Boulder.

Alexander, N. 2002. *Paying for Education: How the World Bank and IMF Influence Education in Developing Countries*. Research Report, 1998, updated 2002. Washington, DC: Citizens' Network on Essential Services.

Alonso i Terme, R. 2002. *The Elimination of User Fees for Primary Education in Tanzania: A Case Study in the Political Economy of Pro-Poor Policies*. Joint Staff Training, June 17, 2002. Washington, DC: World Bank.

Ayres, R. 1983. *Banking on the Poor: The World Bank and World Poverty*. Cambridge: MIT Press.

Barnett, M. and M. Finnemore. 2004. *Rules for the World: International Organizations in Global Politics*. Ithaca: Cornell University Press.

Beardmore, S. and J. Middleton. 2012. "What doesn't the Education Sector Strategy Say? How the Fast Track Initiative and Multisector Operations are Changing the Landscape of World Bank Education Financing," in *Education Strategy in the Developing World: Revising the World Bank's Education Policy*, edited by C.S. Collins and A.W. Wiseman (*International Perspectives on Education and Society*, Volume 16), 301–335). Bingley: Emerald Group Publishing Limited.

Behar, R. 2012, June 27. "World Bank Mired In Dysfunction: Mess Awaits New Head." *Forbes*. Retrieved from: www.forbes.com/sites/richardbehar/2012/06/27/world-bank-spins-out-of-control-corruption-dysfunction-await-new-president (accessed November 16, 2015).

Bonal, X. 2007. "On Global Absences: Reflections on the Failings of the Education and Poverty Relationship." *International Journal of Educational Development*, 27(1): 86–100.

Bracht, C. 2013, May, 8. "Will the BRICS Delivery a More Just World Order?" *Guardian Weekly*. Retrieved from: www.guardian.co.uk/global-development-professionals-network/2013/may/08/brics-development-bank (accessed November 16, 2015).

Broad, R. 2006. "Research, Knowledge, and the Art of 'paradigm Maintenance': The World Bank's Development Economics Vice-Presidency (DEC)." *Review of International Political Economy*, 13(3): 387–419.

Cammack, P. 2011. "The G20, the Crisis, and the Rise of Global Developmental Liberalism." *Third World Quarterly*, 33(1): 1–16.

Chabbott, C. 2003. *Constructing Education for Development: International Organizations and Education for All*. London: Routledge Falmer.

Colclough, C. 1996. "Education and the Market: Which Parts of the Neo-liberal Solution are Correct?" *World Development*, 24(4): 589–610.

Cornia, G.A., R. Jolly, and F. Stewart. 1988. *Adjustment with a Human Face. A Study by UNICEF. Protecting the Vulnerable and Promoting Growth*. Wotton-under-Edge: Clarendon Press.

El-Erian, M.A. 2014, August 25. "Need for a Reality Check on World Bank and IMF." *Gulf News*. Retrieved from: http://gulfnews.com/business/opinion/need-for-a-reality-check-on-world-bank-and-imf-1.1376270 (accessed November 16, 2015).

Finnemore, M. 1996. "Norms and Development: The World Bank and Poverty," in *National Interests in International Society*, edited by M. Finnemore, 89–127. Ithaca: Cornell University Press.

Gershberg, A., P.A. Gonzalez, and B. Meade. 2012. "Understanding and Improving Decentralization in Education. A Conceptual Framework and Guideposts from Three Decentralization Reform Experiences in Latin American." *World Development*, 40(5): 1024–1041.

Güven, A.B. 2012. "The IMF, the World Bank and the Global Economic Crisis: Exploring Paradigm Continuity." *Development and Change*, 43(4): 869–898.

Haas, P.M. 2004. "When Does Power Listen to Truth? A Constructivist Approach to the Policy Process." *Journal of European Public Policy*, 11(4): 569–592.

Heyneman, S.P. 2003. "The History and Problems in the Making of Education Policy at the World Bank, 1960–2000." *International Journal of Educational Development*, 23(3): 315–337.

Heyneman, S.P. 2012. "When Models Become Monopolies: The Making of Education Policy at the World Bank," in *Education Strategy in the Developing World: Revising the World Bank's Education Policy*, edited by C. Collins and A. Wiseman, 43–63. Bingley: Emerald Publishers.

Hinchliffe, K. 1993. "Neo-Liberal Prescriptions for Education Finance: Unfortunately Necessary or Inherently Desirable?" *International Journal of Educational Development*, 13(2), 183–187.

Hinchliffe, K. 2004. *Notes on the HIPC Debt Initiative on Education and Health Public Expenditure in African Countries*. African Human Development Department. Washington DC: The World Bank.

IEG (Independent Evaluation Group). 2004. *From Schooling Access to Learning Outcomes: An Unfinished Agenda: An Evaluation of World Bank Support to Primary Education*. Washington, DC: The World Bank Group.

IEG (Independent Evaluation Group). 2011a. *Trust Fund Support for Development: An Evaluation of the World Bank's Trust Fund Portfolio*. Washington, DC: Independent Evaluation Group, the World Bank Group.

IEG. (Independent Evaluation Group). 2011b. *A Portfolio Note: World Bank Support to Education Since 2001*. Washington, DC: The World Bank Group.

IMF, OECD, World Bank, and UN. 2000. *A Better World for All*. Washington, DC: Communications Development.

Jimenez, E. 1987. *Pricing Policy in the Social Sectors: Cost Recovery for Education and Health in Developing Countries*. Washington, DC: The Johns Hopkins Press for the World Bank.

Jones, P. 1992. *World Bank Financing of Education: Lending, Learning and Development*. New York: Routledge.

Jones, P. 2006. *Education, Poverty and the World Bank*. Rotterdam: Sense Publishers.

Kapur, D., J. Lewis, and R. Webb (eds). 1997. *The World Bank: Its First Half Century. Volume 1: History. Volume 2: Perspectives*. Washington, DC: Brookings Institution Press.

Katten, R. and N. Burnett. 2004. *User Fees in Primary Education*. Washington, DC: Education Sector, Human Development Network, World Bank.

Lincove, J.A. 2006. "Efficiency, Equity and Girls Education." *Public Administration and Development*, 26: 339–357.

Lowrey, A. 2014, May 27. "World Bank Revamping is Rattling Employees." *The New York Times*. Retrieved from: www.nytimes.com/2014/05/28/business/international/world-bank-revamping-is-rattling-employees.html?_r=0 (accessed November 16, 2015).

Marshall, K. 2008. *The World Bank: From Reconstruction to Development to Equity*. London: Routledge.
Middleton, J. 1988. "Changing Patterns in World Bank Investments in Vocational Education and Training: Implications for Secondary Vocational Schools." *International Journal of Educational Development*, 8(3): 213–225.
Miller-Adams, M. 1999. *The World Bank: New Agendas in a Changing World*. London: Routledge.
Mingat, A. and J. Tan. 1984. *User Charges for Education: The Ability and Willingness to Pay in Malawi*. Washington, DC: World Bank.
Mundy, K. 2002. "Education in a Reformed World Bank." *International Journal of Educational Development*, 22(5): 483–508.
Mundy K. 2006. "Education for All and the New Development Compact." *Review of Education*, 52: 23–48.
Mundy, K. and F. Menashy. 2012. "The role of the International Finance Corporation in the Promotion of Public Private Partnerships for Educational Development," in *Public Private Partnerships in Education: New Actors and Modes of Governance in a Globalising World*, edited by S. Robertson, K. Mundy, A. Verger, and F. Menashy, 81–103. London: Edward Elgar.
Mundy, K. and F. Menashy. 2014a. "Investing in Private Education for Poverty Alleviation: The Case of the World Bank's International Finance Corporation." *The International Journal of Educational Development*, 35: 16–24.
Mundy, K. and F. Menashy. 2014b. "The World Bank and Private Provision of Schooling: A Look through the Lens of Sociological Theories of Organizational Hypocrisy." *Comparative Education Review*, 58(3): 401–427.
Nehru, V. 2012. *The World Bank and the Asian Development Bank: Should Asia Have Both?* ADBI Working Paper No. 385. Tokyo: Asia Development Bank Institute.
Nelson, J. 1999. *Reforming Health and Education: The World Bank, the IDB and Complex Institutional Change*. Political Essay No. 26. Washington, DC: The Overseas Development Council.
Nielson, D., M. Tierney, and C. Weaver. 2006. "Bridging the Rationalist-Constructivist Divide: Re-Engineering the Culture of the World Bank." *Journal of International Relations and Development*, 9: 107–139.
Noel, A. 2005. *The New Politics of Global Poverty*. Retrieved from: www.uni-bielefeld.de/soz/personen/Leisering/pdf/Noel%20globale%20Armut.pdf (accessed November 18, 2016).
Nordtveit, B.H. 2012. "World Bank Poetry: How the Education Strategy 2020 Imagines the World," in *The World Bank and Education Critiques and Alternatives*, edited by S.J. Klees, J. Samoff, and N.P. Srtomquist, 21–32. Rotterdam: Sense.
O'Brien, R., A.M. Goetz, J.A. Scholte, and M. Williams. 2000. *Contesting Global Governance: Multilateral Economic Institutions and Global Social Movements*. Cambridge: Cambridge University Press.
OECD/DAC. 1996. *Shaping the 21st Century: The Contribution of Development Cooperation*. Paris: OECD.
Ornstein, M. 2008. *Privatizing Pensions: The Transnational Campaign for Social Security Reform*. Princeton: Princeton University Press.
Patrinos, H., F. Barrera-Osorio, and J. Guaqueta. 2009. *The Role and Impact of Public-Private Partnerships in Education*. Washington, DC: World Bank.
Pritchett, L. 2013. "The World Bank and Public Sector Management: What Next?" *International Review of Administrative Sciences*, 0(0): 1–7.
Putnam, R. 1988. "Diplomacy and Domestic Politics: The Logic of Two-Level Games." *International Organization*, 42(3): 427–460.
Rittberger, V. and B. Zangl. 2006. *International Organization. Polity, Politics and Policies*. New York: Palgrave.
Robertson, S., M. Novelli, R. Dale, L. Tikly, H. Dachi, and N. Alphonce. 2007. *Globalisation, Education and Development: Ideas, Actors and Dynamics*. London: DFID.

Robertson, S.L. 2009. "Market Multilateralism, the World Bank Group and the Asymmetries of Globalising Higher Education: Toward a Critical Political Economy Analysis," in *International Organization and Higher Education Policy: Thinking Globally, Acting Locally*, edited by R. Bassett, and A. Maldonado, 113–131. London and New York: Routledge.

Rodrik, D. 2012, January 19. "Leaderless Globalization." *Alwatan Daily*, p. 7.

Ruggie, J.G. 2003. "The United Nations and Globalization: Patterns and Limits of Institutional Adaptation." *Global Governance*, 9: 301–321.

Samoff, J. and B. Carrol. 2003. *From Manpower Planning to the Knowledge Era: World Bank Policies in Higher Education in Africa*. UNESCO Forum Occasional Paper 2. Paris: UNESCO.

Samerasekera, U. 2012. "Jim Kim Takes the Helm at the World Bank." *The Lancet*, 380(9836): 15–17.

Schultz, T. 1971. *Investment in Human Capital: The Role of Education and of Research*. New York: Free Press.

Severino, J.M. and T. Moss. 2012. *Soft Lending without Poor Countries: Recommendations for the Future of IDA. Report of the Future of IDA Working Group*. Washington DC: Center for Global Development.

Stern, N. 1997. "The World Bank as Intellectual Actor," in *The World Bank, Its First Half Century, II*, edited by D. Kapur, J. Lewis, and R. Webb, 523–609. Washington, DC: Brookings Institution Press.

Stiglitz, J. 2003. *Globalization and its Discontents*. New York: W.W. Norton and Company.

Stone, D. and C. Wright. 2007. *The World Bank and Governance: A Decade of Reform and Reaction*. London: Routledge.

Talley, I. 2014. "World Bank Shapes Overhaul Towards "Solutions Bank."" *New York Times Blog*, April 1, 2014, Retrieved from: http://blogs.wsj.com/economics/tag/jim-yong-kim (accessed November 16, 2015).

Tarabini, A. and J. Jacovkis. 2012. "The Poverty Reduction Strategy Papers: An Analysis of a Hegemonic Link Between Education and Poverty." *International Journal of Educational Development*, 32(4): 507–516.

The Economist. 2014, July 19. "The BRICS Bank an Acronym with Capital: Setting up Rivals to the IMF and World Bank is Easier Than Running Them." *The Economist*. Retrieved from: www.economist.com/news/finance-and-economics/21607851-setting-up-rivals-imf-and-world-bank-easier-running-them-acronym (accessed November 16, 2015).

Thérien, J.P. 2002. "Debating Foreign Aid: Right Versus Left." *Third World Quarterly*, 23(3): 449–466.

Thérien, J.P. 2004. "The Politics of International Development: Towards a New Grand Compromise?" *Economic Policy and Law: Journal of Trade and Environmental Studies Special Issue*. Retrieved from: www.ecolomics-international.org/epal_2004_5_therien_towards_new_grand_compromise....pdf (accessed November 19, 2015).

United Nations General Assembly. 2000. *United Nations Millennium Declaration*. UN Resolution A/RES/55/3. New York: United Nations.

Vavrus, F. and C. Kwauk. 2012. "The New Abolitionists? The World Bank and the 'Boldness' of Global School Fee Elimination Reforms." *Discourse: Studies in the Cultural Politics of Education*, 34(3): 351–365.

Verger, A. 2012. "Framing and Selling Global Education Policy: The Promotion of PPPs in Education in Low-Income Countries." *Journal of Education Policy*, 27(1): 109–130.

Verger, A., D.B. Edwards Jr, and H.K. Altinyelken. 2014. "Learning from all? The World Bank, Aid Agencies and the Construction of Hegemony in Education for Development." *Comparative Education*, 50(4): 381–399.

Vetterlain, A. 2012. "Seeing Like the World Bank on Poverty." *New Political Economy*, 17(1): 35–58.

Wade, R. 1996. "Japan, the World Bank, and the Art of Paradigm Maintenance: The East Asian Miracle in Political Perspective." *New Left Review*, I(217). Retrieved from: http://newleftreview.org/I/217/robert-wade-japan-the-world-bank-and-the-art-of-paradigm-maintenance-the-east-asian-miracle-in-political-perspective (accessed November 16, 2015).

Wade R. 2002. "US Hegemony and the World Bank: The Fight Over People and Ideas." *Review of International Political Economy*, 9(2): 215–243.

Weaver, C. 2008. *Hypocrisy Trap: The Rhetoric, Reality, and Reform of the World Bank*. Princeton: Princeton University Press.

Williamson, J. 1993. "Democracy and the "Washington Consensus." *World Development*, 21(8): 1329–1336.

Woods, N. 2000. "The Challenge of Good Governance for the IMF and the World Bank Themselves." *World Development*, 28(5): 823–841.

World Bank. 1980. *World Development Report*. Washington, DC: World Bank.

World Bank. 1986. *Financing Education in Developing Countries: An Exploration of Policy Options*. Washington, DC: World Bank.

World Bank. 1988a. *World Development Report 1988*. New York: World Bank/Oxford University Press.

World Bank. 1988b. *Education in Sub-Saharan Africa: Policies for Adjustment, Revitalization and Expansion*. Washington, DC: World Bank.

World Bank. 1995. *Priorities and Strategies for Education*. Washington, DC: World Bank.

World Bank, 1999. Education Sector Strategy Paper. Washington, DC: World Bank.

World Bank. 2002. *Achieving Education for All by 2015: Simulation Results for 47 Low-Income Countries*. Washington, DC: World Bank.

World Bank. 2004. *Making Service Work for the Poor: World Bank World Development Report*. Washington, DC: The World Bank Group.

World Bank. 2005. *Review of World Bank Conditionality*. Washington, DC: The World Bank Group.

World Bank. 2011a. *Education Sector Strategy 2020*. Washington, DC: The World Bank Group.

World Bank. 2011b. "World Bank Lending 2011 Presentation." Retrieved from: http://go.worldbank.org/7HL2KJMMG0 (accepted November 16, 2015).

World Bank. 2013a. *Financing for Development Post-2015*. Washington, DC: The World Bank. Retrieved from: www.worldbank.org/content/dam/Worldbank/document/Poverty%20documents/WB-PREM%20financing-for-development-pub-10-11-13web.pdf (accepted November 16, 2015).

World Bank. 2013b. *World Bank Group Strategy*. Washington, DC: The World Bank.

World Bank and UNESCO. 2000. *Higher Education and Developing Countries: Peril and Promise*. Washington, DC: The World Bank.

Chapter 19

The Changing Organizational and Global Significance of the OECD's Education Work

Bob Lingard and Sam Sellar

Introduction

This chapter analyses the education work of the Organisation for Economic Co-operation and Development (OECD), an intergovernmental organization that focuses on economic policy and currently comprises 34 member nations.[1] By way of introduction, we provide a brief history and backdrop to the OECD. We then focus on the changing place of education within the organization. The success of the Programme for International Student Assessment (PISA) has cemented the place of education within the OECD and has become a prototype for subsequent developments such as PISA Tests for Schools, PISA for Development, and the Programme for International Assessment of Adult Competencies (PIAAC). We then explore the catalyzing impact and influence of education within the organization and specifically consider the expanding scope, scale, and explanatory power of PISA and related programs. OECD statistics have become more significant in the global governance of education, which is the focus of the fourth section of the chapter, where we analyze the role of the OECD's education work in what we characterize as *epistemological* and *infrastructural* governance, developed beyond Woodward's (2009) account of the OECD's role in global governance.[2]

A Brief History and Overview of the OECD

The OECD was created in 1961 from the Organisation for European Economic Co-operation, which was established to facilitate the reconstruction of Europe under the USA Marshall Plan. It originally had 20 member countries, all of which were European except for the USA. Japan acceded in 1964 and since that time the USA

The Handbook of Global Education Policy, First Edition.
Edited by Karen Mundy, Andy Green, Bob Lingard, and Antoni Verger.
© 2016 John Wiley & Sons, Ltd. Published 2016 by John Wiley & Sons, Ltd.

and Japan have provided a significant percentage of the core funding of the organization, with commensurate influence over its program of work. Haas (1990, 5) described the OECD in its early days as "a rather incoherent compromise between the United States and the European members," with the USA potentially "capable of playing a hegemonic role." From the outset, the OECD was seen as an international organization focused on economic policy – a rich countries' club and a bulwark against Soviet communism in the Cold War era. In that context, it was regarded as an economic NATO, given its focus on economic growth and productivity in capitalist economies.

Membership of the OECD requires commitment to three broad values: a market economy, liberal democracy, and more recently human rights. With the end of the Cold War, many more nations clearly became eligible for membership. Since that time, membership has broadened and the OECD has also strengthened its relationships with so-called "non-member economies," including developing nations.

The Constitution of the OECD sets out its chief aims as enhancing economic growth, international trade, and economic development. These aims have taken on a different hue in the post-Cold War context of globalization. The OECD has been an important bearer of, but also a response to, neo-liberal globalization. Bourdieu (2003) suggested that one usage of the term globalization has been a performative one, helping to constitute that to which it refers. This applied from the early 1990s to the OECD's usage of globalization to describe a commitment to neo-liberal, market economics. This neo-liberal policy proclivity could perhaps best be seen in the failure of the Multilateral Agreement on Investment (MAI), an OECD initiative to have national governments treat foreign and national investors according to the same terms. Opposition to the MAI focused on the challenge of this development to the sovereignty of nations. Nonetheless, support for a global market economy and free trade remains an important aim of the OECD. However, concerns are now being raised about the negative economic impact of growing inequality in the post global financial crisis period.

The end of the Cold War precipitated a minor crisis of purpose for the OECD. We would suggest that in the post-Cold War context, the OECD has become an important global center for the production of statistics for policy-making, particularly international comparative data. Computational capacities and the development of data infrastructure assisted this new policy focus and the OECD was ahead of other international organizations in this respect (Carroll and Kellow 2011).

From 2008, the financial crises in Europe and globally have precipitated another challenge for the OECD, in relation to its earlier stance of proselytizing a neo-liberal version of market economics. In the wake of the financial crises, and in particular the austerity policies being put in place in various nations of Europe, the OECD has begun once again, perhaps somewhat tentatively, to rethink its economic policy position. The *New Approaches to Economic Challenges* initiative represents a high-level attempt to consider the possibility of a new meta-framing for the OECD's analyses, including moving beyond GDP as the primary growth indicator to focus on issues of well-being, inequality, and social cohesion (see Chapter 9, this volume). In this context, education has become even more important inside the organization, linked to the launch of the cross-committee OECD Skills Strategy (2012), which is an attempt to create and ensure policy coherence across the work of the OECD's various directorates.

It should be stressed, however, that while the organization has a coherent policy position, it also consists of a complex committee structure involving policy actors from member nations, as well as an influential secretariat that undertakes much of the organization's work program. The multiple voices, stances, and, of course, political orientations of the member nations have given rise to the organization's considerable complexity, and the ensuing necessity to walk a fine policy line to manage these competing orientations. The organization is also characterized as a "non-academic university," with a policy-focused research agenda across all of its directorates, but each with different foci adding to complexity. We can see the OECD as an important node in a network of relationships, including member and non-member countries and relationships with other international organizations. Elsewhere, the OECD has been variously described as "a geographical entity, an organizational structure, a policy-making forum, a network of policy-makers, researchers and consultants, and a sphere of influence" (Henry *et al*. 2001, 7).

Two recent publications have provided insightful accounts of the history, *raison d' être*, and functioning of the OECD. Carroll and Kellow (2011) characterize the OECD as an institution adept at adaptation, changing in the face of shifting contexts and pressures, and draw attention to the organization's committee structure through which member nations influence its work program. This elaborate organizational structure is overseen at the apex by the OECD Council, chaired by the Secretary-General and comprising representatives from all member nations. The adaptive character of the OECD is also commented on by Woodward (2009), where he speaks of the OECD's chameleon nature and adeptness at "carving out niches" for itself across the policy domains covered across its various directorates. The OECD, according to Woodward (2009), complements rather than competes with other international organizations. In terms of policy effects, Carroll and Kellow (2011) demonstrate that the OECD exerts soft power through epistemic influence on politicians and policy-makers. This soft power is exerted through processes of mutual surveillance and peer pressure, and has grown with the enhancement of the OECD's statistical work from the mid-1990s. The latter involved the creation of the Indicators of Education Systems (INES), a compendium of data from member countries now published annually, as well as the move to develop PISA from the late 1990s.

Woodward (2009) argues that the OECD has become an influential international organization because "it sows the seeds of international consensus and cooperation that allow humankind to reap a greater capacity to manage our common affairs" (Woodward 2009, 5). He focuses on the role of the OECD in global governance, which he argues, occurs through four modes, namely cognitive, normative, legal, and palliative. Cognitive governance functions through the alignment of values across member nations. Normative governance "is the vaguest dimension of the OECD's policy work but it is arguably through challenging and changing mindsets of the people involved that the Organisation achieves its greatest influence" (Woodward 2009, 8). This is the move toward consensus and commonality across the assumptive worlds of OECD and national policy-makers, perhaps reflected in an emergent global policy actor habitus. Cognitive and normative governance, which we might see as epistemological forms of governance aligned to the creation of epistemic communities (Kallo 2009), together constitute the soft power of the OECD in policy-making globally. Legal governance is not a common mode in the work of the OECD, particularly in education. Palliative governance refers to the OECD's function in lubricating "the wheels of global governance." For example, the OECD can provide a forum for discussing policy matters that do not fit easily within the mandates of other international forums and it supports the work of the World Trade Organization and the Group of Eight (G8) and Group of Twenty (G20) nations. We will utilize and extend Woodward's framework in our analysis of the role of the OECD's education work in global educational governance.

The Changing Place of Education at the OECD: PISA and the Directorate for Education

From 1961 until the late 1990s education had an "inferred role" at the OECD. Papadopoulos (1994) noted:

> There is ... an inferred role for education, both for the contribution it can make to economic growth and as a means by which the purposes of such growth, namely an increase in general well-being, can be given reality; which, in turn, implies that education has its own proper dynamics and must be handled as such if it is to fulfil its role adequately. (p. 11)

In the early days, education was seen in terms of the need to strengthen science and mathematics education to support the production of knowledge workers for advancing economies. Accordingly, it was located within the Office for Scientific and Technical Personnel. Much of the Office's work involved documenting the technological gap between Europe and the USA in the Cold War context of the post-Sputnik period (Istance 1996, 1). The establishment of the Centre for Research and Innovation (CERI) in 1968 gave education a firmer organizational location. The Education Committee was created in 1971, with a new focus on the contribution of education to quality of life issues. The Committee was supported by the Directorate for Scientific Affairs, and this is where CERI was located, but in 1975 education became part of the new Directorate for Social Affairs, Manpower and Education. In 1991 this Directorate was renamed the Directorate for Education, Employment, Labour and Social Affairs (DEELSA) and this remained education's organizational location until the Directorate for Education was established in 2002.

Papadopoulos (1994) suggests that the move from science broadened the conception of education underpinning the OECD's education work at the time, yet others argue that this relocation linked education inextricably to labor markets and employment trends (Istance 1996). Within DEELSA, education work was overseen by the Education Committee, consisting of representatives from all member nations, whereas CERI's governing board consisted of non-governmental persons as well. Until the creation of the Education Directorate, education had no permanent status within the OECD, and its work had to be mandated every five years by the OECD Council. While Papadopoulos (1994) notes that through the 1970s education was framed by progressive concerns about schooling and inequalities derived from sociology, we need to acknowledge the influence exerted on this work by the economic rationale of the organization. The OECD's work in education has always been framed by economic concerns, while at the same time seeking some independence from these with concerns for equity and social justice. Nonetheless, changing conceptions of human capital theory have been a deep structural underpinning of the OECD's education work from 1961 through until the present.

From the 1990s, there was a considerable push inside the OECD from member nations and other international organizations for the development of comparative educational statistics. We note, though, that the OECD has always had an interest in educational statistics, particularly during the 1960s in respect of educational planning. The OECD's work in relation to the educational performance of member nations during its early phases was largely through reviews of national systems conducted at the request of member nations. From the late 1990s, there was a focus on more thematic reviews and international comparisons. Statistical data became increasingly significant in relation to these country reviews and comparative thematic reviews, but they also drew on qualitative data.

Regarding the growing focus on educational statistics, Papadopoulos (1994, 50) comments on a European Ministers of Education meeting in London in 1964, where they recommended that the OECD:

> ...whose work in this field is greatly appreciated, be invited to formulate clearly in a model handbook the various factors involved in effective educational investment planning, so that countries may have basis for the compilation of comparable statistics.

This recommendation was subsequently endorsed by the OECD Council and served as an impetus for the expansion of statistical work, extended further in the 1970s through advanced mathematical modeling and increasing computational capacities. In the early 1970s, the OECD began serious work on educational indicators, which initially involved attempts at collaboration with the United Nations Educational, Scientific and Cultural Organization (UNESCO). Henry et al. (2001) have documented a granular narrative of the increasing significance of quantitative data at the OECD across this time and especially into the 1990s, with strong encouragement from the USA. CERI was not initially as enthusiastic as others about this statistical and indicators work. Heyneman (1993, 375) has written about an acrimonious CERI Board of Directors meeting in 1984 at which the US delegate strongly stressed the necessity of the indicators work and the need to develop input–output measures, yet there was still internal opposition to this development because of perceived technical and conceptual difficulties (Papadopoulos 1994, 190). These oppositions were finally overcome and in 1988 the CERI Governing Board created the INES project.

The initial INES indicators were released in draft form in September 1991, and along with accompanying analyses, have become a more significant part of the OECD's work since that time. Henry et al. (2001, 90) summarize this shift in the OECD's stance on educational indicators and their enhanced role:

> In short, the 1990s saw some remarkable shifts in the development of educational indicators within the OECD: from philosophical doubt to statistical confidence; from covering some countries to covering most of the world; from a focus on inputs to a focus on outputs; and from occupying an experimental status to being a central part of the Organisation's work.

These developments were, of course, set against the backdrop of globalization, the restructuring of the bureaucratic state within nations under new public management (OECD 1995), the growing focus on educational outcomes as opposed to policy inputs, and the enhancement of computational capacities. They were also set against what has been referred to more recently as the rise of policy as numbers that accompanied the new managerialist state (Rose 1999; Ozga 2009; Lingard 2011). The globalization of the economy encouraged an economistic framing of education policy within nations and a focus on the production of more and better human capital. International comparative performance data became central to assisting nations in assessing their potential economic competitiveness globally; in effect data on human capital became surrogate measures of the competitiveness of a nation's economy (Brown et al. 1997). It was in this context that the OECD launched in 1997 what was to become PISA (see OECD 1999). The USA was again an important player in the pressures toward this development of an international comparative measure of national schooling system performance, as they had been with the earlier INES work. This involvement was fueled by internal concerns about educational standards in the USA driven by reports such as *A Nation at Risk* and linked to the view of economists that more sophisticated measures of educational outputs were required, rather than using years of education as a proxy for achievement.

The PISA tests were first administered in 2000, with the analyses and performance rankings released in 2001. This led to the now well-documented PISA shock in Germany (Ertl 2006; Grek 2009), which performed much worse than German self-perceptions of the quality and equity of their schooling system would have suggested. There have been subsequent PISA shocks as well, including in Japan (Takayama 2008) and following the release of the 2009 results showing Shanghai-China as a top performing system (Sellar and Lingard 2013b; Waldow et al. 2014). The impact and mobilization of PISA within nations for policy-making, though, is differentiated – its effects have varying "form, content, amplitude, and intensity" (Carvalho and Costa 2014, 3).

Since 2000, PISA has been conducted every three years with an increasing number of participants. The tests measure reading, mathematical, and scientific literacy, and putatively test what all 15 year olds ought to know and be able to apply in real-world situations, although we note that the test is of the classic paper and pencil variety. While not based in national curricula, the test, at a deep structural level, assumes an isomorphism across the curricula of different national schooling systems, somewhat akin to the assumptions of the world polity theorists such as Meyer and colleagues (1997). This assumption of isomorphism and commensurative work underpin what psychometricians refer to as "differential item functioning" (Zumbo 2007), and the exclusion from analyses of PISA of test items for which there is too much variance across national cultural contexts. These decisions about test construction reflect Rose's (1999) more general point that numbers for policy hide this deep and complex technical work.

We would argue that PISA is helping to create a global educational policy field through its work in constituting the globe as a commensurate space of measurement (Lingard and Rawolle 2011), and in so doing helps to make educational systems across the globe legible for governing (Scott 1998). These developments are part of a global move toward standardization and it has been argued that authority for this move has been "increasingly lodged in the global-level organizations" (Loya and Boli

1999, 176). We might see this occurring at the OECD through PISA, other tests, and educational statistics, with alignments between statistical categories being achieved across nations and international organizations. We note, as well, the voluntarism in these developments and the nature of the processes involved in extending what have come to be seen as "universal, consensually derived standards of unimpeachable technical merit" (Loya and Boli 1999, 181).

National schooling system performance on PISA is ranked according to quality (scores on the tests) and equity (the spread of the scores and strength of the effect of socioeconomic background on performance). The latter has helped to rearticulate notions of social justice in schooling as equity within a meritocratic system based on test performance (Lingard *et al.* 2014). PISA has also had differing impacts on national schooling systems and their policy frames (Carvalho and Costa 2014; Simons 2014), with many nations developing complementary national testing regimes in acceptance of the axiom that one can only improve what one can measure. We must see the relationships between the OECD and nations, though, as reciprocal, involving the "circulation of PISA as part of multidirectional processes that involve reinterpretation, de-contextualisation, and re-contextualisation, and where national, local, regional and international agencies intertwine" (Carvalho and Costa 2014, 3).

The analyses of equity enabled by PISA are important and show the growing impact of socioeconomic background on school performance across OECD countries since the first tests were conducted. Yet, at the same time the OECD's media strategy and national media pressure for PISA league tables give emphasis to quality of national mean performance and not to equity (Wiseman 2013), even though the OECD's PISA reports give emphasis to both issues and indeed stress that quality demands equity. We also note that OECD analyses of PISA tend to overplay the significance of policy in the etiology of systemic performance and downplay societal inequalities (Meyer and Schiller 2013).

With the creation of the Directorate for Education in 2002 the position of education within the OECD was consolidated, but we would suggest it has been strengthened further with the creation of the Education and Skills Directorate in 2012 and the associated launch of the OECD's Skills Strategy aimed at organizational policy coherence. The OECD argues that, "Skills have become the global currency of 21st-century economies" (OECD 2012) and that "The OECD Skills Strategy provides an integrated, cross-government strategic framework to help countries understand more about how to invest in skills in a way that will transform lives and drive economies" (OECD 2012, 3). We would argue that the Skills Strategy reflects an intensification of human capital framing of education, with the concept being broadened to include non-cognitive skills, as we discuss below. This Strategy has enhanced the position of the OECD's education work, with PISA, PIAAC, and other education data now being included, for example, in the organization's *Going for Growth* reports.

It is important to understand the funding arrangements for the OECD's education work. There are two elements to the OECD budget: Part I comes from member nations' contributions, while Part II is funded by participants in specific projects. For example, nations pay to participate in PISA, which is funded out of Part II of the budget. Education relies heavily on Part II budget contributions, which some suggest has led to more efficiency and effectiveness in securing support for and the delivery of specific projects such as PISA. CERI receives Part I budget support, as well as project-based funding.

Education at the OECD is becoming increasingly central and Andreas Schleicher, head of PISA and now Director of Education and Skills, has become a very powerful policy player, both within the organization and in education globally. Here we are in agreement with Woodward's (2009) assessment that the OECD's education policy work has become increasingly important and that the OECD has overtaken UNESCO as the major international organization for education. We also acknowledge Eccleston's (2011, 248) point that an "international organisation's political authority is at its zenith when its rational/technical agenda aligns with prevailing social values and sentiments," and we suggest that this is the case with the OECD's education work today.

PISA: Expanding the Scope, Scale and Explanatory Power

The OECD's education policy work is currently expanding along three interrelated fronts: the scope of its educational assessment programs is widening to generate data about a broader set of skills; the scale of these assessments is expanding to include a larger number of participants; and efforts are being made to increase the explanatory power of these assessments by linking different datasets and by providing data in formats that are easily accessible and useful for policy-makers. This expansion involves growing the infrastructure through which the OECD produces, analyses, and disseminates education data, including the ongoing development of well-established programs such as PISA and the introduction of a suite of new programs. The strategy of building on the PISA brand has been reflected in the description of new programs as "PISA for adults" (PIAAC) or "PISA for schools." The expansion of the OECD's education data infrastructure is thus helping to cement the place of PISA as the best known and most widely influential international large-scale assessment, at least in terms of its media and policy impact.

The OECD's position as a node in a network of intergovernmental and international relations ensures that it is well connected to developments across a range of policy areas. The ability to tap into the zeitgeist and remain "ahead of the curve" in terms of policy ideas and technical expertise is a striking feature of the organization. The expanding scope of the OECD's educational assessments reflects its ability to keep pace with developments, and even set trends, in the fields of psychometrics and economics of education. More than a decade ago the OECD identified the need to widen the concept of human capital that informs its educational assessments and to measure the diverse set of dispositions and personality traits that contribute to the value of human capital. In 2002, the OECD argued that "there is more to human capital than the readily measurable – and very important – literacy, numeracy and workplace skills" (OECD 2002, 124). Drawing on economic research into factors that influence job performance and earnings (e.g. Bowles *et al.* 2001; Heckman *et al.* 2006), the OECD has argued that education policy analyses require conceptions of human capital that include both cognitive and *non-cognitive* skills.

The past decade has witnessed a growing interest in non-cognitive skills among economists and psychometricians, including attention to metacognition, motivation, and personality traits such as grit (Levin 2013). PISA has been collecting student self-reports relating to motivation, self-belief, and engagement with learning since the first round in 2000, and a large volume of the PISA reports is dedicated to the analysis of non-cognitive skills (e.g. OECD 2013a). Similarly, PIAAC, which was conducted for the first time in 2011/12, includes a background questionnaire with measures of social outcomes such as social trust and political efficacy, as well as generic skills such as task discretion, influence on others, and dexterity (OECD 2013b). The OECD holds the view that "a range of non-cognitive skills, such as the capacity to work collaboratively or as a member of a team, communication skills, and entrepreneurship, is also of importance in the modern workplace, and there is considerable interest in comparative information on both the supply of and demand for such skills" (OECD 2013b, 41). The assessment of generic skills in PIAAC was used to infer whether certain non-cognitive skills are involved in the workplace tasks of respondents. In 2013, the OECD also published a report on the measurement of subjective well-being (OECD 2013c), reflecting a broader interest in expanding its economic measurement work beyond GDP and developing cross-country comparisons in new domains relating to well-being.

We can see the expanding scope of the OECD's educational assessments into non-cognitive domains as an expansion of what counts and what is counted as a "skill." This agenda is drawing more aspects of learning, personality, and social life into human capital models and is facilitating the quantification and comparison of these domains, thereby opening them up to new kinds of policy intervention. Beyond a concern with non-cognitive skills, we might also see the expanding scope of OECD education assessments reflected in moves to conduct PISA online in OECD member countries in 2015, which will generate a range of new metadata relating to young people's interaction with computers and the test instrument.

The expanding *scale* of the OECD's education assessment work is being driven by the growth of the PISA program and the development of programs such as PISA for Development, which would extend PISA-comparable assessment into a new set of developing countries. This is increasing the global coverage of the OECD's education work. PISA is one of the OECD's most successful policy "products," and the changing scale of PISA and related programs reflects the capacity of the OECD to generate interest for these data among a range of new users: national and subnational governments, school systems, and individual schools.

Participation in PISA has grown substantially. There were initially 32 participants in PISA 2000, including 28 member countries and 4 non-members, and a further 11 non-member countries later participated in this first round. The 65 participants in the 2012 round thus reflects a doubling of the program's size and includes all 34 member countries and 31 non-members. The OECD now promotes PISA as representing 80% of the world economy (OECD 2013d). Efforts to bring China into the assessment, with Shanghai, Hong Kong, and Macau participating in the publication of results (although assessments have been conducted in other Chinese provinces), have been important to expanding this coverage and building relations with a major non-member economy at the outset of the so-called "Asian century."

The expanding scale of PISA must be set against the post-Cold War reworking of the OECD's role, the expansion of membership, and efforts to engage non-member economies. In 2007, the OECD launched its Enhanced Engagement program to develop the organization's relationship with five major non-member nations: Brazil,

China, India, Indonesia, and South Africa. The program includes the aim of integrating these countries into the OECD's statistical collection and reporting. To date, South Africa is the only Enhanced Engagement "key partner" that has not participated in PISA. The OECD is also currently piloting PISA for Development in the context of the expiry of the UN Millennium Development Goals in 2015 and the establishment of a new post-2015 framework. PISA for Development promises to offer a more relevant instrument to developing countries, while enabling them to collect baseline data that can be used to assess post-2015 progress in education and to compare education performance with countries and systems participating in main PISA. In the context of globalization, PISA might be seen for these nations, but also for those participating in main PISA, as a global positioning device for national schooling systems (Simons 2014).

A particularly interesting development with respect to expansions of scale has been the recent introduction of PISA-based Tests for Schools. This program was trialed in the USA, England, and the Canadian province of Manitoba in 2012, and is currently being implemented in the USA (with moves toward implementation elsewhere, including England and Spain). PISA-Based Tests for Schools are based on PISA items and allow schools to benchmark their performance against others schools, nationally and globally, and against other participants in PISA (nations and subnational systems). This program marks an innovation in the OECD's assessment work insofar as it is not being funded by member nations, but is instead made available directly to schools, which must pay an accredited private supplier to conduct the analysis and reporting of results (currently CTB/McGraw-Hill in the USA).

There are at least two important implications for the OECD's soft power in relation to PISA-based Tests for Schools. First, this program involves new contractual relationships with education companies, who are accredited as national suppliers of data analytics services and thus provide one example of the development of new modes of network governance in education (Ball and Junemann 2012). Second, the program enables the reporting of OECD data at a level that increases the relevance and usefulness of these data for polities and institutions for which PISA has not previously been seen as a relevant policy tool. For example, by providing school-level assessments in the USA, the OECD is able to bypass the national level at which PISA data are currently collected (although the states of Florida, Connecticut, and Massachusetts participated individually in 2012), in order to provide data directly to schools and systems, which can then mobilize these data as evidence of performance and to support claims on funding within the current accountability relations through which US schooling is governed (see Rutkowski 2014).

The final front of expansion is that of *explanatory power*, which involves efforts to improve the claims about educational performance that can be sustained on the basis of OECD data. Here again it is important to recognize the organization's ability to stay abreast of technical developments that enable new kinds of data analysis and representation. For example, the OECD is currently developing methods to match student and teacher data gathered through different assessment programs. The Teaching and Learning International Survey (TALIS) was introduced in 2008 and was conducted again in 2013 with 34 countries. The OECD is linking PISA data with TALIS data to enable student performance to be understood in relation to teaching environments (Kaplan and Turner 2012). The OECD's CERI is also engaged in other projects related to TALIS, such as its *Innovative Teaching for Effective Learning* project, which aims to generate knowledge about classroom teaching practices and which could ultimately be used to provide a fuller picture of relationships between teaching practices and student competencies. Such efforts to enhance explanatory power by linking up different education datasets are part of a broader governance trend "to create standardized, interoperable and dynamic databases to support evidence-based policy, enable individually tailored and targeted services, reduce costs, and provide robust population statistics for analysis and research" (Ruppert 2012, 118–119).

Another example of the expansion of explanatory power is the introduction of data visualization tools, such as the Education GPS portal, which enables PISA, PIAAC, *Education at a Glance* indicators, and other data to be actively explored by users. The Directorate for Education and Skills also publishes regular notes, such as *PISA in Focus*, that present data with policy relevant analysis and commentary. These notes often garner media coverage and reflect the Education Directorate's savvy when it comes to the impact that it has been able to generate from PISA and related products. Indeed, PISA is the largest media event for the organization and now attracts substantial media coverage globally. Media coverage of national performance has played an important role in PISA's impact but has varied from nation to nation (Martens and Niemann 2013). Efforts to sustain and increase explanatory power are also reflected in the ongoing psychometric and statistical work, often in partnership with private contractors and national research organizations, to sustain the comparability of PISA items across countries and cultures and to ensure the viability of trend analyses across each triennial round of PISA.

Each front of expansion – scope, scale, and explanatory power – is clearly interrelated. Increasing the scope of the assessment to include non-cognitive skills enables the analysis of a wider set of factors that contribute to human capital and thus potentially increases the explanatory power of the OECD's data for understanding economic growth. Increasing the scale of the assessment to include a wider set of participants, particularly non-members, potentially increases the explanatory power of the comparisons that can be made between educational performance across different countries and regions. And the desire to increase explanatory power, in turn, encourages expansion of the scope and scale of the OECD's data infrastructure. These fronts of expansion make clear the successes of PISA and related programs over the past 15 years, in terms of influencing policy thinking in education, and point to the ways in which the OECD is building on this influence to expand its measurement work and its influence in education globally.

The OECD's Education Work and Global Educational Governance

There have been a number of important analyses of the OECD's governance mechanisms, both in general (e.g. Woodward 2009) and specifically in relation to education (e.g. Jakobi and Martens 2010). Jakobi and Martens (2010) observe that, "[g]overnance by international organizations ... changes over time, and the recent development of internationalization processes might be a result of changed mechanisms of governance." In relation to the OECD, they argue that "[t]he OECD today not only defines the problem, but also offers the solution... With the new generation of indicators, the Organization has therefore gained an important status in several stages of national policy-making, ranging from agenda setting to policy formulation and implementation" (p. 176). Drawing on the work of Jakobi and Martens (2010), Woodward (2009) and others (e.g. Anagnostopoulos *et al.* 2013; Carroll and Kellow 2011), we argue that the OECD now exerts influence in education globally through the linked mechanism of *epistemological* and *infrastructural* governance.

Reviewing the 50-year history of the OECD, Carroll and Kellow (2011) argue that "the largely voluntary nature of the measures that are the products of the OECD can be seen to be more effective [than binding obligations] because they can embody clarity and higher quality that give rise to fewer concerns by members, precisely because they rarely threaten members' key interests" (p. 264); this is perhaps an example of "the unimpeachable technical merit" (Loya and Boli 1999) of the OECD's metrics. Carroll and Kellow (2011) conclude that the soft power exerted by the organization has been the key to its success and that its substantial influence has been "epistemic in nature" (p. 264). We agree that the OECD's global governance role must be understood in terms of this epistemic influence and we see this as linked to the development of the organization's data infrastructure, or the range of practices, instruments, and technological capacities it has developed for undertaking statistical work. Thus, we argue that the OECD operates through epistemological modes of governance that are linked to modes of infrastructural governance. We expand upon both of these concepts in what follows.

Weiss (2013, 2) defines global governance as "the sum of the informal and formal values, norms, procedures, and institutions that help all actors – states, intergovernmental organizations, civil society, transnational corporations, and individuals – to identify, understand and address trans-boundary problems." We find this definition useful because of its emphasis on the exercise of soft power – the shaping of values, norms, and procedures – in formulating policy problems and solutions. Woodward (2009) reminds us that the OECD is "devoid of the sticks and carrots available to other global institutions" and points to its success in establishing rapprochement between members and non-members through four dimensions of governance: cognitive, normative, palliative, and legal. Woodward (2009) defines cognitive governance as "the incarnation of a community of countries sharing overarching values" (Woodward 2009, 6). Normative governance relates to "the realm of research, knowledge and ideas," and palliative governance is defined as "a lubricant to the wider processes of global governance" (Woodward 2009, 6). This typology of governance modes provides a useful framework for understanding how the OECD exerts influence, and we see it as describing facets of two interrelated modes of governance: *epistemological* governance, which brings together the cognitive and the normative, linked to a form of *infrastructural* governance, which includes the palliative, in the sense that the development of infrastructure can contribute to and shape wider global governance processes. However, infrastructural governance also involves a type of logistical power that, we would argue, is quite active in the OECD's governance mechanisms.

We are drawing here on Mukerji's (2010) distinction between strategics and logistics. Mukerji argues that "[s]trategic power works because people respond to favors and threats (and by extension surveillance), aligning their behaviours to regimes" (p. 402). The OECD produces few legally binding instruments and it seldom exercises strategic power in this way, as do other international organizations and national governments. However, it does exercise strategic power through the system of peer pressure and surveillance that membership involves – the means through which the organization's normative and cognitive governance mechanisms operate. This strategic power is combined with the logistical activity through which the organization '"shapes social life differently, affecting the environment (context, situation, location) in which human action and cognition take place" (p. 402). Drawing on the work of Holland *et al.* (1998), Mukerji describes logistics as productive of "figured worlds": "a politically infused culture that shapes cognition as well as action. The culture consists not only of a constellation of ideas, but also physical forms systematically infused with meaning. It is a physical arrangement of the material environment that intentionally ratifies cultural conceptions of reality" (pp. 406–407). Here we see the OECD's development of data or information infrastructure as central (Bowker *et al.* 2011; Star and Ruhleder 1996) and as enabling a particular combination of logistical and strategic power, which Anagnostopoulos *et al.* (2013) term "informatic" power.

We argue that the epistemological governance role of the OECD must be understood as being linked to the infrastructure that has developed and become embedded to support its data generation and analyses. This infrastructure involves modifications of the environment in which politics and policy-making take place and thus creates the conditions for cognitive/normative governance. At the same time, shared values regarding the need for data to inform governance and policy create an ongoing demand for the expansion of data infrastructure. This is in line with Sassen's (2007) argument that globalization is the creation of global infrastructures that enable global flows of various kinds. The OECD's data infrastructure is important in the globalization of education policy, framing global education policy discourses.

We see the expansion of PISA and related programs as an infrastructural expansion, but one that is closely linked to the OECD's capacities to promote a cohesive set of norms and values (cognitive) and to generate research and knowledge that shifts perceptions and supports particular policy agendas (normative). For example, the implementation of PISA required the establishment of a data infrastructure that includes a multiplicity of elements: the physical paper and pencil tests and the technical work of development embedded within them, the technological capacities of organizations that manage the testing inside nations, the proliferation of particular testing methodologies and standards, the alignment of the categories of measurement, and so on. This infrastructure supports the OECD's work in relation to national governments and other international organizations, contributing to its palliative governance function. At the same time, it is restructuring the professional and technical environments of education research and education policy-making globally, which creates conditions in which the OECD can encourage an alignment of values (e.g. the need for education performance data as a tool for governing systems; the usage of particular psychometric techniques) and can draw on "evidence" to shift perceptions (e.g. creating "shocks" and "policy windows" when performance data can be used to argue the need for reform).

Infrastructural and epistemological governance are thus closely linked and mutually reinforcing. It is for this reason that we see the expansion of the OECD's assessment work in education as both an infrastructural expansion and an expansion of its global governance role. Increasing the scope, scale, and explanatory power of PISA and related programs increases the usefulness of the data generated for a range of international organizations and national governments and helps to shape values and norms, as well as education research practices, political debate, policy-making and, ultimately, practices in schools and other educational institutions. In this sense, the post-Cold War reworking of the organization's role to strengthen its position as a global "centre of calculation" (Latour 1987) provides an important entry point into analyzing its current governance mechanisms, which look set to grow further and in new ways during the post-financial crisis period. This data work now extends to a new array of economic indicators relating to well-being, citizenship, and so on, and efforts are being made to draw new sets of actors into this work, with the potential further to shape the way we think about and view education today.

Conclusion

In this chapter, we have traced the ways in which the OECD has adapted successfully to changing global changes and pressures, from the Cold War context through the post-Cold War period, then through the recent financial crises and subsequently. Set against those changes, we have provided a cartography of the developing place of education inside and outside the organization and its location in new global geographies of governance. From education's inferred role up until the Directorate for Education was established in 2002, through to the location of the education work of the OECD today in the Directorate for Education and Skills, the significance and influence of this work has continued to grow. While statistical analyses have been important to education from the establishment of the OECD, this work has taken on greater salience, particularly from the 1990s with the creation of INES, the publication of *Education at Glance*, and, more influentially, with the rise of PISA and the introduction of related assessments. Inside the organization today, the cross-committee Skills Strategy, in which education is central, seeks to establish policy cohesion across the organization.

In the 21st century, the OECD has become the major international organization in respect of education policy and is helping to constitute a global educational policy field through its soft power. Here the establishment and expansion of its data infrastructure has been very important in making the globe legible for governing. This infrastructural governance is linked to its constitution of a global epistemic community, and through both its data infrastructure and this community the organization exerts a form of epistemological governance in education. It is the OECD's nimble capacities to adapt to changing contexts and to grasp the zeitgeist which have also been important in the enhanced significance of its education work in global educational governance that we have adumbrated here.

Notes

1 Australia, Austria, Belgium, Canada, Chile, the Czech Republic, Denmark, Estonia, Finland, France, Germany, Greece, Hungary, Iceland, Ireland, Israel, Italy, Japan, Korea, Luxembourg, Mexico, The Netherlands, New Zealand, Norway, Poland, Portugal, the Slovak Republic, Slovenia, Spain, Sweden, Switzerland, Turkey, the UK, the USA.
2 In providing this analysis, we draw on two research projects, one conducted late last century (Henry et al. 2001), the other more recently (Sellar and Lingard 2013a).

References

Anagnostopoulos, D., S.A. Rutledge, and R. Jacobsen (eds). 2013. *The Infrastructure of Accountability: Data Use and the Transformation of American Education*. Boston: Harvard Education Press.

Ball, S.J. and C. Junemann. 2012. *Networks, New Governance and Education*. Bristol: Policy Press.

Bourdieu, P. 2003. *Firing Back: Against the Tyranny of the Market*. London: Verso.

Bowker, G.C., K. Baker, F. Millerand, and D. Ribes. 2011. "Toward Information Infrastructure Studies: Ways of Knowing in a Networked Environment," in *International Handbook of Internet Research*, edited by J. Hunsinger, L. Klastrup, and M. Allen, 97–117. Dordrecht: Springer.

Bowles, S., H. Gintis, and M. Osborne, 2001. "The Determinants of Earnings: A Behavioral Approach." *Journal of Economic Literature*, 39: 1137–1176.

Brown, P., A.H. Halsey, H. Lauder, and A. Stuart Wells. 1997. "The Transformation of Education and Society: An Introduction," in *Education: Culture, Economy and Society*, edited by A.H. Halsey, H. Lauder, P. Brown, and A. Stuart Wells. Oxford: Oxford University Press.

Carroll, P. and A. Kellow. 2011. *The OECD: a Study of Organizational Adaptation*. Cheltenham: Edward Elgar.

Carvalho, L.M. and E. Costa, 2014. "Seeing Education with One's Own Eyes and through the PISA Lenses: Considerations of the Reception of PISA in European countries." *Discourse: Studies in the Cultural Politics of Education*, 36: 638–646. DOI:10.1080/01596306.2013.871449.

Eccleston, R. 2011. "The OECD and Global Economic Governance." *Australian Journal of International Affairs*, 65: 243–255.

Ertl, H. 2006. "Educational Standards and the Changing Discourse on Education: the Reception and Consequences of the PISA Study in Germany." *Oxford Review of Education*, 32: 619–634.

Grek, S. 2009. "Governing by Numbers: The PISA 'Effect' in Europe." *Journal of Education Policy*, 24: 23–37.

Haas, E.B. 1990. *When Knowledge is Power: Three Models of Change in International Organisations*. Berkeley: University of California Press.

Heckman, J.J., J. Stixrud, and S. Urzua, S. 2006. "The Effects of Cognitive and Noncognitive Abilities on Labor Market Outcomes and Social Behaviour." *Journal of Labor Economics*, 24: 411–482.

Henry, M., B. Lingard, F. Rizvi, and S. Taylor. 2001. *The OECD, Globalisation and Education Policy*. Oxford: Pergamon Press.

Heyneman, S.P. 1993. "Quantity, Quality and Source." *Comparative Education Review*, 37: 372–388.

Holland, D.C., W. Lachicotte Jr, D. Skinner, and C. Cain. 1998. *Identity and Agency in Cultural Worlds*. Cambridge: Harvard University Press.

Istance, D. 1996. Education at the Chateau de la Muette. *Oxford Review of Education*, 22: 91–96.

Jakobi, A. and K. Martens. 2010. "Expanding and Intensifying Governance: The OECD in Education Policy," in *Mechanisms of OECD Governance: International Incentives for National Policy-Making?* edited by K. Martins and A.P. Jakobi, 162–179. Oxford: Oxford University Press.

Kallo, J. 2009. *OECD Education Policy: A Comparative and Historical Study Focusing on the Thematic Reviews of Higher Education*. Jyvaskyla: Jyvaskyla University Press.

Kaplan, D. and A. Turner. 2012. "Statistical Matching of PISA 2009 and TALIS 2008 Data in Iceland." *OECD Education Working Papers No. 78*. Paris: OECD.

Latour, B. 1987. *Science in Action: How to Follow Scientists and Engineers through Society*. Cambridge: Harvard University Press.

Levin, H.M. 2013. "The Utility and Need for Incorporating Noncognitive Skills Into Large-Scale Educational Assessments," in *The Role of International Large-Scale Assessments: Perspectives from Technology, Economy, and Education Research*, edited by M. von Davier, E. Gonzalez, I. Kirsch, and K. Yamamoto, 67–86. Dordrecht: Springer.

Lingard, B. 2011. "Policy as Numbers: (Ac)counting For Educational Research." *The Australian Education Researcher*, 38: 355–382.

Lingard, B. and S. Rawolle. 2011. "New Scalar Politics: Implications for Education Policy." *Comparative Education*, 47: 367–377.

Lingard, B., S. Sellar, and G.C. Savage. 2014. "Test-Based Accountabilities and Data Infrastructures: Rearticulations of Social Justice as Equity in Education Policy." *British Journal of Sociology of Education*, 35: 710–730.

Loya, T.A. and Boli, J. 1999. "Standardization in the World Polity: Technical Rationality over Power," in *Constructing World Culture: International Nongovernmental Organizations Since 1875*, edited by J. Boli and G.M. Thomas, 169–197. Stanford: Stanford University Press.

Martens, K. and D. Niemann. 2013. "When Do Numbers Count? The Differentiated Rating and Ranking on Education Policy in Germany and the US." *German Politics*, 22: 314–332.

Meyer, J., J. Boli, G.M. Thomas, and F.O. Ramirez. 1997. "World Society and the Nation State." *American Journal of Sociology*, 103: 144–181.

Meyer, H.-D. and K. Schiller. 2013. "Gauging the Role of Non-Educational Effects in Large-Scale Assessments: Socio-Economic, Culture and PISA Outcomes," in *PISA, Power, and Policy: The Emergence of Global Educational Governance*, edited by H.-D. Meyer and A. Benavot, 207–224. Oxford: Symposium Books.

Mukerji, C. 2010. "The Territorial State as Figured World of Power: Strategies, Logistics and Impersonal Rule." *Sociological Theory*, 28: 402–424.

OECD. 1995. *Governance in Transition: Public Management Reforms in OECD Countries*. Paris: OECD.

OECD. 1999. *Measuring Student Knowledge and Skills. A New Framework for Assessment*. Paris: OECD.

OECD. 2002. *Education Policy Analysis*. Paris: OECD.

OECD. 2012. *Better Skills, Better Jobs, Better Lives: A Strategic Approach to Skills Policy*. Paris: OECD.

OECD. 2013a. *PISA 2012 Results: Ready to Learn: Students' Engagement, Drive and Self-Beliefs (Volume III), PISA*. Paris: OECD Publishing.

OECD. 2013b. "What the Survey of Adult Skills (PIAAC) measures." *The Survey of Adult Skills: Reader's Companion*. Paris: OECD.

OECD. 2013c. *OECD Guidelines on Measuring Subjective Well-being*. Paris: OECD.

OECD. 2013d. *PISA 2012 Results in Focus: What 15-Year-Olds Know and What They Can Do With What They Know*. Paris: OECD.

Ozga, J. 2009. "Governing Education through Data in England: From Regulation to Self-Evaluation." *Journal of Education Policy*, 24: 149–162.

Papadopoulos, G.S. 1994. *Education 1960–1990 the OECD Perspective*. Paris: OECD.

Rose, N. 1999. *Powers of Freedom: Reframing Political Thought*. Cambridge: Cambridge University Press.

Ruppert, E. 2012. "The Governmental Topologies of Database Devices." *Theory, Culture and Society*, 29: 116–136.

Rutkowski, D. 2014. "The OECD and the Local: PISA-Based Test for Schools in the US." *Discourse: Studies in the Cultural Politics of Education*, 36: 683–699.

Sassen, S. 2007. *Sociology of Globalization*. New York: W.W. Norton.

Scott, J.C. 1998. *Seeing Like a State: How Certain Schemes to Improve the Human Condition Have Failed*. New Haven: Yale University Press.

Sellar, S. and B. Lingard. 2013a. "The OECD and the Expansion of PISA: New Global Modes of Governance in Education." *British Educational Research Journal*, 30: 917–936.

Sellar, S. and B. Lingard. 2013b. "Looking East: Shanghai, PISA 2009 and the Reconstitution of Reference Societies in the Global Policy Field." *Comparative Education*, 49: 464–485.

Simons, M. 2014. "Governing Education Without Reform: The Power of the Example." *Discourse: Studies in the Cultural Politics of Education*, 36: 712–731.

Star, S.L. and K. Ruhleder. 1996. "Steps Toward an Ecology of Infrastructure: Design and Access for Large Information Spaces." *Information Systems Research*, 7: 111–134.

Takayama, K. 2008. "The Politics of International League Tables: PISA in Japan's Achievement Crisis Debate." *Comparative Education*, 44: 387–407.

Waldow, F., K. Takayama, and Y.-K. Sung. 2014. "Rethinking the Pattern of External Policy Referencing: Media Discourses Over the 'Asian Tigers'' PISA success in Australia, Germany and South Korea." *Comparative Education*, 50: 302–321.

Weiss, T.G. 2013. *Global Governance: Why? What? Whither?* Cambridge: Polity Press.

Wiseman, A.W. 2013. "Policy Responses to PISA in Comparative Perspective," in *PISA, Power, and Policy: The Emergence of Global Educational Governance*, edited by H.-D. Meyer and A. Benavot. Oxford: Symposium Books.

Woodward, R. 2009. *The Organisation for Economic Co-operation and Development*. London: Routledge.

Zumbo, B.D. 2007. "Three Generations of DIF Analyses: Considering Where it Has Been, Where it is Now, and Where it is Going." *Language Assessment Quarterly*, 4: 223–233.

Chapter 20

The Policies that Shaped PISA, and the Policies that PISA Shaped

Andreas Schleicher and Pablo Zoido

In the Dark, All Schools and Education Systems Look the Same

The world is rapidly becoming a different place, and the challenges to individuals and societies imposed by globalization and modernization are widely acknowledged. Increasingly diverse and interconnected populations, rapid technological change in the workplace and in everyday life, and the instantaneous availability of vast amounts of information represent but a few of these new demands.

In contrast to this global reality, education still remains a very local and often inward-looking business. This is not just because much of the educational process centers around local human interaction, but also because different types of "walls" tend to separate educators, institutions, and education systems.

Some of these walls are "natural," established by language or culture, but others result from poor knowledge management in education systems and because education often remains dominated by beliefs, traditions, and sometimes ideologies. As a result, education systems can face difficulties in enabling schools and teachers to share, jointly develop, and implement knowledge about their work and performance. While those who run education systems may have access to some evidence on school performance, those who deliver educational services at the frontline in school often do not, or face obstacles in translating available knowledge into effective classroom practices.

Similar walls exist between education systems and countries, with few instruments for countries to look outwards to educational policies and practices developed and implemented beyond their immediate experience and control. This is a particular challenge since, in the field of education, ethical and practical considerations limit the use of experimental methods to explore alternative policies and practices. Education systems could be much further advanced if they were to effectively integrate and build

---

The Handbook of Global Education Policy, First Edition.
Edited by Karen Mundy, Andy Green, Bob Lingard, and Antoni Verger.
© 2016 John Wiley & Sons, Ltd. Published 2016 by John Wiley & Sons, Ltd.

on the knowledge base that lies in their global workforce, as is the case in other economic and social sectors. Education has always been a knowledge industry in the sense that it is concerned with the transmission of knowledge, but it is still far from becoming a knowledge industry in the sense that its own practices are being transformed by knowledge about their efficacy. This is in contrast to many other fields, where people enter their professional lives expecting their practice to be transformed by evidence and research.

International comparisons can show what is possible in education, in terms of the quality, equity, and efficiency of educational services achieved by the world's top performing education systems, they can foster better understanding of how different education systems address similar problems, and they can help set meaningful targets in terms of measurable goals achieved by the world's educational leaders. Not least, in the face of rapidly improving education systems, even those who claim that the relative standing of countries mainly reflects social and cultural factors must concede that educational improvement is possible.

While cross-sectional international comparisons alone cannot identify cause-and-effect relationships between inputs, processes, and educational outcomes, they can shed light on key features in which education systems show similarities and differences, and make those key features visible to educators, policy-makers, and the general public.

This chapter examines the merits of international comparisons as drivers for educational change, illustrating this with the example of the Programme for International Student Assessment (PISA), which the Organisation for Economic Co-operation and Development (OECD) launched in 2000 to monitor learning outcomes across countries. The example of PISA is interesting in this context because the OECD has no legislative or financial powers through which it could exert any direct influence on public policy. All the OECD provides is evidence, analysis, and advice of the type that PISA generates. Nevertheless, in countries as diverse as Brazil, Japan, Germany, and Mexico, PISA has spurred educational reform and in some cases transformational change in ways that had been unprecedented in preceding decades.

The Design and Impact of PISA

For some, internationally comparative evidence has become the Holy Grail of modern educational policy (Douglass *et al.* 1992). Within less than a decade, it seems that international comparisons such as PISA have established themselves as indispensable for educational reform, which used to be conceived as an essentially domestic domain. By shifting the focus from the inputs and the ways in which education systems are run toward the outputs and outcomes of education systems, and by making these outcomes publicly visible within an internationally comparative framework, they have made the work of education systems and its main stakeholders globally transparent. Indeed, the example of PISA suggests that comparative evidence feeding peer pressure and public accountability may now have greater impact on educational change than legislation, rules, and regulations. But there are skeptics too, who compare the search for comparative data and assessments with the Alchemist's stone, which was sought by medieval chemists to transmute ordinary metal into gold, producing untold riches, assuming that the laws of supply and demand would no longer hold. Their argument is typically that weighing the cow does not make the cow fatter

(Eisner 1996, 4). There are also questions on the extent to which policy lessons derived from international comparisons can be transferred to different socioeconomic and cultural contexts (Meyer and Schiller 2013).

The Holy Grail was a well-defined and described object, and there was only one true grail. The Alchemist's stone was to be recognized by the transformation of all metal into gold. When it comes to comparing educational outcomes, there are many competing visions of what the desirable outcomes of education systems are. Governments therefore had to make difficult choices when they established the scope and nature of PISA. Similar difficulties arise with regard to the methodologies that are used to make educational outcomes amenable to quantitative assessment and to compare and analyse their results. The medieval alchemists were no doubt consistent in following the dictates of their science. But their science was wrong. The search for the Holy Grail was overburdened by false clues and cryptic symbols. Here too, researchers and educators had to make difficult choices when designing the methodologies for PISA, which are discussed in detail in the PISA technical report (OECD 2011) and it is noteworthy that some of these methodological issues remain yet to be resolved. They include, for example, the role of school weights in different estimation methods, the dimensionality of different Item Response Theory models used in the estimation of plausible values or questionnaire indices, the possibility to use items to estimate more than one dimension of competency, whether imputing values for questionnaire items is feasible or not, etc.

Governments (OECD member states working with partner governments outside the OECD) established PISA in the late 1990s to compare the quality, equity, and efficiency of their school systems on a regular basis, in terms of the learning outcomes achieved by students toward the end of compulsory schooling. The heart of PISA is an internationally agreed test that is administered to representative samples of school students in the participating countries. The age of 15 years was chosen as the point of comparison because it represents the last point at which schooling is still largely universal. PISA is closely aligned with the Programme for the International Assessment of Adult Competencies (PIAAC), OECD's assessment of adult competencies, which begins at age 16, where PISA ends, and extends to the age of 65 years. While PISA is looking backwards to establish how effectively school systems establish the foundations for success in life, PIAAC is looking forward to how initial skills feed into further learning and important economic, employment, and social outcomes.

Some general principles were agreed among countries to guide the development and use of PISA:

- PISA is *policy-oriented*. It focuses on providing data and analysis that can help guide decisions on education policy. By linking data on students' learning outcomes with data on key factors that shape learning in and out of school, PISA highlights differences in performance patterns and identifies features common to high-performing students, schools, and education systems.
- PISA is carried out every three years to enable countries to *monitor their progress* in meeting key learning objectives. The basic survey design has remained constant to allow for comparability from one PISA assessment to the next and thus to allow countries to relate policy changes to improvements in education outcomes.

- PISA assesses both subject matter *content knowledge*, on the one hand, and the capacity of individuals to *apply that knowledge creatively*, including in unfamiliar contexts, on the other.
- PISA is designed to provide *comparable data* across a wide range of countries, currently comprising over 70 education systems that cover over 80% of the world economy. Considerable efforts are devoted to achieving cultural and linguistic breadth and balance in assessment materials. Stringent quality-assurance mechanisms are applied in the test design, translation, sampling, and data collection. An age-based rather than a grade-based target population is used to ensure valid international comparisons of educational performance. The PISA for Development project, which provides support to the least developed countries, is an effort aimed at enhancing the PISA instruments so as to make them available and more relevant for countries that have thus far been excluded from global educational comparisons. The PISA-based test for schools allows individual schools to assess where they stand among the world's most successful schools.
- PISA is *a collaborative effort*. Decisions about the scope and nature of the PISA assessments and the background information collected are undertaken by leading experts in participating countries. Governments oversee these decisions based on shared, policy-driven interests.

Seeing what is Possible in Education

The impact of international comparisons is naturally largest when they reveal that a country performs comparatively poorly. The level of public awareness raised by comparisons like PISA has in some countries created an important political momentum and engaged educational stakeholders, including teacher or employer organizations, in support of policy reform.

Equally important, international comparisons have had a significant impact in countries that did not do poorly in absolute terms, but that found themselves confronted with results that differed from how educational performance was generally perceived. In Germany, the education policy debate and changes in light of PISA 2000 were intense (e.g. Ertl 2006; Grek 2009). Confronted with lower than expected results in student performance, PISA triggered a sustained public debate about education policy and reform that came to be known as "PISA shock." For example, equity in learning opportunities across schools had often been taken for granted, as significant efforts were devoted to ensuring that schools were adequately and equitably resourced. The PISA 2000 results, however, revealed large socioeconomic disparities in educational outcomes between schools. Further analyses that separated equity-related issues between those that relate to the socioeconomic heterogeneity within schools and those that relate to socioeconomic segregation through the school system, suggested that German students from more privileged social backgrounds are directed into the more prestigious academic schools, which yield superior educational outcomes, while students from less privileged social backgrounds are directed into less prestigious vocational schools, which yield poorer educational outcomes, even where their performance on the PISA assessment was similar. This raised the specter that the education system was reinforcing, rather than moderating socioeconomic background factors. These results, and the ensuing public debate, inspired a wide range of equity-related reform efforts in Germany, some of which have been transformational in nature. This includes giving early childhood education, that had hitherto been considered largely an aspect of social welfare, an educational orientation; establishing national educational standards in a country where regional and local autonomy had long been the overriding paradigm; or enhancing the support for disadvantaged students, such as students with a migration background.

For many educators and experts in Germany, the socioeconomic disparities that PISA had revealed had not necessarily been surprising. However, it was often taken for granted and outside the scope of public policy that disadvantaged children would fare less well in school. The fact that PISA revealed that the impact which socioeconomic background has on students and school performance varied so considerably across countries, and that other countries appeared to moderate socioeconomic disparities so much more effectively, showed that improvement was possible and provided the momentum for policy change.

Showing that strong educational performance, and indeed improvement, is possible seems to be one of the most important merits of international comparisons. Whether in Asia (like Japan, Korea, Singapore, or Shanghai-China), in Europe (like Finland) or in North America (like Canada), many countries displayed strong overall performance in PISA and, equally important, showed that poor performance in school does not automatically follow from a disadvantaged socioeconomic background. Some countries showed that success can become a consistent and predictable educational outcome: In Finland, the country with the strongest overall results in PISA, the performance variation between schools amounted in 2009 to only 5% of students' overall performance variation, such that parents can rely on high and consistent performance standards in whatever school they choose to enrol their children. Last but not least, some countries have shown that significant educational improvement can be achieved within a limited time span. As noted before, Germany saw significant improvements both in quality and equity of its school systems between 2000 and 2009. Korea's average performance was already high in 2000, yet the Koreans were concerned that only a small elite achieved levels of excellence in the PISA reading assessment back then. Within less than a decade, Korea was able to double the share of students demonstrating excellence. A major overhaul of Poland's school system helped to dramatically reduce performance variability among schools, turn around the lowest performing schools, and raise overall performance by more than half a school year. Portugal was able to consolidate its fragmented school system and improve both overall performance and equity, and so did Hungary. Even those who claim that the relative standing of countries in PISA mainly reflects social and cultural factors had to concede that educational improvement is possible.

Considerable research has been invested into the features of these education systems. In some countries, governments have used knowledge provided by PISA about their relative standing internationally as a starting point for a peer review to study policies and practices in countries operating under similar circumstances that achieve better results. Such peer reviews, each resulting in a set of specific policy recommendations for educational improvement, are now also being carried out regularly by the OECD.

As a result of all of this, the yardsticks for public policy in education are no longer national goals or standards alone, but increasingly the performance of the most successful

	Response percent	Response count
Extremely	5.4%	2
Very	64.9%	24
Moderately	24.3%	9
Not very	5.4%	2
Not at all	0.0%	0
Don't know	0.0%	0

Figure 20.1 To what extent is PISA performance seen by policy-makers in your country as an important indicator of the effectiveness of the school system?
Source: Breakspear (2011).

education systems internationally. Public visibility of international comparisons has sometimes transformed a specialized educational debate into a public debate, with citizens recognizing that their country's educational performance will not simply need to match average performance, but that they will need to do better if their children want to justify above-average wages.

In 2011 researchers carried out a survey on the impact of PISA in countries. The survey was sent to representatives from the 65 countries and economies that participated in PISA 2009. These representatives are formally appointed by their governments to serve in the PISA Governing Board, the body that steers PISA. They are typically high level public officials, many of them the directors of national education evaluation agencies. In this survey, respondents from 16 countries/economies judged that PISA had been "very" influential (Austria, Belgium (French community), Estonia, Germany, Greece, Hungary, Ireland, Israel, Latvia, Mexico, Norway, Poland, the Slovak Republic, Slovenia, Sweden, and Wales-UK), and respondents from a further 11 countries/economies (Australia, Canada, Chile, Hong Kong-China, Italy, Netherlands, Portugal, Scotland-UK, Singapore, Spain, and the USA) judged PISA to be "moderately" influential. The respondents from England-UK, Denmark, and Japan rated PISA as "extremely" influential, whilst respondents from Finland, France, Indonesia, Luxembourg, and Turkey rated PISA as "not very" influential (Breakspear 2011). Respondents were also asked to rate the extent to which policy-makers in their education system see PISA performance as an important indicator of the effectiveness of the school system. These results are illustrated in Figure 20.1.

Putting National Targets into a Broader Perspective

International comparisons can also play an important role in putting national performance targets into perspective. Educators are often faced with a dilemma: if the percentage of students obtaining good degrees in school increases, some will claim that the school system has improved. Others will claim that standards must have been lowered, and behind the suspicion that better results reflect lowered standards is often a belief that overall performance in education cannot be raised. International comparisons allow us to relate those perceptions to a wider reference framework, by allowing schools and education systems to look at themselves in the mirror of the performance of schools and education systems in other countries. Some countries have actively embraced this perspective and systematically related national performance to international performance comparison, by providing a role for PISA within normative national/federal policies: assessment and evaluation, curriculum standards, and performance targets. These normative policy instruments function to set, measure, and reinforce what the education system aims to achieve and its desired improvement trajectory.

According to the above-mentioned survey, PISA-based national or subnational performance targets or indicators have been set in 18 countries/economies, namely: Australia, Belgium (Flemish and French communities), Canada, Denmark, Finland, France, Hungary, Ireland, Israel, Ireland, Japan, Mexico, The Netherlands, Poland, Slovenia, the Slovak Republic, Turkey, and Wales-UK. The responses to the survey reveal the diversity of target types, number of targets, the stakeholders who set them (e.g. the Prime Minster or a national assessment institute), and the documents in which those targets have been elaborated (e.g. White Paper, growth strategy, etc.). Examples of the specific country targets are given in Table 20.1. Target types included the relative rank of a country in international performance, which is dependent on the relative performance of other countries/economies; specific national PISA scores, ranges of scores in each domain, or performance at the OECD average; increases in number of high performers and decreases in percentage of students scoring at or below PISA proficiency Level 2, the baseline proficiency level; and equity goals, including variance between schools. Some countries/economies also use a range of target types and indicators.

Assessing the Pace of Change in Educational Improvement

A third important aspect is that international comparisons provide a frame of reference to assess the pace of change in educational development. While a national framework allows us to assess progress in absolute terms, an internationally comparative perspective allows us to assess whether that progress matches the pace of change observed elsewhere. Indeed, while all education systems in the OECD area have seen quantitative growth over past decades, international comparisons reveal that the pace of change in educational output has varied markedly. For example, among 55–64 year olds, the USA is well ahead of all other OECD countries in terms of the proportion of individuals with both school and university qualifications. However, international comparisons show that this advantage is largely a result of the "first-mover advantage," which the USA had gained after World War II by massively increasing enrolments. It has eroded over past decades as more and more countries have reached and surpassed qualification levels in the USA in more recent cohorts. While many countries are now close to ensuring that virtually all young adults leave schools with at least a high school degree/qualification, which the OECD comparisons highlight as the baseline qualification for reasonable earnings and employment prospects, the USA stood still on this measure and, among OECD countries, only New Zealand, Spain, Turkey, and Mexico now have lower high school completion rates than the USA. Even when including qualifications that people can acquire later in life to make up for unsuccessful school completion, the USA has slipped from rank 1 among OECD countries for adults born in the 1940s to rank 12

Table 20.1 Overview of PISA-referenced performance targets and indicators

Country	Targets/indicators
Australia	PISA used as key national performance measures of numeracy, science literacy, and literacy. These are expressed in the Measurement Framework for Schooling in Australia The proportion of students achieving at or above the proficient standard (defined as Level 3) on the OECD PISA combined mathematics, reading, and science scale. No numeric target is set
Belgium – (Flemish community)	The indicator "Share of 15 year olds performing at level or below in reading literacy" is used in the Flemish "Pact2020" – a future-oriented action plan that was agreed by all Flemish social partners in 2009. The indicator is used to monitor an overarching goal of improving the quality of life and reducing poverty. Specifically, the PISA indicator is referred to in the context of literacy. As the target concerns literacy of the whole population, no specific target has been set for the PISA indicator
Belgium (French community)	In the *Contrat pour l'école*, which is a set of goals assigned to the education system on the basis of a broad consultation of the educative community, PISA is mentioned several times. Some of the targets for 2013 are linked to PISA: - The students' results in reading, mathematics, and science should at least reach and preferably surpass the OECD average, and the proportion of weak students should decrease - The between-school variance in student performance should decrease from 56% to 40% and the school segregation level should be less than 40% - The variance in results in the main subjects explained by the track should progressively be reduced
Canada	Some Canadian provinces have expressed PISA-related performance targets in general terms, such as "improving PISA score" or "improving PISA ranking"
Denmark	Rank – a goal of Denmark is to be in the top five in PISA. The goal was set by the Danish Prime Minister in January 2010
Finland	The goal for national performance for each domain, expressed as a range of PISA scores. The goal is set in the state budget by the government and approved by the parliament
France	For PISA 2012, the target is 17% for low-achieving readers
Ireland	In the national literacy and numeracy strategy, target-setting on the basis of PISA is included as follows: - Increase the percentage of 15-year-old students performing at or above Level 4 (i.e. at the highest levels) in PISA reading literacy and numeracy tests by at least five percentage points by 2020 - Halve the percentage of 15-year-old students performing at or below Level 1 (the lowest level) in PISA reading literacy and numeracy tests by 2020
Israel	Improve Israel's absolute and relative standing on the PISA scale. Increase the percentage of students at the upper part of scales, and reduce the percentage of students at the lower end of the scales
Japan	The government established the "New Growth Strategy" on June 18, 2010, which included various goals to be achieved by the year 2020. PISA is referred to in one of the strategy's goals: to see Japan's overall student performance at the top level among the participating countries. The aim is also to reduce the number of poor performers and increase the number of high performers; make the mean scores of each domain close to those of the top performing countries; and increase the proportion of students who respond positively to the attitudes- and interest-related items to above-average levels

(Continued)

Table 20.1 (Continued)

Country	Targets/indicators
Mexico	Objective 1 of the Education Sector Programme 2007–2012 establishes as a goal for 2012 to raise performance on PISA to 435 points as an average for both mathematics and reading, taking the average score of 392 points, attained in PISA 2006, as the base. The Agreement for the Articulation of Basic Education asserts that the whole curriculum should set a vision for 2021 that includes generalizing the competencies described at PISA Level 3; eliminating the gap between the students who perform below Level 2 and those who perform at or above that level
Poland	Polish education strategy seeks to reduce the number of low achievers in reading, math, and science as defined by the ET 2020 benchmark
The Netherlands	Raise average scores in three PISA domains and increase number of students at highest proficiency levels
Slovak Republic	The Ministry of Education sets its performance targets in relation to performance of the country on PISA. The Ministry, as sole stakeholder, sets the targets with the aim of achieving the OECD average or better in the following round
Slovenia	There are no officially set performance targets based on PISA. However, the 2011 White Paper on Education states that Slovenia should rank in the top third of developed countries/economies in PISA-like assessments
Turkey	National performance targets are determined according to the country's score on PISA and the OECD average
Wales	The Minister has voiced aspirations for improvement in PISA performance and PISA-related skills

among those born in the 1970s. That is not because completion rates in the USA declined, but because they have risen so much faster in many other countries. Two generations ago, South Korea had the economic output of Afghanistan today and was at rank 24 in terms of schooling output among today's OECD countries. Today it is the top performer in terms of the proportion of successful school leavers, with 96% of an age cohort obtaining a high school degree/qualification. In college education, the pace of change has been even more dramatic, and so has been its impact on the relative standing of countries. Within less than a decade, the USA has slipped from first to 15th rank in terms of the proportion of the relevant age cohort graduating from college. The point is that, while progress in a national perspective matters, in a global framework, an internationally comparative perspective is having a growing impact not just on public policy, but on institutional behavior too.

A Tool for the Political Economy of Reform

Last but not least, international comparisons can support the political economy of reform. For example, in the 2007 Mexican national survey of parents 77% of parents interviewed reported that the quality of educational services provided by their children's school was good or very good even though, measured by OECD's PISA 2006 assessment, roughly half of the Mexican 15 year olds who are enrolled in school performed at or below the lowest level of proficiency established by PISA (OECD 2010a). There may be many reasons for such a discrepancy between perceived educational quality and performance on international comparisons. For example, in part this may be due to the fact that the educational services which Mexican children receive are significantly enhanced over the quality of schooling that their parents experienced. However, the point here is that justifying the investment of public resources into areas for which there seems no public demand poses difficult challenges for the political economy of reform. One response by the Mexican presidential office has been to include a "PISA performance target" in the new Mexican reform plan. This internationally benchmarked performance target will serve to highlight the gap between national performance and international standards and monitor how educational improvement feeds into closing this gap. It is associated with a reform trajectory and delivery chain of support systems, incentive structures as well as with improved access to professional development to assist school leaders and teachers in meeting the target, with much of this drawing on the experience of other countries. Brazil has taken a similar route, providing each secondary school with information on the level of progress that is needed to perform at the OECD average performance level on PISA in 2021.

Japan is one of the best performing education systems on international comparisons. However, PISA revealed that while students tended to do very well on tasks that require reproducing subject matter content, they did much less well on open-ended constructed tasks requiring them to demonstrate their capacity to extrapolate from what they know and apply their knowledge in novel settings. Conveying that to parents and a general public who are used to certain types of tests poses a challenge for the political economy of reform too. The policy response in Japan has been to incorporate "PISA-type" open-constructed tasks into the national assessment, with the aim that skills that are considered important become valued in the education system. Similarly, Korea has recently incorporated advanced PISA-type literacy tasks in its university entrance examinations, in order to enhance excellence in the capacity of its students to access, manage, integrate, and evaluate written material. In both countries, these changes represent transformational change, which would have been much harder to imagine without the challenges revealed by PISA.

Conclusions

In a globalized world, the yardsticks for public policy in education are no longer national goals or standards alone, but increasingly the performance of the most successful education systems internationally. International comparisons can be a powerful instrument for policy reform and transformational change as they allow education systems to look at themselves in the light of intended, implemented, and achieved policies elsewhere. They can show what is possible in education, in terms of quality, equity, and efficiency in educational services, and they can foster better understanding of how different education systems address similar problems. Most importantly, by providing an opportunity for policy-makers and practitioners to look beyond the experiences evident in their own systems and thus to reflect on some of the paradigms and beliefs underlying these, they hold out the promise of transformational change. The example of PISA shows that data can be more influential than administrative control or financial subsidy through which we traditionally shape education policy and practice.

Knowing what successful systems are doing does, of course, not yet tell how to improve education. That is where the limits of cross-sectional comparisons like PISA are and where other forms of research need to advance the field. International comparisons are never easy and they are not perfect; in fact numerous academics have pointed out the limits of international large-scale assessments such as PISA (e.g. Pedró 2012). But that is why PISA does not venture into telling countries what they should do, but its strength lies in telling countries what everybody else around is doing and with what success.

Governments cannot simply copy and paste policies and practices that are successful in other contexts, but they can and do learn from studying and analyzing what their peers have labored with and successfully adapted to their own context. While some times countries share more with neighbors or those with a common language and culture, the experience of all countries is fertile ground for useful and important experiences for those that are quick to learn and adapt.

While the development of international comparisons is fraught with difficulties and their comparability remains open to challenges, cultural differences among individuals, institutions, and systems should not suffice as a justification to reject their use, given that the success of individuals and nations increasingly depends on their global competitiveness. The world today is indifferent to tradition and past reputations, unforgiving of frailty and ignorant of custom or practice. Success will go to those individuals, institutions, and countries that are swift to adapt, slow to complain, and open to change. The task for governments will be to ensure that their citizens, institutions, and education systems rise to this challenge and international comparisons can provide useful instruments to this end.

References

Breakspear, S. 2012. *The Policy Impact of PISA: An Exploration of the Normative Effects of International Benchmarking in School System Performance*. OECD Education Working Papers, No. 71. Paris: OECD.

Eisner, E.W. 1996. *Cognition and Curriculum Reconsidered (second edition)*. New York: Teachers College Press.

Ertl, H. 2006. "Educational Standards and the Changing Discourse on Education: The Reception and Consequences of the PISA Study in Germany". *Oxford Review of Education*, 32(5): 619–634.

Douglass, J.A., Thomson, G., and Zhao, C. 2012, February. *Searching for the Holy Grail of Learning Outcomes*. CSHE.3.12. Retrieved from: www.cshe.berkeley.edu/sites/default/files/shared/publications/docs/ROPS.JD.GT.MZ.CLA&AHELO.2.21.2012.pdf (accessed November 30, 2015).

Grek, S. 2009. "Governing by Numbers: the PISA 'Effect' in Europe." *Journal of Education Policy*, 24(1): 23–37.

Meyer, H.D. and K. Schiller. 2013. "Gauging the Role of Non-Educational Effects in Large-Scale Assessments: Socio-Economics, Culture and PISA Outcomes." *PISA, Power, and Policy. The Emergence of Global Educational Governance*, edited by H.D Meyer and A. Benavot, 207–224. Oxford: Symposium Books.

OECD. 2011. *PISA Technical Report*. Paris: OECD.

OECD. 2010a. *PISA 2009 Results: What Students Know and Can Do. Student Performance in Reading, Mathematics and Science. Volume I*. Paris: OECD.

Pedró, F. 2012. "Deconstructing PISA's Bridges: From Results Analysis to Political Prescriptions." *Revista Española de Educación Comparada*, 19: 139–172.

Chapter 21

Dragon and the Tiger Cubs: China–ASEAN Relations in Higher Education

Rui Yang and Jingyun Yao

Introduction

Since the late 1980s, there has been a resurgence of regionalism in global politics. Fresh challenges are created and prospects for new alliances are opened up, often on a regional basis (Hurrell 1995; Jayasuriya 2003). As a symptom of a broader rescaling of the governance of higher education institutions (Jayasuriya and Robertson 2010), regionalism is becoming evident in East and South East Asian higher education, as shown by a rising ASEAN+3 higher education community.[1] Higher institutions in the region build up their community via alliances in a context of the existing "hegemonic" global system (Mundy and Iga 2003). They have shown signs of rescaling through regulatory regionalism (Jayasuriya and Robertson 2010). Their pragmatic and effective approaches in regional integration challenge conventional conceptions of international relations (Mundy 2007).

Realizing the benefits inherent in regional integration, China has taken a role in strengthening regional organizations and in energizing the region's economy (Vogel 2010). With US foreign policy turning toward Asia, China adjusts its policy on South East Asia to give priority to working closely with its ASEAN neighbors. Since the late 1990s, China's diplomatic efforts began to pay more attention to ties with neighboring countries, expanding the traditional *mu lin you hao* (good neighbor and friendliness) approach to the *you lin*, *an lin*, *fu lin* (amicable, peaceful, and prosperous neighborhood) approach. The shift becomes more evident, as China claims it is "a member of the Asian family" and "committed to the policy of building good-neighborliness and friendship and will be a good friend and good partner of Asian countries forever" (Wu 2009).

China's policy toward ASEAN is more political than economic. Strong "natural" economic complementarities between China and South East Asia are absent (Wong and Chan 2003), and China's trade and investment in the region is much less than in

The Handbook of Global Education Policy, First Edition.
Edited by Karen Mundy, Andy Green, Bob Lingard, and Antoni Verger.
© 2016 John Wiley & Sons, Ltd. Published 2016 by John Wiley & Sons, Ltd.

Japan, South Korea, and Taiwan, for instance (UNCTAD 2004). It is the desire to dispel the impression of China as a threat in the region that has moved Beijing to develop its "good neighborliness" policy (Chin and Stubbs 2011). Demonstrating benign international economic leadership and providing tangible and rhetorical support to the region became an essential element of China's strategy from the late 1990s and early 2000s (Solis and Katada 2007).

Despite some recent work (Welch and Yang 2011; Welch 2012), China–ASEAN relations in higher education have remained under-researched since contemporary theories of higher education internationalization (Knight and de Wit 1995; Knight 2008) tend to focus on Western developed countries as prime movers and their relations with national flagship institutions in developing countries. The interactions between China and ASEAN states are, however, multidimensional, often involving "quiet achiever" institutions in China's less developed South West. Most collaboration and exchange in higher education between China and ASEAN countries (except Singapore) are found in the provinces neighboring ASEAN countries (Welch and Yang 2011). Such layered scenarios of China–ASEAN integration in higher education could be better discussed by borrowing theories of regionalism and global governance.

This chapter selects China's disadvantaged Guizhou province to depict a lively picture of regionalization in higher education. It argues that internationalization of higher education between China's South West and ASEAN has been facilitated by supranational and regional initiatives. In addition to the literature and governmental and institutional policy documents, it relies on empirical data collected via 19 semi-structured interviews conducted in Guizhou by the authors during October–November 2013 with actors directly involved in educational cooperation and exchange between Guizhou and ASEAN countries. They included 11 senior and middle level university administrators, two departmental heads from the provincial education bureau, three Chinese teachers, two teachers from ASEAN countries, and one course coordinator. Among them 11 were female.

East and South East Asian Regionalism under Substantial Chinese Influence

Regionalism is, like globalization, one of the phenomena that shape more determinately today's world order. Driven by regional governments, it refers to the expression of a particular regional identity and collective action within a geographical region.[2] It means increased transactions in a defined geographical space combined with the development of collective institutions and a common identity (Fawcett 2004). In contrast, *regionalization* is a bottom-up approach, often spontaneous and driven by interest. It is the development of increased commercial and human transactions in a certain geographical region that gradually transform perceptions of regional operations. The development of both regional and global governance structures has given it increasing impetus (Robertson 2008).

East and South East Asians have felt a strong need to institutionalize regional cooperation. Ideas about East Asian regionalism emerged in 1990 when the then Malaysian Prime Minister, Mahathir proposed the East Asian Economic Group, which later changed into the East Asian Economic Caucus. East Asia here covers what is conventionally defined as East and South East Asia. Former Singaporean Prime Minister, Goh Chok Tong, acknowledged in his address at the East Asia Economic Summit in 2002 that "a nascent sense of an East Asian community" was growing. According to him, ASEAN and three North East Asian countries should be committed to crystallizing a common vision on the nature and direction of East Asian cooperation and regionalism (Terada 2004). After decades of commercial and industrial regionalization, regional networking, and experimentation with regional institutions, regional cooperation in East and South East Asia has entered a new era of community building. ASEAN+3 and the East Asia Summit are the main forums of Asian regionalism.

However, East Asian regionalism has not been immune from controversies. Some describe it as a moving train with no clear final destination. According to some accounts, the train even appears to have stalled (Zhang 2010). Characterized by its bottom-up process and market forces (Hastiadi 2011), it is driven mainly by the need for economic and security cooperation. East Asia's increased economic interdependence over the past few decades has been heavily dominated by the markets rather than by government policies. Coordinated intergovernmental initiatives for cooperation, including the creation of regional institutions, have lagged behind (Capannelli 2011). Its economic integration has not been guided by a clear strategy for creating a unity across the countries in the region (ADB 2008). Regional integration relies much on non-state actors.

South East Asia, home to one of the most enduring intergovernmental organizations outside Europe, displays a much greater interest in developing a wider, more ambitious and inclusive institutional architecture than history might lead one to suspect. It is very much a product of the geographical circumstances. A core paradox of its regionalism is that leaders of four or five South East Asian nations, acting in the name of ASEAN and with the acquiescence of ASEAN's other members, control the basic tone, scope, speed, and direction of the integration movement. Under its roof some very creative diplomacy is taking place (Frost 2008). It hopes to envision its region as "One Vision, One Identity, One Community" in the near future. Well positioned in the trend toward regionalism, it is an indispensable actor at the time of political compromise especially against a backdrop of competition for influence between China and Japan.

Nevertheless, South East Asia faces a number of difficulties in regional integration and its institutional architecture is still not adequate. External forces hastened the birth of the South East Asian regionalism after the Cold War. Even the term South East Asia as a region is fundamentally a colonial and Cold War construct (Acharya 2000). The implementation of regionalism has been much hindered by the lack of willingness of ASEAN states due to their domestic politics. Political stability has always been the first priority for ASEAN states, even at the expense of economic gains. Its bottom-up process alone is not sufficient. A more institutionalized approach is needed in order to make the regionalism solid and sustainable. Although the leaders of ASEAN+3 countries have repeatedly held meetings, the top-down process has still not reached its potential, as observed by an interviewee (an expert on ASEAN) in our study as follows:

> In Asia, regionalization has been achieved most by ASEAN, and Indonesia has been the leader of ASEAN. Indonesian long-term political instability made ASEAN a host of dragons without a head (*qun long wu shou*) ... regionalization has never been more important for all partners, not only in trade, but also in culture, health and education. (Interview 4)

Regional relations matter, and have particular resonance in East and South East Asia, given their dynamic relations with China: a heady mix of cooperation and competition, including in higher education. One reason for the wave of East and South East Asian regionalism is the rise of China (Liu 2008). China is becoming the leading player in the process of regionalism; despite this, ASEAN and other Asian countries hope that the region will not be dominated by a single big power. Meanwhile, some hedging against China's rise is evident, as illustrated in China's border disputes with some immediate South East Asian neighbors.

With a long history of communicating with ASEAN countries, China realizes ASEAN's pivotal role in regional groupings, values ASEAN's regional integration effort, and adheres to it with keen commitments such as the ASEAN–China Free Trade Agreement. It pushes the regional agenda forward, engages bickering parties within the regional multilateral context, and initiates deeper and more comprehensive cooperation. China's recent improvement in its integration with ASEAN countries helps China advance well into the region. Over the past decade or so, China has developed systematic ways of interacting with ASEAN countries. As China's economic growth becomes an engine of regional economic development, the region has benefitted from trading with China.

Most recently, China has conducted new ways of providing foreign aid to ASEAN members without any penalties attached, and reduced difficulties for those who are in need and previously could apply only to Western-dominated international financial institutions for aid. China's acceptance by ASEAN has dramatically broadened the landscape of regionalism. Its strategic advance into the region is to lead to transformation of geopolitical landscape in the region, with profound regional and even global implications, and strong impact on the direction of long-term strategic development for decades to come.

Characterized by dynamic economic cooperation and both strategic cooperation and competition, East and South East Asian regionalism is entering into another phase to develop new intra-Asian mechanisms, while the old trans-Pacific mechanisms continue to exist. Although the USA retains its dominance in the region, the rise of China and the emergence of East and South East Asian regionalism provide much of the momentum and direction for regional development. Since the turn of the new century, the growing power of China and the repositioning of ASEAN have undoubtedly shifted the center of gravity of East Asian regionalism from the USA to China.

Higher Education Integration in East and South East Asia

Higher education institutions worldwide face increasingly similar issues that breach national borders, and require concerted regional efforts. Over the past decade or so, higher education has explicitly been incorporated into regional economic and political agendas, with the emergence of regional-scale higher education visions, policies, and programs (Olds and Robertson 2011). The development of regional higher education in world regions challenges national values and cultures. It calls for new regional instruments that can promote mutual understanding while helping to boost economic and educational competitiveness in emerging knowledge economies. Countries in a region can collaborate to enhance higher education quality and facilitate student mobility through mechanisms such as quality assurance, accreditation, credit transfer, and qualifications recognition.

Regional associations, governments and higher education institutions seek to extend opportunities for educational cooperation. Regional organizations are an expression of educational coordination. ASEAN has increased its members from five to ten, with China as one of the associated "+3." Asia-Pacific Economic Cooperation (APEC) membership increased from 12 in 1989 to 21 in 1997. Each organization includes elements devoted to higher education. Founded in 1961, the United Nations Educational, Scientific and Cultural Organization (UNESCO) Regional Bureau builds networks and capacity in regional higher education, including promoting greater mobility and recognition of higher education qualifications, often in tandem with the Southeast Asian Ministers for Education Organization-Regional Institute for Higher Education. The World Bank and the Asian Development Bank also play influential roles in coordinating regional approaches to higher education (Jakobi 2007).

Some non-regional international organizations are influential in South East Asia. *Education at a Glance*, published by the Organisation for Economic Co-operation and Development (OECD) annually, is an important source of educational indicators covering non-member Asian countries. While the OECD is yet to take an interest in China–ASEAN linkages, their emphasis on international standards provides an impetus for greater convergence in East Asia. Its rating and ranking activities, scientifically researched by experts and presented in an accessible manner, put some Asian states under pressure to import and apply models for education developed in other (usually developed) countries (Martens 2007). UNESCO's Institute for Statistics, based in Montreal, performs a similar function. It is, however, important to note that the traffic is increasingly less one way.

Another form of regionalization in higher education is through establishing associations within the Asia-Pacific. The University Mobility in the Asia-Pacific was established in 1993 to boost cooperation among countries in the Asian Pacific through enhanced international understanding and increased university student and staff mobility. Its activities strengthen cooperation among higher education institutions in the region. The Asia-Pacific Association for International Education was established in 2004 to advocate international education and extend its development. It promotes closer relations and exchanges among Asia-Pacific universities. The Asia-Pacific Quality Network, founded in light of the Brisbane Communiqué, includes Malaysia, Singapore, Vietnam, and China.

Realizing that the creation of a common higher education space is a critical step toward their greater regional integration objective, ASEAN members have explored regional collaboration in higher education (de Prado Yepes 2007). The 1992 summit reaffirmed ASEAN studies and an ASEAN University as priorities for education cooperation, and urged implementation of student exchanges at secondary and tertiary levels as a strategy for promoting ASEAN awareness. A key element was the ASEAN University Network as an inter-university cooperation network with member from ten ASEAN countries (ANU 2008). The Association of Pacific Rim Universities was established in 1997 as a consortium of major research universities in the Asia-Pacific region, with 42 higher education institutions as members, including eight from China (Welch 2011). Its initiatives include important components that act as epistemic and, to a degree, cultural bridges between China and ASEAN.

Based on the agreement on trade in services signed by China and ASEAN in 2007 under the ASEAN–China Free Trade Zone, education can be "traded" transnationally within the region. Meanwhile, non-governmental organizations (NGOs) such as the Association of Southeast Asian Institutions of Higher Learning foster cooperation among member institutions, particularly through regional fellowships and academic exchange programs. The annual Asian University Presidents Forum serves as a platform for the presidents of the member institutions to discuss matters relating to the promotion of international academic collaborations as well as exchange of information and expertise. China's Guangdong University of Foreign Studies hosted the Forum in 2003. Since then, it has been organized annually, hosted and chaired by member universities on a rotational basis. Similarly, the Presidents' Forum of Southeast and South Asia and Taiwan Universities was set up to provide a venue for academics to share their experiences and to improve higher education and international cooperation in the region. In 2008, the Southeast Asian Higher Education Area was launched, pointing to the desire to frame and construct regional agendas and architectures (Olds and Robertson 2011).

China–ASEAN Relations in Higher Education

China pays increasing attention to its South East Asia neighbors. Since the 1990s, China has strengthened its relations with ASEAN states in the fields of foreign aid, trade, finance, infrastructure, business, labor, the environment, and development, as well as in tourism. Its cultural and educational diplomacy is intricate and comprehensive, operating at various levels: establishing firm political and financial connections with South East Asian governments through development aid; exploring a comprehensive cooperative framework through FTA-plus development plans; enhancing cultural attractiveness and promoting pro-China understanding among ASEAN states by means of quasi-governmental projects; and expanding the influence of the private sector and its relations with Chinese overseas and local business networks in South East Asia. Our study finds a surprisingly open attitude of the Chinese toward political issues, as one senior provincial official remarked:

> Working with ASEAN (countries) is politically significant for us. After the Cold War, ASEAN countries have become more independent in their foreign policy. They could be our strategic partners. (Interview 6)

As the social and economic links between the two sides continue to strengthen, exchange and cooperation deepen, moving beyond the higher education sector. Recently, China is projecting its educational services into ASEAN members. China–ASEAN interactions in higher education have increased in both quantity and quality. China offers programs either independently or in collaboration with local institutions in nearly all ASEAN countries. Both the quantity and quality of Chinese language use continue to increase. Since 2004 the number of ASEAN students in China has increased by at least ten times, to about 40,000 in 2012 (Li 2013). The Chinese government provides scholarships to foreign citizens to study in China. The overwhelming majority of the foreign students enrolled in Chinese universities and colleges came from Asia, including South East Asia.[3]

Echoing the mainstream internationalization practice in higher education that focuses on educational exchange with developed countries, there is a hierarchy of internationalization between China and ASEAN members: while Singapore's relations with China are strongest, with dozens of partnerships with key Chinese institutions, other ASEAN members are positioned less favorably with much less well known institutions in China, although they all see China as a major priority (Welch 2011). Within China, the most substantial collaboration and exchange in higher education between China and ASEAN countries other than Singapore are found in the provinces neighboring ASEAN members. Although remaining low profile, China's regional higher institutions in the less economically developed South Western region have been increasingly involved in international cooperation activities.

For ASEAN countries, regional integration in higher education grows in importance, as China becomes a global force in science. China is currently ranked second after the USA in international indices of scientific output (UNESCO 2010). Thus ASEAN members and their higher education institutions see China as an attractive partner, especially its top tier universities. An example of China's wider strategy of strengthening itself through human capital, substantial investment in fostering a few elite research-intensive universities via national projects such as *211* and *985* has paid off,[4] and offers great opportunities for extending cooperation with ASEAN.

The Case of Guizhou

China's interactions with ASEAN are concentrated in its South West. Previously, ASEAN students were concentrated in Guangdong, Guangxi, and Yunnan provinces. While students from Thailand, Burma, Vietnam, and Laos preferred Yunnan, those from Indonesia, the Philippines, Malaysia, and Cambodia tended to choose Guangdong, and those from Vietnam tended to choose Guangxi. With its fast development, Guangdong has shifted its attention to wealthy Western countries. Costs have also increased considerably in Guangdong. ASEAN members thus prefer cheaper supplies and similar developmental needs in Guangxi, Yunnan, and Guizhou.

Located in China's South West, Guizhou has the frontier character of other South Western plateau lands: rough topography, difficult communication, and consequent isolation. It is demographically one of China's most diverse provinces, with ethnic minority groups accounting for more than 37% of its population. Many of such ethnic minority groups share the same or similar cultural traditions and religious beliefs with the peoples in ASEAN countries. It has been one of China's poorest and most disadvantaged provinces. Its nominal GDP for 2012 and per capita GDP ranked last amongst China's 31 provinces. However, Guizhou's economic development has accelerated recently. Its GDP grew by 13.6% in 2012 (Gao and Yang 2012). Excepting Brunei and Cambodia, all ASEAN countries have invested in Guizhou. ASEAN countries are Guizhou's largest trade partner.

Guizhou has one of the highest rates of illiteracy in China, especially among its many minority peoples. There are 47 higher education institutions located in various parts of the province with the best ones concentrated in Guiyang. Eighteen institutions offer undergraduate degrees and above. Among them, Guizhou University is the only national key institution, gaining approval from the Ministry to offer doctoral programs in 2013. Guizhou Normal University and Guizhou Nationalities University each has one program at doctoral level. Guiyang Medical University has the only doctoral program in medical sciences. Guizhou University of Finance and Economics, Guiyang College of Traditional Chinese Medicine, and Zunyi Medical University offer Master's programs. There are 29 institutions offering two to three-year associate degree programs. Among them three are private.

Strategic Policy Design

Limited by various factors, internationalization has long been the weakest link of Guizhou's higher education. However, with Guizhou University taking the lead, Guizhou has recently identified regional integration with ASEAN countries as an important breakthrough (Gao 2012) and the strategy has won support from both the central and provincial governments. Guizhou aims to become a launchpad for China's integration with ASEAN countries in higher education. By so doing, it hopes to exploit fully its resources and upgrade its level of internationalization of higher education.

The annual China–ASEAN Education Cooperation Week is a clear example of Guizhou's strategic policy-making. From 2008, Guizhou has successfully implemented and encouraged ASEAN countries to participate in the event. Participants come from all ASEAN countries. Many ASEAN higher education institutions send their senior administrators and established scholars to attend the forums organized during the week. The inaugural China–ASEAN Education Minister Roundtable Conference was held as part of the third event in 2010. During these events, ASEAN education ministers discussed with China how to widen cooperation and exchanges in higher education and strengthen regional development. Described as a mark of a new stage in China–ASEAN educational exchanges, the event's sub-themes included improving the quality of higher education and promoting regional economic development and talents cultivation. Higher education was to play its part in the sustainable development of a low-carbon economy, and in strengthening China–ASEAN education cooperation and exchange measures, including inter-collegiate cooperation, student exchanges, and language teaching (Xinhua News 2010).

While the week was hosted mainly by Guizhou University, other local universities had the chance to take initiatives. During the fourth event in 2012, Guizhou Normal University co-hosted the China-ASEAN Youth and Sports Culture Festival with the Asian University Sports Federation. The University also established a sister school relationship with Dhurakij Pundit University in Thailand. At the same time, Guizhou University of Finance and Economics hosted the China–ASEAN Government, Industry and Academia Cooperation Forum, and signed agreements on educational exchange with four Thai universities. Guizhou Nationalities University hosted a China–ASEAN Cross-Cultural Forum and proposed to establish professional associations for studies in regional economy, language, and culture between China and ASEAN countries (Gao 2012).

Strategic planning of educational exchange and cooperation with ASEAN countries has always been tailor-made in Guizhou. A number of other measures have been employed to implement the strategy. The China–ASEAN Information Network, for example, is a dedicated website set up for China–ASEAN communication. Strategically designed policy measures have achieved success. A Lao student enrolled in an undergraduate program in law at Guizhou University was reported as making the following remarks:

> I am grateful for my study opportunity provided by China government. I am also grateful for the education I receive at Guizhou University and for the care for ASEAN students. The annual Week works as a bridge between Chinese and ASEAN students to understand and learn from each other. (Fu 2011, 28)

Views from the Chinese side are equally positive, as shown by the following remarks by a senior administrator from the provincial education bureau:

> Even within China, we are not the most internationalized. So we identify ASEAN as our target. China is integrating actively with ASEAN, and this creates great opportunities for us. However, even compared to others in the region, we are not the closest to ASEAN, neither geographically nor culturally. We have to figure out our ways to highlight Guizhou. With strong support from our governments, Guizhou has invented a number of approaches such as China–ASEAN Education Cooperation Week and China–ASEAN Information Network. By far, we are happy with the effects. We are expecting far more in the future. (Interview 6)

Win–win Cooperation Based on Complementary Relations

Guizhou–ASEAN educational cooperation is based on complementary relations. Ranging from climate to habits and customs, ASEAN countries share much with Guizhou. ASEAN students find it easy to live and study in Guizhou. Low cost of living is another reason. Most ASEAN countries are not industrialized, with great demand for professional personnel in agriculture, forestry, animal husbandry, and tourism. Guizhou has strengths in these fields and can provide them with appropriate educational services. A further factor is shared cultural roots. Most ASEAN countries have been influenced by Confucianism and Buddhism, with Chinese characters widely used. Their festivals and customs are similar to those of Guizhou ethnic minority groups. This explains why numbers of ASEAN students studying in China grow fast. The cultural and geographical proximity has led to great demand for the China-related subjects including language, economy, and law. These factors work together to create a combined effect.

On the Chinese side, benefits are evident and go beyond the economic dimension. Indeed, although China's approach to South East Asian integration is largely economic, its purpose is mainly political, directed at enhancing cultural and political influence (Chin and Stubbs 2011). ASEAN has become politically significant for Chinese national and provincial governments as well as for China's regional higher education institutions. Such an understanding has been widely shared in Guizhou among those directly involved in education integration with ASEAN countries, as illustrated by the following remarks from a senior and a middle-level university administrator, respectively:

> We are geographically well positioned to integrate with ASEAN countries. But more importantly, we have long historical links and cultural kinship with them. Many of our ethnic minorities in this region share the same or similar language and culture with them. (Interview 2)

> We have great difficulty in collaborating with the most developed countries such as the US. They don't pay attention to us. Working with them is on one hand too remote for us, and on the other expensive. There's a big gap between us. It's a different story with ASEAN countries, except the National University of Singapore who sees itself a crane standing among chickens. We have already built a good platform and foundation to work with ASEAN universities based on mutual willingness and recognition. It's much easier – we accept each other easily, cost is low, and cultures and values are similar. (Interview 1)

Talking more specifically from an education perspective, one senior university administrator in charge of international exchange expressed similar opinions:

> Our educational cooperation with ASEAN countries is based on mutual benefits. Our engineering and science are better, but in environmental studies, oceanography, agriculture, forestry and fishery, much could be learned mutually. We share so much. Unlike Westerners who eat and study wheat, for example, people in ASEAN countries eat and study rice, just like us. We should not focus only on the West. We need a more balanced view, to have the entire world in perspective. So, ASEAN countries are important. (Interview 2)

However, China has often sacrificed economic benefits for political gains. Its discrepancy between economic approaches and political purposes adds complexity to South East regionalization and creates difficulties for sustainable cooperation with ASEAN, as shown by the following comments:

> Although cost of living in Guizhou is low by Chinese standards, it appears to be too high for many ASEAN citizens. Similarly, at institutional level, some Vietnamese and Laos universities could not start or sustain our proposed collaboration simply because of the cost, although we have already offered substantial discount and waiver of tuition and even accommodation. (Interview 8)
>
> We face a number of difficulties in our cooperation with ASEAN countries. Our students are not very keen to study there. If so, their target would be first Singapore and second Malaysia. Their ideal destination is still Western countries. Finance is a major reason. Our students are usually from less wealthy families. There have been few scholarships by ASEAN countries, and our government scholarships are still limited in number. (Interview 3)

Training and Research Bases

Universities in Guizhou are aware that in order to attract ASEAN students and institutions, they have to build up their own strength. With support from government, recent developments have been reoriented to ASEAN societies. In May 2005, Guizhou University was designated by the Ministry of Education as one of the bases for China's foreign education aid, with a special focus on ASEAN countries. As such it coordinated programs with ASEAN states, and provided those preparing to go to ASEAN countries with language training. Supported strongly by the Ministry of Education and the provincial governments, Guizhou University took concerted action to establish China's first center for ASEAN studies. With a concentration of nationally and internationally renowned ASEAN experts, the center now conduct studies on ASEAN countries from political, economic, cultural, educational, and religious perspectives. Over time it has become an important knowledge base for national and provincial policy-making, and was designated by the Ministry of Education in 2012 as the national base for ASEAN studies, with substantial funding. Other universities have followed suit. In 2012, Guizhou Electric Vocational College was designated as one of the nation's first ten China–ASEAN training bases. These bases also promote economic cooperation between China and ASEAN countries. For instance, they recently worked with Chinese enterprises to donate 10 million RMB worth of sport equipment to ASEAN societies.

Flows of Students and Teachers

Flows of people facilitate regional integration. Regionalism has the capacity to deliberately shape patterns of human mobility (Olds and Robertson 2011). The most evident development in Guizhou–ASEAN higher education integration is the rapid increase in the flow of people across borders. The Chinese government is increasing scholarships to foreign citizens to study in China. For example, 36,943 (9.8%) of the 377,054 international students China hosted in 2014 were on Chinese government scholarships, which were 3621 more than the number in 2013 (CAFSA 2015). As stated repeatedly by the Chinese officials, China plans to expand its numbers of international students to 500,000 by 2020, and promises to offer more scholarships to foreign citizens (Hao 2009). Many of these would go to ASEAN students. Starting from 2008, China has encouraged ASEAN students to study in the universities in their neighboring Chinese provinces or in the best universities in China's inland. A recently announced scheme often called the "Double 100,000 Program" aims to increase the number of ASEAN students in China and Chinese students in ASEAN to 100,000 (Liu 2011).

Since 2008, Guizhou University, entrusted by the Ministry of Education to manage Chinese government scholarships for ASEAN students, started to enroll ASEAN students to study for degrees and in the period normally had a current enrolment of around 230 ASEAN students, of whom over 35% were studying for degrees. Tongren Polytechnic, responding to central government's call for the double 100,000 goal, also established Fanjing Mountain scholarships for ASEAN students. In 2011, the Polytechnic offered the scholarship to 12 Lao students. By 2012, the number had increased to 160 (Zhang and Yang 2012).

The traffic in students is increasingly two-way. Chinese students studying in ASEAN countries grew from 68,510 in 2008 to 82,431 in 2010, while ASEAN students studying in China increased from 3300 in 2000 to 34,735 in 2008, 49,580 in 2010 (Liu 2011), and 54,800 in 2011 (Li 2013). During 2007–2008, Guizhou University sent 450 students to ASEAN countries to study. Among them, 116 were in exchange programs and 205 were on Chinese government scholarships. Priority in selecting candidates to be sent to ASEAN countries include: (a) those with proficiency in a language spoken by ASEAN countries; (b) nominees by institutions with substantial collaboration with ASEAN countries; and (c) special support for ASEAN countries' language and culture programs offered by institutions in China's South Western region.

Another part of the China–ASEAN flow of people is teachers. China proposes, by 2020, to invite 10,000 young teachers, academics, and students from ASEAN countries to participate in exchange activities in language, culture, sports, and arts (Liu 2011). China traditionally dispatches teachers overseas to teach the Chinese language.

Higher institutions in Guizhou have been participating in this exercise. Their destinations are ASEAN countries, in particular Thailand, the Philippines, and Nepal. This includes volunteer Chinese language teachers, who numbered 12 in 2011 and 53 in 2012 (Zhang and Yang 2012).

Flows of people can create profound effects. For instance, a Thai student in tourism management at Guizhou University on a full Chinese government scholarship was reported as describing China as "a passionate, friendly and rapidly-developing country with a rich culture," and said "I am glad to be here to see what the real China is like, as I used to watch Chinese sitcoms to learn Chinese at Siam University" (Wang 2011). However, the flow of people also leads to various challenges as shown by the following comment:

> In general, not many of our students are willing to go to ASEAN (countries) to study. More ASEAN students come to study here. As for teachers, it's difficult for us to send our staff there, and it's even more difficult to have their teachers here at Guizhou. (Interview 7)

Institutional Partnership and Joint Programs

Institutional level exchange and collaboration are becoming regular and frequent. China has agreed to mutually recognize qualifications with Malaysia and Thailand, and plans to clear barriers by further mutual recognition of academic degrees (Liu 2011). It has also signed educational exchange agreements with Singapore, Vietnam, Brunei, Myanmar, Laos, Cambodia, and the Philippines.

Since the 1990s, higher education institutions in Guizhou have inked formal agreements with a wide range of their ASEAN counterparts, covering teacher and student exchange, joint programs, and research collaboration. Guizhou University as the flagship in the province has institutional partnerships with at least 50 ASEAN universities in Brunei, Singapore, Thailand, Vietnam, Malaysia, and Laos.

Recently, there have also been initiatives to set up joint degrees with ASEAN countries to encourage exchange of high level talents enrolled in Master's and doctoral programs. Starting from the field of English language and literature, Guizhou University has had various exchange programs with Siam University and Dhurakij Pundit University in Thailand. It has joint degree programs in English language and literature, animal genetics and animal nutrition with Suranaree University of Technology in Thailand at Master's and doctoral levels. The university has provided the National University of Laos with good breeds of pigs and trains professional farming personnel for Laos (Gao 2012). On the basis of mutual recognition of qualifications, Guizhou University has recently agreed with Hanoi University of Foreign Studies in Vietnam, President University in Indonesia, and Temasek Polytechnic in Singapore to accept students from these countries who are on Chinese government scholarships to study for postgraduate degrees at Guizhou University. It has also signed a number of agreements with the National University of Singapore and Nanyang Technological University in Singapore, and with some Malaysian universities on academic exchange and collaboration (Zhang and Yang 2012).

Benefits of joint programs are evident on both sides. For instance, the joint degree programs in English language and literature with Suranaree University of Technology originally started from Guizhou University. Now similar programs have expanded to other universities and other subject areas. Over ten academic staff members at Guizhou University graduated from such programs, including the Dean of Science with a Thai PhD. Considering the imbalanced academic developments among ASEAN countries, it is not entirely surprising to see the following comments:

> We have cooperation with all ASEAN countries, but our work with Thai universities has been achieving most. (Interview 2)

Concluding Discussion

Although still in its early stages, higher education regionalization in East and South East Asia has demonstrated strong reciprocity, based on deepening relationships, driven by local needs and markets rather than political agreements. However, given the asymmetry of global market, this regionalization has not been able to counterbalance the overall adverse environment for ASEAN higher education development. The flow of students within the region has had little impact on the global movement of students from the South (including ASEAN states) to the North. The quantity and quality of ASEAN regionalization activities cannot be mentioned in the same breath as those achieved in Europe. Indeed, the differences are so striking that they are almost of a different nature.

Aiming at providing rich food for further thought through detailed description, this chapter makes the following observations.

First, since China's first dialogue with ASEAN in 1991, a mutually beneficial China–ASEAN cooperation pattern took shape within two decades. Achievements are reflected in various dimensions including education. They demonstrate that regional and global integration are not replacing multilateralism. Instead, they complement each other. Regional institutions in its less developed areas have mainly achieved China's projection of influence in higher education in South East Asia. Such experiences highlight that internationalization is not always confined to elite higher education institutions. As third- and even fourth-tier institutions within the Chinese system, such "quiet achievers" are hardly visible in global and domestic ranking exercises. Instead, they are largely ignored. However, their down-to-earth contribution to bridging peoples between China and ASEAN countries speaks loudly, and warns us not to lose sight of the bulk of higher education systems.

Second, the progression of South East Asia's regionalism has implications for the way the world governs itself (Liu 2008). Despite some substantial achievements, regional integration in higher education is not immune to challenges. The China–ASEAN experience shows that both state and non-state actors need to be mobilized. While ASEAN countries rely overwhelmingly on non-state actors, China's remarkable success is clearly based on the concerted efforts of both, as well reflected in Liu's (2011) words: "government sets the stage," "higher education institutions act," "mobilizing both the governmental and the non-governmental" to achieve "mutual benefits" and to create "win–win" situations.

Third, over the past five years or so, the China–ASEAN relationship has been held hostage by the conflict over sovereignty in the South China Sea. Bringing in the USA, Japan, or even India to counterbalance China leads to more conflict. The picture for the future does not look necessarily rosy at the moment. China's inconsistency in its

ASEAN policy and its discrepancy between economic means and political purposes adds further complexities. As history shows, the key is to increase the levels of interaction and trust between China and ASEAN. To do so, both sides need to emphasize the aspects of interaction that bind them, such as cultural exchanges and educational ties, to build long-term trust. It is therefore erroneous to overlook integration activities within the region.

Last, but not least in importance, both the practices and their analyses of South East Asian regionalization in higher education are influenced by the European experience. Consciously and unconsciously, the Bologna standards are used as the frame of reference. However, as Verger and Hermo (2010) argue, regional processes such as Bologna and the Southern Common Market (MERCOSUR)-Educativo, are contingent on the distinctive forms of economic and political institutions and forms of educational governance found in these regions. Regional political projects are deeply rooted in domestic structures and tend to respect the interests of domestic coalitions more (Jayasuriya 2003). South East Asian challenges and complexities could not be fully explained by existent European-based theories. This raises questions about the appropriateness of benchmarking the South East Asian experience against the European one.

Notes

1. ASEAN stands for the Association of Southeast Asian Nations. Formed by Indonesia, Malaysia, the Philippines, Singapore, and Thailand on August 8, 1967, it is a political and economic organization of ten countries located in South East Asia. Since its inception, membership has expanded to include Brunei, Cambodia, Laos, Myanmar, and Vietnam. Set up to advance mutual interests in the region, including the acceleration of economic growth, social and cultural progress, and regional peace and stability, it also aims to unite the region and promote greater cross-cultural understanding through various educational and social programs. The "3" refers to ASEAN's associated members in North East Asia – China, Japan, and Korea.
2. The focus of this chapter is on both infra- and supranational levels. The former refers to China's South Western provinces neighboring ASEAN, while the latter points to the interactions among the ASEAN members and between them and China. This is precisely where current theory of higher education internationalization falls short.
3. In 2014, the largest sending countries included Korea, the USA, Thailand, Russia, Japan, Indonesia, India, Pakistan, Kazakhstan, France, Vietnam, Germany, Mongolia, Malaysia, and the United Kingdomin that order (CAFSA 2015).
4. Project 211 is a major initiative, seeking to create a body of around 100 Chinese universities and programs, on which the governments will focus investment in order to catch up with or approach the most advanced level in the world during the 21st century. Initiated on May 4, 1998, Project 985 (code-named after the date year 98 month 5) is a project to promote the Chinese higher education system by founding world class universities in the 21st century.

References

Acharya, A. 2000. *The Quest for Identity: International Relations of Southeast Asia*. Singapore: Oxford University Press.
ASEAN University Network (ANU). 2008. *ASEAN University Network: The Special 12th Anniversary Report*. Bangkok: AUN.

Asian Development Bank (ADB). 2008. *Emerging Asian Regionalism: A Partnership for Shared Prosperity*. Manila: Asian Development Bank.

Capannelli, G. 2011. *Institutions for Economic and Financial Integration in Asia: Trends and Prospects* (ADBI Working Paper 308). Tokyo: Asian Development Bank Institute.

CAFSA (China Association for International Education). "Statistics of International Students 2014." Retrieved from: www.cafsa.org.cn/research/show-1564.html (accessed November 22, 2015).

Chin, G. and R. Stubbs, 2011. "China, Regional Institution-Building and the China-ASEAN Free Trade Area." *Review of International Political Economy*, 18(3): 277–298.

de Prado Yepes, C. 2007. "Regionalization of Higher Education Services in Europe and East Asia." *Asia Europe Journal*, 5(1): 83–92.

Fawcett, L. 2004. "Exploring Regional Domains: A Comparative History of Regionalism." *International Affairs*, 80(3): 429–446.

Frost, E. 2008. *Asia's New Regionalism*. Boulder: Lynne Rienner.

Fu, S. 2011. "Guizhou Deepens Educational Cooperation with ASEAN." *Contemporary Guizhou*, 30: 28–29.

Gao, C. and J. Yang. 2012. "Citibank Praises Guizhou's Economic Growth." *China Daily*, November 30, 2012.

Gao, Y. 2012. "Guizhou University Leads Higher Education Internationalization in Guizhou." Retrieved from: www.gzcpc.com/2012/01/10/33642.html (accessed November 18, 2015).

Hao, P. 2009. "Let's Join Hands for Cooperation and Mutual Benefit." *Form on Education and Culture*, 1: 1–4.

Hastiadi, F. 2011. "The Determinants of East Asian Regionalism." *Finanzas y Política Económica*, 3: 13–26.

Hurrell, A. 1995. "Explaining the Resurgence of Regionalism in World Politics." *Review of International Studies*, 21(4): 331–358.

Jakobi, A. 2007. "Converging Agendas in Education Policy-Lifelong Learning in the World Bank and the International Labor Organization," in *New Arenas of Education Governance*, edited by K. Martens, A. Rusconi, and K. Leuze, 95–114. New York: Palgrave MacMillan.

Jayasuriya, K. 2003. "Governing the Asia Pacific-Beyond the New Regionalism." *Third World Quarterly*, 24(2): 199–215.

Jayasuriya, K. and S. Robertson. 2010. "Regulatory Regionalism and the Governance of Higher Education." *Globalisation, Societies and Education*, 8(1): 1–6.

Knight, J. 2008. "The Internationalization of Higher Education: Are We on the Right Track?" *Academic Matters: The Journal of Higher Education*, October: 5–9.

Knight, J. and H. de Wit. 1995. "Strategies for Internationalization of Higher Education: Historical and Conceptual Perspectives," in *Strategies for Internationalization: A Comparative Study of Australia, Canada, Europe and the United States of America*, edited by Hans de Wit, 5–32. Amsterdam: The EAIE.

Li, T. 2013. "ASEAN Students in China as Public Diplomacy." *Social Sciences in Yunnan*, 5: 29–33.

Liu, B. 2011. "Government Sets the Stage and Higher Education Institutions Act to Mobilize both the Governmental and the Non-governmental to Achieve Mutual Benefits and Win-win Situation." Retrieved from: www.bbght.net/HtmlContent/Detail/a81e0c61-e69e-464c-a8da-3c92a872ec24 (accessed November 18, 2015).

Liu, F.-K. 2008. *Asian Regionalism Strategic Evolution and US Policy in Asia: Some Prospects for Cross-Strait Developments*. Washington DC: Center for Northeast Asia Policy Studies, Brookings Institution.

Martens, K. 2007. "How to Become an Influential Actor," in *New Arenas of Education Governance*, edited by K. Martens, A. Rusconi and K. Leuze, 40–56. New York: Palgrave MacMillan.

Mundy, K. 2007. "Global Governance, Educational Change." *Comparative Education*, 43: 339–357.

Mundy, K. and M. Iga. 2003. "Hegemonic Exceptionalism and Legitimating Bet-Hedging: Paradoxes and Lessons from the US and Japanese Approaches to Education Services under the GATS." *Globalization, Societies and Education*, 1(3): 281–319.

Olds, K. and S. Robertson. 2011. "Regionalism and Higher Education." *Trends and Insights for International Education Leaders*, October: 1–5.

Robertson, S. 2008. "Regionalism, 'Europe/Asia' and Higher Education." *Policy Futures in Education*, 6(6): 719–729.

Solis, M. and S.N. Katada. 2007. "Understanding East Asian Cross-Regionalism: An Analytical Framework." *Pacific Affairs*, 80(2): 229–257.

Terada, T. 2004. "Creating an East Asian Regionalism: The Institutionalization of ASEAN + 3 and China-Japan Directional Leadership." *The Japanese Economy*, 32(2): 64–85.

UNCTAD. 2004. *Trade and Development Report, 2004: Overview*. New York and Geneva: UNCTAD/TDR.

UNESCO. 2010. *UNESCO Science Report 2010*. Paris: UNESCO.

Verger, A. and J.P. Hermo. 2010. "The Governance of Higher Education Regionalization: Comparative Analysis of the Bologna Process and MERCOSUR-Educativo." *Globalization, Societies and Education*, 8(1): 105–120.

Vogel, E. 2010. "Regionalism in Asia." Presentation made to the Japan Institute of International Affairs Conference on the East Asian Community idea in Tokyo, 17 March.

Wang, Y. 2011. "China-ASEAN Education Collaboration on Fast Track." Retrieved from: http://news.xinhuanet.com/english2010/indepth/2011-08/18/c_131058805.htm (accessed November 18, 2015).

Welch, A. 2011. *Higher Education in South East Asia*. London: Routledge.

Welch, A. 2012. "China-ASEAN Relations in Higher Education: An Analytical Framework." *Frontiers of Education in China*, 7(4): 465–485.

Welch, A. and R. Yang. 2011. "A Pearl on the Silk Road? Internationalizing a Regional Chinese University," in *Globalization's Influence upon the Internationalization of East Asian Higher Education Institutes*, edited by J. Palmer, A. Roberts, Y.H. Cho and G. Ching, 63–89. New York: Palgrave Macmillan.

Wong, J. and S. Chan. 2003. "China-ASEAN Free Trade Agreement: Shaping Future Economic Relations." *Asian Survey*, 43(3): 506–526.

Wu, X. 2009. "Chinese Perspectives on Building an East Asian Community in the Twenty-First Century," In *Asia's New Multilateralism*, edited by M.J. Green and B. Gill, 55–77. New York: Columbia University Press.

Xinhua News. 2010. "Chinese State Councilor Proposes Integrated Education with ASEAN Countries." Retrieved from: http://news.xinhuanet.com/english2010/china/2010-08/03/c_13428618.htm (accessed November 18, 2015).

Zhang, C. and X. Yang. 2012. "Promoting Mutual Understanding to Enhance Education Cooperation." *Forum on Education and Culture*, 6: 113–117.

Zhang, Y. 2010. *China and Asian Regionalism*. Singapore: World Scientific Publishing.

Chapter 22

An Analysis of Power in Transnational Advocacy Networks in Education

Ian Macpherson

Introduction

Using two theoretical frameworks – Foucault's theory of power, and a schema of "spaces" of power – this chapter explores the experiences of two transnational advocacy networks – the Global Campaign for Education and the Inter-Agency Network for Education in Emergencies – in order to understand the power of transnational advocacy networks in education and some of the challenges they have faced over the past decade.

Advocacy is the power to define, to resist, and to affect change. Transnational advocacy networks build on the power of organizations and individuals whose experiences transcend national borders, who are united by common purpose, and who are driven by the energy of the collective. These organizations seek to influence the global governance of education at regional and global scales by influencing the policies and discursive frames advanced by apex organizations, including institutions such as the development banks, the United Nations (UN) bodies and bilateral donors, who remain the most powerful agenda-shapers in international education. In 2000, the World Education Forum in Dakar was profoundly shaped by a remarkable rise in the power of civil society and transnational advocacy networks to shape global education policy. As this chapter suggests, in order to continue to exert such power, transnational advocacy networks must retool their strategic goals and adjust their structure based on reaffirmed common cause in response to changes in the environments in which they operate.

Orienting Theoretical Frameworks

Foucauldian Power

Foucault contends that knowledge and truth are produced out of power struggles and are used to authorize and legitimate the workings of power (Foucault 1980). Power creates the sites where knowledge and truth are created; thus power and knowledge are mutually constitutive. Truth, morality, and meaning are therefore *created* through discourse. For Foucault, discourse is the "tactical dimension" (Peterson 2001) of how power relations work between institutions, groups, and individuals. The reciprocal nature of the power/knowledge synergy lies in his thesis that "the production of knowledge and the exercise of administrative power intertwine, and each begins to enhance the other" (Allen 1999: 70).

Implicit in this synergy is the economy of discourse: those with the power of communication and information are those more able to generate knowledge that, in turn, generates more power. Thus he claims that "[p]ower only exists when it is put into action… In effect, what defines a relationship of power is that it is a mode of action which does not act directly and immediately on others. Instead, it acts upon their actions: an action upon an action, on existing actions or on those which may arise in the present or future" (Foucault 1982, 219).

Discourse therefore *acts* upon subjects and conditions their behavior by creating the universe of what is thinkable (knowledge) whilst the exercise of power "consists in guiding the possibility of conduct and putting in order the possible outcome" (Foucault 1982, 221) on the basis of that knowledge. It is in this sense that he argues that power is about "government," the ability to structure the field of possibilities of others; it "both *describes* observed realities and *prescribes* desired outcomes" (Petit and Wheeler 2005, 7).

Foucauldian governmentality applies to transnational advocacy networks both internally and externally. Internal governmentality shapes structures within the network and prescribes the actions of its members, highlighting the fact that networks are not spontaneous – and are characterized by internal struggles over the discursive frames through which they develop their transnational reach and power. External governmentality shapes the actions of networks and their engagement in different spaces.

"Spaces" of Power

Transnational advocacy networks are valuable because they campaign on a set of ideas in spaces where dialogue and policy-making may otherwise comprise only military, government, or economic powers. Such networks "provide a voice for civil society in the otherwise *closed space* of international politics" (CLG 2014a, emphasis added). Not all transnational advocacy networks are social movements, nor are they necessarily oppositional. All, however, vie in some way or other for "cultural supremacy" by promoting or refuting contested narrative frames (Tarrow 1998).

Spaces of power relate to the institutional channels, decision-making arenas, and forums of action as well as opportunities and moments where citizens and organizations affect discourses, decisions, and relationships. These have alternatively been discussed as *political opportunity structures* (Tarrow 1992; 1998), *policy spaces* (McGee 2002), and *democratic spaces* (Cornwall and Coelho 2006). Spaces convey the imagery of boundaries and power relations shape the boundaries of space, what is possible within them, who enters with what identities, discourses, and interests. Broadly speaking three types exist: closed, invited, and claimed (Hughes *et al.* 2003).

Closed spaces are decision-making arenas occupied by elites without any pretense to inclusion, such as government bureaucracies, and concern issues such as fiscal policy. *Invited* spaces are those that, largely as a result of demands for participation, have been opened by governments, supranational organizations, and non-governmental organizations (NGOs). With the growth of participatory governance, invited spaces are multi-scalar, from the local through to the global. *Claimed* spaces are those created by social movements and civil society organizations (CSOs) outside institutionalized policy arenas.

Cornwall (2002) argues that spaces for participation are not neutral but shaped by power relations that both surround and enter them; certain voices or issues may be more or less dominant (visible or hidden) in any space (whether invited or claimed), and invisible power may shape what is said in place of a critical consciousness. Further, the relationship between spaces is dynamic and any one may open or close through struggles for legitimacy, resistance, co-optation, and transformation.

While "transnational advocacy networks prise open democratic space within an elite arena" (CLG 2014), their enduring success is contingent on their ability to continually navigate dynamic spaces. They must manage space within networks themselves. Thus the metaphor of space applies first and foremost *outwardly*, representing the types of spaces they aim to prise open, create, or engage in, but also *inwardly*, representing the different channels, decision-making arenas, and moments when discourse is created and relationships formed.

Civil Society and Education

Participation and the Rights-Based Approach

Beginning in the 1980s, the failure of top-down approaches to alleviate poverty combined with disillusionment in former colonies and leftist academic circles led to a rising focus on "participation" as a mean and ends in international development (Chambers 1983; Cernea 1985; McGee 2002). This emphasis on participation intersected with a rising interest from Southern organizations and UN bodies in the ability of communities to claim basic human rights – rights that had been undermined by Structural Adjustment Policies (SAPs) that aimed to tackle the obstacles to growth perceived, *inter alia*, as bloated bureaucracies and poor governance. Cuts in government spending in social service sectors led to a drop in both access and quality of education in many developing countries, and service-delivery NGOs were more frequently engaged in education service gap-filling.

In contrast to instrumental participation in the great project of the modern, the rights-based approach re-politicized participation by conceiving it as a right and dealt explicitly with issues of power, governance, and democratization. It promised to reclaim its counter-hegemonic (state-driven) and anti-paternalistic (Northern-driven) force, and was viewed by many as "qualitatively different" because it suggested a "more active notion of citizenship – one which recognized the agency of citizens as '*makers and shapers*' rather that 'users and choosers' of interventions or services designed by others" (Gaventa 2004, 29, italics original; Holland *et al.* 2004; Waddington and Mohan 2004). Civil society organizations were also positioned as "major new actors" (McGee 2002, 103).

Rights-based approaches to participation were quickly adopted by apex organizations in international development. SAPs were replaced by Poverty Reduction Strategy Papers (PRSPs) and Sector Wide Approaches (SWAPs), which gave new emphasis to involvement of citizens and civil society institutions in policy-making (Bretton Woods Project 2006; Minogue and Kothari 2002). In Foucauldian terms, these new policy discourses created subject positions, including those of "civil society," "duty-bearers," and "rights-holders," whose roles were defined by apex development organizations. Yet at the same time, they opened up new spaces for participation and effective use of discursive power.

This new environment presented an auspicious opening for civil society in the lead up to the Dakar World Forum on Education in 2000. A large number of national and regional NGOs and civil society organizations gradually joined forces to focus on two core advocacy objectives: the *civic-political process* of securing the right to participate in the democratic governance of education; and *technico-policy aims* focused on equity and the right to education. It was in this auspicious environment that the Global Campaign for Education (GCE) and the Inter-Agency Network for Education in Emergencies (INEE) came into being.

Two Transnational Advocacy Networks

The Global Campaign for Education (GCE)

GCE is the best-known transnational advocacy network in education. It works toward ensuring the realization of the entire Education for All (EFA) agenda at global, regional, and national levels, and comprises over 120 members in more than 100 countries.

Initially conceived as a short-term campaign to raise awareness of the EFA commitments made in Jomtien 1990, GCE was founded in 1999 by ActionAid, Oxfam, Education International (the international body representing teachers' organizations), and the Global March against Child Labour. GCE undertook a range of advocacy activities in the run up to the Dakar 2000 forum, including convening a regional African conference on EFA in South Africa in December 1999 and arranging the first Global Week of Action in April 2000.

These activities created a new internal space for transnational advocacy in education. Because this space was "rooted" in local realities represented through the range of collaborating national and international organizations (Florini 2000; Tarrow 2005), it generated internal cohesion and external legitimacy. Yet as Cornwall (2002) argues, spaces for participation are not neutral but are shaped by power relations. Thus, "those who create it are likely to have more power within it" (PPSC 2011, 17). By the Dakar meeting in April 2000, GCE comprised 30 national coalitions, eight regional members, and eight international NGOs (INGOs). Its work coalesced around: securing global education financing commitments (inherited from Oxfam); establishing national education NGO networks in the South (from ActionAid); reinvigorated roles for teachers as advocates for education change at national level (from Education International); and, set within a broader framework on the rights of the child, a focus on education as a means to end child labor and, therefore, poverty (Mundy and Murphy 2002; Mundy 2012). GCE gained the support of most of the 300 NGOs in Dakar, "became the de facto representative of the NGO position" (Murphy and Mundy 2002, 6) and succeeded in its effort to prise open previously closed external policy spaces, securing meetings with key international actors in the

UN and at the World Bank. Its positions led to "clear and substantial changes" to initial drafts of the Dakar framework (Archer and Anyanwu 2005, 5) and representatives were elected to the drafting committee to determine future EFA structures. Further, without consultation yet in the name of GCE, Oxfam endorsed support for the World Bank's EFA Fast Track plan, which grew out of Oxfam's Global Plan of Action. This caused tensions within the GCE yet secured it a place in what was later to become the EFA-Fast Track Initiative (FTI) advisory committee in 2002.

Complex power dynamics beset GCE and it swiftly faced challenges of representation and accountability, echoing the views of Clark, who suggests that southern voices "often feel like second class citizens among their Northern partners. They feel welcomed as sources of information and legitimation but not as equals" (Clark 2003, 24). The founding of the African Network Campaign on Education for All (ANCEFA) on May 19, 2000 was significant as it was pointedly a response to the domination of the Northern voices at the Dakar meeting – including within GCE (Tomlinson and Macpherson 2007).

Post-Dakar – the Growth of GCE

GCE held its first General Assembly in Delhi in 2001, establishing a constitution and governance structures that sought to embed southern ownership. The campaign was extended and expanded to press Group of Seven (G7) governments and international organizations for better funding and coordination whilst stimulating civil society participation in national EFA policy work through the GCE School Reports (which identified where progress on EFA had been made) and mass mobilization through the Global Action Week (GAW) (from 2003). Both the GAW and the GCE School Reports (GCE-SR) were innovative approaches that combined internal and external civic-political and technico-policy objectives.

The GAW aimed to generate public awareness and pressure national governments on specific EFA targets set within a right to education framework. GAWs raised the profile of education at country level and mobilized pressure on parliamentarians and policy-makers, with millions of people taking part in dozens of countries (see Culey *et al.* 2007). GAW topics were agreed in general assemblies, where members collectively framed the agenda and strengthened cooperative ownership. The fact that the events were undertaken simultaneously in a huge range of countries reinforced solidarity politics within GCE. Additionally, the collective practice of GAWs combined what Keck and Sikkink (1999) refer to as *information, symbolic,* and *leverage* politics, whereby the GCE secretariat was able to move politically useful information about the GAWs into external invited international spaces, leveraging the experience of the smaller and weaker members of the network.

The GCE-SRs, whereby national coalitions graded domestic governments against a range of EFA-related indicators that were then published in an annual report epitomized *accountability* politics; obliging more powerful actors to act on vaguer policies or principles they formally endorsed (Keck and Sikkink 1999). Yet the value of a name-and-shame approach that called out national heads of state and governments was increasingly questioned by national members, who felt an accusatorial and antagonistic approach did little to foster dialogue between states and national coalitions (Culey *et al.* 2007). GCE-SRs ceased after 2008. Shifting tactics were needed to confront and move between closed, claimed, and invited spaces.

Big Funding, Rapid Growth

In 2003 the Dutch Government awarded GCE a seven-year grant of €15 million. The Real World Strategies (RWS) program sought to strengthen the collaboration between GCE and its regional counterparts; the Asia South Pacific Association for Basic and Adult Education (ASPBAE), the Africa Network Campaign on Education for All (ANCEFA), and the Coalition for the Right to Education in Latin America (CLADE). With collaboration across the international regional and national levels, the RWS aimed to "build a movement ... and strengthen the advocacy and campaigning potential of civil society organizations in the global South" (Castillo 2011, 2) and "included a very explicit expectation that civil societies would eventually empower the poor so that they had a say in decision-making at the national level" (Verger *et al.* 2012, 12).

In the same period (2002–2008) the UK government established the Commonwealth Education Fund (CEF) to support 16 national education coalitions in Africa and Asia. While GCE benefitted from CEF funding it did not administer it, which was undertaken collaboratively by ActionAid, Oxfam, and Save the Children, three organizations that had been central to the establishment and growth of the GCE. CEF drove civic-political objectives through national civil society coalition building. A key proposal emanating from the CEF was the Civil Society Education Fund (CSEF) model that sought to generate funds for national coalitions through domestic and international sources including government, private sector, and a 3% automatic trigger on in-country aid grants.

The original CSEF model, taken up by ActionAid and Oxfam under the auspices of both CEF and GCE, proved unsuccessful in creating funds at the national level yet gained traction within the then-named EFA-Fast Track Initiative (renamed as the Global Partnership for Education in 2011). In a landmark development, in 2009 the GPE granted US$17.6 million to GCE for two years to support the development of national education coalitions in 45 GPE-recipient countries through the CSEF.

CSEF secretariats were established within GCE and its regional structures, yet this blurred the relationship between the regional bodies and national coalitions. Previously characterized by solidarity on a shared political, social movement "logic," the move to regional bodies distributing competitive funds downwards to national coalitions created a paradoxical donor "logic": "the relationship gets reversed, there begins to be a tension that undermines the political alliances that should be there (GCE Board)" (cited in Verger *et al.* 2012, 39).

Broadly speaking, where national coalitions were already functioning well (as in many Asia-Pacific and some African contexts), CSEF greatly strengthened their work by increasing the number and capacity of members, expanding their boards and the regularity of board and general assemblies. Where coalitions were nascent or brought into being as a result of CSEF funding (such as in a number of African contexts) it had a mixed effect, sometimes greatly increasing strength, in others swamping small or fragile coalitions that lacked the absorptive capacity to spend, account, and monitor effectively, or considered the CSEF coalition "model"[1] prescriptive and inappropriate to the context. There was also a sense within the regional bodies that CSEF management compromised their ability to engage in regional level advocacy.

In contrast to the collaboration model of RWS, the CSEF had been designed at the apex of GCE, between its board and secretariat and the FTI/GPE on behalf of the members, and epitomized Foucauldian governmentality. By creating knowledge of ideal national coalitions and cascading this via regional structures to the national level, the action of agents – the coalitions themselves – confirmed the picture the discourse drew for them, intertwined through the production of knowledge and administrative power and typifying the power/knowledge synergy. Yet the architecture of CSEFs led to dissonance within GCE and signaled a growing power at the international secretariat and board level. Further, while GCE had claimed space for civil society at national level, the approach was felt by some members to be prescriptive and for some of the coalitions to be "inauthentic" (Culey *et al.* 2007, 47).

Internecine tensions were exacerbated by the *1 Goal: Education for All* campaign. In June 2009 following a unilateral decision by the GCE board, an agreement was signed with the Department for International Development (DFID) and the Fédération Internationale de Football Association (FIFA) for a global campaign leading to a meeting of world leaders at the 2010 Football World Cup in South Africa. The British government committed £1 million and £650,000 of CSEF funds were channeled toward it. A host of celebrities and footballers were enlisted to mobilize an online sign-up designed to reach 35 million people worldwide and the GCE secretariat swelled from 25 people in 2009 to 47 in March 2010. Ultimately, however, the campaign had limited impact, reaching only 14 million people by the time the competition kicked off[2] and securing only a ceremonial breakfast meeting of available world leaders the day before, at which no substantial commitments were pledged. While GCE's media presence was greatly amplified, the confidence in the secretariat of some of its key members was significantly weakened (Mundy and Haggerty 2010). The lack of policy objectives in place of visibility was a key shortcoming (Culey *et al.* 2007) and led some commentators to analogize the campaign as a "firework"; lots of noise and color but ultimately short-lived. The campaign also eroded the confidence of stakeholders in international spaces with one commentator referring to it as GCE's "own goal campaign."

In 2013 GCE was granted a second round of CSEF with various caveats designed to ensure better governance of the funds. Tensions notwithstanding, many national coalitions have now been integrated into the Local Education Groups (LEGs),[3] which act as a central policy table in many developing countries, comprising Ministry of Education representatives, donor countries, teachers' representatives, private providers, universities, and NGOs (Verger *et al.* 2012, 13).

Internal Discourses, Interior Spaces

While Foucault offers insight into how discourse shapes action, Johnston and Noakes (2005) argue that the extent to which discourses resonate with constituents and motivate them into collection action depends heavily on the ability of the "frame makers" (discourse shapers) to resonate with the ideological, attitudinal, and moral orientations – the "cultural stock" – of the "frame receivers," which depends on the "credibility of the promoters and their organisational and professional credentials and expertise" (Johnston and Noakes 2005, 11), their charismatic authority, and their strategic and marketing orientations.

The GCE "frame" was anchored on a rights-based approach (from ActionAid and the Global March Against Child Labour) and specified global financing commitments for public education (from Oxfam), NGO engagement in policy formation (ActionAid), and the role of teachers as change makers (from Education International). The positions articulated were congruent with members' experience, empirically credible, and "meshed, drew upon and synchronized with the dominant culture of the target audience, its narratives, myths and basic assumptions" (Johnston and Noakes 2005, 11–12). They also drew heavily on the credibility and expertise of the promoters.

As the GCE campaign and board grew, ActionAid, Oxfam, Education International, and Global March, along with the regional bodies, exerted power, controlling interior spaces (closed board meetings and invited general assemblies) within which discourses were created not only about GCE's agenda but the advocacy tools through which to achieve it. The board and the secretariat created "the truth" of GCE. Further, the control of interior spaces set the operational structure of GCE, as illustrated by the decision-making around the 1 Goal Campaign and the setting of terms for the CSEF.

External Discourses, Exterior Spaces

In the Foucauldian sense, the participatory development and the human rights discourses created a role for civil society and the invited exterior spaces for GCE to occupy. GCE was both product and producer of these discourses, and its meteoric growth led to the prising open of previously closed spaces, and the creation of new invited spaces. In addition to raising the profile of education and EFA, there is no question that GCE achieved remarkable gains on its governance aims, its first core objective, opening space for civil society participation in the FTI/GPE, and more recently in decision-making bodies for the post-2015 education agenda. It has further been instrumental in supporting the development of regional and national coalitions through the GAW and the professionalization of national coalitions through the CSEF.

In terms of policy influence, GCE's second core objective, its impact has been varied. More children are in school, the gender gap is closing in many countries, user fees have been formally dropped in many countries, and more are monitoring quality. While GCE has succeeded in raising international aid pledges to education, this has not been sufficient to meet all the EFA goals and increased national expenditure as a result of coalition pressure is difficult to attribute (Culey *et al.* 2007). Policy gains at national level have varied from highly significant to still pending (see Verger *et al.* 2012; Civil Society Education Fund 2014).

The Inter-Agency Network for Education in Emergencies (INEE)

INEE is a network of agencies and organizations concentrated on the provision of quality education in emergencies working at multi-scalar levels. INEE comprises over 11,000 members in over 170 countries.

In the lead up to Dakar 2000, the United Nations Education, Scientific and Cultural Organization (UNESCO) convened a group of UN agencies and NGOs to ensure that humanitarian assistance and rapid educational interventions linked to post-conflict or post-crisis reconstruction efforts. This led to several outcomes. First, wording was suggested for Strategy Five of the Dakar Framework that pledged attending governments, organizations, and agencies to meet the needs of education systems affected by conflict. Second, UNESCO, the United Nations Children's Fund (UNICEF), and the United Nations High Commissioner for Refugees (UNHCR) committed to work together toward this goal. Third, the group determined that education had to become part of the humanitarian agenda and the definition of "emergencies" needed to include natural disasters.

UNHCR, UNESCO, and UNICEF convened the first Global Consultation on Education in Emergencies in Geneva in November 2000 to advance Strategy Five of the Dakar framework. Participating civil society, governments, NGOs, and UN agencies determined to share resources, develop consensual guidelines, and work collectively. And considerable effort was taken to avoid creating new coordination mechanisms, with emphasis placed on collaboration rather than formal coordination of agencies' programs.

Shortly afterwards, the first Steering Group was established with representatives from the three UN agencies and three NGOs (CARE, the International Rescue Committee, and the Norwegian Refugee Council), a decision that reflected the "inclusive, collaborative culture embedded in the very foundations of the network" (Mendizabal and Hearn 2009, 21). INEE was thus established as an open, global network to professionalize the field of education in emergencies, was explicitly non-operational and sought to engage in "advocacy, knowledge sharing and the distribution of materials to promote improved collaboration and effectiveness in the context of education in emergencies for the agencies involved in emergency response and post-crisis recovery" (Mendizabal and Hearn 2009, 1). At the outset, INEE sought to be an internal space created for a group of specialist organisations working in emergencies.

The Development of INEE

Its first activity was to review, collate, and distribute learning materials and resources to agencies active in education in emergencies. This was done through the first inter-agency task team in 2001 – Learning Materials and Resources – convened by UNHCR and including representatives from the International Rescue Committee, Jesuit Refugee Service, Save the Children, UNESCO, and UNICEF. Task teams were internal spaces created with the specific intention of supporting a limited program of work centered on a member-identified topic. They depended on member organizations establishing and coordinating a specific team, had only to be endorsed by the Steering Group to be established, and were open to all members on an individual basis, requiring only informal commitment to the team's activities. Additionally, once a task was complete, the team would either dissolve or retool a new task. They were therefore open, fluid, and democratic spaces within the network led and coordinated by members with no overt intention to influence policy.

In the same period three other task teams were established (Information Sharing and Networking; Monitoring and Evaluation; and Post-primary Education), the steering group was expanded to include the Save the Children Alliance and a secretariat established within UNESCO Paris.

While the post-primary and monitoring and evaluation teams atrophied, in 2003 the steering group endorsed the decision to develop the progressive debates within learning materials task team into a substantive work stream and produce the *INEE Minimum Standards for Education in Emergencies, Chronic Crises and Early Reconstruction*. Such a program required a structure that enabled members to collaborate fully, which in turn required greater levels of support from the Secretariat. The development of the Working Group on Minimum Standards "signified a new role for the network: influencing high level policy processes by convening donors, policy makers and researchers" (Mendizabal and Hearn 2009, 29).

Targeted, High-level Advocacy

The first Working Group on Minimum Standards operated from 2003 to 2005, motivated by the commitment to ensure a minimum level of quality and accountability in situations of crisis and the recognition that education must be seen as a priority humanitarian response (INEE 2014a). Comprising 13 organizations[4] coordinating and delivering education in emergency contexts, the working group operated for two years with funding from the Canadian International Development Agency (CIDA), the International Rescue Committee, the International Save the Children Alliance, UNHCR, UNICEF, and the United States Agency for International Development (USAID).

Given its intention to influence policy, the group made "special efforts to ensure that representatives from a variety of levels, including households, schools and communities, local authorities, ministry officials, funding agencies and implementers, were actively involved throughout the consultative process in order to ensure relevance to and buy-in from all education stakeholders" (INEE 2014a). Over 110 consultations were conducted at local and national levels in 47 countries, drawing on information from over 1900 representatives including affected communities, parents, teachers, civil society organizations, governments, and donors. These were further developed with inputs from over 800 members on INEE's listserv at consultations in Africa, Asia-Pacific, Latin America and the Middle East, North Africa, and again at high-level workshops in London, New York, Washington, and Oslo in 2004. Further, the working group continually developed and disseminated knowledge products. Eight reports, concept notes, minutes, and draft standards were shared among the INEE membership for review. Additionally, the draft standards were reviewed through a process involving 40 organization representatives, after which they were reviewed by members of the broader humanitarian community including the health and protection communities, as well as civil society, UN and government agencies, and research and academic institutions. The first set of Minimum Standards was released in 2005.

As a result, in 2006 the UN requested UNICEF and Save the Children, as members of the working group, to develop an operational mechanism to coordinate the on-the-ground activities of multiple organizations responding to emergencies. INEE established an Education Cluster Advisory Group to organize the technical and advocacy activities of its members; Steering Group members engaged in high-level fora advocating for education to be included as part of humanitarian responses and the Minimum Standards working group produced an Adoption Strategies Checklist for inter-agency coordination. In the same year INEE held a policy roundtable at UNICEF in New York on "Education in Emergencies, Fragile States and Reconstruction: Addressing Challenges and Exploring Alternatives," bringing together civil society, academics, UN, and donor representatives. Not only did the event directly engage policy-makers at the height of global practice; by focusing on the institutionalization of the Minimum Standards it began to significantly shape the discourse around emergencies, fragile states, and reconstruction. A second roundtable was hosted in 2006 at the World Bank, led by the International Rescue Committee (IRC), Save the Children, and the Women's Refugee Commission, which focused on teacher compensation in emergency settings. The outcomes included a set of guidelines that would be implemented by practitioner organizations, contributing directly to work of the Education Cluster, which INEE had helped to create.

Activities of the working group in subsequent years focused on the promotion, training in, and implementation of the standards, key to which was the development in 2008 of a "companion agreement" between the Sphere Project and INEE minimum standards, ensuring that all organizations working in emergences viewed education as an essential component of humanitarian responses. Additionally, the group developed an updated version of the Standards in 2011. The group also produced over 17 reports, policy papers, and updates on how the standards were used globally. Currently, the working group, which is still operational, comprises 33 members representing 21 international organizations.

A second Working Group on Education and Fragility was established in 2008 in response to an Organisation for Economic Co-operation and Development-Development Assistance Committee (OECD-DAC) commissioned study on service delivery in fragile states. As a then-emergent area of discourse, the working group purposefully included researchers and academics in addition to practitioners, donors, and government representatives, and aimed to establish research and evidence as the basis for planning in fragile states. Comprising 20 civil society and donor organizations, it convened a high-level policy roundtable hosted by the European Commission to examine emerging aid modalities to support education in fragile contexts. The group produced four texts designed to influence policy at the European Commission, the European Training Foundation, and Gesellschaft für Technische Zusammenarbeit (GTZ), and developed three in-depth analyses of financing modalities in fragile states complemented by six country case studies. In a similar fashion to the work of the Minimum Standards working group, members of the Fragility group conducted regional consultations to assess in-conflict and post-conflict reconstruction on the ground. The first was in Addis Ababa, Ethiopia, in 2010, which developed strategies to enhance the positive role of education in mitigating fragility. The second took place in Juba, South Sudan in early 2011 and analyzed how education could be incorporated into the sector planning process. The third was later in 2011 in Sarajevo, Bosnia-Herzegovina, and parsed how education was able to mitigate fragility in the region. This work was complemented by a series of meetings and side events organized around the development and launch of the 2011 EFA Global Monitoring Report (Global Monitoring Report 2011) and the World Bank's Development Monitoring Report.

At the end of 2011, the group developed a new two-year mandate that explicitly linked to the overall driving goal of INEE on the basis of three factors. One was the concern that fragile states would receive decreasing amounts of overseas funding support following the macro-economic shock of 2008. Second was the influence that the first working group was having on shaping the discourse and practice of education in fragile states. Third was the effect of the strengthened alignment of the different

INEE structures on its overall goal. The working group preserved a closed internal space focused on research that correspondingly aimed to create external policy spaces to influence discourse at national and international levels. By combining knowledge gathering and dissemination the group explored learning opportunities and moments for advocacy to influence policy formation and decision-making (INEE 2014b).

A third working group was formed in 2012 in response to research by the Education Cluster demonstrating that over half of the 57 million out-of-school children lived in conflict-affected contexts, that the number of out-of-school children had risen from 2008 to 2011 (Save the Children 2013) and that the share for humanitarian funding for education has declined from 2.4% in 2011 to 1.4% in 2012 (Global Monitoring Report 2012). The Education Cannot Wait Advocacy Working Group was established to secure sustained funding from donors and planning support by southern governments for education in emergencies. Comprising 17 NGO, private sector and donor organizations, the working group developed the "Education Cannot Wait: Call to Action" agenda, which argued for action on three fronts: (a) *plan* for emergency prevention, preparedness, and response in education sector plans and budgets; (b) *prioritize* education in emergencies by increasing the education share of humanitarian funding from 2% to 4%; and (c) *protect* children, teachers, and education facilities from attack (INEE 2014c). By invitation from the UN Secretary General the group established a direct link to the Global Education First Initiative (GEFI) in 2012 and in 2013 gained high-level endorsement at the UN General Assembly through a panel hosted by the head of UNICEF, Tony Lake, and attended by figures including Gordon Brown, UN Special Envoy for Education, Alice Albright, CEO of the Global Partnership for Education, and education ministers from Somalia and Afghanistan.

Internal Discourses, Interior Spaces

The central tenet of INEE resonated strongly with members' ideological, attitudinal, and moral orientations, while the credentials of the frame "makers" was never in doubt (see Johnston and Noakes 2005). Yet in contrast to GCE, the constituents of INEE were not engaged in frames of protest against dominant discourse but in frames of professionalization in order to create a discourse. Critically, the constituents of all of INEE structures – the Steering Group, the working groups, and the task teams – comprised those that sat both inside *and* outside national and global policy spaces. This was immensely significant for the creation and control of interior spaces and the development of discourses within them.

For instance, the working group structure was different to that of the task team and developed for "consensual advocacy, policy analysis, research and tool development" (Mendizabal and Hearn 2009, 33). Additionally, while task teams were fluid and had one or two individuals sharing coordination, working groups had a chairperson, subgroups – each with a focal point representative – and a full time secretariat staff member to manage the group. Working groups required a two-year commitment of member institutions that had to be applied for and approved by the Steering Group, which also approved working group work plans. In contrast to open and fluid task team spaces created around information exchange and networking therefore, working groups were closed, formal spaces focused around knowledge production, tool development, and policy influence, deliberately comprising a mix of apex international organizations, INGOs, and academic and research institutions who collaboratively engage in the task of co-constructing discourse.

Thus while the Steering Group acts as the governing body of INEE, its control has been light-touch and the real power of INEE occurs within semi-autonomous working groups that have their own institutional structures and include some of the same organizations that sit on the Steering Group.

External Discourses, Exterior Spaces

The discourse on Education in Emergencies has been transformed through the knowledge products of the working groups on Minimum Standards and Education and Fragility. Its assessment has changed from traditional "conflict" or "natural" disasters through the understanding of the structural drivers of emergencies including social cohesion and social justice analyses, and structural inequities and exclusions (Smith 2010). Equally, goals around peacebuilding, human rights promotion, and economic growth are being pursued through new means including protection, safeguarding education investments, disaster risk reduction, and safe learning environments within frameworks of "resilience" (see Nicolai et al. 2014; Smith 2010; Save the Children and UNICEF 2012; and Winthrop and Matsui 2013). More widely still, the entire subsector is subject to ongoing professionalization and the use of evidence-based tools.

Such influence is largely attributable to the purposeful collaboration of apex organizations that epitomize Foucault's power/knowledge synergy; knowledge and truth were created by INEE's discourse, which the subsequent action of agents – practitioner and policy actors in the field – affirmed. Further, these same organizations were able to open closed spaces and invite not only new actors but new "professional" discourses. These external spaces were not claimed in the social movement sense but merely opened by hegemonic organizations, permitting the four frame alignment strategies that Snow (1986) proposes; INEE has been able to *bridge* different frames by connecting humanitarian relief, education, and peacebuilding, as well as social protection, education, and resilience (see Rosenkranz 2014) among others. It has *amplified* its messages by using captivating slogans such as "Education Cannot Wait," and it has *extended* the importance of education to non-educationists, such as by companioning the Sphere Project. Finally, it has also *transformed* the frame by "changing old understanding and meaning [of the frame] and/or generating new ones" (Benford and Snow 2000, 625).

The fact that apex member organizations have created discourse that has subsequently been picked up and advanced by one another is significant. Not only does it epitomize Foucault's power/knowledge synergy where "the production of knowledge and the exercise of administrative power intertwine, and each begins to enhance the other" (Allen 1999, 70), but also those with power of communication and information – those who develop the economy of discourse – are those more able to generate knowledge that, in turn, generates more power. Such discourse creation is truly an exercise in Foucauldian governmentality in that it "both *describes* observed realities and *prescribes* desired outcomes" (Petit and Wheeler 2005, 7). Thus the discourse at once professionalizes at the same time as generates more power through expert knowledge.

Conclusion

In the framework of Mendizabal (2006a; 2006b) both GCE and INEE have been effective in six areas of network functioning: (a) *building community* by promoting and sustaining the values of the members; (b) *filtering*, organizing, and managing information for members; (c) *amplifying* and making public little-known and new ideas, giving them weight and making them understandable; (d) *facilitating* members to carry out their functions more efficiently and effectively; (e) *investing* in its members by providing resources that allowed them to carry out their functions; and (f) *convening* different groups with strategies to support them. Yet parsing the experiences of GCE and INEE through the frameworks of Foucault and the metaphor of spaces reveals different dynamics of power and suggests differential impacts.

The experiences suggest that GCE has been most effective as network "agents" that "draw resources from the members to take the lead in a change process on their behalf" (Mendizabal and Hearn 2009, 12), whereas INEE has functioned more as a network "supporter" that "facilitates and helps its members to bring about change in their own spheres of influence" (Mendizabal and Hearn 2009, 12). Accordingly, GCE created "tangible" value (Allee 2002) through the CSEF process more than "intangible" value of knowledge or experience leading to changed discourse and practice of supranational organizations. Within this tangible value, GCE has fashioned a narrative on the structure and function of national coalitions, a discourse in the Foucauldian sense that has shaped the actions of national members with prescribed outcomes. By contrast, while INEE's value creation is in part tangible (through the creation of resources), its greatest value creation is intangible (through knowledge and processes) developed via optimal interactions of a mix of prime members who co-construct and extend value with one another (see Allee 2002).

What insights do these experiences offer to explain these differences and what questions do they raise for transnational advocacy networks?

From an internal discourse/interior space perspective, it is clear that a frame's resonance with constituents is largely shaped by the credibility of the frame maker and that frame "makers" have left discernible imprints on the agendas of both networks. From an outside discourse/external space the picture is more complex. The transition of GCE from a claimed space pre-Dakar (in which issues were framed and collective action planned) into invited spaces following Dakar (which resulted from challenging closed spaces) illustrates the fluidity of spaces and the challenges of civil society organization shifting from one type to another. Not only must invited spaces be held open by ongoing demands growing out of social movements in claimed spaces, but civil society organizations in invited spaces must shift from more confrontational advocacy methods to negotiator–collaborator methods with other actors in the space, or otherwise risk assimilative-cooptation, on the one hand, or issue/organization exclusion on the other. Spanning these spaces thus requires different strategies, skills, and resources, and civil society organizations must have "staying power" (Pearce and Vela 2005) and the capacity to form effective horizontal alliances if they are to effectively move between them over time.

Further, GCE today faces new challenges that arise, paradoxically, from its successes. While the CSEF in one light is an extraordinary civic-political achievement, it runs the risk of de-politicizing the engagement of civil society by driving its inclusion in national processes as a collaborative rather than contentious "development partner." CSEF may remove the political force of national coalitions by framing them as technical collaborators, especially when coupled with irresistible donor pressure on governments to open invited spaces for civil society. Indeed, as the Institute of Development Studies opines: "invited spaces of participation may not have much potential for change unless there is a strong mobilization from outside the space, and strong political will on the inside to hold the space open and ensure that it is listened to" (PPSC 2011, 17).

We may draw lessons to inform this challenge from INEE, which over time, "has continuously developed its approach to facilitating inter-agency cooperation, informing policy and practice, and has found new and effective ways of engaging an ever broadening membership" (Mendezabal and Hearn 2009, 18). The internal structures of INEE have responded with an evolving strategy for creating discursive influence in a way that GCE has struggled to do. It has also, critically, ensured the formative participation of organizations at the apex of international decision-making. Straddling this insider/outsider role has allowed INEE to avoid the internecine struggles experienced by GCE and to continually exert power as a result of its adaptive capacity to retool its strategic goals and adjust its structure based on reaffirmed common cause in response to environmental shocks within which it operates. Nonetheless, INEE contends with tension between its members; INGOs and apex supranational organizations are not always comfortable bedfellows and can be imperfect allies, yet overall they seem to accept the contradictions, ambiguity, and compromises as a means to a larger end.

Together these experiences give glimpses of the simultaneous objectifying power of discourse acting on agents and the subjective ability of agents in creating discourse. The subjective ability of networks to exercise Foucauldian governmentality and create knowledge and truth seems to be greatly influenced by collaboration with apex, supranational organizations that retain control of invited spaces of power in which new discourses are created and disseminated. Such struggles for "cultural supremacy" are of course greatly shaped by a frame's intent: frames of protest, professionalization, or substantiation engage apex organizations differently. Much better understanding of the power/knowledge synergy of transnational advocacy networks and how they control spaces will be essential to assuring the implementation of an inclusive and democratic post-2015 education agenda.

Notes

1. Including formal registration as an organization, a board that met regularly, annual general assemblies, and a broad and inclusive membership.
2. This has subsequently risen to 18 million.
3. See Verger *et al.* 2012, 63, for a useful disaggregation of how national coalitions have been included in LEGs.
4. CARE Canada; CARE USA; Catholic Relief Services; IRC; Norwegian Church Council; Norwegian Refugee Council and the Norway United Nations Association; Save the Children UK; Save the Children USA; Refugee Education Trust; UNICEF; UNESCO-IIEP; UNHCR; and World Education.

References

Allee, V. 2002. "A Value Network Approach for Modelling and Measuring Intangibles. White Paper." Paper presented at Transparent Enterprise, Madrid, November 2002.

Allen, B. 1999. "Power/Knowledge," in *Critical Essays on Michel Foucault*, edited by K. Racevskis. New York: GK Hall & Co.

Archer, D. and C. Anyanwu. 2005. *The Evolution of Civil Society*. Unpublished.

Benford, R. and D. Snow. 2000. "Framing Processes and Social Movements: An Overview and Assessment." *Annual Review of Sociology*, 26: 611–639.

Bretton Woods Project. (2006). *SAPs/PRSPs*. Retrieved from: http://old.brettonwoodsproject.org/item.shtml?x=537814 (Accessed December 1, 2015).

Castillo, R. 2011. *Enabling South-South and Triangular Cooperation among Civil Society Organisations: The ASPBAE Experience*. Retrieved from: http://www.iiz-dvv.de/index.php?article_id=1318&clang=1 (accessed November 18, 2015).

Center for Law and Globalization (CLG). 2014. *Transnational Advocacy Networks and International Policy*. Retrieved from: https://clg.portalxm.com/library/keytext.cfm?keytext_id=113 (accessed November 18, 2014).

Cernea, M. (ed.). 1985. *Putting People First: Sociological Variables in Rural Development*. Oxford: Oxford University Press for the World Bank.

Chambers, R. 1983. *Rural Development: Putting the Last First*. London: Longman.

Clark, J.D. (ed.). 2003. *Globalizing Civic Engagement: Civil Society and Transnational Action*. London: Earthscan.

Cornwall, A. 2002. *Making Spaces, Changing Places: Situating Participation in Development*, IDS Working Paper No. 173. Falmer: Institute of Development Studies, University of Sussex.

Cornwall, A. and V.S. Coelho. 2006. *Spaces for Change? The Politics of Participation in New Democratic Arenas*. London: Zed Books.

Culey, C., A. Martin, and D. Lewer. 2007. *Global Campaign for Education – 2007 Mid-term Review*. London: Firetail Ltd. Retrieved from: www.firetail.co.uk/GCEMidTermReview.doc (accessed December 1, 2015).

Florini, A.M. 2000. *The Third Force: The Rise of Transnational Civil Society*. New York: Carnegie Endowment.

Foucault, M. 1980. *Power/Knowledge: Selected Interviews and Other Writings, 1972–1977*. Edinburgh: Pearson.

Foucault, M. 1982. "Afterword: The Subject and Power," in *Michael Foucault: Beyond Structuralism and Hermeneutics*, edited by H.L. Dreyfus and P. Rabinow. Brighton: Harvester.

Gaventa, J. 2004. "Towards Participatory Governance: Assessing the Transformative Possibilities," in *Participation: From Tyranny to Transformation?*, edited by S. Hickey and G. Mohan. London: Zed Books.

Global Monitoring Report. 2011. *The Hidden Crisis: Armed Conflict and Education*. Paris: UNESCO.

Global Monitoring Report. 2012. *Youth and Skills: Putting Education to Work*. Paris: UNESCO.

Holland, J., M. Brocklesby, and C. Abugre. 2004. "Beyond the Technical Fix? Participation in Donor Approachs to Rights-Based Development," in *Participation: From Tyranny to Transformation?*, edited by S. Hickey and G. Mohan. London: Zed Books.

Hughes, A., J. Wheeler, R. Eyben, and P. Scott-Villiers. 2003. *Rights and Power Workshop: Report*. Falmer: Institute of Development Studies, University of Sussex.

Inter-Agency Network for Education in Emergencies. 2014a. *Minimum Standards Working Groups*. Retrieved from: www.ineesite.org/en/minimum-standards/working-group (accessed November 18, 2015).

Inter-Agency Network for Education in Emergencies. 2014b. *INEE Working Group on Education and Fragility*. Retrieved from: www.ineesite.org/en/education-fragility/working-group (accessed November 18, 2015).

Inter-Agency Network for Education in Emergencies. 2014c. *Education Cannot Wait Advocacy Working Group*. Retrieved from: www.ineesite.org/en/advocacy/working-group (accessed November 18, 2015).

Johnston, H. and J. Noakes. 2005. *Frames of Protest: Social Movements and the Framing*. Oxford: OUP.

Keck, M. E. and K. Sikkink. 1999. *Transnational Advocacy Networks in International and Regional Politics*. Oxford: Blackwell Publishers.

McGee, R. 2002. "Participating in Development," in *Development Theory and Practice*, edited by U. Kothari and M. Minogue, 92–116. London: Palgrave.

Mendizabal, E. 2006a. *Building Effective Research Policy Networks: Linking Function and Form*. London: ODI.

Mendizabal, E. 2006b. *Understanding Networks: The Functions of Research Policy Networks*. London: ODI.

Mendizabal, E. and S. Hearn. 2009. *Inter-Agency Network for Education in Emergencies: A Community of Practice, A Catalyst for Change*. London: ODI.

Minogue, M. and U. Kothari. 2002. *Development Theory and Practice: Critical Perspectives*. Basingstoke: Palgrave.

Mundy, K. 2012. "The Global Campaign for Education and the Realization of 'Education for All,'" in *Campaigning for "Education for all", Histories, Strategies and Outcomes of Transnational Advocacy Coalitions in Education*, edited by A. Verger and M. Novelli. Rotterdam: Sense Publishers.

Mundy, K. and M. Haggery. 2010. *The Global Campaign for Education January 2008 February 2010: A Review*. Unpublished.

Mundy, K. and L. Murphy. 2001. "Transnational Advocacy, Global Civil Society? Emerging Evidence from the Field of Education." *Comparative Education Review*, 45(1): 85–126.

Nicolai, S., L. Wild, J. Wales, S. Hine, and J. Engel. 2014. *Unbalanced Progress: What Political Dynamics Mean for Education Access and Quality*. Development Progress Working Paper 5. London: ODI.

Pearce and Vela. 2005. *Colombia Country Report in "Assessing Civil Society Participation as supported in-country by CORDAID, HIVOS, NOVIB and Plan Netherlands"*. The Netherlands: NFP Breed Network.

Peterson, R. 2001. *Michel Foucault: Power/Knowledge*. Boulder: Colorado State University Resource Centre for Communications Studies.

Petit, J. and J. Wheeler. 2005. "Developing Rights? Relating Discourse to Context and Practice", in 'Developing Rights?' *IDS Bulletin*, 36(1): 1–8.

Power, Participation and Social Change (PPSC). 2011. *Power Pack: Understanding Power for Social Change*. Retrieved from: www.powercube.net/wp-content/uploads/2011/04/powerpack-web-version-2011.pdf (accessed November 18, 2015).

Rosenkranz, R. 2014. *Resilience goes Mainstream*. Retrieved from: https://www.devex.com/news/resilience-goes-mainstream-84317 (accessed November 18, 2015).

Save the Children. 2013. *Education Cannot Wait: The Impact of Conflict on Children's Education and Futures*. London: Save the Children.

Save the Children and UNICEF. 2012. *Comprehensive School Safety: A Toolkit for Development and Humanitarian Actors in the Education Sector*. Retrieved from: www.preventionweb.net/files/29491_29491comprehensiveschoolsafetytoolk.pdf (accessed November 18, 2015).

Smith, A. 2010. *The Influence of Education on Conflict and Peace Building. Background Paper for EFA Global Monitoring Report 2011*. Background paper prepared for the Education for All Global Monitoring Report 2011.

Snow, D.A., R. Burke Jr, S. Worden, and R. Benford. 1986. "Frame Alignment Processes, Micromobilization, and Movement Participation." *American Sociological Review*, 51: 464–481.

Tarrow, S. 1992. "Mentalities, Political Cultural and Collective Action Frames: Constructing Meaning through Action," in *Frontiers of Social Movement Theory*, edited by A. Morris and C. McClurg Mueller, 174–202. New Haven: Yale University Press.

Tarrow, S. 1998. *Power in Movement: Social Movements and Contentious Politics (second edition)*. New York: Cambridge University Press.

Tarrow, S. 2005. *The New Transnational Activism*. New York: Cambridge University Press.

Tomlinson, K. and I. Macpherson. 2007. *Funding Change: Sustaining Civil Society Advocacy in Education*. London: Commonwealth Education Fund.

Verger, A., X. Rambla, X. Bonal, N. Bertomeu, C. Fontdevila, A. García-Alba, M. Acebillo, B. Edwards, B. Talavera, and T. van Koolwijk. 2012. *Regional and National Civil Society Education Funds – CSEF Evaluation Report*. Retrieved from: www.campaignforeducation.org/docs/csef/CSEFev_FINAL_REPORTv4_complete.pdf (accessed November 18, 2015).

Waddington, M. and G. Mohan. 2004. "Failing Forward: Going Beyond Imposed Forms of Participation," in *Participation: From Tyranny to Transformation?*, edited by S. Hickey and G. Mohan. London: Zed Books.

Winthrop, R. and E. Matsui. 2013. *A New Agenda for Education in Fragile States*. Centre for Universal Education, Working Paper 10. Washington, DC: Brookings Institute.

Chapter 23

The Business Case for Transnational Corporate Participation, Profits, and Policy-Making in Education

Zahra Bhanji

> Traditional approaches to aid are not enough to address the great global challenges of our time. Market-based solutions show incredible promise to solve these daunting problems on a systemic and widespread level. These approaches, however, are still in a nascent stage. Corporations are researching and developing better business practices that meet social and environmental bottom lines while producing profits. Non-profits are pioneering enterprise-based models that offer potential for long-term sustainability. Governments are contributing their resources to encourage and support market-based approaches. (Clinton Global Initiative 2010)

Even though it is well-known that for-profit motivations drive philanthropic investments in education (Bhanji 2012; Van Fleet 2012b), international organizations and governments are calling for an increasingly important role for the private sector in education financing (Rose and Steer 2013). Increasingly, the methods, motivations, and giving practices of wealthy philanthropists and heads of large transnational corporations (TNCs) are changing. "Philanthrocapitalism" has emerged as a new generation of individuals and companies are using business models and techniques to guide their social investments (Bishop 2008), including a greater focus on short-term giving toward specific issues or problems with measureable, outcomes-based results. In addition, there is also a shift, referred to as "new philanthropy," toward greater involvement of givers in philanthropic action and policy communities. "New philanthropists" tend to be personally involved in overseeing grants and expect results from educators and schools (Colvin 2005).

Corporate executive officers (CEOs) are now highly motivated to invest in education and develop a strong workforce. The United Nations Educational, Scientific and Cultural Organization (UNESCO) *et al.* (2013) state that this could potentially be

The Handbook of Global Education Policy, First Edition.
Edited by Karen Mundy, Andy Green, Bob Lingard, and Antoni Verger.
© 2016 John Wiley & Sons, Ltd. Published 2016 by John Wiley & Sons, Ltd.

the largest "skill-less population in history" (UNESCO *et al.* 2013, 31), with roughly one-sixth of the world's population being aged 15 to 24, and one billion living in the developing world (UNESCO 2012). PricewaterhouseCooper's (2011) 14th Annual Global CEO Survey found that 65% of CEOs reported that their biggest talent challenge was the lack of the right skills in their employees. On their part, one-third of the 38,000 employers surveyed in the ManpowerGroup's 2012 Talent Shortage Survey reported that they weren't able to fill jobs because of the lack of technical competences and hard skills (ManpowerGroup 2012).

Corporate philanthropists and CEOs are gaining interest and ever-growing influence over schools and systems of education around the world (Ball 2012). In this chapter, I showcase how TNCs are operating as global governors in education policy through corporate social engagement mechanisms. They are increasingly blending business and social goals. Global governors, according to Avant *et al.* (2010), are "authorities who exercise power across borders for purposes affecting policy. Governors thus create issues, set agendas, establish and implement rules or programs, and evaluate and/or adjudicate outcomes" (Avant *et al.* 2010, 2). Global corporate social engagement (Bhanji 2008) refers to the varying motivations and variety of modes through which corporations operate within social sectors. I will highlight how forms of private authority (cf. Cutler *et al.* 1999) are transnational in scope and mobilize corporate social responsibility (CSR) norms to legitimize their influence over the broad frame and direction of their activities in education. They require the extra economic benefits of engaging in social sectors like education in order to reproduce themselves globally (Bhanji 2012). Corporate social engagement approaches are facilitating corporate leaders to set new policy agendas and are creating new solutions to educational challenges (Ball 2012, 4).

This chapter presents an overview of the multilateral and other global mechanisms through which corporate social engagement norms and activities have entered the education sector. The chapter provides an updated global corporate social engagement typology (Bhanji 2008) and case examples outlining philanthropic and profit motivations and activities of corporations in education policy. The typology highlights new models of corporate giving that incorporate "doing good" within existing business practices. The chapter concludes with a discussion on TNCs and global policy-making in education.

"Market Multilateralism," Forums, and Coalitions Facilitating Corporate Social Engagement in Education

Market multilateralism, referring to the interlinked role of private companies and nation states, plays a coordinated multilateral role within new generalized principles of conduct (Bull and McNeil 2007). These new principles of conduct are based on the global corporate social engagement discourse that is also mediating the work of the private sector within multilateral institutions. In this section, I show how this discourse has been forged in the context of a range of global spaces, with a focus on the United Nations (UN) and the World Economic Forum. As we will see, these organizations have promoted a range of initiatives to instigate the engagement of corporations in education politics.

The United Nations Global Compact

> Corporate philanthropy is critical, but we need more companies to think about how their business policies and practices can impact education priorities. You understand investment. You focus on the bottom-line. You know the dividends of education for all. (Ban Ki-Moon, UN Secretary-General; UNESCO, UNICEF, UN Global Compact, UN Special Envoy for Global Education 2013)

Developed in 1999, the UN's Global Compact is the world's largest voluntary initiative in CSR. The platform encourages the development, implementation, and disclosure of responsible and sustainable corporate policies and practices. The program is based on a learning model to encourage corporations to report their good corporate practices based on ten UN principles, including the protection of human rights, the abolition of child labor, and the promotion and implementation of greater environmental responsibility. The aim of this initiative is make the ten UN principles part of business strategies, culture, and operations, as well as to mobilize support for broader UN goals, including the Millennium Development Goals (United Nations 2006; 2013). Beginning with 50 participating corporations in July 2000, Global Compact has grown to nearly 8000 corporate participants in over 140 countries in 2013. In addition, 4000 civil society signatories play an important role in partnering with businesses and holding companies accountable to their commitments (UN 2013).

The World Economic Forum

The World Economic Forum (WEF) is an interesting case of how global social corporate engagement (Bhanji 2008) discourse and norms have mediated the entrance of TNC involvement into the education sector. It was through its Global Corporate Citizenship Initiative in the early 2000s that the WEF first began to raise awareness amongst its membership of the importance of integrating corporate citizenship into their core business strategies. The WEF infused new norms about the overall business benefits of using corporate citizenship models and sharing cases of businesses that have mainstreamed these norms into their core business activities.

More than ten years later, Gordon Brown, the UN Special Envoy for Global Education, chaired a special session on education at the 2013 World Economic Forum in Davos. The session focused on how the international community could work together to educate the over 60 million children out of school, build the needed four million classrooms, and train the necessary two million teachers. Hikmet Ersek, President and CEO of Western Union Company USA, was one of four panelists. He confirmed his belief that education is a compelling business investment that correlates with the long-term goals of shareholders. It is illustrative of the greater trend of corporate philanthropy norms being recognized as meeting business goals that he stated, "Education means growth. Education means potential. Educated people create jobs" (World Economic Forum 2013).

Reports, Frameworks, and Business Coalitions

There have been numerous prominent reports developed over the years by multilateral organizations that outline specific strategies and frameworks for business to further develop products and new markets in the education sector. For instance, a joint initiative by UNESCO, the United Nations Children's Fund (UNICEF), UN Global Compact, and the UN Special Envoy for Global Education was launched in 2013 with the release of A Framework for Business Engagement in Education. The framework provides corporations with a three-part process to: (a) make the business case to engage in education that aligns with the companies' business strategy and long-term growth; (b) identify activities that improve education and benefit business, and apply best practices; and (c) use education best practices to engage responsibly in business activities (UNESCO et al. 2013).

A stream of The Brookings Institute's work in recent years has focused on business and education. In one report, they offer "five principles to guide future business engagement in education to help business play a more sustainable and scalable role" (Van Fleet 2012a, 3). The interest that the Brookings research and reports have generated has been instrumental in the establishment of a Global Business Coalition for Education in 2012 (GBCE). GBCE is a business-led and action-oriented organization that aims to accelerate progress in delivering quality education for all of the world's children and youth. The Coalition is a network of corporate leaders who initially represented 20 influential global companies (Global Business Coalition for Education 2013). GBCE aims to facilitate collaboration between corporations and other sectors. They also aim to conduct research to share best education practice strategies and highlight their research on business being an active partner in educating the world's children and youth (Global Business Coalition for Education 2013, 1). The Coalition has also organized high-level events, bringing together global decision makers and leaders (Global Business Coalition for Education 2013).

Global Corporate Social Engagement

Increasing numbers of corporate leaders are investing substantive amounts in education. Overall, corporate giving has increased significantly in the USA from US$5 billion in the late 1960s and early 1970s to $17.61 billion in 2005 (Giving USA Foundation 2008, 211). It is estimated that, in addition to passing on a significant amount of money to their heirs, Americans will give an estimated $1.7 trillion to charities and endowed foundations by 2025. Bill Gates, whose personal worth is estimated to be $46 billion, has stated that he will give away 95% of his assets during his lifetime (Colvin 2005).

Philanthropists are spending approximately $1.5 billion on K-12 education in the USA. The largest contributors to education come from the technology, consumer discretionary, and energy sectors, according to the 2007 Corporate Giving Standard Survey, which polled 155 companies (Coady 2008). Most foundation funding remains in the USA. The annual US corporate contribution to education in developing countries is estimated to be $497 million. The majority of the cash contributions to education comes directly from companies and not their corporate foundations. This highlights the direct relationship for private companies between investing in education and the best interest of businesses, irrespective of their foundation's philanthropic activities (Van Fleet 2012b).

Corporate philanthropy is influencing K-12 education worldwide through these significant investments and the increasing policy role played by wealthy philanthropists and heads of TNCs. Colvin (2005) offers some examples of this changing role, including involvement in creating new schools, conducting research, funding scholarships, testing hypotheses, generating new curricula, invoking ideals, setting agendas, bolstering training, and building a case for policy changes (Colvin 2005, 36). Ball (2012) further explains,

> Business is now directly engaged with education policy in a number of different ways and these engagements are part of a broader set of complex processes affecting education policy, which include new modes of philanthropy and aid for educational development, market processes of capital growth and expansion and the search by business for new opportunities for profit. (Ball 2012, 11)

The "rules that hang the world together" (Ruggie 1998, 3) – the different modalities through which corporations are participating in education – are changing from previous forms of involvement by the private sector in education. This is particularly the case in developing countries where TNCs have entered previously highly contested terrain through new social engagement norms. Business literature on corporate social engagement explores the increasing participation of TNCs in the social sector through a broad spectrum of motivations that integrate philanthropic motivations based on purely moral and ethical grounds without clear business rationale (Waldman and Sully de Lunque 2006) to those vested in self-interest that aim to link their corporate social engagement to business performance and profits (Martin 2002; Porter and Kramer 2002; Rowley and Berman 2000).

In Table 23.1, the author's original Global Corporate Social Engagement taxonomy (Bhanji 2008) has been updated and is used to explore the different ways in which business actors are working within the social sector with specific case examples. The case examples provide a glimpse into the diverse type of activities that foundations and corporations are engaged in through the corporate social engagement rubric in education. Each case example provides a brief overview of the foundation/organization, its governance structure (within company or a separate entity), an overview of its recent funding activities in education, and its motivations in education (profit/philanthropic). As I develop in this section, it is clear that business motivations are increasingly becoming more explicit and central in global social engagement frameworks.

Table 23.1 Taxonomy of Global Corporate Social Engagement activities, interests, and governance structure

Type of GCSE activity	Interests (philanthropic or business)	Governance structure
Private foundation philanthropy	Philanthropic	Separate foundation external to business entity
Corporate social responsibility	Business and philanthropic	Foundation or corporate giving department within company
Shared value/business sustainability	Primarily business and philanthropic	Within company marketing department or other business department

Source: Updated from Bhanji (2008).

Private Foundations

There are many different types of foundations. Some of the largest private foundations have been set up by private funds of wealthy business people to be completely separate from the business entity. These foundations are not profit oriented, are not part of the public sector, use their own financial resources (unlike non-governmental organizations (NGOs)), are led by an independent board of trustees or CEO, and aim to improve issues for the common good (e.g. development, the environment, etc.) (Marten and Witte 2008, 5). There are some foundations that operate as grant-makers that finance projects and programs implemented by other actors (typically NGOs) (see below example of the Hewlett Foundation). There are other foundations that are operational actors that finance and implement their own company projects and programs, either alone or in cooperation with other actors (see section on the ICICI Bank) (Marten and Witte 2008, 5).

Case Example of the William and Flora Hewett Foundation

The Hewlett-Packard Company was co-founded in 1939. It was Silicon Valley's first major start-up company and was ranked as the 13th largest business in the USA at the time of William Hewlett's death in 2001. The William and Flora Hewlett Foundation awarded 609 grants valuing approximately $304 million and disbursed approximately $380 million in grant and gift payments in 2012. The Foundation's assets were approximately $7.74 billion as of December 31, 2012 (Hewlett Foundation 2014). The governance and operations of the Hewlett Foundation are separate from the Hewlett-Packard Company.

The investments and work of the Foundation in education have evolved to play a more substantive policy role in recent years. In 2008, Barbara Chow was appointed as the new Director of the Foundation's Education Program. During an interview when first hired, Chow stated,

> I'm a policy person, so I tend to think in terms of leverage. The amounts that state and local governments spend on education outstrip what the federal government or philanthropy can spend to an amazing degree. (Hewlett-Foundation 2008)

Hewlett's education program aims to direct the majority of its resources towards "organizations that will work to make deeper learning the norm in US schools in order to reach our ultimate goal: students' success in work and civic life" (Hewlett Foundation 2012, 7). The Foundation has adopted the term "deeper learning," referring to "higher-order skills and academic knowledge that are the surest path to post-secondary education and that students will need to succeed in the twenty-first century work and civic life" (Hewlett Foundation 2012, 4).

In recent years through its focus at a policy level, the foundation has outlined a series of areas of investment and effort under the "Resetting Learning Goals and Requirements for School" banner. Here the foundation states that

> The Program's policy investments support organizations that promote state and federal policies that can help remove barriers to – and provide incentives for deeper learning goals throughout the K-12 and postsecondary education systems. Grants are focused on

helping state and federal policy makers first articulate a commitment to deeper learning and then identify and implement initiatives that systematically support this vision. (Hewlett 2012, 10)

Interestingly, in a footnote to the above text, the foundation clarifies that:

The Hewlett Foundation does not expend funds or earmark its funding for prohibited attempts to influence legislation (i.e., lobby) within the meaning of the federal tax laws. The Foundation's funding for policy work is limited to permissible forms of support only, such as general operating support grants grantees can allocate at their discretion and project support grants for nonlobbying activities (e.g., public education and nonpartisan research). (Hewlett 2012, 10)

One of the specific goals of the Foundation is to support five to ten states in adopting policy changes that support deeper learning by 2017. Hewlett is aggressively working toward realizing its goals through a suite of funding opportunities. Grants will be provided to these states to

...access to ideas, research, and educational outreach to policymakers in implementing the Common Core[1] standards with fidelity to deeper learning, supporting changes to accountability systems and graduate requirements, and experimenting with innovations and new models in schools and districts. (Hewlett 2012, 11)

Hewlett's policy influence is not directly aligned to the business goals of its corporate entity, Hewlett-Packard. However, there is growing concern among corporate leaders about the limited hiring pool of qualified potential employees with the necessary skills to meet business goals. The Hewlett Foundation is explicit that it hopes through its deep learning policy work to support students to be successful in "the 21century work and civic life" (Hewlett Foundation 2012, 7).

Corporate Social Responsibility (CSR)

CSR activities are actions taken by a firm beyond their direct business interests with the aim to further social goods (McWilliams and Siegel 2001). CSR initiatives are usually distinct from business interests and are run by a philanthropic corporate foundation or separate corporate giving department within a company (Doh and Guay 2006; Himmelstein 1997). CSR activities are also distinct from other forms of giving, which include cash contributions, in-kind donations of products or services, volunteerism, employee-matching programs, employee-giving campaigns, and cause marketing. Cash contributions can come from foundation operating budgets or directly from a company. Corporate operating foundations and trusts enable companies to write off financial profits as charitable contributions for tax purposes. These entities tend to share the same name as the company, are located within the company's headquarters, and are tasked to carry out the company's philanthropic activities; in addition, the majority of the members on the board are corporate senior executives (Van Fleet 2012a).

Case Example of ICICI Foundation

ICICI Bank is India's largest private sector bank, with a network of over 3600 branches and 11,160 ATMs in India, and presence in 19 countries. Its total assets for the fiscal year 2013 were Rs.5367.95 billion (US$99 billion) and the profit after tax was Rs.83.25 billion (US$ 1533 billion). The Bank provides a variety of financial services and banking products to retail and corporate entities through various delivery channels and through its specialized subsidiaries (ICICI Bank 2014).

Some companies have CSR departments within their organization. In this case, the ICICI Foundation is the corporate giving arm of ICICI Inc. ICICI Foundation was established and is governed by ICICI Foundation's president and a council of senior executives from ICICI Group (ICICI Foundation 2013). There are close ties between the company and Foundation. The Foundation received Rs.100 million from ICICI Bank and its affiliated companies from April 2012 to March 2013. Over Rs.65 million was targeted to its elementary education initiatives, and Rs.3.3 million was for the Rural Self Employment Training Institute (ICICI Foundation 2013).

The Foundation states that it seeks to ensure systematic and sustainable impact in better teaching–learning outcomes in schools and classrooms by directly embedding its initiatives within government spaces. Their focus has been to support efforts toward child-centric and child-friendly environments. Their work is rooted within government mandates, including the Right of Children to Free and Compulsory Education Act, 2009 (RtE); the National Curriculum Framework (NCF), 2055; and the National Curriculum Framework for Teacher Education (NCFTE), 2009.

ICICI Foundation has launched elementary education programs with the state governments of Rajasthan and Chhattisgarh. In Rajasthan, the School and Teacher Education Reform Programme is being implemented through a six-year partnership with the state government of Rajasthan that included the establishment of a Unit of Teacher Education within the State Institute for Educational Research and Training (ICICI Foundation 2014). In Chhattisgarh, the ICICI Bank has worked with its partners and developed new curricula and textbooks for Classes 1 to VIII for the newly formed state since 2002. The Foundation signed a Memorandum of Understanding in 2012 with the State Council Educational Research and Training, Government of Chhattisgarh, which included the development of District Institutes of Training and Education (ICICI Foundation 2014).

The Foundation also provides skill training to youth at residential sites in the Udaipur and Jodhpur districts of Rajasthan as part of the ICICI Bank's Rural Self Employment Training Institute. There were over 3200 beneficiaries in 2013 at the centers in Jodphur and Udaipur, with approximately 70% of the trainees having either been placed in jobs or set up their own businesses with an income of Rs.250 to Rs.500 per day (ICICI Foundation 2013).

Although CSR activities are to be distinct and beyond the direct business interests, this case does highlight that some of the Foundation's activities do aim to create goodwill amongst families whose children attend schools that are supported by ICICI Foundation. In addition, the Foundation's youth training support aims for youth to set up businesses or earn income, thus creating new business opportunities for ICICI Bank. The indicators used to evaluate their vocational training programs include the number of bank accounts set up, which is the core business of the Bank.

Shared Value

The shared value approach refers to "creating economic value in a way that also creates value for society by addressing its needs and challenges" (Porter and Kramer 2011, 65). The shared value concept extends earlier corporate citizenship, strategic philanthropy, and "bottom of the pyramid" frameworks, which first introduced the idea that voluntary social initiatives can also meet the strategic business needs of companies. The shared value approach is used within company marketing departments or other business departments. Porter and Kramer (2011) explain that,

> ...value is defined as benefits relative to costs, not just benefits alone. Value creation is an idea that has long been recognized in business, where profit is revenue earned from customers minus costs incurred. (Porter and Kramer 2011, 66)

This notion is not as common in the social sector, where government and NGOs usually measure success in terms of resources used or benefits achieved. Extending the notion of value creation to societal issues makes business sense given the high internal costs incurred by companies resulting from social weaknesses or harms such as the need for remedial training to compensate for inadequacies in education (Porter and Kramer 2011). There have been a variety of initiatives and reports written recently that promote shared value approaches (see section on Reports, Frameworks, and Business Coalitions).

Case Example of Pearson Inc.

Pearson is the largest multinational education and publishing company in the world. Pearson's Chief Executive Officer, John Fallon states

> Pearson now operates in virtually every sphere of the education landscape, from schools to higher and professional education; from publishing textbooks to operating entire institutions. We are the world's leading learning company. With that evolving and more active role in education comes the privilege of insight and a weight of responsibility to prove our impact. (Barber and Rizvi 2013)

The company develops and sells curriculum under a range of respected imprints and electronic learning programs and is a provider of test development, processing, and scoring services to educational institutions, corporations, and professional bodies around the world. Pearson is a British company headquartered in London and operates in 70 countries around the world with approximately 60% of its sales coming from North America and 11% from developing markets. The business generated US$1 billion in revenue for the first time in 2011 (Pearson Inc. 2014b).

Pearson's purpose, as outlined in their 2011 "Pearson PLC: Our Impact on Society" report, is "to help people of all ages to progress through their lives through learning" (Pearson Inc. 2012, 42). The company is explicit in its reports and website that this purpose "is both a social purpose and our core business" (Pearson Inc. 2012, 42), explaining that "our commercial success provides the investment capacity for us to continue to innovate and expand into new geographic markets and new kinds of learning" (Pearson Inc. 2012, 42).

The company's aligned approach to corporate responsibility and commercial priorities is further demonstrated through its governance:

> Corporate responsibility cannot be separated from our financial performance and reputation. As such, our board of directors has ultimate responsibility for considering issues of business responsibility in setting business strategy. (Pearson 2014, 7)

It has prioritized three key issues of economic and social importance: raising literacy levels, improving learning outcomes, and contributing to competitiveness (Pearson Inc. 2012, 6). Pearson states that their commitment to education is also extended through their philanthropic arm, the Pearson Foundation. The Foundation receives a grant each year from Pearson Inc. for its operating budget, which is used to develop partnerships and hands-on programs around the world (Pearson Inc. 2014a).

Pearson also has a strong focus on policy and research activities to measure the effectiveness of their products, programs, and services within pre-kindergarten to Grade 12, higher education, and assessment programs. The company is trying to be a thought leader in this arena by heavily investing in research and policy activities, such as the efficacy framework, a new global research network, and the Pearson's Learning Curve Data Bank, which aggregates internationally comparable education data (Pearson Inc. 2012; Barber and Rizvi 2013).

The company in recent years has also gotten involved in the management of the Programme for International Student Assessment (PISA), where it is advising the Organisation for Economic Co-operation and Development (OECD) on the implementation of computer adaptive testing for PISA (Pearson 2011). Pearson also signed a US$35 million (£22 million) contract with New York state education officials and contracts worth $500 million (£318 million) in Texas and other states including Arizona, Florida, Kentucky, Virginia, and Maryland to provide high stakes testing for schools (Mansell 2012).

There is increasing awareness and criticism of Pearson's influence over education policy. The *Guardian* published an article titled "Should Pearson, a Giant Multinational, Be Influencing Our Education Policy?" that questioned, "how great an influence over education policymaking can and should a private organization have?" (Mansell 2012). Pearson claims that their business and social priorities are the same. It is however apparent that the company is deeply tied to their growing business priorities.

Discussion: Corporate Global Governors and Education Policy-Making

Corporate philanthropists and CEOs are gaining ever-growing influence over schools and systems of education around the world (Ball 2012). The case examples under the rubric of global corporate social engagement illustrate how corporate foundations and TNCs are operating as global governors (Avant et al. 2010) in education policy. They are creating new issues, setting policy agendas, creating new solutions to education challenges within and outside education ministries and departments of education. They are pursuing research activities to generate and share new ideas in education. They are all instigating new policy directions and networks with education decision-makers and leaders around the world. Hewlett's new focus on deep learning and Pearson's learning outcomes activities are, for instance, setting new directions that aim to shift the priorities of government and other educational stakeholders. They are bringing together decision makers within and outside government to share their ideas and co-create new realities and priorities for education. These networks are at their core being driven by corporations. Policy networks do constitute a new form of governance that become new sources of authority or "market authorities" (Shamir 2008, 10) within policy processes. Their policy work is outcome-based with the aim to ultimately influence and shape education.

Like many, Rose and Steer (2013) ask whose interests are they promoting – students' or shareholders'? Business investments in education tend to be small, short-term (Van Fleet 2011), and focused on specific issues or problems (Colvin 2005). Many questions still remain unanswered. To what extent are corporate philanthropic activities meeting the needs of teachers and students? What and whose knowledge is being promoted? Whose worldview and approaches are informing the significant investments for instance in curriculum and teacher training programs (Bhanji 2008)? In addition, the multitude of different programs and activities within the rubric of CSR are not regulated or always focused on the priorities of governments working in education. Greater coordination is also required amongst the recent proliferation of corporate philanthropic or social investment in education to yield greater impacts (GBCE 2013, 1).

For companies, their investments often lack legitimacy, which often leads to significant obstacles in the design and implementation of effective corporate social engagement programs (Bhanji and Oxley 2013). To overcome this, the private sector aims to enhance its legitimacy through activities such as the strategic recruitment of education policy influencers. The appointment by the Hewlett Foundation of Barbara Chow, who formerly served under the Clinton administration, and by Pearson of Sir Michael Barber, the former advisor to the UK Prime Minister and Head of Education at McKinsey, highlights the increasing importance of the education sector for the private sector.

New forms of private authority (Cutler *et al.* 1999) are transnational in scope and mobilize CSR norms to legitimize their influence over the broad frame and direction of their activities in education. It is ultimately their expertise and material authority that have enabled TNCs to operate as policy actors in education. These are new sites of mobilization by corporate actors within new forms of policy and policy expertise (Ball 2012).

Corporations and corporate foundations are shaping education through significant investments in key areas that were traditionally financed by government. ICICI, for instance, has invested in curriculum development and teacher training. Although they are explicit that their investments and activities are within state policy mandates and curriculum frameworks, their influence is shifting the education landscape to meet their core business goals. Further study is required to fully unveil their motivations and the extent to which they are using their material power to influence policy and programmatic directions. It is clear that the metrics ICICI uses to measure its success include those that are closely aligned to their business priorities, including the amount of credit support provided to entrepreneurs and the number of people that want to start their own businesses. This clearly illustrates ICICI's potential interest in supporting the skills development and training to work activities that also generate income and in turn develop a greater banking demand for its products.

The typology and cases presented highlight the diverse and strategic modalities through which corporations are creating new areas of focus and business within social spaces that were previously out of reach. The explicit narrative that corporate responsibility and commercial priorities are not in conflict with each other, but rather are in alignment, is legitimizing the strategic action in education politics of a range of companies around the world. Pearson's statement that "corporate responsibility cannot be separated from our financial performance" (Pearson Inc. 2012, 7) creates a strategic space from which to operate. As Frunkin (2006, 1) argues, "philanthropy allows private actors to act in public ways." The shift toward shared value approaches poses significant risks to education. Education products and services under this perspective would be considered a commodity or asset that would undergo business strategies and be measured by the same systems of value – new interests and new bottom lines. Probably for this reason, Ball (2012, 140) concludes that, "in the world of business shareholders, investors and stock market value – profitability is what counts in the final analysis."

Note

1 The Common Core is a set of college- and career-ready standards in the USA for kindergarten through 12th grade in English language arts/literacy and mathematics.

References

Avant, D., M. Finnemore, and S.K. Sell. 2010. "Who Governs the Globe?," in *Who Governs the Globe?*, edited by D. Avant, M. Finnemore, and S.K. Sell, 1–31. Cambridge: Cambridge Studies in International Relations.

Ball, S. 2012. *Global Education Inc.: New Policy Networks and the Neo-liberal Imaginary*. London: Routledge.

Barber, M. and Rizvi, S. 2013. *The Incomplete Guide to Delivering Learning Outcomes*. Pearson. Retrieved from http://efficacy.pearson.com/wp-content/uploads/2013/11/The-Incomplete-Guide-to-Delivering-Learning-Outcomes-high-res1.pdf (accessed November 25, 2015).

Bhanji, Z. 2008. "Transnational Corporations in Education: Filling the Governance Gap Through New Social Norms and Market Multilateralism?" *Globalisation, Societies and Education*, 6(1): 55–73.

Bhanji, Z. 2012. "Transnational Private Authority in Education Policy in Jordan and South Africa: The Case of Microsoft Corporation." *Comparative Education Review*, 56 (2): 300–319.

Bhanji, Z. and J.E. Oxley. 2013. "Overcoming the Dual Liability of Foreignness and Privateness in International Corporate Citizenship Partnerships." *Journal of International Business Studies*, 44(4): 290–311.

Bishop, M. 2008. *Philanthrocapitalism: How the Rich Can Save the World*. New York: Bloomsbury Press.

Bull, B. and D. McNeill. 2007. "The Rise of Public-Private Partnerships in the Multilateral System," in *Development Issues in Global Governance: Public-Private Partnerships and Market Multilateralism*, edited by B. Bull and D. McNeil, 1–22. New York: Routledge.

Clinton Global Initiative. 2010. "Strengthening Market-Based Solutions." Retrieved from: www.clintonglobalinitiative.org/ourmeetings/2010/action_areas.asp?action_area=Strengthening_Marketbased_Solutions (accessed November 18, 2015).

Coady, M. 2008. *Giving in Numbers: 2008 Edition*. New York: Committee Encouraging Corporate Philanthropy.

Colvin, R. 2005. "The New Philanthropists." *Education Next*, 5(4): 34–41.

Cutler, A.C., V. Haufler, and T. Porter. 1999. "The Contours and Significance of Private Authority in International Affairs," in *Private Authority and International Affairs*, edited by C. Cutler, V. Haufler, and T. Porter, 333–376. Albany: State University of New York.

Doh, J. and T. Guay. 2006. "Corporate Social Responsibility, Public Policy, and NGO Activism in Europe and the United States: An Institutional-Stakeholder Perspective." *Journal of Management Studies*, 43(1): 47–73.

Frunkin, P. 2006. *Strategic Giving: The Art and Science of Philanthropy*. Chicago: University of Chicago Press.

Giving USA Foundation. 2008. *Giving USA 2009: The Annual Report on Philanthropy for the Year 2008*. Glenview: Giving USA Foundation.

Global Business Coalition for Education. 2013. "Connecting Business to Make a Lasting Impact." Retrieved from: http://gbc-education.org/wp-content/uploads/2012/09/GBC-Education-Value-Proposition.pdf (accessed November 18, 2015).

Hewlett Foundation. 2008. "Foundations" A Q&A with Barbara Chow, Education Program Director. Retrieved from: www.hewlett.org/newsroom/news/ foundations-qa-barbara-chow-education-program-director (accessed November 26, 2015).

Hewlett Foundation. 2012. "Deeper Learning Strategic Plan Summary Education Program: December 2012 Update." Retrieved from: www.hewlett.org/uploads/documents/EducationProgram_Deeper_Learning_Strategy.pdf (accessed November 18, 2015).

Hewlett Foundation. 2014. "About The William and Flora Hewlett Foundation." Retrieved from: www.hewlett.org/about (accessed November 18, 2015).

Himmelstein, J. (ed.). 1997. *Looking Good and Doing Good: Corporate Philanthropy and Corporate Power*. Indiana: Indiana University Press.

ICICI Bank. 2014. "About Us." Retrieved from: www.icicibank.com/aboutus/about-us.html (accessed November 18, 2015).

ICICI Foundation. 2013. "ICICI Foundation Launches ICICI Academy for Skills." Retrieved from: www.icicibank.com/aboutus/article/icici-foundation-launches-icici-academy-for-skills.html (accessed November 18, 2015).

ICICI Foundation. 2014. "Elementary Education." Retrieved from: www.icicifoundation.org/read_more/2/8 (accessed November 18, 2015).

Lagemann, E.C. (ed.). 1999. *Philanthropic Foundations: New Scholarship, New Possibilities*. Bloomington: Indiana University Press.

ManpowerGroup. 2012. "Talent Shortage Survey." Retrieved from: www.manpowergroup.us/campaigns/talent-shortage-2013 (accessed November 18, 2015).

Mansell, W. 2011. "Should Pearson, a giant multinational, be influencing our education policy?" *The Guardian*. Retrieved from: www.theguardian.com/education/2012/jul/16/pearson-multinational-influence-education-poliy (accessed November 25, 2015).

Marten, R. and J.M. Witte. 2008. "Transforming Development: The Role of Philanthropic Foundations in International Development Cooperation." Retrieved from: http://dspace.cigilibrary.org/jspui/bitstream/123456789/26599/1/GPPi%20Research%20Paper%20No%2010.pdf?1 (accessed November 18, 2015).

Martin, R. 2002. "The Virtue Matrix: Calculating the Return on Corporate Responsibility." *Harvard Business Review*, 80(3): 68–75.

McWilliams, A. and D. Siegel. 2001. "Corporate Social Responsibility: A Theory of the Firm Perspective." *Academy of Management Review*, 26(1): 117–127.

Pearson. 2011. "Pearson to Develop Frameworks for OECD's PISA Student Assessment for 2015." Accessed August 19, 2014. Retrieved from: http://uk.pearson.com/home/news/2011/september/pearson-to-develop-frameworks-for-oecds-pisa-student-assessment-for-2015.htm (accessed November 18, 2015).

Pearson Inc. 2012. "The Learning Curve: Lessons in Country Performance in Education (2012 Report)." Retrieved from: http://thelearningcurve.pearson.com/the-report (accessed November 18, 2015).

Pearson Inc. 2014a. "Education." Retrieved from: www.pearson.com/about-us/education.html (accessed November 18, 2015).

Pearson Inc. 2014b. "More Low-Income Students in Achieving College Readiness and Success." Retrieved from: www.pearsoned.com/pearson-joins-president-and-mrs-obama-education-secretary-duncan-for-white-house-higher-education-summit/#.UtvTFfYo5hA (accessed November 18, 2015).

Porter, M. and M. Kramer. 2002. "The Competitive Advantage of Corporate Philanthropy." *Harvard Business Review*, 80(12): 56–68.

Porter, M. and M. Kramer. 2011. "The Big Idea: Creating Shared Value." *Harvard Business Review*, 89(1/2): 62–77.

PricewaterhouseCooper. 2011. "14th Annual Global CEO Survey: Growth Reimagined. The Talent Race is Back On." Retrieved from: www.pwc.com/gx/en/hr-management-services/assets/CEO-survey-talent-race.pdf (accessed November 18, 2015).

Rizvi, F. and B. Lingard. 2010. *Globalizing Education Policy*. London: Routledge.

Rose, P. and L. Steer. 2013. *Financing for Global Education: Opportunities for Multilateral Opportunities*. Paris: UNESCO and Brookings Institute.

Rowley, T. and S. Berman. 2000. "A Brand New Brand of Corporate Social Performance." *Business and Society*, 39(4): 397–418.

Ruggie, J.G. 1998. "What Makes the World Hang Together? Neo-Utilitarianism and the Social Constructivist Challenge," in *Constructing the World Polity: Essays on International Institutionalization*, edited by J.G. Ruggie, 1–39. New York: Routledge.

Shamir, R. 2008. "The Age of Responsibilitization: On Market-Embedded Morality." *Economy and Society*, 37(1): 1–19.

UNESCO. 2012. *Education for All Global Monitoring Report*. Paris: UNESCO.

UNESCO, UNICEF, UN Global Compact and UN Special Envoy for Global Education. 2013. *The Smartest Investment: A Framework for Business Engagement in Education*. New York: UN Global Compact Office.

United Nations (UN). 2006. "The Global Compact: Advancing Corporate Citizenship in the World Economy." Retrieved from: www.unglobalcompact.org/docs (accessed November 25, 2015).

United Nations (UN). 2013. "Corporate Sustainability in the World Economy: United Nations Global Compact." Retrieved from: www.unglobalcompact.org/docs/news_events/8.1/GC_brochure_FINAL.pdf (accessed November 18, 2015).

Van Fleet, J. 2011. *A Global Education Challenge: Harnessing Corporate Philanthropy to Educate the World's Poor*. Washington, DC: The Brookings Institution.

Van Fleet, J. 2012a. *Scaling up Corporate Social Investments in Education: Five Strategies that Work*. Washington, DC: The Brookings Institution.

Van Fleet, J. 2012b. "A Disconnect Between Motivations and Education Needs: Why American Corporate Philanthropy Alone Will Not Educate the Most Marginalized," in *Public Private Partnerships in Education: New Actors and Modes of Governance in a Globalizing World*, edited by S.L. Robertson, K. Mundy, A. Verger, and F. Menashy, 158–181. London: Verger.

Waldman, D. and M. Sully de Lunque. 2006. "Cultural and Leadership Predictors of Corporate Social Responsibility Values of Top Management: A GLOBE Study of 15 Countries." *Journal of International Business Studies*, 37: 823–837.

World Economic Forum. 2013. "The Global Education Imperative." Retrieved from: www.weforum.org/sessions/summary/global-education-imperative (accessed November 18, 2015).

Chapter 24

New Global Philanthropy and Philanthropic Governance in Education in a Post-2015 World

Prachi Srivastava and Lianna Baur

Introduction

Institutionalized philanthropy in education in the Global South is not new. However, the macro- and domestic policy contexts characterized by the tail-end of Education for All (EFA), the post-2015 discourse, the disenchantment with official development assistance (ODA), and the growing presence of an increased array of international and Southern non-state private actors (including those with for-profit and commercial motives) constitute an arguably different context from earlier studies that examined the work of (largely American) private foundations in colonial or post-colonial contexts (Arnove 1980; Berman 1983; Davis 1976; King 1971). These developments intimate a new "moment of the politics of education" (Robertson and Dale 2013), in which the current philanthropic buzz is embedded. It is, however, both empirically under-researched and conceptually under-theorized.

This chapter addresses some of those gaps. It is part of an ongoing line of inquiry in view of one of the author's (Srivastava) earlier calls to establish a renewed research interest in global philanthropy in education, particularly in and stemming from the Global South (Srivastava and Oh 2010). The chapter is based on the results of a literature review on philanthropic and private foundation engagement in the Global South by international and Southern philanthropic actors, and emerges from one area of research in a larger research project.[1] Results of the review were extended by conducting a discourse analysis of strategy documents and frameworks of some of the most immediate post-2015 international fora and strategies impacting education, and comparing these with previous frameworks to locate the articulated roles of the private sector and of philanthropic actors over time.[2] The chapter aims to sketch the beginnings of a conceptual analytic on *new*

The Handbook of Global Education Policy, First Edition.
Edited by Karen Mundy, Andy Green, Bob Lingard, and Antoni Verger.
© 2016 John Wiley & Sons, Ltd. Published 2016 by John Wiley & Sons, Ltd.

global philanthropy in education and philanthropic governance in education in the new moment of the politics of education intimated above.

In short, what is termed here as new global philanthropy in education, is based on an apparent "win–win" approach that favors more hands-on interventions by philanthropic actors than in the past who are in search of measurable, tangible, scalable results to tackle issues, seemingly consensually defined as global social problems; and crucially, to insert the market in the public social sphere, specifically in education. The primacy of market-based solutions (e.g. competition, choice, narrowly defined assessment metrics, etc.) is espoused by the new global philanthropy in education. Simultaneously, the increased use of complex multi-stakeholder and public–private partnerships (PPPs) as mechanisms for education provision in many countries of the Global South opens up and creates formal and non-formal spaces for constellations of philanthropic and other non-state private actors to act. These fundamentally alter education governance structures by surreptitiously embedding forms of privatization in education systems, though this may not be the intention of all actors involved.

Extending Ball and Olmedo's (2011) conceptualization of "philanthropic governance," the argument here is that discourse, meanings, and actors gain their legitimacy by manipulating and intertwining three claims associated with philanthropic and/or non-state private actors. These claims can ultimately mute contestation and depoliticize action in this mode of education governance. These are: (a) normalizing long-standing taken-for-granted assumptions of philanthropy with benevolence, goodness, and altruism; (b) extending claims of private sector efficiency and effectiveness; and (c) stressing claims of neutrality to the philanthropic sector as the "third sector," i.e. neither state nor purely private/commercial. The bulk of the chapter presents a conceptual analytic in this area. It must be noted, that as a dynamic field and new line of inquiry, this is the first iteration of the conceptualization.

Philanthropic Engagement in the New Moment of the Politics of Education

Robertson and Dale (2013) provide a useful framework to analyze evolutions in education governance. Based on Dale's (2006) previous work, they outline a range of questions over four levels. For the purposes of the analysis here, the "moment of the politics of education" is most relevant (Table 24.1). This is "where we find the kinds of 'rules of the game' or 'paradigmatic settings' that set basic limits to what is considered possible and desirable from education" (Robertson and Dale 2013, 434). Thus, the new moment of the politics of education is, in essence, the framing architecture (both formal and informal) or the "big picture setting" within which current global philanthropic engagement in education in the Global South is occurring. It is significantly influenced by: (a) macro- and domestic policy contexts characterized by the tail-end of EFA; (b) the post-2015 discourse; (c) the disenchantment with ODA, and (d) the growing presence of increasing arrays of international and Southern non-state private actors, including those with for-profit and commercial motives. These are considered below.

As 2015 approaches, we are told that we are entering an era of transformative paradigmatic shifts in global development. The High Level Panel's Report on the Post-2015 Agenda states: "Perhaps the most important transformative shift is

Table 24.1 Robertson and Dale's questions guiding analysis of the moment of the politics of education

- Issues of "social contract" (how does education contribute to it?) (values of modernity + core problems)
- *Logic of intervention* (how is education's contribution to be delivered?) (grammar of schooling + national focus)
- *What forms are taken by the "architecture of education"?*
- In what ways are the core problems of capitalism (accumulation, social order, and legitimation) reflected in the mandate, capacity, and governance of education? How and at what scales are contradictions between the solutions addressed?
- How are the boundaries of the "education sector" defined and how do they overlap with and relate to other sectors? How is the education sector related to the citizenship and gender regimes?
- How, at what scale and in what sectoral configurations does education contribute to the extra-economic embedding/stabilization of accumulation?
- What is the nature of intra- and inter-scalar and intra- and inter-sectoral relations (contradiction, cooperation, mutual indifference?)
- What functional, scalar, and sectoral divisions of labor of educational governance are in place?

Source: Robertson and Dale (2013), 433 (emphases added).
Note: Italicized questions were used for analysis here.

towards a new spirit of solidarity, cooperation, and mutual accountability that must underpin the post-2015 agenda" (United Nations 2013, 3). Within this broader context, the post-2015 global education agenda is being framed within two articulated crises – one of funding, the other of learning. Six out of ten bilateral donors to basic education cut their aid between 2010 and 2011, which has reportedly stagnated since (UNESCO 2013).[3] As a result, what was reported as a US$16 billion annual funding gap for basic education just three years prior (in 2010), had risen to US$26 billion if we were to reach the goal by 2015 (UNESCO 2014). Globally, 250 million children cannot read or write despite having attended school for four or more years (UNESCO 2014). There is undoubtedly an urgent need to address these gaps and resulting inequities.

While there remains a tacit acknowledgment that ODA to education must increase in the post-2015 scenario, the broader discussion on aid has been marred by its perceived inefficiency and ineffectiveness. The most vehement critics claim that it has further impoverished poor countries and should be dismantled (Moyo 2009). The less severe, nonetheless, seem to accept that there will be scarce resources for aid, and for aid to education, because of constrained budgets in an age of global economic austerity. Though not the focus of discussion here, elsewhere Srivastava (2010) argues that this latent acceptance of scarce resources is indicative of a serious lack of global and domestic political will to address persistent funding gaps, and is used to mobilize increased action from non-state private actors.

In the tail-end of EFA and impending post-2015 engagement, there is, thus, a growing buzz around the potential of philanthropic actors, particularly international and domestic "mega-donors," and the purportedly growing numbers of local Southern foundations, not only to fill resource gaps, but also substantive gaps in scaling up "solutions." Philanthropic actors are idealized as at once, non-market and non-state

(Zoltán and Desai 2007), and as naturally flexible, brisk, agile, and well-suited partners in complex "multi-stakeholder" arrangements to address areas most in need.

Examples of this view in high-level post-2015 exercises can be seen in the High Level Report (United Nations 2013) and in the World Bank's Education Strategy 2020 (World Bank 2011), some of which are presented later in the chapter. On the other hand, the report by the Commonwealth Ministerial Working Group on the Post-2015 Development Framework for Education (2012) is less enthusiastic, highlighting that not all governments may agree to greater non-state private action (p. 9). Nonetheless, increased philanthropic participation, particularly through "newer" forms of philanthropy (e.g. corporate philanthropy, venture philanthropy, social impact philanthropy), have gained currency. Ball and Olmedo (2011) claim this is because "This new conception of philanthropy and aid intentionally blurs the line between business, enterprise, development and the public good, and poses fundamental questions about the methods and future role of traditional development agencies" (Ball and Olmedo 2011, 84). Of interest here is how it alters education governance structures.

The Logics of Intervention and the Contours of Philanthropic Engagement in Education

Nearly all the literature reviewed took as its starting point the rise of a "new" style of philanthropy emerging worldwide. Bishop and Green (2008) famously labeled this style "philanthrocapitalism," or the application of capitalist business practices to philanthropic endeavors. While much of the literature reviewed here noted similar shifts regarding philanthropic engagement in education in the Global South, there is a dearth of literature attempting to conceptualize this engagement, with a few exceptions, most notably the work of Stephen Ball and his colleagues (e.g. Ball 2008; 2012; Ball and Olmedo 2011; Ball and Youdell 2007; Nambissan and Ball 2010).

The analysis here similarly wishes to transcend the limits of characterizing current philanthropic engagement in education in the Global South as philanthrocapitalism. This latter conceptualization does not sufficiently engage with the structural impacts on education systems, the notions of scale and scope of action, the inter-connectedness and hybridity of actors, or the formal and informal institutional rules (global and domestic) that frame action – in short, it does not sufficiently engage with the "stuff" of education governance. Thus, the aim is to provide the beginnings of analysis on the politicized contours of current forms of philanthropic engagement in education in the Global South, against a broader, generally accepted depoliticized frame of neutrality (see Morvaridi 2012; Srivastava and Oh 2010 in a similar vein).

The obvious implication of such a conceptualization when assessing particular action/actors is recognition that there will be differences within and across contexts, i.e. that individual and different types of philanthropic actors will not behave in a similar way in all contexts at every point of time. There may be conflicting or unintentional motives and consequences. Despite this, the overarching legitimizing discourse and the peculiarities of the philanthropic buzz embedded in the new moment of the politics of education favor a particular kind of philanthropic engagement, referred to here as the new global philanthropy in education.

Returning to Robertson and Dale's framework, the analysis here was primarily interested in assessing the logics of intervention guiding philanthropic action in the Global South, and the potential forms of an emerging post-2015 architecture, i.e. the potential governance structure for and resulting from philanthropic engagement in education. Four themes emerged from the review (Table 24.2). The first three are most closely tied to the logics of intervention. These showed a propensity for the logics of intervention of philanthropic engagement to be market-oriented, results-oriented and metrics-based, and top-down. The fourth theme intimates the potential shape and characteristics of an emerging post-2015 architecture for philanthropic engagement in education. This was found to be framed by blurring corporate, philanthropic, and domestic and international development activities and actors, operating in new formal and non-formal global policy spaces.

The analysis in Table 24.2 teases out the embedded accepted logic and contestation for each of the logics of intervention and for the emerging post-2015 architecture, and provides examples of philanthropic engagement for each uncovered during the review. It also provides the basis of conceptual abstraction presented further below.

New Global Philanthropy in Education and Philanthropic Governance in Education

New global philanthropy in education is based on an apparent "win–win" approach that favors more hands-on interventions by philanthropic actors than in the past, who are in search of measurable, tangible, scalable results to tackle education issues that are seemingly consensually defined, primarily by inserting the market in education. This is akin to Ball and Olmedo's (2011) characterization of new philanthropy as "creative capitalism," or "an approach where governments, businesses, and non-profits work together to stretch the reach of market forces so that more people can make a profit, or gain recognition, doing work that eases the world's inequities" (Microsoft 2008, cited in Ball and Olmedo 2011, 84). The "strategic" or "win–win" approach (Craig and Kane 2001) is predicated on market-oriented characteristics of new philanthropy. New philanthropy, thus, rests on a predisposition to quick, short-term, "silver bullet" solutions to meet the "grand challenges" of development; to do more with less; and crucially, to insert the market in the public social sphere (e.g. Ball and Olmedo 2011; Brooks *et al.* 2010). In education, philanthropic actors financing school choice vouchers and investing in purportedly low-fee private school chains are two prominent examples of market-oriented action.

One such example of the latter is the IDP Foundation's Rising Schools Program. The IDP Foundation, an American private foundation established in 2008, started the Rising Schools Program as a micro-finance initiative in 2009 with Sinapi Aba Trust, a Ghanaian micro-finance institution, for low-fee private schools in Ghana:

> IDPRSP [IDP Rising Schools Program] invests in communities through assisting existing schools not well reached by the public education system. It is a realistic market driven program which respects, recognizes and empowers the efforts of the poor who want to be included in MDG goal #2, the Education for All initiative and the Education First initiative, as well as complementing the Government's efforts to educate all children. (IDP Foundation 2013a, section "The Need," para 2)

Table 24.2 Logics of intervention and potential framing of post-2015 architecture for philanthropic engagement in education

	Description	Accepted logic/contestation	Examples[a]
Market-oriented	Shift toward "strategic" choices made by newer Northern and Southern philanthropic actors, many of whom benefited from the global technological boom Application of market-oriented skillset and the same expertise that led to business success to philanthropic engagement in education (Inderfurth et al. 2012; Johnson 2003; Sidel 2008)	**Accepted logic:** Market logic will lead to effective and efficient, targeted education initiatives **Contestation:** The traditional private foundation role of "correcting for" social inequities created by the market has been transformed into one of "connecting to" the market (Brooks et al. 2010)	Government schools compete for funding based on learning levels and teacher performance, e.g. Learning Guarantee Program, Azim Premji Foundation, India (Barnhardt et al. 2009) Emphasis on school choice as the harbinger of competition, and therefore, increased quality, e.g. investment in voucher schemes (Mital 2009) Investments in low-fee private schooling (Ball 2012; Nambissan and Ball 2010), e.g. IDP Foundation in Ghana; Promoting Equality in Africa Schools (PEAS) schools in Uganda and Zambia Establishing "model" schools for scalable, replicable "quality" education, e.g. Satya Bharti School Program, India (Bharti Foundation 2013) "Adoption schemes" in which private foundations and corporations assume the operation and/or management of public schools with the aim of correcting inefficiencies, e.g. Amber Trust adopted schools in Rajasthan, India (Pachauri 2012);
Results-oriented and metrics-based	Shift from project implementation processes or completion to results on investment (Brest 2012) Tendency to promote measurable results, and preference silver bullet solutions (Ball 2012; Brest 2012; Brooks et al. 2010) Investment sometimes seen as "contingent on organisations demonstrating impact and raising confidence in the returns on giving" (Bain and Company 2012, 8)	**Accepted logic:** Input-output model to address education "problems" Straightforward, quick, and measurable inputs that can be replicated in other contexts Focus on quantifiable indicators will increase quality (e.g. achievement testing, infrastructure inputs, student enrolment, teacher attendance) **Contestation:** Quantitative focus can devalue important qualitative indicators of positive school performance and social cohesion which are less easily measurable (e.g. better teacher–student relationships, heightened student confidence) (Edwards 2011; Hess 2005) Narrow solutions paradoxically proposed for particularly poor education systems as "quick fixes" where in fact, context is paramount and change is gradual (Hess 2005)	Gray Matters Capital quality rating system for low-fee private schools (India)

Top-down	Stronger emphasis on business expertise and closer alliance with parent industry causing more hands-on, direct, and "top-down" involvement

Shift from grant-making to implementing education programming including in Global South (Mital 2009; Turitz and Winder 2005)

Contrasted with older (largely grant-making) foundations which were relatively more hands-off and relied on governments, civil society organizations, and other intermediaries to design and implement programmes (Ball 2012; Bernard 2012) | **Accepted logic:**
Direct involvement by successful leaders (often from business) can lead to more effective and efficient ways of implementing education initiatives than through traditional intermediaries (e.g. civil society organizations, governments)

Direct intervention will avoid complex processes of mediation and intervention associated with government and multi-stakeholder partnerships (Mangaleswaran and Venkataraman 2013)

Contestation:
Bypasses local intermediaries and can drive out or neglect the knowledge and expertise of local communities and organizations, limiting the sustainable impact of education initiatives (Ko 2009)

Impedes the incorporation of initiatives into institutional structures required for long-term systemic change (Mangaleswaran and Venkataraman 2013) | Governing bodies of foundations (e.g. board of governors, board of trustees) populated with leading executives and close corporate partners of parent companies (van Fleet 2012), e.g. Intel Foundation Board of Directors composed entirely of Intel employees and senior executives (Intel Foundation 2014)

Private foundations being established as offshoots of corporate social responsibility units/policies and running their own programmes, e.g. local Vodafone Foundations "exist in the Vodafone Local Operating Companies" in 23 countries including the Democratic Republic of Congo, India, Lesotho, Mozambique, South Africa, Tanzania, and Turkey (Vodaphone Group 2014, para 3) |

(Continued)

Table 24.2 (Continued)

	Description	Accepted logic/contestation	Examples[a]
Blurring of corporate, philanthropic, and domestic and international development activities and actors	Strategic involvement in the creation of new global policy spaces which bring together governments, donors, and business to address global education challenges of funding, quality, access, and skills leading up to post-2015 (Ball 2012; Bhanji 2012; Robertson 2012; van Fleet 2012) Development of partnerships and networks in education between businesses and traditional development actors which blend for-profit and non-for-profit approaches (Ball and Olmedo 2011; Brest 2012) and create "shared value" (Mital 2009, 36)	**Accepted logic:** Corporate and philanthropic actors should be given an increasingly prominent voice in global policy discussions on education due to their unique expertise and innovative potential in the sector (ECOSOC 2012; van Fleet 2012) Greater coordination between philanthropic actors, governments, corporate actors, and donors will lead to alignment of education initiatives and avoid duplicative efforts (van Fleet 2012) Education initiatives will be more relevant for development of local businesses by providing skilled future workers creating "shared value" **Contestation:** Corporate actors can exploit these new policy spaces to expand the privatization and marketization of education (Ball 2012; Robertson 2012) Can lead to furthering corporate actors' commercial interests (Bhanji 2012) Strategically designed "partnerships" with governments and donors can be used to neutralize controversial profit-making motives and activities (Robertson 2012; Srivastava and Oh 2010)	Global advocacy campaigns which blend for-profit and non-for-profit approaches to tackling global education problems, e.g. Business Backs Education initiative (supported by UNESCO and the Global Business Coalition for Education), encouraging businesses to collectively spend 20% of their global corporate social spending on education by 2020 through both philanthropy and "social impact investing" (Global Education and Skills Forum 2014); Shared Value Initiative's roundtable at 2014 World Economic Forum, Davos with corporate leaders to discuss business's role in global education and "how companies can create shared value by improving education while driving shareholder returns" (Kramar et al. n.d.) PPPs as strategic entry points for corporations to gain new market information and access, e.g. Microsoft Corporation's Partners in Learning (PiL) program (Bhanji 2012)

Note: [a] Examples are indicative not exhaustive.

The IDP Foundation succinctly defines the problem (access to public education), proposes a "realistic" and straightforward solution (a market-driven program to "empower" the poor), and links it to the grand challenge of meeting Education for All. It further outlines goals for the low-fee private schools to improve quality, and for the micro-finance institution to reap returns on economic investment and have social impact. Finally, the IDP Foundation showcases letters of support from UNESCO and the Ghanaian Ministry of Education, and its special consultative status to the United Nations in July 2012 (IDP Foundation 2013b, para 4), thus entering an elite transnational policy space. In short, everyone's a winner.

The win–win approach of the new global philanthropy in education builds a business case for investing in education, particularly for corporate philanthropic actors (Ball 2008). It encourages international and Southern foundations to capitalize on and gain value from primary or secondary education as profitable investments for their parent or affiliated industry. Proponents assert that corporate and other private foundations can and should connect their support of education with business and with short- and long-term core interests, which can include good community and government relations, a more competent and skilled future workforce, and the creation of new markets (Bronfman and Soloman 2010; Mital 2009; Porter and Kramer 2002).

These goals are furthered in networks that provide spaces for connecting multiple actors (business, philanthropic, civil society, INGOs, etc.), and sometimes the same actors with different simultaneous roles, as new venues for setting and mobilizing policy (Ball 2008; Nambissan and Ball 2010). These spaces are nominally inclusive, i.e. they are portrayed as opening avenues for different and newer actors to enter the global and domestic education space, but in the case of philanthropic actors, tend to select those backed by or closely associated with "big" capital.

For example, the Global Business Coalition for Education (GBCE) describes itself as a "business-led, action-oriented organization" (GBCE 2012, para 5) based on principles of social responsibility through coordinated social investment and philanthropic action to "accelerate progress" in basic education in Afghanistan, Bangladesh, Ethiopia, India, Nigeria, and Pakistan (para 2). However, it builds a case for philanthropic action in education by using capitalist logic to harness value in education to further business ends, i.e. investing in markets for future employment, increasing income potential to create new consumers, and increasing the ease of doing business. It further stresses the involvement of elite business and opportunities to interact in exclusive spaces:

> For companies, investing in education promotes economic growth, leads to more stable societies, fosters healthy communities and makes it easier to do business. Education spurs innovation and increases the skills of employees, the income potential of consumers and the prosperity of communities where business operates [...] In the first year of operation, 20 of the world's most influential companies joined the Coalition, and we are expanding significantly. Our members believe that their influence, core business, social responsibility, strategic investments, thought leadership and philanthropy – when used in collaboration with peer companies, government, nonprofit and the educational community – are powerful tools to increase the number of children and youth who are in school and learning [...] While many companies already engage in education through philanthropic or social investment programs, these actions require coordination to have greater impact. GBC-Education's forum increases companies' effectiveness by creating "members-only" spaces for company leaders to connect and identify cutting-edge opportunities for collaboration. (GBCE 2012, para 2, 3 and 6)

By using the logic to provide greater coordination between corporate actors and philanthropic activities, the GBCE attempts to organize a network of actors by blurring corporate and philanthropic lines. While the coalition may indeed provide a space for actors hitherto operating outside of or excluded from the education space, the "members only" spaces, which are reserved for companies willing to make a $10,000–60,000 annual contribution, successfully preserve access for big business.

Ball and Youdell (2007) argue that philanthropic involvement resting on the blurring of corporate and philanthropic lines leads to "hidden privatisation" in education. The contention here is that privatization in and of education, hidden or otherwise, may or may not be the explicit or sole intentional outcome for every philanthropic actor (e.g. Dulany and Winder 2001), particularly those in networks or coalitions. Rather, the primacy of market-based solutions espoused by the new global philanthropy in education, and the simultaneous increased use of complex multi-stakeholder and PPPs as mechanisms for education provision in many countries of the Global South (Draxler 2008; Srivastava et al. 2013; Verger 2012), open up and create non-formal and formal spaces for constellations of philanthropic and other non-state actors, and fundamentally alter education governance structures by surreptitiously embedding forms of privatization in education systems.

One example is the Promoting Equality in African Schools (PEAS) network in Uganda, which self-describes as "a global charity/social enterprise hybrid" (PEAS, 2012a, para 1). PEAS runs a network of private secondary schools that are meant to be free at the point of entry. At the time of initial writing, at least eight private foundations and trusts invested in PEAS in addition to DFID, the Ugandan Ministry of Education, consulting and business firms, and NGOs/CSOs.[4] This arrangement was enabled by the Ugandan Ministry of Education's 2007 PPP policy to universalize secondary education. Similar developments extending private provision with the involvement of philanthropic and other private actors can be seen in India and Pakistan as a response to different government PPP initiatives in education (e.g. Fennell and Malik 2012; Srivastava et al. 2013).

Ball and Olmedo (2011) argue that such action is indicative of "philanthropic governance," or "the ways in which, through their philanthropic action, these actors are able to modify meanings, mobilise assets, generate new policy technologies and exert pressure on, or even decide, the direction" (Ball and Olmedo 2011, 85) of global education policy. This is somewhat similar to analyses explaining the dynamics of transnational framing of global education policy (Mundy and Murphy 2001; Srivastava 2010; Tota 2014; Verger 2012), and to analyses on the insertion of increased arrays of non-state private actors in education through broader forces of globalization (e.g. Dale and Robertson 2002; Robertson and Dale 2013; Verger et al. 2012).

But, philanthropic governance in education differs in at least one significant way. Discourse, meanings, and actors in this mode of governance gain their legitimacy by manipulating and intertwining three claims associated with philanthropic and/or non-state private actors, which can ultimately, mute contestation, and depoliticize action. These are: (a) normalizing long-standing taken-for-granted assumptions of philanthropy with benevolence, goodness, and altruism; (b) extending claims of private sector efficiency and effectiveness; and (c) stressing claims of neutrality to the philanthropic sector as the "third sector," i.e. neither state nor purely private/commercial. This is best encapsulated in the view propagated in the High Level Report:

> Foundations, other philanthropists and social impact investors can innovate and be nimble and opportunistic, forming bridges between government bureaucracies, international institutions and the business and CSO sectors. Foundations and philanthropists can take risks, show that an idea works, and create new markets where none existed before. This can give governments and business the confidence to take the initiative and scale up successes. Social impact investors show that *there can be a "third way" for sustainable development – a hybrid between a fully for-profit private sector and a pure grant or charity aid programmes. Because they make money, their efforts can be sustainable over time. But because they are new, neither business nor charity*, they do not fall neatly into traditional legal frames. Some countries may need to consider how to modify their laws to take better advantage of this sector. (United Nations 2013, 11, emphases added)

This is not to imply that the underlying claims are not contested. In fact, there is a strand of literature that mounts criticisms on assumptions of altruism (Ball 2008; Bhanji 2008; Lorenzo-Molo 2009; Morvaridi 2012; Rajak 2011), the efficiency and effectiveness (Steer and Wathne 2010; van Fleet 2011; 2012, Watkins 2011), and the neutrality of philanthropic actors (Srivastava and Oh 2010; Zhou 2011). There is further literature that highlights the heterogeneity of actors and modes of action dubbed "philanthropic" (Bhanji 2012; Ball 2008; OECD 2003). Despite this, the array of philanthropic actors and their different modes of operation are easily conflated among themselves, and often, with other non-state private actors. They can be further neutralized by allying them with broader transnational or domestic frameworks of action in education aiming to address persistent inequities.

For example, the World Bank Education Strategy 2020 embeds philanthropic actors (i.e. Hewlett, MasterCard, Qatar foundations) in its description of "private sector" activity in education to build a case for further private investment in education:

> ...the Bank works with the private sector, including enterprises, local and global technical institutions, private donors (such as philanthropic foundations and business networks), and civil society groups as critical partners in a variety of development programs. In many cases the private-sector entities contribute directly as providers of education services at different levels, while in others they partner with governments on service provision or push for education system reforms. The private sector also includes users of the skills produced by the education sector, prompting it to help sharpen the relevance and quality of curricula and modes of delivery. For example, the spread of ICT use in jobs is one reason why schools and students are eager to be proficient in ICT. Private donors, such as the Hewlett, MasterCard, and Qatar foundations, among others, have partnered with the Bank on a variety of knowledge generation and exchange activities that have wide applicability. And as previously mentioned, since 2001 the IFC has been working with private investors to expand education investments in the Global South. (World Bank 2011, 72)

In other cases, philanthropic governance in education may embed the conflation into the institutional structure of influential organizations. For example, the Global Partnership for Education (GPE) recently reformed its structure to allocate one seat out of the 19 on its Board of Directors to a representative of "private sector/foundations."

> Private sector, think tanks and foundations partners[sic] provide strategic, technical and fundraising advice to help the partnership expand its activities and explore innovative

opportunities to achieve education results. Private sector corporations and private foundations are the newest members represented on the Global Partnership Board of Directors. Their commitment to advance our objectives include[sic] working with communities to advocate for education rights, monitoring education sector reform, and increasing awareness of gender equality issues or child labor. They participate with other GPE partners in the elaboration of education strategies in developing country partners and help develop policies to overcome the worst barriers to quality education. (GPE 2014)

In sum, the framing power of philanthropic governance in education stems from its ability to enable actors to fuse and draw on and from characteristics associated with philanthropy and the private sector, and to provide them with a broader repertoire of discourses, symbols, and networks to legitimize action, modify meanings, and mobilize assets. It is precisely the "Cheshire cattishness" of philanthropic governance in education, that is, the ability to selectively bring in and out of sight desired characteristics of the private and philanthropic sectors (and the range of actors therein) to suit the persuasions of the particular audience, that can obscure the specific logics and motivations that guide them, destabilize opposition, and neutralize conceptual dissonance, thus helping to build a narrative to frame international development and global education policy. This ultimately reinforces the private sector and inserts the market in global education to a greater degree than would perhaps be possible by relying exclusively on other types of non-state private and/or state actors.

Notes

1. The broader research project is on the right to education and the role of non-state private actors. It is funded by a grant from the Social Sciences and Humanities Research Council of Canada (SSHRC).
2. In sum, the search yielded 120 documents published from 1990 onwards. Documents from the following forums were reviewed for this chapter: Bellagio Institute, Commonwealth Ministerial Working Group on the Post-2015 Development Framework for Education, Dakar, EFA-FTI, Global Partnership for Education, High Level Report on the Post-2015 Agenda, Jomtien, World Bank 1995 Priorities and Strategies, World Bank Education Strategy 2020.
3. These were: the USA, France, Japan, Norway, The Netherlands, and Canada. The UK, Germany, Australia, and Sweden increased aid to education.
4. The PEAS website lists the following organizations as its partners: DFID, Ministry of Education and Sports, Government of Uganda, ARK, The Best Practice Network, Build it International, Costa Foundation, COINS Foundation, Danson Foundation, Equitable Charitable Trust, Foundation Eagle, Waterloo Foundation, Laura Case Trust, Teach First, Venture Partnership Foundation (VPF), Oliver Wyman, Straight Talk Foundation (PEAS 2012b). As of 2012, PEAS is reported to have opened schools in Zambia.

References

Arnove, R. 1980. *Philanthropy and Cultural Imperialism: The Foundations at Home and Abroad*. Bloomington: Indiana University Press.
Bain & Company. 2012. *India Philanthropy Report 2012*. Mumbai: Bain & Company, Inc.
Ball, S.J. 2008. "New Philanthropy, New Networks and New Governance in Education." *Political Studies*, 56(4): 747–765.

Ball, S.J. 2012. *Global Education Inc.: New Policy Networks and the Neo-Liberal Imaginary*. London: Routledge.

Ball, S.J. and A. Olmedo. 2011. "Global Social Capitalism: Using Enterprise to Solve the Problems of the World." *Citizenship, Social and Economics Education*, 10(2): 83–90.

Ball, S.J. and D. Youdell. 2007. *Hidden Privatisation in Public Education*. Report prepared for the Education International 5th World Congress. Retrieved from: http://old.ei-ie.org/annualreport2007/upload/content_trsl_images/440/Hidden_privatisation-EN.pdf (accessed November 19, 2015).

Barnhardt, S., D. Karlan, and S. Khemani. 2009. "Participation in a School Incentive Programme in India." *Journal of Development Studies*, 45(3): 369–390.

Berman, E. 1983. *The Ideology of Philanthropy: The Influence of the Carnegie, Ford and Rockefeller Foundations on American Foreign Policy*. New York: SUNY Press.

Bernard, B.R. 2012. *Ngo-Business Partnerships: Risk, Trust and the Future of Development*. PhD Dissertation, Department of Peace Studies. Indiana: Notre Dame University.

Bhanji, Zahra. 2008. "Transnational Corporations in Education: Filling the Governance Gap Through New Social Norms and Market Multilateralism?" *Globalisation, Societies and Education*, 6(1): 55–73.

Bhanji, Z. 2012. "Microsoft Corporation: A Case Study of Corporate-led PPPs in education," in *Public Private Partnerships in Education: New Actors and Modes of Governance in a Globalizing World*, edited by S. Robertson, K. Mundy, A. Verger, and F. Menashy, 132–201. Cheltenham: Edward Elgar.

Bishop, M. and M. Green. 2008. *Philanthrocapitalism: How the Rich Can Save the World*. New York: Bloomsbury Press.

Brest, P. 2012. "A Decade of Outcome-Oriented Philanthropy." *Stanford Social Innovation Review*, Spring: 42–47.

Bronfman, C. and J. Soloman. 2010. *The Art of Giving: Where the Soul Meets a Business Plan*. San Francisco: Jossey-Bass.

Brooks, S., M. Leach, H. Lucas, and E. Millstone. 2010. *Silver Bullets, Grand Challenges and the New Philanthropy*. STEPS Working Paper No. 24. Brighton: STEPS Centre. Retrieved from: www.ids.ac.uk/idspublication/silver-bullets-grand-challenges-and-the-new-philanthropy (accessed November 19, 2015).

Commonwealth Ministerial Working Group on the Post-2015 Development Framework for Education. 2012. *Commonwealth Recommendations for the Post-2015 Development Framework for Education*. Background paper. London: Commonwealth Secretariat.

Craig, P. and M. Kane. 2001. *Expanding Public/Private Partnerships for Improving Basic Education through School Sponsorship in the Dominican Republic*. Washington, DC: The United States Agency for International Development.

Dale, R. 2006. "From Comparison to Translation: Extending the Research Imagination." *Globalisation, Societies and Education*, 4(2): 179–192.

Dale, R. and S. Robertson. 2002. "The Varying Effects of Regional Organizational as Subjects of Globalization of Education." *Comparative Education Review*, 46(1): 10–36.

Davis, R.H. 1976. "Charles T. Loran and an American Model for African Education in South Africa." *African Review*, 19(3): 87–99.

Draxler, A. 2008. *New Partnerships for EFA: Building Experience*. Paris: UNESCO International Institute for Educational Planning.

Dulany, P. and D. Winder. 2001. *The Status of and Trends in Private Philanthropy in the Southern Hemisphere: A Discussion Paper for the Executive Session on the Future of Philanthropy*. New York: International Network on Strategy Philanthropy and Synergos.

ECOSOC. 2012. *Issues Note*. Development Cooperation Forum: UN Special Policy Dialogue on "Private Philanthropic Organizations in International Development Cooperation: New Opportunities and Specific Challenges." 27 February 2012, 10 a.m. – 1 p.m. Retrieved from: www.un.org/en/ecosoc/newfunct/pdf/dcf_philanthropy_issues_note.pdf (accessed November 29, 2015).

Edwards, M. 2011. "The Role and Limitations of Philanthropy." Commissioned paper for the Bellagio Initiative. Washington, DC: The Institute of Development Studies, the Resource Alliance, and the Rockefeller Foundation.

Fennell, S. and R. Malik. 2012. "Between a Rock and a Hard Place: The Emerging Educational Market for the Poor in Pakistan." *Comparative Education*, 48(2): 249–261.

Global Business Coalition for Education (GBCE). 2012. "About Us." Retrieved from: http://gbc-education.org/about-us (accessed November 20, 2015).

Global Education and Skills Forum. 2014. "Business Backs Education: A Global Advocacy Campaign Rallying the Private Sector to Support Education." Retrieved from: https://educationandskillsforum.org/business-backs-education/#.U0tWvrQyza4 (accessed November 20, 2015).

Global Partnership for Education (GPE). 2014. "Private Sector and Foundations." Retrieved from: www.globalpartnership.org/private-sector-and-foundations (accessed November 20, 2015).

Hess, F.M. 2005. "Inside the Gift Horse's Mouth: Philanthropy and School Reform." *Phi Delta Kappan*, 87(2): 131–138.

IDP Foundation. 2013a. "About IDP Rising Schools." Retrieved from: www.idpfoundation.org/idp-rising-schools/about-idp-rising-schools (accessed November 20, 2015).

IDP Foundation. 2013b. "Irene D. Pritzer." Retrieved from: www.idpfoundation.org/idp-biography (accessed November 20, 2015).

Inderfurth, K.F., P. Khambatta, N. Lombardo, and M. Stokes. 2012. "Bridging the Gap? New Philanthropy in India UID Helping Those in Need." *U.S.-India Insight*, 2(5): 1–2. Washington, DC: Center for Strategic and International Studies.

Intel Foundation. 2014. "Intel Foundation Board of Directors." Retrieved from: www.intel.com/content/www/us/en/citizenship/citizenship-foundation-board-directors-corporate-information.html (accessed November 20, 2015).

Johnson, P.D. 2003. *Achieving Universal Primary Education: Preliminary Observations on US Philanthropy's Global Role*. Boston: Harvard University's Global Equity Initiative.

King, Kenneth. 1971. *Pan Africanism and Education: A Study of Race, Philanthropy and Education in the Southern States of America and East Africa*. Oxford: Clarendon Press.

Ko, Y.K. 2009. *Interrogating the One Laptop Per Child Project*. Dissertation presented to the Communication and Culture Department. Toronto: York University.

Kramar, M.K., G. Hills, K. Tallani, M. Wilka., and A. Bhatt. n.d. *The New Role of Business in Global Education: How Companies Can Create Shared Value by Improving Education While Driving Shareholder Returns*. A report by FSG.

Lorenzo-Molo, M.C.F. 2009. "Why Corporate Social Responsibility (CSR) Remains a Myth: The Case of the Philippines." *Asian Business and Management*, 8(2): 149–168.

Mangaleswaran, R. and R. Venkataraman. 2013. *Designing Philanthropy for Impact: Giving to the Biggest Gaps in India*. Social Sector Practice Report. McKinsey & Company. Retrieved from: www.mckinsey.com/~/media/McKinsey%20Offices/India/PDFs/Designing_Philanthropy_for_Impact.ashx (accessed November 20, 2015).

Mital, K.M. 2009. "Bringing Education to Children of Lesser Gods: Bharti Foundation's Satya Bharti School Programme." *Management and Change*, 13(1): 1–4.

Morvaridi, B. 2012. "Capitalist Philanthropy and Hegemonic Partnerships." *Third World Quarterly*, 33(7): 1191–1210.

Moyo, D. 2009. *Dead Aid: Why Aid is Not Working and How There is a Better Way for Africa*. Madeira Park: Douglas & McIntyre.

Mundy, K. and L. Murphy. 2001. "Transnational Advocacy, Global Civil Society? Emerging Evidence from the Field of Education." *Comparative Education Review*, 45(1): 85–126.

Nambissan, G.B. and S.J. Ball. 2010. "Advocacy Networks, Choice and Private Schooling of the Poor in India." *Global Networks*, 10(3): 1–20.

OECD. 2003. "Philanthropic Foundations and Development Co-operation." *Off-print of the DAC Journal*, 4(3). Retrieved from: www.oecd.org/development/stats/22272860.pdf (accessed November 29, 2015).

Pachauri, A. 2012. *Multistakeholder Partnerships under the Rajasthan Education Initiative: If Not for Profit, Then for What?* Unpublished doctoral thesis. Brighton: University of Sussex.

PEAS. 2012a. "About Us." Retrieved from: www.peas.org.uk/about-us (accessed November 27, 2015).

PEAS. 2012b. "Our Partners." Retrieved from: www.peas.org.uk/about-us/our-partners (accessed November 20, 2015).

Porter, M.E. and M.R. Kramer. 2002. "The Competitive Advantage of Corporate Philanthropy." *Harvard Business Review*, RO212D: 14–20.

Rajak, D. 2011. *In Good Company: An Anatomy of Corporate Social Responsibility*. Stanford: Stanford University Press.

Robertson, S.L. 2012. "The Strange Non-Death of Neoliberal Privatisation in the World Bank's Education Strategy 2020." *Comparative and International Education*, 14: 189–206.

Robertson, S.L. and R. Dale. 2013. "The Social Justice Implications of Privatisation in Education Governance Frameworks: A Relational Account." *Oxford Review of Education*, 39(4): 426–445.

Sidel, M. 2008. *New Economy Philanthropy in the High Technology Communities of Bangalore and Hyderabad, India: Partnership with the State and the Ambiguous Search for Social Innovation*. University of Iowa College of Law and Obermann Center for Advanced Studies.

Srivastava, P. 2010. "Privatization and Education for All: Unravelling the Mobilizing Frames." *Development*, 53(4): 522–528.

Srivastava, P. and S. Oh. 2010. "Private Foundations, Philanthropy, and Partnership in Education and Development: Mapping the Terrain." *International Journal of Educational Development*, 30(5): 460–471.

Srivastava, P., C. Noronha, and S. Fennell. 2013. *Private Sector Study: Sarva Shiksha Abhiyan*. Report submitted to DFID (India). Retrieved from: www.prachisrivastava.com/uploads/1/9/5/1/19518861/srivastava_et_al._private_sector_study_ssa_india.pdf (accessed November 20, 2015).

Steer, L. and C. Wathne. 2010. "Donor Financing of Basic Education: Opportunities and Constraints." *International Journal of Educational Development*, 30(5): 472–480.

Tota, P.M. 2014. "Filling the Gaps: The Role and Impact of International Non-Governmental Organisations in 'Education for All'." *Globalisation, Societies and Education*, 12(1): 92–109.

Turitz, S. and D. Winder. 2005. "Private Resources for Public Funds: Grantmakers in Brazil, Ecuador, and Mexico," in *Philanthropy and Social Change in Latin America*, edited by C.A. Sanborn and F. Portocarrero, 255–261. Cambridge: Harvard University.

UNESCO. 2013. *Trends in Aid to Education: Lessons for Post-2015*. Education for All Monitoring Report Policy Paper No. 11. 2013/ED/EFA/MRT/PP/11. Retrieved from: http://unesdoc.unesco.org/images/0022/002253/225300E.pdf (accessed November 20, 2015).

UNESCO. 2014. *Teaching and Learning: Achieving Quality for All. EFA Global Monitoring Report 2013/4*. Paris: UNESCO.

United Nations. 2013. *A New Global Partnership: Eradicate Poverty and Transform Economies through Sustainable Development. The Report of the High-level Panel of Eminent Persons on the Post-2015 Development Agenda*. New York: United Nations. Retrieved from: www.un.org/sg/management/pdf/HLP_P2015_Report.pdf (accessed November 20, 2015).

van Fleet, J.W. 2011. *A Global Education Challenge: Harnessing Corporate Philanthropy to Educate the World's Poor*. Working Paper No. 4. Center for Universal Education at Brookings. Retrieved from: www.brookings.edu/reports/2011/04_corporate_philanthropy_fleet.aspx (accessed November 20, 2015).

van Fleet, J.W. 2012. "A Disconnect Between Motivations and Education Needs: Why American Corporate Philanthropy Alone Will Not Educate the Most Marginalized," in

Public Private Partnerships in Education: New Actors and Modes of Governance in a Globalizing World, edited by S.L. Robertson, K. Mundy, A. Verger, and F. Menashy, 158–181. Cheltenham: Edward Elgar.

Verger, A. 2012. "Framing and Selling Global Education Policy: The Promotion of Public–Private Partnerships for Education in Low-Income Contexts." *Journal of Education Policy*, 27(1): 109–130.

Verger, A., M. Novelli, and H. Kosar Altinyelken. 2012. "Global Education Policy and International Development: An Introductory Framework," in *Global Education Policy and International Development: New Agendas, Issues, and Policies*, edited by A. Verger, M. Novelli, and H. Kosar Altinyelken, 3–32. London: Bloomsbury.

Vodaphone Group. 2014. "Local Foundations." Retrieved from: www.vodafone.com/content/index/about/foundation/local_foundations.html (accessed November 20, 2015).

Watkins, K. 2011. *Corporate Philanthropy and the "Education for All" Agenda*. Commissioned paper for the Bellagio Initiative. Washington DC: Institute of Development Studies, the Resource Alliance, and the Rockefeller Foundation.

World Bank. 1995. *Priorities and Strategies for Education: A World Bank Review*. Washington, DC: World Bank. Retrieved from: http://siteresources.worldbank.org/EDUCATION/Resources/278200-1099079877269/547664-1099080118171/Priorities_and_Strategies_for_Ed_WB_Review.pdf (accessed November 20, 2015).

World Bank. 2011. *Learning for All: Investing in People's Knowledge and Skills to Promote Development. World Bank Group Education Strategy 2020*. Washington, DC: World Bank. Retrieved from: wwwr.worldbank.org/educationstrategy2020 (accessed November 20, 2015).

Zhou, H. 2011. "The Role of Private Non-Profit Organizations in Promoting Compulsory Education in Rural China: Applying the Public-Private Mix Model." Unpublished doctoral dissertation. Philadelphia: University of Pennsylvania.

Zoltán, A.J. and S. Desai. 2007. *Democratic Capitalism and Philanthropy in a Global Economy*. Jena Economic Research Papers Series. Jena: Max Planck Institute of Economics.

Part IV Critical Directions in the Study of Global Education Policy

Part IV Introduction

Karen Mundy

The past decade has seen the flourishing of new scholarship on global policy processes in education. This part of the Handbook features chapters that explore new methodological, conceptual, and theoretical approaches to studying global education policy. To do so, authors draw on international relations theory; new theories of policy borrowing and diffusion; new approaches to ethnography; new methodological approaches to the study of networks and organizations; exploit postcolonial and postmodern theories; and rework international relations theories. Each chapter raises critical questions about how to make sense of power and politics in global policy processes, inviting readers to trouble and dispute taken-for-granted notions of power, rationality, and control. As in other chapters of this Handbook, the focus is on carefully understanding and tracing meaning making and discursive practices in order to question the directionality of power, influence, and decision-making in international educational relationships.

Opening this part are two chapters that trouble and complicate more traditional rational actor theories from political science and international relations. In Chapter 25, Timm Fulge, Tonia Bieber, and Kerstin Martens draw on current theories of international relations and political power to ask why international actors have become so prominent in education policy. They suggest that national policy actors sometimes see international organizations and their educational prescriptions as a viable way to overcome political gridlock and historical path dependencies in their own systems. Nonetheless, the reception of global level policies and benchmarking exercises is somewhat unpredictable because it is highly contingent on the political economy of domestic policy processes, where local stakeholders interface with the prescriptions and solutions provided by the international organizations. And the international organizations themselves typically develop forms of authority and policy direction that cannot be easily managed by national policy-makers. Using the European Union (EU) and the Organisation for Economic Co-operation and Development (OECD) as examples, the chapter shows that despite national efforts to instrumentalize and control international organizations, they can often play a role in reshaping domestic political economies and the trajectories of systems in ways originally not planned by national leaders.

In Chapter 26, Patricia Bromley introduces organizational sociology as a counterpoint to more traditional approaches to the study of power and politics in educational policy making. Drawing on neo-institutionalism, Bromley discusses how the rapid expansion of policy agents and actors in education, including non-profit

The Handbook of Global Education Policy, First Edition.
Edited by Karen Mundy, Andy Green, Bob Lingard, and Antoni Verger.
© 2016 John Wiley & Sons, Ltd. Published 2016 by John Wiley & Sons, Ltd.

and private sector actors, has been constructed and legitimized through the spread of institutional cultures that privilege rationalized notions of administrative efficiency, individual agency and rights, and scientific efficacy. Unlike more traditional neo-institutionalists, however, Bromley argues that as organizational actors proliferate they not only diffuse and consolidate common policy scripts, but also generate considerable complexity and pluralism in terms of the kinds of actors engaged in education policy making and the final menu of solutions chosen in different venues. This chapter highlights the importance of studying how different types of educational organizations spread putatively rationale cultures of administration and policy action, and in doing so redefine the goals and structure of educational systems.

A number of chapters in this volume take up theoretical and conceptual frameworks drawn from different disciplines in order to chart new approaches to the study of educational policy. In Chapter 27, Amy Stambach considers how anthropology and ethnography, which have traditionally been concerned with the local and its specificities, have become increasingly engaged in the localization and reconstitution of global education policy processes. Through two case studies – one of an online diasporic community and the other of US university administrators' use of international studies programs, Stambach explores how two different sets of actors understand themselves and their roles as affected by, or as products of, educational systems and their policies. Each case demonstrates how the interface between global processes and specific actors leads to the construction of new social norms and aspirations. At the same time, connections across the two cases demonstrate how educational aspirations are both cultivated and found wanting by the very actors that purvey them.

In a different vein, two chapters in this part utilize post-foundational theories as the backdrop for new approaches to the study of global education policy. Chapter 28 by Stephen Carney explores postmodernity and post-foundational theories – and the way in he has adapted such theories to inform his approach to studying global education policy. Drawing from his work in Zambia, Nepal, Denmark, Tibet, and South Korea, Carney describes how inherent tensions and contradictions in global educational policyscapes collide in the lived experiences and cultures of policy-makers and youth in each setting. In particular, Carney draws out the interplay between neo-liberal concerns with efficiency and accountability and advanced liberal notions of individual rights, liberty, and entitlements – and how these lead to dynamic contestations of identity and educational purpose. Carney considers de- and reterritorialization and the analytical strategies of assemblage and network, in order to provide fresh entry points for theorizing space in global education policy. Ultimately he argues for a movement away from studying global education policy as the search for policy solutions – toward a more reflexive practice that seeks to delve into the submerged drama that occurs as educational policy moves between global and more local spaces and actors.

In Chapter 29, Fazal Rizvi uses postcolonial theory as a lens through which to view the rise of Asian higher education in the social imaginary of education policy-makers in the West (and more specifically among higher education leaders in Australia). Rizvi focuses on the ways in which the success of Asian higher education is understood through an East–West binary, which in turn shapes policies and approaches to engagement that are deeply ambivalent and born out of a history of colonial conquest. The tendency to imagine Asia as a singular socially and culturally "other," rather than as a diverse and evolving set of cultures, peoples, and societies limits the potential for constructive dialogue and engagement. As Rizvi concludes, we need to understand how particular representations of the "other" are constructed in order to develop relations that transcend instrumentalism.

One area of growing interest in the study of global education policy is the development of new methodological approaches to the study of global policy processes, to better capture more pluri-lateral and networked forms of governance and influence. In Chapter 30, Carolina Junemann, Stephen Ball, and Diego Santori look at the emergence of a network of actors and entrepreneurs who promote privatization of educational provision as a solution to problems of inequality in national educational systems. Using network theories and a discourse analysis, the chapter begins with the case of Bridge International Academies (BIA), a for-profit chain of low-cost private schools in sub-Saharan Africa started by an American entrepreneur. Network analysis demonstrates the widening global chain of supporters and brokers of the BIA model and other approaches to franchising of educational services. This chapter suggests a very different form of policy influence and policy diffusion to that mobilized by international organizations – one that is not only more difficult to study because of its globally diffuse and networked nature, but also for the same reasons less susceptible to political and public contest and oversight.

Chapter 31, by Lesley Bartlett and Frances Vavrus, continues this focus on new methodological approaches. Bartlett and Vavrus are well known for their development of the "vertical case study" as an approach to the study of global education policy processes, which employs ethnographic and critical discourse analysis to examine the interface between global and national, and local policy processes and actors. In this chapter, Bartlett and Vavrus are principally concerned with the evolution of global policies on children and children's literacy. They use as a case study the way in which early grade literacy has been redefined and narrowed to a focus on early grade reading by a network of global education policy actors. Bartlett and Vavrus focus here in particular on the way early grade reading has become part of a package of policy solutions that have shaped national level policy formation in Zambia. In doing so, they illustrate how comparison across scales, discursive texts, and policy enactments can enrich our understanding of policy diffusion and its localization.

As a conclusion to this Handbook, senior scholar of global education policy Gita Steiner-Khamsi draws on her groundbreaking work on policy attraction and policy adaptation to explore the spread of global policies on teachers in Central Asia. As Steiner-Khamsi discusses, the global apparatus counts specific items and neglects others, sometimes leaving off the table major issues or gaps in local systems. This is precisely the case with global measures of teacher shortage used in Central Asia. The chapter shows that global policies are more than prescriptive: they are also generative, creating opportunities for local actors to redefine or neglect problems in ways that extend the fault lines among local education policy stakeholders. Steiner-Khamsi concludes with a broad set of questions about the utility of global indicators for identifying and measuring educational problems. As she argues, global indicators are often accompanied by "scripts" that list best practices for resolving policy issues. They create a powerful yet problematic closed circuit of problem recognition and problem solution that narrows the analysis of local policy issues in the direction of already existing global solutions.

Chapter 25

Rational Intentions and Unintended Consequences: On the Interplay between International and National Actors in Education Policy

Timm Fulge, Tonia Bieber, and Kerstin Martens

Since the turn of the century, education policy has increasingly become an internationalized field (Martens *et al.* 2007). While traditionally under the firm control of the nation state, international initiatives have become important triggers for the reformulation of education policies. Considering the natural resistance of education systems to change, their contribution to the introduction of highly consequential and even paradigm-altering reforms in many countries is quite puzzling. In order to understand the internationalization of education policy, in this chapter we focus on the interplay between international initiatives and national actors, concentrating especially on the behavior of relevant actors in recent reform processes and the corresponding policy outcomes. We argue that the internationalization process is strongly driven by rationalist and strategic considerations of national governments who seek to instrumentalize international organizations in order to overcome political gridlock and crowd out opposition in their own countries.

However, international organizations are not simply agents who fulfill the aims of domestic actors. They also pursue their own interests and develop their own norms. Such behavior, in turn, often results in unintended consequences, including rather profound changes to the traditional functioning of the nation state. In addition, once policy reforms are fed back to the domestic level for adoption and implementation, it is sensible to expect an adverse reaction by previously circumvented actors. We therefore anticipate the impact of internationalization to be mediated by what we call national transformative capacities, including the number of veto players on the one hand and national guiding principles in education policy on the other (Nagel *et al.* 2010).

Our empirical evidence is derived from case studies of two international initiatives for which we trace the interplay of national actors and international initiatives and corresponding impacts in different countries. More expressly, we investigate the Organisation for Economic Co-operation and Development's (OECD) Programme for International Student Assessment (PISA) in secondary education and the Bologna Process for a common European Higher Education Area. These initiatives share a set of important characteristics. They were started at similar times (PISA in 2000, Bologna in 1999) and have a comparable approach to education, relying on an economically oriented framework and championing human capital perspectives of education. They emphasize evidence-based policy-making and scientification, focus on life-long learning, and claim to support greater efficiency and accountability (Münch 2009; Parreira do Amaral 2006). Without a doubt, the OECD and the Bologna Process have changed the world's education landscape, inducing remarkable transformations in many countries – despite idiosyncratic national configurations in education.

Theoretical Considerations

For the purpose of this article, we ask a set of consecutive questions. First, how did international actors become so prominent in education policy? Second, what consequences did the internationalization of education policy trigger? Third, how does the impact of internationalization produce meaningful policy change on the domestic level, and what factors mediate its impact? We thus examine the interplay between national and international actors in education policy as a metaphorical boomerang (Martens and Wolf 2009): national policy-makers deliberately threw the boomerang of internationalizing education policy in order to circumvent path-dependent stasis and persistent political opposition to change. Whether it lands where these national actors envisioned – or how it "strikes back" on domestic politics – however, depends significantly on possible unintended consequences and the moderating impact of existing institutional structures.

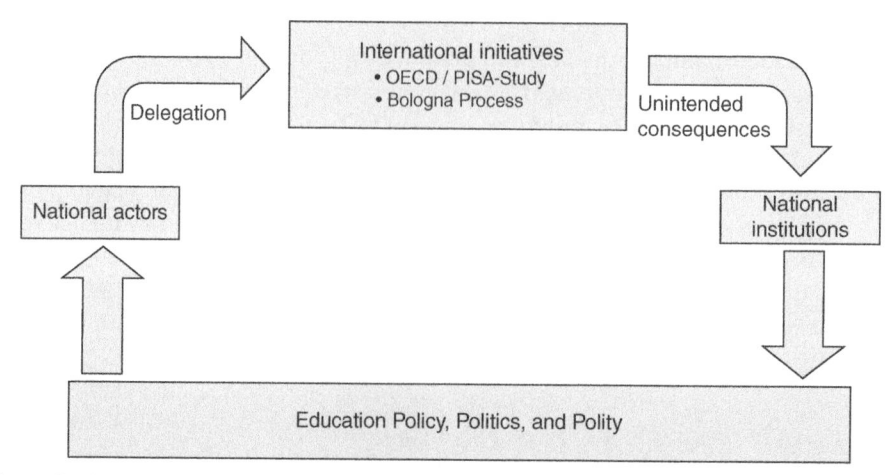

Figure 25.1 Internationalization of education as a boomerang in the domestic arena.

In order to answer these questions, we draw from theories of international relations and public policy analysis in eclectic fashion. Crucially, actors are conceptualized at both the national and the international level as rational actors strategically pursuing their interests. Building on this assumption, liberal intergovernmentalism (Moravcsik 1993a; 1993b) offers a plausible account of why national governments may choose to internationalize education policy despite an implied loss of state control. According to this approach, national governments are willing to enter the intergovernmental arena to pool their problem-solving resources not only to reduce transaction costs, but also to gain leverage at the domestic level. We supplement insights from principal-agent theory in order to analyze the output dimension of the interplay between national and international actors and assert the (un)intended consequences from delegation. While liberal intergovernmentalism is adept at explaining the motivational impetus of internationalization from the perspective of national governments, principal-agent theory expressly focuses on incentives presented to actors carrying out a mandate and generates assumptions about when and why deviations from that mandate can be expected.

The Impetus of Internationalization – a Liberal Intergovernmentalist Account

Trapped in path dependencies of existing institutional structures and domestic cleavages, education policy in most countries has for a long time been very resistant to any kind of change. For example, education secretaries in Germany had repeatedly tried to reform the three-tiered school system, hoping to reduce the effect of social class on academic performance. However, in order to be able to do so a nationwide consensus among all federal states was needed – a condition that was never met because of divergent interests in the German *Länder* (Niemann 2010). Likewise, in France, efforts to streamline degree structures and align the higher education system with an output-orientated paradigm have been stymied by the rapid mobilization of highly politicized reform opponents (Dobbins 2014). We argue that the internationalization of education policy – understood as addressing, involving, or creating international bodies with the intent of developing a transnational frame for education policies – can be understood primarily as an attempt to overcome this political gridlock by reshuffling the distribution of domestic competences. For this reason, national executives pursue intergovernmental governance arrangements to gain decision-making control over other domestic actors.[1]

In analyzing the origin and design of international institutions, Liberal intergovernmentalism takes into account both domestic preferences and strategic interstate interaction (see Moravcsik 1993b for a detailed elaboration). Principally, national governments are constrained by domestic political and societal actors and thus cannot act independently. However, intergovernmental cooperation enables governments to enhance their autonomy vis-à-vis influential domestic actors. As Wolf (1999, 336) puts it, intergovernmental cooperation "can strengthen the executive by establishing an additional political arena which is dominated by government representatives [because] they alone are able to operate simultaneously at the intergovernmental and domestic level." In other words, domestic interests and institutional hurdles can effectively be weakened or even circumvented by resorting to self-binding intergovernmental cooperation.

Intergovernmental cooperation can take many forms and designing an institutional structure that conforms to the interests of a number of national governments is a delicate task. While mutual self-commitment among national governments to intergovernmental arrangements may not necessarily imply a loss of sovereignty (as is the case with supranational institutions such as the European Union, (EU)), it inevitably entails the delegation of competences such as agenda-setting power to the international level. As a consequence, intergovernmental self-commitment has to be designed in a balanced fashion. On the one hand, the strength of intergovernmental self-commitments must be substantial enough to be able to manipulate the domestic context of policy-making. On the other hand, equipping intergovernmental arrangements with too much formal power could undermine governmental autonomy. Thus, national governments have to ensure the stability of self-commitments but at the same time allow withdrawal in case national autonomy is adversely affected (Martens and Wolf 2009).

With regard to the subject at hand, from this perspective the involvement of international initiatives such as PISA or Bologna are rational strategies of national governments aiming to enhance their autonomy vis-à-vis domestic actors and induce policy change. However, since governments are also interested in retaining as much control as possible, they choose intergovernmental arrangements that emphasize soft governance mechanisms over formal authority or even supranational decision-making.

Principal-agent Theory and the Production of Unintended Consequences

The relationship between national governments and international initiatives can be described as a principal-agent relationship in which governments delegate authority to international actors. Delegation is defined as "a conditional grant of authority from a principal to an agent that empowers the latter to act on behalf of the former" (Hawkins et al. 2006, 7). In other words, national governments (as principals) entrust international initiatives (as agents) with a task that they themselves could not accomplish or were not willing to bear the costs of.

However, preferences of principals and agents are seldom perfectly congruent, and agents, conceptualized as actors in their own right, opportunistically pursue their own interests within the constraints imposed on them by their principals. Since control mechanisms are cost-intensive and imperfect, agents often find room for independent action – called *agency slack*. This divergent behavior may not necessarily be a problem as long as agents continue to produce outcomes that are broadly consistent with what their principals intended. Over the long term, however, agents are likely to produce outcomes unintended and unanticipated by the principals. As Pierson (1996, 123) famously stated, agency slack tends to increase over time because of "member-state preoccupation with short-term concerns, the ubiquity of unintended consequences, and the instability of member-state policy preferences."

Principal-agent relationships are further characterized by information asymmetries. While principals are occupied with many tasks at the same time, agents are able to devote their resources exclusively to the task at hand (Hawkins et al. 2006, 24–26). As a result, agents develop expertise that they in turn can use to influence the future preferences of their principals; for example, through lobbying or disseminating norms. Therefore, agency slack may not only lead to deviations from the original mandate (which in itself may be formulated vaguely and thus afford agents room to maneuver), but it may altogether re-define the outcome intended by the principals.

With the introduction of international initiatives as new players in education policy, governments delegated agenda-setting power in order to achieve their policy goals. As a consequence, these international initiatives shape national debates and have become successful policy entrepreneurs in their own right. Equipped with expert knowledge and external legitimacy, international initiatives may compel their principals into extending their competences, further strengthening their role in the discourse or even influence what principals deem to be the optimal outcome of delegation.

Catching the Boomerang – the Impact of Domestic Institutional Settings

So far, it has been argued that national governments resorted to international actors in order to trigger self-transformation processes. A central component of this strategy was to overcome entrenched domestic interests in order to introduce policy reform. While domestic interests and institutional configurations were circumvented in the initiation phase of the transformations, they re-enter the reform process once policy recommendations are hurled back into the domestic setting for implementation. In this context, two factors may help to account for the national variations of change as promoted by international initiatives. These *national transformation capacities* include (a) the number of national veto players in education policy and (b) guiding principles of education as ideational modifiers.

First, veto players – defined as "individual or collective actors whose agreement is necessary for a change of the status quo" (Tsebelis 1995, 301) – are reflective of a country's ability to execute policy reforms. The more players possess veto power over a given policy process, the less likely are far-reaching reforms. Given the fact education policy was internationalized precisely because veto players had previously blocked meaningful reform, they constitute a powerful factor mediating the actual policy impact of international initiatives on national education systems.

The second modifier – guiding principles of education – denotes a country's ideological background. More expressly, guiding principles represent the interpretative framework governing the domestic discourse about education policy and specify criteria for distinguishing right from wrong (Goldstein and Keohane 1993, 9). As such, they are deeply entrenched in the history of nation states and serve as "national schemes of reference to judge the plausibility of policy proposals from IOs" (Nagel *et al.* 2010, 16). Crucially, they may greatly diverge from the market-oriented understanding of education as purported by the international initiatives. For instance, the guiding principle of education as a means to achieve social cohesion certainly yields a different set of beliefs about education policy from a guiding principle emphasizing education as a means to boost individual productivity (see Clark 1983; Dobbins 2011; Nagel *et al.* 2010). As a consequence, where guiding principles embedded within the institutional structure of a nation state are different from those propagated by international initiatives, incorporation of new prescriptions are expected to be contested and ineffective.

In sum, national transformation capacities mediate the impact of international initiatives on education policy. The domestic conflict – circumvented by resorting to the international level in the initial phase of the reform process – resurfaces later on and impedes the faithful implementation of policy prescriptions. On the one hand, national transformation capacities thus constitute a further source of unintended consequences from the perspective of national governments. On the other hand, we find that through transferring discursive authority to the international level, domestic conflicts are much less pronounced than they would have been otherwise.

The OECD as a Shaper of Secondary Education Policies

The PISA Study is one of the most influential studies of the OECD at the beginning of the 21st century. It is also an example of the rational intentions of national governments to provide for more internationally comparative data and how this objective was delegated to an existing international organization. In fact, the idea of providing internationally comparative quantitative data for education systems developed within the OECD with great reluctance and resistance, but gradually became one of the facets of the organization for which the OECD is best known today.

Internationalization of Secondary Education Through the PISA Study

PISA is the acronym for the global testing of student skills: the OECD's "Programme for International Student Assessment" proved to be the most advanced internationally standardized survey for measuring student performance in secondary education on a worldwide scale (Lingard and Grek 2007, 14). The PISA Study was first conducted in 2000 and is the largest international comparative education study surveying the competencies and skills of 15 year olds. It is a major education study both in terms of its budget and the scope of partaking nations. According to the OECD, it assesses "how far students approaching the end of compulsory education have acquired some of the knowledge and skills that are essential for full participation in society" (OECD 2007). Unlike other comparative surveys, PISA covers three different subjects, namely reading, mathematical skills, and scientific literacy; a particular emphasis is made on one of these subjects in each assessment cycle.

Since its inception, it has been conducted every three years with the results being published the following year. PISA goes far beyond the reach of the OECD's membership. While the OECD comprised 34 industrialized countries in 2013, 70 countries participated in the latest PISA evaluation round in 2012. Thus, the PISA Study not only evaluates the secondary school system of all its member states but also those of other nations. As a consequence, countries as diverse as Thailand, Qatar, and Uruguay are taking part in the examination.

The OECD's development of education indicators started in the mid-1980s through rational intentions of national actors. Domestically motivated political interests of a few countries, particularly the USA and France, pressured the OECD to produce better and more comparable educational data. Both countries played a very active and critical role in pushing the OECD to modify its program on international education indicators. They were concerned about their respective national education systems and about the domestic obstacles to reform, but for very different reasons. The USA feared losing the Cold War technology race; education gained importance on the US political agenda after the report "A Nation at Risk" had been published in

1983, describing the appalling state of education in the USA in alarming language. France's left-wing government, on the other hand, was concerned about educational opportunities for socio-economically disadvantaged children. Minister Chevènement aimed at making a more egalitarian education system with equal access a new priority in French education policy. These national governments wanted comparable quantitative data to back up their envisioned national reform processes (Lundgren 2011). Therefore they aimed to instrumentalize the OECD to promote national educational reforms and overcome domestic opposition (Martens and Wolf 2009).

Unintended Consequences

Due to the pressure from these states, the OECD started to develop quantitative indicators designed to measure the effectiveness of national education systems. However, it did not simply carry out that task as envisioned by the interested member states. Rather, institutional dynamics that were unforeseen by the states developed. The OECD developed its own agenda for education data generation and resulting policy recommendations. OECD member countries wanted comparable data on education inputs, but they did not initially anticipate that the international organization would develop its own tool (the PISA Study) for regular testings and rankings (Martens 2007).

Most strikingly, in its PISA Study the OECD evaluates participating states according to their performance in education – and sometimes reveals embarrassing results. Most importantly, the assessments' findings resulted in the so-called "PISA shock" in countries that had always believed they had good education systems. The German system, for instance, was shown to have failed in integrating children from immigrant families and evening out achievement gaps due to differences in socio-economic background. It was one of the OECD findings with the PISA Study most heavily discussed in the German discourse on education reforms (Niemann 2010).

The PISA Study initiated heated debates about the effectiveness and efficiencies of the secondary school system in various countries (Martens *et al.* 2014; Grek 2009; Martens and Niemann 2013) by raising questions of "best practice." As a result, policy-makers in many countries started to critically assess national educational systems concerning their ability to function in an integrative manner. In Germany, poor PISA results prompted a public discussion about reforming the German educational system, while Swiss policy-makers were unsatisfied with the unexpectedly average results of their students. Despite lacking any coercive means of influence, the PISA Study – combined with other factors, such as high school dropout rates, youth criminality, deficient migrant integration, countries' own domestic studies, and national problem pressure – provoked various reform attempts in the OECD world, transition countries, and developing countries (Breakspear 2012).

Through the successful spread of the PISA ideology, the OECD gained standing and reputation as an organization (Sharman 2007). Today it is counted as the "éminence grise" (Rinne *et al.* 2004) in the field of education: its studies serve as reference point when it comes to demonstrating strengths and weaknesses of individual education systems. The OECD has established itself as an international authority in education policy (Bogdandy and Goldmann 2008), and manages to exercise governance, despite its lack of legal authority, by effectively influencing public and policy-makers' opinion formation and putting pressure on domestic actors. This is remarkable because the OECD is not an organization with a proper education mandate, such as the United Nations Educational, Scientific and Cultural Organization (UNESCO) or the International Association for the Evaluation of Educational Achievement (IEA). Rather, the OECD's primary goal has always been to improve economic cooperation.

Additionally, PISA represents a stronger shift toward outcomes and performance measures: its framework presents a tool for the evaluation of education systems that makes comparisons possible. Since existing data from other sources were not sufficient, the OECD's technical staff decided that it needed to develop outcome indicators of its own. The impetus for PISA's design came from these independent analysts, not the states themselves. Consequently, its secretariat gradually broadened the program, hiring new personnel with the appropriate qualifications and experience, some of whom came from the IEA, where they had conducted similar studies (Martens 2007).

The countries did not realize that by pushing the OECD to conduct more research on education indicators they would put themselves under pressure, namely to conduct regular assessments of their national education systems' performance. Professionals who subscribed to the logic of quantitative empirical methods of data collection were given the authority for the project and eventually dominated the discourse. The introduction of these new actors and modes of governance allowed the OECD to generate a new suite of comparative indicators of learning outcomes, and to escape direct governmental control. Whereas the OECD's original work on education indicators was *intentionally* initiated by the states, PISA was the *unintended* consequence of having forced the OECD to develop expertise in education indicators.

Today, international comparative evaluations are accepted as a norm. Even with their soft governance mechanisms, the OECD has proved its capacity to influence national education policy-making and direct policies toward the common model it promotes. Thus, the organization has not only become a successful entrepreneur in education policy, but with its PISA Study it has also the potential to act as a driver of policy convergence in this field.

To sum up, PISA exhibits a typical case of the concept of *agency slack*. By moving the discussion to the international sphere, policy-makers originally aimed to increase their leverage on this policy field and introduce long-needed reforms (Martens and Wolf 2009). Under the influence of the study, however, the policy field of secondary education in many OECD states was comprehensively reoriented toward competence-oriented learning, evidence-based policy-making, education standards, liberalization, accountability, and efficiency orientation. In addition, the substantial empowerment of the OECD as an independent actor not only concerning the PISA study, but also as a renowned authority in a variety of education political issues was not foreseen by the countries, such as France and the USA, demanding the provision of PISA data by the OECD at the end of the 1990s.

Domestic Responses

In secondary education, the effect of domestic political institutions mediating the internationalization of this field has turned out to be rather constrained, and diverse countries adopted several PISA-based OECD recommendations. For example, despite their guiding ideas being rather incompatible with the economic view of the OECD and a multitude of veto players, Switzerland and Germany showed great responsiveness to the PISA-based OECD policy recommendations (Bieber 2016; Niemann 2010).

There are several reasons for the weak blocking effect of transformation capacities. First, countries used the additional international policy-making level to play the two-level game and gain influence. In Switzerland, for example, PISA results provided international legitimacy to surmount the excesses of federalism (Bieber 2016). The related veto power of strong cantonal competencies as well as of the Swiss People's Party (SVP) resulted in structural-conservative education policy-making and temporarily blocked education reforms such as the harmonization of cantonal structures. However, reforms were increasingly required due to changes to the overall socio-economic context, such as the enhanced need for intercantonal labor mobility and commuting (Bieber 2016).

Second, the PISA Study demonstrated strong deficits in national secondary education systems. In France, for example, PISA manifested three major problems: financial inefficiencies, high educational inequality, and pedagogical weaknesses (Dobbins 2014, 117). As a consequence, the normative and economic pressure to act efficiently and effectively increased, and helped to push for the needed reforms. With reference to the top performers, above all Finland and Canada, French politicians justified the greater emphasis on the promotion of equality as well as of pedagogical autonomy. At the same time, in France the relationship between the state and education providers has been redefined. While originally attempting to conceal the poor PISA results from the public, the state-centric French system was forced to engage in a stronger public consultation process with students, teachers, and parents regarding the future aims of education in France (Dobbins 2014, 122).

The Bologna Process and Reforms in Higher Education

The internationalization of education policy is most advanced in Europe in part because the existing institutional structure of supranational and multi-level governance most readily permits governance beyond the nation state. However, countries have been skeptical of ceding control to the EU for fear of a loss of national autonomy, particularly with regard to education policy. As a consequence, the EU was deliberately left out in early internationalization efforts (the initiation of the Bologna Process) but has since gained considerable influence in higher education policy.

Internationalization of Higher Education Through the Bologna Process

The Bologna Process is the prime example of the internationalization of higher education policy. Initiated by the education secretaries of Germany, Italy, France, and the UK in 1998 through the signing of the Sorbonne Declaration, its overarching goal is the creation of the European Higher Education Area. The corresponding policy prescriptions for many countries represent nothing less than a paradigmatic shift in the provision of higher education. For instance, participating countries need to adopt a three-cycle degree structure that distinguishes between undergraduate, graduate, and doctoral students. In addition, mutual recognition of academic records is facilitated by the European Transfer and Accumulation System (ECTS) by awarding credit points according to specified learning outcomes and student workload in hours. Bologna aims to enhance the quality of higher education institutions by promoting competition between universities and compelling them to adopt systems of quality management and assurance. Taken together, these prescriptions aim to achieve higher education policy convergence and improve the competitiveness of European universities vis-à-vis their counterparts abroad.

It is important to emphasize that the Bologna Process is not an initiative within the framework of EU but an intergovernmental self-commitment to cooperate. It takes an inclusive approach, and, as a consequence, today Bologna has 47 signatory states spanning all EU member countries, large portions of Eastern Europe, and even some Eurasian countries. The proportion of students who are enrolled in a three-cycle degree program and under the umbrella of the ECTS is steadily increasing, indicating extensive compliance with Bologna prescriptions in the vast majority of participating states (Bologna Process Implementation Report 2012). Given the fact that Bologna – taken at face value – is little more than a series of biannual ministerial meetings and has not been supplied with any formal authority to ensure compliance, the degree of policy change it has induced is remarkable.

How was this possible? In accordance with our theoretical framework, the instrumentalization of the international level can be explained by the strategic motives of the education secretaries that initiated the Bologna Process. Faced with increasing levels of problem pressure such as high rates of youth unemployment, high dropout rates, as well as underfunded, fragmented, and non-transparent higher education sectors, substantial policy reform was a mutual goal for the national countries of the four founding countries (Germany, France, Italy, and the UK). At the same time, domestic policy-makers had failed in inducing reforms for a variety of reasons and therefore resorted to the international level. For example, in Germany, the responsible subnational *Länder* could not agree on a reform and since the role of the federal executive (namely the Ministry of Education and Research) is quite limited, then-secretary Jürgen Rüttgers co-initiated the Bologna Process with the aim to put international pressure on the domestic opposition (Schriewer 2007). In France, on the other hand, the national government had the formal authority to make reforms, but in the face of deeply entrenched domestic interests, the political capital cost of doing so seemed prohibitive (Cole 2001). Therefore, French secretary Claude Allègre deliberately linked domestic reform to the international level, allowing him to shift responsibility and avoid political backlash by being able to "blame it on Europe" (Martens and Wolf 2009). Interestingly (and perhaps paradoxically), another component of Allègre's calculation was that a proactive intergovernmental commitment by education secretaries might preclude similar ambitions by the European Commission from realization (Witte 2006). In doing so, Allègre's interests were preserving national policy-making authority on the one hand, and to "establish a cultural counterbalance to the dominance of economic motives in the European Union" (Witte 2006, 125) on the other.

By initiating the Bologna Process, national governments were thus able to circumvent domestic opposition to induce substantial reform. Resorting to the international level was only possible because policy goals were roughly congruent[2] and it had the added benefit of changing the distribution of informal competencies for education in favor of the national executives (rather than federal subunits, parliaments, or autonomy-minded universities). At the same time, national governments – at least overtly – did not have to pay for the increased policy authority within their own educational systems with new external constraints since the Bologna Process was designed as an intergovernmental (rather than supranational) initiative that relied purely on soft governance rather than hard law (Abbott and Snidal 2000).

Unintended Consequences

However, the very reason for the success of the Bologna Process is also the greatest source of unintended consequences: By augmenting domestic political discourses about higher education policy with an international, comparative perspective, the nation states perhaps unwillingly conceded their agenda- and norm-setting power to the international level. Where higher education systems used to be self-referential, they were now confronted with a universal model that became the new benchmark for higher education policy. In other words, legitimacy was no longer provided by nation states and their idiosyncratic higher education traditions, but was defined at the international level by the Bologna Process. Over the course of implementation, this discourse increasingly emphasized economic rationales of higher education (see, for example, Münch 2009; Fejes 2008). While the Sorbonne Declaration as the founding document of the Bologna Process does not propagate economic considerations, subsequent documents such as the Bologna Declaration or the Prague Communiqué include key words such as employability and competitiveness as rationales for establishing the European Higher Education Area (Huisman and van der Wende 2004). This view is supported by a sizable body of neo-institutionalist literature conceptualizing the Bologna Process as a manifestation of a larger, global movement toward marketization and standardization in education (e.g. Meyer and Ramirez 2000; Schriewer 2009; Torres and Schugurensky 2002; Marginson, Chapter 16, this volume).

In addition to the self-reinforcing effect of the Bologna Process on higher education discourse, another important unintended consequence was a gradually increasing involvement of the EU in education policy. As mentioned, Bologna was deliberately initiated outside of the EU framework for fear of a loss of state autonomy, with the inclusion of non-EU members as a protective strategy to guard against EU influence. However, in 2001, the European Commission was awarded consultative member status and has been a full participant in follow-up meetings since. Thus over time, the Commission gained leverage to put education policy on its agenda and pursue its interests. While it had started out just as a financier of ministerial meetings and – in the case of France – as an instrumental scapegoat, it subsequently started to link Bologna reforms to activities regularly carried out by the EU. For instance, expertise on indicators to monitor the effectiveness of reforms (e.g. implementation of three-cycle degree structures) is provided by EU institutions such as Eurostat and Eurydice. By 2005, the declaration of a Bologna follow-up meeting even noted the complementarity between the overarching framework for the European Higher Education Area and the European Union (Bergen Communiqué 2005, 2) and its Lisbon strategy for growth and jobs. Given the fact the Bologna Process had originally been designed to escape EU influence, this apparent change of attitude among member states is startling.

Supplementing its growing influence within the Bologna Process, the Commission leveraged its newfound involvement to become a powerful player in education policy in its own right. While prior efforts to put education policy on its agenda had been curtailed by member states, Bologna emboldened the Commission to prioritize education policy and embed it within the larger context of making Europe the "world's leading knowledge-based economy" (European Council 2000; see also Corbett 2003). The newfound role of the EU can be illustrated by the Copenhagen Process, a virtual mirror image of the Bologna Process for vocational education. Initiated in 2002, it aims to enhance cooperation in vocational education and training throughout Europe by furthering recognition, permeability, and mobility (Copenhagen Declaration 2002). In contrast to the Bologna Process, this reform strategy has been fully embedded within the EU from the start. The Commission is not only a member but also the organizer and overseer of the Process and there is little skepticism from member states regarding the Commission's role (Balzer and Rusconi 2007).

In conclusion, agency slack can thus be observed on two interrelated dimensions. First, internationalization has shifted the discursive logic of higher education policy in Europe toward marketization, output-orientation, standardization, and transnationality (Keeling 2006). Given the fact the Bologna Process was actually initiated in part to counterbalance economic motives penetrating the EU, this is a major deviation from the original mandate. Second, subsequent EU involvement – first in the Bologna Process, then in education policy overall – was not intended by the four initiating countries.

Domestic Responses

When it comes to the response of domestic institutional structures to the internationalization of higher education policy, high compliance rates suggest that their mediating impact is surprisingly limited. The observable convergence toward one common higher education model (Dobbins *et al.* 2011) further supports the notion of a uniform impact of the Bologna process, irrespective of domestic factors such as veto players or national guiding principles. In fact, as two of the countries that had both a high number of veto players and diverging guiding principles, Germany and Switzerland were among those who most swiftly and completely implemented the Bologna prescriptions (see Niemann 2010; Bieber 2010, respectively).

So why have domestic actors and institutional configurations not altered the trajectory of the Bologna boomerang? Several components may have contributed to this surprising finding: first, as Börzel and Risse (2000) have argued with regard to European integration, the consensus-oriented political culture[3] present in most European countries is conducive to the effective implementation of externally brought policies because it spreads adaptational costs across multiple stakeholders and compensates dissenting actors in exchange for their approval (see also Witte 2006). For example, in Switzerland the *Schweizerische Universitätskonferenz* (SUK), a common organ of the federal government and cantons possessing one or several universities monitoring Swiss higher education policy, was provided with the single responsibility for the implementation of reforms in the wake of the Bologna Process (Bieber 2016). Likewise, in Germany federal university funding has been increased substantially in recent years (Hartmann 2006).

Second, policy reforms brought about by the Bologna Process may have improved the political leverage of universities and academic professionals – a group of actors intimately involved in the implementation of reforms. As Keeling (2006, 213) puts it, through Bologna reforms "higher education institutions can access new sources of both financial and political support, mobilizing a different constellation of stakeholders, including employers and industry." Finally, as the discursive logic of marketization and standardization has taken root in domestic settings, potential veto players subscribing to traditional guiding principles may have come to the conclusion that the costs of opposing reforms would outweigh the benefits of retaining the status quo (Münch 2009, 39–53).

Conclusion

The Bologna Process and the OECD's PISA Study are among the most powerful of existing international initiatives in education policy. By providing data about the effectiveness of national secondary education systems, PISA has reoriented policy discourses and educational reform agendas toward standard understandings of quality and market needs, and has brought about manifold reforms trying to address respective shortcomings. The pan-European Bologna Process has transformed the higher education systems of many countries by introducing convergent higher education degree program structures and establishing a new paradigm of output-orientated education.

The increasing involvement of international actors in education policy is a new and surprising phenomenon that can be helpfully understood using both conceptual tools from both international relations and public policy research. In this chapter, we explained this internationalization by sequentially utilizing three theoretical approaches. First, we analyzed the motivational impetus of domestic policy-makers to empower international actors and the institutional design of these initiatives. Drawing on liberal intergovernmentalism, which regards national governments as autonomy-seekers, national governments – confronted with domestic opposition to policy reform – are conceptualized as willing to enter the intergovernmental arena not only to pool resources and reduce transaction costs but also to enhance their autonomy vis-à-vis domestic actors such as parliaments or interest groups. Since actors that are embedded only within the national political system are not part of decision-making processes at the international level, governments no longer have to consider their interests or pay political capital costs associated with reform.

This can be clearly illustrated with the Bologna Process. It was initiated because attempts to reform higher education systems in Germany, France, and Italy had repeatedly failed. With problem pressure high, national governments recognized they could only achieve change if they resorted to the international level involvement; thus, they made a self-commitment to cooperate. Concerning PISA, the argument holds true. In particular, the USA and France faced reform pressures, which motivated the engagement to develop comparative quantitative data in secondary education. Contrary to the previous two initiatives, the same cannot be stated for the case of Copenhagen, as this process was the sole enterprise of the European Commission.

Second, we assessed whether international actors acted as envisioned by national governments or whether their involvement produced unintended consequences. We argue that principal-agent theory provides fruitful insights, because this approach posits that the delegation of authority from principals (national governments) to agents (international initiatives) seldom results in perfect compliance with the principal's goals. There is always room for independent action on the part of agents, meaning that international initiatives may deviate from their mandate and potentially influence the interests of their principals. This is certainly the case with the OECD and the PISA Study. In giving the OECD the authority to carry out comparative assessments, national governments did not anticipate that the results would serve as an important reference point in public discourse creating problem pressure that could not go unanswered. In the case of Bologna, unintended consequences of delegation are even more severe. Originally designed to escape influence of the EU, the Commission managed to become a vital player shaping the implementation of agreed-upon reforms and embedding the Bologna Process within a larger strategy of creating a so-called "Europe of knowledge." The Copenhagen Process as a parallel strategy of the Bologna Process in vocational education and training – has not only been designed to allow for EU influence, it is even embedded within the institutional setup of the EU.

Third, we asked how the boomerang of internationalization strikes back on domestic politics. Since internationalization often takes place to circumvent domestic opposition, it would be reasonable to expect that implementation of the reform measures be hotly contested and further unintended consequences should occur. Two analytical concepts help to assess the domestic reactions: veto players and national guiding principles. Veto players represent the actors who need to agree in order to execute reforms, and national guiding principles can be seen as the institutionalized paths countries were following prior to the reforms induced or supported by internationalization. We find that the impact of these mediating variables is surprisingly limited, at least with regard to Bologna and PISA. There was little backlash to the PISA Study as such, only outcry over the bad results that some countries got. Today, the market-oriented principles represented by the OECD have become the norm, and the results serve as reference points for evaluating new policies. Regarding the Bologna Process, countries where there were a high number of veto players and diverging education traditions most swiftly implemented new study structures. Likewise, compliance rates are high and there is observable convergence toward one common European model.

In sum, the internationalization of education has brought about manifold changes in all education sectors. Resorting to the intergovernmental level seems to be a viable way to overcome political gridlock and path-dependencies, but it has also produced a number of unintended consequences. Today, the OECD and the EU are shaping policies and discourses alike, and national governments have increased their autonomy in education matters, as they are the principals of the international actors. However, where there are winners, there are also losers. Actors operating at the national level are being pushed out of the policy-making process, and national traditions lose legitimacy.

Notes

1 For example in many countries (such as Germany, Switzerland, the USA, or Canada), education policy is primarily carried out by the federal subunits, with the national executive having little control.
2 As Witte (2006, 376) puts it, "in all four countries, massification of higher education and the demands of the knowledge economy on the function of HE provided important incentives for bringing different institutional types closer together."
3 For example, components of such a consensus-oriented culture include the presence of multi-partyism, corporatist decision-making, and cooperative federalism.

References

Abbott, K. and Duncan Snidal. 2000. "Hard and Soft Law in International Governance." *International Organization* 54(3): 421–456.

Balzer, C. and A. Rusconi. 2007. "From the European Commission to the Member States and Back? A Comparison of the Bologna and Bruges-Copenhagen Process," in *New Arenas of Education Governance. The Impact of International Organizations and Markets on Educational Policymaking*, edited by K. Martens, A. Rusconi, and K. Leuze, 57–75. Houndmills, Basingstoke: Palgrave.

Bergen Communiqué. 2005. *The European Higher Education Area – Achieving the Goals*. Communiqué of the Conference of European Ministers Responsible for Higher Education, Bergen, May 19–20. 2005.

Bieber, T. 2010. "Playing the Multilevel Game in Education: The PISA Study and the Bologna Process Triggering Swiss Harmonization," in *Transformation of Education Policy*, edited by A.K. Nagel, M. Windzio and A. Weymann, 105–131. New York: Palgrave MacMillan.

Bieber, T. 2016. *Soft Governance, International Organizations and Education Policy Convergence. Comparing PISA and the Bologna and Copenhagen Process*. Basingstoke: Palgrave.

Bogdandy, A. von, and M. Goldmann. 2008. "The Exercise of International Public Authority through National Policy Assessment: The OECD's PISA Policy as a Paradigm for a New International Standard Instrument." *International Organizations Law Review*, 5: 241–298.

Bologna Process Implementation Report. 2012. "The European Higher Education Area in 2012: Bologna Process Implementation Report" Retrieved from: www.ehea.info/Uploads/%281%29/Bologna%20Process%20Implementation%20Report.pdf (accessed November 20, 2015).

Börzel, T.A. and T. Risse. 2000. "When Europe Hits Home: Europeanization and Domestic Change." *European Integration Online Papers*, 4(15): 1–24.

Breakspear, S. 2012. "The Policy Impact of PISA: An Exploration of the Normative Effects of International Benchmarking in School System Performance." *OECD Education Working Papers*, No. 71. Paris: OECD.

Clark, B.R. 1983. *The Higher Education System: Academic Organization in Cross-National Perspective*. Berkeley: University of California Press.

Cole, A. 2001. "The New Governance of French Education?" *Public Administration*, 79(3): 707–724.

Copenhagen Declaration. 2002. *Declaration on Enhanced European Cooperation in Vocational Education and Training*. Declaration of the European Ministers of Vocational Education and Training, and the European Commission in Copenhagen, November 29–30, 2002.

Corbett, A. 2003. "Ideas, Institutions and Policy Entrepreneurs: Towards a New History of Higher Education in the European Community." *European Journal of Education*, 38(3): 315–30.

Dobbins, M. 2011. *Higher Education Policies in Central and Eastern Europe: Convergence towards a Common Model?* New York: Palgrave Macmillan.

Dobbins, M. 2014. "French Education Politics after PISA and Bologna – Rupture or Continuité?," in *Internationalization in Education Policy – A New Constellation of Statehood in Education?*, edited by K. Martens, P. Knodel, and M. Windzio, 115–141. Basingstoke: Palgrave MacMillan.

Dobbins, M., C. Knill, and E. Vögtle. 2011. "An Analytical Framework for the Cross-Country Comparison of Higher Education Governance." *Higher Education*, 62(5): 665–683.

European Council. 2000. *Presidency Conclusions*. Lisbon European Council, March 23–24, 2000.

Fejes, A. 2008. "Standardising Europe: The Bologna Process and new modes of governing." *Learning and Teaching*, 1(2): 25–49.

Goldstein, J. and R.O. Keohane. 1993. *Ideas and Foreign Policy: Beliefs, Institutions and Political Change.* Ithaca: Cornell University Press.

Grek, S. 2009. "Governing by Numbers: the PISA effect in Europe." *Journal of Education Policy,* 24(1): 23–37.

Hartmann, M. 2006. "Die Exzellenzinitiative – Ein Paradigmenwechsel in der Deutschen Hochschulpolitik." *Leviathan,* 34(4): 447–465.

Hawkins, D.G., D.A. Lake, D. Nielson, and M.J. Tierney. 2006. "Delegation under Anarchy: States, International Organizations, and Principal-Agent-Theory," in *Delegation and Agency in International Organizations,* edited by D.G. Hawkins, D.A. Lake, D. Nielson, and M.J. Tierney, 3–38. Cambridge: Cambridge University Press.

Huisman, J. and M. Van der Wende. 2004. "The EU and Bologna: Are Supra- and International Initiatives Threatening Domestic Agendas?" *European Journal of Education,* 39(3): 349–357.

Keeling, R. 2006. "The Bologna Process and the Lisbon Research Agenda: The European Commission's Expanding Role in Higher Education Discourse." *European Journal of Education,* 41(2): 203–223.

Lingard, B. and S. Grek. 2007. "The OECD, Indicators and PISA: An Exploration of Events and Theoretical Perspectives." *Fabricating Quality in European Education,* Working Paper 2.

Lundgren, U. 2011. "PISA as a Political Instrument. One History Behind the Formulating of the PISA Programme," in *PISA under Examination: Changing Knowledge, Changing Tests, and Changing Schoools,* edited by M.A. Pereyra, H.-G. Kotthoff, and R. Cowen, 17–30. Rotterdam: Sense Publishers.

Martens, K. 2007. "How to Become an Influential Actor: The "Comparative Turn" in OECD Education Policy," in *New Areas of Education Governance: The Impact of International Organizations and Markets on Educational Policy Making,* edited by K. Martens, A. Rusconi and K. Leuze, 40–56. Basingstoke: Palgrave Macmillan.

Martens, K. and D. Niemann. 2013. "When Do Numbers Count? The Differential Impact of Ratings and Rankings on National Education Policy in Germany and the US." *German Politics,* 22(3): 314–332.

Martens, K. and K.D. Wolf. 2009. "Boomerangs and Trojan Horses: The Unintended Consequences of Internationalizing Education Policy Through the EU and the OECD," in *European Integration and the Governance of Higher Education and Research,* edited by A. Amaral, G. Neave, C. Musselin, and P. Maassen, 81–108. New York: Springer.

Martens, K., A. Rusconi, and K. Leuze (eds). 2007. *New Arenas of Education Governance: The Impact of International Organizations and Markets on Educational Policy Making: Transformations of the State.* Basingstoke: Palgrave Macmillan.

Martens, K., P. Knodel, and M. Windzio (eds). 2014. *Internationalization in Education Policy: A New Constellation of Statehood in Education?* Basingstoke: Palgrave MacMillan.

Meyer, J.W. and F.O. Ramirez. 2000. "The World Institutionalization of Education," in *Discourse Formation in Comparative Education,* edited by J. Schriewer, 111–132. Frankfurt am Main: Peter Lang.

Moravcsik, A. 1993a. "Introduction: Integrating International and Domestic Theories of International Bargaining," in *Double-Edged Diplomacy,* edited by P.B. Evans, H.K. Jacobson, and R.D. Putnam, 3–42. Berkeley: University of California Press.

Moravcsik, A. 1993b. "Preferences and Power in the European Community: A Liberal Intergovernmentalist Approach." *JCMS: Journal of Common Market Studies,* 31(4): 473–524.

Münch, R. 2009. *Globale Eliten, Lokale Autoritäten: Bildung und Wissenschaft unter dem Regime von PISA, McKinsey & Co.* Frankfurt am Main: Suhrkamp.

Nagel, A.-K., K. Martens, and M. Windzio. 2010. "Introduction – Education Policy in Transformation," in *Transformation of Education Policy,* edited by K. Martens, A.K. Nagel, M. Windzio, and A. Weymann, 261–276. Basingstoke: Palgrave Macmillan.

Niemann, D. 2010. "Turn of the Tide: New Horizons in German Education Policymaking through IO influence," in *Transformation of Education Policy*, edited by K. Martens, A.K. Nagel, M. Windzio, and A. Weymann, 77–104. Basingstoke: Palgrave Macmillan.

OECD. 2007. "PISA – The OECD Programme for International Student Assessment." Retrieved from: www.oecd.org/pisa/pisaproducts/37474503.pdf (accessed November 20, 2015).

Parreira do Amaral, M. 2006. *The Influence of Transnational Organizations on National Education Systems*. Frankfurt am Main: Peter Lang.

Pierson, P. 1996. "The Path to European Integration: A Historical Institutionalist Analysis." *Comparative Political Studies*, 29(2): 123–163.

Rinne, R., J. Kallo, and S. Hokka. 2004. "Too Eager to Comply? OECD Education Policies and the Finnish Response." *European Educational Research Journal*, 3(2): 454–485.

Schriewer, J. 2007. "Bologna – Ein Neu-Europäischer Mythos?" *Zeitschrift für Pädagogik*, 53(2): 182–199.

Schriewer, J. 2009. "Rationalized Myths in European Higher Education: The Construction and Diffusion of the Bologna Model." *European Education*, 41(2): 31–51.

Sharman, J.C. 2007. "Rationalist and Constructivist Perspectives on Reputation." *Political Studies*, 55(1): 20–37.

Torres, C.A. and D. Schugurensky. 2002. "The Political Economy of Higher Education in the Era of Neoliberal Globalization: Latin America in Comparative Perspective." *Higher Education*, 43(4): 429–455.

Tsebelis, G. 1995. "Decision Making in Political Systems: Veto Players in Presidentialism, Parliamentarism, Multicameralism and Multipartyism." *British Journal of Political Science*, 25(3): 289–325.

Witte, J. 2006. *Change of Degrees and Degrees of Change: Comparing Adaptions of European Higher Education Systems in the Context of the Bologna Process*. Enschede: CHEPS.

Wolf, K.D. 1999. "The New Raison d'État as a Problem for Democracy in World Society." *European Journal of International Relations*, 5(3): 333–363.

Chapter 26

Policy and Administration as Culture: Organizational Sociology and Cross-National Education Trends[1]

Patricia Bromley

Over the 20th century, education emerged as a central social, political, and economic concern in countries worldwide. Today its structures span government, business, and civil society sectors and bridge local, national, and international levels. Education is a core administrative and policy task of every government, and it is the focus of a great many intergovernmental and non-governmental organizations (NGOs), including rising numbers of private businesses.[2] Despite the central role of education in countries around the world and in the international system, our understanding of recent transnational administrative and policy trends pushing privatization and new forms of regulation has been handicapped by a conceptual narrowness.

Theories of public policy and administration emerged from political science and management, and research remains dominated by the questions and assumptions of these disciplines. The study of politics typically focus on causal explanations rooted in power and agency, while management research focuses on economic emphases on function and efficiency; one or both of these views characterize most public administration and policy research, including studies of education. While useful in some ways, these approaches overlook important elements of administration and policy that are best understood through a cultural lens. In particular, the behaviors of actors, including individuals and the organizations and countries they inhabit and construct, are often largely shaped by beliefs about appropriate and legitimate actions rather than by their power (or lack of it), *a priori* self-interests, or certainty about the efficacy of their actions. Global education policy is, at best, boundedly rational (Baker and LeTendre 2005; Wiseman and Baker 2005).

In a pointed call for scholars of all public issues to broaden their intellectual terrain, Kelman recommended turning to sociological studies of organization: "The emergence of organization studies in social psychology and sociology created a need and an

The Handbook of Global Education Policy, First Edition.
Edited by Karen Mundy, Andy Green, Bob Lingard, and Antoni Verger.
© 2016 John Wiley & Sons, Ltd. Published 2016 by John Wiley & Sons, Ltd.

opportunity for public administration scholars to reach out... The field failed to do this; instead, it retreated inward" (2007, 232). In part, this chapter is a response to Kelman's appeal. It seeks to bring the insights of sociological analyses of organizations to bear on issues of public administration and policy. It diverges, however, in that he advocates a turn toward managerial emphases on performance in public organizations. Perhaps unlike other public sectors, in the context of education there is a thriving body of work focused on performance, especially in the form of studies of achievement and attainment. The conceptual limitations of studies of educational policy and administration are not related to a lack of attention to performance; instead they come from an overemphasis on power and efficiency and an underemphasis on culture as explanations of core features of educational policy and administration.

This chapter gives a sociological explanation for emergent transnational features of contemporary educational policy and administration. In the next section, I provide a brief overview of early and recent conceptual tenets of sociological or organizational institutionalism, which has become one of the most dominant approaches to the study of organizations in sociology.[3] Subsequently, I outline how recent developments in this view shed light on contemporary trends in global educational policy and administration. Following, I discuss why institutionalism is relatively unknown in policy and administration research and conclude with an overview of the insights it can provide.

The Neo-institutional Approach

Neo-institutionalism emerged in the 1970s mainly in opposition to functional economic and power-based views of organization that imagine social structures to be the optimal solution for achieving some end, be it efficiency or elite interests. It argues that features of formal organization, such as educational policies and administrative practices, diffuse as a cultural matter. As culture, formal structures spread beyond functional requirements and in ways that are not obvious reflections of aggregated self-interests or to the benefit of elites and not necessarily most efficient. And, with social and cultural globalization, formal structures diffuse worldwide (Meyer *et al.* 1997).

This approach calls attention to how the external environment socially constructs actors, providing templates or blueprints for legitimate formal structures and policies.[4] As explained by DiMaggio and Powell: "The new institutionalism in organization theory and sociology comprises a rejection of rational-actor models, an interest in institutions as independent variables, a turn toward cognitive and cultural explanations, and an interest in properties of supraindividual units of analysis that cannot be reduced to aggregations or direct consequences of individuals' attributes or motives" (1991, 8). In a foundational paper, Meyer and Rowan (1977) set out a view of complex organizations in post-industrial society as reflecting cultural beliefs in the institutional environment rather than the technical demands of production. As the environment impinges on organizations, they develop similar formal structures (a process called "isomorphism"). As a consequence of balancing external demands with internal technical requirements, there are routinely gaps between formal structures and daily practices (a process called "decoupling"). A second seminal paper outlined how institutional isomorphism occurred through coercive (including cultural norms and resource dependency), normative (mainly professional influences), and mimetic (copying in the face of uncertainty) channels (DiMaggio and Powell 1983).

As an example of this research applied to global education, a seminal contribution of early scholarship was to show that schooling expands beyond what can be accounted for by the needs of industrialization and across countries with hugely diverse economic, political, and social arrangements (Ramirez and Boli 1987; Boli et al. 1985; Meyer et al. 1992).[5] A number of neo-institutional studies emphasize the global expansion of schooling (for a review, see Ramirez and Meyer 1980) and isomorphism in formal structures such as the creation of ministries of education, curricula, and policies (Frank et al. 1994; 2000; McEneaney and Meyer 2000; McNeely 1995; Wong 1991). In this body of work, educational systems are a manifestation of universalistic cultural principles of progress and justice that grew out of Western roots to become cornerstones in a world society (Meyer et al. 1997).[6] It is expected that there is a gap between the formal policies espoused in these documents and actual educational access and quality (Meyer and Rowan 1977).

New Directions

These core neo-institutional concepts of isomorphism and decoupling continue to offer great purchase for understanding phenomena that are weakly explained by rational action arguments rooted in efficiency or power. But at least since the 1990s, these early emphases on top-down processes, structural similarities, and decoupling between policies and practices have been augmented by new insights.

To begin, institutional theorists have grown increasingly sophisticated in their conceptualization of actors and agency. Early studies were criticized for depicting individuals as "cultural dopes" who unthinkingly enacted social scripts. Contemporary scholars reject this characterization, emphasizing that agency is socially constrained and socially constituted (see Westphal and Zajac 2013 for a review). The numbers and types of social actors exercising agency on various fronts has increased dramatically over time (Drori et al. 2006). The essence of these new social structures has been described as "actorhood," where actors are entities that carry rights and responsibilities on an array of dimensions and seek to act in purposive, legitimate ways (Brunsson and Sahlin-Andersson 2000). Meyer and Bromley (2013) provide an explanation for this trend. Three broad and interconnected cultural trends are most important: the rise of human rights, the decline of the nation state, and the expansion of scientific thought. Issues of rights, justice, and equality expand dramatically (Lauren 2003; Stacy 2009), undermining traditional notions of authority such as the divine right of kings and absolute sovereignty (Bendix 1980). And medieval religious polities are transformed into the secular, administrative, and legal structures of modern nation states (Tilly 1990). Evolving in parallel, Enlightenment-era philosophy expanded alternative bases of authority rooted in secular individualism and scientific thinking; it is difficult to overstate the authority of scientific principles in contemporary world society (Drori et al. 2006). This process, called cultural rationalization, involves the efforts of hugely empowered individuals to define the natural and social world in terms of linear causal chains, where means and ends, inputs and outputs, or causes and effects, are explicitly specified (sometimes in theory more than in fact).[7] Overall, traditional forms of authority decline and new actors become endowed with many rights and capacities.

An additional core change in institutional theories of organization is in the expansion of thinking related to contradictions and pluralism generated by institutional pressures.

As expanding arenas of the natural and social world are re-imagined as subject to human abilities to understand and control, the external environment becomes increasingly complex and any given entity is subject to an expanding array of rationalized pressures (Meyer and Bromley 2013). Due to the expansion of rational human initiative into new realms, the external environment is altered and it becomes possible and necessary for individuals and organizations to attend to increasingly diverse concerns within the same formal structure. Thus, businesses appear more like responsible citizens, and non-profits and government agencies attend to issues of evaluation and accountability (Bromley and Meyer 2014). Within literature on public and non-profit organizations, the trend is toward discussing "blurring" between sectoral boundaries, as well as "hybrids" and "social enterprises" (Billis 2010; Pache and Santos 2010b). In organizational research this phenomenon is evident in the burgeoning literature using terms like "multiple" or "conflicting" "institutional logics" and "institutional pluralism" (Friedland and Alford 1991; Greenwood et al. 2011; Kraatz and Block 2008; Pache and Santos 2010a; Thornton et al. 2012).

Linked to emphases on contradictions and inconsistencies, some speculate that an alternative form of decoupling, between means and ends, may become increasingly common as scientized activities such as evaluation and monitoring increase on all sorts of dimensions, pushing new concerns into existing social structures and pressing for greater alignment between policy and practice (Bromley and Powell 2012). A central focus of early institutional research was in explaining why adopted policies might not be implemented. In public administration and policy, the issue of implementation failures continues to be a core concern (O'Toole 2000; for a classic case see Pressman and Wildavsky 1984). According to neo-institutional arguments, the gap between policy and practice was expected to be largest when formal external evaluation, inspection, and monitoring were weak or conducted informally (Meyer and Rowan 1977, 356–357). But in the contemporary, highly rationalized environment, activities such as formal evaluation are increasingly common, suggesting that this decoupling between formal structures and actual practices may become temporary or less common (Haack et al. 2012).

However, organizations, in theory conceived of as structures designed to efficiently achieve some end goal, in practice come to take on a multitude of additional goals and become more elaborate than pure function demands (Greenwood et al. 2011). Cultural rationalization generates high levels of scientized monitoring and evaluation, pressing organizations to implement (at least in part) the new elements they adopt. It also generates increasing domains that require an organizational response. Whereas early studies of decoupling mainly focused on settings in which formal policies were not implemented, means–ends decoupling describes situations where policies and practices may be quite closely aligned but are opaquely related to an organization's key goal. Under conditions of cultural rationalization, idealized expectations of human capacities and rights expand beyond actual abilities for measurement and control, regardless of how extensive the monitoring. So, for example, even if a foundation's "theory of change" is thoroughly monitored and evaluated and implemented, the theory itself is often built on a rather uncertain knowledge base and may not lead to stated goals.

A main point is that the rationalization of culture generates increasingly complex entities. This has implications for neo-institutional understandings of isomorphism. At the macro level organizations or countries may become more similar in that a particular structure or practice may diffuse over time. For example, more countries may adopt education ministries. But the menu of structures available in the environment is also expanding, leading to an exponential increase in the possible combinatorial patterns. Thus, when looking holistically at any two given units they can diverge over time in terms of the set of structures and practices they adopt, even while the macro-level pattern for a practice is one of diffusion. In short, in contemporary neo-institutional studies the central observation is increasing complexity and elaboration of social structures, driven by the social construction of human ability for agentic behavior on a growing number of fronts. Overall, contemporary organizational institutionalism focuses on the social construction of actors and agency rather than thinking solely in terms of top-down pressures, and gives attention to how institutional pressures can generate complexity and pluralism as well as similarities.

Understanding Trends in Global Education Policy and Administration

Recent developments in institutional theory bridge the fields of organizational sociology and public administration or management, and can provide greater purchase on understanding global policy and administration in education. The scope and scale of the global education sector is now so large that it touches most, if not all, people alive today by virtue of their inclusion/exclusion and the quality of schooling they receive. As mentioned earlier, initial neo-institutional insights are valuable for explaining the global expansion of education. But it is not simply the case that education systems have expanded. They have also changed remarkably in terms of who provides services and how they are governed.

Core trends in contemporary global educational policy and administration are privatization and a shift from bureaucratic, hierarchical government authority to post-bureaucratic, diffuse, shared-power forms of governance. Using examples from Latin America, the USA, India, Africa, South East Asia, and England, Ball explains:

> Arguably, the two main axes of global trends in education policy are those of parental choice and the role of "private" schooling, and the reform of state education systems along managerialist/entrepreneurial lines. The first rests on a set of neo-liberal arguments about more or less radical destatisation, subjecting state organisations to competition and/or the handing over of education service delivery to the private sector. The second is more post-neo-liberal in the sense of reasserting the role of the state but in a new form and with new modalities involving a shift from government to governance; that is from bureaucracy to networks; from delivery to contracting. (Ball 2012, 11)

Educational expansion amplifies the consequences of policy and administrative shifts that have gained credence especially since the 1990s; namely, privatization and the decentralization of state authority over social service provision. These contemporary global trends in education policy and administration can be accounted for by recent neo-institutional emphases on the social construction of actors and growing environmental complexity.

The Rise of New Actors and Interests

Globally, the welfare state has not disappeared, but its growth has slowed with the diffusion of public-sector downsizing rhetoric (Lee and Strang 2006). It is commonly observed that neo-liberalism, and attendant terms such as "New Public Management," "post-bureaucratic," and "reinventing government," indicate a reconstitution of ideas of sovereignty and territoriality, fundamentally altering the historical relationships between public and private, local and global (Christensen and Lægreid 2001; Kernaghan 2000; Osborne and Gaebler 1992; Ong 2006). These neo-liberal fashions in education reform and public sector governance are part of a broader movement that has been called the "denationalization" of the state (Jessop 2004; Sassen 2006). As recent neo-institutional theory explains, the decline of traditional forms of authority, combined with the expansion of individual rights and capacities, provide a cultural foundation for the construction of new actors (Meyer and Bromley 2013). These new actors are built around principles of expanded human rights and scientific thinking rather than older structures, which more often reflected tradition or charisma. Private organizations, both non-profit and for-profit, have emerged as key service providers and policy influentials in the education arena.

The rise of private, for-profit organizations is often widely noted, although it is difficult to obtain reasonable estimates of the scope or scale of business influence and activities in education in any country, let alone worldwide. In part, this is because many for-profit educational activities are outside the formal system. For instance, Bray (1999, 2001) describes the expansion of a "shadow system" of education in the form of private tutoring in countries around the world. In an extreme case, Korea, he estimates that parents spent 150% of the amount of government investment in education (1999, 9). In the USA, there is a large market for test preparation (e.g. to provide training for the exams used for entrance to college and graduate schools) and various other kinds of private educational consultants have emerged (e.g. to provide advice on writing college application letters or any sort of educational decision-making). The numbers of students pursuing higher education in private, for-profit organizations is on the rise. As an example, in the USA, enrolment at for-profit institutions has increased by roughly 225% since 1990, and in the 2010–2011 academic year these institutions comprised 12% of all postsecondary enrollments – about 2.4 million students (National Conference of State Legislatures 2013). These numbers may wane in light of mounting evidence of the relative failure of these for-profit institutions to help students graduate (Blumenstyk 2012), but there is no sign of their disappearance.

Evidence of the rising prevalence of civil society actors in education is somewhat more available. Education has become a main concern for NGOs around the world. In a study of 36 countries, education represents the largest part of domestic non-profit sectors, as shown in Figure 26.1. In the USA, education non-profits have made up 12–13% of all registered voluntary associations each year over the period 1995 to 2012 (National Center for Charitable Statistics 2012). Often, these non-profits work as service providers, existing in partnership with the state through contracting arrangements. At the global level, 238 of the 382 (62%) NGOs with official consultative status with the United Nations are part of the education sector program sector, while 172 (45%) identify themselves by the keywords "education" or "schooling," and 45 (12%) have the word "education" or its translation in their name (UNESCO 2013).

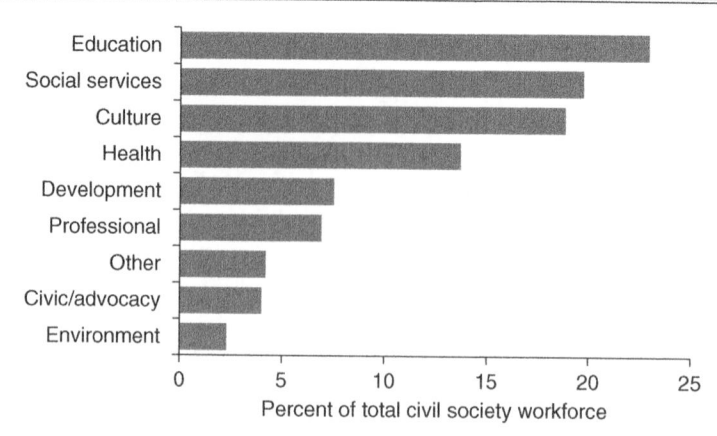

Figure 26.1 Civil society full-time equivalent workforce by field across 36 countries, 1995–2000.
Source: Adapted from Salamon et al. (2004).

An important, but often overlooked, feature of contemporary schooling is that as the range of actors socially authorized to influence schooling expands and scientific knowledge reconstitutes new domains, the sorts of concerns schools must attend to expand as well. In a study of international NGOs (INGOs) working in the field of educational development, Bromley (2010) documents that in addition to continuing their original work as service providers they increasingly work on scientized activities such as monitoring, evaluation, and research. This point is very much in line with contemporary neo-institutional thought, which points out that as cultural rationalization proceeds the social milieu becomes thick with empowered actors in all sorts of domains. New concerns are pushed and pulled into existing organizations, making them more complex. For example, in many countries around the world curricula increasingly include emphases on human rights, environmentalism, and diversity, in addition to traditional topics such as national history (Meyer et al. 2010; Bromley et al. 2011; Bromley 2014). Schools today not only socialize citizens, provide job training, and contribute to equal opportunity, increasingly they also attend to issues of student and teacher safety, consider nutritional needs of their students, and perhaps have initiatives related to protecting the natural world. They must do this while improving test scores on a growing array of assessments, and while reporting (often formally) to governments, communities, donors, and other stakeholders.

The Rise of Managerial Governance

Overall, education has expanded, while government authority over schooling has weakened and private organizations and individuals have become more legitimate voices in school provision and regulation. In the neo-institutional view, new governance mechanisms, such as emphases on accountability and transparency through monitoring, standards, and reporting, emerge to protect rights of a growing number of groups and on a growing number of topics in a systematic and objective (i.e. scientific) way. These new forms of governance underpinned by principles of science and rights in part replace former emphases on hierarchical and imperative authority or absolute loyalty to a sovereign (Drori *et al.* 2006). Older social structures, which were imagined to serve the interests of a principal, now become populated with sovereign and sacred individuals, all of whom have rights and capacities to be respected (Elliott 2007). Schools are no longer envisioned as distinct social structures; instead they become instances of organization where general principles of rights and scientific management should be applied (Bromley and Meyer, 2014). Several oft-observed trends result:

First, with the expansion of social scientific thinking, it becomes assumed we can measure learning through test scores that are comparable across country settings and over time, and that factors influencing test scores (e.g. principal leadership, teacher quality, hours of schooling, socioeconomic status) in one setting may influence it in another. To wit, cross-national educational assessment is becoming a global phenomenon; while only 43 economies participated in the Programme for International Student Assessment (PISA) in 2000, the number increased to 65 by 2012, and 71 are signed up to participate in 2015 (PISA 2014).

Second, the legitimation of quantitative test scores as an outcome of schooling combined with the creation of economics as a scientific field created a setting ripe for the application of market-based theories of incentives, competition, choice, and efficiency/effectiveness. Framed as science rather than ideology, issues of parental choice, vouchers, privatization, accountability, evaluation, and the like are now central educational concerns in countries all over the world, and much policy research (also sometimes described as the economics of education) analyzes the effectiveness of these reforms worldwide (e.g. see Akabayashi and Arakia 2011 for vouchers in Japan; Angrist *et al.* 2006 for vouchers in Colombia; Barrera-Osorio and Raju 2011 for private school subsidies in Pakistan; Böhlmark and Lindahl 2008 for vouchers in Sweden; Bravo *et al.* 2010 for vouchers in Chile; Himmler 2007 for school choice in The Netherlands). By cultural fiat, the best way to improve schooling is using scientific approaches, and economics provided a framework for doing so.

Third, beyond the evolution of economics, the general rise of management as a scientific endeavor has contributed to an additional set of new influences that provide schools with abstract strategies for improving efficiency and effectiveness (in theory if not in practice). Principals and administrators become leaders and managers, sometimes trained in collaboration with business schools.[8] An extreme example is found in a data collection effort known as the World Management Survey, where scholars created context-free definitions of proper management that applied across countries (developed and developing), sectors (education, health care, retail, manufacturing), and ownership type (public or private) (World Management Survey2013; for a detailed methodology see Bloom and Van Reenen 2007). Using this data to study the effect of management on school achievement in Canada, Italy, Germany, Sweden, the UK, and the USA, one study describes how "measuring management requires a definition of 'good' and 'bad' managerial practices which is possibly not contingent on the specific production environment (firms, hospitals, schools) and applicable to different units" (Di Liberto *et al.* 2013, 7).[9] It finds better management is linked to higher test scores, but notes few differences between public versus private schools. Another study examines whether education, manufacturing, retail, or health care have better or worse managerial practices across countries, as shown in Figure 26.2. The authors find that government ownership is associated with worse management

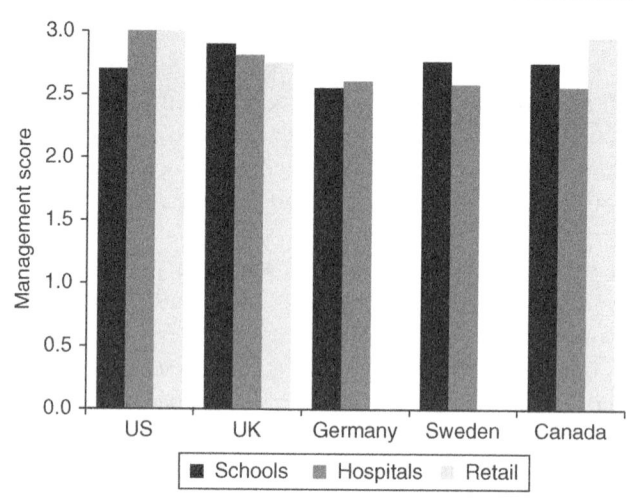

Figure 26.2 Management scores across countries and sectors.
Source: Estimates adapted from Bloom *et al.* (2012), 20.

practices and poor use of incentives in hiring, firing, and promotion practices, and that the USA outperforms other countries in terms of scores in retail and hospital management (Bloom *et al.* 2012, 20). The core point is to illustrate a growing body of research focusing on efficiency and effectiveness in education, where these are thought of as outcomes that can be measured and managed using economic notions of employee incentives and school competition.

Fourth, the decline of traditional forms of authority and expansions in science and rights creates space for new actors to become involved in educational governance. A nascent body of literature also points to the growth of advocacy activities in education. Path-breaking research on the rise of Transnational Advocacy Networks (TANs) notes they may bring the potential to democratize global educational governance. As Mundy and Murphy(2001) describe, TANs are a new and qualitatively different wave of transnational regulation, in that NGOs, citizen's associations, trade unions, and others, come together to influence nation states. These efforts are most recognizable in the genesis of the Global Campaign for Education and the Education for All movement. Parallel to the rise of TANs, it is plausible that domestic advocacy and lobbying by both non-profit and for-profit education consortiums have become a powerful influence on governments, although relatively little research has been done on the topic.[10] One government watchdog group, the Center for Responsive Politics, has tracked spending on education lobbying in the USA over time, as shown in Figure 26.3. At its peak, spending exceeded US$100 million annually. Interestingly, in the 1990s the top spenders were well-known universities, such as Columbia, Harvard, and Johns Hopkins. But by 2013, for-profit corporations such as Warburg Pincus (a private equity firm that is the largest shareholder of Bridgepoint Education) and the Apollo Group (owner of the University of Phoenix) were among the largest spenders on education lobbying (Center for Responsive Politics 2013). In the USA, the vast resources that lobbyists and huge private foundations (such as the Gates Foundation) spend do seem to have a significant influence on education policy (Reckhow 2013).[11]

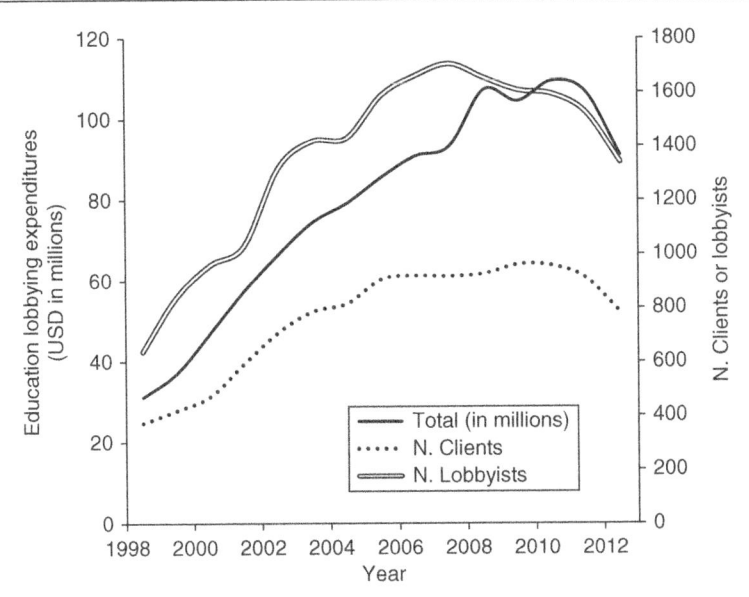

Figure 26.3 Size of education lobbying in the USA, 1998–2012.
Source: Data from Center for Responsive Politics (2012).

Many describe the new forms of authority and governance as a network rather than a hierarchy (Ball 2012; O'Toole 2000; Provan and Kenis 2008). In his study of cross-national policy networks in education, Ball eloquently discusses the "increasing role of business, social enterprise and philanthropy in education service delivery and education policy, and the concomitant emergence of new forms of 'network' governance ... [and] the advocacy and dissemination of 'private' and social enterprise solutions to the 'problems' of state education" (Ball 2012, 1). The imagery of authority and governance structures as becoming more like networks is central in both New Public Management discussions (emphasizing principal–agent interactions) and a discourse of New Public Governance (emphasizing more collaborative and stewardship-like relations among actors).

But in existing accounts of New Public Management trends and New Public Governance, there is little explanation for *why* these changes to traditional governments are occurring. The present social and cultural context is taken as a given, with little attempt to account for why we might see the rise of new types of stakeholders or the development of a plural/pluralistic world (e.g. Osborne 2010). Neo-institutional theory provides an explanation for the emergence of network governance and new stakeholders as rooted in cultural shifts, especially expansion of individual rights and capacities (for who needs to be addressed) and science (for how to address problems). The rise of science and rights along with the decline of the state have flattened older authority structures and led to the inclusion of new actors, creating what some have described as a "multi-stakeholder" and "shared power" world (Crosby and Bryson 2005).

Two additional points are important. First, network imagery only captures part of the picture, as the underlying cultural basis of authority stems from principles of individual rights and scientific thinking that have influence beyond any particular pattern of relations. Descriptively, it makes sense to discuss mechanisms of "governance" rather than the traditional authority of "government" (Rosenau and Czempiel 1992). Forms of rationalized governance, which include mechanisms like formal evaluations, ratings, rankings, certifications, standards, and accreditations, certainly involve multiple players (e.g. non-profits, government, and businesses). But the source of their legitimacy is rooted in an underlying perception of scientific objectivity and/or promotion of human rights. Based in these universalistic principles, the influence of rationalized governance mechanisms can extend even to units outside their formal scope of inclusion or to persons and actors with whom there is no direct network contact.

Second, the rise of rationalized interests in an array of domains (e.g. student and parent rights, safety, environmentalism, privacy, health) presses education organizations to respond in substantial ways on multiple fronts. The ceremonial adoption of policies or structures becomes less feasible in a rationalized cultural environment. Outside stakeholders press for evidence of accountability, and internal participants often themselves prefer to align policies and practices. For example, in a recent study of US schools, Rowan (2006) points out that the context for schooling has become highly rationalized. He points to the rise of large testing agencies, increasing credentialing for education professionals, and stronger policy instruments designed to support particular curricular reforms and hold teachers and schools accountable for student performance. Rowan concludes "institutional governance ... can, in fact, result in more than ceremonial conformity and loose coupling, even in regulated organizations such as schools" (2006, 24). Others have similarly noted how the heightened salience of external accountability measures has resulted in accounts of the recoupling of school practices to formal policies (Spillane et al. 2011). Related, a recent study of the use of strategic planning in non-profits concludes that many plans are faithfully implemented by staff although their utility is unknown, creating a situation better described as "symbolic implementation" than "symbolic adoption" (Bromley et al. 2012). Along these lines, Mundy and Menashy (2014) highlight the inconsistency in the World Bank's simultaneous pursuits of economic returns on loans and poverty alleviation. The means and ends of schooling are continually decoupled and recoupled as waves of reform redefine both the goals of education and how to achieve these goals.

Discussion and Conclusion

Neo-institutional studies of the 1970s and 1980s were largely characterized by emphases on isomorphism and decoupling between policies and practices. Recent advancements emphasize the social construction of great numbers of new actors constituted by principles of rights and science, and an attendant complication of the external environment surrounding those actors. These new directions in institutional theory have mainly developed in the study of organizations, but they apply equally to dominant trends in global educational policy and administration; namely, the rise of new actors in service provision and governance and the increasingly complex structure of schooling. Due to cultural rationalization, layers of administration and management are increasing on multiple fronts. But this is no simple expansion of hierarchical bureaucracy designed to transmit the will of a centralized sovereign down to lower levels of society. Instead organizational expansion in education is the result of increasing authority, empowerment, and rationalization of actors in multiple domains.

As a general comment, all of the perspectives discussed (power/politics-based, managerial/economics-based, and cultural/institutional-based) are huge categories of thought with much internal variation. At the margins, there is often overlap between them. For instance, in more Foucaultian formulations, a power-based view considers "expertise" a sort of influence, and imagines that experts are socialized into their profession and follow its tenets independent of their own self-interest. This is quite similar to many neo-institutional ideas of influence. In the words of Sahlin and Wedlin, "it appears to be not so much a case of ideas flowing widely because they are powerful, but rather of ideas becoming powerful as they circulate" (Sahlin and Wedlin 2008, 223). Moreover, these lenses are not always mutually exclusive. At times, an institutional lens complements, rather than competes with functional views of global education policy and administration.

Neo-institutional theory, however, generates different sorts of research questions and provides explanatory purchase in the wide swathes of social life where explanations of self-interest or efficiency are weak. For example, in critical conceptions new forms of governance are depicted as reflecting the interests of international organizations, wealthy core countries, and transnational elites, who use educational policy to gain wealth and/or power (Altbach 1977; Arnove 1980). It remains uncertain, however, whether transnational advocacy by global civil society groups serves as a counterbalance to hegemonic forces or is yet another vehicle for consolidating power (Mundy and Murphy 2001). Parallel to the ambivalence among comparative education researchers about the democratizing effects of TANs, those looking at the USA are unsure whether the growing influence of private actors serve as a counterbalance to government or represent a new form of oppression (Tompkins-Stange 2013).

A common challenge of power-based explanations is that it can be very unclear whose interests are being served in what way, and conflicting predictions emerge (e.g. regarding whether INGOs are a democratizing force in education or serve to reproduce existing power structures). These views often ignore the public good motives of many individuals and organizations working in the field of education, implicitly assuming the interests of educational experts stem from rather narrow views of personal or national gain. Furthermore, while raw power and interests certainly matter at times, recent trends likely have a taming influence on older forms of authority because it is no longer a legitimate basis for action. In more nuanced applications, critical research notes that the arbitrary, raw execution of power by individual elites or the state is increasingly difficult to justify as authority becomes distributed among multiple types of actors and individuals. For example, in a study of global literacy policy and UNESCO, Jones (1988) describes how use of the raw coercive force of aid or sanctions is rare, indicating that contemporary hegemons more commonly work through external experts that shape policy and administrative formulations in weaker states. Others similarly note the power of global educational policy networks, which stem from core countries and international organizations like the United Nations Educational, Scientific and Cultural Organization (UNESCO) and the World Bank, and act to limit the autonomy of less powerful countries to shape their educational priorities (Ball 2012; Mundy 1998; Jones 1988, 1992). While education experts certainly have influence, they often seem to spread dominant principles as a cultural matter more than in clear pursuit of their own interests in terms of accumulating power or money.

Alternatively, from an economic view, changes in policy and administration are assumed to occur because other actors can provide education more effectively and efficiently than the state (Friedman 1955; Hoxby 2003; Neal 2002). A recent World Bank-sponsored study, for instance, describes the benefits of private provision of schooling as competition in the market for education, autonomy in school management, improved standards through contracts, [and] risk-sharing between government and providers. The study claims:

> Engagement of the private sector is often promoted as an innovative means of improving school quality. It is argued that competition for students will lead to efficiency gains, as schools – state and private – compete for students and try to improve quality while reducing cost… The idea is that, when private schools are encouraged to attract students who otherwise would be educated in state schools, they become innovative and thereby bring improvement to the learning process. Likewise, state schools, to attract students and the resources that come with them, seek to improve and provide an education at least as good as the private schools. Thus, it is argued that school choice will lead to improved learning outcomes and increased efficiency in both types of schools. (Lewis and Patrinos 2012, 6)

In this economic approach, the ideological underpinnings of educational reforms are hidden. Policies are depicted as instrumentally rational, apolitical, and acultural. That is, the starting point is to examine the effects of neo-liberal policies based on the assumption that they spread because they are effective, rather than examining the political and cultural reasons such policies exist. Managerial approaches, such as those of the World Management Survey described in the previous section, share this assumption. Social structures are assumed to be functional and their appropriate design optimizes performance, which is routinely linked to finding the proper incentives to motivate managers and employees to be productive. These assumptions are, rightly or wrongly, generalized to any type of organization.

There is evidence, however, that the assumption of functionality may be misplaced in educational policy and administration. It is increasingly difficult to support arguments that the policies associated with neo-liberalism generate across-the-board improved educational outcomes, as indicated by poor outcomes in settings where these policies are most extreme (e.g. for-profit universities in the USA). Diane Ravitch, once an advocate of such reforms, describes how her views have changed on the use of accountability, choice, and market-based solutions for improving education: "standardized testing, vouchers, charter-schools, and the No Child Left Behind Act have not delivered on their promises. In fact, many of the reforms have had little or no effect. And in many cases, the reforms have backfired" (Ravitch 2011, 2). Similarly, in an extensive review of empirical research of market mechanisms in education commissioned by the the Organisation for Economic Co-operation and Development (OECD), Waslander et al. (2010) find little supporting evidence.

Given its utility in explaining arational characteristics of contemporary governance, it is somewhat odd that sociological neo-institutionalism has not made inroads into mainstream studies of public administration and policy.[12] In part, this stems from a disciplinary split between management and public administration. Critically, Kelman observes this disciplinary divide means public administration scholars are "fixating on the unique 'public' part of public organizations and neglecting, even proudly, the 'organization' part connecting the field to a larger world. Thus, the central separatist theme is opposition to what is designated as 'generic management' – the view that organizations share enough common features about which generalizations may be made to make it useful to study agencies and firms together" (Kelman 2007, 233).

As a matter of history, explanatory emphases on power and function in public policy and administration make sense. But as a matter of modern theory and practice, this two-part focus overlooks at least 60 years of insights from social and organizational theory, limiting the evolution of policy and administration to develop constructivist insights into public phenomena. At a minimum, the classic twofold characterization of administration/policy-as-politics and administration/policy-as-function should be made threefold to include a view of administration/policy-as-culture.

Notes

1 Thanks to John W. Meyer, Francisco O. Ramirez, David Suárez, and the editors of this volume for their comments, and to Jenny Reese for editorial assistance. Work on this chapter was supported by the Public Administration Program at the University of Utah and by a Junior Faculty Leave grant from the College of Social and Behavioral Sciences at the University of Utah.
2 For the purposes of this chapter policy and administration are treated synonymously. Historically, they have been thought of as distinct, even dichotomous, phenomena (see, e.g. Wilson 1887). Policy was the realm of elected officials and politics, while administration and effective policy implementation was the domain of unelected career bureaucrats. Especially since World War II, however, the interconnections between policy and administration have been widely noted (e.g. Denhardt 1990; Gaus 1950). Unelected officials have expertise and influence that is sought after in policy formulation and their decisions on how to interpret, implement, and apply policies at the "street-level" are far from apolitical (Lipskey 1980). Moreover, the major trends discussed here, linked to educational expansion and neo-liberalism, influence policy and administration alike.
3 Roughly 40% of submissions to the Organization and Management Theory section of the Academy of Management's 2012 annual meeting were on the topic of institutional theory, and over half of reviewers self-identified as having relevant expertise (Academy of Management 2013). The two most cited papers in the *Administrative Science Quarterly* are two canonical neo-institutional theory pieces (DiMaggio and Powell 1983; Meyer and Rowan 1977) and these two articles are also among top four most cited works in both the *American Sociological Review* and the *American Journal of Sociology*, as reported by Caren 2012 at http://nealcaren.web.unc.edu/the-most-cited-articles-in-sociology-by-journal/ (accessed November 23, 2015).
4 Although it is not the focus here, a rich tradition of neo-institutional research also focuses on causality in the opposite direction with an eye to understanding how individuals construct and alter institutions (DiMaggio 1988; Zucker 1988). For instance, Hallett (2010) emphasized the individual-level turmoil and conflict involved in a recoupling process in schools. Over time, causality can run in both directions (Padgett and Powell 2012).
5 When applied to the global level, neo-institutional theory is often called world polity or world society theory (Meyer *et al.* 1997).
6 Contrasting functionalist arguments suggest that schooling grows because industrializing economies need workers with more specific differentiated skills (Clark 1962). Alternatively, others emphasize the role of schooling in facilitating class and status competition (Collins 1979) or the maintenance of elite hegemony in society (Bourdieu and Passeron 1977; Bowles and Gintis 1976; Carnoy 1982). Such arguments are hard-pressed to explain trends toward structural similarity worldwide and the prevalence of decoupling between formal policies and daily practices.

7 Rationalization is defined as "the cultural accounting of society and its environments in terms of articulated, unified, integrated, universalized, and causally and logically structured schemes" (Meyer and Jepperson 2000, 102). This definition builds on Weber's ideas of instrumental rationality as the restructuring of social entities around clear rules and toward explicit purposes (Weber 1968).
8 Stanford University, for example, offers a joint Master of Arts in Education/Master of Business Administration degree.
9 The full questionnaire (accessed on November 23, 2015) is available at: http://worldmanagementsurvey.org/wp-content/images/2011/01/Education_Survey_Instrument_20110110.pdf. It comprises five sections. (a) Operations: concerned with the standardization of instructional processes, personalization of teaching and adoption of best practices within the school). (b) Monitoring: focuses on the monitoring of performance and reviewing the results, the dialogue between components within the school and the consequences of anomalies in the processes. (c) Targets: assessment of the managerial capacity of school principals to identify quantitative and qualitative targets, their interconnection and their temporal cascade. (d) People: concerned with human resource management, ranging from promoting and rewarding employees based on performance, removing poor performers, hiring the best teachers, and trying to keep the best ones. (e) Leadership: the leadership capacity of the principal jointly with a clear definition of roles and responsibilities within the school.
10 For an exception in transnational education advocacy, see Verger and Novelli (2012). Outside the realm of education, in a study of non-profits in Kenya, Brass (2012) shows changes in both policy and administration as the government service provision agencies hire former non-profit staff, are influenced by non-profit lobbying, and mimic non-profit service provision strategies.
11 I focus mainly on primary and secondary schooling, but parallel trends are found in higher education through the rise of rankings, models of competition between and within universities, and increasing layers of administration to deal with things like safety, health, protecting the natural world, student rights, and so on.
12 This characterization applies far more to scholarship in North America than elsewhere. In Europe there is a vibrant strand of "Scandinavian institutionalism" that has many parallels to sociological neo-institutionalism and is widely known in European studies of public administration. This body of work builds on insights of March and collaborators such as Olsen, Cohen, and Christiansen, documenting that public organizations are often far from rational (e.g. March and Olsen 1984). More recent formulations emphasize the "translation" and "editing" of external models into organizational settings (e.g. Czarniawska and Sevón 1996; Sahlin and Wedlin 2008) and the reformulation of organizations as "actors" (e.g. Brunsson and Sahlin-Andersson 2000).

References

Academy of Management. 2013. "2013 Organization and Management Theory Division Business Meeting." Retrieved from: www.slideshare.net/OrganizationTheory/2013-business-meeting-slides (accessed November 23, 2015).
Akabayashi, H. and H. Arakia. 2011. "Do Education Vouchers Prevent Dropout at Private High Schools? Evidence from Japanese Policy Changes." *Journal of the Japanese and International Economies*, 25(3): 183–198.
Altbach, P. 1977. "Servitude of the Mind? Education, Dependency and Neo-colonialism." *Teachers College Record*, 9(2): 187–203.
Angrist, J., E. Bettinger, and M. Kremer. 2006. "Long-Term Educational Consequences of Secondary School Vouchers: Evidence from Administrative Records in Colombia." *American Economic Review*, 96(3): 847–862.
Arnove, R.F. 1980. "Comparative Education and World Systems Analysis." *Comparative Education Review*, 24: 48–62.

Baker, D. and G.K. LeTendre. 2005. *National Differences, Global Similarities: World Culture and the Future of Schooling.* Stanford: Stanford University Press.

Ball, S.J. 2012. *Global Education Inc.: New Policy Networks and the Neoliberal Imaginary.* London: Routledge, Taylor and Francis Group.

Barrera-Osorio, F. and D. Raju. 2011. "Evaluating Public Per-Student Subsidies to Low-Cost Private Schools: Regression – Discontinuity Evidence from Pakistan." World Bank Policy Research Working Paper 5638. Washington, DC: World Bank.

Bendix, R. 1980. *Kings or People: Power and the Mandate to Rule.* Berkeley: University of California Press.

Billis, D. (ed.). 2010. *Hybrid Organizations and the Third Sector: Challenges for Practice, Theory and Policy.* London: Palgrave Macmillan.

Bloom, N. and J. Van Reenen. 2007. "Measuring and Explaining Management Practices Across Firms and Countries." *The Quarterly Journal of Economics*, 122(4): 1351–1408.

Bloom, N., C. Genakos, R. Sadun and J. Van Reenen. 2012. "Management Practices Across Firms and Countries." *The Academy of Management Perspectives*, 26(1): 12–33.

Blumenstyk, G. 2012. "Nation's Biggest For-Profit Colleges Suffer Enrollment Declines." *Chronicle of Higher Education.* Retrieved from: http://chronicle.com/article/Big-For-Profit-Colleges-Suffer/131120 (accessed November 23, 2015).

Böhlmark, A. and M. Lindahl. 2008. "Does School Privatization Improve Educational Achievement? Evidence from Sweden's Voucher Reform." IZA Discussion Paper No. 3691. Bonn: Institute for the Study of Labor. Retrieved from: http://ftp.iza.org/dp3691.pdf (accessed November 24, 2015).

Boli, J., F. Ramirez, and J.W. Meyer. 1985. "Explaining the Origins and Expansion of Mass Education." *Comparative Education Review*, 29(2): 145–170.

Bourdieu, P. and J. Passeron. 1977. *Reproduction in Education, Society and Culture.* Beverly Hills: Sage Publications.

Bowles, S. and H. Gintis. 1976. *Schooling in Capitalist America.* New York: Basic Books.

Brass, J.N. 2012. "Blurring Boundaries: The Integration of NGOs into Governance in Kenya." *Governance*, 25(2): 209–235.

Bravo, B., S. Mukhopadhyay, and P.E. Todd. 2010. "Effects of School Reform on Education and Labor Market Performance: Evidence from Chile's Universal Voucher System." *Quantitative Economics*, 1(1): 47–95.

Bray, M. 1999. *The Shadow Education System.* Paris: UNESCO; International Institute for Educational Planning.

Bray, M. 2001. "Private Supplementary Tutoring: Comparative Perspectives on Patterns and Implications." *Compare*, 36(4): 515–530.

Bromley, P. 2010. "The Rationalization of Educational Development: Scientific Activity among International Nongovernmental Organizations." *Comparative Education Review*, 54(4): 577–601.

Bromley, P. 2014. "Legitimacy and the Contingent Diffusion of World Culture: Diversity and Human Rights in Social Science Textbooks, Divergent Cross-National Patterns (1970–2008)." *Canadian Journal of Sociology*, 39(1): 1–44.

Bromley, P. and J.W. Meyer. 2014. "'They Are All Organizations': The Cultural Roots of Blurring Between Nonprofit, Government, and Business Sectors." *Administration and Society.*

Bromley, P. and W.W. Powell. 2012. "From Smoke and Mirrors to Walking the talk: Decoupling in the Contemporary World." *The Academy of Management Annals*, 6(1): 483–530.

Bromley, P., J.W. Meyer, and F.O. Ramirez. 2011. "The Worldwide Spread of Environmental Discourse in Social Studies, History, and Civics Textbooks, 1970–2008." *Comparative Education Review*, 55(4): 517–545.

Bromley, P., H. Hwang, and W.W. Powell. 2012. "Decoupling Revisited: Common Pressures, Divergent Strategies in the US Nonprofit Sector." *M@n@gement*, 15(5): 468–501.

Brunsson, N. and Sahlin-Andersson, K. 2000. "Constructing Organizations: The Example of Public Sector Reform." *Organization studies*, 21(4): 721–746.

Caren, N. 2012. "The Most Cited Articles in Sociology by Journal." Retrieved from: http://nealcaren.web.unc.edu/the-most-cited-articles-in-sociology-by-journal (accessed November 23, 2015).

Carnoy, M. 1982. "Education for Alternative Development." *Comparative Education Review*, 26(2): 160–177.

Center for Responsive Politics. 2013. "Annual Lobbying on Education." Retrieved from: www.opensecrets.org/lobby/indusclient.php?id=W04 (accessed November 23, 2015).

Christensen, T. and P. Lægreid. 2001. *New Public Management: The Transformation of Ideas and Practice*. Farnham: Ashgate.

Clark, B. 1962. *Educating the Expert Society*. San Francisco: Chandler.

Collins, R. 1979. *The Credential Society*. New York: Academic Press.

Crosby, B. and J.M. Bryson. 2005. *Leadership for the Common Good: Tackling Public Problems in a Shared-Power World* (Vol. 264). Oxford: John Wiley and Sons.

Czarniawska, B. and G. Sevón (eds). 1996. *Translating Organizational Change* (Vol. 56). Berlin: Walter de Gruyter.

Denhardt, R.B. 1990. "Public Administration Theory: The State of the Discipline." *Public Administration: the State of the Discipline*, edited by N.B. Lynn and A. Wildavsky, 43–72. Chatham: Chatham House Publishers.

Di Liberto, A., F. Schivardi, and G. Sulis. 2013. *Managerial Practices and Students' Performance* (No. 49). FGA Working Paper.

DiMaggio, P. 1988. "Interest and Agency in Institutional Fields," in *Institutional Patterns and Organizations*, edited by L. Zucker, 3–21. Cambridge: Ballinger.

DiMaggio, P. and W.W. Powell. 1983. "The Iron Cage Revisited: Collective Rationality and Institutional Isomorphism in Organizational Fields." *American Sociological Review*, 48: 147–160.

DiMaggio, P.J. and W.W. Powell (eds). 1991. *The New Institutionalism in Organizational Analysis*. Chicago: University of Chicago Press.

Drori, G.S., S.Y. Jang, and J.W. Meyer. 2006. "Sources of Rationalized Governance: Cross-National Longitudinal Analyses, 1985–2002." *Administrative Science Quarterly*, 51(2): 205–229.

Drori, G.S., J.W. Meyer, and H. Hwang. 2009. "Global Organization: Rationalization and Actorhood as Dominant Scripts." *Research in the Sociology of Organizations*, 27: 17–43.

Elliott, M. 2007. "Human Rights and the Triumph of the Individual in World Culture." *Cultural Sociology*, 1(3): 343–363.

Frank, D.J., E. Schofer, and J.C. Torres. 1994. "Rethinking History: Change in the University Curriculum, 1910–90." *Sociology of Education*, 231–242.

Frank, D.J., S.Y. Wong, J.W. Meyer, and F.O. Ramirez. 2000. "What Counts as History: A Cross-National and Longitudinal Study of University Curricula." *Comparative Education Review*, 44(1): 29–53.

Friedland, R. and R.R. Alford. 1991. "Bringing Society Back in: Symbols, Practices and Institutional Contradictions." In *The New Institutionalism in Organizational Analysis*, edited by W.W. Powell and P.J. DiMaggio, 232–263. Chicago: University of Chicago Press.

Friedman, M. 1955. "Role of Government in Education," in *Economics and the Public Interest*, edited by R. Solo, 123–144. New Brunswick: Rutgers University Press.

Gaus, J.M. 1950. "Trends in the Theory of Public Administration." *Public Administration Review*, 10: 161–168.

Greenwood, R., M. Raynard, F. Kodeih, E.R. Micelotta, and M. Lounsbury. 2011. "Institutional Complexity and Organizational Responses." *The Academy of Management Annals*, 5(1): 317–371.

Haack, P., D. Martignoni, and D. Schoeneborn. 2012. "Corporate Responsibility as Myth and Ceremony: Bad, But Not for Good." *University of Zurich, Department of Business Administration, UZH Business Working Paper*, 305.

Hallett, T. 2010. "The Myth Incarnate Recoupling Processes, Turmoil, and Inhabited Institutions in an Urban Elementary School." *American Sociological Review*, 75(1): 52–74.

Himmler, O. 2007. *The Effects of School Choice on Academic Achievement in the Netherlands.* Göttingen: Georg-August-Universität.

Hoxby, C.M. (ed.). 2003. *The Economics of School Choice.* Chicago: University of Chicago Press.

Jessop, B. 2004. "Hollowing Out the Nation-State and Multilevel Governance," in *A Handbook of Comparative Social Policy*, edited by P. Kennett, 11–25. Boston: Edward Elgar.

Jones, P. 1988. "Unesco and the Politics of Global Literacy." *Comparative Education Review*, 34(1): 41–60.

Jones, P. 1992. *World Bank Financing of Education.* New York: Routledge.

Kelman, S. 2007. "Public Administration and Organization Studies." *The Academy of Management Annals*, 1: 225–267.

Kernaghan, K. 2000. "The Post-Bureaucratic Organization and Public Service Values." *International Review of Administrative Sciences*, 66(1): 91–104.

Kraatz, M.S. and Block, E.S. 2008. "Organizational Implications of Institutional Pluralism." *The SAGE Handbook of Organizational Institutionalism.* London: Sage, 840.

Lauren, P. 2003. *The Evolution of International Human Rights (second edition).* Philadelphia: University of Pennsylvania Press.

Lee, C.K. and D. Strang. 2006. "The International Diffusion of Public-Sector Downsizing: Network Emulation and Theory-Driven Learning." *International Organization*, 60(4): 883.

Lewin, K. and H.A. Patrinos. 2012. *Impact Evaluation of Private Sector Participation in Education: Research Report.* World Bank and CfBT Education Trust. Retrieved from: http://siteresources.worldbank.org/EDUCATION/Resources/PPP_impact_evaluation_report.pdf (accessed November 24, 2015).

Lipsky, M. 1980. *Street-Level Bureaucracy: Dilemmas of the Individual in Public Services.* New York: Russell Sage Foundation.

March, J.G. and J.P. Olsen. 1984. "The New Institutionalism: Organizational Factors in Political Life." *The American Political Science Review*, 78(3): 734–749.

McEneaney, L.H. and J.W. Meyer. 2000. "The Content of the Curriculum," in *Handbook of the Sociology of Education*, edited by M.T. Hallinan, 189–211. New York: Kluwer Academic/Plenum Publishers.

McNeely, C. 1995. "Prescribing National Educational Policies: The Role of International Organizations." *Comparative Education Review*, 39(4): 483–507.

Meyer, John W. and P. Bromley. 2013. "The Worldwide Expansion of 'Organization.'" *Sociological Theory*, 31(4): 366–389.

Meyer, J.W. and B. Rowan. 1977. "Institutionalized Organizations: Formal Structure as Myth and Ceremony." *American Journal of Sociology*, 83(2): 340–363.

Meyer, J.W., F.O. Ramirez, and Y.N. Soysal. 1992. "World Expansion of Mass Education, 1870–1980." *Sociology of Education*, 65: 128–149.

Meyer, J.W., J. Boli, G.M. Thomas, and F.O. Ramirez. 1997. "World Society and the Nation-State." *American Journal of Sociology*, 103(1): 144–181.

Meyer, J.W., P. Bromley, and F.O. Ramirez. 2010. "Human Rights in Social Science Textbooks Cross-national Analyses, 1970–2008." *Sociology of Education*, 83(2): 111–134.

Mundy, K. 1998. "Educational Multilateralism and World (Dis) order." *Comparative Education Review*, 42(4): 448–478.

Mundy, K. and F. Menashy. 2014. "The World Bank and Private Provision of Schooling: A Look through the Lens of Sociological Theories of Organizational Hypocrisy." *Comparative Education Review*, 58(3): 401–427.

Mundy, K. and L. Murphy. 2001. "Transnational Advocacy, Global Civil Society? Emerging Evidence from the Field of Education." *Comparative Education Review*, 45(1): 85–126.

Meyer, J. W. and R.L. Jepperson. 2000. "The 'Actors' of Modern Society: The Cultural Construction of Social Agency." *Sociological theory*, 18(1): 100–120.

National Center for Charitable Statistics. 2012. "Download Data on US Nonprofit sector." Retrieved from: http://nccs.urban.org/database/index.cfm (accessed November 23, 2015).

National Conference of State Legislatures. 2013. "For-profit Colleges and Universities." Retrieved from: www.ncsl.org/research/education/for-profit-colleges-and-universities.aspx (accessed November 23, 2015).

Neal, D. 2002. "How Vouchers Could Change the Market for Education." *Journal of Economic Perspectives*, 16(4): 25–44.

Ong, A. 2006. *Neoliberalism as Exception: Mutations in Citizenship and Sovereignty.* Durham: Duke University Press.

O'Toole, L.J. 2000. "Research on Policy Implementation: Assessment and Prospects." *Journal of Public Administration Research and Theory*, 10(2): 263–288.

Osborne, S.P. (ed.). 2010. *The New Public Governance?: Emerging Perspectives on the Theory and Practice of Public Governance.* London: Routledge.

Osborne, D. and T. Gaebler. 1992. *Reinventing Government: How the Entrepreneurial Spirit is Transforming Government.* Reading: Adison Wesley Public Comp.

Pache, A.C. and F. Santos. 2010a. "When Worlds Collide: The Internal Dynamics of Organizational Responses to Conflicting Institutional Demands." *Academy of Management Review*, 35(3): 455–476.

Pache, A.C. and F. Santos. 2010b. "Inside the Hybrid Organization: An Organizational Level View of Responses to Conflicting Institutional Demands." *Research Center ESSEC Working Paper 1101.* Retrieved from: http://papers.ssrn.com/sol3/Delivery.cfm/SSRN_ID2328257_code2040019.pdf?abstractid=2328257&mirid=1 (accessed November 24, 2015).

Padgett, J.F. and W.W. Powell. 2012. *The Emergence of Organizations and Markets.* Princeton: Princeton University Press.

Pressman, J.L. and A.B. Wildavsky. 1984. *Implementation.* Berkeley: University of California Press.

Programme for International Student Assessment (PISA). 2014. "PISA FAQ." Retrieved from: www.oecd.org/pisa/aboutpisa/pisafaq.htm (accessed November 23, 2015).

Provan, K.G. and P. Kenis. 2008. "Modes of Network Governance: Structure, Management, and Effectiveness." *Journal of Public Administration Research and Theory*, 18(2): 229–252.

Ramirez, F.O. and J. Boli. 1987. "The Political Construction of Mass Schooling: European Origins and Worldwide Institutionalization." *Sociology of Education*, 60: 2–17.

Ramirez, F.O. and J.W. Meyer. 1980. "Comparative Education: The Social Construction of the Modern World System." *Annual Review of Sociology*, 6: 369–399.

Ravitch, D. 2011. *The Death and Life of the Great American School System: How Testing and Choice are Undermining Education.* New York: Basic Books.

Reckhow, S. 2013. *Follow the Money: How Foundation Dollars Change Public School Politics.* Oxford: Oxford University Press.

Rosenau, J.N. and E.O. Czempiel (eds). 1992. *Governance without Government: Order and Change in World Politics (Vol. 20).* Cambridge: Cambridge University Press.

Rowan, B. 2006. "The New Institutionalism and the Study of Educational Organizations: Changing Ideas for Changing Times," in *The New Institutionalism in Education*, edited by H.D. Meyer and B. Rowan, 15–32. Albany: State University of New York Press.

Sahlin, K. and L. Wedlin. 2008. "Circulating Ideas: Imitation, Translation and Editing." *The SAGE Handbook of Organizational Institutionalism.* London: Sage.

Salamon, L.M. and S. Wojciech Sokolowski. 2004. *Global Civil Society: Dimensions of the Nonprofit Sector, Volume Two.* Bloomfield: Kumarian Press. Retrieved from: http://ccss.jhu.edu/wp-content/uploads/downloads/2013/02/Comparative-data-Tables_2004_FORMATTED_2.2013.pdf (accessed November 23, 2015).

Sassen, S. 2006. *Territory, Authority, Rights: From Medieval to Global Assemblages (Vol. 7).* Princeton: Princeton University Press.

Spillane, J.P., K. Healey, L.M. Parise, and A. Kenney. 2011. "A Distributed Perspective on Learning Leadership," In *Leadership and Learning*, edited by J. Robertson and H. Timperley, 159–171. London: Sage.

Stacy, H. 2009. *Human Rights for the 21st Century*. Stanford: Stanford University Press.

Tilly, C. 1990. *Coercion, Capital, and European States, AD 990–1990*. Cambridge: Basil Blackwell, Inc.

Thornton, P.H., W. Ocasio, and M. Lounsbury. 2012. *The Institutional Logics Perspective: A New Approach to Culture, Structure, and Process*. Oxford: Oxford University Press.

Tompkins-Stange, M. 2013. *"Big Think" or "Bottom-Up"? How Private Philanthropic Foundations Seek to Influence Public Education Policy*. Unpublished doctoral dissertation, Stanford University, School of Education.

UNESCO. 2013. "Organizations Maintaining Official Relations with UNESCO." Retrieved from: http://ngo-db.unesco.org/s/or/en (accessed November 23, 2015).

Verger, A. and M. Novelli. 2012. *Campaigning for "Education For All": Histories, Strategies and Outcomes of Transnational Advocacy Coalitions in Education*. Rotterdam: Sense.

Waslander, S., C. Pater, and M. van der Weide. 2010. "Markets in Education: An Analytical Review of Empirical Research on Market Mechanisms in Education." *Organisation for Economic Co-operation and Development*, 52. EDU/WKP(2010)15.

Weber, M. 1968. *Economy and Society*. Totowa: Bedminster.

Westphal, J.D. and E.J. Zajac. 2013. "A Behavioral Theory of Corporate Governance: Explicating the Mechanisms of Socially Situated and Socially Constituted Agency." *The Academy of Management Annals*, 7(1): 607–661.

Wilson, W. 1887. "The Study of Administration." *Political Science Quarterly*, 2(2): 197–222.

Wiseman, A.W. and D.P. Baker. 2005. "The Worldwide Explosion of Internationalized Education Policy." *Global Trends in Educational Policy*, 6: 1–21.

Wong, S.Y. 1991. "The Evolution of Social Science Instruction, 1900–86: A Cross-National Study." *Sociology of Education*, 64(1): 33–47.

World Management Survey. 2013. "Homepage." Retrieved from: http://worldmanagementsurvey.org (accessed November 23, 2015).

Zucker, L.G. 1988. "Where Do Institutional Patterns Come From?" in *Institutional Patterns and Organizations*, edited by L. Zucker, 23–52. Cambridge: Ballinger.

Chapter 27

Ethnography and the Localization of Global Education Policy[1]

Amy Stambach

Now that debates about globalization have subsided and policy-makers and scholars alike acknowledge that the world is, indeed, connected, it is worth asking: What does the global terrain look like? How is global education policy configured and constituted? Who directs education policies, and how can we study education comparatively?

This chapter explores the localization of global education policy as anthropologists have approached the topic. Before the late 1990s, anthropologists focused largely on cultural transmission and classroom learning (for examples, see the works of Mehan 1993; Spindler 1997 [1967]; Whiting and Whiting 1975). Little research examined the historical or political-economic contexts of education policy or practice (for exceptions, see Foley 1991; Scudder and Colson 1980). Yet since at least the early 2000s, a body of scholarship has theorized education in relation to questions of politics, policy, and governance (e.g. Hall 1999; Levinson and Pollock 2011; Ortner 2003; Tuchman 2009; Vora 2013). Indeed, most anthropologists today agree that education and linked social and economic outcomes must be studied and theorized in relation to an "increasingly interconnected world" (Weis 2008, 4; see also Weis 2014). However, this point raises the central question that is the focus of this essay: *How does ethnography, which seems to be concerned with the local and its specificities, shed light on education in an era of global flows, connections, and communities?*

In the following pages, I first define key concepts of ethnography, localization, and global policy, as anthropologists generally see them. I describe these terms in relation to a body of scholarship that conceptualizes culture as a way of doing things, and as a relational social space of action, not "a people" living in a geography. I then present a model of global norm-making (and norm-breaking) that builds on the idea of culture as people's more-or-less planned social arrangements that enable further arrangements and social infrastructure, and I show how this model relates to comparativists' and policy-makers' understanding of the localization of global education policy.

In discussing the localization of global education policy, I draw on research recently conducted in the areas of international development studies and higher education. Anthropologists working within a "policy and politics" framework analyze relationships of *economic exchange and value* that secure and unravel markets through higher education; *policies, laws, and protocols* that often rest, paradoxically, on limited and illiberal commitments to liberalism; *social policies and humanitarian efforts* that sit at the crossroads of "what is" and "what ought to be"; and *religious and humanistic ideas* or notions that people mobilize to transcend borders and connect humanity. Such approaches increasingly focus on higher education as a field site, arguing that the university "serves as a capital sector within education as a whole" (Wernick 2006, 557).

Ethnography: From Case-in-Point to Contexts and Connections

Anthropologists today speak of ethnography as a mode of knowing, an episteme, or an approach to understanding how people see and understand the world. Writing about the use of ethnography for understanding aspects of education, Mills and Morton argue that ethnography is "a technique that emphasizes disjunction and fragmentation, rather than coherence" (2013, x). And in a classic essay titled "Culture is a Verb," Brian Street (1993) challenges the idea that anthropologists' job is to typify "a people," arguing that "culture is an active process of meaning making and contest over definition, including its own definition" (Street 1993, 25). These authors and others (e.g. Biehl and McKay 2012; Pina-Cabral 2013) stress that ethnography is not a watertight representation of "a culture." Rather, it is an organized arrangement, a planned yet sometimes rough-hewn exercise in understanding and portraying how people themselves go about making sense of the world.

Seen as a relational space for enacting and interpreting social worlds, the *local*, as anthropologists conceive it, is – like ethnography – not place-bound but a social context. It is a set of conditions and social relations connected to wider contexts. As such, the local and the global elide. Or, as Inderpal Grewal and Caren Kaplan put it many years ago: "How one separates the local from the global is difficult to decide when each thoroughly infiltrates the other" (Grewal and Caren 1994, 11). Drawing on Deleuze and Guattari's (1987) imagery of the rhizome, Michael Kearney intimated that the local does not so much traverse a geography as it links like "a hypertext" to other places and moments (Kearney 1995, 558). So, too, anthropologists working within a policy and politics vein regard the localization of global education policy not like a tree with roots, or a map with roads, but as an intra-textual field of activity characterized by iterative moments that link back to themselves.

For that matter, even before the 1950s, anthropologists reflected on the ways in which local conditions were connected to wider processes of industrialization, colonialism, or international commerce. Monica Hunter's account "Reaction to Conquest: Effects of Contact with Europeans on the Pondo of South Africa" (Hunter 1936) argued that even "to the most casual observer," the "effect of contact with Europeans" on the Pondo community, and vice versa, is evident. And Bronislaw Malinowski's final published work – "The Pan-African Problem of Culture Contact" –

argued that Kikuyu and Chagga and other communities living in eastern Africa desired practical training in cooperatives and accountancy, in their countries and abroad (Malinowski 1943, 659). Such accounts attest that anthropologists have long attuned questions about ethnography as a "case in point" to analyses of transnational contexts and international connections. Michael Burawoy (2000, 26) pointed this out almost two decades ago, when he noted anthropologists' studies of culture "have always sought to explain how education is shaped by and at the same time influences wider patterns of social inequality." "There never was any isolated tribe here!" he remarked of anthropologists' analysis of industrialization involving African communities (2000, 16).

Certainly, some classic ethnographic accounts focused primarily on culture in geographic places. Examples are Meyer Fortes' (1938) "Social and Psychological Aspects of Education in Taleland" and Enid Schildkrout's (1978) "Age and Gender in Hausa Society: Socio-Economic Roles of Children in Urban Kano." However even these works, though regarding education as primarily reproducing and defining "a people," analyze labor relations and learning as activities that drive transformations. They illuminate connections of many sorts, including what George Marcus would later refer to as "the circulation of cultural meanings, objects, and identities in diffuse time-space" (Marcus 1995, 96).

Such focus on studying processes and connections brings to the foreground of anthropological analysis consideration of how "hidden terrains of ambiguity, contradiction, and struggle" lie "under a veneer of common-sense and seemingly 'natural' ideas about space and time" (Harvey 1990, 205). Anthropologists' contributions to analyzing these hidden terrains are to focus on how *people* (not texts or policies) shape, and are shaped by, education translocally, including examining who writes and circulates texts and policies, and who attributes their actions to them. Key terms within this "policy and politics" approach are circulation, negotiation, and interaction (Shore and Wright 1997; Sutton and Levinson 2001). Indeed, to emphasize people's contributions to the making of their own social worlds, anthropologists today retain a strong commitment to conducting field research. Increasingly, this field research is conducted virtually or translocally, though it still involves a close connection with people as agents of culture. The anthropologist George Marcus (1995) purportedly first coined the term *multi-sited ethnography* to capture the sense that anthropologists work with people in many places simultaneously, and that the place of ethnography is, again, not a geographic place but social space of relational orientation among people engaging with one another.

Marcus' concept of multi-sited ethnography is similar to the anthropological genre of *extended case method* about which Burawoy (2000) writes. However, Marcus and others (e.g. Appadurai 1996; Burawoy 2000; Hannerz 2003; Miller 1995) emphasized that there may be several, sometimes competing clusters of people and agencies that contribute to the creation of a social field, and that this social field may be geographically decentered or extended. Many anthropological studies of education today draw on this extended methodological framework of multi-sitedness to analyze simultaneous centers of cultural production (see, for examples, Fong 2011; Stambach 2010; Woronov 2007). Such works approach education not in terms of "culture contact" or "Westernization" as did some of the classic studies focusing on cultural psychology or child development, but in terms of people's competing interests and activities that transform the social landscape of education.

If indeed capital accumulation is a key means by which people link themselves across space and time, then commodification, too, is logically key to the organization of knowledge and intellectual life. Slaughter and Rhoades (2004) famously referred to the alignment of academic knowledge with markets as *academic capitalism*. Their analysis of universities' commodification focused mainly on the effects of the 1980 Bayh-Dole Act on US higher education institutions. However, with the 1995 founding of the World Trade Organization, which regulates international commercialization of research and education through its General Agreement on Trade in Services, the logic of capitalism now characterizes academic life on an international scale. Today, higher education is a transnational space of global norm-making even though, as Verger (2009) illustrates, higher education is sometimes shaped more by economic than education interests (see also Rizvi and Lingard 2010; Brown *et al.* 2011).

Such a scale – what Roger Dale (2000) refers to as a globally structured educational agenda – presents new challenges and possibilities for people-centered anthropological approaches to ethnography. One of those challenges is to avoid seeing all policies as "traveling," as though globalization means open borders. The other is to avoid the objectification of a globally structured educational agenda; that is, to avoid seeing globalization as natural or a logical consequence of history. In examining how people shape and are shaped by education translocally, anthropologists working in a policy and politics vein analyze how "the logic of contemporary capitalism came to saturate social and intellectual life" (Urciuoli 2011, 362). Aligning education policies with market logic is a rational, if reductive, abstraction. What anthropology offers, as Renato Rosaldo puts it, "is a concrete attentiveness to human agency, to the practices of everyday life, in short to how subjects mediate the processes of globalization" (Inda and Rosaldo 2008, 7).

Ethnographic Accounts

To grasp the reality that people define and exchange knowledge across large tracts of space often quickly and simultaneously – while also recognizing that people live in local realities that practically speaking are circumscribed – I find Halliday and Carruthers' (2009) concept of global norm-making to be useful. Global norm-making refers to the production and transformation of rules that govern educative activity. Framed as an action verb presented as a noun, global norm-*making* (and *un-making*, because *making* invites breaking) exemplifies that people objectify their actions and intentions within an also objectified yet collectively produced social structure.

In expressing policy as an assemblage or confluence of activity, global norm-making enables analysis of three aspects of education policy. One, how people, working within institutions, embody and selectively advance competing ideas or programs of education. Two, how context matters for assembling ideas but not in ways that devolve infinite possibility to all cases; in other words, to say that policy is always localized, or that it always reflects someone's local norms (or hegemony), is not to say that everything is relative. Likewise, to say that education and policy travel is not to say they are the same everywhere. And three, analysis of present-day education policy requires understanding how people know and remember the past and imagine their futures through education. In other words, policy analysis is about understanding how people see themselves, moving forward, as effected by or products of education (Rizvi and Lingard, 2010). A global norm-making analysis thus calls for thinking about education as a field of social activity where people assert and build norms that they also use and re-shape to enable other activities and arrangements. Understanding this field, and how people situated in very different social and political economic locations break and set new norms, is a subject of ethnography.

As a thought exercise, I propose to use a model of global norm-making to examine two sets of ethnographic materials. The first concerns an online diasporic community that the late George Malekela and I analyzed several years ago (Stambach and Malekela 2006). The second concerns US university administrators' uses of international studies programs to link people and places through higher education. Although these sets are separate in space and time, they illustrate the effects and contours of global education policy today.

Bongoland

Bongoland.net is a non-profit, all-volunteer web space that hosts approximately 1600 registered users, who, as of March 2006, posted more than 3000 messages. Established in 2002 and sponsored by Kabissa (kabissa.org), a non-profit capacity-building organization funded by the Small Grants Program of the World Bank, bongoland.net combines technical assistance and internet capacity-building services with opportunities for people to talk about education, politics, and community. Bongoland's "About Us" page notes that the site "bring[s] together Tanzanians from around the globe to share ideas" and "provide[s] a platform for open-source software development through online collaboration of developers located in various places." Both Bongoland.net and Kabissa present their project as a blending of humanitarianism and technical assistance. Both frame "underdevelopment in Africa" as a problem resulting from technological illiteracy, and both provide information and training as a means to advance development and democracy.

Bongoland is also the name of a residential area located near the University of Dar es Salaam – a neighborhood whose official name is Ubungo, in the capital of Tanzania. But even there, Bongoland is not primarily a geographic location. Rather, it is a popular Tanzanian term that means a general place where life is hectic, stressful, and almost always slightly crazy or bonkers. Bongoland represents the desires and hopes of talented and highly educated Tanzanians who live in East Africa and around the world – in the UK, the USA, Australia, Canada, South Africa, and elsewhere. To borrow from cultural geographers, Bongoland is a heterotopic space that reflects an alternate mode of social ordering (Held 2005; Hetherington 1997, viii). It is more sociological than geographic, more conceptual than localizable. In the virtual world of the internet, Bongoland is electronic home to educated East Africans. As a sociological place, Bongoland is peopled by intelligent "residents." Yet the site – both literal and figurative – is often perceived as a place that is stymieing and challenging.

The problems Bongonians face are fourfold. Foreigners are moving into paid positions in Africans' home countries that these foreigners once deemed undeveloped and embryonic. Bongoland is just one of many places for the educated to work but it does not offer many opportunities. Bongonians cannot get research positions in foreign especially US universities because these universities prefer to hire students from China and India, thus making it harder for Bongonians to get jobs. The quality of schooling in Bongoland is poor and no one is willing to fund it. The following four quotes from the website illustrate each of these themes.

> We who are currently here now tend to feel that your places are being taken over – as they say "coup d'état" – by the Foreigners. When asked, we are informed that our Society lacks the intelligentsia and experts, and therefore the needs arise to "approve" the same [i.e., to hire foreign experts].
>
> For me, Bongo will be a place of opportunity just like any other when I am done with my studies. Should an opportunity arise there, I'll take it, but if there is a sweeter deal somewhere else, I'll have to go for it. Like I always tell my friends, if I get a good job for a couple of million [Tanzanian shillings] per month ☺, an apartment ☺, and a car (nothing fancy, Mark II *mayai inatosha* ☺), I'll be back in Bongo so fast.
>
> I think the question remains, who will be doing the research? Is it the Indians, the Chinese or the American[s] themselves? I think it is more likely that there will be more and more Chinese and Indians in labs. You can see it in graduate schools – more than sixty percent of Masters and PhD Engineering students [in US universities] are foreigners, mostly from India and China.
>
> We are all aware that our educational syllabi in all levels are still not in line with the current science and technology… Taking the example of [the] industrial sector, we hardly have any matching syllabus for the current production techniques unless you are taken for further study abroad by the company, but gosh, who will want to incur those extra costs for sending you abroad … when there are plenty of qualified people at the tip of your finger. ☹ ☹ The same applies to computer studies… So you see the kind of education we have proven to produce only the mismatch between the worker and the type of job provided at the labour market out there.

These direct quotes give a human voice to some of the outcomes and effects of higher education. Bongonians recognize that they themselves hold less power than others do, and they name the powerful actors as they see them:

> Gates says Microsoft won't relocate research… Microsoft will always keep its research headquarters in Redmond [Washington], even though countries such as China and India are producing growing numbers of computer scientists.

Taken together, these quotes illustrate (a) that people recognize they are differentially empowered to advance themselves through education; (b) that social locations matter but not always fruitfully; and (c) that until we triangulate the insights agents have into their own place within a globalized system against the structure of that system itself, we cannot see that people "in" universities experience and create the world at large through their own very differently located "politics of hope." Ethnographic analysis of this virtual dialogue holds still, for a moment, the discussion about higher education without ignoring that the conversation occurs in parallel times and places and in relation to history and the future.

The "Global" University

Fast-forward chronological time about a half-dozen years to a three-day summit held at a Midwestern US university. The Summit involved representatives from four US public research universities; the Gates Foundation; the United States Agency for

International Development (USAID); a senior professional staff member of the US Senate on the Committee on Agriculture; the rock star Bono; and an American faith-based non-governmental organization (NGO) called ONE that presented a concert to aid the poor and hungry. It also included private donors who were connected to international food and agricultural industries, including the main private donor of an organization called the Tanzania Partnership Program, a US university-sponsored development project located in rural Tanzania. These actors and this summit are significant for ethnographically illustrating the localization of global connections through higher education policy.

Founded in 2007 as the Partnerships for Sustainable Community Development (PSCD) and fully functional by 2011, the Tanzania Partnership Program (TPP) began by working in two rural Tanzanian communities, one in the south east, and one in the north. Early partners included Michigan State University, the University of Dar es Salaam's Institute of Resource Investment and College of Education, and the Aga Khan Foundation, a non-sectarian Ismaili development organization that has partnered with USAID for many years. TPP's 2011 and 2012 annual reports identify five areas of initiative: clean water access, building and equipping schools, providing human and animal health care, organizing community development sessions, and promoting research collaborations between Michigan State University and Tanzanian partners. Donor funds in 2010–2011 totaled US$472, 213, including funds forwarded from the previous year; Michigan State University contributions were about half the amount. The following year, donor funds totaled $539,387 plus $257,288 from Michigan State University. All of the latter plus half of the donor funds were expended, with $312,000 carried forward to the next year (Michigan State University 2011; 2012).

The Summit convened representatives from "stakeholders" who are frequently identified, as categories, in today's calls for federally funded research proposals: private foundations, civil society organizations, universities, and research and teaching experts. The Gates Foundation's role was to inform universities about the Gates' African commitments and experiences partnering with NGOs to advance African development. Universities' roles were to provide scientific expertise for the proposals and, in serving as hosts for such events as this summit (other summits were held before and after), to provide a platform for educating the public about the value of spending public tax monies and working with for-profit corporations to support infrastructural development outside the USA. A director for agriculture at the Bill and Melinda Gates Foundation spoke on a panel with a Foods Resource Bank representative and a staff member of the Partnership to Cut Hunger and Poverty in Africa. All three speakers framed their goal as working with ONE to cut hunger and end poverty in Africa. And all collaborated to develop research capacity overseas while simultaneously funding faculty and researchers to generate new knowledge and potentially patentable technologies. In exchange, universities would gain research funding, access to overseas locations for university students' internships, as well as new sources of "supply" for overseas students enrolling in US universities, and potential access to new patentable technologies discovered or created through the partnerships.

University administrators were invited to participate on a panel of invited guests; they lent weight to the host university's credibility in demonstrating as a precondition to receiving federal grants that the host university had the ability to convene – and had already convened – a diverse range of partners dedicated in some way to the project. The ONE and U2 components were intended to rally public support for the host university's projects in Africa. The rock concert was intended to invite this public to the football stadium to show them how they too are connected to Africa and can help cut extreme poverty in Africa without giving up a single penny, except to see Bono. Pre-dinner discussion (open to invited guests) focused on the costs and benefits of harvesting certain hardwood trees in Malawi; weighing potential profit from mining against environmental degradation and harm to African farmers; the "farm aid" bill pending in the US Congress that would give taxpayers' money to US agro-industry for shipping surplus to hungry Africa; and the need to mobilize the American public around the cause to help "the poor in Africa," which Bread for the World and Foods Resource Bank representatives agreed was a role faith-based NGOs could play.

Even before the main course was served, one could see a tension in the summit – between using this event and the rock concert as a "just-so" story about universities, and using the event as an alibi to feed the poor when the larger conversation was about building US investment conditions overseas. But the generous meal and gracious dinner glued the guests together, and the evening's conversation was hopeful and heady. And at a workshop the next day, speakers emphasized that all Americans could make a difference in ending extreme poverty.

Analysis

Although the people and location of the summit are different from those of Bongoland, there are important connections. Bongonians and summit members share a commitment to open exchange of ideas and equal opportunity. They all imbue higher education with the possibility of improving and expanding their own and others' futures – even if these are more ideals than realities. Bongonians hope that "should an opportunity arise" their computer science skills will deliver millions of dollars to them and to their families. Administrators hope that convening diverse stakeholders within a university function will pay off in the medium term, when it comes to funding and connecting with US government, industry, and higher education. There are also important connections involving actors and communities, though the actual individuals who represent certain interests are not the same across these settings. The Gates Foundation connects Bongonians' and Summit members' worlds, as do US universities. And all imagine Tanzania as a place of opportunity yet uncertainty.

Such high hope in higher education is a reflection of an education market that involves gamble and long-term management (cf. Brown *et al.* 2011). Administrators' plans to "globalize their campuses" and Bongonians' sense that their home countries are being "taken" by foreigners suggest these parties have a future-oriented view of higher education that requires short-term risks. For Bongonians, the risk is that their higher education may not pay off in terms of jobs; for administrators, the risk is that their loosely orchestrated plan will not play out beyond their own institutional settings. The measure and the currency of risk is capital: the accumulation of unexpended wealth acquired for the purposes of accumulating more capital (cf. Wallerstein 1983, 13–14). Higher education integrates people and capital. It welcomes all but favors some, as indicated in (to take a slightly different example) a special report titled "Chinese Students in Undergraduate Programs: Understanding and Overcoming the challenges," published by a US international educators' organization:

> In recent years many institutions of higher learning have pursued an Asian recruitment strategy to fulfill plans to globalize their campuses and curricula, with the long-term goal of preparing U.S. graduates to compete in an interconnected global economy – one which will be increasingly dominated by China. (www.nafsa.org)

Bongonians, too, recognize that higher education is unequal. They recognize that preferences are given to students from India and China, and that universities favor students from different countries. But Bongonians' uncertainty of employment contrasts with administrators' power to reproduce the economic capital of universities. Bongonians' and university administrators' respectively low and high economic capital marks them as differently able to change a global higher education system. Bongonians seek to increase personal wealth; administrators, to reinvest it in the university. Administrators are able to reinvest "the foreign" at home, while Bongonians are divested by it.

Anthropologists' job is to portray the tensions in the system, and to do so from an always people-centered (i.e. ethnographic) perspective. When it comes to studying global education ethnographically, the local, then, is not a place but it is a form of social inter-digitation. Universities are indicative but not unique sites for studying the localization of global education policy, not least because they embed a nest of culturally productive or generative tensions. Wernick, citing Malinowski, talks about these tensions.

> On one side the university is a *charter* institution (Malinowski 1954), claiming a transcending legitimacy and autonomy, in terms of its axial values of truth, wisdom, science, and so on. On the other side, those who "control the means of material production control the means of mental production"; and the dominant ideas are the ideas of those who dominate (Marx and Engels 1976). (Wernick 2006, 558).

Global norms, seen here in the space of higher education, are constantly made and sometimes challenged. Whereas scholars who focus on policy directly might talk about norms as not made but *set* – as in, set goals and set agendas within policy organizations – anthropologists stay focused on the concept of making in order to stress the ongoing project of social activity.

Understood as the production rather than as the set of rules that govern activity, norm-making thus helps us to see that education is itself both domain, or stage, and medium for effecting and often contesting shared ideas of interaction. In an illustrative essay titled "The Normativity of Numbers," Anders (2008) demonstrates how desk managers and directors in Washington, DC transform numbers into arguments about global policy. Not about education specifically, the essay's focus on economic development nonetheless has implications for education policy. Appropriately interpreted, numbers justify loans and funds for country development: Numbers acquire normativity first by being a "part of the conditions attached to the loan" and second, when they are standardized by loan recipients, whose power of agreement paradoxically but legally cements recipients' subordinate positions (Anders 2008, 195). Numbers are not powerful in themselves; authorities make numbers powerful by making loan recipients seem – and in seeming to be – autonomous and willing agents. In handing loan conditions in the form of numbers, representatives set the conditions of possibility for government representatives. Likewise, government representatives set the terms of their loan agreements: Malawi's Governor of the Reserve Bank and Minister of Finance, an example given in Anders' study, stipulates a Special Drawing Right of 65% of quota and debt relief under the Heavily Indebted Poor Country Initiative. Anders' point is that conditions of requesting a loan are, in legal terms, "set by the government requesting a loan" (Anders 2008, 187). Ownership thus is in the hands of the recipient, though certainly the economic power is not.

In an account of how Rwandan government leaders hope to use entrepreneurial creativity to develop the national economy, Catherine Honeyman (2016) illustrates the important point that there are many different centers of global norm-making. She illustrates how Rwandans turn to South East Asia for a particular model of government. "Rwanda is one of the many countries that have become 'clients' of the Singapore Cooperation Enterprise," Honeyman writes, "and Rwandan President Paul Kagame has often cited Singapore as his development ideal, remarking that 'Singapore's rapid socioeconomic transformation' provides 'an inspiration for Rwanda'" (*Times* 2008 in Honeyman 2016). Honeyman's "theory of *governance as negotiated social learning*" (original emphasis) highlights how policy-making occurs in interaction and in a manner always connected to social infrastructure.

In other words, global norms, seen through an anthropological lens, are made, not already existing; and they are aspirational, not bench-setting. Extending this logic to questions of place, ethnographers examine disjunct-yet-linked social spaces simultaneously. To understand Bongonians' community, one must also know something about Dar es Salaam, in Tanzania. To know something about the Tanzania Partnership Program, one must know something about US higher education and how US higher education operates and funds research and training that depends on Bongonians' engagement.

Examining these kinds of disjunct-yet-linked social spaces does not mean literally comparing them. Frederick Barth (2002, 12), writing about the mobilization of different forms of knowledge, quotes Franz Boas on comparison: "If anthropology desires to establish the laws governing the growth of culture, it must not confine itself to comparing the results of growth alone, but whenever such is feasible, it must compare the processes of growth" (Boas 1940, 280). And years ago Bourdieu and Passeron argued against place-based comparison, favoring instead a model of education that is both trans-historical *and* state-particular (Bourdieu and Passeron 2000 [1977], 188). To get around strict case-by-case comparisons, which are themselves deeply rooted in traditions of school inspection (Jullien 1816–17, see Fraser 1964) and in today's league tables and global rankings, anthropologists – again in the vein that Brian Street recommends – analyze the many and sometimes competing modes of operation that animate education.

All of this is to say that ethnographers' focus on the localization of global education policy is not without attention to a particular soil, village, or landscape. But overall, ethnographic emphasis is on relations and people, and how peoples' social arrangements set the stage for other arrangements – or else ethnography would be geography.

Ethnography as Argument and Artifact

To answer the question posed above – *How does ethnography, which seems to be concerned with the local and its specificities, shed light on education in an era of global flows, connections, and communities?* – ethnographers today (as many always have) approach the local not as geography but as a social location. Ethnographers focus on how people interact and build social institutions that they then hold up and objectify as natural forms that define and describe social life. Education is one such often-naturalized social institution. But anthropologists do not stop with institutions. They investigate how people make and contest and change institutions, and how different institutions in different places compete and interact. This is to say, anthropologists, particularly those working in a policy and politics vein, focus on people as a social entity, not on individuals.

Anthropologists' disquiet about overdoing cross-cultural comparison may come as surprise to some, particularly those who still see anthropologists as focused on "the unique" or "local." But such a position not only mischaracterizes anthropology of the past, it also overlooks that anthropologists theorize education as not unlike culture. Education, like culture, is a way of doing things *and* an objectified set of practices that people mobilize. Education as a social field is always open to powerful assertions about the way the world is and ought to be, but it is also a medium or generative venue for waging change and transforming social building blocks. Anthropologists studying education thus face a unique challenge in producing ethnography. Ethnography is a mode of representation that, like culture, is both an argument and an artifact.

All of this is to agree that education and social and economic outcomes must be studied and theorized in relation to an interconnected world yet also to call for attention to matters of social localization that ethnography helps to illuminate. As the cases of the Bongonians and the Summit illuminate, today's global terrain is risky and incongruous. People paradoxically assume and act as though education has broad and equal reach, but they also acknowledge and feel its limitations. In this regard, global education policy does not travel as freely or openly as either policymakers or some scholars have postulated. It has many loci. Seeing education as both promise and compromise, as opportunity and sorting machine, ethnographers seek to understand what we might more generally think of as multiple centers and recursive cycles of knowledge and power production. A confluence of norms superimpose onto one another uneasily. Ethnographers' job is to trace connections across a human-conceptualized space and time, to follow the turns and trajectories of people's relations and arguments, and to see where arguments intersect, how they stop and fragment, and when, by whom, and how they are diverted. By offering ethnographic references to Bongonians and the Summit in this chapter, I hope to have indicated that ethnography is more than case-in-point but less than analysis of free flowing or "traveling" policy.

Note

1 I am grateful to Christina Cappy for her careful reading and feedback on an earlier version of this chapter.

References

Anders, G. 2008. "The Normativity of Numbers: World Bank and IMF Conditionality." *Political and Legal Anthropology Review*, 31(2): 187–202.

Appadurai, A. 1996. *Modernity at Large: Cultural Dimensions of Globalization*. Minneapolis: University of Minnesota Press.

Barth, F. 2002. "An Anthropology of Knowledge." *Current Anthropology*, 43(1): 1–18.

Biehl, J. and R. McKay. 2012. "Ethnography as Political Critique." *Anthropological Quarterly*, 85(4): 1209–1288.

Boas, F. 1940. "The Limitations of the Comparative Method of Anthropology," in *Race, Language, and Culture*, by Franz Boas, 270–280. New York: Free Press.

Bourdieu, P. and J.-C. Passeron. 2000 [1977]. *Reproduction in Education, Society, and Culture*. London: Sage.

Brown, P., H. Lauder, and D. Ashton. 2011. *The Global Auction: The Broken Promises of Education, Jobs, and Incomes*. New York: Oxford University Press.

Burawoy, M. 2000. "Introduction: Reaching for the Global," in *Global Ethnography: Forces, Connections, and Imaginations in a Postmodern World*, edited by M. Burawoy et al., 1–40. Berkeley: University of California Press.

Dale, R. 2000. "Globalization and Education: Demonstrating a 'Common World Educational Culture' or Locating a 'Globally Structured Educational Agenda.'" *Educational Theory*, 50(4): 427–448.

Deleuze, G. and F. Guattari. 1987. *A Thousand Plateaus: Capitalism and Schizophrenia*. Minneapolis: University of Minnesota Press.

Foley, D. 1991. "Rethinking School Ethnographies of Colonial Settings: A Performance Perspective of Reproduction and Resistance." *Comparative Education Review*, 35(3): 532–551.

Fong, V. 2011. *Paradise Redefined: Transnational Chinese Students and the Quest for Flexible Citizenship in the Developed World*. Palo Alto: Stanford University Press.

Fortes, M. 1938. *Social and Psychological Aspects of Education in Taleland*. London: Oxford University Press.

Fraser, S. 1964. *Jullien's Plan for Comparative Education (1816–17)*. New York: Teachers College Press.

Grewal, I. and C. Kaplan (eds). 1994. *Scattered Hegemonies: Postmodernity and Transnational Feminist Practices*. Minneapolis: University of Minnesota Press.

Hall, K.D. 1999. "Understanding Educational Processes in an Era of Globalization: The View from Anthropology and Cultural Studies," in *Issues in Education Research: Problems and Possibilities*, edited by E.C. Lagemann and L.S. Shulman, 121–156. San Francisco: Jossey-Bass.

Halliday, T.C. and B.G. Carruthers. 2009. *Bankrupt: Global Lawmaking and Systemic Financial Crisis*. Palo Alto: Stanford University Press.

Hannerz, U. 2003. "Being There ... and There ... and There! Reflections on Multi-site Ethnography." *Ethnography*, 4(2): 201–216.

Harvey, D. 1990. *The Condition of Postmodernity: An Enquiry into the Origins of Cultural Change*. Cambridge: Blackwell Publishing.

Held, D. 2005. "National Culture, the Globalization of Communication and the Bounded Political Community," in *Planetary Politics*, edited by S.E. Bronner, 48–58. Maryland: Rowman and Littlefield Publishers, Inc.

Hetherington, K. 1997. *The Badlands of Modernity: Heterotopia and Social Ordering*. London: Routledge.

Honeyman, C.A. 2016. *Educating the Orderly Entrepreneur: Creativity, Credentials, and Controls in Rwanda's Post-Developmental State*. Palo Alto: Stanford University Press.

Hunter, M. 1936. *Reaction to Conquest: Effects of Contact with Europeans on the Pondo of South Africa*. London: Oxford University Press.

Inda, J.X. and R. Rosaldo. 2008. "Tracking Global Flows," in *The Anthropology of Globalization: A Reader (second edition)*, edited by J.X. Inda and R. Rosaldo, 3–46. Maldan: Blackwell Publishing.

Kearney, M. 1995. "The Local and the Global: the Anthropology of Globalization and Transnationalism." *Annual Review of Anthropology*, 24: 547–565.

Levinson, B. and M. Pollock (eds). 2011. *Companion to the Anthropology of Education*. Hoboken: Wiley-Blackwell.

Malinowski, B. 1943. "The Pan-African Problem of Culture Contact." *The American Journal of Sociology*, 48(6): 649–665.

Malinowski, B. 1954. *Magic, Science, and Religion*. Garden City: Doubleday.

Marcus, G. 1995. "Ethnography in/of the World System: The Emergence of Multi-sited Ethnography." *Annual Reviews in Anthropology*, 24: 95–117.

Marx, K. and F. Engels. 1976. *The German Ideology*. Moscow: Progress Publishers.

Mehan, H. 1993. "Beneath the Skin and between the Ears: A Case Study in the Politics of Representation," in *Understanding Practice: Perspectives on Activity and Context*, edited by S. Chaiklin and J. Lave, 241–698. New York: Cambridge University Press.

Michigan State University. 2011. "The 2011 Annual Report, Tanzania Partnership Program." Retrieved from: www.isp.msu.edu/pscd/resources/docs/2011_Annual_Report.pdf (accessed November 23, 2015).

Michigan State University. 2012. "The 2012 Annual Report, Tanzania Partnership Program." Retrieved from: www.isp.msu.edu/pscd/resources/docs/2012_Annual_Report.pdf (accessed November 23, 2015).

Miller, D. 1995. "Introduction: Anthropology, Modernity, and Consumption," in *Worlds Apart: Modernity through the Prism of the Local*, edited by D. Miller, 1–22. New York: Routledge.

Mills, D. and M. Morton. 2013. *Ethnography in Education*. New York: BERA/Sage.

Ortner, S.B. 2003. *New Jersey Dreaming: Capital, Culture, and the Class of '58*. Durham: Duke University Press.

Pina-Cabral, J. 2013. "The Two Faces of Mutuality: Contemporary Themes in Anthropology." *Anthropological Quarterly*, 85(1): 257–276.

Rizvi, F. and B. Lingard. 2010. *Globalizing Education Policy*. New York: Routledge.

Schildkrout, E. 1978. "Age and Gender in Hausa Society: Socio-Economic Roles of Children in Urban Kano," in *Sex and Age as Principles of Social Differentiation*, African Studies Association Monograph 17, edited by J.S. La Fontaine, 109–137. London: Academic Press.

Scudder T. and E. Colson. 1980. *Secondary Education and the Formation of an Elite: The Impact of Education on Gwembe District, Zambia*. New York: Academic Press.

Shore, C. and S. Wright. 1997. *Anthropology of Policy: Critical Perspectives on Governance and Power*. New York: Routledge.

Slaughter, S. and G. Rhoades. 2004. *Academic Capitalism and the New Economy: Markets, State, and Higher Education*. Baltimore: The Johns Hopkins University Press.

Spindler, G.D. 1997 [1967]. "The Transmission of Culture," in *Education and Cultural Process: Anthropological Approaches*, edited by G.D. Spindler, 50–76. Prospect Heights: Waveland Press.

Sutton, M. and B.A.U. Levinson. 2001. *Policy as Practice: Toward a Comparative Sociocultural Analysis of Educational Policy*. Westport: Ablex Publishing.

Stambach, A. 2010. *Faith in Schools: Religion, Education, and American Evangelicals in East Africa*. Palo Alto: Stanford University Press.

Stambach, A. and G.A. Malekela. 2006. "Education, Technology, and the 'New' Knowledge Economy: Views from Bongoland." *Globalization, Societies, and Education*, 4(3): 321–336.

Street, B. 1993. "Culture is a Verb: Anthropological Aspects of Language and Cultural Process," In *Language and Culture*, edited by D. Graddol, L. Thompson, and M. Byram, 23–43. Clevedon: British Association of Applied Linguistics in association with Multilingual Matters.

Tuchman, G. 2009. *Wannabe U: Inside the Corporate University*. Chicago: The University of Chicago Press.
Urciuoli, B. 2011. "Review Essay: The Political Economy of Higher Education: The View from Inside and Outside." *Political and Legal Anthropology Review*, 34(2): 362–368.
Verger, A. 2009. "The Merchants of Education: Global Politics and the Uneven Education Liberalization Process within the WTO." *Comparative Education Review*, 53(3): 379–401.
Vora, N. 2013. *Impossible Citizens: Dubai's Indian Diaspora*. Durham: Duke University Press.
Wallerstein, I. 1983. *Historical Capitalism*. New York: Verso.
Weis, L. 2008. "Introduction." *The Way Class Works: Readings on School, Family, and the Economy*, 1–9. New York: Routledge.
Weis, L. 2014. "Series Editor Introduction." *Confucius and Crisis in American Universities*, by A. Stambach, vii–viii. New York: Routledge.
Wernick, A. 2006. "University." *Theory, Culture and Society*, 23: 557–563.
Whiting, B. and J. Whiting. 1975. *Children of Six Cultures: A Psycho-Cultural Analysis*. Cambridge: Harvard University Press.
Woronov, T.E. 2007. "Chinese Children, American Education: Globalizing Child Rearing in Contemporary China," in *Generations and Globalisation*, edited by J. Cole and D. Durham, 29–51. Bloomington: Indiana University Press.

Chapter 28

Global Education Policy and the Postmodern Challenge

Stephen Carney

Introduction

Even though many education policy scholars engage with elements of a postmodern critique – a set of intellectual incursions that emerged most forcefully in continental (especially French) philosophy – they often struggle to break free of modernist commitments to explanation and order. In part this is because the field of education retains an "orthodoxy of vision" (Paulston 2000, 361–362) essential to the "war against mystery and magic" (Bauman 1992, x). In part it is because the postmodern critique has become domesticated in Western social science *as* globalization theory through primarily Anglo-American appropriations of the French genre (Lizardo and Strand 2009). This move has rescued a significant and problematic approach to theorizing the social and made it amenable to policy scholars as a tool with which to understand (and engage with) the present complex phase of capitalism. In the process, though, much of the potential for establishing alternative ways to conceptualize and respond to contemporary conditions in the educational sphere is compromised.

In this chapter I explore the contours of a postmodern[1] heuristic and consider how this manifests in education policy research, especially in relation to the question of space. In particular, I consider how the concept of de- and re-territorialization (Deleuze and Guattari 1987), and the analytical strategies of assemblage and network, provide fresh entry points for theorizing space in globalizing education policy, but how they are being interpreted through the lens of modernist concerns. I outline some limitations in these analytical strategies before illustrating how I have drawn on postmodern themes in my own work on global education reform in order to explore processes of reconfiguration, rupture, and indeterminacy as important forces shaping the present phase of modernity. Such work is problematic from the

The Handbook of Global Education Policy, First Edition.
Edited by Karen Mundy, Andy Green, Bob Lingard, and Antoni Verger.
© 2016 John Wiley & Sons, Ltd. Published 2016 by John Wiley & Sons, Ltd.

perspective of Anglo-American policy *science* (Robertson and Dale, 2015) but seems unavoidable if one shows "respect for the social significance of the unintelligible" (Ferguson 1999, 210) and acknowledges the impossibility of uncovering authenticity from the "speaking subject" (Lather 2001, 483). I outline some of the critiques leveled against my own approach before, finally, sketching out some elements of what Lather (2007, x) calls "the science possible after our disappointments in science." This opens the way not only for a "defiant" research imagination (Kenway and Fahey 2009), but one that makes possible reinvention and renewal.

A Postmodern Sensibility

Although problematic to attempt a single definition of such a broad movement, one can certainly identify a number of well-rehearsed themes. That one known best to us is captured by Lyotard's (1984) questioning of the grand Enlightenment metanarratives of reason, progress, and emancipation, and the alleged universality they embody. Anticipated by Foucault (1970) in his analysis of the baroque challenge to classical forms of representation (Lambert 2006a), this is a challenge to all truth and knowledge claims. Postmodernism is also associated with attempts to decenter the subject "whose sense of identity and biographical continuity give way to fragmentation and superficial play with images (and) sensations" (Featherstone 1995, 44). Aligned here is the so-called "death of the author," where a text is "not a line of words releasing a single 'theological' meaning (the 'message of the Author-God'), but a multidimensional space in which varieties of writing, none original, blend and clash" (Barthes 1977, 146). As such, any effort to replace the author with a higher transcendentalism is doomed. By contrast, education policy scholarship usually presents us with the "'total text': that form of writing which combines evidence, concepts, argument, conclusion and rhetoric in as tight and 'persuasive' a rhetoric as is possible" (Stronach 2010, 18).

A postmodern sensibility would thus view reality as "fragmentary, heterogeneous and plural," where the nature of the subject and individual consciousness is "inherently unstable and shifting" (Green 1997, 9). Here, the Cartesian subject is replaced by contingent actors confronted with an "ethical paradox" to exercise "moral choice and responsibility" without the "comfort of the universal guidance that modern self-confidence once promised" (Bauman 1992, xxii). This dilemma is exacerbated if we view the contemporary era as being beyond realist representations and reduced to spectacle (Debord 1995).

Whilst equally concerned with the nature of human experience, others question the idea that Western consciousness is approaching an end point. For example, Deleuze and Guattari (1987), in rejecting the humanist orientation of Western thought, especially its preoccupation with a holistic understanding of man as *being*, prioritize the notions of *becoming* and *immanence*. Viewing life (including the mind) as a machine situated in a range of open systems, humans are constantly engaged in processes of de- and re-territorialization, making and transforming connections and proliferations in order to avoid an endless theatre of images (Colebrook 2002). Such flows suggest that our identities, subjectivities, and ethics, rather than reaching a predictable end state, are actively and always becoming something other than themselves. This view challenges the seemingly singular understanding of neo-liberalism as a process of decline that runs through much education policy scholarship.

With inspiration from Deleuze and Guatarri (1987), Hardt and Negri (2000) observe that global capitalism contains a plethora of proliferations making possible the transformation of life beyond the singular meaning system of economic exchange. Even though the commodity form has the power to disrupt the de-territorialized flow of connections, forms, and desires, and to reterritorialize them in the limited logic of capital, the multiple connections and free flow of forms it makes possible have the potential to disrupt this logic. Baudrillard (2001) devotes much energy to the question of value in late capitalism, viewing the current age as one of "diabolical indeterminacy" (Baudrillard 2001, 9–10) that not only disrupts the flow of meaning, but perverts and ultimately disables the logic of exchange on which the capitalist order is based. Confusion, mystification, and information overload, far from being catastrophic indicators of a social world in freefall, actually make possible a re-enchantment of the symbolic order; a system of meaning that remains always beyond the grasp of capitalist exchange (Gane 2004). For those seeking "critical" purpose and a direction for action, this amounts to "difference without intelligibility," "incommensurability," and, ultimately, "indifference" (de Sousa Santos 1999, 39). However, for those who remain "suspicious" of everyday language and its complicity in "ideology critique," the question is: "How can we continue to live and work in a world where truth appears fleetingly and at once begins to decay?" (St. Pierre 1997, 175).

One starting point for a postmodern sensibility is to destabilize and invert dominant understandings of things where notions of becoming, multiplicity, and indeterminacy disrupt the comfortable preoccupations of modernist theorizing. A "post-secular, post-critical, post-Enlightenment undecidability" is thus about "deferral while entire problematics are recast and resituated away from standard logics and procedures" (Lather 2001, 480). A postmodern orientation might be wistful, playful, and even self-ironic. It should seek to unframe, even estrange (MacLure 2006a), our understandings and experiences of the social world and be performative rather than representative (Stronach 2010). This demands a commitment to anti-hegemonic thought (Paulston 2000) and a form of "apprenticeship" (Wallin 2012) that may require the "rupture of fealty" toward one's intellectual masters necessary to maintain "independence as a thinker" (Lotringer et al. 2007, 8).

The Postmodern in Education Policy Research

Post-classical theorizing in education makes a vibrant contribution to the study of teaching and curriculum (Lather 2009; Luke and Luke 1990; Webb 2009), educational subjectivities (Armstrong 2003; Davies 1989) and research methodology (Davies 2010; Lather 2007; MacLure 2006a; Coleman and Ringrose 2013; Stronach 2010). Even though its presence in education policy research is limited, the understanding of globalization as the spatialization of modernity (Featherstone and Lash 1995), has led to growing and promising interest in the philosophy of Deleuze and Guattari (Webb and Gulson 2013; Simons et al. 2009). In particular, their notion of re- and de-territorialization provides a heuristic for exploring state power and reach, policy flows and context in education reform and opens up, at least in "theory," for a focus on a number of Deleuzean themes including: the machinic nature of life; transcendence, immanence, and becoming; the notion of minor literature and its application as non-state philosophy and; finally, to a notion of writing as invention. Much of this richness finds nascent form as an interest in the study of educational flows, assemblages, and networks, and draws on their notion of rhizomic thinking in order to transcend the "arborescent linearity," "binary oppositions," and "Cartesian dualisms" of Western thought (Gale 2007, 477).

This approach to exploring institutional transformation and human subjectivity in education policy can be found in studies of the teacher as nomad (Gale 2007; Honan 2004; Roy 2003), the school as assemblage (Gulson 2011), and education as event (Krejsler and Staunæs 2013). Such work takes direct and deep inspiration from Deleuzean philosophy and aims to subvert the "colonized spaces" of education that limit what can be thought and said (Roy 2003, iv). However, with notable exceptions (Gorur 2011; Webb and Gulson 2013), the assemblage concept in education policy studies is usually read through the lens of Anglo-American anthropology (Marcus and Saka 2006; Ong and Collier 2004; Sassen 2007). Exemplary here is Rizvi and Lingard's (2010) study of social equity in Australian higher education policy, where the "performative politics" of neo-liberal reform bring together "diverse and competing considerations within a single policy framework" (Rizvi and Lingard 2010, 20). This work is part of a larger effort to reimagine education policy research, especially in terms of the emergence of a post-Westphalian "reality" and the role of "state and policymakers (in seeking) to manage and rearticulate global pressures" (Rizvi and Lingard 2010, 21). Such work is grounded in a "value position" to strive "progressively towards a more equal and democratic future that recognizes and respects differences" (Rizvi and Lingard 2010, 69). In such work, postmodern insights are reworked not only to highlight the "global dominance of the neoliberal policy paradigm," but to "resist its negative effects and forge a different, more just and democratic globalization" (Rizvi and Lingard 2010, 3).

Resistance is also central to Ball's (2012, 2) efforts to understand the "how" of neo-liberalism. Identifying the notion of global assemblage as a neglected dimension in the policy transfer literature, he explores the increasing role being played by business, social enterprise, and philanthropy in education, and via the study of policy networks and communities and provides fascinating examples of emerging social relations in their historical and geographical complexity, suggesting (and condemning) a "purposeful agenda which is translated into policy proposals, lobbying and influence in government, the media and academia" (Ball 2012, 26). One case study centers upon the "nomadic, rhizomatic connector," James Tooley, a British educationalist, who has extensive interest (and interests) in low-fee schooling for the poor of the global south (Ball 2012, 50). Here, efforts to connect supranational development agencies, private sector investors, and civil society groups are viewed as undermining the natural order of publically provided, equitable, and socially just education, and speak to a huge mainstream readership concerned about the growing negative effects of neo-liberalism in education.

Such work is notable for attempting to capture some of the "temporality of processes, and the dynamic character of the interrelationships between heterogeneous phenomena" (Ball 2012, 143, citing Rizvi and Lingard 2010, 7). Nevertheless, this approach to network analysis is viewed by Ball himself as being essentially "flawed" as it "inevitably fixes flows, flattens asymmetries, and lags behind the dynamics of exchange" (Ball 2012, 143–144). Such work is typical of education policy research that seeks to explore global dynamics with post-foundational inspirations. Typically, however, a postmodern insight is read in ways that "reinscribe(s) it back into modernist categories of political struggle" (Lather 2007, 103), making possible the perpetuation of a scholarship of loss, longing, and resistance. How can we understand the appropriation of key postmodern ideas into the field of education policy research but in ways that reassert central modernist concerns?

Realizing the Post-Modern Challenge

The Origins of Globalization Theory

In their comparative survey of different "knowledge-geographical traditions" Lizardo and Strand (2009, 39) view Lyotard's epistemological critique of Western thought systems and Baudrillard's attack on the "mythology of the rational mass" (Lizardo and Strand 2009, 42) as essential to a particular "project" that questioned the very premises of the social and thus the future of the nation state and party politics. Baudrillard is especially central to the interest in the social, viewing contemporary consumer and media society as having delivered an "abyss of meaning" (Baudrillard 2007, 40). Rather than investing the "multitude" (in the terminology of Hardt and Negri's "Empire") with political potential, this "place of absorption and implosion" gives rise to a silent "mass" that refuses to be spoken for (Baudrillard 2007, 48–49).

From the standpoint of German theorizing, however, the assumed death of the social is little more than ahistorical speculation laced with "anti-statism." With Habermas its most articulate voice, modernity from the German tradition is viewed as a "frame of mind or subjective stance" toward the social world (Lizardo and Strand 2009, 44). This orientation, or *will*, has a direct lineage in the philosophy of Hegel and prioritizes the state in theories of society. Unsurprisingly, the French/epistemological position is viewed from this perspective as failing to acknowledge the power of progressive politics to shape social life, and harbors a repeat of Germany's actual postmodern moment of 20th-century fascism. By contrast, the British tradition, accepting neither French claims of epoch change nor German visions of progress through the state, prioritizes a gradual intensification and inevitability of "sociostructural changes" in the economy (Lizardo and Strand 2009, 49). This is a crucial move that enables a "bone fide (and epistemologically 'moderate'), *sociology of the postmodern*" (Lizardo and Strand 2009, 50, original emphasis). Here, the concepts of reflexivity and choice (Giddens 1990), risk and uncertainty (Beck 1992), and social diagnosis (Bauman 2000) speak to a British "gradualist" approach (Lizardo and Strand 2009, 54) quite different from French or German understandings of the potential for an active politics of social renewal.

Such considerations are far removed from, but connectable to, the American incursion into postmodern theorizing. This started primarily as an aesthetic movement (Jameson 1984/1991), but was quickly appropriated into discussions about the "trajectory of capitalism" (Lizardo and Strand 2009, 58), in large measure to consolidate the primacy of "alliance politics" in American intellectual debates (Lambert 2006b, 3). For our purposes, the most significant line of thought is that established in Jameson's (1984/1991) seminal text, which deploys postmodern art and architecture as a parallel meaning form to the economy and which served to "corral" together Barthes, Derrida, Foucault, Lyotard, Baudrillard, and even Althusser; a "diverse and mutually exclusive" group of philosophers who he saw as representing "the principal 'rival hermeneutic' to the ascendancy of Marxian interpretation in the United States" (Lambert 2006b, 16–17). Here, Jameson deploys the term postmodern in political rather than epistemological terms, in order to establish "which 'ideology of the text' would be dominant in American cultural and ideological life for the next twenty years and up to the present" (Jameson 1984/1991, cited in Lambert 2006b, 17). Whilst this connects to the British and French traditions (at least that represented by Baudrillard), it nevertheless "draw(s) back to the safe house of neo-Marxism" (Featherstone 1995, 78) and remains a strategy of representation, and thus modernist "repetition" (Spivak 1999, 317), aimed at *anticipating* certain types of changes in political economy, rather than charting what has become, or of thinking anew. As such, "discourse" (Foucault), "desire" (Deleuze and Guattari), and "simulation" (Baudrillard), to name but three key post-foundational thoughts, are marginalized in favor of analyses that are "solemn in their politics, almost humorless (and) still addressing the virtuality of political emancipation from the position of class guilt and/or sadness" (Lambert 2006b, 5).

Whilst many would view such a politico-geographical mapping as "errant essentialism" (Wallin 2012, 149), the notion that we must think in terms of different postmodernisms makes it possible to suggest that the "Anglosaxon theorists of the aesthetics-economy nexus" were well-placed "to easily reconvert the theoretical capital that had been previously honed in the battle to understand postmodernism into sophisticated entries into the globalization problematic" (Lizardo and Strand 2009, 66). This made possible an approach to postmodernism that rejects the "nihilism, incommensurability and simulation" associated with various French contributions to the debate; orientations now viewed as being of limited "practical and theoretical" relevance (65). Where postmodern insights have been maintained in studies of globalization, we thus see a particular domestication and integration with mainstream concerns: re-reading capitalism in ways that enable us to "grasp the whole" in order that we not "lose the capacity to act to change the world" (Featherstone 1995, 79).

Embracing Disjuncture: Experiments in Global Education Policy

How then might we explore actual educational practices, and their significance, when many of our conceptual tools are reworked with the certainties of Enlightenment ideology? With an empirical reach spanning educational actors and contexts from both the Global North and South; I have attempted to explore becoming subjectivities in and around national ministries, universities, and classrooms, and connect these to individual and collective efforts to create meaning. Without being beholden to one overarching meta-theoretical vision, I have sought to problematize global dynamics in terms of a range of effects on subjectivities and subject positions, always being cautious about re-stabilizing the subject as a coherent being.

The first iteration of this complexity found form as an explicitly tentative piece of writing that took inspiration from Appadurai's (1996) imagery of global scapes and flows. In particular, I was struck by his thesis that any attempt to comprehend the global political economy "must take into account the deeply disjunctive relationships among human movement, technological flow, and financial transfers." Together with pervasive "mediascapes" and "ideoscapes," the "lines between the realistic and the fictional" become "blurred" such that "the farther away these audiences are from the direct experiences of metropolitan life, the more likely they are to construct imagined worlds that are chimerical, aesthetic, even fantastic" (Appadurai 1996, 35). Education seemed the perfect stage on which to explore the globalization of experience.

I viewed Appadurai's essay as unsettling dominant modernist narratives about the potential of the nation state and progressive politics to engineer planned change, and was especially drawn to his fleeting reference to Deleuze and Guattari's influential *A Thousand Plateaus* (Deleuze and Guattari 1987), not least the concept of deterritorialization. The notion of an educational "policyscape" – a deliberate reference to this seminal text – was one way to explore new processes of connectivity and exclusion in the global *cultural* economy (Carney 2009). My primary interest was to seek out globalization as it was being experienced through the "ideoscape" of Western-inspired educational policy where neo-liberal concerns for efficiency and accountability meet advanced liberal notions of individual liberty, rights, and entitlements.

Whilst others have problematized the tendency for "methodological nationalism" in education policy research (Robertson and Dale 2008), my particular move was to operationalize this insight via empirical study across contexts that many would view as incompatible (higher education reform in Denmark, community schooling in Nepal, and teacher education in Tibet). Deploying Gupta and Ferguson's (1997) understanding of state spatiality and reach, I attempted to illustrate empirically how the state was "simultaneously decentered by the multiple voices that claim authority to speak about education" (Carney 2009, 65) *and* strengthened by its new mandate in "organizing the field of possibilities, and laying the boundaries for local policy" (Kamat 2002, 116).

For example, whilst Danish policy-makers and administrators were notionally "in charge" of the higher education sector and engaged in a dramatic program of change, they appeared to be swept along on currents established far beyond Danish territorial boundaries. As a state that thoroughly embodied global discourses about knowledge economies and "world class" universities, there seemed no position from which to direct a distinctive "Danish" response to circulating policies. By contrast, whilst the contours of community schooling reform in Nepal were being defined by external actors and their locally situated partners, actual practices could be described as a master class in "The art of not being governed" (Scott 2009). Here, skillful political and bureaucratic maneuvering was able to conflate the predominately donor-driven, politically motivated project of local ownership of schooling with ongoing *decentralization* efforts that were little more than strategies of political *deconcentration* where central authorities passed on responsibilities and obligations to the lower levels but maintained control of vision, purpose, and funding. Nepal must surely be a "weak state" if one reads the literature on these things, but appeared to act with sufficient strength to avoid (or at least defer) the crude client-state models and relations being offered by international donors and regional political powers.

In the study of Chinese teacher education reform in Tibet, it was clear that new national frameworks for learner-centered teaching in primary schools would be implemented, albeit more slowly than Beijing's optimistic timetable. However, at the same time as Chinese education appeared to be in tune with the global fad of the child-friendly classroom, national economic imperatives aimed at securing a productive and skilled workforce for the next phase of Chinese development meant that Tibetan children were now being taught in Chinese and, thus, more able to progress through the demanding exam system, more likely to become "educated," and, one could ponder, well on the way to incorporation into the Han-Chinese political project. History and context, but also powerful but disjunctive global reform messages (i.e. right to locally meaningful education *and* the imperative of economic relevance) enabled a strong state to enhance its reach in the most distant of extremities!

As a research orientation, all three cases were marked by a reluctance to submit to dominant narratives about what neo- and advanced liberalism means in practice, an openness to explore hybridity, rupture, and disjuncture as this emerged in globalizing cultural forms, and a refusal to allow a particular notion of the state to shape my engagement with it. Like Ferguson (2006, 112), I understood that research on the role of the state under global conditions needed to "treat its verticality and encompassment not as a taken-for-granted fact, but as a precarious achievement – and as an ethnographic problem."

This orientation led me to problematize social action, especially the nature of resistance in the context of individualizing ideologies. Here, I attempted to indicate that the potential for contest and protest was shaped by the political logic in a particular context and the resultant, always dynamic, subjectivities of actors who attempted to negotiate the meaning of education. Whilst politicians, administrators, teachers, parents, and students were active subjects in these dramas, their subjectivities were both relational *and* "scalar" (Gomes *et al.* 2012, 223); being shaped both by global and national-level political messages of "how to act," *and* historic and contingent ones about what constituted an appropriate subject position in that time and place. In Nepal, for example, the physical premises of community schools became important public rallying points for newly empowered citizens to critique the state, thus finding a new platform from which to reiterate ancient injustices. At the same time, parents spoke about "community" schooling as a place to learn English in order to escape the community in which they now perceived their children to be trapped! In Denmark, the business-oriented government that had enacted a wide-ranging reform of higher education, ostensibly to integrate the sector into the commercial domain, now found itself being challenged by business leaders who viewed universities in relation to global elite institutions where funding for basic and disinterested research and institutional autonomy were identified as crucial to success on a competitive international playing field. In the case of Tibet, and China more generally, one can only revisit Appadurai's original thesis and wonder how the national legislative vision for an innovative but compliant workforce will eventually intersect with emerging (globalizing) flows that inscribe subjectivities with radically different personal and political potentials.

Most importantly, this work led me to problematize the concept of "culture" by focusing instead on similarly dynamic contestations of locality. Noting that place and space had been thoroughly under-theorized in education policy research, my move was to introduce a spatial dimension to the study of places but to transcend the usual space/society binary. Here, a *spatial determinism* insists that space has its own qualities (e.g. neo-liberalism) that people ultimately come to embody. At the other extreme we find a *social determinism*, where the characteristics of places are determined largely by phenomena such as class, ethnicity, race, gender, and so forth (Gulson 2007, 42). In line with Massey's (2004) notion of place as *event*, I viewed localities as "articulated moment(s) of social space" where "conflict, discursive manoeuvring, and compromise" (Gulson 2007, 45) produced multiple subject-becomings.

This notion was further explored in a second piece of experimental writing emerging from a study of youth in Denmark, South Korea, and Zambia: once again a set of comparative "cases" aimed at evoking discomfort (Carney 2010). With my colleague Ulla Ambrosius Madsen, empirical work has unfolded Appadurai's "theory of rupture," taking media and migration as "major, and interconnected, diacritics" that work on and elevate the *imagination* to the position of "a constitutive feature of modern subjectivity" (Appadurai 1996, 3, original emphasis). Elaborating on Baudrillard's (1981) notions of hyper-reality, simulation, and radical uncertainty, we viewed the current moment as one marked by an increasingly general "disorientation of the saturated space" that gives rise to a "new and historically original dilemma"; one that Jameson (1984/1991) suggests as involving our "insertion as individual subjects into a multidimensional set of radically discontinuous realities, whose frames range from the still surviving spaces of bourgeois private life all the way to the unimaginable decentering of global capital itself" (Jameson 1984/1991, 413). This work focused on youth experiences of education and questioned the orientation of much comparative education policy research toward the seemingly transparent and coherent (institutional) spaces of ministries, agencies, schools, and classrooms, all of which were understood in ways that provided little more than a partial glimpse of the multiple imagined worlds being encountered by global and globalizing subjectivities.

In Denmark, for example, schooled identities involved the acceptance and embodiment of certain dominant narratives about personal freedom *and* collective responsibility which serve to make apparent subtle forms of "othering" that minority groups saw as ensuring their difference and alienation from society: the more they are brought into the fold; the more they are identified as necessarily separate from it; essential to the task of fabricating a distinctive *Danish* identity. In urban Zambia, it was remarkable to observe how schooling was legitimated and normalized in the absence of teachers, facilities, books, or futures: a simulation fueled by distorted association with some abstract Western "original." For many Korean youth, already made docile by extreme surveillance and social control, the institutionalized hell of school was perceived as little more than preparation for the inevitable hell of the corporation. It was cruelly ironic that whilst teachers encouraged students to be the *best* in the world, students imagined lives in the *rest* of world.

In this work we deliberately questioned the confidence with which education policy researchers approached such spaces, suggesting that they should delve deeper into them in order to seek out the complex, submerged drama between the forces of modernity as progress, order, and hope, and modernity's "other": entanglement, disruption, and recalcitrance. Rather than develop "hierarchies, frameworks, abstractions or other methodological crows' nests from which to look down from a distance on the details of educational life" (MacLure, 2006a, 733) we argued that educational policy research must address its "clarity-and closure-seeking tendencies" and give proper weight to those things that are usually marginalized, avoided, or trivialized in order that the "science" of educational research can remain loyal to the enlightenment ideals of truth, coherence, and progress (MacLure, 2006b, 730).

This notion of "otherness" was also central to a third piece of work that focused on the intersection of multiple and disjunctive flows in a *single* place rather than across multiple ones. Through long-term engagement with young people and schooling in urban Nepal, once again undertaken with my colleague Ulla Ambrosius Madsen (Madsen and Carney 2011), we attempted to give form to Appadurai's (1996) claim that "imagination" must be viewed as "central to all forms of agency" and *the* "key component of the new global order" (Appadurai 1996, 31, emphasis added). Using insights gained from close engagement with youth, parents, teachers, and public officials, we focused on the ways in which young people communicate and *consume* the ideologies of consumer modernity, often in ways disconnected from or marginally aligned with intended global messages. Here, the imagination shapes processes of enactment, simulation, resistance, *and* confusion as actors of all types attempt to find and read coherent scripts for life and work in contexts marked by connectivity, contingency, alienation, and ambivalence. We hinted that a reading of the world from the perspective of a particularly vulnerable "developing" state – what some call a "non-convergent holding tank" (Ferguson 2006, 184) – represents more than a foray into exotic wonder or horror. Rather, the processes at work and subjectivities on display here provide important keys to deepening our understanding of education reform in the so-called stable and "developed" North, where the "work of the imagination" is, similarly, "neither purely emancipatory nor entirely disciplined but (is) a space of contestation in which individuals and groups seek to annex the global into their own practices of the modern" (Appaduari 1996, 4). We were especially struck by how teachers trained in reform pedagogy by donor agencies embraced but ultimately fumbled their scripts in the classroom; in the process enabling the new teaching ideologies to further alienate historically marginalized groups such as girls and ethnic caste minorities. Who could have imagined that the rhetoric of student-centered teaching could be deployed to identify and stigmatize female students, who, in adhering to sacred social norms, were reluctant to be visible as "active," "engaged," and thus "successful" learners? Who could have imagined that "modern" pedagogical reform, connected to abstract images of the "good life" elsewhere, would radicalize young people to join the Maoist guerilla movement in search of social justice, only to leave it because of the very lack of social justice on which it is based but, also, to reject cosmopolitan alternatives (including local higher education, employment in service roles, etc.) that were viewed as hollowed-out parodies of the global media-driven referent? This is the Western academic fixation with human mobility applied to the immobile. Processes of "antimembership" (Ferguson 1999, 212) expose young people's feelings of desire and attachment, confusion, and alienation, and, ultimately, their active strategies of non-belonging, and shed a very different light on the role of formal schooling in identity construction.

The grounding in Appadurai's notions of flows and disjuncture led to predictable charges of spatial fetishism and thus ahistoricalism that radically undervalued the role of history, context, and geo-politics in shaping the possibilities *for social action* (Robertson 2012). Viewed as part of the "first enthusiastic embrace of the disembedding tendencies of globalization" (Bude and Dürrschmidt 2010, 496), these writers suggest that Appadurai undervalues "the material and institutional conditions that underpin the reproduction of global culture" (Bude and Dürrschmidt 2010, 482). Others acknowledge the heuristic value of Appadurai's (1996) focus on "the multiplicity of flows," but suggest greater weight be given to those connected to finance and capital (Heyman and Campbell 2009, 132). Ong (1999), for example, asks whether "imagination as social practice can be so independent of national, transnational, and political-economic structures that enable, channel, and control the flows of people, things, and ideas" (Ong 1999, 11). These writers take Appadurai to task for viewing contemporary cultural forms as "fundamentally fractal," and possessing "no Euclidean boundaries, structures or regularities" (Heyman and Campbell 2009, 132, citing Appadurai 1996, 46). Here, the broader anthropological project of finding alternatives to a "bounded, localistic sense of culture" leads to a simplified understanding of geography as comprising either "places or placeless flows" and a view of history that is therefore seriously "distorted" (Heyman and Campbell 2009, 136–137).

Much of this criticism obscures Appadurai's (1996) own "tentative" understanding of the "dynamics of global cultural systems" (Appadurai 1996, 47) and ignores his call for theory generation and empirical research that might elaborate these dynamics. However, rather than being emboldened by the response to "Modernity at Large" (1996), as I was, Appadurai's subsequent display of "atonement" (Appadurai 2013, 1), deep engagement in activist politics (Appadurai 2006), and an eventual return to the disciplinary security of area studies (Appadurai 2013) suggest a sober strategy of revision. Paying homage to Weber and Marx, he now appeals to anthropology to move away from its traditional role in analyzing the "cabinet of curiosities" and to engage, "full-scale," in rethinking how best to "design humanity" (Appadurai 2013, 4–5). Here, this "anthropology of the future" demands an "ethics of possibility which can offer a more inclusive platform for improving the planetary quality of life" (Appadurai 2013, 299–300). Notwithstanding the legitimate ambition to transcend the tension between theory and politics, Appadurai's reframing of global dynamics through the lens of classical social theory suggests yet another expansive intellectual project "tamed and safely integrated into the current social order" (Lizardo and Strand 2009, 39).

Conclusion: Embracing Disappointment

> This is "the science possible after our disappointments in science". (Lather 2007, x)

The dominance of certain American and British intellectual concerns has consolidated modernist knowledge production projects where issues of political and economic power, state authority, and social solidarity are centered in contemporary debates about globalization. Whilst globalization has become important in social theory and education policy research, it has effectively neutralized the critical potential of the anti-foundational ideas on which it is based. As such, we are primarily left with varying approaches to education policy research as "science" that seek to solve problems in the service of rationalized "policy desires" (Webb and Gulson, 57). By contrast, a post-foundational orientation acknowledges a positioning between "an impossible certainty and an interminable deconstruction," and therefore approaches intellectual work with both "reverence and mistrust" (Lather 2007, x). What type of "science" remains possible from this vantage point?

The empirical work outlined here reflects a type of policy problematization (Webb 2014). Rather than a presentation of solutions to problems, this builds upon a "recursive methodology *that seeks difference and complexity* in thinking and practice" (6, original emphasis) by trying to "de-familiarize present practices and categories, to make them seem less self-evident and necessary, and to open up spaces for the invention of new forms of experience" (Ball 1995, 266, cited in Webb 2014, 370). The focus on flows, intensities, and becoming(s) in the research described here was one way to "endorse complexity, partial truths, and multiple subjectivities" (Lather 2007, 136). Here, I took little for granted and refused to assume that subjects "knew their place" or acted accordingly. In this regard, a recursive methodology requires something akin to an "emergentist" understanding of epistemology (Osberg *et al.* 2008) where "knowledge reaches us not as something we receive but as a response, which brings forth new worlds because it necessarily adds something (which was not present anywhere before it appeared) to what came before" (Osberg *et al.* 2008, 225). By viewing subjects as expansive machines with unlimited but unpredictable potentialities (Deleuze), often beyond the grasp of decaying modernist projects of inclusive politics (Baudrillard), research offers the possibility for a form of empirical engagement that is not circumscribed by political ideology about how the world ought to be or the strictures of disciplinary tribalism or intellectual fashion that mediate what can be said, and by whom. Whether such work succeeds in avoiding the politics of representation is open to debate. Like others, I am "less concerned with representing the real than … with living it out in different ways" (Osberg *et al.* 2008, 214). To achieve this I have experimented with social poetics (Brown 1977), "lyrical sociology" (Abbott 2007, 72), baroque method (MacLure 2006a), and sought interconnections with non-Western philosophy (Davies 2011) as ways to "break the hegemonies of meaning and presence that recuperate and appropriate the lives of others into consumption" (Lather, 2007, 136). But there is much more that can be done to explore the "post" in education policy research.

Given the prevailing institutional frames within which education policy research is presently conducted, we must assume that post-foundational approaches will continue to be marginalized or re-appropriated to serve modernist interests. However, the inability of modern scientific projects like education policy studies to capture either the complexity of (globalizing) social dynamics or to totally silence the "otherness" at their core (MacLure 2006b) is the surest indication of the ongoing promise of a postmodernity sensibility.

Note

1. I resist the temptation to provide a singular definition of the postmodern. However, Eagleton (2004) considers it as "the contemporary movement of thought which rejects totalities, universal values, grand historical narratives, solid foundations to human existence and the possibility of objective knowledge." It is "sceptical of truth, unity and progress, opposes what it sees as elitism in culture,

tends towards cultural relativism, and celebrates pluralism, discontinuity and heterogeneity" (Eagleton 2004, 13). We could distinguish this from the related movement known as post-structuralism, which views "structures as historically and reciprocally affected by practice within contingent conditions of time, particularly conceptual practices and how they define disciplinary knowledge" (Prado 1995, 154 in Lather 2001, 479).

References

Abbott, A. 2007. "Against Narrative: A Preface to Lyrical Sociology." *Sociological Theory*, 25(1): 67–99.
Appadurai, A. 1996. *Modernity at Large: Cultural Dimensions of Globalization*. Minneapolis and London: University of Minnesota Press.
Appadurai, A. 2006. *Fear of Small Numbers: An Essay on the Geography of Anger*. Durham: Duke University Press.
Appadurai, A. 2013. *The Future as Cultural Fact: Essays on the Global Condition*. London: Verso.
Armstrong, F. 2003. *Spaced Out: Policy, Difference and the Challenge for Inclusive Education*. Dordrecht: Kluwer Academic Publishers.
Ball, S. 2012. *Global Education Inc.: New Policy Networks and the Neo-Liberal Imaginary*. London, Routledge.
Bauman, Z. 1992. *Intimations of Postmodernity*. London: Routledge.
Bauman, Z. 2000. *Liquid Modernity*. Cambridge: Polity Press.
Beck, U. 1992. *Risk Society: Towards a New Modernity*. London: Sage.
Barthes, R. 1977. "The Death of the Author," in *Image, Music, Text: Roland Barthes*, edited by S. Heath, 146–151. New York: Hill and Wang.
Baudrillard, J. 1981. *For a Critique of the Political Economy of the Sign*. (C. Levin, Trans.). St. Louis: Telos Press.
Baudrillard, J. 2001. *Impossible Exchange*. London: Verso.
Baudrillard, J. 2007. *In the Shadow of the Silent Majority*. Los Angeles: Semiotext(e).
Brown, R.H. 1977. *A Poetic for Sociology*. Cambridge: Cambridge University Press.
Bude, H. and J. Dürrschmidt. 2010. "What's Wrong with Globalization?: Contra 'Flow Speak' – Towards an Existential Turn in the Theory of Globalization." *European Journal of Social Theory*, 13(4): 481–500.
Carney, S. 2009. "Negotiating Policy in an Age of Globalization: Exploring Educational "Policyscapes" in Denmark, Nepal and China." *Comparative Education Review*, 53(1): 63–88.
Carney, S. 2010. "Reading the Global: Comparative Education at the End of an Era," in *New Thinking in Comparative Education: Honouring the Work of Dr. Robert Cowen*, edited by M. Larsen, 125–142. Amsterdam: Sense Publishers.
Colebrook, C. 2002. *Gilles Deleuze*. London: Routledge.
Coleman, R. and J. Ringrose. 2013 (eds). *Deleuze and Research Methodologies*, Edinburgh: Edinburgh University Press.
Davies, B. 1989. *Frogs and Snails and Feminist Tales. Preschool Children and Gender*. Sydney: Allen and Unwin.
Davies, B. 2010. "The Struggle Between the Individualised Subject of Phenomenology and the Multiplicities of the Poststructuralist Subject: The Problem of Agency." *Reconceptualizing Educational Research Methodology*, 1(1): 54–68.
Davies, B. 2011. "Intersections Between Zen Buddhism and Deleuzian Philosophy." *Psyke and Logos*, 32(1): 28–45.
Debord, G. 1995. *The Society of the Spectacle*. New York: Zone Books.
Deleuze, G. and F. Guattari. 1987. *A Thousand Plateaus: Capitalism and Schizophrenia*. Minneapolis: University of Minnesota.

de Sousa Santos, B. 2006. "Globalizations." *Theory Culture Society*, 23: 393.

Eagleton, T. 2003. *After Theory*. New York: Basic Books.

Ferguson, J. 1999. "Global Disconnect: Abjection and the Aftermath of Modernism," in *Expectations of Modernity: Myths and Meanings of Urban Life on the Zambian Copperbelt*, 234–254. Berkeley: University of California.

Ferguson, J. 2006. *Global Shadows: Africa in the Neo-Liberal World Order*. Durham: Duke University Press.

Featherstone, M. 1995. *Undoing Culture: Globalization, Postmodernism and Identity*. London: Sage.

Featherstone, M. and S. Lash. 1995. "Globalization, Modernity and the Spatialization of Social Theory: An Introduction," in *Global Modernities*, edited by M. Featherstone, S. Lash, R. Robertson, 1–24. London: Sage.

Foucault, M. 1970. *The Order of Things: An Archeology of the Human Sciences*. New York: Random House.

Gale, K. 2007. "Teacher Education in the University: Working with Policy, Practice and Deleuze." *Teaching in Higher Education*, 12(4): 471–483.

Gane, N. 2004. *Max Weber and Postmodern Theory: Rationalization Versus Re-Enchantment*. London: Palgrave Macmillan.

Giddens, A. 1990. *The Consequences of Modernity*. Stanford: Stanford University Press.

Gomes, A., S. Robertson, and R. Dale. 2012. "The Social Condition of Higher Education: Globalization and (Beyond) Regionalization in Latin America." *Globalisation, Societies and Education*, 10(2): 221–245.

Gorur, R. 2011. "Policy as Assemblage." *European Educational Research Journal*, 10(4): 611–622.

Green, A. 1997. *Education, Globalization and the Nation State*. London: Macmillan Press.

Gulson, K.N. 2007. "Mobilizing Space Discourses: Politics and Educational Policy Change," *Spatial Theories of Education: Policy and Geography Matters*, edited by K.N. Gulson and C. Symes, 37–56. New York: Routledge.

Gulson, K.N. 2011. *Education Policy, Space and the City: Markets and the (In)Visibility of Race*. New York: Routledge.

Gupta, A. and J. Ferguson. 1997. "After 'people's and 'cultures'," in *Culture, Power and Place: Explorations in Critical Anthropology*, edited by A. Gupta and J. Ferguson, 1–29. Durham: Duke University Press.

Hardt, M. and A. Negri. 2000. *Empire*. Cambridge: Harvard University Press.

Heyman, J. and H. Campbell. 2009. "The Anthropology of Global Flows: A Critical Reading of Appadurai's 'Disjuncture and Difference in the Global Cultural Economy'." *Anthropological Theory*, 9(2): 131–148.

Honan, E. 2004. "(Im)plausibilities: A Rhizo-textual Analysis of Policy Texts and Teachers' Work." *Educational Philosophy and Theory*, 36(3): 267–281.

Jameson, F. 1984/1991. *Postmodernism; or the Cultural Logic of Late Capitalism*. London: Verso.

Kamat, S. 2002. "Deconstructing the Rhetoric of Decentralization: The State in Education Reform." *Current Issues in Comparative Education*, 2(2): 110–119.

Kenway, J. and J. Fahey. 2009. (eds) *Globalizing the Research Imagination*. London: Routledge.

Krejsler, J. and D. Staunæs. 2013. "Desire and (Self-)Management in Education. Post-Lenses on Nordic Intakes of Transnational Tendencies." Special Issue of *International Journal of Qualitative Studies in Education*, 26(9): 1097–1100.

Lambert, G. 2006a. *The Return of the Baroque in Modern Culture*. London: Continuum.

Lambert, G. 2006b. *Who's Afraid of Deleuze and Guattari?* London: Continuum.

Lather, P. 2001. "Postmodernism, Post-structualism and Post(Critical) Ethnography: Of Ruins, Aporias and Angels." in *Handbook of Ethnography*, edited by P. Atkinson, A. Coffey, S. Delamont, J. Lofland, and L. Lofland, 475–492. London: Sage.

Lather, P. 2007. *Getting Lost: Feminist Efforts Towards a Double(d) Science*, Albany: SUNY Press.

Lather, P. 2009. "Getting Lost: Social Science and/as Philosophy." *Educational Studies*, 45(4): 342–357.

Lizardo, O. and M. Strand. 2009. "Postmodernism and Globalization." *Protosociology*, 26: 38–72.

Lotringer, S. 2007. "Introduction: Requiem for the Masses," in *In the Shadow of the Silent Majorities*, edited by J. Baudrillard, 7–31. Los Angeles: Semiotext(e).

Luke, A. and C. Luke. 1990. "School Knowledge as Simulation: Curriculum in Postmodern Conditions." *Discourse*, 10(2): 75–91.

Lyotard, J.F. 1984. *The Postmodern Condition: A Report on Knowledge*. Manchester: Manchester University Press.

MacLure, M. 2006a. "The Bone in the Throat: Some Uncertain Thoughts on Baroque Method." *International Journal of Qualitative Studies in Education*, 19(6): 729–745.

MacLure, M. 2006b. "A Demented Form of the Familiar: Postmodernism and Educational Research." *Journal of Philosophy of Education*, 40(2): 221–239.

Madsen, U.M. and S. Carney. 2011. "Education in an Age of Radical Uncertainty: Youth and Schooling in Urban Nepal." *Globalisation, Societies and Education*, 9(1): 115–133.

Marcus, G. and E. Saka. 2006. "Assemblage." *Theory Culture* Society, 23: 101–106.

Massey, D. 2004. *Space, Place and Gender*. Cambridge: Polity.

Osberg, D., G. Biesta, and P. Cilliers. 2008. "From Representation to Emergence: Complexity's Challenge to the Epistemology of Schooling." *Educational Philosophy and Theory*, 40(1): 213–227.

Ong, A. 1999. *Flexible Citizenship: The Cultural Logics of Transnationality*. Durham: Duke University Press.

Ong, A. and S. Collier. 2004. *Global Assemblages: Technology, Politics, and Ethics as Anthropological Problems*. London: Blackwell.

Paulston, R. 2000. "Imagining Comparative Education: Past, Present, Future." *Compare*, 30(3): 353–365.

Rizvi, F. and B. Lingard. 2010. *Globalizing Education Policy*. London: Routledge.

Robertson, S. 2012. "Researching Global Education Policy: Angles In/On/Out…," in *Global Education Policy and International Development: New Agendas, Issues and Practices*, edited by A. Verger, M. Novelli, and H. Altinyelken, 33–52. London: Continuum Books.

Robertson, S. and R. Dale. 2008. "Researching Education in a Globalising Era: Beyond Methodological Nationalism, Methodological Statism, Methodological Educationism and Spatial Fetishism," *The Production of Educational Knowledge in the Global Era*, edited by J. Resnik, 19–32. Rotterdam: Sense Publishers.

Robertson, S. and R. Dale. 2015. "Toward a 'Critical Cultural Political Economy' Account of the Globalising of Education." *Globalisation, Societies and Education*, 13(1): 149–170.

Roy, K. 2003. *Teachers in Nomadic Spaces: Deleuze and Curriculum*. New York: Peter Lang.

Sassen, S. 2007. *A Sociology of Globalization*. New York: Norton & Co.

Scott, J. 2009. *The Art of Not Being Governed*. New Haven and London: Yale University Press.

Simons, M., M. Olssen, and M. Peters. 2009 (eds). *Re-reading Education Policies: A Handbook Studying the Policy Agenda of the Twenty-First Century*. Rotterdam: Sense Publishers.

St. Pierre, E. 1997. "Methodology in the Fold and the Irruption of Transgressive Data." *Qualitative Studies in Education*, 1(19): 175–189.

Stronach, I. 2010. *Globalizing Education, Educating the Local: How Method Made Us Mad*. New York: Routledge.

Spivak, G. 1999. *A Critique of Postcolonial Reason: Toward a History of the Vanishing Present*. Cambridge: Harvard University Press.

Wallin, J. 2012. "Bon Mots for Bad Thoughts." *Discourse: Studies in the Cultural Politics of Education*, 33(1): 147–162.

Webb, P.T. 2009. *Teacher Assemblage*. Amsterdam: Sense.

Webb, P.T., 2014. "Policy problematization." *International Journal of Qualitative Studies in Education*, 27(3): 364–376.

Webb, P.T. and K. Gulson. 2013. "Policy Intensions and the Folds of the Self." *Educational Theory*, 63(1): 51–68.

Chapter 29

Policy Reponses to the Rise of Asian Higher Education: A Postcolonial Analysis

Fazal Rizvi

Introduction

Consider the following media headlines:

- University rankings show Asian rise and Australian slip.
- Foreign students will desert Britain as Asian universities rise, vice-chancellor warns.
- Enter the dragon: The rise of higher education in Asia.
- Rising in the east, setting in the west: Asian universities climb THE world university rankings.
- China's top universities will rival Oxbridge, says Yale President.

In Australia, Europe, and North America, such headlines have become commonplace – largely predictable. Each time global university rankings are released, the media invariably points to the rapid rise in these ranking of Asian universities with alarm, bemoaning a decline of the quality of higher education in the more established systems in Western countries. That they may no longer be so dominant is assumed to be a source of major concern. Some even call it "a looming crisis" that could result in the West losing its dominance in the emerging global economic and political order. This sense of crisis is given further impetus with the release of comparative data relating to the academic performance of secondary school students in Asia on international tests such as the Programme for International Student Assessment (PISA).

The idea that Asian systems of education have witnessed experienced rapid rise over the past two decades is no longer contested. There is a great deal of empirical evidence to demonstrate spectacular growth in the number of students participating in formal

The Handbook of Global Education Policy, First Edition.
Edited by Karen Mundy, Andy Green, Bob Lingard, and Antoni Verger.
© 2016 John Wiley & Sons, Ltd. Published 2016 by John Wiley & Sons, Ltd.

education in most parts of Asia, at all levels. Literacy and school completion rates have gone up in most Asian countries, often exceeding the targets set for the United Nations' Millennium Development Goals. The performance of many educational systems in Asia on international tests has been most impressive. PISA scores by students in Shanghai and other East Asian systems, for example, attract a great deal of critical attention (see, for example, Jensen 2012; Tan 2012; Sellar and Lingard 2013). At the level of higher education, the number of students enrolled in universities in Asia has increased exponentially, while the research performance of some of these universities has been equally noteworthy, with an enormous rise in the number of high status research publications and patents, particularly in East Asia and Singapore (Marginson 2011).

In this chapter, I take these indictors of success as largely uncontested, but focus instead on the ways in which this success is interpreted in the more established systems of higher education. I want to consider how the spectacular rise of Asian education is understood in "Western" countries, such as the USA, the UK, and Australia; and reflect upon the accounts that are presented to explain this success. In the second part of this chapter, I turn to a range of policy initiatives that the Australian government and universities have pursued in response to Asia's growing significance in the rapidly shifting geopolitical order in higher education. I view the Australian case as illustrative, acknowledging, however, that to treat Australia as illustrative of the broader trends may be misleading, since Australia is geographically located within the Asian region and most of its trade is with Asian countries; and therefore its approach to the rise of Asian higher education can be expected to be markedly different from North American and European countries. While this is true to some extent, in my view, Australian discourses concerning the rise of Asian education nonetheless represent an emerging global pattern, continuous with Australia's historical and political alignment to a broader "Western" imaginary of Asia.

To elaborate an understanding of this imaginary, I draw upon resources from postcolonial theory. In particular, I suggest that the postcolonial notion of ambivalence, as developed, for example, by Homi Bhabha (1994), is most helpful in showing how current "Western" anxieties about the rise of Asian education are, to a large extent, continuous with the colonial representations of Asia, both as an object of desire and derision. In this chapter, I want to argue that "Western" perceptions of the changing geopolitical architecture of higher education remain located within an East–West binary, which imagines Asia to be the West's "other" – admittedly no longer viewed as culturally inferior, but nonetheless framed in terms that display a deep anxiety. The economically robust Asia is interpreted both as a threat, and an opportunity in a fast-integrating global economy. As a result, policy responses to the rise of Asian education in most Western countries are linked both to an evolving logic of global competition in education, as well as a desire to pursue new possibilities of collaboration.

The Rise of Asian Higher Education

The evidence demonstrating the rise of Asian higher education is now overwhelming. The increase in the enrollment in undergraduate programs has been explosive across Asia. Most of the increase in global enrollments-, from 32.6 million in 1970 to 182.2 million in 2011-, has been in East, South East, and South Asia (ADB 2011). Most

Asian countries, at all income levels, have made enormous progress in widening access to bachelor's degree programs. According to the Planning Commission of India (2012), for example, the number of Indian students enrolled in an undergraduate degree program has increased from 8 million in 1995 to almost 23 million in 2012. Graduation rates have also been significant. In Thailand, the gross graduate ratio for undergraduate degree programs has improved from 15% in 2000 to 31% in 2008 (Chapman and Chien 2014, 38). In Korea and Japan, this ratio has now surpassed every European country, and is only marginally behind the USA (UIS 2013).

This growth has been fueled by a combination of factors, ranging from demographic trends, improved economic circumstances, and public aspirations and preferences, to increased investment and other policy decisions. In most Asian countries, both public and private investment in higher education has more than doubled over the past two decades (ADB 2011). Also driving this growth in higher education participation rates is basic education – higher progression rates through primary and secondary education. More students than ever are now graduating from secondary schools and seeking to continue their education, assuming this to be necessary for improved career and life opportunities. There is a growing recognition throughout Asia that the changing economy and the labor market require specialized knowledge-oriented human resources. As a result of these perceptions, there is intense competition for educational success. This is reflected in the growth of private provision of education. There has been a spectacular rise, for example, in the number of international and corporate schools throughout Asia (Ball 2012). It is estimated, for example, that on average, every week, an international school is established in India alone (Prasad 2011). The growing popularity of International Baccalaureate and Cambridge International programs is an indication of the extent to which parents in Asia are now prepared to invest heavily in the education of their children, hoping to prepare them to enter higher education and thrive in an intensively competitive global economy.

To accommodate rapid increases in student demand for higher education, governments throughout Asia have created new universities, diversified delivery mechanisms, and encouraged the entry of private providers. A recent United Nations Educational, Scientific and Cultural Organization (UNESCO) report (2014, 15) has noted that such rapid "expanding out" has created a serious shortage of appropriately qualified instructors. Both public and private universities have faced the escalating demand for instructional staff to serve the fast growing number of undergraduate students. Higher education systems have consequently had to "expand up" – investing in the provision of graduate education in an effort to create a pool of better qualified instructors, who are also able to carry out research. At the same time, research is increasingly viewed as a major driver of economic productivity. Until recently, in most Asian countries, gross enrolment ratios for Master's and doctoral level programs were negligible, but, in the past decade, they have risen to around 10% of all students enrolled in higher education. This has resulted in an increasing proportion of faculty with doctoral and Master's degrees (UIS 2013).

Throughout Asia, expansion of graduate education and university-based research are considered essential both for improving the quality of instruction at undergraduate education and for furthering programs of research and innovation with the potential to accelerate national economic development. Furthermore, Asian systems of higher education now readily acknowledge that to acquire prestige, attract investment, and appeal to international students, they need to be perceived as "excellent" on various systems of international university rankings (UNESCO 2014, 65). While various ranking regimes differ in the factors they include in their assessment technologies, they all regard scholarly publications in top tier international journals as a key indicator of success. This has led universities throughout Asia to pressure their faculty, not only to conduct high-level research, but also to publish widely. Many governments in Asia have developed elaborate schemes to fund research projects helpful to their national interests. They have also established relatively stringent layers of accountability. To enhance their international standing, many governments in Asia have also encouraged their universities to recruit international students. Governments such as Hong Kong, Singapore, and Malaysia have developed comprehensive strategies to position their universities as "regional research hubs" created to attract international students and to enhance international status.

These and a range of other strategies have begun to pay dividends. An increasing proportion of universities throughout Asia have become research active. Simon Marginson (2011; 2014) has compiled a rich portrayal of the rapid rise of East Asian universities in international ranking systems. Recent data indicates, for example, that the number of Chinese universities in the top 500 of world universities has increased from eight in 2008 to 28 in 2012 (UIS 2013). According to Levin (2010), China has built the largest higher education sector in the world in less than a decade, with universities such as Tsinghua, Fudan, Peking, and Jiaotong now able to hold their own with leading American and British universities. Other Asian universities are not all that far behind. The publication output of leading universities in East Asia and Singapore has grown rapidly, as indeed have their research links with prestigious universities around the world. In fields such as chemistry and computer science and materials, the research performance of universities such as Tsinghua University, Hong Kong University of Science and Technology, and the National University of Singapore is now as good as leading US research universities (UNESCO 2014). These universities now aspire to become the world's leading centers of research and innovation. Supported as they are by public and corporate funds, as well as institutional plans designed to meet ambitious expectations and timelines, this appears to be a goal that has already been realized.

Accounting for the Rise

Many journalists and scholars, not only within Asia, but also increasingly in the "West," have attempted to make sense of the recent global ascendency of Asia – and relatedly the rise of its systems of higher education. In Asia, scholars such as Pankaj Misra (2012) and Kishore Mahbubani (2013) have written persuasively about the ways in which Asia's global prominence represent a historical recovery of a past that was undermined by the forces of colonialism. They point to an emerging "postcolonial confidence" in most parts of Asia, which has created the conditions conducive for rapid economic growth. Misra (2012) has suggested that there is now emerging a new more confident Asia from "the ruins of empire". From the perspective of Misra's confident reading of history, colonialism is viewed as an historical exception in the grand narrative of Asian civilizations. In contrast, for Mahbubani (2013), the rise of Asia is best understood in terms of the strategic and carefully crafted policy decisions by its governments to engage with the world, taking full advantage of the emerging norms of global trade and economy. This view is in line with the influential work of Jagdish Bhagwati (2007), who has argued that globalization, when properly governed, is in fact the most powerful force for social good in the world, and has greatly benefited those countries in Asia which have been able to take advantage of the opportunities it offers.

Influential American journalists such as Tom Friedman have had no difficulty embracing Bhagwati's narrative. His book, *The World is Flat* (2007), is focused largely on the ways in which both China and to a lesser extent India have better understood recent global shifts and the opportunities that they present. Through a range of anecdotes, he insists that mobile technologies have made the world "flatter," and have opened up Chinese and Indian entrepreneurs to the possibilities of globalization, enabling their nations to become centers of production of manufacturing goods and informational services, respectively. To do this, they have recognized the importance of education and research, and have invested strategically in fields of learning that most directly benefit their national interests.

In his subsequent book, co-authored with Mandelbaum, *That Used to Be Us*, Friedman's (2011) analytical gaze shifts to the USA. He insists that the USA will inevitably fall behind Asian economies unless it fully understands the challenges and opportunities of globalization in ways that countries in East Asia in particular have. He argues that the end of the Cold War has blinded the USA to the need to take issues of cultural and institutional reform more seriously. Its global position, he argues, cannot endure without the renewal of its institutions, which he regards as the major historical sources of its prosperity and strength. In both of his books, Friedman thus addresses the centrality of the modern university in America's dominance. He argues that American universities have become remarkably conservative, take few risks, and offer a largely homogenous product to their audience. In this sense, he views with alarm America's declining educational system and culture of learning, which he is convinced are the major drivers of the rise of Asian economies.

Across the Atlantic, another influential journalist, Martin Jacques (2009), also points to the Asian culture of learning in his attempts to explain the rise of Asia. In his provocatively titled book, *When China Rules the World*, Jacques shows how China has closed the gap with the world's most developed economies faster than anticipated. Indeed it is now the world's second largest economy, and its rates of growth do not show any sign of decline. Its rapid emergence is changing the world in many ways, from its diplomatic alliances in Africa to the globally rising status of its currency. According to Jacques, within two decades, not only will China displace the USA as the most important economic power, it might also marginalize the "West" in history and require us all to reimagine what it means to be modern. This bold claim rests on Jacques's assumption that nothing will derail the political stability and economic dynamism that China enjoys today. This assumption rests on Jacques's reading of Chinese culture. He regards China to be a civilization state, rooted in unbending norms of Confucianism. Although China may display many signs of embracing Western modernity, Jacques insists that its recent success is due to its commitment to Confucian principles that include respect for authority, hard work, and a constellation of responsibilities to preserve the unity of the Chinese state. In this narrative, education plays a major role, developing citizens who are culturally confident and globally strategic.

Australian accounts of the rise of Asia have similarly underlined the importance of education and culture in the economic rise of Asia. For example, in his book, *There Goes the Neighborhood*, Michael Wesley (2011) has argued that the Confucian philosophy of society, based on the principles of order and stability, as well as deference to superiors, stretches across most of East Asia, Vietnam, and Singapore; and at least partially explains the ways in which these countries now engage with global forces, taking advantage of both the discipline predicated on social hierarchies and the freedom provided by global markets. The social discipline found in most Asian societies has become a source of their strength and of the aspirations they have to return to the position of global prominence they once enjoyed. For the fast-growing Asian middle class, education is a vehicle for realizing their individual and collective aspirations. This is a cultural approach to education, which views it not only as an investment in economic outcomes but also as a collective good, necessary for civilizational advancement.

Anxieties and Ambivalence

While these "Western" accounts of the rise of Asia, found in both popular and academic writings, differ in many respects, what is perhaps most striking are some of the assumptions they share. The discursive framework within which these analyses are located points uniformly to a language of anxiety. For example, Peerenboom (2008, 2) contrasts two different views of China that exist today. On the one hand, China is viewed as "a rising superpower predicted to have the largest economy in the world by mid-century," on the other hand, and perhaps more widely, it is assumed to be "a brutal, anachronistic and authoritarian regime, a threat to geo-stability and to the economies of the industrial world." The rise of China, according to MacDonald and Lemco (2011) is "a wake-up call to the West," "a fierce competitor to western interests" – set on a path to "economic and political ascendancy." Simpfendorfer (2014) suggests that the various factors, from politics to economics to demographics, which affect Asia now will continue to do so in the future, causing the decline of the West. The rise of the new East is thus interpreted as a "powerfully disruptive force" that is likely to have "unexpected economic, political, and social outcomes."

Theoretical resources provided by postcolonialism are helpful in understanding this sense of anxiety (O'Riley 2007). A fundamental tenet of postcolonial theory is that anxiety lies at the heart of the colonial project. Historically, postcolonialism suggests, the exercise of colonial power was never entirely confident about its own normative practices, and was always anxious about the political agency of the colonial subject, and its capacity to resist and undermine colonial authority. While colonial discourses of Asia involved various stereotypes, such as timeless, strange, exotic, feminine, morally inferior, degenerate, tricky and untrustworthy, they equally acknowledged the capacity of Asians for hard work, discipline, and strategic intelligence. Ironically, it is these latter attributes that led colonial powers to be fearful of Asians, to view them as competitors, capable of undermining Western interests and ways of life. Indeed, it is this assumption that, for more than a century, led countries such as the USA and Australia to regard Asian migration as a major source of disruption to their civilizational authority – "an enemy within."

Tchen and Yeats (2014) have compiled a great deal of historical and contemporary material to demonstrate the diverse ways in which this anxiety of the possibilities of the Asian ascendency is expressed. The notion of the "yellow peril," they argue, is one of the oldest and most pervasive ideas in the Western tradition of speaking about Asians – dating back to the birth of European colonialism during the Enlightenment. Yellow "perilism," they insist,

> …is neither misinformation nor the figment of an overactive imagination. It is a structured tradition of concepts and practices hard-wired into the political culture of Western enlightenment modernity itself. Globalized especially by British and Anglo American expansionism, its patterning is a relational and recurrent process of identity formation and disidentification. (Tchen and Yeats 2014, 357)

So embedded is the idea of the yellow peril in the Western "social imaginary" (Taylor 2004) that it is hard to dislodge, even as economic and political conditions change. This is so because it constitutes a framework of ideas, practices, and institutions that are at once descriptive and prescriptive of how things work and ought to be. It is based on a widely held sense of legitimacy, without which it might not be possible for people to work collectively toward common goals. Just the same, its forms are not constant across time and space: its articulations change in response to emerging historical and political conditions, as communities seek to develop new ways of relating to others in order to meet their shifting strategic objectives.

So, in the contemporary era, while some of the crude representations of "yellow perilism" are no longer tolerated, and attempts are made to revise some of the orientalist (Said 1983) constructs of Asia, frequently turning "on what is undoubtedly a well-intended desire to relate to the other," the dominant discourses of the rise of Asia in the West continue to be broadly filtered through a social imaginary that assumes Asians to be socially distant, as well as unreliable and capricious competitors. Invariably, while most accounts of the rise of Asian economies recognize Asians to be culturally and politically confident, and suggest that the abundant economic opportunities in Asia demand new ways of imagining Asia, they remain trapped within colonial constructions. The colonial history of the Western conquests of Asian lands and cultures continues to haunt the current efforts to forge new equal and symmetrical encounters. This is so because a fundamental binary between the "West" and its Asian others continues to be the ghost that refuses to be exorcised.

Despite almost three decades of scholarship in postcolonial studies (see, for example, Loomba 2005), which has problematized such constructions, the binary between "us" and "them" persists, no longer framed in biological terms, but in terms that regard Asians as culturally mysterious and economically distrustful. Such a view of Asia rests on a deep ambivalence. According to Homi Bhabha (1994), the colonial discourse traded on an indeterminacy that treated the other as an object both of desire as well as derision. It encouraged both colonizers and colonized to regard one another in ways that were ambiguous. The colonizer often treated the colonized as both inferior and exotic, while the colonized regarded the colonizer as both enviable yet corrupt. Bhabha argues that colonial power carefully established highly sophisticated strategies of control and dominance; that, while it was aware of its transient nature, it was always anxious to create the means that guaranteed its economic, political, and cultural endurance.

In Bhabha's theory, ambivalence disrupts the authority of colonial domination, because it disturbs the relationship between the colonizer and the colonized. Bhabha suggests that, while the colonial relationship is always ambivalent, it contains sources of its own destruction. Since the colonized do not lack political agency, the colonizer needs to develop strategies to contain and control. As a consequence, forms of ambivalence are themselves dynamic and always emergent. In the postcolonial era, ambivalence thus often remains inherent in attempts to transcend colonial discourses. In what follows, I want to show how this is so in Australian policy attempts to develop new ways of responding to the rise of Asian higher education. I argue that the colonial discourses once produced around the exercise of colonial power have not entirely "self-destructed," as Bhabha suggests, but have become residualized in the contemporary characterizations of cultural difference. To meet the requirements of the changing historical conditions, new discourses of Asia have been created, though not in a conceptual vacuum; rather they are set against the backdrop of the continuing use of colonial ideas. In this sense, the contemporary ambivalent discourses of Asia contain both elements of colonial understanding, as well as conceptual constructions that recognize the realities of Asia rising, and opportunities associated with it.

Asia Literacy

In recent decades, Australia has developed a range of policy initiatives in higher education to engage with Asia. Many of these initiatives have been couched in the symbolic language of Asia literacy – the notion that all Australian students should develop deeper understanding of Asian languages and cultures. Since the mid-1980s, a large number of policies and programs in Australia have highlighted the importance of Asia literacy in schools and universities alike. Stephen Fitzgerald (1988), who first coined the term, argued that knowledge of Asia was essential for Australians to operate successfully in the global economy, since it "will not help our performance just at the margins. It will be central to our ability to perform" (Fitzgerald 1988, 12). In 1989, the Garnaut Report (Garnaut 1989) suggested that as North East Asia becomes "ascendant," Australians need to better understand the linguistic and cultural diversity of the region, and develop new forms of cultural sensibilities that enable them to communicate with Asians more effectively. Five years later, the Rudd Report (Rudd 1994) developed a comprehensive strategy for the teaching of Asian languages, in line with a growing political consensus in Australia that an understanding of Asian societies was fundamental to the enhancement of Australia's economic interests.

More recently, the Melbourne Declaration on Educational Goals for Young Australians – perhaps the key authoritative policy statement on educational values in Australia – declares that "Australians need to become 'Asia literate', engaging and building strong relationships with Asia" (MEECDYA 2008, 4). The Australian curriculum (ACARA 2012) has identified "Asia literacy and Australia's engagement with Asia" as one of its three cross-curricular priorities, suggesting that "an understanding of Asia underpins the capacity of Australian students to be active and informed citizens working together to build harmonious local, regional and global communities, and build Australia's social, intellectual and creative capital." Institutions of higher education have largely accepted this logic, and have taken measures to promote the teaching of Asian languages and cultures (Walker and Sobocinska 2012).

This discursive construction of Asia–Australia relations has been further reinforced in the recent White Paper, "Australia in the Asian Century" (Australian Government 2012), with the underlying premise that the 21st century will be an "Asian Century." The report suggests that by the middle of the century, the Asian region will account for over half of the global output; and that a fast-growing middle class in Asia will largely drive the global economy. It emphasizes the contribution that higher education will need to make to help Australians navigate the Asian Century – a period of transformative economic, political, strategic, and social change.

What is common to these reports is that they uniformly couch their understanding of Asia literacy within a broader instrumentalist logic – a conviction that Australia's integration into Asia is essential for its national prosperity, as well as for its social and economic vibrancy and its security. The recent White Paper, for example, does not depart in any significant ways from the Garnaut and Rudd Reports, insisting that Asia literacy is much more than language fluency, and should involve initiatives that "encourage effective engagement with Asia, deepen interpersonal relationships, augment Australia's security strategy and capitalize on the economic potential of the Asian Century" (Australian Government 2012, 11). Repeatedly, the White Paper asserts its belief that the growing middle class in Asia has created enormous commercial opportunities for Australia; and for Australia to take advantage of these opportunities, it needs to develop appropriate economic policy settings, with respect not only to trade and taxation, but also education, skills formation, and migration.

In a sense, this line of argument about the importance of Asia to Australia's future appears quite respectful of Asian cultural traditions. The White Paper is full of admiration for what many Asian countries have been able to achieve in a short period of time. Also recognized is the plurality and cultural dynamism of Asian societies. While these are clearly new elements in Australian representations of Asia, older colonial assumptions have not entirely faded away. The new discourse is ambivalent, and arguably still located within a fundamental binary between Australians and their Asian others. While postcolonial theorists, such as Loomba (2005), have problematized such constructions, the dualism dividing "us" from "them" persists, encouraging Asia to be viewed instrumentally – as means to *our* ends. As I have argued elsewhere (Rizvi 2013), this instrumentalism "necessarily invokes conceptions of the Asian 'others' whose cultures must be understood, whose languages must be learnt, and with whom closer relationships must be developed – in order for us to realize *our* economic and strategic purposes" (Rizvi 2013, 80, original emphasis).

Student Mobility

The White Paper, "Australia in the Asian Century" (Australian Government 2012) was commissioned by the Australian Labor government, which lost office in late 2013. Some educationists committed to the idea of Asia literacy feared that the new

Conservative government might abandon this policy focus. However, this was never likely, because to abandon the focus on Asia would have involved denying certain fundamental facts about Australia's geography, its shifting demographic composition, and its economic future. It would have implied a rejection of recent attempts to finally abandon the nation's historically embedded Euro-centric imaginary of itself. Indeed this is how it turned out, with the new government reaffirming its commitment to learning about Asia in Australian universities, not so much through its curricular priorities, but through its commitment to encourage more Australian students to participate in mobility programs – to spend up to one year studying in an Asian country, or undertaking internships, mentorships, practicums, and research.

The Australian government regards its "New Colombo Plan" as its signature initiative in promoting a broader understanding of Asia. The New Colombo Plan (NCP) is essentially a scholarship program, which in 2014 is supporting around 1300 undergraduate students and 40 scholarship holders to study in four pilot locations – Indonesia, Japan, Singapore, and Hong Kong. The government's policy rhetoric around NCP is largely predicable. It suggests that NCP is intended to be "transformational, deepening Australia's relationships in the region, both at the individual level and through expanding university, business and other stakeholder links." Its website asserts that "over time, the Australian Government wants to see study in the Indo-Pacific region become a rite of passage for Australian undergraduate students, and as an endeavour that is highly valued across the Australian community." It imagines NCP will forge closer partnerships between governments, universities, and business across the region, enabling Australians to derive maximum social and economic benefits from the opportunities now available in Asia.

While NCP's approach toward learning about Asia is somewhat different, the assumptions upon which it is based are broadly similar to the Labor government's policy priorities as articulated in the White Paper. So, for example, investment in NCP is largely driven by an economic instrumentalism which is linked to Australia's interest in developing a system of higher education that enhances the nation's economic competitiveness within the region by enabling its students to have lived experiences of the cultures of the countries with whom Australians will continue to trade. Effective engagement with Asia, through interpersonal relationships, is considered to be a way of augmenting Australia's security interests and capitalizing on the economic potential of rising Asia. Cynically, perhaps, NCP may also be viewed as consolidating Australia's position within the global market in higher education, countering the widely held perceptions that Australian universities have an asymmetrical relation with full-fee paying international students from Asia on their campuses. The name "New Colombo Plan" is itself suggestive of a new era in Asia–Australia relations. The old Colombo Plan provided students from poorer Asian countries educational aid in order to attend Australian universities to acquire the knowledge and skills they needed to meet the development needs of their countries (Oakman 2004). In contrast, NCP reverses this logic, and is designed to help Australian students go to universities in Asia in order to learn about Asian languages and cultures. It is not an overseas aid program, but may be seen as an exercise in Australia's public diplomacy in the region.

It appears abundantly clear that, like the previous Labor government's focus on Asia literacy, the policy objectives of NCP continue to rest on a binary between

Australia and its Asian others. It is assumed that Asian cultures must be understood in order to manage relationships across two fundamentally different worldviews. In this way, the policy objectives of NCP, no less than the White Paper, presuppose a crude social distance between the Australian "us" and the Asian "them." This sharp distinction in cultural traditions rests on a belief that Australia is a "Western country," differentiated from Asia by history, language, culture, and tradition, and perhaps also religion. It perpetuates the broader East–West dichotomy that has been promoted by authors such as Samuel Huntington (1996). The main problem with such a dichotomy is that it frames cross-cultural links and intercultural relations from the position of radical ontological difference, rather than through differences that are produced historically and politically across shifting relations of power. It fails to acknowledge, for example, that most social practices and institutions in Asia have been shaped by the colonial experience, but rearticulated through aspirations of national development and the operations of global capitalism.

Research Collaboration

A third set of policy responses in Australia to the rise of Asian higher education involves government support of Australian universities to forge closer links with leading Asian universities in research collaborations. Of course, individual collaborations among scholars across national borders have always existed, but most of these links have in the past been between Australian researchers and researchers in the USA and Europe. Australia is now encouraging research links with the fast-growing and well-resourced universities in Asia. Australian foreign policy has begun to pay more attention to the strategic significance of research collaborations for a whole variety of reasons, from improving mutual understanding, to sharing resources to address common problems, to developing strategic advantages over competing powers. It is argued that Australia is part of a dynamic region for research investment and output, and that therefore Australia's research engagement with regional universities needs to be strengthened. The expectation is that regional research engagement will attract increased levels of foreign research investment especially in those areas in which Asian economies have become dominant.

Through programs such as Australia-China Science and Research Fund and Australia-India Strategic Research Fund, successive Australian governments have sought to help Australian researchers to participate in cutting edge scientific projects and workshops with Chinese and Indian scientists, respectively. The policy focus of these programs has been on the development of strategic alliances between Australian and Asian researchers, not only at individual, but also institutional levels. And indeed they have enabled researchers to access expertise, equipment, datasets, research subjects, or sites that are not easily accessed in other ways. They have also helped provide research training, attract international funding streams, and develop regional networks of scholars. These programs have also created conditions for joint publication of scholarly papers, with the potential to enhance the global reputation both for an institution's positioning in global ranking schemes and for its capacity to attract high-quality faculty and students. More broadly, research collaborations have the potential for intellectual communities to build trust, helping to develop common understanding of critical issues through the collection of mutually beneficial information and insights.

While Australia's commitment to develop research links with Asian universities – for reasons both principled and instrumental – cannot be doubted, its symbolic and financial investments have only generated marginal benefits. Many of the links developed with Chinese and Indian researchers, for example, have involved diasporic networks, while the number of collaborations with American and British researchers continues to significantly outnumber links with Asian universities. According to the data produced by the National Science Foundation (2013), while the number of co-authored papers between Chinese and Australian scholars has grown in the past decade, this represents less than half of papers between Australian and American researchers. Australian scientists continue to show a marked preference for working with American and British scholars. Of course, the challenges faced in establishing effective and sustainable research links with Asian universities are considerable. These range from lack of clarity around policies and rules governing the operation of universities across national borders, differences in academic cultures and practices, contentions around distribution of resources and ownership of intellectual property, uneven support from institutional and national leadership, and different perceptions about the benefits of collaborations and conditions of their sustainability.

Beyond these practical problems, there are deeper historical reasons why research collaborations between Australian and Asian universities are hard to establish and sustain. In a project completed for Australia India Education Council, Rizvi *et al.* (2013) found the colonial history and the history of Australian policies toward Asia continue to lead some Indian universities to fear the possibilities of neo-colonial exploitation. Some university leaders view approaches by Australian universities to collaborate suspiciously, assuming asymmetry of knowledge and power. Others feel that mutual trust and respect required in nurturing of effective relationships take a longer period to nurture than is possible in the eagerness of Australian researchers for "quick outcomes."

Miscommunication, lack of attention to cultural nuances, differences in the pace of work, and conflicting expectations often undermine what might otherwise be highly productive collaborations. According to a senior researcher in India, "the Australians came to us with a whole lot of stereotypes about India and Indians, and even a larger bunch of expectations." His colleagues believed that the Australians had assumed a position of cultural superiority and had perceptions of Indian research practices that were both outdated and woefully patronizing. Of course, this Indian example may not apply to most other successful attempts at forging research collaborations with Asian universities, but it does suggests how the social imaginary of Asia as culturally alien is much more persistent that many Australian policy-makers are prepared to admit.

Discussion and Conclusion

What is clear from this discussion is that the three major policy initiatives pursued by Australia to respond to the rise of Asian higher education have produced significant gains. It needs to be noted, however, that such initiatives are not unique to Australia. North American and European countries have made similar efforts, even if their policy initiatives in higher education have not been as robust and systematic. The rise of Asian universities has produced anxiety in most Western countries with established systems of higher education, demanding policy responses. One such response is the European Union-Asia Higher Education Platform (EAHEP), created by the EU to promote cooperation in higher education between Asian and European countries through sharing of information on higher education systems in Europe and Asia, study and research opportunities, cooperation projects and initiatives, events, and funding schemes. Similarly, US-based Asia Society has encouraged deeper USA–Asia connections in higher education by holding a number of conferences and promoting the study of Asian cultures and languages in American universities.

Of course, these policy initiatives should be welcomed, since in an increasingly globalized system of higher education Asian universities are likely to play a major role. However, the discussion in this chapter has suggested that policy approaches adopted by Australia and other Western countries are deeply ambivalent, born out of a history of colonial conquest that now seeks to establish educational relations that are predicated on a more symmetrical set of power relations. This is a most challenging task, because policy-makers across Australia, the USA, and Europe find it difficult to escape the instrumentalist logic within which Australian initiatives such as Asia literacy and NCP are embedded. The need to learn Asian languages and cultures in Australia appears predicated on the belief that this is necessary in order to realize the nation's strategic and economic interests. Of course, there is always an element of instrumentalism in most social relations. However, against the historical backdrop of colonial encounters, instrumentalist ways of articulating policy responses to the rise of Asia involve considerable risks of misinterpretation.

This possibility is further reinforced by the historical legacy of the East–West binary within the framework of which Asia is often imagined, as socially and culturally alien. The persistence of theories such as Huntington's "clash of civilizations" does not help, because they view the basic source of conflict across regions of the world to be cultural rather than economic or political. Such theories encourage the rise of Asia to be explained in terms of an ontological contrast; for example, between Confucian values and liberal, Western, democratic, individualistic, capitalist values, rather than as differences that have have never been absolute, and are often grounded in specific political conflicts. The rise of Asian higher education is often assumed to be sourced in a set of values that supposedly does not bear much resemblance to Western moral precepts. It is assumed, for example, that the so-called Asian values, such as an emphasis on social stability and continuity, a belief in discipline and hard work, an acceptance of social order and authority, a commitment to traditional values, and a prioritization of obligations ahead of rights can readily explain the rapid rise of Asian universities.

Of course, there are major cultural differences within and across societies, both Eastern and Western, but, as Chen (2012) has pointed out, this is a contrast between an *imagined* East and an *imagined* West. Theoretically, the East–West binary encourages cultures to be named as homogenous and monolithic structures in ways that elide specific considerations of cultural, historical, and economic exchange. It risks static representations of Asian societies, potentially overlooking the vast differences that exist within and across regional, religious, gender, and political divides. And it ignores the level of intercultural contact between various regions of the world that has taken place over centuries. In the end, the talk of core Eastern and Western traditions masks the irrefutable fact that all cultures are dynamic, changing through their engagement with other cultures, resulting in the development of new hybridized cultural forms.

In an era of globalization, the East–West binary has become increasingly hard to justify for a number of reasons. Increased global mobility and cultural exchange have made differentiation across absolute cultural categories hard to sustain. The new media and communication technologies have enabled ongoing connections across national and cultural boundaries, recasting any real distinction between "here" and "there," resulting in major shifts in people's sense of identity and belonging. The contemporary processes of globalization have potentially transnationalized the spaces in which an increasing proportion of us now live and work (Rizvi 2011). Global flows of ideas, capital, and people have created conditions in which fluid and hybrid cultural forms have become ubiquitous. Without an understanding of these new forms, the recent rise of Asian higher education cannot be adequately understood, reducing the possibilities of forging effective modes of engagement.

In most Western countries, people now recognize the new Asia to be culturally dynamic, and changing rapidly; but have yet to develop a more dynamic understanding of intercultural relations. The East–West binary is now hard to justify because it rests on a dated conception of how economic, political, and cultural relations across cultural and national borders work. With the various new requirements of transnational cooperation and collaboration, while the policy responses to the rise of Asian higher education, such as Asia literacy, NCP, and research collaboration are apt enough, they need to be interpreted against the history of colonial encounters, in order to transcend such unhelpful constructions as the East–West binary within the framework of which even the most well intentioned of policy proposals are couched (Rizvi 2012).

A historically informed approach to engagement with Asia must acknowledge that all societies are at least in part shaped by diverse and uneven experiences of colonialism, which have positioned them differently (Spivak 2007). While the importance of colonial legacies in the constitution of contemporary social institutions, such as higher education, has often been overlooked in the past, in a politically confident Asia, it is not possible to overlook the "new" or "emergent" forms of cultural practices, which are simultaneously a product of cherished local traditions, colonial relations of power, and transnational cultural exchange alike. If this is so then, as Chen (2010, 255) has pointed out, policy approaches to Asia demand open-ended imagination and dialogue that involve a critical examination of the emerging contours of global interconnectivity and interdependence, and their implications for questions of identity and culture. We need to understand how our practices of the representations of the "other" reflect particular relations of power, and how this understanding is necessary to develop relations that transcend instrumentalism and are informed instead by a moral discourse that views Asian cultures in their own terms and not simply as a means to our economic and strategic ends.

References

ACARA (Australian Curriculum and Reporting Authority). 2012. *The Australian Curriculum.* Canberra: ACARA.

ADB (Asian Development Bank). 2011. *Higher Education across Asia: Issues and Strategies.* Manila: ADB.

Australian Government. 2012. *Australia in the Asian Century* (White Paper). Canberra: Commonwealth Government of Australia.
Ball, S. 2012. *Global Education Inc.: New Policy Networks and the Neoliberal Imaginary.* London: Routledge.
Bhabha, H. 1994. *The Location of Culture.* London: Routledge.
Bhagwati, J. 2007. *In Defense of Globalization.* Oxford: Oxford University Press.
Chapman, D and C.L. Chien (2014) "Expanding Out and Up: What are the System level Dynamics in Malaysia and Thailand," in *Higher Education in Asia: Expanding Out, Expanding Up*, UNESCO Institute of Statistics. Montreal: UNESCO Institute of Statistics.
Chen, K.H. 2010. *Asia as Method: Towards Deimperialization.* Durham: Duke University Press.
Fitzgerald, S. 1988. *Towards an Asia-Literate Society.* Melbourne: Asian Studies Association of Australia.
Friedman, T. 2007. *The World is Flat: A Brief History of the 21st Century.* New York: Farrer, Straus & Giroux.
Friedman, T. and M. Mandelbaum. 2011. *That Used to be Us: How America Fell Behind in the World It Invented and How We can Come Back.* New York: Picador.
Garnaut, J. 1989. *Australia and the Northeast Asian Ascendancy.* Canberra: Australian Government Printing Service.
Huntington, S. 1994. *Clash of Civilizations and the Remaking of the World Order.* New York: Simon and Schuster.
Jacques, M. 2009. *When China Rules the World: The End of the Western World and the Birth of a New World Order.* New York: Penguin.
Jensen, B. 2012. *Catching Up: Learning from the Best School Systems in East Asia.* Melbourne: Grattan Institute.
Levin, R. 2011. "Top of the Class; The Rise of Asia's Universities." *Foreign Affairs*, May–June.
Loomba, A. 2005. *Colonial/Postcolonial.* London: Routledge.
MacDonald, S. and J. Lemco. 2011. *Asia's Rise in the 21st Century.* New York: Praeger.
Mahbubani, K. 2013. *Great Convergence: Asia, the West and the Logic of One World.* New York: Perseus Press.
Marginson, S. 2011. "Higher Education in East Asia and Singapore: Rise of the Confucian Model." *Higher Education*, 61(5): 587–611.
Marginson, S. 2014. "University Rankings and Social Science." *European Journal of Education*, 49(1): 45–59.
Misra, P. 2012. *From the Ruins of Empire: The Revolt Against the West and the Remaking of Asia.* London: Picador.
Ministerial Council on Education, Employment, Training and Youth Affairs (MCEETYA) 2008. *The Melbourne Declaration on Educational Goals for Young Australians.* Canberra: MCEETYA.
National Science Foundation. 2013. *Catalyzing New International Collaborations.* Retrieved from: https://www.nsf.gov/funding/pgm_summ.jsp?pims_id=12815 (accessed December 1, 2015).
Oakman, D. 2004. *Facing Asia: A History of the Colombo Plan.* Canberra: ANU Press.
O'Riley, M.F. (2007) "Postcolonial Haunting: Anxiety Affect and the Situated Encounter." *Postcolonial Text*, 3(4): 35–49.
Peerenboom, R. 2008. *China Modernizes: Threat to the West or the Model for the Rest.* London: Oxford University Press.
Planning Commission of India. 2012. *12th Five Year Plan (2012–2017).* New Delhi: Planning Commission of India.
Prasad, D. 2011. "The Rise of International Schools in India." *International Journal of Education, Economics and Development*, 4(2): 190–201.
Rizvi, F. 2011. "Mobilities and the Transnationalization of Youth Cultures," *Keywords in Youth Studies*, edited by N. Lesko and D. Tarbut. New York; London: Routledge.

Rizvi, F. 2012. "Engaging the Asian Century." *Access: Critical Perspectives on Communication, Cultural and Policy Studies*, 31(1): 73–80.

Rizvi, F. 2013. "Asia Literacy and Beyond." *Curriculum Perspectives*, 33(3): 80–82.

Rizvi, F., R. Gorur, and C. Reyes. 2013. *India-Australia Institutional Collaborations in Higher Education: Potential, Problems and Promises*. Canberra: Australia India Education Council.

Rudd, K. 1994. *Asian Languages and Australia's Economic Future*. Brisbane: Queensland Government Printer.

Said, E. 1979. *Orientalism*. London: Penguin Press.

Sellar, S. and B. Lingard. 2013. "Looking East: Shanghai, PISA 2009 and the Reconstitution of Reference Societies in the Global Education Policy Field." *Comparative Education*, 49(4): 464–485.

Spivak, G. 2007. *Other Asias*. London: Wiley-Blackwell.

Simpfendorfer, B. 2014. *The Rise of the New East: Business Strategies for Success in a World of Increased Complexity*. London: Palgrave MacMillan.

Tan, C. 2012. *Learning from Shanghai: Lessons in Achieving Educational Success*. Amsterdam: Springer.

Taylor, C. (2004) *Modern Social Imaginaries*, Durham: Duke University Press.

Tchen, J and D. Yeats (eds). 2014. *Yellow Peril: An Archive of Anti-Asian Fear*. London: Verso.

UIS (UNESCO Institute of Statistics) (2013) "Higher Education." Retrieved from: www.uis.unesco.org/Education/Pages/tertiary-education.aspx (accessed November 24, 2015).

UNESCO (2014) *Higher Education in Asia: Expanding Out, Expanding Up*. Montreal: UNESCO Institute of Statistics.

Walker, D. and A. Sobocinska (eds). 2012. *Australia's Asia: From Yellow Peril to Asian Century*. Perth: University of Western Australia Press.

Wesley, M. 2011. *There Goes the Neighborhood: Australia and Rise of Asia*. Sydney: Allen and Unwin.

Chapter 30

Joined-up Policy: Network Connectivity and Global Education Governance

Carolina Junemann, Stephen J. Ball, and Diego Santori

Introduction

Building on previous work on policy networks and the analysis of global policy communities (Ball 2012; Ball and Junemann 2012), in this chapter we want to think further about how global policy networks work. We focus on network relationships or more generally connectivity; that is, on what connects the nodes in a policy network and what is connected – what flows through the network. We are interested in understanding, first, what is the substantive tissue that both joins up and provides some durability to these mostly distant and fleeting forms of social interaction both in a socioeconomic sense and a discursive sense? Second, and relatedly, we want to think about network animation and network building or in other words the *work* of networking.

To do this, we are going to focus on a set of organizations and actors connected up around the issue of low cost private schooling in Africa and, more specifically, on Bridge International Academies, a for-profit Low Fee Private School (LFPS) chain in Kenya (see Figure 30.1).[1] Through the analysis of a policy network configured around a chain of LFPSs in sub-Saharan Africa, we explore some of the networking processes, relationships, and exchanges through which new policy ideas involving the advocacy and dissemination of private and social enterprise solutions to the "problems" of state education in developing countries, are disseminated and established, bringing new forms and modalities of governance into play. In this way, we hope that our analysis contributes to the understanding of some of the new "microspaces" in which global education policy is currently being made, beyond the national state, by new actors and organizations. We begin by offering some of the conceptual and methodological starting points that underpin our work.

The Handbook of Global Education Policy, First Edition.
Edited by Karen Mundy, Andy Green, Bob Lingard, and Antoni Verger.
© 2016 John Wiley & Sons, Ltd. Published 2016 by John Wiley & Sons, Ltd.

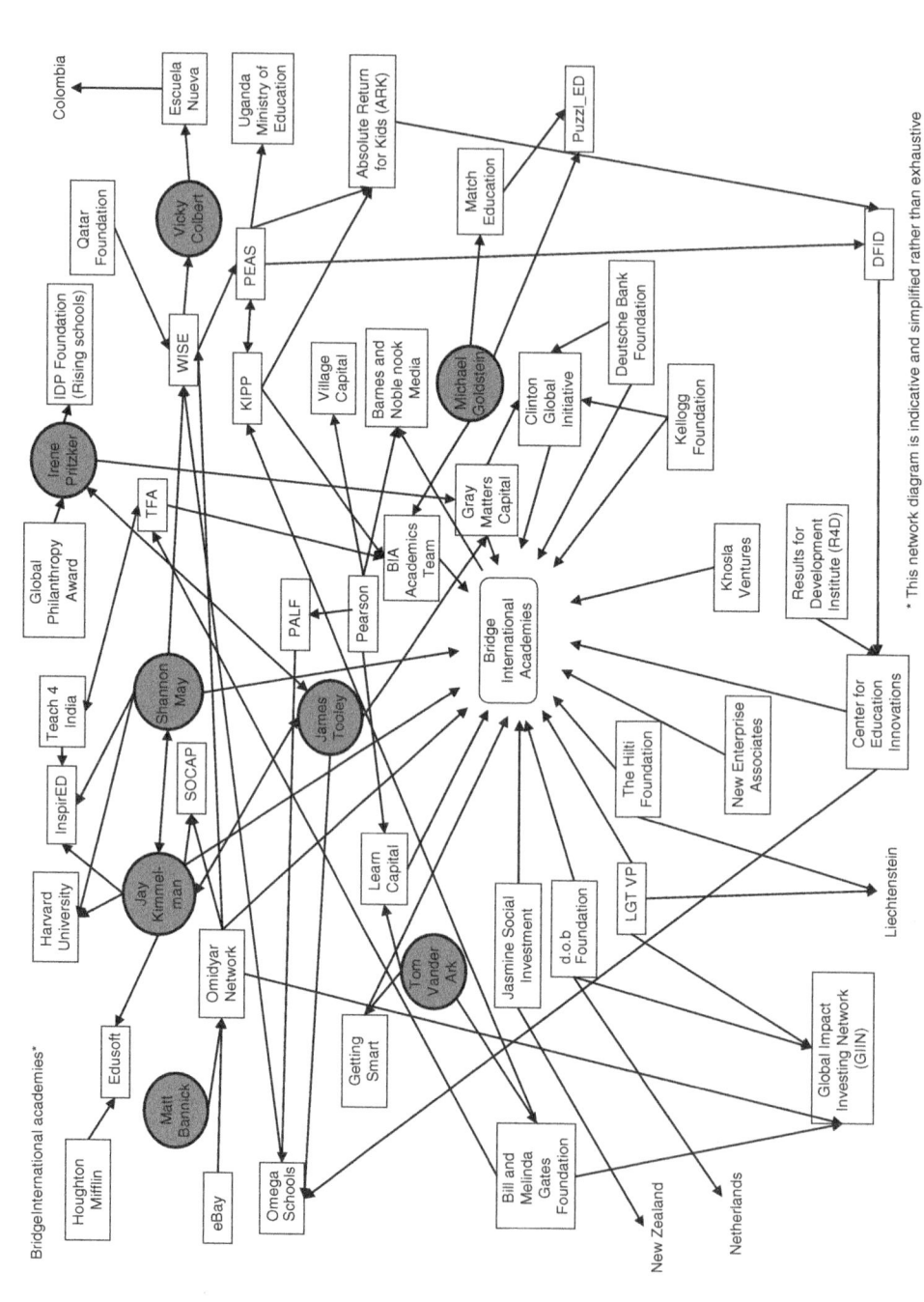

Figure 30.1 Network of organizations and actors connected around Bridge International Academies.

*This network diagram is indicative and simplified rather than exhaustive

Neo-liberal Policy Networks and Global Policy Communities

Much of the recent research on the global governance of education focuses on the "hegemonic influence of formal intergovernmental organizations ... as these directly influence domestic educational policies" (Mundy and Murphy 2001, 85) and how more recently the "legitimacy deficits that plagued UN and Bretton Woods organizations in the 1990s have propelled them to act more cooperatively than ever before" (Mundy 2010, 353). This has given rise to what Mundy (2010) called "mutually reinforcing forms of authority" around UN Education for All goals, whereby civil society coalitions and private sector actors have been increasingly significant players in national and global education policy arenas. As a result, Florini (2000) argues that "civil society's role in global governance is changing from that of gadfly to that of direct participant in the management of global issues" (Florini 2000, 236).

In this context, new partnerships between governments, and civil society and private sector organizations have increasingly been incorporated as a key governance mechanism in addressing entrenched problems of educational development, quality, and access (Draxler 2008). Robertson and Verger (2012) argue that education public–private partnerships (PPPs) have been brought in to address perceived inefficiencies in the delivery of public education and point out the significant role of international organizations and "policy entrepreneurs" (in particular, a group of "experts" within the World Bank, the Asian Development Bank, the International Finance Corporation, the Centre for British Teachers, and Harvard University) in advancing this agenda of governance by partnership. We have explored this in two recent books, one on new governance of education in England (Ball and Junemann 2012), and the other on global education policy networks (Ball 2012). However, in our analyses, we have extended our focus beyond partnerships and beyond the state and the role of multilateral agencies and non-governmental organizations (NGOs) to include the multifaceted and increasing participation of transnational edu-businesses (either as free-standing, competitive, commercial activities or through the outsourcing of state services) and philanthropies in processes of policy. Both in the UK and overseas, private providers are now involved at different levels and on different scales, through advice, consultation, evaluation, philanthropy, partnerships, representation, program delivery, and outsourcing, in the provision, monitoring, and evaluation of public sector services. As we have argued, these new forms of private sector and philanthropic participation in public sector education, and the concomitant new forms of public sector organization, have brought new players, voices, values, and discourses into policy conversations. These new forms constitute what in political science is called "network governance" or governance by networks – that is, "webs of stable and ongoing relationships which mobilize dispersed resources towards the solution of policy problems" (Pal 1997). They are indicative of the increasing complexity of government and at the same time the process that Jessop (2002, 199) calls "destatization," which involves "re-drawing the public-private divide, reallocating tasks, and rearticulating the relationships between organizations and tasks across this divide."

Alongside and as part of these changes, global education policy communities are being reconstituted and are evolving, and new policy discourses and narratives are flowing through them. These new global policy networks, integrated by a diverse set of think tanks, consultants, multi-lateral agencies, donors, education businesses, and philanthropies, constitute policy communities that are based upon shared conceptions of social problems and their solutions. They give space to new voices within policy talk that instill new sensibilities and values, and new forms of social relations associated with neo-liberalism (see Ball 2012). New narratives about what counts as a "good" policy are articulated and validated (see Ball 2007). The "market" is portrayed as the almost ineluctable answer to social and economic problems and existing state solutions are problematized. For example, the establishment of PPPs as the privileged tool for increasing access to basic education in developing countries (a new common sense of "development"), has relied on the discursive construction of state failure (e.g. the main source of limited access and poor quality) accompanied by, as Robertson and Verger (2012) explain, a purposeful framing of causes and issues (failing state, lazy teachers, lack of incentives, lack of accountability, dysfunctional schools) and a selective use of evidence. They have been articulated by neo-liberal rationalities that link market mechanisms such as choice and fee payment to greater accountability and education quality (Watkins 2011) (a matter we pursue further below). Here, the private sector is the model to be emulated. These neo-liberal policy networks work both locally and globally through "policy entrepreneurship" and processes of policy transfer and convergence, by bringing privatizing and market-based ideas, relationships, and money to bear (see Ball 2012).

Researching Global Policy Networks

Education policy is therefore currently being done in new ways, in different places, by a diverse range of actors with varied forms of participation, relationships, and interests involving advocacy, business interests, and "new" forms of philanthropy (see below). The methods and practices of policy are changing along with these shifts and, thus, the way in which we do policy research has to change too, to enable us to analyze beyond the state and beyond the limits of the nation state, to address these global policy networks and the flows of policy within them. Thus, the primary task of policy community and network research is to identify and analyze the operation of these networks, as well as the connections that constitute them.

Provan and Kenis (2008) claim that despite the incredible volume of recent writing on network governance and policy networks, "there is still a considerable discrepancy between the acclamation and attention networks receive and the knowledge we have about the overall functioning of networks" (Provan and Kenis 2008, 229). Furthermore, Dicken et al. (2001, 89) emphasize the need for methodological approaches that can "identify actors in networks, their on-going relations and the structural outcomes of these relations." Our own research methods have been designed to address these limitations and expand the understanding of the form and functioning of education policy networks, of the connections between the participants that animate them and how they work to expand neoliberal sensibilities and practices. Our methods are based on what might be called "network ethnography" (Howard 2002); that is, a mapping of the form and content of policy relations in a particular field, a variation of what Bevir and Rhodes (2003) present as "ethnographic analyses of governance in action." It draws on a combination of internet search material, social media including Facebook, Twitter, and blogs, interviews with network participants, and attendance to network events.

Howard (2002, 550) points out that "whereas social network analysis renders an overarching sketch of interaction, it will fail to capture detail on incommensurate yet meaningful relationships." Thus, we focus our analysis on meanings and transactions rather than subjecting the networks to the more quantitative measures offered by social network analysis. Our aim is to pin down the content, nature, and meaning of the exchanges and transactions between network participants, the roles, actions, motivations, discourses, and resources of the different actors involved, and the extent of their influence on processes of policy.

The setting up of LFPS chains in developing societies by lone entrepreneurs, local businesses, and multinational education companies are all examples of the increasing involvement of non-state actors, in particular, of social enterprises and edu-businesses, in the delivery of educational services. These sorts of initiatives are significant both in terms of what happens in local schools as they interact directly with the local landscape of policy, and, increasingly, with national policy in the sense of contributing to Education for All policy goals or presenting themselves as alternatives to state schools. The LFPS sector is rapidly growing and highly heterogeneous (see Srivastava 2013) but research has tended to focus on individual village entrepreneurs who make up "the vast majority of these new private schools [which] are not the result of shareholders investing money in schools because they see that as the way to obtain the highest financial return" (Walford 2001, cited in Srivastava 2013, 12). However, chains of LFPSs like BIA are beginning to become significant players at the local level in some urban settings and are attracting financial "investment" from both business and business philanthropy (edu-businesses, venture capital, and venture philanthropists, see below). They also participate in new types of relationships (investment as opposed to contracting) and bring new sensibilities and rationalities into play that blur traditional distinctions between public, voluntary, philanthropic, and for-profit provision (as we shall see below).

Through the analysis of a network focused around LFPSs in Africa, in this chapter, we suggest that it is possible to think about global education policy networks both as forms of socioeconomic relationship, based on both affect and exchange, and as epistemic-discursive communities. The different connectivities involved (financial, discursive, facilitative, and social) are what make the flow of policy ideas, policy modalities, and policy technologies possible and contribute to the dissemination of "causal stories" (Stone 1989) and silver bullet solutions to entrenched policy problems. We want to indicate the variety of types of organizations involved in the setting up and development of our example; their global scope; their rationales and purposes; their modalities and aspirations; and their inter-relations.

Money and Meaning

BIA is a for-profit chain of low cost nursery and primary schools in Kenya. It was founded in 2009 by Jay Kimmelman (a Harvard Business School graduate and founder and one time CEO of Edusoft[2]), his wife Shannon May (another Harvard University graduate with a PhD in anthropology from the University of California, Berkeley), and Phil Frei (a Massachusetts Institute of Technology mechanical engineer, and ex-product designer at design consultancy IDEO). The company website claims that "Prior to Bridge International Academies, no one had put together a viable business model that demonstrated that educating the world's largest market was possible."

In 2008, the Clinton Global Initiative Annual Meeting produced a US$8 million commitment over two years, involving Deutsche Bank America's Foundation in partnership with New Globe Schools (which later became Bridge International Academies in Kenya, see below), Gray Ghost Ventures, and the Kellogg Foundation to fund emerging affordable private schools in Kenya and India, "developing scalable systems that will use new capital to strengthen local expertise to extend the reach of low-cost private schools to poor children in India and Kenya." (Stanfield 2010). BIA got off the ground the following year (2009), with a further $1.8 million investment from the Omidyar Network, which led its Series A investment round – and participated in second and third rounds of funding in 2010 and 2012 (Series B and C).

The Omidyar Network describes itself as a philanthropic investment firm. It was established in 2004 by billionaire eBay founder Pierre Omidyar and his wife Pam to "harness the power of markets to create opportunity for people to improve their lives" (company website). As of January 2013, the Omidyar Network has made impact investments in for-profit companies which are addressing social problems totaling $260 million. According to the Omidyar Network, BIA:

> Is an attractive investment opportunity to Omidyar Network because it is a compelling example of a high-impact, scalable, and entrepreneurial solution that addresses one of the most urgent demands of the developing word: low-cost access to quality education. Bridge demonstrates how for-profit innovation can drive social change by employing a unique business model that can be easily replicated in other emerging markets.[3]

Pearson, the world's largest edu-business, has also invested in BIA (see Ball 2012, 124–128). In 2012, Pearson launched the Pearson Affordable Learning Fund (PALF), "supporting mission-driven education entrepreneurs who deliver high quality, for-profit education solutions for the low-income segment in the developing world ... with a goal to help improve access to quality education for the poorest families in the world" (company website). The fund was created with $15 million of initial Pearson capital and made its first multi-million dollar investment in another LFPS chain, Omega Schools in Ghana. In 2010, before the creation of PALF, Pearson had already invested in the LFPS sector, leading BIA's Series B investment round, through the Learn Capital fund, an education venture capital firm that concentrates on education technology startups, in which Pearson is the biggest limited partner.[4] As indicated on the Pearson's website, "the Bridge schools are part of recent moves to expand its education business in Africa."[5] According to PALF, profit is not the only aim: the fund also aspires to "Demonstrate to governments and donors that low-cost private education can help educate the poor in a cost-effective way" (company website). This exemplifies what Bill Gates refers to as "creative capitalism" (as in Clinton Global Initiative Forum 2009), investments that address social challenges and result in sustainable business.

Up to 2011, BIA had raised a total of $15 million through two rounds of funding (A and B). Aside from the above-mentioned, the funders included a mix of foundations, venture philanthropists, and commercial capital investors. Venture capital firms like Spring Hill Equity Partners, interested in investing in businesses that provide both "double-digit financial returns" and "large scale measurable social benefit to low-income consumers, in addition to creating jobs and expanding the local tax base,"⁶ was one of the earlier BIA investors, with a pre-A-round commitment of an undisclosed sum. Further minority funders included LGT Venture Philanthropy, part of the LGT group of the Princely Family of Liechtenstein, which invests in "organizations that were coming up with scalable solutions to social and environmental challenges" (company website); The Hilti Foundation, a Liechtenstein-based charitable foundation that "embraces the integration of entrepreneurial initiatives that can be multiplied and that can offer measureable results" and "invests in projects that contribute to a basic and sustainable improvement of the living conditions of disadvantaged persons"[7]; Jasmine Social Investment, a New Zealand family foundation that made a US$700,000 equity investment in BIA between May 2009 and May 2010, and that invests in organizations that can create "lasting change through social enterprise" and "expect to see measurement of true impact"[8]; and d.o.b, a Dutch family private equity fund "that is aligned with the principles of impact investing and supports innovative private sector initiatives that enhance the quality of life of low income communities, families and people in Africa" (company website). Saskia van der Mast, an investment manager at d.o.b said in an interview that:

> We want to prove that it is possible to create income and valuable products and services for low-income people but, at the same time, that we also can get our money back and also do well financially. And prove to other more commercial players that, in our case Africa, is somewhere where you can make money and where it's valuable to invest in and attractive to invest in. (project interview)

BIA has more recently been able to attract the interest of two large US venture capital firms. New Enterprise Associates (NEA), one of the largest venture capital firms in the world with reportedly US$13 billion in committed capital, led its Series C investment round (closed in the first quarter of 2012), with a significant but undisclosed investment. Jon Sakoda, one of its partners, has indicated in a blog post that "a crisis in education is a terrible thing to waste,"[9] and Khosla Ventures, a California-based venture capital firm that is interested in investing in "large problems that are amenable to technology solutions" (company website).

In several respects BIA exemplifies the predominance of Philanthropy 3.0 (Resource Alliance 2011), impact or investment philanthropy and *philanthrocapitalism* (Brilliant et al. 2007) in the field of education and development; that is, the idea that philanthropy needs to start to resemble a capitalist economy in which benefactors become consumers of social investment, and which operates as for-profit markets with investors and social returns.[10] This in itself is an indication of the work of neo-liberal discourse and practices of "financialization" (Lazzarato 2009). BIA illustrates this blurring of distinctions between philanthropy and business, and profit and social purpose. Here "backers" are looking for both financial and social "returns." Philanthropies speak and act like businesses and businesses like philanthropic organizations. "The 'economic politics' of enterprise appears to know no boundaries, either in terms of where it might be applied" (du Gay 2004, 40) or to what. Business is taking on the moral responsibilities normally associated with the state.

Discursive Connections

As will be already apparent, companies like BIA and its international investors are part of a discursive community connected through a set of shared perspectives and discourses. These privilege the market form and profit incentives as the "one best way" of addressing the provision of universal basic education, raising the quality of education, and providing educational opportunities for the poor in developing societies, together with a critical common sense of state failure and the "dysfunctional" government school (that is unaccountable and lacks incentives to improve), etc. BIA describes itself in recruitment notices as "a for-profit company that deeply believes that financially sustainable solutions are the long-term answer to development in emerging countries."[11] The argument here is for "double bottom lines" or impact investment – investment that has a social as well as a financial return, combining profit and purpose, the idea of doing good by doing well. This in turn relates to a broader discursive ensemble that celebrates the role of enterprise and entrepreneurship. The figure of the hero entrepreneur is very evident on the websites and in the documents of BIA funders. For example:

> Omidyar will focus on high-impact entrepreneurs – those with proven business models and the ability to scale their operations to serve hundreds of thousands or millions of the world's poorest individuals – with the ultimate goal of fostering a more entrepreneurial culture and improving the quality of life for more than ten million people living in extreme poverty.[12]
>
> Pearson, the world's leading learning company, today announced a partnership with innovative funding firm Village Capital to support and invest in education entrepreneurs in India who are serving some of the world's less privileged students.[13]
>
> Village Capital explains: "At Village Capital, we create the space for entrepreneurs to work together across the boundaries of their organizations, to help lift one another's performance." (company website)

In the most straightforward sense, such statements rest upon and reproduce the tenets and methods of neo-liberalism, which Harvey (2005, 2) describes as "a theory of political economic practices that proposes that human well-being can best be advanced by liberating individual entrepreneurial freedoms and skills within an institutional framework characterized by strong private property rights, free markets and free trade." These tenets and methods, as a "standardized narrative" (Barnett 2010) are circulated and celebrated through formulations of policy (see below), by network nodes (brokers and incubators – like Village Capital, Sankalp, Skoll Forum, Clinton Global Initiative), at network events and in publications. They appear both as a political-economic rationality and more explicitly through examples and as "success stories" (McCann 2004).

BIA is increasingly cited as a model of good practice in developing LFPSs (see, for example, Harvard Business School case study, Rangan and Lee 2013; and E.G. West Centre, EFA Working Paper No. 10) exemplifying innovative "inclusive" business models that are "transforming education around the world" (defined as "sustainable organizations that increase access to goods and services in low income communities, while at the same time providing them with new sources of revenue and employment" (Stansfield 2013). Furthermore, BIA's founders speak frequently at international events about their schools and the performance of their students. Only recently, Shannon May was a speaker at the Qatar Foundation's World Innovation Summit Education (WISE) 2013 in Doha, an event described by the President of the Institute of International Education, A. Goodman, as "the Davos of Education" and which convenes international leaders to explore innovative solutions to the world's major educational challenges. Both Shannon May and Jay Kimmelman spoke at Teach for India's annual conference InspirED 2013–2014 (November 30–December 1, Hyderabad), one of India's biggest education-based conferences. These are opportunities to rehearse rationalities, critiques, and causal stories – sharing and dissemination of policy discourse.

These shared discourses and values are reproduced, reiterated, and performed in some forums and events where the networks come together. Events like the annual Social Capital Markets (SOCAP) conference, which is "dedicated to accelerating a new global market at the intersection of money & meaning"[14] or the Clinton Global Initiative annual meetings, are committed to "strengthening market-based solutions":

> Traditional approaches to aid are not enough to address the great global challenges of our time. Market-based solutions show incredible promise to solve these daunting problems on a systemic and widespread level... At the 2010 Annual Meeting, members will discuss the best strategies for bringing these solutions to scale, so the benefits can be felt by more of the four billion people who subsist on less than $3 a day.[15]

At these events people share stories, get to know each other, and establish social and professional relationships. More concretely these are events at which "deals are done" and investment secured. They also provide particular modes of legitimation through the awarding of prizes and the recognition of "achievements." For example, Irene Pritzker, the co-founder and president of the IDP Foundation, received the Global Philanthropy Award at the World Leadership Forum Dinner for her work with the IDP Rising Schools Program in Ghana. One of the WISE awards 2013 for innovative practices that transform education and society was awarded to Promoting Equality in African Schools (PEAS), a chain of affordable secondary schools in Uganda and Zambia that involves a PPP with the Ugandan Ministry of Education. In the same summit, Vicky Colbert, the founder of Escuela Nueva, Colombia, was awarded the 2013 WISE Prize for Education for improving the quality of basic education in low income schools through an innovative educational model. In these moments, what Urry (2003) calls "meetingness"[16] is multi-functional.

> What happened in the end was that Jay [Kimmelman, the BIA co-founder and CEO] was able to get an anchor investor, again through his connections at SOCAP, and that anchor investor then put together a substantial proportion of the Series A requirements. (Samuel Ssenyimba, Investment Manager, LGT Venture Philanthropy, project interview)

There is of course an informality to this, intrinsic to network functioning and very difficult for research to access. The "Omidyar Network was seeking compelling investment opportunities in sub-Saharan Africa and someone within the organization's network made an introduction."[17]

The work of discursive elaboration and dissemination is also done by policy entrepreneurs like James Tooley (see Ball 2012) and other organic intellectuals of neo-liberalism. Tooley explained:

> Three years ago, I began advocating that investors and entrepreneurs should set up chains of low cost private schools. Jay Kimmelman came to visit me and my team in Newcastle and then went to Kenya to set up NewGlobe Schools, a low cost chain of schools with finance from Deutsche Bank and Kellogg Foundation. (Tooley 2009, 7).

The role of personal relationships in all of this should not be underestimated; they play their part in animating and maintaining policy networks and facilitating, discursively and financially, neo-liberal innovations. Awards dinners, social events, and policy tourism (McCann 2013) all play their part in fostering a virtually invisible social infrastructure for these policy networks that should not be left out when accounting for the effectivity of the networks. Some of these relationships are glimpsed in our data.

Policy and Profit

Despite the agonistic relationships between neo-liberalism and government (see Ball 2012), the state is still important here. International aid budgets remain as a significant factor in funding educational development. Individual governments and aid agencies can facilitate or hinder the effectivity of policy networks. Indeed governments are increasingly significant as market-makers, partners, target setters, and monitors and funders of neo-liberal innovations. In all these aspects, states are reworking their modalities of governance. In this case we can see this in the adaptation and assimilation by the UK government of the discourse and methods of enterprise as the basis for a new paradigm for international aid and new kinds of relationships to development. This is evident both in who is being funded and on what basis. The Department for International Development (DFID) increasingly makes aid commitments (or investments) on the basis of outcome requirements and measures, and funds directly private, social enterprise, and third sector providers and infrastructural developments to facilitate local market forms and enterprise solutions. A number of initiatives and moves illustrate this shift. For example, DFID is providing £18.5 million funding for the Developing Effective Private Education Nigeria program (2013–2018) to improve the quality of education in Lagos by supporting change and innovation in the private education market (DFID 2013). DFID is also supporting the Punjab Schools Reform Roadmap in Pakistan, which includes as one of its initiatives the provision of vouchers to out-of-school poor children to attend LFPSs (through the newly created Punjab Education Foundation) (Barber 2013); and is funding the Center for Education Innovations (2012–2016) to document market-based education innovations that can "increase access to quality, affordable and equitable education for the world's poor" (CEI website) with the aim of collaborating more closely with the private sector in development (DFID 2013). DFID is now explicitly interested in supporting private organizations, like BIA, in the effort to achieve international development goals. Policy entrepreneurs, like James Tooley, commonly attend DFID seminars and events.

"Britain will help to foster a revolution in private investment into projects to improve the health, education and future chances of more than five million people across Africa and Asia."[18] This was made clear at a Group of Eight (G8) Social Impact Investment Event in June 2013, where UK's International Development Secretary Justine Greening said:

> The way we think about development is changing. The landscape is shifting. Many of the countries that DFID works in are becoming our trading partners. Governments are focused on market development, trade and growth. A shift has happened. We need innovative financing approaches to meet these changing needs and the changing landscape… It is for this reason that in December I launched the DFID Impact Fund,[19] DFID's first ever returnable capital program, which aims to catalyze the growth of the impact investment market in Africa and South Asia over the next 13 years.[20]

In the same speech, Greening announced that DFID is also supporting the Global Impact Investing Network (GIIN) through the Impact Program – a partnership with Rockefeller Foundation, the United States Agency for International Development (USAID), and the Omidyar Network – "to facilitate the use of standard metrics for measuring development outcomes. This will enable investors and development practitioners to at last share a common language for the shared outcomes we seek."[21]

This is a new conception of aid that blurs the line between business, enterprise, development, and the public good and private interests, and poses fundamental questions about the methods and future role of traditional development agencies and public-sector service providers. BIA becomes an example for DFID (see, for example, the DFID-funded Centre for Education Innovations profile of BIA as one of the successful interventions in the area). Through this, they become linked to other organizations within a shared discourse. It is important to recognize this, as indicated above, as part of a more general shift in the form and modalities of governance. As one project respondent explained:

> The whole, kind of, business planning approach to aid goes back to the early years of the Labour government, particularly when they introduced "public service agreements" whereby each government department had to bid for its budget allocation and negotiate with Treasury and set up performance targets, for which they were then held accountable in subsequent allocations. What was important for us in that change was that it gave us three-year rolling budgets rather than annual budgets, so it was much easier from a development point of view to plan longer term programs.

Social enterprise and business methods bring new actors, energies, and sensibilities to bear upon the problem of access to education.

McBridge – the School in a Box

According to one of BIA's major funders, the Omidyar Network, BIA's "innovative for-profit model has been designed and successfully tested to provide a sustainable, scalable approach to education."[22] As indicated above, the efficiency and scalability claims of the model have made it possible for the company to attract substantial interest from both venture capital and venture philanthropy ("new" forms of philanthropy which draw upon the methods of finance capital, see Frumkin 2010). It is a model based on standardization, what the founders call an "Academy-in-a-box," and which they compare to companies like Starbucks and McDonald's, which offer a seamless experience anywhere in the world. As Kimmelman explains, "We've systematized every aspect of how you run a school. How you manage it. How you interact with parents. How you teach. How you check on school managers, and how you support them."[23] This standardization, it is argued, enables academies to be operated at an extremely low cost, charging less than US$6 a month per child and still being profitable. Technology is a central element of the business model: a standardized curriculum is turned into scripted lessons, which are placed in tablets that also record pupil attendance, track assessments and sync with BIA's headquarters in real time. The tablet used is Barnes and Noble's Nook – in 2012 Pearson took a 5% equity stake in Nook Media investing US$89.5million. An electronic M-Pesa mobile phone system is used to collect fees and make payments to contractors and suppliers (so schools remain cashless). All of this enables BIA to keep the number of non-teaching staff at each academy low (schools are run by a school manager, who in most cases is the only non-teaching staff member). It is, as Kimmelman describes it, a "vertically integrated" model that involves the in-house running of all aspects of the operation, including market research, real estate and construction, technology, curriculum, recruiting, teacher and academy manager training, and quality assurance.[24] Teachers are hired from the local communities and are subject to an eight-week training program (they are high school graduates rather than government-certified teachers). Each school is funded 100% by school fees and it is claimed that individual schools break even within a year or when they reach 200 to 300 students (Rangan and Lee 2013), but that the company will not be profitable until at least 2015, when it aims to have over half a million students enrolled.

Here again in very practical terms the language and values of impact investing – sustainability, scalability, catalytic change – are deployed and scale and scaling-up is key to financial return. Matt Bannick, managing partner of the Omidyar Network, said about BIA in an interview in the *New York Times* (August 20):

> Education is generally where there should be sector-level change. Bridge can scale up and affect millions. The real breakthrough is if others say, "How do we bring this to Nepal or Cameroon?" It's quite possible we will get a nice return, but that wasn't the objective.[25]

Having established their first school in 2009, BIA's expansion has been dramatic: it opened 51 new schools within a week in January 2013 and another 78 in September 2013, when it reached over 200 schools with an enrollment of around 50,000 pupils and reportedly plans to open another 50 schools in January 2014.[26] The growth of the school network has been supported by an increase from three to over 2300 employees between 2009 and March 2013 (according to figures provided by the Center for Education Innovations website), including 1725 teaching staff, 282 non-teaching school staff, and 300 non-school staff.

There is another governance dimension here: BIA is moving toward a multi-country model, having opened seven branches in Uganda and two in Nigeria in 2015 (in May 2013, the company was recruiting expansion directors for India, Nigeria, and Uganda) and reported that it aimed to operate in at least 12 countries by 2025 and have 10 million students enrolled. In July 2013, BIA was recruiting curriculum, teacher training, and teacher recruitment specialists for a Boston-based Academics Team "with roughly fifteen superstars in curriculum, training and measurement"[27] and that is led by Michael Goldstein. Increasingly, key strategic educational planning decisions are going to be made by the Academics Team at the Boston office.

Through its funding and its US team, BIA has various connections with the US charter school movement. Tom Vander Ark, Managing Partner in Learn Capital (a BIA investor, see above), was an Executive Director of Education for the Bill and Melinda Gates Foundation, and Michael Goldstein, BIA's Chief Academic Officer, is the founder of Match Education, a high performing Boston-based charter school provider, named Entrepreneurial Organization of the Year, 2012 by the New Schools Venture Fund. In October 2013, a BIA's recruitment notice for the Boston-based Academics Team stated that they were looking for people "with a proven record of making educational gains, particularly someone with an education reform background (KIPP, Uncommon, TFA, similar),"[28] or, as prolific blogger Michael Goldstein put it in another online post, "the number one thing to me is references, preferably by people I know or one degree of separation from No Excuses people I know (which is a very long list)."[29] These links are already evident in the people that have been recruited so far. BIA's Math Curriculum Director, Sean Geraghty, is a Teach for America (TFA) Alumnus who has coached in the Match Teacher Residency. BIA's Teacher Training Director (a role that includes overseeing the teacher and Academy manager training) is Brittney Fields, another TFA Alumnus, who has recently moved from Kenya to join the Boston-based Academics Team. As Michael Goldstein concedes, "the teacher prep actually looks borderline familiar to any No Excuses educators – i.e., Cold Call and Right is Right are in the mix, Doug Lemov [in reference to the founder of Uncommon Schools, another charter school operator in the USA with a tough approach to teaching and discipline] type stuff in there."[30] Alex Smith, the Early Childhood Director, taught at Knowledge is Power Program (KIPP) and worked as a coach for TFA.

Indeed, the language and modes of operation of BIA have, again, much in common with US charter schools. The BIA website claims that "time-on-task has been proven to be the most important tenet in delivering education;" that is, a longer school day, six days a week (7.30am to 5.30pm, including a slightly shorter day on Saturday). Also, as in charter schools and academies, alternative qualifications and faster routes into teaching are preferred. As described, BIA hires non-teachers, unqualified, who are quickly trained in-house. There is no autonomy and "trust" vested in them, technology replaces creativity and teacher individuality, with a scripted curriculum, and the tablets connected to headquarters enable instant monitoring and analysis of teacher and student performances. Again here the discursive dimension to these network relations is very clear. These charter school organizations share a set of common critiques and commitments and in many cases, either directly or via their funders, an ideological commitment to neo-liberalism.

There is also a second order business and education dimension to the networks of which BIA is a part. This relates to technological "solutions" to educational problems, and concomitant new mobile education (mEducation) business opportunities (see McKinsey and Company (2012) report *Transforming Learning through mEducation*). Khosla Ventures is interested in investing in "large problems that are amenable to technology solutions" (company website). The Nextbillion website notes that "electronic payment mechanisms, provided they are convenient, cheap and secure enough, can propel new business models which in turn can make serious inroads in the delivery of products and services at the base of the pyramid." Pearson's investment in Barnes and Noble's Nook also signals their interest in technology platforms for their software materials. Companies like Microsoft, News Corporation, and Telefonica are also exploring the use of mobile technology devices to "deliver" educational services.

"Causal Stories," Silver Bullets and a "Moral Economy of Hope"

Stone (1989) argues that the translation of specific situations into social or policy problems involves the "strategic portrayal of causal stories" (Stone 1989, 295), which "implicitly call for a redistribution of power by demanding that causal agents cease producing harm and by suggesting the types of people who should be entrusted with reform" (Stone 1989, 300). Endemic problems of "poor" state provision: lack of accountability, corruption, inefficiency, the failing state, and the lazy teacher are also, as noted already, all a part of the "causal story" deployed by BIA and similar neo-liberal actors. This works to capture and define educational problems in a particular way. Over and against this, LFPSs are presented as a silver bullet solution to the "grand challenges" of educational access, raising quality, and achieving development goals (see Ball and Olmedo 2012). BIA has all the elements of a silver bullet. As Samuel Ssenyimba (Investment Manager at LGT Venture Philanthropy, see above) summarized it, BIA "really ticked all the boxes when it came to innovation, when it came to scalability, when it came to replicability, when it came to impact" (project interview). And in similar terms: "This is a highly adaptable and scalable model that could revolutionize education for the world's poor" (Mulago Foundation website). In these ways, a moral economy of hope is articulated, one "in which ignorance, resignation, and hopelessness in the future is deprecated" (Rose and Novas 2004, 5).

BIA is frequently profiled on Tom Vander Ark's (see above) *Getting Smart* blogs, which "look for ways that innovation can help reframe historical problems and suggest new solutions" (particularly related to digital technology). It is portrayed as a successful model of "frugal" innovation, of cost-effectiveness, of doing more (e.g. providing better quality) at lower costs (e.g. as noted above, Shannon May, BIA's co-founder and Chief Strategy Officer, led a "Frugal Innovation" panel at the World Innovation Summit Education 2013 in Doha[31]). It is widely portrayed as a model that is "making education cheaper and more available" Baumard 2013). Baumard (2013) goes on to say that, "Its academic results show pupils outperforming their peers in public and other private schools: a demonstration of the steamroller effect of low-cost schooling in the world of education."

However, the hope vested in the power of the LFPS sector and of BIA in particular to revolutionize access to quality education by the poor is at odds with the significant lack of reliable data on their effectiveness (Srivastava 2013). "There is little agreement, and contradictions and conflicts of interpretation abound" (Walford 2013, 199). Issues of affordability, costs, quality, effectiveness and equity have been raised (Rose 2011; Walford 2013; Oketch and Dgware 2011; UNESCO 2009; Watkins 2004). "Initial understandings of the low-fee private sector in the literature thus far are tentative, and should be interpreted with caution and nuance, attuned to the changing contexts in specific countries over time, and to the potential interests shaping future activities of and in the sector" (Srivastava 2013, 28). Likewise, a recent DFID-commissioned, rigorous review of the evidence on the impact of private schools in developing countries points again to significant gaps in the evidence, e.g. on the capacity of LFPSs to reach the poorest, and on whether there is a positive contribution of private schools to learning outcomes, suggesting that the claims for their effectiveness might therefore be over-emphasized. The report also indicates that "the effect of international companies or chains of private schools has not yet found its way into the literature, except in the claims of those organizations."[32]

What we glimpse here are some of the limits and boundaries of this particular policy community, as well as the ways in which evidence works differently inside and outside the network. In one sense the claims and beliefs, which connect up the network members, are immune to refutation or critique from "outsiders," despite the important role played by measurement-driven funding models. A shared commitment to the charter/LFPS model is crucial to the maintenance of the network, and the assertion of evidenced-based effectiveness is crucial to continued funding of different kinds. Some of those we have interviewed in our research have commented on BIA's reliance on its own measurements and evaluations.

Conclusion

The policy network of which BIA is a part is multifaceted and complex. It is global in scope and has large and diverse "membership" – including business, governments, third sector, NGOs, philanthropies, brokers, etc. It is joined up by methods and money and beliefs and ideology focused on a commitment to "corporate social capitalism." The connectivities involved are political, financial, discursive, technological, and social. Networking is driven by diverse relationships and various exchanges. Funding is fundamental but so too, in a different way, are social relations. The network is animated by brokers, policy entrepreneurs and major funders, who come together at key sites and moments of meetingness. This is a new form of educational governance – connectivity as governance – that is done by new actors, in new places, in new ways. It changes who gets to define and make what is education, who gets to be educated and what it means to be educated. As suggested by Sellar and Lingard (2013) drawing on Woodward, this new form of governance is both epistemological and infrastructural. In regard to the former it has the "capacity to shape the views of key actors in education across local, national and global scales" (Sellar and Lingard 2013, 16) and in regard to the latter, there are both specific (BIA) and general (LFPS, US charters and British academies) developments in school provision, as well as the establishing of new sites of control and decision-making, which are also global in scale. The nation state is no longer an adequate framework for policy analysis of this kind. The relations and boundaries between state, economy, and civil society are being reconfigured, and the conditions of possibility for the economy are reworked, producing new opportunities for profit and a redistribution of moral responsibilities. This is also a reinvention of the state itself and a reconstitution of power relations and technologies of governance. In all of this there is the potential for new kinds of dysfunctions and externalities particularly when the private sector participants make decisions on the basis of the interests of shareholders over and against the interests of the state.

There is also pointed up here a whole new agenda for research, and challenges for researchers. Policy network analysis would have use and relevance in tracing policy export and policy borrowing generally, but also more specifically the advocacy, movement, and take up of assessment and quality policies, education technology "solutions" (see Santori *et al.* 2014), and inclusion and health education policies, among others. Old methods, old problems, and old concepts are no longer fit for purpose.

Notes

1. This is one part of a more complex global education policy network which Stephen Ball has been working on since 2008 (Ball 2012; Ball and Junemann 2012) and which we are developing further in an ongoing Leverhulme Trust-funded research project.
2. Edusoft is an assessment management platform that Kimmelman sold to Houghton Mifflin in 2003 (valued at US$20 million).
3. www.thegiin.org/knowledge/profile/bridge-international-academies
4. www.learncapital.com
5. www.pearson.com/news/2011/march/bridge-international-academies-in-kenya-quality-schooling-for-les.html?article=true (last accessed January 2014).
6. http://springhillequity.com/investments/bridge_international_academies
7. www.hiltifoundation.org/en/who-we-are/approach.php
8. http://www.jasmine.org.nz
9. http://50.57.73.192/blog/a-crisis-in-education-is-a-terrible-thing-to-waste
10. See www.ssireview.org/point_counterpoint/philanthrocapitalism
11. Omidyar Network press release September 22, 2009, available at http://jobs.omidyar.com/jobdetail.php?jobid=184717
12. www.philanthropynewsdigest.org/news/omidyar-network-commits-30-million-at-clinton-global-initiative-to-support-global-entrepreneurship#sthash.jbDrHjZN.dpuf
13. Press release: Pearson and Village Capital Will Fund Education Entrepreneurs in India Using Peer Review, July 17, 2013, available at: http://yourstory.com/2013/07/pearson-and-village-capital-announce-fund-to-support-education-entrepreneurs-in-india/
14. http://socialcapitalmarkets.net
15. https://www.clintonfoundation.org/clinton-global-initiative/meetings/annual-meetings/2010
16. Meetingness, according to Urry, are the occasional face-to-face encounters that are central to the functioning of networks "in order both to 'establish' and to 'cement' at least temporarily those weak ties" (2003, 161).
17. www.thegiin.org/knowledge/profile/bridge-international-academies
18. https://www.gov.uk/government/news/business-uk-impact-investments-to-boost-development
19. This is a £75 million fund managed by CDC on behalf of DFID that "must generate reasonable financial returns and also must achieve strong development impact (defined as creating jobs, directly and indirectly)" (www.cdcgroup.com/dfid-impact-fund.aspx#sthash.PDzLQudH.dpuf).
20. https://www.gov.uk/government/speeches/g8-impact-investment-event
21. www.publications.parliament.uk/pa/cm201012/cmselect/cmintdev/1557/1557we10.htm
22. https://www.omidyar.com/news/bridge-international-academies-launches-affordable-schools-kenya
23. www.wired.com/design/2013/11/schoolinabox
24. www.tilsonfunds.com/Bridge/
25. www.nytimes.com/2012/09/29/your-money/measuring-the-impact-of-impact-investing-wealth-matters.html?_r=0

26 www.npr.org/blogs/parallels/2013/11/12/243730652/do-for-profit-schools-give-poor-kenyans-a-real-choice
27 www.ventureloop.com/ventureloop/jobdetail.php?jobid=168285
28 BIA job description available at: www.idealist.org/view/job/x9tKMGtK4sXd (last accessed January 2014).
29 https://mailman.stanford.edu/pipermail/interestingjobs/2013-May/000179.html
30 https://mailman.stanford.edu/pipermail/interestingjobs/2013-May/000179.html
31 WISE (World Innovation Summit for Education): *Reinventing Education for Life*, October 29–31, 2013, Doha.
32 *The Role and Impact of Private Schools in Developing Countries: A Rigorous Review of the Evidence*. University of Birmingham, Institute of Education and Overseas Development Institute, Draft Report, July 2013 (unpublished).

References

Ball, S.J. 2007. *Education Plc: Understanding Private Sector Participation in Public Sector Education*. London: Routledge.
Ball, S.J. 2012. *Global Education Inc.: New Policy Networks and the Neoliberal Imaginary*. London: Routledge.
Ball, S.J. and C. Junemann. 2012. *Networks, New Governance and Education*. Bristol: Policy Press.
Ball, S.J. and A. Olmedo. 2012. "Global Social Capitalism: Using Enterprise to Solve the Problems of the World." *Citizenship, Social and Economics Education*, 10(2&3): 83–90.
Barber, M. 2013. *The Good News from Pakistan*. London: Reform.
Barnett, C. 2010. "Publics and Markets: What's Wrong with Neoliberalism?" in *The Sage Handbook of Social Geography*, edited by S.J. Smith, M. Pain; S.A. Marston, and J.P. Jones III, 269–296. London: Sage.
Baumard, M. 2013. "Reinventing the Teacher." *Le Monde WISE 2013*.
Bevir, M. and R.A.W. Rhodes. 2003. *Interpreting British Governance*. London: Routledge.
Brilliant, L., J. Wales, and J. Rodin. 2007. "The Changing Face of Philanthropy". *Global Philanthropy Forum 6th Annual Conference. Financing Social Change: Leveraging Markets and Entrepreneurship*, April 11–13. Mountain View, California.
DFID. 2011. *The Engine of Development: The Private Sector and Prosperity for Poor People*. London: Department for International Development.
DFID. 2013. *Education Position Paper: Improving Learning, Expanding Opportunities*. July. London: DFID.
Dicken, P., P.F. Kelly, K. Olds, and H. Wai-Chung Yeung. 2001. "Chains and Networks, Territories and Scales: Towards a Relational Framework for Analysing the Global Economy." *Global Networks*, 1: 89–112.
Draxler, A. 2008. *New Partnerships for EFA: Building on Experience*. Paris: UNESCO-IIEP/World Economic Forum.
du Gay, Paul. 2004. "'Against 'Enterprise' (but not against 'enterprise, for that would make no sense)'." *Organization*, 11(1): 37–57.
Florini, A. 2000. "Lessons Learned", in *The Third Force: The Rise of Transnational Civil Society*, edited by A. Florini. Washington, DC: Carnegie Endowment for International Peace.
Frumkin, P. 2010. *The Essence of Strategic Giving: A Practical Guide for Donors and Fundraisers*. Chicago: University of Chicago Press.
Harvey, D. 2005. *A Brief History of Neoliberalism*. Oxford: Oxford University Press.
Howard, P.N. 2002. "Network Ethnography and the Hypermedia Organization: New Media, New Organizations, New Methods." *New Media and Society*, 4: 550–574.

Jessop, B. 2002. *The Future of the Capitalist State*. Cambridge: Polity Press.
Lazzarato, M. 2009. "Neoliberalism in Action: Inequality, Insecurity and the Reconstruction of the Social." *Theory, Culture and Society*, 26(6): 109–133.
Martin, G. and O. Pimhidzai. 2013. *Education and Health Services in Kenya: Data for Results and Accountability. Service Delivery Indicators*. Washington DC: World Bank. Retrieved from: http://documents.worldbank.org/curated/en/2013/07/18031388/education-health-services-kenya-data-results-accountability (accessed November 25, 2015).
McCann, E. 2004. "'Best Places': Interurban Competition, Quality of Life and Popular Media Discourse." *Urban Studies*, 40(10): 1909–1929.
McCann, E. 2013 "Policy Boosterism, Policy Mobilities, and the Extrospective City." *Urban Geography*, 34(1): 5–29.
McKinsey and Company. 2012. *Transforming Learning through mEducation*. Retrieved from http://mckinseyonsociety.com/downloads/reports/Education/mEducation_whitepaper_April%201_vFINAL.pdf (accessed December 1, 2015).
Mundy, K. 2010. "'Education for All' and the Global Governors," in *Who Governs the Globe*, edited by M. Finnemore, D. Avant, and S. Sell, 333–355. Cambridge: Cambridge University Press.
Mundy, K. and L. Murphy. 2001. "Transnational Advocacy, Global Civil Society: Emerging Evidence from the Field of Education." *Comparative Education Review*, 45(1): 85–126.
Oketch, M. and M. Ngware. 2011. "Free primary education still excludes the poorest of the poor in urban Kenya," in *Achieving Education for All through Public-Private Partnerships: Non-state Provision of Education in Developing Countries*, edited by P. Rose, 131–138. London: Routledge.
Pal, L.A. 1997. "Virtual Policy Networks: The Internet as a Model of Contemporary Governance?" *Proceedings of ISOC*. Retrieved from: www.isoc.org/inet97/proceedings/G7/G7_1.HTM (accessed November 25, 2015).
Provan, K.G. and P. Kenis. 2008. "Modes of Network Governance: Structure, Management, and Effectiveness." *Journal of Public Administration Research and Theory*, 18(2): 229–252.
Rangan, V.K. and K. Lee. 2013. *Bridge International Academies: A School in a Box*. Boston: Harvard Business School Case 511-064.
Resource Alliance. 2011. *Philanthropy: Current Context and Future Outlook*. Bellagio Report. Brighton: IDS, Bellagio Initiative.
Robertson, S. and A. Verger. 2012. "Governing Education through Public Private Partnerships," in *Public Private Partnerships in Education: New Actors and Modes of Governance in a Globalizing World*, edited by S. Robertson et al., 21–42. Cheltenham: Edward Elgar.
Rose, N. and C. Novas. 2004. "Biological Citizenship," in *Global Assemblages: Technology, Politics and Ethics as Anthropological Problems*, edited by A. Ong and S. Collier, 439–463. Oxford: Oxford University Press.
Rose, P. 2011. "Achieving Education for All through Public–Private Partnerships?" in *Achieving Education for All through Public-Private Partnerships: Non-state Provision of Education in Developing Countries*, edited by P. Rose, 1-11. London: Routledge.
Santori, D., S.J. Ball, and C. Junemann. 2015. "mEducation as a Site of Network Governance," in *Mapping Corporate Education Reform: Power and Policy Networks in the Neoliberal State*, edited by W. Au and J. Ferrare, 23–42. Abingdon: Routledge.
Sellar, S. and B. Lingard. 2013. "The OECD and Global Governance in Education." *Journal of Education Policy*, 28(5): 1–16.
Srivastava, P. (ed.). 2013. *Low-Fee Private Schooling: Aggravating Equity or Mitigating Disadvantage?* Oxford: Symposium Books.
Stanfield, J. 2010. *Self Help and Sustainability in Education in Developing Countries*. E.G West Centre EFA Working Paper No. 10, August 2010, Newcastle University.
Stansfield, J. 2013. "All Inclusive: 'Inclusive Business Models' are Transforming Education Around the World." *Education Investor*, (4 February 2013).

Stone, D. 1989. "Causal Stories and the Formation of Policy Agendas." *Political Science Quarterly*, 104(2): 281–300.

Tooley, J. 2009. "Low Cost Private Schools as Part of the Solution for Education for All." *African Technology Development Forum Journal*, 6(1–2): 7.

UNESCO. 2009. *Education for All Global Monitoring Report. Overcoming Inequality: Why Governance Matters*. Oxford: Oxford University Press.

Urry, J. 2003. "Social Networks, Travel and Talk." *British Journal of Sociology*, 54(2): 155–175.

Walford, G. 2013. "Low-Fee Private Schools: A Methodological and Political Debate," in *Low-Fee Private Schooling: Aggravating Equity or Mitigating Disadvantage?* edited by P. Srivastava, 199–213. Oxford: Symposium Books.

Watkins, K. 2004. "Private Education and 'Education for All' – or How Not to Construct an Evidence-Based Argument: A Reply to Tooley." *Economic Affairs*, 24(4): 8–11.

Watkins, K. 2011. *Corporate Philanthropy and the "Education for All" Agenda*. Commissioned Paper, The Bellagio Initiative. Washington, DC: Center for Universal Education, Brookings Institution.

Chapter 31

A Vertical Case Study of Global Policy-Making: Early Grade Literacy in Zambia

Lesley Bartlett and Frances Vavrus

The vertical case study offers a multi-level, multi-sited approach to educational policy research. As illustrated elsewhere (e.g. Bartlett and Vavrus 2014; Vavrus and Bartlett 2012, 2013), a vertical case study traces the course by which policy is formulated and appropriated across space and time by groups of actors in distinct assemblages. One of its goals is to analyze how particular understandings of educational problems are produced and become "globalized" through multilateral policy-making institutions, while simultaneously exploring how these understandings are "localized" by social actors in different locations. In this chapter, we look specifically at the "problem" of early grade literacy, and how it gets articulated in one specific place: Zambia. We show how Critical Discourse Analysis (CDA), which illuminates the way the global literacy agenda is established, can be used in vertical case study research in ways that productively connect the study of global policy-making and national or local educational policy-as-practice. CDA, we contend, provides for a more refined analysis of policy discourse than one frequently finds in the study of global policy because it hones in on the building blocks of discourse, namely, the words and phrases that cohere to produce broader meanings and representations in a social field. Unlike our previous illustrations of vertical case studies that have included a substantial ethnographic component, we focus in this chapter on CDA as an important methodological tool for global policy analysis; in the conclusion, we outline the essential qualitative, multi-site fieldwork that could be done to elaborate a vertical case study of early grade literacy in Zambia.

Vertical Case Study Approaches and CDA

Though dubbed "vertical case study" due to our initial conceptualization of it (Vavrus and Bartlett 2006), this approach incorporates vertical, horizontal, and transversal elements (Bartlett and Vavrus 2014). First, the vertical axis insists on simultaneous attention to and across micro-, meso-, and macro levels, or scales, which constitute the verticality of comparison (see also Bray and Thomas 1995). As Susan Robertson has demonstrated, "scale enables us to trace movements in multiple directions, as new nodes of power and rule are constructed and invigorated, struggled over and legitimated" (Robertson 2011, 24). This axis is also informed by the "spatial turn" in the social sciences, and the including a relational notion of space and attention to the social production of space (see Larsen and Beech 2014). As shown in Figure 31.1, the vertical element of the case study requires attention to influential international organizations, such as (in global educational policy) the World Bank, the United Nations Educational, Scientific and Cultural Organization (UNESCO), or the United States Agency for International Development (USAID); inquiry regarding the formation and implementation of national policies, such as medium of instruction policies, exam policies, and curricular documents; and local appropriation of these policies. Second, the horizontal axis compares how similar policies unfold in distinct locations that are socially produced (Massey 2005) and "simultaneously and complexly connected" (Tsing 2005, 6). For global educational policies, that might entail comparison across schools, as shown in Figure 31.1; alternately, it might involve comparison across district educational offices or community-based organizations. Third, the approach emphasizes the importance of transversal comparison, which historically situates the processes or relations under consideration and traces their creative appropriation through educational policies and practices across time and space. In other words, the transversal element incorporates attention to change over time. It also reminds us to study *across and through* levels to explore how globalizing processes intersect and interconnect people and policies that come into focus at different scales.

Vertical case studies can be developed by engaging a range of research tools, including surveys, focus groups, interviews, participant and non-participant observations, archival research, oral histories, and CDA (see, e.g. the studies in Vavrus and Bartlett 2013b). Such studies attend to the meaning social actors make of the phenomena around them and the ways they continuously culturally produce social structures through everyday engagement and enactment. In our previous work, we have incorporated aspects of Marcus's multi-sited ethnography (1995, 1998) and Feldman's "nonlocal ethnography" (2011) to promote qualitative, field-based educational policy research that expands its reach across place and scale. In this chapter, however, we seek to illustrate how one methodological strategy – CDA – can reveal the ways that policy actors are related through specific historical contingencies that connect disparate social sites in the production of "global policy."

Critical discourse analysis is an approach that reveals how social and political power relations are produced and reproduced in talk and text (Fairclough 1992a; 2000; 2003). CDA involves critically analyzing how policies and "best practices" become inscribed with meanings through particular forms of social practice. For example, CDA can show how, through the construction and circulation of norms

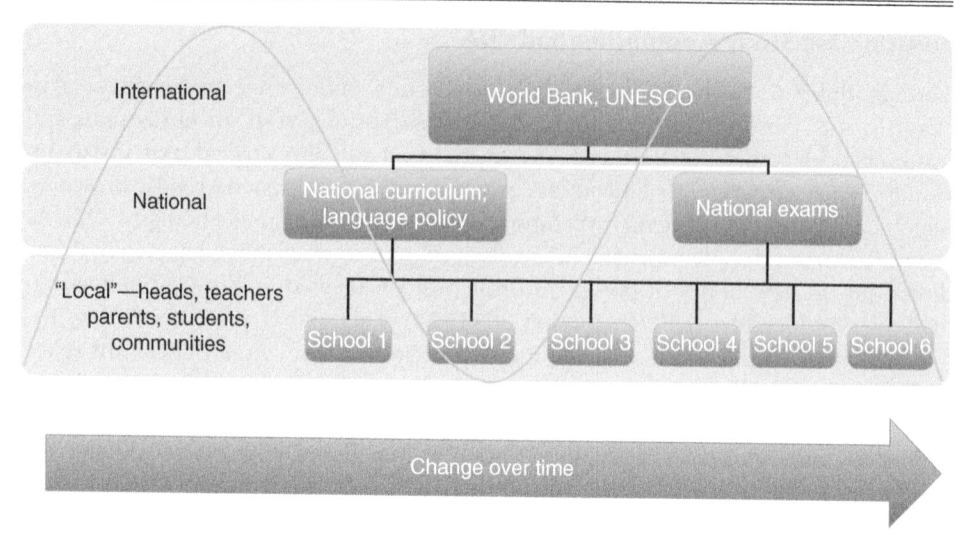

Figure 31.1 Example of a multi-sited vertical case study design.
Source: Bartlett and Vavrus (2014).

through policy documents, powerful donors delimit the parameters of the global educational agenda, influencing the projects that national governments and local implementing partners develop (see, e.g. McCormick 2012). From this point of view, language and social practices are not fixed but rather "articulate" and "disarticulate" at different historical moments. In the process of being (re)articulated, discursive elements that have been brought together in a specific moment of practice are transformed, some achieving stabilization or permanence, others becoming disjunctive and ambiguous (Moretti 2014; Vavrus and Kwauk 2013; Vavrus and Seghers 2010). The fullest CDA entails analysis of the sociopolitical processes of document or discourse production, as well as the assumptions embedded in the content (McCormick 2012). Thus, CDA attends simultaneously to linguistic elements in spoken or written texts, such as grammar, vocabulary, and cohesion, and to the broader socio-cultural and political context that shapes the formation of texts and how people think, feel, and act in response to them. In short, CDA sets as its task a twofold process of "revealing the relationship between linguistic means, forms and structures and concrete linguistic practice, and making transparent the reciprocal relationship between discursive action and political and institutional structures" (Wodak et al. 2000, 9). This is an especially useful approach for global policy studies because it links micro-level textual analysis and macro-level exploration of the authoritative knowledge generated by national and international policy-making institutions.

In this chapter, we use a vertical case study approach to explore how global policy aimed at promoting literacy has narrowed over time to "early grade reading;" we consider how this has been taken up in Zambia; and we address some of the challenges of the reading framework that dominates the field of international development at this time. To do that, we first engage in CDA to examine a set of global policy documents related to literacy and reading. We aim to "make transparent"

(Wodak *et al.* 2000, 9) the consolidation of "early grade reading" as a global problem. To do so, we selected as the corpus key global policy documents:

- *Education for All (EFA) Declaration* (1990)
- *Dakar Framework for Action* (2000)
- World Bank's *Education Sector Strategy* (1999)
- World Bank's *Education Sector Strategy Update* (2005)
- World Bank's *Learning for All: Investing in People's Knowledge and Skills to Promote Development* (2011)
- USAID's *Education Strategy: Improving Lives Through Learning* (2005)
- USAID's *Education Strategy* (2011)

In analyzing these texts, we draw most specifically on one of the three dimensions of CDA described by Fairclough (1992a): discourse-as-text.[1] Therefore, we focus our linguistic analysis on the semantic and lexical relations in the corpus. The semantic relations draw attention to how the meaning between clauses and sentences may differ depending on the actors and institutions that produced the text, while the lexical relations highlight how certain words co-occur in some documents and how the vocabulary in the corpus varies or remains constant across the texts. To do this, we used the "search" feature in Adobe Reader to identify key terms in these documents and to compile lists of the sentences and paragraphs in which they appeared. We searched for relevant lexical items, such as *education*, *literacy*, and *reading*, as well as variants, such as *edu-* and *read-*, to ensure a complete list of terms. Once they were identified, we examined the compilation of clauses and sentences for markers of semantic relations, such as cause/effect, problem/solution, and commitment or assertion through the use of modal auxiliary verbs (may, might, will, should, etc.). We coded the data by reading each document individually and noting recurring linguistic patterns. We then focused on specific patterns and themes within each document through a more detailed syntactic and semantic examination.

Global Policy-Making: Major Shifts

Examining global policy documents from the 1990s through 2011, several key trends become apparent. First, a broad agenda of "Education for All," including youth and adults, has narrowed significantly over time to focus on children enrolled in schools. Second, the broad notion of literacy has similarly contracted to focus on early grade reading, and, moreover, on a very tightly defined notion of reading. Third, there is a noticeable shift in this period toward an emphasis on quality as determined by measurement.

The 1990 *Education for All (EFA) Declaration* established education as a human right and defines education in terms of "basic learning needs" as spelled out in Article 1:

> Every person – child, youth and adult – shall be able to benefit from educational opportunities designed to meet their basic learning needs. These needs comprise both essential learning tools (such as literacy, oral expression, numeracy, and problem solving) and the

basic learning content (such as knowledge, skills, values, and attitudes) required by human beings to be able to survive, to develop their full capacities, to live and work in dignity, to participate fully in development, to improve the quality of their lives, to make informed decisions, and to continue learning. (75)

Of these "basic learning needs," it is only "literacy" that receives further treatment, and literacy in the mother-tongue is specifically mentioned. For instance, in Article 5, where the scope of basic education is explored, the *Declaration* states: "literacy programmes are indispensable because literacy is a necessary skill in itself and the foundation of other life skills. Literacy in the mother-tongue strengthens cultural identity and heritage" (76). It is important to note that the term "reading" is not used in the *Declaration*, and assessment is described only vaguely, as when the document asserts that the "focus of basic education must, therefore, be on actual learning acquisition and outcome, rather than exclusively upon enrollment [...]. It is, therefore, necessary to define acceptable levels of learning acquisition for educational programmes and to improve and apply systems of assessing learning achievements."

Ten years after its initial mandate, the World Education Forum released a far more extensive follow-up document, the *Dakar Framework for Action*. Similar to the 1990 EFA Declaration, the 2000 *Framework* does not mention reading; instead, its focus remains on "literacy," which is mentioned 83 times, far more often than other key terms such as "life skills" (18 times) and "numeracy" (5 times). In addition, literacy is almost entirely associated with adults and adult learning, with "education" being used primarily in conjunction with "children." The *Framework* maintains the largely unspecified stance on assessment, but it goes further to question whether it is even possible to measure educational outcomes across different contexts for comparative purposes, stating: "Many countries continue to face the challenges of defining the meaning, purpose and content of basic education in the context of a fast-moving world and of assessing learning outcomes and achievement. Many of the qualitative and informal aspects of education have still not been clearly assessed. The huge diversity of contexts makes performance and achievements difficult to measure and compare" (13).

The 1999 World Bank's *Education Sector Strategy* (1999) maintains a focus on a broad notion of "education" (551 occurrences), variously describing it as a "cornerstone," "endeavor," "human right," "goal," "area," "attainment," "vision," "investment," and "mission," among other terms. Education contributes to "poverty reduction," creates "populations who can operate in democratic societies," contributes to "building social cohesion," "social development," and "social inclusion," and affects future income, fertility, and health. In contrast, literacy is mentioned only 18 times, most frequently in relation to adults, but also more metaphorically, as in the phrase "technologically literate professionals" (two mentions). Reading receives only four mentions in the text – once in relation to the International Reading Association, and once as an important skill. The document features an emerging emphasis on "quality," with 152 mentions of that term.

Earlier reservations about assessment, explicitly open notions of education, complex views of literacy, and the association of literacy with adults that were visible in the EFA documents of the 1990s and 2000 had changed by the mid-2000s. In addition, careful attention to the documents shows the gradual emergence of an assessment imperative, reading as the central definer of quality basic education, and the idea that quality will be measured by reading.

In 2005, USAID published an *Education Strategy*. The word "education" appears 210 times in the 19 pages of the main text; "literate" or its variants appear 14 times, and "reading" only once. "Education" in this document is defined as a "strategy" to "improve lives." It is also considered an "investment," a "force for development," the "foundation of development and democracy," and one of the central "keys to economic growth and poverty reduction." Education not only "builds human capital" but also "encourages political participation, enhances governance, strengthens civil society" and supports "U.S. interest in states of geostrategic interest." This document features a concern with "quality," a term that appears 35 times. It also shows a shift to a focus on basic education, which consists of "facilitating the acquisition of basic skills, such as literacy, numeracy, and critical thinking that enable people and nations to thrive in an economic environment."

The focus on assessment and reading are more pronounced in the World Bank's 2005 *Education Sector Strategy Update* (ESSU). The Bank has played an important role in EFA since its inception, and it was mentioned in the 2000 *Framework* eight times as a partner organization. Thus, its framing of both educational problems and solutions warrants particular consideration. The ESSU carries forward the goal of EFA, but it introduces an "audit" discourse (Strathern 2000) through its emphasis on "results" and "outcomes," with a major "strategic priority" being the "linkages between education and labor markets" (Strathern 2000, 13). An excerpt from the fourth chapter, entitled "Instilling a Results Orientation," illustrates this discursive shift:

> In many parts of the world, there is a surprising lack of data about student learning. Even though the benefit of education is really a function of the skills and competencies students acquire, rather than the duration of their schooling, most studies of educational outcomes are limited to analysis of years of schooling completed. Such studies can provide only a broad approximation of the increased earning potential, better livelihoods, and poverty reduction that are the result of the education enterprise. (66)

The justification for intensified quantitative assessment is elaborated throughout the chapter:

> Getting children to school is only a first step; what matters is acquisition of knowledge, skills, and values. Learning assessments are crucial for measuring education quality and relevance, diagnosing system weaknesses, and motivating policy reform. While many countries have developed school-based assessments and public exams, few have national assessments in place; no low-income countries have participated in the various international assessments. (71) All countries must have access to, and use, technically valid and reliable objective measures of student learning. (67)

Throughout the ESSU one finds an emphasis on creating a "reliable objective" tool to measure "learning," with reading serving as proxy for learning. As stated in the fourth chapter, creating a reliable tool is the "first goal" and depends upon establishing an "agree[d] upon measure of reading literacy that can be tracked on a country-by-country basis over time and subsequently to develop measures of mathematics, science, and other competencies at the primary level, while simultaneously working to develop adequate indicators at other grade levels" (67). The use of such a tool is justified in the ESSU by noting the increased use of such measures in "industrialized countries," and it cites the "need for global partnerships" to expand those "measures" worldwide (67). Notably, the ESSU contends that the Bank "should play a lead role in establishing such a partnership and in ensuring global consensus on appropriate indicators" (68). In the same chapter, the subsection "Establishing key outcomes and indicators" describes what should be measured: "for primary education, basic outcomes and indicators could include enrollment rates, Grade 1 intake rate, projected and actual primary completion rates (PCR), and reading literacy" (69). In sum, the ESSU emphasized results, outcomes, measurement, primary education, and "reading literacy." However, in short order, "literacy" is dropped in favor of "reading" alone.

The most recent World Bank education sector strategy, *Learning for All: Investing in People's Knowledge and Skills to Promote Development*, was published in 2011 and is intended to guide the work of the Bank through 2020. The title indicates a shift from education as a process to learning as an outcome that can be measured by a number of international student assessments. The document includes explicit and frequent references to assessment; keywords highlight the "results" (50 times) oriented nature of the project that relies on an effort to "invest" (136 times) in "assessment" (53 times) to measure "outcome(s)" (60 times). In addition, "reading" (undefined, cited 10 times) and "literacy" (cited 8 times) are mentioned most frequently and used synonymously, often in conjunction with "math" (cited 11 times) or "numeracy." Though this is a "learning for all" approach, children (and especially girls) are its target: "Children" appears 94 times, "girls" 18 times, "boys" 7 times, "women" 6 times, "adult" 5 times, and "men" not at all. The term "adult literacy" appears only once.

Published in the same year as the World Bank strategy, the USAID *Education Strategy* (2011) shows remarkable consistency with the Bank's document in its emphasis on assessment and early grades; it is distinct, however, in the centrality awarded to early grade reading. The executive summary notes that "[a]ccess to education is a crucial precondition to educational impact, but what matters most thereafter is the quality of education." Citing two documents, one from the World Bank and one from USAID, the strategy claims that in "low-income countries, very little learning is occurring in the classroom" (*USAID 2011, Strategy* 9). In short order, quality of education becomes focused on early grade reading as the "necessary precondition" for other "skills" (10). "Reading" becomes the primary association for "education," appearing 73 times in the document, with other terms like "math" (3 times) trailing well behind. The first of the three strategic goals is "improved reading skills for 100 million children in primary grades by 2015," to be assessed by the Early Grade Reading Assessment (discussed below) (1, 9). Even though the document makes clear in multiple places that it is drawing on the EFA mandate, among other texts, "adult literacy" is only mentioned twice, (compared to 54 mentions of "children") and one of those references states that, though "important," if it did not support USAID's goals it would be "traded off" for more relevant "programming" (8). Notably, reading is not defined in this document; the indicator recommended for assessing the achievement of Goal 1 is the "percentage change in proportion of students in primary grades who, after two years of schooling, demonstrate sufficient reading fluency and comprehension to 'read to learn'" (16). Interventions to achieve Goal 1 include improved "(1) teaching and learning in the classroom, (2) effective school management, (3) national policy and structural reforms to support school and classroom level changes, and (4) engagement and accountability by communities and the public at large" (10). According to the document, reading skills are to be calculated by an Early Grade Reading Assessment that "will measure the performance of our programs primarily though the improvement of reading skills for primary grade students after two years of schooling" (10). It is to this assessment that we now turn.

The Early Grade Reading Assessment (EGRA) was developed in 2006 for USAID by Research Triangle Institute International (RTI), a research institution that works on a wide range of development-related projects, many of which are funded by USAID. As a foundation for EGRA, RTI adopted from the US National Reading Panel (NRP) a restricted definition of reading that focuses on five "core components": phonemic awareness, phonics, vocabulary, fluency, and comprehension. Notably, many language and literacy scholars have criticized the NRP for the ways it defined these components, the way it portrayed their interaction, and the elements of learning to read that were excluded (Allington 2002; Cunningham 2002; Krashen 2002; Garan 2002; Hoffman 2008). While the importance of phonics, phonemic awareness, vocabulary, fluency, and comprehension for learning to read alphabetic writing is indisputable, scholars have critiqued the definition of "scientific evidence" and the way that research results have been represented in the NRP report and subsequent policies that have drawn upon it (Allington 2002, 4). For instance, the report does not consider factors like motivation; it does not prioritize some features of reading, such as print concepts; and it offers an abridged representation of core components like fluency and comprehension (Krashen 2002; Garan 2002). Further, there are debates about the relationship between fluency and comprehension. Finally, there have been serious debates over how the report has been interpreted. While some reading scholars favor a stage-wise approach, insisting on starting with the "parts" like letters and phonemes, most concur that oral vocabulary must be built from the earliest ages for reading success, that writing is essential to literacy learning, and that literacy is best promoted through "balanced" approaches that incorporate explicit skills instruction with authentic texts and a focus on comprehension (Samuels and Farstrup 2011). As Goodman (2006) explains, reading is ultimately a qualitative practice of making meaning from text, but the version of reading represented in the NRP report and EGRA reduces reading to discrete skills and then condenses those skills to isolated, quantitative measures.

Further, as its measurement tool, RTI adopted the influential and controversial US classroom-based continuous assessment tool known as Dynamic Indicators of Basic Early Literacy Skills, or DIBELS. DIBELS consists of a set of short, timed tests meant to measure phonemic awareness, sound–symbol correspondence, accuracy and fluency, reading comprehension, and vocabulary. From its inception, DIBELS was roundly criticized by respected literacy researchers for making claims not based in evidence; distorting the skills required to read and then testing only a fragment of those skills; emphasizing speed over accuracy; and proving difficult to administer consistently (see, e.g. Goodman 2006; Riedel 2007; Samuels 2007). It is rather surprising, given the solid and widespread critiques of DIBELS, that it has become the foundation of a multi-million dollar international campaign for early grade reading

(Hoffman 2012). In the late 2000s, RTI slightly modified several DIBELS subtests and field-tested them, resulting in a suite of short, adaptable, timed tests that have come to be known as EGRA (Gove and Cvelich 2010; RTI 2009). EGRA includes tests such as letter naming, the pronunciation of letter sounds, nonsense word reading, familiar word reading, and comprehension questions based on a short passage; different subtests can be adapted or excluded in different locations. As of 2011, EGRA had been applied in 50 countries and 70 languages by RTI, the World Bank, USAID missions, and a few non-governmental organizations (NGOs) (Gove and Wetterberg 2011; for a more detailed critique of EGRA, see Bartlett *et al.* 2015).

Overall, critical discourse analysis of this corpus helps to identify four critical moves in global policy discourse since the 1990s: (a) the narrowing of literacy to a very specific definition of reading that is based on research conducted in the USA, primarily with monolingual English speakers, which may not be appropriate for other languages, scripts, or orthographies; (b) the contraction from the global agenda of learning for all, including literacy for adults, to the targeting of children's reading in early grades; (c) the shift from access and inputs to quality and outcomes; and (d) the concomitant rise of an audit culture, based on assessments developed for one specific place, time, language, and purpose that have spread globally with limited attention to cultural, historical, and linguistic contexts. Our analysis is aimed at tracking global trends in policy discourses as they have changed over time; it does not seek to determine whether previous or current literacy/reading assessments are more efficacious in a universal sense. However, we remain concerned about the current trend toward, simultaneously, more of a narrow understanding of literacy and more widespread adaptation of this restricted meaning of literacy in multilingual contexts. We turn now to such a case – Zambia – to examine how this global trend is articulating with literacy policy in this multilingual country with a relatively robust history of language and literacy policy.

Language And Literacy Policies and Practices in Zambia

A Historical Lens

Zambia has long been a diverse country with at least 40 recognized indigenous languages (Miti and Monaka 2006; Kashina 1994); however, Serpell argues that there are 14 major language groupings with important similarities in phonology, morphology, and grammar; "seven of those clusters are represented by one of the official languages adopted for basic education [in current policy], and two particular varieties from within two of the clusters [Town Nyanja and Town Bemba] are also widely recognized as *lingua franca*" (Serpell 2014, 75).

The history of primary schooling in Zambia is in part a story of borrowed language policies. From the 1920s through the 1960s, Zambian schools followed the general pattern of other British colonies in sub-Saharan Africa by providing mother-tongue education for two years and then shifting to a widespread vernacular through Standard 5 before shifting to English (Linehan 2004). In 1966, two years after independence, the new Zambian government adopted English as the sole medium of instruction from Grade 1 through tertiary schooling, allowing pupils to select one of seven regional languages to study as a subject. This policy was consistent with

UNESCO recommendations at the time, which reflected fears that privileging certain national languages might be divisive. While various reports, such as the Zambian 1977 *Educational Reform: Proposals and Recommendations*, acknowledged that English as the medium of instruction was detrimental to literacy learning, the documents also framed mother-tongue education as impractical. Evidence of the problems with this approach was presented in a 1993 study by Britain's Overseas Development Agency showing that most Zambian children could not read even two levels below their grade level. A study conducted in 1995 (published in 1997) by the South African Consortium for Monitoring Educational Quality (SACMEQ) showed a similar pattern, with only a quarter of Zambian children reading at "minimum levels," and less than 53% at "a desirable level" (Sampa 2005, 30). Reflecting on the failure of English medium of instruction policies, Sampa wrote:

> Zambia had almost 30 years of experience using English as a medium of instruction from Grade 1 onwards. Children who had very little contact with English outside the school had been required to learn how to read and write through and in this language, which was quite alien to them. This was a major contributory factor to the backwardness in reading shown by many Zambian children. (Sampa 2005, 34)

In the late 1990s and through the 2000s, thanks in part to pressure from the EFA movement but also due to local concerns about educational performance, Zambia adopted a series of education policies and programs focused on literacy. In 1996, the comprehensive education policy document *Educating Our Future* stated: "There is strong evidence that children learn literacy skills more easily and successfully through their mother tongue, and subsequently, they are able to transfer these skills quickly and with ease to English" (Republic of Zambia Ministry of Education 1996, 39). In 1998, under the aegis of the Primary Reading Program, the government began piloting the Breakthrough to Literacy (BtL) program. BtL began in the UK in the 1970s; it was adapted by a South African NGO, Molteno, for use in various southern African contexts. The African versions of BtL used a "familiar-tongue" literacy approach, indicating that the medium of instruction is an indigenous language widely used in the region, but it may not be the "mother-tongue" of all students, especially in a linguistically diverse country such as Zambia. With support from Irish Aid, Zambia piloted BtL in Grade 1 in two districts (Kasama and Mungwi) in the Northern province; results suggested that literacy levels rose significantly (Sampa 2003; 2005). After slightly modifying the program to fit local social and material realities, the Ministry of Education implemented the Zambian New Breakthrough to Literacy (NBTL) program in Grade 1 in various locations. The approach recognized seven official indigenous languages (Bemba, Nyanja, Kaonde, Lozi, Lunda, Luvale, and Tonga, which all belong to the Bantu language family) for initial literacy instruction in Grade 1, and it delayed introduction of English until Grade 2 (Miti and Monaka 2006; Ministry of Education, Government of Republic of Zambia/ Molteno Project 2001).

By 2004, NBTL had spread through most of the country (Sampa 2005; Mwila 2009; 2011). Under NBTL, literacy in the primary grades is supposed to proceed as follows: Grade 1 "is taught in a familiar language while English and a Zambian language are additional school subjects. From Grade 2, literacy is taught in English while Zambian language literacy skills continue to be enhanced. Thereafter children are expected to continue developing their reading and writing skills in both Zambian languages and English in each subsequent grade up to Grade 7" (Nkolola-Wakumelo 2013, 131). Over the course of the 2000s, Zambia added several other literacy components under the NBTL banner, including "Pathway 1 and 2 (oral courses for Grades 1and 2), Step In To English (literacy course for Grade 2) and the Read On Course (an English literacy course for Grades 3–7)" (Sampa 2005, 23–24).

Thus, since the turn of the millennium, Zambia has demonstrated a clear and consistent concern with literacy quality, borrowing models from abroad but also adapting them to maintain a fairly comprehensive view of literacy as a process that includes oral and written skills development in addition to reading. However, as discussed below, the focus has increasingly zeroed in on early grade reading as one finds in global policy-making, especially during the past few years. What might lead a country like Zambia to make this shift from well-established policies and programs with a more holistic view of literacy to a more narrow focus on reading in the early grades? An instrumentalist approach to policy studies would suggest that it is due to inefficiencies in literacy policies; a critical approach, in contrast, assumes that the political economy plays a role, especially in heavily indebted countries like Zambia. Thus, to understand this shift, one could examine policy efficacy, but it is equally important to consider the politics of policy adoption. For instance, Zambia relies heavily on external funds for recurrent education costs, and the US is among the top donors (Beuran *et al.* 2011). In 2009, 44% of Zambia's budget came for external sources, down from 83% in 2000 but still a very high figure when one considers the ways that external influence may affection policy-making (ActionAid 2011).

Contemporary Policy

In the summer of 2011, as part of the USAID Education Quality Improvement Program 2 (EQUIP 2) program, the EGRA was administered to Grade 2 and 3 primary school students in 40 schools in four Bemba speaking provinces in Zambia. The test consisted of five subtasks: letter sound knowledge, unfamiliar word reading fluency, connected text oral reading fluency, reading comprehension, and listening comprehension; all subtasks except reading and listening comprehension were timed as a measure of automaticity. Results were reported as follows:

> For the oral reading fluency task, pupils were asked to read a short narrative story for one minute. A majority (91%) of grade 2 pupils and 78% of grade 3 pupils were unable to read a single word in this passage. For those grade 3 pupils who read more than one word, the average number of words read was about 21 words per minute... This performance is not surprising given weak performance in both letter naming tasks (50% of grade 2 and 42% of grade 3 pupils were unable to name a single letter sound) and decoding tasks (88% of grade 2 and 75% of grade 3 pupils were unable to read a single unfamiliar word). Pupils' performance on these foundational skills was strongly correlated with reading fluency. These findings show that pupils' limited knowledge of letter sounds and weak decoding skills must be addressed to improve their oral reading fluency. (RTI/USAID 2012, ix)

On this basis, the RTI/USAID report concluded, "The curriculum for early grade literacy needs the development of standards and milestones for pre-reading and early reading based on the stages of learning to read, including oral language development, phonological awareness, print awareness, phonetics, reading fluency and comprehension" (2012, 51).

The recommendations resulting from the USAID study are currently being implemented through an intensive EGRA-driven multilingual early grade reading reform in Zambia called Read to Succeed (RTS), one of several education projects in Zambia currently funded by USAID. The project aims for improved student performance in reading in approximately 1300 government basic schools in six provinces of Zambia, and it employs familiar strategies borrowed from USAID reforms elsewhere, including a tight scope and sequence for reading and scripted lessons that emphasize phonemic awareness and phonics. Other familiar features are the centrality of formative assessments, reading materials, school–community partnerships, and Parent Teacher Associations (PTAs) that developed school level Learner Performance Improvement Plans (LPIPs).

The influence of current global policy-making in the area of early grade reading is further evident in Zambia's latest literacy policy, the National Literacy Framework (2013). According to one USAID report, RTS was "instrumental to the development of the National Literacy Framework (NLF) ... [which] provided a roadmap on phonic approach to reading instruction" (USAID 2013, 2). In explaining "the importance of literacy" and justifying the focus on "early grade reading" on pp. 5–7, the framework cites 17 documents: all of them are published in English, most of them are published in the USA, several of them are affiliated with the US NRP efforts, and none of them discusses literacy or reading in Africa broadly or in Zambia specifically. The NLF's privileging of early grade reading with a strong focus on phonics is not surprising, given that so many of the references cited in the framework were produced by scholars who work for or have been affiliated with the World Bank, RTI, USAID, and the US NRP. As the NLF states in acknowledging those who influenced its development:

> *Scholars in reading acquisition* in multiple languages ... have found that learning to decode print – that is, breaking apart or "sounding out" written words into letter sounds – can be done in almost any alphabetic language and requires five key skills, which have been *endorsed by the US National Reading Panel.* (2000)
>
> Gathering *the best practices* from *the international reading community*, together with a multi-leveled efforts and a realization that literacy is crucial to improving education in Zambia, we believe that progress will be made. (Ministry of Education, Science, Vocational Training and Early Education (MESVTEE) 2013, 6, 14; emphasis added)

The notion of "best practices" documented by "the international reading community" is used to support an approach that emphasizes decoding in the early grades. Like NBTL, the Framework urges early literacy instruction in a familiar tongue, though the NLF extends the use of familiar languages as medium of instruction through Grade 4, with English taught as a subject from Grade 2 before using it as the medium of instruction from Grade 5 to the tertiary level. (Notably, the approaches adopted here and by NBTL are problematic for students who do not speak one of the country's seven major languages when they enter Grade 1.)

To justify the emphasis on early grade reading, the NLF cites "the Matthew effect," a term first popularized in reading research by Stanovich (1986) and frequently cited in RTI documents on reading. This effect, as stated in the NLF, provides a clear rationale for early grade reading interventions:

> Children who fall behind in learning to read typically become entangled in a cycle of failure. Low performing readers read less, and as a consequence, they do not gain vocabulary, background knowledge, and information about how reading material is structured. Children below a certain level by the end of Grade 1 are more likely to stay behind, and the gap widens. (MESVTEE 2013, 7)

This passage demonstrates how priorities for literacy interventions are established in global policy-making discourses and get taken up at the national level through the process of intertextuality (Fairclough 1992b). For instance, in this excerpt, the NLF paraphrases (but does not directly quote or cite) documents from RTI.[2] From the same RTI materials, the NLF borrows verbatim a graph to visually represent the Matthew effect. Such moments of intertextuality are significant because, as Fairclough argues, "the text responds to, reaccentuates, reworks past texts, and in so doing helps to make history and contributes to wider processes of change" (1992b, 270). Texts are not borrowed and reworked randomly; intertextuality "is socially limited and constrained, and conditional upon relations of power" (1992b, 270).

Thus, the Zambian NLF is illustrative of discursive practices in national policies that have clear global antecedents. The NLF adopts from international policy documents and policy initiatives a narrow definition of literacy, based on research from a particular group of mostly American, US-based scholars and practitioners; the utility of a "five core components" model of reading regardless of the child's first language and the multilingual context; and the validity of EGRA to measure learning outcomes around the world despite its questionable foundations in DIBELS. Elsewhere we have referred to this sort of policy adaptation as *inter/national policy* to draw attention to the difficulty of separating "national" policy and practice in many countries from the "international" or global institutions that fund or provide other support to federal institutions (Vavrus and Bartlett 2013a).

Discussion

What are the specific implications for Zambian policy-making and educational practice of the analysis presented above? Here we focus on three areas of particular concern: conceptualization of reading, language, and timing (see also Bartlett *et al.* 2015).

Conceptualization of Reading

The new NLF focuses extensively on early grade reading in a manner that reduces literacy to a cognitive psychological model of reading and prioritizes phonics and phonemic awareness. For example, the NLF states:

> In terms 2 and 3 of year one, literacy instruction will transition to teaching letter sounds, sound blends and syllables in a progression to teaching the components of

language. Teaching pre-reading skills and teaching sounds through both phonemic awareness and phonics should be taught daily as a foundation for building reading skills. A direct instruction, synthetic approach to teaching phonics, in which learners are taught letter sounds in a sequence of most frequently used sounds in their language characterizes the first year of instruction... It is suggested that phonemic awareness (defined as the ability to listen to, recognize and manipulate the sounds of the oral language) and phonics (sound/letter relationships) be taught every day in the initial stage following pre-reading and pre-writing. After all the initial sounds in a particular language have been taught, phonemic awareness and phonics should be used for review and remediation as needed, until children can decode new words with ease. At this point, learners will acquire skills to combine vowel sounds and consonant sounds to form syllables; combine vowel sounds and syllables to form words and use the words to form sentences and read them.

Although the NLF does mention the importance of building vocabulary and giving students oral and aural experiences with language, and while it does mention writing (at least handwriting and punctuation), the extensive appendices with individual letter sounds specified to be taught on particular days of the week indicate the priority given to phonics and phonemic awareness in ways that de-emphasize vocabulary, oral language development, comprehension, and broader language experiences thought by many critical literacy scholars to be essential. There is a need for further research to examine the impact of this focus on phonics and phonemic awareness on broader literacy skills and their development over time.

Language

One fundamental challenge of implementing EGRA in multilingual countries like Zambia emerges from the fact that DIBELS/EGRA was developed on the basis of research with primarily monolingual populations reading in English. It is worth pausing to ask: To what extent is the assessment appropriate for other languages? Are the core components of reading (and the expectations for performance on the reading assessment) the same for learning to read in languages and scripts other than English? For example, EGRA concentrates on syllables as units of words, when for some languages it may be far more appropriate to focus on morphology, and specifically the identification of root words, affixes, and suffixes. Given that different alphabetic languages require different reading strategies, a single reading assessment across languages may not be appropriate. Benson (2013), for one, points out that "different languages have different types of meaning encoded in different [parts] of words," such as prefixes and suffixes, and therefore the "idea that words per minute can be an accurate indicator of literacy development" is "questionable" (Benson 2013, 11). As Schroeder (2013) concludes about EGRA, "actual adaptations based on the linguistic characteristics of individual languages are still quite limited, and it will be important to establish developmental benchmarks for assessments like the EGRA that reflect the orthographic and linguistic contexts where they are used" (Schroeder 2013, 259). There is a need for a rigorous peer or specialist review process regarding the reliability and validity of EGRA in other languages, and for extensive discussion of how to blend oral reading assessments with specific language in education policies.

Timing

Although EGRA is only beginning to be used in Zambia, it is likely to become a widely used assessment tool. Yet the decision in EGRA assessments to time each sub-task is quite controversial. For instance, EGRA uses words per minute as a measure, but the concept of a word differs greatly from language to language. However, large claims are being made. For example, the RTS "Reading Tools in a Box" Launch Highlights (USAID 2013) assert: "[a]s the result of the holistic approach and using the scripted lessons in the new reading instruction, beneficiary schools showed incredible positive progress. Anecdotal data obtained through monitoring visits to the schools, classroom observations and information from head teachers, teachers and standard officers indicate that, in just three to four weeks, pupils in grade 1 showed a positive progress towards learning to read. Many pupils moved from non-readers to struggling to read" (USAID 2013, 2). Most literacy scholars would question how three weeks of instruction could have such results, unless either the baseline was flawed or students have spent the weeks being drilled in precisely the kind of tasks that they are then tested upon.

Education scholars working in Zambia have shown that, absent the timing requirement, students are able to show more of what they are able to do, thus calling into question the zero scores (Dr Robert Serpell, personal communication, 2014). Timing may also interfere with performance, especially for those who are not accustomed to such tasks, and it can interfere with certain subtasks. Given such limitations, why does the timing of items persist? It is possible that timing facilitates the rapid assessment of large numbers of children, and this is essential to creating a global measure of learning outcomes that is now central to global educational policy-making discourse. The necessity of getting through the assessment process in a timely fashion is interfering with documenting what children can read, further reinforcing a deficit model of literacy.

In sum, further research is needed on the reading model that is currently being held up as "the best practices from the international reading community" (MESVTEE 2013, 14). EGRA, as a central component of this model, runs the risk of reifying performance on simple decoding tasks as evidence of a much larger and more complex set of literacy skills; it is an imperfect fit, at best, with many of the languages in the countries where it is being employed; and the insistence on timing possibly invalidates several items. It would be beneficial to have more research of the kind conducted by Dubeck *et al.* (2012), in which they conducted observations and interviews to document literacy instruction in lower-primary Kenyan classrooms. We need to know more about existing models of reading pedagogy, as well as how the current push for early grade reading in policy and curricular documents is being interpreted and implemented by teachers.

Conclusions

It is a critical period for literacy in the field of international educational development. Millions of dollars will be invested over the next few years in early grade reading interventions and assessments in Zambia and other countries. According to the Learning Metrics Task Force, which is a global group convened by the Brookings

Institution's Center for Universal Education and UNESCO's Institute for Statistics to develop new education goals, there is an emerging consensus around a reading indicator in the post-2015 goals as a central measure of educational quality. Many expect that EGRA will be selected as the tool to measure reading. Much has been accomplished with the realignment of the international educational agenda toward reading, but significant problems with this shift remain. Without adequate oversight and critical attention, the field has embraced an assessment based on a narrow model of reading that does not adequately address literacy and language diversity. And yet this assessment is being used to drive global policy-making and pedagogy. As stated bluntly by literacy scholar James Hoffman:

> Why not invest millions of dollars and stake the next decade of USAID efforts to promote literacy on the EGRA framework that reduces literacy to letter naming and the rate of correct word reading? Why not, beyond the fact that there is little scientific evidence for EGRA's reliability, validity or effectiveness? (Hoffman 2012, 349)

The vertical case study, which draws upon diverse research techniques that include but are not limited to CDA, surveys, observations, and interviews, offers a valuable approach to study the formation and appropriation of global educational policies like early grade reading. The vertical axis of the approach invites comparison across micro-, meso-, and macro levels in order to see how developments at one level are influencing developments at another, or (on the contrary) how developments at one level are appropriating or ignoring developments at another. In this chapter, we have engaged CDA to trace the travel of early grade reading from international organizations to an NLF in Zambia. Transversal comparison includes historical analysis of change in policy over time, such as the tracing of the shift from literacy for all to early grade reading and its assessment through EGRA. The transversal element also reminds us to study *across and through* levels to explore how globalizing processes intersect and interconnect people and policies that come into focus at different scales.

Future research should expand this initial analysis and complement it with comparative case studies of the implementation and appropriation of these policy frameworks. The horizontal axis of vertical case studies compares how similar policies unfold in distinct locations, such as different countries or different regions within one nation state. In the future, we hope to conduct interviews and observations in Zambian early grade classrooms across the country as the NLF and a new curriculum are rolled out. We also seek to compare such a vertical case study in Zambia to at least one other country in order to examine the challenges of implementing EGRA-based reading policies in diverse contexts. Drawing on these three axes of comparison, we assert that the vertical case study approach offers a fruitful analytical frame for studies of global policy-making.

Notes

1 The other two dimensions in his framework are (a) *discourse-as-discursive-practice*, which he identifies as the meso-level analysis of textual production, distribution, and consumption of texts; and (b) *discourse-as-social-practice*, or the macro level analysis of power/knowledge relations focused on but not limited to institutions that produce policy (Vavrus and Seghers 2010).

2   Those documents include the Guidance Notes for Planning and Implementing EGRA, prepared in 2011 by RTI and IRC and a Powerpoint presentation given by Amber Gove of RTI at the CIES in Charleston South Carolina in 2009 titled, *Why Focus on the Early Grades? The Rationale and Development of the Early Grade Assessments.*

References

ActionAid. 2011. *Real Aid 3: Ending Aid Dependency*. London: ActionAid.

Allington, R. (ed.), 2002. *Big Brother and the National Reading Curriculum: How Ideology Trumped Evidence*. Portsmouth: Heinemann.

Bartlett, L. and F. Vavrus. 2014. "Transversing the Vertical Case Study: Methodological Approaches to Studies of Educational Policy-as-Practice." *Anthropology and Education Quarterly*, 45(2): 131–147.

Bartlett, L., A.J. Dowd, and C. Jonason. 2015. "Problematizing Early Grade Reading: Should the Post-2015 Agenda Treasure What is Measured?" *International Journal of Educational Development*, 40: 308–314.

Benson, C. 2013. *L1-based Multilingual Education and EGRA: Where Do They Meet?* PRAESA Occasional Papers No. 40. Cape Town: PRAESA.

Beuran, M, G. Raballand, and J. Revilla. 2011. *Improving Aid Effectiveness in Aid-Dependent Countries: Lessons from Zambia*. Paris: Centre d'Economie de la Sorbonne.

Bray, M. and R.M. Thomas. 1995. "Levels of Comparison in Educational Studies: Different Insights from Different Literatures and the Value of Multilevel Analyses." *Harvard Educational Review*, 65(3): 472–490.

Cunningham, J. 2002. "The National Reading Panel Report: A Review," in *Big Brother and the National Reading Curriculum*, edited by R. Allington, 49–74. Portsmouth: Heinemann.

Dubeck, M., M. Jukes, and G. Okello. 2012. "Early Primary Literacy Instruction in Kenya." *Comparative Education Review*, 56(1): 48–68.

Fairclough, N. 1992a. *Discourse and Social Change*. Cambridge: Polity.

Fairclough, N. 1992b. "Intertextuality in Critical Discourse Analysis." *Linguistics and Education*, 4: 269–293.

Fairclough, N. 2000. "Discourse, Social Theory, and Social Research: The Discourse of Welfare Reform." *Journal of Sociolinguistics*, 4(2): 163–195.

Fairclough, N. 2003. "'Political Correctness': The Politics of Culture and Language." *Discourse and Society*, 14(1): 17–28.

Feldman, G. 2011. "If Ethnography is More than Participant-Observation, then Relations are More than Connections: The Case for Nonlocal Ethnography in a World of Apparatuses." *Anthropological Theory*, 11(4): 375–395.

Garan, E. 2002. *Resisting Reading Mandates: How to Triumph with the Truth*. Portsmouth: Heinemann.

Goodman, K. 2006. *The Truth about DIBELS: What It Is, What It Does*. Portsmouth: Heinemann.

Gove, A. and P. Cvelich. 2010. *Early Reading: Igniting Education for All. A Report by the Early Grade Learning Community of Practice*. Research Triangle Park: Research Triangle Institute.

Gove, A. and A. Wetterberg (eds). 2011. *The Early Grade Reading Assessment: Applications and Interventions to Improve Basic Literacy*. Research Triangle Park: RTI Press.

Hoffman, J. 2008. "In Search of a "Simple View" of Reading Comprehension," in *Handbook of Research on Reading Comprehension*, edited by S. Israel and G. Duffy, 54–66. New York: Routledge.

Hoffman, J. 2012. "Why EGRA – a Clone of DIBELS – Will Fail to Improve Literacy in Africa." *Research in the Teaching of English*, 46(4): 340–357.

Kashina, K. 1994. "The Dilemma of Standard English in Zambia: Pedagogical, Educational and Sociocultural Considerations." *Journal of Language, Culture and Curriculum*, 7(1): 17–29.

Krashen, S. 2002. "More Smoke than Mirrors: A Critique of the National Reading Panel Report on Fluency," in *Big Brother and the National Reading Curriculum*, edited by R. Allington, 112–124. Portsmouth: Heinemann.

Larsen, M. and J. Beech. 2014. "Spatial Theorizing in Comparative and International Education Research." *Comparative Education Review*, 58(2): 191–214.

Linehan, S. 2004. "Language of Instruction and the Quality of Basic Education in Zambia." Paper commissioned for the *EFA Global Monitoring Report 2005, The Quality Imperative*. Retrieved from: http://unesdoc.unesco.org/images/0014/001466/146659e.pdf (accessed November 25, 2015).

Marcus, G. 1995. "Ethnography in/of the World System: The Emergence of Multi-Sited Ethnography." *Annual Review of Anthropology*, 24: 95–117.

Marcus, G. 1998. *Ethnography through Thick and Thin*. Princeton: Princeton University Press.

Massey, D. 2005. *For Space*. London: Sage.

McCormick, A. 2012. "Whose Education Policies in Aid-Receiving Countries? A Critical Discourse Analysis of Quality and Normative Transfer through Cambodia and Laos." *Comparative Education Review*, 56(1): 18–47.

Ministry of Education, Government of Republic of Zambia/The Molteno Project. 2001. *Zambian New Breakthrough to Literacy*. Lusaka: Longman Zambia.

Ministry of Education, Science, Vocational Training and Early Education [MESVTEE] of Zambia. 2013. *National Literacy Framework*. Lusaka: Curriculum Development Centre.

Miti, L.M. and K.C. Monaka. 2006. "The Training of Teachers of African Languages in Southern Africa with Special Reference to Botswana and Zambia," in *Languages and Education in Africa: A Comparative and Transdisciplinary Analysis*, edited by B. Brock-Utne and I. Skattum, 213–222. Oxford: Symposium Books.

Moretti, F. 2014. *The World According to the Bank: An Analysis of World Bank Reports, 1946–2010*. Lecture conducted from the Institute for Advanced Study, University of Minnesota, Minneapolis, Minnesota.

Mwila, C.M. 2009. *Language and Literacy in Multilingual Communities: An Investigation into the 'National Breakthrough to Literacy Initiative' in Zambia*. Unpublished doctoral dissertation, University of Bath.

Mwila, C.M. 2011. *Indigenous Languages in Initial Literacy in Zambia*. Presentation at the meeting of the British Association of Applied Linguistics Languages in Africa SIG, Coventry, UK. Retrieved from: http://liasig.wordpress.com (accessed November 25, 2015).

Nkolola-Wakumelo, M. 2013. "A Critical Analysis of Zambia's Language-in-Education Policy: Challenges and Lessons Learned," in *Multilingual education in Africa*, edited by H. McIlwraith, 127–146. London: British Council.

Republic of Zambia Ministry of Education. 1996. *Education our Future: National Policy on Education*. Lusaka: Zambia Educational Publishing House.

Riedel, B. 2007. "The Relation between DIBELS, Reading Comprehension, and Vocabulary in Urban First-Grade Students." *Reading Research Quarterly*, 42: 546–567.

Robertson, S. 2011. "'Spatializing' the Sociology of Education: Stand-Points, Entry-Points, Vantage-Points," in *The Routledge International Handbook of Sociology of Education*, edited by M. Apple, S. Ball, and L. Gandin, 15–26. London: Routledge.

RTI. 2009. *Early Grade Reading Assessment Toolkit*. Research Triangle Park: RTI.

RTI/USAID. 2012. *Pupil Performance, Pedagogic Practice, and School Management: An SSME Pilot in Zambia*. Research Triangle Park: RTI.

Sampa, F. 2003. "Mother Tongue Literacy in the Zambian New Breakthrough to Literacy Programme," in *Reading for All in Africa*, edited by A.E. Arua, 173–178. Newark: International Reading Association.

Sampa, F. 2005. *Zambia's Primary Reading Program (PRP): Improving Access and Quality Education in Basic Schools*. Paris: Association for the Development of Education in Africa.

Schroeder, L. 2013. "Teaching and Assessing Independent Reading Skills in Multi-lingual African Countries: Not as Simple as ABC," in *Language Issues in Comparative Education: Inclusive Teaching and Learning in Non-Dominant Languages and Cultures*, edited by C. Benson and K. Kosonen, 245–264. Rotterdam: Sense Publishers.

Samuels, S.J. 2007. "Is Speed of Barking at Text What We Mean by Fluency?" *Reading Research Quarterly*, 42: 563–566.

Samuels, S.J. and A. Farstrup. 2011. *What Research Has to Say about Reading Instruction*. Newark: International Reading Association.

Serpell, R. 2014. "Growth of Communicative Competence in a Dynamic African Context: Challenges for Developmental Assessment," in *Educating for Language and Literacy Diversity*, edited by M. Prinsloo and C. Stroud, 73–96. New York: Palgrave Macmillan.

Stanovich, K. (1986). "Matthew Effects in Reading: Some Consequences of Individual Differences in the Acquisition of Literacy." *Reading Research Quarterly*, 21(4): 360–406.

Strathern, M. 2000. *Audit Cultures*. New York: Routledge.

Tsing, A.L. 2005. *Friction: An Ethnography of Global Connections*. Princeton: Princeton University Press.

USAID. 2011. *Education Sector Strategy: Education Opportunity through Learning*. Washington, DC: USAID.

USAID. 2005. *Education Sector Strategy: Improving Lives through Learning*. Washington, DC: USAID.

USAID Read to Succeed. 2013. *Reading Tools in a Box Launch Highlights*. Washington, DC: USAID.

Vavrus, F. and L. Bartlett. 2006. "Comparatively Knowing: Making a Case for the Vertical Case Study." *Current Issues in Comparative Education* 8(2). Retrieved from: www.tc.columbia.edu/cice/Archives/8.2/82vavrus_bartlett.pdf (accessed November 25, 2015).

Vavrus, F. and L. Bartlett. 2012. "Comparative Pedagogies and Epistemological Diversity: Social and Material Contexts of Teaching in Tanzania." *Comparative Education Review*, 56(4): 634–658.

Vavrus, F. and L. Bartlett (eds). 2013a. *Teaching in Tension: International Pedagogies, National Policies, and Teachers' Practices in Tanzania*. Rotterdam: Sense Publishers.

Vavrus, F. and L. Bartlett (eds). 2013b. *Critical Approaches to Comparative Education: Vertical Case Studies from Africa, Europe, the Middle East, and the Americas*. New York: Palgrave Macmillan.

Vavrus, F. and C. Kwauk. 2013. "The New Abolitionists? The World Bank and the 'Boldness' of Global School Fee Elimination Reforms." *Discourse: Studies in the Cultural Politics of Education*, 34(3): 351–365.

Vavrus, F. and M. Seghers. 2010. "Critical Discourse Analysis in Comparative Education: A Discursive Study of 'Partnership' in Tanzania's Poverty Reduction Policies." *Comparative Education Review*, 54(1): 77–103.

Wodak, R., R. de Cillia, M. Reisigl, and K. Liebhart. 2000. *The Discursive Construction of National Identity*. Edinburgh: Edinburgh University Press.

Chapter 32

Global Indicators and Local Problem Recognition: An Exploration into the Statistical Eradication of Teacher Shortage in the Post-Socialist Region

Gita Steiner-Khamsi

Introduction

Research on policy borrowing and lending contributes to a better understanding of *why* local actors adopt global education policies, and *how* they reframe, modify, or adapt them once transferred to a new context. This dual focus on reception and translation enables researchers to analyze and understand the spread of global education policies in great detail. When examining agency, context, and networks, the question of which policy actors benefited, and who lost in the wake of a policy import, attains the utmost relevance. Naturally, this emphasis has extensive methodological consequences. Among them is the necessity to follow up 5, 10, or 15 years later to see what impact a borrowed policy had on the local policy process. Unsurprisingly, the project of understanding cross-national policy attraction and adaptation has piqued the interest of those who study globalization.

In this chapter I look at a particular case in the process of global policy attraction and adaptation. Looking specifically at global indicators of teacher shortage, I problematize the fact that they function as a "problem recognition filter" at the local and national levels. That is, global indicators narrow the perspective of local actors and determine what they recognize, or do not recognize, as a problem requiring a solution. At times this operates as a vicious cycle, because the (global) solutions are created before the (local) problem has been well understood and defined. Also, because global indicators are used as a tool to measure and define local problems, the interplay between local and global actors, and the overlap between problem recognition and solution, does not account for local realities, even as it propels the spread of global education policy. In an age of globalization and evidence-based policy planning, these two features generate a closed circuit that leaves very limited room for local problem recognition and local problem solution.

The result of this closed circuit is that, more often than not, the solution is packaged in the form of international standards, 21st-century skills, or best practices. Curiously, what occurs in practice, both in developing and developed countries, is an inversion of the decision-making process. Rather than first defining the problem and seeking an answer, the formulation of the (local) problem is aligned with the pre-existing (global) solution. Problems tend to be redefined in terms of quality, accountability, equity, and other global buzzwords. The language changes but the approach – aligning local problem analysis with available global reform packages – remains the same. For example, just as ten to 15 years ago project proposals had to address the issue of "building civil society," today international consultants are hired to formulate education sector reviews that focus on low student achievement in early literacy and numeracy, or lack of teacher accountability.

Therefore, the question addressed in this chapter is how, and to what extent, do internationally generated indicators about teachers generate global norms about teachers; that is, determine globally, for example, what their standard qualification should be, how many hours they should teach, how much they should earn, etc. in their respective countries? More specifically, by addressing the use of indicators in the policy process, we may ask what is lost or gained by the heavy reliance on indicators developed by international knowledge banks, such as the World Bank, the Organisation for Economic Co-operation and Development (OECD), and the United Nations Educational, Scientific and Cultural Organization (UNESCO).

The Use of Global Indicators for Local Problem Recognition

Until now, a great deal of research on policy borrowing and lending has focused on how the "global" is used as an argument to generate reform pressure at the local and national levels. The "semantics of globalization" is a well-explored research topic (Schriewer and Martinez 2002). Translated into the language of comparative policy studies, this means that the early work on borrowing and lending focused on the use of the "global" for local agenda setting. Many researchers found that policy actors refer to globalization as a quasi-external force that is internally induced at critical moments of heightened policy conflict (see Steiner-Khamsi 2002). In other words, domestic policy actors sometimes portray themselves as victims of external forces, such as financial crisis, an emergency situation, or globalization to carry through unpopular reforms. In effect, the semantics of globalization function as a coalition builder, producing the desire for policy change. However, agenda setting is only one stage in the process where the global leaves its imprint. In this chapter, I attempt to investigate another: the impact of global indicators on local problem recognition.

In a recent publication on comparative policy studies, I explored the curious phenomenon of retroactive problem definition in greater detail (Steiner-Khamsi 2013). In this chapter, I attempt to take the argument a step further. Not only are the existing (global) solutions, fueled by funding from international organizations, spread to every corner of the globe, but the indicators for identifying the (local) problem and measuring success are also determined at the global level. The closed circuit of problem definition and solution has led to a self-reinforcing, global governance system, in which international organizations diagnose, prescribe, and evaluate progress toward what they had earlier prescribed as the solution for the local problem. In addition to their financial stature as loan and grant providers, international organizations like the World Bank, the United Nations Children's Fund (UNICEF), and bilateral aid agencies, collect massive amounts of data, and promote particular reform packages, that typically reflect the mission of their organization. Operating as databanks, they document the status quo and amass baseline information to substantiate the need for particular reforms. Then, in the capacity of knowledge banks, they "lend" policy ideas by disseminating their own portfolio of "best practices" that work in different countries.

The three properties of international organizations – money, statistical data, and policy knowledge – account for the type of governance that international and bilateral aid agencies exert vis-à-vis the recipient governments. The self-reinforcing feature of global norm setting rests on the discursive power of global indicators that define the problem, determine the solution, and measure progress toward it. Even though multilateral agencies compete to spread or sell their own package of "best practices" to grant or loan recipient governments, their use of global development indicators is remarkably similar. The indicators used by UNESCO (World Education Indicators) and the World Bank (World Development Indicators) are nearly identical not just in what they measure, but also in what local problems they ignore, or choose not to measure. The indicators tend to focus on problem areas for which international organizations or businesses have solutions, reform packages, or best practices to offer or to sell. Local problems that are generalizable and de-territorializable, and for which *one* (global) solution could be implemented cross-nationally, are given preference.

The consequences of an economy of scale should not be underestimated. It is relevant for state bureaucracies that are concerned with routinizing and standardizing interventions, and it is even more a priority for international businesses concerned with profits, large margins, and low implementation costs. Problems that are seen as too specific, that is, confined to a particular context, are of little interest, because they are difficult to remedy by means of a wholesale policy import. They may as well not exist as far as international donors are concerned, because there is no statistical tool to measure them, and no global solution to lend.

A good case in point, documented elsewhere (Steiner-Khamsi and Stolpe 2006), is international organizations' lack of interest in nomadic education. With a few exceptions, they are unable to identify and measure the challenges associated with schooling the children of nomadic pastoralists, who, in search of greener pastures, must seasonally change their place of residence. How do schools provide education to children of families with a non-sedentary lifestyle? The issue of school access for children of cattle breeders is actually not as exotic as it may sound, and greater attention to this particular segment of the rural population, which is widespread in places like Mongolia, Niger, Nigeria, several Eastern Africa, Middle Eastern, and Arab countries, would be highly desirable. Nevertheless, nomadic education has been ignored, and there is no global agenda on increasing access to education for children in remote rural areas, or indicators to measure access and education quality for children in non-sedentary settings.

The case discussed in this chapter is situated at the opposite end of the spectrum. Unlike educational access for children of herders, teacher shortage is acknowledged to be a pressing issue worldwide, and numerous international organizations have directed their attention and funding to remedy it. The UNESCO Institute of Statistics asserts that millions of teachers will be needed worldwide to achieve universal primary education by 2030. For example, South and West Asia would need an additional 3.5 million teachers, and countries in sub-Saharan Africa would need to recruit 145,000 annually to increase primary enrolment to a universal level by the year 2015. In addition, at the lower secondary school level, 5.1 million teachers are needed to ensure that countries continue to expand compulsory education beyond the primary level (UNESCO 2013). Naturally, the issue is of great interest to teacher unions and civil society organizations. Without any doubt, economists are also preoccupied with teacher salary reform, because in over half of all developing countries, personnel remuneration absorbs at least 75% of the national education budget (UNESCO 2009).

Measuring Teacher Shortage Globally: Wrong Assumptions and Even Worse Solutions

The global figures on teacher shortage, produced by UNESCO (2013) and presented above, grossly understate the magnitude of the problem. Though many education systems have policies and practices in place to cope with chronic teacher shortage, these remedies obscure and invalidate the statistical measure. In many parts of the world, teacher shortage is tackled by relying on double shifts, assigning additional teaching hours, or hiring underqualified or unqualified instructors.

Closer examination reveals that the global education indicator of teacher shortage is biased toward educational systems of developed countries, and does not reflect the complexity of the problem in developing countries. The measurement rests on the following three assumptions that, while possibly valid for developed countries, are inapplicable to the rest of the world: Every teacher works full-time, is qualified, and is paid equitably.

False Assumption 1: Every Teacher Works Full-time

In many developing countries, teachers work in two shifts due to a lack of classrooms, teachers, or both. "Teacher utilization" is thus a notion that is relevant for national level data, but disappears when statistical information is provided at a global level. Teachers who take on a morning and afternoon shift mask the extent of actual teacher shortage.[1]

It is notable that the opposite also applies in many developed countries, where teachers work part-time or teach, to use the concept from the development context, "half a shift." In Switzerland, for example, four out of five teachers are women, and the majority chooses to work part time (Wolter *et al.* 2003; Fuchs 2009). Two-thirds of all teachers work either 50% or less of the full 40 hours per week workload because they can live comfortably on half a paycheck. In poorer countries the opposite applies: teachers work a few hours per week at school because they cannot afford to live on a teacher salary alone.

For example, in several post-socialist countries in Central and Eastern Europe, and the Commonwealth of Independent States, teachers deliberately keep their teaching commitment to the bare minimum to remain employed, so they can work a second job as a municipal employee, merchant, or farmer. The part-time job enables them to remain connected to the profession, draw on the social benefits that public service entails, and serve their country. Armenia and Tajikistan stand out as countries that employ a large number of teachers who work only a few hours per week; that is, less than the statutory teaching load (UNICEF CEECIS 2012). As a principal in a rural school of Kyrgyzstan noted: "There are many teachers in our village but they have other jobs. Only patriots end up working as teachers" (UNICEF Kyrgyzstan 2009).

False Assumption 2: All Teachers are Qualified

Each education system determines the minimum qualification required for teaching. All over the world, the standard qualification has been continuously raised over the past few decades or century, respectively. Today, pre-service teacher education is typically offered at the lower tertiary level for primary school teachers, and upper tertiary level for secondary school teachers. However, there is a huge gap in developing countries between supply and demand for qualified teachers. There are simply not enough qualified teachers to fill vacancies that promise little more than unattractive salaries and onerous work conditions. As a result, only underqualified (e.g. teachers with a vocational degree in teacher education, rather than with a degree at tertiary level), or unqualified teachers (e.g. employees without any teacher education degree) get hired.

In Pakistan, for example, the concept of "life-long learning for teachers" denotes the most common career path. The previous generation of teachers began working with only a short teacher training certificate (Primary Teacher Certificate or Certificate of Teachers), and then, over the course of their career, earned a Bachelor's degree (BA or BSc). With higher education expansion, the inverse now applies. The new generation of teachers begins with a BA or BSc degree in hand but then, because they cannot find a more interesting job, end up working as teachers. They then enroll, sometime during their career, in a teacher education program (Certificate of Teachers, Diploma of Education, or BEd), to complete the standard qualification that is needed for a solid salary. The principle of life-long learning is reflected in the promotion scheme: teachers are promoted and increase their salary with every additional qualification, certificate, or degree that they manage to secure. The salary schemes of provincial governments reflect this pathway to teacher qualification: the higher salary levels distinguish between promotions and new entrants and reserve quotas for both types of personnel actions. In other words, teachers in Pakistan typically start work as unqualified or underqualified teachers and work, or rather study, their way up.

Clearly, the global measure of teacher shortage does not account for whether or not a teacher is qualified. As a result, the problem disappears. For example, in Lesotho, the standard qualification for teachers is 12 years of schooling, as well as a three-year program to earn an Education Diploma. However, only 20% of the practicing teachers fulfill the requirement (Phamotse 2009). Thirty-three percent of practicing teachers are considered underqualified (hold a Primary Teacher Certificate or equivalent), 41% are unqualified (only completed lower or upper secondary school and hold no pedagogical certificate/qualification), and 6% have other types of qualification that are not directly related to the teaching profession. From a national perspective, the unfilled positions (80%) are considerable, when the distinction between qualified, underqualified, and unqualified teachers is taken into account.

False Assumption 3: All Teachers of the Same Salary Rank are Paid Equitably

Of all the three assumptions, the third is the least discussed in the research literature. In the former Soviet Union and Mongolia, teachers work according to a *stavka* system, where they are paid based on the number of hours that they teach, and compensated for any additional task, such as grading student work, serving as class teacher, or taking charge of a science or language laboratory. This is in stark contrast to the weekly workload system, in countries such as in countries of North America and the European Union, where teachers are paid for 35–40-hour weekly workloads. In the workload system, a teacher's job includes teaching, preparation, grading, administrative work, and parent–teacher conferences. The divide is large, and repercussions so considerable, that I will discuss them in a separate section of this chapter.

The point is that in the *stavka* system, teachers are able to boost their income by taking on additional teaching hours and tasks. In practice, the teaching load system benefits teachers in urban or large schools, as well as experienced teachers. They are usually the ones best able to secure additional teaching hours and tasks for which they are paid extra. On the other hand, the *stavka* system has a detrimental effect on secondary school teachers in rural schools, who barely manage to secure a full 18–22-hour teaching load in their subject area.

The smallest common denominator of teacher shortage – measured globally in terms of unfilled positions – is, at best, meaningless and inaccurate. At worst it is harmful, because it obscures important local realities that might otherwise be addressed. In fact, the global indicator of teacher shortage masks the "crisis of the teacher workforce" (*Russian: krizis pedagogicheskogo kadra*) that exists not only in the post-Soviet region, but also other parts of the world. The exclusive focus on teacher quality, and the neglect of massive teacher shortage, has far-reaching effects on policy. It perpetuates the belief that educational systems are populated with poorly performing teachers who by means of teacher licensing, "optimization" (reduction) of schools, or a per capita financing mechanism, need to be pushed out of the system. Most prominently, the global teacher accountability reform movement has turned a blind eye to the root causes of low teacher morale, motivation, and performance: poor work conditions, meager salaries, and lack of teaching qualification. Nevertheless, managerial reforms, such as the teacher accountability reform, are very popular with non-educators and bureaucrats (see Verger *et al.* 2013). For them, greater regulation and control – nowadays reframed as "accountability" measures – will remedy the problem of the low quality of instruction. Teacher performance evaluation is typically part of a teacher accountability reform. However, any additional layer of control introduced in a highly centralized and hierarchical setting, such as putting the school director or inspectors in charge of evaluating the performance of teachers, may be used as a source for bribes in contexts where corruption is seen as a way to boost the income of director and other civil servants.

In half the world, teacher accountability is the cause of, rather than the solution to, low quality instruction. Teachers are regulated and controlled too much, not too little. For example, the educational systems of Eastern Europe, the Caucasus, Central Asia, China, and Mongolia have a rigid accountability system, as a well as a relatively domineering central government structure in place. In fact, inspectors and school directors see it as their professional duty to closely monitor the work of teachers and, if necessary, deduct salary supplements if they have not graded student assignments, punish them if the students in their class are unruly or have broken equipment, and humiliate them in front of their peers. In these countries, teachers spend too many hours documenting their work and filling out reports, rather than working with students, parents, and their peers. Oblivious to the magnitude of the professional crisis in the post-Soviet region, and some other parts of the world, many international organizations are enamored with teacher accountability that, regardless of circumstances and context, is supposed to improve the quality of education (Bruns *et al.* 2011; see Klees *et al.* 2011). Driven by inaccurate data, and dwelling on false assumptions, teacher accountability is a managerial reform that donors pursue with great zeal and conviction. As a result, the adoption of teacher accountability measures is a programmatic conditionality for the approval of grants or loans.

Measuring Teacher Shortage Globally, Regionally, Nationally, and at School Level: The 10+1 Indicators of Teacher Shortage

The talk about the "crisis of the teacher workforce," mentioned above, has been ubiquitous in the post-socialist education space for quite some time, leading governments and international agencies to seriously explore ways to lift the salary of teachers and attract teacher education graduates to the profession. Given this heightened interest in the situation of teachers, UNICEF funded a series of "SITAN" (situation analyses) of teachers in Mongolia, the CEECIS region (Central and Eastern Europe and the Commonwealth of Independent States), and in the Eastern and Southern Africa Region (see UNICEF CEECIS 2012; UNICEF Kyrgyzstan 2009; UNICEF Mongolia 2012). The most ambitious comparative research project was the six-country study in the CEECIS region. It included situation analyses of teachers in the following six countries: Armenia, Bosnia and Herzegovina, the Former Yugoslav Republic of Macedonia, Kyrgyzstan, Moldova, and Uzbekistan. The six research teams collected multilevel data (school, district/province, central level) from the following sources: statistics, policy documents, human resource information (salary tables, staff lists, salary slips), and interview of administrators, school directors, teachers, and students.

The six-country study set out to explore and explain the following contradiction: in all six countries there was public talk of the "teacher crisis" and yet the official teacher shortage statistics only suggested a shortage of 0.2–4.5% in the respective countries. The research project attempted to understand how exactly the official indicator of teacher shortage (defined as unfilled positions) helped to obscure real teacher shortage that in some countries was massive *if* measured at school and district/province level. The national statistics on teacher shortage lead to the erroneous conclusion that teacher shortage is not a problem in the region. However, the magnitude of the teacher shortage crisis surfaces, once the central-level data are juxtaposed with school-level and district/province-level data and, in particular, when coping mechanisms of schools and district/province-level authorities are investigated in greater detail.

As a result of the inadequate global measure of teacher shortage, we started to differentiate between overt teacher shortage (using the global indicator of unfilled positions) and covert teacher shortage (using regional indicators) in the CEECIS region. In collaboration with researchers from the six countries, we developed ten regional indicators that reflect the specific features of communist and post-communist education systems. These include extremely low base salary, supplemented by additional payments for specific tasks, school location, and teacher experience. Finally, we used the 10+1 indicators (ten indicators of covert teacher shortage, plus one indicator of overt teacher shortage), to produce single case studies that helped us to understand which regional indicators apply to which countries, and which do not.

In terms of our methods, we began by comparing every country (global indicator), a few countries (regional indicators), and single case studies (national indicators), to measure the phenomenon of teacher shortage at different levels. We found that with each higher level of analysis – even moving from a provincial to a national level within a country – the teacher shortage rate diminishes. In addition, the period of the school year in which teacher shortage is measured is important. The highest rate is in the spring, when schools report their staffing needs to the district level authorities. That rate drops dramatically once the school year begins in the fall, for an obvious reason. Schools have learned to cope with teacher shortage by using ten different strategies, which ensure that each class period is taught by someone, regardless of whether they are qualified, already have a full teaching load, or have already retired.

The following two examples provide a glimpse into how schools deal with teacher shortage. The first example is from a school in Jalal-Abad, Kyrgyzstan, which uses Kyrgyz, Russian, and Uzbek as languages of instruction. The school employs 48 teachers, and, in the spring, officially reported 25 vacancies, which prevented them from offering physics in Grades 7–11. Asked how the school copes with teacher shortage, the principal replied:

> First of all, we don't divide the classes in Kyrgyz, English, and Russian into two groups even though we would be entitled to do so. This is bad for the quality of teaching in these classes, but we do not have any other choice. Second, we invited four teachers from the surrounding schools to teach at our school. Third, we begged our own retired teachers to come back and teach for us. Seven of our teachers are at retirement age, but are still working. Finally, we received permission from the District Department of Education to assign a double teaching load for our teachers. Twenty teachers at our school teach more than two teaching loads (that is, more than thirty-two to thirty-eight hours). Many of them teach subjects for which they never received any training. The highest teaching load/week at our school is fifty hours. Teaching so many hours is inhuman for teachers, but there is no choice. (UNICEF Kyrgyzstan 2009)

As a follow-up question, we asked: "How many of your teachers that took on additional hours teach subjects for which they weren't trained?" The principal answered:

> It is easier to answer which teachers only teach subjects for which they have a specialist diploma, a degree, or a certificate. Most of our teachers end up taking on additional hours in subjects for which they never took preparatory courses.... [Deputy principal goes through the list of teachers, listed in the salary forms]. From the forty-eight teachers in our school, twenty-two teachers teach subjects other than the ones they have been trained to teach. (UNICEF Kyrgyzstan 2009)

The greatest indicator of covert teacher shortage is the number of teachers that are assigned to teach additional hours in subjects for which they are not trained or qualified. Naturally, this particular indicator has great repercussions for the quality of instruction. The 2006 Programme for International Student Assessment (PISA) study mentions the shortage of qualified teachers in Kyrgyzstan explicitly, and attributes the low student outcomes in science to the lack of qualified science teachers. In Kyrgyzstan, 62% of all schools report vacancies in science. Almost all of these schools (59% countrywide) deal with the shortage by filling their vacancies with teachers who take on additional lessons in science, or by assigning non-qualified teachers (that is, teachers qualified in other subjects, but with no training in science) to teach science (CEATM 2008).

Redistribution of vacant hours is the most common strategy used at the school level to cope with teacher shortage. Kyrgyzstan participated in two PISA surveys (2006 and 2009), and received the lowest rank in the league table. Even though the redistribution strategy is detrimental to the quality of instruction, it is very popular among teachers. They depend on receiving extra payment from the additional teaching hours. Given the inadequate teacher salaries that existed in Kyrgyzstan prior to the salary reform of 2011, this particular coping strategy helped to retain effective teachers at the school, and in the profession (for more detail, see Steiner-Khamsi *et al.* 2011).

Table 32.1 is a summary of the 10+1 indicators grouped into three categories that affect the quality of instruction.

The ten indicators were regionally developed, and characterize core features of post-communist education systems. The research teams in the six countries of the CEECIS region adapted them nationally to reflect contextual differences. The indicator "+1," listed last in Table 32.1, is the final, overt measure of teacher shortage. It represents the global indicator that measures unfilled positions. Since the global indicator "unfilled positions" does not at all capture the reality in the CEECIS region (only 0.2–4.5% of positions are unfilled), we adapted it regionally, and measured canceled subjects and lessons. Even the regional adaptation of the global indicator (canceled subjects and lessons due to teacher shortage), proved to be insufficient. It was only at the school level where the full picture of teacher shortage emerged. This is why it is important to pursue a system theory perspective that explains how a system regulates itself; that is, how it copes with a problem. In this case, the problem being how systems cope with a lack of qualified teachers.

Table 32.1 10+1 Indicators of teacher shortage: the case study of Kyrgyzstan

Indicators			Measurement/examples
1	A. Para-teachers (non-qualified teachers)	Number of professionals (without pedagogical training) who teach at a school	For example, electrician who teaches physics, accountant who teaches math, etc. (professionals without pedagogical training)
2		Number of pedagogical specialists who teach subjects for which they were not trained	For example, Kyrgyz language and literature teacher (with a pedagogical specialist degree) who teaches biology or subjects other than Kyrgyz language and literature
3		Number of university students who teach at a school	This includes both part-time correspondence students (*zaochnik*) as well as full-time university students (*ozchnik*) who teach at the school
4	B. Qualified teachers who teach beyond the permissible or advised retirement age, teaching load, or class/group size	Number of teachers at retirement age	Teachers who continue to teach or are brought back to the school to fill vacancies; the retirement age is 63 years for men, and 58 for women.
5		Number of teachers hired from another school	To circumvent the regulation on the maximum teaching load (24–27 hours per school), teachers are hired from another school to teach at the school. At times these teachers are also hired because the school lacks teachers with the needed qualifications
6		Number of teachers teaching at the same school with more than 24–27 teaching hours/week	Schools need to request permission from the District Education Department if their teachers teach more than 1.5 teaching loads. Some districts officially lifted the ceiling for the maximum amount of teaching hours from 1.5 to two teaching loads (*stavka*)
7		Number of teachers who do not split the class into groups despite the entitlement to do so	In a few subjects (foreign language courses, IT, etc.), schools are permitted to split the class into two groups to allow for more effective learning. Schools with teacher shortage typically do not split classes into groups to avoid increasing the teacher shortage
8	C. Mismatch between what is taught on paper and what is taught in practice	Number of teachers with prolonged absences or absenteeism	Absences can be seasonal or permanent, and can be related to other non-school related economic activities/work (harvesting, trade, etc.), or other school-related obligations (e.g. principals or deputy principals in charge of teaching classes, but because of other obligations neglect their teaching commitment)

Table 32.1 (*Continued*)

Indicators		Measurement/examples
9	Number of teachers who teach for a shorter duration than officially prescribed	The duration of the instructional hours is shortened regularly to save on human resources (which are lacking). The reduction in instructional time applies both to lessons (35 minutes instead of 45) as well as to the school year (shorter school year than prescribed)
10	Number of teachers that are listed in the lesson plan without holding the actual lessons	This indicator includes teachers who are kept on the payroll, but who have recently, or long ago, quit and moved to another location
+1	Canceled subjects and lessons	Measures those subjects that were reported as having a vacancy (or lessons within a subject that had a vacancy) that were not taught in the past school year

Source: Steiner-Khamsi *et al.* (2011); see also UNICEF CEECIS (2012), 19.

Comparing Many Countries, Few Countries, and Single Case Studies

We can now understand, in a more systematic manner, why global indicators constitute policy tools of limited use. Aside from political and economic reasons, they are literally *meaningless* when applied to a particular education system, or a specific context. Naturally, the field of comparative policy studies is not alone in facing the challenge of having to balance the depth, versus the breadth, of its assertions. This problem is inherent to the comparative method.

As researchers, we constantly make choices on whether to sacrifice depth for breadth, or vice-versa. When we investigate and carefully tease out the contradictions between the different levels of analysis, we must decide whether we also need to explain them. In this particular example of teacher shortage, the ultimate goal should be to develop a theory of systems that explains the distinct patterns that we find at global, regional, national, district, or institutional levels. The reason why the global indicator of teacher shortage is meaningless in the post-communist region, is that there is a wide divide between the teacher management, teacher employment, and teacher education systems of the (post-) communist world, and other countries with similarly high literacy rates, as well as between poor and rich countries. Thus discrepancies in teacher shortage statistics motivate us to dig deeper, and bring to light fundamental differences in these systems. Understanding the logic of systems should be the ultimate goal of comparative policy studies. The single case study, in combination with cross-national and regional comparison, is the most effective method of inquiry for fully disclosing the inner workings of an educational system.

The academic question of whether single case studies qualify as comparative becomes moot when considered against the backdrop of studies that pursue contextual comparison (see Little 2000). Case studies are a *sine qua non* of contextual comparison. It is indispensable to carry out case studies to explain similarities and differences between various units of analysis, whether they are cases, countries, contexts, or systems. Researchers should not be pressured by colleagues in their discipline to choose one comparative method or another. Ideally, a comparative study draws on several cases, a few cases, or a single case, as part of the same study. Furthermore, a case study must produce a "thick" description and is, by definition, both horizontal and vertical. It draws on many variables and rests on a sample size of one. Therefore, I find the term "vertical case study" not just tautological, but to some extent misleading, because it suggests that it is possible to produce a case study that is flat or non-vertical (see Vavrus and Bartlett, Chapter 31, this volume). Nevertheless, it may be useful as a reminder that the greatest strength of case studies is their depth, and ability to explain the causal web of actors that interact in a bounded system.

The advantages and disadvantages of case-oriented versus variable-oriented comparative research, as well as between large-N (many countries) versus small-n (few countries) comparisons, are accurately presented in Todd Landman's textbook on comparative methodology (Landman 2003; see also Ragin 1997). Landman systematically discusses the key characteristics of comparative studies that draw on single cases, comparison of a few countries, and comparison of many countries. He should also be credited for acknowledging the value of case studies for contextual comparison. For Landman, single case studies "are by nature not comparative, but may have comparative merits" (Landman 2003, 25). Landman presents a figure that illustrates the depth versus breadth dilemma. Figure 32.1 shows how every increase in sample size results in a greater level of abstraction.

The example of teacher shortage demonstrates that the level of abstraction, reflected in global indicators, creates not only a validity problem, but also an interpretation challenge. For example, the global indicator of teacher shortage may suggest a virtually non-existing shortage rate of 0.2% in a given country. However, the low rate conceals the fact that schools in that country must rely on teachers who work double shifts, take on additional hours, or engage in other local practices that help the system to cope with massive teacher shortage. The high level of abstraction found in large-N studies leads to generalizations, as well as speculations or false interpretations. Single case studies suffer from the inverse problem, resulting from

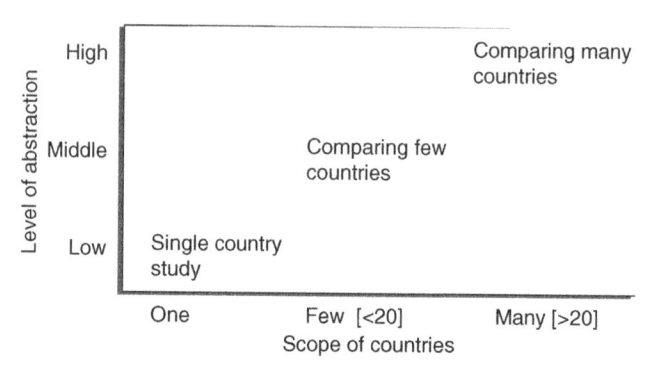

Figure 32.1 Methods of comparison.
Source: Landman (2003), 25.

the lack of comparison with other contexts, cases, systems, or countries. As a result, practices may be attributed to culture rather than to general processes, beliefs, and practices that also exist elsewhere.

The insufficiencies of the teacher shortage indicator are found in other global indicators that, by virtue of having to focus on the smallest common denominator across a wide spectrum of countries, gloss over contextual differences. It should be taken for granted that the level of abstraction and, by implication, the magnitude of imprecision and extent of de-contextualization, increases with every additional case, context, country, or system added onto a comparative study. In fact, the level of abstraction may increase to the extent that the global indicator becomes devoid of any context-specific or country-specific meaning. It becomes literally *meaningless*.

The "Data Revolution": Problems of Transition?

It appears on the surface that we moved in the policy process from politics to statistics and, within statistics, from ad hoc evaluation studies to constant and continuous data mining. Naturally, coalition- and consensus building remain at the very heart of every policy process. Evidence-based policy planning or the "data revolution" represents a political strategy to make the policy process *seem* less political and more rational. In this chapter, I attempted to show that global indicators encounter so many different country-specific or contextual interpretations that they become in fact meaningless or uninterpretable.

Having demystified the use of global indicators for local problem recognition, the question becomes: why amass so much meaningless data? The answer is: it allows for more actors, including non-state actors, international organizations and businesses, to participate in, and benefit from, educational reform. Everyone is invited to participate as long as standards are followed and progress measured and documented. Judging from the debates surrounding the post-2015 development agenda, the trend toward data mining is likely to proliferate over the next few years.

The report of the High-Level Panel of Eminent Persons on the Post-2015 Development Agenda (United Nations 2013), lists five thematic priorities[2] to be pursued in the post-2015 development environment, and concludes with a call for a "data revolution" to help monitor progress toward global development targets.

> We also call for a **data revolution** [bold in original] for sustainable development, with a new international initiative to improve the quality of statistics and information available to citizens. We should actively take advantage of new technology, crowd sourcing, and improved connectivity to empower people with information on the progress towards the targets. (Executive Summary, n.p.)

The High-Level Panel recommends establishing a Global Partnership on Development Data, that ensures that "baseline for post-2015 targets is in place by January 2016," because they expect that the frenzy to collect data will reach a new level in the immediate future. Development projects are already under pressure from funding agencies to collect baseline data and then, a few months or years later, an impact evaluation with quasi-experimental design. The indicators used for the baseline and impact studies are global indicators. As mentioned in the introductory section, the local problem definition and solution, as reflected in baseline and impact studies, are driven by international knowledge banks that, in the case of international educational development, also happen to be agencies that provide grants and loans, as well as reform packages or "solutions," to low income countries.

The fact that global agendas effectively eclipse local needs, there is a functional overlap between description and prescription, and the disappointing realization that much of development statistics hides behind a "façade of precision" (Samoff 1999), does not seem to concern the High-Level Panel of Eminent Persons. For the Panel, the data revolution entails collecting and analyzing more and better data. It envisions the ability to increase data collection with new technologies. In fact, it has been suggested that "mobile technology and other advances" will "enable real-time monitoring of development results." Better data is equated with data that is disaggregated by gender, geography, income, disability, and other categories, "to make sure that no group is being left behind."

The High-Level Panel statement should be interpreted as an unwavering belief in the validity of global indicators. Arguably, every revolution is followed by a transition period, characterized mostly by chaos. In fact, the transition argument is often used as an explanation for why data are imprecise or unavailable. It is notable that back in the very early stages of the "data revolution" in educational development, the Global Partnership in Education (at the time, Education for All Fast Track Initiative (EFA-FTI)) conceded that reliance on statistical data is nearly impossible. The 2007 annual report identifies incongruence of statistical data between international and national databanks, inconsistencies between the international Indicative Framework and the national education sector plans, and an inability to measure – among other questions of top priority – *good* primary education.

First, according to the EFA-FTI Secretariat (2007), the gap between what Ministries of Education report in terms of enrolment figures, and what the UNESCO Institute for Statistics determines, is more than three percentage points. In some cases it is as high as 20. For a donor strategy that relies so heavily upon benchmarking and monitoring annual targets, the incongruence of statistical information is a problem so grave that it calls into question the very foundation of evidence-based planning. The contradictions addressed in this paper deal with indicators that are, at first glance, simpler and uncontested such as, for example, student enrolment or teacher shortage.

Needless to say, the situation is far more complicated when organizations attempt to measure more complex concepts such as poverty, dropout, or teacher absenteeism. Upon closer examination, the statistical information provided at not just country, but also at the international level, is not simply imprecise, it is deeply entrenched in political and economic agendas. In Mongolia, for example, poverty measures swing back and forth several times; usually just before the start of an election season. Similarly, dropout statistics vary dramatically, depending on which government agency has manufactured the data. Surprisingly, there is also a big difference between two departments within the same ministry. Whereas the Nonformal Education Department reported 40,000 dropouts in 2003/4, the department in charge of educational statistics at the Ministry of Education only counted 11,953 (see Steiner-Khamsi and Stolpe 2003, 181).

Many attempts are currently being made to develop global indicators that capture the complexity of a phenomenon in different contexts and countries. An example of a sophisticated analysis demonstrating the scope of the problem is the methodological study on out-of-school children prepared by the Education Policy and Data Center (Omoeva *et al.* 2013). The Out of School Children (OOSC) Initiative, launched by UNICEF and UNESCO in 2010, is another noteworthy attempt to agree on a broader conceptual framework at the global level, which researchers could use to develop indicators at the national level. The OOSC Initiative, for example, defines five dimensions of exclusion (5DE), which are subsequently narrowed down and detailed at the national level.

In other words, there are efforts made to refine global agendas with evidence collected at national and local levels. The purpose is to increase the validity of global indicators by making them more sensitive to a variety of contexts. Why is there such a deep concern with transforming global indicators into a useful policy tool for national and local actors? To return to the questions raised earlier in this section, global indicators may be invalid measures of national and local realities and therefore qualify as "junk;" that is, are decontextualized to an extent that they do not make sense and are devoid of meaning. Nevertheless, decision-makers use them as effective political and economic tools for transferring educational reform packages from one context to another.

As the authors of this volume have pointed out, we are dealing today with the phenomenon of global norm-setting in education. It is not so much the fact that this phenomenon exists, but rather that the processes, mechanisms, and agencies that perpetuate it should be subject to scrutiny. There is indeed a "globally structured agenda for education" (Dale 2000; Verger 2014; Sahlberg, Chapter 7, this volume), and global indicators have been used as tools not only to measure, but also to disseminate a portfolio of "best practices," international standards, and global education policies, at great benefit to those international agencies that lend or sell their packages to recipient countries (see Verger, Lubienski and Steiner-Khamsi 2016).

Notes

1 For a detailed discussion of the various forms of teaching shifts see Bray (2008) and Ndalama and Chidalengwa (2010).
2 The five priorities or "five big, transformative shifts" (see Executive Summary) are: (a) leave no one behind; (b) put sustainable development at the core; (c) transform economies for jobs and inclusive growth; (d) build peace and effective, open and accountable institutions for all; and (e) forge a new global partnership.

References

Bray, M. 2008. *Double-Shift Schooling: Design and Operation for Cost-Effectiveness*. Paris: UNESCO IIEP.
Bruns, B., D. Filmer, and H.A. Patrinos. 2011. *Making Schools Work. New Evidence on Accountability Reforms*. Washington, DC: World Bank.
CEATM (Centre for Educational Assessment and Teaching Methods). 2008. *We Study for Life: The Results of the International Comparative Study of Functional Literacy of 15-Year-Old Pupils, PISA 2006*. Bishkek: CEATM.

Dale, R. 2000. "Globalization and Education: Demonstrating a 'Common World Educational Culture' or Locating a 'Globally Structured Educational Agenda?'" *Educational Theory*, 50(4): 427–448.

Education for All-Fast Track Initiative (EFA-FTI) Secretariat. 2007. *Quality Education for All Children: Meeting the Challenge. Annual Report 2007*. Washington, DC: EFA-FTI Secretariat.

Fuchs, S. 2009. "Mini-Pensen: Ein Drittel der Lehrer mit weniger als 50 Prozent." *Tagesanzeiger*, May 15.

Klees, S.J., J. Samoff, and N.P. Stromquist (eds). 2012. *The World Bank and Education. Critiques and Alternatives*. Rotterdam: Sense.

Landman, T. 2003. *Issues and Methods in Comparative Politics*. New York: Routledge.

Little, A. 2000. "Development Studies and Comparative Education: Context, Content, Comparison and Contributors." *Comparative Education*, 36(3): 279–296.

Ndalama. L. and G. Chidalengwa. 2010. *Teacher Development, Utilization and Workload in Primary Schools in Malawi: Policy and Practice*. Lilongwe: Association of Christian Educators in Malawi.

Omoeva, C., B. Sylla, R. Hatch, and C. Gale. 2013. *Out of School Children. Data Challenges in Measuring Access to Education*. Washington, DC: Education Policy and Data Center/ FHI 360.

Phamotse, P. 2009. *Composition and Status of Primary School Teachers in the Context of EFA. The Case of Contract Teachers in Lesotho*. Maseru: MoET.

Ragin, C.C. 1997. "Turning the Tables: How Case-Oriented Research Challenges Variable-Oriented Research." *Comparative Social Research*, 16: 27–42.

Samoff, J. 1999. "Education Sector Analysis in Africa: Limited National Control and Even Less National Ownership." *International Journal of Educational Development*, 19(4/5): 249–272.

Schriewer, J. and C. Martinez. 2002. "Constructions of Internationality in Education," in *The Global Politics of Educational Borrowing and Lending*, edited by G. Steiner-Khamsi. New York: Teachers College Press.

Steiner-Khamsi, G. (ed.). 2002. *The Global Politics of Educational Borrowing and Lending*. New York: Teachers College Press.

Steiner-Khamsi, G. 2013. "What is Wrong with the 'What-Went-Right' Approach in Educational Policy?" *European Educational Research Journal*, 12(1): 20–33.

Steiner-Khamsi, G. and I. Stolpe. 2006. *Educational Import in Mongolia: Local Encounters with Global Forces*. New York: Palgrave Macmillan.

Steiner-Khamsi, G., N. Teleshaliyev, G. Sheripkanova-MacLeod, and A. Moldokmatova. 2011. "Ten-Plus-One Ways of Coping with Teacher Shortage: A School-Level Analysis of Teacher Shortage in Kyrgyzstan," in *Globalization on the Margins. Education and Postsocialist Transformations in Central Asia*, edited by I. Silova, 203–232. Charlotte: Information Age Publishing.

UNESCO. 2009. *High-Level Group on Education for All. Tenth Meeting. Paris: December 9–11, 2009*. Paris: UNESCO.

UNESCO Institute of Statistics (UIS). 2013. "Global Shortage of Teachers." Retrieved from: www.uis.unesco.org/Education/Pages/world-teachers-day-2013.aspx (accessed November 19, 2015).

UNICEF Kyrgyzstan. 2009. *Survival Strategies of Schools in the Kyrgyz Republic: A School-Level Analysis of Teacher Shortages*. Bishkek: UNICEF Kyrgyzstan.

UNICEF CEECIS. 2011. *Teachers: A Regional Study on Recruitment, Development and Salaries of Teachers in the CEECIS Region*. Geneva: UNICEF CEECIS regional office.

UNICEF Mongolia. 2012. *Teachers in Mongolia: An Empirical Study on Recruitment into Teaching, Professional Development, and Retention of Teachers*. Ulaanbaatar: UNICEF Mongolia.

United Nations. 2013. *A New Global Partnership: Eradicate Poverty and Transform Economies through Sustainable Development. The Report of the High-Level Panel of Eminent Persons on the Post-2015 Development Agenda.* New York: United Nations.

Verger, A. 2014. "Why Do Policy-Makers Adopt Global Education Policies? Toward a Research Framework on the Varying Role of Ideas in Educational Reform." *Current Issues in Comparative Education*, 16(2): 14–29.

Verger, A., H. Kosar Altinyelken, and M. de Koning (eds). 2013. *Global Managerial Education Reforms and Teachers. Emerging Policies, Controversies and Issues in Developing Contexts.* Brussels: Education International.

Verger, A., C. Lubienski, and G. Steiner-Khamsi (eds.). 2016. *The Global Education Industry. World Yearbook of Education 2016.* London and New York: Routledge.

Wolter, S., S. Denzler, and B. Weber 2003. "Betrachtungen zum Arbeitsmarkt der Lehrer in der Schweiz." *Vierteljahreshefte zur Wirtschaftforschung*, 72(2): 1–15.

Name Index

Notes: Page numbers in italics refers figure, bold refers table, page numbers with "n" refers single note numbers and page numbers with "nn" refers multiple notes numbers.

Altbach, Philip, 29, 32, 481
Anderson, Benedict, 2, 59
Anderson-Levitt, Kathryn, 45
Appadurai, Arjun, 8, 265, 492, 509–514

Ball, Stephen J., 5–8, 14, 65, 66, 71, 72, 129, 135, 267, 275, 282, 366, 420, 423, 428–430, 434, 436–443, 452, 474, 479, 481, 507, 515, 521, 535–551
Benavot, Aaron, 9, 13, 129, 140, 164, 166, 241–256, 324, 329, 330
Bhabha, Homi, 520, 525, 526
Blaug, Mark, 99
Bonal, Xavier, 24, 66, 97–108, 343
Bourdieu, Pierre, 4, 101, 102, 267, 297, 298, 358, 483n.6, 499
Bray, Mark, *50, 52*, 475, 555, 587n.1
Bromley, Patricia, 10, 47, 48, 60, 68, 450, 451, 470–484

Carney, Stephen, 8, 10, 69, 451, 504–516
Carnoy, Martin, 5, 10, 22, 25, 27–40, 71, 130, 309n.4, 483n.6
Castells, Manuel, 4, 27, 28, 37
Chabbott, Colette, 13, 43, 53, 326, 341

Colclough, Christopher, 103, 340, 341
Collins, Randall, 100, 483n.6
Cornwall, Andrea, 68, 212, 402–404

Dale, Roger, 8, 9, 13, 45, 69, 70, 75, 276, 433, 434, **435**, 437, 442, 493, 505, 510, 587
de Koning, Mireille, 578
Deleuze, Gilles, 491, 504–506, 509, 510
Durkheim, Emile, 2, 176

EFA-FTI Secretariat, 586

Fairclough, Norman, 555, 557, 566
Ferguson, James, 505, 510, 511, 513
Fine, Ben, 99–101
Finnemore, Martha, 70, 336–338
Friedman, Thomas, 27, 482, 523
Fullan, Michael, 129, 130, 282

Giddens, Anthony, 27, 508
Green, Andy, 1–16, 22–26, 151, 164, 165, 169–185, 292, 309n.4, 436, 505
Grek, Sotiria, 7, 8, 12, 128, 276, 362, 377, 458, 459
Guattari, Félix, 491, 504–506, 509, 510

The Handbook of Global Education Policy, First Edition.
Edited by Karen Mundy, Andy Green, Bob Lingard, and Antoni Verger.
© 2016 John Wiley & Sons, Ltd. Published 2016 by John Wiley & Sons, Ltd.

NAME INDEX

Hanushek, Eric, 5, 24, 29, 34, 55, 81–94
Hargreaves, Andy, 129–132
Heyneman, Stephen P., 53, 99, 101, 140, 323, 329, 339, 340, 361
Hirsch, Fred, 297

Jakobi, Anja, 6, 13, 44, 53, 68, 367, 368, 389
Jessop, Bob, 65, 70, 75, 475, 537
Jones, Philip W., 8, 12, 97, 98, 105, 118, 214, 215, 225, 319, 322, 325–327, 329, 330, 339, 341, 344, 481

Kimmelman, Jay, 536, 539, 543, 544, 546, 550n.2
Klees, Steven J., 118, 579
Kosar Altinyelken, Hülya, 442, 579

Landman, Todd, 584
Levin, Ben, 32, 39, 40, 82, 130, 364, 522
Levin, Henry, 32, 39, 40, 130, 364, 522
Levy, Daniel, 32
Lewin, Keith, 189
Lingard, Bob, 4, 9, 10, 12, 13, 55, 164–168, 244, 276, 305, 314, 315, 362, 363, 458, 493, 494, 507, 520, 549

Marginson, Simon, 32, 164, 167, 168, 291–309, 463, 520, 522
Martens, Kerstin, 8, 13, 367, 368, 389, 450, 453, 454, 456, 459, 460, 462
Marx, Karl, 498, 514
May, Shanon, 114, 262, 263, 265, 394, 398n.4, 405, 541, 543, 546, 548
Meyer, Heinz-Dieter, 140, 363, 376
Meyer, John, 23, 27, 31, 43–61, 64, 68, 209, 278, 305, 362, 463, 471–473, 476, 477, 483nn.1, 3, 5, 484n.7
Mundy, Karen, 1–16, 48, 74, 105, 118, 191, 208, 212, 278, 315, 322, 323, 325–327, 329, 335–352, 385, 404, 407, 442, 450–452, 478, 480, 481, 537
Murphy, Lynne, 8, 13, 48, 208, 212, 404, 442, 478, 481, 537

Novelli, Mario, 14, 170, 192, 193, 200, 484n.10

Ong, Aihwa, 475, 507, 514

Patrinos, Harry A., 66, 67, 107, 251, 345, 482
Pennycook, Alistair, 259, 261, 263, 268
Pritzker, Irene, 536, 543
Psacharopoulos, George, 83, 97, 100, 206, 251, 340

Putnam, Robert, 28, 170, 171, 174, 178–180, 337

Ramirez, Francisco, 10, 23, 43–61, 68, 463, 472, 483n.1
Ravitch, Diane, 137, 140, 482
Robertson, Susan, 8, 13, 14, 45, 47, 70, 71, 74, 107, 164, 167, 275–288, 344, 352n.7, 385, 386, 388, 390, 395, 433, 434, **435**, 437, **440**, 442, 505, 510, 514, 537, 538, 555
Rodrik, Dani, 15, 347

Sahlberg, Pasi, 5, 25, 128–143, 282, 587
Said, Edward, 525
Samoff, Joel, 344, 586
Schleicher, Andreas, 9, 281, 282, 316, 364, 374–384
Schriewer, Juergen, 45, 462, 463, 574
Shirley, Dennis, 130, 131
Sikkink, Kathryn, 70, 218, 405
Smith, Adam, 82, 170, 193, 200, 303, 413
Soysal, Yasemin N., 27, 31, 68, 209, 472
Spivak, Gayatri, 509, 532
Steiner-Khamsi, Gita, 10, 11, 69, 75, 452, 573–586
Stone, Diane, 337, 343, 539, 548
Stromquist, Nelly, 104, 219n.1

Tooley, James, 507, 536, 544
Trow, Martin, 297, 309n.2

Unicef CEECIS, 577, 579, 583
Unterhalter, Elaine, 13, 14, 25, 112, 113, 115–122, 218, 241, 243
Urry, John, 543, 550n.16

Vavrus, Frances, 219n.2, 345, 452, 554–556, 566, 569n.1, 584
Verger, Antoni, 1–16, 23, 45, 64–76, 102, 105, 106, 314–317, 335–352, 398, 406–408, 415n.3, 442, 484n.10, 493, 537, 538, 579, 587

Weber, Max, 2, 262, 288, 484n.7, 514
Wiseman, Alexander, 135, 363, 470
Woessmann, Ludgar, 5, 34, 84, 89–91, 93nn.2, 4, 6, 7, 13, 14, 16, 94nn.20, 22
Wolfensohn, James, 343, 344, 346–350
Woodhall, Maureen, 97

Zajda, Joseph, 132
Zhao, Yong, 129, 140, 270

Place Index

Notes: Page numbers in italics refers figure, bold refers table, page numbers with "n" refers single note numbers and page numbers with "nn" refers multiple notes numbers.

Afghanistan, 166, **190**, 191, 192, 200, 201, 206, 209, 210, **211**, 214, 215, 218, 219, 220n, 382, 412, 441
Albania, **87**, 89
Angola, 191
Arab countries, 237, 575
Argentina, **87**, 89, 294, **349**
Armenia, 577, 579
Asia, 1, 5, **190**, 209, 264, 266, 267, 331, 341, 378, 385, 387, 390, 406, 451, 519–532, 545
Australia, 25, 72, 130, 131, 133, 134, 136, 140, *141*, 260, 267, 285, *295*, *301*, 303, 305, **306**, 370n.1, 379, 380, **381**, 444n.3, 451, 494, 519, 520, 525–531
Austria, 153, **306**, 370n.1, 379
Azerbaijan, **87**, **190**

Bangladesh, 118, 121, 166, 206, 210, **211**, 213, 218, 219, 264, 267, **349**, 441
Belgium, 131, *182–184*, *295*, *301*, 305, **306**, 307, 370n.1, 379, 380, **381**
Bhutan, 166, 206, 210, **211**, 216, 217
Bosnia and Herzegovina, 68, 196, 579

Brazil, 14, 15, 29, 33, 40, 69, **87**, 89, 94n.21, 105, 108, 179, 299, *301*, **301**, 309n.4, 347, 348, **349**, 365, 383
Brunei, 391, 396, 398n.1
Bulgaria, **87**, *295*
Burma, 391

Cambodia, 284, 391, 396, 398n.1
Canada, 13, 25, 57, 129, 130, 135, 140, *141*, 151, 181, *182–184*, 195, 197, 237, 238n.1, 285, 294, *295*, 300, *301*, **306**, 370n.1, 378–380, **381**, 415n.4, 444nn.1, 3, 461, 466n.1, 477, 478, 494
Caribbean, 247, 248, **294**, *294*
Catalonia, 75
Caucasus, 579
Central Asia, 235, 248, 249, **294**, *294*, 452, 579
Central Europe, 232
Chad, 192
Chile, 14, 35, 39, 66, 94n.21, 130, 133, 136, 284, **294**, 300, 305, **306**, 307, 370n.1, 379, 477
China, 6, 15, 29, 33, 45, 56, 57, 236, 260, 264, 267, 270, 275, 280, 292, **294**, *296*, *296*, 297, 300, *301*, **301**, *302*, 304, **306**,

The Handbook of Global Education Policy, First Edition.
Edited by Karen Mundy, Andy Green, Bob Lingard, and Antoni Verger.
© 2016 John Wiley & Sons, Ltd. Published 2016 by John Wiley & Sons, Ltd.

309n.4, 347, **349**, 365, 366, 385–398, 495, 498, 511, 522–524, 529, 579
Colombia, **87**, 89, **190**, 191, 230, **349**, 477, 536, 543
Costa Rica, **349**
Croatia, *295*, 300

Dakar, Senegal, **54**, 118, 119, 166, 197, 207, 215, 242, 244–246, 249–255, 323, 327, 344, 401, 404, 405, 408, 409, 414, 444n.2, *557, 558*
Dar es Salaam, 494, 496, 499
Democratic Republic of Congo, 189, **190**, 191, 201, 236
Denmark, 74, 131, 149, 151, 153, *182–184*, 293, *301*, 305, **306**, 370n.1, 379, 380, **381**, 451, 510–512

East Africa, 218, 235, 494
East Asia, 131, 136, 247–249, **294**, 294, 297, 300, 303–307, 385–390, 397, 398n.1, 474, 499, 520, 522–524, 526
Eastern Europe, 129, 131, 136, 181, 185, 225, 234, 249, 260, **294**, 294, 305, 344, 347, 462, *577, 579*
England, 3, 25, 130, 131, 134–136, 140, *141*, 292, 366, 379, 474, *537*
Eritria, 195, 201
Estonia, *182–184*, 370n.1, 379
Ethiopia, 118, **190**, 200, 201, **349**, 411, 441
Europe, 22, 25, 29, 48, **51**, 59, 68, 94n.19, 98, 114, 128, 130, **190**, 248, 259, 262, 264, 266, 281, 292, 294, 300, 302, 304, 305, 307, 357, 358, 360, 378, 387, 397, 461, 462, 464, 466, 484n.12, 519, 529, 531
European Union, 1, 44, **52**, 68, 128, 231, 260, 450, 456, 462, 463, 531, 578

Finland, 13, 26, 55, 58, 68, 76n.1, 129, 131, 142, 143, *182–184*, 282, 283, 293, 299, **306**, 370n.1, 378–380, **381**, 461
France, 3, 25, **56**, **57**, 129, 152, 161, *182–184*, 232, 300, *301*, **306**, 308, 370n.1, 379, 380, **381**, 398n.3, 444n.3, 452, 455, 458–463, 465
FYR Macedonia, 579

Gambia, 121
Germany, 3, 25, 26, 40, **55**, **57**, 129, 131, 134, 145, 148–150, 153–155, 172, *182–184*, 251, 294, *295*, *301*, 304, 305, 307, 362, 370n.1, 375, 377–379, 398n.3, 444n.3, 455, 459, 461, 462, 464, 465, 466n.1, 477, *478*, 508
Ghana, 119, 122, **349**, 437, **438**, 540, 543
Guinea, 192
Gulf State, 303

Honduras, 195
Hong Kong, 264, 293, 300, 365, 522, 528
Hungary, 370n.1, 378–380

India, 15, 29, 33, 116, 121, 166, **190**, 192, 206, 209, 210, **211**, 212, 218, 219, 220n.13, 260, 294, 299, *301*, 309n.4, 347, **349**, 366, 397, 398n.3, 426, **438**, **439**, 441, 442, 474, 495, 498, 521, 523, 530, *536*, 540, 542, 546, 550n.13
Indonesia, **87**, 89, 236, 266, 348, **349**, 366, 379, 387, 391, 396, 398nn.1, 3, 528
Ireland, 9, *182–184*, *295*, 305, **306**, 307, 370n.1, 379, 380, **381**
Israel, **190**, 300, *301*, 370n.1, 379, 380, **381**
Italy, 172, *182–184*, 227, *295*, *301*, **306**, 370, 379, 461, 462, 465, 477

Japan, 3, 29, 46, **55**, **57**, 83, 131, 150–152, 181, *182–184*, 251, 264, 292, *295*, 299, 300, *301*, 305, **306**, 306, 308, 338, 357, 358, 362, 370n.1, 375, 378–380, **381**, 383, 386, 387, 397, 398nn.1, 3, 444n.3, 477, 521, 528

Kazakhstan, **87**, 398n.3
Kenya, 116, 119, 120, 122, 201, 236, **349**, 484n.10, *535*, 539, 540, 544, 547
Korea, 29, **57**, 61n.1, *182*, *183*, 252, 299, 305, **306**, 306, **349**, 370n.1, 378, 383, 398nn.1, 3, 475, 521
Kosovo, 192
Kyrgyzstan, **87**, 89, *577*, *579–581*, **582–583**

Laos, 391, 394, 396, 398n.1
Latin America, 1, 7, 66, 93n.14, 131, 247, 248, **294**, 294, 305, 410, 474
Latvia, 94n.21, *295*, 379
Liberia, 191
Luxembourg, 370n.1, 379

Malaysia, **57**, 264, 300, *301*, 389, 391, 394, 396, 398nn.1, 3, 522
Maldives, 166, 206, 210, **211**, 216, 217, 219
Mexico, 40, 69, 105, 115, 252, **306**, 307, 341, 348, **349**, 370n.1, 375, 379, 380, **382**

Middle East, 1, 15, 132, 136, **190**, 347, 410
Moldova, 579
Mongolia, 398n.3, 575, 578, 579, 586
Montenegro, **87**, 251
Myanmar, **190**, 396, 398n.1

Nepal, 166, 192, 193, 200, 206, **211**, 216, 218, 219, 396, 451, 510, 511, 513, 546
The Netherlands, 25, 26, **56**, 74, 129, 141, *141*, 181, *182–184*, *295*, *301*, **306**, 370n.1, 379, 380, **382**, 444n.3, 477, *536*
New Zealand, 26, 66, 131, 136, 140, *141*, 284, *295*, 303, 305, **306**, 370n.1, 380, *536*, 541
Nicaragua, 195
Niger, 121, 575
Nigeria, 122, **190**, 441, 544, 546, 575
Nordic countries, 168, 227, 298, 304, 307
North America, 2, 25, 130, 248, **294**, 300, 378, 427, 484n.12, 519, 578

Pakistan, 120, 166, **190**, **200**, 206, **209**, 210, **211**, 213, 214, 218, 219, 220n.13, 260, 264, **301**, 348, **349**, 398n.3, 441, 442, 477, 544, 577, 578
Panama, **87**, 89
Peru, 87, *88*, 88, 89, 93n.14
Philippines, *88*, 88, **190**, 299, **349**, 391, 396, 398n.1
Poland, *182–184*, *295*, *301*, 305, **306**, 349, 370n.1, 378–380, **382**
Prussia, 2, 292

Rwanda, **190**, 196, 499

Sarajevo, 196, 411
Scotland (UK), 379
Senegal, 242, 323
Serbia, **87**, 300
Shanghai (China), 362, 378
Sierra Leone, 191, 193, 200
Singapore, 26, 29, 55, **57**, 58, 142, 143, 260, 264, 293, 300, **301**, 304, 322, 378, 379, 386, 387, 389, 391, 394, 396, 398n.1, 499, 520, 522, 524, 528
Slovak Republic, *184*, **306**, 370n.1, 379, 380
Slovenia, *295*, 300, **301**, 370n.1, 379, 380, **382**
Somalia, **190**, 191, 412
South Africa, 15, 83, *88*, 88, 119–121, 136, 236, 260, 309n.4, 347, 366, 404, 407, **439**, 491, 494

South Asia, 66, 164, 166, 206–220, 294, 390, 520, 545
South Korea, 15, 26, **55**, 131, 142, 143, 245, 264, 294, *295*, 300, *301*, **301**, 305, 382, 386, 451, 512
Soviet Union, 12, 131, 277, 322, 578
Spain, **56**, 72, 136, *182–184*, *295*, *301*, **306**, 366, 370n.1, 379, 380
Sri Lanka, 166, 206, 210, **211**, 212, 215, 217–219
Sub-Saharan Africa, 101, 166, 206, 220n.13, 237, 247, 248, 250, 251, 255, **294**, 294, 351n.2, 452, 535, 543, 562, 576
Sudan, **190**, 192, 193, 195, 200, 352n.6
Sweden, 11, 25, 26, 129, 131, 133, 136, 140, *141*, 141, 152, 175, 179, *182–184*, *295*, 305, **306**, 370n.1, 379, 444n.3, 477, *478*
Switzerland, 153, 157, 293, *301*, 305, **306**, 370n.1, 461, 464, 466n.1, 576
Syria, 190, **190**, 191, 194

Taiwan, 29, 55, **56**, **57**, **294**, 300, *301*, **301**, 386, 390
Tanzania, 14, 122, 195, 236, 253, 345, **439**, 494, 496, 497, 499
Thailand, 85, **87**, **190**, 234, 236, 241, 300, **301**, 323, 391, 392, 396, 398nn.1, 3, 458, 521
Trinidad and Tobago, 87
Tunisia, **87**, 89, 300, **301**
Turkey, 15, 46, 179, **190**, *295*, *301*, **301**, 305, **306**, 307, **349**, 370n.1, 379, 380, **382**, **439**

Uganda, 116, 201, **349**, **438**, 442, 444n.4, *536*, 543, 546, 547
United Kingdom, *184*, 266, 285, *301*, 398n.3
United States, 131, *184*, **190**, 277, *301*, 358, 509
Uruguay, **87**, 458
Uzbekistan, 579

Venezuela, 294
Vietnam, 6, 192, 264, 389, 391, 396, 398nn.1, 3, 524

Wales (UK), 379

Zambia, **438**, 444n.4, 451, 452, 512, 543, 554–570

Subject Index

Notes: Page numbers in italics refers figures, bold refers table, page numbers with "n" refers single note numbers and page numbers with "nn" refers multiple notes numbers.

absolute direct effects, 165, 171, 172, 179, 181
access to education, 98, 116, 117, 120, 146, 165, 193–197, 200, 201, 208, 213, 220n.12, 247, 256n.3, 266, 545, 576
accountability, 5, 6, 10, 22, 23, 25, 35, 39, 128, 131, 133, 136, 137, **139**, 140, 142, 167, 208, 210, 218, 219, 252, 256, 267, 277, 282, 283, 287, 288, 305, 329, 330, 343, 349, 366, 375, 405, 410, 425, 435, 451, 454, 460, 473, 476, 477, 480, 482, 510, 522, 538, 548, 561, 574, 578, 579
accreditation, **56**, 133, 302, 388, 480
ActionAid, 119, 404, 406–408
adult literacy, **211**, 212, 242, 244, 249, 560
African Network Campaign on Education for All (ANCEFA), 405, 406
ANCEFA *see* African Network Campaign on Education for All (ANCEFA)
agenda-setting, 8, 314, 315, 337, 338, 351, 368, 456, 457, 574
aid, 3, 4, 9, 15, 113, 117–119, 122, 165, 166, 194, 198, 200, 206, 207, 209, 212, 214, 216, 218, 241–256, 315, 319, 320, 322, 323, 326, 331, 342–345, 347, 388, 390, 394, 408, 411, 419, 423, 435, 436, 443, 444n.3, 481, 496, 497, 528, 543, 545, 563, 575 *see also* donor aid
ambivalence, 244, 481, 513, 520, 524–526
A Nation at Risk, 25, 55, 130, 362, 458
anthropology, 451, 493, 499, 500, 507, 514, 539
ASEAN (organization, countries) *see* Association of Southeast Asian Nations (ASEAN) (organization, countries)
Asia literacy, 526–528, 531, 532
aspirations for tertiary education, 297
assessment, 5, 7, 12, 24, 29, 34, 39, 55, 71, 84–87, **87**, 89, 92, 93nn.6, 7, 10, 12, 13, 21, 103, 129, 132, 133, 135, 137, 140–142, 185, 236, 241, 247, 249, 255, 265, 267, 276, 280–282, 284, 287, 292, 315, 330, 349, 357, 364–367, 369, 370, 375–378, 380, **382**, 382–384, 413, 428, 434, 454, 458–460, 466, 476, 477, 484n.9, 519, 522, 546, 550, 550n.2, 558–562, 565, 567–569, 570n.2, 581
Association of Southeast Asian Nations (ASEAN), 1, 7, 16, 316, 385–398

The Handbook of Global Education Policy, First Edition.
Edited by Karen Mundy, Andy Green, Bob Lingard, and Antoni Verger.
© 2016 John Wiley & Sons, Ltd. Published 2016 by John Wiley & Sons, Ltd.

Back on Track (UNICEF), 200
basic learning needs, **54**, 196, 557, 558
basic needs, 97, 103, 325, 338
benchmarking, 12, 49, 129, 281, 302, 304, 337, 398, 450, 586
best practices, 9, 44, 49, 53, 58, 60, 348, 422, 444n.4, 452, 459, 484n.9, 555, 565, 568, 574, 575, 587
BIA *see* Bridge International Academies (BIA)
bilateral agency, 34, 278
bilateral aid, 323, 342, 347, 575
Bologna process, 9, 48, 51, 75, 308, 454, 461–466
Bongoland, 494–495, 497
Brazil, Russia, India, China, and South Africa (BRICS), 347
BRICS *see* Brazil, Russia, India, China, and South Africa (BRICS)
Bridge International Academies (BIA), 452, 535, 536, 539–543, 545–549, 550nn.3, 5, 6, 17, 22, 551n.28
business, 1, 28, 56, 66, 99, 122, 137, 145, 167, 178, 267, 276, 292, 316, 325, 335, 374, 390, 419–430, 436, 470, 507, 528, 537, 575
business studies, 296

case study(s), 57, 153–157, 207, 212, 219n.2, 284, 315, 411, 451, 452, 454, 507, 542, 554–570, 580, **582–583**, 583–585
causal story, 539, 543, 548–549
CDA *see* critical discourse analysis (CDA)
CEECIS *see* Central and Eastern Europe and the Commonwealth of Independent States (CEECIS)
CEF *see* Commonwealth Education Fund (CEF)
Center for Education Innovations (CEI), 544, 546
Centre for Educational Research and Innovation (CERI), 360, 361, 364
Central and Eastern Europe and the Commonwealth of Independent States (CEECIS), 577, 579–581, **583**
Central Emergency Response Fund (CERF), 254, 255
centralization, 11
CERF *see* Central Emergency Response Fund (CERF)
CERI *see* Centre for Educational Research and Innovation (CERI)
change management, 112

child protection, 194, 196, 325 *see also* protection of children
civic engagement, 171
Clinton Global Initiative (Forum), 540, 542, 543, 550n.15
CME *see* coordinated market economy (CME)
cognitive skills, 24, 81, 82, **84**, 85, 89, **90**, 91, 92, 364
Cold War, 3, 4, 117, 165, 191, 207, 209, 214, 241, 322, 323, 342, 358, 360, 365, 370, 387, 390, 458, 523
collective skill formation, **152**, 152, 153
colonization, 100, 101, 261
commercialization, 167, 260, 267, 305, 307, 493
Commonwealth Education Fund (CEF), 406
comparative methods, 583, 584
comparison, 1, 12, 34, 47, 55, 129, 140, 153, 157, 207, 282, 284, 285, 287, 292, 293, 299, 308, 320, **329**, 330, 361, 365, 367, 375–380, 382–384, 452, 460, 499, 500, 555, 569, 584, **584**, 585
competition, 3, 5, 12, 22, 25, 27–29, 34–36, 72, 73, 102, 128–130, 133–135, 137, **138**, **139**, 140–142, 147, 175–177, 179, 260, 275, 282, 287, 291, 292, 295, 298, 299, 302–308, 315, 344, 348, 387, 388, 407, 434, **438**, 462, 474, 477, 478, 482, 483n.6, 484n.11, 520, 521
competition in education, 134, 298, 520
conflict-affected, 189–192, 196, 199, 200, 218, 250, 253–255, 327, 335, 347, 350, 351, 352n.6, 412
conflict-sensitive education, 194, 197
Confucianism, 393, 523
connectivity, 300, 510, 513, 535–551, 585
constructivism (critical constructivism), 23, 65, 69, 70, 76, 282, 336
Convention on the Elimination of All Forms of Discrimination Against Women (CEDAW), 54, 115, 195
Convention on the Rights of Children (CRC), 54, 195, 196, 208, 210, 241, 320, 327
Convention relating to the Status of Refugees, 196
coordinated market economy (CME), 26, 147–151
corporate citizenship, 421, 427
corporations, 4, 14, 122–124, 128, 130, 276, 281, 316, 325, 345, 348, 368, 419–423, 427, 429, 430, **438**, **440**, 444, 478, 496, 512, 537, 548

cosmopolitan, 46, 292, 513
cost-recovery, 101, 103, 344
cost-sharing, 22, 23, 32, 33
counter terrorism, 192
CPE *see* cultural political economy (CPE)
CRC *see* Convention on the Rights of Children (CRC)
credentialism, 100, 297
credentials, 152, 175, 283, 295, 307, 407, 412, 480
crime, 170, 176
critical discourse analysis (CDA), 120, 452, 554–557, 562, 569
cultural political economy (CPE), 23, 65, 69, 70, 76
cultural rationalization, 10, 472, 473, 476, 480
culture
  institutional, 27, 329, 451
  organizational, 304, 315, 329, 336, 337, 346, 350
cumulative effects, 165, 171–173, 176, 179–181
customer focus, 305

Dakar Framework for Action, **54**, 166, 197, 235, 242, 250, 255, 557, 558
data, 7, 24, 37, 47, 81, 120, 130, 166, 170, 190, 215, 237, 248, 266, 276, 292, 314, 330, 339, 358, 375, 386, 428, 458, 477, 519, 544, 557, 575
data revolution, 585–587
decolonization, 195, 209
deconcentration, 510
decontextualization (recontextualization), 9, 69, 363, 585
decoupling, 52, 57, 471–473, 480, 483n.6
Deleuzean, 506, 507
demand for education, 5, 28–30, 99, 103, 104, 307, 348
Department for International Development (DFID), 122, 195, 267, 407, 442, 544, 545, 549
deterritorialization, 4, 506, 510
developing countries, 4–6, 12, 24, 32, 34, 38, 39, 64, 73, 74, 81–94, 97–102, 123, 131, 170, 235, 247, 251, 252, 283, 298, 307, 317, 340, 365, 366, 386, 403, 407, 422, 423, 459, 535, 538, 549, 551n.32, 576, 577
development approach to education in conflict, 198
DFID *see* Department for International Development (DFID)

DIBELS *see* Dynamic Indicators of Basic Early Literacy Skills (DIBELS)
diffusion, 9, 10, 15, 22, 23, 27, 31, 32, 43, 64–76, 145, 450, 452, 474, 475
distributional effects, 165, 171, 176–177, 179, 181
diversity, 5, 22, 25, 46, 53, 57, 58, 131, 172, 180, 181, 216, 228, 232, 236, 262, 265, 269, 270, 278, 303–308, 351, 380, 476, 526, 558, 569
d.o.b., 541
donor aid, 206, 209, 216, 218 *see also* aid
dual apprenticeship, 148, 150–154
Dynamic Indicators of Basic Early Literacy Skills (DIBELS), 561, 562, 566, 567

EAHEP *see* European Union-Asia Higher Education Platform (EAHEP)
early child development (ECD), 224–226, 228–231
Early Childhood and Care (ECEC), 166, 224–228, 230–238
Early Childhood Education and Care (ECEC), 164, 166, 224–238
early grade reading, 452, 556, 557, 560–562, 564–566, 568, 569
ECD *see* early child development (ECD)
ECEC *see* Early Childhood Education and Care (ECEC)
Economics
  development, 4, 15, 55, 97–99, 198, 207, 208, 264, 267, 328, 358, 388, 391, 392, 498, 522
  impact, 24, 358
  languages, 267
ECTS *see* European Transfer and Accumulation System (ECTS)
Education
  attainment, 29, 33, 34, 129, 217
  change, 9, 15, 31, 36, 39–40, 130–132, 135, **139**, 375
  in conflict, 165, 189–201, 254, 255, 327, 335
  expansion, 29, 31, 39, 98, 100, 217, 295, 474, 483n.2
  multilateralism, 3, 308, 397, 420–421
  policy analysis, 364
  policy studies, 507, 515
  as a private good, 39
  privatization, 64–76, 317
  professions, 1, 2, 47, **56**, 60, 115, **138**, 139, 167, 208, 220n.7, 427
  as a public good, 74

Education (cont'd)
  quality, 22, 29, 31–37, 107, 108, 323, 382, 563, 569
  and skills, 5, 12, 176, 185, 281, 316, 363, 364, 367, 370, **440**
Education and Emergencies and Post-Crisis Transition (EEPCT), 200
Education at a Glance, 12, 285, 359, 361, 367, 389
Education First Initiative, 197, 437
Education for All (EFA), 9, 13, 25, 48, **51**, 53, **54**, 71, 85, 89, 90, 92, 93n.8, 113, 117–122, 133, 164, 166, 192, 195–197, 199, 207–210, 212, 214–217, 219, 225, 234–237, 241–256, 320, 321, 323, 324, 326–328, 330, 341, 344, 345, 404–408, 411, 421, 422, 433–435, 437, 441, 478, 537, 539, 542, 557–560, 563, 586
Education for All Declaration, 210
Education for All Fast Track Initiative (EFA-FTI) Secretariat, 586
Education International, 242, 281, 404, 408
Education policy, 1–16, 22, 64, 98, 118, 130, 164–169, 206–220, 226, 241, 267, 283, 314, 319–332, 340, 362, 400, 442, 450–466, 470, 490–500, 504–516, 535, 563
Education Reform Act (ERA), 25, 130
Education Sector Strategy Update (ESSU), 559, 560
EFA *see* Education for All (EFA)
elite power, 27
elites, 22, 23, 27, 30–33, 38, 39, 57, 59, 68, 120, 121, 123, 124, 209, 216, 297–299, 307, 309n.2, 340, 378, 391, 397, 402, 403, 441, 471, 481, 483n.6, 511
emergency phase of conflict, 194
employers' associations, 147, 148, 150, 153, 157
engineering, 43, 44, 59, 235, 295, 296, 394, 495
English, 25, 131, 134, 167, 168, 201, 232, 260–270, 299, 300, 303–306, 396, 430n.1, 511, 562–565, 567, 580
English as a global language, 167
English as a medium of instruction (EMI), 264, 563
epistemological governance, 368–370
equality, 10, 23, 25, 30, 31, 43, 103, 104, 106, 107, 112–124, 170, 171, 179, 229, 231–234, 242, 243, 246, 249, 303, 343, **438**, 442, 444, 461, 472, 543
equal opportunities, 232, 321, 476, 497

ERA *see* Education Reform Act (ERA)
ESSU *see* Education Sector Strategy Update (ESSU)
ethnography, 450, 451, 490–500, 538, 555
EU *see* European Union (EU)
Europe, 2, 22, 29, 48, 66, 94n.19, 98, 114, 128, 147, **190**, 234, 248, 259, 281, 292, 338, 357, 378, 387, 461, 484n.12, 519, 577
European Commission, 6, 13, **56**, 169, 200, 238n.3, 264, 266, 275, 281, 411, 462, 463, 465
European Higher Education Area, 454, 461, 463
European Transfer and Accumulation System (ECTS), 461–462
Europeanization, 128
European Union (EU), 1, 7, 9, 12, 44, 48, 51, 52, 68, 69, 128, 169, 231, 252, 260, 264, 266, 307, 450, 456, 461–464, 466, 531, 578
European Union-Asia Higher Education Platform (EAHEP), 531
Evidence-based policy, 72, 218, 244, 268, 279, 367, 413, 454, 460, 573–574, 585
extended case method, 492

faculty mobility, 304
feminist activism, 121
fieldwork, 554
financial crisis, 164, 245, 346–350, 358, 574
foreign languages, 264, 266–267, **582**
fragility, 191, 199, 411, 413
fragmentation, 252, 293, 491, 505
French, 152, 201, 263, 266, 300, 379, 380, 381, 459, 461, 462, 504, 508, 509
functionalism, 31, 32, 36, 38, 482
functionalist, 31–33, 45, 483n.6

G8 *see* Group of Eight (G8)
GATS *see* General Agreement on Trade in Services (GATS)
GAW *see* Global Action Week (GAW)
GBCE *see* Global Business Coalition for Education (GBCE)
GCE *see* Global Campaign for Education (GCE)
gender, 10, 13, 14, 22, 25, 31, 44, 103, 111–124, 170, 175, 213–217, 219, 229, 231–234, 242, 243, **246**, 247–249, 323, 326, 327, 408, **435**, 444, 492, 512, 531, 586

General Agreement on Trade in Services(GATS), 14
GERM *see* Global Educational Reform Movement (GERM)
German, 37, 149, 151, 153, 154, 157, 263, 266, 300, 303, 304, 362, 377, 455, 459, 508
Girls' schooling, 111, 113–115, 117–119, 123, 214
Global Action Week (GAW), 405, 408
Global Business Coalition for Education (GBCE), 422, 442
Global Campaign for Education (GCE), 14, 242, 404–408, 412, 414, 415
global competition, 140, 275, 292, 295, 298, 302, 307, 520
global educational policy (global education policy), 2–9, 11–16, 22–24, 27–40, 43–61, 64–76, 105, 107, 118, 135, 164, 166, 201, 207–209, 314, 315, 319–332, 345, 362, 369, 370, 401, 442, 444, 450–452, 471, 474–481, 490–500, 504–516, 535, 537, 539, 550n.1, 555, 568, 569, 573, 587
Global Educational Reform Movement (GERM), 22, 25, 26, 128–143
global elite, 22, 31, 39, 511
global governance, 8, 9, 167, 275–288, 314, 316, 335–352, 357, 359, 360, 368, 369, 386, 430, 537, 575
global indicators, 452, 573–587
globalization, 1–16, 22, 25–40, 43–61, 65, 106, 128–129, 148, 149, 153, 164, 166, 167, 180, 206, 208, 218, 219n.1, 260, 264, 267, 270, 277, 291, 292, 298–300, 307, 308, 316, 343, 347, 358, 362, 366, 369, 374, 386, 442, 471, 490, 493, 504, 506–510, 514, 523, 532, 573, 574
globally mobile graduates, 298
global norm(s)/global norm-making/global norm-breaking, 23, 320, 490, 493, 494, 498, 499, 574, 575, 587
global partnership for education (GPE), 13, 122, 165, 195, 197–199, 245, 252, 253, 335, 348, 406, 408, 412, 443, 444, 444n.2
global policy, 1, 22, 60, 64, 111, 164, 190, 207, 224, 281, 314, 337, 359, 450, 467, 535, 554–570, 573
global policy flows, 305
global policy networks, 535–551
global politics, 67, 260, 263, 267, 269, 270, 385

global polity, 8, 15, 67, 76, 111–124, 164, 167, 259–270, 385
global science system, 300
global South, 206, 209, 210, 226, 230, 234, 237, 317, 319, 406, 433, 434, 436, 437, 439, 442, 443, 507
global standards, 3, 10, 44
global university ranking, 56, 293, 302, 519
glonacal, 168, 291, 308
GNH *see* gross national happiness (GNH) index
Google, 307
governance, 8, 9, 167, 268–270, 275–288, 314, 316, 335–352, 357, 359, 360, 366, 368–370, 386, 401, 479, 537, 538, 575
see also epistemological governance; global governance; infrastructural governance; network governance
GPE *see* global partnership for education (GPE)
GPE Fragile States Policy, 199
graduate jobs, 296, 297
graduate premium, 293
graduate qualifications, 293
gross national happiness (GNH) index, 216
Gross Tertiary Enrolment Ratio (GTER), 294, 296–298
Group of Eight (G8), 1, 15, 250, 342, 360, 545
Group of 20 (G20), 15, 347, 360
GTER *see* Gross Tertiary Enrolment Ratio (GTER)
Guizhou, 386, 391–397

HCT *see* human capital theory (HCT)
health, 44, 83, 115, 117, 118, 120, 121, 123, 142, 152, 165, 169, 170, 176, 178, 181, 185, 194, 197, 216, 227, 229, 235, 237, 253, 254, 323, 325, 326, 335, 339, 344, 345, 348, 387, 410, 441, 477, 480, 484n.11, 496, 545, 550, 558
hegemony, 100–102, 314, 316, 338, 346–351, 483n.6, 493, 515
Hewlett Foundation, 424, 425, 429
higher education, 2, 24, 27, 46, 75, 81, 101, 114, 145, 164, 170, 195, 208, 264, 291–309, 316, 324, 340, 385–398, 428, 451, 454, 475, 491, 507, 519–532, 577
higher education systems, 33, 167, 168, 251, 291, 293, 299, 300, 303–305, 309n.2, 397, 398n.4, 455, 463, 465, 498, 521, 531
high participation higher education systems, 293

high participation systems (HPSs), 168, 292–299, 307
historical institutionalism, 11, 26, 146
history of education in conflict, 190, 195
homogenization, 59, 134, 308
HPSs *see* high participation systems (HPSs)
human capital, 4, 12, 22, 24, 30, 57, 60, 81–94, 97, 100–102, 134, 149, 151, 164–166, 209, 217, 226, 229, 231, 232, 236, 237, 264, 267, 295, 296, 326, 339, 340, 362–365, 367, 391, 454, 559
human capital theory (HCT), 22, 24, 97–108, 206, 297, 351n.1, 361
humanist/humanism, 322, 505
humanitarian approach to education in conflict, 165, 198, 199
humanitarianism/humanitarian, 114, 165, 190, 194, 196–199, 254, 255, 320, 326, 327, 408–413, 491, 494
humanities, 46, 57, 238n.1, 277, 296, 308, 309n.3, 444n.1, 491, 514
human rights, 1, 10, 13, 14, 23, 27, 30, 31, 44–46, 50, **51**, 52, 53, **54**, 113, 115, 164–166, 198, 206–220, 241, 319–321, 323, 327, 328, 331, 358, 403, 408, 413, 421, 472, 475, 476, 480, 557, 558 *see also* rights
human rights frameworks, 165, 206, 207
Humboldtian, 304
hybridity, 436, 511
hyper-languaging, 260, 269

IBRD *see* International Bank For Reconstruction and Development (IBRD)
ICICI (Group, Foundation), 317, 424, 426, 429
ICT *see* information and communications technology (ICT)
ideationalism, 69
ideological convergence, 22, 27, 31–39
IDP Foundation, 437, **438**, 441, 543
impact investment, 540, 542, 545, 550n.18, 20
income contingent tuition loan, 306
Independent Evaluation Group (IEG), 349
indicators, 12, 25, 34, 49, 69, 84, 113, 119, 154, 181, 195, 199, 210, 215–217, 242, 247, 249, 253, 278, 280, 281, 286, 300, 303, 358, 359, 361, 367, 370, 379, 379, 380, **381**, **382**, 389, 405, 426, **438**, 452, 458–460, 463, 506, 522, 560, 561, 567, 569, 573–587
Industrial Training Board (ITB), 156
INEE *see* Inter-Agency Network for Education in Emergencies (INEE)

inequality/inequalities, 176, 177, 179, 181, 185
  of income, 5, 32, 176, 177, 179, 181, 183, 185
  of skills, 176, 177, 181–185
information and communications technology (ICT), 36–39, 443
Information Technology (IT), 27, 122, **582**
infrastructural governance, 357, 368, 370
infrastructure, 7, 92, 189, 191, 216, 243, 253, 260, 296, 300, 306, 338, 339, 358, 364, 367–370, 390, **438**, 491, 499, 544
INGO *see* International Non-Governmental Organization(s) (INGO)
InspirED, 543
institutionalism, 10, 11, 26, 69, 100, 105, 146, 321, 336, 450, 471, 474, 484n.12
institutionalization, 70, 74, 75, 411
institutional pluralism, 473
institutional theory, 319, 472, 474, 475, 479, 480, 483n.3
Inter-Agency Network for Education in Emergencies (INEE), 195, 197, 408–415
Internally Displaced Person (IDP) Foundation, 437, 438, 441, 543
International Bank For Reconstruction and Development (IBRD), 338, 344, 347, 348
international comparisons, 1, 55, 129, 140, 153, 292, 361, 375–380, 382–384
International Covenant on Economic, Social and Cultural Rights, 115, 208, 320
international development, 15, 34, 130, 251, 267, 319, 331, 335, 337, 338, 342, 347, 403, 437, **440**, 444, 491, 544, 545, 556
international economy, 28
international education, 3, 8, 52, 129, 133, **138**, 243, 297, 302, 304, 305, 326, 389, 401, 458, 543
internationalization of education policy, 453–455, 461
International Non-Governmental Organization(s) (INGO), 47, 48, 48, 68, 166, 224, 228, 237, 404, 413, 415, 441, 476, 481
international organization, 1, 3, 4, 6, 9, 11, 14, 34, 36, 47–49, 53, 60, 67–69, 81, 108, 116, 166, 208, 212, 224, 225, 227, 228, 237, 242, 278, 314–316, 320, 321, 327, 336, 337, 341, 348, 350, 352n.6, 358, 359, 361, 363, 364, 367–370, 389, 404, 405, 411, 413, 419, 450, 452, 453, 458, 459, 481, 537, 555, 569, 575, 576, 579, 585

international testing, 6, 34, 54, 55, 55
internet, 31, 32, 36–38, 131, 292, 300, 307, 494, 538
interpellate/interpellation, 74
Islamic fundamentalist militantism, 347
isomorphism, 10, 68, 362, 471, 472, 474, 480

Keynesianism, 99, 100
knowledge
  economy, 5, 22, 28, 29, 56, 71, 264, 282, 288, 344, 466n.2
  society, 56–58, 60

labour market, 495
language
  and development, 268
  ideology(s), 261
  and migration, 265
language policy and planning (LPP), 260, 262
latent phase of conflict, 193
law, 44, 52, 53, 112, 114, 121, 155, 213, 215, 219, 220nn.6, 8, 10, 11, 279, 293, 295–298, 375, 393, 425, 443, 463, 491, 499
LCPS *see* Low Cost Private School (LCPS)
legitimacy, 22, 28, 33–39, 44, 45, 48, 73, 177, 195, 213, 314, 315, 319–331, 337, 341, 403, 404, 429, 434, 442, 457, 461, 463, 466, 480, 498, 525, 537
  epistemic, 329–331
  normative, 320, 325, 331
  output, 321, 325, 328, 329
  performative, 329–331
  state, 29, 31–32, 34, 37, 39
LGT Venture Philanthropy, 541, 543, 548
liberal arts colleges, 305, 309n.2
liberal intergovernmentalism, 455, 465
liberalization, 14, 65, 106, 149, 212, 225, 340, 341, 460
liberal market economy (LME), 26, 146, 148, 149, 155, 358
life long learning, 454, 577
life sciences, 296
linguistic capital, 267
literacy, 50, 88–90, **90**, 93n.17, 116, 118, 119, 131, 133, 135, 137, 181, **183**, 193, 211, 212, 215, 217, 220n.12, 242–244, 247–249, 255, 256n.3, 278, 322, 323, 330, 341, 362, 364, **381**, 383, 428, 430n.1, 452, 458, 481, 494, 520, 526–528, 531, 532, 554–570, 574, 583
LME *see* liberal market economy (LME)

local (the), 6, 45, 47, 60, 201, 207, 230, 231, 403, 407, 451, 490, 491, 498, 500, 539, 541, 546, 573–575, 586
localization, 8, 47, 215, 219, 270, 451, 452, 490–500
loose coupling, 23, 45, 480
Low Cost Private School (LCPS), 102, 452, 540, 544

managerial governance, 476–490
Manpower Planning Forecast (MPF), 99, 100
Manpower Services Commission (MSC), 156
market in international education, 302
marketization, 5, 131, 291, 292, 299, 305–308, **440**, 463–465
market reforms, 11, 73
mass education, 29, 31, 54, 57–59, 216, 298
mass higher education, 295, 300
massification of education, 196
Mass Open Online Courses (MOOCs), 14, 32, 37, 293, 307
McKinsey, 131, 276, 280, 429, 547
MDGs *see* Millennium Development Goals (MDGs)
measurement, 9, 24, 31, 32, 34–36, 47, 81–86, **138**, 140, 243, 267, 362, 365, 367, 369, **381**, 473, 541, 547, 549, 557, 560, 561, 576, **582**, **583**
meetingness, 543, 549, 550n.16
methodological nationalism, 167, 291, 510
methods of comparison, 584
Millennium Development Goals (MDGs), 25, 85, 89, 92, 93n.9, 113, 119, 120, 166, 192, 207, 208, 212, 217, 243, 254, 255, 320, 327, 344, 366, 421, 520
minority languages, 236, 260, 263, 265–266, 270
mobile technology, 523, 548, 586
modern apprenticeship (MA), 156
modernity, 22, 23, 27, 34, 35, 44, 46, 278, **435**, 504, 506, 508, 512–514, 523, 525
modernization theory, 192, 200, 287
MOOCs *see* Mass Open Online Courses (MOOCs)
MPF *see* Manpower Planning Forecast (MPF)

national hierarchies, 299
National Reading Panel (NRP), 561, 565
national science system, 299, 300, 303
nation state, 2–4, 6, 12, 23, 27–40, 45, 50, 59, 60, 68, 116, 128, 207, 212, 219, 259, 262, 277, 278, 291–293, 420, 453, 457, 461, 463, 472, 478, 508, 510, 538, 549, 569

NBTL program *see* New Breakthrough to
  Literacy (NBTL) program
NCP *see* New Colombo Plan (NCP)
neoimperial, 308
neoinstitutionalism, 69, 450, 471, 482, 484n.12
neoliberalism, 6, 13, 101, 167, 225, 260,
  263, 267, 270, 279, 282, 287, 350, 475,
  482, 483n.2, 505, 507, 512, 538, 542,
  544, 547
network ethnography, 538
network governance, 366, 479, 537, 538
network society, 37
New Breakthrough to Literacy (NBTL)
  program, 563–565
New Colombo Plan (NCP), 528, 529, 531, 532
New Deal on Aid Effectiveness, 198
New Public Management (NPM), 68, 304,
  305, 343, 362, 475, 479
No Child Left Behind (NCLB), 135, 267, 482
non-alignment, 209
nongovernmental organization, 212
non-state private actors, 433–435, 442,
  443, 444n.1
NRP *see* National Reading Panel (NRP)

OECD *see* Organisation for Economic
  Co-operation and Development (OECD)
Omidyar Network (ON), 540, 543, 545,
  546, 550n.11, 12
opportunity theory of conflict, 192, 200
Organisation for Economic Co-operation
  and Development (OECD), 1, 4, 6, 7, 9,
  11–13, 16, 34, 37, 39, 54, 69, 75, 86–91,
  107, 123, 131, 133, 135, 137, 140–143,
  164–167, 169, 181, 191, 225, 228,
  231–235, 237, 238, 244, 254, 275–277,
  279–288, 305, 306, 308n.1, 315, 316,
  326, 337, 341–344, 346, 351, 357–370,
  375, 376, 378, 380–383, 389, 428, 450,
  454, 458–461, 465, 466, 482, 574
organizational sociology, 450, 470–484
othering, 512
Out of School Children (OOSC), 167, 206,
  210, 248, 251, 412, 587
over education, 46, 297, 428
Oxfam, 199, 242, 404–406, 408

PALF *see* Pearson Affordable Learning
  Fund (PALF)
participation, 12, 23, 59, 65, 66, 72,
  115–117, 119, 121, 168, 178, 213, 230,
  241, 245, **246**, 278, 284, 292–294, *295*,
  300, 302–304, 307, 309n.2, 331, 341,
  345, 365, 403–405, 408, 415, 419–430,
  436, 458, 521, 537, 538, 559
partnerships, 68, 116, 117, 119–124, 196,
  197, 200, 218, 228, 234, 241, 245, 252,
  253, 323, 325, 327, 367, 391, 396–397,
  426, 428, 434, **439, 440,** 443, 460, 465,
  475, 496, 499, 528, 537, 540, 542, 545
path dependency, 11, 21, 26, 59, 145–157,
  321, 337, 450, 455, 466
peacebuilding, 192, 195, 200, 413
Pearson Corporation, 14, 122, 135, 276,
  317, 427–430, 540, 546, 548
Pearson (Foundation), 428
Pearson Affordable Learning Fund (PALF), 540
PEAS *see* Promoting Equality in African
  Schools (PEAS)
performance management, 305
philanthrocapitalism, 419, 436, 541, 550n.10
philanthropy
  impact, 436
  new, 419, 437
  venture, 436, 541, 543, 545, 548
physical sciences, 296
PISA *see* Programme for International
  Student Assessment (PISA)
PISA-based Tests for Schools, 366
pluri-scalar, 7
policy
  adoption, 23, 24, 64–76, 564
  borrowing, 2, 3, 10, 292, 450, 550, 573, 574
  diffusion, 15, 23, 64–69, 75, 76, 145, 452
  studies, 507, 515, 556, 564, 574, 583
  traveling, 493
policy-making, 1–3, 7, 9, 22–24, 27, 60, 67,
  70, 100, 108, 115, 116, 118, 120, 121,
  124, 128, 132, 153, 166, 207, 212, 214,
  215, 218, 219, 234, 244, 319–332, 358,
  359, 362, 368, 369, 392, 395, 402, 404,
  419–430, 450, 451, 454, 456, 460–462,
  466, 499, 554–570
policyscapes, 6, 8, 451, 510
political economy, 65, 69, 70, 145, 147–150,
  232, 260, 265, 292, 297, 307, 308, 351,
  382–383, 450, 509, 510, 564
political engagement, 170, 171, 173–177, 185
positional (relational) effects, 172–175, 177,
  179, 180
post-2015, 165, 189, 219, 256, 317, 331,
  366, 408, 415, 433–444, 469, 485
post-bureaucratic, 474, 475
postcolonial(ism), 450, 451, 519–532
post-conflict reconstruction, 165, 189–201, 411
  see also reconstruction phase of conflict

Post-Confucian, 300, 303, 304
post-2015 development agenda, 165, 189, 317, 585
postmodern(ism), 268, 450, 504–516
poverty, 22, 24, 35, 92, 97–108, 115, 121, 122, 124, 165, 189, 198, 209, **211**, 213, 224, 226, 227, 229, 230, 232, 234, 235, **246**, 251, 308, 326, 338, 340, 343, 344, 348, 350, 352n.7, **381**, 403, 404, 480, 496, 497, 542, 558, 559, 586
power
  informatics, 369
  logistical, 368
  soft, 70, 314, 337, 359, 366, 368, 370
  strategic, 368, 369
PPP *see* public–private partnership (PPP)
principal-agent theory, 455–457, 465
private authority, 420, 429
private sector, 5, 14, 16, 24, 30, 65, 66, 71, 73, 101, 107, 120, 122, 140, 198, 231, 248, 254, 292, 293, 299, 305, 306, 325, 327, 328, 331, 344, 345, 390, 406, 412, 419, 420, 423, 426, 429, 433, 434, 442–444, 451, 474, 482, 507, 537, 538, 541, 544, 548, 549
privatization, 6, 22, 23, 31, 36, 39, 64–76, 130, 131, 167, 225, 260, 267, 305, 317, 340, 345, 346, 434, **440**, 442, 452, 470, 474, 477
profits, 5, 29, 32, 37, 419–430, 437, 575
Programme for International Student Assessment (PISA), 5–7, 9, 24, 34, 54, 71, 86, 129, 276, 281, 282, 292, 315, 357, 374–384, 428, 454, 458, 477, 519, 581
  development, 7, 315, 316, 357, 365, 366, 377
  shock, 362, 377, 459
Progress in International Reading Literacy Study (PIRLS), 7, 9, 129
Promoting Equality in African Schools (PEAS), **438**, 442, 444n.4, 543
protection of children, 194, 196, 325 *see also* child protection
protracted phase of conflict, 194
public administration, 351n.4, 470, 471, 473, 474, 482, 483n.1, 484n.12
public goods, 14, 32–33, 74, 178, 307, 436, 481, 545
public policy, 4, 7, 28, 216, 241, 375, 378, 382, 383, 455, 465, 470, 483
public–private partnership (PPP), 66, 72, 75, 107, 113, 296, 302, 434, 442, 543
Punjab Schools Reform Roadmap, 544

quality, 24, 26, 31–40, 44, **51**, 54–56, 60, 72, 81, 85, 89, 92, 114, 118, 122, 123, 134, **138**, 141, 148, 155, 156, 164, 166, 167, 189, 194, 218, 219, 220n.13, 226, 227, 229, 231–234, 236, 238n.3, 243, 256, 264, 275, 280, 284, 287, 298, 304, 360, 362, 363, 368, 375–378, **381**, 383, 388–390, 392, 397, 410, **438**, **440**, 441, 443, 462, 465, 472, 474, 477, 482, 495, 514, 519, 521, 537, 538, 541, 543, 550, 557–560, 562–564, 574, 575, 580–581, 585
  assurance, 14, 302, 344, 377, 388, 546
  education, 5, 22, 29, 31–37, 39, 45, 104, 107, 108, 113, 117, 132, 133, 136, 137, 198, 199, 201, 208–210, 212, 215, 217, 242, 247, 249, 250, 255, 285, 323, 328, 382, 403, 408, 422, 444, 540, 542, 544, 548, 560, 563, 569, 579
quasi-business organization, 168, 292
quasi-market, 22, 25, 73, 102, 305

rate(s) of return (RoR), 29, 100, 102, 103, 108n.1, 118, 206, 219, 294, 340, 341
rationalism, 23, 65, 67–69, 75
realism, 336
reconstruction phase of conflict, 194 *see also* post-conflict reconstruction
regionalism, 7, 385–388, 395, 397
reinventing government, 475
research and development (R&D), 29, 217, 300, 307
research collaborations, 396, 496, 529–530, 532
research intensive universities, 299, 302, 309n.2, 391
retention, 24, 65, 70, 74–76, 236, 327
Rights, 1, 27, 44, **51**, 113–123, 146, 164, 194, 206–220, 224, 241, 261, 278, 319, 358, 403, 421, 451, 510, 531 *see also* human rights; right to education
rights-based approach to education, 327, 330
right to education, 13, 53, **54**, 58, 115, 166, 195–198, 208, 210, **211**, 212–215, 218, 219, 219n.3, 278, 327, 328, 404–406, 444n.1
role of ideas, 65, 70
Russian, **56**, 263, 300, 303, 351n.6, 578, 580

SABER *see* Systems Approach for Better Educational Results (SABER)
Sarva Shiksha Abhiyan (SSA), 209
SAS *see* Survey of Adult Skills (SAS)

School-Related Gender-Based Violence (SRGBV), 112, 121–123
science, technology, engineering, and mathematics (STEM), 59, 295
scientized, 473, 476
security approach to education in conflict, 165, 198, 200
selection, 24, 28, 65, 70, 72–76, 104, 170, 180, 265, 269, 279, 281, 298
semiosis, 70
silver bullet (policy solution), 111, 437, **438**, 539, 548–549
situational analysis (SITAN), 579
skills, 4–6, 15, 22–24, 26, 27, 29, 30, 37, 38, 81–86, **84**, **90**, 93n.6, 98, 132, 137, **138**, 165, 170, 181–183, *182–185*, **183**, 200, 201, 232, 233, 242, 243, 247–249, 251, 254, 255, 256n.5, 278, 285, 295, 324, 339, 344, 350, 358, 363–365, 370, 376, 382, 383, 414, 420, 424–426, 429, **440**, 441, 443, 458, 483n.6, 497, 527, 528, 542, 557–561, 563–565, 567, 568, 574
  cognitive, 24, 81, 82, 84, 85, 89–92, 364
  collective skill formation, 152, 153
  distribution, 177
  education and, 5, 12, 176, 185, 281, 316, 363, 364, 367, 370, 440
  formation, 11, 145–157
  formation regimes, 145–147
  inequality/inequalities, 176, 177, 179, 181, 185
  shortage, 297
social benefits, 32, 118, 165, 170, 171, 185, 201, 540, 577
social capital, 13, 28, 101, 169, 171
social capitalism, 549
Social Capital Markets (SOCAP), 543
social cohesion, 13, 15, 24, 28, 106, 164, 165, 169–185, 197, 209, 269, 323, 358, 413, **438**, 457, 558
social determinism, 512
social enterprise, 442, 473, 479, 507, 535, 539, 541, 544, 545
social equality, 30
social network analysis, 539
social responsibility, 122, 304, 420, **423**, 425–428, **439**, 441
social sciences, 46, 50, **57**, 99–102, 238n.1, 262, 268, 296, *302*, 308, 309n.3, 444n.1, 504, 555
social selection, 298
South–South cooperation, 212
Sphere Project, 197, 411, 413

SRGBV *see* School-Related Gender-Based Violence (SRGBV)
SSA *see* Sarva Shiksha Abhiyan (SSA)
standardization, 9, 25, 128–132, 134, 137, **138**, 140, 362, 463–465, 484n.9, 546
standardized testing, 6, 130, 134, 137, 142, 482
states, 1, 23, 27–40, 50, 65, 99, 114, 128, 148, 165, 169, **190**, 207, 231, 248, 259, 277, 292, 314, 319, 335, 358, 376, 386, 405, 420, 434, 455, 472, 495, 509, 544, 555, 577
state-university relations, 293, 303
statistics, 60, **84**, **90**, 129, 175, 278, 324, 330, 357, 358, 361, 363, 367, 389, 475, 569, 576, 579, 583, 585, 586
structural adjustment, 101, 117, 228–231, 241, 327, 336, 339–343, 346, 350
structural inequalities, 117, 192
structuralism, 69
student mobility, 388, 527–529
Survey of Adult Skills (OECD), 181, *182*, *183*, **183**, *184*
Systems Approach for Better Educational Results (SABER), 167, 276, 283, 284, 349

TANS *see* Transnational Advocacy Networks (TANS)
TALIS *see* Teaching and Learning International Survey (TALIS)
taxation, 23, 29, 30, 35, 298, 304, 527
Taylorism, 35, 150
teacher(s)
  accountability, 283, 574, 578, 579
  education, 189, 206, 426, 510, 511, 577, 579, 583
  professionalism, 26, 275
  qualifications, 577
  salary, 576, 577
  shortage, 250, 452, 573–587
  training, 47, 193, 243, 254, 280, 429, 547, 577
Teach for America (TFA), 547, 574
Teaching and Learning International Survey (TALIS), 7, 167, 267, 276, 281, 283, 285, 286, 366, 367
technology, 1, 4, 6, 7, 14, 15, 23, 27–29, 32, 37, 49, **51**, **57**, 59, 71, 74, 87, 89–92, 93n.7, 19, 121, 129, 131, 132, **246**, 270, 276, 292, 295, 396, 422, 442, 458, 496, 522, 523, 532, 539–541, 546–550, 585
  computer, 28, 39
  digital, 548

educational, 31, 50
global, 287
information, 27, 122, 582
information and communications technology (ICT), 36–39
military, 287
mobile, 548, 586
science and, 50, 51, 264, 495
spread of, 300
testing, 6, 9, 12, 23, 25, 31–36, 39, 47, 54, 55, 55, 84, 129–131, 133, 134, 137, **139**, 140, 142, 175, 265, 267, 281, 363, 369, 423, 428, **438**, 458, 459, 480, 482, 561
text, 7, 209, 213, 219n.1, 235, 269, 284, 411, 425, 452, 492, 505, 508–510, 555–561, 564, 566
  consumption of, 569n.1
  distribution, 569n.1
  production, 8
Third way (the), 130, 343, 443
TIMSS *see* Trends in Mathematics and Science Study (TIMSS)
TNCs *see* Transnational Corporations (TNCs)
tolerance, 30, 58, 112, 170–173, 197, 208, **246**, 254
translocal(ly), 492, 493
Transnational Advocacy Networks (TANS), 13, 210, 212–214, 218, 316, 401–415, 478, 481
Transnational Corporations (TNCs), 4, 14, 316, 368, 419–423, 428, 429
Transpositional [view], 168, 292
Trends in Mathematics and Science Study (TIMSS), 7, 9, 34, 86, 93n.10, 129
trust, 26, 28, 200, 253, 255, 282, 328, 335, 344, 348, 351–352n.6, 398, 415n.4, 424, 425, 437, **438**, 442, 444n.4, 529, 530, 547, 550n.1
  political, 170, 171
  social, 173, 176–185, 365
tuition, 32, 33, 155, 292, 298, 299, 304–307, **306**, 394

UCDP *see* Uppsala Conflict Data Program (UCDP)
UDHR *see* Universal Declaration of Human Rights (UDHR)
UNESCO *see* United Nations Educational, Scientific and Cultural Organization (UNESCO)
UNESCO Institute for Statistics (UIS), 242, 330, 521, 522, 586

UNICEF *see* United Nations Children's Fund (UNICEF)
UNICEF study on teachers, 587
unintended consequences, 453–466
unions, 12, 40, 47, 48, 73, 106, 131, 147, 148, 150, 152–157, 275, 277–279, 281, 322, 338, 421, 478, 576, 578
United Nations Children's Fund (UNICEF), 3, 4, 13, 53, 117–119, 191, 194–196, 199, 200, 208–210, **211**, 212, 217, 224, 227, 228, 236, 238n.5, 245, 247, 315, 319–321, 323–328, **329**, 330, 331, 341, 409, 410, 412, 413, 415n.4, 421, 422, 575, 577, 579, 581, **583**, 587
United Nations Educational, Scientific and Cultural Organization (UNESCO), 1, 3, 4, 12, 13, 34, 51, 52, 53, **54**, 85, **86**, 89, 112, 116, 119, 120, 166, 189, 191, 192, 194, 197, 201, 206, 210, 212, 213, 225, 227, 228, 232, 234–238, 241, 243, 245, **246**, 252, 254, 256nn.1, 2, 4, 277, 278, 288, **294**, 294, **295**, 296, 315, 319–331, **329**, 332n.1, 341, 344, 361, 364, 389, 391, 408, 409, 415n.4, 419–422, 435, **440**, 441, 460, 475, 481, 521, 522, 548, 555, 563, 569, 574–576, 586, 587
United States Agency for International Development (USAID), 119, 192, 195, 197
Universal Declaration of Human Rights (UDHR), 1, 3, 45, 53, **54**, 115, 166, 195, 206–208, 215, 241, 321
Universal Primary Education (UPE), 31, 85, 166, 189, 234, 242, 248, 250, 255, 326, 344, 576
university ranking, **56**, 58–60, 292, 308, 519, 522
Uppsala Conflict Data Program (UCDP), 190
USAID *see* United States Agency for International Development (USAID)

values
  cultural, 216
  political, 30
  social, 30–32, 73, 176, 298, 364
variation, 13, 23, 24, 26, 30–31, 33, 39, 40, 47, 53, 58–59, 65, 70–72, 75, 76, 82, 85, 91, 94n.20, 130, 156, 179, 185, 251, 252, 291, 292, 303, 305, **306**, 307, 378, 457, 481, 538
varieties of capitalism (VoC), 11, 26, 146–151, 157
venture capital, 539–541, 545
vertical case study, 219n.2, 452, 554–570, 584

VET *see* vocational education and training (VET)
VoC *see* varieties of capitalism (VoC)
vocational education and training (VET), 99, 147, 150–155, 157, 323, 464, 466

Washington consensus/post-Washington consensus, 24, 73, 101, 105, 225, 230, 336, 340, 341, 343, 350
WCT *see* World Culture Theory (WCT)
WCU *see* World Class Universities (WCU)
wellbeing, 217
women's rights, 5, 31, 113–123, 232
World Bank, 1, 3, 4, 6, 12–14, 16, 24, 28, 30, 34, 50, 51, 52, 53, 67, 69, 72, 74, 83, 85, 97–99, 101, 104–106, 111, 118, 132, 164, 166, 167, 192, 209, 210, **211**, 212, 217, 218, 224–226, 228–231, 237, 238, 238n.5, 245, 253, 275–278, 283, 284, 287, 294, 296, 302, 315, 316, 319, 323, 326, 327, 330, 335–352, 389, 405, 411, 436, 443, 444n.2, 480–482, 494, 537, 555, 557–560, 562, 565, 574, 575
World Class Universities (WCU), 29, 55–58, 57, 60, 168, 292, 299, 302–304, 306, 307, 398n.4, 510
world culture, 10, 23, 68
World Culture Theory (WCT), 68, 69
World Development Indicators, 575
World Innovation Summit for Education (WISE), 551n.31, 543, 548
World Management Survey, 477, 482, 489
world science system, 168, 292, 299–303, 307
world society, 23, 43–61, 472, 483n.5
world system, 27, 302, 315, 338
world system theory, 31
World Trade Organization (WTO), 1, 14, 74, 305, 360, 493
World Values Survey, 178, 179

Youth Training Scheme (YTS), 156